D

A NATIVE AMERICAN ENCYCLOPEDIA

A
Native American
Encyclopedia

HISTORY, CULTURE, AND PEOPLES

Barry M. Pritzker

OXFORD
UNIVERSITY PRESS

2000

OXFORD
UNIVERSITY PRESS

Oxford   New York
Athens Auckland Bangkok Bogotá Buenos Aires Calcutta
Cape Town Chennai Dar es Salaam Delhi Florence Hong Kong Istanbul
Karachi Kuala Lumpur Madrid Melbourne Mexico City Mumbai
Nairobi Paris São Paulo Shanghai Singapore Taipei Tokyo Toronto Warsaw

and associated companies in
Berlin   Ibadan

Published by Oxford University Press, Inc.
198 Madison Avenue, New York, New York 10016

Oxford is a registered trademark of Oxford University Press

First published 1998 by ABC-CLIO
Santa Barbara, California

Library of Congress Cataloging-in-Publication Data
Pritzker, Barry.
Native Americans : an encyclopedia of history, culture, and
peoples / Barry M. Pritzker.
p.   cm.
Originally published: Santa Barbara, Calif.: ABC-CLIO, ©1998.
Includes bibliographical references and idex.
ISBN 0-19-513897-X (hb)
ISBN 0-19-513877-5 (pb)
1. Indians of North America—Encylclopedias.   I. Title.
E76.P75   1998
970.00497'003—DC21   99-053677

9 8 7 6 5 4 3 2
Printed in the United States of America
on acid-free paper

To Carol Batker,
for her love and encouragement,
and to our children, Olivia and Aaron,
for their patience

CONTENTS

This encyclopedia is an attempt to illuminate in a comprehensive yet readable way some of the complex cultures of the native peoples of North America. In school, I learned that America was a pristine "wilderness" waiting for the so-called right people to come along and build a "civilization." Of course, the truth is that millions of people were already living here. In fact, they had been here for thousands—perhaps tens of thousands—of years before Eriksson, Cabot, and Coronado. Adapting over millennia to diverse climatic and physiographic environments, Native Americans created and continue to build an astonishing range of complex cultures to fulfill both their material and their spiritual needs.

I have always felt a share of responsibility concerning the basic methods—thievery and murder—that brought this rich land under the control of what we now know as the United States and Canada. As a citizen of the United States, I am implicated in and benefit from the long process of expropriation. It was this awareness, in part, that led to my interest in Indians. A teaching stint at the Taos Pueblo Day School and a fellowship at the Summer Institute of the Newberry Library's D'Arcy McNickle Center for the History of the American Indian reinforced my awareness of Native American cultures.

Today, American Indians still struggle to overcome a complicated legacy of destruction. They have been left with a tiny fraction of their aboriginal domain (many groups remain landless altogether). Neither the U.S. nor the Canadian government has hastened to redress grievances. Yet Indians and Inuit are revitalizing their cultures. In the United States, they are an important part of many local and regional economies. In Canada, native people are reclaiming their land as well as their heritage, as the creation of the new territory of Nunavut so clearly illustrates. Indians and Inuit still face daunting challenges in their efforts to retain a native identity and reestablish sovereignty in the face of relentless assimilationist pressures, but many are meeting these challenges head-on and with success.

It is not too late to learn from Native Americans. In light of past and ongoing injustices and the momentum of Indian and Inuit self-determination movements, I would say that an understanding of Indian and Inuit cultures and concerns is essential. The past cannot be changed, but we can recognize aspects of history commonly deemed unimportant, such as the dynamics of native cultures as well as the vital contributions of Native Americans to contemporary society. We can also create a present and a future in which people work together based on mutual understanding and respect. These are my ultimate goals in writing this encyclopedia.

My research is based on a variety of primary and secondary sources. Most primary information on early native cultures comes from the records of explorers, traders, missionaries, and scientists. There are also anthropological studies of native cultures, including interviews with elders and other tribal members. Native art and other material "texts" are also important source material, as are company and government records. More recent primary information includes native-written books, articles, and electronic texts as well as material culture. I have tried to use official, tribally based material whenever possible. Although accuracy has always remained my primary concern, this encyclopedia doubtless contains errors of omission and commission. For these I take full responsibility and extend a preemptive apology to those who might be offended or misguided by any such flaws.

I would also like to thank those people who (knowingly or unknowingly) inspired me and/or helped make it possible for me to undertake and complete this project: the children, staff, and community of the Taos Pueblo Day School in the fall of 1977; Professor Carol Batker, for careful reading and editing and help with perspective; John Bowman, for inspiration and technical assistance; Professor Emma Cappeluzzo, for initiating the University of Massachusetts program that enabled students to teach at New Mexico pueblos; Karen Turple and Pierre Beaudreau at Indian and Northern Affairs Canada as well as Bill Armstrong at the British Columbia Ministry of Aboriginal Affairs for providing documents and other information; and Professor Lawana Trout, the former director of the D'Arcy McNickle Center for the History of the American Indian's Summer Institute. I would also like to thank ABC-CLIO editors Jeff Serena and Todd Hallman for their invaluable guidance, support, and direction. Connie Oehring, Libby Barstow, and Liz Kincaid saw to the encyclopedia's production, including copyediting and artwork, in a most able, professional, and friendly manner.

Finally, I would like formally to acknowledge and to honor the North American Indians and Inuit, who have struggled, and continue to struggle, in the face of hardship and oppression to retain their cultures and traditions and to live dignified lives. I also hope this encyclopedia may be of some service to people who seek to understand and appreciate the cultures of Native Americans in particular and the marvel of human diversity in general.

Barry M. Pritzker

INTRODUCTION

Indians[1] have lived in North America for a long time. There is no agreement on the precise length of time or even on how and when they first appeared on the continent. According to many Indian creation stories, the people[2] have always been here, having originated either below the earth or, less commonly, in some other nonterrestrial zone. The most widely accepted theory states that ancestral Native Americans walked across the Bering Strait when frozen ocean conditions created a land bridge between what is now Siberia and Alaska. That may have occurred anywhere from 15,000 to 40,000 or more years ago. Some people speculate that even without a land bridge, ancient people may have crossed the Bering Strait in boats. Finally, there is a theory, based on certain fossils found in New Mexico, that ancient people arrived here directly from Europe, via Iceland and Greenland.

In any case, the ancestors of at least some groups were living in their historic territories in 10,000 B.C.E.[3] Over the millennia, people adapted to dramatic climate changes by creating new technologies and migrating when necessary. Some early groups hunted species of big game that are now extinct. People gradually filled in new territory as the glaciers withdrew from northern North America. The Great Plains became populated, depopulated, and then repopulated. Some groups settled down to farm the great American triad of corn, beans, and squash while others continued primarily to hunt and/or fish and/or gather wild plant foods.

Some Indian peoples developed complex mythologies and religions, whereas others made do with relatively simple beliefs. Some groups built great cities, with tens of thousands of residents, whereas others preferred living in small groups. Fighting was endemic among some groups, whereas others lived in relative peace. Many Native Americans were deeply knowledgeable about the land itself. Some groups discovered literally hundreds of plants that could be used for medicinal purposes. Indians were no strangers to travel. Some coastal peoples built sturdy, seagoing vessels that took them 60 or more miles out to sea to hunt marine life. Extensive trade networks were set up, so that items both popular and necessary, as well as ideas, could be exchanged over distances of hundreds and even thousands of miles.

Indians learned to stay reasonably cool in the heat of desert summers and, along with the Inuit, reasonably warm in the frozen northern winters. Many groups had brilliant material arts traditions, and many more raised drama and storytelling to artistic heights. In the realm of government, too, Indians fashioned complex responses to various local situations. Some groups developed councils, some were run by clan associations, and some had separate war and peace governments. Groups had strong leaders, weak leaders, or even no real leaders at all. Confederacies such as the Creek and Iroquois developed particularly sophisticated governmental models. One trait that stands out in this area, however, is the near-universal tendency among Native Americans to make decisions by consensual agreement rather than majority rule.

By now the reader should begin to understand the degree of cultural diversity present among the millions of aboriginal American Indian and Inuit people. Why, then, are Native Americans so often depicted as just a handful of people without any culture at all? One reason has to do with myth: It was, and is, convenient for non-natives to pretend that they did not have to take the land from others. Another concerns population. The aboriginal population of North America is variously estimated at between about 2 million and 18 million at its peak. However, diseases such as smallpox, cholera, typhoid, and measles, brought by non-natives,[4] decimated Indian communities. Many suffered population losses of up to 90 percent or more even before non-natives actually arrived, because the germs far outran explorers, traders, missionaries, and settlers. So it was that so many non-natives spoke of the land as open, pristine, and virgin.

Furthermore, literary and historical depictions of Indians as savage, barbarous, and primitive have distorted the clash between the different Indian and Euro-American ways of being in the world. The Spanish sought gold and other forms of riches. They also demanded conversions to Christianity and were perfectly willing to kill and enslave Indians to get what they wanted. The British wanted land above all and were also interested in religious as well as cultural conversions. The French had their share of missionaries but in general were more willing to accept Indian cultures on their own terms, a fact that accounts for the relatively high rates of interracial marriage in New France.

In the far north, the Russians, too, sent missionaries to convert the Indians, but mainly launched a program of brutal enslavement in order to force Indians and Inuit to acquire pelts for Russian trade companies. Indians, for their part, were happy to trade with the newcomers and even to cede some land willingly. They were not, however, prepared for a wholesale onslaught on their land and way of life. These sorts of struggles are often couched in moralistic dualities, such as "savage" and "civilized," but even the introductory student must move beyond simplistic, ethnocentric explanations in order to achieve any real understanding of cultural conflict.

Indian and Inuit groups encountered non-natives at vastly different times. The Norse probably appeared in the extreme northeast around 1000; Basque and other European fishermen arrived in roughly the same area in the early sixteenth century, about the time of Spanish contact in the south. In contrast, some bands in California and the Plateau region did not directly encounter non-natives until the nineteenth century, and in parts of Arctic America there was no direct interracial contact until the early twentieth century.

The experience of Indian groups with non-natives differed according to time and place, but in general there was a greater or lesser degree of aggression on the part of the latter and resistance on the part of the former. Many Indian groups underwent dramatic transformations during the historical period. The need for increased centralization to fight the newcomers and the need to adapt to the loss of freedom altered governmental structures. New alliances were effected, as Indian groups took sides in the great colonial struggles and became heavily involved in the fur trade. Native manufacture of certain items fell away as people tended to become dependent on non-native goods. Religion changed too, as Christianity mixed with and in many cases subsumed traditional beliefs.

Perhaps the two biggest developments to influence the lives of Indians were the introductions of the horse and of firearms. As already mentioned, diseases from abroad also took a great toll on native populations, as did, increasingly, warfare as well as venereal disease and alcohol.

While individuals were busy seizing Indians' territory and destroying their resources, both the United States and Canada, having coalesced as nations, developed official policies that forced Indian groups to give up vast amounts of land. Many were forcibly removed far from their homelands at a tremendous cost in life and suffering. In the United States, treaties made with sovereign Indian nations were broken almost as soon as they were concluded. Some groups in the United States were resettled on ever-shrinking reservations, which may or may not have been located within their ancestral lands. Patriot leaders (not to mention warriors and noncombatants) were killed or otherwise neutralized, and compliant, ersatz leaders were often installed in their place. Canada favored the creation of numerous small reserves generally within aboriginal territory.

In both countries, Indians were placed under tremendous pressure to abandon their heritage and assimilate into non-native society. Various methods were used to achieve these goals, such as forcible removal of children for education at boarding schools, banning aspects of traditional culture such as language and religious practice, and mandatory participation by nomadic groups in farming schemes. These methods went far to erode strong family bonds and tribal traditions. Officials in charge of Indian affairs were notoriously corrupt, a situation that added to the difficulties of Native Americans.

Both countries also passed a series of laws designed to further their assimilationist goals. In the United States, the General Allotment (Dawes) Act (1887) sought to break up the reservation system and tribalism. Among its provisions were those that called for the government to negotiate with tribes with the goal of allotting Indian lands in severalty. Those lands remaining after certain individuals had received their share would be released for sale to or use by non-natives. Although tribes were able to negotiate under this framework, as a group they lost roughly 90 million acres of land—about two-thirds of the total land base—either through the alienation of "surplus" land or because individual allotments were subsequently lost through mechanisms such as tax foreclosure. By forcibly eliminating so much common land, the United States succeeded in dealing a serious blow to tribal identity and cohesion.

Canada concluded a series of numbered treaties with Indian groups, beginning in 1871. These called on native people to exchange land for reserves, payments, and other considerations. In 1876, Canadian officials consolidated their policies under a single Indian Act. Based on earlier laws aimed at eradicating "Indianness" through the enfranchisement of Indian men, the act empowered the federal government to control native people, even to the point of defining who was an Indian and who was not. Under the act, Indian leaders functioned essentially as government agents. Subsequent amendments expanded the concept of enfranchisement, making it involuntary, and outlawed certain rituals, such as the potlatch. They also allowed the government to seize Indian land the government decided was not being sufficiently exploited economically by the tribes. In the far north, the North-West Mounted Police built posts from which they regulated many aspects of Inuit life.

By the early twentieth century, many Indians and Inuit had fallen into conditions of severe poverty and dependence. Although many resisted it, the United States granted citizenship to Indians in 1924. In 1934, U.S. officials overturned Dawes-era policies and passed the Wheeler-Howard Indian Reorganization Act (IRA). Under the IRA, allotment was halted, and Indians were encouraged to create constitutional, majority-rule–style tribal governments. Decisions made by such governments were, of course, subject to approval by the Bureau of Indian Affairs (BIA). The tribes were also given such presumptive incentives as the opportunity to join in non-native development schemes. Despite the best hopes of policy makers, many tribes rejected the IRA as being antithetical to their customs and beliefs as well as a violation of treaty-protected sovereignty.

It was not long, however, before reaction set in, and New Deal policies were in turn reversed: In the 1950s, the federal government set about severing the special relationship between Indian tribes and the United States in a process known as termination. Related policies also encouraged Indians to leave reservations and live in cities. There, instead of jobs and assimilation, many found only poverty, loneliness, and alienation. At the same time the reservations lost thousands of young people who would have provided the next generation of leadership.

Meanwhile, Indians, led in part by war veterans, were creating important pan-tribal organizations. In 1944, the National Congress of American Indians (NCAI) took the lead in advocating for Indian self-determination. Younger activists created the National Indian Youth Conference in 1961. Both of these groups were instrumental in shaping an Indian agenda for political and social action. What ultimately stopped termination, in fact, in addition to the horrific experience of two terminated tribes, the

Menominee and Klamath, was the ability of Indian leaders to convince Congress of the importance of maintaining the government's treaty obligations and of the potential gains in allowing Indians themselves to determine the course of their own futures.

In Canada, as well, the postwar period marked the emergence of Indian organizations determined to break the cycle of dependence and neglect. The far north took on great strategic importance in the early Cold War period, leading to official attention for the first time. Inuit and some Subarctic Indians were still in the process of consolidating their populations around permanent settlements and abandoning, however unwillingly, their traditional lifestyles. In 1969, Canada proposed its own version of termination, but native resistance forced the government to kill the policy before it was even enacted. Quickly, Canada withdrew Indian agents from all reserves and began funding aboriginal organizations preparatory to entering into serious discussions on aboriginal rights. Among the reforms that followed were local control of education, a process that continues today. In 1995, for instance, 98 percent of on-reserve schools were under the control of First Nations. In the far north, organizations like the Inuit Tapirisat of Canada, founded in 1971, began carving out a path toward self-determination.

The Canadian government formally recognized classes of native claims in 1973. Major concords such as the James Bay and Northern Quebec Agreement of 1975 and the Cree-Naskapi Act of 1984 helped establish the principle that the government would negotiate seriously with Indian groups concerning self-determination. Progress in this area may be illustrated in many ways but perhaps most clearly by the agreement between Canada and the Nisga'a Tribal Council on what amounts to a government-to-government basis. Also, in 1985, Parliament removed the most offensive and discriminatory sections of the Indian Act. Finally, sections recognizing Indian, Inuit, and Métis[5] rights were included in the constitution in 1982.

In the United States, a revolution of rising expectations, combined with the growing militancy of the period, produced the "Red Power" movement of the late 1960s and 1970s. Activist organizations included the Native American Civil Rights Council and the American Indian Movement. The most visible manifestations of direct action were the occupation of Alcatraz Island in 1969 and of the Bureau of Indian Affairs in 1972 and the standoff at Wounded Knee, South Dakota, in 1973. Northwestern and then Great Lakes tribes fought hard, visibly, and ultimately successfully for their fishing rights, guaranteed by treaty but denied in practice.

Progress was also made toward reaching the goal of self-determination. Indians scored important, though still limited, legal victories during the period, winning passage of several bills, including the Indian Civil Rights Act (1968), the Alaska Native Claims Settlement Act (1971), and the Indian Self-Determination and Educational Assistance Act (1975). Some tribes gained greater control over extensive mineral holdings (although leases often remained terribly exploitative). Along with Red Power came Red Pride, as people rediscovered their heritage in language, art, and spirituality. Younger people, especially, began increasingly to embrace the teachings of their elders.

Although poverty and poor health remain endemic to many Indian communities, the worst abuses of the early twentieth century have passed, and Indian populations are generally increasing. The U.S. Census recorded roughly two million Indians in 1990. There were 287 reservations composed of 56 million acres of land. More than 300 tribal governments were officially recognized by the federal government, plus over 200 in Alaska, with over 100 more either seeking recognition or considering such a move. Slightly more than 50 percent of Indians in the United States live in urban areas. According to the 1991 Canada census, there were 1,002,675 self-identified Indians, 608 First Nations Councils (bands), 66 Inuit communities, and 2,370 reserves totaling 7.4 million acres. In 1993 there were 626,000 status[6] Indians, 212,650 Métis, and 49,225 Inuit. Almost half of all status Indians live on a reserve.

All over North America, Native American groups continue to press for self-sufficiency and self-determination, including control over natural resources, fulfillment of treaty rights, just compensation for— or the return of—land, and legal jurisdiction. In the United States, organizations such as the Council of Energy Resource Tribes (CERT) take a leading role in managing Indian energy and natural resources. Although gaming is controversial for a number of reasons, many Indian tribes have made it a centerpiece of their new economies—in the mid-1990s there were over 100 high-stakes operations and over 60 casinos taking in roughly $6 billion a year. Child welfare is largely under Indian control. Indian groups are engaged in cultural revitalization on any number of fronts. Nevertheless, unemployment, poverty, and suicide rates remain higher among Indian people than among any other single racial or ethnic group.

In 1995 there were roughly 18,000 native-owned businesses in Canada. Inuit people maintain active cooperatives, some based on art and craft production, as alternative ways to make a living. They have also developed radio and television programming in their native language (Inuktitut). There is a major effort on the part of local Inuit to prepare for the creation of Canada's newest territory, the mainly Inuit Nunavut, in 1999, and other native groups in Canada are busy working out their own versions of cultural revitalization, economic sufficiency, and political self-determination. In 1995, First Nations and the federal government began formulating a strategy designed ultimately to replace the Indian Act with local self-government.

Once independent sovereign nations, later treated as domestic dependent nations, native North Americans are once again on the road to controlling their own destinies. They face daunting and yet exciting challenges in their quest to create new political, social, and economic structures and ways of being based very much on the old ones. Furthermore, despite the long legacy of oppression, dependence, hatred, and fear, Native Americans and non-natives are working together effectively to resolve old conflicts. The success of these efforts will be based, at least in part, on a thorough understanding of the past and a firm commitment to move forward as full and equal partners into the future.

A few explanatory words about this volume are in order. The relatively little information I provide about early prehistory will be found mainly in the introductions to the regional chapters. The study of ancient aboriginal cultures is more technical and conjectural than that of their late prehistory or history. It is beyond the scope of this encyclopedia to discuss theoretical archaeology or anthropology or to delve deeply into the early prehistory of North America. That said, I hope that in the chapter introductions and in the "History" category of the individual entries I have provided enough information about prehistory for the reader to understand that Indian cultures did evolve over time. Readers who desire to learn more about the ancient North American past might find the information I have provided a helpful starting place from which to expand their research.

Material in the first section of each entry, "Historical Information," is meant to apply to precontact life, except as noted in the text. For example, when discussing the diet of Pueblo Indians I have excluded references to items such as melons, a non-native crop grown in early postcontact southwestern gardens. However, it is also true that in many cases no firm line can be drawn between "aboriginal" and "postcontact." Some groups were radically altered shortly following—or, in some cases, even prior to—direct contact with non-natives, whereas others continued relatively unchanged for decades or even centuries after they met non-natives or felt their influence. This being the case, and since much of the early source material comes from non-native observers, the reader must keep in mind that what is meant to be a snapshot portrait of traditional society may in fact include some nonaboriginal elements.

Similarly, my use of the word "traditional" generally refers to the late prehistoric period, even when, strictly speaking, the prehistoric period might not be very traditional at all. An example: Even though many groups changed slowly and gradually between the period of their ancient past and the time when they first met non-natives, the Lakota altered their culture dramatically in the late prehistoric or even the early historic period as they moved from the forests and prairies onto the plains. Although they were Eastern Woodlands denizens for a far longer period than they were masters of the Great Plains, I have chosen to label the latter period as "traditional" because they are so clearly identified as a Plains group. Another way to think about this is that "traditional" generally refers to the named groups at around the time of contact, even though many of those groups did not technically exist as tribes in the ancient past.

The word "tribe" also requires some explanation. Most people are in the habit of referring to Indian groups, past and present, as tribes. This is partly because many Indians are grouped as tribes today and partly because the word denotes a form of social organization in opposition—with connotations implying both "inferior" and "outmoded"—to that of non-native communities. However, the word "tribe" represents a specific form of social organization. Tribes generally share descent, territory, political authority, history, and culture and consider themselves, to varying degrees, as a single, sovereign people.

Many traditional Indian societies were not tribes at all, in that they may have been highly decentralized or did not conceive of themselves as a unified entity. Many groups were actually organized as bands or as extended families. To refer to all aboriginal groups as tribes is to impose a modern idea retroactively on the past. Most, although not all, tribes were created in the postcontact period, under pressure to develop more centralized, European-style political structures. Although many Indians today use the word "tribe" to refer to their larger political structure, many also use words like "nation" and "people." I have tried to use the appropriate term wherever possible.

For space considerations I have generally excluded extinct groups, but I have included some for their particular historical significance. The Natchez and Yana, for instance, fall into this category, whereas groups like the Apalachee, though important, were omitted. Where I have discussed extinct peoples, I have merely sketched the traditional culture and omitted any reference to the nonexistent present. For tribes such as the Lumbee, about which only postcontact information is known, I have discussed the group's precontact antecedents under the "History" heading and proceeded directly to the contemporary information.

I have also omitted any discussion of mythology, an important and fascinating aspect of native cultures. Mythology occupies a vital place in the worldview of most people, perhaps particularly among those without written traditions. Mythology was essentially indistinguishable from what modern people might call "reality" or "history." Often tied to religious belief, mythology can be a window into the past and the means by which people make sense of the present. It seemed to me that I could discuss Native American religious beliefs and practices reasonably clearly and succinctly, but the task of conveying an understanding of mythology in the space of a few sentences seemed far more elusive. Unable to do justice to the topic, I chose to omit a discussion of mythology altogether. Instead, I commend the interested reader to sources that treat this subject with appropriate depth and perspective.

I would also like to point out that this encyclopedia is biased in favor of Indian groups that reside in the United States. Information on native Canadians is far less accessible, although this is beginning to change with the growth of electronic resources. Furthermore, although I have been able to provide very specific information about some topics, for others I have been less detailed and definitive. In such circumstances I hope the reader will find my material a helpful starting point for further research among more specialized resources. Finally, my aspirations to accuracy notwithstanding, caution is always advised regarding the interpretation of any data. Facts are usually appropriate only to a precise time and place, and the temptation to generalize is often irresistible. My choice of words and selection of material reflect my own particular perspective and biases.

Notes

1. The word "Indian" is, of course, technically a misnomer. Christopher Columbus thought he had reached India when he landed on the island of Hispaniola, so he called the natives Indians. There are many other terms by which the people refer to themselves, such as Native American, American Indian, native, band, and First Nation (used mainly in Canada). The use of one word or another sometimes implies a particular political position. Since the words "Indian" and "Native American" have gained widespread acceptance among the people to whom they refer, I generally use them to the exclusion of other labels.

2. "The people" is another term I often use when referring to Native Americans, since many aboriginal self-designations may be translated in this way.

3. B.C.E. stands for Before the Common Era. It replaces the conventional designation and its religious implications. .

4. The term "non-native" is admittedly awkward. However, other words typically used to refer to those people who came to America after 1000 or 1492, such as "whites," Europeans," "Euro-Americans," and so forth, are factually misleading, and words like "invader" are too emotionally charged. "Non-native," at least, has the advantages of being both reasonably neutral and accurate.

5. Métis (Mā tā) are descendants of Indian women and non-native fur traders. In Canada they are officially considered nonstatus Indians and, with Indians and Inuit, constitute one of the three recognized categories of Native American people. On the prairies they combined Indian-style hunting and the settled habits of their European forebears. Today, most live in Manitoba, Canada, and among Chippewa communities in Montana.

6. Under the Indian Act, Canadian law recognizes several categories of Native Americans. "Status," or official Indians, are those registered under the Indian Act. However, not all Indians are registered; these people are "nonstatus" Indians. Status Indians may also be separated into "treaty" or "nontreaty" Indians, depending on the history of their particular group.

A NATIVE AMERICAN ENCYCLOPEDIA

CHAPTER ONE

The Southwest

Southwest

The southwestern United States, site of the continent's longest continuous human habitation outside of Mesoamerica, is also its most environmentally diverse region. Roughly including the states of Arizona and New Mexico, extreme southwest Colorado, extreme southern Utah and Nevada, and extreme southeast California, the region contains three major river basins: the Rio Grande, Colorado, and San Juan. It features colorful canyons, mesas, buttes, deserts, bluffs, rock formations, caves, plateaus, forests, and some of the highest mountains in the United States. Although some parts receive regular rainfall, the Southwest as a whole is distinguished by its aridity.

In addition to its great topographical variation, the region contains a striking divergence of climate, soils, and plant and animal life. Consequently, people living there evolved numerous traits to adapt to their specific local environment in order to survive and prosper. In time, different cultures grew out of these local adaptations. Thus, the region's environmental diversity is matched by an extraordinary linguistic and cultural mix.

Paradoxically, Southwest Indian cultures, although very diverse, also share several unifying factors. The most notable is a farming tradition and the use of ceramics; also important is the absence, in general, of state-level societies and large urban centers. Southwest Indians today take particular pride in their tenacity in retaining their land, religion, institutions, languages, and aesthetic traditions in the face of vigorous efforts over the centuries to eradicate indigenous culture, not to mention the people themselves.

The first people in what was to become the southwestern United States arrived between roughly 23,000 and 10,000 B.C.E. In about 9500 B.C.E. people hunted mammoth, giant bison, and other big game species now extinct. By around 5000 B.C.E., human activity had switched to hunting small desert animals and gathering seeds and wild plants. Both baskets and a flat milling stone were in use. Approximately 4,000 years ago, corn and other cultivated crops began coming into the region from Mesoamerica.

The Indians had completed a gradual process of agricultural transformation by roughly 500 C.E.; by that time squash, cotton, and beans had been introduced, and pottery was being produced. Farming had little immediate impact on the Southwest, but it did set in motion dramatic social and economic changes. Many peoples settled in villages, at first living in pit houses and later in buildings made of wood and/or adobe. (The pit houses, called kivas, continued to be used for ceremonial purposes, as they still are today.) As village life developed, people used pits and pottery to store foodstuffs, replaced spears and darts with bows and arrows, and used wells for water storage. With these adaptations, the four major southwestern cultural groups, each heavily influenced by Mesoamerican civilizations, were in place and poised to begin their major phases of development. These groups were the Anasazi, the Mogollon people, the Hohokam people, and the Hakataya.

The Anasazi lived on the sandstone plateaus and in the narrow canyons and broad valleys of the present-day Four Corners region, where northeast Arizona, northwest New Mexico, and extreme southeast Utah and southwest Colorado meet. Since the region contains little water, the Anasazi refined techniques for dry farming. After their absorption of another cultural group, the Mogollon, the Anasazi built the well-known cliff dwellings at Mesa Verde, Chaco Canyon, and other sites. By around 1400, the Anasazi had abandoned most such sites, including the cliff dwellings, in the western part of their range in favor of the well-watered highland regions, Colorado Plateau waterways, and the Rio Grande Valley. Archaeologists have proposed several theories to explain why the Anasazi abandoned these sites. These include environmental factors (the region experienced a severe drought in the twelfth century), over-farming, decentralization, and natural migration patterns. The so-called Pueblo Indians of today are descended from the Anasazi.

On the edge of the Colorado Plateau, among the forested mountains, grasslands, and streams of present-day eastern Arizona to southwest New Mexico, lived the Mogollon people. Between roughly 900 to 1200, the Mimbres culture, part of the Mogollon, produced some of the best pottery north of Mexico. Some Mogollon people practiced irrigation. After about 1000, Mogollon culture underwent rapid changes in housing, arts, tools, and ceremonies, in part influenced by the Anasazi. By the fifteenth century, the dominant Anasazi had completely absorbed the Mogollon culture.

Sedentary farming based on large-scale irrigation distinguished the Hohokam people, who entered present-day southern Arizona around 300 B.C.E. They lived in the low desert west of the continental divide, primarily along the Gila and Salt Rivers. This region has extremely hot, dry summers and mild-to-cool winters with light rains. Only cactus and hardy trees like mesquite can survive in this desert. As early as several centuries B.C.E., the Hohokam had constructed an extensive and efficient system of irrigation canals. Unlike other southwestern societies, Hohokam houses were scattered according to no discernible plan. For much of their existence, the Hohokam built and occupied relatively large villages and towns, such as Snaketown (located in present-day Pinal County, Arizona), which was occupied roughly from 300 B.C.E. to at least 1100 C.E. Well-developed platform mounds and ball courts, used for religious and gaming purposes, suggest social ties to Mesoamerica. Concurrent with other southwestern peoples, the Hohokam underwent a significant population contraction around 1400 and, for undetermined reasons, vanished shortly thereafter. Their descendants are thought to be the present-day Pimas.

Finally, the Hakataya occupied an extensive area on both sides of the lower Colorado River. These deserts are even lower and hotter than those in Hohokam territory, although the region as a whole features extensive temperature variation. The Hakataya lived in small camps or villages of scattered units or in pueblos with small farm plots. Most of their structures were made of rock, in contrast to the Hohokam, who favored dirt. Relatively mobile, the Hakataya were culturally influenced by the Hohokam and other peoples. The Indian tribes that have occupied this territory in historic times, such as the Havasupai and the Mojave, probably descended from the Hakataya.

A fifth major southwestern cultural group, the Southern Athapaskans, arrived in the region from their ancestral home in west-central Canada late in the prehistoric period, probably in the 1400s, as bison-hunting nomads. These people settled in abandoned areas formerly populated by the Anasazi and Mogollon, although they eventually crowded other groups out of hunting and potential farming areas. Both Navajos and Apaches, the main groups of Southern Athapaskans, continued their nomadic occupations until the nineteenth century and later. The Navajos took up sheepherding, whereas the Apaches, having been pushed off the plains during the eighteenth century by the Comanche, became the most feared raiders of the Southwest.

Corn, beans, squash, cotton, and tobacco constituted the most important crops among prehistoric southwestern tribes. People living near rivers also ate fish as a major part of their diets. Cacti, mescal, screwbeans, mesquite, and grasses were important food sources in the south of the region; deer, mountain sheep, and small mammals were more important in the north. Those who produced little food or who had limited regular access to food raided, traded, or received agricultural products as gifts. The Athapaskans dominated hunting in the Southwest, but only the Navajo hunted more than they gathered, and even for them, hunting was less important than farming as a source of food. Since growing food in the Southwest often required the use of many different environmental niches, a certain degree of mobility often accompanied even farming-based economies.

Southwestern tribes exchanged goods on a large scale throughout the historic and prehistoric periods. Food, shell beads, turquoise and other minerals, silver jewelry, buckskins, baskets and blankets, ritual items, and even spouses, ritualists, dancers, and medicine people were exchanged both within the region and with tribes in neighboring regions. Means of exchange included trade, mutual assistance, gambling and gaming, ceremonial redistribution, and raiding and plundering. Interestingly, although tribes did engage in localized raiding, they fought few or no organized wars, at least through the prehistoric period. In short, southwestern Indians devised complex systems of exchange to ensure, without risk to their independence and basic egalitarianism, that each community received approximately what it needed to survive and prosper.

The religious beliefs of southwestern Indians were, and are, rooted in the natural environment, as are the belief systems of other Native Americans. Some regional themes include the idea of a multilayered worldview, or cosmos, and a concept that the balance between natural and supernatural forces may be maintained through a specialist's access to power. According to this view, an intimate relationship exists between the natural and supernatural worlds. Time and space organize the former in such a way that it becomes endowed with supernatural, or sacred, meaning. Thus time may be thought of not only as linear but also spiritual, and place becomes something far more than where a certain "thing" is located.

Southwestern Indians probably developed complex annual ceremonies, with the goal of maintaining and promoting both individual and community health, as far back as 2,000 years ago. Such ceremonies, usually performed or orchestrated by specialists, were, and are, often accompanied by chanting, dancing, and music. A shaman might acquire special powers to communicate with and influence the supernatural by way of visions, dreamtrances, or learning rituals. Such an approach offers a confrontation with the supernatural away from the human realm.

Conversely, sandpaintings and katsina performances, central to the ceremonialism of tribes such as the Navajo and Hopi, are designed to bring the supernatural into the human sphere. Katsinas are beings or spirits that live in or near water and may bring blessings such as rain, crops, and healing. According to tradition, katsinas visit various villages seasonally and inspire dances in their honor. Masks also figure prominently in katsina dancing and in other forms of southwestern Indian ceremonialism. Masking traditions are probably both of indigenous and of European origin. Typical ritual objects among Southwest Indians include feathers, tobacco, and corn pollen or meal.

As mentioned earlier, the fourteenth and fifteenth centuries saw the end of major residential use of large areas of the Southwest and significant population redistribution. New and colorful ceramics were also produced and distributed at this time. However, the following century was no less dramatic. In 1540, Francisco Vasquez de Coronado's northern expedition, seeking fabled golden cities, encountered the Zuñi pueblo of Hawikuh and established the first European presence in what is now the United States. Coronado retreated two years later, and no further Spanish exploration occurred until 1581. However, by the middle of the seventeenth century, the precontact southwestern Indian population of several hundred thousand or more had been reduced by 75 to 80 percent as a result of new diseases introduced by the Spaniards.

New Spain established its first regional colony in the Rio Grande Valley in 1598 and began to demand religious conversion, monetary tribute, and slave labor of the Indians. Such abuses led to revolts, culminating in the Pueblo revolt of 1680, led by Popé, which succeeded in expelling the Spanish from the valley for 12 years. When they returned, the Spanish had learned to moderate their demands somewhat, and the Pueblo Indians had learned to practice their own religion in secret while adopting a form of Catholicism.

Unlike the British colonists of North America, the Spanish did not attempt, at least initially, to settle on Indian lands. Still, the Spanish influence throughout the region was enormous. In addition to Catholicism and a legacy of oppression, the Spaniards introduced a variety of technological innovations into the area, such as domestic animals, wool and textiles, wheat and other crops, metal tools, and firearms. Spanish subjugation of Southwest Indians ended in 1821 with the declaration of the modern state of Mexico. However, Mexico soon found itself in conflict with the new United States over land, a situation that led to war in 1845 and the Mexican cession between 1848 and 1853 of what is now the southwestern United States.

In short order, but especially following the Civil War, the United States began a military campaign to confine all Indians to reservations. By the 1880s it had largely achieved this goal. The more settled tribes, such as the Pueblos, fared the best during this period, retaining at least part of their traditional lands and largely avoiding the starvation, mass deportations, and attendant suffering that were the fate of the more nomadic and defiant tribes such as the Apaches and Navajos. Loss of land and liberty was almost always accompanied by new religious persecution, this time at the hands of Protestant missionaries.

Twentieth-century efforts to force southwestern Indians deeper into the margins of U.S. society have been realized in part. Statehood for the western states and the accompanying pressure to "open up" the reservations cut into the land base of many tribes. Government policies specifically encouraging the destruction of Indian identity, such as forced attendance at boarding schools and the criminalization of some ceremonies, presaged a decline of tribal structures as well as of weaving, ceramic arts, and other traditional crafts. Especially since World War II, subsistence-based economies have come under attack, and such limited wage work as exists, such as mining, is often associated with environmental degradation and its attendant health problems. Poverty and substance abuse remain endemic among Southwest Indians. The federal government remains reluctant to honor its treaty obligations.

On balance, however, Indian identity remains relatively strong in the late-twentieth-century southwestern United States. To a greater degree than Indians in most other regions, Southwest Native Americans have retained strong, secure reservations and pueblos, which provide the basis of a continuing and vital culture. The influx of non-Indians into the region has also aided the economy by bringing a boom in Native American arts and crafts. Mining leases often remain exploitative, yet they are an important source of income for many tribes, and Indians continue to seek more favorable lease terms. After decades of struggle, Indian education is coming more under local control, and the federal government is committed to some form of Indian self-determination. Indian populations are on the rise; the Navajo, at roughly 220,000, are the second-largest and one of the fastest-growing U.S. Indian tribes.

The Indians of the Southwest still grapple with the challenges of living and trying to succeed in an increasingly dominant Anglo/Hispanic culture while retaining their own heritage. Pressures on the youth are particularly acute. However, as they have for generations past, these people still demonstrate a marked ability to adapt, accepting what they will, or must, and rejecting much else. It is this dynamism, along with relatively unbroken access to their traditions and culture, that remains the key to their ongoing survival and growth.

Acoma Pueblo

Acoma (`Ä k ə mä) is from the Acoma and Spanish *Acoma,* or Acú, meaning "the place that always was" or "People of the White Rock." "Pueblo" is from the Spanish for "village." It refers both to a certain style of Southwest Indian architecture, characterized by multistory buildings made of stone and adobe, and to the people themselves. The Rio Grande pueblos are known as eastern Pueblos; Zuñi, Hopi, and sometimes Acoma and Laguna are known as western Pueblos.

LOCATION Acoma is located roughly 60 miles west of Albuquerque, New Mexico. The reservation consists of three main communities: Sky City (Old Acoma), Acomita, and McCartys. The traditional lands of Acoma Pueblo encompassed roughly five million acres. Of this, roughly 10 percent is included in the reservation.

POPULATION The pueblo's population was perhaps 5,000 in 1550. In 1990, 2,548 Indians lived at Acoma Pueblo; the tribal enrollment was roughly 4,000.

LANGUAGE Acoma is a Western Keresan dialect.

Historical Information

HISTORY All Pueblo people are thought to be descended from Anasazi and perhaps Mogollon and several other ancient peoples. From them they learned architecture, farming, pottery, and basketry. Larger population groups became possible with effec-

tive agriculture and the development of ways to store food surpluses. Within the context of a relatively stable existence, the people devoted increasing amounts of time and attention to religion, arts, and crafts.

In the 1200s, the Anasazi abandoned their traditional canyon homelands in response to climatic and social upheavals. A century or two of migrations ensued, followed in general by the slow reemergence of their culture in the historic pueblos. Acoma Pueblo was established at least 800 years ago.

Acoma Pueblo was first visited by non-Indians in 1539, probably by Estevan, an advance scout of the Coronado expedition. The following year the people welcomed Hernando de Alvarado, also a member of Coronado's group. In 1598, Juan de Oñate arrived in the area with settlers, founding the colony of New Mexico. However, that year Acomas killed some of his representatives, for which they faced a Spanish reprisal in 1599: The Spanish killed 800 people, tortured and enslaved others, and destroyed the pueblo. The survivors rebuilt shortly thereafter and began a process of consolidating several farming sites near Acoma, which were later recognized by the Spanish as two villages.

Oñate carried on the process, already underway, of subjugating the local Indians; forcing them to pay taxes in crops, cotton, and work; and opening the door for Catholic missionaries to attack the Indians' religion. The Spanish renamed the pueblos with saints' names and began a program of church construction. At the same time, they introduced such new crops as peaches, wheat, and peppers into the region. In 1620, a royal decree created civil offices at each pueblo; silver-headed canes, many of which remain in use today, symbolized the governor's authority. In 1629, the Franciscan Juan Ramirez founded a mission at Acoma and built a huge church there.

The Pueblo Indians organized and instituted a general revolt against the Spanish in 1680. For years, the Spaniards had routinely tortured Indians for practicing traditional religion. They also forced the Indians to labor for them, sold Indians into slavery, and let their cattle overgraze Indian land, a situation that eventually led to drought, erosion, and famine. Popé of San Juan Pueblo and other Pueblo religious leaders planned the revolt, sending runners carrying cords of maguey fibers to mark the day of rebellion. On August 10, 1680, a virtually united stand on the part of the Pueblos drove the Spanish from the region. The Indians killed many Spaniards but refrained from mass slaughter, allowing them to leave Santa Fe for El Paso.

The Pueblos experienced many changes during the following decades: Refugees established communities at Hopi, guerrilla fighting continued against the Spanish, and certain areas were abandoned. By the 1700s, excluding Hopi and Zuñi, only Taos, Picuris, Isleta, and Acoma Pueblos had not changed locations since the arrival of the Spanish. Although Pueblo unity did not last, and Santa Fe was officially reconquered in 1692, Spanish rule was notably less severe from then on. Harsh forced labor all but ceased, and the Indians reached an understanding with the Church that enabled them to continue practicing their traditional religion. Acoma resisted further Spanish contact for several years thereafter, then bowed to Spanish power and accepted a mission.

In general, the Pueblo eighteenth century was marked by smallpox epidemics and increased raiding by the Apache, Comanche, and Ute. Occasionally Pueblo Indians fought with the Spanish against the nomadic tribes. The people practiced their religion, more or less in secret. During this time, intermarriage and regular exchange between Hispanic villages and Pueblo Indians created a new New Mexican culture, neither strictly Spanish nor Indian, but rather somewhat of a blend between the two.

Mexican "rule" in 1821 brought little immediate change to the Pueblos. The Mexicans stepped up what had been a gradual process of appropriating Indian land and water, and they allowed the nomadic tribes even greater latitude to raid. As the presence of the United States in the area grew, it attempted to enable the Pueblo Indians to continue their generally peaceful and self-sufficient ways and recognized Spanish land grants to the Pueblos. Land disputes with neighboring Laguna Pueblo were not settled so easily, however.

During the nineteenth century, the process of acculturation among Pueblo Indians quickened markedly. In an attempt to retain their identity, Pueblo Indians clung even more tenaciously to their heritage, which by now included elements of the once-hated Spanish culture and religion. By the 1880s, railroads had largely put an end to the traditional geographical isolation of the pueblos. Paradoxically, the U.S. decision to recognize Spanish land grants to the Pueblos denied Pueblo Indians certain rights granted under official treaties and left them particularly open to exploitation by squatters and thieves.

After a gap of more than 300 years, the All Indian Pueblo Council began to meet again in the 1920s, specifically in response to a congressional threat to appropriate Pueblo lands. Partly as a result of the Council's activities, Congress confirmed Pueblo title to their lands in 1924 by passing the Pueblo Lands Act. The United States also acknowledged its trust responsibilities in a series of legal decisions and other acts of Congress. Still, especially after 1900, Pueblo culture was increasingly threatened by highly intolerant Protestant evangelical missions and schools. The Bureau of Indian Affairs also weighed in on the subject of acculturation, forcing Indian children to leave their homes and attend culture-killing boarding schools. In 1922, most Acoma children had been sent away to such schools.

Following World War II, the issue of water rights took center stage at most pueblos. Also, the All Indian Pueblo Council succeeded in slowing the threat against Pueblo lands as well as religious persecution. Making crafts for the tourist trade became an important economic activity during this period. Since the late nineteenth century, but especially after the 1960s, Pueblos have had to cope with onslaughts by (mostly white) anthropologists and seekers of Indian spirituality. The region is also known for its major art colonies at Taos and Santa Fe.

RELIGION In traditional Pueblo culture, religion and life are inseparable. To be in harmony with all of nature is the Pueblo ideal and way of life. The sun is seen as the representative of the Creator. Sacred mountains in each direction, plus the sun above and the earth below, define and balance the Pueblo world. Many Pueblo religious ceremonies revolve around the weather and are devoted to ensuring adequate rainfall. To this end, Pueblo Indians evoke the power of katsinas, sacred beings who live in mountains and other holy places, in ritual and dance. Each pueblo contains one or more kivas, religious chambers that symbolize the place of original emergence into this world.

In addition to the natural boundaries, Pueblo Indians created a society that defined their world by providing balanced, reciprocal relationships within which people connect and harmonize with each other, the natural world, and time itself. According to tradition, the head of each pueblo is the religious leader, or *cacique*, whose primary responsibility it is to watch the sun and thereby determine the dates of ceremonies. Especially in the eastern pueblos, most ceremonies are kept secret.

GOVERNMENT Pueblo governments derived from two traditions. Elements that are probably indigenous include the cacique, or head of the Pueblo, and the war captain, both chosen for life. These officials were intimately related to the religious structures of the pueblo and reflected the essentially theocratic nature of Pueblo government. A parallel but in most cases distinctly less powerful group of officials was imposed by the Spanish authorities. They generally dealt with external matters and included a governor, two lieutenant governors, and a council. In addition, the All Indian Pueblo Council, dating from 1598, began meeting again in the twentieth century.

CUSTOMS One mechanism that works to keep Pueblo societies coherent is a pervasive aversion to individualistic behavior. Children were traditionally raised with gentle guidance and a minimum of discipline. Pueblo Indians were generally monogamous, and divorce is relatively rare. The dead were prepared ceremonially and quickly buried. A vigil of four days and nights was generally observed. Acoma Pueblo recognized roughly 20 matrilineal clans. The economy was basically a socialistic one, whereby labor was shared and produce was distributed equally. In modern times photography by outsiders is discouraged. At Acoma, a formal, traditional education system under the direction of the kiva headmen includes courses on human behavior, human spirit, human body, ethics, astrology, child psychology, oratory, history, music, and dance.

DWELLINGS Acoma Pueblo featured three rows of three-story, apartment-style dwellings, facing south on top of a 350-foot-high mesa. The lower levels were reserved mainly for storage. The buildings were constructed of adobe (earth and straw) bricks, with beams across the roof that were covered with poles, brush, and plaster. The roof of one level served as the floor of another. The levels were interconnected by ladders. As an aid to defense, the traditional design included no doors or windows; entry was through the roof. Baking ovens stood outside the buildings. Water was primarily obtained from two natural cisterns. Acoma also features seven rectangular pit houses, or kivas, for ceremonial chambers and clubhouses. The village plaza is the spiritual center of the village, where all the balanced forces of the world come together.

DIET Before the Spanish arrived, people living at Acoma Pueblo ate primarily corn, beans, and squash. *Mut-tze-nee* was a favorite thin corn bread. They also grew sunflowers and tobacco and kept turkeys. They hunted deer, antelope, and rabbits and gathered a variety of wild seeds, nuts, berries, and other foods. Favorite foods as of circa 1700 included a blue corn drink, corn mush, pudding, wheat cake, corn balls, paper bread, peach-bark drink, flour bread, wild berries, and prickly pear fruit. The Acomas also raised herds of sheep, goats, horses, and donkeys after the Spanish introduced these animals into the region.

KEY TECHNOLOGY Irrigation techniques included dams and terraces. Pottery was an important technological adaptation, as was weaving baskets and cotton and tanning leather. Farming implements were made of stone and wood. Corn was ground using manos and metates.

TRADE All Pueblos were part of extensive Native American trading networks that reached for a thousand miles in every direction. With the arrival of other cultures, Pueblo Indians also traded with the Hispanic American villages and then U.S. traders. At fixed times during summer or fall, enemies declared truces so that trading fairs might be held. The largest and best known was at Taos with the Comanche. Nomads exchanged slaves, buffalo hides, buckskins, jerked meat, and horses for agricultural and manufactured pueblo products. Pueblo Indians traded for shell and copper ornaments, turquoise, and macaw feathers. Trade along the Santa Fe Trail began in 1821. By the 1880s and the arrival of railroads, the Pueblos were dependent on many American-made goods, and the Native American manufacture of weaving and pottery declined and nearly died out.

NOTABLE ARTS In the Pueblo way, art and life are inseparable. Acoma women produced excellent pottery; men made fine weavings as well as silver necklaces. Songs, dances, and dramas also qualify as traditional arts. Many Pueblos experienced a renaissance of traditional arts in the twentieth century, beginning in 1919 with San Ildefonso pottery.

TRANSPORTATION Spanish horses, mules, and cattle arrived at Acoma Pueblo in the seventeenth century.

DRESS Men wore cotton kilts and leather sandals. Women wore cotton dresses and sandals or high moccasin boots. Deer and rabbit skin were also used for clothing and robes.

WAR AND WEAPONS Though often depicted as passive and docile, most Pueblo groups regularly engaged in warfare. Weapons included clubs, darts, spears, and stones. The great revolt of 1680 stands out as the major military action, but they also skirmished at other times with the Spanish and defended themselves against attackers such as Apaches, Comanches, and Utes. They also contributed auxiliary soldiers to provincial forces under Spain and Mexico, which were used mainly against raiding Indians and to protect merchant caravans on the Santa Fe Trail. After the raiding tribes began to pose less of a threat in the late nineteenth century, Pueblo military societies began to wither away, with the office of war captain changing to civil and religious functions.

Contemporary Information

GOVERNMENT/RESERVATIONS Acoma Pueblo, located on the aboriginal site in central New Mexico, has been continuously occupied for at least 800 years. The pueblo consists of roughly 500,000 acres of mesas, valleys, arroyos, and hills, with an average altitude of about 7,000 feet and roughly 10 inches of rain per year. Several major land purchases have added considerably to the land base since 1977. Only tribal members may own property; almost all enrolled members live on the pueblo. Acoma has been a member of the All Indian Pueblo Council since 1680. The *cacique* (a theological appointment, from the Antelope clan) appoints tribal council members, the governor, and his staff.

ECONOMY Acomas grow alfalfa, oats, wheat, corn, chilies, melon, squash, vegetables, and some fruits. They also raise cattle. Acoma has coal, geothermal, and natural gas resources. Nearby uranium mines served as major employers until the 1980s. Since then, the tribe has provided most jobs. Tribal income is generated through fees charged tourists to enter Sky City (Old Acoma) as well as the associated visitor's center, and the tribe has plans to develop the tourist trade further. Arts and crafts (pottery, silverwork, leatherwork, and beadwork) also generate some individual income.

LEGAL STATUS The Pueblo of Acoma is a federally recognized tribal entity.

DAILY LIFE Although the project of retaining a strong Indian identity is a difficult one in the late twentieth century, Pueblo people have strong roots, and in many ways the ancient rhythms and patterns continue. Many Pueblo Indians, though nominally Catholic, have fused pieces of Catholicism onto a core of traditional beliefs. Since the 1970s control of schools has been a key in maintaining their culture. Health problems, including alcoholism and drug use, continue to plague the Pueblos. Indian Health Service hospitals often cooperate with native healers.

At Acoma, many of the old ceremonies are still performed; the religion and language are largely intact, and there is a palpable and intentional continuity with the past. Nineteen clans remain, each organized by social function. Almost all people speak Acoma and English; many older people speak Spanish as well. Many people live in traditional adobe houses, with outside ovens, but increasingly one finds cement-block ranch and frame houses with exterior stucco. Most people live below the mesa, in the villages of Acomita or McCartys.

Acoma remains a relatively closed society, like other Keresan pueblos, especially as regards religious matters. Acoma shares a junior/senior high school and a full-service hospital with neighboring Laguna Pueblo. Since the uranium mines closed, Acoma has suffered high unemployment rates. The mines have also left a legacy of radiation pollution, resulting in some health problems and the draining of the tribal fishing lake.

Apache, Chiricahua

Chiricahua (Ch ē r ə `kä wä), a name taken from their stronghold in the Chiricahua Mountains, in southeast Arizona, and Apache (U `pa ch ē), from the Zuñi word *Apachu,* meaning "enemy." The Apache call themselves *Ndee,* or *Dine'é* (Di `n ə), "the People."

LOCATION The Apache arrived in the Southwest from present-day Canada around 1400. By the early 1600s, the Chiricahua were living in southwestern New Mexico, southeastern Arizona, and northern Mexico. Late-twentieth-century Chiricahua communities include the Mescalero Apache Reservation in southeastern New Mexico and a presence at Fort Sill, Oklahoma.

POPULATION Approximately 3,000 Chiricahua Apache lived in their region in the early seventeenth century. Of roughly 25,000 Apaches nationwide in 1992, some 3,500, including Chiricahua, Mescalero, and Lipan Apache, lived on the Mescalero Reservation. Several hundred lived off-reservation. A small number of Chiricahua Apaches still live in Oklahoma.

LANGUAGE Apaches speak Southern Athapaskan, or Apachean.

Historical Information

HISTORY Ancestors of today's Apache Indians began the trek from Asia to North America relatively late, in roughly 1000 B.C.E. Most of this group, which included the Athapaskans, was known as the Nadene. By 1300, the group that was to become the Southern Athapaskans (Apaches and Navajos) broke away from other Athapaskan tribes and began migrating southward, reaching the American Southwest around 1400 and crystallizing into separate cultural groups.

The Apaches generally filtered into the mountains surrounding the Pueblo-held valleys. This process ended in the 1600s and 1700s, with a final push southward and westward by the Comanches. Before contact with the Spanish, the Apaches were relatively peaceful and may have engaged in some agricultural activities.

Thrust into contact with the Spanish, the Apaches, having acquired horses, began raiding Spanish and Pueblo settlements. This dynamic included trading as well as raiding and warfare, but the Spanish habit of selling captured Apaches into slavery led to Apache revenge and increasingly hostile conditions along the Spanish frontier. After 1821, the Mexicans put a bounty on Apache scalps, increasing Apache enmity and adding to the cycle of violence in the region.

Following the war between Mexico and the United States (1848), the Apaches, who did their part to bring misery to Mexico, assumed that the Americans would continue to be their allies. They were shocked and disgusted to learn that their lands were now considered part of the United States and that the Americans planned to "pacify" them. Having been squeezed by the Spanish, the Comanches, the Mexicans, and now miners, farmers, and other land-grabbers from the United States, the Apache were more than ever determined to protect their way of life.

Some Chiricahua bands tried to stay out of trouble in the 1850s by planting fields under the supervision of federal agents, but when raiding resumed as a result of broken promises of food and protection, all sides were caught in a spiral of violence. Mangas Coloradas, a peaceful Mimbreño chief, turned to war after he was bullwhipped by U.S. miners in 1860. Cochise, son-in-law of Mangas Coloradas and leader of the Central Band of Chiricahua, began a guerrilla war along the Butterfield Trail after whites killed some of his men. Cochise began as Central Band war chief, but by force of personality and integrity he eventually claimed authority over other Chiricahua bands as well. Resistance continued until 1874, when Cochise, hungry and exhausted, surrendered. He could no longer control other Chiricahua bands, though, and their raiding continued.

Meanwhile, the U.S. policy of concentration via forced marches resulted in thousands of Chiricahua and Western Apaches living on the crowded and disease-ridden San Carlos Reservation. There, a handful of dissident chiefs, confined in chains, held out for the old life of freedom and self-respect. Victorio fled in 1877, taking 350 Indians with him. He battled the army and Apache scouts until he was killed in Mexico in 1880. Nana, his successor, continued the raids until joining the Mescalero Reservation.

When soldiers killed a White Mountain Apache medicine man in 1881, Geronimo, a Southern Band shaman, led a group of Chiricahua away from San Carlos. In 1883 he agreed to return peacefully, but two years later, when soldiers banned the Indians' ceremonial drink, called "tiswin," the Chiricahua fled again. In 1886 Geronimo surrendered in Mexico but on the way back to the United States escaped with 36 other Apaches. Their final surrender, and the effective end of Apache military resistance, came several months later: General Nelson Miles and one-quarter of the U.S. Army, plus Apache scouts, were needed to find and capture them. Geronimo regretted his surrender until his death as a prisoner of war in 1909.

As punishment for the freedom-fighting activities of some of their group, the U.S. government sent all the Chiricahuas, including those who had been living peacefully at San Carlos, to prison in Alabama and Florida, where roughly one-quarter of them died over the following few years. Since the citizens of New Mexico opposed the return of the Apaches to San Carlos, those Chiricahuas who remained alive were sent in 1894 to the Kiowa Reservation at Fort Sill,

Oklahoma, where they took up cattle raising and farming. In 1913, the Chiricahua were granted full freedom, although no reservation. Although some remained at Fort Sill, most moved back to New Mexico and life on the Mescalero Reservation.

Cattle raising and timber sales proved lucrative in the early twentieth century. Eventually, day schools replaced the hated, culture-killing boarding schools. By the late 1940s, every family had a house, and the economy at Mescalero was relatively strong. The reservation is managed cooperatively with the Mescalero and the Lipan Apache.

RELIGION Apache religion is based on a complex mythology and features numerous deities. The sun is the greatest source of power. Culture heroes, like White-Painted Woman and her son, Child of the Water, also figure highly, as do protective mountain spirits *(ga'an)*. The latter are represented as masked dancers (probably evidence of Pueblo influence) in certain ceremonies, such as the four-day girls' puberty rite. (The boys' puberty rite centered on raiding and warfare.)

Supernatural power is both the goal and the medium of most Apache ceremonialism. Shamans facilitate the acquisition of power, which could be used in the service of war, luck, rainmaking, or life-cycle events. Power could be evil as well as good, however, and witchcraft, as well as incest, was an unpardonable offense. Finally, Apaches believe that since other living things were once people, we are merely following in the footsteps of those who have gone before.

GOVERNMENT Traditionally, the Chiricahua knew little tribal cohesion and no central political authority. They were a tribe based on common territory, language, and culture. As much central authority as existed was found in the local group (35 to 200 people), composed of extended families. Its leader, or chief, enjoyed authority because of personal qualities, such as persuasiveness and bravery, often in addition to ceremonial knowledge. (All the famous Apache "chiefs" were local group leaders.) Decisions were taken by consensus. One of the chief's most important functions was to minimize friction among his people.

Local groups joined to form three Chiricahua bands. One was the Eastern, or Cihene (Red Paint People), also known as Mimbreños, Coppermine, Warm Spring, or Mogollon Apaches; the second was the Central (Chokonen). The third band was the Southern (Nednai, Enemy People, also called Pinery or Bronco Apaches), who lived mainly in Mexico. Some intermarriage occurred between bands.

CUSTOMS Women were the anchors of the Apache family. Residence was matrilocal. Besides the political organization, society was divided into a number of matrilineal clans. Apaches in general respected the elderly and valued honesty above other qualities.

Gender roles were clearly defined but not rigidly enforced. Women gathered, prepared, and stored food; built the home; carried water; gathered fuel; cared for the children; tanned, dyed, and decorated hides; and wove baskets. Men hunted, raided, and waged war. They also made weapons and were responsible for their horses and equipment. They also made musical instruments.

Girls as well as boys practiced with the bow and arrow, sling, and spear, and both learned to ride expertly. Although actual marriage ceremonies were brief or nonexistent, the people practiced a number of formal preliminary rituals, designed to strengthen the idea that a man owed deep allegiance to his future wife's family. Out of deference, married men were not permitted to speak directly with their mothers-in-law. Divorce was relatively easy to obtain.

All Apaches had a great fear of ghosts. Chiricahua who died had their faces painted red and were buried the same day. Their personal possessions were burned or destroyed, including their house and favorite horse.

DWELLINGS Chiricahua Apaches lived in dome-shaped brush wikiups, which they covered with hides in bad weather. The doors always faced east. Eastern Chiricahua sometimes used tipis.

DIET Chiricahua Apaches were primarily hunters and gatherers. They hunted buffalo prior to the sixteenth century, and afterward they continued to hunt deer, elk, antelope, rabbits, and other game. They did not eat bear, turkey, or fish.

Wild foods included agave; cactus shoots, flowers, and fruit; berries; seeds; nuts; honey; and wild onions, potatoes, and grasses. Nuts and seeds were often ground into flour. The agave or century plant was particularly important. Baking its base in rock-lined pits for several days yielded mescal, a sweet, nutritious food, which was dried and stored.

Traditional farm crops were obtained from the Pueblos by trade or raid. The Chiricahua, particularly the Eastern Band, also practiced some agriculture: Corn, for instance, was used to make tiswin, a weak beer.

KEY TECHNOLOGY Items included baskets (pitch-covered water jars, cradles, storage containers, and burden baskets); gourd spoons, dippers, and dishes; and a sinew-backed bow. The people made musical instruments out of gourds and hooves. The so-called Apache fiddle, a postcontact instrument, was played with a bow on strings. Moccasins were sewn with plant fiber attached to mescal thorns.

TRADE Trading partners included Pueblo and Hispanic villages, as well as some Plains tribes, especially before the sixteenth century.

NOTABLE ARTS Traditional arts included fine basketry, pottery, and tanned hides.

TRANSPORTATION The horse was introduced into the region in the seventeenth century.

DRESS The Chiricahua traditionally wore buckskin clothing and moccasins. As they acquired cotton and later wool through trading and raiding, women tended to wear two-piece calico dresses, with long, full skirts and long blouses outside the skirt belts. They occasionally carried knives and, later, ammunition belts. Girls wore their hair over their ears, shaped around two willow hoops. Some older women wore their hair Plains-style, parted in the middle with two braids. Men's postcontact styles included calico shirts, muslin breechclouts with belts, cartridge belts, moccasins, and headbands.

WAR AND WEAPONS Historically, the Apache made formidable enemies. Raiding was one of their most important activities. The main purpose of raiding in which one sought to avoid contact with the enemy, was to gain wealth and honor. It differed fundamentally from warfare, which was undertaken primarily for revenge. Chiricahua Apaches did not generally take scalps, not did they maintain formal warrior societies.

Contemporary Information

GOVERNMENT/RESERVATIONS Most Chiricahua Apaches live on the Mescalero Reservation, in southeast New Mexico. The reservation contains roughly 460,000 acres of land and is home in addition to the Mescalero and Lipan Apaches. The 1992 population was 3,511. Residents gained title to the land in 1922. After 1934, the tribal business committee began functioning as a tribal council. In 1964, a new constitution defined the Mescalero tribe without reference to the original band.

Roughly 100 (as of 1992) Chiricahua Apaches still live at Fort Sill, Oklahoma. They are represented by an elected seven-member business committee formed under the auspices of the Indian Reorganization Act (IRA).

ECONOMY Important industries include logging, cattle raising, and the Inn of the Mountain Gods.

LEGAL STATUS Federally recognized tribal entities include the Mescalero Apache Tribe; the Apache Tribe of Oklahoma; and the Fort Sill Apache Tribe of Oklahoma.

DAILY LIFE Intermarriage between Mescalero and Lipan Apaches has tended to blur the distinction between the once-separate tribes on the Mescalero reservation. Up to three-quarters of the people still speak Apache, although the dialect is more Mescalero than Chiricahua or Lipan. The written Apache language is also taught in reservation schools. Some young women still undergo the traditional puberty ritual, and there is a marked interest in crafts and other traditions. The reservation confronts relatively few social problems, despite its high un- and underemployment. Traditional dancing by costumed mountain spirits now coincides with the July Fourth celebration and rodeo. Fort Sill Apaches participate in pan-Indian activities.

Wendall Chino has been the most important leader of the Mescalero tribe since the 1950s. He is mainly known for diversifying the tribal economy, particularly with a ski slope and a resort. In an extremely controversial 1991 decision, he agreed to study the possibility of accepting high-level nuclear waste on the reservation.

Apache, Cibecue
See Apache, Western

Apache, Fort Sill
See Apache, Chiricahua

Apache, Jicarilla
Jicarilla (H ē kä ˋr ē ä) is from the Spanish for "little basket," or "chocolate basket," and Apache is from the Zuñi word *Apachu,* meaning "enemy." The Apache call themselves *Ndee,* or *Dine'é* (Di ˋn ə), "the People."

LOCATION The Apache arrived in the Southwest from present-day Canada around 1400. By the early 1600s, the Jicarilla were living from the Chama Valley in present-day New Mexico east to present-day western Oklahoma. The Jicarilla Reservation is located in northwest New Mexico, west of the Chama Valley.

POPULATION Approximately 800 Jicarilla Apaches lived in their region in the early seventeenth century. Of roughly 25,000 Apaches nationwide, roughly 3,000 Jicarilla lived on their reservation in 1992.

LANGUAGE Jicarillas spoke a dialect of Southern Athapaskan, or Apachean.

Historical Information
HISTORY Ancestors of today's Apache Indians began the trek from Asia to North America in roughly 1000 B.C.E. Most of this group, which included the Athapaskans, was known as the Nadene. By 1300, the group that was to become the Southern Athapaskans (Apaches and Navajos) broke away from other Athapaskan tribes and began migrating southward, reaching the American Southwest around 1400 and crystallizing into separate cultural groups. Before contact with the Spanish, the Apaches were relatively peaceful and may have engaged in some agricultural activities.

In the mid–eighteenth century, the Apache asked for Spanish protection against the Comanche, who were pressing them from the north and east. Despite a promise to settle down and become Christian, the Spanish refused the request. The Comanche, who had acquired guns from the French (the Spanish did not officially sell or trade guns to Indians), so disrupted Apache agriculture and life on the plains that the Apache migrated into the mountains surrounding the Pueblo-held valleys. One Jicarilla group continued to live as far south as the Texas plains until around 1800.

Having acquired horses, the Apache increased their contact with Spanish and Pueblo settlements. This dynamic included trading as well as raiding and warfare, but the Spanish habit of selling captured Apaches into slavery led to Apache revenge and increasingly hostile conditions along the Spanish frontier, effectively establishing the northern limit of New Spain at about Santa Fe. After 1821, the Mexicans put a bounty on Apache scalps, increasing Apache enmity and adding to the cycle of violence in the region.

In an effort to settle its northern areas, Mexico in the early nineteenth century made large land grants to its citizens. In 1841, one such grant delivered 1.7 million acres of Jicarilla land to two Mexicans. U.S. recognition of this grant was to complicate the establishment of a Jicarilla reservation later in the century.

Following the war between Mexico and the United States (1848), the Apaches, who did their part to bring misery to Mexico, assumed that the Americans would continue as allies. They were shocked and disgusted to learn that their lands were now considered part of the United States and that the Americans planned to "pacify" them. Having been squeezed by the Spanish, the Comanches, the Mexicans, and now miners, farmers, and other land-grabbers from the United States, the Apache were more than ever determined to protect their way of life.

Increased military activity led to a treaty in 1851 that called for the cessation of hostilities on all sides and, in exchange for aid, bound the Jicarilla to remain at least 50 miles from all settlements. When U.S. promises of food and protection went unkept, however, the Jicarilla returned to raiding, and the region was plunged into a spiral of violence. Another treaty in 1855 created agencies: Options for the Jicarilla now included either begging for food at the agency or raiding.

In the 1860s, the tribe escaped confinement at the deadly Bosque Redondo (Fort Sumner) only because the camp failed before they could be rounded up. By 1873 they were the only southwestern tribe without an official reservation. At about this time, leaders of the two Jicarilla bands, the Ollero and the Llanero, began consulting with each other, creating a new tribal consciousness. They sent a joint delegation to Washington, D.C., where they lobbied for a reservation, but in 1883 the tribe was moved to the Mescalero Reservation. Finding all the good land already taken, the Jicarilla began shortly to drift back north to their old lands. In 1887, the government granted them an official home.

Unfortunately, the climate on the new reservation was unfavorable for farming, and in any case non-Indians owned whatever good arable land existed. This, plus the existence of individual allotments and centralized government control, slowed economic progress. The tribe sold some timber around the turn of the century. In 1903, the government established a boarding school in Dulce, the reservation capital, but turned it into a sanatorium in 1918 following a tuberculosis epidemic (90 percent of the Jicarilla had tuberculosis by 1914). The Dutch Reformed Church of America opened a school in 1921.

A major addition to the reservation in 1907 provided the Jicarilla with land appropriate to herding sheep. They began this activity in the 1920s, and the tribe soon realized a profit. Livestock owners and the "progressive," proacculturation group tended to be Ollero, whereas the Llaneros were the farmers, the conservatives, and guardians of tradition. In the early 1930s bad weather wiped out most of the sheep herd, although by 1940 it had largely been rebuilt. Also by this time the people were generally healthy again, and acculturation quickened.

The postwar years saw a huge increase in tribal income from oil and gas development. With part of this money the tribe bought out most non-Indian holdings on the reservation. Education levels, health, and morale all rose. In the 1950s, a decline in the sheep industry brought much of the population to live in Dulce. The tribe began per capita payments at that time, partly to offset a lack of economic opportunities in Dulce. This action kept families going until more help arrived with the federal programs of the 1960s as well as an increasingly diversified economy. In the 1970s the tribe won $9 million in land claims.

RELIGION   Apache religion is based on a complex mythology and features numerous deities. Most deities are seen as personifications of natural forces. The sun is the greatest source of power. Culture heroes, like White-Painted Woman and her son, Child of the Water, also figure highly, as do protective mountain spirits (ga'an). The latter are represented as masked dancers (probably a sign of Pueblo influence) in certain ceremonies, such as the girls' puberty rite. Apaches believe that since other living things were once people, we are merely following in the footsteps of those who have gone before.

Supernatural power is both the goal and the medium of most Apache ceremonialism. They recognize two categories of rites: personal/shamanistic and long-life. In the former, power is derived from an animal, a celestial body, or another natural phenomenon. When power appears to a person and is accepted, rigorous training as a shaman follows. Shamans also facilitate the acquisition of power, which may be used in the service of war, luck, rainmaking, or life-cycle events. Power may be evil as well as good, however, and sickness and misfortune could be caused by the anger of a deity or by not treating properly a natural force. Witchcraft, as well as incest, was an unpardonable offense.

Long-life rites were taught by elders and connected to mythology. The most difficult was the bear dance, a curing rite that lasts for four days and nights and features a bear impersonator, shamans, songs, sacred clowns, and dancing. Another such ceremony is the (young boys') relay race, actually a combined ceremony and harvest festival. It derives from mythological concepts of sun and moon and also the duality of the food supply. The race is between the Olleros—sun—animals and the Llaneros—moon—plants. Other important ceremonies include the four-day girls' puberty ceremony, a five-day holiness or curing ceremony, and hunting, cultivation, and rainmaking ceremonies.

GOVERNMENT   Traditionally, the Jicarilla knew little tribal cohesion and no central political authority. They were a tribe based on common territory, language, and culture. As much central authority as existed was found in the local group, composed of extended families. Local groups were loosely associated as bands, which made up the tribe. Local group leaders, or chiefs, enjoyed authority because of personal qualities, such as persuasiveness and bravery, often in addition to ceremonial knowledge. Decisions were taken by consensus. One of the chief's most important functions was to mitigate friction among his people.

Beginning around the nineteenth century, the Jicarilla recognized two distinct bands. The Llanero lived in the eastern Sangre de Cristo Mountains in adobe houses with nearby farms. From the pueblos, especially Taos, they learned pottery and social and religious customs. The Ollero gave up plains life somewhat later. In addition to hunting buffalo, they had picked up some Plains technology, such as tipis, parfleches, and travois.

CUSTOMS   Women were the anchors of the

Apache family. Residence was matrilocal. Besides the political organization, society was divided into a number of matrilineal clans. Apaches in general respected the elderly and valued honesty above most other qualities. The Jicarilla more than most Apaches were influenced by the Plains and Pueblo tribes.

Gender roles were clearly defined but not rigidly enforced. Women gathered, prepared, and stored food; built the home; carried water; gathered fuel; cared for the children; tanned, dyed, and decorated hides; and wove baskets. Men hunted, raided, and waged war. They also made weapons, were responsible for their horses and equipment, and made musical instruments. For boys, training for the hunt began early; the first hunt was roughly equal to a puberty ceremony.

Girls as well as boys practiced with the bow and arrow, sling, and spear, and both learned to ride expertly. Although actual marriage ceremonies were brief or nonexistent, the people practiced a number of formal preliminary rituals, designed to strengthen the idea that a man owed deep allegiance to his future wife's family. Out of deference, married men were not permitted to speak directly with their mothers-in-law. Divorce was unusual though relatively easy to obtain. The mother's brother played an important role in the raising of his nephews and nieces.

All Apaches had a great fear of ghosts. Jicarilla who died were buried the same day. Their personal possessions were burned or destroyed, including their house and favorite horse. They pictured the afterworld as divided into two sections, a pleasant land for good people and a barren one for witches.

DWELLINGS Jicarilla Apaches lived in dome-shaped, pole-framed wikiups, covered with bark or thatch and with skins in cold weather. They also used hide tipis when on a buffalo hunt.

DIET Jicarilla Apaches were primarily hunters and gatherers. They hunted buffalo into the seventeenth century, and afterward they continued to hunt deer, mountain sheep, elk, antelope, rabbits, and other game. They did not eat bear, turkey, or fish.

Wild foods included agave shoots, flowers, and fruit; berries; seeds; nuts; honey; and wild onions, potatoes, and grasses. Nuts and seeds were often ground into flour. The agave or century plant was particularly important. Baking its base in rock-lined pits for several days yielded mescal, a sweet, nutritious food, which was dried and stored.

In the late 1600s they learned farming from pueblos, and by the early nineteenth century they farmed river bottomlands and built irrigation ditches, growing some corn, beans, squash, pumpkins, peas, wheat, and melons. When supplies ran low, crops were obtained from the Pueblos by trade or raid.

KEY TECHNOLOGY Items included baskets (pitch-covered water jars, cradles, storage containers, and burden baskets); gourd spoons, dippers, and dishes; and a sinew-backed bow. The people made musical instruments out of gourds and hooves. The so-called Apache fiddle, a postcontact instrument, was played with a bow on strings. Moccasins were sewn with plant fiber attached to mescal thorns. The Jicarilla used a sinew-backed bow, which was more effective than the Pueblo wooden bow.

TRADE Trading partners included Pueblo and Hispanic villages, as well as some Plains tribes, especially before the seventeenth century.

NOTABLE ARTS Traditional arts included fine basketry, pottery, and tanned hides. The Jicarilla also excelled in beadwork, buckskin tanning, leather work, pottery, and making ceremonial clay pipes.

TRANSPORTATION The horse was introduced into the region in the seventeenth century.

DRESS The Jicarilla traditionally wore buckskin clothing decorated with beadwork and whitened, Plains-style moccasins. As they acquired cotton and later wool through trading and raiding, women tended to wear two-piece calico dresses, with long, full skirts and long blouses outside the skirt belts. They occasionally carried knives and ammunition belts. Girls wore their hair over their ears, shaped around two willow hoops. Some older women wore hair Plains-style, parted in the middle with two braids. Male hairstyles included a middle part, braids, and bangs with a back knot, Pueblo-style. Men also liked large earrings.

WAR AND WEAPONS Historically, the Apache made formidable enemies. Raiding was one of their most important activities. The main purpose of raiding, in which one sought to avoid contact with the enemy, was to gain wealth, such as horses, and honor. It differed fundamentally from warfare, which was undertaken primarily for revenge. Jicarilla war leaders occasionally took scalps but only after the leaders had been ritually purified. Formal warrior societies did not exist. Like hunting, raiding and warfare were accompanied by complex rituals and rules, to which boys were introduced early. The Jicarillas' traditional enemies included the Comanche, Cheyenne, Arapaho, and Navajo; allies included the Utes and Pueblo peoples.

Contemporary Information

GOVERNMENT/RESERVATIONS The Jicarilla Reservation, established in 1887, is located in northwest New Mexico, west of Chama. It contains about 742,000 acres of land. The 1992 population was 3,100. The reservation headquarters is in Dulce. The tribe organized a formal government and adopted a constitution in 1937. Its first elected tribal council consisted mostly of traditional leaders.

ECONOMY   Oil and gas resources, which the tribe is moving to buy, still provide much income. Other important economic assets include sheep, timber, and big game. The tribe and the government provide some employment opportunities.

LEGAL STATUS   The Jicarilla Apache are a federally recognized tribal entity.

DAILY LIFE   Roughly 70 percent of Jicarillas still practice some form of traditional religion. Fewer than half speak Jicarilla, and most who do are older. There has been some revival of traditional pottery and basketry arts, but Dulce and the reservation are increasingly part of the regional economy. Recreation facilities include an Olympic-sized, heated indoor pool. A large number of Jicarillas are Christian. Indians in Dulce live in relatively modern homes or trailers, with water and sewer hookups. Most tribal members live on the reservation.

Apache, Lipan

Lipan (`L ē pan) may mean "warriors of the mountains." Apache comes from the Zuñi word *Apachu,* meaning "enemy." The Apache call themselves *Ndee,* or *Dine'é* (Di `n ə), "the People."

LOCATION   The Apache arrived in the Southwest from present-day Canada around 1400. By about 1700, the Lipan were living on the south-central Texas plains, as far south as Texas's Colorado River. Today they live on the Mescalero Reservation, in southeast New Mexico.

POPULATION   Approximately 100 Lipan Apache lived in their region around 1900, although possibly up to ten times as many lived there prior to contact with non-natives. Of roughly 25,000 Apaches nationwide in 1990, 3,500, including Chiricahua, Mescalero, and Lipan Apache, lived on the Mescalero Reservation; several hundred lived off-reservation.

LANGUAGE   The people spoke a dialect of Southern Athapaskan, or Apachean.

Historical Information

HISTORY   Ancestors of today's Apache Indians began the trek from Asia to North America in roughly 1000 B.C.E. Most of this group, which included the Athapaskans, was known as the Nadene. By 1300, the group that was to become the Southern Athapaskans (Apaches and Navajos) broke away from other Athapaskan tribes and began migrating southward, reaching the American Southwest around 1400 and crystallizing into separate cultural groups.

Before contact with the Spanish, the Apaches were relatively peaceful and may have engaged in some agricultural activities. By about 1700 the Lipan had become separated from the Jicarilla and had migrated into the central and south Texas plains. They had also acquired horses and had become expert buffalo hunters and raiders of the western plains from Kansas to Mexico. Caddoan villages felt the wrath of Lipan raiders and slavers until they acquired guns from French traders and were able to drive the Lipan back into Texas.

A Lipan request for Spanish protection against the Comanche, who were pressing them from the north and east, resulted in the establishment of a mission in 1757, which the Comanche promptly destroyed the following year. By the late eighteenth century, the Comanche had forced most Lipans from Texas into New Mexico to join other Apache bands there.

By the early nineteenth century, the remaining Lipans had established good terms with the Texans, serving as their scouts, guides, and trading partners. Following the war between Mexico and the United States (1848), the Apaches, who did their part to bring misery to Mexico, assumed that the Americans would continue as allies. Instead, the Texans adopted an extermination policy, and those Lipans who escaped went to live in Mexico. In the late 1870s, some Lipans fought with the Chiricahua leader Victorio in his last stand against the United States and captivity. He and they were killed in Mexico.

In 1873, the U.S. government had granted the Mescalero Apache a small reservation surrounding the Sierra Blanca Mountains. The Mescaleros absorbed Apache refugees and immigrants in hopes that the increased numbers would help them gain the elusive title to their land. In 1903, 37 Mexican Lipan Apaches arrived, followed in 1913 by 187 Chiricahuas from Fort Sill, Oklahoma. Eventually, largely through intermarriage, these peoples evolved into the modern Mescalero community.

The United States engaged in extreme repression and all-out assault on traditional culture at the end of the nineteenth century. Cattle raising and timber sales proved lucrative in the early twentieth century. Eventually, day schools replaced the hated, culture-killing boarding schools. By the late 1940s, every family had a house, and the Mescalero economy was relatively stable. The reservation is managed cooperatively with the Mescalero and the Chiricahua Apache.

RELIGION   Apache religion is based on a complex mythology and features numerous deities. Most deities are seen as personifications of natural forces. The sun is the greatest source of power. Culture heroes, like White-Painted Woman and her son, Child of the Water, also figure highly, as do protective mountain spirits *(ga'an).* The latter are represented as masked dancers (probably an indication of Pueblo influence) in certain ceremonies, such as the girls' puberty rite. Apaches believe that since other living things were once people, we are merely following in the footsteps of those who have gone before.

Supernatural power, which pervades the universe, may be utilized for human purposes through ritual procedures and personal revelations. It is both the goal and the medium of most Apache ceremonialism. The ultimate goal of supernatural power was to facilitate the maintenance of spiritual strength and balance in a world of conflicting forces. Apaches recognize two categories of rites: personal/shamanistic and long-life. In the former, power is derived from an animal, a celestial body, or another natural phenomenon. When power appears to a person and is accepted, rigorous training as a shaman follows. Shamans also facilitate the acquisition of power, which may be used in the service of war, luck, rainmaking, or life-cycle events. Power may be evil as well as good, however, and sickness and misfortune could be caused by the anger of a deity or by not treating properly a natural force. Witchcraft, as well as incest, was an unpardonable offense.

Long-life rites were taught by elders and connected to mythology. They were also closely associated with various song cycles. Among the most important and complex is the girls' puberty ceremony. Lasting for four days and nights, this ceremony involved masked dancers, feasting, games, rituals in a ceremonial tipi, and a long and intricate song cycle. Other important rites included cradle, first steps, first haircut, and boys' puberty ceremonies. Once common, the Native American Church has now declined in popularity.

GOVERNMENT Traditionally, the Lipan knew little tribal cohesion and no central political authority. They were a tribe based on common territory, language, and culture. As much central authority as existed was found in the local group (composed of extended families). Its leader, or chief, enjoyed authority because of personal qualities, such as persuasiveness and bravery, often in addition to ceremonial knowledge. (All the famous Apache "chiefs" were local group leaders.) Decisions were taken by consensus. One of the chief's most important functions was to mitigate friction among his people.

CUSTOMS Women were the anchors of the Apache family. Residence was matrilocal. Besides the political organization, society was divided into a number of matrilineal clans. Apaches in general respected the elderly and valued honesty above most other qualities.

Gender roles were clearly defined but not rigidly enforced. Women gathered, prepared, and stored food; built the home; carried water; gathered fuel; cared for the children; tanned, dyed, and decorated hides; and wove baskets. Men hunted, raided, and waged war, although women sometimes took part in antelope hunts and rabbit surrounds. The men also made weapons and were responsible for their horses and equipment. The male puberty ceremony revolved around war and raiding. Girls as well as boys practiced with the bow and arrow, sling, and spear, and both were expert riders.

Although actual marriage ceremonies were brief or nonexistent, the people practiced a number of formal preliminary rituals, designed to strengthen the idea that a man owed deep allegiance to his future wife's family. Out of deference, married men were not permitted to speak directly with their mothers-in-law. Divorce was relatively easy to obtain. The mother's brother played an important role in the life of his sister and her children.

All Apaches had a great fear of ghosts. Death was repressed as much as possible. So great was their fear of the dead that outsiders sometimes buried their dead. Perhaps paradoxically, however, the elderly were venerated. The afterlife was pictured as twofold in nature: a pleasant land for the good but a barren one for witches. The Lipan pictured the underworld, home of the dead, as the place of their original emergence.

DWELLINGS Lipan Apaches generally lived in hide tipis. Occasionally, and especially when they were moved off the plains, they used dome-shaped brush wikiups, which they covered with grass thatch or with hides in bad weather.

DIET Lipan Apaches were primarily hunters and gatherers. They hunted buffalo into the eighteenth century, and afterward they continued to hunt deer, elk, antelope, rabbits, and other game. They ate few birds and did not eat fish, coyote, snake, or owl.

Wild foods included agave; cactus shoots, flowers, and fruit; berries; seeds; nuts; honey; and wild onions, potatoes, and grasses. Nuts and seeds were often ground into flour. The agave or century plant was particularly important. Baking its base in rock-lined pits for several days yielded mescal, a sweet, nutritious food, which was dried and stored. The Lipan moved often to follow animal migrations as well as the ripening of their wild foods. Traditional farm crops were obtained by trade or raid and by practicing some agriculture.

KEY TECHNOLOGY Like the Plains tribes, the Lipan used hide rather than baskets or pottery for most receptacles. Most of their tools were also buffalo based.

TRADE Trading partners included Plains tribes and Hispanic villages, especially before the eighteenth century. At that time their main surplus item was buffalo meat and hides.

NOTABLE ARTS   Traditional arts included tanned hides and some basketry.

TRANSPORTATION   Lipans acquired horses in the seventeenth century. Prior to that time dogs had drawn the travois. To ford rivers, they used rafts or boats of skins stretched over a wooden frame.

DRESS   Men wore buckskin shirts, breechclouts, leggings, and hard-soled, low-cut moccasins. They braided and wrapped their hair. Women also dressed in buckskin and braided their hair. They also plucked their eyebrows.

WAR AND WEAPONS   Historically, the Apache made formidable enemies. After they acquired horses, raiding became one of their most important activities. The main purpose of raiding, in which one sought to avoid contact with the enemy, was to gain wealth and honor. It differed fundamentally from warfare, which was undertaken primarily for revenge and which, like hunting, was accompanied by complex rituals and rules. From the sixteenth century on, the Lipan were in periodic conflict with Utes, Comanches, Spanish, and Mexicans. The Lipan were less concerned than other Apache about contamination from a dead enemy, and, like Plains Indians, they considered it a virtue to be the first to strike a fallen foe (count coup). Military equipment included shields with painted buckskin covers, bows and arrows, quivers, bow covers, wrist guards, spears, rawhide slings, flint knives, and war clubs.

Contemporary Information

GOVERNMENT/RESERVATIONS   The Mescalero Reservation, in southeast New Mexico, contains roughly 460,000 acres of land and is home to the Chiricahua and Mescalero Apaches in addition to the Lipan. The 1992 population was 3,511. After 1934, the tribal business committee began functioning as a tribal council. In 1964, a new constitution defined the Mescalero tribe without reference to the original band.

ECONOMY   Important industries include logging, cattle raising, and the Inn of the Mountain Gods.

LEGAL STATUS   The Mescalero are a federal corporation and a federally recognized tribal entity. They obtained title to the reservation in 1922.

DAILY LIFE   Intermarriage has tended to blur the distinction between the once-separate tribes on the Mescalero Reservation. Up to three-quarters of the people still speak Apache, although the dialect is more Mescalero than Chiricahua or Lipan. The written Apache language is also taught in reservation schools. Some young women still undergo the traditional puberty ritual, and there is a marked interest in crafts and other traditions. The reservation confronts relatively few social problems, despite its high un-

and underemployment. Traditional dancing by costumed mountain spirits now coincides with the July Fourth celebration and rodeo. Many Mescaleros are Catholic. Children have attended public schools since 1953. A tribal scholarship fund exists to help with college expenses. The Lipan language is virtually extinct.

Apache, Mescalero

Mescalero (Mes kä `l ē  r ō ), from mescal, a food derived from the agave or century plant and an important part of their diet. Apache comes from the Zuñi *Apachu*, or "enemy." The Apache call themselves *Ndee*, or *Dine'é* (Di `n ə), "the People."

LOCATION   The Mescalero traditionally lived from east of the Rio Grande to the Pecos and beyond to the west Texas plains. The Mescalero Reservation is located in southeast New Mexico, northeast of Alamogordo.

POPULATION   Perhaps 3,000 Mescaleros lived in the region prior to contact with non-natives. Of roughly 25,000 Apaches nationwide in 1990, 3,500, including Chiricahua, Mescalero, and Lipan Apaches, lived on the Mescalero Reservation; several hundred lived off-reservation.

LANGUAGE   Mescalero is a Southern Athapaskan, or Apachean dialect.

Historical Information

HISTORY   Ancestors of today's Apache Indians began the trek from Asia to North America in roughly 1000 B.C.E. Most of this group, which included the Athapaskans, was known as the Nadene. By 1300, the group that was to become the Southern Athapaskans (Apaches and Navajos) broke away from other Athapaskan tribes and began migrating southward, reaching the American Southwest around 1400 and crystallizing into separate cultural groups.

The Apaches generally filtered into the mountains surrounding the Pueblo-held valleys. This process ended in the 1600s and 1700s, with a final push southward and westward by the Comanches. Before contact with the Spanish, the Apaches were relatively peaceful and may have engaged in some agricultural activities.

Thrust into contact with the Spanish, the Apaches, having acquired horses, began raiding Spanish and Pueblo settlements. This dynamic included trading as well as raiding and warfare, but the Spanish habit of selling captured Apaches into slavery led to Apache revenge and increasingly hostile conditions along the Spanish frontier. After 1821, the Mexicans put a bounty on Apache scalps, increasing Apache enmity and adding to the cycle of violence in the region.

The Mescalero had moved into southern New Mexico by the early sixteenth century and had acquired horses at about the same time. They and the Jicarilla raided (and traded with) Spanish settlements and pueblos on the Rio Grande, and after 1680 they controlled the Camino Real, the main route from El Paso to Santa Fe. They hunted buffalo on the southern plains and were its de facto masters.

After 1725, the Comanche (who had access to French guns) forced the Apaches into the mountains, ending their life on the plains and inaugurating an era of semipoverty. Still, they battled the Spanish, who alternately tried to fight and settle them. An 1801 treaty, reaffirmed by the Mexicans in 1832, granted the Mescalero rations and the right to land in Mexico and New Mexico. Even so, their relations with the Mexicans were tenuous.

Following the Mexican War (1848), during which they had sided with the Texans, the Mescalero assumed that the Americans would continue as allies. They were shocked and disgusted to learn that their lands were now considered part of the United States and that the Americans planned to "pacify" them. Having been squeezed by the Spanish, the Comanches, the Mexicans, and now miners, farmers, and other land-grabbers from the United States, they were more than ever determined to protect their way of life.

Some Mescalero bands tried to stay out of trouble in the 1850s by planting fields under the supervision of federal agents, but when raiding resumed owing to broken promises of food and protection, all sides became caught up in a spiral of violence. By 1863, General James Carleton forced them off their informal reservation in the Sierra Blanca Mountains to Fort Sumner, at Bosque Redondo, on the Pecos. It was a concentration camp: Living with 9,000 Navajos, the Mescalero endured overcrowding, disease, bad water, and starvation. Two years later they escaped into the mountains, where they lived for seven years.

In 1873, the U.S. government granted the Mescalero a small reservation surrounding the Sierra Blanca, which included their traditional summer territory. This land made a harsh home in winter, however, and in any case it was too small for hunting and gathering. That decade was marked by disease, white incursions, and violence directed against them. In 1880, in retaliation after some Mescaleros joined the Chiricahua in their wars against the United States, the army placed the Mescaleros under martial law, disarmed them, and penned them in a corral filled deep with manure.

By the mid-1880s, gambling had replaced the traditional raiding. Missionaries arrived, as did a day school, which the Indians hated for separating the children from their elders. Meanwhile, their population plummeted from 3,000 in 1850 to 431 in 1888.

These were years marked by dependency, agent thievery, tyranny, disease, starvation and malnourishment, and uncertainty about the status of their reservation. Still, they survived the epidemics and efforts to steal their reservation by turning it into a national park (a move that proved unsuccessful in the long run).

The Mescaleros had absorbed Apache refugees and immigrants in hopes that increased numbers would help them gain the elusive title to their land. In 1883, the Jicarilla arrived, although they left by 1887. In 1903, 37 Lipan Apaches arrived, followed in 1913 by 187 Chiricahuas from Fort Sill, Oklahoma. Eventually, largely through intermarriage, all evolved into the modern Mescalero community.

The United States engaged in extreme repression and all-out assault on traditional culture at the end of the nineteenth century. Cattle raising and timber sales proved lucrative in the early twentieth century. Eventually, day schools replaced the hated, culture-killing boarding schools. By the late 1940s, every family had a house, and the reservation economy was relatively strong. The reservation is managed cooperatively with the Chiricahua and the Lipan Apache.

RELIGION Apache religion is based on a complex mythology and features numerous deities. Most deities are seen as personifications of natural forces. The sun is the greatest source of power. Culture heroes, like White-Painted Woman and her son, Child of the Water, also figure highly, as do protective mountain spirits *(ga'an)*. The latter are represented as masked dancers (probably a sign of Pueblo influence) in certain ceremonies, such as the girls' puberty rite. Apaches believe that since other living things were once people, we are merely following in the footsteps of those who have gone before.

Supernatural power is both the goal and the medium of most Apache ceremonialism. The ultimate goal of supernatural power was to facilitate the maintenance of spiritual strength and balance in a world of conflicting forces. Apaches recognize two categories of rites: personal/shamanistic and long-life. In the former, power is derived from an animal, a celestial body, or another natural phenomenon. When power appears to a person and is accepted, rigorous training as a shaman follows. Shamans also facilitate the acquisition of power, which may be used in the service of war, luck, rainmaking, or life-cycle events. Power may be evil as well as good, however, and sickness and misfortune could be caused by the anger of a deity or by not treating properly a natural force. Witchcraft, as well as incest, was an unpardonable offense.

Long-life rites were taught by elders and connected to mythology. Among the most important and complex was the girls' puberty ceremony. Lasting for four days and nights, this ceremony involved masked dancers, feasting, games, rituals in a ceremonial tipi, and a long and intricate song cycle. Other important rites included cradle, first steps, first haircut, and boys' puberty ceremonies. The Native American Church has recently declined in popularity.

GOVERNMENT Traditionally, the Mescalero knew little tribal cohesion and no central political authority. They were a tribe based on common territory, language, and culture. As much central authority as existed was found in the local group (not more than 30 extended families). Its leader, or chief, enjoyed authority because of personal qualities, such as persuasiveness and bravery, often in addition to ceremonial knowledge. (All the famous Apache "chiefs" were local group leaders.) Decisions were taken by consensus. One of the chief's most important functions was to mitigate friction among his people.

CUSTOMS Women were the anchors of the Apache family. Residence was matrilocal. Besides the political organization, society was divided into a number of matrilineal clans. Apaches in general respected the elderly and valued honesty above most other qualities.

Gender roles were clearly defined but not rigidly enforced. Women gathered, prepared, and stored food; built the home; carried water; gathered fuel; cared for the children; tanned, dyed, and decorated hides; and wove baskets. Men hunted, raided, and waged war. They also made weapons and were responsible for their horses and equipment. The male puberty ceremony revolved around war and raiding. Girls as well as boys practiced with the bow and arrow, sling, and spear, and both were expert riders.

Although actual marriage ceremonies were brief or nonexistent, the People practiced a number of formal preliminary rituals, designed to strengthen the idea that a man owed deep allegiance to his future wife's family. Out of deference, married men were not permitted to speak directly with their mothers-in-law. Divorce was relatively easy to obtain.

All Apaches had a great fear of ghosts. Death was repressed as much as possible. Mescaleros who died had their faces painted red and were buried quickly. Their personal possessions were burned or destroyed, including their house and favorite horse, and their names were not spoken again. The afterworld was pictured as a paradise.

DWELLINGS Mescalero Apaches lived in dome-shaped brush wikiups, which they covered with grass thatch or with hides in bad weather. The doors always faced east. When on the plains they used tipis.

DIET Mescalero Apaches were primarily hunters and gatherers. They hunted buffalo into the eighteenth century, and afterward they continued to hunt deer, elk, antelope, rabbits, and other game. They did not eat fish, coyote, snake, or owl.

Wild foods included agave shoots, flowers, and fruit; berries; seeds; nuts; honey; and wild onions, potatoes, and grasses. Nuts and seeds were often ground into flour. The agave or century plant was particularly important. Baking its base in rock-lined pits for several days yielded mescal, a sweet, nutritious food, which was dried and stored.

Traditional farm crops were obtained from the Pueblos by trade or raid. The Mescalero also practiced some agriculture: Corn, for instance, was used to make tiswin, a weak beer.

KEY TECHNOLOGY Items included baskets (pitch-covered water jars, cradles, storage containers, and burden baskets); gourd spoons, dippers, and dishes; leaf brushes; sheep-horn ladles; rock pounders; and a sinew-backed bow. The people made musical instruments out of gourds and hoofs. The one-stringed, so-called Apache fiddle, a postcontact instrument, was played with a bow. Moccasins were sewn with plant fiber attached to mescal thorns. Mescaleros also used parfleches, which they originally acquired from Plains tribes.

TRADE Trading partners included Pueblo and Hispanic villages, as well as some Plains tribes, especially before the eighteenth century. At that time their main surplus item was buffalo meat and hides.

NOTABLE ARTS Traditional arts included fine basketry, pottery, and tanned hides.

TRANSPORTATION Mescaleros acquired horses in the sixteenth century. Prior to that time dogs had drawn the travois. To ford rivers, the Mescalero used rafts or boats of skins stretched over a wooden frame.

DRESS Men wore buckskin shirts, breechclouts, leggings, and hard-soled, low-cut moccasins. They braided and wrapped their hair. Women also dressed in buckskin and braided their hair. They also plucked their eyebrows.

WAR AND WEAPONS Historically, the Apache made formidable enemies. After they acquired horses, raiding became one of their most important activities. The main purpose of raiding, in which one sought to avoid contact with the enemy, was to gain wealth and honor. It differed fundamentally from warfare, which was undertaken primarily for revenge and which, like hunting, was accompanied by complex rituals and rules. Only the war leader, who had undergone a special purifying ritual, took scalps. The Mescalero did not maintain formal warrior societies. Military equipment included shields with painted buckskin covers, bows and arrows, quivers, bow covers, wrist guards, spears, rawhide slings, flint knives, and war clubs.

Contemporary Information

GOVERNMENT/RESERVATIONS The Mescalero Reservation, in southeast New Mexico, contains roughly 460,000 acres of land and is home in addition to the Chiricahua and Lipan Apaches. The 1992 population was 3,511. After 1934, the tribal business committee began functioning as a tribal council. In 1964, a new constitution defined the Mescalero tribe without reference to the original band.

ECONOMY Important industries include logging, cattle raising, and the Inn of the Mountain Gods.

LEGAL STATUS The Mescalero are a federal corporation and a federally recognized tribal entity. They obtained title to the reservation in 1922.

DAILY LIFE Intermarriage has tended to blur the distinction between the once-separate tribes on the Mescalero Reservation. Up to three-quarters of the people still speak Apache, although the dialect is more Mescalero than Chiricahua or Lipan. The written Apache language is also taught in reservation schools. Some young women still undergo the traditional puberty ritual, and there is a marked interest in crafts and other traditions. The reservation confronts relatively few social problems, despite its high un- and underemployment. Traditional dancing by costumed mountain spirits now coincides with the July Fourth celebration and rodeo. Many Mescaleros are Catholic. Children have attended public schools since 1953. A tribal scholarship fund exists to help with college expenses.

Apache, Mimbreño
See Apache, Chiricahua

Apache, Northern Tonto
See Apache, Western

Apache, San Carlos
See Apache, Western

Apache, Southern Tonto
See Apache, Western

Apache, Western

Apache comes from the Zuni *Apachu,* meaning "enemy." These people are properly known as *Ndee,* or *Dine'é* (Di `n ə), "the People." Western Apache is a somewhat artificial designation given to an Apache tribe composed, with some exceptions, of bands living in Arizona. After 1850 these bands were primarily the San Carlos, White Mountain, Tonto (divided into Northern and Southern Tonto by anthropologists), and Cibecue.

LOCATION Traditionally, Western Apache bands covered nearly all but the northwesternmost quarter of Arizona. Their territory encompassed an extreme ecological diversity. Today's reservations include Fort Apache (Cibecue and White Mountain); San Carlos (San Carlos); Camp Verde, including Clarkdale and Middle Verde (mostly Tonto; shared with the Yavapai); and Payson. Tonto also live in the Middle Verde, Clarkdale, and Payson communities.

POPULATION Perhaps 5,000 Western Apaches (all groups) lived in Arizona around 1500. In 1992 the populations were as follows: San Carlos, 7,562 (including some Chiricahuas); Fort Apache, 12,503; Camp Verde, 650 (with the Yavapai); Payson, 92; Fort McDowell (Apache, Mojave, Yavapai), 765.

LANGUAGE Apaches spoke Southern Athapaskan, or Apachean.

Historical Information

HISTORY Ancestors of today's Apache Indians began the trek from Asia to North America in roughly 1000 B.C.E. Most of this group, which included the Athapaskans, was known as the Nadene. By 1300, the group that was to become the Southern Athapaskans (Apaches and Navajos) broke away from other Athapaskan tribes and began migrating southward, reaching the American Southwest around 1400 and crystallizing into separate cultural groups.

The Apaches generally filtered into the mountains surrounding the Pueblo-held valleys. This process ended in the 1600s and 1700s, with a final push southward and westward by the Comanches. Before contact with the Spanish, the Apaches were relatively peaceful and may have engaged in some agricultural activities. The Western Apache bands avoided much contact with outsiders until the mid–eighteenth century. The People became semisedentary with the development of agriculture, which they learned from the Pueblos.

Having acquired the horse, the Western Apache groups established a trading and raiding network with at least a dozen other groups, from the Hopi to Spanish settlements in Sonora. Although the Spanish policy of promoting docility by providing liquor to Native Americans worked moderately well from the late eighteenth century through the early nineteenth, Apache raids remained ongoing into the nineteenth century. By 1830, the Apache had drifted away from the presidios and resumed a full schedule of raiding.

Following the war between Mexico and the United States (1848), the Apaches, who did their part to bring misery to Mexico, assumed that the Americans would continue to be their allies. The Apaches were shocked and disgusted to learn that their lands were now considered part of the United States and that the Americans planned to "pacify" them. Having been squeezed by the Spanish, the Comanches, the Mexicans, and now miners, farmers, and other land-grab-bers from the United States, some Apaches were more than ever determined to protect their way of life.

Throughout the 1850s most of the anti-Apache attention was centered on the Chiricahua. The White Mountain and Cibecue people never fought to the finish with the Americans; out of range of mines and settlements, they continued their lives of farming and hunting. When Fort Apache was created (1863), these people adapted peacefully to reservation life and went on to serve as scouts against the Tontos and Chiric-ahuas.

The Prescott gold strike (1863) heralded a cycle of raid, murder, and massacre for the Tonto. By 1865 a string of forts ringed their territory; they were defeated militarily eight years later. A massacre of San Carlos (Aravaipa) women in 1871 led to Grant's "peace policy," a policy of concentration via forced marches. The result was that thousands of Chiric-ahuas and Western Apaches lived on the crowded and disease-ridden San Carlos Reservation. There, a handful of dissident chiefs, confined in chains, held out for the old life of freedom and self-respect. The Chiricahua Victorio bolted with 350 followers and remained at large and raiding for years. More fled in 1881. By 1884 all had been killed or had returned, at least temporarily. In general, the Western Apaches remained peaceful on the reservations while corrupt agents and settlers stole their best land.

The White Mountain people joined Fort Apache in 1879. As the various bands were spuriously lumped together, group distinctions as well as traditional identity began to break down. A man named Silas John Edwards established a significant and enduring religious cult at Fort Apache in the 1920s. Though not exactly Christian, it did substitute a new set of ceremonies in place of the old ones, contributing fur-ther to the general decline of traditional life. In 1918 the government issued cattle to the Apaches; lumber-ing began in the 1920s. In 1930, the government informed the Apaches that a new dam (the Coolidge) would flood old San Carlos. All residents were forced out, and subsistence agriculture ended for them. The Bureau of Indian Affairs (BIA) provided them with cattle and let all Anglo leases expire; by the late 1930s these Indians were stockmen.

RELIGION Apache religion is based on a complex mythology and features numerous deities. The sun is the greatest source of power. Culture heroes, like White-Painted Woman and her son, Child of the Water, also figure highly, as do protective mountain spirits *(ga'an)*. In fact, the very stories about these subjects are considered sacred. The latter are repre-sented as masked dancers (probably evidence of Pueblo influence) in certain ceremonies, such as the four-day girls' puberty rite. (The boys' puberty rite centered on raiding and warfare.)

Supernatural power, inherent in certain plants, animals, minerals, celestial bodies, and weather, is both the goal and the medium of most Apache cere-monialism. These forces could become involved, for better or worse, in affairs of people. The ultimate goal of supernatural power was to facilitate the mainte-nance of spiritual strength and balance in a world of conflicting forces. Shamans facilitated the acquisition of power, which could, by the use of songs, prayers, and sacred objects, be used in the service of war, luck, rainmaking, or life-cycle events. Detailed and exten-sive knowledge was needed to perform ceremonials; chants were many, long, and very complicated. Power could also be evil as well as good and was to be treated with respect. Witchcraft, as well as incest, was an unpardonable offense. Finally, Apaches believed that since other living things were once people, we are merely following in the footsteps of those who have gone before.

GOVERNMENT Each of the Western Apache tribes was considered autonomous and distinct, although intermarriage did occur. Tribal cohesion was minimal; there was no central political authority. A "tribe" was based on a common territory, language, and culture. Each was made up of between two and five bands of greatly varying size. Bands formed the most important Apache unit, which were in turn composed of local groups (35–200 people in extended families, themselves led by a headman) headed by a chief. The chief lectured his followers before sunrise every morning on proper behavior. His authority was based on his personal qualities and per-haps his ceremonial knowledge. Decisions were taken by consensus. One of the chief's most important functions was to mitigate friction among his people.

CUSTOMS Women were the anchors of the Apache family. Residence was matrilocal. Besides the political organization, society was divided into a number of matrilineal clans, which further tied fami-lies together. Apaches in general respected the elderly and valued honesty above most other qualities. Gen-der roles were clearly defined but not rigidly enforced. Women gathered, prepared, and stored food; built the home; carried water; gathered fuel; cared for the children; tanned, dyed, and decorated hides; and wove baskets. Men hunted, raided, and waged war. They also made weapons, were responsi-ble for their horses and equipment, and made musi-cal instruments. Western Apaches generally planted crops and gathered food in summer, harvested and hunted in fall, and returned to winter camps for raid-ing in winter.

Girls as well as boys practiced with the bow and

arrow, sling, and spear, and both learned to ride expertly. The four-day girls' puberty ceremony was a major ritual (at which mountain spirits appeared) as well as a major social event. Traditional games, such as hoop and pole, often also involved supernatural powers. Marriages were often arranged, but the couple had the final say. Although actual marriage ceremonies were brief or nonexistent, the people practiced a number of formal preliminary rituals, designed to strengthen the idea that a man owed deep allegiance to his future wife's family. Out of deference, married men were not permitted to speak directly with their mothers-in-law. Divorce was relatively easy to obtain. All Apaches had a great fear of ghosts. A dead person's dwelling was abandoned, and his or her name was never spoken again. Burial followed quickly.

DWELLINGS Women built the homes. Most Western Apache people lived in dome-shaped wikiups, made of wood poles covered with bear grass, which they covered with hides in bad weather. Brush ramadas were used for domestic activities.

DIET Western Apache groups were primarily hunters and gatherers. They hunted buffalo prior to the sixteenth century, and afterward they continued to hunt deer, antelope, mountain lion, elk, porcupine, and other game. They did not eat bear, turkey, or fish.

Wild foods included agave shoots, flowers, and fruit; berries; seeds; nuts; honey; and wild onions, potatoes, and grasses. Nuts and seeds were often ground into flour. The agave or century plant was particularly important. Baking its base in rock-lined pits for several days yielded mescal, a sweet, nutritious food, which was dried and stored. About one-quarter of their diet (slightly more among the Cibecue) came from agricultural products (corn, beans, and squash), which they both grew and raided the pueblos for. They also drank a mild corn beer called *tulupai*.

KEY TECHNOLOGY Items included excellent baskets (pitch-covered water jars, cradles, storage containers, and burden baskets); gourd spoons, dippers, and dishes; and a sinew-backed bow. Storage bags were also made of buckskin. The People made musical instruments out of gourds and hooves. The so-called Apache fiddle, a postcontact instrument, was played with a bow on strings. Moccasins were sewn with plant fiber attached to mescal thorns.

TRADE By the mid–eighteenth century, the horse had enabled the Apache to establish a trading and raiding network with at least a dozen other groups, from the Hopi and other Pueblos to Spanish settlements in Sonora. From the Spanish, the Apache acquired (in addition to the horse) the lance, saddle and stirrup, bridle, firearms, cloth, and playing cards.

NOTABLE ARTS Fine arts included basketry (bowls, storage jars, burden baskets, and pitch-covered water jugs) designed with vegetable dyes, hooded cradle boards, and black or dark gray pottery.

TRANSPORTATION Dogs served as beasts of burden before Spanish horses arrived in the seventeenth century.

DRESS The Western Apache traditionally wore buckskin clothing and moccasins. As they acquired cotton and later wool through trading and raiding, women tended to wear two-piece calico dresses, with long, full skirts and long blouses outside the skirt belts. They occasionally carried knives and ammunition belts. Girls wore their hair over their ears, shaped around two willow hoops. Some older women wore hair Plains-style, parted in the middle with two braids. Men's postcontact styles included calico shirts, muslin breechclouts with belts, cartridge belts, thigh-high moccasins, and headbands; women wore Mexican-style cloth dresses. Blankets as well as deerskin coats were used in winter.

WAR AND WEAPONS Historically, the Apache made formidable enemies. Raiding was one of their most important activities. The purpose of raiding, in which one sought to avoid contact with the enemy, was to gain wealth and honor as well as to assist the needy. It differed fundamentally from warfare, which was undertaken primarily for revenge. Western Apaches raided the Maricopa, Pai, O'odham, and Navajo (trading and raiding). Their allies included the Quechan, Chemehuevi, Mojave, and Yavapai. Since the Apache abhorred mutilation, scalping was not a custom, although a killing required revenge. At least one shaman accompanied all war parties. Mulberry, oak, or locust bows were sinew backed; arrow tips were of fire-hardened wood or cane. Other weapons included lances, war clubs, and rawhide slings.

Contemporary Information

GOVERNMENT/RESERVATIONS San Carlos (1871; 1.87 million acres) and Fort Apache (1871; 1.66 million acres) Reservations were divided administratively in 1897. Both accepted reorganization under the Indian Reorganization Act (1934) and elect tribal councils. Other Western Apache reservations and communities include Camp Verde (shared with the Yavapai; 640 acres), Fort McDowell (a Yavapai reservation also shared with Mojave Indians; 24,680 acres), Clarkdale, and Payson (Yavapai-Apache; 85 acres; established 1972).

ECONOMY Important economic activities at San Carlos include cattle ranching, farming, logging, mining (asbestos and other minerals) leases, basket making, and off-reservation wage work. In general the economy at San Carlos is depressed. At Fort Apache the people engage in cattle ranching, timber harvesting, agriculture, operating the Sunrise resort, selling recreation permits, and leasing summer cabins. Unemployment at Fort Apache is relatively low. Recreation is the main resource at Camp Verde.

LEGAL STATUS The San Carlos Apache Tribe, run as a corporation; the Tonto Apache Indians; and the White Mountain Apache Tribe are federally recognized tribal entities. The Payson Community of Yavapai-Apache Indians is a federally recognized tribal entity.

DAILY LIFE San Carlos remains poor, with few jobs. Still, even if it means continuing in poverty, many Apaches resist acculturation: The ability to remain with family and friends remains paramount. The language and many traditions and ceremonies remain an important part of people's daily lives. Increasing off-reservation work, however, has opened the door to additional serious social problems. Management of San Carlos has remained in BIA hands, leaving Indians with the usual problem of being stripped of their heritage and institutions with no replacement or training or responsibility for their own affairs. The people of San Carlos are fighting a University of Arizona telescope bank on their sacred Mount Graham.

The Cibecue are the most traditional people at conservative Fort Apache. Nuclear families are now more important than extended families and local groups, but clans remain key, especially for the many extant ceremonies. Alcoholism and drug use are a large problem on the reservation. Public schools at both reservations have strong bilingual programs; educated leaders are a high need and priority (education levels remain quite low on both reservations). The Tonto have intermarried extensively with the Yavapai.

Apache, White Mountain
See Apache, Western

Chemehuevi
Chemehuevi (Che m ə `w ā v ē) is Yuman for "nose-in-the-air-like-a-roadrunner," referring to a running style of the original settlers of the Chemehuevi Valley. These Indians traditionally called themselves *Nuwu*, "the People," or *Tantáwats*, "Southern Men."

LOCATION Since the late nineteenth and early twentieth centuries, the people have lived in the Chemehuevi Valley, California (part of the Colorado River Valley east of Joshua Tree National Monument, and southwestern California. Their traditional territory was located in southwestern Utah, the Mojave Desert, and finally the Chemehuevi Valley, near the present Lake Havasu.

POPULATION There were perhaps 500 Chemehuevis in 1600. In 1990, there were 95 Indians at Chemehuevi and 2,345 at the Colorado River Reservation (out of these, perhaps 600 identified themselves as Chemehuevi).

LANGUAGE Chemehuevis spoke Paiute, a group of the Shoshonean branch of the Uto-Aztecan language family.

Historical Information
HISTORY Toward the end of the eighteenth century, the Chemehuevi and the Las Vegas band of Southern Paiutes may have exterminated the Desert Mojave. In the mid–nineteenth century, the Chemehuevi took over their territory as well as that of the Pee-Posh (Maricopa) Indians, who had been driven away by the Mojave Indians and had gone to live on the Gila River. The Mojave either actively or passively accepted the Chemehuevi. On the Colorado River, the Chemehuevi developed a crop-based economy and at the same time began to think of themselves as a distinct political entity. They also became strongly influenced in many ways by the Mojave, notably in their interest in warfare and their religious beliefs. Some Chemehuevis raided miners in northern Arizona from the 1850s through the 1870s.

In 1865 the Chemehuevi and Mojave fought each other. The Chemehuevi lost and retreated back into the desert. Two years later, however, many returned to the California side of the Colorado River, where they resumed their lives on the Colorado River Reservation, established two years earlier. Many Chemehuevi also remained in and around the Chemehuevi Valley, combining wage labor and traditional subsistence. By the turn of the century, most Chemehuevis were settled on the Colorado River Reservation and among the Serrano and Cahuilla in southern California. In 1885, after a particularly severe drought, a group moved north to farm the Chemehuevi Valley. When a reservation was established there, in 1907, the tribal split became official.

The creation of Hoover Dam in 1935 and Parker Dam in 1939 spelled disaster for the Chemehuevi. The Hoover stopped the seasonal Colorado River floods, which the Chemehuevi people had depended upon to nourish their crops. The Parker Dam created Lake Havasu, placing most of the Chemehuevi Valley under water. At that point, most Indians in the Chemehuevi Valley moved south again to join their people at the Colorado River Reservation. A government relocation camp operated on the reservation from 1942 to 1945.

By the end of World War II, 148 Navajo and Hopi

families had also colonized the reservation; they, with the Chemehuevi and Mojave, became known as the Colorado River Indian Tribes (CRIT). As a result of a 1951 lawsuit, the Chemehuevi were awarded $900,000 by the United States for land taken to create Lake Havasu. The tribe was not formally constituted until they adopted a constitution in 1971. At about that time, some Chemehuevis began a slow return to the Chemehuevi Valley, where they remain today, operating a resort on their tribal lands.

RELIGION After migrating to the Colorado River Valley, the Chemehuevi became strongly influenced by Mojave beliefs. Specifically, they acquired both interest and skill in dreaming and in using the power conferred by dreams to cure illness and spiritual imbalance. The Chemehuevi also adopted some of the Mojave song cycles, which referred to dreams as well as mythological events.

GOVERNMENT Before their move to the Colorado River, the Chemehuevi had little tribal consciousness or government per se. They roamed their territory in many bands, each with a relatively powerless chief. They assumed a tribal identity toward the mid–nineteenth century. At the same time, the chief, often a generous, smart, wealthy man succeeded by his eldest son, assumed a stronger leadership role.

CUSTOMS After the early nineteenth century, the Chemehuevi burned the body and possessions of their dead, following preparations by relatives. At this time, they also adopted many Mojave and Quechan customs, such as floodplain farming, dwelling type, an emphasis on dreams, and specific war-related customs. New parents rested on a hot bed for several days. Their mourning ceremony, or "cry," in which a wealthy family gave a feast and destroyed goods, had its roots in Southern Paiute culture.

DWELLINGS The traditional Chemehuevi shelter consisted of small, temporary huts covered with dirt.

DIET Following their move to the river, a diet based on foods obtained by hunting and by gathering desert resources was partially replaced by crops such as corn, beans, pumpkins, melons, grasses (semicultivated), and wheat. The Chemehuevi also ate fish from the river; game, including turtles, snakes, and lizards; and a variety of wild plants, such as mesquite beans (a staple) and piñon nuts.

KEY TECHNOLOGY Chemehuevi technology in the nineteenth century consisted largely of adaptations of Mojave items, such as reed rafts, baskets and pottery, a headring for carrying, gourds for storage and rattles, planting sticks and wooden hoes, and fish and carrying nets. They also adopted Mojave floodplain irrigation methods.

TRADE In the nineteenth century, the Chemehuevi participated in the general regional trade,

extending into southern California, which saw the exchange of agricultural products for shells, feathers, and other items.

NOTABLE ARTS The Chemehuevi made excellent baskets. They also learned pottery arts from the Mojave.

TRANSPORTATION In addition to horses (acquired while they were still leading a nomadic existence in the desert) for basic mobility on land, the Chemehuevi used reed or log rafts for river travel, as well as large pots to hold provisions or even small children for short travels in the water.

DRESS After contact with the Mojaves, men began wearing their hair in thin "ropes" that hung down the back. Generally, men and women wore double aprons. Women also wore willow-bark aprons. Both went barefoot except when traveling, when rawhide sandals were worn.

WAR AND WEAPONS The Chemehuevi did not shy away from fighting. Traditional allies included the Mojave (especially), Quechan, Yavapai, and Western Apache. Enemies included the Cocopah, Pima, O'odham, Pee-Posh, and on occasion their allies, the Mojave. Warriors generally clubbed their sleeping victims in predawn raids. They also used the bow and arrow.

Contemporary Information

GOVERNMENT/RESERVATIONS The Chemehuevi have their own reservation in the Chemehuevi Valley, California. It was created in 1907 and contained 36,000 acres, almost 8,000 of which were subsequently lost to Lake Havasu. Most Chemehuevis live on the Colorado River Reservation, created in 1865, and are members of CRIT. This reservation contains roughly 270,000 acres. It is governed under a constitution approved in 1937 and is dominated politically by the Mojave tribe.

Chemehuevis are also represented on the Morongo, Cabazon, and Agua Caliente Reservations (Cahuilla) in California.

ECONOMY The tribal resort on Lake Havasu provides most of the employment and income for members of that reservation. CRIT, which boasts notably low unemployment (10 percent in 1985), features an 11,000-acre farming cooperative (primarily cotton, alfalfa, melons, and lettuce), a sheep herd, a resort (Aha Quin Park), and employment with the tribe, the Bureau of Indian Affairs, numerous small and large businesses, and the local health center. Long-term leases provide further income. There are also hydroelectric, oil, and uranium resources.

LEGAL STATUS Federally recognized tribal entities include the Chemehuevi Indian Tribe of the Chemehuevi Reservation, California, and the Colorado River Indian Tribes of the Colorado River Indian Reservation, Arizona and California.

DAILY LIFE Intermarriage on the Colorado River Reservation has tended to blur the identities of the individual constituent tribes of CRIT, with the possible exception of the Mojave, which dominate by their sheer numbers. The other tribes both concede Mojave domination and search for ways to maintain their individuality. Toward this end, a museum has been built that details the heritage of the separate tribes. The Colorado River Reservation features motorboat races and a rodeo. Children from both reservations attend public schools.

Cochiti Pueblo

Cochiti (K ō `ch ē t ē) from the original Keresan via a Spanish transliteration. The word "pueblo" comes from the Spanish for "village." It refers both to a certain style of Southwest Indian architecture, characterized by multistory, apartmentlike buildings made of adobe, and to the people themselves. Rio Grande pueblos are known as eastern Pueblos; Zuñi, Hopi, and sometimes Acoma and Laguna are known as western Pueblos.

LOCATION Cochiti Pueblo has been located roughly 25 miles southwest of Santa Fe for at least several centuries.

POPULATION In 1990, 666 Cochitis lived on the pueblo, with perhaps at least as many living off; about 500 Cochitis lived there in 1700.

LANGUAGE Cochiti is a Keresan dialect.

Historical Information

HISTORY All Pueblo people are thought to be descended from Anasazi and perhaps Mogollon and several other ancient peoples, although the precise origin of the Keresan peoples is unknown. From them they learned architecture, farming, pottery, and basketry. Larger population groups became possible with effective agriculture and ways to store food surpluses. Within the context of a relatively stable existence, the people devoted increasing amounts of time and attention to religion, arts, and crafts.

In the 1200s, the Anasazi abandoned their traditional canyon homelands in response to climatic and social upheavals. A century or two of migrations ensued, followed in general by the slow reemergence of their culture in the historic pueblos. For a time the Cochiti lived with the San Felipe people but divided before the Spanish arrived.

In 1598, Juan de Oñate arrived in the area with settlers, founding the colony of New Mexico. Oñate carried on the process, already underway in nearby areas, of subjugating the local Indians; forcing them to pay taxes in crops, cotton, and work; and opening the door for Catholic missionaries to attack their religion. The Spanish renamed the Pueblos with saints' names and began a program of church construction (such as San Buenaventura mission at Cochiti). At the same time, the Spanish introduced such new crops as peaches, wheat, and peppers into the region. In 1620, a royal decree created civil offices at each pueblo; silver-headed canes, many of which remain in use today, symbolized the governor's authority.

The Pueblo Indians, including Cochiti Pueblo, organized and instituted a general revolt against the Spanish in 1680. For years, the Spaniards had routinely tortured Indians for practicing traditional religion. They also forced the Indians to labor for them, sold Indians into slavery, and let their cattle overgraze Indian land, a situation that eventually led to drought, erosion, and famine. Popé of San Juan Pueblo and other Pueblo religious leaders planned the revolt, sending runners carrying cords of maguey fibers to mark the day of rebellion. Antonio Malacate of Cochiti Pueblo was also a prominent leader. On August 10, 1680, a virtually united stand on the part of the Pueblos drove the Spanish from the region. The Indians killed many Spaniards but refrained from mass slaughter, allowing them to leave Santa Fe for El Paso. The Cochiti abandoned their pueblo from 1683 to 1692, joining other Keresan people at the fortified town of Potrero Viejo.

The Pueblos experienced many changes during the following decades: Refugees established communities at Hopi, guerrilla fighting continued against the Spanish, and certain areas were abandoned. By the 1700s, excluding Hopi and Zuñi, only Taos, Picuris, Isleta, and Acoma Pueblos had not changed locations since the arrival of the Spanish. Although Pueblo unity did not last, and Santa Fe was officially reconquered in 1692, Spanish rule was notably less severe from then on. Harsh forced labor all but ceased, and the Indians reached an understanding with the Church that enabled them to continue practicing their traditional religion.

In general, the Pueblo eighteenth century was marked by smallpox epidemics and increased raiding by the Apache, Comanche, and Ute. Occasionally Pueblo Indians fought with the Spanish against the nomadic tribes. The people practiced their religion but more or less in secret. During this time, intermarriage and regular exchange between Hispanic villages and Pueblo Indians created a new New Mexican culture, neither strictly Spanish nor Indian, but rather somewhat of a blend between the two.

Mexican "rule" in 1821 brought little immediate change to the Pueblos. The Mexicans stepped up what had been a gradual process of appropriating Indian land and water, and they allowed the nomadic tribes even greater latitude to raid. As the presence of the United States in the area grew, it attempted to enable the Pueblo Indians to continue their generally peaceful and self-sufficient ways, and recognized Spanish land grants to the Pueblos.

During the nineteenth century the process of acculturation among Pueblo Indians quickened markedly. In an attempt to retain their identity, Pueblo Indians clung even more tenaciously to their heritage, which by now included elements of the once-hated Spanish culture and religion. By the 1880s, railroads had largely put an end to the traditional geographical isolation of the pueblos. Paradoxically, the U.S. decision to recognize Spanish land grants to the Pueblos denied Pueblo Indians certain rights granted under official treaties and left them particularly open to exploitation by squatters and thieves.

After a gap of more than 300 years, the All Indian Pueblo Council began to meet again in the 1920s, specifically in response to a congressional threat to appropriate Pueblo lands. Partly as a result of the Council's activities, Congress confirmed Pueblo title to their lands in 1924 by passing the Pueblo Lands Act. The United States also acknowledged its trust responsibilities in a series of legal decisions and other acts of Congress. Still, especially after 1900, Pueblo culture was increasingly threatened by highly intolerant Protestant evangelical missions and schools. The Bureau of Indian Affairs also weighed in on the subject of acculturation, forcing Indian children to leave their homes and attend culture-killing boarding schools.

In the 1930s, a concrete dam just north of Cochiti made possible new irrigation canals. With a sure water supply, ceremonialism largely based on the uncertainties of local agriculture declined steeply. Completion of a larger dam in 1975 flooded important archaeological sites as well as the best sources of potters' clay and some acreage; however, farming had declined anyway.

Following World War II, the issue of water rights took center stage on most pueblos. Also, the All Indian Pueblo Council succeeded in slowing the threat against Pueblo lands as well as religious persecution. Making crafts for the tourist trade became an important economic activity during this period. Since the late nineteenth century, but especially after the 1960s, Pueblos have had to cope with onslaughts by (mostly white) anthropologists and seekers of Indian spirituality. The region is also known for its major art colonies at Taos and Santa Fe.

RELIGION In traditional Pueblo culture, religion and life are inseparable. To be in harmony with all of nature is the Pueblo ideal and way of life. The sun is seen as the representative of the Creator. Sacred mountains in each direction, plus the sun above and the earth below, define and balance the Pueblo world. Many Pueblo religious ceremonies revolve around the weather and are devoted to ensuring adequate rainfall. To this end, Pueblo Indians evoke the power of katsinas, sacred beings who live in mountains and other holy places, in ritual and dance. All Cochiti men belonged to katsina societies. Cochiti Pueblo contained two circular kivas, religious chambers that symbolize the place of original emergence into this world, and their associated societies, Squash and Turquoise.

In addition to the natural boundaries, Pueblo Indians created a society that defined their world by providing balanced, reciprocal relationships within which people connect and harmonize with each other, the natural world, and time itself. According to tradition, the head of each pueblo is the religious leader, or *cacique,* whose primary responsibility it is to watch the sun and thereby determine the dates of ceremonies. Much ceremonialism is also based on medicine societies, and shamans used supernatural powers for curing, weather control, and ensuring the general welfare. Especially in the eastern pueblos, most ceremonies are kept secret.

GOVERNMENT Pueblo governments derived from two traditions. Elements that are probably indigenous include the *cacique,* or head of the Pueblo, and the war captains. These officials are intimately related to the religious structures of the pueblo and reflected the essentially theocratic nature of Pueblo government. A parallel but in most cases distinctly less powerful group of officials was imposed by the Spanish authorities. Appointed by the traditional leadership, they generally dealt with external and church matters and included the governor, lieutenant governor, and *fiscales.* In addition, the All Indian Pueblo Council, dating from 1598, began meeting again in the twentieth century.

CUSTOMS One mechanism that works to keep Pueblo societies coherent is a pervasive aversion to individualistic behavior. Children were traditionally raised with gentle guidance and a minimum of discipline. Pueblo Indians were generally monogamous and divorce is relatively rare. The dead were prepared ceremonially and quickly buried with clothes, beads, food, and other items. A vigil of four days and nights was generally observed. Cochiti Pueblo recognized matrilineal clans, associated with the seasons, as well as two patrilineal kiva groups, which in turn were associated with clans and medicine societies. The economy was basically a socialistic one, whereby labor was shared and produce was distributed equally. In modern times photography by outsiders is discouraged.

DWELLINGS In the sixteenth century, Cochiti Pueblo featured two- to three-story, apartment-style dwellings as well as individual houses, facing south. The buildings were constructed of adobe (earth and straw) bricks, with beams across the roof that were covered with poles, brush, and plaster. Floors were of wood plank or packed earth. The roof of one level served as the floor of another. The levels were interconnected by ladders. As an aid to defense, the traditional design included no doors or windows; entry was through the roof. Pit houses, or kivas, served as ceremonial chambers and clubhouses. The village plaza, around which all dwellings were clustered, is the spiritual center of the village where all the balanced forces of world come together.

DIET Cochitis were farmers. Before the Spanish arrived, they ate primarily corn, beans, and pumpkins. They also grew sunflowers and tobacco. They hunted deer, mountain lion, bear, antelope, and rabbits. Occasionally, men from Cochiti and Santo Domingo Pueblos would travel east to hunt buffalo. Cochitis also gathered a variety of wild seeds, nuts, berries, and other foods. The Spanish introduced wheat, alfalfa, sheep, cattle, and garden vegetables, which soon became part of the regular diet.

KEY TECHNOLOGY Precontact farming implements were wooden. Traditional irrigation systems included ditches as well as floodwater collection at arroyo mouths (ak chin). The Spanish introduced metal tools and equipment.

TRADE All Pueblos were part of extensive Native American trading networks. With the arrival of other cultures, Pueblo Indians also traded with the Hispanic American villages and then U.S. traders. At fixed times during summer or fall, enemies declared truces so that trading fairs might be held. The largest and best known was at Taos with the Comanche. Nomads exchanged slaves, buffalo hides, buckskins, jerked meat, and horses for agricultural and manufactured pueblo products. Pueblo Indians traded for shell and copper ornaments, turquoise, and macaw feathers. Trade along the Santa Fe Trail began in 1821. By the 1880s and the arrival of railroads, the Pueblos were dependent on many American-made goods, and the Native American manufacture of weaving and pottery declined and nearly died out.

NOTABLE ARTS In the Pueblo way, art and life are inseparable. Cochiti arts included pottery, baskets, drums, and shell and turquoise ornaments. Songs, dances, and dramas also qualify as traditional arts. Many Pueblos experienced a renaissance of traditional arts in the twentieth century, beginning in 1919 with San Ildefonso pottery.

TRANSPORTATION Spanish horses, mules, and cattle arrived at Cochiti Pueblo in the seventeenth century.

DRESS Men wore cotton kilts and leather sandals. Women wore cotton dresses and sandals or high moccasin boots. Deer and rabbit skin were also used for clothing and robes, and sandals were made of yucca.

WAR AND WEAPONS Though often depicted as passive and docile, most Pueblo groups regularly engaged in warfare. The great revolt of 1680 stands out as the major military action, but they also skirmished at other times with the Spanish and defended themselves against attackers such as Apaches, Comanches, and Utes. They also contributed auxiliary soldiers to provincial forces under Spain and Mexico, which were used mainly against raiding Indians and to protect merchant caravans on the Santa Fe Trail. After the raiding tribes began to pose less of a threat in the late nineteenth century, Pueblo military societies began to wither away, with the office of war captain changing to civil and religious functions.

Contemporary Information

GOVERNMENT/RESERVATIONS Cochiti Pueblo consists of over 50,000 acres. Although there is no constitution, the tribal council abandoned consensus-style decision making after World War II in favor of majority rule. Other than that, the Pueblo is governed according to tradition. Headmen of the three medicine societies (one of whom is the *cacique*, leader of the pueblo) annually select from the two kiva groups the war captain and his lieutenant, the governor and his lieutenant, and the *fiscale* and his lieutenant.

ECONOMY Some people still farm, although more work for wages in nearby cities. In 1986, the tribe bought out a bankrupt company with whom they had signed very controversial long-term leases and contracts to develop businesses and schools. A lake associated with this development provides some recreational and other facilities; however, it has not brought a hoped-for prosperity to the tribe. Cochitis are particularly known for their fine aspen and cottonwood drums, ceremonial and tourist, as well as their excellent pottery, silver jewelry, and other arts. Unemployment in the early 1990s hovered around 20 percent.

LEGAL STATUS The Pueblo of Cochiti is a federally recognized tribal entity.

DAILY LIFE Although the project of retaining a strong Indian identity is a difficult one in the late twentieth century, Pueblo people have strong roots, and in many ways the ancient rhythms and patterns continue. Many Pueblo Indians, though nominally Catholic, have fused parts of Catholicism onto a core of traditional beliefs. Since the 1970s control of schools has been a key in maintaining their culture.

Health problems, including alcoholism and drug use, continue to plague the pueblos.

Primarily as a result of intermarriage and the general acculturation process, few Cochitis still speak Keresan or Spanish (before World War II many were trilingual). Furthermore, a growing number of Cochitis live off the pueblo, contributing to a general loss of language, traditions, and culture. Since the 1960s, children have attended a nearby day school, with children of nearby Latino communities; this has also affected the community's homogeneity. Cochitis attend high school in Bernalillo, where they graduate in relatively high numbers. Most houses on the pueblo are built of adobe walls, beam and board under adobe roofs, and packed earth or wood plank floors. Some concrete block and frame housing is beginning to appear. Most houses have running water, sewers, telephones, and televisions.

Occasional clan ceremonies are still held, and two of the three traditional medicine societies remain. The office of *cacique* also remains, though in a weakened form. Traditional medicine has largely given way to modern health centers. Most Cochitis are practicing Catholics. Some still observe traditional ceremonies, but more and more as entertainment than for strictly religious reasons. The principal ceremony and major feast day is San Buenaventuras Day. Except for katsina dances, the tribe generally admits the public for its ceremonies.

Cocopah

Cocopah (ˋK ō k ō pä) from the Mojave kwi-ka-pah. The Cocopah called themselves *Xawil Kunyavaei*, "Those Who Live on the River."

LOCATION The traditional home of the Cocopah is near the Colorado River delta. Presently, many tribal members live in northwestern Mexico and on a reservation near Somerton, Arizona.

POPULATION There may once have been as many as 5,000 Cocopahs. In 1993 there were 712, excluding at least 200 Mexican Cocopahs living in Baja California and Sonora.

LANGUAGE Cocopahs spoke River Yuman, a member of the Hokan-Siouan language family.

Historical Information

HISTORY Ancestors of the Cocopah probably migrated from the north during the first millennium. By 1540 the Mojave and Quechan Indians had forced them down the Colorado River, to a place where they farmed 50,000 acres of delta land, made rich by the annual spring floods. The Cocopah encountered Spanish soldiers and travelers during the mid–sixteenth century but remained in place and relatively unaffected by contact with the Europeans until U.S.

dams stopped the Colorado from flooding in the late nineteenth century.

In 1853, the Gadsden Treaty separated the four bands of Cocopah: Two remained in Mexico, and two moved north to near Somerton, Arizona. By the mid-1800s, with the cessation of warfare with their ancient enemies, the Quechans, the Cocopah lost a certain sense of purpose. A generation of men obtained employment as river pilots and navigators along the Colorado River, whetting their appetite for American goods and foods. Riverboat traffic ended when the railroad reached Yuma in 1877. In 1905, an accidental diversion of the Colorado River (the Salton Sea debacle) led to the Cocopahs' final displacement. Lacking strong political, religious, or social leadership, they quickly fell further into disintegration and impoverishment.

Thanks mainly to the work of Frank Tehanna, the U.S. government established a reservation in 1917 for Cocopahs and some Quechans and Pee-Posh. The government then almost completely abandoned them for the next 60 years. By the end of World War II, fewer than 60 Cocopahs remained on the desolate reservation; the rest lived elsewhere, generally in even worse poverty. In the 1960s, the tribe organized and won electricity and improved housing. It built its first tribal building and rewrote its constitution.

In 1986, the tribe received an additional 615 acres, now known as the North Reservation. In the 1970s and 1980s, the tribe made improvements in education as well as other social and cultural programs. That period also witnessed a revival of crafts such as beadwork and the development of fine arts.

RELIGION The Cocopah creation myth, like that of other Yumans, mentions twin gods living under the waters who emerged to create the world. Cocopahs revered the sun. They believed that life is directed by dreams in nearly every regard and relied on the dreams of shamans for success in war and curing. Most ceremonies, including *karuk*, a six-day mourning rite featuring long, "dreamed" song cycles, centered around death. The onset of puberty was also an occasion for ceremonies.

GOVERNMENT The Cocopah traditionally maintained little political leadership. They lived in small settlements, or rancherias, of 10 to 12 families. Society was organized into clans, with each clan having a leader. Other quasi officials included dance and war leaders and funeral orators. Leadership was generally determined by experience, ability, and, as with everything else, dreams.

CUSTOMS The Cocopah cremated their dead, including their possessions, following a special rite. Relatives cut off their hair in mourning, and the name of the dead person was never spoken. Marriage and divorce ceremonies were informal. Deer-bone blades hung on cords from the arms were used to wipe off perspiration. Dogs were kept as pets.

DWELLINGS Originally concentrated in nine rancherias, the Cocopah built two different types of homes. In winter they built conical, partially excavated (later four-post rectangular) structures, covering the walls of sticks with earth. In summer they built oval-domed, brush-covered huts. They also used a circular, unroofed ramada for dwelling and/or cooking and small granaries with elevated floors for storing food.

DIET Corn, beans, black-eyed peas, pumpkins, and later melons were planted, usually in July. Gathered food, such as the seeds of wild saltgrass, roots, fruits, eggs, and especially mesquite, were also important, as was fish (such as mullet and bass) from the river and the Gulf of California. Wild game included deer, boar, and smaller animals. Much of the food was dried and stored for the winter. In general, the women gathered and cooked food, and the men hunted.

KEY TECHNOLOGY The Cocopah planted seeds in holes rather than rows in order to preserve topsoil. They used pottery (jars, seed-toasting trays), crude baskets, fire drills, vegetable-fiber fishing nets, clubs and bow and arrow for warfare, stone and wooden mortars, and stone and clamshell tools. Their musical instruments included a scraped and drummed basket, gourd rattles, and cane flutes and whistles. They also used small earthen dikes for irrigation.

TRADE Trade contacts stretched west to the Pacific, northwest to northern California, northeast to much of Arizona, and southeast well into the Sonoran Desert.

NOTABLE ARTS Women made pottery that was mostly utilitarian, as was the basketry (made by men and women and used for storage, carrying, and cradles). In later historic times the Cocopah also learned loom weaving.

TRANSPORTATION Cottonwood dugouts (the larger ones featured clay floors) or tule or brush rafts were used for river travel. Large baskets were used to transport small items or children on the river.

DRESS Men wore tanned skin loincloths. Women wore bundles of feathers or willow-bark skirts in front and back. For both, clothing was minimal. People wore rabbit-skin robes or blankets in cold weather. Both men and women painted their faces and bodies for ornamental and ritual purposes. Men wore shell ornaments in pierced ears. Sandals were made of untanned skins. Men wore their hair long and braided. In the early twentieth century they tucked it under a bandanna. Women wore their hair long and straight, with bangs.

WAR AND WEAPONS Warfare united the Cocopah. They observed formalized war patterns and respected special war leaders. They prepared for war by dreaming, fasting, and painting their bodies and underwent purification rituals upon their return. Traditional enemies included the Mojave and the Quechan; allied peoples included the O'odham, Pee-Posh, and Pai. Their weapons were the war club, bow and arrow, lance, and deerskin shield.

Contemporary Information

GOVERNMENT/RESERVATIONS The Cocopah Reservation (established in 1917, roughly 1,700 acres) is located near Somerton, Arizona. The tribe adopted a constitution and elected a tribal council in 1964.

ECONOMY A few people practice subsistence farming, but most Indians work off-reservation for wages. Much land is leased to non-Indian farmers. The Cocopah Bend recreational vehicle park provides numerous public recreation facilities. There are also a bingo hall and casino on the reservation. Unemployment peaked at around 90 percent in the 1970s. Tourists buy fry-bread and crafts such as beadwork and reproductions of ceremonial clothing.

LEGAL STATUS The Cocopah tribe is a federally recognized tribal entity. In 1985, the tribe received 4,000 acres in land claims settlements. American Cocopahs are working to restore dual citizenship for their kin in Mexico.

DAILY LIFE Most Cocopahs speak their language. They still burn and otherwise dispose of the possessions of their dead and perform the mourning ceremony. Children attend public schools. A small health clinic on the reservation attempts to cope with the people's numerous health problems. Local housing, formerly grossly substandard (consisting of cardboard hovels as late as the 1970s), is now generally considered adequate. Elders may live in special housing on the reservation. After at least a thousand years of living on the river, the Cocopah are effectively no longer river people.

Colorado River Indian Tribes (CRIT)

See Chemehuevi; Hopi; Mojave; Navajo

Havasupai

Havasupai (Hä vä `s ū p ī) is a name meaning "People of the Blue-Green Water." With the Hualapai, from whom they may be descended, they are also called the Pai (Pa'a) Indians ("the People"; Hualapai are Western Pai, and Havasupai are Eastern Pai). With the Hualapai and the Yavapai, the Havasupai are also Upland Yumans, in contrast to River Yumans such as the Mojave and Quechan.

LOCATION Since approximately 1100, the Havasupai have lived at Cataract Canyon in the Grand Canyon as well as on the nearby upland plateaus.

POPULATION Of roughly 2,000 Pai, perhaps 250 Havasupai Indians lived at Cataract Canyon in the seventeenth century. Approximately 400 lived there in 1990.

LANGUAGE The Havasupai spoke Upland Yuman, a member of the Hokan-Siouan language family.

Historical Information

HISTORY The Havasupai probably descended from the prehistoric Cohoninas, a branch of the Hakataya culture. Thirteen bands of Pai originally hunted, farmed, and gathered in northwest Arizona along the Colorado River. By historic times, the Pai were divided into three subtribes: the Middle Mountain People; the Plateau People (including the Blue Water People, also called Cataract Canyon Band, who were ancestors of the Havasupai); and the Yavapai Fighters.

The Blue Water People were comfortable in an extreme range of elevations. They gathered desert plants from along the Colorado River at 1,800 feet and hunted on the upper slopes of the San Francisco peaks, their center of the world, at 12,000 feet. With the possible exception of Francisco Garces, in 1776, few if any Spanish or other outsiders disturbed them into the 1800s. Spanish influences did reach them, however, primarily in the form of horses, cloth, and fruit trees through trading partners such as the Hopi.

In the early 1800s, a trail was forged from the Rio Grande to California that led directly through Pai country. By around 1850, with invasions and treaty violations increasing, the Pai occasionally reacted with violence. When mines opened in their territory in 1863, they perceived the threat and readied for war. Unfortunately for them, the Hualapai War (1865–1869) came just as the Civil War ended. After their military defeat by the United States, some Pai served as army scouts against their old enemies, the Yavapai and the Tonto Apache.

Although the Hualapai were to suffer deportation, the United States paid little attention to the Havasupai, who returned to their isolated homes. At this point the two tribes became increasingly distinct. Despite their remote location, Anglo encroachment eventually affected even the Havasupai, and an 1880 executive order established their reservation along Havasu Creek. The final designation in 1882 included just 518 acres within the canyon; the Havasupai also lost their traditional upland hunting and gathering grounds (some people continued to use the plateau in winter but were forced off in 1934, when the National Park Service destroyed their homes).

The Havasupai intensified farming on their little remaining land and began a wide-scale cultivation of peaches. In 1912 they purchased cattle. Severe epidemics in the early twentieth century reduced their population to just over 100. At the same time the Bureau of Indian Affairs, initially slow to move into the canyon, proceeded with a program of rapid acculturation. By the 1930s, Havasupai economic independence had given way to a reliance on limited wage labor. Traditional political power declined as well, despite the creation in 1939 of a tribal council.

Feeling confined in the canyon, the Havasupai stepped up their fight for permanent grazing rights on the plateau. The 1950s were a grim time for the people, with no employment and little tourism. Conflict over land led to deep familial divisions, which in turn resulted in serious cultural loss. Food prices at the local store were half again as high as those in neighboring towns. In the 1960s, however, an infusion of federal funds provided employment in tribal programs as well as modern utilities. Still, croplands continued to shrink, as more and more land was devoted to the upkeep of pack animals for the tourists, the tribe's limited but main source of income. In 1975, after an intensive lobbying effort, the government restored 185,000 acres of land to the Havasupai.

RELIGION The Havasupai performed at least three traditional ceremonies a year, the largest coming in the fall at harvest time and including music, dancing, and speechmaking. They often invited Hopi, Hualapai, and Navajo neighbors to share in these celebrations. One important ceremony was cremation (burial from the late nineteenth century) and mourning of the dead, who were greatly feared. Although the Hopi influenced the Havasupai in many ways, such as the use of masked dancers, the rich Hopi ceremonialism did not generally become part of Havasupai life. Curing was accomplished by means of shamans, who acquired their power from dreams. The Havasupai accepted the Ghost Dance in 1891.

GOVERNMENT Formal authority was located in chiefs, hereditary in theory only, of ten local groups. Their only real power was to advise and persuade. The Havasupai held few councils; most issues were dealt with by men informally in the sweat lodge.

CUSTOMS The Havasupai were individualists rather than band or tribe oriented. The family was the main unit of social organization. In place of a formal marriage ceremony, a man simply took up residence with a woman's family. The couple moved into their own home after they had a child. Women owned no property. Babies stayed mainly on basket cradle boards until they were old enough to walk. With some exceptions, work was roughly divided by gender.

Leisure time was spent in sweat lodges or playing games, including (after 1600 or so) horse racing. The Havasupai often sheltered Hopis in times of drought. Both sexes painted and tattooed their faces. Only girls went through a formal puberty ritual.

DWELLINGS In winter and summer, dwellings consisted of domed or conical wikiups of thatch and dirt over a pole frame. People also lived in rock shelters. Small domed lodges were used as sweat houses and clubhouses.

DIET In Cataract Canyon the people grew corn, beans, squash, sunflowers, and tobacco. During the winter they lived on the surrounding plateau and ate game such as mountain lion and other cats, deer, antelope, mountain sheep, fowl, and rabbits, which were killed in communal hunting drives. Wild foods included piñon nuts, cactus and yucca fruits, agave hearts, mesquite beans, and wild honey.

KEY TECHNOLOGY Traditional implements included stone knives, bone tools, bows and arrows, clay pipes for smoking, and nets of yucca fiber. The Havasupai tilled their soil with sticks. Baskets and pottery were used for a number of purposes. Grinding was accomplished by means of a flat rock and rotary mortars.

TRADE The Havasupai often traded with the Hopi and other allied tribes, exchanging deerskins, baskets, salt, lima beans, and red hematite paint for food, pottery, and cloth. They also traded with tribes as far away as the Pacific Ocean.

NOTABLE ARTS Baskets, created by women, were especially well made. They were used as burden baskets, seed beaters and parching trays, pitch-coated water bottles, and cradle hoods. Brown and unpainted pottery was first dried in the sun, then baked in hot coals.

TRANSPORTATION Horses entered the region in the seventeenth century.

DRESS Buckskin, worked by men, was the main clothing material. Women wore a two-part dress, with a yucca-fiber or textile belt around the waist, and trimmed with hoof tinklers. In the nineteenth century they began wearing ornamental shawls. Moccasins, when worn, were made with a high upper wrapped around the calf. Men wore shirts, loincloths, leggings, headbands, and high-ankle moccasins. Personal decoration consisted of necklaces, earrings of Pueblo and Navajo shell and silver, and occasionally painted faces.

WAR AND WEAPONS This peaceful people needed no war chiefs or societies. In the rare cases of defensive fighting, the most competent available leader took charge. Traditional allies included the Hualapai and Hopi; enemies included the Yavapai and Western Apache.

Contemporary Information

GOVERNMENT/RESERVATIONS The Havasupai Reservation was established from 1880 to 1882, near Supai, Arizona, along the Colorado River, 3,000 feet below the rim of the Grand Canyon. It now consists of roughly 188,000 acres, with year-to-year permits issued for grazing in Grand Canyon National Park and the adjacent National Forest. The tribe adopted a constitution and by-laws in 1939 and a tribal corporate charter in 1946. Men and women serve on the elected tribal council. In 1975, the tribe regained a portion (185,000 acres) of their ancestral homeland along the South Rim of the Grand Canyon.

ECONOMY Tourism constitutes the most important economic activity. The tribe offers mule guides, a campground, a hostel, a restaurant, and a lodge, and they sell baskets and other crafts. Farming has almost entirely disappeared. The tribe owns a significant cattle herd. Some people work for wages at Grand Canyon Village or in federal or tribal jobs. Fearing contamination from a new uranium mine, the tribe has banned mining on tribal lands.

LEGAL STATUS The Havasupai are a federally recognized tribal entity.

DAILY LIFE Life among the Havasupai remains a mixture of the old and the new. Unlike many Indian tribes, their reservation includes part of their ancestral land. Most children entering the tribal school (self-administered since 1975) speak only Pai; again, unlike many tribes that focus on learning tribal identity, Havasupai children are encouraged to learn more about the outside world. Students attend school on the reservation through the eighth grade, then move to boarding school in California or to regular public schools.

People continue to celebrate the traditional fall "peach festival," although the time has been changed to accommodate the boarding school schedule. Some people never leave the canyon; many venture out no more than several times a year. The nearest provisions are 100 miles away. Many still ride horses exclusively, although they may be listening to a portable music player at the time. Havasupai people often mix with tourists who wind up in the village at the end of the Grand Canyon's Hualapai Trail. Some people own satellite dishes and videocassette recorders, but much remains of the old patterns, and intermarriage beyond the Hualapai remains rare. Variants of traditional religion remain alive, while at the same time Rastafarianism is also popular, especially among young men. The people are fighting an ongoing legal battle over uranium pollution of a sacred site in the Kaibab National Forest.

Hopi

Hopi (`H ō p ē) from *Hopituh Shi-nu-mu,* "Peaceful People." They were formerly called the Moki (or Moqui) Indians, a name probably taken from a Zuñi epithet.

LOCATION The Hopi are the westernmost of the Pueblo peoples. First, Second, and Third Mesas are all part of Black Mesa, located on the Colorado Plateau between the Colorado River and the Rio Grande, in northeast Arizona. Of the several Hopi villages, all but Old Oraibi are of relatively recent construction.

POPULATION Hopi population was perhaps 2,800 in the late seventeenth century. It was roughly 7,000 in 1990.

LANGUAGE Hopi, a Shoshonean language, is a member of the Uto-Aztecan language family.

Historical Information

HISTORY The Hopi are probably descended from the prehistoric Anasazi culture. Ancestors of the Hopi have been in roughly the same location for at least 10,000 years. During the fourteenth century, Hopi became one of three centers of Pueblo culture, along with Zuñi/Acoma and the Rio Grande pueblos. Between the fourteenth and sixteenth centuries, three traits in particular distinguished the Hopi culture: a highly specialized agriculture, including selective breeding and various forms of irrigation; a pronounced artistic impulse, as seen in mural and pottery painting; and the mining and use of coal (after which the Hopi returned to using wood for fuel and sheep dung for firing pottery).

The Hopi first met non-native Americans when members of Coronado's party came into their country in 1540. The first missionary arrived in 1629, at Awatovi. Although the Spanish did not colonize Hopi, they did make the Indians swear allegiance to the Spanish Crown and attempted to undermine their religious beliefs. For this reason, the Hopis joined the Pueblo rebellion of 1680. They destroyed all local missions and established new pueblos at the top of Black Mesa that were easier to defend. The Spanish reconquest of 1692 did not reach Hopi land, and the Hopis welcomed refugees from other pueblos who sought to live free of Spanish influence. In 1700, the Hopis destroyed Awatovi, the only village with an active mission, and remained free of Christianity for almost 200 years thereafter.

During the nineteenth century the Hopi endured an increase in Navajo raiding. Later in the century they again encountered non-natives, this time permanently. The U.S. government established a Hopi reservation in 1882, and the railroad began bringing in trading posts, tourists, missionaries, and scholars. The new visitors in turn brought disease epidemics that reduced the Hopi population dramatically.

Like many tribes, the Hopi struggled to deal with the upheaval brought about by these new circumstances. Following the Dawes Act (1887), surveyors came in preparation for parceling the land into individual allotments; the Hopis met them with armed resistance. Although there was no fighting, Hopi leaders were imprisoned. They were imprisoned as well for their general refusal to send their children to the new schools, which were known for brutal discipline and policies geared toward cultural genocide. Hopi children were kidnapped and sent to the schools anyway.

Factionalism also took a toll on Hopi life. Ceremonial societies split between "friendly" and "hostile" factions. This development led in 1906 to the division of Oraibi, which had been continuously occupied since at least 1100, into five villages. Contact with the outside world increased significantly after the two world wars. By the 1930s, the Hopi economy and traditional ceremonial life were in shambles (yet the latter remained more intact than perhaps that of any other U.S. tribe). Most people who could find work worked for wages or the tourist trade. For the first time, alcoholism became a problem.

In 1943, a U.S. decision to divide the Hopi and Navajo Reservations into grazing districts resulted in the loss of most Hopi land. This sparked a major disagreement between the tribes and the government that continues to this day. Following World War II, the "hostile" traditionalists emerged as the caretakers of land, resisting cold war policies such as mineral development and nuclear testing and mining. The official ("friendly") tribal council, however, instituted policies that favored exploitation of the land, notably permitting Peabody Coal to strip-mine Black Mesa, beginning in 1970.

RELIGION According to legend, the Hopi agreed to act as caretakers of this Fourth World in exchange for permission to live here. Over centuries of a stable existence based on farming, they evolved an extremely rich ceremonial life. The Hopi Way, whose purpose is to maintain a balance between nature and people in every aspect of life, is ensured by the celebration of their ceremonies.

The Hopi recognize two major ceremonial cycles, masked (January or February until July) and unmasked, which are determined by the position of the sun and the lunar calendar. The purpose of most ceremonies is to bring rain. As the symbol of life and well-being, corn, a staple crop, is the focus of many ceremonies. All great ceremonies last nine days, including a preliminary day. Each ceremony is controlled by a clan or several clans. Central to Hopi ceremonialism is the kiva, or underground chamber, which is seen as a doorway to the cave world from whence their ancestors originally came.

Katsinas are guardian spirits, or intermediaries between the creator and the people. They are said to dwell at the San Francisco peaks and at other holy places. Every year at the winter solstice, they travel to inhabit people's bodies and remain until after the summer solstice. Re-created in dolls and masks, they deliver the blessings of life and teach people the proper way to live. Katsina societies are associated with clan ancestors and with rain gods. All Hopis are initiated into katsina societies, although only men play an active part in them.

Perhaps the most important ceremony of the year is Soyal, or the winter solstice, which celebrates the Hopi worldview and recounts their legends. Another important ceremony is Niman, the harvest festival. The August Snake Dance has become a well-known Hopi ceremony.

Like other Pueblo peoples, the Hopi recognize a dual division of time and space between the upper world of the living and the lower world of the dead. Prayer may be seen as a mediation between the upper and lower, or human and supernatural, worlds. These worlds coexist at the same time and may be seen in oppositions such as summer and winter, day and night, life and death. In all aspects of Hopi ritual, ideas of space, time, color, and number are all interrelated in such a way as to provide order to the Hopi world.

GOVERNMENT Traditionally, the Hopi favored a weak government coupled with a strong matrilineal, matrilocal clan system. They were not a tribe in the usual sense of the word but were characterized by an elaborate social structure, each village having its own organization and each individual his or her own place in the community. The "tribe" was "invented" in 1936, when the non-native Oliver La Farge wrote their constitution. Although a tribal council exists, many people's allegiance remains with the village *kikmongwi (cacique)*. A *kikmongwi* is appointed for life and rules in matters of traditional religion. Major villages include Walpi (First Mesa), Shungopavi (Second Mesa), and Oraibi (Third Mesa).

CUSTOMS Hopi children learn their traditions through katsina dolls, including scare-katsinas, as well as social pressure, along with an abundance of love and attention. This approach tends to encourage friendliness and sharing in Hopi children. In general, women owned (and built) the houses and other material resources while men farmed and hunted away from the village. Special societies included katsina and other men's and women's organizations concerned with curing, clowning, weather control, and war.

Following a death, the deceased's hair was washed with yucca suds and decorated with prayer feathers. The face was covered with a mask of raw cotton, to evoke the clouds. He or she was then wrapped in a blanket and buried in a sitting position, with food and water. Cornmeal and prayer sticks were also placed in the grave, with a stick for a spirit ladder.

DWELLINGS Distinctive one- or two-floor pueblo housing featured sandstone and adobe walls and roof beams of pine and juniper, gathered from afar. The dwellings were entered via ladders through openings in the roofs and were arranged around a central plaza. This architectural arrangement reflects and reinforces cosmological ideas concerning emergence from an underworld through successive world levels.

DIET Hopis have been expert dry farmers for centuries, growing corn, beans, squash, cotton, and tobacco on floodplains and sand dunes or, with the use of irrigation, near springs. The Spanish brought crops such as wheat, chilies, peaches, melons, and other fruit. Men were the farmers and hunters of game such as deer, antelope, elk, and rabbits. The Hopi also kept domesticated turkeys. Women gathered wild food and herbs, such as pine nuts, prickly pear, yucca, berries, currants, nuts, and seeds. Crops were dried and stored against drought and famine.

KEY TECHNOLOGY Farming technology included digging sticks (later the horse and plow), small rock or brush-and-dirt dams and sage windbreaks, and an accurate calendar on which each year's planting time was based. Grinding tools were made of stone. Men wove clothing and women made pottery, which was used for many purposes. Men also hunted with the bow and arrow and used snares and nets to trap animals.

TRADE The Hopi obtained gems, such as turquoise, from Zuñi and Pueblo tribes. Shell came from the Pacific Ocean and the Gulf of Mexico. They also traded for sheep and wool from the Navajo, buckskins from the Havasupai, and mescal from various tribes.

NOTABLE ARTS Fine arts included pottery decorated with designs based on ancient geometric patterns, made by women. Men spun and wove cotton into costumes and clothing, for domestic use and for trade. Designs were generally asymmetrical but balanced between objects and color to render an idea of harmony. Other fine arts included silversmithing, introduced by the Navajo in 1890; weaving baskets and blankets; painting; and creating katsina dolls.

TRANSPORTATION Horses arrived with the Spanish in the sixteenth century.

DRESS Clothing was usually made of cotton and included long dresses for women and loincloths for men. Both wore leather moccasins and rabbit-skin robes as well as blankets and fur capes for warmth. Unmarried women wore their hair in the shape of a squash blossom; braids were preferred after marriage.

WAR AND WEAPONS The annual war society ceremony is now obsolete.

Contemporary Information

GOVERNMENT/RESERVATIONS The Hopi Reservation was established in 1882. Consisting originally of almost 2.5 million acres, the total land base stood at just over 1.5 million acres in 1995. Thirteen Hopi villages now stand on three mesas. A tribal council was created in 1936, although only two of the villages were represented in 1992.

Hopis are also members of the Colorado River Indian Tribes Reservation (*see* Mojave).

ECONOMY As they have for centuries, Hopis continue to farm for their food. They also raise sheep and cattle. Crafts for the tourist trade—especially silver jewelry, katsina dolls, and pottery—bring in some money. Seventy percent of the tribe's operating budget comes from coal leases, but mineral leases remain exploitative, and their effects include strip mining, radiation contamination, and depletion of precious water resources. The tribal council has also invested in factories and in a cultural center/motel/museum complex.

LEGAL STATUS The Hopi are a federally recognized tribal entity, as are the Colorado River Indian Tribes (CRIT), where some Hopis settled after World War II. The Hopi Reservation was carved in 1882 from traditional Hopi lands plus three villages of Navajos living on Hopi lands (settlers and refugees from U.S. Indian wars).

A major dispute has emerged within the tribe and among the Hopi tribal council, the Navajos, and the U.S. government over the lands around the part of the reservation known as Big Mountain. Technically the land belongs to the Hopis, but it has been homesteaded since the mid–eighteenth century by Navajos because, in their view, the Hopis were just "ignoring" it. The Hopi council wants the land for mineral exploitation. Hopi traditionalists want the Navajos to remain, out of solidarity, friendship with their old enemies, and their inclination to share. They would prefer that the land remain free of mineral exploitation.

In 1986, the United States recognized the squatters' rights by proclaiming 1.8 million acres of "joint use area": Each tribe got half, and those on the "other" side were to move. In effect, the Hopis lost half of their original reservation to the Navajo. More than 100 Hopis moved, but many Navajos remained. This conflict remains ongoing, with the Hopis still trying to hold onto their land. Many Indians believe that coal company profits are at the root of the dispute and forced relocations.

DAILY LIFE The Hopi way continues; they are among the most traditional of all Indians in the United States. Hopis maintain a strong sense of the continuity of life and time. The split between "progressive" and "traditional" factions continues. Hopi High School, between Second and Third Mesas, opened in 1986 with an entirely local board. The school emphasizes Hopi culture and a new written language as well as computers and contemporary American curricula. The first dictionary of written Hopi is in preparation. The Hopi are making progress in solving not only the land dispute with the Navajo but also a host of social problems, including substance abuse and suicide.

Most Hopis live in the traditional pueblos, many of which now have glass windows. Perhaps 1,500 Hopis live and work off the reservation, although many return for ceremonies. Especially in some of the modern villages, houses contain plumbing and electricity and are constructed of cement blocks without benefit of a central plaza.

Hopi-Tewa

The Hopi-Tewa are a small group (roughly 700) of Native Americans living mostly on the Hopi Reservation. These Indians are descended from immigrants who settled at First Mesa (Tewa Village [Hano] and Polacca) following the Pueblo rebellion, around 1700. They speak a variety of Tewa, a Tanoan language, and have some distinct cultural attributes.

See also Hopi.

Hualapai

Hualapai (`Wä lä p ī), or Walapai (*Xawálapáiya*), "Pine Tree People," were named after the piñon pine nut. With the Havasupai, they are called the Pai (Pa'a) Indians ("the People": the Hualapai are the Western Pai, and the Havasupai are the Eastern Pai). They are also described, with the Havasupai and the Yavapai, as Upland Yumans, in contrast to the River Yumans, such as the Mojave and Quechan.

LOCATION Hualapai territory is located along the middle course of the Colorado River in present-day northwestern Arizona. Today, most Hualapai live near Peach Springs, Arizona, which is located near the Grand Canyon.

POPULATION Roughly 1,100 prior to contact with non-natives, the 1993 Hualapai population was 1,872.

LANGUAGE Hualapais spoke Upland Yuman, a member of the Hokan-Siouan language family.

Historical Information

HISTORY The Pai Indians, who traditionally considered themselves one people, probably descended from the prehistoric Patayans of the ancient Hakataya culture. Thirteen bands of Pai originally ranged in northwest Arizona along the Colorado River, hunting, farming, and gathering. By historic times, three subtribes had been organized: the Middle Mountain People, the Plateau People, and the Yavapai Fighters. Each subtribe was further divided into several bands, which in turn were divided into camps and families.

Although the Pai encountered non-natives in 1540, or perhaps as late as 1598, neither the Spanish nor the Mexicans developed Hualapai country, which remained fairly isolated until the 1820s. Around that time, a trail was blazed from the Rio Grande to California that led directly through Pai country. After the Mexican cession (1848), Hualapais began working in white-owned mines. With Anglo invasions and treaty violations increasing and the mines ever exploitative, the Hualapai, in 1865, met violence with violence. A warrior named Cherum forced a key U.S. retreat but later scouted for his old enemy. Later, the United States selected Hualapai Charley and Leve Leve as principal chiefs because they were amenable to making peace. The Hualapai war ended in 1869.

As the Eastern Pai played a minor role in the war, they were allowed to return home afterward; it was at this juncture that the two "tribes," Hualapai and Havasupai, became increasingly separate. The army forced those Hualapai who failed to escape to march in 1874 to the Colorado River Reservation. There, the low altitude combined with disease and poor rations brought the Hualapai much suffering and death. When they filtered back home several years later, they found their land in non-native hands. Still, they applied for and received official permission to remain, and a reservation was established for them in 1883.

The reservation consisted of 1 million acres on the South Rim of the Grand Canyon, a fraction of their original land. Before long, overgrazing by non-Indians had ruined the native food supply, and ranchers and cattlemen were directly threatening the Indians with physical violence. A series of epidemics struck the Hualapai. Most Hualapai lived off the reservation, scrambling for wage work and sending their children to Anglo schools. As the Hualapai formed an underclass of cheap, unskilled labor, their way of life began to vanish. The railroad depot at Peach Springs became the primary Hualapai village. The railroad brought dislocation, disease, and some jobs. Their new condition strengthened their differences with the still-isolated Havasupai.

The Hualapai began herding cattle in 1914, although their herds were greatly outnumbered by those of non-natives. Extensive prejudice against the Indians diminished somewhat after World War I, out of respect for Indian war heroes. Through the middle twentieth century the Hualapai retained a strong sense of their culture, although economic progress was extremely slow.

RELIGION According to the Hualapai creation myth, a spirit prayed life into canes cut from along the Colorado River near Spirit Mountain, in present-day Nevada. An unseen world of gods and demons are in part responsible for the dreams that gave male and female shamans their power to cure. This they accomplished by singing, shaking gourds, and pretending to suck out disease with a tube and herbs. They also used their power to control the weather. If successful with a cure, shamans were paid in buckskins, but they might be killed if a patient died. In general, the Hualapai had few ceremonies or dances. They did accept the Ghost Dance in the 1890s.

GOVERNMENT Traditional political authority was decentralized. Headmen of both a camp (roughly 20 people) and a band (roughly 85–200 people) led by fostering consensus. They served as war chiefs and spokespeople when necessary. The position of headman was occasionally hereditary but more often based on personality and ability. There was little or no tribal identity until the early twentieth century, when the Hualapai created a fledgling tribal council. In the 1930s they adopted a constitution and elected their first tribal president.

CUSTOMS The Hualapai cremated their dead and burned their homes and belongings as well. In the nineteenth century they adopted the Mojave mourning ceremony, in which aspects of warfare were staged to honor the dead. They observed no formal marriage ceremony. Divorce was frequent and easy to obtain.

DWELLINGS Dome-shaped brush wikiups as well as rock shelters served as the major dwelling. The people (men, by and large) also used sweat lodges for curing and as clubhouses.

DIET Occasionally the Hualapai grew the standard American crops (corn, beans, and squash) near springs and ditches. Corn was made into mush, soup, and bread; pumpkins were dried in long strips. In the main, however, they obtained their food by hunting and gathering, leaving their summer camps to follow the seasonal ripening of wild foods. The women gathered piñon nuts, cactus and yucca fruits, agave (mescal) hearts, mesquite beans, and other plants. The men hunted deer, antelope, mountain sheep, rabbits (in drives), and small game. Meat was dried and stored in skin bags. The Hualapai also ate fish.

KEY TECHNOLOGY The Hualapai practiced a number of traditional irrigation techniques, such as ditch digging, crop location near water sources, and flood runoff *(ak chin)*. They used flat pounding-grinding rocks and rotary mortars for grinding. Baskets as well as pottery were used for conveyance and storage.

TRADE The Hualapai were part of an extensive system of exchange that stretched from the Pacific Ocean to the Pueblos. Shell decorations and horses came from the Mojave and the Quechan. Rich red ocher pigment was a key trade item, as were baskets and dried mescal and dressed skins. Meat and skins went for crops; lima beans for Hopi peaches.

NOTABLE ARTS Baskets and pottery, including pots, dishes, jars, and pipes, have been made for centuries.

TRANSPORTATION The Hualapai obtained horses in the seventeenth century.

DRESS Clothing was generally made from buckskin or juniper bark. Men wore shorts and breechcloths. Women wore skirts or aprons. Both wore moccasins or yucca sandals. Rabbit-skin robes and blankets were used in cold weather. In addition, the Hualapai painted their faces for decoration (women tattooed their chins), and both sexes wore shell necklaces.

WAR AND WEAPONS Traditional enemies included the Mojave and the Yavapai; their main ally was the Havasupai. The Hualapai fought with mulberry bows, clubs, and hide shields.

Contemporary Information

GOVERNMENT/RESERVATIONS The Hualapai Reservation consists of almost 1 million acres near Peach Springs, Arizona. The tribe adopted a constitution and by-laws in 1938 and a corporate charter in 1943. A new constitution was ratified in 1970. The tribal council consists of nine elected members and one hereditary chief, although the Bureau of Indian Affairs must still approve all ordinances.

ECONOMY The Hualapai Reservation is marked by very high unemployment (more than 80 percent). U.S. Interstate 40 bypasses the reservation, limiting opportunities for tourism. Important economic activities include forestry and raising cattle, along with some hunting and farming. The people sell some baskets to tourists, and they lease land for mining and lumbering. The tribe also controls hydroelectric, natural gas, oil, and uranium resources. Their hope for economic development based on a proposed Bridge Canyon dam was defeated in 1968 by the Central Arizona Project. The Hualapai plan to develop further what is now small-scale tourism, such as permits and guides, related to the Grand Canyon. Many Hualapai work for wages off the reservation.

LEGAL STATUS The Hualapai are a federally recognized tribal entity.

DAILY LIFE Many Hualapai speak English, but many also retain their native tongue. Most Hualapai who live on the reservation live in individual, modern homes. The shift from extended family to nuclear family living contributed to cultural breakdown. One response to this situation has been the development by Peach Springs Elementary School of a nationally recognized model bilingual/bicultural program. With children grounded in their own culture, their self-esteem has risen, which has translated directly into higher graduation rates. A summer memorial pow-wow honors the dead, whose clothes are still burned, but now they are buried rather than cremated. There are four active Christian churches on the reservation.

Isleta Pueblo

Isleta (Ēs 'l ā tä) from the Spanish missions San Antonio de la Isleta and San Augustin de la Isleta (*isleta* means "little island"). The word "pueblo" comes from the Spanish for "village." It refers both to a certain style of Southwest Indian architecture, characterized by multistory, apartmentlike buildings made of adobe, and to the people themselves. The pueblos along the Rio Grande are known as eastern Pueblos; Zuñi, Hopi, and sometimes Acoma and Laguna are known as western Pueblos. The Tiwa name for Isleta Pueblo is *Shiewhibak,* meaning "flint kick-stick place."

LOCATION Since at least the eighteenth century, Isleta Pueblo has been located on the Rio Grande several miles south of Albuquerque. The pueblo consists of a main village (San Agustín) and two farm villages (Chikal and "town chief") 3 miles to the south.

POPULATION In 1990, 2,700 Isletas lived on the pueblo, out of a total population of 2,900. Perhaps 410 lived there in 1790.

LANGUAGE Isletas spoke Southern Tiwa, a Kiowa-Tanoan language.

Historical Information

HISTORY All Pueblo people are thought to be descended from Anasazi and perhaps Mogollon and several other ancient peoples, although the precise origin of the Keresan peoples is unknown. From their ancestors they learned architecture, farming, pottery, and basketry. Larger population groups became possible with effective agriculture and ways to store food surpluses. Within the context of a relatively stable existence, the people devoted increasing amounts of time and attention to religion, arts, and crafts.

In the 1200s, the Anasazi abandoned their traditional canyon homelands in response to climatic and social upheavals. A century or two of migrations ensued, followed in general by the slow reemergence of their culture in the historic pueblos. The Tiwas were probably the first of the Tanoan Pueblo people to enter the northern Rio Grande region. Isleta itself grew from several prehistoric villages in the area, including Puré Tuay. The Spanish made contact with Isleta in the late sixteenth century, establishing a mission in 1613. Modern Isleta is perhaps an eighteenth-century settlement; many disruptions occurred as a result of constant conquistador attacks.

In 1598, Juan de Oñate arrived in the area with settlers, founding the colony of New Mexico. Oñate carried on the process, already underway in nearby areas, of subjugating the local Indians; forcing them to pay taxes in crops, cotton, and work; and opening the door for Catholic missionaries to attack their religion. The Spanish renamed the Pueblos with saints' names and began a program of church construction. At the same time, the Spanish introduced such new crops as peaches, wheat, and peppers into the region. In 1620, a royal decree created civil offices at each pueblo; silver-headed canes, many of which remain in use today, symbolized the governor's authority.

Isleta did not participate in the general Pueblo revolt against the Spanish in 1680, either out of fear of the Spanish or perhaps a reluctance to take the unusual step of joining an all-Pueblo alliance. They, the Spanish refugees, and people from some pueblos south of Albuquerque went to El Paso. Some Isletas reoccupied the pueblo in 1681; at that time, Spanish troops attacked and burned it and took hundreds of prisoners back to El Paso. Their descendants live today at Tigua Pueblo (Ysleta del Sur), south of El Paso. Some Southern Tiwas who did not go to El Paso went instead to Hopi and established a village (Payupki) on Second Mesa. Two Spanish friars escorted over 400 Tiwa back from Hopi in 1742; the permanent occupation of Isleta Pueblo may date from that time.

The Pueblos experienced many changes during the following decades: Refugees established communities at Hopi, guerrilla fighting continued against the Spanish, and certain areas were abandoned. By the 1700s, excluding Hopi and Zuñi, only Taos, Picuris, Isleta and Acoma Pueblos had not changed locations since the arrival of the Spanish. Although Pueblo unity did not last, and Santa Fe was officially reconquered in 1692, Spanish rule was notably less severe from then on. Harsh forced labor all but ceased, and the Indians reached an understanding with the Church that enabled them to continue practicing their traditional religion.

In general, the Pueblo eighteenth century was marked by smallpox epidemics and increased raiding by the Apache, Comanche, and Ute. Occasionally Pueblo Indians fought with the Spanish against the nomadic tribes. The people practiced their religion but more or less in secret. During this time, intermarriage and regular exchange between Hispanic villages and Pueblo Indians created a new New Mexican culture, neither strictly Spanish nor Indian, but rather somewhat of a blend between the two.

Mexican "rule" in 1821 brought little immediate change to the Pueblos. The Mexicans stepped up what had been a gradual process of appropriating Indian land and water, and they allowed the nomadic tribes even greater latitude to raid. As the presence of the United States in the area grew, it attempted to enable the Pueblo Indians to continue their generally peaceful and self-sufficient ways, in part by recognizing Spanish land grants to the Pueblos.

During the nineteenth century the process of acculturation among Pueblo Indians quickened markedly. In an attempt to retain their identity, Pueblo Indians clung even more tenaciously to their heritage, which by now included elements of the once-hated Spanish culture and religion. By the 1880s, railroads had largely put an end to the traditional geographical isolation of the pueblos. Paradoxically, the U.S. decision to recognize Spanish land grants to the Pueblos denied Pueblo Indians certain rights granted under official treaties and left them particularly open to exploitation by squatters and thieves.

Since the 1700s, Isleta had been without katsina masks owing to the presence and active interference of the Spanish. Shortly after Laguna Pueblo divided around 1880 over factional differences, Isleta accepted a number of Lagunas into their village. Isleta traded homes and land for ceremonial invigoration. Within a few years, most of the Lagunas had returned to a village near their pueblo, but the katsina chief remained, as did his descendants, the masks, and the rituals.

After a gap of more than 300 years, the All Indian Pueblo Council began to meet again in the 1920s, specifically in response to a congressional threat to appropriate Pueblo lands. Partly as a result of the Council's activities, Congress confirmed Pueblo title to their lands in 1924 by passing the Pueblo Lands Act. The United States also acknowledged its trust responsibilities in a series of legal decisions and other acts of Congress. Still, especially after 1900, Pueblo culture was increasingly threatened by highly intolerant Protestant evangelical missions and schools. The Bureau of Indian Affairs also weighed in on the subject of acculturation, forcing Indian children to leave their homes and attend culture-killing boarding schools. Pablo Abeita, a member of the reorganized

All Indian Pueblo Council, fought to defeat the Bursum Bill, a plan to appropriate the best Pueblo lands.

The dynamic tension between Catholicism and traditional beliefs remains in flux at Isleta: As recently as 1965 the Indians evicted a priest regarded as insufficiently sensitive to their traditions. Since the late nineteenth century, but especially after the 1960s, Pueblos have had to cope with onslaughts by (mostly white) anthropologists and seekers of Indian spirituality. The region is also known for its major art colonies at Taos and Santa Fe.

RELIGION   In traditional Pueblo culture, religion and life are inseparable. To be in harmony with all of nature is the Pueblo ideal and way of life. The sun is seen as the representative of the Creator. Sacred mountains in each direction, plus the sun above and the earth below, define and balance the Pueblo world. Many Pueblo religious ceremonies revolve around the weather and are devoted to ensuring adequate rainfall. To this end, Pueblo Indians evoke the power of katsinas, sacred beings who live in mountains and other holy places, in ritual and masked dance. The Isleta katsina cult was reestablished at Isleta around 1880 by refugees from Laguna Pueblo, when Laguna religious society heads banded together at Isleta to form a single curing organization, the Laguna Fathers.

In addition to the natural boundaries, Pueblo Indians have created a society that defines their world by providing balanced, reciprocal relationships within which people connect and harmonize with each other, the natural world, and time itself. At Isleta, each tribal division (Red Eyes/summer and Black Eyes/winter) is in charge of the pueblo's ceremonies for half a year. Each is responsible for one major dance a year. According to tradition, the head of each pueblo is the religious leader, or *cacique*, whose primary responsibility it is to watch the sun and thereby determine the dates of ceremonies. Much ceremonialism is also based on medicine societies, and shamans who derive powers from animal spirits use their supernatural powers for curing, weather control, and ensuring the general welfare. Isleta has one round prayer chamber, or kiva. Ceremonies are held either in there or in the central plaza. Especially in the eastern pueblos, most ceremonies are kept secret.

GOVERNMENT   Pueblo governments derived from two traditions. Offices that are probably indigenous include the *cacique,* or head of the Pueblo, and the war captains. These officials are intimately related to the religious structures of the pueblo and reflected the essentially theocratic nature of Pueblo government. At Isleta, the corn group leaders appointed the town chief *(cacique),* who was never permitted to leave the pueblo. Because of his many ritual obligations he was publicly supported. The *cacique* appointed the war or bow priest. A bow rather than a cane symbolized his office. He was of roughly equal importance with the *cacique* and was primarily responsible for security. Isleta also had a hunt chief, who led rituals for assuring health of animals and directed communal hunts, as well as an advisory group called the council of *principales,* composed of all religious officers and their first assistants.

A parallel but in most cases distinctly less powerful group of officials was imposed by the Spanish authorities. Appointed by the traditional leadership, they generally dealt with external and church matters and included the governor, two lieutenant governors, and two sheriffs. The authority of their offices was symbolized by canes. Nontraditional positions also included a ditch boss, who was in charge of the irrigation ditches, as well as a town crier and sacristan. In addition, the All Indian Pueblo Council, dating from 1598, began meeting again in the twentieth century.

The last correctly installed *cacique* at Isleta died in 1896. After that date, disruptions of installation rituals caused the war chiefs to serve for decades as acting *caciques.* This situation came to a head in the 1940s, when a political revolution split the pueblo into several factions and postponed elections. With the help of the Bureau of Indian Affairs, a constitution was drawn up; elections were held and the proper officers installed in 1950.

CUSTOMS   One mechanism that works to keep Pueblo societies coherent is a pervasive aversion to individualistic behavior. Children were traditionally raised with gentle guidance and a minimum of discipline. Pueblo Indians were generally monogamous, and divorce was relatively rare. The dead were prepared ceremonially and quickly buried with clothes, beads, food, and other items, their heads facing south. A vigil of four days and nights was generally observed.

Isleta Pueblo was organized into seven corn groups. Men led the groups, although there were women's auxiliaries. The groups were ritual units more similar to kiva groups, functioning for personal crises and societal ceremonies. The tribe was also divided into Red Eyes/summer and Black Eyes/winter groups. Each had a war captain and two or three assistants. Four men from each group served for life as grandfathers or disciplinarians. Each group had ceremonial, irrigation, clowning, hunting, ballplaying, and other group responsibilities.

Two medicine societies (for illness due to misbehavior or witchcraft) were the Town Fathers and the Laguna Fathers. A warrior's society consisted of people who had taken a scalp and had been ritually purified. Closely associated with the kiva, this group also had a women's component, with special duties. The economy was basically a socialistic one, whereby labor was shared and produce was distributed equally. In modern times photography by outsiders is discouraged.

DWELLINGS Isleta Pueblo featured apartment-style dwellings as high as five stories, as well as individual houses, facing south. The buildings were constructed of adobe (earth and straw) bricks, with beams across the roof that were covered with poles, brush, and plaster. Floors were of wood plank or packed earth. The roof of one level served as the floor of another. The levels were interconnected by ladders. As an aid to defense, the traditional design included no doors or windows; entry was through the roof. Pit houses, or kivas, served as ceremonial chambers and clubhouses. The village plaza, around which all dwellings were clustered, is the spiritual center of the village where all the balanced forces of the world come together. A track for ceremonial foot races was also part of the village.

DIET Isletas were farmers. Before the Spanish arrived, they ate primarily corn, beans, and squash. They also grew cotton and tobacco. They hunted deer, mountain lion, bear, antelope, and rabbits. Occasionally, men from Isleta would travel east to hunt buffalo. Isletas also gathered a variety of wild seeds, nuts, berries, and other foods and fished in rivers and mountain streams. The Spanish introduced wheat, alfalfa, chilies, fruit trees, grapes (often made into wine for sale to Laguna Pueblo or nearby Spanish-American villages), sheep, cattle, and garden vegetables, which soon became part of the regular diet.

KEY TECHNOLOGY Precontact farming implements were wooden. Traditional irrigation systems used ditches to ferry water from the Rio Grande as well as floodwater collection at arroyo mouths (*ak chin*). Tanning tools were made of bone and wood. The Spanish introduced metal tools and equipment. Men hunted with bows and arrows.

TRADE All Pueblos were part of extensive Native American trading networks. With the arrival of other cultures, Pueblo Indians also traded with the Hispanic American villages and then U.S. traders. At fixed times during summer or fall, enemies declared truces so that trading fairs might be held. The largest and best known was at Taos with the Comanche. Nomads exchanged slaves, buffalo hides, buckskins, jerked meat, and horses for agricultural and manufactured pueblo products. Pueblo Indians traded for shell and copper ornaments, turquoise, and macaw feathers. Isleta in particular traded for Jicarilla baskets; decorated pottery from other pueblos, especially Acoma, Zia, and Santo Domingo; and religious pictures from the Spanish, with whom they were in frequent contact. Trade along the Santa Fe Trail began in 1821. By the 1880s and the arrival of railroads, the Pueblos were dependent on many American-made goods, and the native manufacture of weaving and pottery declined and nearly died out.

NOTABLE ARTS In the Pueblo way, art and life are inseparable. Isleta arts included pottery and woven cotton items. Songs, dances, and dramas also qualify as traditional arts. Isleta pottery became strongly influenced by Laguna immigrants in the 1880s. Many Pueblos experienced a renaissance of traditional arts in the twentieth century, beginning in 1919 with San Ildefonso pottery.

TRANSPORTATION Spanish horses, mules, and cattle arrived at Isleta Pueblo in the seventeenth century.

DRESS Men wore shirts, leggings, and moccasins made of deer hides tanned and colored red-brown with plant dye. Women's wrapped leggings and moccasins were of white buckskin. Clothing was also made of spun cotton. Rabbit skin was also used for clothing and robes.

WAR AND WEAPONS Though often depicted as passive and docile, most Pueblo groups regularly engaged in warfare. The great revolt of 1680 stands out as the major military action, but they skirmished at other times with the Spanish and defended themselves against attackers such as Apaches, Comanches, and Utes. They also contributed auxiliary soldiers to provincial forces under Spain and Mexico, which were used mainly against raiding Indians and to protect merchant caravans on the Santa Fe Trail. After the raiding tribes began to pose less of a threat in the late nineteenth century, Pueblo military societies began to wither away, with the office of war captain changing to civil and religious functions.

Contemporary Information

GOVERNMENT/RESERVATIONS Isleta Pueblo contains roughly 211,000 acres. Its constitution was last revised in 1970. Under it, men vote for the governor and an appointed council.

ECONOMY Many people work for wages at the local air force base, for the tribe, or in Albuquerque. Some arts and crafts are produced, especially silver work and textiles; the pottery is produced with commercial methods and materials and is strictly for the tourist trade. There is some cattle ranching and some farming. Most Pueblo land is leased for oil testing.

LEGAL STATUS The Pueblo of Isleta is a federally recognized tribal entity.

DAILY LIFE Although the project of retaining a strong Indian identity is a difficult one in the late twentieth century, Pueblo people have strong roots, and in many ways the ancient rhythms and patterns continue. Some people still speak Isleta, and traditional ceremonies are still performed. Children are born into ritual corn groups as well as one of the winter/summer ceremonial divisions. Many Pueblo Indians, though nominally Catholic, have fused pieces of Catholicism onto a core of traditional beliefs.

Since the 1970s control of schools has been a key in maintaining their culture. Health problems, including alcoholism and drug use, continue to plague the Pueblos. Furthermore, Isleta is the first community downstream from several highly polluting industries, including a huge landfill. Some nearby lakes have been seriously polluted.

Jemez Pueblo

Jemez (`H ē mish) from the Spanish *Jémez*, taken from the Jemez self-designation. The Jemez name for their pueblo is *Walatowa*, "at the pueblo in the cañada" or "this is the place." The word "pueblo" comes from the Spanish for "village." It refers both to a certain style of Southwest Indian architecture, characterized by multistory, apartmentlike buildings made of adobe, and to the people themselves. Rio Grande pueblos are known as eastern Pueblos; Zuñi, Hopi, and sometimes Acoma and Laguna are known as western Pueblos.

LOCATION   Jemez Pueblo is located along the east bank of the Jemez River, 25 miles north of Bernalillo, New Mexico.

POPULATION   In 1990, almost 1,750 Indians were resident, virtually the entire pueblo population. Perhaps 30,000 people lived there in 1530, and 100 in 1744.

LANGUAGE   The people spoke Towa, a Kiowa-Tanoan language.

Historical Information

HISTORY   All Pueblo people are thought to be descended from Anasazi and perhaps Mogollon and several other ancient peoples. From them they learned architecture, farming, pottery, and basketry. Larger population groups became possible with effective agriculture and ways to store food surpluses. Within the context of a relatively stable existence, the people devoted increasing amounts of time and attention to religion, arts, and crafts.

The Jemez people lived near Stone Canyon, south of Dulce, New Mexico, around 2,000 years ago. They moved to near their present location after the arrival of the Athapaskans, around the fourteenth century. However, some of them moved to the San Diego Canyon–Guadalupe Canyon area, south of Santa Fe, where they estab-

lished numerous large fortresses and hundreds of small houses.

The Spaniards found them in 1540 and built a mission there (at Giusewa Pueblo) in the late sixteenth century. In 1621, they began another mission at the Pueblo de la Congregación, the present Jemez Pueblo. In 1628, Fray Martin de Arvide arrived at the Mission of San Diego de la Congregación with orders to unite the scattered Jemez communities, after which Jemez Pueblo became an important center for missionary activity.

Despite the pueblo's position as a missionary center, the Jemez people actively resisted Spanish efforts to undermine their religion. They joined in rebellion with the Navajo in about 1645, a crime for which 29 Jemez leaders were hanged. They also took a leading part in the Pueblo rebellion of 1680. For years, the Spaniards had routinely tortured Indians for practicing traditional religion. They also forced the Indians to labor for them, sold Indians into slavery, and let their cattle overgraze Indian land, a situation that eventually led to drought, erosion, and famine. Popé of San Juan Pueblo and other Pueblo religious leaders planned the great revolt, sending runners carrying cords of maguey fibers to mark the day of rebellion. On August 10, 1680, a virtually united stand on the part of the Pueblos drove the Spanish from the region. The Indians killed many Spaniards but refrained from mass slaughter, allowing most of them to leave Santa Fe for El Paso.

The Jemez people withdrew to sites on the top of the San Diego Mesa in 1681. When the Spanish left they descended, only to reascend in 1689 when they sighted a new Spanish force. Some returned again to the pueblo in 1692, when they, along with Keresans from Zia Pueblo, arrived at an understanding with the Spanish. Most Jemez, however, still resisted the Spanish, a situation that resulted in fighting between the Jemez and the Keresan pueblos of Zia and Santa Ana. This in turn resulted in a punitive Spanish-Keresan expedition in 1694, ending in the death or capture of over 400 Jemez people. All prisoners were pardoned after they helped the Spanish defeat the Tewas at Black Mesa.

By 1696, Jemez Pueblo had been rebuilt and reoccupied at or near the original site. The following year, however, after joining again with the Navajo in an anti-Spanish revolt, the Jemez returned to their ancestral homeland near Stone Canyon. Others went west to the Navajo country; of these, some eventually returned to Jemez but many remained with the Navajo. Some Jemez also fled to Hopi but were returned several years later by missionaries. The Jemez exile did not end until the early eighteenth century, when members of the tribe returned and settled at Walatowa, 12 miles south of their former mesa homes. At that time they built a new church, San Diego de los Jémez.

The Pueblos experienced many changes during following decades: Refugees established communities at Hopi, guerrilla fighting continued against the Spanish, and certain areas were abandoned. By the 1700s, excluding Hopi and Zuñi, only Taos, Picuris, Isleta and Acoma Pueblos had not changed locations since the arrival of the Spanish. Although Pueblo unity did not last, and Santa Fe was officially reconquered in 1692, Spanish rule was notably less severe from then on. Harsh forced labor all but ceased, and the Indians reached an understanding with the Church that enabled them to continue practicing their traditional religion.

In general, the Pueblo eighteenth century was marked by smallpox epidemics, and increased raiding by the Apache, Comanche, and Ute. Occasionally Pueblo Indians fought with the Spanish against the nomadic tribes. The people practiced their religion but more or less in secret. During this time, intermarriage and regular exchange between Hispanic villages and Pueblo Indians created a new New Mexican culture, neither strictly Spanish nor Indian, but rather somewhat of a blend between the two.

Mexican "rule" in 1821 brought little immediate change to the Pueblos. The Mexicans stepped up what had been a gradual process of appropriating Indian land and water, and they allowed the nomadic tribes even greater latitude to raid. In 1837, a political rebellion by Indians and Hispanics over the issue of taxes led to the assassination of the governor of New Mexico and the brief installation of a Taos Indian as governor. At about the same time, the last 20 or so Towa-speaking Pecos people joined the Jemez after abandoning their own pueblo due to Athapaskan raids, smallpox, factionalism, farming decreases, and land pressures from Hispanics. As the presence of the United States in the area grew, it attempted to enable the Pueblo Indians to continue their generally peaceful and self-sufficient ways; in 1858, Congress approved the old Spanish land grant of over 17,000 acres to Jemez Pueblo.

During the nineteenth century the process of acculturation among Pueblo Indians quickened markedly. In an attempt to retain their identity, Pueblo Indians clung even more tenaciously to their heritage, which by now included elements of the once-hated Spanish culture and religion. By the 1880s, railroads had largely put an end to the traditional geographical isolation of the pueblos. Paradoxically, the U.S. decision to recognize Spanish land grants to the Pueblos denied Pueblo Indians certain rights granted under official treaties and left them particularly open to exploitation by squatters and thieves.

After a gap of more than 300 years, the All Indian Pueblo Council began to meet again in the 1920s, specifically in response to a congressional threat to appropriate Pueblo lands. Partly as a result of the Council's activities, Congress confirmed Pueblo title to their lands in 1924 by passing the Pueblo Lands Act. The United States also acknowledged its trust responsibilities in a series of legal decisions and other acts of Congress. Still, especially after 1900, Pueblo culture was increasingly threatened by highly intolerant Protestant evangelical missions and schools. The Bureau of Indian Affairs also weighed in on the subject of acculturation, forcing Indian children to leave their homes and attend culture-killing boarding schools.

Following World War II, the issue of water rights took center stage on most pueblos. Also, the All Indian Pueblo Council succeeded in slowing the threat against Pueblo lands as well as religious persecution. Making crafts for the tourist trade became an important economic activity during this period. Since the late nineteenth century, but especially after the 1960s, Pueblos have had to cope with onslaughts by (mostly white) anthropologists and seekers of Indian spirituality. The region is also known for its major art colonies at Taos and Santa Fe.

RELIGION In traditional Pueblo culture, religion and life are inseparable. To be in harmony with all of nature is the Pueblo ideal and way of life. The sun is seen as the representative of the Creator. Sacred mountains in each direction, plus the sun above and the earth below, define and balance the Pueblo world. Many Pueblo religious ceremonies revolve around the weather and are devoted to ensuring adequate rainfall. To this end, Pueblo Indians evoke the power of katsinas, sacred beings who live in mountains and other holy places, in ritual and masked dance. There is no katsina organization per se at Jemez, but men and women do perform masked dances personifying supernaturals to bring rain.

In addition to the natural boundaries, Pueblo Indians have created a society that defines their world by providing balanced, reciprocal relationships within which people connect and harmonize with each other, the natural world, and time itself. According to tradition, the head of each pueblo is the religious leader, or *cacique,* who serves for life and whose primary responsibility it is to watch the sun and thereby determine the dates of ceremonies. Much ceremonialism is also based on medicine societies: About 20 men's and women's religious societies, such as curing, hunter, warrior, and clown, form the social and religious basis of Jemez society. Shamans, who derive powers from animal spirits, use their supernatural powers for curing, weather control, and ensuring the general welfare. Each person also belongs to two patrilineal kiva groups, Squash and Turquoise.

GOVERNMENT Pueblo governments derived from two traditions. Offices that are probably indigenous include the *cacique* and the war captains. These officials are intimately related to the religious structures of the pueblo and reflected the essentially theocratic nature of Pueblo government. At Jemez, the leaders of the various religious societies appointed the *cacique* for a lifetime term.

A parallel but in most cases distinctly less powerful group of officials was imposed by the Spanish authorities. Appointed by the traditional leadership, they generally dealt with external and church matters and included, at Jemez, a governor, lieutenant governor, and *fiscales*. The authority of their offices was symbolized by canes. In addition, the All Indian Pueblo Council, dating from 1598, began meeting again in the twentieth century.

CUSTOMS One mechanism that works to keep Pueblo societies coherent is a pervasive aversion to individualistic behavior. Children were raised with gentle guidance and a minimum of discipline. Pueblo Indians were generally monogamous and divorce was relatively rare. Intertribal marriage was also rare before World War II. Afterward, and especially after the Bureau of Indian Affairs (BIA)–sponsored relocation program in 1952, the population became more heterogenous. The dead were buried after being sprinkled with water, cornmeal, and pollen. Two days after death, a prayer feather ceremony was held to send the spirit to the land of the katsinas.

The Jemez tribe recognized two divisions, or kiva groups: Squash and Turquoise. The people were further arranged into matrilineal clans with specific ceremonial functions. In modern times photography by outsiders has been discouraged.

DWELLINGS More than any other pueblo, Jemez was built on the heights of mesas. It featured apartment-style dwellings of up to four stories, containing as many as 2,000 rooms, as well as one- and two-room houses. The buildings were constructed of adobe (earth and straw) bricks, with pine beams across the roof that were covered with poles, brush, and plaster. Floors were of wood plank or packed earth. The roof of one level served as the floor of another. The levels were interconnected by ladders. As an aid to defense, the traditional design included no doors or windows; entry was through the roof. Two rectangular pit houses, or kivas, served as ceremonial chambers and clubhouses. The village plaza, around which all dwellings were clustered, is the spiritual center of the village where all the balanced forces of the world come

together. Jemez people also built cliff dwellings to guard access to important places and monitor trails.

DIET Before the Spanish arrived, Jemez people ate primarily corn, beans, and squash. They also grew cotton and tobacco. They hunted deer, mountain lion, bear, antelope, and rabbits. Twice a year, after planting and again after the harvest, men would travel east to hunt buffalo. The women also gathered a variety of wild foods including piñon seeds, yucca fruit, berries, and wild potatoes. The Spanish introduced wheat, alfalfa, chilies, fruit trees, grapes, sheep, cattle, and garden vegetables, which soon became part of the regular diet.

KEY TECHNOLOGY Precontact farming implements were wooden. Traditional irrigation systems used ditches to ferry water from the Rio Grande as well as floodwater collection at arroyo mouths *(ak chin)*. Tools were made of bone and wood. Men hunted with bows and arrows. Pottery and yucca baskets were used for a number of purposes. The Spanish introduced metal tools and equipment.

TRADE All Pueblos were part of extensive Native American trading networks. With the arrival of other cultures, Pueblo Indians also traded with the Hispanic American villages and then U.S. traders. At fixed times during summer or fall, enemies declared truces so that trading fairs might be held. The largest and best known was at Taos with the Comanche. Nomads exchanged slaves, buffalo hides, buckskins, jerked meat, and horses for agricultural and manufactured pueblo products. Pueblo Indians traded for shell and copper ornaments, turquoise, and macaw feathers. During journeys east for buffalo the Jemez traded with Apaches, Comanches, and Kiowas. They also traded buffalo hides and fur blankets to the Spanish and Mexicans as well as pottery for Keresan *ollas*. Trade along the Santa Fe Trail began in 1821. By the 1880s and the arrival of railroads, the Pueblos were dependent on many American-made goods, and the native manufacture of weaving and pottery declined and nearly died out.

NOTABLE ARTS In the Pueblo way, art and life are inseparable. Jemez arts included pottery and woven cotton items. Songs, dances, and dramas also qualify as traditional arts. Many Pueblos experienced a renaissance of traditional arts in the twentieth century, beginning in 1919 with San Ildefonso pottery.

TRANSPORTATION Spanish horses, mules, and cattle arrived at Jemez Pueblo in the seventeenth century.

DRESS Men wore shirts made of tanned deer hides as well as cotton kilts. Women wore black cotton dresses belted with brightly colored yarn. Both wore moccasins with buckskin leggings. Rabbit skin was also used for clothing and robes.

WAR AND WEAPONS Though often depicted as passive and docile, most Pueblo groups regularly engaged in warfare. Every Jemez man belonged to two societies, Eagle and Arrow, related to defense and war. The great revolt of 1680 stands out as the major military action, but they also skirmished at other times with the Spanish and defended themselves against attackers such as Apaches, Comanches, and Utes. They also contributed auxiliary soldiers to provincial forces under Spain and Mexico, which were used mainly against raiding Indians and to protect merchant caravans on the Santa Fe Trail. After the raiding tribes began to pose less of a threat in the late nineteenth century, Pueblo military societies began to wither away, with the office of war captain changing to civil and religious functions.

Contemporary Information

GOVERNMENT/RESERVATIONS Jemez Pueblo consists of over 90,000 acres. Walatowa is the main village. The traditional government is intact. The *cacique* is the head of the pueblo, followed by a war chief and his assistants. These are lifetime positions. The positions of war captain, lieutenant war captain, and assistant war captain are filled annually by the *cacique* and war chief and their staffs and are responsible for policing the pueblo and supervising the social activities of the two divisions.

The Spanish-style civil government is also in place. A governor and his staff (two lieutenants, a sheriff, aides, and *fiscales*) are selected annually by the *cacique* and his staff; all serve without salary. Spanish, Mexican, and Lincoln canes remain symbols of authority.

ECONOMY Many Jemez people work for wages in Los Alamos, Santa Fe, and Albuquerque. Especially since World War II and the Indian arts revival, Jemez artists have been making excellent pottery, yucca baskets, weaving, embroidery, and painting. Many people keep gardens and grow chilies, some corn and wheat, and alfalfa for animals. The Pueblo owns hydroelectric, natural gas, oil, and uranium resources. There are also jobs with the government and the tribe.

LEGAL STATUS The Pueblo of Jemez is a federally recognized tribal entity. In the 1980s, the tribe successfully fought a geothermal development in the Jemez Mountains that threatened their religious practice. Jemez and Pecos Pueblos were formally consolidated in 1936 and maintain a special connection to the land around abandoned Pecos village, now Pecos National Historic Park.

DAILY LIFE Although the project of retaining a strong Indian identity is a difficult one in the late twentieth century, Pueblo people have strong roots, and in many ways the ancient rhythms and patterns continue. At Jemez, most of the religious societies are still extant and active. Their ceremonialism is largely intact, as is their language. The two divisions, Squash and Turquoise, still race and dance. These ceremonies are generally closed to outsiders, but other dances, with strong Catholic elements, tend to be open to tourists. The people of Jemez still recognize an honorable governor of Pecos Pueblo.

Farming, including grape growing, has dwindled, mainly because of drought, government programs to discourage farming, the people's increasing skills in other areas, welfare, and water usurpation. Children generally attend the BIA day school, mission school, or public school. The Jemez people have been particularly successful in voting tribal members onto the local school board. English has replaced Spanish as a second language. There is a recent tradition of producing first-rate long-distance runners, and the tribe has also produced some notable artists.

Laguna Pueblo

Laguna (L ə `g ū nä), Spanish for "lake," refers to a large pond near the pueblo. The word "pueblo" comes from the Spanish for "village." It refers both to a certain style of Southwest Indian architecture, characterized by multistory, apartmentlike buildings made of adobe, and to the people themselves. The Pueblos along the Rio Grande are known as eastern Pueblos; Zuñi, Hopi, and sometimes Acoma and Laguna are known as western Pueblos. The Lagunas call their pueblo *Kawaika*, "lake."

LOCATION Laguna Pueblo is made up of six major villages in central New Mexico, 42 miles west of Albuquerque.

POPULATION Roughly 330 people lived on the pueblo in 1700, plus about 150 more in four nearby villages. In 1990, 3,600 Lagunas lived on the reservation, with perhaps almost as many living away.

LANGUAGE The people spoke a Keresan dialect similar to that of Acoma Pueblo.

Historical Information

HISTORY All Pueblo people are thought to be descended from Anasazi and perhaps Mogollon and several other ancient peoples, although the precise origin of the Keresan peoples is unknown. From them they learned architecture, farming, pottery, and basketry. Larger population groups became possible with effective agriculture and ways to store food surpluses. Within the context of a relatively stable existence, the people devoted increasing amounts of time and attention to religion, arts, and crafts.

In the 1200s, the Anasazi abandoned their traditional canyon homelands in response to climatic and social upheavals. A century or two of migrations ensued, followed in general by the slow reemergence of their culture in the historic pueblos. Laguna and Acoma Pueblos have a unique descent. They have lived continuously in the area since at least 3000 B.C.E. Tradition has it that their ancestors inhabited Mesa Verde. In any case, Laguna's prehistory is closely connected with, if not identical to, that of Acoma.

In 1598, Juan de Oñate arrived in the area with settlers, founding the colony of New Mexico. Oñate carried on the process, already underway, of subjugating the local Indians; forcing them to pay taxes in crops, cotton, and work; and opening the door for Catholic missionaries to attack their religion. The Spanish renamed the Pueblos with saints' names and began a program of church construction. At the same time, the Spanish introduced such new crops as peaches, wheat, and peppers into the region. In 1620, a royal decree created civil offices at each pueblo; silver-headed canes, many of which remain in use today, symbolized the governor's authority.

The Pueblo Indians, including Laguna, organized and instituted a general revolt against the Spanish in 1680. For years, the Spaniards had routinely tortured Indians for practicing traditional religion. They also forced the Indians to labor for them, sold Indians into slavery, and let their cattle overgraze Indian land, a situation that eventually led to drought, erosion, and famine. Popé of San Juan Pueblo and other Pueblo religious leaders planned the revolt, sending runners carrying cords of maguey fibers to mark the day of rebellion. On August 10, 1680, a virtually united stand on the part of the Pueblos drove the Spanish from the region. The Indians killed many Spaniards but refrained from mass slaughter, allowing them to leave Santa Fe for El Paso.

Although Pueblo unity did not last, and Santa Fe was officially reconquered in 1692, Spanish rule was notably less severe from then on. Harsh forced labor all but ceased, and the Indians reached an understanding with the Church that enabled them to continue practicing their traditional religion. Still, the pueblos of Cochiti, Cieneguilla, Santo Domingo, and Jemez rebelled again in 1692. Over 100 people sought refuge at Acoma and Zuñi and then some continued on to found the present village of Old Laguna at the very end of the century. Peace with Spain was finally achieved in 1698. At that time, the Spanish officially recognized Laguna Pueblo, but questions of boundary, especially with Acoma Pueblo, persisted for over two centuries.

The Pueblos experienced many changes during the following decades: Refugees established communities at Hopi, guerrilla fighting continued against the Spanish, and certain areas were abandoned. By the

1700s, excluding Hopi and Zuñi, only Taos, Picuris, Isleta and Acoma Pueblos had not changed locations since the arrival of the Spanish. In general, the Pueblo eighteenth century was marked by smallpox epidemics and increased raiding by the Apache, Comanche, and Ute. Occasionally Pueblo Indians fought with the Spanish against the nomadic Athapaskan and Plains tribes. The people practiced their religion but more or less in secret. During this time, intermarriage and regular exchange between Hispanic villages and Pueblo Indians created a new New Mexican culture, neither strictly Spanish nor Indian, but rather somewhat of a blend between the two.

Mexican "rule" in 1821 brought little immediate change to the Pueblos. The Mexicans stepped up what had been a gradual process of appropriating Indian land and water, and they allowed the nomadic tribes even greater latitude to raid. By this time, sheep, horses, and mules had become important economically at Laguna. As the presence of the United States in the area grew, it attempted to enable the Pueblo Indians to continue their generally peaceful and self-sufficient ways and recognized Spanish land grants to the Pueblos. Land disputes with neighboring Acoma Pueblo were not settled so easily, however.

By the 1880s, several factors had combined to create a cultural and political explosion at Laguna. These included Spanish settlement in 1700s, Anglo settlement in the 1800s, the proximity to railroad lines, and the presence of Protestant whites living and working on the pueblo as teachers, missionaries, surveyors, and traders. Some of these people married into the tribe. Impatient with Catholic and native traditions, they wrote a constitution and were soon serving as tribal governors. These changes inflamed simmering factionalism and led to charges and countercharges of witchcraft. An Anglo governor in the 1870s had the two big kivas torn down. In the late 1870s, a group of traditionalists moved away to the nearby location of Mesita; some relocated to neighboring Isleta Pueblo.

After a gap of more than 300 years, the All Indian Pueblo Council began to meet again in the 1920s, specifically in response to a congressional threat to appropriate Pueblo lands. Partly as a result of the Council's activities, Congress confirmed Pueblo title to their lands in 1924 by passing the Pueblo Lands Act. The United States also acknowledged its trust responsibilities in a series of legal decisions and other acts of Congress. Still, especially after 1900, Pueblo culture was increasingly threatened by Protestant evangelical missions and schools. The Bureau of Indian Affairs also weighed in on the subject of acculturation, forcing Indian children to leave their homes and attend culture-killing boarding schools.

Following World War II, the issue of water rights

took center stage on most pueblos. Also, the All Indian Pueblo Council succeeded in slowing the threat against Pueblo lands as well as religious persecution. Making crafts for the tourist trade became an important economic activity during this period. In 1950 the Laguna sheep herd stood at 15,000, reduced from 52,000 by government edict in the 1930s as a response to overgrazing. Since the late nineteenth century, but especially after the 1960s, Pueblos have had to cope with onslaughts by (mostly white) anthropologists and seekers of Indian spirituality. The Jackpile Uranium Mine opened at Laguna in 1953, creating an economic boom until it closed in 1982.

RELIGION In traditional Pueblo culture, religion and life are inseparable. To be in harmony with all of nature is the Pueblo ideal and way of life. The sun is seen as the representative of the Creator. Sacred mountains in each direction, plus the sun above and the earth below, define and balance the Pueblo world. Many Pueblo religious ceremonies revolve around the weather and are devoted to ensuring adequate rainfall. To this end, Pueblo Indians evoke the power of katsinas, sacred beings who live in mountains and other holy places, in ritual and dance. At Laguna, all boys were initiated into the katsina society. Laguna Pueblo featured two above-ground kivas, religious chambers that symbolize the place of original emergence into this world.

In addition to the natural boundaries, Pueblo Indians have created a society that defines their world by providing balanced, reciprocal relationships within which people connect and harmonize with each other, the natural world, and time itself. According to tradition, the head of each pueblo is the religious leader, or *cacique*, whose primary responsibility it is to watch the sun and thereby determine the dates of ceremonies. Laguna ceremonialism was controlled by shamans and medicine societies. Each had a specialty, though all participated in ceremonies. Particularly important ceremonies included winter solstice, fertility (which also ensured general health by clowning and making fun of evil spirits), reproduction of game animals and general hunting successes, war and precipitation, and curing.

GOVERNMENT Pueblo governments derived from two traditions. One was indigenous and included, at Laguna, the town chief—"holding the prayer stick"—or *cacique* (although Lagunas speak of all leaders as *caciques*). This official is the overall pueblo leader as well as the religious leader, reflecting the essentially theocratic nature of Pueblo government. Other indigenous officials included the "outside chief" or "white hands," the war captains, and the hunt chief. A parallel but in most cases distinctly less

powerful group of officials was imposed by the Spanish authorities. Appointed by the religious hierarchy, they generally dealt with external and church matters and included, at Laguna, a governor, two lieutenant governors, *capitanes*, and *fiscales*. In addition, the All Indian Pueblo Council, dating from 1598, began meeting again in the twentieth century.

CUSTOMS One mechanism that works to keep Pueblo societies coherent is a pervasive aversion to individualistic behavior. Children were raised with gentle guidance and a minimum of discipline. Pueblo Indians were generally monogamous and divorce was relatively rare. At Laguna, the dead were prepared ceremonially and quickly buried, heads facing east, with food and other items. A vigil of four days and nights was generally observed. Laguna Pueblo recognized seven matrilineal clans, important in marriage control and other secular activities. The clans also owned all farm land. As herd workers, Lagunas often used Navajo "slaves," or people offered by their parents as children, raised with Laguna children, and freed as adults. In modern times photography by outsiders is discouraged.

DWELLINGS Laguna Pueblo featured multistory, apartment-style dwellings. The lower levels were reserved mainly for storage. The buildings were constructed of adobe (earth and straw) bricks, with beams across the roof that were covered with poles, brush, and plaster. The roof of one level served as the floor of another. The levels were interconnected by ladders. As an aid to defense, the traditional design included no doors or windows; entry was through the roof. Baking ovens stood outside the buildings. Water was primarily obtained from two natural cisterns. Laguna also features two rectangular pit houses, or kivas, for ceremonial chambers and clubhouses. Herders stayed in caves, small rectangular houses, logs in a horseshoe shape covered with brush, or dugouts. The village plaza is the spiritual center of the village where all the balanced forces of the world come together.

DIET Before the Spanish arrived, people living at Laguna Pueblo ate primarily corn, beans, and squash. They also grew sunflowers and tobacco and kept turkeys. They hunted deer, antelope, and rabbits and gathered a variety of wild seeds, nuts, berries, and other foods. Favorite foods as of circa 1700 included a blue corn drink, corn mush, pudding, wheat cake, corn balls, paper bread, peach-bark drink, flour bread, wild berries, and prickly pear fruit. The Lagunas also raised herds of sheep, goats, horses, and donkeys after the Spanish introduced these animals into the region.

KEY TECHNOLOGY Lagunas practiced dry farming and ditch irrigation technology. They used mica for window lights. Fine white clay yielded excellent pottery, and wicker baskets were fashioned of red willow shoots.

TRADE All Pueblos were part of extensive Native American trading networks that reached for a thousand miles in every direction. With the arrival of other cultures, Pueblo Indians also traded with the Hispanic American villages and then U.S. traders. At fixed times during summer or fall, enemies declared truces so that trading fairs might be held. The largest and best known was at Taos with the Comanche. Nomads exchanged slaves, buffalo hides, buckskins, jerked meat, and horses for agricultural and manufactured pueblo products. Pueblo Indians traded for shell and copper ornaments, turquoise, and macaw feathers. Lagunas traded black woolen dresses as well as curing fetishes. Trade along the Santa Fe Trail began in 1821. By the 1880s and the arrival of railroads, the Pueblos were dependent on many American-made goods, and the Native American manufacture of weaving and pottery declined and nearly died out.

NOTABLE ARTS In the Pueblo way, art and life are inseparable. Laguna women produced excellent pottery; men made fine weavings as well as silver necklaces. Songs, dances, and dramas also qualify as traditional arts. Many Pueblos experienced a renaissance of traditional arts in the twentieth century, beginning in 1919 with San Ildefonso pottery.

TRANSPORTATION Spanish horses, mules, and cattle arrived at Laguna Pueblo in the seventeenth century.

DRESS Men wore cotton kilts and leather sandals. Women wore cotton dresses and sandals or high moccasin boots. Deer and rabbit skin were also used for clothing and robes.

WAR AND WEAPONS Though often depicted as passive and docile, most Pueblo groups regularly engaged in warfare. The great revolt of 1680 stands out as the major military action, but they also skirmished at other times with the Spanish and defended themselves against attackers such as Apaches, Comanches, and Utes. They also contributed auxiliary soldiers to provincial forces under Spain and Mexico, which were used mainly against raiding Indians and to protect merchant caravans on the Santa Fe Trail. After the raiding tribes began to pose less of a threat in the late nineteenth century, Pueblo military societies began to wither away, with the office of war captain changing to civil and religious functions.

Contemporary Information

GOVERNMENT/RESERVATIONS Laguna Pueblo consists of six major villages on 528,079 acres in central New Mexico, bisected by route I-40. Although part of a whole, the villages enjoy some autonomy. The Indian Reorganization Act (IRA) constitution was most recently revised in 1984. Paid secular officials are elected annually.

ECONOMY Lagunas still practice agriculture as well as sheep and cattle herding. Contemporary arts and crafts include fine embroidery, pottery, and yucca basketry. Wage work is provided by a nearby electronics factory, a commercial center, Laguna Industries, and programs paid for by the tribe and the government. The Pueblo owns coal, natural gas, oil, and uranium resources.

LEGAL STATUS Laguna Pueblo is a federally recognized tribal entity.

DAILY LIFE Laguna is considered a relatively wealthy and highly acculturated pueblo. Most people live in new or remodeled homes. Although the project of retaining a strong Indian identity is a difficult one in the late twentieth century, Pueblo people have strong roots, and in many ways the ancient rhythms and patterns continue. Many Pueblo Indians, though nominally Catholic, have fused pieces of Catholicism onto a core of traditional beliefs. Since the 1970s control of schools has been a key in maintaining their culture. Health problems, including alcoholism and drug use, continue to plague the Pueblos. Indian Health Service hospitals often cooperate with native healers.

The Lagunas never replaced their religious hierarchy after the schism in the 1870s, although there is a growing interest in ceremonialism, and the people have built a modern "kiva." Each village annually holds feast days honoring patron saints as well as sacred ceremonial dances. Facilities include an elementary school, public junior/senior high, outpatient clinic, and outdoor pool. The tribe also maintains a scholarship fund. From 1953 to 1982, the Anaconda Mineral Company (uranium) provided 800 well-paying jobs and brought much money to the tribe. However, yellow radioactive clouds drifted over the pueblo during those years, and people built roads and houses with radioactive ore and crushed rock from the mine. Today the groundwater is contaminated, and cancer rates are rising.

Maricopa
See Pee-Posh

Mojave or Mohave

Originally Tzi-na-ma-a. Mojave (M ō `hä v ē) is a Hispanicization of the Yuman *Aha-makave*, meaning "beside the water."

LOCATION The Mojave traditionally lived in the Mojave Valley and along the northern lower Colorado River. Today, Mojave Indians live primarily on the Fort Mojave Reservation (Arizona) and on the Colorado River Indian Reservation (Arizona and California).

POPULATION Roughly 20,000 Mojaves lived along the river in the early sixteenth century. Their number was reduced to 3,000 by 1770. The 1990 census showed roughly 600 Indians living at Fort Mojave (of a tribal enrollment of 967) and roughly 2,350 Indians living on the Colorado River Reservation, a majority of whom identified themselves as Mojave.

LANGUAGE Mojaves spoke River Yuman, a member of the Hokan-Siouan language family.

Historical Information

HISTORY Ancestors of the modern Mojave Indians settled the Mojave Valley around 1150. These people farmed soil enriched from sediment left by the annual spring floods. The Mojave may have encountered non-natives as early as 1540. Although they served as scouts for Father Francisco Garces's Grand Canyon expedition in 1776, among others, they generally resisted Spanish interference and maintained their independence.

Contact with non-natives remained sporadic until the nineteenth century. At about that time they began raiding Anglo-American fur trappers. They also allowed a band of Paiute Indians called the Chemehuevi to settle in the southern portion of their territory. The Mexican cession and discovery of gold in California brought more trespassers and led to more raids. In 1857, the Mojave suffered a decisive military loss to their ancient enemies, the Pima and Pee-Posh (Maricopa) Indians. Two years later, the United States built Forts Mojave and Yuma to stem Mojave raiding. By this time, however, the Mojave, defeated in battle and weakened by disease, settled for peace.

In 1865, the Mojave leader Irrateba (or Yara Tav) convinced a group of his followers to relocate to the Colorado River Valley area. The same year, Congress created the Colorado River Reservation for "all the tribes of the Colorado River drainage," primarily the Mojave and Chemehuevi. Roughly 70 percent of the Mojaves had remained in the Mojave Valley, however, and they received a reservation in 1880. This split occasioned intratribal animosities for decades.

The early twentieth century was marked by influenza epidemics and non-Indian encroachment. The first assimilationist government boarding school had opened at the Colorado River Reservation in 1879. Legal allotments began in 1904. Traditional floodplain agriculture disappeared in the 1930s when the great dams tamed the Colorado River. During World War II, many U.S. citizens of Japanese heritage were interned on the Colorado River Reservation: For this operation the United States summarily appropriated 25,000 acres of Indian land.

For 19 years after the war, until 1964, the Bureau of Indian Affairs (BIA) opened the reservation to Hopi and Navajo settlement (tribal rejection of this rule in 1952 was ignored by the BIA). Now all members of four tribes call the reservation home, having evolved into the CRIT (Colorado River Indian Tribes) Indians, a difficult development for the few remaining Mojave elders. In 1963 a federal court case guaranteed the tribes title to federal water rights. They received a deed to the reservation the following year.

RELIGION The Mojaves believed, as did all Yumans, that they originally emerged into this world from a place near Spirit Mountain, Nevada. Dreaming was the key to Mojave religious experience. Dreams were seen as visits with ancestors. There were omen dreams and, more rarely, great dreams, which brought power to cure, lead in battle, orate a funeral, or do almost anything. However, dreams were considered of questionable authenticity unless they conferred success. Dreams permeated every aspect of Mojave culture. They were constantly discussed and meditated upon. Shamans had the most elaborate great dreams, which were considered to have begun in the womb. Shamans could cause disease as well as cure it, a situation that made for a precarious existence for them.

The Mojaves performed few public ceremonies or rituals. Instead, they sang song cycles for curing, funerals, and entertainment. The cycles consisted of dreams and tribal mythology and were accompanied by people shaking rattles and beating sticks on baskets. A complete cycle could take a night or more to sing, and the Mojave knew about 30 cycles, each with 100–200 songs.

GOVERNMENT Positions of authority such as subchiefs or local leaders derived from dreaming or oratory. Hereditary chiefs in the male line did exist, although with obscure functions. Despite their loose division into bands and local groups, the Mojave thought of themselves as a true tribe; that is, they possessed a national consciousness, and they came together for important occasions such as warfare.

CUSTOMS Men planted the crops and women harvested them. Leaders addressed the people from rooftops in the morning about proper ways of living. Hunters generally gave away what they killed. Both men and women tattooed and painted their bodies. The dead were cremated, and their possessions and homes were also burned after a special ceremony during which mourners sang song cycles. No formal marriage ceremony existed: Marriages were arranged by the couple, and divorce was easy and common. Women carried babies on the hip, never on the back.

Mojaves often traveled widely for trade and fun, covering up to 100 miles by foot in a day.

DWELLINGS Bands and families lived in scattered rancherias, or farms. In warm weather they lived in flat-roofed, open-sided structures. Cold weather dwellings were low and rectangular, with roofs of thatch-covered poles; sand and earth or river mud were piled over the exterior. Doors faced south against the cold north winds. The people also used cylindrical granaries with flat roofs.

DIET Crops such as corn, beans, and pumpkins (and wheat and melons after the Spanish arrived) constituted 50 percent of the Mojave diet. They also caught fish; hunted game such as rabbits and beaver with bows and arrows, traps, or deadfalls; and gathered wild foods. Mesquite beans in particular were a staple, used for food, drink, flour (pith from pods), shoes and clothing (bark), hair dye, instruments (roots), glue (sap), fuel for firing pottery, and funeral pyres.

KEY TECHNOLOGY Mojaves used reed rafts to cross the river; headrings for carrying; gourds for storage of seeds and water and, with wooden handles fastened with greasewood and arrowweed, for rattles; bows and arrows; planting sticks and wooden hoes; and assorted pottery and baskets. They also caught fish using drip and drag fish nets, traps, and basketry scoops.

TRADE Mojaves traded agricultural products with tribes near the Gulf of California and the Pacific Ocean for shells and feathers. They also acted as brokers between a number of tribes for various indigenous items.

NOTABLE ARTS Men and women working together made coiled pottery, dull red when heated, in an open wood fire. In more recent times Mojaves were known for making glass beadwork.

TRANSPORTATION Reed or log rafts were used for long river trips. Also, swimmers used "ferrying pots" to push food or small children ahead of them while they swam.

DRESS Men and women wore loincloths; women also wore willow-bark aprons. Both went barefoot except when traveling, when they wore badger-hide sandals. Rabbit-skin blankets and robes kept them warm in winter. Both sexes wore their hair long; women's hung loose, and men rolled theirs into strands. Both tattooed their chins and painted their faces.

WAR AND WEAPONS The Mojaves were fierce fighters. A warrior society *(kwanamis)* led three different fighting groups: archers, clubbers, and stick (or lance) men. In addition to those three types of weapons, they also used deer-hide shields, mesquite or willow bows, and arrows in coyote or wildcat quiv-

ers. War leaders experienced dreams conferring power in battle. Traditional enemies included the Pima, O'odham, Pee-Posh, and Cocopah; allies included the Quechan, Chemehuevi, Yavapai, and Western Apache. The Mojave often took girls or young women as prisoners, giving them to old men as an insult to the enemy.

Contemporary Information

GOVERNMENT/RESERVATIONS Most Mojave Indians live on two reservations. The Colorado River Reservation (1865), containing roughly 270,000 acres, has an active tribal council (1937) and several subcommittees. The Fort Mojave Reservation (1870), within sight of Spirit Mountain and on ancestral lands, contains 32,697 acres, exclusive of about 4,000 acres in Nevada. Each reservation has its own tribal council. Both contain extremely irrigable land. Mojaves also live on the Fort McDowell Reservation in Arizona (24,680 acres, 765 population in 1992). The last traditional Mojave chief died in 1947.

ECONOMY Farming remains important on the Colorado River Reservation, where unemployment stood at 10 percent in 1985. An 11,000-acre farming cooperative produces mainly cotton, alfalfa, wheat, melons, and lettuce. Tourism is also important: Facilities include a marina, resort (the Aha Quin Park), gift shop, and restaurant. Motorboat races are held in the spring and a rodeo in November. Some people herd sheep or work for the BIA or the public health service. Long-term leases provide significant income, as do numerous large and small businesses, such as a 10-acre recycling plant that opened in 1992.

Although agriculture (primarily cotton) remains important at Fort Mojave, that reservation is harder to irrigate successfully because it contains a checkerboard of private lands. Unemployment there hovers around 50 percent. There are plans to build a huge residential and commercial development, including a casino, in the Nevada part of the reservation. Fort Mojave also leases some land and caters to a small tourist trade. Some opportunities exist in and around the reservation for wage labor.

LEGAL STATUS The Colorado River Indian Tribes and the Fort Mojave Indian Tribe are federally recognized tribal entities. The latter has the status of a sovereign Indian nation.

DAILY LIFE Both groups of Mojaves still cremate their dead and mourn them with some of the old songs and ceremonies. Few other myths or song cycles are remembered. Although many Mojaves are Christians, over half speak their native language. The Fort Mojave Reservation maintains a police force and court system. A hospital at CRIT struggles to provide adequate health care. The tribes support education with scholarship funds as well as land donations. A tribal museum helps to preserve the cultural heritages of the individual Colorado Indian tribes. Children attend public schools. Both communities are fighting a proposed "low-level" radioactive waste dump for nearby Ward Valley, an environmentally sensitive area on ground sacred to local tribes.

Nambé Pueblo

Nambé (Näm `b ā) is a Spanish rendition of a similar-sounding Tewa name, loosely interpreted as "rounded earth." The word "pueblo" comes from the Spanish for "village." It refers both to a certain style of Southwest Indian architecture, characterized by multistory, apartmentlike buildings made of adobe, and to the people themselves. The pueblos along the Rio Grande are known as eastern Pueblos; Zuñi, Hopi, and sometimes Acoma and Laguna are known as western Pueblos.

LOCATION   Nambé Pueblo is located about 15 miles north of Santa Fe, New Mexico.

POPULATION   In 1993 there were 487 enrolled tribal members living on Nambé Pueblo, out of a total enrollment of 630. The total number of Pueblo residents in 1990 was about 1,400. Roughly 350 people lived there in 1600.

LANGUAGE   Nambé people spoke a dialect of Tewa, a Kiowa-Tanoan language.

Historical Information

HISTORY   All Pueblo people are thought to be descended from Anasazi and perhaps Mogollon and several other ancient peoples. From them they learned architecture, farming, pottery, and basketry. Larger population groups became possible with effective agriculture and ways to store food surpluses. Within the context of a relatively stable existence, the people devoted increasing amounts of time and attention to religion, arts, and crafts. In the 1200s, the Anasazi abandoned their traditional canyon homelands in response to climatic and social upheavals. A century or two of migrations ensued, followed in general by the slow reemergence of their culture in the historic pueblos.

In 1598, Juan de Oñate arrived in the area with settlers, founding the colony of New Mexico. Oñate carried on the process, already underway in nearby areas, of subjugating the local Indians; forcing them to pay taxes in crops, cotton, and work; and opening the door for Catholic missionaries to attack their religion. The Spanish renamed the Pueblos with saints' names and began a program of church construction: The first church at Nambé was established in the early 1600s. At the same time, the Spanish introduced such new crops as peaches, wheat, and peppers into the region. In 1620, a royal decree created civil offices at each pueblo; silver-headed canes, many of which remain in use today, symbolized the governor's authority.

The Pueblo Indians, including those at Nambé, organized and instituted a general revolt against the Spanish in 1680. For years, the Spaniards had routinely tortured Indians for practicing traditional religion. They also forced the Indians to labor for them, sold Indians into slavery, and let their cattle overgraze Indian land, a situation that eventually led to drought, erosion, and famine. Popé of San Juan Pueblo and other Pueblo religious leaders planned the revolt, sending runners carrying cords of maguey fibers to mark the day of rebellion. On August 10, 1680, a virtually united stand on the part of the Pueblos drove the Spanish from the region. The Indians killed many Spaniards but refrained from mass slaughter, allowing them to leave Santa Fe for El Paso.

The Pueblos experienced many changes during following decades: Refugees established communities at Hopi, guerrilla fighting continued against the Spanish, and certain areas were abandoned. By the 1700s, excluding Hopi and Zuñi, only Taos, Picuris, Isleta, and Acoma Pueblos had not changed locations since the arrival of the Spanish. Although Pueblo unity did not last, and Santa Fe was officially reconquered in 1692, Spanish rule was notably less severe from then on. Harsh forced labor all but ceased, and the Indians reached an understanding with the Church that enabled them to continue practicing their traditional religion.

In general, the Pueblo eighteenth century was marked by smallpox epidemics and increased raiding by the Apache, Comanche, and Ute. Occasionally Pueblo Indians fought with the Spanish against the nomadic tribes. The people practiced their religion but more or less in secret. During this time, intermarriage and regular exchange between Hispanic villages and Pueblo Indians created a new New Mexican culture, neither strictly Spanish nor Indian, but rather somewhat of a blend between the two.

Mexican "rule" in 1821 brought little immediate change to the Pueblos. The Mexicans stepped up what had been a gradual process of appropriating Indian land and water, and they allowed the nomadic tribes even greater latitude to raid. A political rebellion by Indians and Hispanics in 1837 over the issue of taxes led to the assassination of the New Mexican governor and the brief installation of a Plains/Taos Indian as governor. As the presence of the United States in the area grew, it attempted to enable the Pueblo Indians to continue their generally peaceful and self-sufficient ways and recognized Spanish land grants to the Pueblos.

During the nineteenth century the process of acculturation among Pueblo Indians quickened markedly. In an attempt to retain their identity, Pueblo Indians clung even more tenaciously to their heritage, which by now included elements of the once-hated Spanish culture and religion. By the 1880s, railroads had largely put an end to the traditional geographical isolation of the pueblos. Paradoxically, the U.S. decision to recognize Spanish land grants to the Pueblos denied Pueblo Indians certain rights granted under official treaties and left them particularly open to exploitation by squatters and thieves.

After a gap of over 300 years, the All Indian Pueblo Council began to meet again in the 1920s, specifically in response to a congressional threat to appropriate Pueblo lands. Partly as a result of the Council's activities, Congress confirmed Pueblo title to their lands in 1924 by passing the Pueblo Lands Act. The United States also acknowledged its trust responsibilities in a series of legal decisions and other acts of Congress. Still, especially after 1900, Pueblo culture was increasingly threatened by Protestant evangelical missions and schools. The Bureau of Indian Affairs also weighed in on the subject of acculturation, forcing Indian children to leave their homes and attend culture-killing boarding schools. Since the late nineteenth century, but especially after the 1960s, Pueblos have had to cope with onslaughts by (mostly white) anthropologists and seekers of Indian spirituality. The region is also known for its major art colonies at Taos and Santa Fe.

RELIGION In traditional Pueblo culture, religion and life are inseparable. To be in harmony with all of nature is the Pueblo ideal and way of life. The sun is seen as the representative of the Creator. Sacred mountains in each direction, plus the sun above and the earth below, define and balance the Pueblo world. Many Pueblo religious ceremonies revolve around the weather and are devoted to ensuring adequate rainfall. To this end, Pueblo Indians evoke the power of katsinas, sacred beings who live in mountains and other holy places, in ritual and masked dance. One round kiva, or ceremonial chamber, stands at Nambé.

In addition to the natural boundaries, Pueblo Indians have created a society that defines their world by providing balanced, reciprocal relationships within which people connect and harmonize with each other, the natural world, and time itself. According to tradition, the head of each pueblo is the religious leader, or *cacique,* whose primary responsibility it is to watch the sun and thereby determine the dates of ceremonies. Much ceremonialism is also based on medicine societies, and shamans who derive powers from animal spirits use their supernatural powers for curing, weather control, and ensuring the general welfare. Especially in the eastern pueblos, most ceremonies are kept secret.

GOVERNMENT Pueblo governments derived from two traditions. Offices that are probably indigenous include the *cacique,* or head of the Pueblo, and the war captains. These officials are intimately related to the religious structures of the pueblo and reflected the essentially theocratic nature of Pueblo government. At Nambé, summer and winter *caciques* were the religious and the political leaders of the pueblo.

A parallel but in most cases distinctly less powerful group of officials was imposed by the Spanish authorities. Appointed by the traditional leadership, they generally dealt with external and church matters and included the governor, two lieutenant governors, and two sheriffs. The authority of their offices was symbolized by canes. Nontraditional positions also included a ditch boss, who was in charge of the irrigation ditches, as well as a town crier and sacristan. In addition, the All Indian Pueblo Council, dating from 1598, began meeting again in the twentieth century.

CUSTOMS One mechanism that works to keep Pueblo societies coherent is a pervasive aversion to individualistic behavior. Children were raised with gentle guidance and a minimum of discipline. Pueblo Indians were generally monogamous, and divorce was relatively rare. The dead were prepared ceremonially and quickly buried with clothes, beads, food, and other items. A vigil of four days and nights was generally observed.

At Nambé, in contrast with most other pueblos, seasons were traditionally delineated not so much by the solstice as by the actual change in seasons. Formerly a summer and a winter *cacique,* appointed for life, oversaw the pueblo. Society was divided into two groups, summer (associated with the Squash kiva) and winter (associated with the Turquoise kiva); membership in a group was patrilineal. These groups were further divided into clans. A number of secret societies also existed. For instance, the warrior society was concerned with hunting, war, crops, fertility, and curing. Each society had its own dances and ritual paraphernalia.

DWELLINGS Nambé people built small, irregular dwellings clustered around a central plaza. The buildings were constructed of adobe (earth and straw) bricks, with beams across the roof that were covered with poles, brush, and plaster. Floors were of wood plank or packed earth. Pit houses, or kivas, served as ceremonial chambers and clubhouses. The village plaza, around which all dwellings were clustered, is the spiritual center of the village where all the balanced forces of the world come together.

DIET Before the Spanish arrived, people from

Nambé Pueblo ate primarily corn, beans, and squash. They also grew cotton and tobacco. They hunted deer, mountain lion, antelope, and rabbits and gathered a variety of wild seeds, nuts, berries, and other foods. The Spanish introduced wheat, alfalfa, chilies, fruit trees, grapes, sheep, cattle, and garden vegetables, which soon became part of the regular diet.

KEY TECHNOLOGY Musical instruments included various rattles, drums, and flutes. Irrigation techniques included canals, dams and ditches, and gravity flow. Pottery was an important technological adaptation, as was weaving baskets and cotton. Farming implements were made of stone and wood. Corn was ground using manos and metates.

TRADE All Pueblos were part of extensive Native American trading networks. With the arrival of other cultures, Pueblo Indians also traded with the Hispanic American villages and then U.S. traders. At fixed times during summer or fall, enemies declared truces so that trading fairs might be held. The largest and best known was at Taos with the Comanche. Nomads exchanged slaves, buffalo hides, buckskins, jerked meat, and horses for agricultural and manufactured Pueblo products. Pueblo Indians traded for shell and copper ornaments, turquoise, and macaw feathers. Trade along the Santa Fe Trail began in 1821. By the 1880s and the arrival of railroads, the Pueblos were dependent on many American-made goods, and the native manufacture of weaving and pottery declined and nearly died out.

NOTABLE ARTS In the Pueblo way, art and life are inseparable. Nambé artists specialized in making embroidered dresses. Songs, dances, and dramas also qualify as traditional arts. Many Pueblos experienced a renaissance of traditional arts in the twentieth century, beginning in 1919 with San Ildefonso pottery.

TRANSPORTATION Spanish horses, mules, and cattle arrived at Nambé Pueblo in the sixteenth century.

DRESS Men wore cotton and buckskin shirts and kilts. Womens' traditional dress featured spun cotton dresses and sandals or high moccasin boots. Rabbit skin was also used for clothing and robes.

WAR AND WEAPONS Though often depicted as passive and docile, most Pueblo groups regularly engaged in warfare. The great revolt of 1680 stands out as the major military action, but they also skirmished at other times with the Spanish and defended themselves against attackers such as Apaches, Comanches, and Utes. They also contributed auxiliary soldiers to provincial forces under Spain and Mexico, which were used mainly against raiding Indians and to protect merchant caravans on the Santa Fe Trail. After the raiding tribes began to pose less of a threat in the late nineteenth century, Pueblo military societies began to wither away, with the office of war captain changing to civil and religious functions.

Contemporary Information

GOVERNMENT/RESERVATIONS Nambé Pueblo consists of roughly 19,000 acres. Like most other pueblos, Nambé has no written constitution. An elected governor and four other officials serve for two-year terms. Voting on tribal decisions is restricted to a group of past governors. Children of male, but not female, members of the tribe who have married outside the pueblo are automatically enrolled.

ECONOMY Wage work may be found primarily at Los Alamos, with local businesses, or with the tribe or the government. Nambé Falls is a tourist attraction, although few craftspeople cater to the tourist trade. The tribe also operates a trailer park. There is some subsistence farming as well as grazing on leased lands. In addition, the tribe earns interest on land claims compensation funds.

LEGAL STATUS Nambé Pueblo is a federally recognized tribal entity. The people are currently seeking the return of roughly 45,000 acres of land near the Santa Fe Ski Basin.

DAILY LIFE Since the Tewas retain fewer traditions than most other pueblos, they are not always successful in preserving a palpable and intentional continuity with the past. Most people, especially the younger ones, speak English and Spanish but little Tewa; the trend is toward only English. Children are bused to schools in nearby towns.

Most Nambé Pueblo Indians are at least nominally Catholic. The festival of Saint Francis, in October, is the only ceremony still performed at Nambé (not including one for the tourists in July at Nambé Falls). The last *cacique* died in 1970. No medicine or other societies remain extant. Clans have virtually disappeared; the basic social unit is now the nuclear family. There is a very high rate of marriage with non-Indians; few marry within the Pueblo or even Tewa Indians. Virtually all people complete high school. Since the 1970s, control of schools has been a key in maintaining their culture. Health problems, including alcoholism and drug use, continue to plague the Pueblos.

Navajo

Navajo (`Nä v ə h ō) is a Tewa word meaning "planted fields." The Navajo call themselves *Dine'é* (Di `n ə), "the People." Like the Apache, they are of Athapaskan descent.

LOCATION Dinetah, the traditional Navajo homeland, is located on the lower Colorado Plateau, between the San Juan and Little Colorado Rivers, about 75 miles northwest of Santa Fe. Today's Navajo Nation occupies a 28,800-square-mile reservation in northern Arizona and New Mexico and southern Utah. This land is mostly plateau (above 5,000 feet) and is marked by deep, sheer-walled canyons. The winters are cold, the summers are hot, and there is little water.

POPULATION   The Dine'é are the most numerous Indian tribe in the United States. In 1990, 144,000 Indians lived on the Navajo Reservation, plus 1,177 at Cañoncito and 191 at Ramah (see "Government/ Reservations" under "Contemporary Information"). Many thousands also live off-reservation. More than 200,000 Indians now qualify for membership in the Navajo Nation (officially 219,198 in 1990). Perhaps 6,000 Navajos lived in the Dinetah in 1800.

LANGUAGE   Navajo is an Athapaskan language.

Historical Information

HISTORY   Roughly 3,000 years ago, the Athapaskans, along with others (all called the Nadene), began a new wave of Asian migration into North America. Nomadic hunter-gatherers, the Southern Athapaskans arrived in the Southwest in roughly 1400 and filled in the mountains around the Pueblo-held valleys. The Northern Athapaskans remained in the subarctic.

To the Athapaskans, Spanish influence (early seventeenth century) meant primarily horses, guns, and places to raid. Consequently their interest in raiding grew, and they effectively established the northern Spanish frontier. Spanish missionaries had little success with the Navajo. Navajos also raided Pueblo Indians for food, women, slaves, and property. Between raids, Navajo and Pueblo people traded with each other. From this contact, the Navajo adopted some Pueblo habits, arts, and customs, especially farming, and settled down. The Navajo became farmers, then herders of sheep, goats, and horses.

Navajos helped the Pueblo people in their great revolt against the Spanish (1680), mainly by accepting, occasionally on a permanent basis, fugitives and refugees. Throughout much of the eighteenth century, the Navajo came in greater contact with Pueblo people and adopted more and more of their ways. Dine'é-Pueblo "pueblitas" became almost a distinct culture in parts of the Dinetah. What is now considered the traditional Navajo culture arose out of this cultural mix.

Animal husbandry, agriculture, hunting, gathering, and weaving wool were the economic base of the Navajo as they began slowly to spread west and south. The early nineteenth century saw much reciprocal raiding with Mexicans, Spaniards, and early travelers on the Santa Fe Trail. Faced with the Mexicans' better

firepower, Navajos, especially children, became targets of slave traders during the first half of the nineteenth century. At this time the Navajo possessed no tribal consciousness. They traveled with their livestock in clans (there were over 60) to summer and winter hogans.

In the 1840s, the Navajos held out against U.S. troops in their sacred stronghold, Canyon de Chelly. However, treaties signed then did not stop conflict over grazing lands; white abuses of Indians, including the slave trade; and U.S. Army depredations. Following the Mexican cession (1848), the Navajo were shocked to learn that the United States considered itself as the "owner" of all traditional Navajo territory. In the face of Navajo resistance, the United States determined to take the land by force.

The great warrior and war chief Manuelito attacked and almost took Fort Defiance in 1860. Kit Carson defeated the Navajos in 1864 through a scorched-earth policy: He destroyed their fields, orchards, and livestock and then invaded Canyon de Chelly. Band by band the Navajos surrendered. Manuelito surrendered in 1866. The United States then forcibly relocated 8,000 Navajos to Bosque Redondo (Fort Sumner) in eastern New Mexico, with plans to transform them into farmers. Hundreds of Navajos died on the 400-mile walk, and 2,000 more died in a smallpox epidemic the following year. Those Navajos who had not been captured hid in and around Navajo country.

In 1868 the Navajos were allowed to return and were granted 3.5 million acres of land for a reservation. Although the treaty called for a U.S. government–appointed tribal chief, local headmen retained their power. Manuelito returned home to serve as a Bureau of Indian Affairs (BIA)–appointed subchief and then head chief of the Navajo. He also served as the head of the "Navajo Cavalry," the local police dedicated to ending Navajo raiding. After their return, the Navajo turned successfully to horse and sheepherding. Navajo culture changed quickly at that time: Trading posts opened, rug weaving for tourists began to take the place of traditional blanket weaving, children were sent to U.S. boarding schools (although this was fiercely resisted at first), Navajos began working for the railroads, missionaries arrived in force, and non-native health care made inroads into traditional cultural practices.

By 1886 the reservation had grown from 3.5 to 11.5 million acres, although much of the best land was taken for railroad rights of way. Tremendous sheep and goat herds made the Navajo relatively prosperous and independent until the mid-1890s, when economic and natural disasters combined to reduce the herds by 75 percent. Following this period the

Navajo switched from subsistence herding to raising stock for market.

The Navajo remained organized primarily by band into the twentieth century and thus knew little or no true tribal consciousness until a business council began to meet in 1922. Local business councils, the first and most important community-level political entities, had been created in 1904 (well over 100 chapters of the councils now exist). In 1915, the BIA divided the Navajo Reservation into six districts (which were in turn reorganized in 1955), each with a non-Indian superintendent. These communities retain their character as government towns. In 1923 the secretary of the Interior appointed a tribal commissioner and a tribal council. In 1923 Henry Chee Dodge, who had assumed the position of head chief after Manuelito, became the first tribal chair. He provided the tribe with valuable leadership until his death in 1947.

Overgrazing was the key issue in the 1930s; a BIA-mandated stock reduction at that time led to dramatically lower standards of living. It also led to rejection by the tribe of the Indian Reorganization Act (IRA), of which the stock reduction plan was a part. World War II was a watershed for the tribe: Navajos traveled off the reservation in numbers for the first time, and those who returned came home not only with some money but also with a sense of honor gained from fighting as well as from using their language as a code the enemy was unable ever to break. Still, a crisis of unemployment, and even starvation, marked the immediate postwar years for the Navajo.

The 1950s brought large-scale energy development and with it jobs, money, and new social problems. Coal, oil, and uranium were the most important resources. The number of tribal programs increased dramatically, as did the power of the tribal council. The tribe adopted its own court system and legal code in 1959. The new programs culminated in 1965 with the Office of Navajo Economic Opportunity (ONEO), led by Peter MacDonald. The ONEO funneled tens of millions of dollars into social programs. MacDonald dominated Navajo politics for 20 years, both as head of the ONEO and as tribal chairman in 1970, 1974, 1978, and 1986.

However, the coal leases of the 1960s included provisions for massive strip mining. Soon the once-pristine region was seriously polluted, and by the late 1970s there was strong sentiment against further development. MacDonald himself was convicted in 1990 and 1992 of several felony corruption-related crimes and later jailed. Peterson Zah served as tribal chairman in 1982, as president of the Navajo Nation in 1990, and as chair of the nation in 1992. The controversy over the degree and type of economic devel-

opment continues today, the Navajo having achieved a large degree of self-determination.

RELIGION "Sa'ah Naaghei Bik'en Hozho," which may be characterized as being grounded to the earth, whole, and in harmony with life, is the Navajo Way. Everything is sacred and interrelated. For instance, religion equals identity equals clan equals place. The chief role of ceremonialism is to maintain or restore this harmony. Therefore, most ceremonies are for curing illness, broadly defined as being off balance for any number of reasons, such as contact with non-natives, ghosts, witches, or the dead.

According to legend, Navajos (and all other beings) came to this world 600 to 800 years ago through a progression of underworlds. They were assisted by powerful and mysterious spiritual beings such as coyote, changing woman, spider woman, spider man, and the hero twins. These beings exist in the natural and supernatural worlds and may be called upon for help with curing. Most ceremonies are held when needed, not according to a calendar.

Many important aspects of Navajo ceremonialism, such as the use of masked dancers, feathered prayer sticks, altars, dry (sand) painting, cornmeal, and pollen, were borrowed from the Hopi and other Pueblo people. Traditional Navajo religion excludes organized priesthoods or religious societies. Instead, ceremonies are conducted by "singers" who have mastered one or more of 24 chantway systems. The systems are divided into six main groups: blessing-way, war, gameway (hunting), and the three curing ceremonials—holyway, evilway (ghostway), and life-way. Each group might be composed of 50 or more chants, which in turn might have hundreds of songs or prayers. Specific sandpaintings and social functions often accompany each chant.

As part of the ceremony, the singers use bundles containing items such as rattles, feathered wands and brushes, various stones, and herbal medicines. The most important is the mountain earth bundle, which contains pinches of soil from the tops of the four sacred (bordering) mountains. Around 1940, the Native American Church took its place in Navajo religious practice.

GOVERNMENT Traditionally, the Navajo were organized in a number of bands, each led by a headman (appointed for life) and a clan leader, who were assisted by one or more war leaders. The leaders met formally only every few years. Decisions were taken by consensus.

CUSTOMS In general, the individual takes precedence over the group. Property ownership is individual. The residence group, which was organized around a head mother, a sheep herd, and a customary land-use area, was the largest traditional Navajo organization. Clans were both matrilineal and matrilocal. Men were not allowed to see or talk with their mothers-in-law, so families lived near the wife's mother but in their own homes. The Navajo had a great fear of death. After the dead were buried, their belongings were destroyed.

The extended family was an important economic and social unit, as was the "outfit" in later times, a grouping that consisted of two or more extended families. Home, crops, pottery, and livestock belonged to women and were considered women's work; men made jewelry and represented the family in public and at ceremonials. A four-day girls' puberty ceremony ranked among the most important occasions.

DWELLINGS Navajos lived in hogans. At first they were cone-shaped structures, framed with logs and poles and covered with earth and bark. Later the hogans had six or eight sides and were covered with stone and adobe. Doorways always faced east. The hogans were grouped in rancherias, or small settlements. Other structures included sweat lodges, brush corrals, and ramadas.

DIET Before the Spanish influence, the Navajo grew corn, beans, and squash. Afterward they added fruit trees, oats, and wheat. They hunted antelope, deer, and bear and gathered wild foods such as pine nuts, cactus fruit, wild potatoes, greens, seeds, and herbs. Grazing by sheep, goats, and cattle, acquired from the Spanish in the sixteenth century, destroyed much of their wild food.

KEY TECHNOLOGY The Navajo used traps and snares for hunting. After the introduction of livestock, they learned to spin and weave. In the nineteenth century they learned silver work from the Mexicans.

TRADE Navajos were part of an extensive Native American trading system. In particular, they traded meat, hides, blankets, and minerals to Pueblo Indians for ceramics and cloth. Extensive trade began after the Civil War, with traders acting in many cases as primary links to the outside world as well as bankers, via a pawn system.

NOTABLE ARTS The arts were traditionally seen as ways to relate to and influence spiritual beings and to be closer to the ancestors; as such they were integrated into Navajo ceremonialism. Oral chants told history, traditions, and mythology and were accompanied by music. The Navajo knew several categories of traditional music, from personal/pleasurable to deeply sacred. The people made paintings on clean sand of mineral powders and pollens, which they destroyed at the end of a ceremony. Weaving, done by women, was learned from Pueblo people around 1700; Navajo weavers created a golden age in the early

nineteenth century. Rugs began to replace blankets after 1890. Women also made pottery. Basketry was more utilitarian than artistic. The Navajo learned the art of making silver and turquoise jewelry in the mid-1800s.

TRANSPORTATION The Navajo acquired horses from the Spanish in the sixteenth century.

DRESS Navajos traditionally dressed in aprons and breechcloths of woven yucca, later buckskin, with feathered headgear. Moccasins were made of juniper bark and yucca, later deerskin and cowhide. By the eighteenth century, women wore belted, black wool dresses with stripes of red, yellow, or blue. Men wore buckskin shirts, leggings, and moccasins. From the 1860s on, women wore long, full, colorful skirts and velveteen blouses. Men wore cotton pants and velveteen shirts. Pendleton blankets became regular items of clothing in the nineteenth century; silver and turquoise jewelry in the twentieth.

WAR AND WEAPONS The Navajo first made points of stone for items such as arrows and lance tips; later they used metal. They made bows of oak and juniper and first acquired guns in the seventeenth century. Beginning about that time the Navajo became inveterate raiders. Their traditional targets included the Spanish and the Ute and Pueblo Indians.

Contemporary Information

GOVERNMENT/RESERVATIONS The Navajo Reservation, established in 1868, consists of almost 14 million acres (28,800 square miles) plus several nearby satellite communities. Cañoncito Reservation (1868; 76,813 acres) near Laguna Pueblo is one such satellite, where roughly 1,700 people (1990) are descended from generally proassimilation, Christian Navajos who moved south in the early nineteenth century under Spanish pressure. Other satellite communities include Utah (6,000 people), Ramah (1868; 146,953 acres; 1,500 people), and Puertocito, or Alamo (1868; 63,109 acres; 2,000 people). Thirty thousand Navajos also live on the "checkerboard" in New Mexico, a region in which each alternate square mile is Indian owned. Navajos are also represented among the Colorado River Indian Tribes (*see* Mojave).

Other official Navajo communities include the following: Aneth, Baca, Becenti, Beclabito, Bread Springs, Burnham, Cameron, Casamero, Cheechilgeetho, Chilchinbeto, Chinle, Church Rock, Coalmine, Copper Mine, Cornfields, Coyote Canyon, Crownpoint, Crystal, Dalton Pass, Dennehotso, Forest Lake, Fort Defiance, Ganado, Greasewood, Houck, Huerfano, Inscription House, Iyanbit, Jeddito, Kaibito, Kayenta, Kinlichee, Klagetoh, Lake Valley, Lechee, Leupp, Little Water, Low Mountain,

Lukachukai, Lupton, Manuelito, Many Farms, Mariano, Mexican Springs, Mexican Waters, Nageezi, Naschitti, Navajo Mountain, Nazlini, Nenahnezad, Oak Springs, Oljatoh, Pinedale, Piñon, Pueblo Plaintado, Red Lake, Red Mesa, Red Rock, Rock Point, Rock Springs, Rough Rock, Round Rock, St. Michaels, Sanostee, Sawmill, Sheep Springs, Shiprock, Shonto, Smith Lake, Standing Rock, Steamboat, Sweetwater, Teecnospos, Teesto, Thoreau, Tohatchi, Tolani Lake, Torreon and Star Lake, Tsaile-Wheatfields, Tsayatoh, Tselani, Tuba City, Twin Lakes, Two Grey Hills, Upper Fruitland, White Cone, White Rock, Wide Ruins, and Whitehorse Lake as well as Dilkon Community and Ojo Encino.

Twenty-five energy-producing tribes, including the Navajo, created the Council of Energy Resource Tribes (CERT) in 1976 to help tribes exert control over their mineral resources. Despite their array of lawyers, the tribes have found it difficult to resist pressure from the major energy companies to sign exploitative leases.

The U.S. government still officially controls the Navajo tribal government. Elections for the tribal council are held every four years. In 1936 the council adopted a set of rules that serve as a constitution (they formally rejected organization under the IRA). The "Navajo Nation" was formally adopted in 1969. In 1990, the government was reorganized to coincide with the U.S. model, and the offices of president and vice-president replaced those of chair and vice-chair.

ECONOMY Peabody Coal remains the largest single employer of Navajos. Mineral (oil, gas, coal, uranium) exploitation continues, although not without some controversy. Navajo Agricultural Products Industries and Navajo Forests Products Industries are also large employers. Some people still farm, herd, and produce wool. Many are engaged in making arts and crafts, especially weavings, jewelry, baskets, pottery, and commercial sandpaintings. There is some retail business as well as some off-reservation employment. One-third of the tribal workforce is often unemployed.

LEGAL STATUS The following are federally recognized tribal entities: Navajo Tribe of Arizona, New Mexico, and Utah; Navajo Tribe of Arizona, New Mexico, and Utah (Alamo); Navajo Tribe of Arizona, New Mexico, and Utah (Cañoncito); Navajo Tribe of Arizona, New Mexico, and Utah (Ramah). The Cañoncito Band of Navajos had petitioned for federal recognition as of 1993.

A land dispute with the Hopi dates back to 1882. At that time, the Hopi Reservation included at least 300 Navajos. The Navajos asked for title to the lands in light of Hopi "nonuse": the issue was Hopi "homesteading" versus Navajo "aggressive exploitation." The

Hopi refused. A 1962 district court decision (Healing v. Jones) ruled that each tribe had joint interest in most of the 1882 Hopi Reservation.

In 1974 Congress passed the Navajo-Hopi Land Settlement Act, under which each tribe was to receive half of 1.8 million acres of jointly held land. Those people on the "wrong" side were to move. One hundred Hopis moved. Thousands of Navajos did too, but many refused to leave, and the issue is still in dispute. The Hopi refuse money for land. Traditional leaders among both tribes oppose the act, preferring to keep the land in question open and unspoiled. They have formed a unity council to resolve the situation and consider the ongoing tension the work of energy companies and prodevelopment factions on both tribal councils.

The Navajos also have other land conflicts outstanding with the Hopi as well as with the recently recognized San Juan Paiutes.

DAILY LIFE Navajo children attend community schools, private schools, and reservation high schools; some of the curricula are in the Navajo language. The Rough Rock Demonstration School (1964), the first to operate under a contract from the BIA, demonstrated the wisdom of local control. Since 1969, the reservation has been home to Navajo Community College (the first tribally controlled college); since 1972, to the College of Ganado (Presbyterian). Many Navajos live away from the reservation, although ties between urban Navajos and the reservation remain generally close. Within the context of traditional Navajo identity, new ideas and types of knowledge continue to be taught. Though many Navajos are Christian, the traditional beliefs and the Native American Church are even more popular.

Economically, herders often depend upon a family member with a local wage job. Older Navajos in particular experience chronic under- and unemployment. The tribe has plans to develop a marina, an electronics assembly plant, shopping centers, and motels. Tourism is a high priority. Energy resources are a mixed blessing: They bring in money, but the leases remain exploitative, and their development is often accompanied by political dissension as well as the ravages of strip mining and radiation poisoning.

Life in the late twentieth century remains a balancing act for all. Some (up to 25,000) traditional people speak only or mostly Navajo, some are thoroughly acculturated, and many are uncomfortably in the middle. Today, native healers practice alongside modern doctors. The reservation was scheduled to receive complete telephone service in 1995 but was still waiting as of early 1998. Homes look more modern every year, but the hogan remains the spiritual center and the only place for ceremonies. Women have generally continued their traditional matriarchal roles. Alcoholism is widespread, and suicide rates are high. The Navajo religion is alive and strong, although, with singers and dancers to be paid and food, baskets, and other equipment to be bought, some ceremonials can be very expensive. The Native American Church has a strong presence on the reservation, as does Christianity. Radio stations broadcast programs in Navajo.

Papago

See Tohono O'odham

Pecos Pueblo

See Jemez Pueblo

Pee-Posh

Pee-Posh (`P ē Posh) or "*Pipatsje*," "the People." These people are also known as the Maricopa. (*See also* Pima.)

LOCATION The Pee-Posh lived for centuries along the lower Colorado River and then began migrating to the Gila River region in the 1600s. Today the majority of Pee-Posh live outside of Arizona and California, although the greatest concentrations live with the Pima on the Gila River and Salt River Reservations in Arizona (none live on the Maricopa Reservation).

POPULATION Perhaps 2,500 Pee-Posh and related groups (see "History") migrated to the Gila River region in early historical times. There were roughly 800 Pee-Posh nationwide in 1990.

LANGUAGE The Pee-Posh spoke a dialect of River Yuman, a Hokan-Siouan language.

Historical Information

HISTORY Those people whom the Spanish called the Opa or the Cocomaricopa were one of several small Yuman tribes (including the related groups— the Halchidoma, Kahwan, Kavelchadom, and the Halyikwamai) who lived along the lower Colorado River. Contact with the Spanish was minimal and sporadic. By the early eighteenth century, these peoples had relocated up the Gila River, owing to an escalation of attacks by the Quechan and Mojave. The Pima offered them land and protection, and the two groups soon formed a confederation. By the early nineteenth century, the Pee-Posh had all but absorbed the smaller tribes.

The Pima-Maricopa confederacy went a long way toward making non-Indian settlement of that part of the desert possible, protecting Anglos from Apaches, starvation, and thirst. For example, the Indians used much of their surplus wheat to provide food for the so-called forty-niners on their way to California. (By 1870, their wheat production had reached 3 million pounds, an achievement that aroused the wrath of Anglo wheat farmers.) The Indians also sold wheat to the U.S. Army. In 1857, the confederacy decisively defeated the Quechans and Mojaves at Maricopa Wells, marking the last major formal battle between Indian nations in the Southwest. Beginning in the 1840s, and continuing throughout the century, epidemics took a heavy toll on the Indian population.

In recognition of its alliance with the confederation, the U.S. government established a reservation on the Gila River in 1863 for the Pima and the Pee-Posh. However, river water levels shortly began to fall so low as a result of upstream diversions by nonnatives that a group of Indians moved to the confluence of the Gila and Salt Rivers. Now known as Laveen, this community was first called Maricopa Colony. Halchidoma descendants soon relocated to the Salt River, around the present site of Lehi. In 1879, the original reservation was enlarged, and the Salt River Reservation was established.

During that decade several factors conspired to ruin the Indians' thriving economy: a decline in rainfall, a doubling of the population, and, in particular, huge diversions of Gila River water by non-Indians. By the 1880s, Indian crops routinely failed and famine threatened. Many Pimas and Pee-Posh were forced into the wage economy at the lowest levels. With the loss of the river, the heart of their culture also disappeared. The U.S. government continued to ignore the key problem of water rights, and Pima and Pee-Posh impoverishment continued well into the twentieth century.

In the late nineteenth century, the Bureau of Indian Affairs (BIA) began a campaign to assimilate local Indians. With its blessing, the Presbyterian Church became very active at Gila River, beginning a day school and in general imposing a religious structure on the tribes. The issue of Christianity proved to be a very divisive one on the reservation. In 1914, allotment hit both reservations (against active Indian opposition), scattering the people and further disrupting community life. In 1926, the BIA formed a Pima Advisory Council in an effort to create a formal body that spoke for the tribe. In 1934, the Pimas created a constitution, which was revised by the Pima and Pee-Posh community two years later.

By 1930, non-native water diversions had effectively ended Gila River surface water flowing to the Pee-Posh. Rather than redress the situation, the BIA forced the Indians to use brackish well water. This water was only suitable for growing cotton and some grains, however, and the people could no longer grow edible crops. Several other factors worked to cancel any benefits that might have come with the well water, including a dependency of Indians on wage work, continued ongoing water shortages, and the hated allotments (heirships), which had destroyed their effective land base.

In 1934, the Pima and the Pee-Posh accepted the Indian Reorganization Act (IRA) and formed the Gila River Indian Community. Following World War II, many Pee-Posh (encouraged by the BIA's relocation program) moved away from the reservation. For years outsiders thought that the Pee-Posh had died out and become a subgroup of the Pima Indians.

RELIGION In general, ceremonialism among River Yumans was not especially well developed, except to honor the dead or to celebrate war exploits. Pee-Posh people believed in the power of dreams to direct life and to reveal the potential for special skills and abilities. Shamans had special powers to cure, control the weather, and detect thieves and enemies.

GOVERNMENT Nominal village chiefs exerted little influence. Recognized specialists had the true authority, as curers, calendar-stick keepers, singers, potters, and dancers. All obtained their power from dreams.

CUSTOMS Entire villages moved when someone died, after the body, residence, and possessions had been burned. Special singers sang elaborate song cycles for funerals and transmitted legends, such as ancestral wanderings or conflicts with other groups. Girls celebrated a special puberty ceremony, after which they were tattooed. Both sexes cultivated a high tolerance of pain. As was true for other River Yumans, farming, including ownership of the farm site, was essentially an individual activity. Boundary disputes were solved by mediation or by controlled fighting. The Pee-Posh recognized patrilineal clan as well as village divisions.

DWELLINGS Flattened-dome houses were built with a frame of mesquite or cottonwood uprights and covered with willow ribs and arrowweed thatch. Walls were packed with earth. Rectangular ramadas often adjoined the houses. All dwellings faced east. Other structures included storage sheds, woven basket granaries, and sweat lodges.

DIET The Pee-Posh used floodwater agriculture in their farming. Their staples were mesquite beans and corn. Men planted and cultivated and women harvested. Much food was also gathered, including seeds, berries, nuts, cactus fruit, honey, caterpillars, and beans. The people also ate jackrabbits and fish (caught with nets or bare hands).

KEY TECHNOLOGY All River Yumans share a similar material culture. Clay for pottery was shaped between a curved paddle and a stone anvil or pottery mold. Grinding stones came from granite or sandstone. Wooden mortars, made by hollowing the end of a cottonwood or mesquite log, were used with stone pestles to pulverize mesquite beans. The people used hides for thongs, quivers, shield coverings, and, occasionally, sandals. After the early 1800s, brush dams and ditches replaced floodwater farming as irrigation methods. O'odham-derived calendar sticks told of ancestors, travels, fights, and deaths.

TRADE Trails linked the Pee-Posh with the Mojave and other southern desert peoples. With them, they traded for goods from the Pacific Ocean and the Gulf of California. Trade articles included hand nets and weirless traps for fishing, Pima baskets, and, after the 1700s, Spanish horses and captives. In times of need, food could be obtained from the O'odham literally for a song.

NOTABLE ARTS Women made a wide variety of pottery, including cooking pots, bowls, and water jars. Both men and women wove blankets, cradle ties, headbands, belts, and skirts for girls' puberty ceremonies. Baskets were made and obtained in trade from the Pima.

TRANSPORTATION The Pee-Posh began using horses in the seventeenth century.

DRESS Men wore breechclouts. Women wore fringed skirts of woven willow bark. Both used cotton and rabbit-skin garments in bad weather and sandals for long journeys.

WAR AND WEAPONS The Pee-Posh fought primarily defensive wars. Their weapons included mesquite or ironwood bows, short clubs, and hide shields.

Contemporary Information

GOVERNMENT/RESERVATIONS The Pee-Posh live on the Salt River Reservation (1879; 50,506 acres), near Lehi, and on the Gila River Reservation (1859; 371,933 acres), west of Laveen ("District Seven" of the reservation, the old Maricopa Colony). They share a tribal government with the Pimas; constitutions and by-laws were approved in 1940 (Salt River) and 1936 (Gila River). It is the Ak-chin O'odham who live on the Maricopa Reservation.

ECONOMY The possibility of subsistence farming was lost because individual allotments mandated by the Dawes Act (1887) divided the land into parcels too small to be farmed. Most reservation land is now leased to non-native farmers, and the reservation suffers from a high unemployment rate. Still, the Maricopa Indian Cooperative Association farms about 1,200 acres. Some Indians work off-reservation for wages, generally in Phoenix. Some pottery, not of original Indian concept, is made for the tourist trade. Industrial and mineral development (Gila River) is growing slowly.

LEGAL STATUS Recognized tribal entities include

the Gila River Pima-Maricopa Indian Community and the Salt River Pima-Maricopa Indian Community.

DAILY LIFE   The ethnic identities of the other River Yuman people who followed the Pee-Posh east remain important. Despite the loss of many pre-Pima traditions, the Pee-Posh think of themselves as a united nation and remain in many ways distinct from the Pimas. They are relatively well educated and attend public school. Most speak only English, though a few still speak Pee-Posh. Water rights and health issues, including substance abuse and diabetes, are ongoing concerns. The cremation and mourning ceremonies remain important. A trade fair is held on the reservation every year.

Frame and cement block houses are replacing a few "Pima-style sandwich houses" of adobe packed between slats and timbers. Some Pee-Posh also live in surplus houses of all kinds, including Japanese internment buildings and trailers. Pee-Posh housing is generally considered substandard.

Picuris Pueblo

Picuris (`P ē kur `ē s) comes from the Spanish *Picurís,* "at the mountain gap." The word "pueblo" comes from the Spanish for "village." It refers both to a certain style of Southwest Indian architecture, characterized by multistory, apartmentlike buildings made of adobe, and to the people themselves. Rio Grande pueblos are known as eastern Pueblos; Zuñi, Hopi, and sometimes Acoma and Laguna are known as western Pueblos. The people call their pueblo *Pingultha,* which means either "mountain warrior place" or "mountain pass place."

LOCATION   Picuris Pueblo is located on the western slopes of the Sangre de Cristo Mountains, 18 miles south of Taos Pueblo. The average elevation is about 7,000 feet, which makes for a relatively short and somewhat precarious growing season.

POPULATION   There were perhaps 2,000 residents of Picuris Pueblo in 1630. In 1990, 147 Indians lived on the reservation out of a total population of 1,882.

LANGUAGE   People from Picuris spoke a dialect of Northern Tiwa, a Tanoan language.

Historical Information

HISTORY   All Pueblo people are thought to be descended from Anasazi and perhaps Mogollon and several other ancient peoples. From them they learned architecture, farming, pottery, and basketry. Larger population groups became possible with effective agriculture and ways to store food surpluses. Within the context of a relatively stable existence, the people devoted increasing amounts of time and attention to religion, arts, and crafts.

In the 1200s, the Anasazi abandoned their traditional canyon homelands in response to climatic and social upheavals. A century or two of migrations ensued, followed in general by the slow reemergence of their culture in the historic pueblos. The Tiwas were probably the first of the Tanoan Pueblo people to enter the northern Rio Grande region. Initial settlement of Picuris Pueblo occurred in the twelfth century. It reached its prehistoric peak in the sixteenth century, then declined, probably as a result of the arrival of the Athapaskans.

In 1598, Juan de Oñate arrived in the area with settlers, founding the colony of New Mexico. Oñate carried on the process, already underway in nearby areas, of subjugating the local Indians; forcing them to pay taxes in crops, cotton, and work; and opening the door for Catholic missionaries to attack their religion. The Spanish renamed the Pueblos with saints' names and began a program of church construction, constructing the Mission of San Lorenzo at Picuris in 1621. At the same time, the Spanish introduced such new crops as peaches, wheat, and peppers into the region. In 1620, a royal decree created civil offices at each pueblo; silver-headed canes, many of which remain in use today, symbolized the governor's authority.

Picuris joined the Pueblo rebellion of 1680. For years, the Spaniards had routinely tortured Indians for practicing traditional religion. They also forced the Indians to labor for them, sold Indians into slavery, and let their cattle overgraze Indian land, a situation that eventually led to drought, erosion, and famine. Popé of San Juan Pueblo and other Pueblo leaders, including Tupatu or Luis Picuri, planned the great revolt, sending runners carrying cords of maguey fibers to mark the day of rebellion. On August 10, 1680, a virtually united stand on the part of the Pueblos drove the Spanish from the region. The Indians killed many Spaniards but refrained from mass slaughter, allowing most of them to leave Santa Fe for El Paso.

When the northern pueblos again revolted in 1696, the Picuris abandoned their pueblo and went to live for 20 years on the plains with the Apaches. Between 1680 and 1716, the Picuris population declined by 90 percent. By the 1700s, excluding Hopi and Zuñi, only Taos, Picuris, Isleta, and Acoma Pueblos had not changed locations since the arrival of the Spanish. Although Pueblo unity did not last, and Santa Fe was officially reconquered in 1692, Spanish rule was notably less severe from then on. Harsh forced labor all but ceased, and the Indians reached an understanding with the Church that enabled them to continue practicing their traditional religion.

In general, the Pueblo eighteenth century was marked by smallpox epidemics and increased raiding by the Apache, Comanche, and Ute. The people practiced their religion but more or less in secret. During this time, intermarriage and regular exchange between Hispanic villages and Pueblo Indians created a new New Mexican culture, neither strictly Spanish nor Indian, but rather somewhat of a blend between the two. In the early part of the century the Picuris fought with the Spanish against the Apaches, Utes, and Comanches. They also welcomed a French trading party to the pueblo in 1739, having first encountered French goods through trade with Plains tribes 80 years earlier. By the late eighteenth century they had achieved peace with the Comanche. Partly as a result, Spanish settlement grew, and Picuris Pueblo became surrounded by Spanish-Americans.

Mexican "rule" in 1821 brought little immediate change to the Pueblos. The Mexicans stepped up what had been a gradual process of appropriating Indian land and water, and they allowed the nomadic tribes even greater latitude to raid. As the presence of the United States in the area grew, it attempted to enable the Pueblo Indians to continue their generally peaceful and self-sufficient ways and recognized Spanish land grants to the Pueblos (the grant to 600-year-old Picuris was recognized in 1858). Picuris spent much of the nineteenth century fighting encroachment. To help them, the people turned to non-native civil authorities (Spanish, Mexican, and U.S.). They achieved some success but lost political autonomy in the process.

The relative isolation of Picuris delayed the assimilationist pressures faced by other pueblos. However, a government day school, in which children learned Anglo ways and values, opened in 1899. Adults were encouraged to engage in wage work off the pueblo. Timber operations also began, damaging the fragile irrigation system. In an attempt to retain their identity, Pueblo Indians clung even more tenaciously to their heritage, which by now included elements of the once-hated Spanish culture and religion. By the 1880s, railroads had largely put an end to the traditional geographical isolation of the pueblos. Paradoxically, the U.S. decision to recognize Spanish land grants to the Pueblos denied Pueblo Indians certain rights granted under official treaties and left them particularly open to exploitation by squatters and thieves.

By the 1920s, land disputes had claimed the people's traditional friendliness toward Spanish-Americans. By the 1930s, government wage work and food had largely replaced the subsistence life. Also, the Bureau of Indian Affairs (BIA) was actively intervening in the people's political affairs. After a gap of over 300 years, the All Indian Pueblo Council began to meet again in the 1920s, specifically in response to a congressional threat to appropriate Pueblo lands. Partly as a result of the Council's activities, Congress confirmed Pueblo title to their lands in 1924 by passing the Pueblo Lands Act. The United States also acknowledged its trust responsibilities in a series of legal decisions and other acts of Congress. Still, especially after 1900, Pueblo culture was increasingly threatened by Protestant evangelical missions and schools. The BIA also weighed in on the subject of acculturation, forcing Indian children to leave their homes and attend culture-killing boarding schools.

Since the late nineteenth century but especially after the 1960s, Pueblos have had to cope with onslaughts by (mostly white) anthropologists and seekers of Indian spirituality. The region is also known for its major art colonies at Taos and Santa Fe.

In 1947, the adult men of Picuris voted to change the name of the pueblo to San Lorenzo; however, the name Picuris was again adopted in 1955.

RELIGION In traditional Pueblo culture, religion and life are inseparable. To be in harmony with all of nature is the Pueblo ideal and way of life. The sun is seen as the representative of the Creator. Sacred mountains in each direction, plus the sun above and the earth below, define and balance the Pueblo world. Many Pueblo religious ceremonies revolve around the weather and are devoted to ensuring adequate rainfall. To this end, Pueblo Indians evoke the power of katsinas, sacred beings who live in mountains and other holy places, in ritual and masked dance.

In addition to the natural boundaries, Pueblo Indians have created a society that defines their world by providing balanced, reciprocal relationships within which people connect and harmonize with each other, the natural world, and time itself. At Picuris, people were divided into two patrilineal ceremonial groups, Northside and Southside. Each had a kiva, or prayer chamber. There were also a number of ceremonial organizations, such as Spring People (responsible for the first of three summer rain ceremonies), Fall People (responsible for the second ceremony), and Winter People (responsible for the third ceremony). All used a round house in the north pueblo for ceremonies, except the Winter People, whose ceremonies took place in the "ice kiva." Other ceremonial organizations included water clowns, a mountain group, a *cacique*'s group, and a women's group.

According to tradition, the head of each pueblo is the religious leader, or *cacique,* whose primary responsibility it is to watch the sun and thereby determine the dates of ceremonies. Much ceremonialism is also based on medicine societies, and shamans who derive powers from animal spirits use their supernatural powers for curing, weather control, and ensuring the general welfare. Especially in the eastern pueblos, most ceremonies are kept secret. The mission church at Picuris also served local Spanish-Americans until the late 1800s.

GOVERNMENT Pueblo governments derived from two traditions. Offices that are probably indigenous include the *cacique,* or head of the Pueblo, and the war captains. These officials are intimately related to the religious structures of the pueblo and reflected the essentially theocratic nature of Pueblo government. At Picuris, a Council of *Principales,* composed of the headmen of ceremonial groups and respected elders, made policy, judged offenses, and appointed civil officers.

A parallel but in most cases distinctly less powerful group of officials was imposed by the Spanish authorities. Appointed by the traditional leadership, they generally dealt with external and church matters and included the governor and four assistant governors. The authority of their offices was symbolized by canes. In 1950, Picuris men voted in the pueblo's first election for governor and other civil officials. At that time, the governor replaced the *cacique* as head of the pueblo. During the 1950s and 1960s, the All Indian Pueblo Council (of eastern villages) became increasingly active in asserting rights and solving problems.

CUSTOMS One mechanism that works to keep Pueblo societies coherent is a pervasive aversion to individualistic behavior. Children were raised with gentle guidance and a minimum of discipline. Pueblo Indians were generally monogamous, and divorce was relatively rare. After birth, the baby remained in bed with the mother for 30 days. Children were christened during this time and then confirmed in church between ages 6 and 12. Girls tended to marry in their late teens or early twenties; men about four years later. A new couple established a new household. At Picuris, the dead were ceremonially prepared (black mica on the face and a prayer feather in each hand), death songs were sung, and a wake and Christian hymns followed. Burial, with a food bag, occurred quickly, followed by a four-day vigil. In modern times photography by outsiders is discouraged.

DWELLINGS Picuris Pueblo featured apartment-style dwellings as high as nine stories. The buildings were constructed of adobe (earth and straw) bricks, with beams across the roof that were covered with poles, brush, and plaster. Floors were of wood plank or packed earth. The roof of one level served as the floor of another. The levels were interconnected by ladders. As an aid to defense, the traditional design included no doors or windows; entry was through the roof. Pit houses, or kivas, served as ceremonial chambers and clubhouses. The village plaza, around which all dwellings were clustered, is the spiritual center of the village where all the balanced forces of world come together.

DIET Before the Spanish arrived, Picuris people ate primarily corn, beans, and squash. They also grew cotton and tobacco. They hunted deer, mountain lion, bear, antelope, and rabbits. Occasionally, men from Picuris would travel east to hunt buffalo. The people also gathered a variety of wild seeds, nuts, berries, and other foods and fished in rivers and mountain streams. The Spanish introduced wheat, alfalfa, chilies, fruit trees, grapes, sheep, cattle, and garden vegetables, which soon became part of the regular diet.

KEY TECHNOLOGY Precontact farming implements were wooden. Traditional irrigation systems included ditches as well as floodwater collection at arroyo mouths *(ak chin).* Tanning tools were made of bone and wood. The Spanish introduced metal tools and equipment. Men hunted with juniper bows and arrows.

TRADE All Pueblos were part of extensive Native American trading networks. With the arrival of other cultures, Pueblo Indians also traded with the Hispanic American villages and then U.S. traders. At fixed times during summer or fall, enemies declared truces so that trading fairs might be held. The largest and best known was at Taos with the Comanche. Nomads exchanged slaves, buffalo hides, buckskins, jerked meat, and horses for agricultural and manufactured pueblo products. Pueblo Indians traded for shell and copper ornaments, turquoise, and macaw feathers. Trade along the Santa Fe Trail began in 1821. By the 1880s and the arrival of railroads, the Pueblos were dependent on many American-made goods, and the native manufacture of weaving and pottery declined and nearly died out.

The Picuris served as a link between Pueblo and Plains tribes. In particular, they were generally friendly with the Jicarilla Apache, exchanging both trade items and visits during ceremonies. Despite the proximity of Taos Pueblo (18 miles by trail), the two peoples interacted relatively infrequently and traded little but mountain plants. Picuris enjoyed generally good relations and trade with the Tewa-speaking pueblos, especially San Juan. Picuris also traded with Spanish-Americans, by whom they were surrounded from the eighteenth century on. They also occasionally worked for wages in Spanish-American fields.

NOTABLE ARTS In the Pueblo way, art and life are inseparable. Picuris arts included pottery, baskets, and woven cotton items. Songs, dances, and dramas also qualify as traditional arts. Many Pueblos experienced a renaissance of traditional arts in the twentieth century, beginning in 1919 with San Ildefonso pottery.

TRANSPORTATION Spanish horses, mules, and cattle arrived at Picuris Pueblo in the seventeenth century.

DRESS Men wore shirts, leggings, and moccasins made of deer hides tanned and colored red-brown with plant dye. Womens' wrapped leggings and moccasins were of white buckskin. Clothing was also made of spun cotton. Rabbit skin was also used for clothing and robes.

WAR AND WEAPONS Though often depicted as passive and docile, most Pueblo people regularly engaged in warfare. The great revolt of 1680 stands out as the major military action, but they also skirmished at other times with the Spanish and defended themselves against attackers such as Apaches, Comanches, and Utes. They also contributed auxiliary soldiers to provincial forces under Spain and Mexico, which were used mainly against raiding Indians and to protect merchant caravans on the Santa Fe Trail. After the raiding tribes began to pose less of a threat in the late nineteenth century, Pueblo military societies began to wither away, with the office of war captain changing to civil and religious functions.

Contemporary Information

GOVERNMENT/RESERVATIONS Picuris Pueblo contains almost 15,000 acres. Tribal officers are elected for two-year terms. The tribe is headed by a governor rather than a *cacique.*

ECONOMY Most of the jobs at Picuris Pueblo are with federal and tribal programs. Little remains of the subsistence economy. Some people make pottery for the tourist trade, which is also served by a restaurant and a small museum and cultural center. The tribe also allows a college to hold an anthropological field school in the pueblo. There are also jobs fighting forest fires with the U.S. Forest Service. In 1991, the tribe opened a major hotel in Santa Fe, backed by non-Indian partners and the BIA. Many people leave the pueblo for outside jobs.

LEGAL STATUS Picuris Pueblo is a federally recognized tribal entity.

DAILY LIFE The project of retaining a strong Indian identity is a difficult one in the late twentieth century. Although Picuris people have strong roots and the rebuilding of four kivas has characterized a renewed interest in traditional celebrations, the pueblo is largely acculturated. Children attend local public schools. San Lorenzo's Day, on August 10, is the main feast day; during the races, the traditional division between Northside and Southside people is largely ignored. The pueblo also holds a mountain dance in late September as well as some other dances under direction of the war captain.

Pima

Pima (`P ē mä), from *pi-nyi-match,* "I don't know" (a reply to early questioners). The Pima were originally called Akimel O'odham, or River People, and they are also known as One Villagers because of their relatively settled lives. The O'odham Indians include the Pima, Tohono O'odham (Papago, or Desert People, also known as Two Villagers because of their traditional migration patterns), Sand Papago (Hia C-ed O'odham, or No Villagers because of their more or less constant migrations in search of food), and the Ak-chin O'odham.

LOCATION Traditionally, the Pima lived in rancherias in present-day southern Arizona and northern Sonora, Mexico (the Sonoran Desert). The Spanish categorized them as the Pima Alto (Upper Pima, who lived near the Gila and Salt Rivers) and the Pima Bajo (or Nevones, Lower Pima, who lived along the Yaqui and Sonora Rivers). Today's (upper) Pima reservations are located in southern Arizona.

POPULATION There were roughly 50,000 Pimas in 1500 and perhaps 3,000 in 1700. The 1990 Pima-Maricopa Reservation population was roughly 12,600. There were also at least several hundred Pimas living on the Ak-chin Reservation and off-reservation.

LANGUAGE Piman is a language of the Uto-Aztecan family.

Historical Information

HISTORY The Pima are probably descended from ancient Hohokam Indians. They lived and farmed in permanent settlements (rancherias) near rivers on the northern edge of the Spanish frontier, which at the time was at present-day Tucson. The first non-Indian to visit the Pimas was Marcos de Niza (1589). In 1684, Father Eusebio Kino organized several missions and introduced livestock, wheat, and metal tools into the region.

An accommodation between the Pima and Spanish masked resentments over religious, political, and cultural imperialism, not to mention forced labor. In 1695 the Lower Pima, under Luis Oacpicagigua and others, revolted against the Spanish, and in 1751 the Upper Pima rebelled. The latter had little support from other tribes or even a majority of Pimas, however, and peace was soon established.

Around 1800 the Pee-Posh (Maricopa) Indians came to live near the Upper Pima. At the same time the area came under more frequent attack by Apache raiders. The twin factors of winter wheat production plus increased conflict with the Apache led to a thorough transformation of Pima society. Pima bands engaged in closer cooperation and began to produce agricultural surpluses. This led in turn to an increased integration of their society. By the mid–nineteenth century the position of governor had become hereditary, and the Pima had become a true tribe. They were also the only effective force in the area against the Apache as well as an important economic power.

Despite Pima food assistance to so-called forty-niners and the U.S. Army, Anglo settlers along the Gila River took the best farmland and diverted water for their own use. After the Gadsden Purchase (1853) split O'odham country in two, Anglos began using the term "Pima" for residents on the Gila River and "Papago" for Piman speakers south of the Gila. The United States established a Pima-Maricopa reservation on the Gila River in 1859. However, as a result of failing water supplies, many Indians moved north, where another reservation was established in 1879 on the Salt River. From the 1850s on, three generations of the Azul family led the Pima-Maricopa confederation.

By 1870, Pima wheat production had reached 3 million pounds. Non-natives reacted to this achievement with fear, envy, and retaliation. Major Anglo water diversions soon left the Pima with little water for their crops. Combined with a drought and population increases, this led to Pima impoverishment in the late nineteenth century and early twentieth century. Many Pimas were forced into the wage economy at the lowest levels. The U.S. government ignored the key problem of Pima water rights.

The loss of the river and the growing influence of Presbyterians brought about a severe decline in Pima culture and traditional religion. The Presbyterians replaced the Pima religious structure with one of their own creation. The Presbyterian Church and the Bureau of Indian Affairs (BIA) opened day and boarding schools respectively. Allotment hit the reservation in 1914, breaking up tribal land patterns and further disrupting community life.

In 1926, the BIA created a Pima Advisory Council to meet the bureau's need for a body that spoke for the tribe. Eight years later the Pimas adopted a constitution and tribal council, which remained quite powerless, as the Pima "tribe" had virtually disappeared. The Pima and Maricopa community revised the constitution and by-laws in 1936. In the 1930s the San Carlos Project began returning irrigation water to the Pimas, but several factors worked to cancel its benefits, including the dependency of Indians on wage work (at that point they were reluctant to return to subsistence farming), a complex water-management bureaucracy that mandated required crops, chronic ongoing water shortages, and the fact that allotments (heirship) had destroyed their effective land base. The postwar period has been a time for Pimas once again to assume a degree of control over their own resources and lives.

RELIGION Pimas worshiped several deities, the most important of which were Earthmaker and Elder Brother (I'itoi). The harvest and victory after battle provided the best occasions for ceremonies. Many O'odhams became Catholics in the eighteenth century, but theirs was a Catholicism with important native variations.

GOVERNMENT A civil leader and one or more shamans presided over economically and politically independent villages. Village ceremonial leaders were known as "keepers of the smoke." Village chiefs elected a tribal chief, who ran council meetings. His other responsibilities included overseeing farm projects and defending against Apache raiders. In the mid–nineteenth century, the chieftainship went from a position of power and no wealth to one of wealth and no power. In 1936 the adoption of a new constitution under the Indian Reorganization Act marked the beginning of the Pima battle for legal rights.

CUSTOMS Each village was divided into two groups, Red Ant and White Ant, who opposed each other in games and other ceremonial functions. The groups were further divided into patrilineal clans. In general, men farmed, fished, hunted, built the houses, and wove cotton; women gathered food and made baskets, pottery, and clothing. They also carried firewood and food on their backs in burden baskets. The Pima used a lunar calendar. Their year began with the rainy season and the appearance of flowers on certain plants, such as the saguaro cactus. *Viikita* was a celebration held every fourth harvest to celebrate and ensure the favor of the gods. The Pima buried their dead in rock crevices or in stone huts, with weapons, tools, and food. The deceased's house was burned. For traveling long distances, the Pima preferred running to walking; a ball was kept in motion to maintain the pace.

DWELLINGS Pimas lived in small, round, flat-topped, pole-framed structures, covered with grass and mud. In warmer weather they moved into simple open-sided brush arbors. They also built cylindrical bins in which they stored mesquite beans. Ramadas, used for clubhouses, also dotted each village.

DIET Farm products such as corn, squash (cut into strips and dried), and tepary beans accounted for up to 60 percent of the Pima diet. The people also grew tobacco and cotton and, after the Spanish arrived, wheat (winter wheat ensured against starvation and made farms very productive) and alfalfa. Wild foods included cactus fruit, mesquite beans, greens, chilies, and seeds, which, with corn, were ground into meal on a cottonwood mortar and used in gruel and cakes. Pimas also ate fish and hunted deer, rabbit, mountain sheep, antelope, and reptiles. They drank saguaro wine for ceremonial purposes.

KEY TECHNOLOGY   To irrigate their crops, Pimas diverted water from rivers with dams of logs and brush. They also built canals and feeder ditches. Farm tools consisted of digging sticks and a flat board used for hoeing and harvesting. Hunting bows were made of Osage orange or willow. After a great meteor shower in 1833, the people used calendar sticks—saguaro ribs with cuts—to mark certain events. The Spanish brought horse- and oxen-drawn wagons and plows and metal picks and shovels into the region.

TRADE   Pimas traded salt, seashells, and ceremonies for River Yuman pottery and food. They also traded with the Lower Pimas for hides, mescal, and pepper.

NOTABLE ARTS   Women made highly prized baskets with abstract designs out of black devil's claw. They also made red-and-black pottery. Men made equally good cotton belts and blankets.

TRANSPORTATION   The O'odham traveled by foot until the introduction of Spanish horses in the seventeenth century.

DRESS   Men wore cotton or deerskin breechcloths. Women wore cloth, willow bark, or deerskin wraparound skirts. Both sexes used hide or fiber sandals and cotton and rabbit-skin blankets. They also grew their hair long, wore ear pendants of turquoise and other stones, and tattooed and painted their bodies.

WAR AND WEAPONS   Pimas placed a high value on peace yet became more oriented toward war with the growing Apache threat after the mid–eighteenth century. Traditional enemies also included Quechans and Yavapais; their main allies were the Pee-Posh. Pimas also fought against Apaches with the Spanish, Mexicans, and U.S. troops. Pimas fought in all U.S. wars beginning with the Civil War. Warriors who had killed an enemy underwent a 16-day purification rite. War bows were made of mulberry. Other weapons included clubs and shields.

Contemporary Information

GOVERNMENT/RESERVATIONS   The Gila River Reservation was established in 1859. It consists of roughly 370,000 acres. A community council of 17 members governs by way of various committees; the governing structure also contains an executive and a judicial element. The Salt River Reservation was established in 1879, in Maricopa County, and contains roughly 52,600 acres. Its constitution and by-laws were adopted in 1940. Some Pimas also live among the Tohono O'odham on the Ak-chin Reservation.

ECONOMY   Almost all farmland is leased to non-Indians for industrial parks and agribusiness, although Gila River Farms produces a number of crops, and the Salt River Reservation has roughly 12,000 acres under cultivation. There is some wage work in the cities and with the tribe. There is also a large retail center on the reservation. Other sources of income include apiary licenses, traders' licenses, industrial parks, a large motor racing park, and sand and gravel sales. Additional highway development may bring in some money. The Gila River Arts and Crafts Center, which includes a restaurant and a museum, is a focus for the local tourist trade.

LEGAL STATUS   The Gila River Pima-Maricopa Community of the Gila River Indian Reservation and the Salt River Pima-Maricopa Community of the Salt River Indian Reservation are federally recognized tribal entities.

DAILY LIFE   Faced with the need to store calories against periodic famines, Pimas traditionally ate in what might today be called binges. The combination of the absence of famine and a diet that contains many highly processed, low-fiber, and junk foods has left Pimas with a marked tendency toward diabetes. A number of health centers, including the private Native American Dialysis Center, help with these problems. The Fiesta de Magdalena, held in the fall in Sonora, Mexico, remains the most powerful connection between the Arizona and Mexican O'odham. Water rights remain a pressing issue—the water table in their area has been lowered some 300 feet over the years—as does creeping urban and suburban sprawl.

Most Pimas are Presbyterians and are relatively assimilated into mainstream U.S. life. Few live any longer in extended families. The loss of most traditions has been difficult for some people: It led in part to the death of Ira Hayes, one of six men who raised the U.S. flag on Iwo Jima during World War II. The Pima hold annual fairs, particularly the *mul-chu-tha* festival, in March as well as a rodeo and parades. Some Pimas continue to make baskets. There is a net outflow of population off the reservations. Students attend BIA schools on the reservations (Gila River) as well as public schools. The Salt River Reservation contains a number of recreational and cultural facilities.

Pojoaque Pueblo

Pojoaque (P ō ˋhwä k ā) is an adaptation of the Tewa *Posuwaegeh,* meaning "drink-water place." The word "pueblo" comes from the Spanish for "village." It refers both to a certain style of Southwest Indian architecture, characterized by multistory, apartment-like buildings made of adobe, and to the people themselves. Rio Grande pueblos are known as eastern Pueblos; Zuñi, Hopi, and sometimes Acoma and Laguna are known as western Pueblos.

LOCATION   Pojoaque Pueblo is located 16 miles north of Santa Fe; it is the smallest of the six Tewa villages.

POPULATION   In 1990, 177 Indians lived on the pueblo out of an overall population of roughly 2,500; 79 lived there in 1712 and possibly as many 500 in 1500.

LANGUAGE   Tewa is a Kiowa-Tanoan language.

Historical Information

HISTORY   All Pueblo people are thought to be descended from Anasazi and perhaps Mogollon and several other ancient peoples. From them they learned architecture, farming, pottery, and basketry. Larger population groups became possible with effective agriculture and ways to store food surpluses. Within the context of a relatively stable existence, the people devoted increasing amounts of time and attention to religion, arts, and crafts. In the 1200s, the Anasazi abandoned their traditional canyon homelands in response to climatic and social upheavals. A century or two of migrations ensued, followed in general by the slow reemergence of their culture in the historic pueblos. Occupation of the Pojoaque area has been constant since about 900, and it grew to be a major political and cultural center.

In 1598, Juan de Oñate arrived in the area with settlers, founding the colony of New Mexico. Oñate carried on the process, already underway in nearby areas, of subjugating the local Indians; forcing them to pay taxes in crops, cotton, and work; and opening the door for Catholic missionaries to attack their religion. The Spanish renamed the Pueblos with saints' names and began a program of church construction. At the same time, the Spanish introduced such new crops as peaches, wheat, and peppers into the region. In 1620, a royal decree created civil offices at each pueblo; silver-headed canes, many of which remain in use today, symbolized the governor's authority.

Pojoaque took an active part in the 1680 Pueblo revolt against the Spanish. For years, the Spaniards had routinely tortured Indians for practicing traditional religion. They also forced the Indians to labor for them, sold Indians into slavery, and let their cattle overgraze Indian land, a situation that eventually led to drought, erosion, and famine. Popé of San Juan Pueblo and other Pueblo religious leaders planned the revolt, sending runners carrying cords of maguey fibers to mark the day of rebellion. On August 10, 1680, a virtually united stand on the part of the Pueblos drove the Spanish from the region. The Indians killed many Spaniards but refrained from mass slaughter, allowing them to leave Santa Fe for El Paso.

Pojoaque suffered greatly in the aftermath of the revolt. Spanish recolonizers took much of their best land. The tribe became decimated and scattered but was able to reestablish itself in 1706. However, by then most of their population had been absorbed by other pueblos. Although Pueblo unity did not last, and Santa Fe was officially reconquered in 1692, Spanish rule was notably less severe from then on. Harsh forced labor all but ceased, and the Indians reached an understanding with the Church that enabled them to continue practicing their traditional religion.

In general, the Pueblo eighteenth century was marked by smallpox epidemics and increased raiding by the Apache, Comanche, and Ute. Occasionally Pueblo Indians fought with the Spanish against the nomadic tribes. The people practiced their religion but more or less in secret. During this time, intermarriage and regular exchange between Hispanic villages and Pueblo Indians created a new New Mexican culture, neither strictly Spanish nor Indian, but rather somewhat of a blend between the two.

Mexican "rule" in 1821 brought little immediate change to the Pueblos. The Mexicans stepped up what had been a gradual process of appropriating Indian land and water, and they allowed the nomadic tribes even greater latitude to raid. A political rebellion by Indians and Hispanics in 1837 over the issue of taxes led to the assassination of the New Mexican governor and his brief replacement by a Plains/Taos Indian. As the presence of the United States in the area grew, it attempted to enable the Pueblo Indians to continue their generally peaceful and self-sufficient ways.

During the nineteenth century the population at Pojoaque became so small (it was recorded as 32 in 1870) that the people could no longer hold their ceremonies. A steady loss of their land base contributed to the tribe's degeneration. Many people left to live at other pueblos or to make their way in the outside world. At the same time, documents attesting to Spanish land grants and water rights were lost, although the United States did confirm their holding in 1858; shortly afterward, leaders traveled to Washington to receive the patent as well as a silver-headed Lincoln cane. Paradoxically, the U.S. decision to recognize Spanish land grants to the Pueblos denied Pueblo Indians certain rights granted under official treaties and left them particularly open to exploitation by squatters and thieves.

By the early twentieth century, Pojoaque Pueblo was all but abandoned, although it had become a small Spanish-American settlement by the 1930s. At that time a handful of Pojoaque families returned, evicted non-Indians, and fenced the land. Antonio José Tapia was instrumental in reestablishing the pueblo during this period. Government payment for losses suffered over the years acted as an incentive for other Pojoaques to return. Partly because of lobbying from the All Indian Pueblo Council, Congress confirmed Pueblo title to their lands in 1924 by passing the Pueblo Lands Act. The United States also acknowledged its trust responsibilities in a series of legal decisions and other acts of Congress. Still, the Bureau of Indian Affairs (BIA) forced Indian children to leave their homes and attend culture-killing boarding schools and in general tried its best to undermine Indian identity and survival.

RELIGION In traditional Pueblo culture, religion and life are inseparable. To be in harmony with all of nature is the Pueblo ideal and way of life. The sun is seen as the representative of the Creator. Sacred mountains in each direction, plus the sun above and the earth below, define and balance the Pueblo world. Many Pueblo religious ceremonies revolve around the weather and are devoted to ensuring adequate rainfall. To this end, Pueblo Indians evoke the power of katsinas, sacred beings who live in mountains and other holy places, in ritual and masked dance.

In addition to the natural boundaries, Pueblo Indians have created a society that defines their world by providing balanced, reciprocal relationships within which people connect and harmonize with each other, the natural world, and time itself. According to tradition, the head of each pueblo is the religious leader, or *cacique*, whose primary responsibility it is to watch the sun and thereby determine the dates of ceremonies. Much ceremonialism is also based on medicine societies, and shamans who derive powers from animal spirits use their supernatural powers for curing, weather control, and ensuring the general welfare. Especially in the eastern pueblos, most ceremonies are kept secret.

GOVERNMENT Pueblo governments derived from two traditions. Offices that are probably indigenous include the *cacique*, or head of the Pueblo, and the war captains. These officials are intimately related to the religious structures of the pueblo and reflected the essentially theocratic nature of Pueblo government. Pojoaque had both summer and winter *caciques*.

A parallel but in most cases distinctly less powerful group of officials was imposed by the Spanish authorities. Appointed by the traditional leadership, they generally dealt with external and church matters and included the governor, two lieutenant governors, and two sheriffs. The authority of their offices was symbolized by canes. Nontraditional positions also often included a ditch boss, who was in charge of the irrigation ditches, as well as a town crier and sacristan. In addition, the All Indian Pueblo Council,

dating from 1598, began meeting again in the twentieth century.

CUSTOMS One mechanism that works to keep Pueblo societies coherent is a pervasive aversion to individualistic behavior. Children were raised with gentle guidance and a minimum of discipline. Pueblo Indians were generally monogamous, and divorce was relatively rare. The dead were prepared ceremonially and quickly buried with clothes, beads, food, and other items. A vigil of four days and nights was generally observed.

At Pojoaque, in contrast with most other pueblos, seasons were traditionally delineated not so much by the solstice as by the actual change in seasons. Formerly a summer and a winter *cacique*, appointed for life, oversaw the pueblo. Society was divided into two groups, summer (associated with the Squash kiva) and winter (associated with the Turquoise kiva); membership in a group was patrilineal. These groups were further divided into clans. A number of secret societies also existed. For instance, the warrior society was concerned with hunting, war, crops, fertility, and curing. Each society had its own dances and ritual paraphernalia.

DWELLINGS Most Pueblos (possibly including Pojoaque) originally featured multistory apartment-style dwellings constructed of adobe (earth and straw) bricks, with pine beams across the roof that were covered with poles, brush, and plaster. Floors were of wood plank or packed earth. The roof of one level served as the floor of another. The levels were interconnected by ladders. As an aid to defense, the traditional design included no doors or windows; entry was through the roof. Pit houses, or kivas, served as ceremonial chambers and clubhouses. The village plaza, around which the church and all dwellings were clustered, was the spiritual center of the village where all the balanced forces of the world come together.

DIET Before the Spanish arrived, people from Pojoaque Pueblo ate primarily corn, beans, and squash. They also grew cotton and tobacco. They hunted deer, mountain lion, antelope, and rabbits. They also gathered a variety of wild seeds, nuts, berries, and other foods. The Spanish introduced wheat, alfalfa, chilies, fruit trees, grapes, sheep, cattle, and garden vegetables, which soon became part of the regular diet.

KEY TECHNOLOGY Pojoaque people used irrigation ditches from a time well before the arrival of the Spanish.

TRADE All Pueblos were part of extensive Native American trading networks. With the arrival of other cultures, Pueblo Indians also traded with the Hispanic American villages and then U.S. traders. At fixed times during summer or fall, enemies declared truces so that trading fairs might be held. The largest and best known was at Taos with the Comanche. Nomads exchanges slaves, buffalo hides, buckskins, jerked meat, and horses for agricultural and manufactured pueblo products. Pueblo Indians traded for shell and copper ornaments, turquoise, and macaw feathers. Trade along the Santa Fe Trail began in 1821. By the 1880s and the arrival of railroads, the Pueblos were dependent on many American-made goods, and the Native American manufacture of weaving and pottery declined and nearly died out.

NOTABLE ARTS In the Pueblo way, art and life are inseparable. Traditional arts at Pojoaque include weaving, songs, dances, and dramas. Many Pueblos experienced a renaissance of traditional arts in the twentieth century, beginning in 1919 with San Ildefonso pottery.

TRANSPORTATION Spanish horses, mules, and cattle arrived at Pojoaque Pueblo in the sixteenth century.

DRESS Men wore cotton and buckskin shirts and kilts. Womens' traditional dress featured spun cotton dresses and sandals or high moccasin boots. Rabbit skin was also used for clothing and robes.

WAR AND WEAPONS Though often depicted as passive and docile, most Pueblo groups regularly engaged in warfare. The great revolt of 1680 stands out as the major military action, but they also skirmished at other times with the Spanish and defended themselves against attackers such as Apaches, Comanches, and Utes. They also contributed auxiliary soldiers to provincial forces under Spain and Mexico, which were used mainly against raiding Indians and to protect merchant caravans on the Santa Fe Trail. After the raiding tribes began to pose less of a threat in the late nineteenth century, Pueblo military societies began to wither away, with the office of war captain changing to civil and religious functions.

Contemporary Information

GOVERNMENT/RESERVATIONS Pojoaque Pueblo consists of roughly 11,600 acres, with some still in dispute. The governor, who may be—and has been—a woman, is elected annually. The tribal council, which may also contain women, meets at least every two weeks.

ECONOMY Many people work for wages in Santa Fe or Española. The tribe owns valuable frontage on U.S. Route 285 and is planning long-term commercial development. It also operates La Mesita restaurant, Nambé Mills (pottery), the Poeh Cultural Center and Museum, and several other businesses, including a shopping center. It owns forestry leases in addition to commercial ones. Uranium is found on

the pueblo. Income is divided among all tribal members. To limit excessive development, the council has insisted on ten-year leases; it also insists that Indians have the top priority for jobs. There is very little farming or livestock activity, but there is some craft activity, especially pottery. Pojoaque Pueblo boasts relatively low unemployment.

LEGAL STATUS Pojoaque Pueblo is a federally recognized tribal entity.

DAILY LIFE Pojoaque is largely assimilated into the local Hispanic-Anglo culture. Nothing remains of the old pueblo. Nor do any traditional ceremonies or the office of *cacique* remain (the last *cacique* died around 1900); cultural identity is maintained through participation in other pueblos' ceremonies, particularly those at Santa Clara.

Most people, especially the younger ones, speak English and possibly Spanish but little Tewa; the trend is toward only English. Most Pojoaque Indians are at least nominally Catholic. An excellent school complex educates both local Indian and non-Indian children, and the tribe provides some scholarships for postsecondary education. Health care is available in Española and Santa Fe. Despite the lack of traditional cultural attributes, Pojoaque is slowly regaining its former position as a center of Tewa culture.

Quechan

Quechan (`K ē chan) from *xam kwatcan*, "another going down" (a reference to their ancestral migration). Quechans are also known as Yuma Indians; Yuma is an O'odham word for "People of the River."

LOCATION The Quechan lived in several small settlements, or rancherias, along the bottomlands of the Colorado River, near the mouth of the Gila. Many Quechans now live on the Fort Yuma Reservation as well as on the Cocopah Reservation with Pee-Posh and Cocopas, having once been allied with these tribes.

POPULATION Perhaps 4,000 Quechans lived on the Colorado River in the sixteenth century. Almost 1,200 Quechans lived at Fort Yuma in 1990; others lived on the Cocopah Reservation and off-reservation. The 1990 Quechan population was roughly 3,000.

LANGUAGE Quechan is a dialect of River Yuman.

Historical Information

HISTORY Quechan farmers began using floodwaters of the Colorado River for irrigation beginning around 2,500 years ago. The Quechans first encountered a non-native person in 1540, in the person of Hernando de Alarcón. Father Eusebio Kino arrived in 1698 and Father Francisco Garces in 1775. The

Quechans generally resisted Spanish missions and settlements. A rebellion in 1781 ended Spanish control of a key river crossing, and the Quechans were able to continue their traditional way of life.

In the mid–nineteenth century, Quechans occasionally raided overland travelers (on the Southern Overland Trail, or Butterfield Route), partly in retaliation for crop thievery. The number of non-Indians passing through their territory increased greatly in and after 1849, due to the California gold rush. At that time, the Quechans provided a ferry service across the Colorado. When Anglos attempted to open a competing service, the Quechans blocked the passage. When the U.S. Army intervened to keep the passage open, the Quechans fought back, driving the U.S. forces away for a year. In 1852, the soldiers returned and built Fort Yuma, effectively ending Quechan resistance in the area. Five years later, the Quechan and their Mojave allies were defeated by the Pima and Maricopa in the last big intra-Indian fight near the Colorado River.

In 1853 the United States established the Fort Yuma Reservation with 45,000 acres, on the California side of the Colorado. Steamship and railroad travel as well as the town of Yuma boomed in the following decades. Quechans worked as steamship pilots and woodcutters until railroads ended the industry and then as laborers and domestics.

By the end of the century the tribe, devastated by disease, was in a state of cultural eclipse. Factionalism also weakened the tribe, and Anglos took the opportunity to appoint Quechan leaders unilaterally. Clan and village affiliations broke down when youths were taken away forcibly to boarding school. The Quechan relinquished most of their land in 1893 and lost the best of what was left to Anglos by 1910. Upstream dams prevented natural flooding, and Quechan farmers, people of the river for centuries, found themselves in the position of having to pay for irrigation water.

Quechans lived in poverty well into the twentieth century. Mandated allotment of their land in 1912 led to endless subdivision and rendered it useless for agriculture; most was leased to non-Indians. The federal War on Poverty arrived in the 1960s, and with it new opportunities for decent housing and economic development. In 1978 the government returned 25,000 acres (minus the vital water rights) and paid for even more in the 1980s.

RELIGION Like those of all Yumans, Quechan religion and knowledge were based on dreaming. Dreams were seen as visits with ancestors. The most powerful dreamer was their religious leader. Dreams also brought power to lead in battle, orate a funeral, or do almost anything. However, dreams were considered of questionable authenticity unless they conferred success. Shamans were specialists who were able to cure using supernatural powers acquired through very powerful dreams, perhaps begun in the womb. They also controlled the weather.

Quechans sang extended song cycles for curing, funerals, and entertainment. The cycles consisted of dreams and tribal mythology and were accompanied by people shaking rattles and beating sticks on baskets. Important Quechan ceremonies included a four-day-long girls' puberty rite and a boy's nose-piercing ceremony (at age seven, which also included racing and fasting). A mesquite harvest festival in summer and a crop harvest festival in fall both featured games, contests, gambling, and songs. Quechans also observed a four-day-long mourning ceremony.

GOVERNMENT All political authority was based on dreams, as was the authority of singers, speakers, and curers. Each rancheria had one or more headmen: Although they might meet in council to discuss tribal matters, decision making was by concensus. Other offices included the war leader and funeral orator.

CUSTOMS The Quechan were organized into patrilineal clans. Little or no status differences existed between family groups. Rancheria leaders addressed the people from rooftops on correct behavior. All possessions of the deceased, even the house, were given away or destroyed. Dung was burned to keep away mosquitoes.

DWELLINGS Rectangular, open, earth-covered structures served as summer houses; in winter people lived in semisubterranean houses covered with sand. Other structures included sunshades and woven granaries.

DIET Quechans mainly farmed for their food. They grew corn, beans, and pumpkins and, after the Spanish arrived, melons and wheat. They also grew tobacco and gourds. They used the seasonal flooding of the river to irrigate their fields, predicting the occurrence of the floods with astrological knowledge. They also fished with nets, traps, and bows and arrows. They hunted small game such as rabbits and gathered foods such as mesquite, screwbeans, nuts, and seeds. They parched the nuts and seeds in trays and then ground them to meal or flour. Squash and pumpkins were cut into strips and dried.

KEY TECHNOLOGY Sowing was accomplished by means of digging sticks. Musical instruments included flutes and gourd and deer hoof rattles. Nets attached to headbands were used for carrying burdens on the back. Women made pottery bowls, dippers, and cooking pots as well as basket trays and storage containers.

TRADE Among other items, the Quechan received blankets from the Hopi and Navajo. They traded agricultural products with tribes near the Gulf of California and the Pacific Ocean for shells and feathers.

NOTABLE ARTS Pottery and basketry ranked among Quechan fine arts.

TRANSPORTATION The Quechan used rafts of cottonwood logs or tule reeds for river travel. They floated children and goods in large pots. Horses arrived in their area by the late eighteenth century.

DRESS Quechan dress was minimal. Women wore willow-bark aprons, and men occasionally wore buckskin or bark breechclouts. Both wore rawhide sandals. Domestically manufactured blankets were of rabbit skin or woven bark. Both sexes kept their hair long (men wore long rolls of hair) and painted their faces for decoration. Men also wore nose and/or ear rings.

WAR AND WEAPONS Quechans considered war essential to the acquisition and maintenance of their spiritual power. They distinguished between raiding, an activity whose main purpose was to acquire horses or captives, and warfare, the purpose of which was revenge. The Mojave were traditional allies; enemies included the Cocopah, Pee-Posh, and Pima. The Quechan warrior hierarchy included the leader, then spearmen and clubmen, archers, horsemen (after contact) with spears, and finally women with clubs. For weapons they used mesquite bows, clubs, stone knives, hide shields, and spears.

Contemporary Information

GOVERNMENT/RESERVATIONS The Fort Yuma Reservation (1884) consists of 43,561 acres. Many Quechans also live on the Cocopah Reservation (6,000 acres; established 1917) near Summerton, Arizona. They adopted an Indian Reorganization Act constitution in 1936 and began electing tribal council two years later. Both men and women are represented in leadership positions.

ECONOMY Tribal businesses include sand and gravel operations, recreational vehicle parks, a bingo parlor, and an irrigation project. Still, there are few jobs on the reservation; federal funding of tribal projects accounts for most economic activity. The tribe would like to establish a closed economy, with no need for jobs in Yuma. Future farming depends on establishing water rights and obtaining water for irrigation. Most prime farming land remains leased to non-Indian interests. Legal fights over these matters are pending. In addition, the Indians of the Cocopah Reservation recently signed an agreement to build a large recreational vehicle park.

LEGAL STATUS The Quechan Tribe of the Fort Yuma Indian Reservation is a federally recognized tribal entity.

DAILY LIFE Older Quechans still speak the language. The mourning ceremony remains, as do some of the songs and dances. Most Quechans still prefer to be cremated along with much of their personal property. A small hospital attempts to cope with many cases of diabetes and substance abuse. The elderly are still revered, as are eloquent speakers of the native language. Children attend local public schools. Quechans are largely acculturated and have high hopes for survival in the modern world.

Sandia Pueblo

Sandia (Sän `d ē ä) from the Spanish for "watermelon," referring to the size, shape, and color of the nearby Sandia Mountains. The word "pueblo" comes from the Spanish for "village." It refers both to a certain style of Southwest Indian architecture, characterized by multistory, apartmentlike buildings made of adobe, and to the people themselves. Rio Grande pueblos are known as eastern Pueblos; Zuñi, Hopi, and sometimes Acoma and Laguna are known as western Pueblos. The Tiwa name for Sandia Pueblo is *Napeya* or *Nafiat*, "at the dusty place."

LOCATION Sandia Pueblo is located 15 miles north of Albuquerque, on the east bank of the Rio Grande. The altitude ranges from 5,000 to 10,670 feet, and the land contains good farmland, game, and wild foods.

POPULATION There were roughly 3,000 people living on Sandia Pueblo in 1680 and 350 people in 1748. The 1993 tribal enrollment was 481; 266 people lived on the pueblo.

LANGUAGE Southern Tiwa is a Kiowa-Tanoan language.

Historical Information

HISTORY All Pueblo people are thought to be descended from Anasazi and perhaps Mogollon and several other ancient peoples. From them they learned architecture, farming, pottery, and basketry. Larger population groups became possible with effective agriculture and ways to store food surpluses. Within the context of a relatively stable existence, the people devoted increasing amounts of time and attention to religion, arts, and crafts.

In the 1200s, the Anasazi abandoned their traditional canyon homelands in response to climatic and social upheavals. A century or two of migrations ensued, followed in general by the slow reemergence of their culture in the historic pueblos. The Tiwas were probably the first of the Tanoan Pueblo people to enter the northern Rio Grande region. Sandia Pueblo was founded around 1300.

Francisco Vasquez de Coronado probably visited Sandia Pueblo in 1540. In 1598, Juan de Oñate arrived in the area with settlers, founding the colony of New Mexico. Oñate carried on the process, already underway in nearby areas, of subjugating the local Indians; forcing them to pay taxes in crops, cotton, and work; and opening the door for Catholic missionaries to attack their religion. The Spanish renamed the Pueblos with saints' names and began a program of church construction, constructing the Mission of San Francisco Sandia in 1617. At the same time, the Spanish introduced such new crops as peaches, wheat, and peppers into the region. In 1620, a royal decree created civil offices at each pueblo; silver-headed canes, many of which remain in use today, symbolized the governor's authority.

Sandia joined the Pueblo rebellion of 1680. For years, the Spaniards had routinely tortured Indians for practicing traditional religion. They also forced the Indians to labor for them, sold Indians into slavery, and let their cattle overgraze Indian land, a situation that eventually led to drought, erosion, and famine. Popé of San Juan Pueblo and other Pueblo religious leaders planned the great revolt, sending runners carrying cords of maguey fibers to mark the day of rebellion. On August 10, 1680, a virtually united stand on the part of the Pueblos drove the Spanish from the region. The Indians killed many Spaniards but refrained from mass slaughter, allowing most of them to leave Santa Fe for El Paso.

The Spanish burned Sandia Pueblo after the revolt. It was then reoccupied but later burned or abandoned several times in the 1680s and 1690s; the pueblo was in ruins in 1692. The Sandias first fled to the nearby mountains and then lived for a time at Hopi. Sandia Pueblo was permanently reoccupied in 1748 by a mixed group of refugees from various pueblos. Meanwhile, Santa Fe was officially reconquered in 1692, although Spanish rule was notably less severe from then on. Harsh forced labor all but ceased, and the Indians reached an understanding with the Church that enabled them to continue practicing their traditional religion.

In general, the Pueblo eighteenth century was marked by smallpox epidemics and increased raiding by the Apache, Comanche, and Ute. During this time, intermarriage and regular exchange between Hispanic villages and Pueblo Indians created a new New Mexican culture, neither strictly Spanish nor Indian, but rather somewhat of a blend between the two. Mexican "rule" in 1821 brought little immediate change to the Pueblos. The Mexicans stepped up what had been a gradual process of appropriating Indian land and water, and they allowed the nomadic tribes even greater latitude to raid.

As the presence of the United States in the area grew, it attempted to enable the Pueblo Indians to continue their generally peaceful and self-sufficient ways and recognized Spanish land grants to the Pueblos. However, Sandia lost thousands of acres during this process as a result of filing, surveying, and other errors. In an attempt to retain their identity, Pueblo Indians clung even more tenaciously to their heritage, which by now included elements of the once-hated Spanish culture and religion. By the 1880s, railroads had largely put an end to the traditional geographical isolation of the pueblos. Still, Sandia Pueblo avoided much Anglo-American influence until after World War II. Paradoxically, the U.S. decision to recognize Spanish land grants to the Pueblos denied Pueblo Indians certain rights granted under official treaties and left them particularly open to exploitation by squatters and thieves.

Sandia and other pueblos had suffered significant population decline by 1900 as a result of wars, disease, and resource loss. After a gap of over 300 years, the All Indian Pueblo Council began to meet again in the 1920s, specifically in response to a congressional threat to appropriate Pueblo lands. Partly as a result of the Council's activities, Congress confirmed Pueblo title to their lands in 1924 by passing the Pueblo Lands Act. The United States also acknowledged its trust responsibilities in a series of legal decisions and other acts of Congress.

Still, especially after 1900, Pueblo culture was increasingly threatened by Protestant evangelical missions and schools. The Bureau of Indian Affairs also weighed in on the subject of acculturation, forcing Indian children to leave their homes and attend culture-killing boarding schools. Since the late nineteenth century, but especially after the 1960s, Pueblos have had to cope with onslaughts by (mostly white) anthropologists and seekers of Indian spirituality.

RELIGION In traditional Pueblo culture, religion and life are inseparable. To be in harmony with all of nature is the Pueblo ideal and way of life. The sun is seen as the representative of the Creator. Sacred mountains in each direction, plus the sun above and the earth below, define and balance the Pueblo world. Many Pueblo religious ceremonies revolve around the weather and are devoted to ensuring adequate rainfall. To this end, Pueblo Indians evoke the power of katsinas, sacred beings who live in mountains and other holy places, in ritual and masked dance.

In addition to the natural boundaries, Pueblo Indians have created a society that defines their world by providing balanced, reciprocal relationships within which people connect and harmonize with each other, the natural world, and time itself. At Sandia, people were divided into two patrilineal ceremonial groups, Squash (summer) and Turquoise (winter). Each had a rectangular kiva, or prayer chamber. There were also a number of ceremonial organizations.

According to tradition, the head of each pueblo is the religious leader, or *cacique,* whose primary responsibility it is to watch the sun and thereby determine the dates of ceremonies. At Sandia the *cacique* served for life. Much ceremonialism is also based on medicine societies, and shamans who derive powers from animal spirits use their supernatural powers for curing, weather control, and ensuring the general welfare. Especially in the eastern pueblos, most ceremonies are kept secret.

GOVERNMENT Pueblo governments derived from two traditions. Offices that are probably indigenous include the *cacique,* or head of the Pueblo, and the war captains. These officials are intimately related to the religious structures of the pueblo and reflected the essentially theocratic nature of Pueblo government.

A parallel but in most cases distinctly less powerful group of officials was imposed by the Spanish authorities. Appointed by the traditional leadership, they generally dealt with external and church matters and included the governor and four assistant governors. The authority of their offices was symbolized by canes. During the 1950s and 1960s, the All Indian Pueblo Council (of eastern villages) became increasingly active in asserting rights and solving problems.

CUSTOMS One mechanism that works to keep Pueblo societies coherent is a pervasive aversion to individualistic behavior. Children were raised with gentle guidance and a minimum of discipline. Pueblo Indians were generally monogamous, and divorce was relatively rare. At Sandia the dead were ceremonially prepared and then buried quickly. Burial was followed by a four-day vigil. In modern times photography by outsiders is discouraged.

DWELLINGS Sandia Pueblo featured multistoried apartment-style dwellings constructed of adobe (earth and straw) bricks, with beams across the roof that were covered with poles, brush, and plaster. Floors were of wood plank or packed earth. The roof of one level served as the floor of another. The levels were interconnected by ladders. As an aid to defense, the traditional design included no doors or windows; entry was through the roof. Pit houses, or kivas, served as ceremonial chambers and clubhouses. The village plaza, around which all dwellings were clustered, is the spiritual center of the village where all the balanced forces of the world come together.

DIET Before the Spanish arrived, Sandia people ate primarily corn, beans, and squash. They also grew cotton and tobacco. They hunted deer, mountain lion, bear, antelope, and rabbits. The people also gathered a variety of wild seeds, nuts, berries, and other foods but ate little or no fish. The Spanish introduced wheat, alfalfa, chilies, fruit trees, grapes, sheep, cattle, and garden vegetables, which soon became part of the regular diet.

KEY TECHNOLOGY Precontact farming implements were wooden. Traditional irrigation systems included ditches as well as floodwater collection at arroyo mouths *(ak chin).* Tanning tools were made of bone and wood. The Spanish introduced metal tools and equipment.

TRADE All Pueblos were part of extensive aboriginal trading networks. With the arrival of other cultures, Pueblo Indians also traded with the Hispanic American villages and then U.S. traders. At fixed times during summer or fall, enemies declared truces so that trading fairs might be held. The largest and best known was at Taos with the Comanche. Nomads exchanged slaves, buffalo hides, buckskins, jerked meat, and horses for agricultural and manufactured pueblo products. Pueblo Indians traded for shell and copper ornaments, turquoise, and macaw feathers. The Sandias enjoyed particularly close ties with Zia, Santa Ana, San Felipe, and Laguna Pueblos. They also had frequent contact with Isleta Pueblo, especially at ceremony times.

Trade along the Santa Fe Trail began in 1821. By the 1880s and the arrival of railroads, the Pueblos were dependent on many American-made goods, and the Native American manufacture of weaving and pottery declined and nearly died out.

NOTABLE ARTS In the Pueblo way, art and life are inseparable. Sandia arts included pottery and willow baskets. Songs, dances, and dramas also qualify as traditional arts. Many Pueblos experienced a renaissance of traditional arts in the twentieth century, beginning in 1919 with San Ildefonso pottery.

TRANSPORTATION Spanish horses, mules, and cattle arrived at Sandia Pueblo in the seventeenth century.

DRESS Men wore shirts, leggings, and moccasins made of deer hides tanned and colored red-brown with plant dye. Womens' wrapped leggings and moccasins were white buckskin. Clothing was also made of spun cotton. Rabbit skin was also used for clothing and robes.

WAR AND WEAPONS Though often depicted as passive and docile, most Pueblo groups regularly engaged in warfare. The great revolt of 1680 stands out as the major military action, but they also skirmished at other times with the Spanish and defended themselves against attackers such as Apaches, Comanches, and Utes. They also contributed auxiliary soldiers to provincial forces under Spain and

Mexico, which were used mainly against raiding Indians and to protect merchant caravans on the Santa Fe Trail. After the raiding tribes began to pose less of a threat in the late nineteenth century, Pueblo military societies began to wither away, with the office of war captain changing to civil and religious functions.

Contemporary Information

GOVERNMENT/RESERVATIONS Sandia Pueblo contains roughly 23,000 acres. The *cacique* is considered the village's true leader—the "mother of his people." He has several assistants, one of which will succeed him. The *cacique* and the assistants annually choose officials such as the governor, who has control over aspects that relate to the outside world, and the war captain, who has authority at ceremonial functions. There is also a council, or advisory body, made up of former governors and war chiefs, as well as several other appointed administrative positions.

ECONOMY Important sources of income include sand and gravel leases, a trading post, a bingo parlor, and several small businesses. Many people work for wages in Albuquerque and Bernalillo and for the tribe itself. They also make jewelry on the pueblo. The Pueblo is also purchasing the local Coronado Airport. Aspects of the traditional economy that remain include gathering piñon nuts and hunting deer and rabbits. Unemployment is quite low, owing in part to the community's highly educated work force.

LEGAL STATUS The Pueblo of Sandia is a federally recognized tribal entity. The Pueblo is also seeking title for traditional forest lands that contain a number of sacred sites. They are opposed by the U.S. Forest Service.

DAILY LIFE Traditional religion and culture remain vital at Sandia. Many of the old ceremonies are still performed, and there is a palpable and intentional continuity with the past. The major feast day, the Feast of Saint Anthony (June 13), is celebrated with a corn dance. The people hold many other dances as well during the year. Sandias guard their traditional religious practices carefully. Catholicism exists, too, but with little or no conflict with traditional religion. The two ceremonial groups, Turquoise and Pumpkin (Squash), have permanent leaders and are responsible for dances. There are also kiva organizations, Corn groups, and curing groups. Once enemies, the Navajo are now welcomed visitors at fiesta time.

Pueblo facilities include a community center, a swimming pool, and tribal offices. Most people live in modern, single-family houses, complete with modern amenities and utilities. Only a few people remain in the old village, although many maintain a home there that they use on feast days. In order to help assure that the people have clean water for religious and health purposes, the Pueblo has both sued the government to make it enforce the Clean Water Act and developed its own EPA-approved water quality standards. Health problems, including diabetes, alcoholism, and drug use, continue to plague the Pueblo, which is planning to build both a clinic and a wellness center.

Since the 1970s, control of schools has been a key in maintaining their culture. Sandia's students are supported by tribal scholarship funds and achieve relatively high education levels. However, well over 50 percent of the people speak no Sandia, and there is much marriage out of the Pueblo. A number of language preservation programs are in place. The traditional clans have largely disappeared. Few people wear traditional dress. There is a large Sandia community in California.

Sand Papago, or Hia C-ed O'odham
See Tohono O'odham

San Felipe Pueblo

The Spanish assigned the patron saint San Felipe (San F ə `l ē p ā) Apóstol to this Pueblo in 1598. The word "pueblo" comes from the Spanish for "village." It refers both to a certain style of Southwest Indian architecture, characterized by multistory, apartment-like buildings made of adobe, and to the people themselves. Rio Grande pueblos are known as eastern Pueblos; Zuñi, Hopi, and sometimes Acoma and Laguna are known as western Pueblos. The native name for this Pueblo is *Katishtya*.

LOCATION San Felipe Pueblo is located at the foot of Santa Ana Mesa on the west bank of the Rio Grande, 6 miles north of its junction with the Jemez River (25 miles north of Albuquerque). One or more other San Felipe pueblos may have existed in the area prior to the sixteenth century.

POPULATION The Pueblo population in 1680 was roughly 600. In 1990, 1,859 Indians lived on the Pueblo, out of a total population of almost 2,500.

LANGUAGE San Felipe people spoke a dialect of Keresan.

Historical Information

HISTORY All Pueblo people are thought to be descended from Anasazi and perhaps Mogollon and several other ancient peoples, although the precise origin of the Keresan peoples is unknown. From them they learned architecture, farming, pottery, and basketry. Larger population groups became possible with effective agriculture and ways to store food surpluses. Within the context of a relatively stable existence, the people devoted increasing amounts of time and attention to religion, arts, and crafts.

Keresans have been traced to an area around Chaco Canyon north to Mesa Verde. In the 1200s, the Keresans abandoned their traditional canyon homelands in response to climatic and social upheavals. A century or two of migrations ensued, followed in general by the slow reemergence of their culture in the historic pueblos. For a time the San Felipe people lived with the Cochitis at several locations, but the pueblos divided before the Spanish arrived.

Francisco Vasquez de Coronado may have visited San Felipe Pueblo. In 1598, Juan de Oñate arrived in the area with settlers, founding the colony of New Mexico. Oñate carried on the process, already underway in nearby areas, of subjugating the local Indians; forcing them to pay taxes in crops, cotton, and work; and opening the door for Catholic missionaries to attack their religion. The Spanish renamed the Pueblos with saints' names and began a program of church construction. Oñate found two pueblos at San Felipe, on either side of the river. A church was built at the eastern village around 1600. At the same time, the Spanish introduced such new crops as peaches, wheat, and peppers into the region. In 1620, a royal decree created civil offices at each pueblo; silverheaded canes, many of which remain in use today, symbolized the governor's authority.

The San Felipes took an active part in the 1680 Pueblo revolt against the Spanish. For years, the Spaniards had routinely tortured Indians for practicing traditional religion. They also forced the Indians to labor for them, sold Indians into slavery, and let their cattle overgraze Indian land, a situation that eventually led to drought, erosion, and famine. Popé of San Juan Pueblo and other Pueblo religious leaders planned the revolt, sending runners carrying cords of maguey fibers to mark the day of rebellion. On August 10, 1680, a virtually united stand on the part of the Pueblos drove the Spanish from the region. The Indians killed many Spaniards but refrained from mass slaughter, allowing them to leave Santa Fe for El Paso.

The San Felipe people abandoned their pueblo in 1681, when the Spanish attempted a reconquest. They fled to the top of Horn Mesa southwest of Cochiti, and the Spanish sacked San Felipe. The people agreed to return and accept baptism in 1692. At that time they lived on top of Santa Ana Mesa. Their friendship with the Spanish alienated them from other pueblos. After 1696, they descended from the mesa top to the site of the present pueblo.

The Pueblos experienced many changes during the following decades: Refugees established communities at Hopi, guerrilla fighting continued against the Spanish, and certain areas were abandoned. By the 1700s, excluding Hopi and Zuñi, only Taos, Picuris, Isleta, and Acoma Pueblos had not changed locations since the arrival of the Spanish. Although Pueblo unity did not last, and Santa Fe was officially reconquered in 1692, Spanish rule was notably less severe from then on. Harsh forced labor all but ceased, and the Indians reached an understanding with the Church that enabled them to continue practicing their traditional religion.

In general, the Pueblo eighteenth century was marked by smallpox epidemics and increased raiding by the Apache, Comanche, and Ute. Occasionally Pueblo Indians fought with the Spanish against the nomadic tribes. The people practiced their religion but more or less in secret. During this time, intermarriage and regular exchange between Hispanic villages and Pueblo Indians created a new New Mexican culture, neither strictly Spanish nor Indian, but rather somewhat of a blend between the two.

Mexican "rule" in 1821 brought little immediate change to the Pueblos. The Mexicans stepped up what had been a gradual process of appropriating Indian land and water, and they allowed the nomadic tribes even greater latitude to raid. A political rebellion by Indians and Hispanic poor in 1837 over the issue of taxes led to the assassination of the New Mexican governor and the brief installation of a Plains/Taos Indian as governor. As the presence of the United States in the area grew, it attempted to enable the Pueblo Indians to continue their generally peaceful and self-sufficient ways and recognized Spanish land grants to the Pueblos. San Felipe remained fairly isolated, and there are few references to the Pueblo in the eighteenth or early nineteenth centuries.

During the nineteenth century the process of acculturation among Pueblo Indians quickened markedly. In an attempt to retain their identity, Pueblo Indians clung even more tenaciously to their heritage, which by now included elements of the once-hated Spanish culture and religion. By the 1880s, railroads had largely put an end to the traditional geographical isolation of the pueblos. Paradoxically, the U.S. decision to recognize Spanish land grants to the Pueblos denied Pueblo Indians certain rights granted under official treaties and left them particularly open to exploitation by squatters and thieves.

After a gap of over 300 years, the All Indian Pueblo Council began to meet again in the 1920s, specifically in response to a congressional threat to appropriate Pueblo lands. Partly as a result of the Council's activities, Congress confirmed Pueblo title to their lands in 1924 by passing the Pueblo Lands Act. The United States also acknowledged its trust responsibilities in a series of legal decisions and other acts of Congress.

Still, especially after 1900, Pueblo culture was increasingly threatened by highly intolerant Protestant evangelical missions and schools. In 1943, a U.S. senator from New Mexico tried, ultimately unsuccessfully, to survey the central plaza at San Felipe as part of plans to build a dam there. The Bureau of Indian Affairs (BIA) also weighed in on the subject of acculturation, forcing Indian children to leave their homes and attend culture-killing boarding schools.

Following World War II, the issue of water rights took center stage on most pueblos. Also, the All Indian Pueblo Council succeeded in slowing the threat against Pueblo lands as well as religious persecution. Since the late nineteenth century, but especially after the 1960s, Pueblos have had to cope with onslaughts by (mostly white) anthropologists and seekers of Indian spirituality. The region is also known for its major art colonies at Taos and Santa Fe.

RELIGION In traditional Pueblo culture, religion and life are inseparable. To be in harmony with all of nature is the Pueblo ideal and way of life. The sun is seen as the representative of the Creator. Sacred mountains in each direction, plus the sun above and the earth below, define and balance the Pueblo world. Many Pueblo religious ceremonies revolve around the weather and are devoted to ensuring adequate rainfall. To this end, Pueblo Indians evoke the power of katsinas, sacred beings who live in mountains and other holy places, in ritual and dance. All San Felipe men belonged to Katsina societies. San Felipe Pueblo contained two circular kivas, religious chambers that symbolize the place of original emergence into this world, and their associated societies, Squash and Turquoise.

In addition to the natural boundaries, Pueblo Indians have created a society that defines their world by providing balanced, reciprocal relationships within which people connect and harmonize with each other, the natural world, and time itself. According to tradition, the head of each pueblo is the religious leader, or *cacique*, whose primary responsibility it is to watch the sun and thereby determine the dates of ceremonies. Much ceremonialism was also based on medicine societies, and shamans used supernatural powers for curing, weather control, and to ensure the general welfare. Especially in the eastern pueblos, most ceremonies are kept secret.

GOVERNMENT Pueblo governments derived from two traditions. Elements that are probably indigenous include the *cacique*, or head of the Pueblo, and the war captains (one from each kiva group at San Felipe). These officials were intimately related to the religious structures of the pueblo and reflected the essentially theocratic nature of Pueblo government. At San Felipe the *cacique* served for life and was

not required to support himself or his family. He chose two war chiefs annually (one from each kiva group), who exercised his power. In turn, the first war chief selected new *caciques*. Pueblo Indians did not typically seek to hold office.

A parallel but in most cases distinctly less powerful group of officials was imposed by the Spanish authorities. Appointed by the traditional leadership, they generally dealt with external and church matters and included the governor, lieutenant governor, and *fiscales*. There was also an advisory council of *principales*, composed of former officeholders. In 1934, San Felipe adopted the Indian Reorganization Act, although without a formal constitution. In addition, the All Indian Pueblo Council, dating from 1598, began meeting again in the twentieth century to assert rights and help solve problems.

CUSTOMS One mechanism that works to keep Pueblo societies coherent is a pervasive aversion to individualistic behavior. Children were raised with gentle guidance and a minimum of discipline. Pueblo Indians were generally monogamous, and divorce was relatively rare. The dead were prepared ceremonially and quickly buried with clothes, beads, food, and other items; their possessions were destroyed. A vigil of four days and nights was generally observed.

Matrilineal clans with recognized heads were very important at San Felipe in governing and ceremonies. Various groups acted to hold the pueblo together, including medicine societies (curing, including witch purging; public welfare; and weather); a hunters' society; a warriors' society; and katsina societies, associated with the two patrilineal kiva groups, Squash and Turquoise, which held masked rain dances. In modern times photography by outsiders is discouraged.

DWELLINGS In the sixteenth century, San Felipe Pueblo featured two- to three-story, apartment-style dwellings, as well as up to 200 individual houses. The buildings were constructed of adobe (earth and straw) bricks, with beams across the roof that were covered with poles, brush, and plaster. Floors were of wood plank or packed earth. The roof of one level served as the floor of another. The levels were interconnected by ladders. As an aid to defense, the traditional design included no doors or windows; entry was through the roof. Pit houses, or kivas, served as ceremonial chambers and clubhouses. The village plazas, around which all dwellings were clustered, was the spiritual center of the village where all the balanced forces of world came together.

DIET Before the Spanish arrived, San Felipe people ate primarily corn, beans, and pumpkins. They also grew sunflowers and tobacco. They hunted deer, mountain lion, bear, antelope, and rabbits. They also gathered a variety of wild seeds, nuts, berries, and other foods. The Spanish introduced wheat, alfalfa, sheep, cattle, and garden vegetables, which soon became part of the regular diet. San Felipe fruit orchards date from after the Spanish contact.

KEY TECHNOLOGY Precontact farming implements were wooden. Traditional irrigation systems included ditches as well as floodwater collection at arroyo mouths *(ak chin)*. The Spanish introduced metal tools and equipment. San Felipes built a bridge spanning the Rio Grande by sinking wooden braces into the riverbed and placing over them rock-filled wicker-woven basketry cribs.

TRADE All Pueblos were part of extensive aboriginal trading networks. With the arrival of other cultures, Pueblo Indians also traded with the Hispanic American villages and then U.S. traders. At fixed times during summer or fall, enemies declared truces so that trading fairs might be held. The largest and best known was at Taos with the Comanche. Nomads exchanged slaves, buffalo hides, buckskins, jerked meat, and horses for agricultural and manufactured pueblo products. Pueblo Indians traded for shell and copper ornaments, turquoise, and macaw feathers. Trade along the Santa Fe Trail began in 1821. By the 1880s and the arrival of railroads, the Pueblos were dependent on many American-made goods, and the Native American manufacture of weaving and pottery declined and nearly died out.

NOTABLE ARTS In the Pueblo way, art and life are inseparable. San Felipe arts included pottery, baskets, and wooden masks. Songs, dances, and dramas also qualify as traditional arts. Many Pueblos experienced a renaissance of traditional arts in the twentieth century, beginning in 1919 with San Ildefonso pottery.

TRANSPORTATION At least as early as the 1600s, San Felipe people used rafts to cross the Rio Grande. They also used canoes, paddled, and hauled by rope, at least as early as the 1700s. Spanish horses, mules, and cattle arrived at San Felipe Pueblo in the seventeenth century.

DRESS Men wore cotton kilts and leather sandals. Women wore cotton dresses and sandals or high moccasin boots. Deer and rabbit skin were also used for clothing and robes, and sandals were made of yucca.

WAR AND WEAPONS Though often depicted as passive and docile, most Pueblo groups regularly engaged in warfare. The great revolt of 1680 stands out as the major military action, but they also skirmished at other times with the Spanish and defended themselves against attackers such as Apaches, Comanches, and Utes. They also contributed auxiliary soldiers to provincial forces under Spain and Mexico, which were used mainly against raiding Indians and to protect merchant caravans on the Santa Fe Trail. After the raiding tribes began to pose less of a threat in the late nineteenth century, Pueblo military societies began to wither away, with the office of war captain changing to civil and religious functions.

Contemporary Information

GOVERNMENT/RESERVATIONS San Felipe Pueblo contains almost 49,000 acres, mostly on the east side of the Rio Grande. The Pueblo is governed in the traditional manner.

ECONOMY Many people work in Albuquerque or Bernalillo. San Felipe also produces some art and crafts, including baskets, woven sashes and belts, and pueblo moccasins with deerskin uppers and cowhide soles. Both large- and small-scale farming is practiced, the latter in combination with other subsistence activities such as hunting, picking piñon nuts, and trading.

LEGAL STATUS San Felipe Pueblo is a federally recognized tribal entity.

DAILY LIFE The project of retaining a strong Indian identity is a difficult one in the late twentieth century, yet Pueblo people have strong roots, and in many ways the ancient rhythms and patterns continue. Many San Felipe people have fused pieces of Catholicism onto a core of traditional beliefs. Their religion, ceremonialism, and social structure are largely intact. Since the 1970s control of schools has been a key in maintaining their culture. Smaller children attend BIA day schools or public schools and either a tribally run or a public high school. Stubbornly high unemployment is partially responsible for the health problems, including alcoholism and drug use, that are present on the pueblo. Many San Felipe people still speak Keresan. There is relatively little intermarriage outside the Pueblo. Most people live in the old pueblo, in traditional adobe houses, and in new government-built frame houses. San Felipe is considered to be one of the most culturally conservative pueblos.

San Ildefonso Pueblo

San Ildefonso (San Ēl dä `fän s ō) is the name of the Spanish mission established in 1617. The Tewa name for the Pueblo, *Powhoge,* means "where the water runs through." The word "pueblo" comes from the Spanish for "village." It refers both to a certain style of Southwest Indian architecture, characterized by multistory, apartmentlike buildings made of adobe, and to the people themselves. Rio Grande pueblos are known as eastern Pueblos; Zuñi, Hopi, and sometimes Acoma and Laguna are known as western Pueblos.

LOCATION Located roughly 22 miles northwest of Santa Fe, San Ildefonso shares a common boundary with Santa Clara Pueblo.

POPULATION In 1990, approximately 350 Indians lived on the pueblo, out of a total population of 1,500. Perhaps 800 people lived there in 1680.

LANGUAGE San Ildefonso people spoke a dialect of Tewa, a Kiowa-Tanoan language.

Historical Information

HISTORY All Pueblo people are thought to be descended from Anasazi and perhaps Mogollon and several other ancient peoples. From them they learned architecture, farming, pottery, and basketry. Larger population groups became possible with effective agriculture and ways to store food surpluses. Within the context of a relatively stable existence, the people devoted increasing amounts of time and attention to religion, arts, and crafts. In the 1200s, the Anasazi abandoned their traditional canyon homelands in response to climatic and social upheavals. A century or two of migrations ensued, followed in general by the slow reemergence of their culture in the historic pueblos. San Ildefonso has been occupied at its present site since before the Spanish arrived.

In 1598, Juan de Oñate arrived in the area with settlers, founding the colony of New Mexico. Oñate carried on the process, already underway in nearby areas, of subjugating the local Indians; forcing them to pay taxes in crops, cotton, and work; and opening the door for Catholic missionaries to attack their religion. The Spanish renamed the Pueblos with saints' names and began a program of church construction. At the same time, the Spanish introduced such new crops as peaches, wheat, and peppers into the region. In 1620, a royal decree created civil offices at each pueblo; silver-headed canes, many of which remain in use today, symbolized the governor's authority.

San Ildefonso played a leading role in the 1680 Pueblo revolt against the Spanish. For years, the Spaniards had routinely tortured Indians for practicing traditional religion. They also forced the Indians to labor for them, sold Indians into slavery, and let their cattle overgraze Indian land, a situation that eventually led to drought, erosion, and famine. Popé of San Juan Pueblo as well as a San Ildefonso official named Francisco and other Pueblo leaders planned the revolt, sending runners carrying cords of maguey fibers to mark the day of rebellion. On August 10, 1680, a virtually united stand on the part of the Pueblos drove the Spanish from the region. The Indians killed many Spaniards but refrained from mass slaughter, allowing them to leave Santa Fe for El Paso.

San Ildefonso was also a leader in the resistance to the Spanish reconquest under Diego de Vargas. The people of San Ildefonso and members of other pueblos moved to the top of Black Mesa and held out there until 1694, two years longer than most other pueblos.

In 1696, San Ildefonso staged another uprising, killing two priests; this was the last of the Pueblo armed resistance. Although Pueblo unity did not last, and Santa Fe was officially reconquered in 1692, Spanish rule was notably less severe from then on. Harsh forced labor all but ceased, and the Indians reached an understanding with the Church that enabled them to continue practicing their traditional religion.

In general, the Pueblo eighteenth century was marked by smallpox epidemics and increased raiding by the Apache, Comanche, and Ute. Occasionally Pueblo Indians fought with the Spanish against the nomadic tribes. The people practiced their religion but more or less in secret. During this time, intermarriage and regular exchange between Hispanic villages and Pueblo Indians created a new New Mexican culture, neither strictly Spanish nor Indian, but rather somewhat of a blend between the two.

Mexican "rule" in 1821 brought little immediate change to the Pueblos. The Mexicans stepped up what had been a gradual process of appropriating Indian land and water, and they allowed the nomadic tribes even greater latitude to raid. A political rebellion by Indians and Hispanics in 1837 over the issue of taxes led to the assassination of the New Mexican governor and his brief replacement by a Plains/Taos Indian. As the presence of the United States in the area grew, it attempted to enable the Pueblo Indians to continue their generally peaceful and self-sufficient ways. Paradoxically, however, the U.S. decision to recognize Spanish land grants to the Pueblos denied Pueblo Indians certain rights granted under official treaties and left them particularly open to exploitation by squatters and thieves.

After the Pueblo revolt, and contrary to tradition, San Ildefonso relocated to the north. In 1923, when mortality rates rose and prosperity fell, the *cacique* led a small group of people back to the original southern village. By this time, however, a flu epidemic had reduced part of the tribe, the winter people (see "Customs"), to two families, so the other division (summer people) divided and absorbed what was left of the winter people. This situation gave rise to intense factionalism that greatly affected the pueblo. The traditional summer-winter division was virtually replaced by an ersatz north-south split. Each group, organized around a plaza, became autonomous but incomplete. By the late 1930s, some offices and societies had been discontinued, and some ritual had been forgotten. Secular authority remained in the hands of the north side for decades, and the situation turned violent in the 1930s when kivas were raided and burned.

Partly because of lobbying from the All Indian

Pueblo Council, Congress confirmed Pueblo title to their lands in 1924 by passing the Pueblo Lands Act. The United States also acknowledged its trust responsibilities in a series of legal decisions and other acts of Congress. Still, the Bureau of Indian Affairs (BIA) forced Indian children to leave their homes and attend culture-killing boarding schools and in general tried its best to undermine Indian identity and survival. Beginning in the 1920s, traditional subsistence agriculture at San Ildefonso began to fail, primarily because of a population decrease and land incursions by non-natives, and malnutrition became a serious problem. At that time the San Ildefonso economy became increasingly based on cash, especially cash derived from the sale of arts and crafts.

RELIGION In traditional Pueblo culture, religion and life are inseparable. To be in harmony with all of nature is the Pueblo ideal and way of life. The sun is seen as the representative of the Creator. Sacred mountains in each direction, plus the sun above and the earth below, define and balance the Pueblo world. Many Pueblo religious ceremonies revolve around the weather and are devoted to ensuring adequate rainfall. To this end, Pueblo Indians evoke the power of katsinas, sacred beings who live in mountains and other holy places, in ritual and masked dance.

In addition to the natural boundaries, Pueblo Indians have created a society that defines their world by providing balanced, reciprocal relationships within which people connect and harmonize with each other, the natural world, and time itself. According to tradition, the head of each pueblo is the religious leader, or *cacique,* whose primary responsibility it is to watch the sun and thereby determine the dates of ceremonies. Much ceremonialism is also based on medicine societies, and shamans who derive powers from animal spirits use their supernatural powers for curing, weather control, and to ensure the general welfare. Especially in the eastern pueblos, most ceremonies are kept secret. San Ildefonso was among the Pueblos least receptive to Christianity, which was not established there until well into the nineteenth century.

GOVERNMENT Pueblo governments derived from two traditions. Offices that are probably indigenous include the *cacique,* or head of the Pueblo, and the war captains. San Ildefonso had both summer and winter *caciques.* These officials are intimately related to the religious structures of the pueblo and reflected the essentially theocratic nature of Pueblo government.

A parallel but in most cases distinctly less powerful group of officials was imposed by the Spanish authorities. Appointed by the traditional leadership, they generally dealt with external and church matters and included the governor, two lieutenant governors, and

two sheriffs. The authority of their offices was symbolized by canes. Nontraditional positions also often included a ditch boss, who was in charge of the irrigation ditches, as well as a town crier and sacristan. The Spanish canes, plus canes given them by President Lincoln, continue to be a symbol of authority. In addition, the All Indian Pueblo Council, dating from 1598, began meeting again in the twentieth century.

CUSTOMS One mechanism that works to keep Pueblo societies coherent is a pervasive aversion to individualistic behavior. Children were raised with gentle guidance and a minimum of discipline. Pueblo Indians were generally monogamous, and divorce was relatively rare. The dead were prepared ceremonially and quickly buried, feet to the north (the original place of emergence). Their possessions were broken and placed on the grave, along with food, to help them on their journey to the spirit land. A vigil of four days and nights was generally observed.

At San Ildefonso, in contrast with most other pueblos, seasons were traditionally delineated not so much by the solstice as by the actual change in seasons. Formerly a summer and a winter *cacique,* appointed for life, oversaw the pueblo. Society was divided into two groups, summer (associated with the Squash kiva) and winter (associated with the Turquoise kiva); membership in a group was patrilineal. These groups were further divided into clans. A number of secret societies also existed. For instance, the warrior society was concerned with hunting, war, crops, fertility, and curing. Each society had its own dances and ritual paraphernalia.

DWELLINGS San Ildefonso Pueblo originally featured two- and three-story apartment-style dwellings constructed of adobe (earth and straw) bricks, with pine beams across the roof that were covered with poles, brush, and plaster. Floors were of wood plank or packed earth. The roof of one level served as the floor of another. The levels were interconnected by ladders. As an aid to defense, the traditional design included no doors or windows; entry was through the roof. Three pit houses, or kivas, two rectangular and one round, served as ceremonial chambers and clubhouses. The village plaza, around which the church and all dwellings were clustered, was the spiritual center of the village, a place where all the balanced forces of world came together. The multilevel dwelling was replaced in historic times at San Ildefonso by one- and two-story adobe houses.

DIET Before the Spanish arrived, people from San Ildefonso Pueblo ate primarily corn, beans, and squash. They also grew cotton and tobacco. They hunted deer, mountain lion, antelope, and rabbits. They also gathered a variety of wild seeds, nuts, berries, and other foods. The Spanish introduced wheat, alfalfa, chilies, fruit trees, grapes, sheep, cattle, and garden vegetables, which soon became part of the regular diet.

KEY TECHNOLOGY San Ildefonso people used irrigation ditches long before the arrival of the Spanish.

TRADE All Pueblos were part of extensive aboriginal trading networks. With the arrival of other cultures, Pueblo Indians also traded with the Hispanic American villages and then U.S. traders. At fixed times during summer or fall, enemies declared truces so that trading fairs might be held. The largest and best known was at Taos with the Comanche. Nomads exchanged slaves, buffalo hides, buckskins, jerked meat, and horses for agricultural and manufactured pueblo products. Pueblo Indians traded for shell and copper ornaments, turquoise, and macaw feathers. Trade along the Santa Fe Trail began in 1821. By the 1880s and the arrival of railroads, the Pueblos were dependent on many American-made goods, and the Native American manufacture of weaving and pottery declined and nearly died out.

NOTABLE ARTS In the Pueblo way, art and life are inseparable. Traditional arts at San Ildefonso included pottery, weaving, songs, dances, and dramas. In 1919, San Ildefonso kicked off a major Pueblo arts revival with its pottery, based on prehistoric designs and styles, and its painting.

TRANSPORTATION Spanish horses, mules, and cattle arrived at San Ildefonso Pueblo in the sixteenth century.

DRESS Men wore cotton and buckskin shirts and kilts. Womens' traditional dress featured spun cotton dresses and sandals or high moccasin boots. Rabbit skin was also used for clothing and robes.

WAR AND WEAPONS Though often depicted as passive and docile, most Pueblo groups regularly engaged in warfare. The great revolt of 1680 stands out as the major military action, but they also skirmished at other times with the Spanish and defended themselves against attackers such as Apaches, Comanches, and Utes. They also contributed auxiliary soldiers to provincial forces under Spain and Mexico, which were used mainly against raiding Indians and to protect merchant caravans on the Santa Fe Trail. After the raiding tribes began to pose less of a threat in the late nineteenth century, Pueblo military societies began to wither away, with the office of war captain changing to civil and religious functions.

Contemporary Information

GOVERNMENT/RESERVATIONS San Ildefonso Pueblo contains roughly 26,000 acres. The *cacique* (summer group) appoints the governor, who is confirmed by the Council of Principales. The governor is assisted by a lieutenant and a 12-member council.

ECONOMY The wage economy is based on work in surrounding cities as well as the sale of art and crafts, particularly pottery and painting.

LEGAL STATUS San Ildefonso is a federally recognized tribal entity.

DAILY LIFE Although the project of holding on to their identity is a strong challenge, Pueblo people have strong roots, and in many ways the ancient rhythms and patterns continue. The tribal schism was formally healed in the 1960s with regard to civil authority, when houses dividing the two plazas were removed, but ceremonialism remains disrupted and diminished. Still, many public and closed ceremonies take place throughout the year. Traditional religion has also merged in some degree with Catholicism; for example, the Pueblo feast day for their patron saint is also celebrated with the buffalo-deer dance and a Comanche dance. Many people are married with both Catholic and traditional ceremonies.

Control of local schools since the 1970s has been a key in maintaining the Pueblo culture. Health problems, including alcoholism and drug abuse, continue to plague the pueblos. Indian Health Service hospitals often cooperate with native healers from two medicine societies. Many people still speak Tewa, and English has served as a common second language since the 1960s. Children attend the pueblo day school and then either the public high school or private (Catholic and tribally run) high schools. Most people live in either the old pueblo, in homes around two plazas, or in outlying adobe-style houses. The houses have modern utilities and conveniences.

San Juan Pueblo

The Tewa name for San Juan (San `Hwän) Pueblo is *Ohke*, the meaning of which is unknown. The word "pueblo" comes from the Spanish for "village." It refers both to a certain style of Southwest Indian architecture, characterized by multistory, apartment-like buildings made of adobe, and to the people themselves. Rio Grande pueblos are known as eastern Pueblos; Zuñi, Hopi, and sometimes Acoma and Laguna are known as western Pueblos. A sacred metaphorical phrase meaning "village of the dew-bedecked corn structure" also refers to the San Juan Pueblo.

LOCATION San Juan Pueblo is located about 25 miles north of Santa Fe, on the east bank of the Rio Grande. The land includes river bottomlands and mountains.

POPULATION In 1990, almost 1,300 Indians lived on the Pueblo, out of a total population of 5,200. Roughly 300 people lived there in 1680.

LANGUAGE The people spoke a dialect of Tewa.

Historical Information

HISTORY   All Pueblo people are thought to be descended from Anasazi and perhaps Mogollon and several other ancient peoples. From them they learned architecture, farming, pottery, and basketry. Larger population groups became possible with effective agriculture and ways to store food surpluses. Within the context of a relatively stable existence, the people devoted increasing amounts of time and attention to religion, arts, and crafts. In prehistoric times, the Tewa were generally north and west of their present locations and have inhabited numerous prehistoric villages on both sides (though mostly the west side) of the Rio Grande and the Rio Chama. In the 1200s, the Anasazi abandoned their traditional canyon homelands in response to climatic and social upheavals. A century or two of migrations ensued, followed in general by the slow reemergence of their culture in the historic pueblos.

When the Spanish arrived in the 1540s, the San Juan people were living at the present pueblo and at a more westerly pueblo. The appearance of Gaspar Castaño de Sosa in 1591 marked the first contact between San Juan and non-natives. In 1598, Juan de Oñate arrived in the area with settlers, founding the colony of New Mexico. Oñate carried on the process, already underway in nearby areas, of subjugating the local Indians; forcing them to pay taxes in crops, cotton, and work; and opening the door for Catholic missionaries to attack their religion. The Spanish renamed the Pueblo San Juan Bautista; it was also known as San Juan de los Caballeros. At the same time, they introduced such new crops as peaches, wheat, and peppers into the region. In 1620, a royal decree created civil offices at each pueblo; silver-headed canes, many of which remain in use today, symbolized the governor's authority.

In 1680 Pueblo Indians organized and carried out a revolt against the Spanish. For years, the Spaniards had routinely tortured Indians for practicing traditional religion. They also forced the Indians to labor for them, sold Indians into slavery, and let their cattle overgraze Indian land, a situation that eventually led to drought, erosion, and famine. Popé of San Juan Pueblo and other Pueblo religious leaders planned the revolt, sending runners carrying cords of maguey fibers to mark the day of rebellion. On August 10, 1680, a virtually united stand on the part of the Pueblos drove the Spanish from the region. The Indians killed many Spaniards but refrained from mass slaughter, allowing them to leave Santa Fe for El Paso.

Although Pueblo unity did not last, and Santa Fe was officially reconquered in 1692, Spanish rule was notably less severe from then on. Harsh forced labor all but ceased, and the Indians reached an understanding with the Church that enabled them to continue practicing their traditional religion.

In general, the Pueblo eighteenth century was marked by smallpox epidemics and increased raiding by the Apache, Comanche, and Ute. Occasionally Pueblo Indians fought with the Spanish against the nomadic tribes. The people practiced their religion but more or less in secret. During this time, intermarriage and regular exchange between Hispanic villages and Pueblo Indians created a new New Mexican culture, neither strictly Spanish nor Indian, but rather somewhat of a blend between the two.

Mexican "rule" in 1821 brought little immediate change to the Pueblos. The Mexicans stepped up what had been a gradual process of appropriating Indian land and water, and they allowed the nomadic tribes even greater latitude to raid. A political rebellion by Indians and Hispanics in 1837 over the issue of taxes led to the assassination of the New Mexican governor and his brief replacement by a Plains/Taos Indian. As the presence of the United States in the area grew, it attempted to enable the Pueblo Indians to continue their generally peaceful and self-sufficient ways. Paradoxically, however, the U.S. decision to recognize Spanish land grants to the Pueblos (they recognized the grant to San Juan in 1858) denied Pueblo Indians certain rights granted under official treaties and left them particularly open to exploitation by squatters and thieves.

San Juan's reputation as a center of trade was enhanced when a general store opened on the Pueblo in 1863 (see "Trade"). Farming and cattle raising were the other economic mainstays of the pueblo during this period.

Partly because of lobbying from the All Indian Pueblo Council, Congress confirmed Pueblo title to their lands in 1924 by passing the Pueblo Lands Act. The United States also acknowledged its trust responsibilities in a series of legal decisions and other acts of Congress. Still, the Bureau of Indian Affairs (BIA) forced Indian children to leave their homes and attend culture-killing boarding schools and in general tried its best to undermine Indian identity and survival. Until the 1940s, the San Juan economy remained almost completely subsistence based.

Since the late nineteenth century, but especially after the 1960s, Pueblos have had to cope with onslaughts by (mostly white) anthropologists and seekers of Indian spirituality. For about 20 years beginning in the 1960s, the people used a number of federal grants to construct various facilities as well as to support a number of social, economic, and cultural programs.

RELIGION   In traditional Pueblo culture, religion and life are inseparable. To be in harmony with all of nature is the Pueblo ideal and way of life. The sun is seen as the representative of the Creator. Sacred mountains in each direction, plus the sun above and the earth below, define and balance the Pueblo world. Many Pueblo religious ceremonies revolve around the weather and are devoted to ensuring adequate rainfall. To this end, Pueblo Indians evoke the power of katsinas, sacred beings who live in mountains and other holy places, in ritual and masked dance. *Cikumu* (Chicoma Mountain) is a particularly sacred location for the people of San Juan.

In addition to the natural boundaries, Pueblo Indians have created a society that defines their world by providing balanced, reciprocal relationships within which people connect and harmonize with each other, the natural world, and time itself. According to tradition, the head of each pueblo is the religious leader, or *cacique,* whose primary responsibility it is to watch the sun and thereby determine the dates of ceremonies. Much ceremonialism is also based on medicine societies, and shamans who derive powers from animal spirits use their supernatural powers for curing, weather control, and ensuring the general welfare. Especially in the eastern pueblos, most ceremonies are kept secret. Since at least the seventeenth century, Catholicism has strongly influenced traditional religion and ceremonialism.

Winter (Turquoise) and summer (Squash) groups divided the pueblo. Each had a cacique and a kiva. There were also eight ceremonial societies, including curing, clowning, hunting, and defense. The *caciques* and the heads of societies, or priests, ran the religious and the political life of the pueblo. All rituals were performed within the winter-summer context. Also, all children were initiated into the masked dance society, Ohuwa.

GOVERNMENT Pueblo governments derived from two traditions. Offices that are probably indigenous include the *cacique* (two at San Juan), or head of the Pueblo, and the war captains. These officials are intimately related to the religious structures of the pueblo and reflected the essentially theocratic nature of Pueblo government.

A parallel but in most cases distinctly less powerful group of officials was imposed by the Spanish authorities. Appointed by the traditional leadership, they generally dealt with external and church matters and included the governor, two lieutenant governors, two sheriffs, and four *fiscales.* The authority of their offices was symbolized by canes. Nontraditional positions also often included a ditch boss, who was in charge of the irrigation ditches, as well as a town crier and sacristan. The Spanish canes, plus canes given them by President Lincoln, were a symbol of authority. In addition, the All Indian Pueblo Council, dating

from 1598, began meeting again in the twentieth century.

CUSTOMS One mechanism that works to keep Pueblo societies coherent is a pervasive aversion to individualistic behavior. Children were raised with gentle guidance and a minimum of discipline. Pueblo Indians were generally monogamous, and divorce was relatively rare. The dead were prepared ceremonially and quickly buried. Their possessions were broken and placed on the grave, along with food, to help them journey to the spirit land. A vigil of four days and nights was generally observed.

At San Juan, a summer and a winter *cacique,* appointed for life, oversaw the pueblo. Society was divided into two groups, summer (associated with the Squash kiva) and winter (associated with the Turquoise kiva); membership in a group was patrilineal. These groups were further divided into more than 30 clans. A number of secret societies also existed. For instance, the warrior society was concerned with hunting, war, crops, fertility, and curing. Each society had its own dances and ritual paraphernalia. Numerous life-cycle rites, as well as songs, crafts, and communal activities such as maintenance of irrigation canals and performing dances, also ensured that one spent one's life "becoming" a Tewa.

People of San Juan further classified themselves into three categories: ordinary earth people, youths, and made people (priests of eight separate priesthoods, half of which admit women as full members). Similarly, their physical world was divided into three corresponding categories. Village, farmlands, and other nearby lowlands, accessible to all and particularly the woman's domain, were delineated by four shrines to ancestors. Hills, mesas, and washes, defined by four sacred mesas and in the spiritual charge of the "youths," were a mediating environment in spatial, social, sexual, spiritual, and even subsistence terms. Mountains, a male realm of hunting and male religious pilgrimages, were in the charge of the made people.

DWELLINGS San Juan Pueblo originally featured multistory apartment-style dwellings constructed of adobe (earth and straw) bricks, with pine beams across the roof that were covered with poles, brush, and plaster. Floors were of wood plank or packed earth. The roof of one level served as the floor of another. The levels were interconnected by ladders. As an aid to defense, the traditional design included no doors or windows; entry was through the roof. Pit houses, or kivas, served as ceremonial chambers and clubhouses. The village plaza, around which the church and all dwellings were clustered, was the spiritual center of the village, a place where all the balanced forces of the world came together.

DIET Before the Spanish arrived, people from San Juan Pueblo ate primarily corn, beans, and squash. They also grew cotton and tobacco. They hunted deer, mountain lion, antelope, and rabbits. They also gathered a variety of wild seeds, nuts, berries, and other foods. The Spanish introduced wheat, alfalfa, chilies, fruit trees, grapes, sheep, cattle, and garden vegetables, which soon became part of the regular diet.

KEY TECHNOLOGY San Juan people used irrigation ditches from well before the arrival of the Spanish.

TRADE All Pueblos were part of extensive aboriginal trading networks. Many, such as San Juan, visited nearby Pueblos regularly to attend festivals and occasionally to intermarry. With the arrival of other cultures, Pueblo Indians also traded with the Hispanic American villages and then U.S. traders. At fixed times during summer or fall, enemies declared truces so that trading fairs might be held. The largest and best known was at Taos with the Comanche. Nomads exchanged slaves, buffalo hides, buckskins, jerked meat, and horses for agricultural and manufactured Pueblo products. Pueblo Indians traded for shell and copper ornaments, turquoise, and macaw feathers.

Trade along the Santa Fe Trail began in 1821. The trader Samuel Eldodt opened a general store at San Juan in 1863. Until it burned down in 1973, it was the oldest continuously operated store in New Mexico and furthered San Juan's reputation as a trade center. By the 1880s and the arrival of railroads, the Pueblos were dependent on many American-made goods, and the native manufacture of weaving and pottery declined and nearly died out.

NOTABLE ARTS In the Pueblo way, art and life are inseparable. Traditional arts at San Juan included pottery, weaving, masks, songs, dances, and dramas. The great Pueblo arts revival, begun at San Ildefonso in 1919, came to San Juan in the 1930s.

TRANSPORTATION Spanish horses, mules, and cattle arrived at San Juan in the sixteenth century.

DRESS Men wore cotton and buckskin shirts and kilts. Womens' traditional dress featured spun cotton dresses and sandals or high moccasin boots. Rabbit skin was also used for clothing and robes.

WAR AND WEAPONS Though often depicted as passive and docile, most Pueblo peoples regularly engaged in warfare. The great revolt of 1680 stands out as the major military action, but they also skirmished at other times with the Spanish and defended themselves against attackers such as Apaches, Comanches, and Utes. They also contributed auxiliary soldiers to provincial forces under Spain and Mexico, which were used mainly against raiding Indi-ans and to protect merchant caravans on the Santa Fe Trail. After the raiding tribes began to pose less of a threat in the late nineteenth century, Pueblo military societies began to wither away, with the office of war captain changing to civil and religious functions.

Contemporary Information

GOVERNMENT/RESERVATIONS San Juan Pueblo contains roughly 12,000 acres. The *cacique* still oversees religious and political matters, appointing the various governmental leaders. The church officers still function as an important level of government. Women's role in pueblo government and religious affairs is severely circumscribed. There is also a tribal court.

ECONOMY Many people work in nearby cities and towns or on the pueblo for federal or tribal programs. Crafts, especially pottery, are an important economic activity. The Pueblo hosts the self-sustaining Oke Oweenge Cooperative for artists. It also collects rent for leased land and buildings. The tribe also owns a gas station near Española, a recreation center, and a bingo operation and contains gas and oil resources.

LEGAL STATUS The Pueblo of San Juan is a federally recognized tribal entity.

DAILY LIFE Although the project of holding on to their identity is a strong challenge, Pueblo people have strong roots, and in many ways the ancient rhythms and patterns continue. Despite the absence of the older generation—still the most important transmitters of traditional culture—in today's nuclear families, many of the old ceremonies are still performed, and the religion and language are largely intact. There is a palpable and intentional continuity with the past. Since the 1950s, San Juan people have also attended festivals as far away as the Plains, the West, and the Midwest. Traditional religion has also merged to some degree with Catholicism.

Control of local schools since the 1970s has been a key in maintaining the Pueblo culture. The San Juan Day School included a fine bilingual and bicultural program until funding was cut off in 1990. Many people still speak Tewa, and English has served as a common second language since the 1960s. However, increasing rates of intermarriage (already high with the Hispanic community) with other Indians and non-natives threaten the culture to some degree; most of these couples live away from San Juan. Health problems, including alcoholism and drug abuse, continue to plague the Pueblos, and there is no professional health care at San Juan Pueblo. Indian Health Service hospitals often cooperate with native healers. The nuclear family is the basic social and economic unit. Several legal cases regarding water rights remain ongoing.

Santa Ana Pueblo

Santa Ana (`San tä `Ä nä) people call their Old Pueblo *Tamaya*. The word "pueblo" comes from the Spanish for "village." It refers both to a certain style of Southwest Indian architecture, characterized by multistory, apartmentlike buildings made of adobe, and to the people themselves. Rio Grande pueblos are known as eastern Pueblos; Zuñi, Hopi, and sometimes Acoma and Laguna are known as western Pueblos. (See "Location" and see "Daily Life" under "Contemporary Information.")

LOCATION The Old Pueblo (Tamaya) is located 27 miles northwest of Albuquerque, on the north bank of the Jemez River 8 miles northwest of its junction with the Rio Grande. This fairly isolated location traditionally kept residents from much contact with non-Indians. The pueblo was all but abandoned in historic times because of low-quality arable land. The people then bought land and moved to a location (Los Ranchitos) about 10 miles to the southeast and just north of Bernalillo.

POPULATION As of 1990, 480 Indians lived on the reservation; roughly 340 lived there in 1700.

LANGUAGE The people spoke a dialect of Keresan.

Historical Information

HISTORY All Pueblo people are thought to be descended from Anasazi and perhaps Mogollon and several other ancient peoples, although the precise origin of the Keresan peoples is unknown. From them they learned architecture, farming, pottery, and basketry. Larger population groups became possible with effective agriculture and ways to store food surpluses. Within the context of a relatively stable existence, the people devoted increasing amounts of time and attention to religion, arts, and crafts.

Keresans have been traced to an area around Chaco Canyon north to Mesa Verde. In the 1200s, the Keresans abandoned their traditional canyon homelands in response to climatic and social upheavals. A century or two of migrations ensued, followed in general by the slow reemergence of their culture in the historic pueblos. Old Santa Ana was probably established in the late sixteenth century.

Francisco Vasquez de Coronado may have visited Santa Ana Pueblo. In 1598, Juan de Oñate arrived in the area with settlers, founding the colony of New Mexico. Oñate carried on the process, already underway in nearby areas, of subjugating the local Indians; forcing them to pay taxes in crops, cotton, and work; and opening the door for Catholic missionaries to attack their religion. The Spanish renamed the Pueblos with saints' names and began a program of church construction. At the same time, they introduced such new crops as peaches, wheat, and peppers into the region. In 1620, a royal decree created civil offices at each pueblo; silver-headed canes, many of which remain in use today, symbolized the governor's authority.

The Santa Anas took part in the 1680 Pueblo revolt against the Spanish. For years, the Spaniards had routinely tortured Indians for practicing traditional religion. They also forced the Indians to labor for them, sold Indians into slavery, and let their cattle overgraze Indian land, a situation that eventually led to drought, erosion, and famine. Popé of San Juan Pueblo and other Pueblo religious leaders planned the revolt, sending runners carrying cords of maguey fibers to mark the day of rebellion. On August 10, 1680, a virtually united stand on the part of the Pueblos drove the Spanish from the region. The Indians killed many Spaniards but refrained from mass slaughter, allowing them to leave Santa Fe for El Paso.

Shortly after the onset of the revolt, the residents had abandoned Santa Ana and were living in the Jemez Mountains. The Spanish burned Santa Ana Pueblo in 1687. By 1693, the Santa Anas had rebuilt their pueblo. They also joined with the Spanish against Pueblo and other Indians after this time.

The Pueblos experienced many changes during the following decades: Refugees established communities at Hopi, guerrilla fighting continued against the Spanish, and certain areas were abandoned. By the 1700s, excluding Hopi and Zuñi, only Taos, Picuris, Isleta, and Acoma Pueblos had not changed locations since the arrival of the Spanish. Although Pueblo unity did not last, and Santa Fe was officially reconquered in 1692, Spanish rule was notably less severe from then on. Harsh forced labor all but ceased, and the Indians reached an understanding with the Church that enabled them to continue practicing their traditional religion.

In general, the Pueblo eighteenth century was marked by smallpox epidemics and increased raiding by the Apache, Comanche, and Ute. Occasionally Pueblo Indians fought with the Spanish against the nomadic tribes. The people practiced their religion but more or less in secret. During this time, intermarriage and regular exchange between Hispanic villages and Pueblo Indians created a new New Mexican culture, neither strictly Spanish nor Indian, but rather somewhat of a blend between the two. Santa Anas began buying and cultivating fields at Ranchitos and spent more and more time there into the next century.

Mexican "rule" in 1821 brought little immediate change to the Pueblos. The Mexicans stepped up what had been a gradual process of appropriating Indian land and water, and they allowed the nomadic tribes even greater latitude to raid. A political rebellion by Indians and Hispanic poor in 1837 over the issue of taxes led to the assassination of the New Mexican governor and the brief installation of a Plains/Taos Indian as governor. As the presence of the United States in the area grew, it attempted to enable the Pueblo Indians to continue their generally peaceful and self-sufficient ways and recognized Spanish land grants to the Pueblos.

During the nineteenth century the process of acculturation among Pueblo Indians quickened markedly. In an attempt to retain their identity, Pueblo Indians clung even more tenaciously to their heritage, which by now included elements of the once-hated Spanish culture and religion. By the 1880s, railroads had largely put an end to the traditional geographical isolation of the pueblos. Paradoxically, the U.S. decision to recognize Spanish land grants to the Pueblos denied Pueblo Indians certain rights granted under official treaties and left them particularly open to exploitation by squatters and thieves. Fierce epidemics swept through Santa Ana around the turn of the century. Those children who escaped the sickness were forced to attend a new Bureau of Indian Affairs (BIA)–sponsored day school designed to strip them of their Indian heritage.

After a gap of over 300 years, the All Indian Pueblo Council began to meet again in the 1920s, specifically in response to a congressional threat to appropriate Pueblo lands. Partly as a result of the Council's activities, Congress confirmed Pueblo title to their lands in 1924 by passing the Pueblo Lands Act. The United States also acknowledged its trust responsibilities in a series of legal decisions and other acts of Congress. Still, especially after 1900, Pueblo culture was increasingly threatened by Protestant evangelical missions and schools. The BIA also weighed in on the subject of acculturation, forcing Indian children to leave their homes and attend culture-killing boarding schools.

Following World War II, the issue of water rights took center stage on most pueblos. Also, the All Indian Pueblo Council succeeded in slowing the threat against Pueblo lands as well as religious persecution. Making crafts for the tourist trade became an important economic activity during this period. Since the late nineteenth century, but especially after the 1960s, Pueblos have had to cope with onslaughts by (mostly white) anthropologists and seekers of Indian spirituality. The region is also known for its major art colonies at Taos and Santa Fe.

RELIGION In traditional Pueblo culture, religion and life are inseparable. To be in harmony with all of nature is the Pueblo ideal and way of life. The sun is seen as the representative of the Creator. Sacred mountains in each direction, plus the sun above and the earth below, define and balance the Pueblo world. Many Pueblo religious ceremonies revolve around the weather and are devoted to ensuring adequate rainfall. To this end, Pueblo Indians evoke the power of katsinas, sacred beings who live in mountains and other holy places, in ritual and dance. All Santa Ana men belonged to Katsina societies. Santa Ana Pueblo contained two circular kivas, religious chambers that symbolize the place of original emergence into this world, and their associated societies, Squash and Turquoise.

In addition to the natural boundaries, Pueblo Indians have created a society that defines their world by providing balanced, reciprocal relationships within which people connect and harmonize with each other, the natural world, and time itself. According to tradition, the head of each pueblo is the religious leader, or *cacique*, whose primary responsibility it is to watch the sun and thereby determine the dates of ceremonies. Much ceremonialism is also based on medicine societies, and shamans used supernatural powers for curing, weather control, and ensuring the general welfare. Important ceremonies at Santa Ana included the winter solstice, several winter dances, San Antonio Day, the summer solstice, San Juan's Day, Santiago's Day, and the harvest dance. Especially in the eastern pueblos, most ceremonies are kept secret.

GOVERNMENT Pueblo governments derived from two traditions. Elements that are probably indigenous include the *cacique*, or head of the Pueblo, and the war chiefs. These officials were intimately related to the religious structures of the pueblo and reflected the essentially theocratic nature of Pueblo government. At Santa Ana the *cacique* served for life and was not required to support himself or his family. He authorized all rituals and made yearly appointments, including two war chiefs (one from each kiva group) who exercised his power. In turn, the first war chief chose new *caciques*. Other traditional offices included the war chiefs' assistants and a ditch boss who, by means of ritual and duties, presided over the Pueblo irrigation system. Pueblo Indians did not typically seek to hold office.

A parallel but in most cases distinctly less powerful group of officials was imposed by the Spanish authorities. Appointed annually by the traditional leadership, they generally dealt with external and church matters and included the governor, lieutenant governor, captains, and *fiscales* (church officials). In addition, a sacristan (another church official) and a *kahéra* (drum roller for certain ceremonies) served for life. There was also an advisory council of *principales,* composed of former office holders. In 1934, Santa Ana adopted the Indian Reorganization Act, although without a formal constitution. In addition, the All Indian Pueblo Council, dating from 1598, began meeting again in the twentieth century to assert rights and help solve problems.

CUSTOMS One mechanism that works to keep Pueblo societies coherent is a pervasive aversion to individualistic behavior. Children were raised with gentle guidance and a minimum of discipline. Pueblo Indians were generally monogamous, and divorce was relatively rare. The dead were prepared ceremonially and quickly buried with clothes, beads, food, and other items; their possessions were destroyed, and they were said to become katsinas in the land of the dead. A vigil of four days and nights was generally observed.

Matrilineal clans with recognized heads determined kiva membership and regulated marriage. Various other groups acted to hold the pueblo together, including medicine societies (curing, including witch purging, which was open to men only; public welfare; and weather); a hunters' society; a clown society; a warriors' society (open to men who had killed or scalped an enemy in battle); and katsina societies, associated with the two patrilineal kiva groups, Squash and Turquoise, which held masked rain dances. At Santa Ana the katsina society was voluntary and open to both sexes. In modern times photography by outsiders is discouraged.

DWELLINGS In the sixteenth century, Santa Ana Pueblo featured two- to three-story, apartment-style dwellings as well as individual houses arranged around several plazas. The buildings were constructed of adobe (earth and straw) bricks, with beams across the roof that were covered with poles, brush, and plaster. Floors were of wood plank or packed earth. The roof of one level served as the floor of another. The levels were interconnected by ladders. As an aid to defense, the traditional design included no doors or windows; entry was through the roof. Two pit houses, or kivas, served as ceremonial chambers and clubhouses. The village plazas, around which all dwellings were clustered, was the spiritual center of the village where all the balanced forces of the world came together.

DIET Before the Spanish arrived, Santa Ana people ate primarily corn, beans, and pumpkins, using dry farming methods and ditch irrigation. They also grew sunflowers and tobacco. They hunted deer, mountain lion, bear, antelope, and rabbits. They also gathered a variety of wild seeds, nuts, berries, and other foods. The Spanish introduced wheat, alfalfa, sheep, cattle, and garden vegetables, which soon became part of the regular diet.

KEY TECHNOLOGY Precontact farming implements were wooden. Traditional irrigation systems included ditches as well as floodwater collection at arroyo mouths *(ak chin).* Textiles were woven of cotton. Other items included baskets, pottery, and leather goods. In more recent times, Santa Anas made jewelry and straw-inlay work. The Spanish introduced metal tools and equipment.

TRADE All Pueblos were part of extensive aboriginal trading networks. With the arrival of other cultures, Pueblo Indians also traded with the Hispanic American villages and then U.S. traders. At fixed times during summer or fall, enemies declared truces so that trading fairs might be held. The largest and best known was at Taos with the Comanche. Nomads exchanged slaves, buffalo hides, buckskins, jerked meat, and horses for agricultural and manufactured pueblo products. Santa Anas traded for numerous daily and ceremonial items, including drums, tortoise rattles, buffalo robes, abalone shell jewelry, bows, arrows, quivers, pottery, and blankets. Trade along the Santa Fe Trail began in 1821. By the 1880s and the arrival of railroads, the Pueblos had become dependent on many American-made goods, and the native manufacture of weaving and pottery declined and nearly died out.

NOTABLE ARTS In the Pueblo way, art and life are inseparable. Santa Ana arts included pottery, baskets, and wooden masks. Songs, dances, and dramas are other traditional arts. Santa Anas learned the art of silversmithing from the Navajo around 1890. Many Pueblos experienced a renaissance of traditional arts in the twentieth century, beginning in 1919 with San Ildefonso pottery.

TRANSPORTATION At least as early as the 1700s, Santa Ana people used canoes to cross the Rio Grande. Spanish horses, mules, and cattle arrived at Santa Ana Pueblo in the seventeenth century.

DRESS Men wore cotton kilts and leather sandals. Women wore cotton dresses and sandals or high moccasin boots. Deer and rabbit skin were also used for clothing and robes, and sandals were made of yucca.

WAR AND WEAPONS Though often depicted as passive and docile, most Pueblo groups regularly engaged in warfare. The great revolt of 1680 stands out as the major military action, but they also skirmished at other times with the Spanish and defended themselves against attackers such as Apaches, Comanches, and Utes. They also contributed auxiliary soldiers to provincial forces under Spain and Mexico, which were used mainly against raiding Indians and to protect merchant caravans on the Santa Fe Trail. After the raiding tribes began to pose less of a threat in the late nineteenth century, Pueblo military societies began to wither away, with the office of war captain changing to civil and religious functions. At Santa Ana, the old warrior society is now made up of men who have killed a bear, mountain lion, or eagle.

Contemporary Information

GOVERNMENT/RESERVATIONS Santa Ana Pueblo contains roughly 62,000 acres. It is governed in the traditional manner with the addition of a modern administrative structure. Most people live at Ranchitos.

ECONOMY Most people work either in Albuquerque or on federal and tribal projects. Farming was revived beginning in the mid-1980s as a commercial endeavor. Products from their Blue-Corn Mill and greenhouse complex are marketed internationally. There are also some crafts as well as a golf course and restaurant, a smoke shop, and some commercial offices. The Pueblo contains geothermal resources.

LEGAL STATUS Santa Ana Pueblo is a federally recognized tribal entity.

DAILY LIFE The project of retaining a strong Indian identity is a difficult one in the late twentieth century, yet Pueblo people have strong roots, and in many ways the ancient rhythms and patterns continue. Santa Ana is more religiously conservative than most pueblos, although Santa Ana people have in general fused pieces of Catholicism onto a core of traditional beliefs. Their religion, ceremonialism, and religious and social structure are largely intact. Many Santa Ana people still speak Keresan. Since the 1970s control of schools has been a key in maintaining their culture. Children attend a nearby pubic school. Facilities at Ranchitos include a clinic, offices, a swimming pool, and a community center.

Tamaya features parallel rows of single-story houses grouped around several plazas, two circular kivas, and an eighteenth-century church. The houses are built of adobe and contain no modern utilities. Tamaya is reserved for ceremonial use, though most families have a home there as well as at Ranchitos. Housing at Ranchitos includes independent adobe structures with modern facilities as well as small, modern wood-frame houses.

Santa Clara Pueblo

The Tewa name for Santa Clara (`San tä `Clä rä) Pueblo is *Capo,* variously translated. The word "pueblo" comes from the Spanish for "village." It refers both to a certain style of Southwest Indian architecture, characterized by multistory, apartment-like buildings made of adobe, and to the people themselves. Rio Grande pueblos are known as eastern Pueblos; Zuñi, Hopi, and sometimes Acoma and Laguna are known as western Pueblos.

LOCATION Santa Clara Pueblo is located on the west bank of the Rio Grande, about 25 miles north of Santa Fe.

POPULATION The Pueblo population was roughly 650 in 1780 and perhaps several thousand in 1500. In 1990, 1,245 Indians lived on the Pueblo out of a total population of over 10,000. Total tribal enrollment was over 2,000.

LANGUAGE The people spoke a dialect of Tewa.

Historical Information

HISTORY All Pueblo people are thought to be descended from Anasazi and perhaps Mogollon and several other ancient peoples. From them they learned architecture, farming, pottery, and basketry. Larger population groups became possible with effective agriculture and ways to store food surpluses. Within the context of a relatively stable existence, the people devoted increasing amounts of time and attention to religion, arts, and crafts. In prehistoric times, the Tewa were generally north and west of their present locations and have inhabited numerous prehistoric villages on both sides (though mostly the west side) of the Rio Grande and the Rio Chama.

In the 1200s, the Anasazi abandoned their traditional canyon homelands in response to climatic and social upheavals. A century or two of migrations ensued, followed in general by the slow reemergence of their culture in the historic pueblos. According to tradition, Santa Claras lived previously in two sites north of the present pueblo. Francisco Vasquez de Coronado found them in the pueblo's present location in 1540.

In 1598, Juan de Oñate arrived in the area with settlers, founding the colony of New Mexico. Oñate carried on the process, already underway in nearby areas, of subjugating the local Indians; forcing them to pay taxes in crops, cotton, and work; and opening the door for Catholic missionaries to attack their religion. The Spanish renamed the Pueblos with saints' names and began a program of church construction. At the same time, the Spanish introduced such new crops as peaches, wheat, and peppers into the region. In 1620, a royal decree created civil offices at each pueblo; silver-headed canes, many of which remain in use today, symbolized the governor's authority.

In 1680 Pueblo Indians organized and carried out a major revolt against the Spanish. For years, the Spaniards had routinely tortured Indians for practicing traditional religion. They also forced the Indians to labor for them, sold Indians into slavery, and let their cattle overgraze Indian land, a situation that eventually led to drought, erosion, and famine. Popé of San Juan Pueblo and other Pueblo religious leaders planned the revolt, sending runners carrying cords of maguey fibers to mark the day of rebellion. On August 10, 1680, a virtually united stand on the part of the Pueblos drove the Spanish from the region. The Indians killed many Spaniards but refrained from mass slaughter, allowing them to leave Santa Fe for El Paso.

Although Pueblo unity did not last, and Santa Fe was officially reconquered in 1692, Spanish rule was notably less severe from then on. Harsh forced labor all but ceased, and the Indians reached an understanding with the Church that enabled them to continue practicing their traditional religion.

In general, the Pueblo eighteenth century was marked by smallpox epidemics and increased raiding by the Apache, Comanche, and Ute. Occasionally Pueblo Indians fought with the Spanish against the nomadic tribes. The people practiced their religion but more or less in secret. During this time, intermarriage and regular exchange between Hispanic villages and Pueblo Indians created a new New Mexican culture, neither strictly Spanish nor Indian, but rather somewhat of a blend between the two.

Mexican "rule" in 1821 brought little immediate change to the Pueblos. The Mexicans stepped up what had been a gradual process of appropriating Indian land and water, and they allowed the nomadic tribes even greater latitude to raid. As the presence of the United States in the area grew, it attempted to enable the Pueblo Indians to continue their generally peaceful and self-sufficient ways. Paradoxically, however, the U.S. decision to recognize Spanish land grants to the Pueblos denied Pueblo Indians certain rights granted under official treaties and left them particularly open to exploitation by squatters and thieves.

Especially after 1821, the Pueblos underwent a steady acculturation. Toward the late nineteenth century, the United States reintroduced religious repression. The government and Protestant missionaries branded Indian religious practices as obscene and immoral, and the Bureau of Indian Affairs forcibly removed Indian children to culture-killing boarding schools.

Partly because of lobbying from the All Indian Pueblo Council, Congress confirmed Pueblo title to their lands in 1924 by passing the Pueblo Lands Act. The United States also acknowledged its trust responsibilities in a series of legal decisions and other acts of Congress. Following World War II, the issue of water rights took center stage on most pueblos. Also, the All Indian Pueblo Council succeeded in slowing the

threat against Pueblo lands as well as religious persecution. Making crafts for the tourist trade became an important economic activity during this period. Since the late nineteenth century, but especially after the 1960s, Pueblos have had to cope with onslaughts by (mostly white) anthropologists and seekers of Indian spirituality. The region is also known for its significant art colonies at Taos and Santa Fe.

RELIGION In traditional Pueblo culture, religion and life are inseparable. To be in harmony with all of nature is the Pueblo ideal and way of life. The sun is seen as the representative of the Creator. Sacred mountains in each direction, plus the sun above and the earth below, define and balance the Pueblo world. Many Pueblo religious ceremonies revolve around the weather and are devoted to ensuring adequate rainfall. To this end, Pueblo Indians evoke the power of katsinas, sacred beings who live in mountains and other holy places, in ritual and masked dance.

In addition to the natural boundaries, Pueblo Indians have created a society that defines their world by providing balanced, reciprocal relationships within which people connect and harmonize with each other, the natural world, and time itself. According to tradition, the head of each pueblo is the religious leader, or *cacique,* whose primary responsibility it is to watch the sun and thereby determine the dates of ceremonies. Much ceremonialism is also based on medicine societies, and shamans who derive powers from animal spirits use their supernatural powers for curing, weather control, and ensuring the general welfare. Especially in the eastern pueblos, most ceremonies are kept secret. Since at least the seventeenth century, Catholicism has strongly influenced traditional religion and ceremonialism.

Winter (Turquoise) and summer (Squash) groups divided the pueblo. Each had a *cacique* and a kiva. Ceremonial societies included curing, clowning, hunting, and defense. The *caciques* and the heads of societies, or priests, ran the religious and the political life of the pueblo. All rituals were performed within the winter-summer context.

GOVERNMENT Pueblo governments derived from two traditions. Offices that are probably indigenous include the *cacique,* or head of the Pueblo, and the war captains. At Santa Clara, both summer and winter *caciques* "ruled" by consensus among the pueblo leaders, meeting in the kiva and having the final say in all matters. Each traded village control every six months. These officials were intimately related to the religious structures of the pueblo and reflected the essentially theocratic nature of Pueblo government.

A parallel but in most cases distinctly less powerful group of officials was imposed by the Spanish authorities. Appointed by the traditional leadership, they generally dealt with external and church matters and included the governor, two lieutenant governors, sheriffs, and *fiscales*. The authority of their offices was symbolized by canes. Nontraditional positions also often included a ditch boss, who was in charge of the irrigation ditches, as well as a town crier and sacristan. Also, a council of *principales* (present and former officers) had justice-related responsibilities. The Spanish canes, plus canes given them by President Lincoln, were a symbol of authority. In addition, the All Indian Pueblo Council, dating from 1598, began meeting again in the twentieth century.

Santa Clara Pueblo experienced a major political schism in the 1890s. The winter division, the more "progressive" for much of the nineteenth century, had resisted the rigid dictates of pueblo life and advocated a separation of religious from secular life. In 1894, the summer division and some winter people applied for and received recognition from the Indian agency in Santa Fe as the legitimate governing authority at the Pueblo. For the next 30 years, the summer division elected all secular officials except the lieutenant governor and tried to enforce the traditionally rigid sacred-secular connection. The winter group resisted and openly defied them.

In the 1930s, each division split along progressive and conservative lines; now there were four factions, each allied with a like-minded group. Their government in shambles, the Pueblo requested arbitration by the Indian Service in Santa Fe, with the result that the Pueblo incorporated under the Indian Reorganization Act (IRA) and turned to a constitution and an elected government. Thus religious and secular affairs were finally split, and participation in ceremonies was made voluntary.

CUSTOMS One mechanism that works to keep Pueblo societies coherent is a pervasive aversion to individualistic behavior. Children were raised with gentle guidance and a minimum of discipline. Pueblo Indians were generally monogamous, and divorce was relatively rare. The dead were prepared ceremonially and quickly buried. Their possessions were broken and placed on the grave, along with food, to help them journey to the spirit land. A vigil of four days and nights was generally observed.

At Santa Clara, a summer and a winter *cacique*, appointed for life, oversaw the pueblo. Society was divided into two groups, summer (associated with the Squash kiva) and winter (associated with the Turquoise kiva); membership in a group was patrilineal. These groups were further divided into clans. A number of secret societies also existed. For instance, the warrior society was concerned with hunting, war, crops, fertility, and curing. Each society had its own

dances and ritual paraphernalia. Numerous life-cycle rites, as well as songs, crafts, communal activities such as maintenance of irrigation canals, prayer retreats, and performing dances, also ensured that one spent one's life "becoming" a Tewa.

People of Santa Clara further classified themselves into three categories: ordinary earth people, youths, and made people (priests of eight separate priesthoods, half of which admit women as full members). Similarly, their physical world was divided into three corresponding categories. Village, farmlands, and other nearby lowlands, accessible to all and particularly the woman's domain, were delineated by four shrines to ancestors. Hills, mesas, and washes, defined by four sacred mesas and in the spiritual charge of the "youths," were a mediating environment in spatial, social, sexual, spiritual, and even subsistence terms. Mountains, a male realm of hunting and male religious pilgrimages, were in the charge of the made people.

DWELLINGS Santa Clara Pueblo originally featured apartment-style dwellings of up to five stories constructed of adobe (earth and straw) bricks, with pine beams across the roof that were covered with poles, brush, and plaster. Floors were of wood plank or packed earth. The roof of one level served as the floor of another. The levels were interconnected by ladders. As an aid to defense, the traditional design included no doors or windows; entry was through the roof. Pit houses, or kivas, served as ceremonial chambers and clubhouses. The village plaza, around which the church and all dwellings were clustered, was the spiritual center of the village, a place where all the balanced forces of the world came together.

DIET Before the Spanish arrived, people from Santa Clara Pueblo ate primarily corn, beans, and squash. They also grew cotton and tobacco. They hunted deer, buffalo, mountain lion, antelope, and rabbits, and they also fished. They also gathered a variety of wild seeds, nuts, berries, and other foods. The Spanish introduced wheat, alfalfa, chilies, fruit trees, grapes, sheep, cattle, and garden vegetables, which soon became part of the regular diet.

KEY TECHNOLOGY Santa Clara people traditionally diverted water from the Rio Grande via irrigation ditches. They used wood shovels and hoes, stone axes, and woven fiber baskets. They fished with pointed sticks and yucca-fiber nets.

TRADE All Pueblos were part of extensive aboriginal trading networks. With the arrival of other cultures, Pueblo Indians also traded with the Hispanic American villages and then U.S. traders. At fixed times during summer or fall, enemies declared truces so that trading fairs might be held. The largest and best known was at Taos with the Comanche. In the seventeenth and eighteenth centuries, Santa Clara Pueblo traded primarily with other Pueblos, Comanches, Kiowas, Jicarillas, and Utes. They traded cornmeal, wheat flour, bread, and woven goods for jerked meat, buffalo robes, pipe pouches, tortoise shells, buckskins, and horses. They also traded for baskets, Navajo blankets, shell and copper ornaments, turquoise, and macaw feathers. Santa Claras sometimes acted as middlemen between Plains tribes and more southern pueblos. Trade along the Santa Fe Trail began in 1821. By the 1880s and the arrival of railroads, the Pueblos were dependent on many American-made goods, and the native manufacture of weaving and pottery declined and nearly died out.

NOTABLE ARTS   In the Pueblo way, art and life are inseparable. Traditional arts at Santa Clara included pottery, weaving, masks, songs, dances, and dramas. The great Pueblo arts revival, begun at San Ildefonso in 1919, came to Santa Clara in the 1930s and 1940s.

TRANSPORTATION   Spanish horses, mules, and cattle arrived at Santa Clara in the sixteenth century.

DRESS   Men wore cotton and buckskin shirts and kilts. Womens' traditional dress featured spun cotton dresses and sandals or high moccasin boots. Rabbit skin was also used for clothing and robes.

WAR AND WEAPONS   Though often depicted as passive and docile, most Pueblo peoples regularly engaged in warfare. The great revolt of 1680 stands out as the major military action, but they also skirmished at other times with the Spanish and defended themselves against attackers such as Apaches, Comanches, and Utes. They also contributed auxiliary soldiers to provincial forces under Spain and Mexico, which were used mainly against raiding Indians and to protect merchant caravans on the Santa Fe Trail. Tewas occasionally raided Navajos for goods. After the nomadic tribes began to pose less of a threat in the late nineteenth century, Pueblo military societies began to wither away, with the office of war captain changing to civil and religious functions.

Contemporary Information

GOVERNMENT/RESERVATIONS   Santa Clara Pueblo consists of almost 46,000 acres. The Pueblo adopted a constitution in 1935. They elect six officials annually, nominated by the kiva groups, plus a tribal council. The *cacique* still runs sacred matters.

ECONOMY   Many Santa Clara Indians work in Santa Fe, Española, and Los Alamos or for federal and tribal programs. Arts and crafts, including textiles, embroidery, and especially pottery, also bring in money. Tourism is an important economic activity. The cliff dwellings at Puye (an ancestral home) and Santa Clara Canyon are well-developed tourist sites, and dances for tourists are held in July. The tribe

leases pumice and timber resources.

LEGAL STATUS   Santa Clara Pueblo is a federally recognized tribal entity.

DAILY LIFE   Although the project of holding on to their identity is a strong challenge, Pueblo people have strong roots, and in many ways the ancient rhythms and patterns continue. Many of the old ceremonies are still performed; the religion is largely intact, and there is a palpable and intentional continuity with the past. Traditional religion has also merged to some degree with Catholicism.

Change has come to Santa Clara Pueblo, but thanks in part to effective political leadership, disruption has been minimal. Control of local schools since the 1970s has been another key in maintaining Pueblo culture. Santa Clara maintains a relatively high regard for Western education. Many people still speak Tewa, and English has served as a common second language since the 1960s. Health problems, including alcoholism and drug abuse, continue to plague the Pueblos. There is a small hospital at Santa Clara. The nuclear family is the basic social and economic unit. A new senior citizens community center helps elders remain vital and purposeful.

Santo Domingo Pueblo

The Santo Domingo (`San tō Dō `mē n gō) people call their pueblo *Kiuw*. The word "pueblo" comes from the Spanish for "village." It refers both to a certain style of Southwest Indian architecture, characterized by multistory, apartmentlike buildings made of adobe, and to the people themselves. Rio Grande pueblos are known as eastern Pueblos; Zuñi, Hopi, and sometimes Acoma and Laguna are known as western Pueblos.

LOCATION   Santo Domingo Pueblo is situated on the east bank of the Rio Grande, 30–35 miles southwest of Santa Fe, near the Camino Real and modern highways.

POPULATION   About 3,000 Indians lived in this largest of the eastern Keresan pueblos in 1990. Roughly 150 people lived there in 1680.

LANGUAGE   The people spoke a Keresan dialect.

Historical Information

HISTORY   All Pueblo people are thought to be descended from Anasazi and perhaps Mogollon and several other ancient peoples, although the precise origin of the Keresan peoples is unknown. From them they learned architecture, farming, pottery, and basketry. Larger population groups became possible with effective agriculture and ways to store food surpluses. Within the context of a relatively stable existence, the people devoted increasing amounts of time and attention to religion, arts, and crafts.

Keresans have been traced to an area around Chaco Canyon north to Mesa Verde. In the 1200s, the Keresans abandoned their traditional canyon homelands in response to climatic and social upheavals. A century or two of migrations ensued, followed in general by the slow reemergence of their culture in the historic pueblos. The original Santo Domingo people lived in at least two villages called Gipuy, several miles north of the present location. These sites were eventually destroyed by flooding, and the people established a village called Kiwa, about a mile west of the present pueblo.

In 1598, Juan de Oñate arrived in the area with settlers, founding the colony of New Mexico. Oñate carried on the process, already underway in nearby areas, of subjugating the local Indians; forcing them to pay taxes in crops, cotton, and work; and opening the door for Catholic missionaries to attack their religion. The Spanish renamed the Pueblos with saints' names and began a program of church construction. Santo Domingo (Saint Dominic) replaced the Pueblo's original name, Gipuy, in 1691. At the same time, the Spanish introduced such new crops as peaches, wheat, and peppers into the region. In 1620, a royal decree created civil offices at each pueblo; silver-headed canes, many of which remain in use today, symbolized the governor's authority.

The Santo Domingos took an active part in the 1680 Pueblo revolt against the Spanish. For years, the Spaniards had routinely tortured Indians for practicing traditional religion. They also forced the Indians to labor for them, sold Indians into slavery, and let their cattle overgraze Indian land, a situation that eventually led to drought, erosion, and famine. Popé of San Juan Pueblo as well as Alonzo Catiti from Santo Domingo Pueblo and other Pueblo leaders planned the revolt, sending runners carrying cords of maguey fibers to mark the day of rebellion. On August 10, 1680, a virtually united stand on the part of the Pueblos drove the Spanish from the region. The Indians killed many Spaniards but refrained from mass slaughter, allowing them to leave Santa Fe for El Paso. The Santo Domingos were forced to retreat north with other Keresan peoples to the fortified town of Potrero Viejo. They returned in 1683, although sporadic rebellion continued until 1696.

The Pueblos experienced many changes during the following decades: Refugees established communities at Hopi, guerrilla fighting continued against the Spanish, and certain areas were abandoned. By the 1700s, excluding Hopi and Zuñi, only Taos, Picuris, Isleta, and Acoma Pueblos had not changed locations since the arrival of the Spanish. Several floods destroyed the original site of Santo Domingo Pueblo; the present pueblo was established in the early eigh-

teenth century. Although Pueblo unity did not last, and Santa Fe was officially reconquered in 1692, Spanish rule was notably less severe from then on. Harsh forced labor all but ceased, and the Indians reached an understanding with the Church that enabled them to continue practicing their traditional religion.

In general, the Pueblo eighteenth century was marked by smallpox epidemics and increased raiding by the Apache, Comanche, and Ute. Occasionally Pueblo Indians fought with the Spanish against the nomadic tribes. The people practiced their religion but more or less in secret. During this time, intermarriage and regular exchange between Hispanic villages and Pueblo Indians created a new New Mexican culture, neither strictly Spanish nor Indian, but rather somewhat of a blend between the two.

Mexican "rule" in 1821 brought little immediate change to the Pueblos. The Mexicans stepped up what had been a gradual process of appropriating Indian land and water, and they allowed the nomadic tribes even greater latitude to raid. A political rebellion by Indians and Hispanic poor in 1837 over the issue of taxes led to the assassination of the New Mexican governor and the brief installation of a Plains/Taos Indian as governor. As the presence of the United States in the area grew, it attempted to enable the Pueblo Indians to continue their generally peaceful and self-sufficient ways and recognized Spanish land grants to the Pueblos (in 1858, the United States recognized a 1689 Spanish land grant to Santo Domingo Pueblo of roughly 70,000 acres).

During the nineteenth century the process of acculturation among Pueblo Indians quickened markedly. In an attempt to retain their identity, Pueblo Indians clung even more tenaciously to their heritage, which by now included elements of the once-hated Spanish culture and religion. By the 1880s, railroads had largely put an end to the traditional geographical isolation of the pueblos. Paradoxically, the U.S. decision to recognize Spanish land grants to the Pueblos denied Pueblo Indians certain rights granted under official treaties and left them particularly open to exploitation by squatters and thieves. In 1886, Kiwa was destroyed by floods, and the people moved to their present location.

After a gap of over 300 years, the All Indian Pueblo Council began to meet again in the 1920s, specifically in response to a congressional threat to appropriate Pueblo lands. Partly as a result of the Council's activities, Congress confirmed Pueblo title to their lands in 1924 by passing the Pueblo Lands Act. The United States also acknowledged its trust responsibilities in a series of legal decisions and other acts of Congress. Still, especially after 1900, Pueblo culture was increasingly threatened by Protestant evangelical missions and schools. The Bureau of Indian Affairs also weighed in on the subject of acculturation, forcing Indian children to leave their homes and attend culture-killing boarding schools.

Following World War II, the issue of water rights took center stage on most pueblos. Also, the All Indian Pueblo Council succeeded in slowing the threat against Pueblo lands as well as religious persecution. Making crafts for the tourist trade became an important economic activity during this period. Since the late nineteenth century, but especially after the 1960s, Pueblos have had to cope with onslaughts by (mostly white) anthropologists and seekers of Indian spirituality. The region is also known for its major art colonies at Taos and Santa Fe.

RELIGION In traditional Pueblo culture, religion and life are inseparable. To be in harmony with all of nature is the Pueblo ideal and way of life. The sun is seen as the representative of the Creator. Sacred mountains in each direction, plus the sun above and the earth below, define and balance the Pueblo world. Many Pueblo religious ceremonies revolve around the weather and are devoted to ensuring adequate rainfall. To this end, Pueblo Indians evoke the power of katsinas, sacred beings who live in mountains and other holy places, in ritual and dance. All Santo Domingo men belonged to katsina societies. Santo Domingo Pueblo contained two circular kivas, religious chambers that symbolize the place of original emergence into this world, and their associated societies, Squash and Turquoise.

In addition to the natural boundaries, Pueblo Indians have created a society that defines their world by providing balanced, reciprocal relationships within which people connect and harmonize with each other, the natural world, and time itself. According to tradition, the head of each pueblo is the religious leader, or *cacique,* whose primary responsibility it is to watch the sun and thereby determine the dates of ceremonies. Much ceremonialism is also based on medicine societies, and shamans used supernatural powers for curing, weather control, and ensuring the general welfare. As at other pueblos, much doctrine and ritual of the Catholic Church has been integrated into the native religion at Santo Domingo. Important ceremonies include church days such as Easter, Christmas, and saints' days as well as corn and harvest dances and other ceremonies related to agriculture and legend. Especially in the eastern pueblos, most ceremonies are kept secret.

GOVERNMENT Pueblo governments derived from two traditions. Elements that are probably indigenous include the *cacique,* or head of the Pueblo, and the war chiefs. These officials were intimately related to the religious structures of the pueblo and reflected the essentially theocratic nature of Pueblo government. At Santo Domingo the *cacique* was the head medicine man; he represented the Corn Mother and was sometimes referred to as *yaya,* or mother. He authorized all rituals and made yearly appointments, including two war chiefs (one from each kiva group) who exercised his power. In turn, the first war chief chose new *caciques.* Other traditional offices included the war chiefs' assistants and a ditch boss who, by means of ritual and duties, presided over the Pueblo irrigation system. Pueblo Indians did not typically seek to hold office.

A parallel but in most cases distinctly less powerful group of officials was imposed by the Spanish authorities. Appointed annually by the traditional leadership, they generally dealt with external and church matters and included the governor, lieutenant governor, captains, and *fiscales* (church officials). Young men were groomed for certain positions. There was also an advisory council of *principales,* comprised of former office holders. In addition, the All Indian Pueblo Council, dating from 1598, began meeting again in the twentieth century to assert rights and help solve problems.

CUSTOMS One mechanism that works to keep Pueblo societies coherent is a pervasive aversion to individualistic behavior. Children were raised with gentle guidance and a minimum of discipline. Pueblo Indians were generally monogamous, and divorce was relatively rare. The dead were prepared ceremonially and quickly buried with clothes, beads, food, and other items; their possessions were destroyed, and they were said to become katsinas in the land of the dead. A vigil of four days and nights was generally observed.

Matrilineal clans also existed at Santo Domingo, although their functions remain unclear. Various other more or less secret societies including medicine, hunters, clown, warriors, and katsina (associated with the two patrilineal kiva groups, Squash and Turquoise) acted to hold the pueblo together. The societies are said to have gained power from supernatural animals, through fetishes and figurines. Santo Domingo societies were traditionally so strong that other pueblos came to them if theirs needed revitalization. Most traditional customs remained relatively intact at Santo Domingo well into the 1940s. In modern times photography by outsiders is discouraged.

DWELLINGS In the seventeenth century, Santo Domingo Pueblo probably contained multistory apartment-style dwellings constructed of adobe (earth and straw) bricks, with beams across the roof that were covered with poles, brush, and plaster. Floors were of wood plank or packed earth. The roof of one level served as the floor of another. The levels were interconnected by ladders. As an aid to defense, the traditional design included no doors or windows; entry was through the roof. Two pit houses, or kivas, served as ceremonial chambers and clubhouses. The village plaza, around which all dwellings were clustered, was the spiritual center of the village where all the balanced forces of the world came together. Floods destroyed previous settlements; the present village dates from 1886.

DIET Before the Spanish arrived, Santo Domingo people ate primarily corn, beans, and pumpkins. They also grew sunflowers and tobacco. They hunted deer, mountain lion, bear, antelope, and rabbits. They also gathered a variety of wild seeds, nuts, berries, and other foods. The Spanish introduced wheat, alfalfa, sheep, cattle, and garden vegetables, which soon became part of the regular diet.

KEY TECHNOLOGY Precontact farming implements were wooden. Traditional irrigation systems included ditches as well as floodwater collection at arroyo mouths (ak chin). Textiles were woven of cotton. Other items included baskets, pottery, and leather goods. The Spanish introduced metal tools and equipment.

TRADE All Pueblos were part of extensive aboriginal trading networks. With the arrival of other cultures, Pueblo Indians also traded with the Hispanic American villages and then U.S. traders. At fixed times during summer or fall, enemies declared truces so that trading fairs might be held. The largest and best known was at Taos with the Comanche. Nomads exchanged slaves, buffalo hides, buckskins, jerked meat, and horses for agricultural and manufactured pueblo products. Trade along the Santa Fe Trail began in 1821. By the 1880s and the arrival of railroads, the Pueblos were dependent on many American-made goods, and the Native American manufacture of weaving and pottery declined and nearly died out.

NOTABLE ARTS In the Pueblo way, art and life are inseparable. Santo Domingo arts included pottery, baskets, and turquoise necklaces. They also excelled at making pump-drilled heishi beads. Songs, dances, and dramas are other traditional arts. Santo Domingos may have taught turquoise work to the Navajos in the 1880s.

TRANSPORTATION Spanish horses, mules, and cattle arrived at Santo Domingo Pueblo in the seventeenth century.

DRESS Men wore cotton kilts and leather sandals. Women wore cotton dresses and sandals or high moccasin boots. Deer and rabbit skin were also used for clothing and robes, and sandals were made of yucca.

WAR AND WEAPONS Though often depicted as passive and docile, most Pueblo groups regularly engaged in warfare. The great revolt of 1680 stands out as the major military action, but they also skirmished at other times with the Spanish and defended themselves against attackers such as Apaches, Comanches, and Utes. They also contributed auxiliary soldiers to provincial forces under Spain and Mexico, which were used mainly against raiding Indians and to protect merchant caravans on the Santa Fe Trail. After the raiding tribes began to pose less of a threat in the late nineteenth century, Pueblo military societies began to wither away, with the office of war captain changing to civil and religious functions.

Contemporary Information

GOVERNMENT/RESERVATIONS Santo Domingo Pueblo contains roughly 70,000 acres. It is governed in the traditional manner, and there is no written constitution.

ECONOMY The Pueblo hosts an annual arts fair; it also contains a service station and a small museum/visitor center. Many Santo Domingos work in nearby cities. Many are also active artists, specializing in traditional turquoise and shell necklace, pottery, other jewelry, woven belts, and leather moccasins and leggings. Santo Domingo people trade widely throughout the Southwest. In keeping with their conservative values, much of their work is unsigned. Farming and grazing are also important economic activities.

LEGAL STATUS Santo Domingo Pueblo is a federally recognized tribal entity.

DAILY LIFE Santo Domingo remains one of the most conservative pueblos. The religion, ceremonialism, and social structure of the Pueblo are largely intact, and the society remains proud and vital. Most Santo Domingo people still speak Keresan, along with English and some Spanish. Many people marry within the pueblo. Changes since World War II include a greater reliance on hospitals, improved sanitation, and fewer school disruptions for religious or ceremonial reasons. Although their appreciation for Western education has increased, high school dropout rates remain very high, in part because of continued opposition from pueblo leaders. They fear that non-Indian education opens up the potential for undesirable, far-reaching change; an example would be to have women sitting on the tribal council. Santo Domingos are well represented in the leadership of pan-Pueblo political organizations.

Taos Pueblo

Also known as San Geronimo de Taos. Taos (`Tä ō s) is from a Tiwa word meaning "in the village."

The word "pueblo" comes from the Spanish for "village." It refers both to a certain style of Southwest Indian architecture, characterized by multistory, apartment-like buildings made of adobe, and to the people themselves. Rio Grande pueblos are known as eastern Pueblos; Zuñi, Hopi, and sometimes Acoma and Laguna are known as western Pueblos. The Taos name for their Pueblo is *Tecuse* or *Ilaphai,* "at the mouth of Red-Willow Canyon."

LOCATION   The northernmost, highest (with Picuris, at about 7,000 feet), and one of the most isolated of the eastern pueblos, Taos is 70 miles north of Santa Fe.

POPULATION   In 1990, 1,200 Indians lived at Taos; the tribal enrollment stood at roughly 1,800. Roughly 2,000 people lived there in the late seventeenth century.

LANGUAGE   Taos Indians spoke Northern Tiwa, a Kiowa-Tanoan language.

Historical Information

HISTORY   All Pueblo people are thought to be descended from Anasazi and perhaps Mogollon and several other ancient peoples. From them they learned architecture, farming, pottery, and basketry. Larger population groups became possible with effective agriculture and ways to store food surpluses. Within the context of a relatively stable existence, the people devoted increasing amounts of time and attention to religion, arts, and crafts. The Anasazi pueblo of Chaco, in northwest New Mexico, is thought by some to be the ancestral home of the Taos Indians.

In the 1200s, the Anasazi abandoned their traditional canyon homelands in response to climatic and social upheavals. A century or two of migrations ensued, followed in general by the slow reemergence of their culture in the historic pueblos. The Tiwas were probably the first of the Tanoan Pueblo people to enter the northern Rio Grande region. The earliest archaeological sites near Taos date from 1000 to 1200; these are not at the site of the present pueblo, however, and most remain unexcavated. "Modern" Taos dates from roughly 1400.

Francisco Vasquez de Coronado visited Taos in 1540. In 1598, Juan de Oñate arrived in the area with settlers, founding the colony of New Mexico. Oñate carried on the process, already underway in nearby areas, of subjugating the local Indians; forcing them to pay taxes in crops, cotton, and work; and opening the door for Catholic missionaries to attack their religion. The Spanish renamed the Pueblos with saints' names and began a program of church construction, establishing the mission of San Geronimo at Taos in the early seventeenth century. At the same time, the Spanish introduced such new crops as peaches, wheat, and peppers into the region. In 1620, a royal decree created civil offices at each pueblo; silver-headed canes, many of which remain in use today, symbolized the governor's authority.

Taos played a leading role in the Pueblo rebellion of 1680. For years, the Spaniards had routinely tortured Indians for practicing traditional religion. They also forced the Indians to labor for them, sold Indians into slavery, and let their cattle overgraze Indian land, a situation that eventually led to drought, erosion, and famine. Popé of San Juan Pueblo and other Pueblo religious leaders planned the great revolt at Taos, sending runners carrying cords of maguey fibers to mark the day of rebellion. On August 10, 1680, a virtually united stand on the part of the Pueblos drove the Spanish from the region. The Indians killed many Spaniards but refrained from mass slaughter, allowing most of them to leave Santa Fe for El Paso.

Santa Fe was officially reconquered in 1692, after which the Taos fled to the mountains and to their Plains friends, the Kiowa. The Spanish sacked Taos Pueblo in 1693, after which the Indians returned and rebuilt. Another short-lived rebellion occurred in 1696. Although Pueblo unity did not last, Spanish rule was notably less severe from then on. Harsh forced labor all but ceased, and the Indians reached an understanding with the Church that enabled them to continue practicing their traditional religion. By the 1700s, excluding Hopi and Zuñi, only Taos, Picuris, Isleta, and Acoma Pueblos had not changed locations since the arrival of the Spanish.

In general, the Pueblo eighteenth century was marked by smallpox epidemics and increased raiding by the Apache, Comanche, and Ute. The people practiced their religion but more or less in secret. During this time, intermarriage and regular exchange between Hispanic villages and Pueblo Indians created a new New Mexican culture, neither strictly Spanish nor Indian, but rather somewhat of a blend between the two.

Mexican "rule" in 1821 brought little immediate change to the Pueblos. The Mexicans stepped up what had been a gradual process of appropriating Indian land and water, and they allowed the nomadic tribes even greater latitude to raid. As the presence of the United States in the area grew, it attempted to enable the Pueblo Indians to continue their generally peaceful and self-sufficient ways and recognized Spanish land grants to the Pueblos. A political rebellion by Indians and poor Hispanics in 1837 over the issue of taxes led to the assassination of the governor of New Mexico and his brief replacement by a Plains/Taos Indian. In 1845, a few Tiwas from Taos, along with local Hispanics, killed the U.S. governor and attacked several officials over depredations committed by U.S. troops as well as long-standing land issues. The troops replied with a slaughter.

In an attempt to retain their identity, Pueblo Indians clung even more tenaciously to their heritage, which by now included elements of the once-hated Spanish culture and religion. By the 1880s, railroads had largely put an end to the traditional geographical isolation of the pueblos. Paradoxically, the U.S. decision to recognize Spanish land grants to the Pueblos denied Pueblo Indians certain rights granted under official treaties and left them particularly open to exploitation by squatters and thieves.

After a gap of over 300 years, the All Indian Pueblo Council began to meet again in the 1920s, specifically in response to a congressional threat to appropriate Pueblo lands. Partly as a result of the Council's activities, Congress confirmed Pueblo title to their lands in 1924 by passing the Pueblo Lands Act. The United States also acknowledged its trust responsibilities in a series of legal decisions and other acts of Congress. Still, especially after 1900, Pueblo culture was increasingly threatened by Protestant evangelical missions and schools. The Bureau of Indian Affairs also weighed in on the subject of acculturation, forcing Indian children to leave their homes and attend culture-killing boarding schools.

In 1906, the U.S. government included Taos's holiest site, the Blue Lake region in the Sangre de Cristo Mountains, as part of a national forest. Under the leadership of longtime governor Severino Martinez and others, the tribe fought to get it back. In 1965 they received title to the land and were offered a cash payment, but they held out for the land. In 1970 the government returned Blue Lake, along with 48,000 surrounding acres. Since the late nineteenth century, but especially after the 1960s, the Pueblos have had to cope with onslaughts by (mostly white) anthropologists and seekers of Indian spirituality. The region is also known for its major art colonies at Taos and Santa Fe.

RELIGION In traditional Pueblo culture, religion and life are inseparable. To be in harmony with all of nature is the Pueblo ideal and way of life. The sun is seen as the representative of the Creator. Sacred mountains in each direction, mountain lakes and other natural places, plus the sun above and the earth below, define and balance the Taos Pueblo world. Many Pueblo religious ceremonies revolve around the weather and are devoted to ensuring adequate rainfall. To this end, Pueblo Indians evoke the power of katsinas, sacred beings who live in mountains and other holy places, in ritual and masked dance.

In addition to the natural boundaries, Pueblo Indians have created a society that defines their world by providing balanced, reciprocal relationships within which people connect and harmonize with each other, the natural world, and time itself. Unlike the situation in most Pueblos, the heads of the kiva societies, rather than the *cacique,* were the most important religious leaders. In fact, the *cacique* had both religious and secular duties.

Seven kiva or ceremonial societies were active at Taos. Each had special functions and separate religious knowledge. Feathers of birds such as eagles, hawks, and ducks, as well as wildflowers, were important ceremonially. Traditionally, all preteen boys underwent religious training, and a select few were chosen for an 18-month initiation, culminating in a pilgrimage to Blue Lake, into one of the kiva societies. Only initiated men could move from "boys" to "elders" and hold secular office.

Much ceremonialism is also based on medicine societies, and shamans who derive powers from animal spirits use their supernatural powers for curing, weather control, and ensuring the general welfare. Corn dances are held in summer and animal dances in winter. Most ceremonies at Taos are still kept secret from outsiders. Although most Taos Indians consider themselves Catholics, it is a form of Catholicism that coexists with their traditional religion. The Native American Church was introduced at Taos in 1907. Although controversial, it remains active.

GOVERNMENT Pueblo governments derived from two traditions. Offices that are probably indigenous include the *cacique,* or head of the Pueblo, and the war captains. These officials are intimately related to the religious structures of the pueblo and reflected the essentially theocratic nature of Pueblo government. At Taos, the *cacique* plus the tribal council (kiva society heads plus secular officials) ruled religious matters.

A parallel but in most cases distinctly less powerful group of officials was imposed by the Spanish authorities. Appointed by the traditional leadership, they generally dealt with external and church matters and included the governor, assistant governors, and *fiscales.* The authority of their offices was symbolized by canes. Community announcements were called out from the roof of the governor's house. During the 1950s and 1960s, the All Indian Pueblo Council (of eastern villages) became increasingly active in asserting rights and solving problems.

CUSTOMS One mechanism that works to keep Pueblo societies coherent is a pervasive aversion to individualistic behavior. Children were raised with gentle guidance and a minimum of discipline. A high value is placed on generosity and reciprocity. Pueblo Indians were generally monogamous, and divorce was relatively rare.

Taos Indians enjoyed regular contact with other Pueblos and Plains Indians, and they have borrowed freely from other cultures over the centuries. However, they are very protective of their own society and have maintained a fundamental cultural isolation. Most people who married out of the Pueblo have stayed away.

Corpses were dressed in their best clothes and buried with food. Household members observed a four-day vigil, after which they set out prayer feathers and cornmeal for the spirit of dead. In modern times photography by outsiders is discouraged.

DWELLINGS Taos was formerly walled, as a defense against the Comanche raids of the 1700s. The Pueblo features two clusters of apartment-style buildings, as high as six stories, on either side of Taos Creek. The buildings are constructed of adobe (earth and straw) bricks, with beams across a roof covered with poles, brush, and plaster. Floors are of wood plank or packed earth. The roof of one level serves as the floor of another. The levels are interconnected by ladders. As an aid to defense, the traditional design included no doors or windows; entry was through the roof. There were also a number of adobe houses scattered around the Pueblo. Seven pit houses, or kivas, serve as ceremonial chambers and clubhouses. The village plaza, around which all dwellings are clustered, is the spiritual center of the village where all the balanced forces of world come together. A racetrack is part of the village, built to accommodate ceremonial footraces.

DIET Before the Spanish arrived, Taos people ate primarily corn, beans, and squash. They also grew cotton and tobacco. A relatively short growing season necessitated a greater dependence on hunting and gathering. They hunted deer, mountain lion, bear, antelope, and rabbits. Men from Taos also traveled east to hunt buffalo. The people also gathered a variety of wild seeds, nuts, berries, and other foods and fished in rivers and mountain streams. The Spanish introduced wheat, alfalfa, chilies, fruit trees, grapes, sheep, cattle, and garden vegetables, which soon became part of the regular diet.

KEY TECHNOLOGY Precontact farming implements were wooden. Most pottery was basically utilitarian. Tanning tools were made of bone and wood. Musical instruments included drums of animal hide. Men hunted with juniper bows and arrows. The Spanish introduced metal tools and equipment.

TRADE All Pueblos were part of extensive aboriginal trading networks. With the arrival of other cultures, Pueblo Indians also traded with the Hispanic American villages and then U.S. traders. Taos Indians traded for cotton since they could not grow it themselves. At fixed times during summer or fall,

enemies declared truces so that trading fairs might be held. The largest and best known was at Taos with the Comanche. In fact, Taos served as a Pueblo trade gateway to the Plains tribes north and east. Nomads exchanged slaves, buffalo hides, buckskins, jerked meat, and horses for agricultural and manufactured pueblo products. Pueblo Indians traded for shell and copper ornaments, turquoise, and macaw feathers.

Despite the proximity of Picuris Pueblo (18 miles by trail), the two peoples interacted relatively infrequently and traded little but mountain plants. Trade along the Santa Fe Trail began in 1821. By the 1880s and the arrival of railroads, the Pueblos were dependent on many American-made goods, and the Native American manufacture of weaving and pottery declined and nearly died out.

NOTABLE ARTS In the Pueblo way, art and life are inseparable. Taos arts included moccasins, drums, songs, dances, and dramas. Many Pueblos experienced a renaissance of traditional arts in the twentieth century, beginning in 1919 with San Ildefonso pottery.

TRANSPORTATION Spanish horses, mules, and cattle arrived at Taos Pueblo in the seventeenth century. Horses were especially important at Taos.

DRESS Men wore Plains-style fringed and beaded buckskin shirts, leggings, and moccasins. Women wore deerskin dresses and white buckskin moccasins (married women). Rabbit skin and buffalo hide were also used for blankets and robes.

WAR AND WEAPONS Though often depicted as passive and docile, most Pueblo groups regularly engaged in warfare. The great revolt of 1680 stands out as the major military action, but they also skirmished at other times with the Spanish and defended themselves against attackers such as Apaches, Comanches, and Utes. They also contributed auxiliary soldiers to provincial forces under Spain and Mexico, which were used mainly against raiding Indians and to protect merchant caravans on the Santa Fe Trail. After the raiding tribes began to pose less of a threat in the late nineteenth century, Pueblo military societies began to wither away, with the office of war captain changing to civil and religious functions.

Contemporary Information

GOVERNMENT/RESERVATIONS Taos Pueblo contains roughly 95,000 acres. Twenty-two civil officers are appointed annually by the traditional religious leadership. The all-male council consists of roughly 60 members (1990).

ECONOMY Most people obtain money by working in Taos and by making and/or selling arts and crafts, especially drums and moccasins but also woodcarvings, weavings, pottery, and rabbit-skin blankets. Tourists also pay parking and camera fees to the Pueblo. There is also some work available with the tribe.

LEGAL STATUS Taos Pueblo is a federally recognized tribal entity.

DAILY LIFE Although holding on to their identity is increasingly a challenge, Pueblo people have deep roots. In general, change has come very slowly to Taos. Many of the old ceremonies are still performed; the religion is largely intact, as is the language and entire worldview; and there is a very palpable and intentional continuity with the past. Community duties include cleaning irrigation ditches, repairing fences, plastering the church, and dance and other ceremonial activities. English is replacing Spanish as the Pueblo's second language. Control of their own day school since the 1970s has been a key in maintaining their culture, although most students go to high school in the town of Taos. Taos Pueblo copes with a number of health problems, including diabetes, alcoholism, and drug use.

Since the 1930s, the traditional multistoried pueblos have contained glass windows and some doorways, although no electricity or running water. Now fewer than 100 people live there, and the buildings are falling into disrepair. Most people live in single-family adobe houses, more and more of which include commercial building materials. Buildings outside the old walls have been electrified since 1971, although indoor toilets are still unusual. Some so-called crackerbox houses put up by the Department of Housing and Urban Development also dot the pueblo. The ruined village walls remain important in Taos thought: Anything within them is considered sacred. A few Indians keep summer homes in nearby towns.

Older people still wear the dress of an earlier era, such as braids, blankets, moccasins, simulated leggings, and brightly colored shawls. The extended family remains important. Birth, death, and marriage rituals reflect the Catholic influence. Divorce is becoming more frequent, and interpersonal conflicts are more likely to be handled outside of the pueblo (in state court, for example). An elaborate kiva initiation for boys begins between ages 7 and 10. San Geronimo Day (September 29–30) is the major harvest/feast day. Taos Indians maintain frequent contact with their non-Indian neighbors, yet they retain firm cultural boundaries.

Tesuque Pueblo

Tesuque (Te `s ū k ē) is a Hispanicization of the Tewa word *tecuge*, which means "structure at a narrow place" or "dry, spotted place." The word "pueblo" comes from the Spanish for "village." It refers both to a certain style of Southwest Indian architecture, characterized by multistory, apartmentlike buildings made of adobe, and to the people themselves. Rio Grande pueblos are known as eastern Pueblos; Zuñi, Hopi, and sometimes Acoma and Laguna are known as western Pueblos.

LOCATION Tesuque Pueblo is located 9 miles north of Santa Fe, on the Tesuque River.

POPULATION Perhaps 200 people lived at Tesuque Pueblo in 1680. In 1990, 232 Indians lived there, out of a total population of almost 700. There were 488 enrolled members of Tesuque Pueblo in 1993.

LANGUAGE Tesuque Indians spoke Tewa, a member of the Kiowa-Tanoan language family.

Historical Information

HISTORY All Pueblo people are thought to be descended from Anasazi and perhaps Mogollon and several other ancient peoples. From them they learned architecture, farming, pottery, and basketry. Larger population groups became possible with effective agriculture and ways to store food surpluses. Within the context of a relatively stable existence, the people devoted increasing amounts of time and attention to religion, arts, and crafts. In prehistoric times, the Tewa were generally north and west of their present locations and have inhabited numerous prehistoric villages on both sides (though mostly the west side) of the Rio Grande and the Rio Chama.

In the 1200s, the Anasazi abandoned their traditional canyon homelands in response to climatic and social upheavals. A century or two of migrations ensued, followed in general by the slow reemergence of their culture in the historic pueblos. Tesuque Pueblo had at least one (unknown) location previous to its present site, which dates from 1694.

In 1598, Juan de Oñate arrived in the area with settlers, founding the colony of New Mexico. Oñate carried on the process, already underway in nearby areas, of subjugating the local Indians; forcing them to pay taxes in crops, cotton, and work; and opening the door for Catholic missionaries to attack their religion. The Spanish renamed the Pueblos with saints' names and began a program of church construction, establishing a mission known as San Lorenzo at Tesuque in the early seventeenth century. At the same time, the Spanish introduced such new crops as peaches, wheat, and peppers into the region. In 1620, a royal decree created civil offices at each pueblo; silver-headed canes, many of which remain in use today, symbolized the governor's authority.

In 1680 Pueblo Indians organized and carried out a major revolt against the Spanish. For years, the Spaniards had routinely tortured Indians for practicing traditional religion. They also forced the Indians to labor for them, sold Indians into slavery, and let their cattle overgraze Indian land, a situation that eventually led to drought, erosion, and famine. Popé of San Juan Pueblo and other Pueblo religious leaders planned the revolt, sending runners carrying cords of maguey fibers to mark the day of rebellion. The revolt began on August 10, 1680, probably at Tesuque. A virtually united stand on the part of the Pueblos drove the Spanish from the region. The Indians killed many Spaniards but refrained from mass slaughter, allowing them to leave Santa Fe for El Paso.

Although Pueblo unity did not last, and Santa Fe was officially reconquered in 1692, Spanish rule was notably less severe from then on. Harsh forced labor all but ceased, and the Indians reached an understanding with the Church that enabled them to continue practicing their traditional religion. Tesuque Indians abandoned their pueblo after 1680 but rebuilt it on the present site in 1694.

In general, the Pueblo eighteenth century was marked by smallpox epidemics and increased raiding by the Apache, Comanche, and Ute. Occasionally Pueblo Indians fought with the Spanish against the nomadic tribes. The people practiced their religion but more or less in secret. During this time, intermarriage and regular exchange between Hispanic villages and Pueblo Indians created a new New Mexican culture, neither strictly Spanish nor Indian, but rather somewhat of a blend between the two.

Mexican "rule" in 1821 brought little immediate change to the Pueblos. The Mexicans stepped up what had been a gradual process of appropriating Indian land and water, and they allowed the nomadic tribes even greater latitude to raid. A political rebellion by Indians and Hispanic poor in 1837 over the issue of taxes led to the assassination of the governor of New Mexico and his brief replacement by a Plains/Taos Indian. As the presence of the United States in the area grew, it attempted to enable the Pueblo Indians to continue their generally peaceful and self-sufficient ways. Paradoxically, however, the U.S. decision to recognize Spanish land grants to the Pueblos denied Pueblo Indians certain rights granted under official treaties and left them particularly open to exploitation by squatters and thieves.

Especially after 1821, the Pueblos underwent a steady acculturation. Toward the late nineteenth century, the United States reintroduced religious repression. The government and Protestant missionaries branded Indian religious practices as obscene and immoral, and the Bureau of Indian Affairs forcibly removed Indian children to culture-killing boarding schools. As part of the effort to retain their traditions, Indians more deeply embraced customs once seen as alien, such as Catholicism. By the 1880s, railroads had ended the traditional isolation of most pueblos. Instead of treaties, the United States recognized old Spanish land "grants" of pueblo land. Ironically, this put them outside official treaty rights and left them particularly open to exploitation by squatters and thieves.

Tesuque ran out of water in the early twentieth century as a result of diversions by recent Anglo settlers. A series of dams and basins restored much of their water by 1935. Partly because of lobbying from the All Indian Pueblo Council, Congress confirmed Pueblo title to their lands in 1924 by passing the Pueblo Lands Act. The United States also acknowledged its trust responsibilities in a series of legal decisions and other acts of Congress. In the late 1950s, Tesuque Pueblo received no tribal income other than the interest from funds on deposit with the government. Since the late nineteenth century, but especially after the 1960s, Pueblos have had to cope with onslaughts by (mostly white) anthropologists and seekers of Indian spirituality. The region is also known for its significant art colonies at Taos and Santa Fe.

RELIGION   In traditional Pueblo culture, religion and life are inseparable. To be in harmony with all of nature is the Pueblo ideal and way of life. The sun is seen as the representative of the Creator. Sacred mountains in each direction, plus the sun above and the earth below, define and balance the Pueblo world. Many Pueblo religious ceremonies revolve around the weather and are devoted to ensuring adequate rainfall. To this end, Pueblo Indians evoke the power of katsinas, sacred beings who live in mountains and other holy places, in ritual and masked dance.

In addition to the natural boundaries, Pueblo Indians have created a society that defines their world by providing balanced, reciprocal relationships within which people connect and harmonize with each other, the natural world, and time itself. According to tradition, the head of each pueblo is the religious leader, or *cacique*, whose primary responsibility it is to watch the sun and thereby determine the dates of ceremonies. Much ceremonialism is also based on medicine societies, and shamans who derive powers from animal spirits use their supernatural powers for curing, weather control, and ensuring the general welfare. Especially in the eastern pueblos, most ceremonies are kept secret. Since at least the eighteenth century, Catholicism has strongly influenced traditional religion and ceremonialism.

Winter (Turquoise) and summer (Squash) groups divided the pueblo. Each had a *cacique* and a kiva. Ceremonial societies included katsina, curing, clowning, hunting, and defense. The *caciques* and the heads of societies, or priests, ran the religious and the political life of the pueblo. All rituals were performed within the winter-summer context.

GOVERNMENT Pueblo governments derived from two traditions. Offices that are probably indigenous include the *cacique,* or head of the Pueblo, and the war captains. These officials are intimately related to the religious structures of the pueblo and reflected the essentially theocratic nature of Pueblo government.

A parallel but in most cases distinctly less powerful group of officials was imposed by the Spanish authorities. Appointed by the traditional leadership, they generally dealt with external and church matters and included the governor, two lieutenant governors, sheriffs, and *fiscales.* The authority of their offices was symbolized by canes. Nontraditional positions also often included a ditch boss, who was in charge of the irrigation ditches, as well as a town crier and sacristan. Also, a council of *principales* (present and former officers) had justice-related responsibilities. The Spanish canes, plus canes given them by President Lincoln, were a symbol of authority. In addition, the All Indian Pueblo Council, dating from 1598, began meeting again in the twentieth century.

CUSTOMS One mechanism that works to keep Pueblo societies coherent is a pervasive aversion to individualistic behavior. Children were raised with gentle guidance and a minimum of discipline. Pueblo Indians were generally monogamous, and divorce was relatively rare. The dead were ceremonially prepared and quickly buried. Their possessions were broken and placed on the grave, along with food, to help them journey to the spirit land. A vigil of four days and nights was generally observed.

At Tesuque, a summer and a winter *cacique,* appointed for life, oversaw the pueblo. Society was divided into two patrilineal groups, summer (associated with the Squash kiva) and winter (associated with the Turquoise kiva), which united in times of crisis and for the welfare of the Pueblo. These groups were further divided into relatively weak and ill-defined clans. A number of secret societies also existed. For instance, the warrior society was concerned with hunting, war, crops, fertility, and curing. Each society had its own dances and ritual paraphernalia. Numerous life-cycle rites, as well as songs, crafts, communal activities such as maintenance of irrigation canals, prayer retreats, and performing dances, also ensured that one spent one's life "becoming" a Tewa.

DWELLINGS Tesuque Pueblo originally featured apartment-style dwellings of up to five stories constructed of adobe (earth and straw) bricks, with pine beams across the roof that were covered with poles, brush, and plaster. Floors were of wood plank or packed earth. The roof of one level served as the floor of another. The levels were interconnected by ladders. As an aid to defense, the traditional design included no doors or windows; entry was through the roof. Pit houses, or kivas, served as ceremonial chambers and clubhouses. The village plaza, around which the church and all dwellings were clustered, was the spiritual center of the village, a place where all the balanced forces of the world came together.

DIET Before the Spanish arrived, people from Tesuque Pueblo ate primarily corn, beans, and squash. They also grew cotton and tobacco. They hunted deer, mountain lion, and antelope, and they also fished. They also gathered a variety of wild seeds, nuts, berries, and other foods. The Spanish introduced wheat, alfalfa, chilies, fruit trees, grapes, sheep, cattle, and garden vegetables, which soon became part of the regular diet.

KEY TECHNOLOGY Tesuque people traditionally diverted water from the Rio Grande via irrigation ditches. They used wood shovels and hoes, stone axes, and woven fiber baskets. They fished with pointed sticks and yucca-fiber nets.

TRADE All Pueblos were part of extensive aboriginal trading networks. With the arrival of other cultures, Pueblo Indians also traded with the Hispanic American villages and then U.S. traders. At fixed times during summer or fall, enemies declared truces so that trading fairs might be held. The largest and best known was at Taos with the Comanche. In the seventeenth and eighteenth centuries, Tesuque Pueblo traded primarily with other Pueblos, Navajos, and Plains tribes. They traded cornmeal, wheat flour, bread, and woven goods for jerked meat, buffalo robes, pipe pouches, tortoise shells, buckskins, and horses. They also traded for baskets, Navajo blankets, shell and copper ornaments, turquoise, and macaw feathers. Trade along the Santa Fe Trail began in 1821. By the 1880s and the arrival of railroads, the Pueblos were dependent on many American-made goods, and the native manufacture of weaving and pottery declined and nearly died out.

NOTABLE ARTS In the Pueblo way, art and life are inseparable. Traditional arts at Tesuque included pottery, weaving, masks, songs, dances, and dramas. Tesuque joined in the great Pueblo arts revival, begun at San Ildefonso in 1919.

TRANSPORTATION Spanish horses, mules, and cattle arrived at Tesuque in the sixteenth century.

DRESS Men wore cotton and buckskin shirts and kilts. Womens' traditional dress featured buckskin or spun cotton dresses and leather sandals or high moccasin boots. Rabbit skin was also used for clothing and robes.

WAR AND WEAPONS Though often depicted as passive and docile, most Pueblo peoples regularly engaged in warfare. The great revolt of 1680 stands out as the major military action, but they also skirmished at other times with the Spanish and defended themselves against attackers such as Apaches, Comanches, and Utes. They also contributed auxiliary soldiers to provincial forces under Spain and Mexico, which were used mainly against raiding Indians and to protect merchant caravans on the Santa Fe Trail. Tewas occasionally raided Navajos for goods. After the nomadic tribes began to pose less of a threat in the late nineteenth century, Pueblo military societies began to wither away, with the office of war captain changing to civil and religious functions.

Contemporary Information

GOVERNMENT/RESERVATIONS Tesuque Pueblo contains roughly 17,000 acres. Government is by tradition, with officers elected annually by the division chiefs. At Tesuque, the office of governor rotates between four men. The *fiscales* have responsibilities outside of the church. The Tesuques have no sheriff, unlike the other Tewa pueblos. The council, consisting of the officers, past governors, and the war chief, acts as liaison to the outside world. Tesuque is a member of the Eight Northern Indian Pueblos Council.

ECONOMY Many people work in Santa Fe or Los Alamos. Some good pottery is produced, but there is generally little art or crafts. Subsistence farming, the basis of the economy into the 1960s, still exists, as does grazing and sales of timber. Income is also derived from leasing land to non-Indian businesses as well as from a bingo parlor.

LEGAL STATUS Tesuque Pueblo is a federally recognized tribal entity.

DAILY LIFE Although the project of holding on to their identity is a strong challenge, Pueblo people have deep roots, and in many ways the ancient rhythms and patterns continue. Many of the old ceremonies are still performed; the religion is largely intact, and there is a palpable and intentional continuity with the past. Almost all Tesuques are Catholic. Tesuque was one of the first pueblos to have electricity and housing put up by the Department of Housing and Urban Development in addition to the traditional adobe houses.

Tesuque is traditionally the most conservative of the Tewa pueblos. Many people still speak Tewa, and English has served as a common second language since the 1960s. Children attend a day school on the reservation and public or private high school in Santa Fe. Health problems, including alcoholism and drug abuse, continue to plague the Pueblos. Indian Health Service hospitals often cooperate with native healers.

The annual katsina dance in October is closed to outsiders. In 1970, the pueblo entered into an extremely controversial, long-term lease with a non-native company to develop thousands of acres of tribal lands. They also gave up some water rights. After years of litigation, Tesuque canceled the lease in 1976. The annual feast day is November 12.

Tigua

This tribe lives on Ysleta del Sur Pueblo, "Isleta of the South," a reference to the ancestral Isleta Pueblo in New Mexico. The Pueblo was formerly known as Tigua (ˋT ē wä) Reservation. The word "pueblo" comes from the Spanish for "village." It refers both to a certain style of Southwest Indian architecture, characterized by multistory, apartmentlike buildings made of adobe, and to the people themselves. (*See also* Isleta Pueblo.)

LOCATION Ysleta del Sur Pueblo is located within the southern boundary of El Paso, Texas.

POPULATION The original—late-seventeenth-century—population of Ysleta del Sur Pueblo may have ranged from 500 to about 1,500. In 1990, 211 Indians out of a total population of 292 lived at Tigua. Tribal enrollment in the mid-1990s was around 1,500.

LANGUAGE The native language of the Tigua people is Southern Tiwa.

Historical Information

HISTORY Ysleta del Sur Pueblo was founded in 1682 by Pueblo refugees from the rebellion of 1680. Its original inhabitants included Indians from Isleta Pueblo as well as Piro, Manso, Apache, Suma, and Tompiro Indians, none of whom joined the revolt. These Indians retreated south with the fleeing Spaniards. They built a church at Tigua, dedicated to Saint Anthony, in 1682. Following the 1692 Spanish reconquest, in which these Indians participated, Governor Diego de Vargas planned to resettle them in their New Mexico homelands, but most preferred to remain. The Piros eventually became absorbed into Tigua Pueblo or the local Spanish-American population. At some point, the Ysleta Indians received a land grant from the king of Spain.

For the next two centuries, Tigua people practiced farming on irrigated fields. Tiguas scouted for El Paso settlements against Comanche and Apache raiders. Tiguas also scouted for the Texas Rangers and the U.S. cavalry during the Indian campaigns. After 1848, however, Tiguas were subject to "legal" and extralegal abuses from rapacious Anglos, and much of their land was lost. When President Lincoln acknowledged the New Mexican Pueblo land grants with a second set of silver-headed canes, Tigua, standing in the

Confederacy, was ignored. In any case, since Texas retained its public lands, the U.S. government was unable to create a reservation for the Tigua.

In the late nineteenth century and into the 1920s the tribe virtually faded away, mixing with the local populace and living in extreme poverty. In 1967, the state of Texas recognized the Ysleta Indian community; federal recognition followed the next year. The receipt of federal money and recognition revitalized the tribe and provided the means through which it was able to reclaim its identity.

RELIGION Tiguas practice Catholicism, with some native elements. The Pueblo's patron saint is Anthony, who was the patron of Isleta Pueblo before the 1680 revolt. A small core of people practice a more traditional religion, featuring a katsinalike entity known as the *awelo,* or grandfather, who oversees all behavior. The tribe also possesses buffalo *awelo* masks and an ancient ceremonial drum.

GOVERNMENT The tribal government is Spanish-style civil. There is a *cacique,* a *cacique teniente* (lieutenant *cacique,* or governor), an *alguacil* or sergeant at arms, a *capitán de guerra* or war captain, and four assistant captains. Except for the first and the last, all are elected annually. Ysleta del Sur Pueblo also possesses the old Spanish canes, symbols of political authority, that were carried by the original settlers.

CUSTOMS Tribal ceremonial items are stored in a *tusla,* generally the home of a tribal officer, where celebrations are often held. There is a high rate of intermarriage with outsiders, particularly with Mexicans and other Indians. The Tigua enjoy a close relationship with Isleta Pueblo, New Mexico, 250 miles away. They are also associated with the Tortugas community of Las Cruces, New Mexico, a Tigua community founded in the late nineteenth century and composed of Tigua, Piro, and Manso Indians. The Tiguas also have relatives in Mexico, at the former Piro pueblo of Senecú, near Juarez. There may have been a clan system in earlier days.

DWELLINGS Originally, adobe houses were arranged around a church plaza. The general neighborhood is shared with Mexican American and Anglo neighbors.

DIET Traditional crops included corn, beans, and squash. The people also hunted buffalo and other wild game.

KEY TECHNOLOGY Women made pottery into the twentieth century. They also made willow baskets, and men wove blankets and braided rope.

TRADE Tiguas traded corn, wheat, fruit, and salt as well as crafts. Most arts and crafts were sold in El Paso and Juarez, although some were traded in Chihuahua City.

NOTABLE ARTS Women made pottery until the last traditional potter died in 1930. Before the early twentieth century, men wove blankets and braided rope, and women made willow baskets.

TRANSPORTATION Baskets were used to transport goods.

DRESS Men wore cotton kilts and leather sandals. Women wore cotton dresses and sandals or high moccasin boots. Buckskin and rabbit skin were also used for clothing and robes.

WAR AND WEAPONS Tiguas supplied soldiers to help the Spanish reconquer New Mexico in the 1680s and 1690s. They also fought against Comanches and Apaches during most of the eighteenth and nineteenth centuries.

Contemporary Information

GOVERNMENT/RESERVATIONS Ysleta del Sur Pueblo, established in 1682, contains 66 acres. The state of Texas is trustee for all tribal lands. Men elect all officials including the *cacique,* war captain, and governor. There is no constitution.

ECONOMY Most people work in El Paso and surrounding cities. Some beadwork, pottery, and other crafts are produced and sold to tourists. Texas has initiated a program to turn the reservation into a tourist attraction. A Tigua tribal museum, restaurant, and gift shop already exist. Gaming is seen as the way of the future.

LEGAL STATUS Ysleta del Sur Pueblo is a federally recognized tribal entity. A land claims case for prehistoric Huenco lands, of great religious significance to the Tigua, is pending.

DAILY LIFE The Tigua community is an urban enclave. In the early 1900s, Spanish largely replaced Tiwa on the Pueblo, with English as a second language. Some tribal revitalization has occurred since the 1960s, including ceremonies, language, and hunts, but the population is overwhelmingly assimilated. Tribal rolls closed in 1984 with 1,124 certified members. The Tiguas use their tribal drum, brought from New Mexico 300 years ago, on the Feast of Saint Anthony.

The officially unrecognized Tortuga community (Gualalupe Indian Village) still exists in Las Cruces, on 40 acres owned by their own incorporated organization. Land is privately owned. No one speaks the native language, but several traditional ceremonies, such as the Rabbit Hunt, attended by the people of Ysleta del Sur Pueblo, are still performed.

Tohono O'odham

Tohono O'odham (T ō h ō n ō `Ō d ə m) are also known as Papago or Desert People. The name Papago is derived from the Pima word *Papahvio-Otam,* meaning "bean people." They are also known as Two Villagers, owing to their traditional migration patterns (see "History" under "Historical Information"). They, along with the Pima (Akimel O'odham, or River People, also known as One Villagers because of their relatively settled lives), the Sand Papago (Hiaced O'odham, also known as No Villagers, because of their more or less constant migrations in search of food), and the Ak-Chin ("mouth of the arroyo") O'odham, constitute the O'odham Indians.

LOCATION The Tohono O'odham lived originally in the Sonoran Desert near the Gulf of California. (The Sand Papago lived in the western and most arid parts of the Sonoran Desert.) Today they live in four reservations in southern Arizona (see "Government/Reservations" under "Contemporary Information").

POPULATION Up to 50,000 Tohono O'odham probably lived in the region in 1500, although their numbers had shrunk to about 3,000 by 1700. In 1990, approximately 8,500 people lived on the main reservation. Another 400 lived at Ak Chin, almost 1,100 lived at San Xavier, about 500 lived at Gila Bend, and several thousand lived off-reservation. The enrolled membership in 1991 was 17,589.

LANGUAGE The native language of the Tohono O'odham is Piman, a Uto-Aztecan language.

Historical Information

HISTORY The O'odham are probably descended from the ancient Hohokam Indians. Unlike the Hohokam or the Pima, the Tohono O'odham were seminomadic. They generally spent summers in their "field villages" in the desert, usually at the mouth of an arroyo, where flash floods would provided needed water. Winters were spent in "well villages," by mountain springs.

The Tohono O'odham may have first met non-natives in the 1500s. They experienced extensive contact with the Spanish in late 1600s when Father Eusebio Kino established numerous Catholic missions and introduced cattle, horses, and wheat (1684). The Spanish also established a series of presidios against the growing Apache threat. Although too isolated to have had to endure harsh forced labor and agricultural taxes as did the Pima, some Tohono O'odham, such as Luis Oacpicagigua and others, participated in the Pima revolt of 1751.

Apaches constituted the major threat from the eighteenth century through the mid–nineteenth century. During this time, the Sand Papago died off or became assimilated with the Spanish or surrounding tribes. From 1840 to 1843, the Papago fought and lost a war against Mexico in an attempt to stop the usurpation of their lands. With the Gadsden Purchase (1853), the Tohono O'odham lost the part of their territory that remained in Mexico, although they tended to ignore the international border for many years. Despite tighter border restrictions today, Tohono O'odham Indians living in Sonora and the United States remain in contact.

In the 1860s, the Papago fought with the Pima, Pee-Posh, and U.S. troops against the Apaches. Still, Anglos appropriated their water holes and grazing land, resulting in conflict and some violence. San Xavier Reservation was founded in 1874, with Gila Bend Reservation following in 1882. The Papago Reservation was established in 1916 and 1917, albeit without most of the Tohono O'odhams' best lands.

The railroad came to Tucson in the 1880s, bringing an increase of cattlemen and miners into O'odham territory. The cattle lost by these people began important O'odham herds. By the end of the century, countless Papago (and other Indian) girls were working as domestics for whites through Bureau of Indian Affairs (BIA) programs at the Phoenix Indian School. About this time, and concurrent with the rise of many Christian schools, the O'odham culture declined markedly.

A field camp at Vecol Wash became the permanent settlement of the Ak Chin O'odham in the 1870s; Pimas and Maricopas lived there too. In the early wage economy, O'odham potters sold and traded water-cooling ollas; men cut firewood; basket makers sold baskets. Cotton picking became the most important economic activity through the 1950s. In the 1970s, a severe drought killed many cattle, reducing the Papago to near starvation.

RELIGION The Tohono O'odham worshiped Earth Maker (*Tcuwut Makai*) and Elder Brother (*I'itoi,* or *Se'ehe*), the heroes of their creation story, whose sacred home is Baboquivari Peak in southern Arizona. Ceremonies encouraged these spirits to bring the rain that made food possible. The people also made annual pilgrimages to salt flats near the Gulf of California, home of the rain spirits, to pray to them.

Their most sacred ceremony was *Nawait,* or the new year's rain ceremony, which they celebrated with saguaro wine. Other important ceremonial occasions included puberty (especially for girls), funerals, the summer cactus wine feast, the "naming" (to honor and entertain other groups), purification following childbirth, sickness, the corn harvest, the deer hunt, the early winter harvest, purification for an eagle killing, warfare, and the annual salt expeditions.

Shamans, both men and older women, derived curing power from dreams. Although many Papagos became Catholic in the eighteenth century, having clustered around Spanish presidios and missions to escape the Apache, it was a Catholicism heavily mixed with traditional beliefs.

GOVERNMENT The Tohono O'odham were organized into autonomous villages. Although each village had a chief (there was no tribal chief), decisions were taken by consensus. Each village also had shamans, a headman who set the agenda for meetings and mediated conflict, and an all-male council. They also recognized a ceremonial leader, akin to the headman, called Keeper of the Smoke. Other officials included a village crier, war leader, hunt leader, game leader, and song leader.

CUSTOMS A universal O'odham concept of the way of life *(Himdag)* centers on family, community, generosity, and modesty. The Papago made annual visits to relatives on the Gila River or in the Sonora River Valleys. In times of famine, families often moved to Pima villages along the Gila River. Every four years the Papago and Pima together celebrated *Viikita,* a holiday dedicated to ensuring their continued fortune, with dancers and clowns dressed in masks and costumes.

Each Tohono O'odham village was divided into two clans, Buzzard and Coyote. Their year began when the cactus fruit ripened. Gifts and wagering were major forms of exchange. Games and races also held cultural importance. With the exception of warriors, who were cremated, the dead were dressed in their best clothing and buried with their personal property in caves, crevices, or stone houses.

DWELLINGS Like those of the Pimas, everyday Papago houses were circular and constructed of saguaro and ocotillo ribs and mesquite covered with mud and brush. Ceremonial houses were similar, but larger. Wall-less ramadas provided shelter for most outdoor activities in good weather. Sand Papagos used small rings of stone as temporary windbreaks.

DIET The key to survival in the desert was diversification. The goal of the Papago was security rather than surpluses. Men grew corn, beans, and squash. Later the Spanish introduced cowpeas, melons, and wheat. Winter wheat especially provided an edge against starvation. The people also hunted, primarily in the winter. Wild foods such as mescal, mesquite beans, ironwood and paloverde seeds, cactus fruits, amaranth and other greens, wild chilies, acorns, and sand root provided about three-quarters of their diet. Saguaro wine was used on ceremonial occasions. During hard times the Papago "hired out" to Pima Indians, exchanging labor for food. The Sand Papago ate shellfish from the Gulf of California, reptiles, insects, and small mammals. A staple was the parasitic plant sand root.

KEY TECHNOLOGY The Desert People baked in pit ovens. They used long poles called kuibits to knock down saguaro fruit. The use of calendar sticks, with carved dots and circles to record important ceremonies, began in the early 1830s. Notches referred to secular events, such as earthquakes or Apache attacks. Other equipment included carrying nets, frame backpacks, and cradle boards. In characteristic *ak chin* farming, men built dams to channel water runoff into one major arroyo. When the flash floods arrived, they would water the fields by erecting brush spreader dams across the arroyo. After contact with the Spanish, the Desert People adopted picks, shovels, and horse- and oxen-drawn plows and wagons.

TRADE Trade occurred mostly in the fall and winter. The Tohono O'odham traded meat, baskets, pottery, salt, shells, mineral pigments, and macaws for corn and, later, wheat from Pimas and Quechans. The Sand Papago also traded with Yuman peoples on the Colorado River.

NOTABLE ARTS Specialized arts included coiled willow, devil's claw, yucca, and bear grass baskets. Older people made a traditional red pottery.

TRANSPORTATION Baskets were used for transporting goods.

DRESS Men wore cotton or deerskin breechcloths. Women wore cloth, willow bark, or deerskin wraparound skirts. Both sexes used hide or fiber sandals and cotton and rabbit-skin blankets. They also grew their hair long, wore ear pendants of turquoise and other stones, and tattooed and painted their bodies.

WAR AND WEAPONS Traditional enemies of the Papago included the Mojave and the Apache.

Contemporary Information

GOVERNMENT/RESERVATIONS The Tohono O'odham live on four reservations in southern Arizona, with a combined acreage of over 2.8 million: San Xavier (1874); Gila Bend (1882, although most of this reservation was lost by flooding caused by the Painted Rock Dam); Ak Chin (1912); and Papago, or Sells (1874). The people are in regular communication with O'odham living in Mexico.

A tribal constitution and by-laws were ratified in 1937, and an elected tribal council, from the Papago Reservation plus San Xavier and Gila Bend, runs tribal political affairs. Decision making is decentralized, with district tribal councils acting to preserve the interests of the community. A 1986 constitutional revision created a tripartite form of government. The BIA still maintains direct influence over the tribe.

ECONOMY Important economic activities include mining (mostly copper) and chemical businesses; license fees paid by traders and hunters; farming; cattle, including both individual subsistence herds and large herds owned by wealthy families; bingo; and fire fighting. Wage work is also provided by the tribe, the BIA, the health service, and businesses in nearby cities and towns. Arts and crafts include world-famous baskets, pottery, wooden bowls, horsehair miniatures, and lariats. The San Xavier Reservation has recently opened an industrial park. Unemployment often remains above 30 percent.

LEGAL STATUS The Ak Chin Indian Community of Papago Indians and the Tohono O'odham Nation of Arizona (formerly the Papago Tribe of the Sells, Gila Bend, and San Xavier Reservations) are federally recognized tribal entities. The Sand Papago won recognition in 1980s but own no land to date.

DAILY LIFE With the advent of drilled wells and a dependable water supply, the O'odham no longer migrate to mountain well villages; thus has their immemorial relationship with their environment and their world been changed forever. The Fiesta de Magdalena, a combination harvest, trade, and religious festival held every fall in Sonora, Mexico, remains the most powerful connection of the Arizona O'odham to Mexico. English has largely replaced Spanish as a second language.

Many O'odham still live in extended families, and they still strive for consensus decision making. More than three-quarters of O'odham Indians are at least nominally Catholic. Schools use local resources to teach native language and culture; the main reservation contains both schools and a hospital. In addition, the tribe works closely with the University of Arizona to develop and institute a wide variety of educational programs available to tribal members. A rodeo and fair are held at Sells in October; the Saguaro Festival is also celebrated. Many, perhaps a majority, of O'odham Indians live off-reservation.

At San Xavier, allotment policies in 1890 gave most of the land to individuals. With division by inheritance, 400–500 people may own an acre today, making individual land use almost impossible. These people practice cooperative farming. The Ak-chin O'odham speak a distinct dialect and consider themselves neither Tohono O'odham nor Pima. Having abandoned subsistence farming in the 1930s, they now operate a cotton cooperative. Acculturation at Ak-chin is far advanced.

Tortugas
See Tigua

Walapai
See Hualapai

Yaqui

Yaqui (`Yä k ē) is a name established by Jesuit missionaries in the early seventeenth century. It was taken from the name of a nearby river. The traditional Yaqui name for themselves is *Yoeme*.

LOCATION The Yaqui originated in the northwestern Mexican state of Sonora. They have lived in southern and southwest Arizona from the late nineteenth century.

POPULATION The Yaqui population stood at perhaps 30,000 at contact (1533), the largest native tribal population in northwest New Spain. Roughly 6,000 now live in U.S. villages out of a total U.S. tribal enrollment (1992) of almost 10,000. About 25,000 Yaquis live in Sonora, Mexico.

LANGUAGE Yaquis spoke a dialect of Cahita, a member of the Uto-Aztecan language family.

Historical Information

HISTORY The aboriginal land of the Yaquis consisted of roughly 6,000 square miles in Sonora, Mexico, approximately between the Rio Mátapa and the Arroyo de Cocoraqui. The Yaqui believe their boundaries were made sacred by singing angels (*batnaataka*) who traversed them in mythological times. Although the Sonora region is primarily a desert, Yaqui lands in the river basin were quite fertile as a result of the annual flood cycles.

A party of Spaniards first encountered the Yaqui in 1533 but were prevented by force from trespassing on Yaqui territory. In 1609, after defeating the Spanish for the third time, the Yaquis arrived at an accommodation with them and accepted Jesuit missionaries in 1617. Over the next seven years almost all Yaquis converted to Catholicism.

The next 150 years were a period of creative cultural and economic growth for the Yaqui. Transformations in agriculture and technology led to increasing agricultural surpluses and economic diversification (mining and sheep herding for the Spanish wool trade). In 1740, the Yaqui staged a major revolt as a result of growing tensions over land incursions, Spanish attempts to secularize and control the missions, and missionary abuses. The Indians' defeat strengthened both Spanish colonial power and the Jesuit missions, until the latter were expelled from the New World in 1767.

The 1800s were a time of semiautonomy, with gradual loss of land and continual resistance against the Mexicans. Juan Ignacio Jusacamea, also known as Juan de la Cruz Banderas or Juan Banderas, emerged as the uncontested leader of the Yaquis and their allies in the early Mexican rebellions until his capture and execution in 1833. Further periodic revolts culminated in the so-called Cajeme era (1875–1885), a period of Yaqui cultural and economic renewal during which Yaqui society made a final defensive stand against Mexico under José María Leyva, called Cajeme.

The defeat of Cajeme in 1885 was followed by military occupation, repression, and mass deportation under the regime of Porfirio Diaz, although Yaqui bands continued guerrilla resistance in the Bacatete Mountains into the twentieth century. Most Yaquis not exiled to the Yucatan dispersed throughout rural Sonora, assisting the guerrillas and working in the mines, on the railroads, and on haciendas. Many also headed north to the United States to begin new Yaqui communities there.

The Mexican Revolution of 1910 offered the Yaqui a chance to regroup and reestablish their identity, with the formation of their own revolutionary army. Following the wars, Yaquis began a gradual return to their traditional lands and a reconstruction of their culture. For Yaquis living in Mexico, the last half of the twentieth century has been marked by the integration, albeit at the lowest levels, into that country's economy. In 1964, the U.S. Congress gave 202 acres of land to the Pascua Yaqui Association. This grant became the basis of New Pascua, which became officially recognized in 1978.

RELIGION The Yaqui Indians have been practicing a heavily Christian-influenced religion for nearly 400 years. They recognize a two-part universe: one is town and church, whose dwellers are mortal; the other is the *Huya Aniya,* spirit world and source of spiritual power, whose dwellers are immortal. The two worlds are integrated ritually. Every Christian ceremony requires participation of ceremonialists, such as Pascola and Deer Dancers, whose power derives from the *Huya Aniya.*

Other important religious elements include honoring of and concern for ancestors, the sharing of accumulated wealth for help in curing (healing), maintaining and distributing the benevolent power of Our Mother (the supernatural), honoring the patron saints of the eight towns (see "Dwellings"), and affirming the sacred relationships between the Yaqui and their traditional territory.

In addition to a number of feast days, the most important and elaborate ceremony of the year is the *waehma,* or the reenactment during Holy Week of Christ's (the great curer) final days. A central theme is the accumulation of evil in the town and the destruction of that evil during a ceremonial battle on Holy Saturday, through the ritual use of flowers, followed by a great celebration.

GOVERNMENT The largest political unit was the town. Authority consisted of five groups: church, civil governors, military, "custom authorities" *(kohtumbre),* and fiesta makers *(Pahkome).* Each had its own clearly defined jurisdiction, but they worked together on matters of the public good. Decision making was by consensus in town meeting except in time of military emergency, and even then the military leader's power in nonmilitary affairs was highly circumscribed. A constant process of interaction and sharing promoted continuity among the towns.

CUSTOMS Traditional Yaqui households consisted of any number of nuclear families related in a variety of ways. Yaqui elders were respected as the tribal spokespeople and maintained schools for young men. The godparent system, introduced by the Jesuits, has evolved into a highly complex and important institution.

DWELLINGS Prior to 1617 the Yaqui lived in roughly 80 rancherias, most containing fewer than 250 people, consisting of clusters of dome-shaped, cane mat–covered adobe houses with flat or gently sloping roofs. Consolidation under the Jesuits of the scattered rancherias into eight towns, each with between 2,000 and 4,000 people, occurred by the mid-1600s. Each town was built around an adobe-walled church, with new civil, military, and ceremonial organizations grouped around the church and central plaza. Houses built near churches always included ramadas as well as walled rooms, surrounded by a cane fence. After 1887, the Mexicans succeeded in imposing the grid plan of settlement on Yaqui towns.

DIET Cultivated crops such as corn, squash, beans, and amaranth were supplemented by abundant wild foods such as mesquite beans, cactus fruits, succulent roots, grass seeds, wild game (including deer and rabbits), and many kinds of shellfish and large saltwater fish from the Gulf of California. By the late seventeenth century, the Jesuits had introduced wheat, pomegranates, peaches, figs, and other crops as well as cattle (including oxen for plowing) and horses.

KEY TECHNOLOGY Rudimentary irrigation ditches were improved by the Jesuits, who also introduced the plow to the region. The Yaquis traditionally fashioned cane into a great number of articles, including mats for roof and wall materials, household compound fences, sleeping mats, cutting instruments, spoons, and shelves as well as numerous ceremonial items.

TRADE Yaquis generally had many items to trade, including crops, cane items, and woven articles.

NOTABLE ARTS Yaqui traditional arts consist of ritual dance (all male) and religious drama, music, wood mask carving, cane mat making, and blanket and mat weaving in both cotton and wool.

TRANSPORTATION Horses were introduced into the region in the seventeenth century.

DRESS Yaquis wore cotton and wool clothing and blankets as well as special ceremonial kilts, masks, rattles, stuffed deer heads, and red ribbons (symbolizing flowers).

WAR AND WEAPONS Members of the military society served for life and had their own rituals, which included flag-bearing ceremonies and dances. Although the elected captains generally tended to dominate Yaqui society in the eighteenth and nineteenth centuries because of the continual state of crisis, community leaders were always consulted for important decisions.

Contemporary Information

GOVERNMENT/RESERVATIONS Significant U.S. Yaqui communities are located in and around Phoenix and Tucson, Arizona (Guadaloupe, Eloy, Old Pascua, New Pascua Pueblo [Yaqui Reservation; population 2,737 in 1992], and Barrio Libre). Village organization is church oriented and controlled by the ceremonial groups. A Bureau of Indian Affairs–approved Yaqui constitution (1988) calls for an elected tribal council. In Mexico, an unofficial tribal structure, created by the Mexican government and loosely based on and operating with the traditional government, has been in existence since the 1930s.

ECONOMY In the United States, tribal members participate in the local economy in a number of urban occupations and professions and as farm or construction workers. In addition, the tribe runs a landscape nursery, a charcoal-packing business, and a bingo enterprise. Unemployment remains very high. In Mexico, government water diversions and rapid development have removed the possibility of subsistence farming.

LEGAL STATUS The Yaqui received official U.S. government recognition in 1978, primarily through the leadership of Anselmo Valencia; the Pascua Yaquis are a federally recognized tribal entity. Many Mexican Yaquis live on their reservation and in the "original eight" and other small towns.

DAILY LIFE Wherever Yaquis have settled, they have maintained some degree of devotion to the ideal of life in the eight towns. Religion remains a distinct blend of Catholic and native beliefs, and the ceremonial cycle still follows the life of Christ. Saints' days are celebrated with fireworks, feasting, and entertainment, such as masked dancing and musicians. Lenten and Holy Week ceremonies remain especially elaborate, culminating in the unique Passion Play.

Yaquis living in the United States enjoy close contact with the Tohono O'odham (Papago) tribe, including mutual attendance of ceremonies and festivals. Children attend public school, where they have access to Yaqui language preservation programs. Contemporary issues include obtaining decent health care and housing, in addition to solving the high unemployment rate. Yaqui arts especially include music, dance, and painting. Rural houses in the United States are built primarily of adobe. Most houses feature a fenced-in yard, with a few trees, small plots of green grass, and flowers. Open ramadas serve as the main living spaces and also as gathering places at fiesta time. Typically, a small white church sits at one end of the village plaza with a fiesta ramada at the other end. Over 50 homes at Old Pascua were rebuilt in the 1980s.

In Mexico, Yaquis are still relatively isolated and more traditional than other Indian groups. In clothing and material culture they are nearly identical to rural Mexican mestiso peasant farmers.

Yavapai

Yavapai (`Yä vä p ī) from the Mojave *Enyaéva Pai,* "People of the Sun." They are sometimes confused with the Apaches, as a result of their long association together, and are occasionally (and erroneously) referred to as Mojave Apaches or Yuma Apaches.

LOCATION Traditionally, the Yavapai controlled roughly 10 million acres in present-day west-central Arizona. This transitional area between the Colorado Plateau and the lower deserts provided them with a salubrious mixture of desert, mountain, and plateau plants and animals. Today, Yavapai Indians live on the Fort McDowell, the Camp Verde, and the Yavapai Reservations, Arizona.

POPULATION In 1992 there were approximately 1,550 enrolled Yavapais on the three reservations. Resident population in 1990 was as follows: Six hundred and forty lived at Fort McDowell, 650 lived at Camp Verde, 130 lived at Prescott, and some lived off-reservation. Roughly 1,500 Yavapai lived in their area in 1500.

LANGUAGE Yavapais spoke a dialect (similar to Pai) of Upland Yuman, a Hokan-Siouan language (though culturally and historically the Yavapai were more closely related to the Tonto Apache).

Historical Information

HISTORY The nomadic Yavapai were probably descended from the ancient Hakataya peoples. Traditionally they consisted of four major divisions: the Kewevkapaya (southeastern), the Wipukpaya (northeastern), the Tolkepaye (western), and the Yavepe (central). Each was further divided into local bands.

Contact between the Spanish and the Yavapais occurred in 1582. After Father Francisco Garces lived with them in 1776, contact became more frequent. Nevertheless the Yavapais lived traditionally until the 1850s, largely because their country was too rough for the Spaniards, Mexicans, or Americans. Some bands, especially the Kewevkapaya, raided with the Apaches. After the Mexican cession, more non-Indian travelers and miners frequented the region, although the Yavapai tried to avoid conflict, owing primarily to their poor weaponry.

Gold was discovered in 1863. Shortly thereafter the frontier arrived and brought the permanent disruption of Yavapai traditional life. Hungry and under continuous attack, the Yavapai fought back. In 1872–1873, General George Crook's bloody Tonto Basin campaign against the Tonto Apaches and Yavapais (won with a heavy reliance on Pai scouts) ended with a massacre of Yavapais. Forced onto the Camp Verde reservation after disease had killed an additional one-third of their number, the Yavapai and Tonto Apaches dug a 5-mile irrigation ditch using discarded army tools and brought in a good harvest. For this they were forcibly relocated (again) in 1875 and settled with the Apaches on the San Carlos Reservation, 180 miles to the east. Many died or were killed on the "March of Tears" (within 25 years, their population fell from 1,500 to 200).

At San Carlos the Yavapai again tried farming. They also scouted for the army against the Chiricahua Apaches and acquired cattle. However, flooding ruined their ditches, miners and ranchers took their land, and they still wanted to go home. By 1900, most Yavapais had left San Carlos. Some returned to the Verde Valley and some to Forts McDowell and Whipple. In 1903, Fort McDowell became a reservation, inhabited mostly by the Kewevkopaya band. Camp Verde (Weepukapa) reservation was established in 1910, with outlying communities such as Middle Verde, Clarkdale, and Rimrock added during the following 60 years. Fort Whipple became a reservation (Yavapai-Prescott) in 1935. The western Yavapai (Tolkepaye) received no reservation and have nearly disappeared.

The Verde River ran through Fort McDowell. The Yavapai tried farming once again, but they were soon involved in a struggle for water rights. Instead of providing funds to improve irrigation and guard against floods, the government wanted to remove the Yavapai to the Salt River Pima Reservation. Largely owing to the efforts of Carlos Montezuma they were able to remain, but they secured little money or water. During this period cattle grazing and wage work, both on and off the reservation, became important sources of income. From the 1950s through the 1980s, the Yavapai also fought off a dam (Orme) that would have flooded most of the Fort McDowell Reservation, refusing $33 million in compensation. Finally, in 1990, the Yavapai won passage of a law granting them sufficient water rights from the Verde River as well as $25 million in compensatory funds.

Yavapais and Apaches leaving San Carlos settled at Camp Verde around the turn of the century. Camp Verde is more Apache than Yavapai in character.

Unable to make a living on the inadequate reservation lands, most people worked in the nearby copper industry until the 1930s and 1940s.

In 1935 a separate reservation, primarily inhabited by the Yavepe band, was created north of Prescott. Rather than organize under the Indian Reorganization Act, this group maintained the traditional governing structure until 1988. Their land base is surrounded by the city of Prescott.

RELIGION Like other Yumans, veneration of the sun, dream omens, and shamanism were key aspects of Yavapai religion. Knowledge of all kinds was acquired by each person through dreaming. Shamans conducted healing rituals by singing, smoking tobacco, and sucking out bad blood. Some Yavapai rituals included the use of sandpaintings. Singing, dancing, and eagle feathers were part of every ritual, as were certain plants and musical instruments such as rattles, drums, and flutes. "Little people" or spirits living in the mountains were thought to help people. The Yavapai place of emergence was considered to be at Montezuma Well, near Sedona.

GOVERNMENT The closest the Yavapai came to centralized authority was each local group's "civic leader." This person would orate each morning on proper ideas and behavior. Leadership was based on personal merit (wisdom, personality, and ability in war).

CUSTOMS The Yavapai were a nomadic people who followed the ripening of wild foods. Bands camped in groups of up to ten families; winter gatherings were even larger. Elders or group leaders orated each morning from the roof of a hut, instructing people on the proper way to live. Social dances were held on occasion. Until the early 1900s the dead were customarily cremated (the house and possessions were also burned). Polygyny was rare, as was divorce. The Yavapai practiced formal puberty rites for women and men.

DWELLINGS People lived in caves or dome-shaped huts, framed with poles and covered with brush, thatch, or mud. Other structures included ramadas and sweat lodges.

DIET Mescal was a staple, along with other wild plants such as cactus fruit, mesquite beans, greens, acorns, piñon nuts, walnuts, seeds, and berries. Women gathered wild foods. Game included deer, quail, fox, antelope, and rabbits; people also ate lizards, caterpillars, yellowjacket nests, and turkeys. Small amounts of corn, beans, and squash were grown or traded, mostly by the western band.

KEY TECHNOLOGY Tools included bows and arrows, baskets, clubs, buckskin ponchos, grinding stones and other stone tools, throwing sticks, and snares or traps for hunting. Food was boiled in clay pots.

TRADE   The Yavapai were active traders in a large local trade network. Baskets were the primary currency. They traded mescal and buckskin to the Navajo for blankets and to the Hopi for jewelry. They occasionally obtained corn from the Pima and the O'odham.

NOTABLE ARTS   Women made pottery, but baskets were one of the most highly developed arts. Color came not from dyes or artificial materials but from the shoots of cottonwood and mulberry trees, the roots of yucca or soapwood, or devil's claw.

TRANSPORTATION   Women made baskets for carrying goods.

DRESS   The Yavapai painted their bodies. Ornaments included necklaces, bracelets, and ear and nose rings (especially warriors). Bangs were worn to the eyebrows. Men wore hide breechclouts, leggings, and moccasins, and blankets or skin ponchos in winter (also boots and mittens). Women wore two buckskins draped over a belt and a buckskin top and moccasins (of buckskin or possibly yucca fiber). Some women tattooed their faces. Men dressed the skins for clothing.

WAR AND WEAPONS   Each local group decided for itself whether or nor to join a war. Yavapai traditional enemies included the Pai, Pima, Pee-Posh, and O'odham. Their allies included the Quechan, Mojave, and Apache. Unlike the Apaches, the Yavapais used few guns; instead, they mostly made do with hunting tools to fight the U.S. Army. Other weapons included clubs, hide shields, mulberry bows, and cane arrows with obsidian points. Although they were inclined toward war, they proved to be more flexible than the Apaches regarding change, adaptation, and coexistence.

Contemporary Information

GOVERNMENT/RESERVATIONS   Yavapai reservations are at Prescott (1935; almost 1,400 acres), Fort McDowell (1901–1904; almost 25,000 acres; 28 miles northeast of Phoenix), and Camp Verde (1914; 1,092 acres in two sections, shared with the Tonto Apache). At Camp Verde intermarriage has produced a new tribe, the Yavapai-Apaches, organized in 1937. Clarkdale (1969; 60 acres, also shared with the Apache) and Payson (Yavapai and Tonto Apache, 1972; 85 acres) are associated with Camp Verde, which, with Fort McDowell, elects a tribal council.

ECONOMY   At Fort McDowell, a gambling establishment brings in much money and provides employment, as does the tribal farm. There is also a large sand and gravel operation and several small businesses. Some people work in surrounding cities and towns, raise stock, or, in a few cases, practice subsistence farming. Under- and unemployment often exceeds 50 percent. A water settlement (1990) provided for both water rights and $25 million in compensatory funds. There is potential for economic development near the Beeline Highway. Some women also produce coiled baskets for the tourist trade.

Verde places most economic hope in tourism associated with Montezuma Castle National Monument; some people also work off-reservation. At Prescott there is an industrial park, a commercial park, a shopping center, a bingo operation, and a hotel complex, and there are plans for a museum. People also raise stock and work off-reservation.

LEGAL STATUS   The Fort McDowell Mohave-Apache Indian Community, Fort McDowell Band of Mohave Apache Indians, Yavapai-Apache Indian Community, and the Yavapai-Prescott Tribe are all federally recognized tribal entities.

DAILY LIFE   Acculturation is well established; the last big Yavapai dance was held in 1924. The language is all but lost. Children attend public schools. Camp Verde is negotiating the purchase of 6,500 additional acres. Some women still make high-quality baskets. The tribes cosponsor Ba'ja days, a cultural celebration. Yavapai-Prescott has also developed a cultural program with a professional staff.

Ysleta del Sur Pueblo
See Tigua

Yuma
See Quechan

Zia Pueblo

Zia (`Ts ē  ä, or `S ē ä) from the Spanish spelling of its Keresan name. The word "pueblo" comes from the Spanish for "village." It refers both to a certain style of Southwest Indian architecture, characterized by multistory, apartmentlike buildings made of adobe, and to the people themselves. Rio Grande pueblos are known as eastern Pueblos; Zuñi, Hopi, and sometimes Acoma and Laguna are known as western Pueblos.

LOCATION   Zia Pueblo is located on the Jemez River, 30 miles north of Albuquerque, New Mexico.

POPULATION   At least 5,000 and as many as 20,000 Indians may have lived on the pueblo in 1540, although fewer than 300 remained in 1690 and fewer than 100 in 1890. In 1990, 637 Zia Indians lived on the pueblo, with perhaps as many living outside of it.

LANGUAGE   Zia Indians spoke a dialect of Keresan.

Historical Information

HISTORY   All Pueblo people are thought to be descended from Anasazi and perhaps Mogollon and several other ancient peoples, although the precise origin of the Keresan peoples is unknown. From them they learned architecture, farming, pottery, and basketry. Larger population groups became possible with effective agriculture and ways to store food surpluses. Within the context of a relatively stable existence, the people devoted increasing amounts of time and attention to religion, arts, and crafts.

Keresans have been traced to an area around Chaco Canyon north to Mesa Verde. In the 1200s, the Keresans abandoned their traditional canyon homelands in response to climatic and social upheavals. A century or two of migrations ensued, followed in general by the slow reemergence of their culture in the historic pueblos. Six thirteenth-century archaeological sites have been identified with Zia. Five of these were occupied between the sixteenth and eighteenth centuries. Antonio de Espejo, who visited in 1583, called these sites Punames and described a large city with eight plazas, over 1,000 two- to three-story houses, and a population of at least 5,000 and perhaps as many as 20,000.

In 1598, Juan de Oñate arrived in the area with settlers, founding the colony of New Mexico. Oñate carried on the process, already underway in nearby areas, of subjugating the local Indians; forcing them to pay taxes in crops, cotton, and work; and opening the door for Catholic missionaries to attack their religion. The Spanish renamed the Pueblos with saints' names and began a program of church construction; the mission at Zia was built about 1610. At the same time, the Spanish introduced such new crops as peaches, wheat, and peppers into the region. In 1620, a royal decree created civil offices at each pueblo; silver-headed canes, many of which remain in use today, symbolized the governor's authority.

The Zians participated in the 1680 Pueblo revolt against the Spanish. For years, the Spaniards had routinely tortured Indians for practicing traditional religion. They also forced the Indians to labor for them, sold Indians into slavery, and let their cattle overgraze Indian land, a situation that eventually led to drought, erosion, and famine. Popé of San Juan Pueblo and other Pueblo religious leaders planned the revolt, sending runners carrying cords of maguey fibers to mark the day of rebellion. On August 10, 1680, a virtually united stand on the part of the Pueblos drove the Spanish from the region. The Indians killed many Spaniards but refrained from mass slaughter, allowing them to leave Santa Fe for El Paso.

Zia suffered a bloody military defeat by Spanish forces in 1687: Six hundred were killed, and many were held captive for ten years. In 1689 Zia received a royal land grant from Spain. In 1692 Zia accepted mass baptism and collaborated with the Spanish in

their campaigns against other pueblos throughout the rest of the decade.

The Pueblos experienced many changes during the following decades: Refugees established communities at Hopi, guerrilla fighting continued against the Spanish, and certain areas were abandoned. By the 1700s, excluding Hopi and Zuñi, only Taos, Picuris, Isleta, and Acoma Pueblos had not changed locations since the arrival of the Spanish. Although Pueblo unity did not last, and Santa Fe was officially reconquered in 1692, Spanish rule was notably less severe from then on. Harsh forced labor all but ceased, and the Indians reached an understanding with the Church that enabled them to continue practicing their traditional religion.

In general, the Pueblo eighteenth century was marked by smallpox epidemics and increased raiding by the Apache, Comanche, and Ute. Occasionally Pueblo Indians fought with the Spanish against the nomadic tribes. The people practiced their religion but more or less in secret. During this time, intermarriage and regular exchange between Hispanic villages and Pueblo Indians created a new New Mexican culture, neither strictly Spanish nor Indian, but rather somewhat of a blend between the two.

Mexican "rule" in 1821 brought little immediate change to the Pueblos. The Mexicans stepped up what had been a gradual process of appropriating Indian land and water, and they allowed the nomadic tribes even greater latitude to raid. A political rebellion by Indians and Hispanic poor in 1837 over the issue of taxes led to the assassination of the New Mexican governor and the brief installation of a Plains/Taos Indian as governor. As the presence of the United States in the area grew, it attempted to enable the Pueblo Indians to continue their generally peaceful and self-sufficient ways and recognized Spanish land grants to the Pueblos.

During the nineteenth century the process of acculturation among Pueblo Indians quickened markedly. In an attempt to retain their identity, Pueblo Indians clung even more tenaciously to their heritage, which by now included elements of the once-hated Spanish culture and religion. By the 1880s, railroads had largely put an end to the traditional geographical isolation of the pueblos. Paradoxically, the U.S. decision to recognize Spanish land grants to the Pueblos denied Pueblo Indians certain rights granted under official treaties and left them particularly open to exploitation by squatters and thieves.

After a gap of over 300 years, the All Indian Pueblo Council began to meet again in the 1920s, specifically in response to a congressional threat to appropriate Pueblo lands. Partly as a result of the Council's activities, Congress confirmed Pueblo title to their lands in 1924 by passing the Pueblo Lands Act. The United States also acknowledged its trust responsibilities in a series of legal decisions and other acts of Congress. Still, especially after 1900, Pueblo culture was increasingly threatened by Protestant evangelical missions and schools. The Bureau of Indian Affairs also weighed in on the subject of acculturation, forcing Indian children to leave their homes and attend culture-killing boarding schools.

Until World War II, however, much of Zia's traditional life remained substantially unchanged. Almost all Zians lived on the pueblo, and all adult members participated in community events. Herding dominated the economy in the mid–twentieth century, although there was a shift from sheep to cattle. Since the late nineteenth century, but especially after the 1960s, Pueblos have had to cope with onslaughts by (mostly white) anthropologists and seekers of Indian spirituality. The region is also known for its major art colonies at Taos and Santa Fe.

RELIGION   In traditional Pueblo culture, religion and life are inseparable. To be in harmony with all of nature is the Pueblo ideal and way of life. The sun is seen as the representative of the Creator. Sacred mountains in each direction, plus the sun above and the earth below, define and balance the Pueblo world. Many Pueblo religious ceremonies revolve around the weather and are devoted to ensuring adequate rainfall. To this end, Pueblo Indians evoke the power of katsinas, sacred beings who live in mountains and other holy places, in ritual and dance. Zia Pueblo contained two circular kivas on its south side, religious chambers that symbolize the place of original emergence into this world. The kiva societies were Wren and Turquoise.

In addition to the natural boundaries, Pueblo Indians have created a society that defines their world by providing balanced, reciprocal relationships within which people connect and harmonize with each other, the natural world, and time itself. According to tradition, the head of each pueblo is the religious leader, or cacique, whose primary responsibility it is to watch the sun and thereby determine the dates of ceremonies. Religious societies were central to the Pueblo's social structure; they helped to ensure the fertility of crops and people, triumph over evil, success in hunting, physical and spiritual curing, and good relations between the living and their dead ancestors. Shamans also used supernatural powers for curing, weather control, and ensuring the general welfare. Especially in the eastern pueblos, most ceremonies are kept secret.

GOVERNMENT   Pueblo governments derived from two traditions. Elements that are probably indigenous include the cacique, or head of the Pueblo, and the war chiefs. These officials were intimately related to the religious structures of the pueblo and reflected the essentially theocratic nature of Pueblo government. The tiyamunyi were the supreme priests of Zia from legendary times until about 1900. Since then, proper installation rituals have been forgotten, and this office has been replaced by the former first assistant, who is now called cacique. Freed from other work, he mostly meditates and invests annual officers.

A parallel but in most cases distinctly less powerful group of officials was imposed by the Spanish authorities. Appointed annually by the traditional leadership, they generally dealt with external and church matters and included the governor, lieutenant governor, captains, and fiscales (church officials). There was also an advisory council of principales, composed of former officeholders. In 1863, President Lincoln presented Pueblo leaders with ebony canes, which were then used with the older Spanish canes as symbols of authority. The All Indian Pueblo Council, dating from 1598, began meeting again in the twentieth century to assert rights and help solve problems.

CUSTOMS   One mechanism that works to keep Pueblo societies coherent is a pervasive aversion to individualistic behavior. Children were raised with gentle guidance and a minimum of discipline. Pueblo Indians were generally monogamous, and divorce was relatively rare. The dead were prepared ceremonially and quickly buried with clothes, beads, food, and other items; their possessions were destroyed, and they were said to become katsinas in the land of the dead. A vigil of four days and nights was generally observed. Matrilineal clans existed but were not linked to memberships in kiva or religious societies. Various other groups acted to hold the pueblo together, including medicine and other religious societies. In modern times photography by outsiders is discouraged.

DWELLINGS   In the sixteenth century, Zia Pueblo featured two- to three-story, apartment-style dwellings arranged around eight plazas. The buildings were constructed of adobe (earth and straw) bricks, with beams across the roof that were covered with poles, brush, and plaster. Floors were of wood plank or packed earth. The roof of one level served as the floor of another. The levels were interconnected by ladders. As an aid to defense, the traditional design included no doors or windows; entry was through the roof. Two pit houses, or kivas, served as ceremonial chambers and clubhouses. The village plazas, around which all dwellings were clustered, was the spiritual center of the village where all the balanced forces of the world came together.

DIET   Before the Spanish arrived, Zians ate primarily corn, beans, and pumpkins, using the flood-waters of the Jemez River as both irrigation and fertil-izer. They also grew sunflowers and tobacco. They hunted deer, mountain lion, bear, antelope, and rab-bits. They gathered a variety of wild seeds, nuts, berries, and other foods. The Spanish introduced wheat, alfalfa, sheep, cattle, and garden vegetables, which soon became part of the regular diet.

KEY TECHNOLOGY Precontact farming imple-ments were wooden. Textiles were woven of cotton. Other items included baskets, pottery, and leather goods. The Spanish introduced metal tools and equipment.

TRADE All Pueblos were part of extensive abo-riginal trading networks. With the arrival of other cultures, Pueblo Indians also traded with the His-panic American villages and then U.S. traders. At fixed times during summer or fall, enemies declared truces so that trading fairs might be held. The largest and best known was at Taos with the Comanche. Nomads exchanged slaves, buffalo hides, buckskins, jerked meat, and horses for agricultural and manu-factured pueblo products. Zians traded for numerous daily and ceremonial items, including drums, tortoise rattles, buffalo robes, abalone shell jewelry, bows, arrows, quivers, pottery, and blankets. Trade along the Santa Fe Trail began in 1821. By the 1880s and the arrival of railroads, the Pueblos were dependent on many American-made goods, and the Native Ameri-can manufacture of weaving and pottery declined and nearly died out.

NOTABLE ARTS In the Pueblo way, art and life are inseparable. Zia arts included pottery, baskets, and wooden masks. Songs, dances, and dramas are other traditional arts. Many Pueblos experienced a renais-sance of traditional arts in the twentieth century, beginning in 1919 with San Ildefonso pottery.

TRANSPORTATION Spanish horses, mules, and cattle arrived at Zia Pueblo in the seventeenth cen-tury.

DRESS Men wore cotton kilts and leather san-dals. Women wore cotton dresses and sandals or high moccasin boots. Deer and rabbit skin were also used for clothing and robes, and sandals were made of yucca.

WAR AND WEAPONS Though often depicted as passive and docile, most Pueblo groups regularly engaged in warfare. The great revolt of 1680 stands out as the major military action, but they also skir-mished at other times with the Spanish and defended themselves against attackers such as Apaches, Comanches, and Utes. They also contributed auxil-iary soldiers to provincial forces under Spain and Mexico, which were used mainly against raiding Indi-ans and to protect merchant caravans on the Santa Fe

Trail. According to tradition, a Zian who touched a dead enemy or anything that belonged to him was required to scalp the corpse and bring the scalp back for purification; he then joined the warriors' society. After the raiding tribes began to pose less of a threat in the late nineteenth century, Pueblo military soci-eties began to wither away, with the office of war cap-tain changing to civil and religious functions.

Contemporary Information

GOVERNMENT/RESERVATIONS Zia Pueblo occu-pies roughly 121,080 tribally owned acres. There are two all-male tribal councils: one concerned with sec-ular matters, the other the more important and secret religious council. There is also an administrative staff.

ECONOMY With wage jobs, sheep and cattle rais-ing is the most important economic activity. Stock raising is conducted by cattle and sheep groups based on clan membership. Many people work in sur-rounding cities. Arts and crafts, especially wool kilts (men) and pottery (women) occupy an important economic niche. Agriculture is served by modern irri-gation systems. Major crops include corn, wheat, alfalfa, oats, beans, chilies, melons, and fruits. Most produce is sold on the open market. The Pueblo con-tains geothermal, natural gas, and oil resources.

LEGAL STATUS Zia Pueblo is a federally recog-nized tribal entity.

DAILY LIFE The project of retaining a strong Indian identity is a difficult one in the late twentieth century, yet Pueblo people have deep roots, and in many ways the ancient rhythms and patterns con-tinue. At Zia, men must still participate in the dances, take care of the *cacique*'s field and food needs, sweep the village plaza, and clean and repair the irrigation ditches. Many Zia people still speak Keresan.

The older Pueblo now has ground-level entries and glass windows, and most homes have electricity and running water. Floors are of packed earth under linoleum. Interior walls are whitewashed. Each household owns a beehive oven. The seventeenth-century mission church is still standing. Modern houses have also been built along and across the river. As of the mid-1990s, a new village located to the east was under construction.

Zia religion and ceremonial and social structure are largely intact, though since World War II Zia has been marked by relatively increased social break-down, with fewer people belonging to religious soci-eties. The governor's power has grown at the expense of the *cacique*'s. Increasing numbers of Zians live off-reservation. Some of the traditional societies, like the katsina, hunters, and warrior societies, now exist much devoid of their former knowledge.

The household is now the primary economic and

social unit. Six modern clans still exist. Many Zians have fused pieces of Catholicism onto a core of traditional beliefs. They distinguish between Indian and Catholic marriages: The former are formed through cohabitation and are easily dissolved, whereas the latter go through the Church and are difficult to dissolve. There has been a written form of the Zia dialect of Keresan since 1990. Facilities include a community building, museum and cultural center, clinic, gymnasium, and offices.

Zuñi

Zuñi (`Z ū n y ē or `Z ū n ē), from the Spanish, is the name of both a people and a pueblo. This Pueblo's original name was *Ashiwi,* which might have meant "the flesh."

LOCATION   Zuñi consisted of six pueblos along the north bank of the upper Zuni River, in western New Mexico, at least 800 years ago. It is presently in the same location.

POPULATION   In 1990, 7,073 Indians lived at Zuñi. Perhaps as many as 20,000 lived there in 1500.

LANGUAGE   Zuni is a language unlike that spoken at other pueblos. Scientists speculate as to a possible link to the Penutian language family.

Historical Information

HISTORY   Zuñis and their ancestors, the Mogollon and the Anasazi, and perhaps Mexican Indians as well have lived in the Southwest for well over 2,000 years. By the eleventh century, the "village of the great kiva," near Zuñi, had been built. In the fourteenth and fifteenth centuries a large number of villages existed in the Zuni Valley. By 1650 the number of Zuñi villages had shrunk to six.

Zuñi was probably the first native North American village visited by Spaniards, who had heard tales of great wealth in the "Kingdom of Cibola." In 1539, Estavinico, a black man in the advance guard of Fray Marcos de Niza's party, visited Zuñi. He was killed as a spy, and his group quickly retreated. The following year, Francisco Vasquez de Coronado visited the pueblos, ranging all the way to present-day Kansas in search of the mythical Cibola. The Zuñis resisted his demands and fled to a nearby mesa top. Other Spanish came in Coronado's wake. The first mission was established at Hawikuh in 1629. In 1632, Zuñis attacked and killed a number of missionaries, but the Spanish built a new mission, Halona, in 1643.

Zuñi participated in the Pueblo revolt of 1680. Their main grievances were being forced to supply the Spanish with corn, women, and labor and being punished harshly for practicing their religion. At that time the Zuñis lived in three of the original six pueblos. They fled to escape the Spanish, and in 1693

returned to the village at Halona on the Zuni River. A new church was built there, but shortly abandoned, the Zuñis preferring their own religion to Christianity. The ancient site of Halona is now modern Zuñi.

Left on their own by the Spanish, Zuñi was open to raids from Apaches, Navajos, and Plains tribes. Zuñi was still self-sufficient as of 1850, although it was on important trade routes and was increasingly raided by both Indians and Anglos. The U.S. government officially recognized a Zuñi reservation in 1877, although one far too small to support traditional agriculture. Three outlying summer villages established in the early nineteenth century became permanent in the 1880s, and a fourth such village was established in 1912 or 1914. In the late nineteenth and early twentieth centuries the Zuñi economy shifted from agriculture to sheep and cattle herding. With the decline of warfare, their Bow society turned to warfare against supposed Zuñi witches. The Bureau of Indian Affairs soon called in troops to suppress witchcraft trials, destroying the power of the Bow priests and the entire traditional government.

The opposition of tribal members as well as the failure of the government's Black Rock Reservation and Dam combined to block implementation of the allotment process at Zuñi. Erosion of arable land has been a considerable problem, especially since the debacle of counterproductive, government-mandated canal irrigation projects in the early twentieth century. By the 1930s, the government was promoting livestock as an alternative to agriculture. After World War II, the continuing shift in political power from priests to politicians led to the growth of political parties and the increased importance of the tribal council.

RELIGION   Religion, including membership in religious and ceremonial organizations, was at the core of Zuñi existence. The sun priest was highly revered: In charge of solstice ceremonies as well as the calendar, he was held responsible for the community's welfare. The Zuñi recognized six points of orientation, which corresponded to the cardinal directions as well as mythological events. Each had its own color, position, kiva group, medicine societies and priesthoods, and ceremonies. Kivas were rectangular and above ground.

Katsinas, or benevolent guardian spirits, played a key part in Zuñi religion. Katsinas represented the rain gods as well as Zuñi ancestors. All boys between the ages of 11 and 14 underwent initiation into the katsina cult. At death, one was said to join the katsinas, especially if one was closely associated with the cult. Both men and women could join the curing cult of the beast gods. Its focus was animals of prey who lived in the east.

The Zuñi new year began at the winter solstice. A 20-day period during this time was known as *Itiwana,* or cleansing and preparing the village for the new year. Winter dances took place from February through April. Summer dances began at the solstice and lasted into September, concluding with the fertility ritual called *Olowishkia.* In late November or early December the Zuñis celebrated *Shalako,* a reenactment by katsina priests of the creation and migration of the Zuñi people. The people built six to eight Shalako houses and attended the Shalako katsinas—giant-sized messengers of the rain gods. This festival was accompanied by spectacular dancing and closed the Zuñi year. *Molawai,* or the ritual dramatization of the loss and recovery of corn maidens, immediately followed Shalako.

GOVERNMENT   Ruled by heads of various priesthoods and societies, Zuñi was a theocracy. Bow priests enforced the rules from at least the seventeenth century on. A tribal council played a minor role in the nineteenth century but a more powerful one in the twentieth century. Zuñi accepted the Indian Reorganization Act (IRA) and an elected tribal council in 1934 (they ratified a constitution in 1970).

During the eighteenth century, a parallel, secular government developed at Zuñi to handle mundane problems. Based on the Spanish model, it was appointed by and responsible to the religious leaders. Offices included a governor, two lieutenant governors, a sheriff, and *fiscales* (church assistants). These officers acted as liaisons between the pueblo and the outside world and kept order within the pueblo. Metal-topped canes with a Spanish cross served as symbols of authority. Through the years, these were augmented by more Spanish canes, Mexican canes, and then canes given by President Lincoln to reward the pueblo for its neutrality in the Civil War.

CUSTOMS   Zuñi was divided into two groups, people of the north (also characterized as winter or rain) and people of the south (also characterized as summer or sun). Matrilineal clans affected ceremonial roles and certain behaviors. In general, however, ritual activity went through the father's family, and economic activity went through the mother's. There were also a number of secret cults and societies, some highly complex, each responsible for certain ceremonies. Zuñis traditionally cremated their dead. In modern times the dead are buried, with their possessions burned or buried after four days, following a ceremony that includes prayer sticks and cornmeal. With the exception of certain clan and family taboos, marriage was a matter between the two people involved and was traditionally preceded by a trial period of cohabitation. Divorce was simple and easy.

DWELLINGS   Like other Pueblo Indians, Zuñis lived in multistoried houses (pueblos). Men built the structures of stone and plaster, not the adobe bricks used in the pueblos to the east. Ladders led to the upper stories. Floors were of packed adobe and roofs of willow boughs, brush, and packed earth. Women kept the outsides whitewashed. Tiny windows and outside beehive ovens were introduced in the sixteenth century.

DIET   Farming was the chief Zuñi mode of subsistence. Men grew at least six varieties of corn plus beans, squash, and cotton. The Spanish introduced crops such as wheat, chilies, oats, and peaches. Zuñis used dams and sage windbreaks for irrigation. Corn was dried, ground into flour or meal, and served as mush or baked into breads. Food was also obtained by hunting (deer, antelope, and rabbits), fishing, and gathering wild plants (women were the gatherers, and they also kept small garden plots).

KEY TECHNOLOGY   Zuñis used dams and sage windbreaks for irrigation.

TRADE   The Zuñi traded in pottery, baskets, textiles, and shell and turquoise ornaments, among other items.

NOTABLE ARTS   Traditional arts included pottery, weaving, and basketry (of willow and yucca leaves). In the 1830s they added brass and copper jewelry, which was in turn replaced around 1870 by silver (a skill learned from the Navajo). The Zuñi began using turquoise around 1890.

TRANSPORTATION   Women made baskets to transport goods.

DRESS   Men wove cotton into ceremonial costumes and clothing. Women wore one-piece black cotton dresses, belted at the waist. Both wore moccasins and deerskin leggings.

WAR AND WEAPONS   Zuñis who killed an enemy could join the Bow priesthood, which served as an important part of the religious hierarchy. The warrior society has deteriorated in recent years.

Contemporary Information

GOVERNMENT/RESERVATIONS   Zuñi is located at the ancient site of the old village of Halona, in McKinley and Valencia Counties, New Mexico. A continuation of the 1689 Spanish land grant, the main reservation was established in 1877. Three other tracts were added later. Despite the return of their most sacred site, Katsina Village, in 1984, the reservation's 636 square miles is less than 3 percent of the tribe's original holdings. Most tribal members live on the reservation.

Zuñis elect their own governors and tribal councils, yet the religious leaders remain powerful. Tribal officers' terms begin during the first week of January and last for two years. Since 1970 the Zuñis have controlled their own reservation.

ECONOMY   The most important economic activities on Zuñi Pueblo are tribal employment and silver and turquoise jewelry manufacture, begun in earnest in the 1920s. People also make pottery, weavings, and baskets. Some Zuñis still farm and raise livestock, although by 1900 the tribe had lost 80 percent of its land base to Anglo settlers. Zuñi Cultural Resources Enterprise provides local archaeological services, and several individuals have established small businesses. There is also work off-reservation, particularly in Gallup, the nearest city. The tribe received $50 million in land claims settlements in 1990. Various water rights cases remain ongoing, as does planning for economic development.

LEGAL STATUS   Zuñi Pueblo is a federally recognized tribal entity.

DAILY LIFE   Most Zuñis live in the old pueblo, which has been rebuilt as single-story houses. There are also almost 1,000 houses in nearby settlements. Modern and traditional associations, such as the Lions Club, American Legion, clans, kiva groups, priesthoods and medicine societies, school boards, and cattle, farm, and irrigation associations all coexist at Zuñi. The result is a modern but close and cohesive community in which heritage remains vital. Much of the traditional religion, customs, social structure, and language remains intact.

Radio stations broadcast programs in Zuñi. Zuñis control their educational system (they received a school district in 1980), in which native language and culture figures prominently. The tribe also provides basic social services. Shalako, celebrating in late fall the connections between modern Zuñis and the spirits of their ancestors, remains a major ceremony. Races are still held between clans and ceremonial groups. An arts and crafts fair is held in mid-May.

CHAPTER TWO

California

California

California," in the context of this chapter, corresponds approximately to the present state of California. It omits the southeastern deserts because the Indian cultures of those deserts are usually considered part of the Southwest. Nor does it cover the region east of the Sierra Nevada (Great Basin), the extreme northeast of the state (Plateau), or Baja California (Mexico). The region contains two great mountain ranges, the Coastal and the Sierra Nevada; two major rivers, the Sacramento and the San Joaquin, and many minor river systems; roughly 1,100 miles of coast; interior semidesert; and, at least before the nineteenth century, huge areas of grassland in the central valleys. Much of California's climate may be categorized as Mediterranean, with the north, west, and highlands in general receiving more precipitation than the south, east, and lowlands.

Today's references to pre-twentieth-century "tribes," such as "Pomo" or "Cahuilla," are nothing more than contemporary conventions. Few, if any, of the roughly 300,000 California Indians (eighteenth century) were organized into true tribes. Instead, the most common form of political organization and the largest autonomous group was the tribelet, or cluster of satellite villages around one or more permanent villages. Perhaps 500 of these groups existed in aboriginal California. Tribelets shared a language, culture, and history. Each contained from some 50 to 500 people. They were often presided over by a headman, or chief, who controlled economic resources and activity. Chiefs were generally very wealthy and greatly respected. Different tribelets were occasionally named and even spoke varying dialects. Members of a tribelet were often related through the male line. Tribelets in northwestern California were, as a rule, less cohesive than in other parts of the region.

With perhaps the highest pre-Columbian population density north of Mexico, California Indians spoke over 300 different dialects of some 100 lan-

guages. The three main language families were the Hokan (from the Great Plains), Penutian (possibly from British Colombia and/or the Yucatan), and Uto-Aztecan (from the Southwest). Algonquian (eastern North America), Athapaskan (from Canada), and Yukian (origin unknown) languages were also spoken in California.

Though in many ways quite diverse, California Indians tended to share a number of cultural similarities. Foremost among these perhaps was a dependence on acorns as a staple food. Others included the use of shamans as religious leaders and doctors, especially doctors who cure by sucking; political organization by tribelet; an emphasis on individual wealth and private property; a reliance on such foods as fish, deer, elk, antelope, buckeye, sage seed, and epos root in addition to the primary food of acorns; the manufacture of numerous types of finely crafted baskets; and the use of datura in religious or rite-of-passage ceremonies. Many California people were subjected to strong mission influences in the eighteenth and nineteenth centuries.

In general, although California Indians suffered terribly from contact with the Spanish, they fared even worse at the hands of non-natives around the time of the gold rush and after. The population of Native Americans in the region fell by more than 90 percent, from upward of 200,000 in the mid–nineteenth century to roughly 15,000, within the span of a generation or two. Today, the descendants of these people, still in the process of regrouping, are fashioning renewed lives and identities as Indians of California.

California being relatively isolated geographically, its original occupation by people was probably not the result of mass migrations of major cultures but rather the slow trickling in of a number of small groups over a long period of time. Archaeologists have determined that people were present in some parts of California at least 19,000 years ago. Some believe that human occupation goes back 50,000 years. About 9000 B.C.E., native peoples began the transition from an economy based mainly on hunting to one that also depended heavily on seed collecting. By about 2000 B.C.E., people had adjusted to local environments to the point that they had evolved several different subsistence patterns.

During the hunting period, people probably used darts powered by throwing sticks to bring down ancient species of camel, bison, and horse as well as several species of big game that still exist. They also hunted smaller mammals and fowl, fished, and ate some shellfish and plant food. They lived in open-air dwellings, although they may also have used caves for shelter. The transition to seed collecting took place between roughly 6000 and 3000 B.C.E., particularly along the south coast. In some areas the changeover evolved directly from the hunting economy, whereas in others it seems to have been a function of the westward migration of interior seed-gathering peoples. Milling stones served as the gatherers' primary tool. During this time, settlements seem to have increased in both size and stability.

After about 3000 B.C.E., Native Americans in California began to show a more pronounced economic and cultural diversity in response to fine-tuned regional and local adaptations. In general, a variety of subsistence strategies was practiced, with one predominating. Tools became more varied, numerous, and well made. At this time, the Windmiller culture flourished in the lower Sacramento Valley. Those people were accomplished artists and craftspeople, having made a number of stone, bone, and wooden tools as well as beads from shells acquired in trade from coastal tribes. They also made pottery, twined baskets, and, most notably, finely crafted charmstones, the exact purpose of which is unclear. The dead were buried prone, with faces down and oriented toward the west. They were decorated with shells and pendants and accompanied by a variety of goods.

Regional and local diversification was sufficiently advanced that by roughly 500 C.E., and in some cases much earlier, the basic patterns and customs of many historical peoples had been established. Population shifts and, in general, increases in village size and complexity also continued during this time, as people continued to take better advantage of food resources. As already mentioned, most California Indians depended on the acorn as a staple food. Acorns were collected on special autumn expeditions organized specifically for this purpose. After removing the kernels from the shell, sun drying them and pounding them into flour, Indian women leached out the bitter tannic acid by a variety of methods, most commonly

by repeatedly pouring hot water over the flour. The meal was then boiled into soup or mush or baked into bread. Other common foods, which of course varied depending on the availability of resources, included big game such as deer, elk, antelope, and bear; fish such as salmon and trout; smaller mammals; a huge diversity of seeds, nuts, berries, roots, bulbs, tubers, and greens; insects and their larvae; waterfowl; sea mammals; shellfish and mollusks. The only cultivated crop was tobacco.

From as early as 1000 B.C.E., many California Indian groups created rock art. Most such art was probably made for ceremonial purposes, such as hunting or puberty rituals. Indians either carved or pecked the rock face (petroglyphs) or painted it (pictographs) to make their drawings. Most designs featured geometric patterns such as crosses, stars, wheels, triangles, and dots as well as stylized representations of people and animals.

Trade was well developed in California. Most trade occurred between close neighbors, although long-distance trading was not uncommon either, as an extensive and continuous trail system crisscrossed the entire region. Items were either bartered or purchased with money such as dentalium shells, clamshell disk beads, and magnesite beads. Among the chief items traded were foods, especially salt, acorns, and fish; shell beads; baskets; hides and pelts; obsidian; and bows. Trading generally took place either as part of friendly visits or on ceremonial occasions.

Organized warfare was rare among California Indians. Reasons for conflict ranged from physical offenses such as murder and rape to trespass and sorcery to simple insult. Surprise attacks were often the preferred method of fighting; in any case, pitched battles were generally avoided, and casualties remained low. Armed conflict was generally resolved after a brief period of fighting, with the headmen of each party forming a peace commission to work out the details. Most groups agreed to compensate the other for all damages incurred, such as loss of life and property.

Ceremonialism played an important role in the lives of most California Indians. For most groups, shamans were the religious leaders as well as the curers, obtaining their powers through intercourse with supernatural spirits. Some peoples had secret religious societies, such as those associated with the Kuksu cult. This cult involved a lengthy and complex instructional period and, by referencing and impersonating supernatural spirits, symbolically restored the group to an original, perfect state. Other groups celebrated a World Renewal cycle of ceremonies, an elaboration of first salmon rituals that provided an opportunity to relate history and mythology and to display wealth.

Most groups practiced well-defined rituals centered around life-cycle events such as puberty and death. Other ceremonial occasions were related to subsistence. Shamanic preparation as well as certain initiation rites or ceremonies frequently included the use of psychotropic drugs such as datura (jimsonweed or toloache) to assist in the attainment of visions. Tobacco was also an important part of most rituals. Music and dance were an integral part of most ceremonies. Catholicism arrived by force with the Spanish. Most peoples were influenced by the Ghost Dances of the 1870s.

Marriage generally took place when the couple was recently postpubescent. Northern California Indians observed a relatively rigid and closed class system, based on wealth and perpetuated by marriage (including the bride price) and custom: People were either elite, common, or poor. Some groups also kept slaves. Chiefs and shamans often had more than one wife, as could any wealthy man. Occupational specialists included craftspeople as well as minor officials such as assistant chief, messenger, and dance manager. Games such as hoop-and-pole, the hand game, cat's cradle, shinny (a form of lacrosse), dice, and athletic contests, as well as music and dancing, were almost universal.

Indians across California first encountered nonnatives at widely different times. Along the southern and central coast, Indians met Spanish and English explorers, for example, as early as the mid–sixteenth century. In some of the interior hills and valleys, face-to-face contact occurred as late as the early to mid–nineteenth century, and in some more remote desert and mountain locations not until the early twentieth century, although indirect contact had been established for some time previously in the form of trade items, diffused customs, and disease. Radical change due to contact with non-natives began in the south and central coastal regions with the establishment of the first missions and in the north and interior with the gold- and/or land-induced invasion of Indian territory.

The long-term presence of the Spanish, beginning in 1769 with the founding of a presidio and Franciscan mission in San Diego, had a profound effect on California. Immediate ramifications were of two kinds. Habitat change occurred when European grasses and weeds replaced the original seed-food grasses; overgrazing accelerated erosion and diminished the amount of available surface water; and the amount of much wild game and marine food was reduced. Direct personal change occurred when large numbers of Indians were forcibly transported and confined to Spanish missions from San Diego to San Francisco. There, disease, torture, overwork, and malnourishment, combined with a policy of cultural genocide, both drastically reduced Indian populations and destroyed many cultures. Indians resisted both actively, through occasional armed revolts, and passively, mainly by escaping into the interior, where they introduced horses, firearms, and other elements of Spanish culture. Indians in southern and central California who remained outside of mission life were generally able to adopt resistance strategies and gradually adapt their lives to the new influences.

The missions came under Mexican control in 1834 and were secularized shortly thereafter. The original intention had been to divide mission lands and wealth between the new administrators and the Indians; in practice, the former kept it all for themselves. Many mission Indians worked on the new ranchos (estates), living lives little different from those in the missions. Others drifted into lives of poverty and misery in the white settlements. Some who still had aboriginal homes returned to them, resuming traditional lives as much as possible in the face of cultural dislocation and regular attacks from Mexican colonists. Many Indian groups, particularly in the Sacramento Valley, abandoned their once-peaceful ways and turned to raiding and guerrilla warfare to protect themselves. Some Indians also fought with the Yankees in the Mexican War.

Further dislocations occurred as the United States took possession of California. The 1848 Treaty of Guadalupe Hidalgo had no provisions protecting Indian land title. Many Indian peoples living in the regions of the mines as well as desirable farmlands in central and northern California were overwhelmed by the crunch of non-native immigrants and were all but exterminated. After 1850, many Indians living in interior California lost their lives to starvation and unchecked—in fact, government-subsidized—massacres. Vigilantes and other criminals kidnapped more than 10,000 Indian men, women, and children and sold them for use as virtual slaves. Furthermore, disease, in part caused by lowered resistance due to hunger and ill-treatment, probably surpassed kidnapping and murder as a cause of village abandonment. In 1833 a major malaria epidemic struck Indian populations. Later smallpox and venereal and other diseases took a huge toll.

In the early 1850s, U.S. treaty commissioners met with 400 or so chiefs and headmen, representing between one-third and one-half of California Indians. At that time several Indian groups signed 18 treaties, but the state of California, asserting its "state's rights" and preferring Indian extinction to a negotiated settlement, pressured the U.S. government not to ratify them. The United States did establish several reservations in the 1850s; however, since federal aid was siphoned off by corrupt bureaucrats, and massacres, kidnappings, and land theft continued even on the reservations themselves, most were abandoned in the following decade. Most California Indians were never restricted to reservations but were left to fend for themselves, their land taken and most of their people destroyed.

In the 1870s, federal administration of Indian affairs in the state was placed under the control of churches, which promptly moved to suppress all traditional religious practices. The United States began granting reservations to so-called Mission Indians in 1875. Throughout the last half of the nineteenth century, Indians struggled to support themselves through farming, raising livestock, and subsistence and ruthlessly exploitative wage labor while receiving few or no government services. This pattern continued well into the twentieth century. At the same time, Indians continued to resist government policies such as the abduction and forced settlement of their children at boarding schools and the breaking up of their reservations under the provisions of the hated Dawes Act (1886), all aimed at detribalization and forced assimilation. Although Indian resistance was partially successful, Anglo pressure was inexorable, and the old ways and knowledge declined steadily during the twentieth century.

Following World War II, government "termination" policies favored ending all services to California Indians, a move that resulted in plunging economic and quality-of-life indicators on the remaining reservations and rancherias. In the 1960s, federal housing, health, education, and training programs and a changing political climate combined to provide an environment within which California Indians began to take greater control over their lives. They created new political organizations to meet the new situations. Eventually, interreservation organizations proliferated to meet the needs of Indians.

Cultural change accompanied political and economic change. The establishment of several museums and language classes reflected a growing interest in native cultures. Increasing Indian interest in and control over their own education resulted in greater Indian participation in the educational process at all levels. Indian morale slowly rebounded. The Native American Historical Society led an effort to replace negative stereotypes in school texts; this organization also created a publishing house and a newspaper, *Wassaja*. Still, in the 1970s, most Indians lived with appalling housing conditions and few job opportunities and were continuing to lose their land base as a result primarily of tax and other government policies.

Today, people once thought to be extinct are in fact still very much present. Many Indian peoples have survived as recognizable, continuous entities. There is much lost ground to be recovered, yet California Indians are tackling the issues of identity, housing, and land within a context of renewed self-determination and pride as well as sophisticated political organizing, economic planning, and communication skills.

Achumawi

Achumawi (Ä ch ū ˋmä w ē , or Ä j ū ˋmä w ē), "River People." Also known, occasionally with the Atsugewi, as Pit River Indians, from their practice of hunting deer by means of pitfalls. These people were organized into 11 bands and shared several cultural characteristics of Indians of the Great Basin.

LOCATION   The Achumawi traditionally lived in the northeastern part of the region, from Mount Shasta and Lassen Peak to the Warner Range. This area of tremendous ecological diversity yielded a huge variety of foods, medicines, and raw materials. In the 1990s, Pit River Indians live on their own or shared reservations and rancherias, plus Pit River trust lands, in Modoc, Shasta, Mendocino, Lassen, and Lake Counties, California (see "Government/Reservations" under "Contemporary Information").

POPULATION   Roughly 3,000 Achumawi lived in California in the mid–nineteenth century. In 1990, 75 Pit River Indians lived on eight rancherias and the Pit River trust lands. Pit River Indians also lived on four reservations with other tribes. Tribal enrollment in the early 1990s was 1,350.

LANGUAGE   With the Atsugewi, their language made up the Palaihnihan Branch of the Hokan language family.

Historical Information

HISTORY   Trappers entering Achumawi territory in 1828 made little impact. However, the flood of non-natives after the gold rush provoked Achumawi resistance, which was brutally repressed by state and private militias as well as extralegal vigilantes. By the end of the century, several hundred Achumawis had been forced onto the Round Valley Reservation. Some remained in their traditional lands, however. Their acquisition of individual allotments after 1897 helped them to retain their band ties and some subsistence activities.

Most of these allotments were lost in the early twentieth century to Pacific Gas and Electric. Major health problems plagued the Achumawi Indians in the 1920s. Seven small rancherias were created between 1915 and 1938. In 1938, some Achumawi families settled on the 9,000-acre XL Ranch. As late as the 1950s, the Achumawi still retained much of their ancient knowledge and carried on a form of their aboriginal existence. It was mostly younger people who began a new activism in the 1960s, focused on the issues of sovereignty and land usurpation. The Pit River Tribe received federal recognition in 1976.

RELIGION By means of vision quests, boys might attract a spirit guide, or supernatural power. Girls acquired their connection to the spirit world through ceremony. This power could strongly influence the quality of daily activities such as hunting, fighting, gambling, or shamanic responsibilities. However, supernatural power could depart at any time for any or no reason.

Shamans, or doctors, provided medical care as well as religious leadership. In fact, the two were closely related. A shaman's power, or medicine, which could be held by man or woman, was similar to the spirit guide, only more powerful. Shamans often used medicinal plants and wild tobacco, curing with the explicit aid of their spirit power. The Achumawi recognized four types of maladies: visible accidents, "bad blood," poisoning by another shaman, or soul-loss (connected with another's death).

GOVERNMENT The Achumawi people were composed of about nine tribelets. Though autonomous, each was connected by language, culture, and intermarriage. Chiefs were chosen on the basis of popularity, ability, and possession of supernatural powers.

CUSTOMS At puberty, boys usually went to mountain retreats in search of a spirit vision that would bestow supernatural powers. They also had their noses pierced. On the occasion of their first menstrual period, girls sang, danced, and feasted with the community all night for ten days. This activity was repeated for nine days on the second month, eight on the third, and so on until the tenth month, when they were considered women.

Corpses were cremated and all their former possessions burned. Mourners cut their hair, darkened their faces with pitch, and refrained from speaking the name of the dead. The soul was said to head for the western mountains. When a chief died, two or three less-liked members of the tribe were sometimes killed to provide the chief with traveling companions.

When within earshot, people were generally addressed by their kin terms, not by their names. Gifts exchanged at marriage were regarded as a price for both spouses. If a married person died, the surviving spouse could still be obligated to marry another suitable person in that family. As with many North American Indians, the Achumawi played the hand game, as well as shinny, wrestling, and footraces.

DWELLINGS Conical three-season houses were made of tule mats over a light pole framework. Wood-frame winter houses were built partly underground and covered with grass, bark, or tule and a layer of earth. Both were entered by means of a ladder through the smoke hole.

DIET The environmentally diverse Achumawi territory, which ranged from mountains to lowland swamps, contained a great variety of foods. The Achumawi regularly burned the fir and pine uplands, meadows, and grasslands in order to augment this richness. The fires stimulated the growth of seed and berry plants, made insects available for collecting, and drove game into accessible areas.

Food staples included fish, such as salmon, trout, bass, pike, and catfish; crawfish; and mussels. Waterfowl were caught with nets, and the people ate the eggs as well. Other important foods included acorns, tule sprouts, various seeds, berries, roots and bulbs, and insects and their larvae. Game included deer, antelope, bear, beaver, badger, coyote, and a variety of small mammals.

KEY TECHNOLOGY Bow wood was either juniper or yew. Most points and blades were made from obsidian. Other building materials included bone and stone, including antler. Baskets were made for a number of purposes, including fish traps. The Achumawi made five kinds of tule or milkweed nets, including dip, gill, seine, and waterfowl. Tule was used for many other products, including mats, twine, shoes, and rafts. Fire drills were made of juniper. Sometimes the people used a cedar rope as a slow-burning match. They also made juniper snowshoes.

TRADE Achumawis had regular and friendly contact with the Atsugewi, who could speak their language. They traded occasionally with the Shasta, Yana, and Paiute.

NOTABLE ARTS Achumawi women made fine flexible twined baskets of grasses and willow, decorated with vegetable dye designs. Beginning about 1000 B.C.E., the people also made petroglyphs, or rock carvings, that were related to hunting large game.

TRANSPORTATION For river travel, the Achumawi used both tule fiber balsa rafts and juniper and pine dugout canoes.

DRESS Clothing included shirts, skirts, belts, caps, capes, robes, leggings, moccasins, and dresses. Clothing was made primarily of deer, badger, coyote, and antelope skin and shredded juniper bark. Colored minerals were used to decorate both objects and people.

WAR AND WEAPONS The slave-raiding Modocs were a traditional enemy. Instead of retaliating in kind, the Achumawi usually hid out until the raiders went away. Weapons included elk hide armor and shields and arrows poisoned with rattlesnake venom.

Contemporary Information

GOVERNMENT/RESERVATIONS Achomawi/Pit River reservations include: Alturas Rancheria (1906; 20 acres; Modoc County); Big Bend Rancheria (1916; 40 acres); Big Valley Rancheria (Pomo and Pit River; Lake County); Likely Rancheria (1922; 1.32 acres); Lookout Rancheria (1913; 40 acres; Modoc County); Montgomery Creek Rancheria (1915; 72 acres; Shasta County); Redding Rancheria (31 acres; 79 Indians in 1990; Shasta County); Roaring Creek Rancheria (1915; 80 acres; Shasta County); Round Valley Reservation (1864; 30,538 acres; 577 Indians in 1990, Mendocino County); Susanville Rancheria (1923; 150 acres; Lassen County); and XL Ranch Reservation (1938; 9,254.86 acres; Modoc County). Most rancherias are governed by elected tribal councils.

The Pit River Tribe was formally recognized in 1976, and a constitution was adopted in 1987. The 1990 population was roughly 1,350. Each of 11 bands is represented by one vote in a tribal council.

ECONOMY Unemployment on the reservations and rancherias remains stubbornly high. Jobs in logging and hay ranching are available at XL Ranch. There is also some money to be made in the tourism trade, especially in basket sales.

LEGAL STATUS The Alturas Indian Rancheria of Pit River Indians; the Pit River Tribe of California (including Big Bend, Lookout, Montgomery Creek, and Roaring Creek Rancherias and XL Ranch); the Big Valley Rancheria of Pomo and Pit River Indians; the Covelo Indian Community of the Round Valley Reservation; and the Susanville Indian Rancheria of Paiute, Maidu, Pit River, and Washoe Indians are all federally recognized tribal entities.

DAILY LIFE Attempts at tribal organization have been largely unsuccessful. Ancient subdivisions are still identifiable and, despite the population decimation and scattered and inadequate land base, the people retain a strong attachment to the land and to their traditions. Pit River Indians work to oppose development of the sacred Mt. Shasta. They also hold an annual powwow.

Barbariño

See Chumash

Cahto

Cahto (`Kä t ō) is Northern Pomo for "lake," referring to an important Cahto village site. The Cahto called themselves *Djilbi*, the word in their language for that same lake and village. The Cahto are sometimes referred to as Kaipomo Indians.

LOCATION The Cahto homeland is in northwest California, south of Rattlesnake Creek, north of the North Fork of the Ten Mile River, and between the South Fork of the Eel River and just west of the Eel River (more or less the Long and Cahto Valleys). Today, most Cahtos live in Mendocino County.

POPULATION Roughly 1,100 Cahto Indians lived in their region in the early eighteenth century. In 1990, 129 Cahto-Pomo people lived at Laytonville. A few Cahto also lived at Round Valley Reservation.

LANGUAGE Cahto was an Athapaskan language.

Historical Information

HISTORY Like other Indian people who were overwhelmed by the sheer numbers and brutality of non-native Californians in the 1850s, the Cahto fought back for a brief period before being defeated. Their population declined by some 95 percent during the nineteenth century. The town of Cahto was founded in 1856, the same year reservations were created at Round Valley and Fort Bragg, in Mendocino County. The town of Laytonville was established in 1880.

RELIGION Cahtos prayed frequently, in part to two original beings, *Nagaicho*, or Great Traveler, and *Tcenes*, or Thunder. They also followed the Kuksu cult, which involved the acquisition of spiritual power through direct contact with supernatural beings. Tribal and intertribal ceremonies were held in winter (such as the Acorn Dance) and summer. A host who had enough food to share invited his neighbors. Then there was dancing for a week, the creation story was told, and the headman made speeches.

GOVERNMENT The Cahto lived in approximately 50 villages. Although most were completely autonomous, six in Long Valley were united to the extent that they called themselves "Grass Tribe." Each village was led by a headman or two. His authority was mainly advisory, and he was generally succeeded by his son.

CUSTOMS Marriage was generally a matter between the couple involved, although girls were generally prepubescent when married. The Cahto practiced polygyny as well as the taboo that prevented a man from addressing his mother-in-law directly. Divorce was easily obtained for nearly any reason. Unlike many California Indians, pregnant Cahto women observed no food taboos. Deformed children and twins were killed at birth.

The six-day girls' puberty ceremony included dietary taboos and then a quiet life for five subsequent months. Boys, at puberty, remained in the dance house all winter to receive admonitions regarding proper behavior; "ghosts" also sang and danced for this purpose. Corpses were buried with their valuables or cremated if away from home. Both men and women mourners cut their hair, and women put pitch on their bodies.

Adult games included shinny, the grass game, stone throwing, and races. Children's games included camping, skipping rope, and playing with acorn tops. Women enjoyed singing in chorus around an evening fire. The Cahto danced the feather and *necum* dances solely for pleasure. Pets included birds, coyotes, and rabbits.

The Cahto knew three types of shamans: sucking doctors, bear doctors, and singing and dancing doctors. Bear doctors were said to be strong enough to kill enemies of the Cahto. Various ceremonies, including magic, were practiced before all important events, such as hunting, war, birth, and funerals. Men owned hunting and war items; women owned their clothing, baskets, and cooking rocks. Men generally hunted and fished. Women gathered all foods except acorns; gathering acorns was a communal activity.

DWELLINGS Living houses, which were privately owned by up to three families, were built over two-foot-deep pits. Slabs, bark, or earth covered wood rafters, which in turn rested on four poles. Most houses were rebuilt after two years as a vermin-control measure. Larger villages contained similarly built but larger dance houses.

DIET Acorns, salmon, and deer served as food staples. Other important foods included other fish; bear; mink, raccoon, and other small game; birds; and some insects. Meat was generally broiled over coals or on a spit. The Cahto also ate a variety of seeds, tubers, and berries. They also used domesticated dogs to help them hunt.

KEY TECHNOLOGY Stone, bone, and shell were the primary tool materials. Baskets were usually twined but sometimes coiled. Hunting tools included traps, snares, bows, arrows, slings, nets, and harpoons. Fish were sometimes poisoned. Musical instruments included whistles, rattles, a foot drum, a musical bow, and a six-hole elderberry flute.

TRADE The Cahto were particularly friendly with the Northern Pomo. Some Cahto even spoke Pomo in addition to their own language. In addition to regular trade with the Northern Pomo, the Cahto gathered shellfish and seaweed in Coast Yuki territory. They also supplied these people with hazelwood bows in exchange for items such as salt, mussels, seaweed, abalone, sea fish, clamshells, and dried kelp. They traded arrows, baskets, and clothing to the Wailaki in exchange for dentalia. They also supplied clam disk beads to the Lassik and received salt from the Northern Wintun as well as dogs from an unknown location to the north.

NOTABLE ARTS Fine arts consisted of fashioning musical instruments and singing.

TRANSPORTATION The Cahto used log rafts for crossing streams.

DRESS Men and women dressed in a similar fashion. They both wore tanned deerhide aprons. They also wore long hair and used iris nets. Both wore bracelets, nose and ear ornaments, and, occasionally, tattoos.

WAR AND WEAPONS The Cahto seldom engaged in large-scale warfare. There were, however, frequent conflicts with the Sinkyone, Yuki, Northern Pomo, Wailaki, and Huchnom, generally over murder or trespass. When fighting occurred, close fighting was avoided whenever possible. War dances were held before each battle. Weapons included the bow and arrow, deer hide sling, and spear. All casualties were indemnified following the fighting.

Contemporary Information

GOVERNMENT/RESERVATIONS Laytonville Rancheria (1906), in Mendocino County, consists of 264 acres. The tribal council consists of three people who serve a one-year term. The term "Cahto" refers to those eligible for tribal membership, even though some Cahtos personally adhere to other tribal affiliations.

ECONOMY Some Cahtos work at a nearby lumber mill. However, unemployment remains high at Laytonville. The tribe has built the Ya-Ka-Ama Indian Center in Sonoma County.

LEGAL STATUS The Cahto Indian Tribe of the Laytonville Rancheria is a federally recognized tribal entity.

DAILY LIFE Laytonville is not an isolated Indian community. Racial intermarriage is common, and Indians compete for scarce job opportunities with other local citizens. Educational levels among Cahtos are relatively low. Little remains of traditional culture, although there are Pomo dancers and basket weavers, and native language classes are held.

Cahuilla

Cahuilla (Kä `hw ē lä), perhaps derived from the Spanish *kawiya,* or "master." The Cahuilla refer to themselves as *Iviatim,* or speakers of their native language.

LOCATION The Cahuilla lived generally southwest of the Bernardino Mountains in the eighteenth century. They ranged over a territory including several distinct environmental zones, from mountain ranges to canyons to desert (11,000 feet to 273 feet). Today they live on ten reservations in southern California.

POPULATION The Cahuilla population may have numbered as many as 10,000 in the seventeenth century, with roughly 5,000 remaining by the late eighteenth century. In 1990, the total Indian population of all reservations on which Cahuilla lived, including those they shared with other peoples, was 1,276.

LANGUAGE Cahuilla was a language from the Cupan subgroup of the Takic division of the Uto-Aztecan language family.

Historical Information

HISTORY New diseases and elements of Spanish culture probably preceded the physical arrival of the Spanish, which occurred when the Juan Bautista de Anza expedition arrived in 1774. The Cahuilla were at first hostile to the Spanish. Since most routes to the Pacific at that time were by sea, the two groups had little ongoing contact, except that a few Cahuillas were baptized at nearby missions.

By the early nineteenth century, some Cahuillas worked seasonally on Spanish cattle ranches, and aspects of Spanish culture such as cattle, wage labor, clothing, and language had significantly changed the traditional Cahuilla lifestyle. The latter maintained their autonomy until the severe smallpox epidemic of 1863. After 1877, they moved slowly on to reservations. Although self-supporting, they grew increasingly dependent on the Americans.

After 1891 the federal government took a much more active role in their lives. Government schools trained Cahuillas to perform menial tasks; influential Protestant missionaries suppressed native religion and culture; allotment under the Dawes Act (1886) destroyed their agricultural capabilities; and Indian Service personnel controlled their political activities, under protest. From roughly 1891 through the 1930s, Cahuillas farmed, raised cattle, worked for wages, sold peat and asbestos, and leased their lands for income. Lack of water was a chronic obstacle to economic activities. Their tourist industry, especially that of the Agua Caliente Band, also dates from the 1920s.

Following World War II, partial termination and the severe curtailment of government services forced the Cahuilla to take a much more active role in their welfare. Renewed federal programs in the 1960s in combination with a vitalized tribal political structure led to a general increase in the quality of life for most Cahuillas.

RELIGION The Cahuilla recognized a supreme power, neither good nor bad, but unpredictable. According to their worldview, the entire universe and everything in it was interconnected. Cahuillas performed a large number of rituals. The most significant ones were an annual mourning ceremony, the eagle ceremony (honoring a dead chief or shaman), rite-of-passage rituals, and food-related rituals. Song cycles were a key part of Cahuilla ritual. They sought to reaffirm the people's place in the universe and their connections with the past and with all things. Ceremonial implements included rattles, headdresses,

wands, eagle-feathered skirts, and especially the *máyswut*, a ceremonial bundle.

GOVERNMENT The Cahuillas lived in about 50 villages aboriginally. The political unit was the clan, or group of between three and ten lineages. Each clan had a leader, usually hereditary, called the *nét*. This person had religious, economic, and diplomatic as well as political responsibilities. The *nét* also had an assistant.

Háwayniks knew and sang the ceremonial songs, including the long song cycles. Shamans (always male) had much power, including curing, through the control of supernatural power. They also controlled the weather; guarded against evil spirits; and, with the *néts*, exercised political authority. Strong as it was, however, the shaman's authority was only maintained by regular public displays of power.

CUSTOMS The Cahuilla recognized two societal divisions, Wildcat and Coyote, each composed of a number of patrilineal clans. Female doctors complemented male shamans as curers; their methods included the use of medicinal plants and other knowledge. When a person died, the spirit was believed to travel to the land of the dead; from there, it could still be involved in the lives of the living. Old age was venerated, largely because old people taught the traditional ways and values, which were themselves venerated.

Reciprocity and sharing were two defining values. The Cahuillas frowned upon hasty behavior; conversely, it was appropriate to do things slowly, deliberately, and cautiously. They enjoyed regular interaction, including intermarriage, with other Indian groups such as the Gabrieleño and Serrano.

Although each extended family had a village site and resource area, land away from the village could be owned by anyone. Mens' games were based on endurance and the ability to withstand physical punishment. Women's games included footraces, juggling, cat's cradle, top spinning, jackstones, and balancing objects. People often bet on games.

Cahuilla songs contained tribal history and cosmology, and they accompanied all activities. Singing was common. Bathing and cleanliness in general were important. Spouses were selected by parents from the opposite division. Divorce was difficult to obtain. Everyone observed specific rules of deference and behavior toward other people.

DWELLINGS Dome-shaped shelters were constructed of brush. Rectangular houses were generally made of thatch. Other structures included acorn granaries, mens' sweat houses, and ceremonial lodges.

DIET Six varieties of acorns constituted a key food source. Other gathered food included pine nuts, mesquite and screwbeans, and a huge variety of cactus, seeds, berries, roots, and greens. Other plants were used in construction and for medicinal purposes. Rabbits, deer, antelope, rodents, mountain sheep, reptiles, and fowl were all hunted, and fish were taken. Meat was roasted, boiled, or sun-dried in strips, with the bones then cracked for marrow or ground and mixed with other foods. Blood was drunk fresh or cooked and stored. Some Cahuilla bands practiced agriculture, although this was a less important activity.

KEY TECHNOLOGY The Cahuilla used a variety of natural materials for their technological needs, including willow or mesquite wood (bows and arrows), grasses (cooking, storage, and carrying baskets), stone (mortars, pestles, manos and metates, arrow straighteners), wood (mortars), clay (pottery for cooking, storage, eating, and pipes), pine pitch (to seal storage bins for food preservation), and mescal (fibers for rope). Other technological innovations included hunting nets, snares and traps, baking ovens or pits, and musical instruments such as elder flutes, whistles, panpipes, and rattles.

TRADE The Cocopah-Maricopa Trail, a major trade route, bisected Cahuilla territory. Two other trade routes, the Santa Fe and the Yuman, passed close by. Cahuillas traded mostly with the Mojave, Halchidoma, Ipai, Tipai, Luiseño, Serrano, and Gabrieleño. The Cahuilla traded food products, furs, hides, obsidian, and salt for shell beads, minerals such as turquoise and tourmaline, Joshua tree blossoms, axes, and other crafts. Rituals and songs were also exchanged.

NOTABLE ARTS Petroglyphs, perhaps beginning as early as 1000 B.C.E., depicted big game hunting. Pictographs, associated with the girls' puberty ceremony, began in the fifteenth century.

TRANSPORTATION Baskets were used to transport goods.

DRESS Women wore basket hats as well as skirts of mescal bark, tule, or skins. Men wore breechclouts of the same material when they wore anything at all. Both men and women wore sandals of mescal fibers soaked in mud and tied with mescal fibers or buckskin. Babies wore mesquite-bark diapers. Blankets or woven rabbit-skin robes were used for warmth.

WAR AND WEAPONS Cahuillas fought other Cahuillas as a last resort, usually over economic disputes. Weapons included war clubs and poison-tipped arrows.

Contemporary Information

GOVERNMENT/RESERVATIONS Cahuilla reservations include Agua Caliente (1896; 23,173 acres; Riverside County; 1957 constitution and by-laws), Augustine (1893; 502 acres; Thermal County),

Cabazon (1876; 1,382 acres; Indio and Riverside Counties; 20 Indians; democratically elected tribal council); Cahuilla (1875; 18,884 acres; Riverside County), Los Coyotes (1889; Cahuilla and Cupeño; 25,049.63 acres; San Diego County), Morongo (1908; 32,362 acres; Cahuilla, Serrano, and Cupeño, Riverside County), Ramona (1893; 560 acres; Riverside County), Santa Rosa (1907; 11,092.6 acres; Kings County), and Torres-Martinez (1876; 24,024 acres; Imperial and Riverside Counties). Each is administered by elected business committees and/or tribal councils in conjunction with the Bureau of Indian Affairs (BIA) and is connected to the others in various formal and informal ways. None have Indian Reorganization Act constitutions.

ECONOMY Important activities include cattle raising, farming, billboard and land leasing, and general off-reservation employment opportunities. Agua Caliente has extensive real estate holdings. The Cabazon Band operates the Fantasy Springs Casino and owns an industrial park; they have no unemployment, though income is fairly low. In general, the Cahuillas' land is far from markets, water, and jobs. Most of the reservations have job development plans. The unemployment rate at Torres-Martines was 78 percent in 1995. There is also some basket making for the tourist trade.

LEGAL STATUS The Agua Caliente Band of Mission Indians of the Agua Caliente Indian Reservation; the Augustine Band of Mission Indians of the Augustine Indian Reservation; the Cabazon Band of Mission Indians of the Cabazon Indian Reservation; the Cahuilla Band of Mission Indians of the Cahuilla Reservation; the Los Coyotes Band of Cahuilla Mission Indians of the Los Coyotes Reservation; the Morongo Band of Cahuilla Mission Indians of the Morongo Reservation; the Ramona Band or Village of Cahuilla Mission Indians; the Santa Rosa Band of Cahuilla Mission Indians of the Santa Rosa Reservation; and the Torres-Martinez Desert Cahuilla Indians are federally recognized tribal entities.

DAILY LIFE Some traditions remain alive, although much diminished, such as the funeral ritual, foods, and kin relationships, as do values like reciprocity. Ceremonies have been greatly modified, but the patterns remain, as do traditional games, relationships with the supernatural, wagering, and songs. People, especially the young, are learning the living language. Most Cahuillas are Catholic. Institutions include the Malki Museum of Cahuilla Culture at Morongo Reservation, the Morongo Indian Health Clinic, and the Torres-Martinez Historical Society. Cahuillas are relatively well educated. Two intertribal powwows are held annually. Tribal autonomy remains an issue, as does resource management and Indian burials. Recently, Cahuillas have been forced to consider the issue of hazardous waste disposal on their lands. An Agua Caliente Cultural Museum is planned for Palm Springs.

Among the Cabazon Band, children receive education grants to attend public or private schools off the reservation. The casino plays a major role in their lives. The people are building 1,000 houses on their reservation.

At Torres-Martinez, extended families often live together. Children attend public school but also learn traditional songs and dances. Seniors meet regularly, and many converse in their native language. Diabetes and substance abuse are significant social problems. Neither the clans nor many traditional ceremonies remain. Most people live in trailers or Housing and Urban Development/BIA housing, little of which is suitable for the desert. Illegally dumped toxic sludge is a local environmental threat and the object of ongoing blockades and other protests.

Chilula

See Hupa

Chukchansi

See Yokuts

Chumash

Chumash (`Ch ū mash), a label chosen by an Anglo anthropologist, comes from the word used by the Coastal Chumash for either the Santa Cruz *(Mitcú-mac)* Indians or the Santa Rosa *(Tcú-mac)* Indians. Each Chumash regional group—Barbareño, Ynezeño, and Ventureño (Eastern Coastal); Obispeño and Purisimeño; Island Chumash; and Interior Chumash—has its own self-designation. The Chumash are sometimes referred to as the Santa Barbara Indians.

LOCATION Traditionally, the Chumash lived along the Pacific coast from San Luis Obispo to Malibu Canyon and inland as far as the western edge of the San Joaquin Valley. There were also Chumash Indians on the Santa Barbara Channel islands of San Miguel, Santa Rosa, Santa Cruz, and Anacapa. Today, the Santa Ynez Band lives at and near Santa Ynez, California.

POPULATION Chumash population was between roughly 10,000 and 18,000 in the late eighteenth century. In 1990, 213 Indians lived on the Santa Ynez Reservation.

LANGUAGE At least six separate groups spoke related Hokan languages: Barbareño, Ventureño, Ynezeño, Purisimeño, Obispeño, and the Island language.

Historical Information

HISTORY The Coastal Chumash were living in their traditional territory by roughly 1000. In 1542, contact was established between the Chumash and the Spanish explorers Juan Cabrillo and Bartolome Ferello. Relations were amiable, and although the Spanish soon began using the Santa Barbara Channel as a stopover for their trans-Pacific voyages, early impact on the Chumash was minimal.

In 1772 the Franciscans built San Luis Obispo mission. Other missions followed soon thereafter. The Chumash entered the mission period willingly, and many became completely missionized (turned into farmers, artisans, and Christians). However, for most Indians, missions were places of slave labor. Smallpox and syphilis were major killers, but even the common cold often turned into a deadly disease. Refusing either to give up their traditional ways or to be mistreated by the Spanish missionaries, some Chumash escaped into the hills either before or during the mission period. In 1824, Indians staged a major rebellion at several missions. Many sought sanctuary with the Yokuts Indians or at other interior communities. Although many ultimately returned to the missions, many others did not.

Mexico seized control of the missions in 1834. Indians either fled into the interior, attempted farming for themselves and were driven off the land, or were enslaved by the new administrators. Alcoholism soon became a large problem among the Chumash. Many found highly exploitative work on large Mexican ranches. After 1849 most Chumash land was lost to theft by Americans and a declining population, mainly as a result of the effects of violence and disease. The remaining Chumash began to lose their cohesive identity. In 1855, a small piece of land (120 acres) was set aside for just over 100 remaining Chumash Indians near Santa Ynez mission. This land ultimately became the only Chumash reservation, although Chumash individuals and families also continued to live throughout their former territory in southern California.

Chumash cemeteries along Santa Barbara Channel were looted extensively in the 1870s and 1880s. By 1900, disease combined with intermarriage had rendered Chumash culture virtually extinct.

RELIGION Little is known about traditional Chumash religion and ceremonialism. The people worshiped a deity, the nature of which is unclear, called *sup, achup,* or *chupu.* Shamans cured disease using chants, herbs, and a tube with which to suck out bad spirits. Their power derived from a guardian angel that appeared to them in a vision. Charmstones were a key part of shamans' work. The Chumash used toloache, a powerful hallucinogen, for ceremonial purposes.

GOVERNMENT   The Chumash were organized by village rather than by tribe. Villages were led by chiefs; their limited authority was based on heredity and wealth. Coast villages maintained patrilineal descent groups. Each contained three or four captains, one of whom was head chief. Women could inherit the position of head chief. A chief's formal power was limited to leading in war, presiding at ceremonies, and granting hunting permissions.

CUSTOMS   After a mourning ceremony, the dead were buried face down (face up on the islands), head to the west, and in a flexed position. Graves were marked with rows of wood or stone. Some babies may have been killed at birth. Also, babies' noses were flattened after birth. At the onset of puberty, girls were subject to dietary restrictions, and boys were given a strong liquor to induce visions. Brides were purchased with gifts. Adultery was taboo, and only a few highly placed men could have more than one wife.

Many people smoked tobacco. Coastal people were generally gentle and slow to anger. Punishment was rare. Transvestitism was common and even esteemed. On the coast, people had more time for games, singing, and dancing

DWELLINGS   The Chumash lived in rancheria-style villages. Their houses, some of which were as large as 50 feet in diameter, were domed. They were built on poles bent inward and covered with grass. A hole in the roof let light in and smoke out. Houses in the interior were generally smaller. Reed mats covered frame beds. Reeds were also used for floor coverings, partitions, and mattresses. Other structures included storehouses, sweat houses, and ceremonial ramadas.

DIET   Live oak acorns were a staple, although fish, shellfish, and marine mammals were more important for coastal and island Chumash. The people also hunted game such as mule deer, coyote, and fox and gathered pine nuts, cherries, and a variety of roots, bulbs, seeds, and berries.

KEY TECHNOLOGY   The Chumash hunted with bow (sinew-backed) and arrow, snares, and deadfalls. They fished with seines, dip nets, and hook and line, killing larger fish and sea mammals with harpoons. They carved wood plates, bowls, and boxes; they wove water baskets and sealed them from the inside with asphaltum. Coastal residents fashioned stools of whale vertebrae.

Other cooking items and tools were made of stone, especially steatite. Musical instruments included elder wood or bone flutes, whistles, and rattles. The Chumash had no drums. For water transportation they used a *tomol*, or planked canoe (see "TRANSPORTATION"). Abalone and shell were used for inlay work. In general, material culture was less developed away from the coast.

TRADE   Trade was active with nearby tribes. The mainland Chumash provided steatite, asphaltum, fish, wooden vessels, beads, and shells, in exchange for black pigment, antelope and elk skins, piñon nuts, obsidian, salt, beads, seeds, and herbs.

NOTABLE ARTS   Fine arts included baskets, sea animals carved in wood and soapstone, and, from roughly 1000 to 1800, ceremonial rock paintings. The latter were generally abstract but also contained highly stylized life forms. The circle was a basic theme. Rock paintings were especially well developed in mountainous regions, although the arts were generally less well developed away from the coast.

TRANSPORTATION   The Chumash are the only native North Americans who built boats out of planks. They split cedar logs with antler or whalebone wedges and smoothed the lumber with shell and stone tools. Planks were lashed together with sinew or plant fibers and then caulked with asphaltum. The resulting boats had 12- to 30-foot double-bowed hulls and were moved with double-bladed paddles. They carried a crew of four and were quite oceanworthy; they traveled at least as far as San Nicholas Island, 65 miles offshore.

DRESS   Most Chumash men wore few or no clothes. Women wore knee-length buckskin skirts ornamented with snail and abalone shell. All wore additional buckskin clothing, blankets, or robes against the cold weather. Men and women tied their long hair with strings interwoven with the hair. They pierced their noses and ears, painted their bodies, and wore shell, bone, and stone necklaces.

WAR AND WEAPONS   Reasons for war included trespass, breach of etiquette, avenging witchcraft, or defense (interior Indian peoples occasionally attacked the Coastal Chumash). Rules of engagement were highly formalized. In general, however, the Chumash seldom engaged in actual warfare. The 1824 revolt against the Mexicans stands out as the major historical conflict.

Contemporary Information

GOVERNMENT/RESERVATIONS   The only formal Chumash reservation is the 127-acre Santa Ynez Reservation (1901; Santa Barbara County). It is governed by a five-member business council (1968 articles of incorporation).

ECONOMY   There is a campground and a bingo parlor at Santa Ynez.

LEGAL STATUS   The Santa Ynez Band of Chumash Mission Indians is a federally recognized tribal entity. The Coastal Band of Chumash Indians had petitioned for federal recognition as of 1997.

DAILY LIFE The last native speaker of a Chumash language died in 1965. Santa Ynez features a tribal hall and a clinic. Although little knowledge remains of their traditional culture, the people perform dances, songs, and storytelling and make crafts for the tourist trade as well as local cultural organizations.

Costanoan

Costanoan (Cos tä `n ō än) is Spanish for "coast people." The term denotes a language family as opposed to a unified political entity such as a tribe. Costanoans are sometimes referred to as *Ohlone*, the name of one tribelet.

LOCATION The Costanoans traditionally lived around and south of San Francisco and Monterey Bays and east to near the central valleys. Today many live in the same area and in Indian Canyon in San Benito County.

POPULATION The Costanoan population was roughly 10,000 in the mid–eighteenth century and about 200 in the late 1970s. There were probably thousands of Costanoan descendants in the mid-1990s.

LANGUAGE Costanoan, a group of about eight languages, belongs to the Penutian language family.

Historical Information

HISTORY Costanoan ancestors reached the Bay areas in roughly 500. They first encountered non-natives in the Sebastián Vizcaíno exploring expeditions of 1602. By the late eighteenth century, the Spanish had built seven missions in their territory and forced most Costanoans to join them.

In an effort to stem and reverse their cultural and physical extinction, the Costanoans in the late eighteenth century organized several incidents of armed resistance. Between 1770 and 1832, the Costanoan population fell by more than 80 percent as a result of disease, hardship, and general abuse. Their aboriginal existence disappeared during this time, as their culture and traditional practices were repressed and they mingled and mixed with other Indian peoples, including Esselen, Miwok, and Yokuts, also brought by force to the missions.

After 1835, when Mexico secularized the missions, many Costanoans worked on ranches or tried to return to a hunting and gathering existence. Most, however, had become mixed with non-natives and other Indians, establishing multiethnic Indian communities in the area. Costanoans were considered ethnologically extinct by the early twentieth century.

However, land claims cases in the 1920s and the 1960s resulted in small monetary payments and, as well, the recognition of Costanoan/Ohlone survival.

Also in the 1960s, Costanoan descendants of Mission San José prevented the destruction of a burial ground that lay in the proposed path of a freeway. These people later organized as the Ohlone Indian tribe and now hold title to a cemetery in Fremont, California. A similar situation occurred in 1975, resulting in the establishment of the Pajaro Valley Ohlone Indian Council. In 1911 and again in 1988, individuals received trust allotments that became the Costanoan refuge of Indian Canyon.

RELIGION The sun was just one of many Costanoan deities that received offerings such as tobacco smoke as well as seeds, tobacco, shell beads, and feathers. Shamans interpreted their dreams in religious terms, which were often used as a guide for future actions. Shamans also controlled weather and cured disease by sucking out offending disease objects and through the use of herbs. They could also bestow luck in economic pursuits. Much of their power depended on the performance of dances and ceremonies, including the Medicine Man's Dance, Devil's Dance, Coyote Dance, Dove Dance, and Puberty Dance.

GOVERNMENT Roughly 50 tribelets, each headed by a chief and a council of elders, spoke Costanoan languages. Each tribelet averaged about 200 people. The larger ones, of up to 500 people, had more than one permanent village.

Although men were usually chiefs, women occasionally held the office in the absence of male heirs. The position of chief was hereditary but subject to village approval. Responsibilities included directing ceremonial, economic, and war activities; feeding visitors; providing for the poor; caring for captured grizzly bears and coyotes; and leading the council of elders. All power was advisory except in time of war. An official speaker also had ceremonial and diplomatic duties.

CUSTOMS Costanoans maintained a clan structure as well as a division into two main groups, Deer and Bear. Small gifts given from groom to bride constituted the marriage formalities. The new couple lived in the groom's father's house. Men might have more than one wife. The dead and their possessions were either buried or cremated; their souls were said to journey across the sea. Widows cut or singed their hair, covered their heads with ashes or asphalt, and battered themselves, sometimes seriously.

Music often accompanied religious and mythological ritual. Both sexes underwent puberty rituals: Girls were confined to their houses and observed food taboos; boys used datura to seek visions. People played games such as ball race, shinny, hoop-and-pole, dice, and the hand game and often bet on the results.

DWELLINGS Most houses were conical in shape and built of tule, grass, or ferns around pole frames. Some Costanoan people substituted redwood slabs or bark. Sweat houses, used by men and women, were dug into the side of a stream. Large houses or brush enclosures served as dance sites.

DIET Costanoans hunted deer using deer-head disguises. They also hunted elk, antelope, bear, mountain lion, waterfowl, small mammals, and reptiles. They caught fish, especially salmon, steelhead, sturgeon, and lamprey in nets and traps. Fish were also speared by the light of a bonfire. Gathered foods included acorns, seeds, berries, nuts, insects, grapes, roots, greens, and honey. The people also ate shellfish as well as beached whales and sea lions.

Costanoans also practiced land management by controlled burning. This activity promoted the growth of seed-bearing plants, consumed dead plant material (a fire hazard), increased the grazing area for game, and facilitated acorn gathering.

KEY TECHNOLOGY Technological innovations included the use of tule balsa canoes; twined baskets; musical instruments, including bird-bone whistles, alder flutes, rattles, and a musical bow; earth ovens (for roasting meat, especially sea lion and whale); a variety of nets for catching rabbits, fish, and fowl; and cagelike traps to capture quail. Milkweed, hemp, or nettle fiber was used for cordage. Bedding was of tule mats and animal skins.

TRADE Significant trading partners included Plains Miwok, Sierra Miwok, and Yokuts Indians. Costanoans supplied mussels, abalone shells, dried abalone, salt, and olivella shells and imported piñon nuts and possibly clamshell beads.

NOTABLE ARTS Arts included music, usually connected with ritual or myth (instruments included whistles, rattles, and flutes) as well as dances and basket making.

TRANSPORTATION Tule balsa canoes were used for fishing and duck hunting.

DRESS Men often wore no clothes; women wore tule or buckskin aprons. Rabbit-skin, deerskin, duck feather, or otter-skin robes were worn in cold weather. Some men wore beards but most plucked facial hair with wooden tweezers or a pair of mussel shells or singed it with a hot coal. Both sexes painted and tattooed their bodies. Ornaments were worn in pierced ears and around the neck.

WAR AND WEAPONS War was not uncommon among the different tribelets and between the Costanoan and the Esselen, Salinan, and Northern Valley Yokuts. Trespass often provoked hostilities, which began either by prearrangement or by surprise attack. Captives, except young women, were usually killed, their heads displayed on a pike in the village.

Raiding parties burned enemy villages. The main weapon was the bow and arrow.

Contemporary Information

GOVERNMENT/RESERVATIONS The (corporate) Ohlone Indian Tribe holds title to a cemetery in Fremont, California. In 1988, a Mutsun descendant acquired land (Indian Canyon) by allotment.

ECONOMY There is complete integration into the mainstream economy.

LEGAL STATUS The Amah Band of Ohlone/Costanoan Indians, the Costanoan Band of Carmel Mission Indians, the Indian Canyon Band of Costanoan/Mutsun Indians and the Ohlone/Costanoan/Muwekma Tribe are all recognized by the state of California. As of 1997, they had not yet attained federal recognition.

In 1971, descendants of the Costanoans formed the Ohlone Indian Tribe, which is still unrecognized. The Pajaro Valley Ohlone Indian Council was formed in the mid-1970s.

DAILY LIFE All Costanoan languages are virtually extinct, although some people are trying to revive Mutsun. Some Costanoans engage in Indian-related activities such as crafts and the recognition struggles of tribes and local sacred sites. *Noso-n* (Mutsun for "in breath as it is in spirit") is a newsletter for the contemporary community of Costanoans and neighboring peoples. In 1989, Stanford University agreed to return all of its Native American skeletal remains to local Ohlone/Costanoan people for reburial. Costanoan descendants established the Carmel Valley Indian Center to promote cultural programs and exhibits about local Indians.

Cupeño

Cupeño (K ū ˋp ā n y ō) is Spanish for "a person who comes from *Kúpa*."

LOCATION The Cupeño traditionally lived in a mountainous area at the headwaters of the San Luis Rey River and the San Jose de Valle Valley. Today most Cupeños live on Pala Reservation in San Diego County.

POPULATION Fewer than 750 Cupeños lived in their region in the mid–eighteenth century. In 1990, 563 Indians lived on the Pala Reservation, some of whom were Cupeño.

LANGUAGE Cupeño belongs to the Cupan subgroup of the Takic family of Uto-Aztecan languages.

Historical Information

HISTORY Specific Cupeño customs and identity were derived from neighboring Cahuilla, Luiseño, Ipai, and other groups in a process that began at least 800 years ago. Non-natives entered the area in 1795.

In the early nineteenth century, the Spanish took over Cupeño lands, building a chapel, a health spa, and a meeting place and grazing their cattle. During this period, Indians worked as virtual serfs for Spanish masters.

Juan Antonio Garra, a clan leader, attempted but failed around 1850 to organize a general revolt of all southern California Indians meant to drive out or kill all non-natives. He was captured by Cahuilla Indians and later shot by a paramilitary court. His village, Kúpa, was also burned. Between 1875 and 1877, the U.S. government created thirteen separate reservations for former "Mission Indians." Around the turn of the century, despite widespread local and even national protest, the California Supreme Court ordered all 250 or so Cupeños to move from their homes at Warner's Hot Springs to the Pala Reservation (Luiseño), awarding title to the former land to a man who was once governor of California. An influential group of non-natives pressured the government in 1903 to purchase a 3,438-acre ranch for the Cupeño at Pala Valley, now known as New Pala. By 1973 fewer than 150 people claimed Cupeño descent.

RELIGION Death ceremonies were perhaps the Cupeños' most important. Corpses were burned almost immediately, possessions were burned several weeks or months later, and images of the dead were burned every year or two as part of an eight-day festival. Also, an annual eagle-killing ritual was held in honor of the dead.

GOVERNMENT Kúpa and Wilákalpa were the two permanent villages prior to 1902. Each was politically independent. Decisions concerning the entire village were taken by consensus of the clan leaders.

CUSTOMS Cupeños recognized two divisions, Coyote and Wildcat, and within them a number of patrilineal clans. Each clan owned productive food-gathering sites. Each had a leader, usually hereditary in the male line, as well as an assistant leader.

Sometimes leaders were also shamans. Shamans were powerful, feared, and respected. They cured, witched, and divined through supernatural powers acquired in trances and dreams. Parents arranged most marriages, with the boy's parents taking the lead in mate selection, gift-giving, and feasting. Girls around age 10 underwent a puberty ceremony. The male initiation ceremony occurred between 10 and 18 years of age and probably involved the use of toloache.

DWELLINGS Family houses were conical in shape, built partly underground, and covered with reeds, brush, or bark. Earth sweat houses were also semisubterranean. People used ramadas for ceremonies and domestic chores. Other structures included acorn granaries, mens' sweat houses, and ceremonial lodges.

DIET Acorns, small seeds, berries, cactus fruit, deer, quail, rabbits, and other small mammals constituted the basic Cupeño diet.

KEY TECHNOLOGY The Cupeño used a variety of natural materials for their technological needs, including willow or mesquite wood (bows and arrows), grasses (cooking, storage, and carrying baskets), stone (mortars, pestles, manos and metates, arrow straighteners), wood (mortars), clay (pottery for cooking, storage, eating, and pipes), pine pitch (to seal storage bins for food preservation), and mescal (fibers for rope). Other technological innovations included hunting and carrying nets, snares and traps, baking ovens or pits, and musical instruments such as elder flutes, whistles, panpipes, and rattles.

TRADE The Cupeño were part of an elaborate southern California network that dealt in economic and ritual items and activities. The Cocopah-Maricopa Trail, a major trade route, as well as the Santa Fe and the Yuman Trails passed close by. The people traded food products, furs, hides, obsidian, and salt for shell beads, minerals such as turquoise and tourmaline, Joshua tree blossoms, axes, and other crafts. Rituals and songs were also exchanged.

NOTABLE ARTS Rock paintings were used in the girls' puberty ceremony. Fine arts also included pottery, coiled baskets, and sandpaintings.

TRANSPORTATION Baskets were used to transport goods.

DRESS Women wore basket hats as well as skirts of mescal bark, tule, or skins. Men donned breechclouts of the same material when they wore anything at all. Both wore sandals of mescal fibers soaked in mud and tied with mescal fibers or buckskin. Babies wore mesquite-bark diapers. Blankets or woven rabbit-skin robes were used for warmth.

WAR AND WEAPONS Cupeño groups generally feuded over women, trespass, and sorcery. Murder also required retribution. Tactics included ambush or simply chasing away an enemy. Weapons included the bow and arrow (possibly with a poisoned tip), poniard, thrusting sticks, and war club. Forced to resist the missions and Mexican imperialism, the people became more aggressive during the early nineteenth century.

Contemporary Information
GOVERNMENT/RESERVATIONS An elected tribal council governs the Cupeño at Pala Reservation (New Pala, which is divided from Old Pala [Luiseño] by the San Luis Rey River). Many Cupeños also live on the Morongo and the Los Coyotes Reservations (Cahuilla) and are intermarried with those people.

ECONOMY There is income from agricultural land and mineral resources, especially sand and gravel.

LEGAL STATUS The Cupeño are a federally recognized tribal entity.

DAILY LIFE The Cupa Cultural Center was dedicated in 1974. Some people still speak the language (there are language instruction programs) and practice several traditions, including some games, funeral rituals, social songs (such as birdsongs), and dances. The people still live in a traditional central village. Major political issues include economic development, sovereignty, health, housing, water availability, protection of sacred sites, gaming, and toxic waste pollution.

Diegueño

See Tipai-Ipai

Hupa

Hupa (`H ū pä), from the Yurok name for the Hoopa Valley. Their self-designation was *Natinook-wa*, "People of the Place Where the Trails Return." The Hupa were culturally and linguistically related to three neighboring groups, the Chilula, Whilkut, and the North Fork Hupa, who lived mainly to their east.

LOCATION The Hupa lived traditionally along the lower Trinity River, a main tributary of the Klamath, and especially in the Hoopa Valley. The Hoopa Valley Reservation is in this region today.

POPULATION Roughly 1,000 Hupa Indians lived in and near the Hoopa Valley in the early nineteenth century. In 1990, 1,732 Indians lived on the reservation out of a total enrollment of roughly 2,140 Indians.

LANGUAGE Hupa is an Athapaskan language.

Historical Information

HISTORY Little is known about Hupa prehistory, although they are culturally related to the Yurok and the Karuk to the north. They arrived in northern California in roughly 1000. Being fairly isolated, they had little contact with non-natives until the mid–nineteenth century. There were few Spanish or Russian inroads or even American trappers. Even in 1849, the Hupa saw some miners but avoided the wholesale displacement experienced by other natives.

After the 1849 gold rush, settlers flooded the region, but the Hupas held their ground. The construction of a fort in 1858 resulted primarily in some liaisons between soldiers and Hupa women. The government created the Hoopa Valley Reservation in 1864. Because of the relative lack of cataclysmic disruption and the location of a reservation in their traditional homeland, the Hupa were generally able to adjust slowly but steadily to their new situation. The period following World War II brought good jobs as lumberjacks and mill workers as well as the end of the traditional subsistence economy. In the 1970s and 1980s, the United States took control of tribal funds and resources for use at the government's discretion.

RELIGION The Hupa celebrated annual World Renewal ceremonies, for which shamans performed secret rites and dances such as the White Deerskin Dance and the Jumping Dance. This ceremony was held in specific locations for ten days in late summer or fall. It included a long narrative about Hupa history and the actions of the supernaturals. Wealthy families provided ceremonial regalia. The people also held other ceremonies for seasonal activities, such as the beginning of the salmon run. Two ceremonial divisions, northern and southern, came together in the ancient village of Takimildin, located in the heart of the Hoopa Valley.

Curing shamans, whose methods included sucking out illness-causing objects, were almost always women. They charged high fees, which were payable in advance but refundable if the cure failed. People also used family-owned medicines for more minor ailments. Hupas also believed that male sorcerers could find many ways in which to harm a person. They recognized many spirits and supernatural beings but gave them little ritual attention. They did observe numerous daily rituals and taboos and recognized the obligation to maintain a healthy mindset.

GOVERNMENT The Hupa recognized no formal political leadership. Instead, people were ranked according to their wealth. The family was a basic unit, but several patrilineally related households formed a larger grouping or a village. The 10 to 15 Hupa villages acted together informally and only for activities like holding religious ceremonies or building communal fish weirs.

CUSTOMS According to Hupa tradition, all customs were formed in an earlier, mythological period of the peoples' existence. One notable custom concerned social status, which was defined by inheritable material possessions such as albino deerskins, large obsidian blades, and headdresses decorated with red-headed-woodpecker scalps. Money, such as shell currency, was slightly different from material wealth and could be used to pay for items such as a dowry, a shaman's fee, or an indemnity to an injured party. Wealth could theoretically be obtained through hard work, but in practice property was difficult to accumulate and there was little movement through class lines. The legal code stated that every wrong had to be compensated for, usually with money but occasionally with blood. Family and individual wealth and power affected the terms of redress.

When a Hupa died, his or her body was wrapped in deerskin and buried. Clothing and utensils were placed on top of a plank-lined grave marked with a board. Close relatives cut their hair as a sign of mourning. After five days, souls departed for a dank, dark underworld (the souls of shamans and singers were fortunate to inhabit a pleasant heaven in the sky).

Hupas observed a number of life-cycle prohibitions and taboos as well as magic and religious observances. Babies remained in the cradle until they walked and were not formally named at least until age five. Children knew only mild discipline. At age eight or so a boy joined his father in the sweat lodge. Pubescent girls were considered unclean and remained secluded, although girls from wealthier families might have a party to mark the occasion. Girls married at 15 or 16; boys slightly later. A feast and an exchange of gifts marked the occasion. Only rich men could afford more than one wife. Sex was generally avoided for a number of reasons, except during the late summer and fall family camping trips. In case of divorce, which was fairly easy to obtain, the bride price was returned if the couple was childless.

Most men and women worked hard and steadily, although time was set aside for diversions. Men played the hand game; women bet on the mussel-shell toss. Other diversions included athletic contests, storytelling, and smoking at bedtime for men. The voice was the most important musical instrument, followed by wooden clappers, bone whistles, and hoof rattles.

DWELLINGS For most of the year, Hupas lived in cedar-planked single-family houses built around a square hole. A stone-lined fire pit sat in the center of the house. Smoke escaped through a hole in the three-pitched roof. Earthen shelves next to the walls served as storage areas. Women and children slept in the family house; men slept in semisubterranean sweat houses, which they also used as clubhouses and workshops. People lived in roofless brush shelters during the autumn acorn-gathering expeditions.

DIET Acorns and fish, especially salmon, were the staples. Women harvested and prepared the former, cooking it into mush or bread. Deer and elk were captured by stalking or driving them into a river and then pursuing them by canoe. Small game was also taken. Other fish included trout, sturgeon, and eel. Fish was sliced thin and smoke dried for storage or broiled fresh. People also gathered a number of food plants, including berries, nuts, seeds, roots, and greens. They did not eat many birds, reptiles, amphibians (except turtles), insects, and larvae. Hupas rarely lacked for an adequate food supply.

KEY TECHNOLOGY Women made baskets for a number of uses. Men made wooden bowls and other items as well as tools of stone and bone. Hupas fished using dip nets, gill nets, and dragnets; weirs; bone-pointed harpoon; and hook and line. Hunters used a sinew-lined bow with stone-tipped arrows. They also used iris-fiber nooses.

TRADE Hupas traded acorns and food with the Coastal Yurok for canoes, dried seaweed (for salt), and ocean fish. They also traded occasionally with other groups. Products were either bartered for or purchased with shell money.

NOTABLE ARTS Fine arts included baskets (women) and horn work (men), particularly elkhorn items such as spoons for men (women used mussel-shell spoons). People made highly abstract petroglyphs from roughly 1600 on.

TRANSPORTATION Hupas traveled the rivers using redwood dugout canoes and paddles.

DRESS Men wore buckskin breechclouts or nothing at all. Women wore a two-piece buckskin skirt. They also had three vertical striped tattoos on their chins. Basketry caps protected their heads against burden basket tumplines. Hide robes were used for warmth. People on long journeys wore buckskin moccasins and leggings. Both sexes wore long hair and ornaments in pierced ears.

WAR AND WEAPONS The Hupa never fought together as a tribe. Even villages rarely united for war, which was generally a matter for individuals or families. Hupas kept their conflicts short, few and far between, with few casualties, except for a particularly harsh war with the Yokuts in the 1830s. Favored tactics included ambushes and surprise raids. Weapons included the bow and arrow, spears, stone knives, and rocks. Wooden or hide "armor" was sometimes worn for protection.

Contemporary Information

GOVERNMENT/RESERVATIONS The 85,445-acre Hoopa Valley Reservation (1876; Humboldt County) is the largest and most populous Indian reservation in California. The Hupa share it with some Karuk, Chilula, Yurok, Whilkut, and other Indians. The Hoopa Valley Tribe adopted a constitution and by-laws in 1950. Some Hupas also live at Elk Valley Rancheria, Del Norte County.

ECONOMY The reservation is generally self-sufficient. Timber, farming, and livestock constitute the main economic activities.

LEGAL STATUS The Hoopa Valley Tribe is a federally recognized tribal entity.

DAILY LIFE Hupas maintain a strong tribal identity and sense of continuity with the past, thanks in part to a continued presence in their homeland. They still practice many traditional customs, such as hunting, fishing, acorn gathering, basket and bead making, and the two World Renewal dances. The language is still spoken, particularly by older people. Children attend public school. The people seek complete political and economic control of their own affairs.

Jamul Indians

See Tipai-Ipai

Juaneño

See Luiseño

Kamia

See Tipai-Ipai

Karuk

Karuk (`Kä ruk) means "upstream," as opposed to the word for their neighbors, Yurok, which means "downstream."

LOCATION In the mid–nineteenth century, the Karuk lived on the middle course of the Klamath River in three main clusters of villages. Today, most Karuk live in Siskiyou County, California, and in southern Oregon.

POPULATION Karuk population in the eighteenth century is estimated to have been around 1,500. In 1990, tribal membership was pegged at 2,900, a number that included 33 Indians living on Karuk trust lands in Siskiyou County, California, as well as the Karuk population of the Quartz Valley Reservation and those living in the region.

LANGUAGE Karuk is a Hokan language.

Historical Information

HISTORY Contact with outsiders was largely avoided until 1850 and the great gold rush. At that time miners, vigilantes, soldiers, and assorted Anglos seized Karuk lands, burned their villages, and massacred their people. Hitherto unknown diseases also decimated their population. Many Karuk were removed to the Hoopa Valley Reservation.

Without a reservation of their own, many survivors drifted away from their traditional lands in search of work. Children were forcibly removed from their families and sent to culture-killing boarding schools. Some people did remain at home, however, and continued to live a lifestyle that included traditional subsistence and religious activities. Ceremonialism fell off after World War II but was reinvigorated beginning in the 1970s.

RELIGION The acorn harvest and the salmon run provided occasions for ceremony and celebration. Specific events included the World Renewal dances: the Jumping Dance, held in spring (associated with the salmon run), and the Deerskin Dances, held in fall (associated with the acorn harvest and the second salmon run). Both featured priestly rituals, displays of wealth, dancing, and singing.

GOVERNMENT No political organization or formal leadership existed within the three main clusters of villages, although wealthy men enjoyed a greater degree of influence. The Karuk regulated their community through shared values.

CUSTOMS Culturally, the Karuk were very similar to the neighboring Yurok and Hupa. In fact, they enjoyed especially close marriage and ceremonial ties with the Yurok. Their main values were industry, thrift, and the acquisition, mostly by hunting and gambling, of property such as dentalium shells, red woodpecker scalps, and large obsidian blades. These forms of wealth were important in and of themselves, not just for their purchasing power.

Woman doctors cured by sucking out the cause of a disease with the help of a "pain," an object, recoverable at will, that she kept within her body. Other kinds of doctors of both sexes cured by using medicinal plants. Corpses were buried in a family plot, along with shell money and valuables. Clothing and tools were hung on a fence around the grave. After five days, the soul was said to ascend to a place in the sky (the relative happiness of the afterlife was said to depend on the level of a person's wealth). A dead person's name remained taboo until or unless given to a child.

Crimes were recognized against individuals only (not against society). As such they could be atoned for by making material restitution. Refusal to pay could lead to death. The Karuk considered sex to be an enemy of wealth and did not often engage in it except during the fall gathering expeditions. Sex and children outside of marriage were acceptable in this scheme: "Legitimacy," like almost everything else, had a price. Marriage was basically a financial transaction, as was divorce. A couple lived with the man's parents.

The Karuk observed many daily magical practices and taboos. They also underwent extensive ritual preparations for the hunt, including sweating, bathing, scarification, bleeding, smoking their weapons with herbs, fasting, and sexual continence. Games included gambling with a marked stick, shinny, cat's cradle, archery, darts, and the women's dice game.

DWELLINGS Dwelling structures (family houses and sweat houses) were made of planks, preferably cedar. Family houses were rectangular and semisubterranean, with an outside stone-paved porch and a stone-lined firepit inside. Doors were small and low. Males from about three years of age slept, sweat, gambled, and passed the time in sweat houses, which women, except for shaman initiates, could not enter.

DIET The Karuk diet consisted mostly of salmon, deer (caught in snares or by hunters wearing deer head masks), and acorns (as soup, mush, and bread). The people also hunted bear, elk, and small game. Meat and fish were usually roasted, although salmon and venison could be dried and stored. The only cultivated crop was tobacco. The following were never eaten: dog, coyote, wolf, fox, wildcat, gopher, mole, bat, eagle, hawk, vulture, crow, raven, owl, meadowlark, blue jay, snake, lizard, frog, caterpillar, and grasshopper.

KEY TECHNOLOGY To catch fish, Karuks stood on fishing platforms holding large dip nets (the platforms were privately owned but could be rented). They also used harpoons and gaffs. They cut planks with stone mauls and horn wedges. Wooden implements included seats, storage boxes, spoons (for men; women used mussel-shell spoons), and hand drills for making fire. Women wove vegetable fiber baskets, containers, cradles, and caps. Bows were made of yew wood, with sinew backings and strings. Meat and bulbs were roasted in an oven of hot stones.

TRADE The Coastal Yurok supplied seaweed (for salt) to nearby tribes.

NOTABLE ARTS Fine arts included woodwork, storytelling (myths, with songs), and highly abstract petroglyphs, made after approximately 1600.

TRANSPORTATION Karuks purchased Yurok boats made from hollowed-out redwood logs.

DRESS Hides, usually from deer, and furs were the basic clothing materials. Women wore hides with the hair on to cover their upper bodies, and they wore a double apron of fringed buckskin. They also had three vertical lines tattooed on their chins. Men wore a buckskin breechclout or nothing at all. Both sexes wore buckskin moccasins with elkhide soles and perhaps leggings for rough traveling. Both sexes also wore basketry caps and ear and nose ornaments. They decorated their ceremonial clothing with fringe, shells, and pine nuts. Snowshoes were of hazelwood with iris-cord netting and buckskin ties.

WAR AND WEAPONS There was no war in a real sense, only retaliatory activity that might involve fellow villagers. Casualties were invariably light, and young women who may have been captured were usually returned at settlement time, when every injured party received full compensation. Weapons included yew bows, obsidian-tipped arrows, and elk hide or rod armor vests.

Contemporary Information

GOVERNMENT/RESERVATIONS The Karuk Tribe of California elects a nine-member tribal council. They adopted a constitution in 1985. Committees oversee the various programs. As of 1995, there was a land base of 300 acres.

The Quartz Valley Reservation, Siskiyou County, has a land base of 300 acres. The 1992 population was roughly 124.

ECONOMY The tribe itself employed about 80 people in 1995. It operates three health clinics and owns a hardware store. Tribal members also work for the U.S. Forest Service. The Karuk Community Development Corporation maintains formal development plans.

LEGAL STATUS The Karuk Tribe of California has been a federally recognized tribal entity since 1979. The Quartz Valley Rancheria of Karok, Shasta, and Upper Klamath Indians is a federally recognized tribal entity.

DAILY LIFE Although hundreds and perhaps thousands of people claim Karuk ancestry, few Karuks remain who have been in direct contact with their elders and traditions. Still, since the 1970s Karuks have revived aspects of their traditional culture, including their language and the World Renewal ceremony (Pikyavish), held in late summer and early fall. The traditional fine art of basket weaving has also been rediscovered.

Medicine men and women usually receive their authority from an elder. Many people live in extended families. Most children attend public schools, and the tribe provides some scholarship money for those who attend college. Several villages have been inhabited since precontact times. There is a pending land claim against the United States. Important contemporary issues include health care, water rights, proper natural resource management, and land acquisition.

Konkow
See Maidu

Konomihu
See Shasta

Lassik
See Wailaki

Luiseño

Luiseño (L ū i `s ā ny ō) is a name derived from the Mission San Luis Rey. Luiseño Indians associated with a nearby mission, San Juan Capistrano, were often referred to as Juaneño Indians. Both of these peoples are included among the groups of so-called Mission Indians.

LOCATION The traditional (eighteenth-century) location of the Luiseño was a region of great environmental diversity, along the coast and inland along streams, south of present-day Los Angeles but north of the Tipai-Ipai. Today most Luiseño live on reservations in San Diego and Riverside Counties.

POPULATION Roughly 10,000 in the late eighteenth century, the 1990 Luiseño population on their reservations stood at 1,795.

LANGUAGE Luiseño and Juaneño belong to the Cupan group of the Takic division of the Uto-Aztecan language family.

Historical Information

HISTORY The Luiseño constituted a distinct culture from at least 1400 or so. They first encountered non-natives in 1796, with the Gaspar de Portolá expedition and the founding of Mission San Diego. Shortly thereafter, the Spanish built Missions San Luis Rey and San Juan Capistrano. Many Luiseños were missionized, and many died during this and succeeding Mexican and U.S. periods of hardship, disease, and murder.

After Mexican secularization of the missions in 1834, many Indians revolted against their continued exploitation by Mexican rancheros. In general, Luiseño villages maintained their traditional subsistence activities, with the addition of wheat and corn agriculture, irrigation, orchards, and animal husbandry. The United States created several Luiseño reservations in 1875; people either lived there or scattered. The 1891 Act for the Relief of Mission Indians led to the placement of federal administrative personnel on the reservations, including police, schools, and courts. The idea was to undermine the traditional power structure and move the people toward assimilation into mainstream U.S. culture.

Throughout the nineteenth and into the twentieth century, Luiseños fought to retain their land and their traditions. For instance, their resistance to government schools culminated in 1895 when a Luiseño burned the school and assassinated the teacher at Pachanga. Luiseños rejected the Indian Reorganization Act (IRA) of 1934 because it provided for too little home rule. They were finally forced to abandon once-prosperous farms and orchards after precious water supplies were taken by non-Indians living upstream.

Still, federal control of the reservations increased, as did pressure to assimilate. The 1950s brought a partial termination of federal services, which stimulated a resurgence of local self-government and self-determination. This trend accelerated in the 1960s with the arrival of various federal economic programs. Today, Luiseños are prominent in state and regional Indian groups.

RELIGION Ritual drama and sacred oral literature controlled their environment and confirmed Luiseños' place in the world. Ritual offices included chief, assistant chief, shamans, councilors, and members of the *Chinigchinich* society (most of the men in the village). A large number of ceremonies revolved around hunting, life-cycle, weather control, and war and peace. Some ceremonies involved questing for visions with the help of a drink prepared from jimsonweed (datura). Religious knowledge/power was carefully guarded.

Sandpaintings were part of the secret *Chinigchinich* cult initiation (the cult may have been in part a response to the Spanish presence): The cosmos, sacred beings, and human spiritual phases were all represented. Sandpaintings never lasted beyond the ceremony. Ritual equipment included stone grinding bowls, clay figurines, sacred wands, head scratchers, and eagle-feather headdresses. Most participants in rituals were paid.

GOVERNMENT The Luiseño were organized into roughly 50 patrilineal clan tribelets, each with an autonomous, semipermanent village led by a hereditary chief. Each village group also had its own food resource area; other resources (raw materials, sacred sites as well as food) could be owned individually or collectively. Trespass was by express permission only.

The chief supervised hunting, gathering, and war activities. He was aided by an assistant, shamans, and a council of advisers (all positions were hereditary). Band specialists managed natural resources using techniques such as controlled burning and water and erosion management. They also led various activities such as rabbit hunts and deer and antelope drives. In the eighteenth century, Spanish-style political offices (such as *generales* and *capitanes*) existed parallel to the traditional religious ones.

CUSTOMS In addition to food and other resource areas, private property might include capital and ritual equipment, eagle nests, and songs. Social status was important and defined by many criteria. Aside from hunting (male) and gathering (female), sexual divisions of labor were ill defined. Aged women taught children crafts, whereas older men were generally more active in ceremonial affairs, including making hunting and ceremonial paraphernalia, and in instructing initiates. Games included dice, the split stick gambling game, the ball and stick game, and cat's cradle.

The Luiseño observed various life-cycle taboos, restrictions, and ritual requirements. Puberty rituals stressed correct conduct, such as dances, ordeals, learning songs and rituals (boys), and rock painting and behavior in married life (girls). Girls married an arranged partner shortly after puberty. Divorce was possible but not easy to obtain. Death ceremonies proliferated. At different times, burning an image of the deceased, purification of the relatives, feasting and gift-giving were all practiced. A person's possessions were generally destroyed when she or he died.

DWELLINGS Family houses were conical in shape, built partly underground, and covered with reeds, brush, or bark. Earth sweat houses were also semisubterranean. People used ramadas for ceremonies and domestic chores.

DIET Six species of acorns served as a dietary staple. Inland groups traveled seasonally to fish along the coast; coastal groups gathered acorns inland. Luiseños also ate a wide variety of seeds, nuts, berries, bulbs, roots, mushrooms, cactus pods, and fruits. Seeds were parched, ground, and cooked into mush. Other foods included small game, deer (stalked or run down), antelope, fowl, fish, sea mammals, crustaceans, and mollusks. Teas as well as tobacco and datura were used medicinally and ceremonially. Most predators as well as reptiles were avoided. Many foods were cooked in clay jars over a fire; game was roasted in coals.

KEY TECHNOLOGY Luiseños practiced controlled burning of certain areas to increase the yield of seed-bearing plants. They hunted with bow and arrow, throwing sticks, snares, and traps. Men used deer-antler flakes to help flake stone points. They built canoes for ocean fishing. Other fishing equipment included seines, basketry traps, dip nets, bone or shell hooks, possibly harpoons, and poison. Utilitarian items included pottery, coiled and twined baskets, carrying pouches of net or skin, stone grinding tools, cooking and eating utensils of wood and stone, and musical instruments, including bone and cane whistles, cane flutes, split-stick clappers, and turtle shell, gourd, or hoof rattles.

TRADE The Luiseño imported steatite bowls (from Santa Catalina Island), obsidian (from northern or eastern neighbors), and other items.

NOTABLE ARTS Fine arts included pottery; coiled baskets, decorated with tan, red, or black geometric designs; sandpaintings; petroglyphs, perhaps associated with hunting, from about 500 B.C.E. to 1000; and pictographs, which featured straight and wavy lines, angles, and people. The pictographs were used in girls' puberty ceremonies after about 1400.

TRANSPORTATION Dugout or balsa canoes were used for ocean fishing.

DRESS Women wore cedar bark aprons. Men generally wore little or no clothing, although both sexes used deer, rabbit, or otter robes in colder weather. They also tattooed and painted their bodies and wore pendants of mica, bone, clay, abalone shell, and bear claws; human hair bracelets and anklets; and yucca-fiber and deerskin moccasins.

WAR AND WEAPONS Trespass was a major cause for war. The Luiseño were also fairly imperialist,

fighting (and marrying) to acquire territory. During war, the chief assumed commander duties along with an initiated warrior class. Weapons included the bow and arrow, small and large war clubs, lances, slings, and thrusting sticks.

Contemporary Information

GOVERNMENT/RESERVATIONS Luiseño reservations include Rincon (1875; 4,276 acres; 379 Indians in 1996; San Diego County), Pala (1875; 11,893 acres; San Diego County; shared with the Cupeño), Pauma and Yuima (1872; 5,877 acres; San Diego County), Soboba (1883; 5,916 acres; Riverside County), Pechanga (1882; 4,394 acres; Riverside County), La Jolla (1875; 8,541 acres; San Diego County), and Twentynine Palms (1895; 402 acres; San Bernardino County). The reservations feature elected chairs and councils, formal membership roles, and articles of association.

ECONOMY A range of jobs may be found on or near the reservations. Many operate campgrounds, orchards, and stores. La Jolla has excellent recreation facilities that also bring in money. Pauma has hydroelectric resources. Planning for resource development is ongoing.

LEGAL STATUS The La Jolla Band, the Twentynine Palms Band, the Soboba Band, the Rincon Band, the Pechanga Band, the Pauma Band, and the Pala Band of Luiseño Mission Indians are federally recognized tribal entities. The Juaneño Band of Mission Indians had not attained federal recognition as of 1997.

DAILY LIFE Many people still speak Luiseño, and language classes are popular among the young. Villiana Hyde has written a language text (1971). Traditional food, games, songs, and dances remain part of people's lives, as do many ideas regarding property and other cultural references. Luiseños are relatively highly educated. Although most Luiseños are Catholics, some traditional ceremonies, such as the initiation for cult members, the installation of religious chiefs, and funerals, are still performed.

Reservations feature libraries as well as senior and cultural programs. Water rights remain an ongoing issue despite the tribe's paper victory in a court case settled in 1985. In general, Luiseños have struck a balance between resisting government intrusion into their lives and becoming politically savvy enough to manipulate public and private organizations to their best benefit.

Maidu

Maidu (`M ī d ū), a group of three languages (Maidu, Konkow, and Nisenan; see "Language") and in modern times a tribe of Indians. Maidu comes from their self-designation and means "person." Konkow comes from the Anglicization of their word for "meadowland." Nisenan comes from their self-designation and means "among us."

LOCATION Traditional Maidu territory is along the eastern tributaries of the Sacramento River, south of Lassen Peak. This country features a great variation in terrain, from river and mountain valleys to high mountain meadows. Today, most Maidus live on two small reservations in Butte County and share one in Lassen County and one in Mendocino County.

POPULATION Roughly 9,000 Maidus lived in the early nineteenth century. In 1990, two lived at Berry Creek and five at Enterprise Rancheria. Also in 1990, 154 Indians of mixed tribes, including Maidu, lived at Susanville, and 577 Maidu and other Indians lived at Covelo. The 1995 Maidu population is considered to be approximately 2,500.

LANGUAGE Maiduan is a Penutian language. Its three divisions—northeastern or mountain (Maidu), northwestern or foothill (Konkow), and southern or valley (Nisenan)—were probably mutually unintelligible.

Historical Information

HISTORY Prior to about 1700, when they abandoned it to the Paiutes, Maidus also controlled territory east of Honey Lake into present-day Nevada. Maidus first met Spanish and U.S. expeditions and trappers in the early nineteenth century. Initial contact was peaceful.

The Maidu were relatively successful in avoiding missions, but many were killed in 1833 by a severe epidemic, possibly malaria. The 1849 gold rush led directly to theft of their land, disruption of their ability to acquire food, more disease, violence, and mass murder. Most survivors were forced into ranch and farm work and onto reservations. Although some groups signed a treaty in 1851, it was never ratified; each Maidu received a land claims settlement payment of about $660 in 1971.

The Konkow Reservation was established as Nome Lackee in 1854, but its residents were forced nine years later to abandon it and march to the Round Valley Reservation. The few surviving Nisenan lived near foothill towns and worked in local low-paying industries at that time. Many Maidu children attended assimilationist boarding schools around the turn of the century. Maidu culture underwent a brief revival in the 1870s under the influence of the Ghost Dance. All rancherias were purchased between 1906 and 1937 under legislation providing for "homeless" California Indians. Following the death in 1906 of the last hereditary headman, much of the people's ceremonial regalia was sold to a local museum.

RELIGION Maidu religion was closely related to their mythology. Konkows and Nisenans, but not the Maidu proper, practiced the Kuksu cult, a ceremonial and dance organization led by a powerful shaman. Only those properly initiated could join. Members followed a dance cycle in which dances represented different spirits.

Shamans trucked with the spirits, cured, interpreted dreams, and conducted ceremonies. Spirits were said to live in natural geographic sites. Shamans had at least one spirit as a guardian and source of power. Female shamans were assumed to be malevolent.

The Nisenan observed an annual fall mourning ceremony and other ritual dances as well. Doctors could be of either sex, although women were considered less likely to hurt a patient (doctors could also poison people). Religious specialists included religious shamans, poison shamans, singing shamans, and weather shamans.

GOVERNMENT Of the three main Maidu divisions, the valley people, or Nisenan, had the largest population and the most number of tribelets (permanent villages). Village communities (consisting of several villages, with size in inverse proportion to elevation) were autonomous. The central village had the largest dance or ceremonial chamber, which doubled as a home to the headman. This office, which was inheritable only among the Nisenan, was chosen by a shaman. He or she (women might become chiefs among Nisenan) was generally wealthy and served primarily as adviser and spokesperson.

CUSTOMS The Maidu observed many life-cycle taboos and restrictions. Gender roles were fairly rigidly defined. There was no formal marriage ceremony other than mutual gift-giving. Couples lived in the woman's home at first and later in a home of their own near the man's family. If a woman gave birth to twins, she and the babies were often killed. The Nisenan practiced cremation; the other two groups buried their dead with food and gifts. All three burned the house and possessions after death and held annual mourning ceremonies for several years thereafter.

Most fishing and hunting areas were held in common. Theft from a neighbor was severely punished, although theft from someone of another community was not punished by the home community. Murder and rape were dealt with by blood revenge (of the guilty party or a near friend or relative) or by payment. Lying was generally avoided. The community policed its boundaries against poachers.

Games include hoop-and-pole, tossing games, dice games, and hand games and often contained wagering, music, and song. Tobacco was their only cultivated plant. It was smoked in elderberry pipes at bedtime and during ceremonies.

DWELLINGS The Maidu settled in small village groups, with the headman, dance hall, and ceremonial chamber in the central village. Hill dwellings were pole-framed, brush- or skin-covered houses in winter and brush shelters in summer. Most mountain people remained in their villages during the winter. In winter, valley people lived in earth-covered, domed pit houses, with door and smoke openings in the roof. They used brush shelters in summer.

DIET Maidus were mainly hunters and gatherers. Their staple was the acorn, from which they made mush, bread, and soup. They also ate pine nuts, manzanita, roots, and insects. Game included deer (hunted in communal drives), elk, antelope, and bear (for hides). Meat was baked, dried, or roasted. Fish included eel, salmon, and trout. Taboo foods among the Maidu proper included coyote, dog, wolf, buzzard, lizard, snake, and frog. Konkows refused to eat bear and mountain lion. The Nisenan ate neither owl, condor, nor vulture. Maidus drank wild mint tea and manzanita cider.

KEY TECHNOLOGY Nets, weirs, and spears served a fishing equipment. The people hunted with bow and arrow and stone (basalt and obsidian) spears and knives. Other tools (stone, grass, and wood) included scrapers, arrow straighteners, pestles, mortars, and pipes. They used a buckeye drill to start fires and tule mats for seats, beds, roofs, doors, skirts, rafts, and beds. Musical instruments included drums, rattles, flutes, whistles, and a bow.

TRADE Little individual travel occurred between villages greater than 20 miles apart, but trade was widespread among nearby villages and groups. Goods also changed hands as a result of gambling games. The Konkow traded arrows, bows, deer hides, and foods for shell beads, pine nuts, and salmon. The Maidu proper traded bows and deer hides to enemy Achumawi for beads, obsidian, and green pigment. The Nisenan traded acorns, nuts, berries, wood, and skins for fish, roots, grasses, shells, beads, salt, and feathers. Goods could also be purchased with shell and baked magnesite cylinder beads.

NOTABLE ARTS Fine arts included baskets; necklaces; shell, bone, and feather earrings; and other bead and feather work. Petroglyphs, mostly circles and dots, with a few people or animals, were created perhaps as early as 1000 B.C.E.

TRANSPORTATION Dugout and tule (rush) canoes were used for water transportation.

DRESS Dress was minimal year-round. In summer, men wore nothing or a buckskin breechclout. Women wore apron skirts of buckskin, bark, or grass. Bear, deer (bird and fowl feather to the south), and mountain lion fur robes and blankets were added in cold weather. Only the northeastern group wore moccasins and snowshoes. Both sexes wore tattoos and shell, bone, feather, and wood ornaments.

WAR AND WEAPONS Posting regular sentries against enemies was a common practice. Although all groups recognized foreign enemies, most warfare occurred between villages or village communities. Favored tactics included raiding and ambush. Arrows were often poisoned. Other weapons included spears, sticks, slings, and elk hide armor. The Konkow tortured captured males, whereas the Nisenan simply killed them. Women prisoners were generally kept in the household.

Contemporary Information

GOVERNMENT/RESERVATIONS Berry Creek (1916; 33 acres; Butte County) and Enterprise (1906; 40 acres; Butte County) are the two Maidu rancherias. Maidus also live on the Greenville Rancheria (Plumas and Tehama Counties), Shingle Springs Rancheria (El Dorado County), the Susanville Rancheria (1923; 150 acres), and the Round Valley Reservation (1864; 30,538 acres) with other tribes. Most rancherias are governed by elected tribal councils.

The Chico Rancheria (Mechoopda Maidu) is governed by an elected tribal government. There were about 70 residents of a population of 400 in the early 1990s.

ECONOMY Unemployment among the Maidu community remains chronically high. Because of the small land base and limited resources, economic development remains extremely limited.

LEGAL STATUS The Berry Creek Rancheria of Maidu Indians; the Greenville Rancheria of Maidu Indians; the Enterprise Rancheria of Maidu Indians; the Mooretown Rancheria of Maidu Indians; the Shingle Springs Rancheria of Maidu Indians; the Susanville Indian Rancheria of Paiute, Maidu, Pit River, and Washoe Indians; and the Covelo Indian Community of the Round Valley Reservation are all federally recognized tribal entities. The Mechoopda Tribe of Maidu Indians was rerecognized in 1992.

The Maidu Nation and the North Maidu Tribe are currently unrecognized.

DAILY LIFE Maidus have generally assimilated with other Indians and with the general population. A few Maidu still speak their language, make baskets, and hold ceremonies. Social problems abound: Education levels are low, whereas levels of crime, alcoholism, and suicide remain stubbornly high. Housing, sanitation, and health care is generally poor. Many Maidus suffer from diabetes. The Maidu hold an annual bear dance in Janesville, and efforts have increased to preserve the language and culture. Maidus are also active in pan-Indian activities.

Mattole

See Wailaki; Wiyot

Mission Indians

See Cahuilla; Luiseño; Serrano; Tipai-Ipai

Miwok

Miwok (`M ē wok) is a word meaning "People" in Miwokan.

LOCATION The Miwok were originally composed of three divisions: Eastern (Sierra), Lake, and Coast. The Miwok lived in over 100 villages along the San Joaquin and Sacramento Rivers, from the area north of San Francisco Bay east into the western slope of the Sierra Nevada. The Lake Miwok lived near Clear Lake, north of San Francisco Bay.

Today the Eastern Miwok live in five rancherias, located roughly between Sacramento and Stockton, and in nearby cities. Lake Miwoks have one small settlement at Middletown Rancheria that they share with Pomo Indians.

POPULATION Miwok population stood at about 22,000 in the eighteenth century, of whom approximately 90 percent (19,500) were Eastern Miwok. In 1990, the total Miwok population was about 3,400.

LANGUAGE There were several dialects and groups of Miwokan, a California Penutian language.

Historical Information

HISTORY Lowland occupation of California by the Eastern Miwok probably began as early as 2,000 years ago or more; occupation of the Sierra Nevada is only about 500 years old. The Eastern Miwok were divided into five cultural groups: Bay Miwok, Plains Miwok, Northern Miwok, Southern Miwok, and Central Sierra Miwok. Sir Francis Drake (1579) and Sebastian Cermeño (1595) may have met the Coast Miwok, but no further record of contact exists until the late eighteenth century and the beginning of the mission period. Russians also colonized the region in the early nineteenth century.

The Spanish had established missions in Coast Miwok and Lake Miwok territory by the early nineteenth century to which thousands of Miwoks were forcibly removed and where most later died of disease and hardship. In the 1840s, Mexican *rancheros* routinely kidnapped Lake Miwok people to work on their ranches and staged massacres to intimidate the survivors. As a result of all this bloodshed, previously independent tribelets banded together and even formed military alliances with other groups such as the Yokuts, raiding and attacking from the 1820s through the 1840s.

Everything changed for the Eastern Miwok in the late 1840s, when the United States gained political control of California and the great gold rush began. Most Miwoks were killed by disease, white violence, and disruption of their hunting and gathering environment. The Mariposa Indian War (1850), led by Chief Tenaya and others, was a final show of resistance by the Eastern Miwok and the Yokuts against Anglo incursions and atrocities. By the 1860s, surviving Miwoks were eking out a living by mining, farm and ranch work, and low-paying work on the edges of towns. Most Miwoks remained on local rancherias, several of which were purchased for them by the U.S. government in the early twentieth century.

Coast Miwok remained for the most part in their traditional homeland in the twentieth century, working at sawmills, as agricultural laborers, and fishing. They were officially terminated in the 1950s, but in 1992 a group called the Federated Coast Miwok created by-laws and petitioned the government for recognition.

RELIGION Eastern and probably also Coast Miwoks believed in the duality (land and water) of all things. Ceremonies, both sacred and secular, abounded, accompanied by dances held in great dance houses. The ceremonial role of each village in the tribelet was determined by geographical and political considerations. Lake Miwoks only allowed men in the dance houses.

Sacred ceremonies revolving around a rich mythology featured elaborate costumes, robes, and feather headdresses. The Miwok recognized several different kinds of shamans, such as spirit or sucking shamans, herb shamans (who cured and helped ensure a successful hunt), and rattlesnake, weather, and bear shamans. Shamans, whose profession was inherited patrilineally, received their powers via instruction from and personal acquisition of supernatural power gained through dreams, trances, and vision quests.

GOVERNMENT The main political unit was the tribelet, an independent and sovereign nation of roughly 100–500 people (smaller in the mountains). Each tribelet was composed of a number of lineages, or settlement areas of extended families. Larger tribelets, those composed of several named settlements, were led by chiefs, who were usually wealthy. Their responsibilities included hosting guests, sponsoring ceremonies, settling disputes, and overseeing the acorn harvest. In turn, chiefs were supplied with food and were expected to conduct themselves with a measure of grandness.

Among the Lake Miwok, special ceremonial officials presided over dances. Among Eastern and Lake Miwok the office of chief was hereditary and was male if possible. Other officials included the announcer (elective) and messenger (hereditary).

The Coast Miwok also included two important female officials who presided over certain festivals and who supervised construction of the dance house.

CUSTOMS All Eastern Miwoks were members of one of two divisions (land or water). Both boys and girls went through puberty ceremonies. Marriage between Lake Miwok was a matter arranged by the parents through gift giving. Intermarriage between neighboring groups was common. The many life-cycle prohibitions and taboos included sex before the hunt or during a woman's period. Fourth and later infants may have been killed. The dead were cremated or buried. Widows cut their hair and rubbed pitch on their heads. Along the coast, property was burned along with the body. The name of the dead was never spoken again. There were no mourning ceremonies.

Men and occasionally women used pipes to smoke a gathered local tobacco. Miwoks possessed a strong feeling for property: Trespass was a serious offense, and virtually every transaction between two people involved payment. The profession of "poisoner" was widely recognized, and many people feared being poisoned more than they feared illness. People often danced, both for fun and ritual. Most songs were considered personal property. Both sexes played hockey, handball, and the grass game. Women also played a dice game. Children played with mud or stick dolls, acorn buzzers, and pebbles as jacks.

DWELLINGS Miwoks built conical houses framed with wooden poles and covered with plants, fronds, bark, or grasses. Hearths were centrally located, next to an earth oven. Pine needles covered the floors; mats and skins were used for bedding. Some winter homes or dance houses, and most houses among the Lake Miwok, were partially below ground. Larger villages had a sweat lodge that served mostly as a male clubhouse.

DIET Acorns, greens, nuts, berries, seeds, and roots were some of the great variety of wild plants eaten by the Miwok. They also ate fish, especially salmon, trout, and shellfish, and hunted elk, deer, bear, antelope, fowl, and small game, especially rabbit. Deer were hunted in several ways, including driving them into a net or over a cliff, stalking while in deer disguise, shooting them from blinds, and running them down over the course of a day or so. Miwoks generally avoided eating dog, coyote, skunk, eagle, roadrunner, and snakes and frogs.

KEY TECHNOLOGY Hunting equipment included traps, snares, and bow and arrow. A variety of baskets served many functions, such as winnowers, seed beaters, cradles, burden baskets, and storage. Fish were caught with nets, hook-and-line, and harpoon. Foods were stored either in granaries (acorns) or baskets. Foods were baked or steamed in earth ovens. Stone and bone provided the raw material for a variety of tools. Cords and string came from plant fibers, especially milkweed and hemp. Coast and Lake Miwok used clamshell beads as money. Musical instruments included elderberry flutes, drums, cocoon rattles, clappers, and whistles. The Lake Miwok used several plants for natural dyes.

TRADE Costanoans supplied the Eastern Miwok with salt. Other items of exchange included obsidian, shells, bows, and baskets. Along the coast, goods were more often purchased than traded. Lake Miwoks often traveled west to collect marine resources such as clamshells and seaweed.

NOTABLE ARTS Fine arts included baskets and representational petroglyphs, consisting mostly of circles and dots and beginning as early as 1000 B.C.E.

TRANSPORTATION The Eastern Miwok used a tule balsa on navigable rivers. Log rafts were used on the coast.

DRESS Eastern and Lake men wore buckskin breechclouts and shirts. Men along the coast wore little or nothing. Most women wore hide skirts and aprons, although in lower elevations they sometimes used grasses for skirts. Hide and woven rabbit-skin robes and blankets kept people warm in winter. Most people also wore ear and nose ornaments as well as face and body paint. They also practiced tattooing and head deformation (flattened heads and noses) for adornment. Young children wore no clothes. Hair was worn long except in mourning (Eastern Miwok). Lake Miwoks braided their hair.

WAR AND WEAPONS The bow and arrow was the most important weapon. Coast Miwoks also used slings.

Contemporary Information

GOVERNMENT/RESERVATIONS Middletown Rancheria (189 acres in Lake County; 18 Indians in 1990) is a Lake Miwok and Pomo community. Eastern Miwok lands include Jackson Rancheria (1893; 331 acres in Amador County; 35–40 families in 1990; tribal council), Sheep Ranch Rancheria (1916; .92 acres [a cemetery] in Calaveras County), and Tuolomne Rancheria (1910; 336 acres in Tuolumne County; some 150 population in 1990). Other rancherias with very small Miwok populations include Shingle Springs, Buena Vista, Chicken Ranch, and Cortina.

ECONOMY Many Miwoks work in logging and related industries. There are also some employment opportunities at Yosemite National Park. There is a bingo parlor on the Chicken Ranch Rancheria.

LEGAL STATUS The Chicken Ranch Rancheria of Me-Wuk Indians, the Jackson Rancheria of Me-Wuk Indians, the Tuolomne Band of Me-Wuk Indians, the

Sheep Ranch Rancheria of Me-Wuk Indians, and the Buena Vista Rancheria are federally recognized tribal entities. The Cortina Indian Rancheria is a federally recognized tribal entity.

The American Indian Council of Mariposa County, the Calavaras Band of Mewuk, the Federated Coast Miwok Tribe, and the Ione Band of Mewuk have petitioned for federal recognition.

DAILY LIFE There is a clinic/health center and a traditional roundhouse at Tuolumne Rancheria. Tuolumne also celebrates an acorn festival as well as a pan-Indian gathering in September. Although most of the religious traditions have been lost, young people are beginning to revive some dances and songs. Many Coast Miwoks have achieved prominence as scholars. Lake Miwoks have developed innovative educational programs in local schools. With native speakers of Miwok almost gone, the people have developed a number of programs to preserve and restore the language. Traditional basket making and weaving are also making comebacks.

Monache

See Mono

Mono

Mono (ˋM ō n ō), or Monache, is a Yokuts term of uncertain meaning. Also known as the Western Mono, they are *Nimi,* or "People," in their own language.

LOCATION Traditionally, the Mono lived in central California along the Sierra Nevada, higher in elevation (mainly 3,000 to 7,000 feet) then the Foothill Yokuts. Today most Mono live on Big Sandy and Cold Springs Rancherias, with other Indians on the Tule River Reservation, and in several northern California communities.

POPULATION Mono population stood at roughly 2,500 in the late eighteenth century. In 1990, 38 lived on the Big Sandy Rancheria; 159 lived on the Cold Springs Rancheria; and probably several hundred are included with the 745 mixed Indians on the Tule River Indian Reservation and in communities in northern California.

LANGUAGE Mono is a language of the western group of the Numic family of the Uto-Aztecan language stock.

Historical Information

HISTORY In the eighteenth century, the Mono included six independent tribal groups (Northfork Mono, Wobonuch, Entimbich, Michahay, Waksachi, Patwisha). They were in general culturally similar to the neighboring Foothill Yokuts. Since they lived in a region not highly desired by miners or non-native

settlers, they enjoyed relatively higher survival rates in the nineteenth century than did most other California Indian peoples.

As "homeless Indians," the Mono received three rancherias from the federal government in the 1910s. Some individuals also acquired parcels of land. Many people retained their traditional subsistence gathering patterns while working as loggers, ranch hands, miners, and domestic help. As was the case with many other Indians, a large number of Mono moved to the cities after World War II.

RELIGION The Mono believed that spirits contained supernatural powers that might be employed by people with the proper knowledge. Supernatural powers were obtained through a connection with nature or by taking datura, a drug, as part of a ritual. Although shamans were especially skilled in these techniques, most people thought it a good idea to possess some powers for general success in life. Shamans used their powers for curing. However, they could also hurt or kill, and various evil activities were often ascribed to them.

Ceremonies included bear dances (by members of the Bear lineage) and the annual mourning ceremony. The Mono brought the Ghost Dance of 1870 west of the Sierra Nevada. This phenomenon ended by 1875, largely because it failed to bring back the dead as promised; the 1890 Ghost Dance revival had no impact on the Mono.

GOVERNMENT Each Mono group was composed of villages or hamlets of between one and eight huts, each led by a (usually hereditary male) chief. Patrilineal lineages, such as Eagle, Dove, Roadrunner, and Bear, were social organizations. The chief (from the Eagle lineage) arranged ceremonies, saw to the needy, and sanctioned the killing of evil shamans or others. He led by suggestion rather than by command. A messenger (Roadrunner lineage) assisted the chief and settled quarrels. They both had a symbol of office, an eight-foot-long cane with red-painted bands and string on top. Only the Northfork Mono had formal intradivision groups (Eagle and Dove), each with its own chief.

CUSTOMS After death, the soul was said to travel west for two days to the land of the dead. The dead were cremated and their remains buried. Mourning took place at the time of death and also at an annual ceremony. The Mono maintained close relations with their neighbors for activities such as trade, intermarriage, ceremonies, visiting, and resource exploitation. They observed no particular hunting or puberty rituals. Most men had only one wife (some wealthy men had more). Marriages were planned by the man's parents; the principals usually agreed. Divorce was possible for cause. Mono married each other as well as Yokuts Indians.

DWELLINGS The Mono built three types of houses: conical with an excavated floor, oval with a ridgepole, and conical with a center pole covered by thatch or cedar bark. Houses were arranged in a semicircle around the village. Most villages also contained a sweat house (male only), an acorn storehouse, and an open area used for dances and ceremonies.

DIET Acorns were the staple food of these hunter-gatherers. They also ate roots, pine nuts, seeds, and berries (and drank cider from manzanita berries). They hunted and trapped deer, bear, rabbits, and squirrels. Good hunters shared their meat. Bears were often killed by blocking egress from their caves and then shooting them. Fish were caught with traps, weirs, nets, and spears.

KEY TECHNOLOGY Items included a variety of fish nets and hunting traps; pottery and soapstone cookware; baskets; juniper and laurel bows; obsidian knives, scrapers, and arrow points; and various tools of stone and wood.

TRADE Trade occurred mainly with the Owens Valley Paiute on the eastern side of the mountains. Most items were natural products, including acorns, obsidian, pine nuts, and rabbit skins. Mono also traded with the Yokuts.

NOTABLE ARTS Traditional arts included basket making and beadwork.

TRANSPORTATION People floated babies and other valuables across rivers in basket boats. They used log rafts with brush or mat decking for crossing streams.

DRESS Men and women wore deerskin or fiber aprons or breechclouts. Some groups wore moccasins. Both sexes pierced their ears and noses and tattooed their faces. Face and bodies were painted for ceremonies only. Woven rabbit-skin blankets were used in cold weather.

WAR AND WEAPONS The usual cause of war was trespass or injuries to individuals (from shamans). Its intent was individual revenge; actual intertribal warfare was rare. People fought with bows and special, occasionally poisoned, arrows. The Monache generally did not take captives. Peacemaking included gifts of presents that were not considered reparations.

Contemporary Information

GOVERNMENT/RESERVATIONS The Mono Tribal Council is located in Dunlap, California. Formal communities include the Tule River Reservation (Tulare County, shared, with a tribal council); the Posgisa community (about 200 people) at Big Sandy Rancheria (Fresno County); the Num (about 600 people), located around the town of North Fork; the Wobonuch community at Dunlap (about 80 people);

and the Holkoma community at Cold Springs Rancheria (Fresno County; 275 people; 155 acres). Populations are as of the early 1990s.

ECONOMY The Tule River Reservation contains hydroelectric resources.

LEGAL STATUS The Tule River Indian Tribe of the Tule River Indian Reservation, the Big Sandy Rancheria of Mono Indians, the Northfork Rancheria of Mono Indians (Num community), and the Cold Springs Rancheria of Mono Indians are all federally recognized tribal entities.

As of 1997, the Dunlap Band of Mono Indians (Wobonuch community) and the Mono Lake Indian community had not attained federal recognition.

DAILY LIFE There is a regional health center at North Fork, as well as a seniors' lunch program and a Head Start program. The Sierra Mono Museum is located at North Fork. It features displays, collections, and classes in traditional arts and language. Indian Days are held in August. The community at Big Sandy uses federal grant money for programs to preserve language and traditional culture.

Nisenan
See Maidu

Nomlaki
See Wintun

Nongatl
See Wailaki

Obispeño
See Chumash

Okwanuchu
See Shasta

Patwin
See Wintun

Pit River Indians
See Achumawi

Pomo
Pomo (`P ō m ō), a group of seven culturally similar but politically independent villages or tribelets. This Pomo word means roughly "those who live at red earth hole," possibly a reference to a local mineral.

LOCATION Traditionally, the Pomo lived about 50 miles north of San Francisco Bay, on the coast and inland, especially around Clear Lake and the Russian River. Today there are roughly 20 Pomo rancherias in northern California, especially in Lake, Mendocino, and Sonoma Counties. Pomo Indians also live in regional cities and towns.

POPULATION   Roughly 15,000 in the early nineteenth century, the Pomo population stood at 4,766 in 1990. About one-third of these lived on tribal land.

LANGUAGE   "Pomo" was actually seven mutually unintelligible Pomoan (Hokan) languages, including Southern Pomo, Central Pomo, Northern Pomo, Eastern Pomo, Northeastern Pomo, Southeastern Pomo, and Southwestern Pomo (Kashaya).

Historical Information

HISTORY   Pomo prehistory remains murky, except that the people became a part of a regional trading system at about 1500. By the late 1700s, the Spanish had begun raiding Southern Pomo country for converts, and Hispanic influence began to be felt in Pomo country. Russian fur traders also arrived to brutalize the natives during this time. Their primary method of attracting Indian help was to attack a village and kidnap the women and children, who were then held as hostages (slaves) while the men were forced to hunt fur-bearing animals. In 1811 the Russians established a trading post at Fort Ross, on Bodega Bay (abandoned in 1841).

Hundreds of Pomos accepted the Catholic faith at local Spanish missions after 1817. In 1822, California became part of the Mexican Republic. Mexicans granted land to their citizens deep within Pomo country and enforced the land grants with strict military control. Thousands of Pomos died of disease (mainly cholera and smallpox) during the 1830s and 1840s, and Mexican soldiers killed or sold into slavery thousands more. Deaths from disease were doubly killing: Since the Pomo attributed illness to human causes, as did many native peoples, the epidemics also brought a concurrent rise in divisive suspicions and a loss of faith in traditions.

A bad situation worsened for the Pomo after 1849, when Anglos flooded into their territory, stealing their land and murdering them en masse. Survivors were disenfranchised and forced to work for their conquerors under slavelike conditions. A number of Pomos—perhaps up to 200—were killed by the U.S. Army in 1850. In 1856, the Pomo were "rounded up" and forced to live on the newly established Mendocino Indian Reserve. The government discontinued the reserve eleven years later, however, leaving the Indians homeless, landless, and with no legal rights.

Later in the century, Pomos mounted a project to buy back a land base. Toward this end, they established rancherias (settlements) and worked as cheap migrant agricultural labor, returning home in winter to carry on in a semitraditional way. By 1900, however, Pomos had lost 99 percent of these lands

through foreclosure and debt. The remaining population were viewed with hatred by most whites, who practiced severe economic and social discrimination against them. This situation provided fertile ground for Ghost Dance activity and the Bole-Maru (dreamer) cult, an adaptive structure that may have helped ease their transition to mainstream values.

Missionaries in the early twentieth century worked with Indians to promote Indian rights, antipoverty activities, education, and temperance. By that time, Pomos had begun using the courts and the media to expand their basic rights and better their situation. A key Supreme Court decision in 1907 recognized the rancherias as Indian land in perpetuity. More Pomo children began going to school; although the whites kept them segregated, the people mounted legal challenges designed to win equal access. After World War I, Indian and white advocacy groups proliferated, and reforms were instituted in the areas of health, education, and welfare. Indians gained a body of basic legal rights in 1928.

During the 1930s, the Depression forced a return to more traditional patterns of subsistence, which led to a period of relative prosperity and revitalization. At the same time, contact with other, non-Indian migratory workers brought new ideas about industry and labor organization to the Pomo. Intermarriage also increased. Women gained more independence and began to assume a greater role in religious and political affairs around this time.

After World War II, the United States largely relinquished its role in local Indian affairs to the state of California, which was unprepared to pick up the slack. Several rancherias were terminated, and services declined drastically, leading to a period of general impoverishment. Since the 1950s, however, various Indian groups have been active among the Pomo in helping them to become more politically and economically savvy, and some state agencies have stepped in to provide services. The Clear Lake Pomo were involved in the takeover of Alcatraz Island in 1969–1971, reflecting their involvement in the pan-Indian movement. Beginning in the 1970s, many Pomo bands successfully sued the government for rerecognition, on the grounds that Bureau of Indian Affairs promises of various improvements had not been kept.

RELIGION   The Kuksu cult was a secret religious society, in which members impersonated a god (kuksu) or gods in order to obtain supernatural power. Members observed ceremonies in colder months to encourage an abundance of wild plant food the following summer. Dances, related to curing, group welfare, and/or fertility, were held in special earth-covered dance houses and involved the initiation of 10- to 12-year-old boys into shamanistic, ritual, and other professional roles. All initiates constituted an elite secret ceremonial society, which conducted most ceremonies and public affairs.

Secular in nature, and older than the Kuksu cult, the ghost-impersonating ceremony began as an atonement for offenses against the dead but evolved into the initiation of boys into the Ghost Society (adulthood). A very intense and complex ceremony, especially among the Eastern Pomo, it ultimately became subsumed into the Kuksu cult.

The Bole-Maru in turn grew out of the Ghost Dances of the 1870s. The leader was a dreamer, and a doctor, who intuited new rules of ceremonial behavior. Originally a revivalistic movement like the Ghost Dance, this highly structured, four-day dance ceremony incorporated a dualistic worldview and thus helped Indians to step more confidently into a Christian-dominated society.

Other ceremonies included a women's dance, a celebration of the ripening of various crops, and a spear dance (Southeastern, involving the ritual shooting of boys). Shamans were healing or ceremonial professionals. They warded off illness, which was thought to be caused by ghosts or poisoning, from individuals as well as the community. Doctors (mostly men) were a type of curing specialist, who specialized in herbalism, singing, or sucking.

GOVERNMENT   The Pomo were divided into tribelets, each composed of extended family groups of between 100 and 2,000 people. Generally autonomous, each tribelet had its own recognized territory. One or more hereditary, generally male, minor chiefs headed each extended family group. All such chiefs in a tribelet formed a council or ruling elite, with one serving as head chief, to advise, welcome visitors, preside over ceremonies, and make speeches on correct behavior. Groups made regular military and trade alliances between themselves and with non-Pomos. A great deal of social control was achieved through a shared set of beliefs.

CUSTOMS   The Pomo ranked individuals according to wealth, family background, achievement, and religious affiliation. Most professions, such as chief, shaman, or doctor, required a sponsor and were affiliated with a secret society. The people recognized many different types of doctors. Bear doctors, for instance, who could be male or female, could acquire extraordinary power to move objects, poison, or cure. The position was purchased from a previous bear doctor and required much training. Names were considered private property.

Boys, who were taught certain songs throughout their childhoods, were presented with a hair net and a bow and arrow around age 12. For girls, the onset of puberty was a major life event, with confinement to a menstrual hut and various restrictions and instructions. Pomos often married into neighboring villages. The two families arranged a marriage, although the couple was always consulted (a girl was not forced into marriage but could not marry against the wishes of her family). Methods of population control included birth control, abortion, sexual restrictions, infanticide, and occasionally geronticide. The dead were cremated after four days of lying in state. Gifts, and occasionally the house, were cremated along with the body.

DWELLINGS   Along the coast, people built conical houses of redwood bark against a center pole. Inland, the houses were larger pole-framed, tule-thatched circular or elliptical dwellings. Other structures included semisubterranean singing houses for ceremonies and councils and smaller pit sweat houses.

DIET   Hunters and gatherers, the Pomo mainly ate seven kinds of acorns. They hunted deer, elk, antelope, fowl, and small game. Gathered foods included buckeyes, pepperwood nuts, various greens, roots, bulbs, and berries. Most foods were dried and stored for later use. Coastal groups considered dried seaweed a delicacy. In some communities the good food sources were privately owned.

KEY TECHNOLOGY   Items included baskets (cooking pots, containers, cradles, hats, mats, games, traps, and boats); fish nets, weirs, spears, and traps; tule mats, moccasins, leggings, boots, and houses; and assorted stone, wood, and bone tools. Feathers and beads were often used for design. Hunting tools included the bow and arrow, spear, club, snares, and traps.

TRADE   The Pomo participated in a vast northern California trade group. Both clamshell beads and magnesite cylinders served as money. People often traded some deliberately overproduced items for goods that were at risk of becoming scarce. One group might throw a trade feast, after which the invited group was supposed to leave a payment. These kinds of arrangements tended to mitigate food scarcities.

Exchange also occurred on special trade expeditions. Objects of interest might include finished products such as baskets as well as raw materials. The Clear Lake Pomo had salt and traded it for tools, weapons, furs, and shells. All groups used money of baked and polished magnesite as well as strings of clam shell beads. The Pomo could count and add up to 40,000.

NOTABLE ARTS   Pomo baskets were of extraordinarily high quality. Contrary to the custom in many tribes, men assisted in making baskets. Pomos also carved highly abstract petroglyphs beginning about 1600.

TRANSPORTATION   Coastal residents crossed to islands on driftwood rafts bound by vegetal fiber. The Clear Lake people used boats of tule bound with split grape leaves.

DRESS   Dress was minimal. Such clothing as people wore they made from tule, skins, shredded redwood, or willow bark. Men often went naked. Women wore waist-to-ankle skirts, with a mantle tied around the neck that hung to meet the skirt. Skin blankets provided extra warmth. A number of materials were used for personal decoration, including clamshell beads, magnesite cylinders, abalone shell, and feathers. Bead belts and neck and wrist bands were worn as costume accessories and as signs of wealth.

WAR AND WEAPONS   Poaching (trespass), poisoning, kidnapping or murder of women or children (usually for transgressing property lines), or theft constituted most reasons for warfare. Pomos occasionally formed military alliances among contiguous villages. Warfare began with ritual preparation, took the form of both surprise attacks and formal battles, and could end after the first casualty or continue all the way to village annihilation. Women and children were sometimes captured and adopted. Chiefs of the fighting groups arranged a peace settlement, which often included reparations paid to the relatives of those killed. Hunting or gathering rights might be lost or won as a result of a battle. Pomos often fought Patwins, Wappos, Wintuns, and Yukis. They made weapons of stone, bone, and wood.

Contemporary Information

GOVERNMENT/RESERVATIONS   In addition to cities and towns in and around northern California, Pomos live at the following rancherias: Big Valley (Pomo and Pit River, Lake County; 38 acres; 90 Indians), Cloverdale (Mendocino County; no formal land base; 1 resident), Dry Creek (Sonoma County; 1906; 75 acres; 38 Indians), Coyote Valley (Mendocino County), Sulphur Bank (Lake County; 1949; 50 acres; 90 Indians), Grindstone (Glenn County), Lytton (Sonoma County), Hopland (Mendocino County; 1907; 48 acres; 142 Indians), Stewart's Point (Sonoma County; 40 acres; 86 Indians [Kashia Band]), Manchester–Point Arena (Mendocino County; 1909; 363 acres; 178 Indians), Middletown (Lake County; 1910; 109 acres), Potter Valley (Mendocino County; 200 tribal members; 10 acres; 1 Indian resident), Redding (Shasta County; 31 acres; 79 Indians), Redwood Valley (Mendocino County; 58 acres; 14 Indians), Robinson (Lake County; 103 acres; 113 Indians), Sugar Bowl (Scott's Valley Band of Pomo Indians [Pomo and Wailaki], Lakeport County), Sherwood Valley (Mendocino County; 350 acres; 9 Indians), Upper Lake (Lake County; 1907; 19 acres; 28 Indi-

ans), Guidiville (Mendocino County), and Laytonville (Cahto-Pomo, Mendocino County; 200 acres; 129 Indians). They also live at the Pinoleville Reservation (1911; Mendocino County; 99 acres [almost half owned by non-natives]; 280 members) and the Round Valley Reservation (1864; 30,538 acres; Achomawi, Concow, Nomlaki, Wailaki, Wintun, Yuki, and Pomo; Mendocino County; 577 Indians). Population figures are as of 1995. Rancherias and reservations are generally governed by elected tribal councils.

The Pinoleville Band of Pomo Indians lives on the Pinoleville Reservation, which is located north of Ukiah, Mendocino County. The reservation was "unterminated" and its boundaries reestablished in the 1980s.

ECONOMY   Pomo country is still relatively poor. People engage in seasonal farm work as well as skilled and unskilled work. Some work with federal agencies, and some continue to hunt and gather their food.

LEGAL STATUS   The Big Valley Rancheria of Pomo and Pit River Indians, the Cloverdale Rancheria of Pomo Indians, the Coyote Valley Band of Pomo Indians, the Dry Creek Rancheria of Pomo Indians, the Elem Indian Colony of Pomo Indians of the Sulphur Bank Rancheria, the Grindstone Rancheria, the Guidiville Rancheria, the Hopland Band of Pomo Indians of the Hopland Rancheria, the Kashia Band of Pomo Indians of the Stewart's Point Rancheria, the Laytonville Rancheria (Cahto-Pomo), the Lytton Rancheria, the Manchester Band of Pomo Indians of the Manchester–Point Arena Rancheria, the Middletown Rancheria of Pomo Indians, the Pinoleville Reservation of Pomo Indians, the Potter Valley Rancheria of Pomo Indians, the Redding Rancheria of Pomo Indians, the Redwood Valley Rancheria of Pomo Indians, the Robinson Rancheria of Pomo Indians, the Round Valley Reservation, the Scott's Valley Band of Pomo Indians, the Sherwood Valley Rancheria of Pomo Indians, and the Upper Lake Band of Pomo Indians of Upper Lake Rancheria are all federally recognized tribal entities.

The Sherwood Rancheria, the Yokayo Rancheria, and the Yorkville Rancheria are all privately owned; their Pomo communities are seeking federal recognition.

DAILY LIFE   Despite the years of attempted genocide and severe dislocation, Pomo culture remains alive and evolving. The extended family is still the main social unit. Pomo languages are still spoken, and some traditional customs, including ritual restrictions, traditional food feasts, some ceremonies, intercommunity ceremonial exchange, singing and dancing, and seasonal trips to the coast, are still performed. Pomo doctors cure illness caused by poisoning; non-Indian doctors are called in for some other medical problems. Pomo basket weavers enjoy an international reputation.

Many Christian Pomos practice a mixture of Christian and traditional ritual. Some Pomos would like to unite politically, but the lack of such a tradition acts as a brake on the idea. However, various transgeographic (not limited to one formal or even informal community) social and political organizations do exist to bring the Pomo people together and advance their common interests. The relatively large number of non-natives on some of the Pomo rancherias may be explained by the effects of termination and the loss of individual Pomo land (to taxes and foreclosure) and its subsequent sale to whites. The struggle continues to reacquire a land base and to win recognition (or rerecognition) for some bands. Pinoleville must deal with environmentally hazardous industries established within its borders.

The pan-Pomo Ya-Ka-Ama Indian Center features a plant nursery among other economic development, educational, and cultural projects. The intertribal Sinkyone Wilderness Council works to restore heavily logged areas using modern native techniques.

Purisimeño

See Chumash

Salinan

Salinan (Sä `l ē n ə n) consisted of two divisions, Northern (Antoniaño) and Southern (Migueleño). A third division, extreme Coastal, may also have existed.

LOCATION The people traditionally lived along the south-central California coast, inland to the mountains. Today's Salinan descendants live mainly in the Salinas Valley between Monterey and Paso Robles.

POPULATION Roughly 3,000 in the late eighteenth century, the contemporary population consists of hundreds of Salinan descendants.

LANGUAGE Salinan was a Hokan language.

Historical Information

HISTORY Little is known about Salinan prehistory. In 1771 the Spanish constructed San Antonia de Padua, the first mission in Salinan territory. By 1790 this was the largest mission in California. Mission San Miguel followed in 1797 and also expanded rapidly. The northern division of Salinans became associated with the former mission; the southern with the latter mission.

Under some pressure, most Salinans abandoned their aboriginal customs and became acculturated to mission life. After 1834 and the secularization of the missions, the Salinan experienced a rapid depopula-

tion, primarily as a result of intermarriage and assimilation. Survivors either worked on the large *rancheros* or else remained in their original homeland as small-scale ranchers and hunters and gatherers. By the 1880s, most of the few remaining Salinan worked on the large cattle ranches that overspread the area, retaining a memory of their Indian heritage as well as close contact with each other. Until the 1930s there was a Salinan community not far from Mission San Antonia known as The Indians.

RELIGION The Salinan offered prayer to the golden eagle, the sun, and the moon. Shamans controlled the weather. Souls went to a western land of the dead. Initiation into religious societies was important, probably within the context of the Kuksu and/or the toloache cults.

GOVERNMENT Salinan political organization by tribelet was typical of California Indians.

CUSTOMS Clans as well as a Deer-Bear ceremonial division may have existed in aboriginal times. Although generosity with property was considered a virtue, loans of currency came with high rates of interest. Girls did not undergo a formal puberty ceremony. The boys' puberty ceremony involved the use of datura. (Datura was also used for pain relief.) Although the Salinan observed no formal marriage ceremony, marriage was formalized by gift giving and other customs. Divorce was relatively easy to obtain. The dead were cremated. The people played the bone game, shinny, ball races, games of strength, and possibly hoop-and-pole games. Shamans cured. They also poisoned and specialized in black magic. Medical treatments included bleeding, scarification, herbs, and sweat baths.

DWELLINGS Houses were domes, about 10 feet square, with a pole framework covered with tule or rye grass. Other buildings included communal structures and dance houses.

DIET Acorns were the staple food. The people also gathered wild oats, sage seeds, berries, mescal, and wild fruits. They hunted deer, bear, and rabbit, and they fished. They ate snakes, lizards, and frogs but not skunks.

KEY TECHNOLOGY Both coiled and twined baskets were used for a number of purposes. Stone tools included scrapers, choppers, points, mortars, pestles, and bowls. Bone and shell tools included awls, wedges, and fish hooks. Wooden tools included mortars, combs, and spoons. Musical instruments included cocoon rattles, elderwood rattles and flutes, musical bows, rasps, bone whistles, and drums. The Salinan also had calendars, numerical and measuring systems, and some knowledge of astronomy. They cooked basket-leached acorn meal in an earth oven.

TRADE Salinans and Yokuts enjoyed friendly

relations, including visiting, mutual use of resources, and trade. The former traded beads and unworked shells for salt-grass salt, seeds, obsidian, lake fish, and possibly tanned hides. They also traded with other groups for wooden dishes, steatite vessels, and ornaments. Trade competition for the inland market for shells led to much enmity, particularly with the Costanoan. Beads of mussel and shell formed the basis of a local currency.

NOTABLE ARTS Pictographs, mostly angles, with some people and animals, appeared from about 1000 to 1600. Baskets were produced in aboriginal times.

TRANSPORTATION Baskets were used to transport goods.

DRESS Men wore few or no clothes. Women wore tule aprons, cloaks of rabbit or otter skin, and basket hats. Both sexes painted and possibly tattooed their bodies and wore abalone shell earrings.

WAR AND WEAPONS Frequent combatants included Chumash and Costanoan Indians. Allies included the Yokuts. Salinans fought with sinew-backed bows and cane arrows.

Contemporary Information

GOVERNMENT/RESERVATIONS The Salinans have neither tribal land nor a formal organization. Most Salinan descendants live in the Salinas Valley between Monterey and Paso Robles.

ECONOMY Salinan descendants work as ranchers and in the local economy.

LEGAL STATUS The Salinan Nation had not received federal recognition as of 1997.

DAILY LIFE An informal network keeps Salinan identity alive. In recent years there has been a renewed interest in heritage and traditional culture.

Santa Barbara

See Chumash

Serrano

Serrano (S ə `rä n ō) is a name taken from the Spanish term for "mountaineer" or "highlander."

LOCATION In the late eighteenth century, the Serrano lived in small, autonomous villages, near water sources in the San Bernardino Mountains and Mojave Desert. Today most live mainly on two reservations in Riverside and (especially) San Bernardino Counties, California.

POPULATION Serrano population stood at roughly 2,000 in the late eighteenth century. In 1990, 56 Indians lived on the San Manuel Reservation, and 526 Serrano and members of other tribes, mostly Cahuilla, lived on the Morongo Reservation.

LANGUAGE Serrano belongs to the Takic division of the Uto-Aztecan language family and includes lan-

guages such as Kitanemuk, probably Vanyume, and possibly Tataviam.

Historical Information

HISTORY The Serrano may have encountered the Spanish as early as the 1770s, but the latter exerted little influence until 1819, when they constructed a settlement in the area. Most Western Serrano were removed by force to the missions between then and 1834; at that point, too few remained to carry on a traditional lifestyle. The Vanyume, a group associated with the Serrano and possibly living just to their north, became extinct well before 1900.

RELIGION The Serrano recognized a hierarchy of supernatural beings and spirits. Shamans conducted their ceremonies. They acquired their powers through dreaming and datura-induced visions.

GOVERNMENT Autonomous lineages, the main political unit, claimed specific local territory. Larger social units included clans, headed by *kikas* who provided political, economic, and religious leadership. *Kikas* also had assistants.

CUSTOMS All people belonged to one of two divisions, Wildcat and Coyote, each of which was composed of a number of patrilineal clans. In addition to conducting religious ceremonies, shamans also interpreted dreams and cured both by sucking out disease objects and by administering medicinal plants.

Both young men and women undertook puberty ceremonies. *Waxan,* the female ceremony, was public in the case of wealthy families and included dietary restrictions and instructions on how to be good wives. During *Tamonin,* the boys' ceremony, initiates ingested a datura drink and danced around a fire in the ceremonial house. After they experienced their visions, they learned special songs. The ceremony was followed by feasting and gift giving. A new mother and child lived in a heated pit for several days, observing food taboos. The dead were cremated, and most of their possessions were burned. A month after the death, a second burning of possessions was held, accompanied by singing and dancing. There was also an annual seven-day mourning ceremony.

DWELLINGS Parents, unmarried daughters, married sons, and sometimes extended family members lived in circular, domed tule-mat houses built around willow frames. Most household activities took place in nearby ramadas. Other structures included granaries, semisubterranean sweat houses, and a large ceremonial house where the *kika* lived. Men, women, and children all sweated and bathed together.

DIET Women gathered acorns, pine nuts, yucca roots, and mesquite and cactus fruit. Men hunted deer, antelope, mountain sheep, and small game using bow and arrow, traps, and curved throwing sticks. They also hunted birds, especially quail, and occasionally fished. Meat was baked in earth ovens, boiled in watertight baskets, or parching in trays with hot coals. The people also ate bone marrow. Blood was either thickened and cooked or eaten cold.

KEY TECHNOLOGY Food utensils included flint knives, stone or bone scrapers, pottery trays and bowls, baskets, and horn and bone spoons and stirrers. Most tools, including awls, arrow straighteners, bows, arrows, fire drills, pipes, and musical instruments, were made of wood, bone, stone, shell, or plant fiber.

TRADE Desert and mountain villages traded with each other for foods unavailable in the other's area.

NOTABLE ARTS The Serrano made fine decorated coiled basketry. They also carved petroglyphs, beginning perhaps as early as 1000 B.C.E., that depicted big game hunting. Pictographs, consisting of geometric designs, straight and wavy lines, and people, were painted as part of the girls' puberty ceremony as early as 1400 C.E.

TRANSPORTATION Goods were carried in baskets.

DRESS Serrano Indians wore little clothing except for some rabbit and otter fur blankets.

WAR AND WEAPONS Their traditional enemies included the Mojave and Chemehuevi.

Contemporary Information

GOVERNMENT/RESERVATIONS The San Manuel Reservation (1893; San Bernardino County; 658 acres) had an early-1990s population of 25 Indians (out of 85 enrolled Serranos). Serranos also share the Morongo Reservation with other tribes, particularly the Cahuilla. Serrano descendants also live on the Soboba Reservation.

ECONOMY People on the San Manuel Reservation work primarily at bingo facilities and other wage-paying jobs. Many Morongo people are cattlemen and farmers. They also have a bingo facility.

LEGAL STATUS The San Manuel Band of Mission Indians is a federally recognized tribal entity.

DAILY LIFE Today's Serrano participate in pan-Indian ceremonies and events. Many residents of Morongo are Moravian. A very few people still speak Serrano. Although their culture has largely disappeared, the few people who claim Serrano ancestry remain proud of their heritage and identity. Some sacred and secular songs are sung on social occasions.

Shasta

Shasta (`Shas t ə) were one of four Shastan tribes, the other three being Konomihu, Okwanuchu, and New River Shasta. The origin and meaning of the word "Shasta" is obscure. The approximate translation for their word for their homeland, *kahusariyeki*, is "among those who talk right."

LOCATION Traditionally, the Shasta lived on both sides of the modern California-Oregon border, roughly in Oregon's Jackson and Klamath Counties and California's Siskiyou County, regions mostly of mountains and forest. Today most Shastas live on the Quartz Valley Rancheria in Siskiyou County, California; the Shasta Nation in Yreka, California; and among the general population.

POPULATION Roughly 3,000 Shastas lived in their region in the eighteenth century. In 1990, 19 Indians (Karuk, Shasta, and Upper Klamath) lived at the Quartz Valley Rancheria. The Shasta had roughly 600 enrolled members at that time.

LANGUAGE Shasta, Konomihu, Okwanuchu, and New River Shasta make up the Shastan division of the Hokan language family.

Historical Information

HISTORY Fur trappers in the 1820s constituted the first non-native presence in the Shasta region. Their influence was relatively benign, in sharp contrast to that of the settlers who soon followed in their wake. Although Shastas often fought each other and their neighbors, they all banded together in the 1850s to resist the Anglo invaders. In 1851, a treaty called for a Shasta reservation in Scott Valley, but the state of California refused to let the treaty be ratified. After the signing, Indians ate a meal at which the food had been poisoned with strychnine; thousands more Indians died during the ensuing attacks by white vigilantes.

The few surviving Shastas were forced onto the Grande Ronde and, later, Siletz Reservations. Among the other treaties that included Shastas was the 1864 Klamath Treaty, in which, unbeknownst to them, their aboriginal homeland was ceded. Shastas participated in the late-nineteenth-century religious revivals, including the Ghost Dance, Earth Lodge cult, and Big Head cult.

RELIGION The most important ceremony centered around girls' puberty. There were also war dances and doctor-making ceremonies as well as several personal rituals for luck and protection.

GOVERNMENT Shastas lived in villages of one or more families. Larger villages as well as each of the four divisions had a headman (loose hereditary succession) whose duties included mediating disputes among men and preaching correct behavior. The headman's wife had similar responsibilities among women.

CUSTOMS Shamans were usually women. They

cured through the use of supernatural powers, which were also the source of all disease and death (except ill will). They acquired these powers through dream trances, during which a spirit or "pain" taught the shaman its song. An extended training period followed the trance experience. Each shaman acquired certain paraphernalia over the years. They diagnosed by singing, dancing, or blowing tobacco smoke and cured by sucking. If a shaman lost too many patients, she was killed. Shamans' services were also available to kill an enemy (by throwing a "pain") and to find lost or stolen objects and people. Doctors, who cured by using medicinal plants, were also women.

The Shasta observed numerous life-cycle food and behavior taboos. Puberty activities for boys included an optional vision-seeking quest, which ensured success in male activities such as hunting, fishing, gambling, and racing. The girls' puberty ceremony and dance were the group's most important. Marriage required the payment of a bride price. Wealthy men occasionally had more than one wife. Divorce was unusual. The dead were buried in family plots; their possessions were burned or buried. Widows cut their hair (widowers singed it), covered their head and face with a pitch and charcoal mixture until remarriage, and observed several taboos. Souls were said to travel east along the Milky Way to the home of Mockingbird, a figure in Shasta mythology.

Both bitter feuds and friendships characterized Shasta intragroup relations. Payment usually resolved interpersonal differences. Families (through the male line) owned exclusive rights to specific hunting or fishing places within the village territory at large. Money and wealth were measured in olivella, haliotsis, deerskins, clamshell disks, dentalia, and woodpecker scalps. Games included ring-and-pin, shinny, target games, and the men's grass (hand) and women's many-stick games.

DWELLINGS Rectangular winter homes were set about three feet into the ground. With earth side walls and wood end walls, they held between one and four families. All houses faced the water. Furnishings included tule pillows and wooden stools. Some groups used tule or raccoon-skin bed coverings; others used elk or deerskin blankets or imported buffalo hides. The community house was similar, but larger. Boys past puberty and unmarried men slept in the sweat house if their village contained one. The menstrual hut was generally located on the west side of the village. Other structures included brush shelters in spring and summer and bark houses during the fall acorn-gathering season.

DIET Shastas generally ate two meals a day. Venison was a staple. Hunters also brought in bear, fowl, turtles, and various small game. Their methods included stalking and the use of drop pits and traps. Various hunting rituals and taboos included not eating one's first kill. Meat was boiled, baked (in earth ovens), broiled, or dried. Insects were parched or baked.

Men also fished for salmon, mussels, trout, and eels, using spears, nets, and traps. There were several first-fish-run rituals and taboos. Fresh salmon was generally roasted. Acorns were another staple. In addition to acorns, gathered foods included pine nuts, roots, seeds, greens, bulbs, and berries. Dried foodstuffs were ground into flour. Men were often served before women.

KEY TECHNOLOGY Most tools were made of wood, bone, stone, and obsidian. The Shasta also used rawhide and basket containers, bowls of wood and soapstone, imported and domestic baskets, and adhesives made of fish glue, pine pitch, and chokecherry pitch.

TRADE The four Shasta groups traded with each other as well as within the different villages of each group. They traded acorns (Achumawi, Wintun) and acorn paste (Rogue River Athapaskans), clamshell beads (northern peoples), and buckskin, obsidian, and dentalia (Warm Springs Indians). They obtained obsidian (Achumawi), buckskin clothing (Warm Springs Indians), otter skins (northern peoples), dentalia (Rogue River Athapaskans), and pine nut necklaces (Wintun). Trade with their northern neighbors generally excluded the Klamath and the Modoc. From their California neighbors, the Shasta received acorns, baskets, dentalia, obsidian blades, juniper, and Wintun beads.

NOTABLE ARTS The Shasta specialized in making deerskin containers. Their relatively few musical instruments included deer-hoof rattles, bone and elder flutes, and hide drums.

TRANSPORTATION They used pine dugout canoes and tule rafts to navigate waterways.

DRESS Clothing was made of deerskin and shredded bark. People also wore shell necklaces, ear and nose ornaments, face and body paint, and tattoos. Heads were flattened for aesthetic reasons. Caps were of basketry (women) and buckskin (men). Footgear included buckskin ankle-length moccasins and snowshoes.

WAR AND WEAPONS The four groups occasionally fought with each other. They also engaged in intragroup feuds, primarily for revenge of witchcraft, murder, rape, and insult to a headman. Other occasional enemies included the Achomawi, Wintun, and Modoc (retaliation for the latter's raiding). Weapons included the bow and arrow, knives, and rod armor vests. Peace settlements included disarmament and payments. Young women occasionally accompanied a Shasta war party. They might be taken captive but were usually returned as part of the settlement.

Contemporary Information

GOVERNMENT/RESERVATIONS The Quartz Valley Rancheria (1939; rerecognized in 1983; Siskiyou County) had an early-1990s Shasta population of two.

Shasta descendants also live on the Grande Ronde and Siletz Reservations (*see* Upper Umpqua entry in Chapter 3).

ECONOMY Most people work in the timber industry or at local small businesses.

LEGAL STATUS The Shasta Nation had not received federal recognition as of 1997. The Quartz Valley Rancheria of Karok, Shasta, and Upper Klamath Indians is a federally recognized tribal entity.

DAILY LIFE Today's Shasta have little knowledge of aboriginal culture. No Shasta languages are currently spoken. The people are primarily interested in federal recognition, archaeology, and the return of grave items. Residents of the Quartz Valley Rancheria suffer from poor health care. Some Shastas possess heirloom family artifacts.

Sinkyone

See Wailaki

Smith River Indians

See Tolowa

Tache

See Yokuts

Tipai-Ipai

Tipai-Ipai (`T ē p ī -`Ē p ī) is the common name since the 1950s of two linguistically related groups formerly known as Kamia (Kumeyaay) and Diegueño. Both terms mean "People." "Diegueño" comes from the Spanish mission San Diego de Alcala. "Kamia" may have meant "those from the cliffs." The Tipai-Ipai are sometimes referred to as Diegueño Mission Indians.

LOCATION As of the late eighteenth century, the Tipai-Ipai lived in southern California and Baja California, along the coast and inland almost to the Colorado River. Today, many live on 13 reservations in San Diego County, California.

POPULATION The late-eighteenth-century Tipai-Ipai population stood between 3,000 and 9,000. In 1990, roughly 1,200 Tipai-Ipais lived on the reservations and perhaps 2,000 more lived off-reservation.

LANGUAGE Diegueño is a member of the Yuman division of the Hokan language family.

Historical Information

HISTORY People have been living in traditional Tipai-Ipai territory for roughly 20,000 years. A proto–Tipai-Ipai culture had been established by about 5000 B.C.E., and the historic Tipai-Ipai were in place about 1,000 years ago.

In 1769, the Spanish built the presidio and mission of San Diego de Alcala and began rounding up local Indians, especially those to the north and on the coast. The latter revolted regularly. In 1775, about 800 people from some 70 villages united to burn the mission. It was later rebuilt, however, and the missionization process continued. After the Mexicans secularized the missions in 1834, they treated the resident Tipai-Ipai as trespassers or rebels and continued many of the same oppressive practices that characterized mission life.

In 1852, shortly after the United States gained control of California, the Senate ratified a treaty with "the nation of Diegueño Indians," under which the latter lost their best lands. Overgrazing and water diversions soon destroyed their remaining grassland and woodland. By the late 1870s, the Tipai-Ipai were settled on about 12 small, poor reservations, although many were at least located on the site of native villages. Coastal Ipais also lived in San Diego slums or camped in nearby hills.

At the turn of the century many Tipai-Ipais could be found working for low wages on ranches and in mines and towns or starving on the inadequate reservations. Traditional government was disrupted by Indian agents who required the Indians to select a "captain." Bitter political factions had emerged by the 1930s with the formation of the rival Mission Indian Federation and the Southern Mission Indians. Frequent cross-border visits and ceremonies became difficult after 1950 and impossible after the 1970s, owing to U.S. immigration policies. In recent times, the bands have been reviving the traditional governing structure.

RELIGION Shamans were the religious leaders. They performed ceremonies, interpreted dreams, controlled weather, and cured the sick. Evil shamans might also produce disease. Named song cycles were associated with certain ceremonial dances. Ground paintings, a feature illustrating the connection with southwestern cultures, featured symbols of colors and their associated directions. Their most important religious ceremony was *kaurk*. This clan-based mourning ceremony lasted from four to eight days. It included gift giving, dancing with images of the dead, and feasting and culminated with the burning of effigies of the dead. Toloache, a hallucinogenic root, was used by adolescent boys and adult men for spiritual strengthening.

GOVERNMENT The Tipai-Ipai consisted of over 30 autonomous bands or tribelets, usually made up of a single patrilineal clan and headed by a clan chief and an assistant. Neither the tribe nor the band had a formal name. Positions of authority were sometimes inherited by eldest sons, brothers, and, rarely, widows. Two tribal chiefs directed ceremonies, advised about proper behavior, and appointed war or gathering leaders. Band leaders and councils saw to resource management. In historic times, some chiefs ordered assistants to beat nonconformists. The Imperial Valley Tipai had a tribal chief but no clan chief.

CUSTOMS The Tipai-Ipai observed numerous life-cycle rituals, obligations, and taboos. Reaching puberty was a public affair. Girls underwent special rites; boys often had their nasal septa pierced. Most marriages, arranged by parents when children reached puberty, were monogamous. Divorce was relatively easy to effect. Twins were considered a blessing and supernaturally gifted. The dead were cremated along with their possessions. Souls were said to inhabit a region somewhere in the south. Wailing, speech making, the singing of song cycles, and gift exchange might accompany cremation. Mourners cut their hair, blackened their faces, and never mentioned the deceased's name again.

All tribal members shared certain lands. In addition, each band claimed specific communal land, some of which was apportioned to individual families, as well as the right to kill thieves and trespassers. Certain rights were also preserved for the needy. Mockingbirds and roadrunners were caged as pets. Before hunting, a man studied his dreams, fasted, and avoided women and corpses. He usually gave away his first deer.

DWELLINGS Dwellings varied with season and environment. In winter, people built dome-shaped houses with a pole framework, covered with bark, thatch, or pine slabs. Openings faced east. The people also lived in mountain caves. Brush shelters and pole and palm-leaf thatch houses served in the summer.

DIET The food staple was flour made from six varieties of acorn as well as from mesquite beans and seeds of sage, pigweed, peppergrass, flax, and buckwheat. Flour was cooked into mush and cakes and stewed with meat and vegetables. Other wild foods included cactus, agave, clover, cherries, plums, elderberries, watercress, manzanita berries, piñon nuts, and prickly pear. People fished where fish were available. Animal foods, which were generally roasted on coals or in ashes, included rodents and an occasional deer. The people also ate lizards, some snakes, insects, larvae, and birds. They also cultivated tobacco, which only men smoked. Imperial Valley Ipais planted maize, beans, and teparies, but they placed greater emphasis on gathering.

KEY TECHNOLOGY Men hunted with a bow and arrow and throwing sticks. A variety of basketry and pottery items served food-related functions. Other tools were made of stone, bone, and wood.

TRADE The Tipai-Ipai traded most frequently among themselves, but since major trails crossed their territory, they also interacted with others as far inland as Zuñi. Coastal people traded salt, dried seaweed, dried greens, and abalone shells for acorns, agave, mesquite beans, and gourds. Other items traded included granite for pestles, steatite for arrow straighteners, red and black minerals for paint, and eagle feathers.

NOTABLE ARTS Tipai petroglyphs, which were produced perhaps as early as 1000 B.C.E., depicted big game hunting. The Ipai produced theirs from roughly 500 B.C.E. to A.D. 1000. Pictographs, which featured geometric designs, were used as part of the girls' puberty ceremony as early as circa 1400.

TRANSPORTATION Most fishing boats were either balsa rafts or dugout canoes.

DRESS Dress was minimal. Children and men often went naked. Women wore an apron. Both sexes wore caps against head-carried items and sandals of agave leaves. Bedding and robes were of rabbit skin, willow bark, or buckskin. Men plucked whiskers with their fingers. Women tattooed their chins and painted their bodies.

WAR AND WEAPONS Clans generally feuded over women, trespass, murder, and sorcery. Tactics included ambush or simply chasing away an enemy. Weapons included the bow and arrow, poniard, and war club. Forced to resist the missions and the Mexicans, the people became more aggressive during the early nineteenth century.

Contemporary Information

GOVERNMENT/RESERVATIONS The following were Tipai-Ipai (Diegueño) reservations in 1990: Barona (1875; 5,902 acres; 450 members), Campo (1893; 15,480 acres; 213 enrolled members), Capitan Grande (1875; 15,753 acres), Cuyapaipe (1893; 4,103 acres; 16 enrolled members), Inaja and Cosmit (1875; 852 acres; 16 enrolled members), Jamul (1975; 6 acres; 120 enrolled members), LaPosta (1893; 4,500 acres; 13 enrolled members), Manzanita (1893; 3,579 acres; 52 enrolled members), Mesa Grande (1875; 1,000 acres; roughly 300 enrolled members), San Pasqual (1910; 1,379.58 acres; roughly 200 enrolled members), Santa Ysabel (1893; 15,527 acres; 950 enrolled members), Sycuan (1875; 640 acres; 120 enrolled members), and Viejas (1875; 1,609 acres; 180 members). All are located in San Diego County. Membership figures may exclude children. Most reservations are governed by elected councils and chairs. Bands are attempting to revive a tribal-level organization. Populations are as of 1990.

ECONOMY Sycuan Reservation operates restaurants, a casino, a bingo parlor, and an off-track betting establishment. Other reservations are planning development along these lines.

LEGAL STATUS The Barona Group of Capitan Grande Band, the Campo Band, the Capitan Grande Band, the Cuyapaipe Community, the Inaja Band, the LaPosta Band, the Manzanita Band, the Mesa Grande Band, the Santa Ysabel Band, the Sycuan Band, and the Viejas Group of Capitan Grande Band of Diegueño Mission Indians are all federally recognized tribal entities. The Jamul Indian Village of California is a federally recognized tribal entity. The San Pasqual General Council is a federally recognized tribal entity.

DAILY LIFE Major contemporary issues include sovereignty, the status of tribal land, water rights, and economic independence. Tipai-Ipai Indians are also interested in issues concerning education, housing, health care, traditional culture, and the environment. Most Indians are Catholic or observe a combination of Catholic and native religious traditions. Most religious ceremonies are closed to the public. Major feasts, such as the Fiesta de Las Cruces on November 14, celebrate the fusion of Indian, Spanish, Mexican, frontier, and contemporary American customs and beliefs. Many dialects of Diegueño are still spoken. The traditional art of basket making has been revived.

Most reservations have tribal halls, programs for seniors, and various cultural programs. Some have libraries, preschools, and police and fire departments and provide scholarship assistance to students.

Tolowa

Tolowa (`To l ə wä) is an Algonquian name given to these people by their southern neighbors, the Yurok. Cultural and linguistic relatives in Oregon are known as Chetco and Tututni. Tolowas are presently associated with the Tututni. Their name for themselves is *Xus,* or "person."

LOCATION Traditionally, the Tolowa lived in approximately eight permanent villages in northwestern California, from Wilson Creek north to the Oregon border. The area included coast, rivers (especially the Smith River), and interior marshes, hills, and mountains. Today many Tolowa live in and around Humboldt and Del Norte Counties, California.

POPULATION From perhaps 2,400 in the early nineteenth century (out of roughly 4,000 Tolowa/Chetco/Tututnis), by 1990 59 Indians lived on the Trinidad Rancheria and 32 Indians lived on the Elk Valley Rancheria (mostly Tolowa). Roughly 400 people identified themselves as Tolowa in 1990.

LANGUAGE The people spoke several dialects of Tolowa, an Athapaskan language.

Historical Information

HISTORY During the late eighteenth century, probably before the Tolowa had yet encountered non-natives face to face, an epidemic contracted from non-native explorers in the region destroyed one of their villages. The first direct contact came in June 1828 in the person of Jedediah Smith and his exploring party. However, the Tolowa continued to live relatively unaffected by outside influences until about 1850.

More than half of the Tolowa population died during that decade alone from disease and the effects of Anglo mass murders. In 1860, following the Chetco/Rogue River Indian War (begun in 1852), 600 Tolowas were forced to march into reservations in Oregon. Some of those people were later removed to the Hoopa Valley Reservation. The 1870 Ghost Dance revival reached them in about 1872 and lasted about ten years.

Around the turn of the century, the Tolowa suffered further dramatic population reduction as a result of disease, mostly measles and cholera. Their population at this time had been reduced by roughly 95 percent, to some 200 people. Individual Tolowas had received a few allotments in the late nineteenth century. In 1906, the government purchased tracts of land near the mouth of the Smith River that later became the Smith River and Elk Valley Rancherias. By 1913, most Tolowas were living in and around Crescent City and on the Hoopa Valley and Siletz Reservations. Beginning in 1923 and lasting for at least 30 years, owing to the government crackdown and confiscation of regalia, people held their traditional religious observances secretly.

The Indian Shaker Movement, which supported traditional healing and spiritual practices, arrived around 1930 and remained popular for a generation. About the same time, the Del Norte Indian Welfare Association was founded as a community and self-help organization. The two rancherias were terminated in 1960, with devastating cultural results. As a response to termination, Tolowa landowners in 1973 created the Nele-chun-dun Business Council and filed for federal acknowledgment ten years later as the Tolowa Nation. The rancherias were reinstated in 1983.

RELIGION Most important Tolowa ceremonies were connected with diet, such as catching the season's first salmon, smelt, or sea lion. The *Naydosh* (Feather Dance) was performed as part of a World Renewal ceremony.

GOVERNMENT The wealthiest man in the village was usually the leader. There was no formal chief or overall political organization.

CUSTOMS Prestige, in the form of gaining and displaying wealth, or treasure (such as large obsidian knives, necklaces of dentalium shell beads, and red woodpecker scalp headdresses) was of prime concern to the Tolowa. Treasure was not normally used for utilitarian purposes except for bride prices. Besides marrying off daughters, other ways to get wealth were shrewd trading, fines and indemnities (there were many occasions for this, which were watched for carefully), infant betrothal, and gambling. Wealthy men might have several wives.

Shamans were mostly women or transvestite men. They were paid a high fee for curing disease. Their methods included dancing, trances, and sucking with the assistance of a spiritual power, or "pain." Although Tolowa villages did not closely cooperate among themselves, intermarriage and ceremonial interaction between the Tolowa and their neighbors (Yurok, Karuk, Hupa, Tututni) was common. Male activities mostly revolved around hunting, boat building, and fishing; women generally collected and transported food, especially acorns, and prepared it for eating and storage. Corpses were removed through a loose plank in the house, wrapped in tule mats, and buried with shell beads and other objects.

DWELLINGS Tolowas lived in square redwood-plank houses with two-pitched roofs. The central area was slightly excavated for cooking and sleeping. An interior ground-level ledge was used for storage. Men and boys slept, gambled, and made nets and weapons in semisubterranean sweat houses. The people lived in their permanent villages about nine months a year, leaving in late summer to fish for smelt on sandy beaches and continuing on inland to catch salmon and gather acorns through the fall.

DIET Salmon, smelt, and sea lion were the staples. Other foods included seaweed, shellfish, shore bird eggs, and acorns. The people may have cultivated tobacco.

KEY TECHNOLOGY Technological innovations included wild iris fishnets; tule mats; baskets of various fibers; stone, fiber, bone, and wooden tools such as bow and arrow, harpoons, fishing nets, woodworking wedges (antler), stone pounders, and pestles; and bone needles for weaving tule items. Deer hooves were used as musical instruments. Tolowas counted by fives.

TRADE Local trading networks extended into interior California and Oregon and along the coast at least as far north as Puget Sound.

NOTABLE ARTS Highly abstract petroglyphs date from roughly 1600. Locally, complex twined basket design depended on techniques such as overlay. The design was characterized by a large variety of geometric elements and the use of three colors.

TRANSPORTATION The people built and used 40-foot redwood canoes from which to fish and hunt sea lions.

DRESS Men wore buckskin breechclouts or nothing at all. Women wore a two-piece buckskin skirt. They also had three vertical stripes tattooed on their chins. Basketry caps protected their heads against burden-basket tumplines. Hide robes were used for warmth. People on long journeys wore buckskin moccasins and leggings. Both sexes wore long hair and ornaments in pierced ears.

WAR AND WEAPONS Each village defended its land, occasionally against other Tolowa villages. There were few pitched battles; most fights consisted of individual attacks or village raids. Young women were sometimes taken captive but usually returned at settlement time. Every injured party received a settlement, with the winners paying more than the losers.

Contemporary Information

GOVERNMENT/RESERVATIONS Tolowas live at the following locations: the Cher-ae Heights community of the Trinidad Rancheria (47 acres; about 60 Yurok, Wiyot, and Tolowa Indians in the mid-1990s) in Humboldt County; the Big Lagoon Rancheria (20 acres; 19 Yurok and Tolowa in 1996) in Humboldt County; the Smith River Rancheria (1906; 30 acres; 72 Indians) in Del Norte County, rerecognized in the 1980s and governed by the constitution of the Howonquet Indian Council; and the Elk Valley Rancheria (1906; Del Norte County; roughly 30 Tolowa, Yurok, and Hupa, governed by a nine-member tribal council). Tolowas also live on the Siletz Reservation (*see* Upper Umpqua entry in Chapter 3).

ECONOMY Unemployment at Elk Valley in 1995 stood at about 40 percent. Economic activities there include casino gambling and a casket company. Access to jobs is relatively difficult.

LEGAL STATUS The Cher-ae Heights Indian Community of the Trinidad Rancheria, the Smith River Rancheria, and the Big Lagoon Rancheria are federally recognized tribal entities. The Elk Valley Rancheria of Smith River Tolowa Indians is a federally recognized tribal entity. The Tolowa Nation, derived from the nineteenth-century Jane Hostatlas allotment and the 1973 Nele-chun-dun Business Council, had not received federal recognition as of 1997. The Tolowa-Tututni Tribe of Indians is also federally unrecognized.

DAILY LIFE Although few know and practice the old traditions, the Tolowa do perform ceremonies such as the *Naydosh* (Feather Dance). Indian Shaker religious practices are also popular. At Elk Valley, extended families live together or nearby. Children attend public school, although the people are working toward setting up tribal schools. Health care facilities are considered inadequate, despite the presence of a clinic at Smith River. Diabetes, heart disease, and substance abuse are chronic problems. Tolowas have written dictionaries and conduct classes in their native language. Like most rural people, they garden, fish, and hunt for subsistence.

Tubatulabal

Tubatulabal (T ə ˋbät ə l ˋä b ə l), "pine nut eaters." These people originally lived in three autonomous bands: the Pahkanapil, Palagewan, and Bankalachi, or Toloim.

LOCATION In the early nineteenth century, the Tubatulabal lived in the southern Sierra Nevada and their foothills and in the Kern, South Fork Kern, and Hot Springs Valleys. Today many live on reservations in Tulare County.

POPULATION A population of up to 1,000 Tubatulabal lived in their region in the early nineteenth century. In 1990, roughly 400 Tubatulabal Indians live in the Kern River Valley, and possibly another 500 live elsewhere.

LANGUAGE Tubatulabal was a subgroup of the Uto-Aztecan language family.

Historical Information

HISTORY This group of Indians entered the region at least around 1450 and perhaps as early as 2,000 years ago. They first encountered Spanish explorers in the late eighteenth century. By the mid–nineteenth century, miners, ranchers, and settlers began taking their land. The Kern River gold rush began in 1857. In 1862, a few Tubatulabals joined the Owens Valley Paiutes in antiwhite fighting in the Owens Valley. In the following year whites massacred Tubatulabals in the Kern River Valley.

By 1875, most male survivors were working for local ranchers. In 1893, survivors of the Pahkanapil Band, the only one left of the original three, were allotted land in the Kern and South Fork Kern Valleys. The people experienced severe epidemics of measles and influenza in 1902 and 1918. During the twentieth century, many Tubatulabals moved to the Tule River Reservation and throughout California. After the last hereditary leader died in 1955, a council of elders carried on leadership through the 1960s. In the 1970s, the Tubatulabal, Kawaiisu, and Canebrake area Indians formed the Kern Valley Indian Community and Council, a goal of which is to obtain federal recognition.

RELIGION According to traditional belief, numerous supernatural spirits often took human or animal form. They were treated with respect, in part because they could be malevolent. Shamans used jimsonweed, believed to have special powers, as an aid in curing. They also used singing, dancing, herbs, blowing tobacco smoke, and sucking techniques, calling upon their supernatural guardian helpers for assistance. Shamans could be either men or women, but only men could cure: Female shamans were witches, the most feared members of the community (men could also be witches). Chronically unsuccessful shamans might be accused of witchcraft and killed. Shamanism was considered an inborn quality that could not be acquired.

GOVERNMENT The three bands were composed of several family groups, mobile throughout much of the year except during winter, when they settled in hamlets of between two and six extended families. Each band was headed by a chief, generally hereditary, occasionally female. He or she arbitrated disputes, represented the band, and organized war parties. A "dance manager" or "clown" instigated public criticism of the chief preparatory to the appointment of a new chief. He also acted the clown at ceremonies. Although the three bands were politically autonomous, people often visited and intermarried.

CUSTOMS Neither men nor women underwent formal puberty rites. Marriages were formalized by gift exchanges or groom service to his in-laws. Corpses were wrapped in tule mats and buried. A six-day mourning ceremony was held within two years, during which time a tule effigy of the dead was destroyed along with most of his or her possessions.

Each band claimed formal but unexclusive possession of a specific territory. The people played several games, most of which involved gambling on the outcome. They included a women's dice game, a men's shinny game, and a men's hoop-and-pole game (in which an arrow was shot through a rolling hoop). String figure making and storytelling provided entertainment on winter evenings. Professional male dancers performed at various ceremonies and occasions. Also, both sexes danced for enjoyment.

DWELLINGS Winter houses were circular, dome-shaped structures of brush or mud. In summer, people used open-sided pole-and-beam brush shelters. Bedding consisted of tule mats and skins. Most villages also contained a brush-and-mud sweat house. Special structures, in which several families slept, ate, and stored supplies, were constructed at the autumn gathering grounds. These buildings were between 30 and 50 feet in diameter and featured three- to four-foot-high brush walls.

DIET Food staples were acorns, piñon nuts, and fish. People either caught fish individually or drove them into stone corrals, where other people waded in and tossed them out. Sun-dried and stored, acorns and piñons were eventually ground into meal and mixed with water to form gruel or mush. The Tubatulabal also ate seeds, berries (juniper, manzanita, goose), roots (tule, cattail), and bulbs. Plant foods were boiled, parched, roasted, or baked in pit ovens. Berries were eaten fresh, boiled, or pounded or were mixed with water, shaped into cakes, sun-dried, and stored.

Men hunted deer, bear, antelope, mountain lion, mountain sheep, birds, and small game. They also participated in annual communal antelope drives with neighboring tribes. Large game was broiled, roasted, or stewed immediately or salted and sun-dried for storage. Sugar crystals came from cane; salt from plants and rock salt. Both men and women used wild tobacco as an emetic before bed.

KEY TECHNOLOGY The Tubatulabal made coiled and twined baskets. Coiled baskets often had human, snake, or geometric designs. Local red clay was used to make pottery. Other technological items included the sinew and self-backed bow (strung with native twine); numerous nets, snares, traps, and throwing sticks for hunting small game; fishing baskets, traps, nets, harpoons, hooks, and stone-and-wood corrals; a barrel cactus spine awl for sewing and basket making; and soaproot fiber brushes. Many such tools were made of stone. Musical instruments included rattles, quill whistles, elderberry flutes, and musical bows.

TRADE Small groups of men and women traded piñons, balls of prepared tobacco, and other items for clamshell disks, which served as money. Their trading expeditions took them as far as the coast or as close as the next hamlet. During winter, when supplies were low, people bought goods with their own or borrowed lengths of disks.

NOTABLE ARTS Fine baskets were their major art. They also made pictographs on local rock faces.

TRANSPORTATION Fishermen hurled harpoons from tiny floating tule platforms.

DRESS In summer, men went naked, and women wore tanned deerskin aprons. Other clothing, worn during various times of the year, included deerhide moccasins, vests, aprons, and coats. Only women, clowns, and shamans decorated their bodies.

WAR AND WEAPONS The Tubatulabal engaged in regular hostilities against their neighbors for revenge against previous attacks. These wars lasted between one and two days and produced only light casualties. The preferred fighting method was to attack the whole village by surprise at dawn. Peace was arranged through negotiation and was generally accompanied by mutual nonaggression promises.

Contemporary Information

GOVERNMENT/RESERVATIONS Tule River Reservation (Tule River Tribe; Tulare County; 1873; 55,356 acres, shared with the Monache and the Yokuts) had a 1990 population of roughly 750. It is governed by a tribal council.

The Kern Valley Indian Community (KVIC) and Council is a member of the Confederated Aboriginal Nations of California. KVIC tribes signed four unratified treaties in 1852 and never received any compensation for their aboriginal lands.

ECONOMY People obtain employment as cowhands, secretaries, and loggers and in local businesses. The Tule River Economic Development Council works to provide economic opportunities there. Economic resources include timber and a campground.

LEGAL STATUS The KVIC had not received federal recognition as of 1997. The Tule River Tribe is a federally recognized tribal entity.

DAILY LIFE Outmigration and intermarriage have diminished the people's tribal identity. The lives of today's Tubatulabals are similar to those of their non-Indian neighbors. The Valley Cultural Center is a symbol of their active rebuilding of their culture and spirituality. The Monache Gathering is a three-day event that includes sweat lodge ceremonies. The Tule River Reservation has its own health center. Some elders continue to make baskets and dig for traditional roots.

Ventureño

See Chumash

Wailaki

Wailaki (`Wī lä kē) is a Wintun term meaning "north language." The tribe had three main subdivisions: Tsennahkenne (Eel River Wailaki); Bahneko (North Fork Wailaki); and Pitch Wailaki (located farther up the North Fork of the Eel River). The Wailaki are culturally related to four other small tribes—the Mattole, Lassik, Sinkyone, and Nongatl—who lived just to their north and west.

LOCATION In aboriginal times, the Wailaki lived in northwestern California, along the Eel River and the North Fork Eel River. Today, descendants of these people live in and near Mendocino County.

POPULATION Roughly 2,700 Wailaki lived in their region in the mid–nineteenth century; the population of all five tribes may have exceeded 13,000. In 1990, 577 Indians, including some Wailaki, lived on the Round Valley Reservation. The enrolled tribal membership in 1990 was 1,090.

LANGUAGE With the Mattole, Lassik, Sinkyone, and Nongatl, the Wailaki spoke a Southern Athapaskan language.

Historical Information

History Although human occupation of the region is at least 4,000 years old, the Southern Athapaskans appear to have come to California around 900. They had little contact with non-natives until the mid–nineteenth century. The Anglo extermination raids of 1861 and 1862 were fairly successful.

Survivors fiercely resisted being placed on reservations. Most stayed in the hills working on Anglo sheep and cattle ranches. Others worked on small parcels of land. At one point around the turn of the century, so many of their young were being kidnapped and indentured that parents tattooed their children so they would always know their ancestry.

RELIGION The Wailaki believed that spirits were present in all objects, inanimate as well as animate. The source of shamans' power was their ability to communicate with *Katanagai* (Night Traveler), the creator god. The Wailaki recognized various types of shamans, both men and women, who might attend special schools to receive visions and practice on patients. They cured the sick by sucking or with herbs and could find lost souls. Sucking and soul-loss doctors could also foretell the future and find lost people or objects. Singing, dancing, and smoking tobacco accompanied most shamans' rituals. Other ceremonies were connected with salmon fishing, acorn gathering, and girls' puberty.

GOVERNMENT Traditionally, the Wailaki consisted of at least 19 tribelets and 95 villages. Tribelets were presided over by hereditary chiefs, who settled disputes and provided food for ceremonial occasions. Chiefs were entitled to extra wives.

CUSTOMS The nuclear family was the primary social unit. Gift exchange formed the basis of the marriage formalities. Mothers-in-law and sons-in-law did not speak directly to each other out of respect. Herbal abortion was practiced and probably infanticide, especially in the case of twins, one of whom was generally killed. Divorce was relatively easy to obtain for the usual reasons: unfaithful, barren, or lazy wife; unfaithful or abusive husband. Corpses were buried with their heads facing east; the grave was later piled with stones. Wives and husbands were generally buried together. The house was destroyed, and possessions were buried or otherwise disposed of.

Wealth was important but not as much as with the Klamath River people to the north. Most property except land was individually owned. Childrens' games included jumping rope, swinging, running races, dolls, tops, and buzzer or hummer toys. Adult games included shinny, archery contests, the hand game, and the women's dice game.

DWELLINGS In winter, people lived in circular houses with conical roofs, made of redwood slabs or bark. A cooking fire was located in the center of a dugout floor. Two or more families occupied a single house. Hide bedding was most common. Brush shelters served as summer houses. Villages also contained circular sweat houses.

DIET Acorns and game, including deer and elk, were the major food source. The Wailaki also ate fish, particularly salmon and trout. Summer was a time for migration following acorns and other ripening plant food sources.

KEY TECHNOLOGY Women coiled and (mostly) twined hazel shoots and conifer root fibers, decorated in bear grass, into basket containers, bowls, caps, traps, and other items. Musical instruments included drums, rattles, clappers, whistles, and flutes. Elkhorn and wooden wedges with groundstone mauls were used to split wood. Spoons were made of elkhorn or deer skull. Other raw materials included hide, horn, and stone. Fire came from buckeye or willow fire drills with moss for tinder.

TRADE Regular trade partners included the Yuki and Cahto Pomo.

NOTABLE ARTS Fine arts included basket making, woodworking, and the manufacture of ceremonial clothing and items.

TRANSPORTATION Although the Mattole, Lassik, Sinkyone and Nongatl used dugout canoes, the Wailaki made do with log rafts. Goods and children were towed in baskets by swimmers.

DRESS Clothing, especially in summer, was minimal. When they did wear clothes, men wore deer hide shirts and buckskin breechclouts. Women wore a one-piece bark skirt or a double apron of buckskin. Both sexes wore their hair shoulder length or longer, combed it with soaproot brushes, and cut it with a stone knife.

WAR AND WEAPONS Retaliation or revenge for murder, witchcraft, insult, or rape could lead to war among tribelets or families. Most Southern Athapaskans fought little and then usually only among themselves. Battles consisted mainly of surprise attacks. Ceremonial dances preceded and victory dances followed hostilities. All casualties and property loss were compensated for. Weapons included the sinew-backed bow and arrow, knives, clubs, sticks, slings, spears, and rocks. The Wailaki also used elk hide armor and shields.

Contemporary Information

GOVERNMENT/RESERVATIONS Some Wailaki Indians live on the Round Valley Reservation (1864; 30,538 acres) as well as on the Sugar Bowl Rancheria (Lakeport County). Their constitution and by-laws were approved in 1936. Other California Southern

Athapaskans also live among and have become mixed with Athapaskan Hupa or with other Indians. The Rohnerville Rancheria (Humboldt County) is home to some Southern Athapaskans.

ECONOMY Important economic activities include cattle and sheep ranching, logging, and local small business employment.

LEGAL STATUS The Covelo Indian Community of Round Valley Reservation (Wailaki, Yuki, Pit River, Achumawi, Pomo, Konkow, Nomlaki, Wintun) is a federally recognized tribal entity. The Wailaki are federally recognized as part of the Covelo Indian Community and have applied for separate recognition as well.

DAILY LIFE Today's Wailakis are known for their healers and doctoring schools. Local plants are used in traditional arts, such as basket weaving and woodworking, as well as for curing and subsistence. They are in the process of reacquiring their own land base; part of this project includes the struggle for access to aboriginal locations.

Whilkut

See Hupa

Wintun

Wintun (`Win tun), "person." The Wintun people consisted of three subgroups: Patwin (Southern); River and Hill Nomlaki (Central); and Wintu (Northern).

LOCATION Wintuns traditionally lived west of the Sacramento River, from the valley to the Coast Range. Today most Wintuns live on reservations and rancherias in Colusa, Glenn, Yolo, Mendocino, and Shasta Counties.

POPULATION The eighteenth-century population of Wintuns was roughly 15,000, including perhaps 2,000 Nomlaki. In 1990, 147 Indians lived on the four Wintun rancherias, and more lived off-reservation. Also, Wintuns were among 656 Indians who lived on two other shared reservations. The enrolled membership figures were 2,244 Wintu, 332 Nomlaki, and no Patwin.

LANGUAGE The three Wintun language groups—Wintu, Nomlaki, and Patwin—are Penutian languages.

Historical Information

HISTORY In aboriginal times, the Wintuns consisted of nine major groups within the three main subgroups. Some Nomlakis encountered the Spanish as early as 1808, although in general the Nomlaki were outside the sphere of Spanish influence.

By 1800, Patwins were being taken by force to the missions. Wintus first met non-natives in 1826, when the Jedediah Smith and Peter Ogden expeditions entered the region. Malaria epidemics killed roughly 75 percent of Wintuns in the early 1830s. Severe smallpox epidemics followed in 1837. By the mid–nineteenth century, most of their land had been stolen. Ranchers' cattle and sheep destroyed their main food sources. Miners polluted the fresh water. Then came the massacres. Captain John C. Frémont killed 175 Wintu and Yana in 1846; in 1850, whites gave a "friendship" feast with poisoned food, killing 100 Wintu. In 1851, 300 Indians died when miners burned the Wintu council house.

The so-called Cottonwood Treaty, ratified in 1852, acknowledged 35 square miles of Wintu land, but from 1858 to 1859, California regular and irregular troops killed at least 100 Wintus and displaced hundreds of others. Throughout the 1860s, Wintuns were hunted down and either killed or used as laborers. The 25,000-acre Nome Lackee Reservation was established in 1854 in the foothills of western Tehama County. Indians created a stable existence there based on farming, but by 1863, the reservation had been taken over by whites, and its residents were sent to Round Valley. Many surviving Nomlakis eventually returned to their old territory, working as farm hands and establishing a number of settlements, or rancherias. Most Patwins who survived the missions, military forays, raids, epidemics, and massacres either became assimilated into white society or were forced onto small reservations during the 1850s and 1860s, most of which have since been terminated.

A period of religious revival occurred in the 1870s, during which much traditional practice was replaced with Ghost Dance and, later, Big Head ceremonies. Wintus gathered en masse for the last time at the end of the nineteenth century. Copper-processing plants around the turn of the century poisoned what decent land and water remained in the region. Cortina, Colusa, Paskenta, and Grindstone Rancherias were created between 1906 and 1909. Wintu children were formally excluded from local schools until 1928. Termination and allotment policies during 1952 and 1953 further broke up Wintun culture; only three rancherias survived this period. In the 1930s, and again in the 1970s, dam construction flooded much of their remaining land. Despite an agreement with the Wintu people, the U.S. government removed people from and destroyed the Toyon-Wintu site in 1984.

RELIGION The rich Wintun mythology included recognition of a supreme being as well as numerous spirits. Wintuns prayed to the sun before washing in the morning, smoking, and eating. Spirits, present in all things, could be acquired by dreaming and going to a sacred place and engaging in ritual behavior.

Among the Nomlaki, they could also be influenced by prayer, charms, magic, and ritual. Shamans provided overall religious leadership. Bear shamans could destroy enemies. They received their powers during an annual five-day initiation period of fasting, dancing, and instruction from other shamans. Their curing methods included massage, soul capture, and sucking out a disease-causing object. Some Wintuns practiced the Kuksu cult, in which one or more secret societies, open by initiation to men and some high-status women, performed their own dances and rituals to restore the people to a perfect aboriginal state.

Wintuns did not adopt the 1870 Ghost Dance but rather the 1871 Earth Lodge cult, which preached return of the dead, the end of the world, and protection of the faithful. The Bole-Maru religion came in 1872, and dream dancing was popular toward the end of the century. Among the Nomlaki, virtually every activity and life-cycle phase carried with it ritual restrictions and ceremonies.

GOVERNMENT Like many California peoples, Wintuns were organized into tribelets. The village was the main social, economic, and political unit. Villages were autonomous and had clearly defined territory. Each village was led by a chief, often hereditary, who arbitrated disputes, hosted ceremonies and gatherings, and engaged in diplomatic relations with chiefs of other villages. The chief, who was materially supported by his followers, had to be a good singer and dancer and generally well liked. The Nomlaki recognized a secret society of higher-status men. These people had a higher degree of authority in public matters and controlled most of the skilled crafts and professions.

CUSTOMS The complex girls' puberty ritual involved seclusion for up to seven months in a special hut, a special diet and behavior, and, later, a dance. Boys had no puberty ceremony, but after killing their first deer they gave away the meat and then bathed. Marriage and cohabitation were synonymous; premarital relations were frowned upon. Wealthy men might have more than one wife. Mother-in-law taboos were present but not absolute. Both men and women observed many food and behavioral taboos related to pregnancy and birth. When a person died, mourners dressed his or her body in good clothes, removed it through a special opening in the rear of the house, and buried it with acorn meal, water, and personal items. The Patwin wrapped their dead with long hemp cords. Souls were said to travel along the Milky Way.

Murder and rape or other sexual transgressions were generally capital crimes. Most intentional crimes could be atoned for by compensating the injured party. Dances were more often social than religious and were often given when food was plentiful. Gambling was also a part of social dances; activities included the grass game (men), hand games, shinny (women), football, hoop and pole, ring and pin, and other contests of skill. Songs could also be social or religious.

DWELLINGS Four to seven pole-framed, bark-covered conical houses made up a village. Among the Patwin, dwellings as well as the ceremonial and domed menstrual huts were semisubterranean and earth covered. The men's clubhouse and sweat lodge was semisubterranean and circular, 15–20 feet in diameter, with one center pole. In cold weather single men also slept there.

DIET Men hunted deer and rabbits both communally in drives and individually. They also smoked bear (except grizzly) out of their dens and captured fowl, birds, and rodents. Communal drives were held to catch salmon and trout. Women gathered grubs, grasshoppers, acorns, greens, and seeds. Men and women cooperated in gathering acorns, with men shaking acorns out of trees for women to gather. The acorns were then dried and pounded into meal, after leaching them to remove their bitter taste.

KEY TECHNOLOGY Material items included bows (seasoned yew, reinforced with shredded deer sinew and containing twisted deer backbone sinew string), arrowheads (obsidian, pressure-flaked), arrows, and fishing nets, poles, and traps. Iris, hemp, grapevine, and milkweed were used for cordage. Other tools were made from bone, horn, and stone. Baskets served a number of functions. Fire drills were made of buckeye. Grass, boughs, or deer hides served as mattresses.

TRADE Trade was more frequent between villages or tribelets than with other peoples. Wintus obtained salmon flour, body paints, yew wood for bows, and obsidian for deer hides, woodpecker scalps, and salt. The Nomlaki traded for highly prized black bear pelts. They also traded in items made from Oregon to San Francisco Bay. Patwins traded freely and intermarried with some Pomo groups. Bows were a common item of exchange. In general, strings of clamshell disks, dentalia, and magnesite cylinders served as money. Men bartered mostly in clamshells and dentalia, women in baskets.

NOTABLE ARTS Basket making constituted the main Wintun fine art.

TRANSPORTATION People used rafts to cross streams and floated children or supplies in large baskets. River Patwin used tule balsa boats that exceeded 20 feet in length.

DRESS Dress was minimal. Adult women wore shredded maple bark aprons. Capes and blankets for warmth were of deer, fox, and rabbit skin. Decorations included earrings, headdresses, and tattooing (mainly women). The Nomlaki wore elk hide sandals.

WAR AND WEAPONS In addition to fighting neighboring villages and tribelets, Wintun enemies generally included the Shasta, Klamath, Modoc, and Yana. The Nomlakis' main enemy was the Yuki. Wintus took no prisoners. Typical provocations for feuds or war included murder, theft of women, poaching, and trespass. Among the Nomlaki not all men fought; those who did underwent special practical and magical training. Seers determined the proper course of action, and poisoners used magic as a weapon. Wars were usually limited, and casualties were minimal. Weapons included the bow and arrow, clubs, spears, daggers, slings, and wooden rod armor. Hand-to-hand fighting was avoided if possible. When the fighting stopped, an assembly of important men decided on just compensation.

Contemporary Information

GOVERNMENT/RESERVATIONS Wintuns currently live at Grindstone Creek Rancheria (Glenn County; 1906; 80 acres), Cortina Rancheria (Colusa County; 1907; 640 acres [Miwok]), Colusa Rancheria (Colusa County; 1907; 273 acres), Redding Rancheria (Shasta County), Rumsey Rancheria ("Yocha-De-He"; Yolo County; 1907; 185 acres), and the Round Valley Reservation/Covelo Indian Community (Mendocino County; 1864; 30,538 acres [Wailaki, Yuki, Nomlaki, Pomo, Concow, Pit River, and Little Lake peoples]). The Rumsey Rancheria elects a tribal council based on a constitution and by-laws approved in 1976. Other communities are governed by tribal councils as well.

ECONOMY The Rumsey Rancheria's diversified businesses include agricultural enterprises and a grocery store, service station, and bingo casino. They are financially self-sufficient.

LEGAL STATUS The Colusa Rancheria (Cachil DeHe Band of the Colosa Indian Community); Cortina Indian Rancheria; Grindstone Indian Rancheria (Wintun-Wailaki); and the Rumsey Indian Rancheria are federally recognized tribal entities. The Covelo Indian Community of the Round Valley Reservation is a federally recognized tribal entity. The Hayfork Band of Nor-El-Muk Wintu Indians, the Wintoon Indians, and the Wintu Indians of Central Valley had not received federal recognition as of 1997.

DAILY LIFE In the 1970s, the residents of Grindstone Rancheria, in combination with local non-Indians, successfully fought the Story–Elk Creek Dam. Today's Wintus work to protect ancient burial sites as well as the sacred Mt. Shasta. The Nomlaki have been forced to deal with the issue of toxic waste dumping. Although much traditional culture has been lost,

their heritage, transmitted in large measure by dedicated elders, remains very important to Wintu people.

Wiyot

Wiyot (`Wē yut) is the name of one of three culturally and linguistically related groups on the Eel River Delta in the early nineteenth century. They were culturally similar to the Yurok.

LOCATION The Wiyot traditionally inhabited the vicinity of Humboldt Bay, California, from the Little River south to the Bear River and east about 25 miles. This environment is coastal lowlands, an unusual one in California. Today, most Wiyots live in and around Humboldt County.

POPULATION As many as 3,500 Wiyot may been living in their region in the early nineteenth century. In 1990, roughly 50 Indians who consider themselves Wiyot lived on rancherias, with perhaps another 400 in local cities and towns.

LANGUAGE Wiyot was an Algonquian language related to Yurok.

Historical Information

HISTORY Humboldt Bay was first occupied around 900 by either Wiyots or Yuroks. In 1806, the first non-native explorers came into the region. The first systematic murders of Wiyots began around 1852 during the Chetco/Rogue River Indian War. Regular killings of Indians led to wholesale massacres shortly thereafter. In 1860, a massacre at Gunther Island, perpetrated by white residents of Eureka during a Wiyot religious celebration, killed as many as 250 Indians. Survivors were forced onto reservations on the Klamath and Smith Rivers. Wiyot culture never recovered from this event; their identity became mixed with whites and other local Indian peoples.

RELIGION The creator was known as "that old man above." The Wiyot practiced World Renewal ceremonies and dances. Although other peoples celebrated the World Renewal religion in a showy and complex manner, which involved recitations, displays of wealth, costumed dances, and various decorations, the Wiyot observed it irregularly and with less flair. Men and women also performed victory dances when an enemy was killed and conducted an elaborate girls' puberty ceremony. They did not observe a first salmon ritual. Female berdaches played an important role in Wiyot ceremonialism.

GOVERNMENT In place of formal tribal organization, each Wiyot group was autonomous and self-governing.

CUSTOMS Wealth was valued as the source of social stratification and prestige, although not to the degree of the Klamath River peoples. There was no debt slavery. Most of the common menstrual taboos were absent among the Wiyot. Married couples generally lived with the father's family, except in the case of "half-marriages" (when a man worked to cover part of the bride price). Corpses were carried by stretcher to the cemetery and buried in an extended position in plank-lined graves along with money and valuables. Relatives and undertakers observed various taboos following the funeral.

Both women and men hunted. Disease was considered to be caused either by the intrusion of poison objects, soul loss, or breaches of taboo. Herb doctors and especially sucking doctors (shamans) cured disease. Unlike most northwest California peoples, the Wiyots did not penalize shamans for declining a curing case.

DWELLINGS   Two or more families, including men, slept in rectangular houses of split redwood planks. Each unnamed house had a two- or three-pitch roof and a smoke hole at the top. The sweat house, built like a dwelling, only smaller, was used for gambling, ceremony, and occasionally sleeping. The Wiyot built no separate birth or menstrual huts.

DIET   Acorns were both traded for and gathered on special inland expeditions. The people also gathered berries and various other foods. Salmon, the main food staple along with other fish, was caught with traps, nets, weirs, on platforms, and with the use of fish poisons. Other foods included mollusks, sea lions, stranded whales, deer, elk, and other game. They did not eat wolf, fox, bear, and skunk.

KEY TECHNOLOGY   Tools and utilitarian items were made from bone, shell, stone, and wood. Twined baskets served a large variety of purposes.

TRADE   Wiyots participated in a regional trading complex.

NOTABLE ARTS   Wiyot baskets were particularly well made.

TRANSPORTATION   The Wiyot used large redwood dugout canoes.

DRESS   Women generally wore twined basket hats and either fringed and embroidered buckskin double-aprons that hung to between the knee and the ankle or one-piece, inner-bark skirts or aprons. Men wore buckskin breechclouts. Robes were of deer hide and woven rabbit skin. Both sexes wore moccasins.

WAR AND WEAPONS   Murder, insult, or poaching were the typical causes of war. The Wiyot fought by surprise attack or prearranged battle and used elk hide armor, rawhide shields, and bows and arrows. Women and children were not killed in war. After the fighting, both sides paid compensation for damaged property.

Contemporary Information

GOVERNMENT/RESERVATIONS   Today, Wiyot live on the Blue Lake Rancheria (Wiyot, Yurok, Hupa; Humboldt County), the Rohnerville Rancheria (Wiyot-Mattole; Humboldt County), the Table Bluff Rancheria (Humboldt County), and the Trinidad Rancheria (Yurok, Wiyot, Tolowa; Humboldt County). Government is by tribal council.

ECONOMY   All four rancherias are working to promote economic development. Logging and fishing are important economic activities.

LEGAL STATUS   The Bear River Band of the Rohnerville Rancheria is a federally recognized tribal entity (Wiyot/Mattole). The Blue Lake Rancheria, the Trinidad Rancheria, and the Table Bluff Rancheria are federally recognized tribal entities.

DAILY LIFE   The Wiyot support the traditional culture of their neighbors. They also hold an annual vigil in memory of the victims of the 1860 massacre. There is some semitraditional basket making among the people.

Yana

Yana (`Yä nä), "People."

LOCATION   In the early nineteenth century, the Yana lived in the upper Sacramento River Valley and the adjacent eastern foothills. The elevation of their territory ranged between 300 and 10,000 feet.

POPULATION   The aboriginal population of Yana probably numbered fewer than 2,000. Few, if any, Yana remain alive today.

LANGUAGE   Yana was a Hokan language. Its four divisions were Northern, Central, Southern, and Yahi.

Historical Information

HISTORY   Members of an 1821 Mexican expedition may have been the first non-natives to encounter the Yana. Hudson's Bay Company trappers almost certainly interacted with the Yana from about 1828 on, and some Mexicans received land grants in Yana territory during that time. The first permanent Anglo settlement in the area came in 1845.

By the late 1840s, Anglo trails crossed Yana territory. With Anglo encroachment came increased conflict: Attacks by U.S. soldiers (John C. Frémont in 1846, for example) led to retaliations, and as food became scarcer the Yana began raiding cabins. In the 1860s, Anglos set out to exterminate the Yana. Though massacres, disease, and starvation, their population was reduced by 95 percent in about 20 years.

In 1911, a Yana man named Ishi walked out of the foothills of Mt. Lassen to a nearby town, where two anthropologists were able to communicate with him. Ishi eventually communicated his story, which began at the time when Anglo invaders and murderers began to destroy the Yahi. Only about a dozen or so Yahis remained alive after a massacre in 1868, six years after Ishi's birth. These people remained in the wilderness until 1908, when only four were left. Three died shortly thereafter, leaving Ishi as the only remaining Yahi in 1911. After leaving the woods, he lived and worked at the University of California Museum of Anthropology (San Francisco), demonstrating traditional crafts, providing a wealth of information about his culture, and learning some English. Ishi died of tuberculosis in 1916.

RELIGION Little is known about Yana ceremonial life. They may have practiced the Kuksu cult. The few surviving Yana danced the Ghost Dance in 1871.

GOVERNMENT Yana tribelets consisted of a main village with several smaller satellite villages. Each village probably had a hereditary chief or headman, who lived in the main village. Chiefs were wealthy and often had two wives. They led the dances, orated from the roof of the assembly house on proper behavior, and were the only ones permitted to keep vultures as pets. The villagers provided food for chiefs and their families.

CUSTOMS Shamans, mostly male, received their power by fasting in remote places or swimming in certain pools. Trained by older shamans, they cured by singing, dancing, or sucking. Unsuccessful shamans might be accused of sorcery and killed. Various roots and teas were also used as medicines.

Girls had a more significant puberty ritual and greater restrictions around puberty than did boys. Parents arranged most marriages. The Yana observed a strong mother-in-law taboo. Yahi dead were usually cremated; the other groups buried their dead after four days, wrapped in deerskin, along with personal items, and burned their house and other possessions.

Land was privately owned. Men played double-ball shinny (usually a woman's game). Other games included ring and pin, cat's cradle, stick throwing at a stake, and the grass or hand game.

DWELLINGS Northern and Central groups lived in earth-covered multifamily houses. The Southern and Yahi groups preferred smaller, conical bark-covered houses. An assembly house was located in a tribelet's main village. All groups lived in temporary brush shelters or caves while hunting.

DIET Acorns, fish, and venison were the staples. Men climbed trees to shake acorns down while women gathered, shelled, and dried them. After leaching the acorn flour, it was used for mush, bread, and a soup with meat, berries, and other foods. Women also gathered roots, tubers, bulbs, berries, pine nuts, and grasshoppers. Men stalked deer using a deer-head decoy and bow and arrow. Salmon was broiled on heated rocks, roasted over an open fire, or

dried and stored. Rabbits were hunted in community drives. The Yana also took other game.

KEY TECHNOLOGY Yanas hunted with bow (preferably of yew wood) and arrow, as well as snares. They used spears, nets, and traps to catch fish. Other technological items included stone grinding tools; baskets of hazel, willow, pine roots, and sedge; milkweed fiber, peeled bark, and hemp ropes; mahogany and oak digging sticks; and buckeye fire drills. Musical instruments included rattles and elderwood flutes.

TRADE Typical exports included deer hides, salt, baskets, and buckeye fire-making drills. Imports included obsidian (Achumawi and Shasta); arrows, wildcat-skin quivers, and woodpecker scalps (Atsugewi); clam disk beads and magnesite cylinders (Maidu or Wintun); dentalium shells (Wintu); and barbed obsidian arrow points from the north.

NOTABLE ARTS Yana women made fine baskets.

TRANSPORTATION People used rafts to cross streams and floated children or supplies in large baskets. Regional Indians also used dugout and tule (rush) canoes for water transportation.

DRESS Women wore shredded bark or tule aprons or skirts. Wealthy women wore braids of human hair and skirts with leather and grass tassels. Men who could afford them wore buckskin leggings in winter; others made do with a simple apron. Men also wore eelskin hats and deerskin moccasins. Adornments included necklaces, feather headbands, woodpecker-scalp belts, and body paint. Hide robes provided warmth in winter. Men plucked facial hair with a split piece of wood. Both sexes pierced their ears.

WAR AND WEAPONS The Yana often fought their neighbors. Poaching and avenging the abduction of women were common reasons for war.

Ynezeño

See Chumash

Yokuts

Yokuts (`Yō kutz), a linguistic term meaning "person" or "People." The three divisions were the Northern Valley Yokuts, the Southern Valley Yokuts, and the Foothill Yokuts. Contemporary Yokuts tribes include the Choinumni, the Chukchansi, the Tachi (or Tache) and the Wukchumni.

LOCATION The Yokuts traditionally lived along the San Joaquin Valley and the Sierra Nevada foothills. Specifically, the Southern Yokuts inhabited a lake-slough-marsh environment in the southern San Joaquin Valley; the Northern Yokuts' territory was wetlands and grassy plains in the northern San Joaquin Valley; and the Foothill Yokuts lived approximately on the western slopes between the Fresno and

Kern Rivers. Today, Yokuts live on two rancherias in Tulare and Kings Counties and in nearby communities.

POPULATION The Yokuts population stood between 18,000 and 50,000 in the early eighteenth century. They had one of the highest regional population densities in aboriginal North America. In 1990, about 1,150 Indians lived on two Yokuts rancherias. At least several hundred more live on other rancherias and are scattered nearby and around California.

LANGUAGE Yokuts people spoke various dialects of Yokuts, a California Penutian language.

Historical Information

HISTORY The San Joaquin Valley has been inhabited for some 11,000 years. Yokuts culture is probably about between 600 and 2,000 years old, with direct cultural antecedents dating back perhaps 7,000 years. Aboriginal population density was extremely high, relatively speaking. The Spanish came into the region of the Southern Yokuts in the 1770s and were warmly received.

In the early nineteenth century, serious cultural destruction began as the northern valleys were drawn into the exploitative mission system. Yokuts resistance and retaliation brought further Spanish repression and even military expeditions. Foothills Yokuts communities were protected by their relative isolation, but they sheltered escapees and began raiding for horses to ride and eat, activities that they continued into the Mexican period. Yokuts became excellent cattle breeders and horse breakers during this period.

In the early 1830s, malaria and cholera epidemics killed roughly three-quarters of all Indians in the region. Mexicans established land grants in the San Joaquin Valley. By then, traditional flora, fauna, and subsistence patterns had all been severely disrupted. After the United States annexed California in 1848, its citizens began a large-scale campaign of slaughter and land theft against the Yokuts. The latter, along with their Miwok allies, resisted Anglo violence and land theft by force (such as the Mariposa Indian War of 1850–1851). In 1851, the tribes signed a treaty to relinquish their land for a reservation and payment, but pressure from the state of California kept the U.S. government from ratifying the agreement.

Dispossessed, some Yokuts worked on local ranches, where they were poorly paid and kept practically in peonage. The 1870 Ghost Dance revival provided a straw of hope to a beaten people. It lasted two years; its failure probably prevented the 1890 Ghost Dance from gaining popularity. The Tule River Reservation was established 1873. The Santa Rosa Rancheria was established in 1921.

Yokuts found minimal employment in the logging industry, as ranch hands, and as farm laborers into the twentieth century. Their children were forcibly sent to culture-killing boarding schools in the early part of the century. By the 1950s, most Indian children were in (segregated) public schools. A cultural revival took place beginning in the 1960s.

RELIGION The Yokuts' most important festival was their annual six-day ritual in honor of the dead. They also celebrated the arrival of the first fruit of the season. Group ceremonies were always conducted in the open and included shamanic displays of magic powers. Many men and older women also had spiritual helpers that conferred good fortune or specific abilities. The Northern Yokuts may have practiced the Kuksu cult. Men and women of this group also drank datura annually as part of a spring cleansing and curing ritual. Among the central Foothills group, datura was drunk once in a lifetime, by adolescents.

GOVERNMENT The Yokuts were organized into about 50 named tribelets, each with its own semipermanent villages, territory, and dialect. Each tribelet also had several hereditary chiefs (often at least one per village, usually from among the Eagle lineage). The chief, usually a wealthy man, sponsored ceremonies, hosted guests, aided the poor, mediated disputes, and authorized hunts as well as the murder of evil people such as sorcerers. Other offices included chief's messenger.

CUSTOMS Corpses, often along with their material possessions, were traditionally cremated. Most undertakers were berdaches. Public and private mourning ceremonies were observed. The afterworld, to the west or northwest, was a mirror image of this world, only better.

Shamans derived power from spirit animals via dreams or vision quests. They cured and presided over ceremonies. Large fees were charged for cures. Chronically unsuccessful shamans might be accused of sorcery and killed.

Various patrilineal lines existed among the Yokuts. Each had a totem symbol, such as a bird or an animal, which had certain ceremonial functions. Also, many tribelets had a dual division (Eagle and Coyote).

Among both men and women, various restrictions and taboos were associated with pregnancy and childbirth. The girls' puberty ceremony also involved certain restrictions and taboos. Families arranged the marriages with the couple's consent. Most men had only one wife. After living for a year with the woman's parents, a couple lived in or near the husband's parents' home. The Yokuts observed parent-in-law taboos. Divorce was relatively easy to obtain. After their infant cradle of soft tule, babies were confined to a forked-stick frame for almost a year.

Among the Foothill Yokuts, everyone swam at least daily, with adolescents also swimming several times at night during the winter for toughening. The divisions competed against each other in games, with men and women often gambling on the results. Both sexes played the hand game. Women also threw dice or split sticks. Leisure activities also included dancing and storytelling. Men smoked tobacco, usually at bedtime. Rattles accompanied most singing, which usually occurred during rituals. Other instruments included bone and wood whistles, flutes, and a musical bow.

DWELLINGS   The Southern Yokuts built both single-family oval-shaped and ten-family dwellings, in which each family had its own door and fireplace. Both featured tule mats covering pole frames. Mats also covered the floor and raised beds. Men sweated and sometimes slept in sweat houses.

The Northern Yokuts built similar single-family and possibly ceremonial earth lodges. Conical huts thatched with grass or bark slabs characterized dwellings of the Foothills Yokuts. Beds were of pine needles. Other structures included sweat houses, gaming courts, and mat-covered granaries and ramadas. Among Foothills Yokuts, women might use the sweat houses when no men were present.

DIET   The wetland home of the Southern Valley Yokuts contained an enormous variety and quantity of wildlife. They hunted fowl, rabbits, squirrels and other rodents, turtles, and occasionally big game. They gathered tule roots, manzanita berries, pine nuts, and seeds. Seafood included lake trout, salmon, perch, and mussels. Fresh fish was broiled on hot coals or sun-dried for storage. They also raised dogs for eating but did not eat frogs. Their salt came from salt grass.

In addition to many of the above foods, Northern Valley Yokuts depended on fish, mussels, turtles, elk, antelope, and smaller mammals. Salmon and especially acorns were staples. The Foothills Yokuts ate a lot of deer, quail, acorns, and fish. They also ate pine nuts, wild oats, manzanita berries, duck, trout, wasp grubs, squirrels, and rabbits. Iris bulb and tule root were important sources of flour. Men stalked deer by using deer disguises, or they ambushed them and shot them with bow and arrow. Quail were trapped. Salmon and other fish were caught with spears, weirs, and basket traps. The Yokuts also planted tobacco and may have engaged in basic horticulture or plant management.

KEY TECHNOLOGY   Baskets alone included water bottles, seed beaters, burden baskets, cooking vessels, winnowing trays, cradles, and caps. People fished with traps, nets, baskets, and spears from scaffolds built over river banks. Other types of snares and nets were used to capture fowl, as were spring poles with underwater triggers, stuffed decoys, and special water-skimming arrows.

Cords and ropes were fashioned from milkweed fiber. Ovens were made of earth. Northern Valley Yokuts' tools were made more often of stone and bone. Foothills Yokuts used stone, obsidian, granite, and quartz, and they had basic pottery. Southern Valley Yokuts made most of their crafts of tule, although there were a few wood, stone, and bone tools. The Yokuts burned wild seed plant areas to improve the following year's crop.

TRADE   Yokuts Indians traded widely with peoples of different habitats. Southern Valley people imported obsidian for arrowheads and sharp tools, stone mortars and pestles, wooden mortars, and marine shells for money and decoration. Northern Valley people traded dog pups for Miwok baskets and bows and arrows. They also traded with other tribes for mussels and abalone shells. Hunting, gathering, or fishing rights were occasionally exchanged as well.

NOTABLE ARTS   Basketry was considered a fine art as well as a craft. Representational petroglyphs, mostly circles and dots, were made perhaps as early as 1000 B.C.E. The Yokuts also drew pictographs, similar to those of the Chumash, into the historic period.

TRANSPORTATION   Valley Yokuts used wide, flat rafts made from lashed tule rushes. They floated belongings across rivers on log rafts. Some Foothills groups also used small basket boats. Women carried burdens in baskets anchored by tumplines.

DRESS   Dress was minimal. Men wore skin breechclouts at most. Women's clothing consisted of skin, grass, or tule aprons. Blankets and bedding were often made from the skins of rabbits or mud hens. Women tattooed their chins and used ornaments in pierced ears and noses.

WAR AND WEAPONS   Yokuts tribelets would occasionally fight one another or neighboring groups, but they were generally peaceful. Motives for fighting included trespass, theft of food, or the adventurous raiding by young men. They generally did not take captives. The peace conference included presents that were not considered reparations.

Contemporary Information

GOVERNMENT/RESERVATIONS   Many Yokuts live on the Santa Rosa Rancheria (1921; 170 acres; about 400 people in 1990 [Tachi tribe]) and the Tule River Reservation (1873; 55,356 acres; 750 people in 1990 [Tule River tribe]). Both are governed by tribal councils. Some Foothills Yokuts live in hamlets or scattered dwellings on or near their former territories.

The Choinumni tribe is governed by a tribal council and affiliated with the Choinumni Cultural

Association. Their 1990 population was about 250.

The Wukchumni tribe, population about 300 (1990), is governed by a tribal council.

The Picayune Rancheria (Chukchansi tribe) was founded in 1912 and "unterminated" in 1984. There is no land base for the population of about 800.

Table Mountain Rancheria (Chukchansi and Monache; 1916; 100 acres) had a 1990 population of about 100 people.

ECONOMY Primary economic activities include lumbering; ranching, including the leasing of lands; and farming. Many people, especially off-reservation Yokuts, receive government assistance. The Tule River Economic Development Corporation is a local planning agency. There are bingo parlors on the Table Mountain and Santa Rosa Rancherias.

LEGAL STATUS The Santa Rosa Indian Community (Tachi Tribe) is a federally recognized tribal entity. The Picayune Rancheria of Chukchansi Indians is a federally recognized tribal entity. The Table Mountain Rancheria is a federally recognized tribal entity. The Tule River Indian Tribe of the Tule River Indian Reservation is a federally recognized tribal entity. The Choinumni Tribe and the Wukchumni Tribe had not received federal recognition as of 1997.

DAILY LIFE Some Yokuts dialects are still spoken. Much of Yokuts traditional culture, other than on a scattered individual level, has disappeared. Some spiritual leaders belong to the Native American Cultural Association. Educational levels among the Yokuts is generally low, and the people suffer from recurring social and health problems. Important contemporary concerns include health care, education, land rights, the protection of sacred sites, and federal recognition.

The Tule River Reservation has its own health center. It also sponsors an elders' gathering in August and San Juan's Day in June. The Choinumni Tribe celebrates a traditional harvest gathering. The Wukchumni Tribe holds a spring dance. Chukchansi Indians are working to establish a land base. The Santa Rosa Rancheria celebrates a festival for spiritual renewal on March 1. Yokuts also attend many intertribal gatherings.

Yurok

Yurok (`Yū̄ rə k) is a Karuk word meaning "downstream" and refers to the tribe's location relative to the Karuk people. The Yurok referred to themselves as *Olekwo'l*, or "persons."

LOCATION Traditionally, the Yurok lived in permanent villages along and near the mouth of the Klamath River, in northern California. Today, many live on several small rancherias in Humboldt County.

POPULATION The aboriginal Yurok population was roughly 3,000 (early nineteenth century). In 1990, 1,819 Indians, not all of them Yurok, lived on four Yurok reservations. Other Yurok lived off-reservation. The official Yurok enrollment in 1991 was about 3,500.

LANGUAGE Yurok is an Algonquian language.

Historical Information

HISTORY Some Yurok villages were established as early as the fourteenth century and perhaps earlier. Their first contact with non-natives came with Spanish expeditions around 1775. The first known contact was among Hudson's Bay Company trappers and traders in 1827. However, the Yurok remained fairly isolated until about 1850, when a seaport was created in Yurok territory to make travel to the gold fields more accessible. The rush of settlers after 1848 led to a wholesale slaughter and dispossession of the Yurok. An 1851 treaty that would have established a large Yurok reservation was defeated by non-Indian interests. Shortly after the first white settlement was founded, Yuroks were working there as bottom-level wage laborers.

President Franklin Pierce established the Klamath River Reservation in Yurok Territory in 1855. Congress authorized the Hoopa Valley Reservation in 1864. In 1891, the Klamath River Reservation was joined to the Hoopa Reservation in an extension now called the Yurok Reservation. This tract of land consisted of 58,168 acres in 1891, but allotment and sale of "surplus" land, primarily to Anglo timber companies, reduced this total to about 6,800 acres. Three communal allotments became the rancherias of Big Lagoon, Trinidad, and Resighini.

From the mid–nineteenth century into the twentieth, many Yuroks worked in salmon canneries. Yuroks formed the Yurok Tribal Organization in the 1930s. Indian Shakerism was introduced in 1927, and some Yuroks joined the Assembly of God in the 1950s and 1960s. In a landmark 1988 case, the U.S. Supreme Court declined to protect sacred sites of Yurok and other Indians from government road building. Also in 1988, the Hoopa-Yurok Settlement Act partly resolved a long-standing dispute over timber revenues and fishing rights.

RELIGION With other northern California Indians, local Yurok groups practiced the World Renewal religion and the accompanying wealth-displaying white deerskin and jumping dances. Other ceremonies included the brush dance, kick dance, ghost dance, war dance, and peace dance. People who performed religious ceremonies were drawn from the ranks of the aristocracy (see "Government"). In general, religious training was related to acquiring not spirits, as in regions to the north, but rather real items, such as dentalia or food.

GOVERNMENT The wealthiest man was generally the village leader. About 10 percent of the men made up an aristocracy known as *peyerk,* or "real men." Selected by elder sponsors for special training, including vision quests, they lived at higher elevations, spoke in a more elaborate style, and acquired treasures such as albino deerskins, large obsidian knives, and costumes heavily decorated with shells and seeds. They also wore finer clothing than most Yuroks, imported special food, ate with a different etiquette, hosted ceremonial gatherings, and occasionally spoke foreign languages. The *peyerk* occasionally gathered as a council to arbitrate disputes. "Real women" went through a similar training experience. Since children were considered a financial drain, "real women" and their husbands practiced family limitation by sexual abstinence.

CUSTOMS Social status was a function of individual wealth, which was itself a major Yurok preoccupation. Only individuals owned land, although other resources might be owned as well by villages and descent groups. Poor people could voluntarily submit to the status of slave in order to acquire some measure of wealth. Imported dentalia shells were a major measure of wealth; they were engraved, decorated, and graded into standard measures for use as money. Other forms of wealth included large obsidian blades (also imported), pileated woodpecker scalps, and albino deerskins.

Via prayer and elicitation of wrongdoing, women doctors cured by gaining control of "pains," small inanimate, disease-causing objects within people. The misuse of curing power (sorcery) could cause individual death or group famine. Intertribal social and ceremonial relations with neighbors were frequent and friendly. Yurok villages often competed against each other in games. Unlike most offenses, certain sex crimes may have been considered crimes against the community.

The basic unit of society was small groups of patrilineally related males. Marriage was accompanied by lengthy haggling over the bride price. Most couples lived with the husband's family. Illegitimacy and adultery, being crimes against property, were considered serious. Corpses were removed from the home through the roof and buried in a family plot. If a married person died, the spouse guarded the grave until the soul's departure for the afterworld several days after death.

DWELLINGS Yuroks lived in over 50 semipermanent villages; late summer and early fall were devoted to gathering expeditions. Village dwellings were small rectangular redwood-plank houses with slanted or three-pitched roofs and a central excavated pit. Platforms lined the interior. A small anteroom was located immediately inside the entrance. They housed individual biological families. Houses of people of standing were named. People lived in temporary brush shelters while away on the gathering trips.

Rectangular plank sweat houses served as dormitories for the men and boys of a kinship unit. A "rich man," or head of a paternal kin group, built this structure for himself and his male relatives. The walls lined the sides of a deep pit, within which there was a fire for providing direct heat. Men often sweated in the afternoon, alternating sweats with immersion in chilly river water, scrubbing with herbs, and reciting prayers for good fortune. Space inside the sweat house was apportioned according to rank.

DIET Acorns and salmon were riverine staples; other fish and shellfish were also eaten along the coast. Yuroks also ate sea lions, elk, deer, small game, and various roots and seeds.

KEY TECHNOLOGY Baskets were used for a number of purposes. Many items, including houses and canoes, were fashioned of wood. Salmon were taken with weirs, poles, and nets as well as with harpoons. Yuroks may have had systems of higher mathematics.

TRADE Yuroks traded canoes to the Karuk and other neighboring peoples.

NOTABLE ARTS Baskets were particularly well made, as were wood products such as sweat house stools and headrests; dugout canoes with seats, footrests, and yokes; and hollowed treasure chests.

TRANSPORTATION Yuroks traveled both river and ocean on square-ended, dugout redwood canoes.

DRESS Ceremonial regalia included headdresses with up to 70 redheaded-woodpecker scalps. Every adult had an arm tattoo for checking the length of dentalia strings. Everyday dress included unsoled, single-piece moccasins, leather robes (in winter), and deerskin aprons (women). Men wore few or no clothes in summer. They generally plucked their facial hair except while mourning.

WAR AND WEAPONS The Yurok were not a hostile people by nature, but they feuded constantly. An elaborate wergild system, intimately connected to social status, was used to redress grievances. In their occasional fighting among themselves or with neighboring tribes—for offenses ranging from trespass and insult to murder—they avoided pitched battles, preferring to attack individuals or raid villages. Their fighting seldom resulted in many casualties. Young women were sometimes taken captive but were usually returned at the time of settlement. All fighting ended with compensation for everyone's losses.

Contemporary Information

GOVERNMENT/RESERVATIONS Yuroks may be found on the Hoopa Extension (Yurok) Reservation (1891; roughly 7,800 acres), the Berry Creek Rancheria (Butte County; 1916; 33 acres [Maidu]), the Resighini Reservation (Del Norte County; 1938; 228 acres [Coast Indian Community]), the Trinidad Rancheria (Humboldt County; 1917; 47 acres [Cher-Ae-Heights community]), the Big Lagoon Rancheria (Humboldt County; 1918; 20 acres; 19 Yurok and Tolowa in 1996), the Blue Lake Rancheria (Humboldt County), and the Elk Valley Rancheria (Del Norte County; 1906; 100 acres, with Tolowa and Hoopa). The first election for a Yurok Tribal Council was scheduled for 1997.

ECONOMY Logging and fishing (commercial and subsistence) are the most important local economic activities. People also leave the communities for work in the Bay area and elsewhere. Trinidad Rancheria owns a bingo parlor, and Big Lagoon Rancheria has invested in a major hotel. The Yuroks also manage two fish hatcheries.

LEGAL STATUS The Yurok Tribe, the Big Lagoon Rancheria (Yurok and Tolowa), and the Coast Indian Community of Yurok Indians of the Resighini Rancheria are federally recognized tribal entities, as are the Hoopa Extension Reservation, the Trinidad Rancheria, the Blue Lake Rancheria, the Berry Creek Rancheria, and the Elk Valley Rancheria. In 1983, the Yuroks and the Tolowas won a protracted battle with the United States for control of a sacred mountainous site in the Six Rivers National Forest.

DAILY LIFE Many Yuroks live semisubsistence lives of hunting, fishing, and gathering. Some still speak the Yurok language. Since the 1970s there has been a revival of traditional arts such as basket weaving and woodworking, along with some traditional ceremonies, such as the Jump and Brush Dances. Sumeg, a re-created traditional plank hamlet, was dedicated in 1990. The few *peyerk* who survive are almost all elderly.

The Tsurai Health Center (Trinidad Rancheria) serves the Yurok population. The application of dioxin by the U.S. Forest Service and timber companies to retard the growth of deciduous trees poses a major health problem in the area. Important ongoing issues include increasing the land base, construction of decent and affordable housing, the institution of full electrical service, protection of Indian grave sites and declining salmon stocks, and economic development.

CHAPTER THREE

The Northwest Coast

Northwest

For the purposes of this book, the Northwest Coast geographic region extends from just north of Yakutat Bay in southwest Alaska more or less to the California-Oregon border, including lands west of the Coast and Cascade Mountains. Its length is roughly 1,500 miles, but its width averages less than 100 miles. It is a territory dominated and defined by water. Especially in the north, great sounds, inlets, and fjords bring the maritime world to people well away from the coast and islands, and numerous rivers further contextualize their liquid world. Depending on elevation and precise distance from the coast, it is an area of seemingly endless fog and rain, fierce winter storms, dense forest, and giant trees. The climate is generally moderate.

The tribes that are spoken of today are modern inventions. Aboriginally, perhaps 165,000 Indians of the Northwest Coast lived in autonomous villages; these and their lineage constituted their political identities. Thus, for example, the people now referred to as the Tlingit tribe were once about 14 separate and distinct Tlingit tribes, such as Chilkat Tlingit, Hoonah Tlingit, and Stikines Tlingit, each of whom shared a dialect, territory, natural resources, and certain inherited rights and obligations. In the north, autonomous local groups occasionally formed military and/or ceremonial alliances. Northwest Coast Indians spoke at least 40 dialects of languages in the Nadene (Athapaskan), Haida, Tsimshian, Wakashan, Chimakuan, Salishan, and Penutian language families.

Almost all Northwest Coast Indian groups shared certain aspects of material culture. Not surprisingly, the sea and/or rivers played a central role in their lives. Fish, especially salmon, was the most important food for most Northwest Coast Indians. Since transportation for most of these groups was by canoe, they were great builders of canoes as well as other finely constructed and carved wooden objects. Trees, espe-cially the red cedar, were the raw materials for everything from canoes to clothing to plank houses. The people generally lived in permanent winter villages but had one or more small permanent, semipermanent, or seasonal villages or camping sites as well.

Aside from life's necessities, their most important activity was to acquire and maintain wealth and social status. Especially in the north, society was carefully ranked according to hereditary status. The region's classic ceremonial activity—the potlatch—was both a reflection of and a means to perpetuate this system of social inequality. Religion was based on an individual's relationship with one or more guardian spirits acquired from the nonhuman world.

With the arrival of non-natives (Spaniards, Russians, British, and, later, Americans) in the late eighteenth and the nineteenth centuries, native Northwest Coast peoples suffered a fate similar to that of other Native Americans. Across the board, populations declined by as much as 90 percent, mostly owing to disease as well as destruction and appropriation of subsistence areas. However, the effects of these changes were uneven; in general, southern and coastal peoples fared worse than northern and more interior peoples.

In the late twentieth century, longhouse kin ties had endured in many places, and tribes in general were moving toward increasing levels of self-government. In the United States, the 1974 Boldt decision (see later discussion of fishing rights in western Washington) secured native fishing rights, although the status of native rights in British Columbia is far less clear. Northwest Indians in general are full participants in contemporary U.S. and Canadian life while at the same time retaining strong native identities.

The first humans entered the Northwest Coast region about 10,000 years ago. Early prehistoric cultures probably came from the interior via the Columbia River and, somewhat later, down the coast and up the river valleys. Technology was characterized by flaked stone industries. Little else is known about the very earliest inhabitants of the region, other than that they adapted quite successfully to the region.

In southwestern Alaska, a new and much better documented stage of cultural development began around 3000 B.C.E. Items of that period, including adzes, labrets, and beads, were fashioned of ground stone and bone. These people ate shellfish and some sea mammals. Later, around 1000 B.C.E., bark mats and poles appear, as do signs of extensive fish and land mammal consumption, more complex tools, and seasonal site occupation. Items consistent with early historic culture date from roughly 1000 C.E.

In northern and central British Columbia as well, changes in the archaeological record, particularly the presence of shellfish middens, indicate that the basic subsistence technology for the following 5,000 years was in place by at least 3000 B.C.E. Sedentary villages appear around 700 B.C.E., and social ranking, woodworking, and distinctive regional art styles shortly thereafter. Intergroup trade was also well established by this time.

Southern British Columbia and northern Washington show a somewhat different pattern. Several distinct cultural periods preceded the final prehistoric pattern, which began in roughly 400 C.E., although in many respects life in the region was little changed from that around 3000 B.C.E. Cultural continuity can be demonstrated along Washington's ocean coast for at least the past 4,000 years and around Puget Sound for roughly 2,000 years.

Separate and distinct cultures evolved in the Lower Columbia and Willamette Valleys as early as 1560 B.C.E. (Lower Columbia) and 5800 B.C.E. (Willamette Valley). The former featured a fishing economy and larger villages; the latter was based on more diverse subsistence activities and smaller villages or camps. Finally, along the Oregon coast, people moved from a premarine to a marine-based economy early in the first millennium B.C.E., with the marine and riverine culture becoming fully developed by about 500 C.E.

Descriptions of traditional Northwest Coast Indian culture are heavily influenced by what non-Indians observed in the late eighteenth and the nineteenth centuries, by which time many aboriginal elements had been altered. However, what follows is a portrait of aspects probably common to many aboriginal Northwest Coast cultures.

The use of two resources above all defined Northwest Coast Indians: fish, especially salmon, and cedar. Many peoples caught all five kinds of salmon: pink, coho, chum (dog), chinook, and sockeye. Many groups celebrated rituals concerning the season's first salmon run. Up to 12 methods of salmon fishing were employed, including varieties of nets, spears, and traps. Other important fish included halibut, eulachon (candlefish), smelt, herring, and sturgeon.

Also, many groups availed themselves of abundant quantities of shellfish. Seafood was generally eaten fresh or dried and stored for the winter. Eulachon was used primarily for its oil. Other common foods, in addition to fish and shellfish, included sea mammals, some land mammals, and plants, especially berries (mashed and dried into cakes) and roots such as camas, wapato, and bracken fern. Food was generally eaten fresh, or grilled, boiled (in a basket with hot rocks), or steamed or baked in a pit oven. Mountain goat was hunted for its hair and horn.

The other primary resource, red cedar (redwood in the south), was the backbone of Northwest Coast technology. People used it for clothing, baskets, houses, and canoes as well as for art, ceremonial, and utilitarian objects such as bent-corner boxes, bowls, masks, and heraldic poles. Men worked it with tools such as adzes, chisels, wedges, hammers, drills, and knives. Blades were made of rock, shell, horn, bone, and a small amount of iron. Most carved wood objects were of extremely fine craftsmanship. Although most men could craft objects of wood, canoe making was a distinct profession. Northwest Coast Indians built several types of canoes for specialized activities.

In general, Northwest Coast Indian people fished for eulachon in late winter; gathered seaweed, cedar bark, and herring spawn and fished for halibut in early spring (May); moved to their summer camps around June, where they gathered sea bird eggs and caught salmon; fished and gathered berries, roots, and shoots throughout the summer; preserved the fish and hunted in the fall; and gathered shellfish, hunted sporadically, observed their ceremonies, gambled, told stories, wove, and carved in winter.

Most Northwest Coast societies were ranked according to social status. Status was generally inherited and carried with it certain rights and obligations. Chiefs of local (kin) groups, for instance, tended to be both wealthy and of high birth. They directed large-group activities and wore finer and special clothing. Since it concerned the interests of two kin groups, marriage was a function more of social organization than of life cycle.

Typically, four groups existed: nobility, upper class free, lower class free, and slaves (actually not members of society at all). Each individual was also ranked within the group. Because they were largely based on inheritance, the groups were fairly immutable, although some transfer was possible through acquiring (by trade, purchase, marriage, or war) some inherited rights. These rights, or privileges, owned by the kin group, included songs, dances, performances, and control of subsistence areas and were identified by crests, or design patterns, reflecting real and mythical histories of family lines and associated incidents, animals, and spirits.

All such items were originally obtained by an ancestor from a supernatural spirit. All present members of an opposite division received payment to view a crest, because in so doing they legitimated both the display and the crest's associated privileges. Resource areas were often "owned" or controlled by kin groups. Among the nobility, status—indeed, the entire system of ranking and kin groups—was confirmed and reaffirmed by a ceremonial obligation called the potlatch.

Potlatching, although it probably increased in intensity during the nineteenth century, was almost certainly part of aboriginal culture. The potlatch was held on varying occasions, such as the succession of a chief, an important life-cycle event, or to save or regain face. Nobles, or chiefs, and their groups invited other chiefs and their relatives from other villages to a feast that lasted for several days. Seating was strictly according to social position. The host and his family would recite their myths and genealogies and give gifts, also according to social position, the acceptance of which also indicated acceptance of the social order.

All potlatches included feasting, socializing, speeches, songs, displays of wealth (such as hammered pieces of copper, pelts, robes, and dentalium shell) and crests, and dances. The original purpose of the institution may have been to exchange goods for food during lean times. Potlatches were held in winter. Around the turn of the century, the "rivalry potlatch," a bitter scene in which the object was to humiliate a rival, was brought about in part because of population decline and consolidation.

Northwest Coast religion centered around the phenomenon of a guardian spirit. Such spirits came from both animate and inanimate objects. They could be individually acquired or inherited; they occasionally arrived uninvited. Individual acquisition of guardian spirits came as the result of spirit quests—bathing, fasting, and praying in remote places—that began when a person was prepubescent and culminated as many as 10 or 20 years later when the spirit power revealed itself. The spirit, associated with a particular song and dance that was displayed during the winter ceremonials, imparted some kind of skill or luck or some special knowledge. Shamans received special spirits that enabled them to cure and/or harm people.

Large rectangular plank houses were the norm along the Northwest Coast. Roof types (shed, gambrel, gable) varied according to location. Several families generally lived in a house, each partitioned off

from another, with a particular family's position in the house determined by rank. Temporary seasonal shelters were built of mats, planks removed from the main house, or bark. House posts were frequently carved and painted with heraldic or crest designs. In fact, most Northwest Coast art was heraldic in nature. In addition to house posts, beams, and fronts, this kind of art was often displayed, especially in the north, in the form of totem (mortuary, memorial, portal) poles.

Weaving was an important nonwood craft. Raw materials included spruce root, cedar inner bark, cattail, tule, mountain goat and dog wool, and bird down. Most women used the twining method to weave baskets (including watertight baskets), clothing (capes, hats, robes), and mats. Coast Salish women spun wool on a full loom. Some clothing was also made of dressed skins, although these were more generally traded for than made locally.

Aboriginally, intragroup conflict was minimal, with the exception of witchcraft, which was a capital offense along with clan incest (among those groups with clans). Intergroup conflict took place within the framework of feuds and wars: The former entailed conflict for a legalistic purpose, whereas the latter existed solely for material gain (land, booty, slaves). In general, the north saw more warfare than the south. Chiefs were the nominal war commanders, and soldiers often undertook practical as well as ritual preparations before fighting. Night raids were the preferred war strategy. Victims' heads were often displayed on poles as proof of fighting prowess. Defensive tactics included the use of sentries and fortifications.

The first non-natives may have appeared on the Northwest Coast as early as the sixteenth century. However, it was not until Captain James Cook's crew realized in 1778 the enormous profit in selling Northwest Coast sea otter pelts in China that contact began in earnest. Land-based fur trade operations by Russians, Spaniards, British, and Americans followed shortly after the onset of the maritime fur trade. By about 1850 sea otter stocks had become depleted, and the great non-native fur trade era along the Northwest Coast had come and gone.

During this relatively brief period, diseases such as smallpox and malaria destroyed up to 80 percent or more of some Indian villages. Alcoholism and venereal disease killed more slowly but just as surely. Indians also acquired firearms, iron, sugar, flour, rum, and sails for their canoes during this period. Some strategically placed chiefs became wealthy by monopolizing parts of the fur trade. With the exception of the effects of depopulation, however, and the concentration of remaining populations around trading posts, basic cultural patterns were little disrupted. One significant result of the new wealth accumulated by some groups was the increase in numbers and extravagance of potlatches and the reinvigoration of material culture, including artistic expression.

Though they did not know it, non-native settlers who arrived in the mid–nineteenth century found the Indian population greatly diminished. Perhaps because of the region's relative inaccessibility, all-out war between Indians and Anglos was largely avoided on the northern Northwest Coast. The United States having only acquired Alaska from the Russians in 1867, its nonmilitary presence was minimal there until the late nineteenth century.

Still, throughout the Northwest Coast, Indians in the late nineteenth century saw further outbreaks of infectious disease as well as intensive missionary work, official efforts to encourage assimilation, severe racial prejudice, and regular anti-Indian violence. Their land was increasingly taken over by non-native squatters while the Indians were legally denied the right to squat on, and thus obtain rights to, their own land. Ultimately, their subsistence patterns and cultural traditions under severe attack, and divided among themselves over the merits of change, most Indians became involved in the wage economy, such as canneries and commercial fishing, built without their permission on their lands.

The United States and Britain fixed their western boundary in 1846 at 49 degrees north latitude. Shortly thereafter, Oregon and Washington Territories were created, and the United States set about extinguishing Indian land title. In Oregon white settlers and miners were allowed simply to dispossess Indians. In the 1850s, treaties were concluded with Washington coastal tribes, providing for land cession and removal to reservations. Reservations in Washington were near or within traditional territory. Most Oregon Indians, however, were removed to two distant reservations following the bitter Rogue River wars of 1851–1855. Conditions there were poor and many starved, and in any case the reservations were soon whittled down by the government. Even in Washington, from 1855 to 1856, a coalition of Puget Sound tribes under the leadership of the Nisqually chief Leschi rose up against their poor treatment at the hands of the whites. Education, including missionization, and agriculture were the primary methods to force the Indians to assimilate. By the early twentieth century, Indian populations were still declining, and many traditions continued to unravel.

Unlike most other North American Indians, the Indians of British Columbia were not conquered militarily, nor did they formally surrender title to their land. In 1884, 13 years after British Columbia joined the Canadian Confederation, the Canadian government simply discounted Indian land ownership and passed its first Indian Act, under which it appropriated land and exercised legal control over Indians within Canada. The first of its two main provisions established roughly 200 small reserves to accommodate the different bands. A reserve could consist of a fishing location, a cemetery, or a village site. The thinking was to permit Indians to remain self-sufficient as they made the transition to a capitalist economy, whereas in the United States policymakers forced various groups of Indians to live together on large reservations, where they were strongly encouraged to become farmers and abandon their traditional identities. The other major provision of the Indian Act outlawed the potlatch; that provision was repealed in 1954.

In 1912, a group of Tlingit and Tsimshian men and women formed the Alaska Native Brotherhood (ANB). This group, with the Native American Sisterhood formed 11 years later, was dedicated to progress as defined by non-native society: Anglo-style education, citizenship, and the abolition of native customs, especially languages and the potlatch (which persisted clandestinely despite its de jure ban). During the 1920s, the ANB broadened its activities to include working against the pervasive institutional and individual discrimination against Native Americans. Today they embrace many of their old traditions, and the ANB remains an active and influential player in Tlingit-Haida-Canadian affairs.

Groups like the Tlingit and Haida Central Council fought for years for aboriginal land claims. The landmark resolution of this fight was the Alaska Native Claims Settlement Act (1971). Under its terms, Alaska's Tlingit and Haida Indians were organized into regional corporations. In addition, the act created 200 village corporations. Indians born before 1971 were issued shares of their corporation. As of 1996, they are restricted from selling those shares on the open market unless a majority, and in some cases (Tlingit and Haida, for instance) a supermajority of the tribe agrees to do so.

Indians in western Washington have their own landmark legal case. With the rise of the Indian self-determination movement in the 1960s and 1970s, Indians in that region redoubled their efforts to safeguard their fishing rights under the various treaties. For decades, white-owned commercial fishing had been depleting fish stocks so that the Indians, who were guaranteed by treaty the right to fish at their usual places, were decreasingly able to exercise that right. Often Indians were harassed physically and legally for attempting to fish in their usual way. In 1974, Judge George Boldt ruled definitively that the treaty Indians of western Washington were entitled under their treaties to special fishing rights at their "usual and customary" fishing places and to take 50 percent of the allowable salmon harvest in the state. The impact of this ruling has been profound. It includes an explosive growth of Indian fishing and marine-related industries as well as the reinvigoration of local Indian culture.

Since World War II, Canada has tried through federal funds and programs to increase the socioeconomic status of Indians in British Columbia. Since the 1970s, at least, those Indians have fought, with limited success, for an increased share of self-determination. Regional band organizations ("tribal councils") formed in the mid-1970s to press a range of issues, from land claims to services to national political reforms. Despite the reemergence of potlatching and other aspects of traditional culture such as language, rituals, art, performances, and songs after laws against them were removed in 1950s and 1960s, British Columbia Indians still face severe social and economic challenges.

In keeping with the relatively harsh treatment on the Oregon reservations, the federal government in the United States voted to terminate them in 1951— that is, to sell the land and end the government's relationship with the 61 tribes and bands. Many tribes supported this move. However, when it predictably led to further impoverishment, tribes petitioned for and secured restoration in the 1970s and 1980s. Also in the 1980s, Oregon tribes redoubled their efforts to secure economic development and improved housing and health services.

Bella Bella

Bella Bella (`Be l ə `Be l ə) is a term dating from 1834 that does not refer to an aboriginal self-designation. The Bella Bella (made up of at least three subgroups: the Kokaitk, Oelitk, and Oealitk), Haihais, and Oowekeeno are sometimes referred to as Heiltsuk. The Heiltsuk, along with the Heisla, are today identified as Bella Bella or northern Kwakiutl.

LOCATION   Traditionally, these groups lived in the vicinity of Queen Charlotte Sound, north of Vancouver Island and the Kwakiutl people, in the Canadian province of British Columbia. This is a relatively moderate, wet land marked by inlets, islands, peninsulas, mountains, and valleys.

POPULATION   Roughly 1,700 Bella Bellas lived in their territory in 1835. In 1901 the figure had shrunk to 330, but it climbed to 1,874 in 1995.

LANGUAGE   The Heiltsuk spoke Heiltsuk (Haihai and Bella Bella)-Oowekyala (Oowekeeno), a Wakashan language. The two component languages were virtually mutually unintelligible.

Historical Information

HISTORY   Bella Bellas probably met non-Indians for the first time in 1793, when the explorers George Vancouver and Alexander Mackenzie arrived to prospect for the fur trade. Shortly thereafter, that trade brought more Anglos as well as Anglo-Indian violence. Milbanke Sound was the first local major trade center. In 1833, the Hudson's Bay Company built Fort McLoughlin on Campbell Island as a major trading post. Although it abandoned the fort ten years later, the company opened a small store on the site about 1850. During the fur trade period, the Bella Bellas emerged as middlemen, controlling access to some interior tribes and playing the Americans and British off against each other.

An 1862 smallpox epidemic set off a period of rapid change. Dramatic Indian depopulation led to village consolidation. Missionization followed, as did the growth of the commercial fishing, canning, and logging industries. In 1880, the government separated Indians from their land by unilaterally establishing reserves. The Bella Bella reserve was run by Methodist missionaries. Village centralization and consolidation continued. Around 1900, two Oowekeeno villages were established near a sawmill and a cannery. The Haihais moved from their local villages in about 1870 to Swindle Island, a fuel depot for steamships.

In the twentieth century, northern Kwakiutls were largely displaced from the logging and fishing industries owing to a combination of factors, including competition with non-natives, technological advances, and loss of land rights. Increased unemployment and out-migration has been the result. However, ties remain strong between home communities and those people in regional cities and towns.

RELIGION   Dancing or secret societies performed their ceremonies in winter. Initiation into the societies was by hereditary right. Dances—a first, or shamans', series, including a cannibal's dance; a "coming down again," or second, series, including war dances; and a dog-eating dance—were ranked according to the status of both the dance and the performers. Performances dramatized the encounter of an ancestor with a supernatural being. Wealthy, high-status people sponsored dances, feasts, and potlatches. A council of chiefs managed the winter dances.

GOVERNMENT   As was generally the case along the Northwest Coast, the basic political unit was the autonomous local group or clan. Each such group was presided over by a chief. Parts of several clans often formed a village, where the highest-ranking chief had relative degrees of control over the others. For defensive purposes, some villages congregated to form loose confederations or tribes.

CUSTOMS Distinctive crests and ranked titles identified each of the four crest groups, or clans—Raven, Eagle, Orca, and Wolf. These groups also had heads, or chiefs. Resource sites could be owned by families, local groups, or crest groups and could be rented out for some form of compensation.

In general, society was divided into status-ranked groups, such as chiefs, free commoners, and slaves. Some divisions also added another free group between commoners and slaves, as well as several levels of chief. Symbols of high rank included tattoos, ornamentation, and the possession of wealth and hereditary titles. Commoners had less prestigious names, held smaller feasts, and had no inherited rights to certain dances. The low-class free were orphans or the unambitious, with no wealthy relatives.

Regular intermarriage occurred between the Bella Bella and the Bella Coola. Marriage between close cousins was condoned if it furthered one's status. The bride price was a key ingredient of a marriage; in cases of divorce it was generally refunded.

DWELLINGS Semipermanent winter villages were composed of rectangular cedar plank houses. Features included vertical wall planks, a gabled roof and double ridgepole, carved interior posts, an adjustable central smoke hole, and mat-lined walls in sleeping areas. Summer camp houses were of similar but less elaborate construction. When they were in small or temporary camps, people made do with bark structures.

DIET Fish, especially salmon, was the staple. Other marine foods were also important. The Bella Bella took stranded whales only for their blubber. They ate several varieties of berries and hunted deer, wolf, bear, mountain goat, small mammals, waterfowl, and most birds (except crow and raven) and their eggs. Other than in winter, when food stores were eaten, people migrated seasonally to various resource sites.

KEY TECHNOLOGY Fishing technology included stone and wood stake weirs, traps, harpoons, dip nets, and clubs. Harpoons, clubs, and bow and arrow were used for hunting sea mammals. Land animals were hunted with the help of dogs, snares, spears, and deadfalls. Digging sticks helped people gather roots. Most woodworking tools were of stone. Women made burden and storage baskets.

TRADE The Bella Bella traded shellfish and seaweed with more inland groups (such as the Bella Coola) for eulachon and eulachon products. They also obtained canoes in trade, often from the north.

NOTABLE ARTS Bentwood boxes, chests, canoes, and horn spoons and ladles were items of fine local construction. Also important were relief carved and painted ceremonial/religious items such as totem poles and masks.

TRANSPORTATION The cedar dugout, a shallow-bottom canoe used with round-tipped blades, was the primary means of transportation. The Bella Bella and Haihais also used bark canoes for lake travel.

DRESS In warm weather, women wore cedar-bark aprons; men went naked. Blankets of woven cedar bark, mountain goat wool or dog hair, or tanned, sewn skins kept people warm in cold weather. Women wore waterproof basket caps and cedar-bark ponchos in the rain. Both sexes wore their hair long. Those who could afford it wore abalone nose and ear pendants. High-status women also wore labrets, dentalia bracelets, necklaces, and anklets. They also deformed their babies' heads for aesthetic purposes. The people painted their bodies and faces against sunburn.

WAR AND WEAPONS The Bella Bella fought regularly, mainly against the Bella Coola, Haida, Tsimshian, and Kwakiutl. They were well organized militarily. The Haihais were regularly under attack, but the Oowekeeno were more geographically isolated. Revenge, trespass, violation of custom, and seasonal shortages of food were common causes of war.

Contemporary Information

GOVERNMENT/RESERVATIONS The Heiltsuk Band, formerly the Bella Bella, controls 22 reserves on 1,369 hectares of land on Campbell Island. As of 1995, the population was 1,874. Elections are held under the provisions of the Indian Act, and the band is unaffiliated.

ECONOMY Important economic activities and resources include a shipyard, cable television, fisheries, and small businesses.

LEGAL STATUS The Heiltsuk Band is a federally and provincially recognized entity.

DAILY LIFE Throughout the twentieth century, life for the Bella Bella has been characterized by displacement from local industries, the loss of rights to their land, and slow population increase. One result of these trends has been high unemployment and out-migration, although ties between home communities and populations in Vancouver remain relatively strong. Children attend band and provincial schools. A Heiltsuk cultural-educational center facilitates the rebuilding and promotion of local culture. Other facilities include a community hall and a day care center. The old religion has been largely replaced by Christianity, and much of the traditional culture has been lost.

Bella Coola

Bella Coola (`Be l ə `C ū l ə) is an Anglicization of a Heiltsuk word for the speakers of the Bella Coola language. The native word for the people of the Bella Coola valley was *Nuxalkmx*. They consisted of four or five subgroups linked linguistically, territorially, and culturally, although not politically. These people are known today as the Nuxalt Nation.

LOCATION Traditionally, several permanent villages existed south and east of the Bella Bella and the Haisla, east of the Queen Charlotte Sound coast in British Columbia. These people may also have occupied territory east of the Coastal Range. Beginning around 1800, they consolidated their villages at the mouth of the Bella Coola River. In 1936, a flood forced them to move from the north to the south shore of the river's mouth. Their traditional territory is rugged, with mountains, estuaries, and forests. The climate is cool and wet.

POPULATION Perhaps 1,400 Bella Coolas lived in their villages in 1780. In the 1970s, roughly 600 lived on their reserves and in Northwest cities.

LANGUAGE Bella Coola is a Salishan language.

Historical Information

HISTORY The Bella Coola were latecomers to the region, probably arriving around 1400. In 1793 they encountered the explorers George Vancouver and Alexander Mackenzie; the Indians traded fish and skins to them for iron, copper, knives, and other items. As the fur trade developed, Hudson's Bay Company maintained a local fort/post from 1833 to 1843. During this period, the Bella Coola prevented furs from the Carrier Indians (an eastern group) from reaching the coast, thus maintaining a trade monopoly with the whites.

Shortly after gold was discovered in their area (1851), disease, alcohol, and hunger combined to weaken and kill many Indians. A severe smallpox epidemic in 1863 forced the abandonment of numerous villages. Hudson's Bay Company operated another local trading post from 1869 to 1882, and Protestant missionaries penetrated the Bella Coola territory in the 1870s and 1880s. In 1885, nine Bella Coolas journeyed to Germany for 13 months, dancing and singing for European audiences and inspiring the anthropologist Franz Boas to begin his lifelong study of Northwest Coast Indians. A Norwegian colony, the first local non-Indian settlement, was established in the Bella Coola Valley in 1894.

These changes, combined with the gradual transition to a commercial (fishing and logging) economy and the replacement of traditional housing with single-family structures, weakened descent groups and led to the gradual consolidation of ceremonials and the abandonment of songs. In the 1960s and 1970s, however, the people relearned the old songs, using recordings made by anthropologists. In the 1970s, the revival of traditional culture also included new masks and dances.

RELIGION The Bella Coola recognized four or five worlds, including a center, or human, world. A supernatural being kept this flat center world level and balanced. There were many deities and a supreme female deity, all of whom resided in the sky. All things had spirits that could intervene in the lives of people. Favorable intervention might be gained through prayer and ritual sexual intercourse.

Their extremely rich ceremonialism was dominated by two secret societies as well as the potlatch. Membership in one such society, *Sisaok,* was restricted to the children and relatives of certain chiefs. An extended period of seclusion accompanied initiation, as did songs and the display of carved masks with crests. The ceremony dramatized various kin-related legends. The other society, *Kusiut,* was based on contact with the supernaturals. Its dances, such as cannibal, scratcher, breaker, and fungus, included songs and masks representing supernatural beings. These dances dominated the ceremonial period, which lasted from November through March.

All people had the potential to become shamans; the event occurred when a supernatural being conferred power through a visit, a name, and songs. Some such power could cure sickness. Some shamans received power through ghosts and could see dead people; they cured disease caused by ghosts.

GOVERNMENT Aboriginally, the Bella Coola inhabited between 30 and 60 autonomous villages, each consisting of from 2 to 30 houses arranged in a row along a river or creek bank. Each village had a chief, whose status derived from his ancestral name, prerogatives, and wealth. Chiefs had little direct ruling power. A woman who had been "rebought" several times, and had thus helped her husband accumulate status, was also recognized as a chief.

CUSTOMS Descent groups probably owned fish weirs in aboriginal times. Hunting, too, could only occur in an area claimed by a descent group. Hunters, some of whose ancestral prerogatives allowed them to be known as professionals, underwent ritual preparation.

The units of social organization included the household, village, and descent group, or all those with a common ancestral mythology. A child could inherit both parents' descent groups, but residence with the father's family tended to reinforce the patrilineal line. Social status was important and clearly delineated. The ability (and obligation) to give away gifts on ceremonial occasions (potlatches) was a key component of social status. Social mobility was possible, and even slaves might obtain dance prerogatives and thus achieve some status.

Babies were born with the assistance of midwives in a birth hut in the woods. Their heads were flattened and their bodies massaged daily. Wealthy parents gave naming potlatches. Infanticide and abortion were occasionally practiced. The Bella Coola pierced the nasal septa of high-status children, both boys and girls; the occasion was accompanied by potlatches. Upon reaching puberty, girls were secluded, and their activity and diet were restricted for a year. There were no boys' puberty rituals, although their first hunted game was distributed and eaten ritually as were the first berries gathered by girls.

Although the "ancestral family" was an important source of Bella Coola identity, they did intermarry extensively with other peoples. Parents and elderly relatives arranged marriages, around which there were many rituals and opportunities to increase status. The relatives of high-status brides were expected to "rebuy" the woman (donate goods) every time her husband gave a potlatch. Cruelty, neglect, and infidelity were considered grounds for divorce.

Corpses were buried squatting in a wooden box. Twins' coffins were placed in trees. Coffins may also have been placed in caves, on scaffolds, or on top of memorial poles. They may also have been wrapped in bearskins and left on tree stumps in the forest. Property was also buried at the funeral.

Music could be both sacred and secular. The former was sung by a choir, who used sticks and drums for a beat, and three main performers. Various wind instruments were also used to symbolize the supernaturals.

DWELLINGS Permanent houses were large, planked structures. They were constructed of red cedar and often built on stilts against floods and enemies. Housefronts were decorated with the owner's crest. Houses were inhabited by extended families. Entrance was through carved house posts. Some winter houses were excavated, with only the roofs showing.

DIET The Bella Coola enjoyed a fairly regular food supply. Fish were the staple, including five types of salmon plus steelhead trout, rainbow and cutthroat trout, eulachon, Pacific herring, and others. All fish was boiled, roasted, or smoke dried. Eulachon was very valuable, perhaps more for its grease than as food. The first chinook salmon and eulachon of the season were eaten ritually.

Other important foods included shellfish; seals, sea lions, and beached whales; land mammals, such as mountain goat, bear, lynx, hare, beaver, marmot, and deer; and fowl. More than 135 plants were used for foods, medicines, and raw materials. Important plant foods included berries and the cambium layer of the western hemlock (steamed with skunk cabbage leaves, pounded, dried, and mixed with eulachon grease).

KEY TECHNOLOGY Fish were taken in weirs and also with harpoons, dip nets, rakes, and hook and line. Hunting technology included snares, traps, deadfalls, spears, and bow and arrow. General raw materials included wood and stone (dishes, containers, boxes, spoons), sheep horn (spoons), and cedarbark (mats, clothing, baskets, rope, fishing line). Men built canoes for water transportation, and women made burden and storage cedar-bark baskets.

TRADE The Bella Coola received herring eggs from the Bella Bella as well as some canoes from the Bella Bella and other Kwakiutl groups. They also traded with some Plateau Indians.

NOTABLE ARTS Wood carving was probably the preeminent Bella Coola art. Masks, entry poles, house frontal poles (with entrance through a gaping mouth), and carved posts were often painted and decorated with crest figures. They had no fully developed totem pole. They also made pictographs and petroglyphs.

TRANSPORTATION The Bella Coola used several types of canoes, including long, narrow canoes of a single red cedar log for rivers (most common), plus four types of seagoing canoes. Canoes were decorated with crest designs or painted black. Hunters also wore two types of snowshoes in winter.

DRESS Blankets and moccasins came from seal, sea lion, and caribou skin (although the Bella Coola usually went barefoot). They also made mountain goat wool blankets and fur robes and capes and wore long hair and shell and bone ornaments. Tattooing was common.

WAR AND WEAPONS The people engaged in irregular conflict with neighbors such as the Carrier, Chilcotin, and Kwakiutl. Their lack of political centralization made retaliating against raiding parties difficult. The Bella Coola raided too, attacking at dawn, burning a village, killing all the men, and taking women and children as slaves. Weapons included moose-hide shields, wood armor, the bow and arrow, clubs, and spears.

Contemporary Information

GOVERNMENT/RESERVATIONS The Nuxalt Nation (known before about 1980 as the Bella Coola Band) has seven reserves on 2,024 hectares at the mouth of the Bella Coola River in British Columbia, Canada. Their population in 1995 was 1,140, of whom 718 people lived on the reserve. They are governed according to the provisions of the Indian Act and are affiliated with the Oowekeeno/Kitasoo Tribal Council.

ECONOMY Economic activities and resources include a sawmill smoker plant, commercial fishing, and tree farm license registration.

LEGAL STATUS The Nuxalt Nation is a federally and provincially recognized entity.

DAILY LIFE Nuxalt people retain some ceremonies and make wood carvings for sale to tourists. Children attend both band and provincial schools. The reserve contains two fire houses, a community hall, two administration buildings, a seniors' home, and a clinic. Beginning in the 1970s there was a revival of traditional culture, including new masks, songs, and dances. Their dancers perform throughout British Columbia.

Chehalis

See Salish, Southwestern Coast

Chetco

See Tolowa (Chapter 2); Upper Umpqua

Chinook

Chinook (Shin `uk or Chin `uk), one of a group of Chinookan peoples whose branches included Lower Chinookan (or Chinook proper) and Upper Chinookan. The name came from a Chehalis word for the inhabitants of and a particular village site on Baker Bay.

LOCATION Traditionally, the Chinookan peoples lived along the Pacific Coast around the Columbia River Delta and upstream on both sides for about 150 miles. Lower Chinookans included the Shoalwater Chinook (Shoalwater or Willapa Bay and the north bank of the Columbia from Cape Disappointment to Gray's Bay) and the Clatsop (south bank of the Columbia, from Young's Bay to Point Adams). Upper Chinookans included the Cathlamet (Grays Bay to Kalama), the Multnomah (Kalama to about Portland and up the Columbia just past Government Island), and the Clackamas (southwest of Portland and roughly along the Willamette and Clackamas Rivers). Today, most Chinooks live in southwestern Washington and scattered around the Pacific Northwest.

POPULATION In 1780, roughly 22,000 Chinookans lived in their territory, a figure that declined to less than 100 in the late nineteenth century. Chinook tribal membership stood at more than 2,000 in 1983.

LANGUAGE The Chinookan family of Penutian languages was composed of Lower Chinookan (Chinook proper) and Upper Chinookan, which included the languages of Cathlamet, Multnomah, and Kiksht. In the context of historic Northwest Coast trade, "Chinook," or Oregon Trade Language (consisting of elements of Chinookan, Nootkan, French, and Eng-lish), was considered a trade lingua franca from Alaska to California.

Historical Information

HISTORY Although Chinookans may have spotted Spanish ships off the Columbia River delta, it was early Anglo explorers who first encountered and spread smallpox to the Chinook in 1792. Meriwether Lewis and William Clark lived among and wrote about the Clatsops in 1805.

The fur trade began in earnest during the next decade; Astoria was founded in 1811. During the early days of the fur trade, at least, the Indians played key roles. The acquisition of goods such as musket and powder, copper and brass kettles, cloth, tobacco, and other items increased the relative prestige of downriver groups so much that they tried to monopolize trade to the exclusion of their upriver rivals. Native culture began gradually to change, owing mainly to acquisition of manufactured items and to enduring contact between Indians and Anglos.

Shortly after the initial contacts, Indians began to experience severe population declines due to disease. Alcohol-related disease and deaths took a further toll. They abandoned many village sites and consolidated others, particularly around trading sites. The number of potlatches may have increased during this time, as villages had to rerank themselves within the context of the new trading society. By the 1850s, most survivors were being forced, under treaties that were never ratified, to cede their land in exchange for fishing rights. Survivors drifted to area reservations (Chehalis, Siletz, Grande Ronde, Shoalwater) or remained in their homelands.

By the twentieth century, the (Lower) Chinook had so effectively merged with the Lower Chehalis and the Shoalwater Salish that their language essentially passed out of use. Other groups also lost their identities through merger and consolidation. In 1899, the Chinooks, Clatsops, Cathlamets, and Wahki-akums (Upper Chinookans) presented a land claim to the U.S. government. They were awarded $20,000 (for almost 214,000 acres) in 1912. In 1925, the tribe established a business council to pursue its elusive treaty rights. A 1931 U.S. Supreme Court case (*Halbert v. U.S.*) held that Chinooks and other tribes had formal rights on the Quinault Reservation. Within a few years they had become that reservation's largest landholders. The Bureau of Indian Affairs (BIA), however, blocked their bid to organize a government under the Indian Reorganization Act.

In 1951, the nonreservation Chinookans combined to form the Chinook Nation and press their land claims with the newly created (1946) Indian Claims Commission. Soon, however, and without any official action, the BIA began to treat them as a terminated tribe. In 1971, this group, reconstituted in 1953 as the Chinook Indian Tribe, Inc., received an award of almost $50,000, but no land. Their petition for federal recognition, filed in 1979, is still pending.

RELIGION All Chinookan males and some females sought guardian spirit powers on prepubescent quests alone at night. Special songs and dances accompanied the receipt of such powers. An elaborate ceremonialism, based on the acquisition and display of spirit powers, took place during winter, the sacred period of spiritual renewal. Shamans might rent their powers to inflict harm (bodily injury or soul loss) or to cure someone. Chinookans also observed the first salmon rite.

GOVERNMENT Aboriginally, the Chinookans lived in more than 30 villages. Each village had a hereditary chief, but through the deployment of the proper alliances and methods a chief could exercise his authority over a wider area. The chief arbitrated quarrels, supervised subsistence activities, and provided for his village in time of need. His privileges included taking food, goods, or women at will. The chief was assisted by an orator who spoke directly to the lower-ranked people.

CUSTOMS Chinookan society was clearly stratified; status rankings included slave, commoner, and chief. High status went to those who had and could display wealth (food, clothing, slaves, canoes, high-ranked spouses), such as chiefs, warriors, shamans, and traders, as well as those with hereditary privileges. Slaves were bought, sold, or captured as property. Fishing areas were usually controlled by specific descent groups, although other subsistence areas were not so clearly controlled. Ties between villages were maintained by trade and alliances through wives. Imported dentalium shell was used for money and ornamentation. Later, beads from China were also highly prized.

All life-cycle events, at least among high-status families as well as those of chiefly succession, were marked by wealth display, gift giving, feasting, singing, and dancing. The purpose of the potlatch, a word meaning "giving" in Chinookan, was to reaffirm the lineage system as well as individual and descent group rank and social status, by conferring legitimacy on an occasion. Chinookans observed numerous taboos around girls' puberty (including seclusion for five months) and menstruation. Nonslave infants' heads were flattened at birth for aesthetic reasons. Corpses were placed in cattail mats; burial with possessions took place in canoes. A slave was sometimes killed to serve as a servant in the afterlife. Mourners cut their hair and never again spoke the name of the dead. Lacrosse was a popular game.

DWELLINGS Permanent winter dwellings were rectangular, gable-roofed, cedar plank houses, excavated and framed with cedar logs, with an average length of 50 feet. Decorations were of geometric, animal, and human designs. Floors were mat covered or planked, with an excavated central fireplace and a smoke hole above. Elevated bed platforms ran along the walls. Winter villages generally comprised around 20 houses. A light framework supported shelters of cattail-mat sides and cedar-bark roofs at summer fishing, hunting, or root-gathering camps.

DIET Fish—all five salmon species plus sturgeon, steelhead trout, eulachon, and herring—was the dietary staple. Chinookans fished with nets, especially seine nets, as well as scoops and spears. Fish were usually smoke dried. Rituals attended the season's first salmon run. Other marine foods included stranded whales (which also provided blubber and oil) and other mammals as well as shellfish. Men hunted deer, elk, bear, and other large game, as well as smaller game and fowl, with snares, deadfalls, traps, spears, and bow and arrow. Women gathered roots, especially the wapato tuber, and berries.

KEY TECHNOLOGY Raw materials included wood, bone, shell, cedar bark, spruce roots, bear grass, cattail rushes, antler, and horn. These materials were carved, woven, and otherwise shaped. Especially significant were carved bent wooden boxes, dugout canoes, and twined bear grass baskets. Long poles with bunches of deer hooves served as musical instrument.

TRADE Their strategic location at the mouth of the Columbia, as well as their business skills, enabled the Chinookans to dominate trade as far away as Puget Sound and areas to the west and south. The Dalles, a giant waterfall and rapids on the Columbia, was the site of a great aboriginal trade fair. Participants brought pelts, mountain sheep horn, baskets, woven rabbit-skin robes (interior tribes); slaves (Klamath and Modoc); salmon, bear grass, blubber, canoes, and berries (Chinook); and dentalia (Nootkas). Connections to this trade fair stretched ultimately as far as the Great Plains. As mentioned earlier, the existence of "Chinook jargon," the regional trade language, was testament to the central role the Chinook played in trade. Imported dentalium shells were a standard medium of exchange.

After contact, the Chinook were involved in a triangular trade in which they traded elk-hide cuirasses and other items to non-natives, who traded them to other native people for sea otter pelts, which they in turn traded in China for items such as silk and tea. Meanwhile, the Chinook traded guns, powder, and steel tools obtained from the non-natives to other Indians for fabulous profit. This trade pattern greatly increased the status of Chinook women, who played a more active trading role than men. When land-based trade in items such as beaver and other furs replaced the maritime trade, women continued their dominant roles.

NOTABLE ARTS   Significant art objects included carved wooden boxes and house framework, totem poles, wrap-twined baskets, and carved and decorated mountain sheep horn bowls that were first steamed, boiled, and molded into shape.

TRANSPORTATION   Six types of canoes were carved from a single cedar or fir log. An elaborate manufacturing process included harrowing, carving, and painting the logs and then studding them with shells. Large canoes could hold up to 30 people.

DRESS   Men went naked whenever possible. Women wore at least a skirt of cedar bark or strips of silk-grass. Some wore a deerskin breechclout. In cold weather people wore robes of various furs. Some groups wore a conical rainproof cedar hat as well as tule-mat rain capes. Personal ornaments were made of shell, feathers, and beads.

WAR AND WEAPONS   When diplomacy failed, a regional system of reparations took effect; the system included payment, enslavement, execution, or formalized warfare. War might also serve to establish the relative rankings among villages. Following a war, the losers paid reparations to the victors.

Contemporary Information

GOVERNMENT/RESERVATIONS   Many Chinookans live on the Chehalis Reservation, Grey's Harbor and Thurstron Counties, Washington. The reservation (1864; 2,076 acres) had a 1990 population of 307 Indians. The Chehalis Reservation is governed by a generally elected community council, which in turn elects a business committee. Chinookans also live on the Shoalwater Reservation (1866; 335 acres), Pacific County, Washington. In 1990, 66 Indians lived on this reservation, which is governed by an elected tribal council. Chinook descendants also live on the Grand Ronde and Siletz Reservations (see Upper Umpqua).

ECONOMY   Chinook Indian Bingo operates on the Long Beach Peninsula. Chinooks are also active in the commercial forestry and fishing industries.

LEGAL STATUS   In 1979, the Tchinouk Indians of Klamath Falls, Oregon, and the Chinook Indian Tribe of Chinook, Washington, appealed for federal recognition, based on the unratified 1851 treaty and their unofficial termination in 1955. The government rejected the Tchinouk petition in 1986; the Chinooks' was denied in early 1998.

DAILY LIFE   Chinooks are largely integrated into the mainstream. The language is not spoken. Still,

tribal members are planning a museum and cultural center to keep alive their heritage and spirit. They have taken an active role in local organizations such as the Quinault Allotees Association and the Small Tribes Organization of Western Washington. Some people still speak the so-called Chinook jargon.

Comox

See Salish, Northern Coast

Coosans

Coosans (`K ū s ə ns) consisted of the Coosan proper and Siuslaw peoples. The word is probably southwestern Oregon Athapaskan and refers to Coos Bay and the surrounding region. "Coos" may mean "on the south," "lake," or "lagoon." "Siuslaw" comes from the Siuslaw word for their region.

LOCATION   The Coosans lived around Coos Bay, Oregon, roughly from Twomile Creek in the south to Tenmile Lake in the north. Siuslaw speakers lived north of them along the coast and inland, to about Tenmile Creek. Except for the immediate coast, much of the area is mountainous and densely forested. Today, most of these people live in and around Coos Bay in southwestern Oregon.

POPULATION   The number of Coosans in the mid–eighteenth century may have approximated 4,000. This number had declined to roughly 465 by 1870. In the early 1990s, the Confederated Tribes of Coos, Lower Umpqua, and Siuslaw Indians had an enrolled population of 526. The Siletz Reservation had an official Indian population of 2,000 in 1991.

LANGUAGE   Coosans spoke two Coosan languages, Hanis and Miluk. The Siuslawans spoke the Siuslaw language, which consisted of the dialects Siuslaw proper and Lower Umpqua (Kuitch). Both Coosan and Siuslaw were Penutian languages.

Historical Information

HISTORY   The first regional contact with non-natives occurred in 1792, when Upper Umpquas traded with U.S. and British ships. Occasional trade-based contacts through the 1830s were generally amicable, except for a Kuitch (Lower Umpqua) massacre of the Jedediah Smith party in 1828 and their attack on a Hudson's Bay Company fort in 1838.

Tensions increased with the major influx of non-natives in the 1850s. Although only the southernmost Coosan group, the Miluks (Lower Coquilles), participated in general in the 1855–1856 Rogue wars, all the Coosans and Siuslaws also suffered. An 1855 treaty, signed by Chief Jackson and others, though never ratified, was used to dispossess the Indians of their land and move them the following year to the Lower Umpqua River. Miluks and Kuitch were taken to the

Coast (later the Siletz and the Alsea) Reservation, where about half died of starvation, exposure, and disease.

During these and subsequent years, the military continued to round up groups of Indians living in remote areas. As was the case nearly everywhere, Indian agents stole mercilessly from the Indians. Indians who practiced their traditional customs were whipped at a post. Easy access to alcohol corrupted, demoralized, and sickened the people.

In 1860, both groups were forcibly marched to the Siletz Reservation, which had been created five years earlier. In 1861, people on the southern part of Siletz, including Coos and Kuitch, were moved to or near the Yachats River on the coast, home of the Alsea Indians. They remained there until 1875, dying of illness and starvation from trying to farm in a rain forest. In 1865, a central strip was removed from the reservation and opened for white settlement. The northern part then became the Siletz Reservation (Miluk) and the southern half became the Alsea Reservation (Coosans, Kuitch, and Alseans).

In 1875, when the Alsea Reservation was made available for non-Indian settlement, many people refused to go to Siletz. Some joined the Siuslaws while others filtered back to their original homelands and received 80-acre homesteads from the government in 1876. As their culture and language languished, tribal members worked as loggers, laborers, clam diggers, and cranberry harvesters. Women specialized in making baskets and cattail fiber mats.

Those Coosans who did live at Siletz worked at subsistence activities around the turn of the century. Indian loggers cut trees that stood on their former, plundered reservation. Siletz Indians won several small land claims judgments in the 1930s and 1950s. However, the tribe and reservation were "terminated" in the mid-1950s, with devastating result. They were restored in 1977 and given a 3,630-acre reservation three years later.

The Confederated Tribes of Coos, Lower Umpqua, and Siuslaw organized formally in 1916. They have spent the rest of the century petitioning the government for compensation for their aboriginal lands, in vain to date. The Coos obtained a 6.1-acre "reservation" at Coos Bay in 1940. They were involuntarily terminated in 1954 and restored 30 years later.

The Dream Dance, a local variation of the Ghost Dance, was popular in the 1870s. By the twentieth century, most native languages were no longer spoken. In 1917, Coosans and Siuslaws created the Coos–Lower Umpqua–Siuslaw Tribal Government. A schism in the Coos tribe occurred in 1951 after a court ruled that some Miluks were eligible to share in money awarded in a land claims suit to the (Upper) Coquille (Mishikhwutmetunne) Indians. These Miluks then became affiliated with the Coquille Indian Tribe.

RELIGION Individuals could acquire power, mostly used to ensure luck in gaining wealth, through dreams and spirit quests. Unlike more northerly tribes, few other than shamans were actively involved with the supernatural; most people were much more interested in obtaining wealth. The most common kind of shaman was rigorously trained as a curer of disease (caused either by intrusion of a disease-causing object, often sent by a hostile shaman, or, less often, by soul loss). The second kind of shaman was more ritualistic; in addition to curing, these shamans also found thieves and promulgated evil. This type of shaman was involved in the numerous life-cycle taboos and especially in the elaborate girls' puberty ceremony and various other rituals of purification.

The people regularly held large-scale ceremonies featuring dancing, feasting, games, and gambling. Their mythology included stories of a primordial trickster, of legends, and of supernatural beings of forest and water. First salmon and first elk ceremonies were also held.

GOVERNMENT The basic political unit was the winter village group, usually a group of paternally related men with their families. Each major village had a chief and often an assistant chief. An informal council of wealthy men and women advised the chief. Succession was mainly hereditary, at least among the Coosans. Women might succeed if there were no eligible males. Chiefs arbitrated quarrels, supervised communal activities, and saw that no one went hungry. Villagers contributed food to the chief's family.

CUSTOMS Coosan and Siuslaw society consisted of four classes: chiefly and wealthy families, a socially respectably majority, poor people, and slaves (obtained by capture or trade). The classes enjoyed similar subsistence levels; their main difference lay in nonfood wealth and status. Marriage occurred when a groom's family paid a bride price, which was later returned in a lifelong cycle of mutual gift giving and responsibilities. The dead were buried. Their goods were broken and placed in and around the grave.

DWELLINGS Permanent houses ranged between 20 and 50 or more feet long and half as wide and were excavated to a depth of about 3 to 6 feet. Two or more center posts supported a single ridgepole. Rafters sloped to the ground or to side supports. Walls and gabled roofs were of lashed cedar planks. Tule mats lined the inside walls, mat partitions divided the several families within the house, and mats or hides covered the floors. Bed platforms ran along the walls.

Among the Siuslaw, two or more houses were sometimes joined together.

Camp houses were of thatched grass with a gabled or one-pitch roof. Two types of sweat houses existed. One doubled as a men's clubhouse and boys' dormitory. It was square, plank-walled, excavated, and covered with dirt. The other, for use by both men and women, was in a beehive shape and heated by steam.

DIET The staple food was fish, primarily salmon. Fishing gear, used from shore and canoes, included dip nets, clubs, weirs, and harpoons. Other important food resources included shellfish, marine mammals, deer, and elk as well as various roots, shoots, and berries, such as camas, skunk-cabbage roots, and wapato. Both Coosans and Siuslaws cultivated tobacco. Most groups wintered near the ocean and moved upstream in summer to fish for salmon, hunt, and trap.

KEY TECHNOLOGY Women made cattail and tule mats and various twined, decorated baskets. Men made weapons and hunting and fishing gear, including canoes. Most tools were made of wood, plant fiber, shell, or bone.

TRADE Both groups traded mainly with their immediate neighbors.

NOTABLE ARTS Baskets and carved wood items were the principal arts.

TRANSPORTATION Most transportation was by water and therefore by canoe, of which there were three main types. One was 15–20 feet long and flat bottomed, with both ends slightly raised. Another, often obtained in trade from the north, was larger and favored for ocean fishing; it was flat bottomed, with an undercut bow and pointed prow. The third type was a shovelnose canoe for bay and river travel. Most canoes were made of red cedar.

DRESS Most clothing was made by women from skins and various fibers. Both sexes wore leggings and moccasins but usually only for travel and in cold weather. On such occasions, they also wore headbands and waterproof fur or fiber capes. Men generally wore breechclouts or shorts and often shirts and caps. Women wore shirts and skirts or one-piece dresses and woven hats. Everyone wore rain capes of cattail or shredded bark. Wealthy people were likely to decorate their clothing. Some people wore tattoos, primarily for measuring dentalia strings. The Kuitch wore large beads in their noses and flattened the heads of their infants.

WAR AND WEAPONS Some hunting gear doubled as weapons.

Contemporary Information

GOVERNMENT/RESERVATIONS The Confederated Tribes of Coos, Lower Umpqua, and Siuslaw Indians,

Inc., is based in Coos Bay, Oregon. The Coos tribe adopted its first constitution and by-laws in 1938 and has its own land (6.1 acres) and cemetery.

Federal recognition was restored in 1977 to the Confederated Tribes of Siletz Indians of Oregon, and in 1980 they received 3,630 acres of federal land. The mid-1990s tribal enrollment was roughly 2,900. A nine-member Tribal Council governs these Indians.

The Coquille Indian Tribe, composed of Miluks and Upper Coquilles, is also based in Coos Bay and has a land base of 6.2 acres. The 1993 population was 630.

ECONOMY The Confederated Tribes of Coos, Lower Umpqua, and Siuslaw Indians work with the federal government on excavating and preserving archaeological projects. Logging, lumber, fishing, and service industries constitute major economic activities. Economic activity at Siletz is overseen by the Siletz Tribal Economic Development Corporation (STEDC) and centers on the timber industry. There are also a smokehouse and a bingo parlor. A casino is in the planning stages.

LEGAL STATUS The Confederated Tribes of Coos, Lower Umpqua, and Siuslaw Indians is a federally recognized tribal entity. The Coquille Tribe received federal rerecognition in 1989. The Confederated Tribes of the Siletz Reservation is a federally recognized tribal entity. The Coos Tribe of Indians is federally recognized within their confederation with the Lower Umpquas and the Siuslaws.

DAILY LIFE Over the past 30 years, the Coos tribe has formed several organizations to preserve its culture, the most prominent of which may be the Oregon Coast Indian Archaeological Association. The research center/museum is open on the Confederated Tribes of Coos, Lower Umpqua, and Siuslaw Reservation, which also sponsors a salmon feast in August. With the Bureau of Land Management, they are planning a $20 million interpretive center. In the mid-1970s, Indians influenced local schools to adopt programs and curricula relating to native culture. The Siletz Reservation holds a powwow in August; a museum/archive is in the process of being established.

Coquille (Mishikhwutmetunne)
See Coosans; Upper Umpqua

Cow Creek Band of Umpqua Indians
See Upper Umpqua

Cowichan
See Salish, Central Coast

Cowlitz
See Salish, Southwestern Coast

Duwamish

See Salish, Southern Coast

Grand Ronde, Confederated Tribes of

See Upper Umpqua

Haida

Haida (`H ī dä) is an adaptation from their self-designation. In the late eighteenth century, Haidas lived in a number of towns, politically unorganized but distinguishable as six groups by geography, tradition, and speech. These groups included the Kaigani people, the people of the north coast of Graham Island, the Skidegate Inlet people, the people of the west coast of Moresby Island, the people of the east coast of Moresby Island, and the southern (Kunghit) people. The west coast Pitch-town people stood outside this classification system.

LOCATION Haida territory included the Queen Charlotte Islands and Alexander Archipelago of British Columbia. This is a region of considerable environmental variation, including coastal lowlands, plateau, and mountains. The area is fairly wet, especially in the west.

In the 1990s, most Haida live in Masset and Skidegate on the Queen Charlottes and Hydaburg (established in 1911 as a specifically acculturated Haida town) on Prince of Wales Island, Alaska. Many also live in the cities of Ketchikan, Alaska, and Seattle, Washington.

POPULATION The Haida population was roughly 9,000–10,000 in the late eighteenth century. This number dropped by almost 95 percent, to about 550, in 1915. In 1996 there were 1,076 members of the Skidegate band, of whom 478 were a resident population; 2,300 members of the Masset band; and 342 Indians at Hydaburg. The total U.S. Haida population was about 1,800.

LANGUAGE Haidas spoke various dialects, including Skidegate and Masset, of the Haida Athapaskan language.

Historical Information

HISTORY Haida country was settled more than 9,000 years ago. The natives first saw a non-Indian when the Spanish explorer Juan Pérez Hernandez arrived in 1774. Numerous trading ships followed in the late eighteenth and early nineteenth centuries. The Haida traded sea otter pelts for European and U.S. manufactured goods. They also began cultivating potatoes at this time. By the late eighteenth century the Haida were rich and powerful.

Early trade was generally peaceful except for some hostilities in 1791, the probable year they first contracted smallpox. The sea otter trade ended about 1830. It was replaced by land-based fur operations and the Hudson's Bay Company; its 1830s post at Fort Simpson (Coast Tsimshian country) became the central trading location for Tlingit, Haida, and Tsimshian traders for the next 40 years. The Haida also traded in Victoria beginning in 1858, drawn by the local gold rush. During this period, however, they fought with rival Kwakiutls and fell victim to drinking and prostitution. More disease, especially smallpox, hit hard in 1862 and led to widespread village abandonment and consolidation. By the mid-1870s, Haida culture was in full collapse.

Christian (Methodist) missionaries arrived in Haida country in 1829. The Anglican church was active at Masset from the early 1880s on; shortly thereafter the Haida ceased erecting grave posts and memorial totem poles. Dancing and the power of shamans also declined. In 1883, Haida villages were divided between Methodists (central and southern) and Anglican (northern) missionaries.

Under government auspices, the Presbyterian Church established Hydaburg, Alaska, around the turn of the century. It was meant to facilitate the transition among Haidas from traditional to dominant culture. In 1936, the Haida became the first Indian group in Alaska to adopt a constitution under the Indian Reorganization Act. They succeeded in obtaining a large reservation in 1949, but under pressure from the salmon industry, a judge invalidated the reservation several years later.

Haidas in Canada were granted almost 3,500 acres of land in 1882 and another 360 in 1913. By the twentieth century, Haidas were migrating seasonally to work in the commercial mining, fishing, and canning industries. Acculturation proceeded rapidly. The potlatch was outlawed in 1884, although many Indians continued clandestinely to observe this central aspect of their culture. Government land allotments without regard to traditional lineages undercut the latter's power, as did the growth of single-family housing.

Canada passed its first comprehensive Indian Act in 1884. Among other things, the act established numerous small reserves for Indian subsistence and other activities. In 1912, Presbyterian Tlingits formed the Alaska Native Brotherhood (the Alaska Native Sisterhood was founded 11 years later), which worked for the abandonment of tradition, the mitigation of racial prejudice, increased educational opportunities, and land rights. These organizations reversed their stand against traditional practices in the late 1960s. Severe overt economic and social discrimination against Indians continued, however, including a virtual apartheid system during the first half of the twentieth century.

After World War II, Masset experienced a brief

boom in carpentry and boatbuilding. Most villagers in the 1960s worked in the canning and processing industries for half the year and were otherwise unemployed. In general, Alaska Indians campaigned for self-government and full citizenship. Canadian Indian policy favored integration into mainstream society after World War II. In the 1960s, the government granted Indians a measure of self-determination, which sparked a period of cultural renewal. Tlingits and Haidas received a $7.5 million land claims settlement in 1970. Under the terms of the Alaska Native Claims Settlement Act (1971), the Haidas set up several corporations, although one, the Haida Corporation, declared bankruptcy in 1986.

RELIGION Haidas believed that animals possessed intelligence and humanlike souls, had a hierarchical ranking, lived in villages, and could change their form at will. Haidas offered prayers, grease, tobacco, and flicker feathers to the spirits of game animals. They also conceived of three worlds: sky, sea, and land. Their ceremonies were directly related to the system of social stratification. Potlatches, feasts, and dance performances, given by high-ranking people, were the main ceremonial events. Shamans, with multiple supernatural powers, were considered to be more powerful than chiefs.

GOVERNMENT People lived in autonomous villages, some consisting of a single lineage. The basic social and political unit was the lineage, or clan; each contained up to 12 households and was presided over by a hereditary chief. He gave permission for others to access the lineage's subsistence area and could declare war. Household chiefs (owners of plank houses) exercised control over their households, deciding when members left for fishing or hunting camps. In multilineage towns, the wealthiest, highest-ranking house chief was the town master, or town mother.

CUSTOMS The Haida divided most labor along sex and class lines. Women gathered, processed, and preserved all foods; prepared animal skins; and made clothing and baskets. Men fished, hunted, built houses and canoes, carved, and painted. Canoe making and carving, as well as sea otter hunting, were high-prestige occupations. Economically important slaves, captured during war, did much of the fishing.

Ambition, success in hunting and fishing, and industry were highly valued qualities. Haida society was divided into two matrilineal divisions, Raven and Eagle, each composed of lineages, or clans. Lineages had mythological origins and controlled property such as subsistence areas and names, dances, songs, and crest figures. Crests were the identifying symbols of lineages and an indication of personal rank within the lineage. They were carved on totem poles and

other wooden items and tattooed on the body.

At feasts and potlatches, guests were seated according to their rank. Feasts, although always part of potlatches, were also held separately to name a child, at a marriage or death, to honor a visitor, or to enhance prestige. In addition to personal rank, there was a class system. Upper-class people bore many potlatch names, because when they were children their parents had given potlatches in their honor; they owned houses and were heirs to high-ranking names and chieftainships.

The Haida observed a number of life-cycle rituals and taboos. Children were regarded as reincarnated ancestors. Uncles toughened boys by, for example, making them take winter sea swims. There was no boys' puberty ceremony, but girls were secluded for a month or longer and followed many behavioral restrictions. Marriages were arranged in childhood or infancy. Property exchange and gift giving marked the marriage. Death among high-status people was a major ceremonial occasion. After bodies were washed, costumed, and painted, they lay in state for several days. Then they were placed in bent-corner coffins constructed by men of the father's lineage and removed through a hole in the wall. Burial was either in a lineage grave or in a mortuary column, followed by a potlatch and the raising of a memorial pole. Commoners had no poles erected in their honor. Slaves were thrown into the sea.

DWELLINGS There were two basic types of red cedar–plank houses, one with seven roof beams, a central smoke hole, and corner posts, and the other with four beams and four internal posts. Both types were roofed with cedar bark. Larger houses (houses could be as large as 60 by 100 feet) featured a centrally excavated pit and terraced tiers leading down to the base. Sleeping places were arranged by tier according to rank. Corner and interior posts were carved and painted. They were set along the tree line and facing the beach.

House names were considered personal property and might be attributes of the owner or related to the construction or physical features of the house. At one time, towns were probably composed of one lineage only. Many Haida towns had a "forest" of totem poles along the beachfront. Entry into the house was either through a hole in the bottom of a pole or through elliptical doorways cut into the front facade.

DIET Fish, especially halibut and salmon, and shellfish (gathered by men and women) were the staples. They were sliced and sun dried or smoked. Other important foods included sea mammals (seals, porpoises, sea otters, sea lions, and stranded whales), wild foods (seaweed, berries, and shoots), and land mammals (deer and beaver [Alaska], caribou [the

Queen Charlottes], and bear). Meat was also preserved by smoking and drying. Some groups also ate birds (hunted by men and women) and their eggs. The Haida also grew tobacco.

KEY TECHNOLOGY   The Haida were a seafaring people. Fishing technology included hook and line (of gut), traps, and harpoons. Hunting equipment included snares, bows and arrows, and clubs. Women made twined basketry (for quivers and other items) of split spruce roots and cedar-bark mats and bags. Building tools included wooden wedges, stone adzes, and basalt or jade hammers. Dugout cedar canoes were up to 70 feet long and 8 feet wide, carved and painted. The Haida had a fire bow drill and began working their own iron in the late eighteenth century.

TRADE   At least in the early historic period, the Haida gained wealth from their skill as traders. They traded canoes, slaves, and shell to the Tlingit for copper, Chilkat blankets, and moose and caribou hides. Canoes, seaweed, chewing tobacco, and dried halibut went to the Tsimshian for eulachon grease, dried eulachons, and soapberries. They acquired slaves from the Kwakiutl. There was some intravillage trade. In the mid-1830s they traded furs, dried halibut, potatoes, and dried herring spawn to the Hudson's Bay Company for blankets, rice, flour, and other staples.

NOTABLE ARTS   The Haida were outstanding wood-carvers. Their masterpieces included canoes, totem (mortuary) poles, house fronts, walls, screens, weapons, bentwood boxes, ceremonial masks, tools, and implements. Totem pole carving burgeoned during the nineteenth century with the acquisition of metal tools; the Haida built some of the best such poles in world history.

Designs included zoomorphic crest figures as well as mythological beings and events. Black, red, and blue-green were traditional colors. Other arts included basketry, especially hats, and other excellent woven items, such as robes, capes, and blankets. They may have carved argillite in prehistoric times, but certainly for the curio trade from the nineteenth century on, at which time they also took up silver engraving.

TRANSPORTATION   The Haida built several forms of red cedar dugout canoes.

DRESS   Clothing came from otter and other furs, cedar bark, and other fibers. Upper-class people wore tattoos. Wooden labrets were placed in the lips of upper-class girls at puberty; the size depended on rank and age.

WAR AND WEAPONS   The Haida enjoyed fighting. Their enemies included the Coast Tsimshian, Bella Bella, and Southern Tlingit as well as the Kwakiutl, Coast Salish, and Nootkans. There were also internal conflicts. Plunder and revenge were the main reasons

for fighting. Weapons included the bow and arrow, bone-tipped spears, clubs, wooden helmets, and armor.

RELATIONS WITH NON-NATIVES   Early trade relationships were positive, except for one violent incident directed against them in 1791 and subsequent revenge attacks. Non-native "culture" rather than weapons "triumphed" over the Haida as they fell to social vices as well as disease. Missionaries had success among the Haida, although the latter secretly retained many elements of their culture. Thorough acculturation took place during the last quarter of the nineteenth century.

Contemporary Information

GOVERNMENT/RESERVATIONS   The centers of contemporary Haida culture are Masset and Skidegate on the Queen Charlottes, British Columbia, and Hydaburg (established in 1911 as a specifically acculturated Haida town), Alaska. A 101,000-acre reservation there was invalidated in 1952. The city of Hydaburg remains, at least for now, under the general control of Haida Indians.

In Canada, bands (an administrative entity created by the Indian Act) manage most resources. Although not self-governing, they elect councils every two years. Since the 1980s the Council of the Haida Nations, from Masset and Skidegate, has pursued common goals and interests.

The Old Masset Village Council Band, formerly known as the Masset Band and located seven kilometers west of the village of Masset, British Columbia, is commonly known as Haida Village. The band controls 26 reserves on 907 hectares. Their population in 1995 was 2,201, of which 600 people lived in 260 houses on the reserves. They are affiliated with the North Coast Tribal Council in addition to the Council of the Haida Nation. Officials are elected by custom.

The Skidegate Band is located in southeast Graham Island, British Columbia. Eleven reserves are located on 670 hectares of land. The band is affiliated with the North Coast Tribal Council as well as the Council of the Haida Nation. The 1996 population was 1,076, of which 478 people lived in 239 houses.

ECONOMY   The Sealaska Corporation, which includes Haidas since they were a party to the Alaska Native Claims Settlement Act, owns large timber, fishery, and other interests. The Haida Corporation also owns timber and oil and seafood interests. Residents of Hydaburg are engaged in subsistence economies as well as some commercial fishing and timber jobs. Most skilled jobs are held by outsiders. Unemployment among the Haida is a major problem.

Economic activities and resources of the Old Masset Village Council Band include a pizza parlor, a taxi service, a bed-and-breakfast, a jewelry casting company, stores, a boat charter, seasonal logging, and commercial fishing. Economic activities and resources of the Skidegate band include the Gwaala-gaa Naay Cooperative grocery and a number of small businesses as well as seasonal logging and commercial fishing.

Hydaburg features a municipal government and a small urban economy, in addition to a reliance on the logging industry.

LEGAL STATUS   The Hydaburg Cooperative Association is a federally recognized tribal entity. With the Alaska Native Claims Settlement Act (1971), hundreds of native corporations formed, including Sealaska (the Tlingit-Haida Central Council), which is a federally recognized tribal entity.

The Old Masset Village Council Band and the Skidegate Band are federally and provincially recognized entities. Tlingit and Haida native villages include Angoon, Craig, Hoonah, Hydaburg, Juneau (Juneau Fishing Village), Kake, Klawok, Klukwan, Saxman, Sitka Village, and Yakutat. The government of British Columbia and Native Canadians continue to struggle over the issue of aboriginal rights.

DAILY LIFE   In Canada, native towns have regular and constant interaction with other nearby towns, yet life in the communities still centers around kinship, rank, and traditional ceremonial activities. The major church denominations are Anglican, Pentecostal, and United Church of Canada. The cultural renaissance of the 1970s was based in part on the emergence of several major artists.

Facilities at Masset include offices, a community hall, a counseling center, a warehouse, a longhouse, an elders' center, and a group home. Those at Skidegate include a community hall, a recreation hall, offices, a senior citizens center, and a gift shop. Children of both bands attend both and provincial schools.

Among the Alaska Haida, the elders and clan heads are churchgoers and serve as city officials and corporate directors. Extended families are still important, as are Christian churches, especially Presbyterian and the Assembly of God. Schools include classes in native language, drawing, and carving.

Mortuary potlatches and feasting are still part of Haida culture. In the 1980s, Canadian Indians began an initiative to enshrine native rights in the new constitution.

Haihais
See Bella Bella

Hoh
See Quileute

Kikiallus
See Salish, Southern Coast

Klallam
See Salish, Central Coast

Kuitch (Lower Umpqua)
See Coosans

Kwakiutl

Kwakiutl (Kw ā g ē ` ū tl) was originally the name of a local group and may mean "beach on the other side of the water." Once roughly 30 autonomous tribes or groups, the Kwakiutl did not think of themselves as a people until about 1900. They are sometimes referred to as Kwakwaka'wakw (Kwakiutl-speaking people) or Kwakwala (Kwakiutl language).

LOCATION   Many Kwakiutls continue to live in or near their aboriginal territory, which is located around the Queen Charlotte Strait on the central coast of British Columbia.

POPULATION   The Kwakiutl population in the early nineteenth century was about 8,000. In 1991, roughly 2,300 Kwakiutl lived on local reserves, and perhaps another 1,800 lived in regional cities and towns.

LANGUAGE   Kwakiutl is a member of the northern (Kwakiutlan) branch of the Wakashan language family. The three related languages were Haisla, Heiltsuk-Oowekyala, and Kwakiutl proper.

Historical Information

HISTORY   The area around the Queen Charlotte Strait has probably been occupied for 10,000 years or longer. During the last 5,000 years, two distinct cultures arose. One was based on simple obsidian technology and featured a broad-based subsistence economy. People of the second, or Queen Charlotte Strait culture (post–500 b.c.e.), used bone and shell technology and ate mostly salmon, seal, and other marine foods.

Spanish, British, and U.S. explorers arrived in the region in the late eighteenth century. By early in the next century the local sea otter trade was in full swing. The Hudson's Bay Company became active when the sea otter trade diminished, around the 1830s. At that time the Kwakiutl began serving as middlemen in the fur trade. They and many other Indian peoples were frequent visitors to the company's post at Fort Victoria.

Changes in Kwakiutl culture during the fur trade

period included the substitution of iron and steel for native materials in tools as well as Hudson's Bay blankets for the older style of robes. Disease epidemics leading to depopulation also took a heavy toll at that time. In the 1850s, several Kwakiutl villages consolidated around a Hudson's Bay Company coal mine at Fort Rupert; this was the genesis of the Kwakiutl tribe. In general, the 1850s and 1860s were terrible years for the Kwakiutl, marked as they were by the destruction of several villages by the British Navy and Bella Coola raiders as well as smallpox epidemics. In the late 1880s, Canada established reserves for some Kwakiutl bands while claiming much of their aboriginal territory.

Aboriginally, trade partners were also often raiding targets. The enforced cessation of intertribal hostilities about 1865 precipitated an explosion of potlatching activity, as all Kwakiutl tribes became part of the system of social alliances and tribal ranking. The potlatch flourished despite legislation outlawing it in 1885 and 1915, as did traditional artistic expression.

Acculturation was proceeding rapidly by the 1880s. The Kwakiutl were giving up their traditional dress, subsistence activities, and many customs and were entering the local wage economy. Around 1900, Alert Bay, site of a cannery, a school, and a sawmill, superseded Fort Rupert as the center of Kwakiutl life. The early twentieth century was a period of economic boom for Kwakiutls owing to the growth of the commercial fishing and canning industries. Another boom in the fishing industry occurred after World War II. Many people abandoned the potlatch and traditional culture during the Depression and converted to the Pentecostal Church. Potlatching was not significantly reestablished until the 1970s.

RELIGION In traditional Kwakiutl belief, everything had a supernatural aspect that commanded respect from people in the form of individual daily prayer and thanks. Guardian spirits, which provided luck and certain skills, might be obtained through prayer or fasting. Associated with each spirit was a secret ceremonial society, such as Cannibal, Grizzly Bear, and Warrior, as well as specific dances and ceremonies.

Shamans formed an alliance with a supernatural helper and were initiated into their craft by other shamans. The Kwakiutl recognized several degrees of shamanic power, the highest being the ability to cure and cause disease; these most powerful people were usually attached to chiefs. Shamans used songs, rattles, and purification rings (hemlock or cedar) in public curing ceremonies. Witches could harm or otherwise control people without recourse to supernatural power, although knowledge similar to theirs

was available to guard against such practices.

The winter ceremonials were based on complex mythological themes and involved representations of supernatural beings and stories of ancestral contact with them. Principal winter ceremonies, including the Cedar Bark Dance and the Weasel Dance, involved feasting, potlatching, entertainment, and theater. Winter was considered a sacred season because the supernaturals were said to be present at that time. People attempted to be on better behavior and even took on sacred names.

GOVERNMENT Each of the roughly 30 autonomous tribes (local groups) had its own hereditary chief, subsistence area, winter village, and seasonal sites. Tribes consisted of between one and seven (usually at least three) kin groups (numayms), each having perhaps 75–100 people aboriginally and roughly 10–15 in the late nineteenth–early twentieth century. In early historic times, some tribes formed joint winter villages without losing their individual identities.

CUSTOMS Kin groups (tribes) owned resource areas, myths, crests, ceremonies, songs, dances, house names, named potlatching positions, and some inheritable guardian spirits. Crests, privileges, and rights were transmitted through marriage. The Kwakiutl recognized many forms of permissible marriages. Preserving the existence of crests and privileges remained all important, and rules were bent or broken over time to accommodate this need. There were four traditional classes or status groups: chiefs, nobles, commoners, and slaves. Society became much more equal in the mid–nineteenth century: As the population declined, the number of privileged positions remained constant, so that more people could rise to such positions.

Potlatches, once modest affairs, became highly complex, elaborate, and more culturally central in the late nineteenth century, helping to integrate and drive Kwakiutl society by validating social status and reciprocities. The size of a potlatch varied according to the event being marked: Life-cycle events for high-status children and wiping out casual mistakes received small potlatches; receipt of a first potlatch position, dancing the winter ceremonial, and the occasion of girls' puberty received moderate-sized potlatches; and the assumption of a chiefly name and/or position within a kin group, a grease feast, the buying and selling of coppers, the erection of crest memorial poles, and marriage received the largest potlatches. All included feasting, socializing, speeches, songs, displays of wealth and crests, and dances. Such potlatches were occasionally given on credit; that is, on borrowed goods (blankets), usually lent at 100 percent interest.

Traditionally, the Kwakiutl practiced blood revenge, in which one or more people might be killed upon the death of a close relative. Corpses were buried in trees, caves, or canoes (chiefs), although northern groups cremated their dead.

DWELLINGS Rows of cedar beam and plank houses with shed roofs faced the sea in traditional villages. The central house posts were carved and painted with crests. A sleeping platform extended around walls. Four families of the same kin group occupied most houses, each in a corner with its own fireplace. Private areas were partitioned off. Each village also had one or more ceremonial houses, similarly constructed. By the late nineteenth century, houses were built with milled lumber and gabled roofs.

DIET The Kwakiutl ate mostly seafood: clams, salmon, halibut, and other marine life. Fish were smoke dried. The people traveled to their widespread resource areas in canoes. Fish (eulachon) oil was also an important dietary supplement. They also ate berries, sea grass, roots, mountain goat, elk, and deer.

KEY TECHNOLOGY Fish were taken with dip nets, weirs, and rakes. Harpoons were used for seals and sea lions and bow and arrow for land mammals. Kelp tubes, baskets, wooden boxes, and chests served as containers. In general, men worked wood and women wove fibers. There were no full-time craftspeople. The Kwakiutl had an abundance of material goods such as boxes, mats, spoons, dishes, and canoes. Most craft production took place in winter. A few tools, such as the mortar and pestle, were made of stone.

TRADE The Kwakiutl engaged in widespread intertribal trading for specific items such as eulachon oil, dried halibut, and herring roe.

NOTABLE ARTS As a people, the Kwakiutl were artists. Even in utilitarian items, visual art was joined with rhetoric, mythology, and performance art to glorify the kin groups. Wooden objects, such as massive houseposts, totem and commemorative poles (nonaboriginal), masks, rattles, feast dishes, and other objects used for crest displays were carved and/or painted. The point of most Kwakiutl art was social—to display ancestral rights—rather than specifically religious, although the two are basically inseparable.

Their basic colors were black and red. The Kwakiutl experienced a golden age of art from about 1890 to 1920. They also produced some excellent twined, spruce root, and cedar bark hats.

TRANSPORTATION Most travel took place over water in a number of different style of dugout cedar canoes. Skin sails were used from the nineteenth century on.

DRESS In warm weather, women wore cedar-bark aprons and men went naked. Women wore waterproof basket caps and cedar-bark ponchos in the rain. Blankets of woven cedar bark, mountain goat wool or dog hair, or tanned, sewn skins served as cold-weather protection. Long yellow cedar-bark robes were particular to Kwakiutl people. Both sexes wore their hair long. Some men let their facial hair grow. Those who could afford them wore abalone nose and ear pendants. Women also wore dentalia bracelets, necklaces, and anklets. People also painted their bodies and faces against sunburn.

WAR AND WEAPONS The Kwakiutl often fought each other (other Kwakiutl tribes) for revenge and fought neighboring peoples such as the Coast Salish for plunder, land, heads, and slaves. One group, the Lekwiltok, were particularly aggressive. The Kwakiutl had guns as early as the late eighteenth century.

Contemporary Information

GOVERNMENT/RESERVATIONS Canadian band councils have municipal power (over roads, water, sewers, and so on) and manage various economic activities. An administrative tribal organization, the Kwakiutl District Council, was organized in 1974. In 1982, four bands (later five) left the council to form the Musga'makw Tribal Council. See "Daily Life" for profiles of individual bands as of 1995.

ECONOMY Various bands are associated with different activities, such as marinas, oyster hatcheries, tourism, laundromats, cafeterias, and shipyards. General band operating funds come from the federal government. Most people also engage in semitraditional seasonal pursuits, such as hunting and commercial fishing. Some jobs are also available within band enterprises.

LEGAL STATUS Bands may pass laws binding upon members and visitors; overall law enforcement is assumed by the Royal Canadian Mounted Police.

DAILY LIFE Most Kwakiutl children are educated in provincial schools, although there are some band-administered schools. All have well-established programs to teach traditional language and culture. The Kwaguilth Museum (1979; Cape Mudge, Quadra Island, British Columbia) and the U'Mista Cultural Center (1980; Alert Bay, British Columbia) both hold ceremonial objects returned by the government in 1978. They also record oral histories, prepare school curricula and display exhibits, and organize classes.

Bands still reflect traditional family alliances and allegiances. Many traditional practices remain, such as potlatches for girls' puberty, memorials, and other purposes; dance societies; and the inheritance of ceremonial prerogatives. The Kwakiutl never experienced a dramatic artistic revival, mainly because their artistry was never significantly interrupted. The elderly now maintain their own households, baptism is common, and most marriages and funerals take place in church. Soccer tournaments are popular, and an annual sports weekend is held in June. English is the first language of most Kwakiutl.

Campbell River Band: Their reserve was established in 1888. Population is 495, of whom 176 live on the reserve. They are governed under the provisions of the Indian Act and are affiliated with the Kwakiutl District Council. Children attend provincial schools. Economic activities include commercial fishing, tourism, logging, pulp and paper, and mining. Facilities include offices and a community hall.

Cape Mudge Band: Five reserves are located on about 665 hectares of land. Population is 761, of whom 314 live on the reserve. They are governed under the provisions of the Indian Act and are affiliated with the Kwakiutl District Council. Children attend band and provincial schools. Economic activities include salmon fishing, commercial fishing, tourism, logging, pulp and paper, trapping, and mining. Facilities include offices, a community hall, a museum, and the Tsaw-Kwa-Luten Resort and Conference Center.

Gwa'sala-Nakwaxda'xw Band: Twenty-six reserves are located on 752 hectares of land near Port Hardy, British Columbia. Population is 502, of whom 374 live in 91 houses on the reserve. They are governed by custom and are affiliated with the Kwakiutl District Council. Children attend band and provincial schools. Economic activities include commercial fishing, forestry, tourism, and mining. Facilities include offices, a community hall, and an arts and crafts building.

Kwa-wa-aineuk Band: Ten reserves are located on 205 hectares of land on Watson Island. The main community is also known as Hopetown. The reserves were allotted in 1916. Population was 28, of whom 19 lived in six houses on the reserve. They are governed by custom and are affiliated with the Musga'makw Tribal Council. Children attend provincial schools. Facilities include offices and a workshop.

Kwakiutl Band: Eight reserves are located on 295 hectares of land near Port Hardy, British Columbia. Population is 536, of whom 279 live in 68 houses on the reserves. They are governed by custom and are affiliated with the Kwakiutl District Council. Children attend band and provincial schools. Economic activities include commercial fishing, forestry, tourism, and mining. Facilities include offices and a community hall.

Kwiakah Band: Two reserves are located on 69 hectares of land. The reserves were allotted in 1886. Most people live on the Campbell River Indian Reserve. Population is 17, of whom none live on the reserve. They are governed by custom and are affiliated with the Kwakiutl District Council.

Kwicksutaineuk-ah-kwaw-ah-mish Band: Ten reserves are located on 172 hectares of land 40 miles east of Port Hardy, British Columbia. The reserves were allotted in 1886. Population is 251, of whom 144 live in 22 houses on the reserves. They are governed under the provisions of the Indian Act and are affiliated with the Musga'makw Tribal Council. Children attend provincial schools. Facilities include offices, a longhouse, and a community hall.

Mamaleleqala-Que'Qua'Sot'Enox Band: Three reserves are located on 233 hectares of land. The reserves were allotted in 1886. This band was formerly known as the Mamalillikulla Band. Population is 295, of whom none live on the reserve. They are governed by custom and are affiliated with the Kwakiutl District Council.

Namgis First Nation, formerly the Nimkish Tribe: Eight reserves are located on 388 hectares of land south of Port McNeill, British Columbia. The reserves were allotted in 1884. Population is 1,346, of whom 714 live in 121 houses and 15 apartment units on the reserve. They are governed by custom and are affiliated with the Musga'makw Tribal Council. Children attend band and provincial schools. Economic resources include a salmon hatchery. Facilities include offices, a museum, a longhouse, community buildings, and a community health center.

Oweekeno Band: Three reserves are located on 712 hectares of land on the Wanuk River, British Columbia. Population is 204, of whom 60 live in 23 houses on the reserve. They are governed under the provisions of the Indian Act and are affiliated with the Oweekeno-Nuxalk Tribal Council. Children attend band and provincial schools. Economic resources include logging and salmon enhancement. Facilities include offices, a community center, and a drop-in center.

Quatsino Band: Nineteen reserves are located on 346 hectares of land south of Port Hardy, British Columbia. The reserves were allotted in 1886. Population is 316, of whom 214 live on the reserve. They are governed under the provisions of the Indian Act and are affiliated with the Kwakiutl District Council. Children attend provincial schools. Economic resources include mining, forestry, tourism, and fishing. Facilities include offices, a community center, and a fire station.

Tanakteuk Band: Seven reserves are located on 318 hectares of land 270 kilometers northwest of Vancouver, British Columbia. The reserves were allotted in 1866. Population is 150, of whom 22 live on federal land at Whe-la-la-u, Alert Bay. They are governed by custom and are affiliated with the Kwakiutl

District Council. Economic resources include mining, tourism, and fishing. Facilities include offices.

Tlatlasikwala First Nation, formerly known as the Nuwilti Band: Six reserves are located on 3,474 hectares of land. The reserves were allotted in 1916. Population is 37, of whom all live on federal land at Whe-la-la-u, Alert Bay. They are affiliated with the Kwakiutl District Council, the Kwakiutl First Nation Treaty Society, and Kwakiutl Territorial Fisheries. Economic resources include commercial fishing.

Tlowitsis-Mumtagila Band, formerly Turnour Island Band: Eight reserves are located on 188 hectares of land 260 kilometers northwest of Vancouver, British Columbia. The reserves were allotted in 1916. Population is 293, of whom 3 live on the reserve. They are governed by custom and are affiliated with the Whe-la-la-u Area Council and the Musga'makw Tribal Council. Economic resources include forestry, mining, fishing, and tourism.

Tsawataineuk Band: Five reserves are located on 218 hectares of land 290 kilometers northwest of Vancouver, British Columbia. The reserves were allotted in 1886. Population was 447, of whom 113 live in 41 houses on the reserve. They are governed by custom and are affiliated with the Musga'makw/Tsawataineuk Tribal Council. Children attend band and provincial schools. Economic resources include commercial logging, fishing, and silviculture. Facilities include offices, a community hall, a longhouse, and a church.

Lower Umpqua

See Coosans

Lummi

See Salish, Central Coast

Makah

Makah (M ə ˋkä) is a Klallam word for "the People." The Makah word for themselves is *Kwe-net-che-chat,* "People of the Point." They were a whaling people, culturally similar to the Nootkans of Vancouver Island.

LOCATION   The Makah lived around Cape Flattery on the northwest tip of the Olympic Peninsula, a region of fierce, rainy winters and calm, sunny summers. The Makah Reservation is in Clallam County, Washington, within their aboriginal lands.

POPULATION   Makah population was roughly 2,000 in the late eighteenth century. In 1990, 940 Indians lived on the Makah Reservation, and perhaps another 1,000 Makahs lived in regional cities and town.

LANGUAGE   Makah is a southern or Nootkan language of the Wakashan language family.

Historical Information

HISTORY   People have lived around Cape Flattery for roughly 4,000 years. The Makahs emigrated from Vancouver Island about 500 years ago, although some Makah villages were occupied as early as 1500 B.C.E. The Makahs first encountered non-natives around 1790, when British and Spanish ships entered the area, and the Spanish built a short-lived fort. Around 1809, the Makah detained several shipwrecked Russians and Inuit and also detained three shipwrecked Japanese in 1833. They traded occasionally with Hudson's Bay Company.

Results of early contact included an intensification of trade and the use of non-native goods as well as disease epidemics. By the 1850s, villages were being abandoned as a result of depopulation. The Makah signed the Treaty of Neah Bay in 1855, ceding land in return for "education, health care, fishing rights," and a reservation (subsequently enlarged). The Indian Service soon moved in and tried to eradicate Makah culture. They prohibited the native language and customs in government schools and tried, but failed, to replace maritime traditions with agriculture.

During the 1860s and 1870s, Makahs hunted fur seals for the non-native market. In the 1880s, Makahs were hunting on white-owned ships, at a profit so great that they temporarily abandoned whaling. By the 1890s, some Makahs had their own boats and were hiring both Indian and white crews. At this time, however, the seal population began to decline owing to overhunting. As international treaties began to restrict seal hunting, Makahs turned to poaching and then abandoned the activity altogether. By this time, in any case, many of their maritime-related ceremonies had disappeared.

In 1896, when the boarding school closed, many families moved to Neah Bay, which became the Makahs' primary village. In 1911, a treaty gave the Makah and some other Indian groups the right to hunt seals using aboriginal methods, a practice that continued for several decades. Commercial logging began in 1926. A road connecting the reservation with the outside world opened in the 1930s, as did public schools, which replaced the hated boarding schools. Tourism and the general local cash economy increased. In the 1940s, the Army Corps of Engineers completed a breakwater that provided a sheltered harbor for tourist boats and fishing vessels.

Major postwar economic activities were commercial fishing, logging, and tourism. Makah cultural life began to reemerge with the relaxation of the more severe anti-Indian government policies. In any case, some aspects of traditional culture, such as the potlatch and the language, had never been eradicated. In 1970, archaeological excavations at the village of

Ozette revealed much about the aboriginal life of the Makah. This site has yielded over 50,000 artifacts as well as other valuable information and has encouraged many young Makahs to study anthropology.

RELIGION The acquisition of guardian spirits was central to Makah religion and ceremonialism. Adolescent boys acquired them by fasting in remote places. Shamans, both male and female, who had acquired several guardian spirits cured people and provided ceremonial leadership.

Except for ritual hunting preparations, most ceremonies took place in winter. Carved wooden masks figured prominently in a four-day Wolf ritual, during which members were initiated into the secret *klukwalle* society. A healing ceremony and complex whaling rituals follow Nootka patterns.

GOVERNMENT The Makah lived in five permanent, semiautonomous villages, with one or more lesser satellite village in the same general area.

CUSTOMS Social groups included headmen, commoners, and slaves. The headmen regularly affirmed their rank through the institution of the potlatch. Commoners could advance or fall back slightly through marriage or by acquiring privileges. Alliances were formed and privileges and subsistence areas were inherited through ranked patrilineal lineages.

Whaling and fur seal hunting were particularly prestigious occupations. Only the former was an inherited privilege, but both involved substantial ritual components. Only men hunted and fished aboriginally; women gathered shellfish and plants and cleaned, cooked, and otherwise prepared food products.

At the onset of puberty, girls were secluded and observed certain rites. Gifts from the man's to the woman's family constituted a marriage; such gifts were then redistributed to extended family and friends. Corpses were removed through house roofs and buried in boxes, along with possessions. Slaves were sometimes killed when a chief died.

DWELLINGS Permanent houses were built on wooden frames as large as 60 by 30 by 15 feet high. Platforms along the wall served as sleeping and storage areas. Planks from nearly flat roofs, on which fish drying racks were located, could be easily removed for ventilation. Several families lived in one house. Privacy was provided by removable partitions. House fronts and posts were carved or painted. In summer, some people left the permanent villages for summer residences.

DIET The region supported abundant land and sea life, including mammals, fish and shellfish, birds, and flora. Sea mammals were the most important staple, followed by fish, particularly halibut. Oil, especially from whales and fur seals, was used to flavor dried foods. The Makah ate some land mammals. Plant foods included several varieties of berries, roots (especially sand verbena, surf grass, and buttercup), and greens. Plants were also used medicinally, for raw materials, and in entertainment.

KEY TECHNOLOGY Makah women wove spun dog wool or bird skin and fiber cordage on a two-bar loom. Women also made baskets of cedar as well as of cattail, tule, and cherry bark. Whaling equipment included mussel shell–tipped harpoons, line made of whale sinew and pounded cedar boughs, and skin floats for floating the dead whales and towing them ashore. Fishing equipment included hooks and kelp lines, weirs, traps, and gaffs. Land mammals provided additional raw material, such as antler and bone, for manufactured items. Shell was used for cutting and eating tools and for adornment. Mats for canoe sails, blankets, and cargo wrap were made from cedar bark. Wooden implements, such as bent-corner boxes (steamed and bent), bowls, dishes, containers, clubs, harpoon and arrow shafts, and bows, were fashioned from yew, red cedar, spruce, alder, and hemlock.

TRADE The Makah were actively involved in trade and social intercourse with all neighbors, including Klallam, Quileute, and Nitinaht. Makahs often served as middlemen, handling items such as dried halibut and salmon, sea otter skins, vermilion, whale and sea oil, dentalium shells, dried cedar bark, canoes, and slaves. They made an especially good profit selling whale oil. Camas, a favorite food, was obtained in trade from the north. They both imported and exported canoes.

NOTABLE ARTS Basketry and wood carving were the two most important Makah arts.

TRANSPORTATION Several different types of canoes were used for hunting marine mammals and for war, trade, carrying freight, and other activities.

DRESS Men wore little or nothing in warm weather. Such clothing as men and women did wear was generally made from cedar bark and woven bird down feathers, as were diapers and other such items. Blankets, skins, and cloaks provided warmth in colder weather. People also wore conical hats and bearskin robes in the rain. Personal adornment included nose and ear ornaments and face paint.

WAR AND WEAPONS Makahs occasionally fought the Quileute, Klallam, Hoh, and others as well as their Nootkan relations to the north. Weapons included bone and horn-tipped clubs, yew-wood bows, arrows with stone or bone tips, knives, spears, and slings.

Contemporary Information

GOVERNMENT/RESERVATIONS The Makah Reservation (1855; 27,244 acres) is located in Clallam

County, Washington. The tribe accepted the Indian Reorganization Act in 1934 and adopted a constitution and by-laws in 1936. They provide for a five-member tribal council, elected for staggered three-year terms, with various appointed committees. In 1984, the Makah retook possession of Tatoosh and Waadah Islands. A one-square-mile reservation has also been established around the Ozette archaeological site.

ECONOMY   The Makah Cultural and Research Center (1979) is home to the Ozette artifacts. This major institution administers a highly successful language preservation program and is largely responsible for reinvigorating the Makah language. Commercial fishing, including a side business renting cabins to other fishers, remains important. Other economic activities include some logging and production of olivella-shell jewelry. The government (health services and schools) and local retail businesses provide some stable employment. Unemployment hovers around 50 percent.

LEGAL STATUS   The Makah Indian Tribe is a federally recognized tribal entity.

DAILY LIFE   Radio station KRNB (1975) broadcasts from Neah Bay with some programs in Makah. Makah Days, a two-day celebration, is held at the end of August. The Makah are the only tribe in the United States with a treaty right to hunt whales. In 1995 they took their first whale in 80 years. In October 1997 they received permission from the International Whaling Commission to resume subsistence whaling. Some people still dance the family dances. Most Makahs are literate in their language.

Muckleshoot

See Salish, Southern Coast

Nisqually

See Salish, Southern Coast

Nooksack

See Salish, Central Coast

Nootkans

Nootkans (`N ū t k ə ns) were a linguistic group of Vancouver Island Indians consisting of more than 22 tribes, confederacies, or sociopolitical local groups. Captain James Cook, who thought it was the native name for what came to be called Nootka Sound, originated the term.

LOCATION   Many Nootkans continue to live in or near their aboriginal territory, which was the western half of Vancouver Island, British Columbia, roughly 125 miles north and south of midcoast. The geography features a rocky coast and a coastal plain ("out-

side") as well as a series of inlets penetrating deep into the hilly interior ("inside"). The climate is wet and moderate with fierce winter storms.

POPULATION   The Nootkan population was at least 15,000 in the mid–eighteenth century. In 1984, roughly 4,700 Nootkans lived in the region.

LANGUAGE   Nootka and Nitinaht, together with Makah, constitute the southern or Nootkan branch of the Wakashan language family.

Historical Information

HISTORY   Nootkan culture changed relatively little during the 5,000 years preceding contact with non-natives. In the late prehistoric period they had acquired iron and other metals through trade and salvage from shipwrecks. In 1778, Captain Cook remained with the Nootkas for a month, acquiring a large collection of sea otter pelts. Cook's crew later sold the pelts to Chinese merchants at great profit, thereby laying the basis for the northwest maritime fur trade.

A few Nootkan chiefs, such as Maquinna, whose power was maintained in part by the Spanish, became very wealthy by controlling that trade. Partly by means of firearms, they established themselves as intermediaries between whites and other Indian peoples. During that time, Indians began to suffer significant population decline owing to increased warfare (competition over the fur trade) as well as epidemics, including venereal disease. By the end of the century, hunters had so depleted the sea otter stock that the local fur trade was in sharp decline. In its wake, Indians began attacking trade ships, which in turn greatly diminished their contact with non-natives for several decades.

Population decline and general dislocation led to the formation of new tribes and confederacies in the early nineteenth century. Continued Nootkan attacks on trade ships in midcentury brought retaliation from the British navy. Gradually, without being formally conquered, the Nootkans became integrated into the new commercial economy. There was a continuing trade in the furs of animals such as deer, elk, mink, marten, and northern fur seal. Throughout the late nineteenth century, Nootkans were important suppliers of dogfish oil, which was used in the logging industry. They also became involved in the pelagic sealing industry, hunting from canoes as well as schooners. Some Nootkans became wealthy during that period and even purchased their own schooners. Commercial fishing was another important local industry, providing jobs and drawing people to canneries from their villages. Crafts for the tourist trade also became important around that time, as did seasonal hop picking in the Puget Sound area.

When British Columbia joined Canada in 1871, Nootkans became part of the federal Indian reserve system. Villages still in use received small reserves in the 1880s, though without having formally surrendered any land to the government. Missionaries arrived to carry out government health and education programs. Such programs included the establishment of Indian boarding schools, where native culture was ruthlessly suppressed.

After World War II, further consolidation and centralization of the Nootkan population paralleled similar trends in the fishing industry. Potlatching and other forms of traditional culture continued, despite government opposition. Beginning in the 1960s and 1970s, Nootkans focused on fostering a positive self-identity and achieving control over their own destinies. In 1978, a political organization called the West Coast District Council (formerly the West Coast Allied Tribes) proclaimed the name *Nuu-chah-nulth* ("all along the mountains") for all Nootkan peoples and renamed the organization the Nuu-chah-nulth Tribal Council.

RELIGION Numerous categories of spirit and mythological beings were recognized as ubiquitous. They could be obtained and controlled through rituals or by spirit quests. Rituals, especially as practiced by chiefs, helped to ensure bountiful salmon runs, the beaching of dead whales, and other food resources. Long-haired shamans dived to the bottom of the sea to battle soul-stealing sea spirits. Chiefs also engaged in spirit quests (commoners' spirit help came through minor rituals and charms). One obtained power from a spirit being by seizing it, rather than by establishing a relation with it as with a guardian spirit. Such power provided special skills, luck, or other achievements.

Nootkans prayed for power to the Four Chiefs of Above, Horizon, Land, and Undersea. They observed two primary winter ceremonies: the Dancing, or Wolf ritual, and the Doctoring ritual (central and southern Nootkans only). Although the former was an initiation and the latter a curing ceremony, the ultimate purpose of both was to confirm the social order. The Wolf ritual, several of which might be held in a village each winter, involved masks and dramatization.

GOVERNMENT Local groups held defined territories, the legitimacy of which came from a particular legendary ancestor. The chiefly line of descent was the group's nucleus. The highest-ranking man in a local group was its chief; the position was inheritable.

Local groups sometimes united to form tribes, with ranked chiefs and common winter villages and ceremonials. Some northern Nootkan tribes also came together to form confederacies, with each local group retaining its identity, territory, and ceremonies.

CUSTOMS Inherited rights formed the basis of social rank and governed the ownership and use of practically everything of value. Inheritance was generally patrilineal. Nootkan social classes consisted of chief, commoners, and slaves. Chiefs did not work; they directed their followers, who in turn supported and were taken care of by them. A chief's close male relations were secondary chiefs (such as war chiefs and speakers). Chiefs received tribute for the use of resource sites. When goods accumulated, they held a feast or a potlatch. Other occasions for potlatches included life-cycle and public events such as status transfer and confirmation. The participation in all life-cycle rituals and ceremonies was commensurate with social rank.

Pregnancy and birth carried numerous rituals and restrictions, especially regarding twins. Infants' heads were flattened to achieve an aesthetic ideal. Children were regularly instructed on correct behavior, such as industry, peacefulness, and social responsibility, and on ritual knowledge. For high-status families, the onset of female puberty was the occasion for a great potlatch. It also entailed rituals and seclusion for the woman herself. Along with warfare, marriage was the means by which local groups sought to maximize access to subsistence areas. As such, it was mostly an alliance between families and was accompanied by great ritual, depending on rank. Although divorce was possible, adultery, unless chronic or within the chief's family, was generally smoothed over.

Corpses were placed in a flexed position and buried away from the village, in boxes or canoes placed in trees or caves. Valuables were also interred, and belongings, including the house, might be burned. Memorial poles were erected to chiefs. Sometimes slaves were killed as companions to the dead.

DWELLINGS Multifamily cedar houses between 40 and 150 feet long, 30 and 40 feet wide, and 8 and 10 feet high lined the beaches. Planks were removable for use in smaller camp dwellings. Roofs were of both shed (primarily in the south) and gabled style. Individual family areas, each with its own fireplace, were set off from the others by storage chests. Sleeping platforms ringed the walls. Posts and beams were carved with hereditary designs. Local groups had house frames standing at three sites: permanent village, summer fishing and sea hunting areas, and a main salmon stream.

DIET Salmon, smoked and dried, was the staple. Nootkans also ate herring, halibut, cod, snapper, flounder, and other fish. Other important foods included roots, berries, bulbs, ferns, crabapples, and eelgrass; shellfish, mollusks, kelp, and sea cucumbers; waterfowl; and sea mammals such as harbor seals, porpoises, sea lions, sea otters, and whales. The ritual preparation by whalers, who were always chiefs, included bathing, praying, and swimming and began months in advance of the whaling season. Land mammals included deer, elk, black bear, and small mammals. Most food was dried, smoked, steamed in pits, or broiled in wooden boxes with red-hot stones.

KEY TECHNOLOGY Fish were taken with dip nets, rakes, floating fences, and weirs; waterfowl with nets, nooses, bow and arrow, and snares; marine inverte-brates with yew digging and prying sticks; sea mam-mals with clubs, harpoons, stakes hidden in seaweed, and nets. Special whaling equipment consisted of harpoons with musselshell blades, two 40- to 60-fathom lines, floats, and lances. Nootkans used six types of canoes, some with cedar bark–mat sails. The uses of wood, a key raw material, included hunting and war tools, canoes, houses, utensils, buckets, and storage boxes. Mattresses and other such items were made of cedar bark.

TRADE Nootkans enjoyed a virtual monopoly on dentalia shell, an item highly prized by many peo-ples along and surrounding the Northwest Coast. They also supplied sea otter pelts and canoes. Their primary trading partners were the Nimpkish Kwaki-utl and the Makah. Nootkans received eulachon oil and grease from the Tsimshian, Chilkat goat-hair blankets from the Tlingit, and furs from the Coast Salish (who obtained them from interior peoples).

NOTABLE ARTS Music and dance were important Nootkan arts. Vocal music, often containing compli-cated structures, patterns, and beats, was accompa-nied by drumming and rattles. Songs were sung for many different occasions, both sacred and secular.

Drama regularly included masks to represent supernatural beings. People told long, complex sto-ries on winter evenings. House posts and fronts and many wooden objects were elaborately carved with crests designs. The decorated conical, onion-domed cedar-bark and spruce-root whaler's hat was a classic Nootkan basketry item. Painting was highly devel-oped in the historic period.

TRANSPORTATION Red cedar dugout canoes came in various sizes. Paired canoes bridged with house planks served to move large loads.

DRESS Men went naked in warm weather. Women wore shredded cedar-bark aprons, and both sexes wore bark robes and conical rain capes as well as hats (which varied according to social class) of tightly woven cedar bark and spruce root. Long yellow cedar-bark robes were distinctive to Nootkan people. Faces were painted for decoration and sunburn pro-tection. Ornaments of dentalium, abalone, horn, and other items were worn in the nose and ears and as bracelets and anklets.

WAR AND WEAPONS The Nimpkish Kwakiutl and the Makah were regular objects of Nootkan military attention. War chiefs wore elk hide armor with painted designs. Raiding took place primarily to acquire booty, including slaves. Weapons included bone and horn-tipped clubs, yew-wood bows, arrows with stone or bone points, knives, spears, and slings. Many Nootkans had guns as early as the late eigh-teenth century.

Contemporary Information

GOVERNMENT/RESERVATIONS As of 1995, 15 Nootkan bands lived in their traditional territory in British Columbia. The Nuu-chah-nulth Tribal Coun-cil is elected by all Nootkans and funded by most bands. See "Daily Life" for summaries of bands.

ECONOMY Economic activities and band resources are described under "Daily Life." Since the nineteenth century, Nootkans have made baskets for commercial sale.

LEGAL STATUS All of the following bands are federally and provincially recognized entities.

DAILY LIFE The following are extant Nookan bands (as of 1995):

Ahousaht Band: The band was formed in 1951 from the Ahousaht and Kelsemaht Bands. It controls 25 reserves on 592 hectares of land. The reserves were allotted in 1889. The 1995 population was 1,415, of whom 487 lived in 105 houses on the reserve. The band is governed under the provisions of the Indian Act and is affiliated with the Nuu-chah-nulth Tribal Council. Economic activities and resources include a seabus service, freight services, a bakery, and a camp-site. Facilities include a community hall, a church, a cultural center, administrative offices, and two gym-nasiums.

Ditidaht Band: The band controls 17 reserves on 727 hectares of land. The reserves were allotted in 1890. The 1995 population was 481, of whom 141 lived in 34 houses on the reserve. The band is gov-erned by custom and is affiliated with the Nuu-chah-nulth Tribal Council. Children attend provincial schools. Economic activities and resources include forestry and a gravel pit. Facilities include a commu-nity hall, a cultural center, administrative offices, and recreational facilities.

Ehattesaht Band: The band controls nine reserves on 136 hectares of land. The reserves were allotted in 1889. The 1995 population was 193, of whom 91 lived in 21 houses on the reserve. The band is governed by custom and is affiliated with the Nuu-chah-nulth Tribal Council. Economic activities and resources include fishing, logging, mining, tourism, and aqua-culture. Facilities include a community center.

Hesquiaht Band: The band controls five reserves on 320 hectares of land on the west coast of central

Vancouver Island. The reserves were allotted in 1886. The 1995 population was 543, of whom 149 lived in 24 houses on the reserve. The band is governed by custom and is affiliated with the Nuu-chah-nulth Tribal Council. Economic activities include fishing. Facilities include a community hall, a privately owned store, and a sawmill.

Kyuguot Band: The band controls 20 reserves on 382 hectares of land on northwest Vancouver Island. The reserves were allotted in 1889. The 1995 population was 393, of whom 133 lived in 31 houses on the reserve. The band is governed by custom and is affiliated with the Nuu-chah-nulth Tribal Council. Economic activities include fishing and logging. Facilities include a community hall.

Mowachaht/Muchalaht Band, formerly the Nootka Band: The band controls 17 reserves on 263 hectares of land at the mouth of Nootka Sound. The 1995 population was 390, of whom 119 lived in 28 houses on the reserve. The band is governed by custom and is affiliated with the Nuu-chah-nulth Tribal Council, which administers its schools. Economic activities include forest products and a boat launch. Facilities include offices, a playground, and a tourist center.

Nuchatlaht Band: The band controls 11 reserves on 92 hectares of land on the northwest coast of Vancouver Island. The reserves were allotted in 1889. The 1995 population was 127, of whom 27 lived in eight houses on the reserve. The band is governed by custom and is affiliated with the Nuu-chah-nulth Tribal Council. Economic activities include forestry and fishing. Facilities include offices and a clinic.

Ohiaht Band: The band controls 13 reserves on 816 hectares of land on the southwest coast of Vancouver Island. The reserves were allotted in 1882. The 1995 population was 474, of whom 101 lived in 33 houses on the reserve. The band is governed by custom and is affiliated with the Nuu-chah-nulth Tribal Council. Children attend provincial schools. Economic resources include a campsite. Facilities include offices, a cemetery, and a recreation hall.

Opetchesaht Band: The band controls five reserves on 215 hectares of land near Port Alberni. The reserves were allotted in 1882. The 1995 population was 206, of whom 90 lived in 33 houses on the reserve. The band is governed under the provisions of the Indian Act and is affiliated with the Nuu-chah-nulth Tribal Council. Economic activities and resources include logging and a pulp mill. Facilities include offices, a cemetery, a community hall, and a cultural center.

Pacheenaht Band: The band controls four reserves on 174 hectares of land on the southwest coast of Vancouver Island. The reserves were allotted in 1882.

The 1995 population was 214, of whom 82 lived in 24 houses on the reserve. The band is governed under the provisions of the Indian Act and, although unaffiliated, is part of the Nuu-chah-nulth people. Children attend provincial schools. Economic activities and resources include a campsite and a ferry service. Facilities include offices and a longhouse.

Tla-o-qui-aht First Nations (formerly called Clayoquot): The band controls ten reserves on 220 hectares of land near Pacific Rim National Park. The reserves were allotted in 1889. The 1995 population was 618, of whom 264 lived in 60 houses on the reserve. The band is governed under the provisions of the Indian Act and is affiliated with the Nuu-chah-nulth Tribal Council. Economic activities and resources include fishing and tourism. Facilities include offices, a store, an arts and crafts store, a community hall, a clinic, and a marina.

Toquaht Band: The band controls seven reserves on 196 hectares of land on the southwest coast of Vancouver Island. The reserves were allotted in 1882. The 1995 population was 115, of whom 12 lived in eight houses on the reserve. The band is governed by custom and is affiliated with the Nuu-chah-nulth Tribal Council. Economic activities and resources include fishing and building supplies. Facilities include offices.

Tsesaht Band: The band controls eight reserves on 584 hectares of land near Port Alberni. The reserves were allotted in 1882. The 1995 population was 735, of whom 406 lived in 115 houses on the reserve. The band is governed by custom and is affiliated with the Nuu-chah-nulth Tribal Council. Children attend provincial schools. Economic activities and resources include fishing and forestry. Facilities include a community hall, a recreation building, and a cultural center.

Uchucklesaht Band: The band controls two reserves on 232 hectares of land 30 kilometers west of Victoria. The reserves were allotted in 1882. The 1995 population was 135, of whom 25 lived in 13 houses on the reserve. The band is governed by custom and is affiliated with the Nuu-chah-nulth Tribal Council. Economic activities include a water freight service. Facilities include a clinic.

Ucluelet Band: The band controls nine reserves on 199 hectares of land 60 kilometers east of Port Alberni. The reserves were allotted in 1882. The 1995 population was 538, of whom 193 lived in 67 houses on the reserve. The band is governed under the provisions of the Indian Act and is affiliated with the Nuu-chah-nulth Tribal Council. Economic activities include fishing, fish processing, a minimall, a laundromat, and a video arcade. Facilities include a community center, a museum, a nursery school, and a marina.

Oowekeeno

See Bella Bella

Puyallup

See Salish, Southern Coast

Quileute

Quileute (`Kwil ē̄ ū t) is taken from the name of a village at the site of La Push. The Hoh Indians, formerly considered a Quileute Band, now have independent federal recognition.

LOCATION Traditionally, the Quileute lived along the coast from south of Ozette Lake to just south of the Hoh River and west to Mt. Olympus, on the Olympic Peninsula. Most of the region is rain forest. Today, many Quileute live on reservations on the Pacific coast of the Olympic Peninsula, in the state of Washington.

POPULATION In the late eighteenth century, about 500 Quileutes lived on the Olympic Peninsula. Tribal enrollment in the early 1990s was about 875. In 1990, 302 Indians lived on the Quileute Reservation; another 74 on lived on the Hoh Reservation.

LANGUAGE Quileute is a Chimakuan language.

Historical Information

HISTORY In late-prehistoric times, the Quileute were members, with the Hoh and the Quinault, of a confederation that controlled most tribes from Cape Flattery to Grey's Harbor. Quileutes either killed or enslaved the first non-natives they met (Spanish in 1775; British in 1787; Russian in 1808). They had little contact with whites until 1855, when the Indians signed a treaty agreeing to move to the Quinault Reservation. They had not yet moved, however, by 1889, the year the one-square-mile La Push Reservation was created. Four years later, a reservation was established for the people of the Hoh River.

In the interim (1860s–1880s), Quileutes tried as best they could to resist the invading non-natives. Most declined to send their children to an Anglo school that opened at La Push in 1882. Symptomatic of the interracial hostility that reigned during that time was the fire set by a white person at La Push in 1889 that destroyed 26 houses and almost all precontact artifacts.

In 1895, the Quileutes embraced the Indian Shaker religion. In 1912, whites appropriated ancient fishing sites to open a canning industry on the Quillayute River. Indians were declared ineligible to obtain fishing licenses. They gave up whaling in 1904 and sealing in the 1930s. In 1936, shortly after 165 Quileutes were each allotted 80 acres of timbered land on the Quinault Reservation, the tribe adopted a constitution and by-laws.

RELIGION The Quileute universe was peopled with a creator-transformer and a variety of ghosts, spirits, monsters, and creatures. This interplay gave rise to a rich mythology. Entrée to one of five ceremonial societies—warrior, hunter, whaler, shaman, and fisher—might be obtained by holding a potlatch or showing evidence of an appropriate guardian spirit power. Initiations, which included dances with carved wood masks, took place primarily in winter. Potlatches also accompanied life-cycle events.

Individuals could claim guardian spirits, from nature or ancestors, through special quests or by being adopted by the power. Such powers could also be lost or stolen, perhaps through the intercession of a shaman, or simply depart, in which case a shaman might bring them back (this was the lost soul cure—shamans could also cure disease). Adolescents quested after spirit powers by fasting and visiting remote places. The Quileute also observed first salmon rites.

GOVERNMENT A village, made up of extended families, was the basic political unit. Each village had two hereditary chiefs.

CUSTOMS Quileute society was divided into the hereditary groups that were usual for Northwest Indians: chiefs, commoners, and slaves (acquired in raids or trade). Much social activity was devoted to maintaining and pursuing status. With rank came the rights to names, dances, songs, designs, guardian spirit powers, and membership in certain secret societies.

The traits of cleanliness, moderation, and generosity were especially prized. At puberty, girls were confined to a section of the house for five days. Boys began spirit questing in their late teens. Perhaps because pre- and extramarital sex were taboo, the Quileutes recognized ten different types of marriage, including polygamy. Quileutes intermarried regularly with Makahs and Quinaults. Divorce was common.

Both parents were subject to behavioral restrictions around pregnancy and childbirth. The birth of twins subjected parents to eight months of additional taboos. Babies were kept in cradle boards. Noble families flattened their babies' heads. The dead were wrapped in mats or dog-hair blankets and buried in canoes or hollow logs. Mourners cut their hair and painted their faces. Widows observed special taboos, such as not sleeping lying down. The name of the dead was not spoken for some time, and mourners asked those with similar names to change them. On the second anniversary of death, remains of high-status people were reburied, and a memorial potlatch was given.

DWELLINGS Winter camps of multifamily, permanent plank houses were located at stream mouths.

Houses were roughly 60 feet by 40 feet and had single-pitch roofs, sleeping platforms, and fireplaces for each family. In summer, groups would divide into families and range in hereditary subsistence areas. During this time they lived in cattail-mat or brush lean-tos.

DIET Quileutes ate all five species of salmon. Other important fish included steelhead, halibut, smelt, trout, flounder, dogfish, skate, and octopus as well as shellfish. They gathered 16 types of fruits and berries, roots, sprouts, and seaweed as well as bear-berry (kinnikinnick) for smoking. They also hunted marine mammals and land mammals, especially deer and elk, as well as small game and birds, with bow and arrow, snares, and deadfalls.

KEY TECHNOLOGY Men and women fashioned most items from spruce roots, hemlock, cedar, willow bark, kelp, reeds, and grasses. Woman made water-tight burden and storage twined baskets. They also wove rain hats, mats, skirts, and capes.

Men made bent-corner wooden boxes as well as wooden platters, dishes, bailers, fishhooks, rattles, and masks. When building red-cedar canoes, they used yew-wood wedges to split the trees and adzes to carve and hollow the logs. Hunting equipment included harpoons, lances, bow and arrow, and clubs. Other tools included stone hammers, mortars, and scrapers; mussel shell knives and harpoon points; and antler awls and scrapers.

TRADE Trade was primarily with the Makah and the Quinault. The Quileute traded camas and sea mammal blubber for oysters, sockeye salmon, and eulachon grease. They traded Makah dentalia and blankets for Quinault salmon. They also obtained woven blankets of goat wool in trade.

NOTABLE ARTS The many Quileute arts and crafts included basketry, weaving, and wood carving.

TRANSPORTATION Most transportation was by canoe.

DRESS Women often wore shredded cedar-bark skirts and capes. Rain gear included spruce-root rain hats. Tattoos and ear and nose ornaments were popular. The nobility flattened their babies' heads.

WAR AND WEAPONS The Quileute regularly fought their trade partners, the Makah and the Quinault, as well as other coastal peoples, especially over trespass or insult. They retreated to a fortress atop James Island when attacked.

Contemporary Information

GOVERNMENT/RESERVATIONS The Quileute (La Push) Reservation (594 [originally 837] acres) was established in 1889. In 1936, the tribe adopted a constitution and by-laws. Members of an elected five-person tribal council serve three-year terms. The tribe has relatively wide legal powers on the reservation.

The Hoh Reservation (443 acres) was created in 1893. That tribe adopted a constitution in 1969. It is governed by a five-member tribal council on which members serve two-year terms.

ECONOMY Important economic activities include a tribally owned fish-buying company, a fish hatchery, a cooperative store, a trailer park, and a fishing gear store. Tourism, including a restaurant and a resort, provides some jobs, as does the logging industry and the tribal government. Many people still fish.

LEGAL STATUS The Hoh Indian Tribe and the Quileute Indian Tribe are federally recognized tribal entities.

DAILY LIFE Only a handful of Quileute speakers remain, but a Quileute dictionary and a nationally recognized instructional program are helping people to learn the language. People still practice some traditional crafts, including canoe making. Potlatches, and their accompanying focus on cultural identity and traditions, have become popular again since the 1980s, after having virtually disappeared during the 1960s.

Most Hohs are Protestants or Shakers; their children attend school in nearby Forks. La Push students either attend school in Forks or the tribal school (K-8).

Quileutes have been actively involved in the resurgence of the Northwest cedar canoe culture since the 1980s, which includes regular canoe trips to Seattle and a Heiltsuk festival at Bella Bella. Annual Quileute days are usually held on the first weekend in August. The *Quileute Indian News* is published regularly. Elders Week celebrations are held in May.

Quinault

See Salish, Southwestern Coast

Salish, Central Coast

Central Coast Salish (`Sal ish), a group of Indians that shared a common language family and a related culture. Central Coast Salish tribes and villages included Squamish (at least 16 villages), Nooksack (at least 20 villages), Klallam (about a dozen villages), Halkomelem, and Northern Straits. Halkomelem had three divisions: Island (Nanoose, Nanaimo, Chemainus, Cowichan, and Malahat), Downriver (Musqueam, Tsawwessen, Saleelwat, Kwantlen, Coquitlam, Nicomekl, and Katzie), and Upriver (Matsqui, Sumas, Nicomen, Scowlitz, Chehalis, Chilliwak, Pilalt, and Tait). Northern Straits had six divisions: Sooke, Songhees, Saanich, Semiahmoo, Lummi, Samish. The discussions that follow do not apply to every group or tribe.

LOCATION   Traditionally, the lands inhabited by the Central Coast Salish in Canada and the United States included both sides of the southern Strait of Georgia, the San Juan Islands, extreme northwest Washington east of the strait, and parts of the northern Olympic Peninsula. The region is generally wet and moderate, although it includes some drier and cooler regions.

Most contemporary Central Coast Salish Indians live on reserves or reservations in or around their aboriginal lands or in cities of the Northwest.

POPULATION   The Central Coast Salish population stood at roughly 20,000 in the mid–eighteenth century. In the 1990s it was around 16,000.

LANGUAGE   Central Coast Salish, which includes the Squamish, Nooksack, Klallam, Halkomelem, and Northern Straits (Lkungen) languages, is a member of the Central division of the Salishan language family.

Historical Information

HISTORY   Some Central Coast Salish may have had contact with the Spanish explorer Juan de Fuca in 1592, or in 1787 an Anglo fur trader may have been the first non-Indian inside the Strait of Juan de Fuca. Regular Spanish explorations of Coast Salish territory began in the early 1790s. Smallpox epidemics also began about that time, if not earlier.

Land-based Anglo fur traders established themselves at the mouth of the Columbia River in 1811. The Hudson's Bay Company built a fort on the Fraser River in 1827. That post, Fort Langley, became the local center of interracial contact and trade. Indians supplied materials, labor, and goods, and Indian women married or otherwise became involved with Anglo traders. Fort Victoria, built in 1843, drew Indian trade from Puget Sound to as far north as Alaska.

The Treaty of Washington (1846) split Central Coast Salish country between the United States and Canada. The British subsequently created small reserves for every village (which they called bands). On the U.S. side, the Point Elliot and Point No Point Treaties in 1855 ceded Indian land and created a few regional reservations. However, most Indians remained in their own territories rather than remove to the designated reservations. Some groups were left landless by this process. Anglo settlers began trickling in during the 1850s. The trickle turned into a flood in 1858 when gold was discovered in the Fraser River.

Christian missionaries, present since 1841, became more active after 1858. During the following decades a number of bands became thoroughly Christianized. By the 1860s, many Central Coast Salish Indians were working in the new industries: logging, farming, shipping, and commercial fishing. They also found seasonal work picking berries and hops. Nooksacks were expected under the terms of the Point Elliot Treaty to move to the Lummi Reservation, but few did. They continued to function as a tribe, although the government no longer considered them one, and finally received federal recognition in 1973.

The Lummi Reservation was established in 1855. Gold seekers around this time inflicted great personal harm on the Lummi and other tribes. Still, despite pressure to adopt agriculture, many Lummis continued to practice a semitraditional lifestyle based on reef-netting. They lost key lands as a result of white encroachment in 1890s, although by the 1930s they had acquired and cultivated new land. They lost over one-third of their population during the 1950s as a result of the official government policy of relocating reservation Indians to urban areas. In the 1970s they received a land claims settlement for the loss of their reef netting locations, which they have refused to accept because they consider it far too low.

According to the terms of the Point No Point Treaty (1855), Klallams were to remove to the Skokomish Reservation. However, most remained in their traditional villages. In 1874, some Klallam Indians purchased land and called their settlement Jamestown. When the United States purchased about 1,600 acres for the Klallam in 1936, they were separated into the Lower Elwha Tribal Community and the Port Gamble Indian Community (the former sawmill settlement of Little Boston). Some Klallams also went to the Puyallup Reservation.

According to the Point Elliot Treaty (1855), the Samishes were supposed to move onto various local reservations, but few did. Many moved in the 1870s to Guemes Island, built a longhouse (almost 500 feet long) and continued their traditional customs as best they could. By 1912, however, whites had forced them off this land. Some people occupied traditional villages while other simply scattered. Many received allotments on the Swinomish Reservation. They adopted a constitution and by-laws (subsequently revised) in 1926 and were awarded a land claims settlement in 1971, which they refused.

By the turn of the century, Indian material culture had been significantly changed, but some groups retained traditional activities, such as the potlatch. For these Indians, the early twentieth century was marked by economic decline, increased cultural suppression in boarding schools, the spread of the Shaker religion, and the revival of spirit dancing. Meanwhile, the Northwestern Federation of American Indians (formed in Tacoma in 1914) pushed for fulfillment of treaty rights. In *U.S.* v. *Washington* (1974), the U.S.

Supreme Court ruled that half of the harvestable salmon and steelhead in Washington waters were reserved for federally recognized, land-based treaty tribes.

RELIGION Central Coast Salish recognized a mythological time when their legendary ancestors lived. They believed that people are composed of several components, one or more of which might occasionally get lost or lured away and would have to be restored by shamans. In their everyday lives, they made a distinction between what was considered normal and anything that might connote danger or power (such as a deformed person, a menstruating woman, or a corpse). People sought luck or skills from an encounter with a spirit. An accompanying song provided direct access to the spirit's power.

Shamans' spirit helpers gave special powers. Men and women could be shamans. Curing, the province of shamans, entailed singing, drama, and extracting a harmful entity with the hands and mouth. Some shamans could also foretell the future. Spells or incantations were also believed to carry power. Most people used them to help perform a task, but people highly skilled in such matters could be hired for special occasions.

Intra- and intervillage spirit dances took place in winter. The host provided food, and dancers danced their spirit songs, of which there were several categories. Dances and songs were accompanied by much ritual paraphernalia. Secret societies also held their dances in winter. Their main ceremony was initiating new members; the right to membership was hereditary. Central Coast Salish people also observed first salmon ceremonies (the ritual preparation and consumption of the season's first catch). Cleansing rituals were made both to erase a disgrace and to enhance a festive occasion.

GOVERNMENT Each group lived in a number of villages. Heads of the leading or established household served as local group chiefs. As such, they had little or no power to govern; they were wealthy and influential men who entertained guests, made decisions about subsistence activity, and arbitrated disputes.

CUSTOMS Several extended families made up a household, which owned particular subsistence areas and tools, such as clam beds and fowl nets. Some particularly prestigious households, or "houses" (in the European sense), descended from a notable ancestor and shared resources, names, ceremonies, and other valuables. Some local groups may have had their own winter villages, although larger villages included several local groups. Members of different households cooperated in some activities such as deer drives, building a salmon weir, ceremonies, and defense, but they were not necessarily culturally homogeneous. There was little intervillage cooperation. Social groups included worthy people (those with wealth, ancestry, manners, and guardian spirits), worthless people, and slaves.

The Central Coast Salish intermarried from within and without. Marriages involved ritual exchanges and promoted trade. They were initiated by men; women could refuse, but they felt pressure to marry "well." A wedding usually entailed the exchange of gifts (material and/or hereditary privileges) and a cleansing ceremony. Exchanges of food and gifts between families-in-law continued throughout the marriage.

From an early age, children were "toughened" by swimming in icy water and running in storms. This process culminated in the adolescent spirit quest. Boys marked puberty by making their first kill. If possible, girls were feted with a feast and a display of hereditary privileges. They were secluded during their periods. Among the Cowichan, a girl undertook a solitary vigil; if she was joined by a boy, and their parents agreed, they could be married. Corpses were wrapped in blankets and placed in canoes or grave boxes. Among the worthy, bones were rewrapped several years later with an accompanying display of privileges.

Potlatches, as opposed to feasts, were usually held outdoors in good weather. Occasions included life crises and important life-cycle or ceremonial events. Usually all or part of a village held the potlatch, with each house marking its own occasions. Goods were not expected to be returned: The point was status—that is, good relations with neighbors and good marriages for children.

Some hunters, both land and sea, achieved a professional status and spent whole summers hunting. People generally spent the summers traveling in small groups, following seasonal food cycles and living in temporary dwellings. They enjoyed several gambling games, including the hand and disk games. Sports included shinny, races, athletic competitions, and games of skill. Singing for pleasure was common.

DWELLINGS Winter villages consisted of from one house to several rows of houses built on the beach. Houses were up to several hundred feet long. They had a permanent wooden framework with a shed roof and removable roof and wall planks. Each family had a separate fire. House posts were decorated with painted and carved images of ancestors and spirit powers. These people also built some fortified war refuges (stockades). Other structures included summer mat houses, wooden grave houses, and pole and mat sweat lodges.

DIET Fish, especially salmon (all five species),

were the staple food, although they were available to different people in different places at different times of the year. The leaner, fall runs were dried for storage; otherwise they were eaten fresh. Other important foods included sea mammals (seal and porpoise, used mostly for oil; sea lions; whales [Klallam]); shellfish; land mammals such as deer, elk, black bear, mountain goats, and beaver (smaller game as well as grizzlies, cougars, and wolves were generally avoided); waterfowl; and a large variety of plants. Camus, brake fern, wapato, and wild carrots were especially important, but other bulbs, roots, berries, sprouts, and stems were also used. Camus fields were burned and reseeded. Potato husbandry became important after 1800.

KEY TECHNOLOGY Fish were taken with reef nets, dip nets, trawl nets, harpoons, gaff hooks, spears, basket traps, weirs, tidal pounds (rows of underwater stakes), hooks, and herring rakes and in rectangular nets suspended between two canoes, a method by which several thousand fish a day might be captured. Harpoons, seal nets, and clubs served as marine mammal hunting equipment; land mammals were taken with pitfalls, snares, bow (2.5 to 3 feet, made of yew) and arrow, and spears. Waterfowl were snagged in permanent nets stretched across flyways. They were also hunted with bow and arrow, flares and nets at night, and snares.

Important raw materials included wood, hides, antler, horn, mountain goat wool, beaver teeth, wood stone, and shell. Wooden items included house materials, canoes, bent-corner boxes, dishes, tools, weapons, and ceremonial items. Shredded bark was used for towels, mattresses, and similar items. Sewn mats of cattail leaves and tule lined interior house walls, covered frames of summer shelters, and were made into mattresses, rain covers, and sitting or kneeling pads. Women made several types of baskets, including wrapped lattice, coiled, twined, and woven. They practiced a distinctive form of weaving, spinning wool from a special breed of dog (now extinct) plus mountain goat wool, waterfowl down, and fireweed cotton on a large spindle and weaving it on a two-bar loom.

TRADE All groups engaged in local and regional trade and intermarriage. The Klallam, in particular, were great traders as well as warriors. Salish people imported Chilkat blankets, among other items.

NOTABLE ARTS Wooden items such as house posts, canoes, grave monuments, and household and ritual items were artistically carved and/or painted. Designs featured humans, animals, and/or vision powers. Lummi and other women wove cedar-bark baskets and mountain goat and dog wool blankets.

TRANSPORTATION Most travel was by canoe.

There were five distinct types, depending on the activity, not including those obtained in trade.

DRESS Men often went naked or wore buckskin shorts or robes (skin or shredded bark). Women wore short aprons or skirts and robes. Some men and women wore conical basketry hats, and some men wore fur caps. In cold weather, both sexes wore down-and-nettle shirts, robes, and perhaps ponchos. There were also fine blankets made of mountain goat and coyote wool as well as plant fibers. Hunters wore hide outfits and moccasins or snowshoes. Ponchos of woven cedar bark or cattail leaves served as rain gear.

Free people had flattened heads. Personal adornments included pierced ears and often pierced noses, tattoos, and body paint (which was also applied against insects). Headgear included women's Plateau-style basketry hats and mushroom-shaped, brimmed spruce-root hats worn by both sexes. Both men and women wore their hair long.

WAR AND WEAPONS The Central Coast Salish fought wars among themselves, with their neighbors, and with more distant neighbors. Injury and death, intentional or not, demanded compensation. Refusal to pay might lead to fighting, and some groups, such as the Klallam, saw compensation as dishonorable. The Klallam were particularly aggressive; the impaled heads of their foes, often Snohomish, Cowichan, or Duwamish, often decorated their beaches. There was some naval warfare, in which canoes rammed and sank other canoes. At least in the early nineteenth century, the Lekwiltok (Kwakiutl) were a common enemy.

Raids, for loot, territory, vengeance, or a show of power, were led by professional warriors with special powers. Raids featured surprise attacks. Men were killed, and women and children were captured, later to be ransomed or sold as slaves. Warriors wore elk hide armor.

Contemporary Information

GOVERNMENT/RESERVATIONS In 1984, 235 reserves (approximately 62,000 acres) were connected with 52 Central Coast Salish bands (approximately 13,000 people) in British Columbia. See "Daily Life" for summary descriptions of selected bands in Canada.

The Nooksack Reservation (12 acres) was created in 1973. Most Nooksacks live in and near Deming, Nooksack, and Everson, Washington. They are governed by a tribal council. A further 60 acres of reservation land is expected. The 1991 tribal population was 1,168.

The Jamestown S'klallam Reservation (1980; 12 acres; population 240) is located at the upper Strait of Juan de Fuca. The Klallam are governed by an elected tribal council. Also, with the Port Gamble, the Lower Elwha Klallams, and the Skokomishes (Twana), the Jamestown S'klallam make up the Point No Point Treaty Council, an administrative body.

The Elwha S'klallam Reservation (1968; 427 acres; 530 population) is located in Clallam County, Washington. The Lower Elwha Tribal Community began in 1936. They adopted a constitution and by-laws in 1968. The Lower Elwha Community Tribal Council is composed of all qualified voters. Members of a business committee are elected to two-year terms.

The Port Gamble Reservation (1936; 1,303 acres; 860 population) is located on the Kitsap Peninsula in Washington. The Port Gamble Indian Community adopted a constitution in 1939. A business committee appoints various standing committees. Many Klallams also live on the Skokomish Reservation.

The Lummi Reservation (1849; 7,073 acres allotted, 12 acres tribally owned) is west of Bellingham, Washington. The Lummi adopted a new constitution in 1970. The 11 members of an elected business council serve three-year terms. The tribal council elects officers and establishes committees. The Lummi are the dominant group on this mixed-group reservation. The enrolled membership in 1992 was 3,200, about half of whom lived on the reservation.

ECONOMY The Lummi run fish hatcheries and an aquaculture program. They also have a salmon-rearing facility, a huge fishing fleet, a restaurant-boating complex, and a fish-processing plant. Nevertheless, the unemployment rate there in the early 1990s approached 70 percent. There are several community-owned businesses, including a gas station, store, and mobile home park, and crafts enterprises on the Port Gamble Reservation. Klallams and Nooksacks are also active in the commercial fishing industry. Other important economic activity includes subsistence gardening, fishing, logging, and seasonal farm work.

LEGAL STATUS The Nooksack Indian Tribe has been federally recognized since 1973. The Jamestown Klallam Tribe is a federally recognized tribal entity. The Lower Elwha Tribal Community of the Lower Elwha Reservation (Klallam) is a federally recognized tribal entity. The Port Gamble Indian Community of the Port Gamble Reservation (Klallam) is a federally recognized tribal entity. The Lummi Tribe is a federally recognized tribal entity. The Samish Indian Tribe is seeking federal recognition.

DAILY LIFE Central Coast Salish Indians in both the United States and Canada are still linked socially through festivals, canoe racing, games, winter dancing, and the Indian Shaker Church. The Nooksack have a tribal center complex at Deming. They work closely with federal and state entities to manage local natural resource areas and are engaged in redressing housing and health care shortages. Cultural preservation is carried out mainly by means of identifying and preserving cultural sites. Although these people are largely assimilated, they maintain strong family connections to a greater Indian identity. Funerals, in particular, are important occasions on which to express that identity, as are longhouse ceremonials and local pantribal celebrations.

Most Klallams are Protestant. Their children attend public schools. There are several tribal community programs at Lower Elwha and Port Gamble, including a substance abuse program, health clinic, housing department, hatchery-fisheries department, and a higher adult–vocational education department. The Port Gamble Reservation enforces most of its own laws. The Jamestown Klallam have an annual gathering, "S'klallam Qwen Seyu."

Many of the roughly 600 Samish live on the Tulalip, Lummi, or Swinomish Reservations as well as near the tribal headquarters in Anacortes, Washington. They operate a gift shop as well as an archaeological consulting service and participate in spirit dancing and other local Indian activities.

The Lummi Reservation features childrens' programs as well as a K-8 school and Northwest Indian College. Some Lummi children attend Catholic school. The local Indian Health Service provides medical and dental care. The annual Lummi Stommish water carnival in June features canoe racing. Few speak the tribal language, but some traditional ceremonies and festivals are still held. Some tribes began a revival of blanket weaving in the 1980s. Many Lummis are Christian, although traditional spirit dancing and the Indian Shaker Church are also important.

Selected Central Coast Salish bands in British Columbia (statistics as of 1995):

Chehalis Band controls two reserves on 907 hectares of land 10 miles west of Agassiz. The population is 775, of whom 400 people live on the reserves. The band is governed under the provisions of the Indian Act and is currently unaffiliated. Children attend band and provincial schools. Important economic resources and activities include small businesses, forestry, and fishing. Facilities include two recreation buildings, a cultural center, a longhouse, and offices.

Chemainus Band controls four reserves on 1,225 hectares of land about 30 kilometers south of Nanaimo. The reserves were allotted in 1877. The population is 882, of whom 690 people live on the reserves. The band is governed under the provisions of the Indian Act and is affiliated with the Mid-Island Tribal Council. Children attend band and provincial schools. Important economic resources and activities include a construction company, a campsite, and a general store. Facilities include an administration building and a clinic.

Coquitlam (Kwayhquitlim) Band, formerly part of the Chilliwack Tribe, controls two reserves on 89 hectares of land. The population is 81, of whom seven people live in five houses on the reserves. The band is governed by custom and is currently unaffiliated. Important economic resources and activities include a proposed residential and golf course development.

Cowichan Band controls nine reserves on 2,493 hectares of land near the city of Duncan. The population is 2,972, of whom 1,922 people live on the reserves. The band is governed under the provisions of the Indian Act and is currently unaffiliated. Children attend band and provincial schools. Important economic resources and activities include a construction company, a fish hatchery, land leasing, wood carving, and several small businesses. Facilities include nine recreation buildings, two cultural centers, a community hall, and offices.

Cowichan Lake Band controls one reserve on 39 hectares of land on the north shore of Cowichan Lake. The population is 12, of whom 10 live on the reserve. Elections are by custom. The band is affiliated with the First Nations South Island Tribal Council (FNSITC).

Malahat Band, formerly part of the Saanich Tribe, controls one reserve on 237 hectares of land 40 kilometers north of Victoria. The reserve was allotted in 1877. The population is 220, of whom 81 live in 13 houses on the reserve. Elections are held under the provisions of the Indian Act. The band is affiliated with the FNSITC. Children attend provincial schools. Facilities include a longhouse and a recreation building.

Musqueam Band controls three reserves on 254 hectares of land near the Point Grey area of Vancouver. The population is 925, of whom 454 live in 110 houses on the reserves. Elections are held under the provisions of the Indian Act. Children attend band and provincial schools. Important economic resources include a shipyard and a hotel. Facilities include a community and recreation hall, offices, a longhouse, and a church.

Nanaimo Band controls six reserves on 26 hectares of land near the city of Nanaimo. The reserves were allotted in 1876. The population is 1,089, of whom 409 live in 122 houses on the reserves. Elections are held under the provisions of the Indian Act. The band is affiliated with the Alliance Tribal Council. Children attend band and provincial schools. Important economic activities include forest industries. Facilities include a recreation center, a cultural center, a store, and offices.

Katzie Band controls five reserves on 340 hectares of land west of Port Hammond. The population is 396, of whom 201 people live in 75 houses on the reserves. Elections are held according to custom. The band is affiliated with the Alliance Tribal Council. The economy is based on commercial fishing and land leases. Facilities include offices.

Pauquachin Band, formerly part of the Saanich Tribe, controls two reserves on 319 hectares of land in the southwest part of Vancouver Island. The reserves were allotted in 1877. The population is 265, of whom 177 live in 56 houses on the reserves. Elections are held under the provisions of the Indian Act. The band is affiliated with the FNSITC. Schools are administered by the Saanich Indian School Board. Important economic activities include a recreational vehicle park. Facilities include a recreation center, offices, and a longhouse.

Pehelakut Band controls four reserves on 635 hectares of land near Chemainus, British Columbia. The reserves were allotted in 1877. The population is 657, of whom 421 live in 101 houses on the reserves. Elections are held under the provisions of the Indian Act. The band is affiliated with the Mid-Island Tribal Council. Children attend band and provincial schools. Important economic activities include a general store. Facilities include a community hall, offices, and a longhouse.

Semiahmoo Band controls one reserve on 129 hectares of land southeast of White Rock. The population is 60, of whom 26 live in seven houses on the reserve. Elections are held under the provisions of the Indian Act. The band is unaffiliated. Children attend provincial schools. Economic activities include a campsite. Facilities include a church.

Skwah Band controls four reserves on 342 hectares of land near Chilliwack, British Columbia. The reserves were established in 1879. The population is 354, of whom 171 live in 58 houses on the reserves. Elections are held under the provisions of the Indian Act. The band is unaffiliated. Children attend band and provincial schools. Important economic activities include local agriculture and businesses in Chilliwack. Facilities include a community hall, offices, and a recreation room.

Songhees Band controls three reserves on 126 hectares of land near Esquimault Harbor. The reserves were allotted in 1878. The population is 330, of whom 206 live in 60 houses on the reserves. Elections are held under the provisions of the Indian Act. The band is unaffiliated. Children attend band and provincial schools. Important economic activities include a boat ramp, a mobile home park, and a store. Facilities include a community hall, offices, and a sports field.

Sooke Band controls two reserves on 67 hectares of land on the south end of Vancouver Island. The reserves were allotted in 1877. The population is 160, of whom 78 live on the reserves. Elections are held under the provisions of the Indian Act. The band is affiliated with the FNSITC. Children attend provincial schools. Important economic activities include forestry and off-reservation businesses. Facilities include a community hall, offices, a cultural center, and a park.

Squamish Band controls eight villages from the north shore of Burrand Inlet to the head of Howe Sound. The population is 2,554, of whom 1,627 live in 350 houses. Elections are held by custom. The band is affiliated with the Alliance Tribal Council. Children attend band and provincial schools. Important economic activities include land developed and leased by the band and several small businesses. Facilities include a community hall, a cultural center, a library, an arts and crafts building, a group home, a seniors' home, a longhouse, and offices.

Tsartlip Band, formerly part of the Saanich Tribe, controls three reserves on 324 hectares of land 25 kilometers north of Victoria. The reserves were allotted in 1877. The population is 695, of whom 419 live in 98 houses on the reserves. Elections are held under the provisions of the Indian Act. The band is affiliated with the FNSITC. Schools are administered by the Saanish Indian School Board. Important economic activities include a boat ramp, a campsite, and a store. Facilities include a cultural center and offices.

Tsawout Band, formerly part of the Saanich Tribe, controls two reserves on 258 hectares of land about 30 kilometers north of Victoria. The reserves were allotted in 1877. The population is 567, of whom 402 live in 80 houses on the reserves. Elections are held under the provisions of the Indian Act. The band is affiliated with the FNSITC. Important economic activities include small businesses, hotels, and trailer parks. Facilities include a cultural center, longhouse, community hall, and offices.

Tsawwassen Band controls one reserve on 750 acres of land. The population is 173, of whom 109 live in 55 houses on the reserve. Elections are held under the provisions of the Indian Act. The band is affiliated with the Alliance Tribal Council. Children attend band and provincial schools. Important economic activities include a recreational park and a proposed hotel/marina complex. Facilities include a recreation center, a church, and offices.

Tseycum Band, formerly part of the Saanich Tribe, controls one reserve on 28 hectares of land on Saanich Inlet. The reserves were allotted in 1877. The population is 124, of whom 75 live in 22 houses on the reserves. Elections are held under the provisions of the Indian Act. The band is affiliated with the FNSITC. Important economic activities are mostly off-reserve. Facilities include a cemetery, a sports field, and offices.

Salish, Northern Coast

The constituent groups of the Northern Coast Salish (`Sal ish) included Island Comox, Mainland Comox (Homalco, Klahoose, and Sliammon), Pentlatch, and Sechelt. The Comox called themselves *Catlo'ltx.*

LOCATION Traditional Northern Coast Salish territory, all in Canada, included roughly the northern half of the Strait of Georgia, including east-central Vancouver Island. The climate is wet and moderate. In the 1990s, Northern Coast Salish Indians live in villages and reserves in their traditional territory and in regional cities and towns.

POPULATION The Comox population in 1780 was about 1,800. In 1995, about 2,750 Northern Coast Salish from six bands (Comox, Homalco, Klahoose, Sliammon, Qualicum [Pentlatch], and Sechelt) lived in the region.

LANGUAGE Northern Coast Salish, which includes the Comox, Pentlatch, and Sechelt languages, is a member of the Central division of the Salishan language family.

Historical Information

HISTORY Juan de Fuca may have encountered the Northern Coast Salish in 1752. British and Spanish trade ships arrived in 1792 to a friendly reception. Owing to the lack of sea otter in the Strait of Georgia, however, most Northern Coast Salish did not participate in the local maritime fur trade.

Miners and other non-natives founded Victoria in 1843. By this time local Indians had experienced severe epidemics with some concomitant village abandonment and consolidation. Catholic missionaries arrived in the 1860s, and many natives converted and renounced their ceremonials, including potlatching. Some self-sufficient overtly Christian villages were established, complete with a missionary-imposed governing structure. By the end of the century, the missionaries, along with Catholic boarding schools, had largely destroyed the native language and culture.

With their traditional economy severely damaged, many Indian men took jobs as longshoremen, loggers, and migrant farmers. They also worked in commercial fishing, including canneries. Canada officially established Indian reserves in 1876, by which time Indians had already lost much of their aboriginal land. In the early twentieth century, several Indian organizations, such as the Allied Tribes and the Native

Brotherhood of British Columbia, formed to pursue title to aboriginal lands. The Alliance of Tribal Councils continued this work in the 1970s and worked to foster a positive self-image as well as political unity. Partly as a result of its activity, in 1986 the Sechelt Band became the first self-governing Indian group in Canada.

RELIGION People sought guardian spirits (from animate or inanimate objects) to confer special powers or skills. Spirits were acquired in dreams or by fasting or other physical tests. The Northern Coast Salish Indians celebrated two forms of winter ceremonials: spirit dancing, which was inclusive and participatory, and masked dancing, which was reserved for only certain high-status families. Shamans as well as various secret societies provided religious leadership.

GOVERNMENT Villages were headed by chiefs, who were the heads of the leading or established households. Chiefs had little or no power to govern; they were wealthy and influential men who entertained guests, made decisions about subsistence activity, and arbitrated disputes.

CUSTOMS Among most groups, the "local group" consisted of members who traced their descent patrilineally from a mythical ancestor; it was identified with and controlled certain specific subsistence areas. The right to hold potlatches and certain ceremonies, including dances and songs, was also inheritable. Northern Coast Salish people were either chiefs, nobles, commoners, or slaves.

Both parents, but especially the mother, were subject to pregnancy and childbirth taboos and restrictions. Infants' heads were pressed for aesthetic effect. Pubescent girls were secluded and their behavior was restricted, but boys were physically and mentally trained to seek a guardian spirit. Those who embarked on extended training and quests became shamans.

People were considered marriageable when they reached adolescence. Men, accompanied by male relatives, first approached women in a canoe. Polygyny was common, and multiple wives resided in the same household. Corpses were washed, wrapped in a blanket, and placed in a coffin that was in turn set in a cave or a tree away from the village. Possessions were burned. The Comox and Pentlatch erected carved and painted mortuary poles.

DWELLINGS Northern Coast Salish people built three types of permanent plank houses (semiexcavated and with shed and gabled roofs). Planks could be removed and transported to permanent frameworks at summer villages. Some houses were up to 60 or 70 feet long and half as wide. Most were fortified with either stockades or deep trenches. The Pentlatch

and Island Comox had enclosed sleeping areas and separate smoke-drying sheds. Structures housed several related households, including extended families and slaves.

DIET Fish was the staple, especially salmon. Fall salmon were smoke dried for winter storage; the catch from summer salmon runs was eaten fresh. The people practiced ritual preparation and consumption of the season's first salmon. They also ate lingcod, greenling, steelhead, flounder, sole, and herring roe.

Other important foods included sea mammals (sea lion, harbor seal, porpoise); shellfish; land mammals, such as deer, bear, and some elk and mountain goat; birds and fowl; and plant foods, including berries, shoots and leaves, roots, bulbs, and cambium.

KEY TECHNOLOGY Fish were taken with gill nets, basket traps and weirs, gaffs and harpoons, tidal basins of stakes or rocks, dip nets, and rakes (herring). Seal nets, clubs, and harpoons with an identifiable float served as marine mammal hunting equipment. Land mammals were taken with pitfalls, snares, bow (2.5 to 3 feet long, made of yew) and arrow, nets, knives, traps, and spears. Waterfowl were snagged in permanent nets stretched across flyways. They were also hunted with bow and arrow, flares and nets at night, and snares.

Important raw materials included wood, hides, antler, horn, mountain goat wool, beaver teeth, wood, bone, stone, and shell. Wooden items included house materials, canoes, bent-corner boxes, dishes, tools, weapons, and ceremonial items. Shredded bark was used for towels, mattresses, and similar items. Sewn mats of cattail leaves and tule lined interior house walls, covered frames of summer shelters, and were made into mattresses, rain covers, and sitting or kneeling pads. Women made several types of baskets of cedar limb splints or roots, including wrapped lattice, coiled, twined, and woven.

TRADE Goods such as fish oil, dentalia, baskets, berries, furs, and deer hides were traded among local groups as well as with neighboring Coast Salish peoples.

NOTABLE ARTS Wooden items such as house posts, canoes, grave monuments, and household and ritual items were artistically carved and/or painted. Designs featured humans, animals, and/or vision powers.

TRANSPORTATION Several different types of red cedar canoes, from narrow trolling canoes to 20-person war canoes, served as water transportation.

DRESS Men often went naked in warmer weather and added a woven down and nettle-fiber shirt in winter. Women wore long skirts made of cedar-bark strips and sometimes added a shirt similar to that of the men. Extra clothing, often made of skins, was worn on trips into the interior. The people also made blankets of mountain goat and coyote wool as well as fibers of various plants.

WAR AND WEAPONS Regular enemies included the Lekwiltok (Kwakiutl) and Nootkans. Wars consisted of armadas of warriors armed with bow and arrow and spears. Warriors wore a long protective robe at least two heavy skins thick.

Contemporary Information

GOVERNMENT/RESERVATIONS In 1984, 234 reserves (approximately 25,000 hectares) were connected with 52 Canadian Coast Salish groups. Most Mainland Comox people lived on the Sliammon Indian Reserve. The Sechelt Indian Band Self-governing Act (1986) provided them with municipal constitutional and legislative powers. See profiles of selected bands under "Daily Life."

ECONOMY The people currently engage in various activities. See profiles of selected bands under "Daily Life" for details.

LEGAL STATUS Bands listed under "Daily Life" are all federally and provincially recognized.

DAILY LIFE Mainland Comox is still viable and spoken by about one-third of the population. See the following profiles of selected bands for further detail.

Selected Northern Coast Salish Bands in British Columbia (statistics are as of 1995):

Comox Band controls four reserves on 285 hectares of land on the east coast of Vancouver Island. The reserves were allotted in 1877. The population is 243, of whom 103 people live on the reserves. Elections are held under the provisions of the Indian Act. The band is affiliated with the Kwakiutl District Council. Children attend provincial schools. Important economic activities and resources include fishing, logging, and tourism. Facilities include a recreation building, a longhouse, and offices.

Homalco Band controls 11 reserves on 624 hectares of land near Calm Channel. The population is 346, of whom 130 people live on the reserves. Elections are held by custom. The band is affiliated with the Alliance Tribal Council. Children attend provincial schools. Important economic resources include a fish hatchery. Facilities include a recreation building and offices.

Klahoose Band controls ten reserves on 1,357 hectares of land on Cortes Island. The population is 242, of whom 45 people live in 16 houses on the reserves. Elections are held under the provisions of the Indian Act. The band is affiliated with the Alliance Tribal Council. Children attend provincial schools. Important economic activities include forestry and shell fishing. Facilities include a community center, a church, and offices.

Qualicum Band controls one 77-hectare reserve on the southeast coast of Vancouver Island. The reserve was allotted in 1876. The population is 91, of whom 50 people live in 16 houses on the reserves. Elections are held under the provisions of the Indian Act. The band is unaffiliated. Children attend provincial schools. Important economic resources include a fish hatchery and a campsite/store. Facilities include a sports field and offices.

Sechelt Band controls 33 reserves on more than 1,000 hectares of land 50 kilometers north of Vancouver. The population is 910, of whom 477 people live on the reserves. Elections are held under the provisions of their own constitution. The band is unaffiliated. Economic plans include a marina/hotel complex, a condominium complex, small businesses, and a fish hatchery. Facilities include a preschool.

Sliammon Band controls six reserves on 1,907 hectares of land near Powell River. The population is 775, of whom 569 people live in 165 houses on the reserves. Elections are held under the provisions of the Indian Act. The band is affiliated with the Alliance Tribal Council. Children attend band and provincial schools. Important economic activities and resources include a salmon hatchery, seafood products, forestry, land leases, and small businesses. Facilities include a gymnasium, a movie house, a clinic, group homes, a church, and offices.

Salish, Southern Coast

Southern Coast Salish (`Sal ish) refers to over 50 named, autonomous Indian groups or tribes inhabiting the Puget Sound region and speaking one of two languages. The component groups included (but were not limited to) Swinomish, Skagit (Lower Skagit or Whidby Island Skagits), Upper Skagit, Stillaguamish, Skykomish (perhaps once a subdivision of the Snoqualmie), and Snohomish (speakers of Northern Lushootseed); Steilacoom, Snoqualmie, Suquamish, Duwamish, Puyallup, Nisqually, and Squaxin (speakers of Southern Lushootseed); and Quilcene, Skokomish, and Duhlelip (speakers of Twana). Many of these groups themselves consisted of autonomous subdivisions. Little is known of these Indians' lives before their contact with non-natives.

LOCATION Southern Coast Salish people lived in and around the Puget Sound Basin in Washington. The climate is generally wet and moderate, with the northern areas somewhat drier. Although most of the land was timbered, some was kept open by regular burning practices. Most contemporary Southern Coast Salish Indians live on local reservations or in nearby cities and towns.

POPULATION The precontact population was estimated to be around 12,600. In 1990 there were probably over 20,000 self-identified Southern Coast Salish Indians. See individual entries under "Government/Reservations" under "Contemporary Information" for 1990 reservation populations.

LANGUAGE Southern Coast Salish, which includes the Lushootseed (Northern and Southern dialects) and Twana languages, is a member of the Central division of the Salishan language family.

Historical Information

HISTORY The basic Southern Coast Salish culture was in place at least 2,000 years ago. George Vancouver visited the region in 1792. By that time, evidence of metal and smallpox suggested that the Southern Coast Salish might already have encountered Europeans indirectly. Owing primarily to the lack of sea otters in their region, the Salish experienced little further contact for the next 30 years or so.

At least after 1827 and the establishment of the Hudson's Bay Company post on the Fraser River, the Southern Coast Salish were in regular contact with non-native traders. Fort Nisqually was founded in 1833. Among the cultural changes the Indians experienced were the introduction of firearms, the move away from traditional forms of dress, and the beginning of the potato crop. They also experienced new native ideas from remote places, such as the Plateau Prophet Dance.

Catholic missionaries arrived around 1840. The first U.S. settlers followed shortly thereafter, especially after the United States took control of the region by the Treaty of Washington (1846). In 1850, the Donation Land Act of Oregon allowed settlers to invade and claim Indian land. Washington Territory was officially established in 1853.

In 1854 and 1855, Southern Coast Salish Indians signed a number of treaties (Medicine Creek, Point Elliot, and Point No Point) ceding land and creating seven future reservations (Squaxin, Nisqually, Puyallup, Port Madison, Tulalip, Swinomish, and Skokomish). Notable chiefs who signed included Sealth (Suquamish/Duwamish, after whom the city of Seattle was named), Goliah (Skagit), and Patkanin (Snoqualmie). The Nisqually chief Leschi opposed the Medicine Creek Treaty, arguing that his people should settle near the mouth of the Nisqually River and other traditional subsistence areas. He was hanged by the Americans in 1858.

The Steilacooms were denied a reservation because of the planned development of the town of Steilacoom. Most joined other local reservations or remained in their homeland, becoming the ancestors of the modern tribe. Upper Skagits were left landless by the Point Elliot treaty; they later received and then lost several individual allotments.

In 1857, an executive order established the Muckleshoot Reservation (the Muckleshoots were an amalgam of several inland tribes and groups). During subsequent years these lands were whittled away by the Dawes Act and other legal and extralegal coercions (such as the unofficial toleration of illegal whiskey peddlers). Indians rebelled against unfair and dishonest treaty negotiations by engaging in the 1855–1856 Indian war and by refusing to move onto reservations.

However, by the 1850s, most Southern Coast Salish were heavily involved in the non-native economy; most sold their labor, furs, and other resources to non-Indians. Important and growing industries included logging, commercial fishing and canning, and hopyards. Seattle was founded in and grew out of a Duwamish winter village (in 1962, the government paid the members of the Duwamish tribe $1.35 an acre for land that had become the city of Seattle). The Duwamishes moved around the region, refusing to settle on reservations, until some joined the Muckleshoot and Tulalip Reservations. Whites burned them out of their homes in West Seattle in 1893. In 1925, though landless, they adopted a constitution and formed a government. Furthermore, most tribes came under the control of the rigidly assimilationist Bureau of Indian Affairs.

In 1917, the government commandeered most of the 4,700-acre Nisqually Reservation for Camp (later Fort) Lewis. Displaced Nisquallis scattered to various reservations and lands. During the 1960s, clashes between Indians and non-natives over fishing rights sometimes became violent; they were settled in the Indians' favor, however, in the 1970s. Contrary to government desires, they did not farm but maintained their hunting and fishing traditions.

The Puyallups did turn to agriculture during the 1870s. For that reason, they were seen by whites as having made great progress toward civilization. The growth of the adjacent city of Tacoma fueled pressure for the sale of unallotted lands; most of the reservation had been lost by the early twentieth century. The Puyallup were at the forefront of the fishing wars of the 1960s and 1970s. Many Snohomishes left their reservation during the last years of the nineteenth century as a result of overcrowding and oppressive government policies. These Indians, plus those who never moved to the Tulalip Reservation, became the historic Snohomish tribe.

The Tulalip tribes were created in 1855, as was the Tulalip Reservation, which was intended for the Snohomish, Snoqualmie, Stillaguamish, Skykomish, and others. The word "Tulalip" comes from a Snohomish word meaning "a bay shaped like a purse." Many of these Indians refused to settle on the reservation, however, and ended up landless.

By the 1860s, the Squaxins had abandoned their traditional dress but maintained other aspects of their culture. In 1874, about 30 Squaxins went to live at and became assimilated into the Twana community. Some Squaxins also owned allotments on the Quinault Reservation. In 1882, a Squaxin Indian, John Slocum, began the Indian Shaker Church, which emphasizes morality, sobriety, and honesty. This religion soon spread far and wide and continues today. The Snoqualmies were removed to the Tulalip Reservation after the Indian wars; they slowly assimilated into that and nearby white communities.

RELIGION According to the Twana, people were possessed of life souls and heart souls. Illness occurred if the former left the body. At death, life souls went to the land of the dead and were eventually reborn, whereas heart souls just disappeared. The people prayed to the sun and the earth, deities concerned with ethics. They also regarded salmon and other animal species as "people in their own country," complete with chiefs and other such conventions.

A mythological age ended when a transformer fashioned this world. Guardian spirits, both regular (lay) and shamanistic, were believed responsible for all luck, skill, and achievement. Shamans received the same powers as lay people, plus two unique powers as well. Spirit helpers and their associated songs were acquired through quests (or occasionally inheritance), which might begin as early as age eight and which consisted of fasting, bathing, and physical deprivation. Following the quest, nothing happened for up to 20 years, at which time the spirit returned (temporarily causing illness), the person sang and danced, and the power was activated. Shamans cured certain illnesses (such as soul loss) and could also cause illness and death, an explanation of why they were sometimes killed.

Southern Coast Salish Indians celebrated several regular ceremonies. The Winter Dance was sponsored by someone who was ill as a result of a returning spirit. There was much ritual connected with a "cure," including dancing, singing, feasting, and gift distribution. The soul recovery ceremony was an attempt to recapture a soul from the dead. Performers sang their spirit songs and dramatized a canoe search and rescue of soul. The potlatch was given by someone who had encountered a wealthy power and was to become wealthy himself. It was held in summer or early fall. The leading men of nearby villages and their families were invited. Guests brought food and wealth. Potlatches lasted for several days and included games, contests, secular songs, and dances, after which the sponsor gave away gifts and sang his power song.

Among the Twana, Suquamish, and maybe others, the *tamanawas* ceremony initiated new members (adolescents of both sexes with wealthy parents) into a secret religious society.

GOVERNMENT Each local group had one or more winter villages as well as several summer camps and resource sites. Village leaders were generally the heads of the wealthiest households; they had no formal leadership role. In Twana villages, the chief's speaker and village crier delivered brief sermons and awakened people, respectively.

CUSTOMS Villages consisted of one or more houses, which in turn sheltered several families, each within its own special section. Village membership may have been more permanent or stable in the south than in the north. Although they were truly autonomous, neighboring groups were linked by intermarriage, ceremonial and customary activities, and the use of common territories. Fishing sites and equipment could be individually or communally owned. Hunting was a profession among many Southern Coast Salish groups.

Classes, or social groups, included upper free (wealthy, high birth, sponsors of feasts and appropriate ceremonies), lower free (less wealth, common birth, fewer and less prestigious ceremonies), and slave (property). Recognition by the intervillage network was required to confirm or alter status. Possessions of woven blankets, dentalia, clamshell-disk beads, robes, pelts, bone war clubs, canoes, and slaves constituted wealth. House posts and grave monuments of high-status people were carved and/or painted. All except slaves and the very poor had their heads flattened in infancy. Popular games included gambling (dice and the disk and hand games) as well as games of skill and athletic contests. More southerly people smoked tobacco (obtained in trade) mixed with kinnikinnick (bearberry).

There were few proper birth ceremonies, although behavior was restricted for a new mother and father. At adolescence, both sexes were expected to seek visions, although a girl was subject to a greater number of behavioral restrictions, including isolation at her first period (and at all subsequent periods). Upper-class girls had "coming out parties" after their first isolation to announce their marriageability. Marriage was arranged by families, usually to people in different villages. It involved the ritual exchange of gifts. Divorce was possible but difficult, especially among the upper class. Death received the most ritualistic treatment. Professional undertakers prepared the body, which was interred in a canoe or an above-ground grave box. After the funeral there was a feast, and the deceased's property was given away.

DWELLINGS Permanent plank houses had shed

roofs (later, gambrel and gabled roofs) and were very similar to those of the Central Coast Salish. Several families (nuclear or extended, possibly including slaves) shared a house. Each family, or sometimes two, had its own fireplace. Co-wives might also share the house and have their own fireplaces. Cedar long-houses might be as large as 200 by 50 feet.

Some houses were built and used by wealthy men as potlatch houses. Temporary summer camp houses consisted of mats covering pole frames. Most villages had at least one sweat house. Stockades protected some villages. The famous "old man house," a Suquamish dwelling, once stood in the village of Suqua. It was about 500 feet long and 60 feet wide. The government ordered it burned in the 1870s.

DIET   Fish, especially salmon, was the staple for most groups. They also ate herring, smelt, flatfish, lingcod, sturgeon, and cutthroat and rainbow trout. Sea mammals included seals and beached whales. Of the land mammals, most people ate blacktail deer, black bear, elk, and smaller animals. Dogs were used to help in the hunt. Deer and elk were sometimes hunted in community drives. Other important foods included about 20 species of fowl; shellfish; and plants such as bracken, camus, and wapato as well as other roots, bulbs, sprouts, berries, and nuts. From the mid-1850s on, many of these groups raised pota-toes.

KEY TECHNOLOGY   Fishing equipment included seines, gill nets, weirs, traps, trawl nets, dip nets, lift nets, gaffs, harpoons, and herring rakes. For hunting, people used clubs, harpoons, bow and arrow, pitfalls, snares, nets, and flares (for night hunting). Wood-working was the primary male craft. Men used stone mauls, elk antler, yew wedges, and other tools to make canoes, house planks, utensils, bent-corner boxes, containers, dishes, and spoons.

Women worked with shredded cedar bark and cattail leaves, making cordage, mats (bed, canoe, wall), blankets, and baskets (including coiled cedar-root hard baskets) in various shapes and sizes. They also wove blankets of mountain goat wool, dog fur, and bird and fireweed down. Twana women made soft twined decorated baskets of sedge or cattail leaves. The Nisqually, a more interior people, made elk hide parfleches in which to carry food and store meat.

TRADE   The Southern Coast Salish regularly traded among themselves and their immediate neigh-bors as well as with interior groups and Indians east of the Cascade Mountains. Most of their canoes were obtained from outer coast peoples. Items from the east included mountain goat hair and hemp fiber.

NOTABLE ARTS   Wood carving and painting, weaving, and basket making were the most important arts. All men carved wood, but some were specialized craftsmen. Men also pecked or incised stone, bone, and antler. Boards used in the spirit canoe ceremony (a soul recovery ceremony) were elaborately painted.

TRANSPORTATION   Several types of cedar canoes were employed for purposes such as trolling, hunting, moving freight, and warfare. For major travel (such as travel to and from summer camps), people made a sort of catamaran by lashing some boards between two canoes. Upriver peoples used log rafts for cross-ing or traveling down streams. Winter hunters walked on snowshoes. Horses arrived in the area in the late eighteenth century, but only inland groups such as the Nisqually and Puyallup used them extensively.

DRESS   Most clothing was made of shredded cedar bark and buckskin. In warm weather, men wore breechclouts or nothing; women wore a cedar-bark apron and usually a skirt. In colder weather, men and some women wore hide shirts, leggings, and robes of bearskin as well as skins of smaller mammals sewn together. Both wore hide moccasins.

Some groups wore basketry or fur caps. Many wore abalone and dentalia earrings. Women also wore shell, teeth, and claw necklaces as well as leg and chin tattoos. Older men might keep hair on their faces.

WAR AND WEAPONS   Intragroup violence was usually dealt with by compensation and purification. Fighting, usually resulting from revenge, the ambi-tions of warriors, and slave raids, was usually with nonneighboring groups. Professional warriors did exist, although warfare was largely defensive in nature. Weapons included war clubs, daggers, spears, and bow and arrow (possibly poisoned). Hide shirts were worn as armor. Rather than fight, Twanas might hire shamans to harm other groups.

At least in the early nineteenth century, the South-ern Coast Salish had to deal with highly aggressive Lekwiltok Kwakiutl raiders. On at least one occasion the Salish tribes banded together to launch a retalia-tory expedition against the Kwakiutl. Some groups, such as the Skagit and Snohomish, had guns before they ever saw non-Indians.

Contemporary Information

GOVERNMENT/RESERVATIONS   The Skokomish Reservation (1874; 6,300 acres; 431 Indians/183 non-natives) includes Twana, Klallam, and Chimakum Indians. A constitution and by-laws were approved in 1938. They are governed by a tribal council. Their own court regulates hunting, fishing, and other laws.

The Port Madison Reservation (1855; 7,811 acres, less than half of which is Indian owned; 372 Indi-ans/4,462 non-natives) is home to the Suquamish tribe (Suquamish and Duwamish, roughly 800 in the mid-1990s). A 1965 constitution and by-laws call for an elected seven-member tribal council. A large number of non-Indians, not subject to tribal law, live on the reservation. Roughly 400 (1991) Duwamish Indians also live off-reservation.

The Muckleshoot Reservation (1857; 1,275 acres; 858 Indians/2,983 non-natives) adopted a constitution and by-laws in 1836, under the Indian Reorganization Act (IRA). Three new members are elected annually to the Muckleshoot Tribal Council. The tribe is a member of the Intertribal Court System (1978).

The Nisqually Reservation (1854; 941 acres; 363 Indians/215 non-natives) approved a constitution and by-laws in 1946. A council governs the Nisqually Indian Community.

The Puyallup Reservation (1855; less than 1,000 acres, almost none of which is Indian-owned; 906 Indians/31,486 non-natives) is governed by the Puyallup Tribal Council. The reservation is also home to some Nisquallis, Cowlitzes, Muckleshoots, Steilacooms, and other Indians.

The Tulalip (formerly the Snohomish) Reservation (1855; 10,667 acres; 1,193 Indians/5,910 non-natives) is home to the Tulalip tribes, who are mostly of Snohomish, Stillaguamish, Snoqualmie, Skykomish, Skagit, and Samish descent. The original constitution and by-laws were approved in 1936. A six-member board of directors is elected every three years.

The Upper Skagit Reservation (1981; roughly 99 acres; 162 Indians/18 non-natives) was purchased by the tribe. The tribe operates under a constitution and by-laws approved in 1974. A chair, elected annually, presides over the seven-member Upper Skagit Tribal Council. The tribe is also a member (with the Swinomish Indian Tribal Community and the Sauk-Suiattles) of the Skagit System Cooperative, which regulates fishing in the Skagit River system, and (with the Lummi, Nooksack, and Swinomish tribes) of the Northwest Washington Service Unit of the Indian Health Service. Tribal enrollment in 1993 was 552 people.

The Swinomish Reservation (1855; 3,602 acres; 578 Indians/1,704 non-natives) is located in Skagit County. Their constitution was adopted in 1936, under the IRA. Governed by the Swinomish Indian Senate, from which the principal tribal officers are elected, the Swinomish Indian Tribal Community (roughly 625 people in 1993) is composed of Swinomish, Kikiallus, Suquamish, Samish, and Upper and Lower Skagit peoples. They are members, with the Upper Skagit Reservation and the Sauk-Suiattles, of the Skagit System Cooperative.

The Squaxin Island Reservation (1854; 971 acres;

127 Indians/30 non-natives on trust lands) has been abandoned; most of the people live in and around Kamilche, the location of their tribal center, and Shelton, Washington. A constitution was accepted in 1965. The people are governed by a tribal council.

The Sauk-Suiattle Reservation (23 acres; 69 Indians/55 non-natives) separated from the Upper Skagits in 1946. Their constitution and by-laws, featuring a seven-member tribal council, were approved in 1975. They are members, with the Upper Skagit Reservation and the Swinomish Indian Tribal Community, of the Skagit System Cooperative.

The Stillaguamish Reservation (60 acres; 96 Indians/17 non-natives) was purchased with proceeds from a 1966 land claims settlement. The tribe of roughly 185 members is governed by a board of directors. It comanages 700 square miles of the Stillaguamish watershed.

The Snohomish Tribe was incorporated in 1927 and 1974. Its by-laws were written in 1928 and its constitution in 1934. It is governed by councils and chairpersons. Tribal enrollment in the early 1990s was about 900 people.

Most of the roughly 600 members of the Steilacoom tribe live in and around Pierce County. The tribal offices, including a museum, are in the town of Steilacoom. Their constitution and by-laws were originally created in the 1930s. They are governed by a nine-member council with three officers. There is also an honorary chieftain. They are largely assimilated.

ECONOMY Fisheries industries predominate, such as aquaculture, hatcheries, and fishing fleets. There are some traditional crafts as well as retail establishments such as stores, marinas, and restaurants. Tribes receive income from trust lands and leases. The Suquamish are involved in clamming, fishing, plant gathering, and bingo. The Muckleshoot are also involved with bingo, as are the Puyallups and Swinomish, and are planning a casino. Tribal governments also provide some employment. Unemployment, however, remains very high on most reservations.

Upper Skagits manufacture replica Northwest Coast bentwood boxes. They and several other tribes recently reached a multimillion-dollar settlement with Seattle City Light for losses sustained to their fisheries by the erection of dams on the Skagit River early in the century.

Tulalip is beginning to reduce its unemployment rate of greater than 40 percent. Part-time work includes fishing, logging, and crop picking. Tribal income is also derived from land leases to non-Indians, a number of small businesses, a bingo operation, and a casino. Economic plans include construction of a golf course, a business park, and a second casino.

LEGAL STATUS Fishing rights litigation came to a head in the 1960s and 1970s. The main point of contention was the paucity of the salmon run, which was due primarily to river diversions for power and irrigation. Indians were losing out on the competition for the remaining salmon. When the state of Washington regulated the Puyallup fishery in the name of conservation, the Puyallups fished illegally, justifying that activity by their treaty rights. In the landmark 1974 case of *U.S.* v. *Washington* (the so-called Boldt decision, later upheld almost in its entirety by the U.S. Supreme Court), the court held that traditional tribal fisheries are protected by the 1854 and 1855 treaties.

One result of this decision was that tribal governments began enforcing fishing regulations. Taxes went to support the tribal fisheries industries as well as some social services. The decision also helped to promote Indian identity by refocusing it on fishing as a core activity.

Federally recognized tribal entities include the Upper Skagit Tribe, the Sauk-Suiattle Tribe, the Swinomish Tribal Community (Swinomish, Skagit, Samish), the Skokomish Tribe (Twanas), the Suquamish Tribe, the Muckleshoot Tribe, the Nisqually Indian Community, the Puyallup Tribe, the Tulalip Tribes, the Stillaguamish Tribe, and the Squaxin Island Tribe. The Snoqualmie Tribe received full federal recognition in early 1998.

The Snohomish Tribe is a federally recognized political entity and has applied for tribal recognition. The Kikiallus Tribe, formerly a subdivision of the Skagits; the Steilacoom Tribe; the Duwamish Tribe; and the Snoqualmoo Tribe (derived from the Snoqualmies after a factional split in the 1840s) have petitioned for federal recognition. The Samish Tribe has been denied federal tribal recognition.

DAILY LIFE In general, the Southern Coast Salish people come together regularly for intertribal gatherings around traditional ceremonies and activities, such as winter spirit dancing and games.

The Suquamish Museum and Cultural Center (1980) is a center of that tribe's cultural life. The Suquamishes are predominantly Catholic. Their children attend public school. Chief Seattle Days, held in August in conjunction with the American Legion, celebrates local Indian culture, and other festivals are also open to the public. The Duwamish have formed a nonprofit corporation to foster tribal identity and culture. They still seek federal recognition and fishing rights.

The Muckleshoot Tribe has a community center, library, medical-dental clinic, educational training

programs, and police force. Many people are active in the Indian Shaker Church as well as the Pentecostal Church. A land reacquisition program is underway. Their Skopbsh celebration is held in early May.

The Puyallups hold a powwow in late summer. After two physical occupations, they regained title in 1980 to the site of a former Indian hospital. They now operate the Takopid Health Center, which provides a wide range of health care for Indians of hundreds of tribes. They also recently reached a land claims settlement with the government for $112 million for tribal land that illegally became the port of Tacoma. Most Puyallups are Christian, although traditional winter spirit dancing and healing ceremonies are still held. Lushootseed is taught in schools but is not generally spoken.

Numerous services on the Nisqually Reservation include a clinic, programs for the old and young, and a library, trading post, and bingo hall. Nisquallis participate in the Indian Shaker Church and various Christian churches.

Most of the approximately 100 Sauk-Suiattles live in Skagit County. Many work in the fishing and logging industries; unemployment on the reservation exceeds 80 percent. Many also practice spirit dancing, and there are members of the Indian Shaker Church and various Christian denominations.

As a result of dams, diking, and water diversions by public and private interests, the Skokomish lost important pieces of their lands in the twentieth century. They are currently trying to recover some of this land. Most Skokomish children attend public high school, although there is a tribal school for grades K–4. The tribe has native language and curriculum projects, plus a basketry project in conjunction with neighboring tribes. Most Skokomishes are either Pentecostals or Shakers, and some people practice the traditional *tamanawas* religion. The tribe observes several festivals, most connected with traditional activities such as personal naming and the first salmon run.

The Stillaguamish work mainly in Snohomish County. They are assembling a tribal history in order to learn more about their heritage. The tribal center features courses in arts and language, and the tribe operates a fish hatchery. Children of the Swinomish Indian Tribal Community attend public school. Most Swinomishes are Catholics. They hold the Swinomish festival, featuring traditional games, dances, and food, on Memorial Day. They also observe Treaty Days in late January and participate in local canoe races and powwows.

The Steilacoom Tribe is creating an activities learning center on five acres of land they lease from Fort Steilacoom Park (in Pierce County). The center emphasizes both traditional (basketry, wood carving) and modern (such as energy conservation) technology. Fort Steilacoom Community College coordinates programs with the tribe. There is an annual Elders Feast Day.

Most of the 1,000 or so Snoqualmies live on non-Indian lands throughout the Puget Sound area. A very few people still speak the native language. The tribe sponsors arts and crafts classes and trains traditional dancers.

Many Upper Skagits, on the Upper Skagit, the Swinomish, or the Sauk-Suiattle Reservation, retain elements of their traditional culture. The language is still spoken; shamans still practice; and traditional dances, music, and ceremonials, particularly pertaining to funerals, spirit powers, and the giving of inherited Indian names, are still important. A tribal center and a library are on the Upper Skagit Reservation.

Tulalip children attend public schools, including an elementary school on the reservation. Tribal members are attempting to revive the traditional crafts of basketry and wood carving. Instruction in Lushootseed is also offered. They celebrate First Salmon ceremonies as well as other traditional festivals, and much of the traditional social structure remains intact. Primarily as a result of intermarriage, assimilation, and allotment, the Skykomishes no longer constitute an identifiable tribe. The Snohomish continue to seek tribal recognition and a land base.

Squaxin Island people retain the use of the island for various activities. Most are Protestant, although some celebrate the First Salmon ceremony. The tribe is active in local environmental management programs and manages a hatchery and a salmon and steelhead fishery program.

Salish, Southwestern Coast

Southwestern Coast Salish (`Sal ish) is a term used to refer to the speakers of four closely related Salishan languages. Its component groups are Queets, Copalis, and Quinault, who are speakers of Quinault; Humptulips, Wynoochee, Chehalis, and Shoalwater Bay, who are speakers of Lower Chehalis; Satsop and Kwaiailk, or Upper Chehalis, who are speakers of Upper Chehalis; and Cowlitz, who are speakers of Cowlitz.

LOCATION   Traditionally, the Southwestern Coast Salish lived along the Pacific coast from just south of the Hoh River delta to northern Willapa Bay, including the drainages of the Queets, Quinault, Lower Cowlitz, and Chehalis River systems, all in the state of Washington. Local environments included rain forest, mountains, open ocean, sheltered saltwater bays, forest, and prairies. Today, most of these Indians live on local reservations or in Northwest cities and towns.

POPULATION   There were perhaps 2,500 Quinault and Lower Chehalis and about 8,000 Kwaiailks and (mostly Lower) Cowlitzes around 1800. In 1990, there were roughly 2,000 Southwestern Coast Salish Indians living on reservations (see "Government/Reservations" under "Contemporary Information") and at least half as many living in local cities and towns.

LANGUAGE   Southwest Salish, which includes the Quinault, Lower Chehalis, Upper Chehalis, and Mountain and Lower Cowlitz languages, is part of the Tsamosan (formerly Olympic) division of the Salishan language family. The Upper and Lewis River Cowlitz spoke dialects of Sahaptian.

Historical Information

HISTORY   In 1775, Southwestern Coast Salish encountered and killed Spanish explorers and salvaged their ship for iron. By the late 1780s, Indians were used to trading with Europeans and had already experienced population loss from European diseases.

The Lower Chehalises were among the people who traded with Meriwether Lewis and William Clark in 1805–1806. Contact with non-natives was commonplace after Astoria was founded on the Columbia estuary in 1811. The Hudson's Bay Company founded local posts such as Fort Vancouver (1825), Fort Nisqually (1833), and Cowlitz Farm (1839). Some Cowlitz groups became mixed with the Klickitats, an inland group, during the early nineteenth century. As access to European goods increased, Indians also skirmished among themselves for control of the inland trade.

A malaria epidemic devastated Indian populations in the 1830s and resulted in significant village abandonment and consolidation. For instance, the Chinook and Lower Chehalis people combined in a bilingual tribe known as Shoalwater Bay Indians; the Salishan-Chinook language (as well as the tribe's later adoption of Lower Chehalis) eventually died out altogether. The Treaty of Washington (1846) and the Donation Land Act (1850) allowed non-natives to appropriate Indian land. Many Indians, especially inlanders, were driven away, exterminated, and/or had their food resources destroyed or taken.

Cowlitzes refused to sign the 1855 treaty because it did not provide a reservation in their homelands. Along with many other tribes, they fought the United States in the Indian wars of 1855–1856. After inflicting severe dislocations, the government ordered them to remove to the Chehalis Reservation, but they refused, continuing to hold out for their own reservation. Many groups refused to sign treaties or accept goods from Indian agents, fearing that such action would be seen as evidence of forfeiture of land title.

The Quinault River Treaty in 1855 did provide that tribe with a reservation in exchange for vast areas of their traditional lands. In 1864, the Chehalis Reservation was created—without treaties or the formal Indian cession of land—for Chehalis, Cowlitz, and some southern coastal people, but most remained near their homes. These people either became assimilated into white population or joined the Chehalis Confederated Tribes or other tribes. Most Chehalis Reservation land was later reappropriated; the rest was homesteaded by 36 Indians and set aside for school purposes.

The Shoalwater Bay Tribe and Georgetown Reservation were created in 1866. The tribe was composed mainly of Chehalis and Chinook families living on Willapa (formerly Shoalwater) Bay. By 1879, these Indians all spoke the Lower Chehalis dialect.

All reservation Indians experienced pressure to Christianize, take up farming, and give up their culture. Corrupt agents profited on their rations. Of necessity and desire, hunting, fishing, and gathering continued, although Indians increasingly became involved in the cash economy (logging, farming, and railroads).

The Quinaults remained relatively isolated until the late 1880s. During the early twentieth century, a legal ruling allowed members from various non-Quinault tribes to claim allotments on that reservation and to apply for (and receive) status as Quinaults. This process first resulted mostly in environmental degradation and a sharply decreased salmon run as a result of clearcutting and then in the attendant relocation of people off the reservation.

RELIGION Southwestern Coast Salish religion centered around the relation of individuals, including slaves, to guardian spirits. Spirits lived either in the land of the dead or in animate and inanimate objects. They provided wealth, power, skill, and/or luck. Songs, dances, and paraphernalia were associated with particular spirits. Spirits not properly honored could be dangerous. Training (such as bathing, fasting in lonely places, and other physical tests) to acquire a spirit began as early as about age seven and culminated in a formal spirit quest at adolescence.

Shamans, who might be men or women, had especially powerful spirits. They diagnosed and cured disease. They could also cause illness or death and were occasionally hired for this purpose. Feasts involved only local people; potlatches were intertribal. The latter, held in winter, were given at life-cycle events or at the perceived bequest of a spirit. Social status was closely related to potlatching activity.

Spirit song ceremonials were observed in winter, accompanied among some tribes by gift giving. Some coastal groups also had secret societies. Most groups celebrated first salmon rituals during which they burned the salmon's heart and distributed some of the fish to all villagers.

GOVERNMENT Politically independent villages were each composed of between one and ten households, each household consisting of several families. A nonpolitical "tribe" was recognized as several villages that shared a language and a territory. Village leaders tended to come from certain families, with the eldest son often inheriting the leadership position. Leaders were wealthy and often owned several slaves so they would not have to work as hard as others did. Their power was limited to giving advice and settling disputes. In some villages (the Quinault, for example), speakers announced the chief's decisions and negotiated with other villages. This office was obtained by merit. Some villages also had official jokers or buffoons.

CUSTOMS Property rights, such as the control of subsistence areas and even the use of particular parts of a whale, were inheritable and carefully controlled. One's work and social activities depended on gender, talent, status, and the possession of an appropriate spirit power. Shamans had especially powerful spirit powers.

The basic social distinction was between slave and free, although some free people were wealthier and more influential than others. Houses were owned by the man who contributed the most labor and materials to its construction. He also directed certain subsistence activities such as weir building. Upon his death, the house would be torn down; it might be rebuilt nearby, or else the former members would each build a new house.

Girls were secluded for up to several months at the onset of puberty. Marriage, especially among the wealthy, began a permanent cycle of mutual gift and food giving. Families of deceased spouses generally provided replacements. Free people were interred in a box or double canoe (one over the other) that was placed in a tree or on posts. Their possessions were either given away or interred with them. The house was purified or destroyed. Among the wealthy, reburial might take place after a year or two.

DWELLINGS Cedar-planked, gabled houses were arrayed along a river. A door was set at one or both ends. From two to four families, or sometimes more, lived in a house. Partitions divided sections for menstruating women. Sleeping platforms with storage space underneath ran along the interior walls. Shorter benches in front of the houses were used for sitting and as a place for men to talk and work. Interior walls might be lined with mats.

Temporary summer shelters were made of cedar-bark slabs or mat- or bough-covered pole frames.

People also occasionally stayed in temporary bark or brush hunting shelters.

DIET Fish, especially all five types of salmon, was the food staple. Besides salmon, the people used sturgeon, trout, eulachon (or smelt), halibut, herring, and cod. Fish were eaten fresh or smoke dried. Eulachon was used mainly for its oil. Other important foods included shellfish; land mammals (especially in the Quinault highlands and among the Kwaiailks) such as deer, elk, and bear; water fowl and birds; sea mammals; and plants, especially inland, such as camas, berries, crabapples, roots, and shoots. Inland people burned prairie land every two to three years.

KEY TECHNOLOGY Fishing equipment included nets (trawl, gill, drift, dip), weirs, clubs, traps, harpoons, hook and line, herring rakes, and gaffs. People hunted with bow and arrow, deadfalls, nooses, snares, and nets. Professional woodworkers made most houses and canoes as well as bent-corner and bent-bottom boxes, utensils, and tools. The basic woodworking tool was the adz. Women shredded bark and sewed and twined mats. They also made baskets, mostly of spruce root along the coast.

TRADE Neighbors regularly traded and intermarried. Dentalium shells served as currency for durable goods. Food and raw materials were usually exchanged for the same. Canoes were widely exchanged. The Copalises provided many groups with razor clams. The local trading complex stretched from Vancouver Island to south of the Columbia River and also east of the Cascades.

NOTABLE ARTS Baskets (especially Cowlitz coiled baskets), carved and painted wooden items, and Quinault spirit masks were the region's most important art objects.

TRANSPORTATION Canoes were the predominant travel mode. Men made and traded for canoes of varying shapes and sizes, depending on function. Rafts were kept at river crossings. Inland groups acquired horses by at least the early nineteenth century.

DRESS Men went naked in the summer; women wore knee-length shredded bark skirts. Both wore fur or skin clothing in colder weather, with robes of dog or rabbit fur or bird skins. The wealthy might wear sea otter–skin robes. Hunters wore leggings and moccasins in winter. Waterproof rainwear was made of cattail fiber. The Quinault wore twined split spruce-root rain hats. Body paint and tattooing were customary, as was infant head flattening, especially with groups nearest the lower Columbia River. Many men along the coast wore mustaches.

WAR AND WEAPONS Most disputes between villages were usually settled by some form of economic arrangement such as formal compensation or marriage. In general, the Cowlitz were on unfriendly terms with coastal groups, and the Queets fought the Quileute and sometimes the Quinault. The Chehalis killed many Queets and burned their villages around 1800; they also regularly attacked the Copalises. Queets, Quinaults, Hohs, and Quileutes occasionally confederated to oppose the Klallams, Makahs, Satsops, and others.

Fighting was more regulated in the south, and there no slaves were taken. Weapons included mussel-shell knives, whalebone daggers, yew spears with shell or bone points, whale-rib and stone clubs, and the bow and arrow. Elk hide shirts and helmets and cedar shields (Chehalis), as well as slatted wood breast-plates, provided protection in war.

Contemporary Information

GOVERNMENT/RESERVATIONS In 1990, 942 Quinault, Quileute, Chinook, Hoh, Chehalis, Queets, and Cowlitz Indians lived on the Quinault Reservation, in Taholah, Washington (1855; 340 square miles). These people adopted by-laws in 1922. A new constitution in 1975 gave decision-making powers to an 11-member business committee. Much of the reservation is owned by non-Indian timber and milling companies. Quinault tribal enrollment in the early 1990s was about 2,400.

The Shoalwater (Georgetown) Reservation (1866; 1,035 acres; about 100 residents and 150 enrolled members in 1993) is located in Pacific County, Washington. The people rejected the Indian Reorganization Act but adopted a constitution and became formally organized in 1971. They elected a tribal council shortly thereafter.

In 1990, 307 Chehalis, Quinault, Muckleshoot, Nisqually, Klallam, and other Indians lived on the Chehalis Reservation, Oakville, Washington (1864; 1,952 acres). A constitution and by-laws were adopted in 1939. They are governed by the generally elected Chehalis Community Council, which then elects a business committee.

The Cowlitz Tribe of Indians is an unincorporated association formed to press land claims and maintain traditions. Their constitution and by-laws provide for a five-member executive committee. They have a small (17.5 acres) land base along the Cowlitz River. The tribe divided in 1973 over a $1.55 million land claims settlement when a small group, subsequently calling itself the Sovereign Cowlitz Tribe, preferred to hold out for land. The 1990 population of the Cowlitz Indian Nation was 1,689.

ECONOMY Important economic activities include fishing and related industries, government-related jobs, logging and related industries, building trades, and social services. There is a restaurant at

Shoalwater Bay and a bingo parlor at Chehalis. Some income is earned from allotment leases. An arts and crafts manufacturing factory, a fish-processing plant, restaurants, and food markets are on the Quinault Reservation.

LEGAL STATUS   The Cowlitz Indian Tribe is recognized by the state of Washington and won preliminary approval for federal recognition in early 1998. The Confederated Tribes of the Chehalis Reservation, the Quinault Indian Nation, and the Shoalwater Bay Tribe are federally recognized tribal entities.

DAILY LIFE   The Quinaults exercise sovereignty over their territory, participating in a federal self-governance project and rehabilitating depleted and destroyed natural resources. A tribal police force and court system help to maintain order on the Quinault Reservation. There is some dissension over jurisdiction between the tribe and the Quinault Allottees Association, composed of members of other tribes with allotments on the Quinault Reservation. Children attend classes in the Indian-oriented Taholah schools. The contemporary style of Quinault art is influenced by South Sea Island art forms. Although most Quinaults are Protestant, some older members attend the Indian Shaker Church. An annual trout derby, featuring canoe races, is held in late May. Talolah Days take place on the Fourth of July.

The Chehalis Reservation maintains a water system and river clean-up operations. They have a tribal center, a health clinic, a meeting room for the elderly, a library, classrooms, and tribal offices. The county sheriff enforces laws. Most children attend public schools. Programs exist to preserve native language and culture. A tribal history was published in 1980. Tribal Days at the end of May feature games, dances, and feasting. Assembly of God and the Indian Shaker churches have a strong presence on the reservation.

The Shoalwater Bay people run a restaurant and work with non-Indians in the surrounding area. Children attend public school. Funds from a land claims settlement have been invested in reacquiring land. Health care is quite poor. Ongoing traditions include the passing on of hereditary names, annual fishing and gathering, and involvement in the Indian Shaker Church.

Cowlitz Indians have maintained their government and tribal authority since aboriginal times. The native languages have been lost, however, with the possible exception of some Sahaptian among those enrolled on the Yakima Reservation. Recently, they have been involved in several efforts to protect their ancestral lands from the ravages of dams. Many Cowlitzes continue to seek personal spirit guidance through vision quests. The system of extended family networks, so characteristic of traditional life, remains intact.

Samish
See Salish, Central Coast

Sauk-Suiattle
See Salish, Southern Coast

Shoalwater Bay
See Salish, Southwestern Coast

Siltez, Confederated Tribes of
See Coosans; Upper Umpqua

Siuslawans
See Coosans

Skagit
See Salish, Southern Coast

Skokomish (Twana)
See Salish, Southern Coast

Snohomish
See Salish, Southern Coast

Snoqualmie
See Salish, Southern Coast

Snoqualmoo
See Salish, Southern Coast

Squaxin
See Salish, Southern Coast

Steilacoom
See Salish, Southern Coast

Stillaguamish
See Salish, Southern Coast

Suquamish
See Salish, Southern Coast

Swinomish
See Salish, Southern Coast

Tillamook

Tillamook (`Til ə m ū k) is a Chinookan word for a Tillamook place-name, possibly meaning "land of many waters" or "People of Nehalem." These people were formerly referred to by other names, such as Calamoxes.

LOCATION   The Tillamook traditionally lived along a coastal strip from roughly Tillamook Head to the Siletz River, in present-day Oregon.

POPULATION   The Tillamook population stood

at about 2,200 in 1805. In 1950 it was under 250. In 1990 roughly 50 Tillamook descendants lived in and around Oregon.

LANGUAGE Tillamook is a Salishan language. Its dialects included Nehalem, Nestucca, Salmon River (Nechesnan), and Siletz (Tillamook proper).

Historical Information

HISTORY History records the first contact between the Tillamook and non-natives as occurring in 1788, although iron knives and smallpox scars told of at least indirect encounters previously. They were also visited by Meriwether Lewis and William Clark. Regular contact with traders began after 1811. Epidemics of malaria, syphilis, smallpox, and other diseases, as well as guns and liquor, diminished the Tillamook population by around 90 percent in the 1830s and greatly reduced the number of their villages.

In 1850, the Donation Land Act opened Tillamook lands for white settlement. Indians ceded land in an unratified 1851 treaty, and the few surviving Tillamooks either remained in place, officially landless, or were removed to the Siletz or Grand Ronde Reservations. Under the leadership of the peaceful Kilchis, Tillamooks refused to participate in the wars of the 1850s. Awards from the Indian Land Claims Commission in 1958 and 1962 did little to reunite a scattered and unorganized people. Congress officially terminated its relationship with the Tillamook in 1956.

RELIGION Tillamooks attempted to gain power from spirits, whom they believed were more active and closer to humans in winter. Shamans renewed their power in January or February by sponsoring a ceremony that included singing a power song and dispensing food and presents to guests. During the course of this 5- to 15-day ceremony, all other "knowers" (those with spirit powers) sang their songs too. Winter was also the time for relating myth narratives. Mythological characters were particularly important because social status was dependent on one's ability to form a relationship with a mythological personage, a natural feature, or a guardian spirit. Rituals also accompanied the first seasonal consumption of various foods.

GOVERNMENT Society was divided into the many free and the few slave people as well a majority of people who had acquired guardian spirits and a minority of those who had not. The elite were wealthy and experts in doctoring, war, and hunting. Women received status from their own guardian spirits or from those of their close relatives. Older women were accorded higher status.

Depending on the particular activity, different people, including shamans, headmen, and warriors, played leadership roles in the numerous small villages. Headmen were particularly skilled orators and negotiators. Most disputes, up to and including murder, were settled by arbitration and involved payment. This was often the case even with people from other villages.

CUSTOMS After a baby's birth, the mother remained confined and taken care of for 15 days while the father forfeited sleep for 10 nights. Free infants' heads were deformed. Infants were fed on demand and sucked elk sinew pacifiers. Children were formally named at an ear-piercing ceremony; boys also had their nasal septa pierced. This ceremony included feasting and dancing and varied according to the family's wealth. Children were rarely punished corporally. A boy's first food kill and a girl's first gathered food were reserved for the elderly.

Girls were secluded at the onset of puberty and underwent a series of ritual behaviors and food taboos. One such ritual was an all-night guardian spirit vigil in the woods, during which the girl repeatedly bathed in a cold stream. Any spirits gained during this quest remained inactive until middle age. At puberty, boys fasted and undertook guardian spirit quests that also included bathing. A boy's personal power and adult occupation were equated with the spirit song he obtained at that time. Boys, too, activated their spirit powers only at middle age.

Although marriages were arranged, the principals were consulted and respected. Bride and groom prices were commensurate with their family's status. Initial residence was in the groom's parents' village. High-status men might have more than one wife. Infanticide was a common result of illegitimate births.

Corpses were painted, dressed, wrapped in a blanket, and bound with cedar bark. After a two- to three-day wake, they were buried in raised canoes. Wealthy families might reopen the grave after a year, clean the bones, and replace the grave goods.

The Tillamook recognized five types of shamans: healers (men, by drawing with the hands, and women, by sucking), poison doctors (men, with much ritual paraphernalia to send and extract poisons), spirit doctors (men who personally retrieved lost spirits from the spirit world), love doctors (women); and baby diplomats (men who foretold events by conversing with babies).

DWELLINGS Winter villages were usually built at the mouths of rivers or streams. They typically consisted of several houses, at least one work-and-menstrual hut, sweat houses, and a graveyard. Rectangular houses, which were occupied by up to four families, were constructed of cedar planks tied together with peeled and steamed spruce roots. Roofs were gabled with overlapping planks. Each had several fires in a center pit and sleeping platforms along the sides. Some houses were built aboveground and some were semisubterranean (with a door in the roof and entrance via a ladder). Mat partitions separated families and multiple wives. Floors were covered by ferns and rush mats. Pitch torches or fish-head or whale-oil lamps provided extra light. Roots were kept in pits beneath the floor.

DIET Salmon and other fish were the staples. Other seafood included sea lions, seals, and shellfish. Women gathered salmonberries, huckleberries, strawberries, camas, ferns, and other plant foods. Men hunted elk, beaver, muskrat, bear, and waterfowl. Many foods were either steamed in earth ovens, stone-boiled in baskets or bowls, or dried on racks.

KEY TECHNOLOGY Canoes, bone needles and awls, and baskets were among the most important material items. Fish were caught in weirs, traps, and seine and gill nets. They were also clubbed or harpooned.

TRADE The Tillamook were part of a flourishing regional trade. In general, they traded tanned beaver hides, canoes, and baskets to northern Columbia River peoples for abalone shell, dentalia, buffalo hides and buffalo horn dishes, and dried salmon. The Tillamook bought wapato roots and other items from Columbia River peoples east of the Coastal Range. They traded and intermarried with the Kalapuyas, and they also raided their southern neighbors for slaves, which they sold in the north.

NOTABLE ARTS Women made excellent wrap-twined baskets.

TRANSPORTATION Canoes of several sizes and shapes were used for travel and fishing. They were single-log dugouts, painted black on the outside and red on the inside, and coated with pitch.

DRESS Women wore large grass, tule rush, or shredded-bark back aprons, small front aprons, and buckskin leggings. Men wore fur or basketry caps, breechclouts, buckskin shirts, and hide pants. Beaver and painted buckskin capes and rabbit, bobcat, or sea otter fur blankets kept people warm in the winter. Footgear included both moccasins and snowshoes. Items such as menstrual pads and diapers were made of cedar bark. Both sexes painted their hair part red and wore ear pendants. Men also wore nose pendants. Women wore decorative tattoos, but men's tattoos were only to measure dentalium.

WAR AND WEAPONS Weapons included hunting equipment as well as elk hide armor. The Tillamook painted themselves for war with red and black stripes. Their enemies may have included the Chinook and

the Kalapuyans. Slave raiding may have been a primary object of war.

Contemporary Information

GOVERNMENT/RESERVATIONS Since termination, Tillamook descendants have declined to organize or to seek a reversal of their unrecognized status. Some are members of the Confederated Tribes of Siletz and the Grande Ronde community.

ECONOMY Tillamooks have no distinct economic activities.

LEGAL STATUS The Tillamook people are not recognized as a distinct native entity by any state government or by the federal government.

DAILY LIFE Tillamooks are integrated within their native and non-native communities. There are few reminders in their daily lives of their Native American heritage.

Tlingit

Tlingit (`Tl ē n git or `Kl ē n kit), meaning "human beings," is taken from the group's name for themselves. The Coastal Tlingit were a "nationality" of three main groups—Gulf Coast, Northern, and Southern—united by a common language and customs. The Interior Tlingit have never considered themselves a cohesive tribe.

Of the three major groups of coastal Tlingits, the Gulf Coast group included the Hoonah of Lituya Bay; the Dry Bay people at the mouth of the Alsek River, who were established in the eighteenth century by a conglomeration of Tlingits and Athapaskans; and the Yakutat, who were composed of Eyak speakers from the Italio River to Icy Bay. In 1910 the Yakutat merged with the Dry Bay people. Northern Tlingits included the Hoonah on the north shore of Cross Sound, the Chilkat-Chilkoot, Auk, and Taku; the Sumdum on the mainland; and the Sitka and Huntsnuwu, or Angoon, on the outer islands and coasts. The Southern Tlingit included the Kake, Kuiu, Henya, and Klawak on the islands and the Stikine or Wrangell, Tongass, and Sanya or Cape Fox along the mainland and sheltered waters.

LOCATION Coastal Tlingit groups lived along the Pacific coast from roughly Icy Bay in the north to Chatham Sound in the south, or roughly throughout the Alaskan panhandle. This country, no more than 30 miles wide, but roughly 500 miles long, is marked by a profusion of fjords, inlets and bays, and islands, most of which are mountainous. The climate is marked by fog, rain, snow, and strong winds in fall and winter. Most Coastal Tlingits live in Alaska and in cities of the greater Northwest.

Interior Tlingits lived along the upper Taku River, although during the nineteenth and twentieth centuries, and in response both to the fur trade and the gold rush, most moved to the headwaters of the Yukon River. Many contemporary Interior Tlingit live in Teslin Village (Yukon Territory) and Atlin (British Columbia). Some also live in Whitehorse (Yukon) and Juneau (Alaska).

POPULATION Total Tlingit population was at least 10,000 in 1740. Inland Tlingits probably never numbered more than 400. In the early 1990s there were roughly 14,000 Tlingits in the United States and 1,200 in Canada.

LANGUAGE Tlingit is remotely related to Athapaskan languages.

Historical Information

HISTORY Humans have lived in Tlingit country for at least 10,000 years; continuous occupation of the region began around 5,000 years ago. People probably came from the south, with Tlingit culture perhaps having its origins near the mouths of the Nass and Skeena Rivers about 800 years ago. The earliest Tlingit villages had disappeared by historic times, however, and a new migration into the area began in the eighteenth century, as the Haida displaced southern Tlingit groups.

Russian explorers in 1741 were the first non-natives to enter the region. Spanish explorers heralded the period of regular interracial contact in 1775. The Russians had established a regular presence in 1790. They built a fort at Sitka in 1799 that fell to the Indians three years later. The Russians rebuilt in 1805, however, and made the fort the headquarters of the Russian-American Company from 1808 until 1867. Although the Tlingits maintained their independence during the Russian period, they did acquire tools and other items. Many fell to new diseases (a particularly severe smallpox outbreak occurred from 1835 to 1839), and some were converted to the Russian Orthodox Church.

In 1839, when the Hudson's Bay Company acquired trading rights in southeastern Alaska from the Russian-American Company, the region saw an influx of European-manufactured goods. The advent of steel tools had a stimulating effect on traditional wood carving. During this time, the Tlingit successfully resisted British attempts to break their trade monopoly with the interior tribes. By the 1850s, Tlingits were trading as far south as Puget Sound and had regular access to alcohol and firearms from the Americans.

Tlingits protested the U.S. purchase of Alaska in 1867, arguing that if anyone were the rightful "owner" of Alaska, it was they and not the Russians. In any case, the soldiers, miners, and adventurers who arrived after the purchase severely mistreated and abused the Indians. For much of the last half of the nineteenth century, U.S. naval authorities persecuted shamans thought to be involved with witches. Although Tlingits owned southeast Alaska under aboriginal title, they were prevented from filing legal claims during, and thus profiting from, the great Juneau gold rush of 1880. The mines ultimately yielded hundreds of millions of dollars worth of gold, of which wealth the Tlingit saw little or none.

Commercial fishing and canning as well as tourism in the area became established in the 1870s and 1880s, providing jobs (albeit at wages lower than those earned by white workers) for the Indians. The Klondike gold rush of 1898–1899 brought more money and jobs to the region. Meanwhile, Christian missionaries, especially Presbyterians, waged an increasingly successful war against traditional Indian culture.

By 1900 many Tlingit had become acculturated. They had given up their subsistence economy and abandoned many small villages. Many worked in canneries in British Columbia or picked hops in Washington. Potlatches began to diminish in number and significance, and many ceremonial objects were sold to museums. Despite this level of acculturation, however, some mid–nineteenth century Tlingit villages continued to exist into the twentieth century.

In 1915, Alaska enfranchised all "civilized" natives, but severe economic and social discrimination continued, including a virtual apartheid system during the first half of the twentieth century. Some villages incorporated in the 1930s under the Indian Reorganization Act and acquired various industries. After World War II the issue of land led to the formation of the Central Council of Tlingit and Haida, which in 1968 won a land claims settlement of $7.5 million ($0.43 an acre).

Despite Tlingit efforts, Alaska schools were not integrated until 1949. The Alaska Native Brotherhood (ANB), founded in Sitka in 1912 by some Presbyterian Indians, was devoted to rapid acculturation; economic opportunity, including land rights; and the abolition of political discrimination. The Alaska Native Sisterhood (ANS) was founded soon after. Both organizations reversed their stand against traditional practices in the late 1960s.

RELIGION Animals and even natural features had souls similar to those of people. Thus they were treated with respect, in part to win their help or to avoid their malice. Hunters engaged in ritual purification before the hunt, and during the hunt the hunter as well as his family back home engaged in certain formal rules of behavior.

Shamans were very powerful. Most were men. Shamans could cure, control weather, bring success in hunting, tell the future, and expose witches, but only if they were consulted in time and not impeded by another shaman. Their powers came from spirits that could be summoned by a special song. A shaman underwent regular periods of physical deprivation to keep spiritually pure. Neither he nor his wife could cut their hair.

GOVERNMENT The basic political units were matrilineal clans of two divisions, Raven and Eagle. Each clan was subdivided into lineages or house groups. Thus, the tribes, or groups, listed above lacked any overall political organization and were really local communities made up of representatives of several clans. All territory and property rights were held by the clans. Clan and lineage chiefs, or head-men, assigned their group's resources, regulated subsistence activities, ordered the death of trespassers, and hosted memorial ceremonies.

CUSTOMS The two divisions served as opposites for marriage and ceremonial purposes. Some clans and lineages moved among neighboring groups such as the Haida, Tsimshian, and Eyak. A clan's crest represented its totem, or the living things, heavenly bodies, physical features, and supernatural beings associated with it. Crests were displayed on house posts, totem poles, canoes, feast dishes, and other items. All present members of an opposite division received payment to view a crest, because in so doing they legitimated both the display and the crest's associated privileges. All clan property could be bought and sold, given as gifts, or taken in war.

In general, spring brought hunting on the mainland, halibut fishing in deep waters, and shellfish and seaweed gathering. Seal hunting began in late spring, about the time of the first salmon runs. Summer activities generally included catching and curing salmon, berrying, and some sealing. Summer was also the time for wars and slave raids. Fall brought some sea otter hunting (land otter were never killed). In the late nineteenth century, fall was also the time for more salmon fishing and curing, potato harvesting, and hunting in the interior. Winter villages were established by November. Winter was the season for potlatches and trading.

Individuals as well as lineages were ranked, from nobility to commoners. Slaves were entirely outside the system. (Slaves were freed after the United States purchased Alaska and were brought into the social system on the lowest level.) Women had high status, probably because they controlled the food supply (not catching fish but the much harder and more laborious jobs of cutting, drying, smoking, and baling it). Any injury to someone in another clan required an indemnity. Clan disagreements were usually but not always settled peacefully. The three important feasts were the funeral feast, memorial potlatch feast, and childrens' feast.

All babies were believed to be reincarnations of maternal relatives. At about age eight, a boy went to live with his maternal uncle, who saw that he toughened and purified himself and learned the traditions and responsibilities of his clan and lineage. Girls were confined in a dark room or cellar for up to two years (according to rank and wealth) at their first period, at which time they learned the traditions of their clan, performed certain rituals, and observed behavior restrictions. At the end of this time their ears were pierced, high-status families gave a potlatch, and girls were considered marriageable.

Only people of opposite divisions but similar clans and lineages could marry. Marriage formalities included mutual gift giving. Southerners erected tall mortuary totem poles near their houses. Death initiated a mourning period and several rituals, including singing and the funeral. Cremation occurred on the fourth day, except possibly longer for a chief. Widows observed particularly restrictive mourning rituals. A person's slaves were sometimes killed. The evening after the cremation, mourners held a feast for their division opposites. Dead slaves were simply cast onto the beach. Burial was adopted in the late nineteenth century.

DWELLINGS Tlingits usually lived in one main (winter) village and perhaps one or more satellite villages. In the early nineteenth century, the former consisted of a row of rectangular, slightly excavated, gable-roofed planked houses facing the water. Each house could hold 40–50 people, including about six families and a few unmarried adults or slaves. Each family slept on partitioned wooden platforms that could be removed to make a larger ceremonial space.

Other features included a central smoke hole and a low, oval front doorway. The four main house posts were carved and painted in totemic or ancestral designs. Palisades often surrounded houses or whole villages. Other village structures included smokehouses, small houses for food and belongings, sweat houses, and menstrual huts.

In the nineteenth century, Inland Tlingits lived in rectangular houses similar to those of the coastal people. They also built brush lean-tos that could shelter up to 10 or 15 people.

DIET Fish was the staple, especially all five species of salmon, as well as eulachon, halibut, and herring. Fish was boiled, baked, roasted, or dried and smoked for winter. Whole salmon might be frozen for winter use. Other important seafoods included shellfish, seaweed, seal, sea lion, sea otter, and porpoise.

The people also ate land mammals such as deer, bear, and mountain sheep and goat. Dogs assisted in the hunt. Inland Tlingit hunted caribou, moose, and some wood bison. Beaver were speared or netted under ice. Migrating waterfowl provided meat as well as feathers, eggs, and beaks. Some groups gathered a variety of berries, plus hemlock inner bark, roots (riceroot, fern), and shoots (salmonberries, cow parsnips). They began cultivating potatoes after the Russians introduced the food in the early nineteenth century.

People sucked cultivated tobacco mixed with other materials; they began smoking it when the Russians introduced leaf tobacco and pipes in the late eighteenth century.

KEY TECHNOLOGY   Salmon were caught in rectangular, wooden traps; trapped behind stone walls; or impaled on wooden stakes in low water. Other fishing equipment include hook and (gut) line, harpoons, and copper knives. Men hunted with spears, bow and arrow, a whip sling, and darts. Raw materials included horn (spoons, dishes, containers), wool (blankets), and wood (fire drill, watertight storage and boiling boxes). Tlingits began forging iron in the late eighteenth century, although some iron was acquired from intercontinental trade or drift wreckage in aboriginal times. Some foods were baked in earth ovens.

TRADE   Imports included walrus ivory from Bering Sea Eskimos, copper from interior tribes, dentalia shell from the south, Haida canoes, Tsimshian carvings, slaves, furs, skin garments decorated with porcupine quills, and various fish products. Exports included Chilkat blankets, seaweed, leaf tobacco, and fish oil. Intragroup trade was largely ceremonial in nature. When the whites came, Tlingits tried to monopolize that trade, even going so far as to travel over 300 miles to destroy a Hudson's Bay Company post.

Inland Tlingit trade partners included the Tahltan, Kaska, Pelly River Athapaskan, and Tagish.

NOTABLE ARTS   Tlingits excelled at wood carving, especially ceremonial partitions in house chiefs' apartments, bentwood boxes, chests, and bowls, house posts (usually shells fronting the structural posts), masks, weapons and war regalia, and utilitarian and ceremonial items used by nobles.

Chilkat Tlingit blankets were the most intricate and sought-after textiles of the Northwest Coast. They were really ceremonial robes, and the ceremonies, in which myth was dramatized through dance, were fully as artistic as the crafts themselves.

Weaving of shirts, aprons, and leggings may have come originally from the Tsimshian. Rock art probably served functions similar to those of totems. Beadwork was of very high quality. Shamans used many art objects, including carved ivory and antler and bone amulets. Baskets were also an important Tlingit art.

TRANSPORTATION   Tlingits preferred the great Haida canoes that were purchased by wealthy Tlingit headmen. The most common type of canoe was of spruce, except in the south, where they used red cedar. Styles included ice-hunting canoes for sealing, forked-prow canoes, shallow river canoes, and small canoes with upturned ends for fishing and otter hunting. Some Inland Tlingits also used skin canoes, but most used rafts or small dugouts when they could not walk.

Tlingits purchased Eyak and Athapaskan snowshoes. They carried burdens using skin packs with tumplines. Only a few coastal groups used Athapaskan-style sleds.

DRESS   In warm weather, women wore cedarbark aprons, whereas men went naked. Blankets of woven cedar bark, mountain goat wool or dog hair, or tanned, sewn skins kept people warm in cold weather. Women wore waterproof basket caps and cedar bark ponchos in the rain. Conical twined spruce-root hats also served as prestigious crest objects.

Inland Tlingits wore pants with attached moccasins. Tailored shirts were made of caribou or moose skin. Winter clothing included goat wool pants, hooded sweaters made of caribou or hare skin, and fur robes.

WAR AND WEAPONS   War occurred between clans in different groups or tribes for reasons of plunder or, more often, revenge. Warfare included killing, torture, and the taking of women and children as slaves. Settlement involved the ceremonial kidnapping and ransom of high-ranking individuals, dancing, and feasting. Weapons included daggers, spears, war clubs, and bows and arrows. Fighters also wore hide and rod armor over moose-hide shirts as well as head and neck protection.

Although a considerable degree of intermarriage took place between the two groups, Interior Tlingits fought with Tahltans and Kaskas in the nineteenth century, mainly over trapping territory.

Contemporary Information

GOVERNMENT/RESERVATIONS   Many Tlingits live in their traditional villages, although many also live in urban centers in Alaska and the Northwest. In the Yukon, Tlingits form a part of the Carcross Tagish First Nation (Da Ka Nation Tribal Council). The Teslin Tlingit Council Band (part of the Da Ka Nation) controls three reserves on 187 hectares of land in the southwest part of Teslin. The 1993 population was 482 (119 houses). Elections have been mandatory (imposed by the Department of Indian Affairs) since the late 1940s. The clan leadership is composed of a chief and five counselors. Children attend band and provincial schools. Facilities on the reserves include two administration buildings, a longhouse, a clinic, a recreation center, and a drop-in center.

ECONOMY At its founding in the early 1970s, Sealaska Corporation received 280,000 acres of timberland and $200 million. Each native village received surface land rights, and the corporation received subsurface rights to the same land. These corporations became active in logging, fishing, and land development.

Important economic activities of the Teslin Tlingit Council Band include a coin laundry. The band plans to organize a development corporation.

LEGAL STATUS The Sealaska Regional Corporation (Tlingit-Haida Central Council) is a federally recognized tribal entity. The council itself is composed of elected delegates from 14 communities in southeast Alaska and of representatives from other communities. The Hydaburg Cooperative Association is a federally recognized tribal entity.

Under the Alaska Native Claims Settlement Act of 1971, 12 regional for-profit corporations (e.g., Sealaska Corporation) and roughly 200 village corporations were created and given nearly $1 billion and fee-simple title to 44 million acres in exchange for the extinction of aboriginal title to Alaska. The not-for-profit Sealaska Heritage Foundation supports a number of cultural activities.

Tlingit and Haida native villages include Angoon, Craig, Hoonah, Hydaburg, Juneau (Juneau Fishing Village), Kake, Klawok, Klukwan, Saxman, Sitka Village, and Yakutat.

The Teslin and Atlin Bands of Tlingit Indians are formally recognized by Canada.

DAILY LIFE Most villages now have full electric service as well as amenities such as satellite television. Every village has a grade school, some have high schools, and all have at least one church. The traditional clan system still exists but has declined in importance. Relatively few people speak the Tlingit language, although it is now being taught in school. Most Tlingits are Christian. Urban Tlingits show a markedly greater level of assimilation than do those away from cities.

The ANB and the ANS now work toward cultural renewal. Some aspects of traditional culture and ceremonialism, such as potlatching (the memorial for the dead), singing and dancing, and crest arts (especially woodworking and carving) have undergone a revival in recent years.

Inland Tlingits became formally linked with the "outside" world when the Alaska Highway opened in the 1940s and again in the 1960s when radio and television became generally available. Most, especially the younger people, speak only English. There is still some traditional potlatching.

Tsimshian

Tsimshian (`Tsim shin, or `Sim shin) is a Coast and Southern Tsimshian self-designation meaning "inside the Skeena River." The Tsimshian were a group of linguistically and culturally related people. Their four major divisions were the Nishga (Nass River), Gitksan (Upper Skeena River), Coast Tsimshian (Lower Skeena River and adjacent coast), and Southern Tsimshian (southern coast and islands). They were culturally similar to the Haida and Tlingit.

LOCATION Northwestern British Columbia, the home of the Tsimshian, is heavily forested, and the climate is wet, with coastal regions marked by numerous fjords and islands. Most villages were along the mouths of the Nass and Skeena Rivers. Some were in a subalpine zone, where drier land permitted more foot—as opposed to canoe—travel. In the 1990s, Tsimshians live in villages and towns in northwest British Columbia and in cities throughout the Northwest.

Annette Island, on which a reserve is located, is about 16 miles south of Ketchikan, Alaska.

POPULATION The Tsimshian population was about 8,000–10,000 in 1800. In the early 1990s there were about 2,450 Tsimshians in the United States and 4,550 in Canada.

LANGUAGE The various Tsimshian languages (Coast and Southern Tsimshian, Nishga, and Gitksan) and dialects were not all mutually intelligible.

Historical Information

HISTORY Relatively recent arrivals to the Northwest Coast, the Tsimshian began pushing the Tlingit farther north and the Haisla farther south and fighting the Heiltsuk for coastal areas around the mid–eighteenth century. They had already seen European goods when a Southern Tsimshian group met a British trade ship in 1787. Interracial contact remained sporadic until the Hudson's Bay Company founded Fort Simpson in 1831. Many Coast Tsimshian subsequently relocated near the fort in order to strengthen and protect their key role in the local fur trade.

The basic structures of native culture remained intact until the arrival of Christian missionaries. William Duncan, an Anglican, appeared in 1857. Five years later, he and some Indian converts founded the Christian colony of Metlakatla, which grew until it moved in 1887 to Annette Island, Alaska, and was renamed New Metlakatla. Residents there had to renounce traditional life and accept Duncan's utopian principles. Congress established the Annette Island Reserve in 1891. This community prospered until it was beset by factionalism and decline until the 1930s, when it began to recover.

Shortly after the arrival of a Methodist missionary at Fort Simpson in 1874, that community became thoroughly Christianized. As missions spread in the area, Indians replaced many native customs, such as the erection of totem poles, with Euro-Canadian styles and customs. The gold rush of 1867 also brought increased contact with non-natives. Although Indians still practiced some subsistence activities, they also began the switch to a wage economy. The first local salmon cannery was established in 1876, for instance.

During the late nineteenth century, Tsimshian villages became official "bands" with unilaterally imposed reserves under the federal Indian Act. At the end of the century, most coastal bands had been converted to Christianity and the Nass people had abandoned their villages and became largely assimilated into Canadian society; the Gitksan, however, maintained many aspects of traditional culture.

A federal and provincial school system replaced missionary schools in the mid–twentieth century. The enforced enfranchisement of women, air links to the villages (1950s), and television (1960s) and satellite reception (1980s) have generally strengthened the forces of secularization, urbanization, and democratization, although more traditional cultural elements were reestablished after the 1960s.

RELIGION Potlatches, feasts, and secret society dances, all highly ritualistic, were held in winter. The dances were apparently borrowed from Haisla and Heiltsuk-speaking people in about the seventeenth or eighteenth century. House chiefs also served as religious leaders, ensuring that people showed the proper respect for animals and spirits. They also served as "power," "real," and "great" dancers, in which roles they dramatized and validated the powers of their ancestors and their house and initiated young people into ritual roles.

Religious specialists called blowing shamans complemented the chiefs' activities. Their responsibilities included curing as well as controlling the weather. Witches worked in secret to harm people. They had no recourse to spiritual beings but used items such as bits of corpse to make people unclean and thus unready for a supernatural encounter.

GOVERNMENT Each Tsimshian village was as autonomous from another as it was from a Haida or a Tlingit village. Local groups (26 in the mid–nineteenth century) had permanent winter villages as well as spring and summer fishing villages and camps. "Houses" (maternal extended families) were

presided over by (usually male) chiefs, who, in addition to their religious responsibilities, managed the economic resources of the house. Other house members provided for their economic welfare.

Several houses made up a village. Each group of house chiefs had an established rank order, so that the village chief (a position not present in all villages) was the highest-ranking house chief in the village.

CUSTOMS Wolf, Eagle, Raven, and Blackfish or Killer Whale constituted the four matrilineal clans, although traditionally most villages may have had a dual division. The "house" was the basic social unit. It controlled fishing camps and berry and hunting territories and also owned songs, crests, names, and other privileges. Tsimshian people belonged to one of the following groups: chiefs, named families of lesser rank, or free but unnamed people. Slaves were usually imported.

All important life-cycle events necessitated ritual duties and wealth exchanges. Such events included birth, naming, ear (boy) and lip (girl) piercing at about age seven, second naming (and girls' seclusion) at puberty, marriage (arranged with the purpose of advancing social rank), house building, and death. Insults or mistakes, however inadvertent, were occasions for face- (and rank-) saving feasts or potlatches. At puberty, boys sought guardian spirits by bathing and fasting in remote places. Men purified themselves before hunting and fishing. There were also rituals connected with the first seasonal fish catch. Corpses, along with secret society regalia, were generally burned. Ghosts were regarded as possibly being dangerous to the living.

Feasts, such as potlatches, were the glue that held society together; they expressed and maintained the social order, inheritance, and succession. They generally lasted for several days and included dancing, singing, and gift giving. Slaves were often given as gifts; as a wealthy people, the Tsimshian had many of them.

DWELLINGS Winter longhouses were typical of the area. Post and beam structures constructed of red cedar timbers; gabled roofs covered their roughly 2,500 square feet of living space. Inside were central fireplaces and side platforms for sleeping. Cedar-bark mats provided insulation. The door, which occasionally consisted of holes in totem poles, faced the beach. Chiefs' dwellings became dance houses in winter.

The chief and his immediate family occupied the rear of the house. House fronts were painted with crest designs. Other structures included menstrual huts, summer houses, and sweat lodges.

DIET People ate halibut, salmon, herring spawn, water birds and their eggs, seal, sea lion, sea otter, and shellfish. Eulachon oil ("grease") was obtained by boiling rotting eulachon and skimming the fat. Other important foods included dried seaweed, the cambium of several trees, berries, crabapples, deer, elk, mountain goat, mountain sheep, bear, caribou, and moose.

KEY TECHNOLOGY Fishing equipment included traps, bent hook and line (of cedar-bark cord), harpoons, and porpoise lures. The yagatl, an underwater net controlled by a ring and pole, was used to catch eulachon. Women wove clothing and other items from the inner bark of red cedar trees. They also wove plaited and twined baskets from cedar (coast) and maple and birch (inland) bark. Men carved wooden items, including totem poles, storage boxes, chests, canoes, tools, cradles, and fishing and hunting gear. Other tools and implements included bark dishes, stone chisel, and goat horn arrow points. Native copper was used for some tools and ceremonial items.

TRADE The Tsimshian enjoyed a highly profitable monopoly on the grease (eulachon oil) trade. At a huge regional trade fair held every spring at the mouth of the Nass River, Coast Tsimshian peoples traded grease with interior Tsimshians (Gitksans) for furs, dressed deer and moose skins, and porcupine-quill embroidery, which the latter had obtained from interior tribes such as the Carrier. From the Haida the Tsimshians received canoes, carved boxes, dried halibut, and chewing tobacco. Foods, carved horn spoons, and slaves were also traded.

NOTABLE ARTS Carved wood items included painted boxes, rattles, masks and other ceremonial items, and totem poles. House fronts were painted elaborately. Basketry was also an art.

TRANSPORTATION TRANSPORTATION between most sites and activities was by sea canoe, often obtained from the Haida, as well as bark canoe or raft.

DRESS Women wore Chilkat robes (they may have originated the style and technique), woven from mountain goat wool and yellow cedar bark into colored lineage crest designs. They also wore labrets. Both sexes wore skin aprons, cedar-bark robes, conical spruce basketry hats, and fur or skin robes in winter. Snowshoes were used in winter.

WAR AND WEAPONS War occurred between clans in different groups or tribes for reasons of plunder or, more often, revenge. Warfare included killing, torture, and the taking of women and children as slaves. Peace settlements involved the ceremonial kidnapping and ransom of high-ranking individuals, followed by dancing and feasting. Enemies included Tlingit, Haida, Kwakiutl, and Salish groups. The people fought with daggers, bone-tipped spears, war clubs, and bows and arrows. Fighters also wore hide and rod armor over moose-hide shirts as well as wooden helmets.

Contemporary Information

GOVERNMENT/RESERVATIONS In 1984, 255 reserves (roughly 36,000 hectares) were connected with 17 Tsimshian bands from all four major divisions. See "Daily Life" for profiles of the bands.

Metlakatla has had a city council since 1915. There are 12 democratically elected council members. The Annette Island Reserve (86,471 acres; 1,185 Native Americans in 1990) was established in 1891.

ECONOMY Many households still engage in traditional subsistence activities and eat locally harvested foods. Some bands own logging operations. Other sources of jobs include the commercial fishing and logging industries as well as band government, hatchery projects, and fish farms. There are some individual band enterprises, including crafts for the tourist trade. Tsimshians endure relatively high un- and underemployment.

LEGAL STATUS In 1976, the Nisga'a Tribal Council (which represents about 6,000 Nisga'a) began negotiating a comprehensive land claim with the federal government. Provincial officials joined the discussions in 1990. In 1996, the parties reached an Agreement-in-Principle that will form the basis for a final agreement. Provisions include a cash payment of $190 million as well as Indian ownership and self-governance of over 1,900 square kilometers of the Nass River Valley. Also addressed are issues pertaining to taxation, the environment, access to land, land use, mineral rights, and cultural artifacts. This would be the first modern-day treaty in British Columbia.

The Annette Island Reserve is a federally recognized tribal entity. See "Daily Life" for federally and provincially recognized tribal councils.

DAILY LIFE Society and individuals are regulated by a blend of traditional and Anglo institutions. For instance, much ceremonialism was suppressed and replaced over the years by clubs, bands, organizations, and other structures more typical of Anglo society. Tsimshian children receive both English and traditional names, including rank if appropriate. Among some groups, houses still control fishing and hunting places as well as names and privileges.

Most schools contain bilingual-bicultural programs. Port Simpson has the largest concentration of Tsimshian people. Clans still regulate marriage and carry out other roles. Potlatches and other feasts and traditional activities are very much alive. English is the first language for most people.

In 1970, 'Ksan was established, an open-air museum representing a Gitksan village of circa 1800. It also contains an art school and serves as a center for preserving and rebuilding Indian culture. Many of the best contemporary native artists train there. In part because of the existence of 'Ksan, Tsimshian art itself has come back from near obscurity to reclaim its traditions.

Metlakatla remains something of a successful utopian community, based on communal rather than individual values. Since the 1970s, an effort has been underway to reinvigorate traditional culture there.

Tsimshian bands in British Columbia include (statistics are as of 1995):

Gitanmaax Band is located five kilometers west of New Hazelton, British Columbia. The population is 1,632, of whom 665 live in 165 houses on the reserve. Elections are held under the provisions of the Indian Act. Children attend band and provincial schools. The band is affiliated with the Gitksan Wet'suwet'en Local Services Society (GWLSS). Important economic resources and activities include a campground, a taxi service. and lumber activities. Facilities include offices, a community hall, a clinic, an art school, a youth center, and a church.

Gitanyow Band, formerly Kitwancool Band, is located 24 kilometers north of Gitwangah Indian Village. The population is 595, of whom 342 live in 65 houses on the reserve. Elections are held under the provisions of the Indian Act. Children attend band schools. The band is affiliated with the GWLSS. Important economic resources and activities include fishing, logging, and tourism. Facilities include offices, a community hall, a clinic, a longhouse, and churches.

Gitlakdamit Band controls 30 reserves on 2,000 hectares of land 112 kilometers from Terrace. The local community of New Aiyansh was established in 1964. The population is 1,463, of whom 682 live in 178 houses on the reserves. Elections are held under the provisions of the Indian Act. The band is affiliated with the Nisga'a Tribal Council (NTC). Children attend band and provincial schools. Important economic resources and activities include a minimall. Facilities include a newspaper, a radio and local television rebroadcast station, offices, a community hall, a youth center, and a church.

Gitsegukla Band is located 33 kilometers west of New Hazelton. The population is 721, of whom 454 live in 123 houses on the reserve. Elections are held under the provisions of the Indian Act. The band is affiliated with the GWLSS. Children attend band and provincial schools. Important economic resources and activities include a large housing project, logging, and a grocery store. Facilities include offices, a community hall, a clinic, and churches.

Gitwangah Band is located 50 kilometers southwest of New Hazelton. The population is 905, of whom 430 live in 104 houses on the reserve. Elections are held under the provisions of the Indian Act. The band is affiliated with the GWLSS. Children attend

band and provincial schools. Important economic resources and activities include a sawmill, logging, fishing, a grocery store, and a gas station. Facilities include offices, a community hall, a clinic, an alcohol treatment center, and churches.

Gitwinksihlkw Band, formerly Canyon City Band, controls six reserves on 655 hectares of land 120 kilometers from Terrace. The on-reserve population lives in 43 houses on the reserves. Elections are held by custom. The band is affiliated with the NTC. Children attend band and provincial schools. Important economic resources and activities include logging and a campground. Facilities include offices, a community hall, and a fire station.

Glen Vowell/Sikokoak Band is located 12 kilometers north of Hazelton. The population is 322, of whom 141 live in 55 houses on the reserve. Elections are held under the provisions of the Indian Act. The band is affiliated with the GWLSS. Children attend band and provincial schools. Important economic resources and activities include harvesting wood and an upholstery shop. Facilities include offices, a community hall, a clinic, a fire station, and a church.

Hartley Bay Band controls 14 reserves on 520 hectares of land 144 kilometers south of Prince Rupert. The population is 582, of whom 150 live in 78 houses on the reserves. Elections are held by custom. The band is affiliated with the North Coast Tribal Council and the Tsimshian Tribal Council (TTC). Children attend provincial schools on the reserves. Important economic resources and activities include a freight service, fishing, and a store. Facilities include offices and a nursery school.

Kincolith Band is affiliated with the NTC. The population is 1,250, of whom 370 live on reserve land.

Kispiox Band is located 16 kilometers north of Hazelton. The population is 1,184, of whom 525 live in 153 houses on the reserves. Elections are held under the provisions of the Indian Act. The band is affiliated with the GWLSS. Important economic resources and activities include a fish hatchery, an art studio, a cafe, and three grocery stores. Facilities include offices, a community hall, recreation grounds, and churches.

Kitasoo Band controls 14 reserves on 598 hectares of land on Swindle Island. The population is 423, of whom 319 live in 85 houses on the reserves. Elections are held under the provisions of the Indian Act. The band is affiliated with the Oweekeno/Kitasoo Nuxalk Tribal Council. Children attend band schools. Important economic resources and activities include a wood shop, a sawmill, a seafood processing plant, a fish farm, a store, and an ice plant. Facilities include offices, a community hall, a drop-in center, and a church.

Kitkatla Band controls 21 reserves on 1,885 hectares of land 72 kilometers southwest of Prince Rupert. The population is 1,304, of whom 407 live in 125 houses on the reserves. Elections are held by custom. The band is affiliated with the North Coast Tribal Council and the TTC. Children attend band and provincial schools. Important economic resources and activities include fishery, video games rental, and a taxi service. Facilities include offices, a community hall, a recreation hall, and churches.

Kitselas Band controls nine reserves on 1,103 hectares of land east of Terrace. The population is 421, of whom 163 live in 36 houses on the reserves. Elections are held according to the provisions of the Indian Act. The band is affiliated with the TTC. Children attend provincial schools. Important economic resources and activities include plans for large tourism and real estate developments. Facilities include offices, a community hall, and a longhouse.

Kitsumkalum Band controls three reserves on 588 hectares of land 5 kilometers west of Terrace. The population is 540, of whom 191 live in 55 houses on the reserves. Elections are held according to the provisions of the Indian Act. The band is affiliated with the TTC. Children attend provincial schools. Important economic resources and activities include a recreational vehicle park, a boat launch, a guide service, a crafts shop, and a motel. Facilities include offices, a recreation center, and a warehouse.

Lakalzap Band controls three reserves on 1,836 hectares of land 144 kilometers from Terrace. The population is 1,375, of whom 617 live in 110 houses on the reserves. Elections are held according to the provisions of the Indian Act. The band is affiliated with the NTC. Children attend band and provincial schools. Important economic resources and activities include a water taxi service, a bus service, and logging. Facilities include offices, a community hall, a warehouse, and a fire station.

Lax Kw'Alaams Band controls 72 reserves on 1,049 hectares of land. The population is 2,404, of whom 1,049 live in 211 houses on the reserves. Elections are held according to the provisions of the Indian Act. The band is affiliated with the TTC. Children attend band and provincial schools. Important economic resources and activities include a store, a video store, and a motel. Facilities include offices, a community hall, and a seniors' home.

Metlakatla Band controls 16 reserves on 162 hectares of land five kilometers from Prince Rupert. The population is 528, of whom 101 live in 47 houses on the reserves. Elections are held according to the provisions of the Indian Act. The band is affiliated with the North Coast Tribal Council. Children attend provincial schools. Important economic resources and activities include the Metlakatla Development Corporation, a ferry service, industrial real estate, and small businesses. Facilities include offices, a community hall, a museum, and a recreation building.

Tulalip
See Salish, Southern Coast

Tututni
See Tolowa (Chapter 2); Upper Umpqua

Twana
See Salish, Southern Coast

Upper Coquille
See Upper Umpqua

Upper Skagit
See Salish, Southern Coast

Upper Umpqua
Upper Umpqua (`Ump kwä) were one of several Athapaskan-speaking groups of southwest Oregon. The word may have meant "high and low water," "thunder," or "boat over the water." Their self-designation was *Etnemitane*.

LOCATION There were traditionally five bands in southwest Oregon, in the valley of the south fork of the Umpqua River. There were other groups to the west and south, including coastal areas. These included Upper Coquilles (Mishikhwutmetunne), Chetco, Chasta Costa, Tututni (all four so-called Coast Rogue Indians), Galice, and Applegate. Most descendants of these people live on or near reservations in the same area (see "Government/Reservations" under "Contemporary Information").

POPULATION There were roughly 5,600 Oregon Athapaskans in the late eighteenth century. In 1990 there were roughly 3,000 Grande Ronde Indians as well as 850 Cow Creek Indians. There were around 2,900 enrolled Siletz Indians in the mid-1990s.

LANGUAGE Upper Umpqua, Galice-Applegate, the Tututni dialects (Mishikhwutmetunne, Tututni, Chasta Costa), and the Chetco dialect of the Tolowa language are all members of the Pacific branch of the Athapaskan language family.

Historical Information
HISTORY Non-Indian traders first arrived in the area in the late eighteenth century. The fur trade began around 1818, at which time a group of Umpquas was killed by traders, possibly Iroquois in the service of the North West Company. Hudson's Bay Company established Fort Umpqua in 1836.

Around this time, previously unknown diseases began taking a serious toll on the Indians.

Sporadic, trade-based contact continued until the flood of settlers in the late 1840s and the gold rush (Rogue River Valley) of 1852. In 1851, the Tututnis traded 2.5 million acres of land for $28,500. Their bitterness when they subsequently understood the deal fueled their desire to extract revenge. They soon began killing whites and burning settlers' houses. Two years later, when a group of whites attacked some Chetco Indians after persuading them to disarm, the Chetcos attacked some soldiers, and the fighting spread.

Upper Umpquas stayed out of the war, having signed a land cession treaty in 1854 and moved two years later to the Grand Ronde Reservation. Some Upper Umpquas along with villages of different linguistic groups signed a treaty in 1853; in exchange for a land cession of more than 700 square miles, it recognized the existence of and called for a reservation for the Cow Creek Band of the Umpqua tribe. The Rogue River War of 1855–1856 provided an opportunity for whites to destroy game trails and hunting grounds and to appropriate and clear land for farms. Cow Creeks fled the area during this period, hiding in the mountains as refugees.

After the war, local Indians, once fiercely independent, were shattered. Some Upper Umpquas, Tututnis, Chetcos, Coquilles, Chasta Costas, and others were forced to walk over the mountains in winter to the Grand Ronde Reservation. Other groups straggled in until 1857, when many Indians were moved to the Coast (or Siletz) Reservation, created two years earlier. On the way, and once there, several hundred died from exposure, starvation, and disease. Shamans who failed to cure the diseases were persecuted by their people, which gave the government an excuse to step in and disarm the Indians.

Meanwhile, the Grand Ronde Reservation was created in 1857. A school system designed to eradicate Indian culture was promptly set up. Many people left Grand Ronde for the Siletz Reservation or local communities. Those that remained worked as farmers or loggers.

Disparities between treaty and nontreaty Indians as well as agents' promotion of alcohol and thievery spread discord and exacerbated intertribal conflict. Many Indians escaped during this time but were rounded up by soldiers, who further abused them. Meanwhile, intermarriage further weakened tribal identities.

In 1865, a central strip was removed from the Siletz Reservation and opened for white settlement. The northern part then became the Siletz Reservation and the southern half (Coosans, Siuslawans, and Alseans) became the Alsea Reservation. The Bureau of Indian Affairs (BIA) turned all operations over to the Methodists, who worked to eradicate all vestiges of Indian culture. Indians danced the Ghost Dance in 1871; the variant Earth Lodge cult (locally known as the Warm House Dance) began in 1873. The Indian Shaker Church became popular beginning in the 1890s.

By 1894, most of the Siletz Reservation had been ceded to the public domain, and tribal languages had all but disappeared. Remaining residents worked in subsistence activities or in logging, cutting trees on their plundered reservation. By 1928, as a result of both widespread theft and the allotment processes, most of the land base was gone. Eighteen years later, the Confederated Tribes of the Siletz Reservation voted to accept termination of government recognition and services. The former reservation land base of 1.3 million acres had completely disappeared. Most of the allotments were lost shortly thereafter, mainly owing to nonpayment of taxes. Tribal life for most of the former Siletz tribes virtually disappeared. At the same time, although 537 acres of land had been added to the Grand Ronde Reservation in 1936, it, too, was declared terminated.

Meanwhile, the Cow Creek Band had intermarried extensively with other Indians as well as the French-Canadian population. The group created a formal government around 1918. They pressed their case for land claims litigation, but by the time they learned of the existence of the Indian Claims Commission, they had missed the deadline for filing a claim. Officially terminated in 1956, they were formally restored in 1982. Later in that decade they accepted a land settlement of $1.5 million and, over the objections of the BIA, placed the funds in a permanent endowment.

In 1973, the Siletz formed a new council to work for restoration of tribal status, which was obtained in 1977. The new 3,630-acre Siletz Reservation was created in 1980. Grand Ronde was restored in 1983, with all former rights save those pertaining to subsistence activities. A Tribal Council was formed the same year. Five years later, Congress gave the tribe 9,811 acres of timbered land, the income of which was used to purchase a 100-acre administrative land base.

RELIGION There were numerous opportunities for feasts and gift giving, such as birth, naming, first kills, puberty, war, death, and the make-doctor dance for new shamans. Feasts included both sacred and secular elements.

GOVERNMENT Each village had a chief who had several wives and slaves. He acted as an arbiter and received a share of all financial transactions as well as a food tithe. The position of chief was generally inherited through the male line.

CUSTOMS Although they slept in sweat houses, men and boys ate in the family house, where their mothers or wives cooked for them. Women gathered firewood and plants, made baskets, prepared foods, and carried water. Men fished, hunted, tanned hides, tended tobacco, and made nets, planks, and canoes.

Although society was ranked according to wealth, the divisions were not as rigid as they were farther north. Slaves were usually acquired in raids, although a chief could enslave a villager for improper behavior.

Most shamans were women. They cured by extracting a "pain," a small object filled with the patient's blood. Some groups also had common shamans, who blew smoke and waved a flicker feather over the patient. Unsuccessful cures sometimes led to the identification and murder of evil shamans (sorcerers). However, if the patient then died, a murder compensation had to be paid for the dead shaman. A shaman's fee was often paid to her husband. Shamans' powers derived from guardian spirits. Other powers conferred by certain spirits included the ability to cure rattlesnake bites, talk to herbs to receive remedies and love charms from them, and find lost objects.

Numerous rituals were associated with pregnancy and birth. Girls were secluded when they reached puberty and were not permitted to touch their hair or skin nor to eat anything except dry food for a year. They also had to swim twice a day, and their fathers also underwent certain restrictions. Women were purchased for marriage; children were illegitimate if their mothers were not paid for. Jealousy, meanness, and barrenness were acceptable reasons for divorce. Parents could also buy back their daughter, who then had considerable personal freedom.

The various death customs included the deathbed confession of wrongs, carriage of the corpse to the cemetery on a deerskin, and funeral orations. Mourners cut their hair and wore ashes and pitch on their heads and faces

DWELLINGS House size corresponded to the status of its residents. The plank house of a wealthy family was 20 by 30 feet, with three inside fires, fern and grass wall mats, and inside drying racks. Men slept in sweat houses, of which each village had at least one. People lived in brush houses in their summer hunting camps and in windbreaks on beaches in their fall fishing camps.

DIET Women dug roots such as camas and wild carrots beginning in early summer. Roots were steamed in large pits and prepared for storage. Women also gathered berries, which were usually eaten fresh. Men caught salmon, trout, and lamprey in summer. In late summer, young men hunted elk and deer in the mountains; the women then dried the meat on racks. Tututnis gathered acorns.

In fall, people moved to fishing camps to catch salmon and smoke salmon eggs. The first few salmon were eaten ritually. The people also burned berry patches in the fall; hunting grounds were burned every five years. Winter fare was soup of leftover bones and dried and rotted salmon heads and eggs. In spring, people ate seagull eggs and yellowjacket grubs, followed by bear and possibly beached whale. There was some local variation in diet, which was leveled out in part by trade.

KEY TECHNOLOGY Fishing gear included harpoons, fences, clubs, and nets. In general, raw materials included wood (acorn stirrers, paddles, drying racks, drums, canoes, arrows, bows, spears, traps, fire drills, bowls), animal hides (blankets, aprons, capes, drums, quivers, tobacco pouches), stone (points, blades, fire holders, hammers, pestles), and bone (whistles, men's spoons). Women used their fingers or shells instead of bone spoons. Other items included deer hoof rattles, iris-fiber nets, maple-bark string, tule mats, and baskets.

TRADE In general, camas and hides from the interior were exchanged for marine products from the coast. Other important trade items included dentalia shells from Vancouver and obsidian points from the south, both of which were valued as items of wealth.

NOTABLE ARTS Baskets, especially from the Chetco, were of particularly fine execution.

TRANSPORTATION Dugout canoes provided the main mode of transportation.

DRESS Women wore buckskin aprons; capes of tule, deerskin, elkskin, or woven rabbit furs; and basketry caps. Girls' aprons were made of maple bark. Men went naked or wore a front apron; they plucked their facial hair. Both sexes kept their hair long and covered their faces with elk or deer grease. Moccasins were only worn when men went into the brush. Chetco women adorned themselves with olivella beads.

WAR AND WEAPONS Warriors wore very thick elk hide armor, danced a war dance before battle, and fought with bows and arrows. They sometimes paid for a charm to ensure that their arrows might be especially effective. All battlefield deaths were compensated for, a practice that tended to keep the casualty rate down.

Contemporary Information

GOVERNMENT/RESERVATIONS The Coquille Tribe, descendants of the Miluk (Lower) Coosans and the Mishikhwutmetunne, was formed in the aftermath of a land claims settlement (1975). In 1993 the tribe of 630 members was headquartered at Coos Bay, Oregon. It elects a seven-member council and owns 6.2 acres of land.

The Grande Ronde Indian Reservation (Confederated Tribes of Grande Ronde Indians: Shasta, Kalapuya, Rogue River, Molalla, Umpqua), created in 1857, comprises 9,811 acres. The confederation began in 1934 under the Indian Reorganization Act, and the group was incorporated in 1935. In 1974 the Confederated Tribes of Grande Ronde Indians grew out of the old Confederated Tribes of the Grande Ronde Community; they incorporated as a nonprofit organization the following year and were restored to federal status in 1983. The reservation is governed by a nine-member elected tribal council as well as tribal courts.

The Confederated Tribes of Siletz Indians were officially rerecognized in 1977 and received 3,630 acres of federal land in 1980. They are governed by a nine-member tribal council. The mid-1990s enrolled population was roughly 2,900.

The Smith River and Elk Valley Rancherias, home to Chetco and Tututni Indians, were terminated in 1960, only to be rerecognized in the 1980s.

The Cow Creek Band owns land in Canyonville, Oregon.

ECONOMY   The Coquilles are economically integrated with the local population. Timber revenues are the most important economic resource at Grande Ronde. Under the supervision of the Siletz Tribal Economic Development Corporation (STEDC), the tribe features a smokehouse and timber sales and plans to build a casino. The Cow Creek Band is part-owner of a bingo facility. Its members also work in logging and in the service sector.

LEGAL STATUS   The Confederated Tribes of Grande Ronde Indians is a federally recognized tribal entity. The Confederated Tribes of Siletz Indians is a federally recognized tribal entity. The Cow Creek Band of Umpqua Indians, a nonprofit organization, is a federally recognized tribal entity (1984).

In 1983, Chetcos and Tututnis (Oregon Tolowas) formed the Tolowa Nation and petitioned the federal government for recognition, which had not been received as of 1997.

DAILY LIFE   Among the Oregon Tolowas, the Feather Dance remains important, as does the Indian Shaker Church. The native language remains alive. Facilities include a clinic, a tribal center, and a senior center.

Grande Ronde sponsors many social and economic programs, including student financial assistance and an annual powwow. There is a community center, a dental center, and a seniors' center, and there are plans to build housing on the reservation. Siletz features a tribal center, a housing program, and a clinic.

The Cow Creek Band hosts a week-long powwow in July. Members also gather in midsummer to pick blueberries. Many members are Catholic, but traditional burials and reinterments continue to be practiced.

CHAPTER FOUR

The Great Basin

Great Basin

The Great Basin encompasses roughly 400,000 square miles of land between the Rocky Mountains and the Sierra Nevada. Geologically, it includes extreme eastern California, southeast Oregon, all of Nevada but the extreme south, extreme southeast Idaho, extreme southwest Wyoming, and western Utah. This is an area of interior drainage, featuring high deserts and valleys (around 5,000 feet), both freshwater and saltwater lakes, and mountains more than 12,000 feet high. Except for the high mountains, and especially in the south, there is relatively little precipitation.

Although Great Basin Indians share cultural traits and social connections with neighboring groups in other areas, so that the term "Great Basin cultural area" is a somewhat arbitrary convention, sufficient homogeneity existed within a defined region for anthropologists to consider the term legitimate. The boundaries of the Great Basin cultural area considerably exceeded those of the geographical one. Prior to 1600, between 40,000 and 50,000 people lived in an area extending from California east of the Sierra crest into eastern Oregon, central Idaho, extreme southwest Montana, western Wyoming, all of Nevada and Utah, the western two-thirds of Colorado, extreme northern New Mexico, and extreme northern and western Arizona.

Except for the Hokan-speaking Washoe, all late prehistoric Great Basin dwellers spoke dialects of Numic (Shoshonean) languages. Fluidity was a major characteristic of both territory and identity. That is, whereas today we speak of the Western Shoshone or the Northern Paiute, for linguistic and vaguely cultural purposes, these Indians had no such concepts. Since few groups regarded subsistence areas as exclusively controlled, they tended to range over wide distances, mixing and intermarrying with other Numic-speaking and neighboring groups. Social and economic organization, and therefore leadership, was

decentralized, except in eastern groups after the introduction of the horse.

Residents of the Great Basin adapted very successfully to a large number of microenvironments that changed over time. Hunting and especially gathering were the primary activities. Creosote predominated in the southern and western Great Basin; saltbush and sagebrush, as well as many types of seed grasses, in the high deserts; and juniper, piñon, and other trees in the mountains. A few marshes supported cattails and rushes. The region supported a wide variety of animals, although distribution was uneven.

In general, and with the exception of eastern groups of the posthorse era, Indians of the Great Basin were relatively peaceful. Many groups turned briefly to raiding when faced in the mid–nineteenth century with Anglo attacks and the destruction of their habitat. Afterward, they tried to adjust to the new situation. Many people were able to retain strong elements of traditional culture, particularly religion and social structure. Still, they faced the usual severe discrimination and policies aimed at cultural genocide. Despite land claims victories and mineral leases, the economic and social situation for Great Basin Indians today remains difficult.

Archaeological evidence suggests that people first entered the Great Basin roughly 12,000 years ago, probably arriving from the south. These earliest people were probably not Shoshonean; they were displaced or absorbed by Shoshonean people, perhaps as recently as 1000. The basic hunting and gathering way of life for Great Basin Indians changed relatively little from the Early Archaic period (8000–2000 B.C.E.) through about 1600 C.E. The only exception is in southern Idaho (Snake and Salmon Rivers area), where people hunted now-extinct big game from the thirteenth century B.C.E. until about 6000 B.C.E.

In and around Utah, the typical foraging life was partially replaced from about 400 to 1300 by semi-sedentary communities based on farming. These Fremont culture people made containers and artistic figurines of clay. Although distinguished in part by their agricultural traditions, they continued to rely on hunting and gathering, especially in the north and west. Fremont cultures began to break up by around 1000, and by about 1350 the Archaic tradition had reestablished itself throughout the Great Basin, remaining more or less intact until the nineteenth century.

Most groups relied heavily on seed-bearing grasses and piñon seeds as well as roots (camas, yampa, bitterroot) and berries (buckberry, wolfberry, chokecherry). Birds, rabbits, deer, pronghorn antelope, rodents, fish, insects, and other nonplant resources probably made up around 25 percent of their diet, on average. For many groups, piñon seeds were the winter staple. Women extracted the seeds, then parched and ground them to make a mush or gruel. Acorns were another important food; after being leached (north and west), roasted, shelled, and ground, they were also stone boiled into a type of gruel. People in and near the southern deserts used plants such as agave, mesquite, and screwbean. Some southern groups also grew a limited amount of corn, beans, and squash.

Great Basin Indian technology was simple but effective. People used twined and coiled baskets, constructed primarily of willow, grasses, and roots, to carry burdens; to beat, winnow, and parch seeds; and to contain cold and boiling water. Pottery generally appeared with the Shoshonean people. Although plants and animals provided most raw materials, people also made tools and utensils out of stone, obsidian, bone, and wood. Nets, traps, snares, flaked stone knives, and bow and arrow were all used in the hunt. Fish were taken with nets, weirs, hook and line, basket traps, spears, and harpoons. The ubiquitous fire-hardened digging stick was the main root-gathering implement. Fire was started with drills, and the embers were often retained for storage and transportation. Some groups also encouraged certain plants by burning brushlands and forests as well as pruning. Some native irrigation was also practiced, especially in Owens Valley.

Both season and location determined the type of shelter. Brush windbreaks were common in warm weather. Winter houses were typically conical, roughly 10 feet high and 10–15 feet in diameter, and built of brush, bark, grass, and/or tule over piñon and/or juniper pole frames. Some northern groups covered the frame with skins. Doorways generally faced east. Caves were also utilized. As for clothing, most people wore little except in the coldest weather. Women often wore twined sagebrush bark or willow hats and long gowns in winter. Men and women wore fur or twined-bark breechclouts. Fur or sage-bark moccasins were worn in winter, as were twined-bark or skin leggings. Fur (including buffalo) robes and rabbit-skin blankets, consisting of several strips of rabbit skin woven on a frame, were worn as capes during the day and used for coverings at night.

Aboriginal Great Basin society was relatively decentralized. The basic social and economic unit was the camp, or nuclear family, consisting of parents, children, and one or two grandparents, aunts, uncles, or cousins. This group was autonomous and self-governing by consensus, although an older male might be especially influential. Most labor was divided fairly rigidly by gender.

In regions of greater productivity, semipermanent winter villages emerged, which consisted of related family clusters. This type of interaction allowed people to share information about resources, to observe ceremonies and share mythological tales, and to trade. Headmen usually presided over villages; they delivered speeches on and coordinated subsistence activities, but the egalitarian impulse among Shoshonean people rendered their authority tenuous. Some more centralized societies emerged after the introduction of the horse.

Trade routes in the region, featuring Pacific coast shells, appeared at least by 5000 B.C.E. By around 2000 B.C.E., beads, obsidian, and other items were traded in a major network that ran from southern and central California to Nevada and Utah. Shell trade reached its maximum precontact distribution in the Great Basin by 1500. In general, Great Basin Indians exchanged hundreds of items between themselves and their neighbors, especially in the late eighteenth century, including hides, robes, food items, dresses, moccasins, medicinal plants, beads, and horses.

Aboriginal Shoshonean peoples recognized various beings or spirits capable of affecting human existence and may have recognized one or more supreme beings, such as the sun. They practiced both individual and group religious ceremonies. On an individual level, some people acquired supernatural powers, often through dreams or visions, from friendly spirits. Such powers brought them luck or skills. Certain rituals and behavior restrictions were associated with life-cycle events, especially girls' puberty and death. Group activities were mostly associated with the Round Dance. Performed on occasions such as piñon harvests and communal hunts, the Round Dance was associated with fertility, bounty, and rain.

Male or female shamans, although possessing no formal political power, often exercised influence in society owing to their abilities to cure and lead the ceremonies. People formally showed respect for plants and animals they had taken. They ritually disposed of certain animal parts, such as glands or organs, and addressed dead animals in a special way. Plants were often taken with an offering to their spirits and a prayer of thanks. Over 300 plant species were used medicinally. Plants and animals played an important role in mythology and regional cosmology. Rock art as well as small sculptures and figurines, some of which are at least several thousand years old, expressed aspects of prehistoric religion and ritual.

Late-eighteenth-century Spanish explorers of the Great Basin encountered Indians who had already been influenced by Euro-Americans. Utes escaping from Spanish captivity probably brought horses north of the Colorado River by the mid–seventeenth century. By the mid–eighteenth century, many eastern Shoshonean groups had thoroughly adopted the horse and had moved closer—both culturally and physically—to their fellow mounted Indians on the Great Plains. In contrast, some western Shoshoneans, whose environment did not favor mounted exploitation, remained without the horse (except as a food source) until the nineteenth century. Groups like the Goshute Shoshones and the Southern Paiutes became ready targets for Ute and Navajo slave raiders, who in turn were supported by the Spanish and Mexicans into the nineteenth century.

The Spanish explored the region and traded with the Indians, but they did not form colonies. Because of the isolation and relatively harsh environment of the Great Basin, it was the last region in the contiguous United States to be taken over by non-natives. However, change, when it did come, was rapid, largely because the ecology of the region was so fragile. Indians guided and traded with early explorers and trappers; many Indians first received firearms, alcohol, and new diseases during that period. The first Mormon settlers appeared around the time the United States acquired the Great Basin, in the 1848 Treaty of Guadalupe Hidalgo. Ranchers and farmers soon completed the process, begun by explorers, trappers, emigrants, and miners, of resource degradation and destruction of aboriginal habitat.

Livestock were allowed to compact the soil and overgraze, ruining the seed grasses. Anglos appropriated scarce water sources and converted natural resource–rich lands to farms. They prohibited the Indians from managing grasslands through regular burnings and cut down vital piñon groves for firewood. Game animals, deprived of their own resources and increasingly crowded out, either disappeared or retreated to safer though far less accessible regions. In a relatively few years, the environment that had supported tens of thousands of Indians for millennia was gone. Hungry, weakened by disease, and victims of wanton violence, Indian populations began to decline dramatically.

Survivors responded to this new situation in several ways. Many groups withdrew farther from areas of white activity and tried to carry on as best they could. As these areas became increasingly marginal, the camp groups were forced into greater levels of cooperation. Some briefly formed bands to exploit non-Indian "resources" or even to engage in war. Some remained near the trails and simply begged for food. Some people attached themselves to ranches or farms, working for wages but living apart and trying to retain their identities as Indians. The money around mining towns attracted some Indians, but they were always severely discriminated against and forced to undertake the most menial and low-paying work.

In the 1850s, the government created the first of the Great Basin Indian reservations, on which it planned to transform the Indians into Christian farmers (although without providing adequate land or material or technical support). Native culture was ruthlessly suppressed. Children were kidnapped or otherwise forced to attend culture-killing boarding schools away from the reservation. To make matters worse, the extent of Indian land was gradually whittled away, in part as a result of the Dawes Act of 1886. Many Great Plains Indians (up to 40 percent or more) remained away from the reservations altogether, preferring to take their chances on their own.

The Ghost Dance originated among Northern Paiutes, beginning around 1869. According to the visions of a man named Wodziwob, Indians who danced and sang in a specified way could bring about the return of a precontact golden age, including the return to life of deceased Indians. This movement spread rapidly throughout the Great Basin and into California and lasted from a year or two up to several decades. In 1889, another Northern Paiute, named Wovoka, revived the Ghost Dance religion. His visions instructed Indians to perform the Ghost Dance, live in peace among themselves and with whites, work hard, and avoid alcohol. If they would do these things, they would achieve happiness in the next world. As interpreted by its adherents throughout much of the west, however, the religion promised an immediate salvation.

About the same time as the second Ghost Dance gained popularity, the Ute Bear Dance began to spread into southern Nevada, northern and western Arizona, and southern California. Also, as part of Bear Dance ceremonies, some southwestern Great Basin groups began adapting part of the Yuman mourning ceremony. The "cry," like the Ghost Dances, was probably meant to comfort the living under increasingly desperate conditions.

No Great Basin groups danced the Sun Dance before the nineteenth century, but among the Eastern Shoshone, who adopted it from the Comanche about 1800, it did precede reservation life. At the same time that more western groups were adopting and adapting the Ute Bear Dance, the Utes themselves, along with the Eastern Shoshones, were creating a new, modern Sun Dance. As the Sun Dance spread, its focus shifted away from warfare and buffalo hunting toward transcending contemporary problems such as widespread illness and growing poverty and toward restoring harmony. Christian elements also entered the Sun Dance. The Sun Dance today is very popular as an ongoing expression of interreservation religious life.

The Peyote religion, or Native American Church, also appeared in the Great Basin in the late nineteenth century. Originating in prehistoric Mexico, Peyotism today incorporates elements of Christianity while remaining a pan-Indian affair. It is also part of the Traditional-Unity Movement, a recent tradition born of the political struggles of the 1960s and 1970s that incorporates elements of the Sun Dance, Sweat Lodge, and Sacred Pipe ceremonies. This movement and its associated ceremonies are particularly strong at the Fort McDermitt Reservation (Northern Paiute).

By the 1930s, the effort to make Christian farmers out of Great Basin Indians had failed. Instead, Indians had lost much of their land and, even though retaining their Indian identity, were in desperate straits socially and economically. Ranching, a key economic activity, supported only a small minority of reservation Indians. Severe discrimination and lack of language and job skills precluded significant off-reservation employment. Whites succeeded in destroying what viable Indian industry existed, such as the Pyramid Lake fisheries.

Conditions improved marginally into the 1940s as a result of the so-called Indian New Deal, which brought a degree of self-determination as well as increased federal support to the tribes. Land claims victories (over $137 million total) and mineral leases also brought money to selected groups beginning in the late 1930s. However, in a complete reversal of policy, the government began terminating some reservations and treaty responsibilities during the 1950s.

In the 1960s, the government again reversed course and significantly increased support to Indian peoples, helping to alleviate desperate poverty and usher in a renewed period of self-determination. Also, groups like the Northern Paiute and Western Shoshone Indians began a series of actions, such as hunting regardless of local laws and denouncing unfavorable bills before the Nevada legislature, to highlight their push for sovereignty and enforcement of treaty rights. By the 1970s, as a result of federal programs, continued land claims victories, tribal enterprises, and Indian political action, life on Great Basin reservations had improved significantly, if unevenly.

Despite these gains, Great Basin Indians continue to struggle. Chronic poverty and cultural devastation are difficult to overcome. Unemployment, substance abuse, and suicide rates remain high. Health facilities and services remain inadequate. Control over their economic destiny remains elusive. And, as in many Indian tribes, particularly in the west, disagreements between traditionalists and "progressives" divide communities.

Still, pride in Indian identity is at a high point today, as evidenced by the profusion of Indian newspapers and tribal historical and cultural projects. Many tribal governments make decisions in the traditional fashion, by consensus, rather than by majority rule. Traditional activities such as piñon harvesting, ceremonies, and crafts remain important parts of native identity. Women are increasingly participating in tribal government. Tribal businesses include agricultural markets, crafts enterprises, fish hatcheries, and smoke shops. Mineral and ranch leases also provide a large percentage of tribal income, and credit restrictions and cash flows have eased. Despite ongoing challenges, most Great Basin Indians remain committed to prospering as Indians.

Bannock
See Paiute, Northern; Shoshone, Northern

Goshute
See Shoshone, Western

Paiute, Northern

Northern Paiute (`P ī ū t) includes a number of seminomadic, culturally distinct, and politically autonomous Great Basin groups. "Northern Paiute" is a modern construction; aboriginally, these groups were tied together only by the awareness of a common language. Paiute may have meant "True Ute" or "Water Ute" and was applied only to the Southern Paiute until the 1850s. Their self-designation was *Numa,* or "People." Non-natives have sometimes called these people Digger Indians, Snakes (Northern Paiutes in Oregon), and Paviotso. The Bannock Indians were originally a Northern Paiute group from eastern Oregon.

LOCATION. Traditionally, the groups now known as Northern Paiute ranged throughout present-day southeast Oregon, extreme northeast California, extreme southwest Idaho, and northwest Nevada.

Bannock territory included southeastern Idaho and western Wyoming (the Snake River region). The highly diverse environment included lakes, mountains, high plains, rivers, freshwater marsh, and high desert. Elements of California culture entered the region through groups living on or near the Sierra Nevada. Presently, Northern Paiutes live on a number of their own reservations (see "Government/ Reservations" under "Contemporary Information"), on other nearby reservations, and among the area's general population.

POPULATION The Paiute population in the early nineteenth century was roughly 7,500, excluding about 2,000 Bannocks. In 1990, about 6,300 Paiutes, including Paiute-Shoshones, lived on reservations.

LANGUAGE With Mono, Northern Paiute is part of the Western Numic (Shoshonean) branch of the Uto-Aztecan linguistic family.

Historical Information

HISTORY People later called the Bannocks, or Snakes, acquired horses as early as the mid–eighteenth century. They soon joined the Northern Shoshone in southern Idaho in developing fully mounted bands and other aspects of Plains culture, including buffalo hunting, extensive warfare, and raiding for horses.

Early Northern Paiute contacts with fur traders such as Jedediah Smith (1827) and Peter Skene Ogden (1829) were friendly, although a party led by Joseph Walker (1833) massacred about 100 peaceful Indians. When reached by whites, the Indians already had a number of non-native items in their possession, such as Spanish blankets, horses, buffalo robes, and Euro-American goods.

Most Northern Paiutes remained on foot until the late 1840s and 1850s. Around this time, heavy traffic on the Oregon and California Trails (late 1840s) and the gold rush of 1848 brought many non-natives through their territory. These people cut down piñon trees for fuel and housing, and their animals destroyed seed-bearing plants and fouled water supplies. Mining resulted in extensive and rapid resource degradation. New diseases took a heavy toll during this period. Indians responded by moving away from the invaders or attacking wagons for food and materials. White traders encouraged thefts by trading supplies for stolen items and animals. Some Indians began to live at the fringes of and work at white ranches and settlements.

Gold and silver strikes in the late 1850s fueled the cycle of conflict and violence. Local conflicts during this period included the brief Pyramid Lake war in 1860; the Owens Valley conflicts in 1862–1863; and the Coeur d'Alene war (1858–1859), which grew out of the Yakima war over white treaty violations. In the Snake war (1866–1867), Chiefs Paulina and Weawea led the Indians to early successes, but eventually the former was killed and the latter surrendered. Survivors settled on the Malheur Reservation (Oregon) in 1871. Winnemucca, who represented several hundred Northern Paiute in the 1860s and 1870s, participated in the Pyramid Lake war and, with his daughter Sarah, went on to serve as a negotiator and peacemaker. In 1873, he refused to take his band to the Malheur Reservation, holding out for a reservation of their own. The Bannocks, too, rebelled in a short-lived war over forced confinement on the Fort Hall Reservation and white treaty violations.

Beginning in 1859, the United States set aside land for Northern Paiute reservations. Eventually, a number of small reservations and colonies were created, ultimately to lose much of their land to non-Indian settlers. Most Northern Paiutes, however, drifted between reservations, combining traditional subsistence activities with growing dependence on local Anglo economies. Conflict on several reservations remained ongoing for decades (some issues are still pending) over issues such as water rights (Pyramid Lake, Walker River), white land usurpation, and fisheries destruction (Pyramid Lake). Refugees from the Bannock war were forced to move to the Yakima Reservation; from there many ultimately moved to the Warm Springs Reservation.

The government also established day and boarding schools from the late 1870s into the 1930s, including Sarah Winnemucca's school at Lovelock. Sarah Winnemucca, who published Life Among the Paiutes in 1884, also worked tirelessly, although ultimately unsuccessfully, for a permanent Paiute reservation. Northern Paiute children also attended Indian boarding schools across the United States. Most traditional subsistence activities ceased during that period, although people continue to gather certain foods. New economic activities included cattle ranching at Fort McDermitt, stock raising, haying, and various businesses.

In 1889, the Northern Paiute Wovoka, known to the whites as Jack Wilson, started a new Ghost Dance religion. It was based on the belief that the world would be reborn with all Indians, alive and dead, living in a precontact paradise. For this to happen, Indians must reject all non-native ways, especially alcohol; live together in peace; and pray and dance. This Ghost Dance followed a previous one established at Walker River in 1869.

Family organization remained more or less intact during the reservation period. By about 1900, Northern Paiutes had lost more than 95 percent of their aboriginal territory. Most groups accepted the Indian

Reorganization Act (IRA) and adopted tribal councils during the 1930s. Shamanism has gradually declined over the years. The Native American Church has had adherents among the Northern Paiute since the 1930s, and the Sweat Lodge Movement became active during the 1960s.

RELIGION Power resided in any animate or inanimate object, feature, or phenomenon. Any person could seek power for help with a skill, but only shamans acquired enough to help, or hurt, others. A power source would expect certain specific behaviors to be followed. Most power sources also had mythological roles.

Shamans, male and female, were religious leaders. Their power often came in a recurring dream. They cured by sucking, retrieving a wandering soul, or administering medicines. Disease could be caused by soul loss, mishandling power, or sorcery. Some shamans could also control weather. Special objects as well as songs, mandated by the power dream, helped them perform their tasks. Power could also be inherited or sought by visiting certain caves.

The sun was considered an especially powerful spirit, and many people prayed to it daily. Some groups celebrated rituals associated with communal food drives or other food-related events.

GOVERNMENT Nuclear families, led (usually) by senior members, were the main political and economic unit. Where various families came together, the local camp was led by a headman who advised, gave speeches on right behavior, and facilitated consensus decisions. The position of headman was often, although not strictly, inherited in the male line. Camp composition changed regularly. Other elders were selected to take charge of various activities such as hunts and irrigation projects.

The traditional headman system was replaced at least in part by the emergence of chiefs during the mounted, raiding years of the 1860s and 1870s. Headmen returned during the early reservation years, however, followed by elected tribal councils beginning in the 1930s.

CUSTOMS Extended families came together semiannually (on occasions such as the fall piñon harvest) to form communities with distinct but not exclusive subsistence areas. Groups were generally named with relation to a food that they ate, a particular geographical region, or another category. After contact, some bands were named after local chiefs (e.g., Winnemucca).

Parents suggested marriages for children in their mid to late teens. Sometimes two or more siblings married two or more siblings. An exchange of presents and cohabitation formalized a marriage, with the couple usually living with the wife's family for the

first year or so. A man could have more than one wife (additional wives might include his wife's sisters or his brother's widow).

New parents were subject to various food and behavior restrictions. Important ceremonies were the girls' puberty rite and the annual mourning ceremony. The former included running to and from a hill for five to ten mornings and making piles of dry brush along the way, bathing, and ritual food restrictions. Boys performed a ceremony at time of their first large game kill. They stood on a pile of sagebrush and chewed the meat and sage, placing it on their joints to make them strong.

The dead were wrapped in skin blankets and buried with their favorite possessions. Houses and other property were burned. Mourners cut their hair, wailed, and covered their faces with ashes and pitch. The mourning period lasted a year. Suspected witches were burned.

Northern Paiutes held athletic contests and played a number of games, such as the hand game, the four-stick game, and dice games.

DWELLINGS Dwelling style and type was marked by great seasonal and regional diversity. Wickiups, used mostly in summer, were huts of brush and reeds over willow pole frames. Winter houses in the north were a cone-shaped pole framework covered with tule mats and earth. Some western groups included a mat-covered entryway. All had central fires. In the mountains, people built semisubterranean winter houses of juniper and pine boughs covered with branches and dirt. Dispersed winter camps consisted of two or three related families (roughly 50 people). In late prehistoric times, the Bannock used buffalo skin tipis during winter.

DIET Diet also varied according to specific location. Plants supplied most food needs. They included roots, bulbs, seeds, nuts, rice grass (ground into meal), cattails, berries, and greens. Roots were either eaten raw or sun dried and stored. Pine nuts and acorns were especially important. Animal foods included fowl (and eggs), squirrel, duck, and other small game as well as mountain sheep, deer, buffalo, and elk. Rabbits were hunted in communal drives. Small mammals were either pit roasted, boiled, or dried for storage. Lizards, grubs, and insects were also eaten. Trout and other fish were crucial in some areas, less important in others. Fish were usually dried and stored for winter. Some groups cultivated wild seed-bearing plants. The Bannock fished for salmon in the Snake River and hunted buffalo in the fall.

KEY TECHNOLOGY Seed beaters, conical carrying baskets, and twined trays for gathering plant material were just some of the baskets produced by Northern Paiute women. Women shelled and ground seeds and nuts with manos and metates or wood or stone mortars and stone pestles. They used fire-hardened digging sticks to extricate roots. Fish were taken with spears, harpoons, hooks, weirs, nets, basket traps, and poison. Irrigation was carried out with dams of boulders and brush and diversion channels. Diapers and similar items were made of softened bark or cattail fluff.

Some pottery was made after about 1000. Tule and cattails were used for many purposes, such as houses, boats, matting, bags, clothing, duck decoys, and sandals. Hunting technology, which differed according to location, included the bow and arrow, traps, corral, snares, deadfalls, and stone knives. Arrow shafts were straightened, smoothed and polished with stone tools, and kept in skin quivers.

TRADE Northern Paiutes obtained some Shoshone mountain sheep horn bows in trade. They also traded fish, moccasins, and beads for pine nuts, fly larvae, and shells. Their trade partners included the Maidu, other Paiute groups, and the Western Shoshone. The Bannock traded for war horses with the Nez Percé.

NOTABLE ARTS Rock art in the region is at least several thousand years old. People also made various stone, wood, and/or clay art objects. Baskets, mainly twined, were largely utilitarian.

TRANSPORTATION Hunters and travelers wore snowshoes in winter. Water transportation was by tule boat. Some groups, especially the Bannock, used horses from the mid–eighteenth century on.

DRESS Again, there was much regional variation based on the availability of materials. Women tended to wear tule or skin skirts, aprons, or dresses, with rabbit-skin or hide capes in winter, the edges of which were sometimes fringed and beaded. They also wore tule or hide moccasins and basket caps. Men wove the rabbit-skin blankets on a loom.

Men wore breechclouts, buckskin (or rabbit-skin or twined-sagebrush) shirts, and rabbit-skin or hide robes or capes and caps in winter. Other winter wear included rabbit-skin socks and twined-sagebrush-bark or badger-skin boots. Both sexes wore hide or sagebrush-bark leggings during winter or while hunting. They also wore headbands and feather decorations in their hair. Men plucked their facial hair and eyebrows. Shell necklaces and face and body paint were usually reserved for dances.

WAR AND WEAPONS Bannock enemies included the Blackfeet and sometimes the Crow and the Nez Percé. They fought with wood and horn bows and stone-tipped arrows, spears, buffalo hide shields, and clubs.

Contemporary Information

GOVERNMENT/RESERVATIONS The following are reservations, colonies, and rancherias that have significant Northern Paiute populations:

Duck Valley Reservation, Owyhee County, Idaho, and Elko County, Nevada (1877; Shoshone and Paiute): 289,819 total acres (in Nevada and Idaho); 1,021 Indians (1990); organized under the IRA; constitution and by-laws adopted, 1936; tribal council.

Fallon Reservation and Colony, Churchill County, Nevada (1887; Paiute and Shoshone): 5,540 acres; 356 resident Indians (1990); 900 enrolled members (1992); seven-member tribal council.

Fort McDermitt Reservation, Malheur County, Oregon, and Humboldt County, Nevada (1892; Paiute and Shoshone): 35,183 acres; 387 resident Indians (1990); 689 enrolled members (1992); eight-member tribal council.

Lovelock Indian Colony, Pershing County, Nevada (1907): 20 acres; 80 resident Indians (1990); 110 enrolled members (1992); five-member tribal council.

Reno-Sparks Indian Colony, Washoe County, Nevada (1917; Washoe and Paiute): 1,984 acres; 262 resident Indians (1990); 724 enrolled members (1992); seven-member tribal council.

Summit Lake Reservation, Humboldt County, Nevada (1913): 10,500 acres; 6 resident Indians (1990); 112 enrolled members (1992); five-member tribal council.

Pyramid Lake Reservation, Lyon, Strorey, and Washoe Counties, Nevada (1874): 475,689 acres, including all of Pyramid Lake; 959 resident Indians (1990); 1,798 enrolled members (1992), almost all of whom live on the reservation; ten-member tribal council.

Walker River Reservation, Churchill, Lyon, and Mineral Counties, Nevada (1871): 323,406 acres; 822 residents (1993); 1,555 enrolled members (1993); seven-member tribal council.

Winnemucca Indian Colony, Humboldt County, Nevada (1971): 340 acres; 17 enrolled members (1992); five-member tribal council.

Yerington Reservation Colony and Campbell Ranch (Yerington Reservation and Trust Lands), Lyon County, Nevada (1916/1936): 1,653 total acres; 354 resident Indians (1992); 659 enrolled members (1992); organized under the IRA; constitution and by-laws adopted, 1937; seven-member tribal council.

Burns Paiute Indian Colony, Burns Paiute Reservation and Trust Lands, Harney County, Oregon (1863): 11,944 acres; 151 resident Indians (1990); 356 enrolled members (1992); five-member tribal council.

Warm Springs Reservation, Clakamas, Jefferson, Marian, and Wasco Counties, Oregon (1855; Confederated Tribes: Northern Paiute, Wallawalla [Warm Springs], and Wasco Indians): 643,507 acres; 2,818 resident Indians (1990); 123 enrolled members (1993). Decisions of the 11-member tribal council are subject to general review by referendum. The IRA constitution was adopted in 1938 (*see also* Wishram in Chapter 5).

Cedarville Rancheria, Modoc County, California (1914): 17 acres; six resident Indians (1990); 22 enrolled members (1992);

Fort Bidwell Reservation, Modoc County, California (1897): 3,330 acres; 107 resident Indians (1990); 162 enrolled members (1992); five-member community council.

Bridgeport Indian Colony, Mono County, California (1976): 40 acres; 37 resident Indians (1990); 96 enrolled members (1992); five-member tribal council.

Susanville Rancheria, Lassen County, California (1923; Paiute, Maidu, and Pit River Indians): 140 acres; 154 Indians (1990); business council.

Benton (Utu Utu Gwaitu) Paiute Reservation, Mono County, California (1915): 160 acres; 52 resident Indians (1990); 84 enrolled members (1991); five-member tribal council.

Women are generally as active as men on tribal councils.

ECONOMY Economic activities differ at each location. Some have no economic resources at all. Most feature some cattle ranching, agriculture on the larger reservations, and tribal businesses such as smoke shops, minimarts, and especially government (tribal) employment. Fishing and recreational activities dominate the economy at Pyramid Lake. Walker River is a member of the Council of Energy Resource Tribes (CERT). Some Indians work at off-reservation jobs. A few are able to support themselves with crafts work.

LEGAL STATUS The following Northern Paiute bands, locations, and peoples are federally recognized tribal entities: Cedarville Rancheria, Bridgeport Paiute Indian Colony, Burns Paiute Indian Colony, Fort Bidwell Indian Community, Fort McDermitt Paiute and Shoshone Tribes, Lovelock Paiute Tribe, Paiute-Shoshone Tribe of the Fallon Reservation and Colony, Pyramid Lake Paiute Tribe, Reno-Sparks Indian Colony, Shoshone-Paiute Tribes of the Duck Valley Reservation, Summit Lake Paiute Tribe, Susanville Indian Rancheria, Utu Utu Gwaitu Paiute Tribe, Walker River Paiute Tribe, Winnemucca Indian Colony, and Yerington Paiute Tribe. The Confederated Tribes of the Warm Springs Reservation is a federally recognized tribal entity. The Pahrump Band of Paiutes has applied for federal recognition, as have the Washoe/Paiute of Antelope Valley, California.

DAILY LIFE Traditional kinship relations remain relatively strong among the Northern Paiute. Although there are various language preservation programs and activities, such as the dictionary and grammar produced by the Yerington tribe, few young Northern Paiute children outside of Fort McDermitt learn to speak their native language. Health, education, and outmigration continue as significant areas of concern.

Most Northern Paiutes are Christians, although some also practice elements of their traditional religion. Others participate in regional religions such as the Native American Church, the Sweat Lodge Movement, and the Sun Dance. The Sun Dance at McDermitt Reservation, introduced in 1981, varies considerably from sun dances held among Utes and Northern and Eastern Shoshones. It includes a pipe ceremony, a peyote ceremony, and a sweat lodge ceremony. Women can dance unless they are menstruating or are pregnant. Men and women pierce themselves. This ceremony is part of the Traditional-Unity Movement.

In 1991, the Truckee River compact confirmed water rights for Pyramid Lake and Fallon; it also granted compensation for water misappropriated earlier.

Paiute, Owens Valley

Owens Valley Paiute (`P ī ū t) is the name given to a number of Paiute groups distinguished in part by their semisettled, cooperative lifestyle as well as their irrigation practices. They were largely responsible for bringing elements of California culture into the southern Great Basin. Non-natives formerly included them with the Monache or Mono Indians. "Paiute" may have meant "True Ute" or "Water Ute" and was applied only to the Southern Paiute until the 1850s. Their self-designation was *Numa,* or "People."

LOCATION Traditionally, the groups now known as Owens Valley Paiute controlled the Owens River Valley, more than 80 miles long and an average of 7 miles wide. The fertile and well-watered region, east of the southern Sierra Nevada, contains a wealth of environmental diversity. Presently, Owens Valley Paiutes live on a number of their own reservations (see "Government/Reservations" under "Contemporary Information"), on other nearby reservations, and among the area's general population.

POPULATION In the early nineteenth century there were about 7,500 total Paiutes (perhaps

1,500–2,000 Owens Valley Paiutes). In the 1990s, about 6,300 Paiutes, including about 2,500 Owens Valley Paiutes, lived on reservations.

LANGUAGE The Owens Valley Paiutes' dialects of Mono are, with Northern Paiute, part of the Western Numic (Shoshonean) branch of the Uto-Aztecan linguistic family.

Historical Information

HISTORY Owens Valley Paiutes first saw non-natives in the early nineteenth century (although they may have seen Spanish explorers earlier). These early explorers, trappers, and prospectors encountered Indians who were already irrigating wild crops.

Military and civil personnel surveyed the region in the late 1850s with an eye toward establishing a reservation for local Indians. The first non-Indian settlers arrived in 1861. These ranchers grew crops that fed nearby miners and other whites. As the white population increased, so did conflicts over water rights and irrigated lands. Whites cut down vital piñons for fuel. Hungry Indians stole cattle, and whites retaliated by killing Indians. As of early 1862, however, the Indians still controlled the Owens Valley, because they formed local military alliances.

Camp Independence was founded in July 1862 as a military outpost. Fighting continued well into 1863, until whites got the upper hand by pursuing a scorched earth policy. Many Indians surrendered but were back in the valley within a few years. By this time, however, whites had taken over most of their best lands, and a diminished Indian population was left to settle around towns, ranches, and mining camps, working mostly as laborers. Indians on newly reserved lands, increasingly including Western Shoshone families, worked mainly as small-scale farmers.

Indian schools opened in the late nineteenth century, although formal reservations were not established until the twentieth. Too small for ranches, the early reservations supported small-scale farming as the main economic activity. However, many Indians still lived on nonreservation lands and on other, non-Paiute reservations.

From the early twentieth century through the 1930s, the city of Los Angeles bought most of Owens Valley, primarily for water rights. This development destroyed the local economy, eliminating the low-level Indian jobs. The city also proposed new ways to dispossess and consolidate the remaining Indians at that time. Ultimately, most Indian people approved of the series of land exchanges (those at Fort Independence rejected the plans). During the 1940s, the federal government built new housing and sewer and irrigation systems on the new Indian lands.

RELIGION Religious observances centered on round dances and festivities associated with the fall harvest. Professional singers in elaborate dance regalia performed in a dance corral. The girls' puberty ceremony was also important.

The cry was an annual Yuman-derived mourning ceremony for those who had died during the previous year. A ritual face washing (the first time since the death that the face was washed) marked the end of the official spousal year of mourning.

Male and female shamans were primarily doctors and religious leaders. Their power often came in a recurring dream. They cured by sucking, retrieving a wandering soul, or administering medicines. Disease was caused by soul loss, mishandling power, or sorcery. Special objects as well as songs, mandated by the power dream, helped them perform their tasks. They might acquire a good deal of clandestine political power by making headmen dependent on them.

GOVERNMENT Owens Valley Paiutes lived in semipermanent base camps, or hamlets, named for natural features. The camps were semipermanent in that (usually) the same families occupied them intermittently throughout the year and year to year. This level of social organization showed some similarities to California "tribelets." Within the camps families were completely independent. Families might share or coordinate in subsistence activities, but doing so was informal and unstructured.

Hamlets within a given area cooperated in intermarriage, irrigation, rabbit and deer drives, funerals, and the use of the sweat house. The headmen or chiefs directed these communal activities. Their other duties included conducting festivals and ceremonies, overseeing construction of the assembly lodge, and determining the death penalty for a shaman accused of witchcraft. The position was hereditary, usually in the male line.

CUSTOMS Although many people maintained the dams, an elected irrigator was responsible for watering a specific area. In summer, most families pursued hunting and gathering activities. They generally occupied their valley dwelling places in spring, the time of irrigation; fall, the time of social activities; and winter, unless the pine nut or Indian rice grass crops failed.

People held athletic contests and played a number of games, such as the hand game, shinny, the four-stick game, hoop and pole, and dice games.

DWELLINGS The Owens Valley Paiutes built several kinds of structures. The circular, semisubterranean sweat house served as an assembly house, a dormitory for young men, and a place for men to sweat. It was built, under sponsorship and supervision of local chief, of a central ridgepole supported by forked posts. A framework of poles was covered with earth and grass. Heat was by direct fire. The building also contained a central smoke hole, and the doorway faced east.

The winter family dwelling, 15 to 20 feet in diameter, was conical, semisubterranean, and built on a pole framework (no center ridgepole) covered with tule, grass, and sometimes earth. At mountain pine nut gathering winter camps, people built a wooden structure, perhaps with a gabled roof, consisting of poles of dead timber covered with bark slabs and boughs. In summer, ramadas of willow poles supporting a rectangular roof and covered with tule or brush, as well as semicircular brush windbreaks, served as the main living spaces.

DIET Diet also varied according to season and specific location. In general, the staple was pine nuts, harvested in autumn. Other important foods included acorns (prepared California-style); wild seeds, roots, and bulbs; berries; nuts; grasses (such as rice grass, ground into meal); cattails; and greens. Seeds were harvested in summer. Roots were either eaten raw or sand dried and stored. There was also some intentional irrigation of wild roots and seed-bearing plants.

In addition to the all-important plant resources, there was some fishing of suckers, minnows, and pupfish. The larvae and pupae of brine shrimp and fly were gathered, dried, shelled, and stored. People who had the assistance of a supernatural power hunted squirrels, quail, and other small game. The meat of small mammals was either pit roasted, boiled, or dried for storage. Rabbits were hunted in communal drives, deer in hunting teams. Caterpillar larvae were baked and sun dried.

KEY TECHNOLOGY For irrigation, Owens Valley Paiutes used temporary dams and feeder streams of summer floodwaters. Their main tool was a long wooden water staff. They used nets to catch rabbits and fish. Fish were also speared or poisoned and often dried and stored for winter.

Hunting technology differed according to location, but usually featured a sinew-backed juniper bow, arrows, nets, snares, and deadfalls. Twined and coiled basketry included burden baskets with tumplines for distance (even transmountain) carrying and seed beaters. Fire was made with a drill, and smoldering, cigar-shaped fire matches were used to transport it. Roots were dug with mountain mahogany digging sticks. Nuts were ground and shelled with manos and metates or wood or stone mortars and stone pestles. Some women made pottery, from the mid–seventeenth to the mid–nineteenth century.

TRADE The Monache, Miwok, Tubatulabal, and Yokuts of California were important trade, marriage, and ceremonial partners. Strung shell beads served as a medium of exchange. Acorns were usually imported, from the Monache, for example, in exchange for salt and pine nuts. The Owens Valley Paiute also traded shell money to the Western Shoshone for salt and rabbit-skin blankets.

NOTABLE ARTS Local rock art is at least several thousand years old. Art objects were also made from a variety of materials, including stone, wood, and clay.

TRANSPORTATION Some groups plied the lakes and marshes with tule boats.

DRESS Type and style of clothing varied according to location. In general, women wore tule or skin skirts, aprons, or dresses. Some women wore relatively large basket caps. Men favored a breechclout and perhaps a buckskin (or rabbit-skin or twined-sagebrush) shirt.

In winter, both sexes wore rabbit-skin or hide capes, hide or sagebrush-bark leggings, tule or hide moccasins, and fur caps. Other winter wear included rabbit-skin socks and twined sagebrush-bark or badger-skin boots. Both sexes wore sagebrush sandals and socks, headbands, and feather decorations in their hair. Men plucked their facial hair and eyebrows.

Men wove rabbit-skin blankets on a vertical frame. Shell necklaces and face and body paint were usually reserved for dances. Diapers and other such items were made of softened bark or cattail fluff.

WAR AND WEAPONS The aboriginal Owens Valley Paiute seldom fought.

Contemporary Information

GOVERNMENT/RESERVATIONS Significant numbers of Owens Valley Paiutes live on the following reservations:

Bishop Colony, Inyo County, California (1912; Owens Valley Paiute-Shoshone): 875 acres; 934 resident Indians (1990); 1,350 enrolled members (1991); five-member tribal council.

Fort Independence Reservation, Inyo County, California (1915; Owens Valley Paiute and Shoshone): 356 acres; 38 resident Indians (1990); 123 enrolled members (1991); three-member business council.

Lone Pine Reservation, Inyo County, California (1939; Owens Valley Paiute-Shoshone): 237 acres; 168 resident Indians (1990); 296 enrolled members (1991); five-member tribal council.

Big Pine Reservation, Inyo County, California (1939; Owens Valley Paiute and Shoshone): 279 acres; 331 resident Indians (1990); 413 enrolled members (1991); five-member tribal council.

Benton (Utu Utu Gwaitu) Paiute Reservation, Mono County, California (1915): 160 acres; 52 resident Indians (1990); 84 enrolled members (1991); five-member tribal council.

Each Owens Valley reservation is governed by a tribal council. Another administrative body, the Owens Valley Paiute-Shoshone Band of Indians (Big Pine, Lone Pine, Bishop, and Fort Independence) administers grant funds and valley-wide programs.

ECONOMY The museum-cultural complex at Bishop provides some employment. Indians are also employed with the tribes and with a number of tribal businesses. Lone Pine, Fort Independence, and Benton have few current economic resources. There is some employment in local mines as well as some tourism.

LEGAL STATUS The following Paiute bands, locations, and peoples are federally recognized tribal entities: Fort Independence Indian Community, Paiute-Shoshone Indians of the Bishop Community of the Bishop Colony, Paiute-Shoshone Indians of the Lone Pine Community, and Utu Utu Gwaitu Paiute Tribe. The Washoe/Paiute of Antelope Valley, California, have petitioned for government recognition.

DAILY LIFE The Bishop Colony maintains a culture center, a museum, and other facilities and programs. With the Owens Valley Paiute-Shoshone Band, they sponsor a summer powwow and rodeo. In the 1980s, elders persuaded the forest services not to apply pesticides against a Pandora moth infestation of nearby piñon pines; the moth's larvae are still gathered and eaten, as are pine nuts and other traditional foods. Much of the Owens River and its watershed has been diverted to Los Angeles. Few people still speak Owens Valley Mono, although individual reservations sponsor cultural awareness and language programs. Other ongoing traditional activities include the cry ceremony, food gathering, and crafts. Outmigration remains a problem, as are poverty, poor health, and the continuing lack of job opportunities.

Paiute, Southern

Southern Paiute (`P ī ū t) is a designation for approximately 16 seminomadic, culturally distinct, and politically autonomous Great Basin groups, such as Kaibab, Kaiparowits, Panguitch, Shivwits, Moapa, Paranigets, and Panaca. Their self-designation was *Nuwu*, or "Person." The Chemehuevi (*see* Chapter 1) were originally a Southern Paiute group. "Southern Paiute" is a modern construction and is more a linguistic than a cultural convention. "Paiute" may have meant "True Ute" or "Water Ute" and was applied to the Northern Paiute only after the 1850s. To the north and northeast, some Southern Paiute groups merged with the Western and Southern Ute.

LOCATION Southern Paiutes lived and continue to live in southwest Utah, southern Nevada, north-

west Arizona, and southeast California. The San Juan Paiutes lived east of the Colorado River. Southern Paiute territory encompasses a great environmental diversity, including canyons and high deserts of the Colorado Plateau and the Great Basin.

POPULATION The entire early-nineteenth-century Paiute population was roughly 7,500. In 1990, roughly 700 Southern Paiutes lived on reservations.

LANGUAGE Southern Paiute languages belong to the southern Numic (Shoshonean) branch of the Uto-Aztecan language family. Their languages were mutually unintelligible with those of the Northern Paiutes.

Historical Information

HISTORY Numic-speaking Southern Paiutes came into their historic area around 1000, perhaps from around Death Valley. They gradually replaced Hopis in the south and may have learned agriculture from them. They encountered a Spanish expedition in 1776 but adopted neither horses nor much else of Spanish culture. However, diseases and some material items may have preceded actual contact. Some groups were practicing agriculture before 1800.

By 1830, the trail established by the first Spanish explorers was in heavy use. The increased traffic depleted the area's natural resources. The trail also facilitated raiding and trading parties by both Indian and non-native peoples. Mounted Utes and Navajos, and later Spanish expeditions and American trappers, were engaged in raiding and trading for Southern Paiute slaves. Starving Southern Paiutes sometimes sold their children for food. One effect of this situation was the Paiutes' self-removal from areas that were economically productive but close to slave raiders. The loss of a significant percentage of their young also contributed to the population reduction that was well under way by this time.

Mormon settlers arrived in 1847. At first participants in the slave trade, they had it legally abolished by the mid-1850s (although they continued to "adopt" Indian children). However, their practice of establishing settlements and missions on the best land, thereby depleting native resources and squeezing the Indians out, soon left the latter as beggars. Many Mormons alternated between seeing Indians negatively, as did most Americans, and positively, because of a perceived connection to biblical Israelites. About the same time, the Chemehuevi split off and moved down the Colorado River.

Some groups retaliated against whites by raiding their settlements. In a move to head off violence, six Mormon Southern Paiute headmen agreed in 1865 to move their people to the Uintah and Ouray Reservation, the home of their Ute enemies. The treaty remained unratified, however, and was later abandoned. By the 1870s roughly 80 percent of Southern Paiutes had died as a result of starvation and disease (Southern Paiute death rates exceeded birth rates well—in some cases, halfway—into the twentieth century). Survivors had begun the process of acculturation, gathering into larger camps and working in new white towns.

By executive order, a reservation (Moapa) of roughly 3,900 square miles was established in Nevada for the Southern Paiutes in 1872. Although few Indians moved there, it was expanded in 1874 with the idea that Southern Paiutes would be turned into farmers and ranchers. Soon, however, the reservation was greatly reduced in size. When promised federal support was not forthcoming, conditions began rapidly to deteriorate.

Meanwhile, Indians in southern Utah were either seeking wage work or trying desperately to hold on in their traditional locations. In the late 1880s, after a local white rancher persuaded the government to remove the Shivwits from their lands, the Shivwits Reservations was established in southern Utah, Though it was later expanded, the land was never good enough to support the population, even without inevitable conflicts over water and range rights. Many residents eventually moved away. Several small Mormon-affiliated farming communities had also been established by 1885.

Several reservations were created for Southern Paiutes in the twentieth century (although one, the San Juan Paiute Reservation, was returned to the public domain shortly after an oil company expressed an interest in the parcel). In the mid-1950s, the Utah Paiute (Shivwits, Indian Peaks, Koosharem, and Kanosh Bands) were removed from federal control (terminated), although policy dictated that this would not happen until the people were ready and willing to take care of themselves. (The groups were restored in 1980.) The immediate effects of this action included a tremendous loss of the modest land base (through individual allotment sales and nonpayment of taxes), greater impoverishment, exploitative leases to non-Indians, removal of health services, and greatly increased social problems. When people tried to hunt rabbits again for survival, they discovered that many animals had been poisoned by fallout from the Nevada nuclear test site. Perhaps not surprisingly, many people left the reservation during these years.

In 1965, Southern Paiutes were awarded $8,250,000 ($0.27 an acre) as official compensation for their aboriginal land. The bands used their shares in different ways, but nearly all provided for some direct per capita payments as well as long-term concerns. New federal programs during this time also helped lift many Indians out of dire poverty and provide them with decent housing. During the 1960s, many people were poisoned with the insecticide DDT as a result of government and farmer spraying. Women basket makers, who pulled willow twigs through their teeth, were especially hard hit.

RELIGION Shamans provided religious leadership; they cured and conducted ceremonies such as the girls' puberty rite. They could be men or women, although women were more often considered evil. Power dreams, perhaps dreamed in a special cave, also provided instructions and songs.

Disease was attributed to sorcerers, a ghost-inspired poisonous object (necessitating the removal of the object by sucking), or soul loss (cured by the shaman's recapturing the soul). The mourning ceremony, or cry, was undertaken by wealthy relatives of a recently (three months to a year) deceased person so they could eat and sleep well. It was a feast at which many items were destroyed.

In general, groups came together for singing (men) and round dancing on occasions such as the harvest and before a war. Some groups danced the 1890 Ghost Dance.

GOVERNMENT Camp groups were composed of between 1 to 10 or 15 households, many of whom were related. They were led by a headman as well as the best hunters and gatherers. Headmen served in an advisory capacity. This position tended to remain in the family and among men but did not necessarily pass from father to son (except for the Chemehuevi and Las Vegas).

CUSTOMS The basic unit was the nuclear family. Each group generally gathered food, hunted, and camped together. Each was associated with a specific though nonexclusive geographic territory.

People married early; girls might be pre- or postpubescent. Most marriages were monogamous. Gender-determined rituals over infants' navel stumps underscored the priority placed on hunting for men and industry in domestic chores for women. Both new parents observed postpartum behavior and food restrictions.

Meat that a boy killed was given away to the elderly until he reached puberty. Puberty rites for both sexes included bathing, body painting, hair trimming, and physical endurance. Relatives prepared a corpse, then underwent behavior and food restrictions. Most groups cremated their dead. The dead person's possessions were burned or buried, and his or her house was torn down and moved. Some groups occasionally killed a relative as company for the deceased. There was a permanent taboo on using the name of the dead.

Springs were considered inheritable private property. People commonly gambled on hand and other games such as shinny, four-stick, hoop and pole, and target. Other games included ring and pin as well as athletic contests.

DWELLINGS Type of residence varied with season and locale. Winter dwellings included caves; conical houses of cedar bark, rushes, or grass over a tree limb framework; and gabled houses of willow and earth over pole frames. Most summer houses were brush shelters, shades, and windbreaks. Canvas or skin tipis were adapted from the Ute beginning in the mid–nineteenth century.

DIET Southern Paiutes migrated seasonally, following the food supply. Their diet was based on hunting, gathering, and some agriculture (mostly corn, beans, and squash, using floodplain or ditch irrigation). Tobacco patches and grasslands were burned to encourage growth.

Women gathered wild plants, including goldenrod and grass seeds, roots, pine nuts, yucca dates, cactus fruit, agave, nuts, juniper berries, mesquite, and screwbean. Grasshoppers, caterpillars, ant larvae, and insect grubs were also eaten. Seeds were parched, ground, and eaten as mush or as bread. Men hunted small game, the major source of protein, with the assistance of spirits and/or shamans. Rabbits were especially important. They were hunted individually or driven communally into 100-yard-long nets. Big game included deer, antelope, and mountain sheep. Some groups fished occasionally.

KEY TECHNOLOGY Fire-hardened sticks were used to dig roots. Bows were made of cedar, locust, or mountain sheep horn. Basketry was a major craft. Coiled and twined baskets were used for winnowing and parching trays, hats, cradles, burden baskets, and containers. Twined seed beaters were an important gathering implement. Men made nets for hunting and carrying burdens. They also tanned hides, scraping with a sharp bone and rubbing with brain and bone marrow. Some pottery also existed.

TRADE Southern Paiutes mainly traded with each other, although there was some intergroup trade as well as intermarriage and economic and ceremonial cooperation with Western Shoshone groups. The Chemehuevi and Las Vegas people were in direct contact with Indians of southern California, partly in connection with the trade in Pacific Coast haliotis shells. Both, but especially the Chemehuevi, took on the Mojave culture in the nineteenth century. They also hunted in Yavapai and Hualapai territory and intermarried with the former.

Other groups traded buckskins, hides, robes, blankets, and other items to Utes, Navajos, and Hopis for items such as blankets, maize, and beads. The Kaibabs traded buckskins and other items to other Paiute groups for agricultural products, horses, dogs, pipes, robes, beads, and other items.

NOTABLE ARTS Many Southern Paiutes, especially the Moapa and the Kaibab, made fine baskets. Songs and narratives were also aesthetic arts. Most songs were derived from dreams and sung without accompaniment. Men told tales in winter, including songs and some theater. Local rock art is at least several thousand years old. Art objects were made from a variety of materials, including stone, wood, and clay.

TRANSPORTATION Women carried burdens in baskets with head tumplines; men used net and chest tumplines. Southern Paiutes traveled widely for subsistence, trade, and pleasure. Like the Mojave, the Chemehuevi used log rafts and reed balsas.

DRESS Although dress varied with location and available materials, women tended to wear double aprons of skin or vegetable fiber and basket caps. Men wore skin breechclouts, if anything, and skin caps. In colder weather, people wore woven rabbit-fur robes, which also served as bedding, as well as twined-bark leggings.

People generally went barefoot or wore bark or yucca sandals. Hunters used snowshoes in winter. Red body paint was used against the sun and also as decoration for life-cycle occasions. Both sexes tattooed their faces. Pierced ears were decorated with stick, stone, and shell earrings.

WAR AND WEAPONS The Southern Paiutes were generally on friendly terms with each other and with neighboring groups. In early historical times, Utes, Navajos, and non-native New Mexicans aggressively raided Southern Paiutes for slaves. The Chemehuevi–Las Vegas were more warlike. They exterminated the desert Mojave in the late eighteenth century, and the Chemehuevi moved into their territory. Weapons were mostly clubs.

Contemporary Information

GOVERNMENT/RESERVATIONS The following colonies and reservations have significant numbers of Southern Paiutes:

Las Vegas Indian Colony, Clark County, Nevada (1911): roughly 3,850 acres; 52 resident Indians (1992); 71 enrolled members (1992); seven-member tribal council.

Moapa River Reservation, Clark County, Nevada (1875): 71,955 acres; 190 resident Indians (1990); 273 enrolled members (1992); six-member business council.

Paiute of Utah Reservation, Iron, Millard, Sevier, and Washington Counties, Utah (1972; Cedar City, Indian Peaks, Kanosh, Koosharem, and Shivwits Bands): 32,458 acres; 323 resident Indians (1990); 609 enrolled members (1992); six-member tribal council.

Kaibab Reservation, Mohave County, Arizona (1913): 120,413 acres; 102 resident Indians (1990); 212 enrolled members (1992); seven-member tribal council.

San Juan Paiute, Arizona and Utah: no reservation currently; 115 Indians live on traditional land (1992); 221 enrolled members (1992); eight-member tribal council.

Pahrump Band of Paiute Indians, Nevada: no reservation currently; 50 Indians live on traditional lands (1992); 70 enrolled members (1992); five-member tribal council.

Although these communities all have constitutions and by-laws, a more traditional decision-making process generally occurs in practice.

ECONOMY Various economic activities on the different reservations and colonies include a cooperative farm, a gift shop, a minimart, a sand and gravel company, and a fireworks and smoke shop at Moapa. The unemployment rate there approaches 90 percent. Promised jobs at a nearby power plant have failed to materialize. Moapa was granted an additional 70,000 acres in the 1980s.

Las Vegas Colony boasts relatively low unemployment, thanks largely to employment in the city as well as a tribal smoke shop and minimart. They received an additional 3,700 acres northwest of the city in 1983, slated for commercial, industrial, recreational, and residential development.

There is a cattle cooperative and tourist center at Kaibab. The Utah Paiutes were granted 4,770 additional acres of land in 1984, plus a multimillion-dollar trust fund. Activities there include farming, mining leases, cattle leases, and cut-and-sew operations. The San Juan Paiutes have revived their traditional excellence in basket making.

LEGAL STATUS The following Paiute bands, locations, and peoples are federally recognized tribal entities: Kaibab Band of Paiute Indians, Las Vegas Tribe of Paiute Indians, Moapa Band of Paiute Indians, Paiute Indian Tribe of Utah, and San Juan Paiute Tribe. The Pahrump Band of Paiutes has applied for federal recognition.

DAILY LIFE Although the past remains palpable, many' traditional practices have disappeared. Some groups maintain the cry, combining it with funerals, as well as traditional storytelling, the girls' puberty and first child rituals, and some traditional games. A few people still obtain part of their diet from traditional sources. The kinship system remains strong. Except at San Juan, few but the elderly still speak the languages, although there are tribal programs aimed at increasing native language proficiency. Major festive occasions are the Bear Dance, the Ute Sun Dance, and rodeos. Many Kaibabs have been converted to

Mormonism. The Utah Paiute endure very high unemployment and many health-related problems, including high cancer rates likely caused by living downwind from the Nevada (nuclear) test site. Most communities have some form of local health care as well as special assistance programs for the elderly.

The San Juan Paiutes struggled for over 100 years with the Navajo and with white authorities over possession of parts of northern Arizona. For much of this period, they were largely forgotten or counted as Navajos, although the people themselves retained their identities. After the death in 1969 of their longtime chief tribal elder, Alfred Lehi, they began taking action to regain their official status. They received federal recognition in 1989 and continue to work for formal landholdings. This community remains relatively traditional.

Shoshone, Eastern or Wind River

Eastern, or Wind River, Shoshone (Sh ō `sh ō n ē), a group grounded in Great Basin traditions who modified their culture to include elements from Plains and postcontact cultures. The Comanche broke away from the Eastern Shoshone about 1700 and moved south toward Texas (*see* Comanche [Chapter 6]). The term "Shoshone" is of dubious origin and was not a self-designation.

LOCATION The Eastern Shoshone lived in western Wyoming from at least the sixteenth century on, expanded well into the northern Great Plains through the eighteenth century, and then retreated in the nineteenth century. They were loosely divided into two groups: Mountain Sheep Eaters to the north and west and Buffalo Eaters to the east and south. Most Eastern Shoshones now live on the Wind River Reservation, in Fremont and Hot Springs Counties, Wyoming.

POPULATION There were perhaps 3,000 Eastern Shoshones in 1840. In 1990, 5,674 Eastern Shoshones and Arapahos lived on the Wind River Reservation.

LANGUAGE The Eastern Shoshones spoke dialects of Shoshone, a Central Numic (Shoshonean) language of the Uto-Aztecan language family.

Historical Information

HISTORY Beginning at least as early as 1500, the Comanche-Shoshone began expanding eastward onto the Great Plains and adopting wide-scale buffalo hunting. With the acquisition of horses, about 1700, they also began widespread raiding and developed a much stronger and more centralized leadership. It was roughly at this time that the Comanche departed for places south. Armed (with firearms), the Blackfeet and other tribes began driving the Eastern Shoshone off the westward plains beginning in the late eighteenth century. Major smallpox epidemics occurred during that period, and the Eastern Shoshone adopted the Sun Dance introduced around 1800. Extensive intermarriage also occurred with the Crow, Nez Percé, and Métis.

During most of the nineteenth century, the Eastern Shoshone, under their chief, Washakie, were often allied with whites and grew prosperous. During the peak of the fur trade, from 1810 to 1840, the Eastern Shoshone sold up to 2,000 buffalo skins a year. When settlers began pouring into their territory in the 1850s, the Eastern Shoshone, under Washakie, tried to accommodate. In the Fort Bridger Treaty of 1868 they received 44 million acres; this figure was later reduced to fewer than 2 million. During the next 15 or so years they lived in a roughly traditional way on their reservation.

Because the Shoshone fought with the U.S. Army against the Lakota on many occasions, they felt betrayed when the government placed the Arapaho, their traditional enemies, on their reservation in 1878. The disappearance of the buffalo in the 1880s spelled the end of their traditional way of life. From the late nineteenth century and into the mid–twentieth century, the Eastern Shoshone, now confined to reservations, experienced extreme hardship, population loss, and cultural decline. They had no decent land, hunting was prohibited, government rations were issued at starvation levels, and they could find no off-reservation employment because of poor transportation and white prejudice. Disease, especially tuberculosis, was rampant. Life expectancy was roughly 22 years at that time. The Indian Service controlled the reservation

A slow recovery began in late 1930s. Land claims victories brought vastly more land as well as an infusion of cash (almost $3.5 million). Concurrently, the tribal council, hitherto relatively weak, began assuming greater control of all aspects of reservation life. By the mid-1960s, the incidence of disease was markedly lower, owing in large part to the diligent efforts of women. Indicators such as housing, diet, economic resources (such as oil and gas leases), education, and real political control had all increased. Life expectancy had risen to 40–45 years. Traditional religious activity remained strong and meaningful. And yet severe and ongoing problems remained, including continuing white prejudice and a corresponding lack of off-reservation job opportunities, outmigration, slow economic development, and fear of the growing strength of the Arapaho.

RELIGION The Eastern Shoshone knew two basic kinds of religious practice. One was aimed at an individual's obtaining the assistance of supernatural powers from spirits. In exchange for power, such spirits, which could also be dangerous, demanded adherence to strict behavioral taboos. Power was gained either through dances or by sleeping in sacred places. Success in obtaining power was marked by a vision through which the power transferred skills or protections as well as songs, fetishes, and taboos. Power might also be transferred from one shaman to another by blowing. Should a person's power depart, a shaman had to recapture it lest the person die. Shamans did not so much control power as they were dependent on it.

The other kind of religious practice was designed to ensure the welfare of the community and nature as a whole by the observance of group ceremonials. The Father, the Shuffling (Ghost), and the Sun Dances were all addressed toward beneficent beings. The first two, during which men and women sang sacred songs, often took place at night in any season except summer. The Shuffling Dance was particularly important to Mountain Sheep Eaters.

The four-night and three-day Sun Dance was held in summer and featured exhaustion owing to dancing and lack of water. Introduced from the Plains around 1800, it symbolized the power and cohesion of the tribe and of the generations. It was an occasion for demonstrating virility, courage, and supernatural powers. Male dancers first participated in ritual sweats and other preparations, which began as early as the preceding winter. The ceremony itself, held around ten outer poles encircling a buffalo head mounted on a center pole, was followed by a great feast of buffalo tongues. Little boys were charged with grabbing the tongues.

Spirit places, things, and people were inherently dangerous and included ghosts, whirlwinds, old or menstruating women, death, and illness. Illness was seen as coming from either a breach of taboo or malevolent spirits. Sacred items and activities included sweating, burning certain grasses and wood, smoking wild tobacco, eagle feathers, paints, and certain songs. The peyote cult began on the reservation around 1900.

GOVERNMENT Centralization was the key to successful buffalo hunting and warfare and thus to eighteenth- and nineteenth-century Eastern Shoshone survival. During prosperous times (for instance, those with strong chieftainships) and when they came together seasonally as a tribe (for instance, for the spring buffalo hunt and the summer Sun Dance), the Eastern Shoshone numbered between 1,500 and 3,000.

A chief was at least middle-aged and of military or shamanistic training. He had authority over hunting, migration, and other issues. He and his assistants controlled the two military-police societies. His several distinctions included possessing a painted tipi and a special feathered headdress. He also acted as chief diplomat for external disputes.

The Eastern Shoshone separated into between three and five bands in winter, camping mainly in the Wind River Valley. Each band had a chief as well as military societies. Bands were loosely identified with particular geographic regions. Membership fluctuated, with extended family groups joining different Shoshone bands or perhaps even bands of other tribes such as the Crow.

CUSTOMS   Women were in general subordinate to men, chiefly because menstruation set them apart as sources of ritual pollution. The younger wife or wives usually suffered in instances of polygyny. Widows were dispossessed. At the same time, women gained status as individuals through their skills as gatherers, crafters, gamblers, midwives, and child care providers. Particularly during the fur trade, alliances with white trappers and traders were made with daughters and sisters, leading to important interethnic ties.

Social status positions were earned through the use (or nonuse) of supernatural power, except that age and sex also played a role. Infants and small children were not recognized as sexually different. Boys began their search for supernatural power around adolescence. "Men" were those who were married and members of a military society.

Girls helped their mothers until marriage, which was arranged shortly after the onset of puberty. Menstrual restrictions included gathering firewood (a key female chore) and refraining from meat and daytime sleeping. A good husband was a good provider, although he might be considerably older.

Wealth and prestige accrued to curers; midwives; good gamblers; hunters and traders; and fast runners. Property was often destroyed or abandoned at death. Generosity was a central value: Giveaways for meritorious occasions were common. Men cared for war and buffalo horses, women for packhorses. High-stakes gambling games included the hand and four-stick dice game, double-ball shinny (women), and foot races.

DWELLINGS   After the move onto the Plains, women made buffalo skin tipis according to a strenuous, time-consuming procedure. Men decorated the tipis. Beds, a central fireplace, and parfleches filled the inside. The master bed had a decorated antelope hide or two.

DIET   Bands engaged in small-scale hunting and gathering in summer; buffalo were hunted communally in spring and especially in fall. Staples included buffalo, elk, beaver, mule deer, antelope, mountain sheep, moose, bear, jackrabbit, and smaller game. The winter diet relied heavy on dried buffalo (pemmican). Trout and other fish, caught in spring, were also a staple. Fish were eaten fresh or sun dried or smoked for storage. Important plants included camas, wild onion, berries, and sunflower seeds.

KEY TECHNOLOGY   Most goods were made from animal (especially the buffalo) and plant materials as well as minerals such as flint, obsidian, slate, and steatite. Every part of the buffalo was used, including the dung (for fuel). In the historic period, iron from non-native traders became very important.

Fishing equipment included traps, weirs, dams, and spears. Roots in particular were cooked in earth ovens. Food was kept in leather parfleches. Men prepared shields, hide drums, and rattles; women made most other leather work, such as tipis, clothing, containers, and trade items. They also made coiled baskets.

With counting sticks, Eastern Shoshones could keep track of numbers up to 100,000.

TRADE   Perhaps the largest regional intertribal trade gathering was held in midsummer at Green River, Wyoming.

NOTABLE ARTS   Art objects were made from a variety of materials, including stone, wood, and clay. Leather goods included tipis, parfleches, shields, and other items. Elkhides were painted to depict important events such as Sun Dances, buffalo hunts, and warfare. The best-made goods were often decorated with beads or drilled elk's teeth. People made pictographs at the sites of particularly sacred places.

TRANSPORTATION   Eastern Shoshones had the horse from about 1700 on. A horse (formerly dog)-drawn travois transported the infirm as well as households. Dogs aided in transportation, hunting, and war. Snowshoes were worn for winter hunting.

DRESS   Most clothing and blankets were made of buffalo and other hides. With their eastern expansion, the Eastern Shoshone adopted Plains fringed-and-beaded styles.

WAR AND WEAPONS   Beginning in the eighteenth century, the state of war was more or less continuous, and warfare took a great toll on the Eastern Shoshone. There were two military societies. About 100–150 brave young men were Yellow Brows. The recruitment ritual included backwards speech (no for yes, for example). This fearless society acted as vanguards on the march. They fought to the death in combat and had a major role keeping order on the buffalo hunt. Their Big Horse Dance was a highly ritualistic preparation for battle. Logs were older men who took up the rear on the march. Both groups were entitled to blacken their faces.

Shamans participated in war by foretelling events and curing men and horses. As many as 300 men might make up a war party. Traditional enemies included the Blackfeet and later the Arapaho, Lakota, Cheyenne, and Gros Ventre. During the mid– to late nineteenth century, the principal ally of the Shoshone was the U.S. Army.

Spring and especially fall were the time for war. At these times the Eastern Shoshone generally fought as a tribe. Men made handle-held shields from thick, young buffalo bull hide. Rituals and feasting accompanied their manufacture. Each was decorated with buckskin and fringed with feathers. Weapons included sinew-backed bows, obsidian-tipped arrows, and clubs. Successful warriors were entitled to paint black and red finger marks on their tipi. Warriors occasionally committed suicide in combat.

Contemporary Information

GOVERNMENT/RESERVATIONS The Wind River Reservation (1863; Shoshone and Arapaho Tribes), Fremont and Hot Springs Counties, Wyoming, has 2,268,008 acres and a population of 5,674 Indians (1990). Both tribes have business councils.

ECONOMY Major activities are ranching, crafts, and clerical jobs. Some people regularly hunt and fish. There is income from mineral leases; the Eastern Shoshone tribe is a member of the Council of Energy Resource Tribes (CERT). Un- and underemployment is chronically high.

LEGAL STATUS The Arapaho Tribe of the Wind River Reservation and the Shoshone Tribe of the Wind River Reservation are federally recognized tribal entities.

DAILY LIFE Quasi-traditional religion remains important. The Sun Dance has been explicitly Christianized and is now intertribal. Only a few Mountain Sheep Eaters practice the Shuffle Dance. Peyotism is popular. Giveaways, formerly related to public coup counting, are now associated with other occasions. Shoshone language courses are taught at the Wyoming Indian High School, located on the reservation. Housing, most of which consists of modern "bungalows," is considered generally inadequate. The people use canvas tipis for ceremonial purposes.

High rates of substance abuse and suicide plague the reservation; accidents have replaced disease as primary killers. Outmigration remains a problem. Women have more freedom as well as political and social power, obtained in part through their participation in certain musical ceremonies. Wyoming Indian High School is Arapaho-dominated; most Shoshone attend off-reservation public high schools. Traditional games such as the hand game, with its associated gambling, remain popular, especially at powwows. Many people still speak the language.

Shoshone, Northern

Northern Shoshone (Sh ō `sh ō n ē) is a modern, anthropological term used to distinguish a region of Shoshone culture. The Northern Shoshone and Bannock (originally a Northern Paiute group) shared a number of cultural traits with the Paiute and the Ute Indians as well as with so-called Eastern or Wind River Shoshones (there was no aboriginal distinction between Shoshone groups) and Northern Paiutes. Northern Shoshones incorporated elements of Great Basin, Plateau, and Great Plains culture. The term "Shoshone" first surfaced in 1805. Other Indians and non-Indians sometimes referred to some Shoshone and Northern Paiute groups, particularly mounted bands, as Snake Indians (sedentary Shoshone and Northern Paiutes were often referred to as Diggers), but their name for themselves was *Nomo*, or "People."

LOCATION In the early nineteenth century, Northern Shoshones lived mostly in Idaho south of the Salmon River or on the Snake River plains and the mountains to the north. This region, on the border of the Columbia Plateau, has a relatively dry climate. It contains the Sawtooth and Bitterroot Mountains, valleys, river highlands, and the Snake and other rivers and creeks. Today, most Northern Shoshones live in and around Bannock, Bingham, Caribou, and Power Counties, Idaho.

POPULATION The precontact population of up to 30,000 had been cut by 90 percent by the mid–nineteenth century. In 1990, the Fort Hall Reservation population was 3,035 Indians.

LANGUAGE Shoshone is part of the central Numic (Shoshonean) division of the Uto-Aztecan language family. The Bannocks spoke western Numic, also a Shoshonean language, although mutually unintelligible with central Numic.

Historical Information

HISTORY The Paiute-speaking Bannock were among the first local groups to acquire horses, in the late seventeenth century. At that time, they migrated from eastern Oregon to Shoshone territory near the Snake River and organized fully mounted bands and engaged in group buffalo hunts. They and the Northern Shoshones also began to raid for horses and assumed many other aspects of Plains culture, such as tipis and warrior societies, yet the Bannock continued to interact with their Northern Paiute relatives. Sacajawea, a Shoshone woman, served as a guide on the Lewis and Clark expedition of 1804. Her diplomatic and navigation skills saved the party on more than one occasion.

Continuing their move east to the western

extremity of the northern Plains, the Shoshone were soon (mid–eighteenth century) driven back by the gun-wielding Blackfeet. Some Northern Shoshone groups did not become mounted until the nineteenth century or used the horse only as a pack animal. Such groups, particularly those away from the centers in the Snake and Lemhi River Valleys (for example, the so-called Sheepeaters), lived in scattered settlements and remained sedentary and peaceful.

The Lewis and Clark party (1804–1806) may have been the first non-Indians in the area. Anglos soon opened trading posts at Pend Oreille Lake (British, 1809) and the Upper Snake River (Northwest Company, 1810). Throughout the 1810s and 1820s, white trappers ranged across Shoshone territory, destroying all beaver and buffalo west of the Rockies. Other game suffered as well, as did the traditional Northern Shoshone way of life. Indians also acquired much non-native technology during this time, including firearms, iron utensils, and alcohol, and new diseases took a heavy toll.

By the 1840s, the fur trade had collapsed. Non-Indians began arriving en masse after the California gold rush and the opening of the Oregon Trail, further stressing the delicate local ecology. In 1847, the Mormons arrived. By the 1860s, the buffalo had all but disappeared. Relatively quickly, many Northern Shoshone groups faced starvation. They began to raid white settlements and wagons in retaliation, an activity that quickly brought counterraids. This kind of conflict persisted throughout the 1860s and 1870s, although the Fort Hall Reservation (originally 1.8 million acres) was created by treaty in 1868.

The Bannocks, however, had resisted confinement to Fort Hall. Some peoples' resistance was a direct influence of the Dreamers cult founded about 1860 by the Wanapum Smohalla. The continued destruction of their way of life—led by the wholesale slaughter of the buffalo, inadequate rations, white ranchers' crowding, and violence committed against them when they continued subsistence activities guaranteed by treaty—led to a major revolt in 1878. Its immediate cause was Anglo hog herding in a camas root area forbidden to them by treaty. The Bannocks and some Northern Paiute bands, under the Bannock chief Buffalo Born and the Paiutes Egan and Oytes, engaged the soldiers for several months that summer. Ultimately, the Paiutes were settled among the Yakima in Washington, and the Bannocks, held as prisoners of war for a while, were permitted to return to Fort Hall.

The Sheepeater war also took place in 1878, when roughly 50 central Idaho Bannocks and Shoshones, who lived primarily on mountain sheep, began raiding settlers who were encroaching on their subsistence area. At first eluding the army, they were eventually captured and placed at Fort Hall. Other Shoshones, too, fought to retain their traditions; most ended up at Fort Hall.

The United States created the Lemhi Valley Reservation in 1875, but its people were moved to Fort Hall when the reservation was terminated in 1907. Meanwhile, the Fort Hall Reservation itself shrank by more than two-thirds as a result of encroachments by the railroads, timber, mining, highway, and other interests. Dawes Act (1887) allotments further reduced it in size. Life at Fort Hall was marked by irrigation problems; major projects in the early twentieth century benefited white farmers only. Other serious problems included the flooding of good bottomlands by the American Falls Reservoir. Major economic activities during that time included sheep and cattle ranching. A phosphate mine opened after World War II.

Fort Hall Indians acquired the Sun Dance from Plains Indians, via the Wind River Shoshone, during the 1890s. Some also adopted the Native American Church in 1915. The government awarded them a land claims settlement of more than $8.8 million in 1964; another, smaller settlement was received in 1971 by the Lemhi Valley descendants.

RELIGION Northern Shoshones used dreams and visions to acquire helping spirits. Such spirits instructed people on the use of medicines with which to activate their power. Certain food and other restrictions might also be imposed. Spirits might cure illness, protect an individual from arrows, or hurt other people.

Most or all men could cure, although there were also professionals. Their methods included herbs, charms, and sweats. They gained their supernatural power through dreams, visions, and visits to remote, spirit-dwelling places.

There was a concept of a creator, but creative agency was proscribed to mythological characters such as wolf and coyote. Ceremonial occasions that featured round dances included the spring salmon return, the fall harvest, and times of adversity.

GOVERNMENT Loosely organized groups were characteristic of Great Basin culture. Traditionally, the Northern Shoshone were organized into seminomadic bands with impermanent composition and leadership. Some bands had chiefs; others, particularly in the west, had neither bands nor chiefs.

Life on the Plains called for higher forms of organization, both to hunt buffalo and to defend against enemies. In the fall, for instance, the Snake and Lemhi River–area bands came together for councils, feasts, and buffalo hunts. During these times, the more eastern bands were led by a principal chief and several minor chiefs. However, these offices were still nonhereditary, loosely defined, and somewhat transitory. Also, with more complex social organization, band councils arose to limit the power of the chiefs. Some "police" or soldier societies may also have existed to keep order during hunts and dances.

CUSTOMS Equality and individual autonomy were cardinal Shoshone values. Just as social organization was fairly undeveloped, especially to the west, there was also little barrier to social interaction. Many groups often intermarried, visited, and shared ceremonies and feasts. Social networks were wide and strong.

Local groups were named by the foods they ate, but the same band might have several names, and the same name might apply to several bands. Most marriages were monogamous. Both marriage and divorce were simple and common. The dead were wrapped in blankets and placed in rock crevices. Mourners cut their hair, gashed their legs, and killed one of the deceased's horses. Some private property (such as tools and weapons) was recognized, but private ownership of land or subsistence areas was not.

DWELLINGS Fort Hall and Lemhi people lived in Plains-style tipis after about the eighteenth century. Otherwise, Northern Shoshones typically built conical dwellings of sagebrush, grass, or woven willow branches. A similar structure was used for sweat lodges and menstrual huts.

DIET Roots (such as prairie turnips, yampa root, tobacco root, bitterroot, and camas) were steamed in earth ovens for several days or boiled. Berries (such as chokecherries and service berries), nuts, and seeds were also important foods, as were grasshoppers, ants and other insects, lizards, squirrels, and rabbits.

Big game included antelope, deer, elk, and mountain sheep. Buffalo were native to parts of the region but became especially important in the seventeenth century, when people would travel for the fall hunt to the Plains (east of Bozeman) and then back to the Snake River in winter or early spring.

Salmon was the most important fish. In fact, the salmon fishery was one of the key distinguishing features between the Northern Shoshone and the Eastern Shoshone. People also caught sturgeon, perch, trout, and other fish on Columbia and Snake River tributaries.

KEY TECHNOLOGY Fish were caught with nets, weirs, basket traps, harpoons, and spears. They were also attracted at night with torches. Steatite (soapstone) was used for items such as bowls and pipes. Women made coiled and twined sagebrush-bark and -root baskets and containers. They applied pitch to the interior to make them watertight. Boiling was accomplished by dropping hot stones into water baskets. Rawhide containers, perhaps painted with geometric designs, were also used.

Women carried willow stick and buckskin cradle boards on their backs. Digging sticks were hardened and sharpened by fire, which was in turn made with a drill. The Bannock used some pottery, horn utensils, and salmon-skin bags.

TRADE Trade was extensive in the area. Many Plateau as well as northern Plains Indians received the horse by way of the Shoshone. Their main trade partners were the Flathead, Nez Percé, Crow, Umatilla, and Cayuse, with whom they traded buffalo skins, salmon, horses, and mules. There were also friendly relations and trade with the Northern Paiute. Annual trade fairs occurred at places like the Green River (Wyoming), the Cache Valley (Utah), and Pierre's Hole (Idaho).

NOTABLE ARTS The chief art, especially in the late prehistoric and historic periods, was rawhide painted with geometric designs. The Northern Shoshone and Bannock also made beadwork with geometric designs. Their petroglyphs are at least several thousand years old. Various other art objects have been made from a variety of materials, including stone, wood, and clay.

TRANSPORTATION Horses arrived in the mid– to late seventeenth century; before that, dogs helped with transporting goods. Hunters used snowshoes in winter. The Bannock used tule rafts.

DRESS After they entered the mounted period, people dressed similarly to Plains Indians. They wore elk-skin clothing decorated with quillwork or beadwork in summer. Men wore leggings and fringed shirts, and women wore dresses, knee-length leggings, and elk-tooth necklaces. In the winter both sexes wore buffalo-skin, elk-skin, or deerskin moccasins as well as antelope, deer, buffalo, or mountain sheep robes. Otherwise, the traditional dress was breechclouts and rabbit-skin robes. Feathered headdresses were worn for ceremonial purposes.

WAR AND WEAPONS Weapons included cedar, elk, or sheep horn bows; poison-tipped arrows kept in otterskin quivers; and stone war clubs. Obsidian was used for knives and arrowheads. Defensive equipment included antelope-skin armor and buffalo-skin shields. Among the peoples' traditional enemies were the Blackfeet and possibly the Nez Percé. In later aboriginal times, the Shoshone acquired Plains war customs such as counting coup and taking scalps. Their Scalp Dance was also acquired from Plains groups.

Contemporary Information

GOVERNMENT/RESERVATIONS Fort Hall Reservation, Bannock, Bingham, Caribou, and Power Counties, Idaho (1868; Bannock and Northern Shoshone), contains 523,917 acres. The 1990 Indian population was 3,035. A constitution and by-laws were approved in 1936, and a corporate charter was ratified the following year. Government is provided by an elected business council. Most of the land is in Indian hands.

Duck Valley Reservation, Owyhee County, Idaho, and Elko County, Nevada (1877; Shoshone and Paiute), contains 289,819 acres. The 1990 Indian population was 1,021. An Indian Reorganization Act–based constitution and by-laws were adopted in 1936. Government is provided by a tribal council.

The Northwestern Band of Shoshoni Indians (roughly 400 population in 1995) live near Fort Hall, Idaho, although their land base, the Washakie Reservation (184 acres) is in Utah.

ECONOMY At Fort Hall, important economic activities include public fishing and hunting, high-stakes bingo, tribal income from leases and mineral rights, several small businesses, and some agriculture. The tribe operates a 20,000-acre irrigation project. Many people also work for the tribal government. The people also receive interest and investments from a $15.7 million land claims award to the Northern and Eastern Shoshone in 1968. A proposal to open a casino is tied up in court. Un- and underemployment is a major problem.

LEGAL STATUS The Bannock Tribe (Shoshone-Bannock), the Shoshone Indians, and the Northwestern Band of the Shoshoni Nation are federally recognized tribal entities.

DAILY LIFE Despite centuries of intermarriage, many people still identify themselves as Bannock or Shoshone. Both languages are still spoken. Children attend public schools. A new clinic opened in 1990. The museum and library at Fort Hall are just two of the ways by which the people stay in touch with their Indian identities. Other ways include bilingual education, a weekly newspaper, and active religious observances such as the Sun Dance and the Peyote cult. The reservation runs adult education and youth recreation programs. It also hosts many traditional festivals, including a week-long celebration in August and an all-Indian rodeo.

Shoshone, Western

Western Shoshone (Sh ō ˋsh ō n ē) were a number of Shoshonean-speaking groups generally inhabiting a particular area. Many groups were known to whites as Diggers. Their self-designation was "Newe." The Goshute (Gosiute) are ethnic Shoshones, despite considerable intermarriage with the Ute and the existence of a 1962 court ruling legally separating them from the Western Shoshone. Little pre-1859 scientific

ethnographic data exist on the Western Shoshone.

LOCATION Most Western Shoshone bands lived in harsh environments such as the Great Salt Lake area (Goshute) and Death Valley (Panamint). Their territory stretched from Death Valley through central Nevada into northwestern Utah and southern Idaho. Most Western Shoshones today live on a number of reservations within their aboriginal territory. They also live in nearby and regional cities and towns.

POPULATION The aboriginal population of Western Shoshones may have numbered between 5,000 and 10,000, although it had declined to roughly 2,000 by the early nineteenth century. In 1990, 3,815 Paiute-Shoshones, Goshute Shoshones, and Shoshones lived on reservations. This figure does not include 2,078 Te-Moak Shoshones (1992).

LANGUAGE The Western Shoshone spoke three central Numic languages—Panamint, Shoshone, and Comanche—all members of the Numic (Shoshonean) branch of the Uto-Aztecan language family. Since all Shoshones (Western, Northern, and Eastern or Wind River) spoke Shoshone, the term Shoshone is an ethnic rather than a linguistic one.

Historical Information

HISTORY Western Shoshones were first visited by non-natives—the Jedediah Smith and Peter Skene Ogden parties—in the late 1820s. Other trappers and traders passed through during the next 20 years. Despite the willingness of some groups, such as the Walker party, to massacre Indians, the latter were relatively unaffected by early contacts with non-natives.

The Mormons, who ultimately had a huge impact on the Goshute Shoshone, began arriving to stay in 1847. The white presence increased throughout 1840s and 1850s, but the discovery of the Comstock Lode in 1857 turned the stream into a flood. By then, degradation of the natural environment was well under way. New diseases also stalked the region, severely affecting both human and animal populations. Indians responded by either retreating farther from white activity or, less often, by raiding, stealing, and begging.

The Pony Express, established in 1860, passed through the center of Western Shoshone country. Supply depots at important springs displaced Indians, which encouraged attacks and then army reprisals. By 1860, Mormons had invaded Goshute territory, and miners and ranchers were closing in on the rest of Western Shoshone lands. Grazing, plowing, and wood cutting (piñon and juniper pine) destroyed subsistence areas and forage land. Indians began to work for settlers as wage laborers to fend off starvation. Euro-American clothing, technology, and shelter quickly replaced the traditional variety.

Federal negotiations with Great Basin tribes began in the 1850s, in part to check sporadic violence against settlers. The first treaties with Western Shoshone groups were signed in 1863. They called for Indians to give up hostilities, settle down eventually, and receive goods annually worth a total of $50,000. In return, the settlers could stay. Significantly, the Indians never actually ceded any land.

The army soon began rounding up Indians. When no reservations near good land with water were established during the 1870s, some Shoshones joined Northern Paiutes and Bannocks in their wars of resistance. In 1879, Shoshones refused an order to move to the Western Shoshone (Duck Valley) Reservation. Despite the extreme disruption of their lives, elements of traditional culture survived, such as religious beliefs (largely excepting the Goshute) and limited subsistence patterns. Most Shoshones still lived unconfined after 1900.

The percentage of Western Shoshones living on reservations peaked at 50 in 1927. Most carried out semitraditional subsistence activities combined with seasonal or other wage work in mines and on ranches and farms. In an effort to enlarge the reservation population, the United States encouraged Northern Paiutes to settle at Duck Valley. Finally, accepting the fact that most Western Shoshones did not and would not live at Duck Valley, the government created a series of "colonies" during the first half of the twentieth century.

In 1936, the Paiutes and most Shoshone groups organized the Paiute-Shoshone Business Council. Chief Temoak and his descendants were considered the leaders of this effort. The U.S. government refused to recognize the traditional Temoak council, however, and instead organized their own Te-Moak Bands Council. This split culminated when the traditionalist-backed United Western Shoshone Legal Defense and Education Association (1974) argued that the Te-Moak Bands Council did not represent Western Shoshone interests and, further, that the Western Shoshones never ceded their land. The courts rejected their claim in 1979 and ordered them paid $26 million in compensation. In 1985, the Supreme Court ruled that the 1979 payment legally extinguished their title to the disputed 24 million acres.

RELIGION Apo, the sun, was a principal deity. Anyone could obtain supernatural powers through dreams and visions, although medicine men (*bugahant*) served as religious leaders. Most groups recognized three kinds of shamans: curers of specific ailments, general curers, and self-curers or helpers. Curing was effected by sucking and the laying on of hands. In theory, men and women could both be shamans, although only men may have practiced cur-

ing. Shamans were also capable of capturing antelopes' souls and helping to drive them into corrals. Some groups may not have had shamans at all.

People used several hundred herbal remedies to cure nonsupernatural ailments such as cuts and bruises. The round dance was basic to ceremonial celebration. In some areas the dance was associated with courtship or rainmaking. Festivals were often held in times of plenty.

GOVERNMENT Groups in small winter villages were composed of family clusters and named for an important food resource or a local geographic feature. Thus, the territory and not the composition of the group was definitive. Group membership was not fixed and groups were not bands per se. Chiefs or headmen had little authority other than directing subsistence activity.

CUSTOMS Ritual activity focused on birth, girls' puberty, and death. Girls' puberty rituals included isolation as well as instruction on hard work and other proper behaviors. Corpses were cremated or buried in caves or rock slides. Some groups observed an annual mourning ceremony that included singing, speech making, and destroying the deceased's property. Mourners cut their hair and waited at least a year before remarriage. Shamanistic midwives offered supernatural assistance to ensure a baby's welfare. Some infanticide was practiced, especially in the west.

Good hunters might take more than one wife. Groups west of the Humboldt River practiced the bride price. Marriages were meant to establish close family ties. Divorce and remarriage were common. In the Reese River Valley, piñon groves were owned by individual families. Games included shinny, ball race (men), hoop and pole, dice, and four-stick. Most of these games involved betting. Shinny had some religious significance. People also played with jacks and string games. The elderberry flute was the only widespread musical instrument.

DWELLINGS Relatively little subsistence activity in winter meant less population mobility and the chance to establish villages of several families. Winter houses for about six people were conical huts of bark-covered pole frame. The smoke hole served as an entrance. People also lived in caves, brush sun shades, and domed wickiups. Sweat houses were domed in the north and conical in the south. Most groups also built menstrual huts.

DIET The main economic activity was foraging in families or groups of families from spring through fall. Staple plant foods included grasses, pine nuts, seeds, berries, spring greens, and roots. The Panamint ate mesquite pods and screwbeans. Seeds were threshed, roasted on parching trays, winnowed, ground, and boiled. They could then be eaten or cached. Mesquite pods were ground and eaten as cakes. Other desert foods included salvia seeds, cactus, agave, and gourds.

Meat, some of which was dried for winter, included bighorn sheep, antelope, deer, jackrabbits, and rodents. Dogs assisted in summer sheep hunts. Groups of people drove antelope and rabbits into corrals and nets. Antelope were also hunted individually using masks and disguises. Other food sources, depending on location, included fish, birds, waterfowl, larvae, grasshoppers, and crickets.

KEY TECHNOLOGY In general the Western Shoshone adapted very successfully to a relatively harsh environment. They used sticks to beat grasses and dig roots, as well as using seed beaters of twined willow. Coiled and twined baskets were important in grass collection, as was a twined winnowing tray. Waterproof baskets allowed people to forage far from water.

Other tools and equipment included stone metates for grinding seeds; snares, traps, and deadfalls to hunt cottontails and rodents; bows of juniper and mountain mahogany; wildcat skin quivers; stone or horn arrow straighteners; and some pottery.

TRADE Western Shoshones traded items such as salt and rabbit-skin blankets to Owens Valley Paiutes for shell money and buckskins.

NOTABLE ARTS Baskets were of very high quality. The people also made rock art for at least several thousand years as well as art objects from a variety of materials, including stone, wood, and clay.

TRANSPORTATION Western Shoshones possessed few horses even after other Shoshones acquired them (horses competed for their staple grasses).

DRESS Boys and some girls remained nude, especially in summer. Otherwise girls wore a front apron. Even in winter many people wore few clothes other than fur robes. What clothing existed was made of rabbit skin and/or the hides of bighorn sheep, antelope, or deer. If these materials were scarce, people used bark or grass as clothing materials. Women wore twined sage-bark or willow hats and a skin gown in winter. Both sexes wore fur or sage-bark moccasins in winter. They pierced their ears and wore ear and neck ornaments of shell and bone. Face and body painting and tattooing were common, especially among young adults.

WAR AND WEAPONS Other than some historic-era conflict over the Ute propensity to sell Goshutes into slavery, the Western Shoshone practiced little warfare.

Contemporary Information

GOVERNMENT/RESERVATIONS The following reservations and colonies have a significant Western Shoshone presence:

Duck Valley Reservation, Owyhee County, Idaho, and Elko County, Nevada (1877; Shoshone and Paiute): 289,819 acres; 1,701 enrollment (1990); organized under the Indian Reorganization Act (IRA); constitution and by-laws approved 1936; governed by a business council.

Duckwater Reservation, Nye County, Nevada (1940; Shoshone): 3,815 acres; 288 enrollment (1990); governed by a tribal council.

Ely Indian Colony, White Pine County, Nevada (1931; Shoshone): 111 total acres; 274 enrollment (1990); organized under the IRA; constitution and by-laws approved 1966; governed by a council.

Fallon Reservation and Colony, Churchill County, Nevada (1887; Paiute and Shoshone): 69 (colony) and 3,480 (tribal, plus 4,640 allotted) acres; 506 Indians (1990); governed by a business council.

Fort McDermitt Reservation, Humboldt County, Nevada, and Malheur County, Oregon (1892; Shoshone and Paiute): 16,354 tribal acres in Nevada plus almost 19,000 acres of tribal land in Oregon; 387 Indians (1990); governed by a tribal council.

Big Pine Reservation, Inyo County, California (1939; Paiute and Shoshone): 279 acres; 331 Indians (1990).

Bishop Indian Colony, Inyo County, California (1912; Paiute-Shoshone): 877 acres; 934 Indians (1990); governed by a tribal council.

Death Valley Indian Community, Death Valley, California (1982; Timbi-sha Shoshone): 40 acres; 199 Indians (1992).

Fort Independence Reservation, Inyo County, California (1915; Paiute and Shoshone): 234 acres; 38 Indians (1990).

Lone Pine Reservation, Inyo County, California (1939; Paiute-Shoshone): 237 acres; 168 Indians (1990); governed by a tribal council.

Yomba Reservation, Nye County, Nevada (1937; Yomba Shoshone): 4,718.46 acres; 192 Indians (1992).

Goshute Reservation, White Pine County, Nevada, and Juab and Tooele Counties, Utah (1863): 7,489 acres; 98 Indians (1990); 413 enrolled members (1993), 1940 constitution and by-laws; governed by a business council.

Battle Mountain Reservation, Battle Mountain, Nevada (1917; Te-Moak Band of Western Shoshone): 700 acres; 553 Indians (1995); governed by a tribal council.

Elko Indian Colony, Elko, Nevada (1918; Te-Moak Band of Western Shoshone): 193 acres; 1,326 Indians (1995); governed by a band council.

Ruby Valley (Te-Moak) Trust Lands, Elko, Nevada (1887; Te-Moak Western Shoshone Indians): 15,000 acres; approximately 30 Indians (1998); governed by a tribal council.

South Fork and Odgers Ranch Indian Colony, Lee, Nevada (1941; Te-Moak Band of Western Shoshone): 13,050 acres; 257 Indians (1995); governed by South Fork Tribal Council.

Wells Indian Colony (1980; Te-Moak Tribe of Western Shoshone): 80 acres; 182 Indians (1995); governed by a band council.

Skull Valley Reservation, Tooele County, Utah (1917; Goshute Tribe): 17,444 acres; 32 Indians (1990); 111 enrolled members (1993); no constitution.

ECONOMY   In addition to employment with federal and tribal entities and income from leases and land claims funds, significant economic activities on the various reservations include enterprises such as smoke shops, motels, gas stations, and other small businesses. Several reservations and colonies remain in the cattle and farming business. Un- and underemployment are generally very high.

Outside of limited cattle and hay ranching, there are no employment opportunities on the Goshute Reservation. Skull Valley leases land to Hercules (aerospace), and some tribal members work there as well as at a convenience store and a seasonal water project.

LEGAL STATUS   The following are federally recognized tribal entities: the Death Valley Timbi-sha Shoshone Band (since 1982), the Duckwater Shoshone Tribe, the Fort McDermitt Paiute and Shoshone Tribes, the Paiute-Shoshone Indians of the Bishop Community, the Paiute-Shoshone Tribe of the Fallon Reservation and Colony, the Paiute-Shoshone Indians of the Lone Pine Community, the Shoshone-Paiute Tribes of the Duck Valley Reservation, the Yomba Shoshone Tribe, the Confederated Tribes of the Goshute Reservation, and the Skull Valley Band of Goshute Indians of Utah. The constituent bands of the Te-Moak tribe of Western Shoshone Indians make up a federally recognized tribal entity.

DAILY LIFE   Tribal gatherings (fandangos) feature traditional round dances, prayers, and games. Most groups have instituted language preservation programs. In confederation with other Great Basin tribes, several Western Shoshone groups opposed siting the MX intercontinental ballistic missile system on treaty lands. Western Shoshones have rejected the 1985 Supreme Court land claims decision (see "History" under "Historical Information"), holding that by the terms of the 1863 treaty they retain formal title to 24 million acres of aboriginal land. Negotiations are currently in progress.

Communications remain difficult on the remote Goshute and Skull Valley Reservations. Those Goshute Reservation children not attending boarding schools are bused 60 miles to high school; the ride is 16 miles at Skull Valley. Both the Native American Church and the Mormon Church are popular among Goshutes. Reservation crafts include beadwork, basketry, and making buckskin items.

Shoshone, Wind River

See Shoshone, Eastern

Ute

Ute (Y ū t), roughly 11 autonomous Great Basin bands. In the eighteenth century, eastern bands included the Uncompahgre (or Tabeguache), Yampa and Parusanuch (or White River Band), Mouache, Capote, and Weeminuche, and western bands included the Uintah, Timpanogots, Pahvant, Sanpits, and Moanunts. The word "Utah" is of Spanish derivation, probably borrowed originally from an Indian word. Their self-designation was *Nunt'z,* "the People."

LOCATION   Aboriginally, Utes lived in most of present-day Utah, except the far western, northern, and southern parts; Colorado west of and including the eastern slopes of the Rockies; and extreme northern New Mexico. Today, the three Ute reservations are in southwest Colorado, the Four Corners area, and north-central Utah.

POPULATION   From roughly 8,000 in the early nineteenth century, the Utes declined to about 1,800 in 1920. In 1990 approximately 5,000 lived on reservations, and roughly another 2,800 lived in cities and towns.

LANGUAGE   With Southern Paiute, Ute is a member of the southern Numic (Shoshonean) division of the Uto-Aztecan language family. All dialects were mutually intelligible.

Historical Information

HISTORY   The Utes and their ancestors have been in the Great Basin for as many as 10,000 years. They lived along Arizona's Gila River from about 3000 B.C.E. to about 500 B.C.E. At that time, a group of them began migrating north toward Utah, growing a high-altitude variety of corn that had been developed in Mexico. This group, who grew corn, beans, and squash and also hunted and gathered food, is known as the Sevier Complex. Another, related group of people, known as the Fremont Complex, lived to the northeast.

In time, Fremont people migrated into western Colorado. When a drought struck the Great Basin in the thirteenth century, the Fremont people moved into Colorado's San Luis Valley, where they later became known as the Utes. They became one of the first mounted Indian peoples when escaped Spanish captives brought horses home in the mid–seventeenth century. Communal buffalo hunts began shortly thereafter. Mounted warriors brought more protection, and larger camps meant more centralized government and more powerful leaders as well as a rising standard of living. Utes also facilitated the spread of the horse to peoples of the Great Plains.

Southern and eastern Ute bands raided New Mexico Indians and hunted buffalo on the Plains during the seventeenth into the nineteenth centuries. Utes also raided Western Shoshones and Southern Paiutes for slaves (mostly women and children), whom they sold to the Spanish. Moreover, they were forced to defend some hunting territory against the Comanche (formerly an ally) and other Plains tribes around that time. As a result of relentless Comanche attacks, the Southern Utes were prevented from developing fully on the Plains. Driven back into the mountains, they lost power and prestige, and the northern bands, enjoying a more peaceful and prosperous life, increased in importance.

A Spanish expedition in 1776 was the first of a line of non-native explorers, trappers, traders, slavers, and miners. Non-natives established a settlement in Colorado in 1851, and a U.S. fort (Fort Massachusetts) was built the following year to protect that settlement. Utes considered non-native livestock grazing on their (former) land fair game. In the midst of growing conflicts, treaties (which remained unratified) were negotiated in the mid-1850s.

The flood of miners that followed the 1858 Rockies gold strikes overwhelmed the eastern Utes. At the same time, Utes were allied with the Americans and Mexicans against the Navajo. Mormons, fighting the western Utes for land from late 1840s on, had succeeded by the mid-1870s in confining them to about 9 percent of their aboriginal territory. The United States created the Uintah Reservation in 1861 on land the Mormons did not want. They made most Utah Utes, whose population had been decimated, settle there in 1864.

In 1863, some eastern bands improperly signed a treaty ceding all bands' Colorado mountain lands. Five years later, the eastern Utes, under Chief Ouray, agreed to move west of the continental divide provided about 15 million acres was reserved for them. Soon, however, gold discoveries in the San Juan Mountains wrecked the deal, and the Utes were forced to cede an additional 3.4 million acres in 1873 (most of the remainder was taken in 1880). The U.S. government considered Ouray "head chief of the Utes," paid him an annual salary, and supplied him with expensive goods.

The Southern Ute Reservation was established on the Colorado–New Mexico border in 1877. At that time, the Mouache and Capote Bands settled there, merged to form the Southern Ute tribe, and took up agriculture. Resisting pressure to farm, the Weeminuche, calling themselves the Ute Mountain tribe, began raising cattle in the western part of the Southern Ute Reservation (the part later called the Ute Mountain Reservation).

In the late 1870s, a new Indian agent tried to force the White River Utes to give up their traditional way of life and "become civilized" by setting up a cooperative farming community. His methods included starvation, the destruction of Ute ponies, and encouraging the government to move against them militarily. When the soldiers arrived, the Indians made a defensive stand and a fight broke out, resulting in deaths on both sides (including Agent Nathan Meeker and U.S. Army Commander Thomas Thornburgh). Chief Ouray helped prevent a general war over this affair. The engagement was subsequently called by whites the Thornburgh "ambush" and the Meeker "massacre" and led directly to the eviction of the White River people from Colorado.

By 1881, the other eastern bands had all been forced from Colorado (except for the small Southern and Mountain Ute Reservations), and the other eight bands, later known as the Northern Ute, were assigned to the Uintah and Ouray Reservation in northern Utah (the Uintah Reservation was expanded in 1882 to include the removed Weeminuche Band).

Government attempts to force the grazing-oriented Ute to farm met with little success, owing in part to a lack of access to capital and markets and in part to unfavorable soil and climate. Irrigation projects begun early in the twentieth century mainly benefited non-Indians who leased, purchased, or otherwise occupied Ute land. The government also withheld rations in an effort to force reservation Utes to send their children to boarding school. During the mid-1880s, almost half of the Ute children at boarding schools in Albuquerque died. In 1911, the Ute Mountain Utes increased their acreage while ceding land that became Mesa Verde National Park.

The last traditional Weeminuche chief, Jack House, assumed his office in 1936 and died in 1971. Buckskin Charley led the Southern Utes from Ouray's death in 1880 until his own in 1936. His son, Antonio Buck, became the first Southern Ute tribal chair. During the 1920s and 1930s, Mountain Utes formed clubs to promote leadership and other skills. Disease remained a major killer as late as the 1940s.

By 1934, the eastern Utes controlled about .001 percent of their aboriginal lands. In 1950, the Confederated Ute Tribes (Northern, Southern, and Mountain) received $31 million in land claims settlements. During the 1950s, Ute Mountain people began to assume greater control over their own money, and mineral leases provided real tribal income. Funds were expended on a per capita basis and invested in a number of enterprises, mostly tourist related. The 1960s brought federal housing programs and more land claims money, but the effectiveness of tribal leadership declined considerably. A group of mixed bloods, called the Affiliated Ute Citizens, were legally separated from the Northern Utes in 1954.

RELIGION Utes believed that supernatural power was located within all living things. Curing and weather shamans, both men and women, derived additional power from dreams. A few shamans, influenced by Plains culture, undertook vision quests.

One of the oldest of Ute ceremonies, the ten-day Bear Dance was a welcome to spring. Bear is a mythological figure who provides leadership, wisdom, and strength. Perhaps originally a hunting ritual, the dance, directed by a dance chief and his assistants, signaled a time for courtship and the renewal of social ties. It was also related to the end of the girls' puberty ceremony. An all-male orchestra played musical rasps to accompany dancers. The host band sponsored feasting, dancing, gambling, games, and horse racing.

The Sun Dance, of Plains origin, was held in mid-summer.

GOVERNMENT Before the mid–seventeenth century, small Ute hunting and gathering groups were composed of extended families, with older members in charge. There may also have been some band organization for fall activities such as trading and hunting buffalo.

With the advent of horses, band structure strengthened to facilitate buffalo hunting, raiding, and defense. Each band now had its own chief, or headman, who solicited advice from constituent group leaders. By the eighteenth century, the autonomous bands came together regularly for tribal activities. Each band retained its chief and council, and within the bands, family groups retained their own leadership.

CUSTOMS Western Utes were culturally similar to the Paiutes and Shoshones, whereas eastern Utes adopted many Plains traits. The southeastern Utes, in turn, were influenced by the Pueblos and the Jicarilla Apache. Resource areas were owned communally. Games included shinny (women), hoop-and-pole, and dice.

People chose their own spouses with some parental input. Divorce was easy and common. In general, men could have multiple wives. There were various taboos and food restrictions during and immediately after pregnancy for both men and women. Minor rituals were meant to ensure a child's industriousness. Although children were welcomed, twins were considered an unlucky sign, and one or both were often allowed to die. Naming might take place any time, and names were not fixed for life. Nicknames were common.

A menstruating woman was secluded and observed several behavioral restrictions, including the common one of not being allowed to scratch herself with her own hands. There were few puberty customs per se, although girls sometimes danced the Bear Dance, and boys could not eat their first kill. Corpses were wrapped in their best clothes and buried in rock crevices, heads to the east. Their possessions were destroyed (or occasionally given away), and their horses were killed or had their hair cut.

DWELLINGS The western Utes lived year-round in domed willow houses. Weeminuches used them only in summer, and all groups also used brush and conical pole-frame shelters 10–15 feet in diameter, covered with juniper bark or tule. Sweat houses were of similar construction and heated with hot rocks. In the east, after the seventeenth century, people lived in buffalo (or elk) skin tipis, some of which were up to 17 feet high.

DIET Bands generally regrouped into families to hunt and gather during spring and summer. Important plant foods included seeds, pine nuts, yampa, berries, and yucca. Some southeastern people planted corn in the late prehistoric period. Some groups burned areas to encourage the growth of wild tobacco.

Buffalo were native to the entire area and were important even before the horse. Other important animal foods included elk, antelope (stalked or driven over cliffs), rabbit (hunted with throwing sticks or communally driven into nets), deer, bear, beaver, fowl, and sage hens. Meat was eaten fresh, sun dried, or smoked. Coyote, wolf, and bobcat were hunted for their fur only.

Other important foods included crickets, grasshoppers, and locusts (dried with berries in cake form). Some western groups ate lizards and reptiles. Some bands also fished, especially in the west, using weirs, nets, basket traps, bow and arrow, and harpoons. Important fish included cutthroat trout, whitefish, chubs, and suckers.

KEY TECHNOLOGY Musical instruments included flutes, rasps, and drums. Later prehistoric eastern groups obtained shelter, food, clothing, glue, containers, tools, bow strings, and more from the buffalo. Baskets, often made of willow and squaw-bush twigs, were used for a variety of purposes, especially in seed and berry gathering and preparation. Wood, stone, and horn were other common raw materials. People made cedar, chokecherry, or sheep horn bows, flint knives, and coiled pottery, mostly in the west. They wove tule sleeping mats and made cordage of various barks and plant fibers.

TRADE Some southeastern bands traded at Taos and Pecos, perhaps exchanging meat and buckskin for agricultural products. Utes traded with the Spanish when they were not at war. They also acquired blankets and other items from the Navajo for buckskins and buffalo parts.

NOTABLE ARTS Fine and performing arts included music, especially singing and drumming; basket making; leather tanning (by women); rock art; and assorted art objects made from materials such as stone, wood, and clay.

TRANSPORTATION Dogs pulled small travois before horses arrived in the region. Later, goods were moved on full-sized horse-pulled travois made from tipi poles. Winter hunters wore snowshoes, and some western groups used tule rafts or balsas.

DRESS Eastern groups wore tanned buckskin clothing. Shirts were plain before increased contact with Plains groups added beads, fringe, and other designs. Twined sagebrush bark was the preferred material in the west. Blankets were made especially of rabbit and buffalo (especially in the east). Men protected their eyes against the sun with rawhide eye shields. They also wore beaver or weasel caps, and both sexes wore hard-sole moccasins over sagebrush socks in winter. Personal decoration included face painting (mostly for special occasions) tattooing, ear ornaments, and necklaces.

WAR AND WEAPONS Before the horse, warfare was generally defensive in nature. Utes became mounted raiders in the late seventeenth century. Their usual targets were Pueblo, Southern Paiute, and Western Shoshone Indians. Weapons included a three- to four-foot bow (chokecherry, mountain mahogany, or mountain sheep horn was preferred) and arrows. Eastern Utes also used spears as well as buffalo-skin shields.

Some bands were allied with the Jicarilla Apache and the Comanche against both the Spanish and the Pueblos. Utes had generally poor relations with the Northern and Eastern Shoshone, although they were generally friendly with the Western Shoshone and Southern Paiute, especially before they began raiding these groups for slaves in the eighteenth century. Navajos were alternately allies and enemies. Eastern Utes observed ceremonies before and after raids.

Contemporary Information

GOVERNMENT/RESERVATIONS The Southern Ute Reservation is located in Archuleta, La Plata, and Montezuma Counties, Colorado. Established in 1873, it contains 310,002 acres. The 1990 Indians population was 1,044. A constitution adopted in 1936 provides for an elected tribal council.

The Uintah and Ouray Reservation is located in Carbon, Duchesne, Grand, Uintah, Utah, and Wasatch Counties, Utah. Founded in 1863, it contains 1,021,558 acres and had a 1990 Indian population of 2,647. It is governed by a business council.

The Ute Mountain Reservation, including the White Mesa Community, is in La Plata and Montezuma Counties, Colorado; San Juan County, New Mexico; and San Juan County, Utah. Created in 1873, it contains 447,850 acres. The 1990 Indians population was 1,262. A 1940 constitution provides for a tribal council.

ECONOMY Important economic activities include oil and gas leases (all Ute reservations are members of the Council of Energy Resource Tribes), stock raising (Ute Mountain and Uintah and Ouray), some timber sales, interest on tribal funds, tribal and government agencies and programs, and tourism, especially on the Southern Ute and Uintah and Ouray Reservations. The Southern Utes are planning a casino and gambling complex. They have also purchased and operate natural gas wells.

The Ute Mountain high-stakes casino joins a bingo hall and pottery cooperative as important economic activities. Ute Mountain has also been able to restore some of its some year-round hunting rights and to negotiate model mineral leases, including provisions for job training. The Ute Mountain Tribal Park features Anasazi ruins. On the Southern Ute Reservation, the Sky Ute Convention Center has had trouble showing a profit. Up to one-half of Utes work for the tribal or federal government. Unemployment remains high on all Ute reservations, and household incomes remain well below those of neighboring non-natives.

LEGAL STATUS The Southern Ute Indian Tribe, the Ute Mountain Tribe, and the Ute Indian Tribe (of the Uintah and Ouray Reservation) are federally recognized tribal entities.

DAILY LIFE The Ute language is still widely spoken, although less so among the Southern Ute and among young people in general. There are annual performances of the Bear and Sun Dances. Most housing on all reservations is relatively modern and adequate, although it is considered insufficient on the Southern Ute Reservation. The Southern Ute Reservation also holds a fair and a rodeo and features a newspaper, a library, and a Head Start program. It is the most acculturated of the three communities.

All tribes have scholarship programs for college-bound young people. The White Mesa people at Ute Mountain have become mixed with Navajos and

Paiutes. Water there has been contaminated by nearby uranium mills. Most White Mesa people are Mormons. At Ute Mountain, life expectancy remains below 40 years, and alcoholism rates may approach 80 percent. Job discrimination remains a formidable obstacle to employment. Basketry and beadwork remain important artistic activities.

The Animas–La Plata water settlement may mean considerable additional water resources for drinking and possibly farming for the Southern and Mountain Utes. The Native American Church is active among the Southern and Mountain Utes. Factionalism based on tribal membership requirements and deep-seated political disputes, many based on government policy, still threatens the tribes. The quasi-official Affiliated Ute Citizens, with low blood quantums, remain ineligible for most tribal benefits.

Washoe

Washoe (`Wä sh ū), a word derived from *Washiu*, or "Person," their self-designation. Though lacking any formal institutional structures, the Washoe considered themselves a tribe, or a distinct people.

LOCATION   Washoes lived and continue to live around Lake Tahoe, from Honey Lake in the north to about 40 miles north of Mono Lake in the south, on both sides of the California-Nevada border. This mountainous and environmentally rich region was relatively compact (most groups lived within an area of 4,000 square miles, although their range exceeded 10,000 square miles). The Washoe shared many cultural traits of both California and Great Basin Indians.

POPULATION   The Washoe population was at least 1,500 in the early nineteenth century. In 1991, over 1,000 lived on reservations and at least 500 lived off-reservation.

LANGUAGE   Washoe is a Hokan language.

Historical Information

HISTORY   Ancestors of the Washoe arrived in the region roughly 6,000 years ago. Unbroken cultural continuity lasted from around 500 up to about 1800. Although Washoes may have met Spaniards in the late eighteenth century, they were fairly removed from contact with non-Indians until the 1848 California gold rush brought people through their lands. Anglos established trading posts and settlements, complete with fenced lands and water resources, in the 1850s. Indian demands for compensation were met with refusal and/or violence.

When Anglos blamed the Washoe for Northern Paiute resistance, the Indians were forced to turn for protection to the whites who were appropriating their lands. The 1858 discovery of the Comstock silver lode brought a flood of people to nearby Virginia City. They cut the pine forests, and their cattle ate all the wild grasses and scared off the game. Barely ten years after their first substantive contact with white people, around 1850, the Washoes' subsistence areas, and thus the basis for their traditional lives, had been virtually destroyed.

Commercial fishing began in Lake Tahoe by the 1860s. Washoes danced the Ghost Dance in the 1870s. The government repeatedly refused to grant them a reservation on the grounds that there was no good land to give them and that, in any case, their disappearance was imminent. The Washoe were pushed farther and farther into the margins, trying to stay alive as best they could. By the late nineteenth century, whites thought of the "Washoe Tribe" as those groups around Carson City and the Carson Valley; other Washoe groups were unknown or ignored.

The Washoes eventually bought or were allotted some small plots of marginal land. Land for "colonies" was donated or purchased with government funds around 1917 and again in the 1930s. The land was always of poor quality, with little or no water. Some Washoe men worked as ranch hands, women as domestic laborers. Well into the twentieth century, desperate poverty was made even worse by white efforts to repress their culture. The Indians suffered severe discrimination and had no legal civil rights.

Some Washoes embraced the Peyote religion in 1932. Its strenuously opposition by whites and by some traditional shamans brought factionalism to the community. In 1935, the tribe accepted the Indian Reorganization Act and ratified a constitution and by-laws. However, tribal leadership remained ineffective through the 1960s. Throughout the period, most Washoes lived marginally in Carson Valley and around Carson City, although some small groups continued to live in their traditional territory. Public facilities, including schools, were desegregated in the 1950s. The Washoes were awarded a land claims settlement of $5 million in 1970.

RELIGION   Spirits could be related to myths and legends as well as death; those related to death were seen as sources of illness and bad luck. The Pine Nut Dance was the most important ceremony. It was a harvest ceremony that featured prayers, feasting, dances, and games. Other ceremonies were also related to communal subsistence activities.

Male and female shamans acquired supernatural powers through dreams and refined them through apprenticeships. The power imposed strict behavioral and dietary regulations. Shamans used their powers to cure, often by sucking after singing and praying for four days. They also used certain paraphernalia, such as rattles, feathers, and whistles. Shamans collected a fee for curing and participated in hunting and warfare by using their powers. However, they were also regarded with suspicion as potential sorcerers and were regularly killed.

GOVERNMENT In general, the Washoe maintained a strong impulse toward egalitarianism. Small, autonomous, occasionally permanent settlements were composed of family groups. These settlements were fluid in composition, since families regularly moved from one group to another. Each family group was led by temporary headmen (occasionally headwomen) who exercised wider (settlement-wide) influence only occasionally and by dint of accomplishment. Their role as diplomats was assisted by having several wives who might remain with their relatives and establish various family alliances.

Hunt leaders also played leadership roles, and shamans might acquire unofficial influence. Although some concept of a regional community did exist (in the form of local groups that occasionally cooperated), there was probably no formal division into bands, even into the twentieth century when white-imposed leadership created such a perception.

CUSTOMS A weak dual division structure may have existed in camps and for games. Marriage partners were generally arranged. Marriage or sexual relations between relatives was strictly taboo. An exchange of gifts between two families constituted a marriage. Couples generally lived with the woman's family until after the first child was born. Separation and divorce were easily obtained.

The dead were cremated, their unburned bones placed in a creek. They were also buried under logs or left in the open. Mourners cut their hair, and houses of the dead were either burned or abandoned. The Washoe had no concept of exclusive territoriality. Some intermarriage with Northern Paiute groups as well as with Miwoks, Maidus, and Nisenans led to irregular cooperation between various subgroups for purposes of trade, visiting, and defense.

Women gathered, processed, and cooked most foods (although both sexes cooperated in gathering acorns and pine nuts and in some fishing and hunting). There were many life-cycle rites and rituals, all connected with ensuring both individual and community health and well-being. Husbands were not present at birth, although they shared some of their wives' postpartum restrictions. Women nursed babies for up to five years. Babies received their names, which were usually derived from some personal behavior, at around age one. Games, which usually included gambling, included the hand game, races, and athletic contests.

The four-day girls' puberty ceremony was a major event. The young women observed several food restrictions, performed many chores on little sleep, and were prohibited from combing their own hair or scratching themselves. Women friends and relatives chanted songs by a fire while dancing a "jumping dance." Afterward, men and women danced a round dance. The dancing continued throughout the night and was followed by a formal conclusion ceremony. The whole was repeated at a woman's second period, after which she was considered marriageable.

DWELLINGS Mountain winter villages were occupied by at least some members of the family year-round. A conical pole framework between 10 and 15 feet in diameter and set in a shallow pit supported slabs of bark tied on with cordage or sinew. Thatching may also have been used. Doorways faced east. Houses could hold up to about seven people. Temporary, dome-shaped brush shelters, as well as windbreaks and lean-tos, served as seasonal housing while people were away fishing, gathering, or hunting.

DIET Most people moved seasonally with the food supply, but that supply was generally abundant and in predictable locations. Washoes faced little regular hunger until non-natives destroyed their way of life. Each unit made its own decisions about when and where to procure food. The only exceptions to this rule were foods taken collectively, such as acorns, pine nuts, fish, and some animals.

Fish, including trout, suckers, whitefish, and chub, was a staple. Ice fishing was practiced in winter. Fish were caught both individually and communally and were prepared either by pit roasting, stone boiling (in baskets), or drying. Other staples usually included acorns, which were shelled, ground into flour, and leached before being used to make dumplings. Pine nuts, gathered in late fall, were made into flour for soup.

Washoe women gathered a great variety of wild plants, including roots, grasses, seeds, nuts, berries, and bulbs, for food as well as medicine. Tule and cattails were especially important. Women gathered plants with digging sticks. Family groups had traditional harvesting areas. Some rituals were associated with gathering activities.

Deer, antelope, and rabbit were hunted communally in drives. Rabbits, the most important dietary animal, were driven into corrals or over cliffs. The people also hunted mountain sheep and other large and small game, birds, and waterfowl. They collected insects, especially locusts, grasshoppers, and grubs. Men and sometimes women smoked wild tobacco or used it for poultices. Golden eagles were never killed; bears only rarely.

KEY TECHNOLOGY Fishing equipment included

harpoons, nets, dams, weirs, basket traps, and hook and line. Men used the bow and (sometimes poisoned) arrows for hunting. Other technological items included twined and coiled baskets; stone mortars and pestles, metates and manos, and knives; sandstone pipes and arrow smoothers; wooden utensils and cooking items; fire drills; and looms for making beadwork and weaving rabbit-skin blankets.

TRADE The Washoe traded mostly among themselves. When they did trade "outside the family," mainly with groups such as the Miwok, Nisenan, and Northern Paiute, they generally exchanged items such as salt, obsidian, pine nuts, and rabbit skins for sea shells, redbud bark (for baskets), hides, and food items.

NOTABLE ARTS Basketry was utilitarian in form and style but, fueled by white demand, reached artistic heights in the late nineteenth century. Rock art was at least several thousand years old. Art objects were made from a variety of materials, including stone, wood, and clay.

TRANSPORTATION People built cedar-bark and tule rafts for lake fishing and river crossings, circular manzanita or piñon snowshoes for winter hunting, and wooden skis for marsh or snow walking.

DRESS The basic clothing materials were skins, usually deerskin, and sagebrush bark. Men generally wore breechclouts, plus capes and leggings in winter. They also plucked their facial hair. Women wore aprons, adding capes in winter. Both sexes wore moccasins of deer hide lined with sage in winter, although people usually went barefoot. Rabbit-skin blankets or robes were also important for clothing and bedding. Both sexes wore tattoos as well as ornaments of many materials and pierced their ears.

WAR AND WEAPONS Intergroup relations were generally peaceful and cooperative. Most wars (with Maidus, Northern Paiutes, or Miwoks) concerned conflict over the use of subsistence areas. They were small and relatively insignificant. The Achumawi and Atsugewi sometimes raided northern Washoe camps. War leaders were selected for periods of conflict.

Contemporary Information

GOVERNMENT/RESERVATIONS The Washoe Tribe of Nevada and California has 4,300 acres, plus over 60,000 acres of assorted parcels. These include the Wade Property, California (388 acres); Silverado Parcel, Nevada (160 acres); Upper Clear Creek, Nevada (157 acres); and Lower Clear Creek, Nevada (209 acres). They also have public domain allotments. The tribe serves the residential communities of Dresslerville, Carson, and Stewart, Nevada, and Woodfords, California. It is governed by a 14-member tribal council according to a constitution adopted in 1966.

Woodfords Community, Alpine County, California (1970), 80 acres, 338 resident Indians (1991), is governed by a community council.

Carson Colony, Carson City County, Nevada (1917), 160 acres, 275 resident Indians (1991), is governed by a community council.

Dresslerville Colony, Douglas County, Nevada (1917), 90 acres, 348 resident Indians (1991), is governed by a community council.

Stewart Community, Nevada (1990), 2,960 acres, 90 resident Indians (1991), is governed by a community council.

Washoe Reservation (Ranches), Douglas County, Nevada (1982), 794 acres, 65 Indians (1990), is governed by a tribal council.

Reno-Sparks Indian Colony, Washoe County, Nevada (1917; Washoe and Paiute), 1,984 acres, 262 resident Indians (1990), 724 enrolled members (1992), is governed by a seven-member tribal council.

Susanville Rancheria, Lassen County, California (1923; Maidu, Pit River, and Washoe), 150 acres, 154 Indians (1990), is governed by a seven-member tribal council.

ECONOMY There is still some subsistence acorn and pine nut gathering as well as deer and rabbit hunting. Women make baskets and rabbit-skin blankets. Tribal businesses include a smoke shop, crafts shop, park with camping facilities, construction company, and an aquaculture facility.

LEGAL STATUS The Washoe Tribe of Nevada and California (Carson Colony; Dresslerville, Woodfords, and Stewart community councils), the Reno-Sparks Indian Colony, and the Susanville Indian Rancheria are federally recognized tribal entities. The Washoe-Paiute of Antelope Valley, California, have petitioned for government recognition.

DAILY LIFE The Washoe have succeeded in keeping many aspects of their cultural heritage alive. The language is still spoken, although mostly by older people. The girls' puberty rite is still an important ceremony. The tribe hosts an annual tribal picnic, publishes a newsletter, and operates a health center, senior center, housing authority office, and police force. It has jurisdiction of the deer herd as well as other natural resources within their territory. The Stewart Colony maintains a library and archives, and a cultural center is in progress at Lake Tahoe along land long disputed. Children take classes in a wide range of tribal traditions, customs, and arts. The tribe is still creating a land base and seeks to identify sacred sites.

Zuni Pueblo, New Mexico. Like many Indian groups, the Zuni people are committed to succeeding as Indians in the 21st Century. © Nicholas DeVore III/Photographers Aspen

U.S.A. Southeast Alaska; Native Americans at a 1998 celebration in Juneau. Most of them are Tlingit Indians in full ceremonial regalia. © David J. Job/ Ken Graham Agency

Seminole Indian. Big Cypress Reservation, Florida. ©1993 Brenda James/New England Stock

Navajo jewelry on display in Arizona. Navajo Indians are world famous for their silver and turquoise jewelry.
©Photophile

An Inupiat man on a snowmobile in the middle of summer 1996. Many Inupiat survive through a combination of traditional subsistance activities and some involvement with the cash economy. © Mike Swanson/Ken Graham Agency

This pow-wow at the Menominee Indian Reservation, Wisconsin, has been held annually since 1977. The Menominee people are still recovering from the devastating effects of the government's 1950s and 60s era termination policies. © Michael Shedlock/New England Stock

A classroom in Point Hope, Alaska, home to the Chukchi Sea Trading Company. Artists and craftspeople in this isolated village have found a way to market their wares to a worldwide audience. © Clyde H. Smith/New England Stock

A Zuni Indian weaves a blanket on the Zuni Reservation in New Mexico. Zunis both make a living and reinforce cultural values through the manufacture and sale of their craft. © L.L.T. Rhodes/Photophile

Shoshone children work on traditional Indian crafts at a summer workshop in Ethete, Wyoming. © John Easdtcott Associates /YVA Momatiuk/Woodfin Camp & Associates

TOP: Cheyenne Buffalo Skull. The red paint symbolizes the sun's rays. Buffalo skulls were often used by the Plains Indians in "the adoption ceremony." All rights reserved, Photo Archives, Denver Museum of Natural History

ABOVE: Seneca Corn Husk mask. All rights reserved, Photo Archives, Denver Museum of Natural History

LEFT: This is an Iroquois False Face mask. They are often included in medicine bundles used in rituals along with turtle rattles. They need to be kept covered as otherwise, they cannot prevent sickness. They are usually passed along to an heir or buried with the 'owner.' All rights reserved, Photo Archives, Denver Museum of Natural History

This is a Choctaw medicine horn; a ritualistic object often contained in a medicine bundle and used in healing rituals.

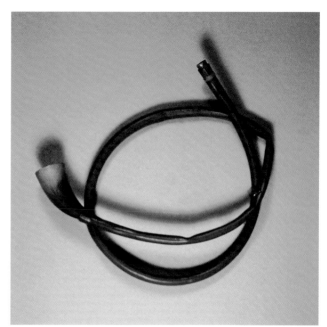

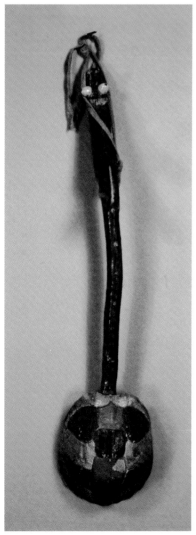

This is a Seminole turtle shell, or Locv-saukv, made by medicine men from the shells of land turtles. During the preparation (dried, filed with gravel), special prayers are said so that the rattles will have voices. These rattles are worn by women in preparatory dances for the Green Corn Ceremony, a Native American New Year. They are passed down from mother to daughter.

A group of Indians in full Indian garb riding through an Indian village. © Archive Photos

Native American rug weaving in Monument Valley, Arizona. © Archive Photos

Native American woman sitting on a car hood and shading her eyes from the sun. © Archive Photos

North Dakota/Mandan. Mandan-Hida tsa Natives, woman and child. © Jeff Greenberg/Archive Photos

Elderly Seminoles. The older women still cling to traditional garb, but the men and the younger generation favor white man's clothing. © Max Hunn/Archive Photos

An Indian family pose in doorway of their adobe hut. © Archive Photos

Mangansutt Indians. © George Dabrawski/Archive Photos

Mangansutt Indians. © George Dabrawski/Archive Photos

Mangansutt Indian. © George Dabrawski/Archive Photos

Mohawk Native American. © Jeff Greenberg/Archive Photos

Taos dancers in New Mexico. © Meston/Archive Photos

Crow or Blackfoot chief, White Buckskin. ©
Hackett/Archive Photos

Indian woman. © Archive Photos

Wisconsin Dells, Stand Rock, Tom Tom
dance. © Meston

Inter-tribal Ceremonial Jemez eagle dancers. © Meston

The Plateau

Plateau

The Plateau region is physically defined by two major river systems, the Columbia and the Fraser. Some 240,000 square miles of land east of the Coast Range (British Columbia) and the Cascade Range (Washington and Oregon) are drained by these rivers. Plateau Indian territory encompassed present-day eastern Washington; eastern Oregon; extreme northeastern California; northern Idaho; extreme western Montana; and interior portions of British Columbia. Aboriginal population estimates for the Columbia Plateau range between 50,000 and 60,000 people.

Climatically, the Plateau is a land of extremes. The northern, or Canadian, Plateau is heavily forested and receives significantly more rain than does the semi-arid southern, or Columbia, Plateau. Summer temperatures may approach those of the deserts, whereas near-Arctic cold regularly grips the region in winter.

Most Plateau tribes spoke dialects of either Sahaptian or Interior Salishan languages; the former, along with Wasco-Wishram (Upper Chinookan [Kiksht]) and Modoc/Klamath, are sometimes grouped as Penutian languages. The Kootenai spoke a linguistically isolated language. Owing to trade and familial considerations, however, many groups were functionally multilingual. Athapaskan-speaking Indians such as the Carrier and Chilcotin, considered Subarctic peoples in this book, are occasionally grouped within the Plateau area.

A dependence on inland fish, particularly salmon, as well as roots and berries, was a defining characteristic of Plateau Indian life. Other typical traits included the use of semisubterranean pit earth houses as well as aboveground mat longhouses, the production of a wide variety of grass baskets, individual relationships with guardian spirit helpers, an appreciation of individual dignity and autonomy, and a reluctance (at least before the early eighteenth century) to engage in warfare.

In the eighteenth and nineteenth centuries, acquisition of the horse made buffalo hunters and raiders out of many groups. Not surprisingly, contact with non-Indians resulted in enormous population and territorial losses as well as significant cultural loss. With the help of land claims awards, favorable legal rulings concerning subsistence rights, and an increasingly well-educated population, Plateau tribes today are attempting with increasing success to rebound from the relative misery of the past 150 years.

People have lived in the Plateau region continuously for at least 10,000 years. Cultural and linguistic continuity dates back at least several thousand years. During much of this period there was no effective cultural boundary between the Plateau and adjacent parts of other regions such as the Great Basin. Although technology changed through the centuries (for example, people adopted specialized grinding tools circa 3000 B.C.E. and the bow and arrow circa 500 B.C.E. at the latest), the basic lifestyle remained similar from the earliest days to the arrival of the horse in the late prehistoric period.

Although salmon and other fish were a staple food for most groups, Plateau Indians also gathered plant foods such as camas, kouse root, bitterroot, and a variety of berries. Roots were often cooked in earth ovens. Plants provided essential medicines and raw materials. Hunting provided additional nourishment: Depending on location, game included deer, elk, antelope, mountain sheep, and bear as well as rabbit, squirrels, and other small game. Most Plateau groups followed a regular migratory route to obtain foods at their greatest productivity. The purpose of Plateau food acquisition was both to meet immediate needs and to built up a surplus for the lean winter months and for trade.

Winter villages, usually located along waterways, were occasionally occupied all year, although generally the dwellings were dismantled and their mats used in temporary summer shelters. Houses generally consisted of semisubterranean lodges (roughly 5 feet deep and 10–16 feet in diameter) of grass, brush, and earth over planks (probably an older style). Roofs were either flat or dome shaped. Entrance was gained through the smoke hole. In summer and perhaps later in time people lived in rectangular tule mat–covered structures with inverted V roofs. Shared hearths ran along the center. These reached lengths of up to 60 feet and accommodated from two to eight families.

In the Thompson River region, circular winter pit houses generally had pyramidal roofs through which one entered and descended on notched ladders. These houses, 20–40 feet in diameter, accommodated 15 to 30 people. Sweat lodges were generally constructed of grass and earth over a wooden frame. Food was stored in pits or on wooden platforms.

Twined "Indian hemp" and tule were two of the most important raw materials for Plateau Indians. The former (along with sagebrush and willow bark) was used to make cordage, baskets, hats, bedding, and nets for fishing and hunting rabbits. Tule, a type of bulrush, was used in the manufacture of mats, which were in turn used as house coverings, flooring, and corpse shrouds. Twined and coiled baskets, often made of spruce or cedar root, were ubiquitous on the Plateau. People used them for household utensils, cooking vessels (boiling by placing heated stones in liquid), water and burden containers, drinking cups, cradles, and numerous other purposes. Bark containers were also used.

Basket weavers and bone carvers, in particular, sometimes reached levels of artistic excellence. Some baskets were decorated with geometric designs, especially in the Thompson River region. In the Middle Columbia region (Sahaptian speakers), Northwest Coast influence revealed itself during the late prehistoric period in art motifs of humans and animals.

The bow and arrow was the principal hunting tool and weapon. Spears were also used and, in war, clubs and armor of rawhide or wooden slats. Arrows were straightened with an elk bone wrench and smoothed with sandstone tools. Fish were speared, netted with weirs and traps, or, especially in the north, caught with hook and line. Women used a stick, sometimes tipped with antler, to dig roots. Other tools, such as pestles and mauls, were made from stone (basalt and granite), bone, and other materials. Dugout as well as bark canoes served as water transportation. Some Indians also regularly burned certain areas to make them more productive and attractive to game.

Before the equestrian tradition became established, clothing was generally made from bark, grass, and fur. Men and women wore breechclouts or aprons and ponchos. Men wore fur leggings in winter; those of women were made of hemp. Ornaments were fashioned from a number of materials, including olivella and dentalium shells from the Pacific Ocean, river clam shells, and various bones.

Plateau Indians traded widely as part of a huge regional network. The largest and most important trading center was located at the Dalles and Celilo Falls, at the head of the Columbia gorge. Surplus salmon—dried, pounded into meal, and stored in salmon skin and cattail bags—was one of the main trade items. Groups from hundreds of miles around brought their specialties: Dentalium and other shells, obsidian, baskets, meat, animal products, clothing, and later slaves and horses were among the most important items. The trade fairs were also centers of cultural exchange.

At least before the advent of the horse, most Plateau societies were relatively egalitarian. That is, villages were politically autonomous, and the authority of village chiefs lay more in their ability to persuade and adjudicate than in their power to make rules and enforce decisions. Women as well as men could be chiefs of many bands. Specialized leaders such as salmon and war chiefs exercised leadership in specific situations. Slavery was hereditary only in far western groups with close ties to Northwest Coast Indians.

In general, Plateau society was held together less by authoritarian means than by an ethic of sharing and obligation as well as by kinship and trade networks and associations. Because people rarely married within their own village, these networks were quite extensive throughout the Plateau. Furthermore, marriage networks generally survived even death, as a widow or widower often married her or his spouse's sibling. Plateau Indians practiced a sexual division of labor, in which women gathered plants, processed and prepared food, and took care of young children, and the men fished, hunted, and had a greater voice in politics, diplomacy, and military affairs.

Aboriginal Plateau religion centered around the relationship between individuals and spirits of animate or inanimate natural things (animals, plants, phenomena, or physical features). Pubescent or prepubescent boys and girls undertook quests in remote places, at which time they often entered into a relationship with a spirit and obtained its song and power, which were revealed indirectly years later. In exchange for respect, which included honor during the winter dances, the spirit was thought to bestow important powers or skills. Shamans, salmon chiefs, and other highly skilled leaders were thought to have attracted one or more particularly powerful spirit helpers.

Non-native influence in the Plateau region

appeared with the introduction of the horse, from Shoshone peoples to the south, as early as 1730. Use of the horse influenced life on the Plateau in many ways. It allowed people to migrate over greater distances and to transport larger quantities of dried food. It generally favored political centralization and the formation of tribal structures. Although most groups, especially those on the Canadian and Upper Columbian Plateau, retained their traditional subsistence patterns, others began to hunt buffalo on the Great Plains (or greatly increased their buffalo-hunting activity) and to adopt other aspects of Plains culture, including full-scale raiding.

The historical period among Plateau Indians began with the 1804–1806 Lewis and Clark expedition. However, as was almost universally true, by the time non-Indians actually appeared, Indian populations had declined substantially (up to 90 percent in some cases) owing to the advance arrival of previously unknown diseases such as smallpox and malaria. Disease epidemics among Indians continued well into the twentieth century. Fur traders followed on the heels of Lewis and Clark, and right behind them came missionaries. Initial relations between Plateau Indians and non-natives were generally friendly.

By the early 1840s, the fur trade in the region had come to an end, and the great tide of non-Indian invaders began to pour in. One of the first major interracial conflicts occurred in 1847 when Cayuse Indians attacked the Waiilatpu Mission and killed its founders, Marcus and Narcissa Whitman, as well as several other whites. The motive behind this action was apparently that the Cayuse held the missionaries responsible for all the sickness and death among the Indians. They also saw the missionaries as symptomatic of the rapidly increasing assault on Indian land and the growing attacks on Indian traditions.

In 1855, several Indian groups, mostly Sahaptian speakers, ceded millions of acres of land in exchange for reservations, financial considerations, and certain subsistence rights (such as fishing) guaranteed in perpetuity. Other Plateau reservations were established by executive order. Between 1855 and 1858, the Yakima and other Plateau groups fought in desperate wars of resistance with the U.S. Army and volunteers. Twenty years later, a Nez Percé band, in a famous and nearly successful act, chose flight to Canada rather than accept the loss of their beloved homeland and a greatly diminished reservation. British Columbia did not establish tribes and reservations per se, but rather created dozens of very small reserves for the individual bands. Although this process allowed most Indians to remain in their traditional territory, it left them with less land overall and discouraged social and political cohesiveness.

Meanwhile, the rise of new Indian religions reflected the extent to which native culture was being altered by the new situation. Around 1860, a Wanapum (Columbia River) Indian named Smohalla had a vision while recovering from a wound. He spoke of the coming end of the world and the resurrection of the Indian dead. He urged Indians to resist Euro-American culture and reservation life and focus instead on attaining salvation through traditional beliefs and practices, including sacred singing and dancing. Smohalla attracted groups of defiant, antireservation Indians to his community near Priest Rapids. He was often jailed for opposing U.S. efforts to encourage farming among Indians.

The teachings of Smohalla and other Plateau prophets were a direct response to the unprecedented destruction of Indian population and traditional lifestyle. They were as well an attempt to bridge the gulf between Indian religion and Christianity, past and present. These beliefs spread rapidly throughout the Plateau and formed the core of the *Wáashat*, Dreamer, Seven Drums, or Longhouse religion.

Few Indians of British Columbia were conquered militarily, nor did they formally surrender title to their land. In 1884, 13 years after British Columbia joined the Canadian Confederation, the Canadian government simply discounted Indian landownership and passed its first Indian Act, under which it appropriated land and exercised legal control over Indians within Canada. Roughly 200 small reserves were created to accommodate the different bands. The thinking was to permit Indians to remain self-sufficient as they made the transition to the capitalist economy, whereas in the United States policymakers forced various groups of Indians to live together on large reservations, where they were strongly encouraged to become farmers and abandon their traditional identities.

Like most North American Indians, Plateau tribes saw increasing difficulty in the late nineteenth and early twentieth century. Few treaty provisions that protected Indians were enforced. For instance, selling alcohol to Indians was prohibited, but offenders were never punished. Indians' land base continued to shrink, sometimes dramatically, owing to a combination of strategies that included the infamous Dawes Act as well as unilaterally imposed "boundary negotiations."

By that time, Indian culture was under full-scale assault at the hands of missionaries and Bureau of Indian Affairs (BIA) boarding schools. Most groups, previously independent and self-sufficient, sank into dependency and poverty. Government officials failed to transform these fishers, gatherers, and hunters into farmers. Job opportunities were minimal, and legal and social discrimination was rampant. Overall health on the reservations was poor.

The tide began to change, ever so slowly, in the mid-1930s, with the passage of the Indian Reorganization Act (IRA). Although many tribes rejected its provisions, the act provided tribes with an opportunity to form governments recognized by the United States (even if the structures were largely alien to native tradition) and to begin to assume greater control over their lives. Unfortunately, the official termination policies of the 1950s undid much of the good of the IRA, and the general postwar economic recovery excluded most Indian reservations.

Revitalization began again in the 1960s, a period of increased federal support to tribes as well as the emergence of a renewed identification with and pride in Indian heritage. In 1974, the issue of fishing rights came to a dramatic head with the so-called Boldt decision reaffirming Indians' right to an active, vital fishery. Corollary concerns such as the effect on native fisheries of potentially destructive actions such as logging, pollution, and dams remain controversial. Fisheries issues may be seen as part of the larger and still controversial question of overall tribal sovereignty. This in turn is bound up with the still deplorable economic situation on most reservations: Although individuals and tribes receive income from timber, mining, grazing leases, and tourism, poverty and its concurrent social ills remain endemic.

On an individual level, many Indians participate in traditional cultural practices. The *Wáashat* (Longhouse or Seven Drums) religion is particularly strong among Sahaptian speakers. Services are conducted in the Sahaptian language, and the religion is an important means for transmitting and affirming Indian identity. The Native American (Peyote) Church and various Christian churches are also represented on the reservations. Like many Native Americans, Plateau Indians face the challenge of retaining a meaningful Indian identity within a culture that cares little about such things. As the tribes become more important decision makers in regional economic matters, this challenge will assume growing importance and poignancy.

Cayuse

Cayuse (`Kī ūz) is a word derived from the French *cailloux,* meaning "People of the Stones or Rocks." Their self-designation was *Waiilatpus,* "Superior People." The Cayuse were culturally similar to the Nez Percé and Wallawalla.

LOCATION   In the eighteenth century, Cayuse Indians lived along the headwaters of the Walla Walla, Umatilla, and Grande Ronde Rivers, in present-day Oregon and Washington. Today, most Cayuse live in Umatilla County, Oregon, and in regional cities and towns.

POPULATION   The Cayuse population was about 500 in the eighteenth century. In 1990, 1,028 Cayuse, Umatilla, and Wallawalla Indians lived on the Umatilla Reservation.

LANGUAGE   Cayuse, or Waillatpuan, may have been associated with the Sahaptian division of the Penutian language family. However, many Cayuse adopted the Nez Percé language in the nineteenth century.

Historical Information

HISTORY   The Cayuse may have lived with the Molala Indians, on the John Day River, until the early eighteenth century. At that time the Cayuse acquired horses, and by the nineteenth century they owned many horses and were very strong and dominating for the size of the tribe. They expanded northward and eastward, into the Grande Ronde and Walla Walla Valleys, subjugating the Wallawalla tribe in the process. They also regularly hunted buffalo on the Great Plains, adapting many Plains cultural attributes.

Largely because of their enormous herds of horses, the Cayuse became so wealthy during this period that they no longer bothered to fish, trading instead for fish and other necessities. They welcomed the Lewis and Clark expedition in 1806 and welcomed as well the fur traders who entered their territory shortly thereafter. They were not especially interested in furs but rather in the goods of non-Indian manufacture that they might trade for. Their openness to non-natives was also due in part to their luck at having so far escaped most of the disease epidemics that ravaged other Indian peoples.

The first Presbyterian missions in the area opened in 1836. In 1843, the first emigrants traveled on the Oregon Trail. In 1847, relations between the Cayuse and whites, hitherto friendly, took a dramatic turn for the worse when a group of Indians destroyed the local mission and killed its founders, Marcus and Narcissa Whitman, and others. They blamed the missionaries for the disease epidemics that were destroying their people. They also resented the Whitmans for their intolerance to the Indians and their new wealth based on sales of former Indian land.

The Whitman "massacre" was the opening salvo in a constant struggle (the Cayuse war) with non-natives that lasted until about 1850. Tiloukaikt, a band chief and former friend of non-native traders, was a leader in this conflict. The tribe was ultimately defeated, and some of its members were hanged by the U.S. government. By this time, disease, warfare, and intermarriage with the Nez Percé had greatly reduced the tribe. Although the Cayuse kept up sporadic resistance into the 1850s, they were assigned by treaty to the Umatilla Reservation in 1855 and most were removed there in 1860. Some Cayuses took up farming on the reservation. Some joined the Yakimas (1855), Nez Percés (1877), and Bannocks (1878) in their various wars against the whites, but some also served with the U.S. Army during these wars.

RELIGION Individuals acquired and maintained relationships with helping nature spirits. Such spirits were obtained during adolescent quests; their powers, which facilitated various skills, were revealed many years later. Shamans acquired particularly strong guardian spirits. They led religious ceremonies and cured illness by blowing, sucking, and chanting. They were also regularly killed for misusing or stealing power. The main religious ceremonies were related to guardian spirits (winter ceremonies), food, and battle.

GOVERNMENT At least in early historic times, each of three autonomous bands was led by a chief and occasionally a war chief. The three chiefs made up a tribal council. Chiefs usually owned many horses and were responsible in part for lecturing their people on proper behavior. The bands, composed of families, were seminomadic. Most subsistence activity was carried out at the family level. By the mid–nineteenth century a single chief had replaced the tripartite structure.

CUSTOMS Wealthy men could have more than one wife. The Cayuse regularly intermarried with the Nez Percé. There were strict sanctions against adultery. Infants' heads were shaped for aesthetic purposes. Twins were often killed at birth. In the eighteenth century, the Cayuse became highly skilled horsepeople and adopted the Plains philosophy of war and raiding.

DWELLINGS Typical Plateau woven reed and mat summer huts and semisubterranean earth-covered winter lodges gave way to hide tipis in the eighteenth century.

DIET Salmon and other fish were the staples. This was supplemented by various plant foods, especially camas and other roots, and berries. Large and small game also contributed to the Cayuse diet.

KEY TECHNOLOGY Woven reed mats and baskets played a major role in Cayuse material culture.

Trade Particularly after the early eighteenth century, the Cayuse dominated trade at the Dalles, site of the region's premier trade fair, as well as at other trade locations. Among other items, salmon products and shells came from the west, and elk and buffalo products came from the east. Horses became the most important trade item: In the early nineteenth century,

the Cayuse commonly exchanged beaver and horses for guns and ammunition. The Cayuse also collected tribute from weaker tribes.

NOTABLE ARTS Cayuse Indians were known for their fine baskets and, later, horse equipment.

TRANSPORTATION Horses arrived in Cayuse country about 1750. In the early nineteenth century, each person had from 10 to 15 to up to as many as 2,000 horses.

DRESS Plateau-style clothing of bark and fur breechclouts, aprons, and ponchos were replaced in the eighteenth century by Plains-style clothing such as long dresses for women, shirts and leggings for men, and moccasins. This late-prehistoric clothing was made of tanned skins, especially antelope and elk, and decorated with fringe and quillwork.

WAR AND WEAPONS In common with most Plateau groups, the Cayuse engaged in little raiding or warfare until they acquired horses. At that time, they quickly subjugated neighbors such as the Umatilla and the Wallawalla. Plains-style raiding for booty and glory became very important, as did secret war societies and ceremonial preparations for combat. Women and children, particularly Shastas and Klamaths, were taken as slaves, and captured men were killed. The prebattle ceremony included fasting, sweating, praying, and dancing. Western Shoshones were traditional enemies of the Cayuse, whereas the Nez Percé were longtime allies.

Contemporary Information

GOVERNMENT/RESERVATIONS Most Cayuses live on the Umatilla Reservation, Umatilla and Union Counties, Oregon (1855; Umatilla, Cayuse, Wallawalla). The reservation contains 95,273 acres; in 1990, its Indian population was 1,028 people. The reservation is governed by a nine-member elected tribal council plus several active committees. The constitution and by-laws were adopted in 1949.

The Umatilla Reservation is a member of the Umatilla Basin Project, the Columbia River Intertribal Fish Commission, the Basalt Waste Isolation Project, the Hanford Environmental Dose Reconstruction Project, the Columbia Gorge Commission, and other environmental and planning organizations.

ECONOMY In the 1960s, each member of tribe was paid almost $3,500 as compensation for fishing sites lost to the Dalles Dam. There have been other land claims settlements as well. The reservation is developing an Oregon Trail Interpretive Center. There is income from farm leases. Tribal programs provide credit as well as seasonal and regular employment. The tribes also own a forest, a range, a store, and a lake (facilities for camping and fishing).

LEGAL STATUS The Confederated Tribes of the Umatilla Reservation is a federally recognized tribal entity.

DAILY LIFE The Confederated Tribes of the Umatilla Reservation value both traditional and modern education. There are some language preservation programs as well as a college scholarship fund. Facilities include a day care center, an arts and crafts organization, and health education and substance abuse programs. Activities include the annual Pendleton Round-up (dances, crafts fair, rodeo) and an annual Indian festival of the arts. The Seven Drum religion is a major force in cultural revitalization. Traditional first salmon and roots ceremonies are also celebrated. The tribes' role in regional economic and political affairs continues to grow.

Coeur d'Alene

Coeur d'Alene (`Kir d ə `l ā n), French for "awl heart," is reportedly a reference by an Anglo trader to the trading skills of these Indians. Their self-designation was *Skitswish*, perhaps meaning "foundling."

LOCATION In the eighteenth century, the Coeur d'Alene lived along the Spokane River upstream from Spokane Falls, including Lake Coeur d'Alene. The region of over four million acres is fertile and well watered. In the early nineteenth century the tribe lived in central Idaho, eastern Washington, and western Montana; the mountains in this area helped to protect their horses against raiders from the Plains. Today's Coeur d'Alene Reservation is located in Benewah and Kootenai Counties, Idaho.

POPULATION The aboriginal (early-eighteenth-century) population of roughly 2,000 had declined to about 500 by 1850. In 1990, 749 Coeur d'Alene and Spokan Indians lived on the reservation, and another 500 or so lived off-reservation.

Language Coeur d'Alene Indians spoke an Interior Salish dialect. They also used a local sign language.

Historical Information

HISTORY Like all Salish peoples, the Coeur d'Alenes probably originated in British Columbia. They migrated to the Plateau during their prehistoric period, keeping some Pacific Coast attributes even after they adopted Plateau culture. They acquired the horse around 1760, at which time they gave up their semisedentary lives to hunt buffalo, Plains-style.

Their traditional antipathy toward outsiders made it difficult for trappers to penetrate their territory. A Jesuit mission was established in 1842, however, foreshadowing the significant role the Jesuits were to play in their later history. At this time, the Jesuits successfully influenced the Indians to give up buffalo hunting and begin farming.

In the meantime, intermittent warfare with Indians and non-Indians, plus disease and crowding, had dropped their population by about 85 percent by 1850. In 1858 they fought the ill-fated Coeur d'Alene war (1858) with the help of tribes such as the Northern Paiute, Palouse, and Spokan. Although the immediate cause of this conflict was white treaty violations, it may be seen as an extension of the Yakima war (1855–1856) and the general Plateau Indian resistance struggle during that time.

The roughly 600,000-acre Coeur d'Alene Reservation was created in 1873, at which time the Indians ceded almost 2.4 million acres. However, pressure from miners soon forced the tribe to cede almost 185,000 more acres in the late 1880s. Most of the rest of their land was lost to the allotment process in the early twentieth century. In 1894, 32 Spokan families joined the reservation. Most Coeur d'Alene Indians became Catholics, farmers, and stock breeders. In 1958, the tribe was awarded over $4.3 million in land claims settlements.

RELIGION Mythical creatures and spirits were all around and in many different forms. Everyone could potentially obtain guardian spirits through vision quests. Furthermore, people prayed for luck to forces of nature. Shamans cured with the help of especially powerful guardians. The few group festivals were held at the beginning of the food season.

GOVERNMENT There were originally three geographical divisions of Coeur d'Alene Indians: Coeur d'Alene River, Spokane River, and Coeur d'Alene Lake. Each was composed of autonomous bands, which were in turn composed of groups of several families, each led by an elected chief. There was no overall tribal organization until the mid–nineteenth century.

CUSTOMS Coeur d'Alenes were fiercely independent. Band territorial rights merited a high degree of respect. The people practiced some polygyny. Descent and residence were generally patrilineal. The dead were wrapped in blankets and buried in the ground or under rocks. In addition, the Coeur d'Alenes engaged in giveaways reminiscent of the coastal potlatch.

DWELLINGS Semiexcavated conical mat houses held between one and three families. Larger, aboveground structures were used for communal activities. Sweat houses were made of bark or grasses over a willow-stick frame. As the tribe became more nomadic, skin tipis gradually replaced mat lodges.

DIET In addition to salmon and other fish, deer was a staple before the time of large-scale buffalo hunting. Other important animal foods included elk, antelope, moose, sheep, bear, and small game. Dogs provided assistance in the hunt. Camas, bulbs, roots, seeds, and berries rounded out the diet.

KEY TECHNOLOGY Fishing technology included assorted gaffs, hooks, traps, and nets. A variety of coiled baskets served different functions. Many utensils were made of stone and bone. Pipes were carved of soapstone. Bows were made of mountain sheep horn.

TRADE The Coeur d'Alene traded in coiled baskets, rabbit-skin clothing, and, especially after the mid–eighteenth century, horses and buffalo-derived items. They were known for their shrewd trading practices.

NOTABLE ARTS Artistic expression may be seen especially in the manufacture of coiled baskets.

TRANSPORTATION Cedar-bark canoes were used to traverse lakes and navigate rivers. Horses were in general use from about 1760 on.

DRESS Traditional clothing was made of woven rabbit skin and the skins of deer, elk, or antelope. Women wore aprons, and men wore leggings, breechclout, and shirt. Beginning in the late eighteenth century, beads and quillwork were added to many clothes. Both sexes wore moccasins and robes in cold weather.

WAR AND WEAPONS Aboriginally, the people enjoyed good relations with their neighbors, only occasionally fighting with the Nez Percés or the Spokan. After they acquired the horse, the Coeur d'Alene were allied with the Nez Percé, the Flathead, and the Kootenai against Plains tribes such as the Crow, Lakota, and Blackfeet. Coeur d'Alenes generally won few wars.

Contemporary Information

GOVERNMENT/RESERVATIONS The Coeur d'Alene Reservation (1873) is located in Benewah and Kootenai Counties, Idaho. It contains 69,176 acres and had a 1990 population of 749 Indians. The constitution, approved in 1949, calls for a seven-member tribal council elected for three-year terms. Reservation residents are mostly Coeur d'Alene but also include some Kalispel, Spokan, and other Indians. The tribe is a member of the Upper Columbia United Tribes and the Affiliated Tribes of Northwest Indians. Some Coeur d'Alene Indians also live on the Colville Reservation (see Colville).

ECONOMY Farming, grazing, and lumbering constitute the most important economic activities. There are also a large tribal farm, a shopping center, a medical center, a construction company, and a service station. Unemployment is chronically high (around 50 percent). Some Indians continue to hunt, fish, and gather foods on and around the reservation. A gam-

bling establishment has been proposed. The tribe received almost $174,000 in land claims settlements in 1981, money that helps the tribe in its goal to purchase lost tribal land.

LEGAL STATUS The Coeur d'Alene Tribe is a federally recognized tribal entity. The people are currently contesting the U.S. claim to Coeur d'Alene Lake.

DAILY LIFE Most Coeur d'Alene Indians are Catholics. Little traditional culture remains, although some language preservation programs have recently been instituted. Children attend a mission school or public schools. People celebrate various Catholic and quasi-traditional ceremonies. There is a tribal college scholarship fund. The tribe is reacquiring non-Indian owned land in order to unify its land base. It is currently engaged in environmental reclamation projects to mitigate the effects of mining devastation. Whaalaa Days, in July, feature traditional games and contests.

Columbia
See Sinkiuse

Columbia River Indians
See Colville; Umatilla; Yakima

Colville

Colville (`K ō l vil) is a name derived from the Colville River and Fort Colville (a Hudson's Bay Company trading post), which in turn were named for Eden Colville, a governor of the company. Whites also called these Indians "Basket People," after their large salmon fishing baskets, and "Chaudière" (kettles), after depressions in the rocks at Kettle Falls and a corruption of their self-designation, *Shuyelpee*. They were culturally similar to the Okanagon and Sanpoil Indians.

LOCATION In the eighteenth century, the Colville Indians lived in northeastern Washington, around the Kettle and Columbia Rivers. Today, most live in Ferry and Okanogan Counties, Washington, and in nearby cities and towns.

POPULATION The eighteenth-century Colville Indian population stood at roughly 2,000. The Colville population reportedly declined to six or seven in 1882. In 1990, 3,782 Indians lived on the reservation.

LANGUAGE Colville Indians spoke a language from the Okanogan group of the Interior division of the Salish language family.

Historical Information

HISTORY As early as 1782, a smallpox epidemic destroyed large numbers of Colville Indians. Colville

Indians became involved with the fur trade shortly after the arrival in the area of the first non-Indians around 1800. By the mid–nineteenth century they were suffering from a sharply declining population and a deteriorating way of life due to new diseases, anti-Indian violence, land theft, and severe disruption of their subsistence habits. Missionaries arrived in 1838. Non-Indian miners flooded into the area in the mid-1850s. Colvilles did not participate in the wars of that time.

Two Colville reservations were established in 1872 for local nontreaty tribes. One, created in April, was considered by local whites to have too-fertile lands, so another reservation with less desirable land was established in July. The early reservation years were marked by conflict with non-Indians and among the tribes. Many Colville Indians converted to Catholicism in the later nineteenth century. In 1900, they lost 1.5 million acres, over half of their reservation. Even so, non-natives continued to settle on the truncated reservation in large numbers until 1935.

The Confederated Tribes of the Colville Reservation were formed in 1938. The government restored some land in 1956. The tribe divided over the issue of termination through the 1950s and 1960s but ultimately decided against it. The tribe won significant land claims settlements in the later twentieth century.

RELIGION Colvilles believed in the presence of spirits in all natural things, animate and inanimate. Individuals sought guardian spirits and their associated songs through the traditional means of singing, fasting, praying, and performing feats of endurance. Prepubescent boys generally undertook a series of one-night vigils. Shamans' especially powerful spirits allowed them to cure illness and perform other particularly difficult tasks.

The five-day first salmon ritual, held under the direction of the salmon chief, was the most important ceremony. Other important religious occasions included the midwinter spirit dances and the first fruits rite. The midwinter dances served the additional purposes of bringing people together and releasing winter tensions.

GOVERNMENT Autonomous villages were each led by a chief and a subchief; these lifetime offices were hereditary in theory but were generally filled by people possessing the qualities of honesty, integrity, and diplomacy. The authority of chiefs to serve as adviser, judge, and general leader was granted mainly through consensus. As judge, the chief had authority over crimes of nonconformity such as witchcraft, sorcery, and assault.

An informal assembly of all married adults confirmed a new chief and oversaw other aspects of village life. All residents of the village were considered citizens. Other village leaders included a messenger, a speaker, and a salmon chief (often a shaman, with the salmon as a guardian spirit, who supervised salmon-related activities). By virtue of their ability to help or hurt people, shamans also acquired relative wealth and power from their close association with chiefs, who liked to keep them friendly.

CUSTOMS Colvilles regularly intermarried with other Salish people. They also very occasionally practiced a form of potlatch. Local villages had associated, nonexclusive territories or subsistence areas. Winter was a time for visits and ceremonies. During that season, women also made mats and baskets, made or repaired clothing, and prepared meals while men occasionally hunted or just slept, gambled, and socialized.

Pacifism, generosity, and interpersonal equality and autonomy were highly valued. Girls fasted and were secluded for ten days at the onset of puberty, except for a nighttime running regime. The exchange of gifts between families constituted a marriage, a relationship that was generally stable and permanent. Corpses were wrapped in tule mats or deerskin and buried with their possessions. The family burned the deceased's house and then observed various taboos and purification rites. Mourners cut their hair and wore old clothes.

DWELLINGS Traditional winter dwellings were semisubterranean, circular pit lodges, with grass, brush, and earth covering a pole frame; they had flat or conical roofs. Entrance was through a ladder in the smoke hole. In the late prehistoric period, the people began building rectangular tule-mat houses. Each of the two to eight families in the house paired off to share a fire in the center of the building.

DIET Food was much more often acquired by the family than by the village. Fish, especially salmon, played a central role in the diet (groups were able to net up to 3,000 a day at Kettle Falls). Men caught four varieties of salmon as well as trout, sturgeon, and other fish. They fished from May through October. Although women could not approach the actual fishing areas, they cleaned and dried the fish. Dried fish and sometimes other foods made up much of the winter diet. People generally ate two meals a day in summer and one in winter.

Women gathered shellfish, salmon eggs, bulbs, roots, nuts, seeds, berries, and prickly pear. Camas was eaten raw or roasted, boiled, or made into cakes. A short ceremony was performed over the first gathered crop of the season. Men hunted most large and small game in the fall. They prepared for the hunt by sweating and singing. Meat was roasted, boiled, or dried. Women came along to help dress and carry the game. Men also hunted birds and gathered mollusks.

KEY TECHNOLOGY Twined and coiled basketry items were heavily represented. These included utensils, cooking tools, containers, bags, and hats. Some items were decorated with geometric designs. Women sewed tule mats with Indian hemp. Hunting tools included spears and the bow and arrow. People also used sandstone arrow smoothers and elk rib arrow straighteners. Fish were speared, netted, and caught in weirs and traps. Women used a slightly curved digging stick with an antler or wood cross handle.

TRADE Trade fairs were held at Kettle Falls and at the mouth of the Fraser River. The level of trade increased with the acquisition of horses.

NOTABLE ARTS Artistic expression was seen mainly in coiled baskets with geometric designs as well as mat weaving. Rock painting had been practiced for thousands of years.

TRANSPORTATION Before the horse, people used two kinds of dugout canoes and snowshoes.

DRESS Standard traditional attire was a bark breechclout or apron, a bark poncho, winter leggings (fur for men, hemp for women), and fur robes. Skin garments became popular beginning in the late prehistoric period. For decoration, people wore Pacific Coast shell ornaments as well as animal teeth and claws.

WAR AND WEAPONS Men used their hunting tools as weapons, plus rawhide or wooden armor. War chiefs were selected on an ad hoc basis. Colvilles were occasionally allied with Okanagon Indians against the Nez Percé and Yakima.

Contemporary Information

Government/Reservations The Colville Reservation (1872) is located in Ferry and Okanogan Counties, Washington. It comprises 1,011,495 acres and had a 1990 Indian population of 3,782. An Indian Reorganization Act constitution approved in 1938 calls for a 14-member business council and various committees. The Confederated Tribes is a member of the Affiliated Tribes of Northwest Indians and other intertribal organizations.

Colville Indians are also members of the Columbia River Indians, a group who lives primarily in Priest Rapids, Cooks Landing, Billieville, and Georgeville, Washington; Celilo, Oregon; and non-Indian communities. The Council of Columbia River Chiefs meets at Celilo, Oregon. The community at Priest Rapids is directly descended from that of Smohalla, a founder of the Dreamer or Longhouse religion.

ECONOMY The reservation economy is largely built around stock raising, farming, logging (including a sawmill) and reforestation, and seasonal labor. There is some mining as well as a meat-packing plant,

a log cabin sales business, and tourism-related businesses such as a trading post and gambling enterprises. There is potential for development of hydroelectric resources.

LEGAL STATUS The Confederated Tribes of the Colville Reservation is a federally recognized tribal entity. The Columbia River Indians are not federally recognized.

DAILY LIFE Colville Indians are largely acculturated. Language preservation programs are hindered by the lack of a common aboriginal language. Recent efforts to reinvigorate disparate tribal cultures and religions include the presence of the Chief Joseph Band of Nez Percé Indians with their Seven Drum Religion, the Indian Shaker Church, and the Native American Church. The reservation hosts an annual powwow and a circle celebration. There is also a program of reacquiring and consolidating the land base and a goal to increase the general levels of education. The Colville Business Council wields growing power in regional and statewide issues.

Flathead
See Salish

Kalispel

Kalispel (`Kal ə s pel), "Camas People," from the name of an important plant food. They are also known as the Pend d'Oreilles, French for "ear drops," a term referring to the Indians' personal adornment. These people were grouped aboriginally into two divisions, lower (Kalispel proper) and upper.

LOCATION In the eighteenth century, the Kalispel lived around Pend d'Oreille Lake and River. Today, most live on their reservation in Pend Oreille County, Washington. Kalispels also live on the Colville and Flathead Reservations.

POPULATION The eighteenth-century Kalispel population was approximately 1,600. In 1990, some 250 Kalispels lived on reservations and in regional cities and towns.

LANGUAGE Kalispels spoke a dialect of Interior Salish.

Historical Information

HISTORY Like other Salish peoples, the Kalispel probably came from British Columbia. The upper division may have moved east and south onto the plains of Montana before the Blackfeet pushed them back, in the eighteenth century, to the Pend d'Oreille Lake region. They especially joined with other Plateau groups to hunt buffalo and organize war and raiding parties after the introduction of the horse.

The North West Trading Company opened a trading post in Kalispel country in 1809. The first

Catholic mission opened in 1846 and relocated in 1854 with the Upper Kalispels to the Lake Flathead area. Kalispels were forced into a major land cession in 1855, and the upper division was assigned to the Flathead Reservation, in Montana, but the lower division refused to relocate, asking instead for a reservation of their own. They remained relatively isolated until 1863, when the British Columbia gold rush brought many miners through their territory.

In 1887, one of the two Lower Kalispel bands moved to the Flathead Reservation. The other, under Marcella, remained in the Pend d'Oreille Valley. Their reservation was created by executive order in 1914: It consisted of 4,629 acres, of which only 150 acres of tribal land remained after individual allotments and white encroachments. The tribe was awarded $3 million in land claims settlements in 1960, and another $114,000 in 1981.

RELIGION Individuals obtained guardian spirits in dreams and visions to provide them with luck and success. Boys began vision quests around the onset of puberty with fasting and praying. Shamans' powerful spirits let them cure illness, see the future, and influence hunting. To honor their spirits, men sang their spirit songs and danced during a midwinter festival. The Kalispel also celebrated other, food-related festivals.

GOVERNMENT In the eighteenth century there were two geographical divisions, Upper Pend d'Oreilles and Lower Pend d'Oreilles, or Kalispelem. The latter were further divided into Lower Kalispel (Kalispel proper), Upper Kalispel, and Chewelah (perhaps a separate tribe). Each division was composed of related families and was led by a chief selected on the basis of merit. Later, a tribal chief presided over a council made up of the band chiefs.

CUSTOMS Games almost always included gambling. Marriage was usually monogamous. People cultivated some tobacco. The dead were dressed in robes, sewn in blankets, temporarily placed on a platform, and then buried. Their possessions were given away, and their names were never spoken again.

DWELLINGS The basic structure was semiexcavated and cone shaped, built of mat and earth covering a wood frame. A larger one was used for communal and ceremonial use, and smaller ones, holding one to three families, for living. Kalispels also built cedar-bark lodges and temporary brush shelters. Decorated hide tipis replaced mat dwellings during the eighteenth century.

DIET Fish was the staple, especially trout, salmon, and whitefish. Important plant foods included camas (from which the Indians made a distinctive bread), bitterroot, other roots, and berries. Some buffalo hunting took place on the Plains after the eighteenth century; other important animal foods included antelope, deer, elk, and small game. Most food was boiled with hot stones in baskets.

KEY TECHNOLOGY In addition to the usual Plateau technological items, Kalispels specialized in making white pine canoes, birch-bark baskets, and woven skin bags.

TRADE Kalispels traded for smoked salmon and other items with people from the west.

NOTABLE ARTS Artistic expression was found mainly in basketry.

TRANSPORTATION The Kalispel were masters of their white pine canoes. The lower division had distinctive low-riding canoes to meet the winds on Pend d'Oreille Lake. Although they were excellent horsemen, they had relatively few horses, even in the mid–nineteenth century.

DRESS Most clothes were made from rabbit or deer skins. Men wore breechclouts and shirts, and women wore dresses. Both wore moccasins, caps, robes, leggings, and shell earrings.

WAR AND WEAPONS The Kalispel were generally peaceful, although they were occasionally allied with the Spokan against the Kootenai.

Contemporary Information

GOVERNMENT/RESERVATIONS The Kalispel Reservation (1914) is located in Pend Oreille County, Washington. It contains 4,557 acres; the 1990 Indian population was 91. The tribal charter and constitution were approved in 1938. The Kalispel Indian Community is descended from Lower Kalispels.

Some Kalispel also live on the Salish-Kootenai Reservation, Montana, as well as on the Colville Reservation, Washington (see Colville; Salish).

ECONOMY Tribal businesses include Kalispel Caseline, Kalispel Agricultural Enterprise, and Kalispel Tribal Bingo. Grazing also provides some income. Other projects, such as a tribal store and a fish and game business, are under consideration. The Kalispel are also attempting to reacquire several thousand acres of land. Income levels on the reservation are chronically low.

LEGAL STATUS The Kalispel Indian Community is a federally recognized tribal entity.

DAILY LIFE Kalispels are trying to remain economically competitive into the twenty-first century while retaining their tribal identity. Kalispel Powwow Days are held in August.

Klamath

Klamath (`Klam uth) is a word of uncertain derivation. The Klamaths' self-designation is Maklak, "People." The Klamath were culturally similar to the Modoc and other northern California Indian peoples.

LOCATION In the early nineteenth century, Klamath people lived on 20 million acres in south-central Oregon and northeastern California. The land included forests and mountains of the Cascade Range, highland lakes and marshes, and the headwaters of the Klamath River. Today the descendants of these people live mostly in Klamath County, Oregon, and in regional cities and towns.

POPULATION Perhaps 1,200 Klamath Indians lived in the early nineteenth century. In 1958, on the eve of termination, the tribal rolls stood at 2,133. In 1993, the tribe had about 2,700 enrolled members.

LANGUAGE Klamath is a dialect of Lutuami, a Penutian language.

Historical Information

HISTORY Klamath Indians were probably spared direct contact with non-natives until the arrival in 1829 of Peter Skene Ogden. The white invasion of the 1850s also brought disease and scattered the game, destroying traditional subsistence patterns. In an 1864 treaty, the Klamath and Modoc people ceded over 13 million acres of land for a 1.1-million-acre reservation on former Klamath lands in southern Oregon. In addition to Klamaths and Modocs, the reservation included Pit River Indians, Shastas, Northern Paiutes, and other groups. These Indians agreed to end the practice of slavery at that time.

Some Modocs left the reservation in 1870 because of friction between themselves and the Klamaths. The latter remained aloof from the 1872–1873 Modoc war. By the end of the nineteenth century, all Indians on the Klamath Reservation were known as the Klamath tribe. In 1901, the government agreed to pay the tribe $537,000 for misappropriated lands. Other land claims settlements, for millions of dollars, followed during the course of the century.

In 1958 the U.S. government terminated the Klamath Reservation. Although the government had long coveted the timber-rich reservation, whereas many Klamaths were strongly against it, termination was hastened by a tribal leader at the time. In 1958, 77 percent of the tribe voted to withdraw from the collective entity and take individual shares of the land proceeds. In 1974, the remaining 23 percent agreed to sell the rest of the reservation for per capita shares. At that time, the Klamaths lost the last of their land base. Termination has had a profoundly negative effect on members of the tribe.

RELIGION Male and female shamans acquired power through fasting, visions, and prayer. The most powerful shamans, able to cure illness as a result of their possession of very strong spirit power, were generally men. Curing itself was dramatic in a literal sense. Shamans also controlled weather, accompanied war parties, affected hunting, and found lost items. They held winter seances to demonstrate their power.

People sought spiritual help at puberty and at other times by going to remote places to fast, pray, and swim. Powers came from spirits that were associated with nature. Spirits conferred power and songs, which might provide luck and skills, in dreams and visions.

GOVERNMENT Traditionally, the Klamath were organized into from four to seven autonomous subdivisions or tribelets. Each tribelet may have consisted of about ten winter hamlets. Each had a chief (chosen either as a consequence of wealth or the ability to provide leadership in war), but shamans probably wielded more authority.

CUSTOMS Acquiring wealth and prestige was the basic goal, although the concept was nowhere near as developed as it was along the Northwest Coast. Klamaths collected items such as skins, food, shells, and weapons. Industriousness and acquisitiveness were valued, and the people practiced little hospitality or sharing. The tribelets were as likely to feud as to intermarry.

Summer was a time for gathering, hunting, and warfare. Exchanging gifts (the bride price) constituted a marriage. Divorce was not uncommon, although it was complicated by property arrangements. Klamaths flattened their babies' foreheads. Corpses were wrapped in tule mats and, with their possessions, carried by canoe to a funeral pyre. The house was also burned. Following the ceremony, relatives of the deceased sweated in the sweat lodge for purification. Dances were generally nonceremonial in nature.

DWELLINGS Permanent winter hamlets were generally built on lake shores and near marshes. Houses were semisubterranean, circular multifamily structures, covered with earth on a wood frame. Entrance was through the roof. Several nuclear families might live in one lodge. Circular, mat-covered wood frame houses served in summer or on hunting trips. Winter and summer sweat lodges were built in a style similar to that of the dwellings.

DIET Fish, mostly freshwater whitefish and suckers, was the food staple. The Klamaths also ate waterfowl. In summer, women gathered roots, berries, and other plant foods, and men hunted deer, antelope, and small game. Wild waterlily seeds (*wokas*) were harvested in late summer; they were eventually ground into flour.

KEY TECHNOLOGY Fishing equipment consisted of nets, traps, and spears. Bows were made of juniper or yew; arrowheads were of obsidian or stone. Twined baskets and mats served a large variety of purposes.

TRADE Klamath Indians participated in local

trade patterns. With the arrival in the region of horses, the Klamath engaged in large-scale raiding for slaves and goods, which they then traded in the north for horses.

NOTABLE ARTS   Basketry was well developed into a fine art.

TRANSPORTATION   Klamath Indians used both dugout canoes and snowshoes.

DRESS   Women wore basketry caps, and moccasins were made of tule before the switch to buckskin. Men and women wore fiber skirts, as well as tule leggings, sandals, and fur mittens in winter. After the Plains influence became stronger, in the nineteenth century, they switched to fringed fiber or buckskin aprons. They also pierced their ears and noses for dentalia shells and wore tattoos.

WAR AND WEAPONS   War leaders were selected on an ad hoc basis. The Klamath were frequently at war with the Achumawi, Shasta, and Kalapuya. They raided these groups, especially in the early nineteenth century, for slaves and goods, which they traded in the north for horses. Raiding parties might consist of men from different tribelets, since war was the main activity that brought people together (women sometimes accompanied war parties). Revenge was a major cause of war. Offensive and defensive equipment included fine bows and arrows and elk hide and slat armor, clubs, and spears. The main strategy lay in surprise attacks. After victory, warriors would collect booty and slaves, mutilate and dismember the dead, and perform a scalp dance that lasted for several nights.

Contemporary Information

GOVERNMENT/RESERVATIONS   The Klamath Reservation is located in Chiloquin, Oregon. The General Council (total enrolled adult population) chooses an eight-member business committee. A constitution, originally adopted in 1929, was reestablished in 1975.

ECONOMY   At least 70 percent of Klamaths live below the poverty level (before termination, Klamaths were one of the most self-sufficient of all U.S. tribes).

LEGAL STATUS   The Klamath Indian Tribe is a federally recognized tribal entity (rerecognized in 1986). In the 1970s, federal courts recognized Klamath hunting and fishing rights, despite the absence of a land base.

DAILY LIFE   The Klamath tribe has a new dental facility and plans for new tribal offices and a cultural center. Cultural revitalization programs include an annual sucker ceremony, basket-weaving classes, and native-language textbooks. Klamath people also practice such traditional crafts as beadwork and bone

work. They host an all-Indian basketball tournament in February and March and a powwow on December 31. Treaty Days in August celebrate the restoration of tribal status.

Klikitat

Klikitat (`Klik i tat) is derived from a Chinook term meaning "beyond" (the Cascade Mountains). Their self-designation was *Qwulh-hwai-pum,* "Prairie People." The Klikitat were culturally similar to the Yakima.

LOCATION   Klikitats lived and continue to live in the vicinity of Mt. Adams in south-central Washington.

POPULATION   The precontact population was roughly 700. Today Klikitat descendants constitute roughly 8 percent of the population of the Confederated Tribes and Bands of the Yakima Indian Nation (about 500 people).

LANGUAGE   Klikitat was a member of the Sahaptian division of the Penutian language family.

Historical Information

HISTORY   The Klikitat may have originated south of the Columbia River, moving north in the prehistoric period to become skilled horsepeople and fighters after they acquired horses around 1700. The 1805 encounter with Meriwether Lewis and William Clark, on the Yakima and Klikitat Rivers, was friendly all around.

Skilled with firearms, the Klikitat sometimes acted as mercenaries for other Indian tribes, taking women and horses as pay. Their effort during the 1820s to expand south of the Columbia was repulsed by the Umpqua. Later, the Klikitats had their revenge by helping whites to conquer the Umpqua. They also scouted for the U.S. Army in the 1850s.

In 1855, the United States asked Klikitats and other local Indians, including Yakimas, to cede 10.8 million acres of land. Most tribes accepted a 1.2-million-acre reservation in exchange. Although Indians retained fishing and gathering rights at their usual off-reservation places and were given at least two years to relocate, the governor of Washington declared their land open to non-Indians 12 days after the treaty council ended.

In anger at this betrayal, a few Yakimas killed some whites. When soldiers arrived, a large group of Indians drove them away. In retaliation for the treacherous murder of a Wallawalla chief and negotiator, the Wallawalla, Klikitat, Cayuse, and Umatilla Indians joined the Yakimas in fighting non-Indians. Yakimas agreed to settle on a reservation in 1859, after the war ended and 24 of their number were executed. The future Yakima Indian Nation included, in addition to Yakima bands, the Klikitat, Wanapam, Wishram, Palus (Palouse), and the Wenatchi.

Reservation Yakimas entered a brief period of prosperity but were soon pressured to sell land; most people were forced into poverty, obtaining some seasonal work at best. In 1891, about one-third of the reservation land had been allotted to individuals, but the Yakima Nation, under Chief Shawaway Lotiahkan, was able to retain the "surplus" usually sold to non-Indians in such cases. Still, many of the individual allotments, including some of the best irrigated land, were soon lost. Around the turn of the century as much as 80 percent of the reservation was in non-Indian hands.

As a result of twentieth-century dam construction (Bonneville, 1938; Grand Coulee, 1941; Dalles, 1956), the number of salmon and steelhead that returned to spawn to the Yakima River declined by between 98–99 percent. The issue of fishing rights remained an important and controversial one from the beginning of the reservation period through its resolution in 1974. Well into the twentieth century, Yakima Nation people continued much of their traditional subsistence and ceremonial activities.

RELIGION   Klikitats believed in a supreme creator and many other deities as well. Adolescent boys undertook spirit quests in the mountains. Shamans, recipients of particularly powerful guardian spirits, cured illness but were sometimes killed themselves if their patient died.

Government   Nomadic bands were led by nonhereditary chiefs with advisory powers. Before the historic period, the tribe created two divisions, eastern and western, of which the latter mixed with Cowlitz Indians west of the Cascades to become Taitnapams.

CUSTOMS   Dogs and women carried most burdens before the horse's arrival. Burial took place in rock slides and gravel pits lined with cedar planks. Occasionally a corpse, along with tools and ornaments, was cremated in such a pit. Klikitats were skilled horse riders.

DWELLINGS   Klikitats traditionally lived in typical Plateau-style semisubterranean circular pit houses with conical earth-covered roofs. Aboveground, mat-covered houses partially replaced the pit houses around 1800.

DIET   Fish, especially salmon, was the dietary staple. Various berries, roots, bulbs, and other plant foods were also important. Men also hunted deer, elk, antelope, and various large and small game.

KEY TECHNOLOGY   The reed mat served a number of purposes, as did coiled and twined baskets. Containers were made out of bark as well as reeds. Hunting weapons included spears and the bow and arrow. Spears, nets, and weirs were used in fishing. Other tools included stone drills, scrapers, and knives. Antler wedges were used to split wood. Bone was used to make awls and needles.

TRADE   Skilled traders, Klikitats served as intermediaries between Northwest Coast and Plateau peoples.

NOTABLE ARTS   Women made fine baskets that were sometimes decorated with geometric patterns. Beginning in the late prehistoric period, they also made clothing decorated with quillwork, shells, and feathers, as well as fine beaded blankets.

TRANSPORTATION   The people used dugout canoes and snowshoes. They acquired horses around 1700.

DRESS   Bark and fur breechclouts, aprons, and ponchos were replaced by Plains-style clothing in the eighteenth century. Women wore twined basket hats.

WAR AND WEAPONS   Weapons of war were generally the same as hunting weapons, with the addition of stone clubs. Klikitat bows and arrows were of particularly high quality.

Contemporary Information

GOVERNMENT/RESERVATIONS   The Yakima Reservation and Trust Lands (1859) are located in Klikitat, Lewis, and Yakima Counties, Washington. They consist of roughly 1.4 million acres. The 1992 enrolled Indian population was 8,315 (of a total reservation population of well over 27,000). The reservation is governed by a 14-member tribal council.

Some Klikitats also live on the Siletz Reservation (*see* Upper Umpqua in Chapter 3).

ECONOMY   Timber and its associated industries, including a furniture manufacturing plant, are the nation's main income producer. The reservation also owns extensive range and farmland, although 80 percent of irrigated land remains leased by non-Indians. The Wapato Project provides control over their own water. The Yakima-Klikitat Fish Production Project, a cooperative effort between the Yakima Nation and Washington State, is a major fishery restoration/conservation venture.

In addition to fishing and small business enterprises, the nation owns an industrial park containing Indian and non-Indian industries. The Yakima Land Enterprise operates fruit orchards and stands and a recreational vehicle park. Government and the tribe provide other jobs. Still, unemployment fluctuates between about 30 and 60 percent, and up to 75 percent of the people live below the poverty level.

LEGAL STATUS   The Confederated Tribes and Bands of the Yakima Indian Nation is a federally recognized tribal entity.

DAILY LIFE   Klikitats are no longer distinct as a tribe. In 1972, the United States restored about 22,000 acres of land, including the sacred Pahto (Mt. Adams). The Longhouse (Seven Drums) religion is active on the reservation, as are sweat house customs and first foods feasts. The longhouse serves as the locus of Indian identity. Longhouse families throughout the Plateau region are tied together, mostly through marriage. The Indian Shaker religion is also active on the reservation, as are Christian churches.

In addition to religious practice, Yakimas maintain many aspects of traditional culture, including family customs, service, and leadership. The language is alive and well, especially as part of religious ceremonies and among more traditional people. There are language classes for adults and childrens. Yakima basketry is still an important art and craft.

The nation operates a huge, full-service cultural center, museum, and restaurant in addition to two community centers and an elders' retirement center. As part of an overall emphasis on education, the nation provides incentives such as scholarships and summer programs. Children attend public school on the reservation. There is also a tribally run school as well as a private, four-year liberal arts college on the reservation. The nation publishes newspapers and operates a radio station. It also hosts an annual summer all-Indian rodeo, a powwow, a huckleberry festival, and basketball tournaments. Lawsuits over water use from the Yakima River system are pending.

Kootenai

Kootenai (ˋK ū t ə n ā), a nomadic people geographically divided into upper and lower divisions after their exodus from the northern Great Plains. The Upper Kootenai remained oriented toward the Plains, whereas the Lower Kootenai assumed a more Plateau-like existence. Their self-designation was *San'ka*, "People of the Waters."

LOCATION The Kootenai may once have lived east of the Rockies, perhaps as far east as Lake Michigan. In the late eighteenth century, the Kootenai lived near the borders of British Columbia, Washington, and Idaho. Today, most live on the Kootenai Reservation, Boundary County, Idaho; on the Flathead Reservation, Flathead, Lake, Missoula, and Sanders Counties, Montana; and on several reserves in British Columbia.

POPULATION The immediate precontact population was about 1,200. In 1990, roughly 900 Kootenai Indians lived in the Northwest, including several hundred intermarried with Salish people. The 1991 Canadian Kootenai population was around 550.

LANGUAGE Kutenaian is unrelated to any language family except possibly Algonquian.

Historical Information

HISTORY During the eighteenth century, the Kootenai acquired the horse and began hunting buffalo on the Plains, adopting much of Plains culture. Shortly after initial contact around 1800, Canadian traders built Kootenai House, a trading post. More traders, including Christianized Iroquois, as well as missionaries soon followed. Despite the Kootenais' avoidance of much overt conflict with whites, they suffered dramatic population declines during these years, primarily as a result of disease and alcohol abuse. The formal establishment of the international boundary in 1846 divided the tribe over time.

The Flathead Reservation was established in 1855 for the Salish and Kootenai people. Some Kootenai refused to negotiate the loss of their land, however, and did not participate in these talks. Some moved to British Columbia rather than accept reservation confinement. When the Kootenai Reservation was established in 1896, about 100 Kootenai Indians moved to the Flathead Reservation. Of the ones who refused to move, those near Bonners Ferry were granted individual allotments in 1895. The tribe won a $425,000 land claims settlement in 1960, and the Kootenai Reservation was officially established in 1974.

RELIGION People believed that every natural thing has a spirit and that there is one master spirit, perhaps the sun. Everyone hoped to acquire the help of guardian spirits they sought on adolescent vision quests. Male and female shamans provided religious leadership, acquiring spirit powers in dreams that allowed them to cure and foretell the future. Curing involved singing power songs, chanting, and shaking rattles. Ceremonies such as the midwinter festival, the Sun Dance, and the War Dance were related to soliciting and/or honoring spirits. There were three religious societies: Crazy Dogs, Crazy Owls, and Shamans.

GOVERNMENT Each of roughly eight autonomous bands was led by a chief and an assistant chief, such as a war, fish, and hunting chief. The chieftainship was hereditary into the historic period, when leadership qualities began to assume the most importance. A council of shamans chose the upper division chief. Decision making was by consensus.

CUSTOMS Games almost always included gambling. Prisoners of war were enslaved. Marriage was usually monogamous. People cultivated some tobacco. The dead were dressed in robes, sewn in blankets, temporarily placed on a platform, and then buried. The family moved the deceased's tipi, gave away all former possessions, and never spoke the person's name again. Kindness was a highly valued quality.

DWELLINGS The Kootenai traditional dwelling, summer and winter, was conical (especially the lower division), made of rushes and mats or hemp over pole frames. During the eighteenth century, that style switched, especially among the upper division, to buffalo-skin or mat tipis. They also used oblong, semisubterranean communal festival houses of mats on a pole frame.

DIET   Although they lived in the mountains west of the continental divide, upper division Kootenais remained oriented toward Great Plains buffalo, whereas the lower division ate mostly fish (trout, salmon, and sturgeon), small game, and roots. Both divisions also hunted big and small game, and both gathered roots and berries, especially bitterroots. Most foods were dried and stored for winter.

KEY TECHNOLOGY   Men fished using weirs, basket traps, and spears. Women made a variety of baskets, including ones that could hold water. Hunting equipment included cherry and cedar bows, clubs tipped with antler points, stone knives, and slingshots. Buffalo were hunted with a bow and arrow or by driving them off cliffs. Leather items were prominent, especially among the upper division, whereas the lower division primarily made items of Indian hemp and tule. Kootenais also made carved wood bowls, clay pots, and stone pipes.

TRADE   Kootenais participated in regional trading complexes and began trading with non-native trappers about 1807.

NOTABLE ARTS   Upper division people especially became very skilled leather workers.

TRANSPORTATION   The Lower Kootenai were oriented toward rivers and lakes, and their water transportation was accomplished by use of bark and dugout canoes. Hunters used snowshoes in winter. Upper division people acquired horses in the eighteenth century.

DRESS   Lower division Indians wore bark, mat, and hemp clothing, whereas upper division people used mostly skins. They switched to Plains-style clothing, including dresses, breechclouts, shirts, and leggings that were decorated with fringe, feathers, quills, and beadwork, in the eighteenth century. Both groups wore moccasins and fur robes.

WAR AND WEAPONS   Although the Kootenai were not especially militaristic, the war chief reigned in the upper division and was second in importance in the lower division. The Blackfeet, Lake, Assiniboine, and Cree were traditional enemies. Hunting equipment was used as weapons.

Contemporary Information

GOVERNMENT/RESERVATIONS   The Kootenai Reservation (1974) is located in Boundary County, Idaho. It contains roughly 2,680 acres, most of which are allotted. The 1990 Indian population was 61, of roughly 200 tribal members, most descended from Lower Kootenais. Residents are closely related to the Kootenai community at Creston, British Columbia. The 1947 constitution calls for a four-member elected tribal council. The Kootenai Tribe is a member of the Upper Columbia United Tribes Organization and the Affiliated Tribes of Northwest Indians.

The Flathead Reservation (1855; Confederated Salish and Kootenai Tribe, which includes Flathead, Kalispel, and Kootenai) is located in Flathead, Lake, Missoula, and Sanders Counties, Montana. It contains 627,070 acres and is governed by a ten-member tribal council. The 1990 Indian population was 5,110; most Kootenais are descended from the upper division. Just under half of the land base is non-Indian owned, and over 80 percent of the reservation population is non-Indian. Kootenais live mainly in the northern part of the reservation.

Four bands (Columbia Lake, Lower Kootenai, Saint Mary's, Tobacco Plains) live on various reserves in British Columbia (see their profiles under "Daily Life").

ECONOMY   On the Flathead Reservation, forestry and associated enterprises as well as ranching are important economic activities. Tourism, including the KwaTaqNuk resort on Blue Bay on Flathead Lake, is also important. The tribes lease the Kerr Dam for $10 million annually and will assume the dam's operating license in 2015. S&K Electronics provides some jobs. Most tribal members work for the tribes. High unemployment (about 50 percent in the late 1980s) remains chronic.

There are a crafts shop, a motel, and a fish hatchery at Bonners Ferry (Kootenai Reservation). Some people continue to hunt, fish, and gather plant foods.

LEGAL STATUS   The Confederated Salish and Kootenai Tribes of the Flathead Reservation is a federally recognized tribal entity. Legal jurisdiction over Flathead Reservation Indians belongs to the tribes. The Kootenai Tribe of Idaho is a federally recognized tribal entity. The four Canadian bands are federally and provincially recognized.

DAILY LIFE   Despite serious economic, social, and health problems on the Flathead Reservation, people try to retain their Indian culture and to transmit it to the younger generations. Salish and Kootenai College and a tribal high school were created around 1977. The reservation hosts two large powwows in July.

The establishment of the Kootenai Reservation in 1974 led to paved roads, improved housing, and a community center. Traditional culture, religion, and language remain strong among the Bonners Ferry Kootenai.

There are four Kootenai bands in Canada (statistics are as of 1995):

Lower Kootenai Band controls eight reserves on 2,443 hectares of land. The reserves were allotted in 1906. The population is 156, of whom 77 live in 32 houses on the reserves. Election is by custom, and the band is affiliated with the Ktunaxa/Kinbasket Tribal Council. Children attend band and provincial schools. Important economic resources and activities include trapping, hay ranching, a bird sanctuary, and small businesses. Facilities include offices, a community hall, and a recreation center.

St. Mary's Band controls four reserves on 7,446 hectares of land. The reserves were allotted in 1884. The population is 231, of whom 163 live in 54 houses on the reserves. Election is by custom, and the band is affiliated with the Ktunaxa/Kinbasket Tribal Council. Children attend band schools. Important economic resources and activities include livestock ranching, a museum, arts and crafts, and individual hay farms. Facilities include offices, a recreation center, a garage, and a church.

Tobacco Plains Band controls one reserve on 4,227 hectares of land. The reserve was allotted in 1884. The population is 138, of whom 88 live in 24 houses on the reserve. Election is by custom, and the band is affiliated with the Ktunaxa/Kinbasket Tribal Council. Important economic resources and activities include livestock ranching, logging, farming, a restaurant, and a duty-free shop. Facilities include offices, a garage, and a fire station.

Columbia Lake Band controls one reserve on 3,401 hectares of land. The reserve was allotted in 1884. The population is 199, of whom 111 live in 44 houses on the reserves. Election is by custom, and the band is affiliated with the Ktunaxa/Kinbasket Tribal Council. Important economic resources and activities include a campground and an individually owned dude ranch. Facilities include a recreation hall and a ceramics shop.

Lake

See Okanagon

Lillooet

Lillooet (`Lil wet), a name meaning "wild onion" or "end of the trail" and once applied only to the lower division of the tribe. The Lillooet exhibited marked characteristics of Northwest Coast culture.

LOCATION Most Lillooets lived traditionally and continue to live in southwest British Columbia, Canada.

POPULATION The eighteenth-century population of approximately 4,000 has recently been exceeded (about 4,500 in 1995).

LANGUAGE Lillooet is an Interior Salish language.

Historical Information

HISTORY Indian groups of the Plateau, including Interior Salishan speakers, have been living in their historic regions for a long time, probably upward of 9,000 years. Early (circa 1809) intercourse with non-native traders was generally friendly, although some non-native diseases had struck the people even before the beginning of the actual contact period. The people were able to live in a relatively traditional way until they were devastated by smallpox epidemics accompanying the gold rushes of the mid–nineteenth century. To make matters worse, famine followed the disease epidemics, striking with particular severity in the mid-1860s. Survivors gradually resettled on reserves delineated by the government of British Columbia.

RELIGION Special guardian spirits helped shamans cure and recover lost souls. Carved wooden masks representing mythological clan ancestors were displayed at clan dances.

GOVERNMENT Lillooets were organized into upper and lower divisions, with each division composed of named bands of one or more villages. In aboriginal times, each village represented a single clan with one hereditary chief. Other leaders included war chiefs, hunting chiefs, orators, and wealthy and generous men.

CUSTOMS Adolescents prepared for adulthood by fasting and engaging in feats of physical endurance. They also sought guardian spirits through vision quests or dreams to give them luck and skills. Girls were isolated at the time of their first menstrual periods. Like coastal groups, the Lillooet observed a caste system and kept slaves. Potlatches commemorated special life-cycle events, at which the host enhanced his prestige by giving away gifts. The dead were wrapped in woven grass or fur robes and placed in painted grave boxes or in bark- or mat-lined graves. Graves were often marked with mortuary poles carved with clan totems (spirit and mythological associates).

DWELLINGS Men built circular winter lodges of cedar bark and earth on a wood frame. Lodges were excavated to a depth of around 6 feet and ranged between about 20 and 35 feet in diameter. The floor was covered with spruce boughs. The clan totem was carved on the center pole or on an outside pole (lower division). Larger log and plank dwellings housed between four and eight families. Oblong or conical mat-covered houses served as shelter in summer.

DIET Salmon and other fish were the food staples. Men hunted both large and small game, including bear, beaver, rabbit, raccoon, and mountain goat. Hunters rubbed themselves with twigs to disguise their human scent. Women gathered assorted roots and berries and dried the foods for storage.

KEY TECHNOLOGY The basic raw materials were bark, tule, and wood in addition to skins and other animal parts. Fishing equipment included nets, weirs, spears, and traps. Men, sometimes assisted by dogs, hunted with bow and arrow, traps, deadfalls, and snares. Many items and utensils were carved from wood. Bags were of bark, twined grasses, or skin. Digging sticks were made of sheep horn or deer antler.

TRADE The Lillooet were great traders in the lower Fraser River region. They served as the main intermediary for coastal trade. Exports included animal skins, cedar bark, berries, hemp, and goat's wool. Imports included sea products, especially shells and salmon, as well as dugout canoes and slaves.

NOTABLE ARTS Men were known for their skill at wood carving. Stone, often soapstone, was also carved for artistic purposes, most often in the shape of a seated person holding a bowl. Women decorated clothing with porcupine quillwork. They also made excellent coiled baskets decorated with geometric motifs and colorful dyes.

TRANSPORTATION People used both bark and cedar dugout canoes to navigate local waterways. They used snowshoes for winter travel. Most Interior Salish people acquired horses in the mid–eighteenth century.

DRESS Most clothing was made from cedar bark or skins. Men wore deerskin breechclouts in summer and added skin leggings and short shirts in winter. Women probably wore wraparound skirts, plus leggings in winter. Moccasins were generally plain. Some people used thongs to tie pieces of fur or hide to their feet. Women wove robes of rabbit skin or goat wool. Personal decorations included dentalium shell ornaments and face paint. Men wore long looped necklaces, often decorated with abalone shell. Women tended to wear abalone in their braids and tattoo their wrists and arms.

WAR AND WEAPONS Lillooets fought with Thompsons and other Salish groups. Defensive equipment included armor of elk skin or rods as well as large shields.

Contemporary Information

GOVERNMENT/RESERVATIONS See "Daily Life" for profiles of contemporary Lillooet bands (all statistics are as of 1995).

ECONOMY Economic activities center around forestry, fishing, hay ranching, and land development.

LEGAL STATUS The bands described under "Daily Life" are federally and provincially recognized.

DAILY LIFE Anderson Lake Band controls 804 hectares of land at the head of Anderson Lake. The reserve was established in 1881. The population is 213, of whom 134 live on the reserve. Elections are held under the provisions of the Indian Act, and the band is affiliated with the Coast Mountain Development Council. Children attend provincial schools. Important economic activities and resources include a campsite, a boat launch, a fast food restaurant, an investment corporation, logging, a sawmill, and a fish factory. Facilities include offices, a community hall, and a church.

Bridge River Band controls three reserves on 3,940 hectares of land. The reserve was established in 1881. The population is 303, of whom 111 live on the reserve. Elections are held under the provisions of the Indian Act, and the band is affiliated with the Lillooet Tribal Council. Children attend band and provincial schools. Important economic activities and resources include forestry management and a hay cooperative. Facilities include offices, a community hall, and a garage.

Cayoose Creek Band controls three reserves on 687 hectares of land near the town of Lillooet. The reserve was established in 1881. The population is 150, of whom 85 live on the reserves. Elections are held by custom, and the band is affiliated with the Lillooet Tribal Council. Children attend band and provincial schools. Important economic activities and resources include a partnership in Lillooet Salish Enterprise, ranching, arts and crafts, and forestry. Facilities include offices and a church.

Fountain Band controls 17 reserves on 1,572 hectares of land north of the town of Lillooet. The population is 706, of whom 489 live in 82 houses on the reserves. Elections are held by custom, and the band is currently unaffiliated. Children attend band and provincial schools. Important economic activities and resources include ranching, arts and crafts, forestry, and a small boat factory. Facilities include offices, a community hall, a day care center, and a church.

Lillooet Band, formerly part of the Fraser River Band, controls six reserves on 700 hectares of land west of the town of Lillooet. The population is 290, of whom 163 live in 44 houses on the reserve. Elections are held by custom, and the band is affiliated with the Lillooet Tribal Council. Children attend band and provincial schools. Important economic activities and resources include land leases and commercial property rentals. Facilities include offices, a community hall, a recreation center, a kindergarten, and a church.

Mount Curie Band controls ten reserves on 2,929 hectares of land 6 miles south of Pemberton. The population is 1,515, of whom 1,053 live in 276 houses on the reserves. Elections are held under the provisions of the Indian Act. Children attend band and provincial schools. The Mount Curie Band has instituted a five-year economic development plan that includes agriculture, forestry, and tourism. Facilities include offices, a community hall, and a group home.

Pavilion Band controls seven reserves on 1,112 hectares of land north of the town of Lillooet. The reserves were established in 1861. The population is 380, of whom 253 live in 43 houses on the reserves. Elections are held by custom, and the band is affiliated with the Lillooet Tribal Council. Children attend band and provincial schools. Important economic activities and resources include a limestone plant and small businesses. Facilities include offices, a recreation center, and a church.

Samahquam Band controls five reserves on 183 hectares of land on Douglas Portage. The population is 220, of whom 12 live in two houses on the reserves. Elections are held by custom, and the band is affiliated with the Coast Mountain Development Council. Children attend provincial schools. Important economic activities and resources include the Coast Mountain Development Corporation. There are no facilities on the reserves.

Seton Lake Band controls six reserves on 1,802 hectares of land on the north shore of Seton Lake. The population is 512, of whom 230 live in 71 houses on the reserves. Elections are held by custom, and the band is affiliated with the Lillooet Tribal Council. Children attend band and provincial schools. Important economic activities and resources include forestry, a sawmill, a store, a restaurant, and a wood products manufacturing shop. Facilities include offices, a community hall, a church, and a garage.

Skookum Chuck Band, formerly part of the Lillooet River Band, controls ten reserves on 676 hectares of land on Douglas Portage. The population is 305, of whom 25 live in 16 houses on the reserves. Elections are held by custom, and the band is affiliated with the Coast Mountain Development Council and the In-SHUCK-ch Council. Important economic activities and resources include the Coast Mountain Development Council. Facilities include offices, a community hall, a church, and a diesel power station.

Modoc

Modoc (`M ō dok), from *Moatokni,* or "Southerners" (Klamath). Their self-designation was *Maklaks,* or "People," as was that of their neighbors and linguistic cousins, the Klamath.

LOCATION Traditionally, Modocs lived around Goose, Clear, Tule, and Klamath Lakes, in northern California and southern Oregon. Today, Modocs live mostly around Oregon and in Northwest cities as well as in Oklahoma.

POPULATION The eighteenth-century Modoc population was roughly 500. There were almost 600 enrolled Modocs in 1990, roughly two-thirds of whom lived in or near Chiloquin, Oregon.

LANGUAGE With the Klamath, the Modoc spoke a dialect of the Lutuami division of the Penutian language family.

Historical Information

HISTORY Modocs obtained horses early in the nineteenth century, about the time they encountered non-natives, and by the 1830s they were aggressively raiding their neighbors for horses, slaves, and plunder. Major disease epidemics in 1833 and 1847 reduced their population considerably. Wagon trains began coming through their territory during the late 1840s, scaring the game away and disrupting their natural cycles. Hungry now, and anxious and resentful, they began attacking the intruders, as well as neighboring Indians, for slaves. When gold was found near their territory in 1851, miners flocked in and simply appropriated Indian land, killing Indians as they liked.

The 1860s Ghost Dance brought them little comfort, and they, especially the women, drifted into debauchery during this period. In 1864, Modocs and Klamaths ceded most of their land and moved to the Klamath Reservation. The Modoc were never comfortable there, however, and matters became worse when a food scarcity exacerbated the level of conflict. They petitioned several times for their own reservation, but to no avail. In 1870, about 300 Modocs under Kintpuash (Captain Jack) reestablished a village in their former homeland on the Lost River. Increasing conflict with white settlers soon led to a military confrontation, after which the Indians escaped to nearby lava beds.

Meanwhile, another group of Modocs under Hooker Jim also fled to the lava beds south of Tule Lake after attacking several ranches in revenge for an unprovoked army attack on their women and children. In a confrontation early in 1873, about 80 Indians held off 1,000 U.S. soldiers and irregulars. At a peace parley later that year, the Modocs killed the U.S. general and one of his negotiators. Later, another white attack was repulsed, but the Indians killed some soldiers during negotiations. However, Modoc unity was failing, and their food was running out. Hooker Jim was captured and betrayed his people, leading troops to the hideout of Kintpuash, who was forced to surrender. At his trial, Hooker Jim's testimony against Kintpuash and others resulted in their being hanged. Most surviving Modocs were sent to the

Quapaw Reservation in the Indian Territory (Oklahoma).

The Oklahoma Modoc became farmers and ranchers, and many adopted Christianity. Modoc tribal land ownership in Oklahoma ended in 1890 when their land was allotted to individuals. A group of 47 Modocs returned to the Klamath Reservation around 1905, but that reservation was terminated in 1954. Its lands were sold in 1964 and 1971. The Oklahoma Modocs lost their tribal status in 1956 as well, but they were restored in 1978.

RELIGION Shamans, usually men, provided religious leadership. They dreamed spirit dreams for five nights and then performed a five-day quest, acquiring a number of guardians and powers. They could cure illness, interpret dreams, control the weather, and harm people at will. Curing was generally accomplished by sucking out a disease object. Adolescent boys and girls also undertook spirit quests.

GOVERNMENT Each of about 25 Modoc villages was led by a civil and a war chief. Civil chiefs were selected on the basis of their wealth as well as their leadership and oratory skills; there were also some hereditary chiefs. An informal community assembly decided most legal matters.

CUSTOMS Corpses were wrapped in deerskin and cremated. The house and possessions were also burned, and the deceased's name was no longer spoken. Widows cut their hair and covered their faces with pitch and ash. Modocs practiced infant head flattening.

DWELLINGS Winter dwellings were permanent, semiexcavated lodges made of willow poles covered with tule mats and earth. Width averaged between 12 and 20 feet. People entered through a smoke hole in the roof. Temporary mat-covered structures were used at seasonal camping sites. Sweat houses were heated with steam; they were a place for cleansing as well as praying.

DIET Modocs followed the food supply in three seasons. They ate fish, especially salmon, trout, perch, and suckers. Men hunted a variety of large animals as well as rabbits and other small game. Antelope were driven into brush corrals. Fowl were taken with nets and decoys. Women gathered camas and other roots, greens, berries, and fruits. Seeds, especially those of the waterlily *(wocus)*, were also important; they were gathered in the fall and ground into flour.

KEY TECHNOLOGY Fishing equipment included nets, spears, hook and line, and basket traps. Many items were made of tule or bulrushes, such as twined baskets, mats, cradles, rafts, and moccasins. The people used stone mullers and metates for grinding seeds, stone arrow straighteners, and basketry seed beaters.

TRADE Modoc Indians were actively involved in the regional trade. They especially obtained horses for slaves and plunder at the Dalles.

NOTABLE ARTS Women made particularly fine baskets.

TRANSPORTATION Traditional means of transportation included cedar dugout canoes, snowshoes, and tule and lashed-log rafts. Horses were acquired in the early nineteenth century.

DRESS Men and women wore skin, grass, or tule aprons. They also wore tule moccasins, leggings, fur robes, and hats in winter. Charcoal black on the face protected against sun and snow. They flattened their infants' heads for aesthetic purposes.

WAR AND WEAPONS The war chief was coleader of the village. Modocs' traditional enemies were the Achumawi and the Shasta.

Contemporary Information

GOVERNMENT/RESERVATIONS The Modoc Tribe of Oklahoma is located in Miami, Oklahoma. Their constitution was approved in 1991. They own an administrative building, a church, a cemetery, and just over nine acres of land.

Many Modoc descendants also live on the Klamath Reservation in Chiloquin, Oregon. The General Council (total enrolled adult population) chooses an eight-member business committee.

ECONOMY Modoc descendants participate in the local economy.

LEGAL STATUS The Modoc Tribe of Oklahoma is a federally recognized tribal entity.

DAILY LIFE Oklahoma Modocs are engaged in a major project to document their history and recover their language and traditions. Some Oklahoma Modocs regularly attend ceremonies with their relatives in the Northwest. They are also involved with pan-Indian activities in Oklahoma.

Nespelem
See Sanpoil
ū

Nez Percé
Nez Percé (`N ā P ū r`s ā , `Nez Pur`s ā , or Nez P ū rs), French for "pierced nose," was a name bestowed by non-Indian traders in the nineteenth century. Ironically, the Nez Percé did not generally pierce their noses as many other local Indians did. Their Salishan neighbors called them *Sahaptin,* or *Sahaptin.* Their self-designation was *Nimipu,* "the People," or *Tsoop-Nit-Pa-Loo,* "the Walking Out People." Their early historic culture also contained Great Plains and Northwest Coast elements.

LOCATION Before contact with non-Indians, the

Nez Percé lived on about 17 million acres between the Blue and the Bitterroot Mountains in southeast Washington, northeast Oregon, and southwest Idaho. Today, most live in Clearwater, Idaho, Lewis, and Nez Percé Counties, Idaho; Ferry and Okanogan Counties, Washington; and in regional cities and towns.

POPULATION The early-nineteenth-century Nez Percé population was about 6,000. In 1990, roughly 3,000 enrolled Nez Percés lived in Idaho.

LANGUAGE Nez Percé is a member of the Sahaptian division of the Penutian language family.

Historical Information

HISTORY Somewhere around 1730, the Nez Percé acquired horses and began their dramatic transformation from seminomadic hunters, fishers, and gatherers to Plains-style buffalo hunters. They quickly became master horse riders and breeders. Several decades of peaceful hunting and trading ended around 1775, when the Blackfeet Indians, armed with guns they received through the fur trade, began a long period of conflict in western Montana. By 1800 or so, Nez Percé Indians had been exposed to Euro-American technology and had heard rumors of a very powerful people to the east.

Their first encounter with non-Indians was with the Lewis and Clark expedition (1805). The Indians welcomed these white people as well as the hundreds of traders, missionaries, and others who poured in in subsequent years. The Nez Percé were involved in fur trade during the 1820s and 1830s; they even helped to outfit settlers in the 1840s. Meanwhile, epidemics were taking a tremendous toll on their population.

In 1855, the Indians ceded several million acres of land but kept over eight million acres for a reservation. Non-Indian miners and other intruders ignored the restrictions and moved in anyway, precipitating a crisis among the Indians over the issue of loyalty toward whites. Following gold strikes in 1860, whites wanted the Wallowa and Grande Ronde Valleys, land that equaled more than 75 percent of the reservation. In 1863, only one chief, with no authority to sell Nez Percé land, signed a treaty. The United States then used that document as an eviction notice, ending years of friendship and cooperation between the Nez Percés and whites. In the meantime, the Dreamer religion had begun influencing the Nez Percé, among others, to resist non-native imperialism.

In 1877, the Wallowa Band were unilaterally given 30 days to leave their homeland. In response to this ultimatum, some younger Indians attacked a group of whites. Young Joseph, chief with his brother, Ollikut, reluctantly sided with the resisters. When soldiers came, firing on an Indian delegation under a flag of peace, the Indians fired back. Joseph's band,

about 450 Indians under the leadership of Looking Glass, knew that they could never return home or escape punishment at the hands of the United States. They decided to head for Canada.

During their two-month flight, the group traveled 1,700 miles, constantly evading and outwitting several thousand U.S. Army troops. They did fight several battles during their journey but never were defeated. They also passed through Yellowstone National Park at one point, encountering tourists but leaving them in peace. Joseph was just one of the leaders of this flight, but he became the most important and well known. Many Indians died along the way.

Tired, hungry, and cold, the group was forced to surrender in early October just 30 miles from Canada. Joseph and other Nez Percé were never allowed to return to their homeland. Those who survived were exiled to Kansas and the Indian Territory (Oklahoma), where many died of disease, and finally to the Colville Reservation in Washington.

The sharply rising death rate among the Nez Percé from tuberculosis after the 1870s stemmed largely from the replacement of their traditional mat houses by "modern" wooden ones. Heavy missionization had by the end of the nineteenth century resulted in factionalism and considerable loss of tribal heritage. In 1971, Nez Percés received land claims settlements of $3.5 million.

RELIGION Spirits were inherent in all of nature. After years of instruction, adolescents sought their protection and power by fasting and visiting remote places. Men and women shamans, with especially strong, heavenly oriented guardian spirits, provided religious leadership. They cured illness, controlled the weather, and presided at ceremonies. They might also inflict harm. Curing methods included smoking, sweats, and herbal medicines. Dreams were also connected to good and evil events. During the winter religious ceremonies, participants dressed as their spirits and sang their spirit songs. There were many intertribal festivals and ceremonials as well, such as scalp dances.

GOVERNMENT Small, local bands each had one or more villages and fishing areas. Civil chiefs led the bands, although war chiefs exercised temporary power during periods of conflict. Chiefs were generally elected, although sons often followed fathers, and wealth (in horses) became more important in the late prehistoric period. They had no power in purely personal matters. Women could neither be nor elect chiefs. Chiefs and old men made up the village and tribal councils; decisions were taken by consensus. Ultimately, tribal cohesion grew out of the necessity to defend against fighters from the Great Plains.

CUSTOMS Bands were called by the names of streams. Each group contained at least one permanent winter village and a number of temporary fishing camps. Some subsistence areas were considered tribal property. All handmade items were the property of the maker, except that the male was entitled to all property in unusual cases of separation or divorce.

Menstruating and late-term pregnant women were strictly segregated. Young, unmarried men slept in the sweat lodges. Young men and women, especially the latter, were married by about age 14. Brides were commonly purchased, and polygamy was common. Abortion was rare, as was birth out of wedlock. Adultery was a capital crime. Women did most domestic work, including dressing skins; men's work revolved around hunting and war.

Immediately after death, corpses were dressed in good clothes and had their faces painted. After several days, they were wrapped in deerskin and buried with their former possessions. Boulders and cedar stakes marked grave sites. The family in mourning cut their hair and wore poor, dirty clothing.

Pipe smoking was an important part of burial and other rites and ceremonies. The murder of a tribe member usually required blood revenge or at least blood money. Theft was punished by public disgrace. Other serious crimes or infractions included adultery, rape, and lying. Prisoners of war might be used as slaves, but their children were free, and the adults were also frequently adopted into the tribe. Some names and songs ran in the male line. Typical games included archery, dice, hoop-and-pole, and the hand game; most included betting. Childrens' games included tops and string games.

DWELLINGS Permanent settlements were located along rivers. Winter dwellings were semisubterranean, circular wood frame structures covered with cedar bark, sage, mats, grasses, and earth. The roof was flat or conical. Mats covered the floors. There were also tipi-like communal longhouses, up to 150 feet long, of similar construction. These houses held up to 50 families. People slept along inner walls and shared fires along the center.

Older boys and unmarried men slept and sweated in grass- and earth-covered sweat lodges; others were built for men and women to sweat in. Circular, underground menstrual huts were about 20 feet in diameter. In summer, people built temporary brush lean-tos. Some groups adopted hide tipis in the eighteenth century.

DIET Nez Percés were seminomadic, moving with the food supply. Fish, especially salmon, was a staple, along with trout, eel, and sturgeon. Salmon was broiled, baked, or boiled or dried, smoked, and stored. Animal food included elk, deer, moose, mountain sheep, rabbits, and small game. After the Nez Percé acquired the horse, parties traveled to the Plains to hunt buffalo. Some meat was "jerked" for winter. Deer were run down or shot, as were other game, with a bow and arrow or killed with a spear. Some animals were hunted with use of decoys.

Women gathered plant foods such as camas, kouse, bitterroot, wild carrot, wild onion, and berries. Camas, dug in midsummer, was peeled and baked in a pit oven. Most berries were dried and stored for winter. Other food included fowl, eggs, and birds. People ate horses, lichens, and tree inner bark when there was nothing else to eat. Most food was either boiled, steamed in pits, or roasted in ashes.

KEY TECHNOLOGY Fish were speared from platforms and caught using nets, spears, small traps, and weirs. Men used various nooses, snares, nets, and deadfalls for hunting as well as bows made of mountain sheep horn. Women made a range of woven and coiled baskets, some watertight, as well as woven reed bags. They also made cups, bowls, winnowing baskets, women's caps, and mats of cattails and tule. Many baskets were made of Indian hemp, bear grass, and other grasses.

Other important raw materials included bone, horn, and wood. Many tools and items, such as mortars, pestles, knives, and mauls, were made of chipping and flaking stone and also obsidian. Mattresses were cottonwood inner bark or dry grass, blankets were elk hides, and folded skins served as pillows.

Nez Percé Indians also used a fire-hardened digging stick, a fire drill, and board and buckskin cradles. Musical instruments included rattles, flageolets, whistles, and drums. They also used a 12-month calendar and named four seasons.

TRADE Relatively early acquisition of horses gave the Nez Percé a trade advantage, although they also traded widely before they had the horse. They acquired items made as far away as British Columbia and the Mississippi Valley. Abalone was among the items they acquired from coastal Indians, as were carved wooden items, dried clams, dentalium shells, and wapato root. Also, by the eighteenth century, the Nez Percé were trading east of the Bitterroots for buffalo products and other Plains items.

NOTABLE ARTS Traditional arts included woven baskets, wallets, petroglyphs, and blankets and tipi skins decorated with pictographs. In the historical period they were known for porcupine-quill embroidery, rawhide painting, and cornhusk basketry.

TRANSPORTATION After acquiring the horse in the mid–eighteenth century, the Nez Percé went on to develop first-rate stock through selective breeding. They also used snowshoes and dugout canoes.

DRESS Clothing was made of cedar bark and the

untailored skin of deer, elk, and buffalo. Men wore moccasins, leggings, breechclouts, shirts, and highly decorated robes. Women wore moccasins, fringed gowns, and basket hats, replaced in the historic period with skin caps decorated with fringe and elks' teeth. People cleaned their clothes with white clay. Men plucked their facial hair. People painted their faces and bodies for decoration and against snow blindness. Tailored, Plains-style skin clothing became popular in the eighteenth century.

WAR AND WEAPONS In general, raiding and war, for booty, glory, and revenge, were very important to the Sahaptians. By virtue of their being the most powerful Plateau tribe, the Nez Percé played a central role in regional peace and war. At least after the late eighteenth century, they fought with the Flathead, Coeur d'Alene, and Spokan against the Blackfeet, Gros Ventre, Crow, and other Plains tribes. They also sometimes fought against these allies. The Cayuse, Umatilla, Yakima, and Wallawalla were also allies against the Shoshone, Bannock, and other northern Great Basin tribes.

Men held intertribal dances before wars and buffalo hunts. Weapons included cedar, ash, or mountain sheep horn bows; obsidian or jasper-tipped arrows, sometimes dipped in rattlesnake venom; and spears. Elk-skin shields, helmets, and armor were used for defense. The eagle-feather war bonnet may or may not have come originally from the Plains. Men and horses were painted and decorated for war.

Contemporary Information

GOVERNMENT/RESERVATIONS The Nez Percé Reservation (1855) is located in Clearwater, Idaho, Lewis, and Nez Percé Counties, Idaho. It contains 92,685 acres; the 1990 Indian population was 1,860. A tribal committee is elected every three years, according to the constitution adopted in 1948. A nine-member executive committee serves staggered three-year terms. The Nez Percé Tribe is a member of the Columbia River Intertribal Fish Commission, the Affiliated Tribes of Northwest Indians, and other state and regional organizations.

The Colville Reservation (1872) is located in Ferry and Okanogan Counties, Washington. It contains 1,011,495 acres and had a 1990 Indian population of 3,782. Under the Indian Reorganization Act constitution approved in 1938, the reservation is governed by a 14-member business council plus various subcommittees. The Confederated Tribes is a member of the Affiliated Tribes of Northwest Indians as well as other intertribal organizations.

ECONOMY The Nez Percé tribe is currently undertaking a major land reacquisition program. Most income comes from farm and timber, and the

tribe runs a printing plant, a marina, and a limestone quarry. Their economic development plans include a forestry management program and gambling and tourist facilities, including the Nee-Mee-Poo Trail and an expansion of the Nez Percé National Historical Park. With other Idaho tribes, they are negotiating for a favorable settlement of the water rights issue. A large percentage of the reservation is leased to non-Indians.

Important economic activities on the Colville Reservation include stock raising, farming, logging (including a sawmill) and reforestation, seasonal labor, mining, and tourism. The reservation contains the potential to develop hydroelectric resources. The tribe owns a meat-packing plant, a log cabin sales business, and various gambling enterprises.

LEGAL STATUS The Nez Percé Tribe of Idaho is a federally recognized tribal entity. The Confederated Tribes of the Colville Reservation is a federally recognized tribal entity.

DAILY LIFE The Nez Percé tribe makes an effort to preserve their native language, since few people under age 30 speak it well. There are dictionaries and other texts in the Nez Percé language. Other ongoing aspects of native culture include traditional dances, root feasts, traditional games, and Seven Drums Society ceremonies. The tribe has attained legal jurisdiction on the reservation. It is actively involved in nuclear and other regional environmental issues, including efforts to reinstate local salmon and steelhead runs. The tribe administers a scholarship fund for deserving students. Among the festivals observed on the reservation are Lincoln's birthday, a spring root festival in May, a Presbyterian camp meeting in early summer, and Pi-Nee-Wau Days in August.

Colville people are largely acculturated. Language preservation programs are hindered by lack of a common language. The Chief Joseph Band of Nez Percés, with their Seven Drum religion, have taken the lead in recent efforts to reinvigorate disparate tribal cultures and religions. The Indian Shaker Church and the Native American Church are also active on the reservation. There is a program to reacquire and consolidate the land base. Educational levels are on the rise. The Colville business council wields growing power in regional and statewide issues.

Okanagon

Okanagon (Ō k ə n `ä g ə n), "seeing the top, or head," or *Isonkva'ili*, "Our People." They were the main tribe of a culturally related group of Indians also including the Senijextee (Lake), Colville, and Sanpoil Indians. They are occasionally known today as the Northern Okanagon (Canada) and the Sinkai-etk (United States).

LOCATION   Okanagons traditionally lived in the Okanagon and Similkameen River Valleys, including Lake Okanagon, in Washington and British Columbia. Today, most Okanagons live on the Colville Reservation, on reserves in British Columbia, and in regional cities and towns.

POPULATION   The late-eighteenth-century Okanagon population was about 2,500. Today roughly 2,000–2,500 Okanagon Indians live mostly in Canada.

LANGUAGE   Okanagon Indians spoke a dialect of Interior Salish.

Historical Information

HISTORY   Okanagons undertook a gradual northward expansion following their acquisition of horses in the mid–eighteenth century. They first encountered non-native traders in the early nineteenth century and Catholic Indians and missionaries shortly thereafter. The tribe was artificially divided when the international boundary was fixed in 1846. The Sinkaietks did not participate in the Yakima war (1855–1856), although some did join in fighting the United States later in that decade.

A gold strike on the Fraser River in 1858 brought an influx of miners and increased the general level of interracial conflict. Most U.S. Okanagons settled on the Colville Reservation in 1872. The Canadian Okanagon were assigned to several small reserves.

RELIGION   Okanagons believed in a chief creator deity as well as the presence of spirits in all natural things, animate and inanimate. Guardian spirits could be acquired by adolescents through physical training, fasting, and seclusion. Shamans' especially powerful spirits allowed them to cure illness and perform other particularly difficult tasks. Okanagon Indians celebrated a girls' puberty ceremony, a first fruits ceremony, and a midwinter spirit festival and dances as well as war, scalp, marriage, and sun dances, some of which were acquired in the historical period.

GOVERNMENT   Two geographical divisions, the Similkameen and the Okanagon proper, were each composed of between 5 and 10 autonomous bands. Each band was led by a (usually hereditary) chief with advisory powers. The true locus of authority was found in a council of older men. War, hunt, and dance chiefs were selected as needed.

CUSTOMS   Corpses were wrapped in matting or robes and then buried in the ground or in rock slides. Sometimes canoes or carvings were placed over the grave site. Mourners cut their hair and wore old clothes. A pleasant land of the dead was recognized as existing to the south or west. Okanagons regularly intermarried with other Interior Salish people, especially Spokan and Thompson Indians. They practiced polygamy. They also very occasionally practiced a form of potlatch.

DWELLINGS   Winter dwelling were of two types. One was a conical, semisubterranean, pole frame lodge covered with earth. This type was about 10–16 feet in diameter, and entrance was gained through the roof. The people also built rectangular, mat-covered, multifamily lodges. In summer they used conical, tule mats on pole frames and, later, skin tipis. Men and women used domed sweat houses for purification; the structures were also used as living quarters for youths in spirit training.

DIET   Salmon was the main staple. Large and small game, including elk, bear, bighorn sheep, and marmot, was also important. Dogs sometimes assisted in the hunt, in which animals were often surrounded and/or driven over a cliff. Meat was roasted, boiled, or dried. Buffalo was always part of the diet but became more important when groups began using horses to hunt buffalo on the Great Plains. Important plant foods included camas, bitterroot, berries, and nuts.

KEY TECHNOLOGY   Men caught fish with dip nets, seine nets, traps, weirs, spears, and hook and line. Stone, bone, and antler provided the raw material for most tools. Women made cedar-bark or woven spruce root-baskets with geometric designs. Some baskets were woven tight enough to hold water. Women also specialized in making woven sacks. They sewed tule mats with Indian hemp.

TRADE   Trade fairs were held at Kettle Falls and at the mouth of the Fraser River. The level of trade increased with acquisition of horses.

NOTABLE ARTS   Basketry and tanning were especially well developed. Rock painting had been practiced for thousands of years.

TRANSPORTATION   Water transportation methods included bark, especially birch-bark, canoes and rafts. People used snowshoes during winter travel. Horses were acquired in the mid–eighteenth century.

DRESS   Beginning in the eighteenth century, dressed skins provided the main clothing material. Men wore shirts and breechclouts, and women wore aprons. Both wore moccasins, leggings, sewn or woven caps, and goat wool or woven rabbit-fur blankets and robes.

WAR AND WEAPONS   War chiefs were selected on an ad hoc basis. Weapons included juniper bows and flint-tipped arrows. Okanagons were occasionally allied with Colville Indians against the Nez Percé and Yakima.

Contemporary Information

GOVERNMENT/RESERVATIONS   The Colville Reservation (1872) is located in Ferry and Okanogan

Counties, Washington. It covers 1,011,495 acres and had a 1990 Indian population of 3,782. An Indian Reorganization Act constitution approved in 1938 calls for a 14-member business council and various committees. The Confederated Tribes is a member of the Affiliated Tribes of Northwest Indians and other intertribal organizations.

Okanagon bands in Canada live on a number of different reserves. See "Daily Life" for profiles of some of these bands (all statistics are as of 1995).

ECONOMY   The reservation economy is built largely around stock raising, farming, logging (including a sawmill) and reforestation, and seasonal labor. There is some mining as well as a meat-packing plant, a log cabin sales business, and tourism-related businesses such as a trading post and gambling enterprises. There is potential for development of hydroelectric resources. The economies of the Canadian bands center on agriculture, farming, forestry, and small businesses.

LEGAL STATUS   The Confederated Tribes of the Colville Reservation is a federally recognized tribal entity. All of the bands described under "Daily Life" are federally and provincially recognized.

DAILY LIFE   Colville Indians are largely acculturated. Language preservation programs are hindered by the lack of a common aboriginal language. Recent efforts to reinvigorate disparate tribal cultures and religions include the presence of the Chief Joseph Band of Nez Percé Indians with their Seven Drum religion, the Indian Shaker Church, and the Native American Church. The reservation hosts an annual powwow and a circle celebration. There is also a program of reacquiring and consolidating the land base and a goal to increase the general levels of education. The Colville Business Council wields growing power in regional and statewide issues.

The Lower Similkameen Band controls 11 reserves on 15,276 hectares of land. The reserves were allotted in 1876. The population is 313, of whom 275 live in 64 houses on the reserves. Elections are by custom, and the band is affiliated with the Similkameen Administration. Children attend band and provincial schools. Important economic resources and activities include agriculture, farming, forestry, and small businesses. Facilities include offices and a church.

The Okanagon Band, composed of seven different communities, controls five reserves on 10,603 hectares of land. The reserves were allotted in 1877. The population is 1,367, of whom 676 live in 224 houses on the reserves. Elections are under the provisions of the Indian Act, and the band is currently unaffiliated. Children attend band and provincial schools. Important economic resources and activities include haying and small businesses. Facilities include offices, a community hall, a fire station, and a church.

The Osoyoos Band controls two reserves on 13,052 hectares of land. The reserves were allotted in 1877. The population is 316, of whom 223 live in 86 houses on the reserves. Elections are under the provisions of the Indian Act, and the band is currently unaffiliated. Children attend band and provincial schools. Important economic resources and activities include a vineyard, a campsite, farming, and land leases. Facilities include offices, a community hall, a church, and a garage.

The Penticton Band controls two reserves on 18,691 hectares of land. The population is 675, of whom 397 live in 120 houses on the reserves. Elections are by custom, and the band is currently unaffiliated. Children attend band and provincial schools. Important economic resources and activities include land leases, forestry, a gravel pit, a billiard hall, and individual hay ranches. Facilities include offices, a community hall, a heritage center, and a church.

The Upper Similkameen Band controls seven reserves on 2,602 hectares of land. The population is 41, all of whom live in 14 houses on the reserves. Elections are held under the provisions of the Indian Act, and the band is affiliated with the Similkameen Administration and the Okanagon Tribal Council. Children attend provincial schools. Important economic resources and activities include a campsite, ranching, and a hairdressing business.

Pend d'Oreille
See Kalispel

Salish

Salish (`Sal ish), or Flathead, from the fact that they did not, like many neighboring peoples, shape their babies' foreheads (they left them "flat"). Their self-designation was *Se'lic,* or "People."

LOCATION   Traditionally, the Salish lived in western Montana, around the Rocky and Little Belt Mountains. Today, most live in Flathead, Lake, Missoula, and Sanders Counties, Montana.

POPULATION   The precontact population of Salish Indians may have been between 600 and 3,000. In 1990, the reservation Indian population, including Kalispel and Kootenai people, was 5,110, with several hundred Salish Indians also living away from the reservation.

LANGUAGE   The Salish spoke a dialect of Interior Salish.

Historical Information

HISTORY   All Salish-speaking Indians probably originated in British Columbia. From their base in western Montana, the Salish may have moved farther east onto the Plains before being pushed back around 1600 by the Blackfeet. The Salish continued moving westward, into north-central Idaho, throughout the following two centuries.

Around 1700 they acquired horses and assumed a great deal of the culture of Plains Indians (including buffalo hunting, stronger tribal organization, and raiding). Ongoing wars with the Blackfeet as well as several smallpox epidemics combined in the eighteenth century to reduce their population significantly. They also encountered Christian Iroquois Indians during this time.

Although disease preceded their physical arrival, non-Indians began trading in Salish country shortly after the 1805 visit of the Lewis and Clark expedition. The missionary period began in 1841. In 1855, a major land cession (the Hellgate Treaty) established the Flathead, or Jocko, Reservation, but most Salish Indians avoided confinement until at least 1872, in part owing to their friendliness with the Americans. During these years, other tribes were placed on the reservation, and the buffalo herds diminished rapidly. Charlot, the leader of one Salish band, held out in the Bitterroot Mountains until 1891, when his people finally joined the Flathead Reservation.

The government considered terminating the reservation in the 1950s but was successfully opposed by tribal leaders. In 1960, the tribe won roughly $4.4 million in land claims settlements.

RELIGION People sought luck from guardian spirits in dreams and visions. Preadolescent spirit quests included fasting and praying. Spirits also conferred songs and objects that became a person's medicine. Shamans' strong guardians let them cure illness, confer hunting success, and see the future. The many dances and ceremonies of the early historic period included the Sun Dance, Medicine Dance, Hunting Dance, first fruit ceremony, Woman's Dance, and war dances. Seasonal religious ceremonies were generally related to food or guardian spirits.

GOVERNMENT Various bands were formed of several related families. Each band was led by a chief and an assistant chief, chosen by merit. The chieftainship may have been hereditary in earlier times. Beginning in the late prehistoric period, as tribal cohesiveness increased, the band chiefs formed a tribal council to advise a tribal chief, and later the band chiefs themselves were relegated to the status of minor chiefs or subchiefs. In addition, individuals were selected as needed to lead various activities such as hunting and war.

CUSTOMS Rule or law breakers were punished by public whipping and/or ridicule. Premarital sexual relations were frowned on; the woman could be whipped if discovered. Marriage was arranged by families, although some people also eloped. It was formalized by cohabitation as well as a formal ceremony. Polygamy was common. Women were responsible for all domestic tasks.

The dead were buried dressed in skins and robes. A mourning feast followed the funeral; it included the disposal of the dead person's former possessions. The mourning period could last a year.

DWELLINGS Winter dwellings were of two types. One was partially excavated, conical mat (cedar bark, hemp) houses on wooden frames; the other was long communal and ceremonial lodges. Brush shelters sufficed during camping and mountain hunting trips. Bark or skin tipis gained popularity after the horse turned the Salish into buffalo hunters.

DIET Beginning in the eighteenth century, buffalo, hunted on the Great Plains, became a key food item. Before this period, however, the Salish ate a number of animals including elk, deer, antelope, and small game. Fish, including trout, salmon, and whitefish, formed an important part of their diet. Plant foods included camas, bitterroot, other bulbs, roots, and berries.

KEY TECHNOLOGY Men used hook and line, nets, traps, and weirs to catch fish. Women made birchbark and woven skin containers as well as coiled cedar baskets. They also made twined grass spoons.

TRADE Salish Indians participated in the regional trade, particularly with the Kalispel. They imported Nez Percé baskets and traded in stolen horses from the early eighteenth century on. They became involved in the fur trade in the early nineteenth century.

NOTABLE ARTS Women decorated their well-made baskets with geometric designs.

TRANSPORTATION Pole rafts served as water transportation. The horse arrived after about 1700, and the Salish soon learned to handle this animal expertly.

DRESS Most clothes were made from rabbit or deer skins. Men wore breechclouts and shirts, and women wore dresses. Both wore moccasins, caps, robes, leggings, and shell earrings.

WAR AND WEAPONS The Salish fought few wars before they acquired horses, at which time warfare became common and serious. They often fought the Blackfeet and Crow with the help of the Kalispel and Nez Percé. Capturing an enemy without using weapons was considered a great coup. Dances preceded and followed wars. War captives became slaves.

Contemporary Information

GOVERNMENT/RESERVATIONS The Flathead Reservation (1855; Flathead, Kalispel, and Kootenai) is located in Flathead, Lake, Missoula, and Sanders Counties, Montana. It contains 1,244,000 acres. The 1990 Indian population was 5,110. Just under half of the land base is non-Indian owned, and over 80 percent of the reservation population is non-Indian. There is a ten-member tribal council.

ECONOMY Forestry, including sawmills, and ranching are important reservation industries. Tourist facilities include the KwaTaqNuk resort on Flathead Lake. The tribe receives $10 million on an annual lease for Kerr Dam, on the Lower Flathead River; it will assume the operating license in 2015. Many people work for the tribe, including its tourist resort on Flathead Lake and its facilities at Hot Springs. S&K Electronics provides some jobs. Income is also generated by gravel sales. Unemployment remains quite high (about 50 percent in the late 1980s).

LEGAL STATUS The Confederated Salish and Kootenai Tribes is a federally recognized tribal entity. Legal jurisdiction over reservation Indians belongs to the tribes.

DAILY LIFE Despite considerable intermarriage with non-Indians, the tribes attempt to retain their culture and transmit it to the young by means of a cultural heritage project. The reservation is plagued with the serious social ills that often accompany poverty, including substance abuse. Salish Kootenai College and a tribal high school were created around 1977. The tribes hold two large powwows in July and various other activities.

Sanpoil

Sanpoil, or San Poil (Sän p ō ` ē l), is derived from a native word possibly referring to what may have been their self-designation, *Sinpauelish (Snpui'lux)*. They were culturally and linguistically similar to the neighboring Nespelem Indians.

LOCATION Late-eighteenth-century Sanpoils lived near the Columbia and the Sanpoil Rivers, in north-central Washington. The environment is one of desert and semidesert. Today, most Sanpoils live in Ferry and Okanagon Counties, Washington, and in regional cities and towns.

POPULATION The Sanpoil population around 1775 was approximately 1,600. Today, perhaps several hundred Indians claim Sanpoil descent.

LANGUAGE With the Nespelem, the Sanpoil spoke a particular dialect of Interior Salish.

Historical Information

HISTORY Severe epidemics in the late eighteenth century, and again in the late 1840s and early 1850s, depleted the Sanpoil population considerably. Sanpoils were among the Indians who visited Catholic missionaries at Kettle Falls in 1838. By avoiding the wars of the 1850s and by consciously eschewing contact with non-Indians, they managed to remain free until 1872, when they were moved to the Colville Reservation. Even after confinement, the Sanpoil refused government tools, preferring to hunt, fish, and gather by traditional means and to conduct small-scale farming.

RELIGION Individuals sought guardian spirits through the traditional means of singing, fasting, praying, and performing feats of endurance. Such spirit quests were considered mandatory for men and optional for women. Prepubescent boys generally undertook a series of one-night vigils. Many people acquired between three and six spirit helpers.

The spirits in question were those of animals; they assured the seeker of luck and various skills. Songs often accompanied received powers, which were generally called upon well after the quest: When one had settled into an adult life, the returning spirit power caused an illness that had to be cured by a shaman.

Male shamans outnumbered female shamans. Their powerful spirits helped them to cure illness; they could also harm people if they chose. Among the causes of illness, in addition to a returning spirit, were breaking taboos and suffering bewitching. Shamans were paid for successful cures.

The five-day first salmon ritual was the most important ceremony. It was held under the direction of the salmon chief. Other important religious occasions included the midwinter spirit dances and the first fruits rite. The midwinter dances served the additional purposes of bringing people together and releasing winter tensions.

GOVERNMENT Autonomous villages were each led by a chief and a subchief; these lifetime offices were hereditary in theory but were generally filled by people possessing the qualities of honesty, integrity, and diplomacy. Unlike some other Plateau groups, only men could be chiefs. The authority of Sanpoil chiefs to serve as adviser, judge, and general leader was granted mainly through consensus. As judge, the chief had authority over crimes of nonconformity such as witchcraft, sorcery, and assault. His penalty usually consisted of a fine and/or lashes on the back.

An informal assembly of all married adults confirmed a new chief and oversaw other aspects of village life. All residents of the village were considered citizens. Village size averaged about 30–40 people, or roughly three to five extended families, although some villages had as many as 100 people. Other village leaders included a messenger, a speaker, and a salmon chief (often a shaman, with the salmon as a guardian spirit, who supervised salmon-related activities). By virtue of their ability to help or hurt people, shamans also acquired relative wealth and power from their close association with chiefs, who liked to keep them allied.

CUSTOMS Local villages had associated, nonexclusive territories or subsistence areas. Any person was free to live anywhere she or he wanted; that is, family members could associate themselves with relatives of their settlement, relatives of a different settlement, or a settlement where they had no relatives. Winter was a time for visits and ceremonies. During that season, women also made mats and baskets, made or repaired clothing, and prepared meals while men occasionally hunted or just slept, gambled, and socialized.

People rose at dawn, winter and summer, and began the day by bathing in the river. In spring, groups of four or five families left the village for root-digging areas; those who had spent the winter away from the main village returned. The old and the ill generally remained in camp.

Pacifism, generosity, and interpersonal equality and autonomy were highly valued. Girls fasted and were secluded for ten days at the onset of puberty, except for a nighttime running regime. The exchange of gifts between families constituted a marriage, a relationship that was generally stable and permanent. Corpses were wrapped in tule mats or deerskin and buried with their possessions. The family burned the deceased's house and then observed various taboos and purification rites. The land of the dead was envisioned as being located at the end of the Milky Way.

DWELLINGS Sanpoil Indians used the typical Plateau-style winter houses. One was a single-family structure, circular and semisubterranean, about 10–16 feet in diameter, with a flat or conical roof. People covered a wood frame with planks or mats and then a layer of grass, brush, and earth. Entrance was gained through the smoke hole, which could be covered by a tule mat. The interior was also covered with a layer of grass.

They also built communal tule-mat houses consisting of a pole framework covered by grass, earth, and tule mats. These houses were about 16 feet wide, between 24 to about 60 feet long, and about 14 feet high, with gabled roofs. Entrance was through matted double doors. Each family had an individual tule-covered section, but they shared a number of fireplaces in the central passage.

Summer houses were similar in construction but smaller, single-family structures. Some more closely resembled a mere windbreak. Some groups built adjoining rectangular, flat-roofed summer mat houses/windbreaks. Mat houses were always taken down after the season. Men also built sweat lodges of grass and earth over a willow frame.

DIET Food was much more often acquired by the family than by the village. Fish was a staple. Men caught four varieties of salmon as well as trout, sturgeon, and other fish. They fished from May through October. Although women could not approach the actual fishing areas, they cleaned and dried the fish. Dried fish and sometimes other foods made up much of the winter diet. People generally ate two meals a day in summer and one in winter.

Women gathered shellfish, salmon eggs, bulbs, roots, nuts, seeds, berries, and prickly pear. Camas was eaten raw or roasted, boiled, and made into cakes. A short ceremony was performed over the first gathered crop of the season. Men hunted most large and small game in the fall. They prepared for the hunt by sweating and singing. Women came along to help dress and carry the game. Men also hunted birds and gathered mollusks. Venison and berries were pounded with fat to make pemmican.

KEY TECHNOLOGY Fish were caught using traps, nets, spears, and weirs. Spearing required the construction and use of artificial channels and platforms. Utensils were carved from wood. Women made woven cedar, juniper, or spruce root baskets, including water containers and cooking pots. Women also made the all-important mats, of tule and other grasses, whose uses included houses, bedding (skins were also used), privacy screens, waterproofing, holding food, and wrapping corpses. There was also some sun-dried pottery covered with fish skin.

TRADE The Sanpoil engaged in extensive local trade, communication, visiting, and intermarriage.

NOTABLE ARTS Artistic expression was seen mainly in carved wood items, coiled baskets with geometric designs, and mat weaving.

TRANSPORTATION Dugout canoes served as water transportation. Horses arrived about the mid–eighteenth century.

DRESS The Sanpoil wore surprisingly little clothing. Woven bark and, later, dressed buckskin provided breechclouts, ponchos, and aprons. Women also wore woven caps. Men wore fur leggings in winter; women's leggings were generally made of hemp. Some winter clothing, such as mittens, caps, woven blankets, and robes, was made from the fur of rabbits and other animals. Men plucked their facial hair. Both sexes plucked their eyebrows and wore earrings, necklaces, and face paint.

WAR AND WEAPONS The Sanpoil were known for their general pacifism, even in the face of attacks by the Shuswap, Coeur d'Alene, and Nez Percé.

Contemporary Information

GOVERNMENT/RESERVATIONS The Colville Reservation (1872) is located in Ferry and Okanogan Counties, Washington. It consists of 1,011,495 acres.

The 1990 Indian population was 3,782. An Indian Reorganization Act constitution, approved in 1938, calls for a 14-member business council and various committees. The Confederated Tribes are members of the Affiliated Tribes of Northwest Indians and other intertribal organizations.

ECONOMY The reservation economy is built largely around stock raising, farming, logging (including a sawmill) and reforestation, and seasonal labor. There is some mining as well as a meat-packing plant, a log cabin sales business, and tourism-related businesses such as a trading post and gambling enterprises. There is potential for development of hydroelectric resources.

LEGAL STATUS The Confederated Tribes of the Colville Reservation is a federally recognized tribal entity.

DAILY LIFE Confederated Colville Indians are largely acculturated. Language preservation programs are hindered by the lack of a common aboriginal language. Recent efforts to reinvigorate disparate tribal cultures and religions include the presence of the Chief Joseph Band of Nez Percé Indians with their Seven Drum religion, the Indian Shaker Church, and the Native American Church. The reservation hosts an annual powwow and a circle celebration. There is also a program of reacquiring and consolidating the land base and a goal to increase the general levels of education. The Colville Business Council wields growing power in regional and statewide issues.

Shuswap

Shuswap (Shus wäp): "to know, or recognize" or "to unfold, or spread." The word may also refer to relationships between people. They may once have called themselves *Xatsu'll*, "on the cliff where the bubbling water comes out." The people currrently refer to themselves as the Great Secwepemc Nation.

LOCATION Shuswaps continue to live in and near their aboriginal territory in the Fraser and North and South Thompson River valleys, British Columbia.

POPULATION The early-nineteenth-century Shuswap population was about 7,000. In 1991 it stood at almost 5,000.

LANGUAGE Shuswap is a dialect of the Interior division of the Salishan language family.

Historical Information

HISTORY Interior Salishan people settled in their historic areas roughly 9,000 years ago. Hudson's Bay Company posts were established in the early nineteenth century. The people soon became active in the fur trade. Intertribal warfare ended in the early 1860s. About that time, the Shuswap were decimated by epidemics, in part brought by gold miners flooding the region. Non-natives squatted on and then claimed

the land of the ailing Shuswap. A Shuswap reserve of 176 square miles was created in 1865; it was soon reduced to 1 square mile. A second reserve was created in 1895. In 1945, with the Chilcotin and other groups, the Shuswap founded the British Columbia Interior Confederation to try to persuade provincial and federal officials to be more responsive to their needs.

RELIGION Adolescent boys sought guardian spirits for luck and skills through fasting, praying, and visiting remote places. Shamans' powerful guardians allowed them to cure illness and restore lost souls. Their methods included massage, blowing, sprinkling water, and prescribing taboos. Feasting, dancing, singing, drumming, and tobacco smoking were included in most religious ceremonies. Masked dances reenacted a person's vision quest.

GOVERNMENT The Shuswap were divided into about seven autonomous bands. All had hereditary chiefs who advised, lectured on correct behavior, and coordinated subsistence activities. There were also specialized chiefs for war, hunt, dance, and other activities.

CUSTOMS Bands were more or less nomadic, according to their food sources. By the nineteenth century, northern and western bands had adopted the Northwest Coast pattern of social stratification. The nobility belonged to hereditary crest groups, and commoners belonged to nonhereditary associations. Slaves were generally acquired in battle or trade. At puberty, boys undertook guardian spirit quests, whereas girls were secluded and practiced basket making and other skills. They also fasted and prayed, and they went out at night to run, exercise, and bathe. Corpses were buried in sand banks or rock slides with their possessions; small mourning houses were sometimes built by the grave.

DWELLINGS Men built circular winter lodges of cedar bark and earth on a wood frame. Lodges were excavated to a depth of around 6 feet and ranged between about 20 and 35 feet in diameter. The floor was covered with spruce boughs. The clan totem was carved on the center pole or on an outside pole (lower division). Larger log and plank dwellings had several rooms and housed between four and eight families. Oblong or conical mat-covered houses served as shelter in summer.

DIET Fish, especially salmon, was the staple in some areas. People away from rivers depended on large and small game and fowl. All groups ate roots and berries.

KEY TECHNOLOGY Men caught fish with nets, basket traps, spears, weirs, and hooks. Hunting equipment included bow and arrow, traps, and spears. Utensils and some baskets were made of birch bark, coiled baskets were fashioned from cedar or spruce roots, and many tools were made of stone. People also made skin or woven grass bags. Digging sticks had wood or antler cross-handles.

TRADE All bands traded for slaves. Other major trade items included dentalium shells, hemp, cedar bark, moose and deer skins, roots, and salmon products.

NOTABLE ARTS Women wove geometric designs into their well-crafted baskets. They also decorated clothing with porcupine quillwork.

TRANSPORTATION People plied the rivers and lakes in bark and dugout canoes. They used snowshoes in winter. Horses arrived in the late eighteenth century.

DRESS Most clothing was made from cedar bark or skins. Men wore deerskin breechclouts in summer and added skin leggings and short shirts in winter. Women probably wore wraparound skirts, with leggings in winter. Moccasins were generally plain. Some people used thongs to tie pieces of fur or hide to their feet. Women wove robes of rabbit skin or goat wool. Fringe, bone, teeth, and shell decoration was used on some items. Personal decorations included dentalium shell ornaments and face paint. Men wore long looped necklaces, often decorated with abalone shell. Women tended to wear abalone in their braids and tattoo their wrists and arms. In the nineteenth century, many people switched to Plains-style skin clothing.

WAR AND WEAPONS All bands acquired slaves by raiding and in war. At least by the eighteenth century, warfare had become a regular band activity. The Shuswap fought at one time with most of their neighbors, including bands of Okanagon, Thompson, Cree, Chilcotin, and Carrier. Defensive equipment included rod armor, elk-skin vests, and shields. Weapons included the bow and arrow; short spears; wood, bone, and stone clubs; and bone knives.

Contemporary Information

GOVERNMENT/RESERVATIONS Some eighteen Secwepemc bands live in British Columbia. Total reserve land equals roughly 59,000 hectares. See selected profiles under "Daily Life." (All statistics are as of 1995 unless otherwise noted.)

ECONOMY Hunting, trapping, and fishing remain important. See profiles under "Daily Life" for additional activities.

LEGAL STATUS The bands profiled under "Daily Life" are federally and provincially recognized.

DAILY LIFE The Adams Lake Band controls seven reserves on almost 3,000 hectares of land. The reserve, then called the Sahkaltkum Band Reserve, was allotted in 1877. The population is 570, of whom

363 live on the reserves. The band is affiliated with the Shuswap Nation Tribal Council. Children attend band and provincial schools. Important economic activities and resources include forestry, land leases, and a laundromat. Facilities include offices, a community hall, a fitness and cultural center, a clubhouse, and a church.

The Bonaparte Band controls six reserves on 1,332 hectares of land. The reserve was allotted in 1878. The population is 631, of whom 204 live on the reserves. Elections are held under the provisions of the Indian Act, and the band is affiliated with the Shuswap Nation Tribal Council.

The Canim Lake Band (Tsqescen) controls six reserves totaling 2,029.6 hectares of land. They are part of the Lake Division of the Shuswap Tribe. Band population in 1996 was 517 members, nearly three-quarters of whom lived on tribal land. The band is affiliated with the Cariboo Tribal Council. Facilities include a K–12 school. The band itself employs between 50 and 150 people, depending on the season. In addition to educating its members, the band operates many social programs, several businesses, and health services. Shuswap is taught in the school.

The Canoe Creek Band includes the communities of Dog Creek and Canoe Creek. The band controls 5,880.4 hectares of relatively poor land; the best local land is owned by non-native ranchers. The band is affiliated with the Cariboo Tribal Council. Fewer than half of the band's 650 members live on the reserve. Housing and jobs are in short supply. Dog Creek children attend public school; Canoe Creek operates a K–3 school. Facilities in Dog Creek include administrative offices, a store/gas station/post office, a gymnasium/community center, and a skating rink. Canoe Creek has the school, a community center, and a church. Band members operate their own small businesses. Sports are popular, as are hunting, gathering, and fishing.

The High Bar Band controls three reserves on 1,506 hectares of land on the Fraser River. The reserve was allotted in 1871. The population is 49, of whom two live in one house on the reserves. Elections are held according to custom, and the band is currently unaffiliated. There is a cattle ranch on the reserve.

The Kamloops Band controls five reserves on 13,249 hectares of land near the city of Kamloops. The reserve was allotted in 1877. The population is 832, of whom 491 live in 138 houses on the reserves. Elections are held according to custom, and the band is affiliated with the Shuswap Nation Tribal Council. Children attend provincial schools. Important economic activities and resources include forestry, mining, ranching, a development corporation, an industrial park, land leases, a museum, and cattle and hay ranching. Facilities include offices and a garage.

The Little Shuswap Band controls five reserves on 3,135 hectares of land. The population is 258, of whom 157 live in 53 houses on the reserves. Elections are held according to custom, and the band is unaffiliated. Children attend band and provincial schools. Important economic activities and resources include forestry, land leases, a resort, and logging. Facilities include offices, a community hall, a boat house, and a machine shop.

The Neskonlith Indian Band controls three reserves. They are currently in the process of forging a ten-year plan for community building and economic development. Along with the Adams Lake and Little Shuswap Bands, they are working on land claims arising from their original 1862 reservation.

The Shuswap Band controls one reserve on 1,106 hectares of land. The reserve was allotted in 1884. The population is 205, of whom 113 live in 49 houses on the reserves. Elections are held according to the provisions of the Indian Act, and the band is affiliated with the Ktunaxa/Kinbasket Tribal Council. Children attend band and provincial schools. Important economic activities and resources include a sand and gravel company, a hay ranch, a recreational vehicle park, and small businesses. Facilities include offices and a community center.

The Skeetchestn Band, formerly Dead Man's Creek Band, controls one reserve consisting of 7,908 hectares of land. The population is 383, of whom 135 live in 45 houses on the reserve. Elections are held according to custom, and the band is affiliated with the Shuswap Nation Tribal Council. Children attend band and provincial schools. Important economic activities and resources include a campsite, a store, tourism, and individual ranches. Facilities include offices, a recreation center, a church, and a community center.

The Soda Creek Band (Xatsu'll First Nation) occupies two reserves totaling about 2,048 hectares. The present population is between 250 and 300 people, almost all of whom are Secwepemc. The band is affiliated with the Cariboo Tribal Council. Economic activities include logging and tourism. The people have received little or no compensation for non-native utility and natural resource extraction on tribal lands.

The Spallumcheen Band controls three reserves on 3,095 hectares of land at Enderby. The reserves were allotted in 1877. The population is 574, of whom 309 live in 84 houses on the reserves. Elections are held according the provisions of the Indian Act, and the band is affiliated with the Shuswap Nation

Tribal Council. Children attend band and provincial schools. Important economic activities and resources include logging, a gas station, a grocery store, and arts and crafts.

The Whispering Pines/Clinton Band controls three reserves on 565 hectares of land 18 kilometers north of Kamloops. The population is 97, of whom 60 live in 11 houses on the reserves. Elections are held according the provisions of the Indian Act, and the band is affiliated with the Shuswap Nation Tribal Council. Children attend provincial schools. Important economic activities and resources include cattle and hay ranching and a rodeo grounds.

The Williams Lake Band has roughly 1,927 hectares of land. Over 60 percent of the approximately 350 band members live on-reserve. The band is affiliated with the Cariboo Tribal Council. Economic activities include agriculture and timber as well as small businesses. Children attend public schools. Members enjoy indoor and outdoor recreational facilities.

Sinkaietk
See Okanagon

Sinkiuse

Sinkiuse (`Sin ku y ū s), "between people," also known as Columbia, Isle de Pierre, and Moses Band.

LOCATION In late prehistoric times, the Sinkiuse lived mainly along the east bank of the Columbia River, although they ranged throughout the plateau south and east of the river. Today, their descendants live on the Colville Reservation, Ferry and Okanogan Counties, Washington, and in cities and towns around central Washington.

POPULATION The late-eighteenth-century Sinkiuse population was at least 800. In 1990, 3,782 Indians lived on the Colville Reservation, perhaps 10 percent of whom were Sinkiuse descendants.

LANGUAGE The Sinkiuse spoke a dialect of Interior Salish.

Historical Information

HISTORY Sinkiuses may have come either from the lower Columbia River area or from a more northerly location. They encountered non-Indians and joined the fur trade in 1811. They fought the United States in the 1850s under their chief, Moses, but adopted a peaceful stance after the war. The Columbia Reservation was established in 1879 and was abolished several years later. Four bands followed Chief Moses to the Colville Reservation; others accepted allotments and lost their geographic identity.

RELIGION Individuals sought guardian spirits

through the traditional means of singing, fasting, praying, and performing feats of endurance. The spirits assured the seeker of luck and various skills. Songs often accompanied received powers, which were generally called upon well after the quest: When one had settled into an adult life, the returning spirit power manifested itself by means of an illness that had to be cured by a shaman.

Shamans' powerful spirits helped them to cure illness; they could also harm people if they chose. Among the causes of illness, in addition to a returning spirit, were breaking taboos and suffering bewitchment. Shamans were paid for successful cures.

Important religious occasions included the first salmon ritual, the midwinter spirit dances, and the first fruits rite. The midwinter dances served the additional purposes of bringing people together and releasing winter tensions.

The Dreamer Cult, a mid-nineteenth-century phenomenon, was a revivalistic cult that celebrated traditional Indian religious beliefs. Although it was explicitly antiwhite, the religious doctrine also contained elements of Christianity. Its adherents thus attempted to remain faithful to their Indian traditions while taking steps to adapt to non-Indian culture.

GOVERNMENT Autonomous villages were each led by a chief and a subchief; these lifetime offices were hereditary in theory but were generally filled by people possessing the qualities of honesty, integrity, and diplomacy. The authority of chiefs was granted mainly through consensus.

An informal assembly of all married adults confirmed a new chief and oversaw other aspects of village life. All residents of the village were considered citizens. Other village leaders included a messenger, a speaker, and a salmon chief (often a shaman, with the salmon as a guardian spirit, who supervised salmon-related activities). By virtue of their ability to help or hurt people, shamans also acquired relative wealth and power from their close association with chiefs, who liked to keep them allied.

Customs The Sinkiuse were seminomadic for nine months a year; during the other three they lived in permanent winter villages. Winter was a time for visits and ceremonies. During that season, women also made mats and baskets, made or repaired clothing, and prepared meals; men occasionally hunted or just slept, gambled, and socialized.

In spring, groups of four or five families left the village for root-digging areas; those who had spent the winter away from the main village returned. People rose at dawn, winter and summer, and began the day by bathing in the river. Men's realm was toolmaking, war, hunting, fishing, and, later, horses.

Pacifism, generosity, and interpersonal equality and autonomy were highly valued. Girls fasted and were secluded for ten days at the onset of puberty, except for a nighttime running regime. The exchange of gifts between families constituted a marriage, a relationship that was generally stable and permanent. Corpses were wrapped in tule mats or deerskin and buried with their possessions. The family burned the deceased's house and then observed various taboos and purification rites.

DWELLINGS The Sinkiuse built typical Plateau-style, semiexcavated, cone-shaped wood frame houses covered with woven matting and/or grass. Longer, lodge-style structures of similar construction were used for communal activities. Villages also contained mat-covered sweat lodges. Temporary brush shelters served as summer houses. Later, skin tipis replaced the aboriginal structures.

They also built communal tule-mat houses consisting of a pole framework covered by grass, earth, and tule mats. These houses were about 16 feet wide, between 24 to about 60 feet long, and about 14 feet high, with gabled roofs. Entrance was through matted doors. Each family had an individual tule-covered section, but they shared a number of fireplaces in the central passage.

DIET Food was much more often acquired by the family than by the village. Fish was a staple. Men caught four varieties of salmon as well as trout, sturgeon, and other fish. They fished from May through October. Women cleaned, dried, and stored the fish. Dried fish and sometimes other foods made up much of the winter diet. People generally ate two meals a day in summer and one in winter.

Women gathered shellfish, salmon eggs, bulbs, roots, nuts, seeds, and berries. Camas was eaten raw or roasted, boiled, and made into cakes. A short ceremony was performed over the first gathered crop of the season. Men hunted most large and small game in the fall. They prepared for the hunt by sweating and singing. Women came along to help dress and carry the game. Men also hunted birds and gathered mollusks.

KEY TECHNOLOGY Men caught fish with nets, weirs, traps, and hook and line. Utensils were carved of wood. Women made coiled baskets of birch bark and/or cedar root; they also wove wallets and bags of woven strips of skin, and they sewed tule mats and other items.

TRADE The Sinkiuse engaged in extensive local trade, communication, visiting, and intermarriage.

NOTABLE ARTS Artistic expression was seen mainly in carved wood items, coiled baskets with geometric designs, and mat weaving.

TRANSPORTATION Dugout canoes and some

pole rafts served as water transportation. Horses arrived about the mid–eighteenth century.

DRESS The Sinkiuse wore surprisingly little clothing for such a northern climate. Woven bark and, later, dressed buckskin provided breechclouts, ponchos, and aprons. Women also wore woven caps. Men wore fur leggings in winter; women's leggings were generally made of hemp. Some winter clothing, such as mittens, caps, woven blankets, and robes, was made from the fur of rabbits and other animals. Both sexes plucked their eyebrows and wore earrings, tattoos, necklaces, and face paint.

WAR AND WEAPONS Sinkiuse were generally friendly with their Interior Salish neighbors.

Contemporary Information

GOVERNMENT/RESERVATIONS The Colville Reservation (1872) is located in Ferry and Okanogan Counties, Washington. It comprises 1,011,495 acres and had a 1990 Indian population of 3,782. An Indian Reorganization Act constitution approved in 1938 calls for a 14-member business council and various committees. The Confederated Tribes is a member of the Affiliated Tribes of Northwest Indians and other intertribal organizations.

ECONOMY Important economic resources and activities include stock raising, farming, logging (including a sawmill) and reforestation, seasonal labor, mining, a meat-packing plant, a log cabin sales business, tourism, and gambling enterprises. The tribe plans to develop its hydroelectric potential.

LEGAL STATUS The Confederated Tribes of the Colville Reservation is a federally recognized tribal entity.

DAILY LIFE Although a small number of Colville residents claim Sinkiuse descent, most people are largely acculturated. Language preservation programs are hindered by the lack of a common language, and few people still speak Sinkiuse (Columbia). Recent efforts to reinvigorate disparate tribal cultures and religions include the Seven Drum religion, the Indian Shaker Church, and the Native American Church. The tribe has undertaken a program of reacquiring and consolidating their land base. Education levels are increasing. The Colville Business Council wields growing power in regional and statewide issues.

Spokan

Spokan (Sp ō `kan), a Plateau tribe having three geographic divisions: upper, lower, and southern, or middle. The Spokan have also been known as Muddy People, as well as Sun People, probably after a faulty translation of their name. Their self-designation was *Spoqe'ind,* "round head."

LOCATION Spokan Indians lived in the mid–eighteenth century along the Spokane River, in eastern Washington and northern Idaho. Today they live on reservations in Washington and Idaho as well as in regional cities and towns.

POPULATION The early-nineteenth-century Spokan population was very roughly 2,000. In 1990, about 2,100 enrolled Spokan Indians lived on the Spokane Reservation as well as on the Coeur d'Alene, Flathead, and Colville Reservations and in regional cities and towns.

LANGUAGE Spokan is a dialect of the Interior division of the Salishan language family.

Historical Information

HISTORY The Spokan Indians probably originated in British Columbia along with other Salish groups. After they acquired horses from Kalispel Indians, around the mid–eighteenth century, they began hunting buffalo on the Great Plains. This was especially true of the upper division. By the time they encountered the Lewis and Clark expedition in 1805, their population had already declined significantly as a result of smallpox epidemics.

Following the Lewis and Clark visit, the North West, Hudson's Bay, and American Fur Companies quickly established themselves in the area. Missionaries arrived in the 1830s: They found the Spokan to be reluctant converts, and the influence of Christianity acted to create factionalism among the tribe. Interracial relations declined sharply in the late 1840s with the Whitman massacre and the closing of the Protestant mission (*see* "History" under Cayuse). Severe smallpox epidemics in 1846 and in 1852 and 1853 helped spur the rise of the Prophet Dance and the Dreamer Cult.

After miners had effectively dispossessed the Spokan from their territory, they joined with Coeur d'Alenes, Yakimas, Palouses, and Paiutes in the short-lived 1858 Coeur d'Alene, or Spokan, war. Spokan Indians then remained on their land as best they could or settled on various reservations. Despite pleas from Chief Joseph, they remained neutral in the 1877 Nez Percé war. In that year, the lower division agreed to move to the Spokan Reservation (1881; 154,898 acres). Ten years later, the other two divisions, as well as some remaining lower Spokans, agreed to move to either the Flathead, Colville, or Coeur d'Alene Reservations. The local fort, Fort Spokan, became an Indian boarding school from 1898 to 1906. There were also conflicts over land with non-natives in and around the city of Spokane at this time.

In the early twentieth century, much tribal land was lost to the allotment process as well as "surplus" land sales to non-Indians. Dams built in 1908 (Little

Falls) and 1935 (Grand Coulee) ruined the local fishery. Uranium mining began in the 1950s. The Spokan tribe successfully fought off termination proceedings begun in 1955. In 1966, the tribe received a land claims settlement of $6.7 million.

RELIGION Preadolescents acquired spirit helpers, through quests and in dreams and visions, to provide them with essential skills. Shamans' particularly strong spirits allowed them to cure illness, foresee the future, and assist hunters. Spokan Indians celebrated the midwinter (spirit) and midsummer religious ceremonies as well as first fruits and harvest ceremonies.

The Dreamer Cult, a mid-nineteenth-century phenomenon, was a revivalistic cult that celebrated traditional Indian religious beliefs. Although it was explicitly antiwhite, the religious doctrine also contained elements of Christianity. Its adherents thus attempted to remain faithful to their Indian traditions while taking steps to adapt to non-Indian culture.

GOVERNMENT Each division was composed of a number of bands, which were in turn composed of groups of related families. Bands were led by a chief and an assistant chief, who were selected on the basis of leadership qualities. The office of band chief may once have been hereditary. Several bands might winter together in a village and at that time select an ad hoc village chief. Decisions were taken by consensus. In the historic period, as authority became more centralized, there was also a tribal chief.

CUSTOMS The Spokan were seminomadic for nine months a year; during the other three they lived in permanent winter villages. Men's realm was tool making, war, hunting, fishing, and, later, horses. The dead were covered with skins and robes and buried after spending some time on a scaffold. A pole marked the grave site.

DWELLINGS The Spokan built typical Plateau-style, semiexcavated, cone-shaped wood frame houses covered with woven matting and/or grass. Longer, lodge-style structures of similar construction were used for communal activities. Villages also contained mat-covered sweat lodges. Temporary brush shelters served as summer houses. Later, skin tipis replaced the aboriginal structures.

DIET Fish, especially salmon, was the staple. Trout and whitefish were also important. These were mostly smoked, dried, and stored for the winter. Men hunted local big game and, later, buffalo on the Plains. A favorite hunting technique was for many men to surround the animal. Important plant foods included camas, bitterroot and other roots, bulbs, seeds, and berries.

KEY TECHNOLOGY Men caught fish with nets, weirs, traps, and hook and line. Women made coiled baskets of birch bark and/or cedar root; they also wove wallets and bags of woven strips of skin, and they sewed tule mats and other items.

TRADE Spokan Indians traded coiled baskets, woven wallets and caps, and tule mats, among other items, with local tribes, particularly the Coeur d'Alene.

NOTABLE ARTS Women wove geometric designs into their well-made baskets. They also decorated clothing with porcupine quillwork.

TRANSPORTATION Spokan Indians used pole rafts for river travel. They acquired horses around the mid–eighteenth century.

DRESS Clothing was made of bark and fur until the advent of widespread buffalo hunting, when styles took on Plains characteristics. Both men and women tattooed their bodies.

WAR AND WEAPONS Spokans were generally friendly with their Interior Salish neighbors, especially the Kalispel. The Coeur d'Alene were occasional enemies until the mid–eighteenth century, when they became allies in wars against the Crow and Blackfeet. As part of these wars, the Spokan counted coups, took scalps, and held war dances.

Contemporary Information

GOVERNMENT/RESERVATIONS The Spokane Reservation (1881) is located in Lincoln and Stevens Counties, Washington. It contains 133,302 acres. The 1990 Indian population was 1,229. The reservation is governed by an elected tribal council.

ECONOMY There is a tribal store on the Spokane Reservation. Income is also generated by land leases, a post mill, a lumber mill, farming, and a fish hatchery. The reservation suffers from chronic high unemployment. There is a casino on the Colville Reservation.

LEGAL STATUS The Spokane Tribe is a federally recognized tribal entity.

DAILY LIFE Spokan Indians are essentially assimilated, although there are some language preservation programs operating through a cultural center on the reservation. Efforts to revitalize traditional religion are controversial owing to the concurrent introduction of religious elements from Great Plains cultures. Water rights, gaming, and control of resource areas remain ongoing issues. The reservation has both Catholic and Protestant churches as well as a community center. It hosts an annual festival over Labor Day weekend.

Thompson

The Thompson (`Tom sun) Indians are also known as *Ntlakyapamuk*.

LOCATION The Thompson Indian homeland is

the Fraser, Thompson, and Nicola River Valleys in southwest British Columbia.

POPULATION The late-eighteenth-century Thompson population was about 5,000. It was approximately 5,700 in 1995.

LANGUAGE Thompson is a dialect of the Interior division of the Salishan language family.

Historical Information

HISTORY Several trading companies became established in Thompson country following the initial visit of non-Indians in about 1809. Miners flooded in after an 1858 gold strike, taking over land, disrupting subsistence patterns, and generally forcing the Indian population to the brink of ruin. Disease, too, took a heavy toll during the nineteenth century, killing as many as 70 percent of the precontact Indian population. The government of British Columbia confined the Thompson Indians to reserves in the late nineteenth century.

RELIGION Guardian spirits, acquired in youth through fasting and seclusion, provided luck and various skills. Shamans cured illness with the help of their especially powerful spirits. Thompson Indians celebrated the arrival of the season's first salmon as well as the Ghost or Circle Dance.

GOVERNMENT Thompson Indians recognized two geographical divisions, located downstream and upstream of about the location of Cisco on the Fraser River. Within the divisions, bands were autonomous, consisted of related families, and were led by hereditary chiefs whose powers were largely advisory. A council of older men wielded real authority.

CUSTOMS The girls' puberty rite consisted of daily prayers, bathing, and rubs with fir branches. The dead were buried in sand pits or rock slides; graves were marked with stakes or posts. People's former ornaments and tools were buried with them. In a reflection of their cultural proximity to Northwest Coast people, slavery was hereditary among the Thompson.

DWELLINGS In winter, people lived in circular, earth-covered pole-frame lodges built in pits. Each lodge was about 20–40 feet in diameter and could hold between 15 and 30 people. Entry was gained via a notched ladder inserted through the smoke hole. In summer, people used oblong or circular lodges consisting of rush mats over a pole frame. Both men and women used domed sweat houses for purification. Sweat houses were also homes for youths during their spirit quest period.

DIET Thompson Indians subsisted on the typical Plateau diet of fish, especially salmon; some large and small game; and plant foods that included many roots, berries, and nuts (especially camas and bitterroot).

KEY TECHNOLOGY Men caught fish by using weirs, seine nets, traps, dip nets, and hook and line. They also carved soapstone (steatite) pipes. Bows were often made of juniper. Women made cedar-root or birch-bark baskets decorated with geometric designs, as well as birch and spruce bark containers. Some were woven tight enough to hold water. Women also wove blankets of goat wool or strips of rabbit fur, and they sewed tule mats with Indian hemp cord. Digging sticks featured antler or wood cross-handles. Other tools and utensils were also made of stone, antler, and bone.

TRADE Thompson Indians traded especially with the Okanagon, Lake, Colville, and Sanpoil people. They received dentalium shell from north of Vancouver Island, across the mountains, and down the Fraser River.

NOTABLE ARTS Women made fine baskets decorated with geometric motifs and natural dyes. The Thompson people developed a distinctive form of "negative" body painting, which involved removing pigment from a painted surface. Deer jaws were used to scratch parallel lines.

TRANSPORTATION Thompson men made both birch-bark and dugout canoes. Snowshoes were worn in winter. Horses arrived around the mid– to late eighteenth century.

DRESS Traditionally, most clothing, such as breechclouts, ponchos, skirts, and robes, was made from cedar bark and fur. Dressed skin clothing, including leggings, breechclouts, and tunics, probably reflected the later influence of the Great Plains. Moccasins were generally plain. Women wove robes of rabbit skin or goat wool. Fringe, bone, teeth, and shell decoration was used on some items. Personal decorations included jewelry of dentalium shell, bone and animal teeth, and face paint. Men wore long looped necklaces, often decorated with abalone shell. Women tended to wear abalone in their braids.

WAR AND WEAPONS Thompsons selected temporary war chiefs, as needed. Stuwiks were a traditional enemy until the Thompsons absorbed them by about 1800, although the people also fought regularly with other Salishan groups. Weapons used in regular raiding included the bow and arrow; spears; wood, bone, or stone clubs; bone daggers; and wooden slat armor.

Contemporary Information

GOVERNMENT/RESERVATIONS Thompson Indians are organized into roughly 16 bands located on about 200 reserves in British Columbia. Their total land base is roughly 42,500 hectares. See band profiles under "Daily Life" (all statistics are as of 1995).

ECONOMY Wage labor and basket sales complement farming, hunting, fishing, and gathering.

LEGAL STATUS All of the bands discussed under "Daily Life" are federally and provincially recognized.

DAILY LIFE The Boston Bar Band, originally the Koia'um Village, controls 12 reserves on 609 hectares of land. The reserves were allotted in 1878. The population is 182, of whom 64 live in 20 houses on the reserves. Elections are held according to the provisions of the Indian Act, and the band is affiliated with the Nlaka'pamux Nation Tribal Council. Children attend provincial schools. Important economic resources include a campsite.

The Boothroyd Band, formerly known as Chomok Band, controls 19 reserves on 1,122 hectares of land. The population is 244, of whom 84 live in 29 houses on the reserves. Elections are held according to the provisions of the Indian Act, and the band is affiliated with the Nlaka'pamux Nation Tribal Council. Children attend provincial schools. Facilities include a church.

The Cook's Ferry Band controls 24 reserves on 4,048 hectares of land. The reserves were allotted in 1878. The population is 267, of whom 75 live on the reserves. Elections are held according to custom, and the band is currently unaffiliated. Children attend provincial schools. Important economic activities include ranching. Facilities include a community hall, a fire station, and a garage.

The Kanaka Bar Band (formerly part of the Lytton Band) was originally composed of gold miners from the Hawaiian Islands. The Kanakas were employed by the Hudson's Bay Company, which had established a trading post in Honolulu in 1834. Many Hawaiians traveled on company ships to the Northwest Coast. Some stayed, especially to mine gold, and intermarried with the Native Americans. The band controls six reserves on 229 hectares of land. The reserves were allotted in 1881. The population is 147, of whom 55 live in seven houses on the reserves. Elections are held according to custom, and the band is affiliated with the Fraser Canyon Indian Administration. Children attend provincial schools. Silviculture is an important economic activity.

The Lower Nicola Band controls nine reserves on 7,096 hectares of land. The reserves were allotted in 1878. The population is 807, of whom 470 live in 121 houses on the reserves. Elections are held according to the provisions of the Indian Act, and the band is affiliated with the Nicola Valley Tribal Council. Children attend band and provincial schools. Important economic activities and resources include an irrigation system, cattle ranching, logging/forest products, and small businesses. Facilities include a community hall, a church, and a cultural club.

The Lytton Band controls 54 reserves on 5,980 hectares of land near the Fraser and Thorpe Rivers. The reserves were allotted in 1881. The population is 1,480, of whom 714 live in 228 houses on the reserves. Elections are held according to the provisions of the Indian Act, and the band is affiliated with the Nklaka'pamux Nation Tribal Council. Children attend band and provincial schools. Important economic activities and resources include a hardware store, a motel, and individual ranches and businesses. Facilities include a community hall, a seniors' home, a group home, a womens' shelter, and an arts and crafts store.

The Neskonlith Band, a South Thompson band, is located six kilometers south of Chase, British Columbia. The reserve was allotted in 1877. The population is 499, of whom 223 live in 54 houses on the reserves. Elections are held according to the provisions of the Indian Act, and the band is affiliated with the Shuswap Nation Tribal Council. Children attend band and provincial schools. Important economic activities and resources include a development corporation, a demonstration farm and silviculture program, and small farms and businesses. Facilities include a community hall, a fire station, and a church.

The Nicomen Band controls 15 reserves on 1,175 hectares of land. The population is 85, of whom 53 live in 14 houses on the reserves. Elections are held according to the provisions of the Indian Act, and the band is affiliated with the Fraser Canyon Indian Administration. Children attend provincial schools. Important economic activities and resources include ranches.

The Nooaitch Band controls two reserves on 1,693 hectares of land. The reserves were allotted in 1878. The population is 171, of whom 116 live in 27 houses on the reserves. Elections are held according to the provisions of the Indian Act, and the band is affiliated with the Nicola Valley Tribal Council. Children attend provincial schools. Important economic activities and resources include small businesses. Facilities include offices, a church, and a fish hatchery.

The North Thompson Band controls five reserves on 1,521 hectares of land 24 kilometers north of Barnere. The reserves were allotted in 1877. The population is 512, of whom 217 live in 71 houses on the reserves. Elections are held according to the provisions of the Indian Act, and the band is affiliated with the Shuswap Nation Tribal Council. Children attend band and provincial schools. Important economic activities and resources include a feed lot, haying, logging, a fish hatchery, farming, a construction company, and a sawmill. Facilities include offices, a recreation hall, a women's club, a church, and an elders' home.

The Oregon Jack Creek Band controls six reserves on 823 hectares of land 17.5 kilometers west of Cache Creek. The reserves were allotted in 1878. The population is 49, of whom 11 live in six houses on the reserves. Elections are held according to custom, and the band is affiliated with the Nlaka'pamux Nation Tribal Council. Important economic activities and resources include cattle and hay ranching.

The Shakan Band controls two reserves on 3,874 hectares of land. The reserves were allotted in 1878. The population is 112, of whom 68 live in 22 houses on the reserves. Elections are unofficially held according to custom as well as according to the provisions of the Indian Act. The band is affiliated with the Nicola Valley Tribal Council. Children attend band and provincial schools. Important economic activities and resources include a campground and individual ranches. Facilities include a community hall and a church.

The Siska Band controls 11 reserves on 319 hectares of land. The reserves were allotted in 1876. The population is 231, of whom 78 live in 24 houses on the reserves. Elections are held according to custom, and the band is currently unaffiliated. Children attend band and provincial schools. Important economic activities and resources include a grocery store and a convenience store. Facilities include a community hall and offices.

The Skuppah Band controls eight reserves on 211 hectares of land. The population is 56, of whom 40 live in 12 houses on the reserves. Elections are held according to custom, and the band is affiliated with the Fraser Canyon Indian Administration. Children attend band and provincial schools. Important economic activities and resources include livestock, a café-restaurant, and individual hay and cattle ranches. Facilities include a community hall.

The Spuzzum Band controls 16 reserves on 636 hectares of land. The population is 152, of whom 37 live in 13 houses on the reserves. Elections are held according to custom, and the band is affiliated with the Fraser Canyon Indian Administration. Children attend provincial schools. Important economic activities and resources include an individual backhoe business. Facilities include offices.

The Upper Nicola Band (Thompson and Okanagon) controls eight reserves on 12,503 hectares of land. The reserves were allotted in 1878. The population is 715, of whom 431 live in 96 houses on the reserves. Elections are held according to custom, and the band is affiliated with the Nicola Valley Tribal Council. Children attend band and provincial schools. Important economic activities and resources include a store, a gas station, a cattle company, and individual small businesses. Facilities include offices, a hotel, a community hall, and a church.

Umatilla

Umatilla (Ū mä `til ä) is a name derived from a village name meaning "many rocks." This group is culturally similar to other Sahaptian people, such as Klikitat, Nez Percé, Wallawalla, and Yakima.

LOCATION The Umatilla homeland was located along the lower Umatilla River and the Columbia River west of the mouth of the Walla Walla River. Today, most Umatillas live in Umatilla and Union Counties, Oregon, and in regional cities and towns.

POPULATION The late-eighteenth-century Umatilla population was roughly 1,500. In 1990, over 1,000 Umatillas, Cayuses, and Wallawallas lived on the Umatilla Reservation, and approximately 700 Umatillas lived off-reservation. The Confederated Tribes of the Umatilla Reservation had a combined enrollment of around 1,900 in the mid-1990s.

LANGUAGE Umatilla was a member of the Sahaptian division of the Penutian language family.

Historical Information

HISTORY As with other regional Indian groups, the Umatillas first encountered non-natives when the Lewis and Clark expedition passed through their territory around 1805. Fur traders quickly moved in shortly thereafter. Severe epidemics began in the mid–nineteenth century, about the same time Catholic and Protestant missionaries flocked to the region.

The Umatillas enjoyed a peaceful relationship with non-Indians until the late 1840s. In 1851 a Catholic mission, previously established in 1847 and then abandoned, was rebuilt. At that time the Umatillas sent warriors to support the Cayuses in their war against whites from the Willamette Valley. In the mid-1850s they were forced, with the Wallawallas and the Cayuses, to cede over four million acres and accept the creation of a reservation. The Umatillas joined the Yakima war of resistance from 1855 to 1856. However, two decades later, they fought against the Indians in the Bannock war. Umatillas were responsible for the death in that war of the Paiute chief Egan. Despite the Indians' possible hopes for better treatment at the hands of the whites, the original reservation of over 245,000 acres was quickly pared to under 100,000 by the process of allotment and sales of "surplus" to non-Indians.

RELIGION After years of instruction, adolescents sought the protection and power of spirits in nature by fasting and visiting remote places. Men and women shamans, with especially strong, heavenly-oriented guardian spirits, provided religious leadership. They cured illness, controlled the weather, and presided at ceremonies. They might also inflict harm. Dreams were also connected to good and evil events. During the winter religious ceremonies, participants dressed as their spirits and sang their spirit songs. Most important ceremonies centered on the first gathered fruit and salmon catch of the season.

GOVERNMENT Small, local bands each had one or more villages and fishing areas. Civil chiefs led the bands, although war chiefs exercised temporary power during periods of conflict. Chiefs were generally selected by a combination of merit, heredity, and wealth. Chiefs and old men made up the village and tribal councils; decisions were taken by consensus. The bands came together under a single chief in times of celebration and danger.

CUSTOMS Each band contained at least one permanent winter village and a number of temporary fishing camps. Some subsistence areas were considered tribal property. Menstruating and late-term pregnant women were strictly segregated. Young, unmarried men slept in the sweat lodges. Young men and women, especially the latter, were married by about age 14. Brides were commonly purchased, and polygamy was common. Abortion was rare, as was birth out of wedlock. Adultery was a capital crime. Women did most domestic work, including dressing skins; men's work revolved around hunting and war.

Immediately after death, corpses were dressed in good clothes and had their faces painted. After several days, they were wrapped in deerskin and buried with their former possessions. Boulders and cedar stakes marked grave sites. The family in mourning cut their hair and wore poor, dirty clothing.

Pipe smoking was an important part of burial and other rites and ceremonies. The murder of a tribe member usually required blood revenge or at least blood money. Theft was punished by public disgrace. Other serious crimes and infractions included adultery, rape, and lying. Typical games included archery, dice, hoop-and-pole, and the hand game; most included betting. Childrens' games included tops and string games.

DWELLINGS Permanent settlements were located along rivers. Winter dwellings were semisubterranean, circular wood frame structures covered with cedar bark, sage, mats, grasses, and earth. The roof was flat or conical. Mats covered the floors. These houses, up to 60 feet long, held up to 50 families. People slept along inner walls and shared fires along the center. In summer, people built temporary brush lean-tos. Some groups adopted hide tipis in the eighteenth century.

DIET Umatillas moved with the food supply. Fish, especially salmon, was the staple, along with trout, eel, and sturgeon. Salmon was broiled, baked, boiled, or dried, smoked, and stored. Animal food included elk, deer, moose, mountain sheep, rabbits, and small game. Parties also traveled to the Plains to hunt buffalo. Some meat was "jerked" for winter. Deer were run down or shot, as were other game, with a bow and arrow or killed with a spear. Some animals were hunted with the use of decoys.

Women gathered plant foods such as camas, kouse, bitterroot, wild carrot, wild onion, and berries. Camas, dug in midsummer, was peeled and baked in a pit oven. Most berries were dried and stored for winter. Other food included shellfish, fowl, eggs, and birds. People ate horses, lichens, and tree inner bark when there was nothing else to eat. Most food was either boiled, steamed in pits, or roasted in ashes.

KEY TECHNOLOGY Fish were speared from platforms and caught using nets, spears, small traps, and weirs. Men used various nooses, snares, nets, and deadfalls for hunting as well as bows made of mountain sheep horn. Women made a range of woven and coiled baskets, some watertight, as well as woven reed bags. They also made cups, bowls, winnowing baskets, women's caps, and mats of cattails and tule. Many baskets were made of Indian hemp, bear grass, and other grasses.

Other important raw materials included bone, horn, and wood. Many tools and items, such as mortars, pestles, knives, and mauls, were made of chipping and flaking stone and also obsidian. Mattresses were cottonwood inner bark or dry grass, blankets were elk hides, and folded skins served as pillows. The ubiquitous digging stick was fire-hardened with a wood or antler cross-handle.

TRADE Relatively early acquisition of horses gave the Umatilla a trade advantage, although they also traded widely before they had the horse. They acquired items made as far away as British Columbia and the Mississippi Valley. Abalone was among the items they acquired from coastal Indians, as were carved wooden items, dried clams, dentalium shells, and wapato root.

NOTABLE ARTS Traditional arts included woven baskets, wallets, petroglyphs, and blankets and tipi skins decorated with pictographs.

TRANSPORTATION The Umatilla used snowshoes and dugout canoes. They acquired the horse in the early eighteenth century.

DRESS Clothing was made of cedar bark and the untailored skin of deer, elk, and buffalo. Men wore moccasins, leggings, breechclouts, shirts, and highly decorated robes. Women wore moccasins, fringed gowns, and basket hats, replaced in the historic period with skin caps decorated with fringe and elks' teeth. People painted their faces and bodies for decoration and against snow blindness. Tailored, Plains-style skin clothing became popular in the eighteenth century.

WAR AND WEAPONS   To counter the threat of attack from Paiutes, their most feared enemy, Umatillas formed a war alliance with the Nez Percés. They often took refuge on Blalock Island, now under water.

Contemporary Information

GOVERNMENT/RESERVATIONS   The Umatilla Reservation (1855; Umatilla, Cayuse, Wallawalla) is located in Umatilla and Union Counties, Oregon. It contains roughly 172,000 acres, most of which are individually allotted. The 1990 Indian population was 1,028. The constitution and by-laws, adopted in 1949, call for an elected nine-member Board of Trustees.

Umatilla Indians are also members of the Columbia River Indians, who live primarily in Priest Rapids, Cooks Landing, Billieville, and Georgeville, Washington; in Celilo, Oregon; and in non-Indian communities. The Council of Columbia River Chiefs meets at Celilo, Oregon. The community at Priest Rapids is directly descended from that of Smohalla, a founder of the Dreamer or Longhouse religion.

The tribes are also members of the Umatilla Basin Project, the Columbia River Intertribal Fish Commission, the Basalt Waste Isolation Project, the Hanford Environmental Dose Project, the Columbia Gorge Commission, and other environmental and planning organizations.

ECONOMY   In 1953, the tribe received almost $4 million in compensation for fishing sites lost to the Dalles Dam. The tribe has won other land claims settlements as well. It is currently developing an Oregon Trail interpretive center. Other sources of income include farm leases as well as a tribally owned forest, range, resort, trailer court, grain elevator, store, and lake (camping and fishing). A golf course and entertainment park are planned. Tribal programs provide credit as well as seasonal and regular employment.

LEGAL STATUS   The Confederated Tribes of the Umatilla Reservation is a federally recognized tribal entity. The Columbia River Indians are not federally recognized.

DAILY LIFE   The tribe values both traditional and modern education. There are some language preservation programs, and there is a college scholarship fund. The Seven Drum religion is a major force in cultural revitalization. People's religious practices also include traditional salmon and roots ceremonies. Facilities include a day care center and an arts and crafts organization. The tribe also operates health education and substance abuse programs. It sponsors an annual Pendleton Round-up, including dances, crafts fair, and rodeo, and an annual Indian festival of the arts. The regional political and economic effectiveness of the Umatillas continues to grow.

Wallawalla
See Umatilla

Warm Springs Reservation, Confederated Tribes of the
See Paiute, Northern (Chapter 4); Umatilla; Wishram

Wasco
See Wishram

Wishram

Wishram (`Wish r ə m), or *Tlakluit,* a Plateau group with many cultural attributes of Northwest Coast Indians. They were culturally similar to the neighboring Wasco people.

LOCATION   Wishram Indians lived along the north bank of the Columbia River, several miles above and below the Dalles. Today, their descendants live on local reservations, especially the Yakima, and in regional cities and towns.

POPULATION   The eighteenth-century Wishram population was about 1,500. A 1962 census listed 10 Wishrams in Washington. The contemporary population is part of the Warm Springs and Yakima Reservation communities.

LANGUAGE   Wishram was a member of the Chinookan (Kiksht) division of the Penutian language family.

Historical Information

HISTORY   Owing to their physical location at the Dalles, the most important trading area in the Northwest, the Wishram traditionally enjoyed favorable trade relations with many neighboring tribes. In the early nineteenth century, however, non-Indian traders threatened this position while at the same time the Wishram population was declining rapidly due to disease. Conflict with traders was one result. Ongoing intertribal warfare also took a population toll.

In 1855, the Wishram and Wasco were forced to sign treaties ceding most of their land (roughly 10 million acres); the treaties established the Warm Springs Reservation in north-central Oregon. Wishram Indians also became part of the Yakima Indian Nation on the Yakima Reservation. A key treaty provision allowing the Indians to fish "at all . . . usual and accustomed stations in common with the citizens of the United States . . ." served as the basis for a landmark legal ruling in 1974 that protected the Northwest Coast Indian fishery. In the 1860s members of the Warm Springs Reservation organized informally into linguistic and cultural divisions: There were Sahaptian-speaking people ("Warm Springs Indians"); Upper Chinookan–speaking Wascos and Wishrams; and Northern Paiutes after 1879.

In 1891, about one-third of Yakima Reservation land was allotted to individuals, but the Yakima Nation, under chief Shawaway Lotiahkan, retained the "surplus" usually sold to non-Indians in such cases. Still, much land that was allotted to Indians was soon lost, including some of the best irrigated land. Around the turn of the century as much as 80 percent of the reservation was in non-Indian hands.

The Warm Springs Boarding School opened in 1897; designed to eradicate Indian culture, it fell short of its goal before it closed in the 1960s. Dams, however (Bonneville, 1938; Grand Coulee, 1941; Dalles, 1956), destroyed the native fisheries. Although the tribes were compensated financially for the fisheries, the spiritual and cultural loss was devastating. During the course of the twentieth century the number of salmon and steelhead that returned to the Yakima River to spawn declined by about 99 percent. The issue of fishing rights remained an important and controversial one from the beginning of the reservation period through its resolution in 1974. Well into the twentieth century, Yakimas continued much of their traditional subsistence and ceremonial activities.

RELIGION Adolescent boys sought guardian spirits by fasting and performing feats of skill or daring associated with remote places. Shamans' guardian spirits, usually several animals, helped them cure the sick. Important ceremonies included first salmon rites as well as midwinter guardian spirit dances.

GOVERNMENT Each of several villages was led by a hereditary chief.

CUSTOMS Wishram Indians observed the system of social stratification typical of Northwest Coast Indians: There were nobles, middle-class, commoners, and slaves; the slaves were acquired in war or trade. Slavery was also hereditary. Marriage was formalized by an exchange of gifts and family visits. Infants were occasionally betrothed for purposes of creating or cementing family alliances. Corpses were wrapped in buckskin and interred in plank burial houses. Remarriage to the dead spouse's sibling was common. Fishing areas were privately owned and inheritable by groups of families.

DWELLINGS Wishrams probably built plank houses characteristic of the coastal style. Beginning about the eighteenth century, they also built circular winter houses, holding between one and six families. These were built of a pole framework over a six-foot pit, covered with mats of grass and dirt or cedar bark. Entrance was through the smoke hole. Bed platforms were located around the walls. In summer, people built gabled-roof mat lodges with several fireplaces. Hunters and mourners purified themselves, and the sick healed, in sweat lodges.

DIET Fish, especially salmon, pike, eels, sturgeon, and smelts, was the most important food. Salmon eggs were also eaten. Fish were either eaten fresh or dried or smoked and ground for long-term storage. Important plant foods included roots, bulbs (especially camas), wild onions, wild potatoes, acorns, and various nuts and berries. Men hunted game to supplement the diet.

KEY TECHNOLOGY In addition to nets, weirs, traps, and spears for fishing, men made a variety of carved wood tools and utensils. Women made twined baskets and bags decorated with geometric figures.

TRADE The Dalles, or Five Mile Rapids, in Wishram territory was the most important trading location in the Northwest; several thousand Northwest Coast and Plateau Indians traded there during various trade fairs. Wishram and Wasco people acted as intermediaries in the trade of a huge amount and variety of items, including blankets, shells, slaves, canoes, fish and animal products, dried roots, bear grass, and, later, horses. Trade connections stretched from Canada to Mexico and from the Rocky Mountains west to the ocean.

NOTABLE ARTS Baskets and some carved wood items were exceptionally well made.

TRANSPORTATION Men built and traded for dugout canoes and snowshoes.

DRESS Most clothing was made of skins. Men wore breechclouts; women wore aprons and basket caps. People also painted their faces and wore dentalium shell ornaments. Plains-style clothing became popular in the nineteenth century.

WAR AND WEAPONS At least in the early to mid–nineteenth century, the Wishram and Wasco fought Northern Paiutes, Bannocks, and Northern Shoshones.

Contemporary Information

GOVERNMENT/RESERVATIONS The Yakima Reservation and Trust Lands (1859) are located in Klikitat, Lewis, and Yakima Counties, Washington. They contain roughly 1.4 million acres. The 1990 Indian population was 6,296, of a total population of well over 27,000. The Yakima Nation is governed by a 14-member tribal council.

The Warm Springs Reservation (1855; Wasco/Wishram, Wallawalla [Warm Springs], and

Northern Paiute) is located in Clakamas, Jefferson, Marian, and Wasco Counties, Oregon. It contains 643,507 acres. The 1990 Indian population was 2,818. The 1993 tribal enrollment was 3,410. Decisions of the 11-member tribal council are subject to general review by referendum. An Indian Reorganization Act constitution was adopted in 1938.

ECONOMY　Warm Springs features the Kah-Nee-Ta resort; the Warm Springs Forest Products Industries, which includes logging, a plywood plant, and a sawmill; herds of wild horses; a salmon hatchery; a tribally owned hydroelectric plant; a museum; a casino; and two radio stations. Tribal government is also a major provider of jobs. The tribe's economy is significantly self-sufficient and reservation based.

Timber is the Yakima Nation's main income producer; its forest products industry includes a furniture manufacturing plant. The nation maintains extensive range and farmland. However, 80 percent of irrigated land remains leased by non-Indians. The Wapato Project provides the Indians with control over their own water.

The Yakima-Klickitat Fish Production Project, a cooperative effort between the Yakima Nation and Washington State, is a major fishery restoration/conservation venture. An industrial park contains Indian and non-Indian industries. The Yakima Land Enterprise operates fruit orchards and stands and a recreational vehicle park. Other employment is provided by the government and the nation as well as by small business enterprises. Still, unemployment fluctuates between about 30 and 60 percent, and up to 75 percent of the people live below the poverty level.

LEGAL STATUS　The Confederated Tribes and Bands of the Yakima Nation and the Confederated Tribes of the Warm Springs Reservation are both federally recognized tribal entities. Lawsuits over water use from the Yakima River system are pending.

DAILY LIFE　The Warm Springs Sahaptians remain the most traditional group on the reservation; this language is spoken on ceremonial occasions. Few people still speak Wishram. Warm Springs children attend public grade school on the reservation and public high school off the reservation. The Seven Drum religion, conducted in Sahaptian, provides a link to other Plateau Sahaptian communities. The Feather Dance religion, which emphasizes ritual healing, is also active on the Warm Springs reservation.

On the Yakima Reservation, many people follow the Longhouse (Seven Drums) religion as well as sweat house customs and first foods feasts. The longhouse serves as the locus of Indian identity and is used for ceremonial occasions. Longhouse families throughout the Plateau region are linked together, mostly through marriage. The Indian Shaker religion is also active on the reservation, as are several Christian churches.

Yakimas maintain many aspects of traditional culture, including family customs, service, and leadership. The language is alive and well, especially as part of religious ceremonies and among more traditional people. Adults and children may take classes to strengthen their native language skills. Yakima basketry is still an important art and craft.

The Yakima Reservation boasts a huge, full-service tribal cultural center, museum, and restaurant in addition to two community centers. There is an emphasis on education, with the tribe providing incentives such as scholarships and summer programs. Children attend public school on the reservation. The reservation also sponsors a tribally run school; a private, accredited, four-year liberal arts college; tribal newspapers; and a radio station. It hosts an annual all-Indian rodeo, a powwow, a huckleberry festival, and several basketball tournaments. In 1972, the government restored about 22,000 acres of land to the Yakima Nation, including the sacred Pahto (Mt. Adams).

Yakima

Yakima (`Ya ku mu), "runaway," the common name for the people who called themselves *Waptailmim*, "People of the Narrow River." The Yakima people may have originated from members of neighboring tribes such as the Palouse and Nez Percé.

LOCATION　The Yakima homeland is located along the Columbia, Wenatchee, and Yakima Rivers in southern Washington. It includes lands from the Cascade summits to the Columbia River.

POPULATION　The late-eighteenth-century (pre-contact) population was about 7,000. By 1805 the population had fallen to half of that. A 1910 reservation census noted the population at 1,362. Today, Yakimas are among the over 6,000 Indians enrolled in the Yakima Nation. Yakimas also live off-reservation and in regional cities and towns.

LANGUAGE　Yakima is a member of the Sahaptian division of the Penutian language family.

Historical Information

HISTORY　Yakima bands acquired horses by the early eighteenth century and began hunting buffalo on the Great Plains. Horses brought them wealth, but even though the people acquired certain aspects of Plains culture, they did not become wholesale buffalo hunters as some other Plateau tribes did. In 1805 the Lewis and Clark expedition arrived; many trappers, missionaries, and traders soon followed. The missionaries found reluctant converts. By the early to mid–nineteenth century, the Yakima had suffered dramatic population reductions owing to disease as well as to warfare with the Shoshone.

In 1855, the governor of Washington forced local Indians to cede 10.8 million acres of land. Most tribes agreed to accept a 1.2-million-acre reservation. Shortly thereafter, gold was discovered north of the Spokane River. Although Indians retained fishing and gathering rights at their usual off-reservation places and were given two to three years to relocate after they signed the 1855 treaty, the governor declared their land open to non-Indians 12 days after the treaty council.

Friction was inevitable at this point. Miners killed some Yakimas, and the Indians retaliated in kind. When soldiers arrived, a large group of Indians drove them away. In response to the treacherous murder of a Wallawalla chief and negotiator, the Wallawalla, Palouse, Cayuse, and Umatilla Indians joined the Yakimas in fighting non-Indians. The war spread in 1856. Seattle was attacked, and southern Oregon tribes joined the fighting; that part of the conflict was called the Rogue River war. The Coeur d'Alene war of 1858, in which Yakimas also participated, was essentially another part of the same conflict.

In 1859, following the end of the fighting and the execution of 24 Yakimas, the Indians agreed to settle on a reservation. The future Yakima Indian Nation included, in addition to the Yakima bands, the Klickitat, Wanapam, Wishram, Palus (Palouse), and the Wenatchi. Reservation Yakimas entered a brief period of relative prosperity under a worthy Indian agent. Soon, however, facing the usual pressures to sell their land, most Indians were forced into poverty, mitigated in part by some seasonal work.

By 1891, about one-third of the reservation land had been allotted to individuals, but the Yakima Nation, under Chief Shawaway Lotiahkan, retained the "surplus" usually sold to non-Indians in such cases. Still, much land that had been allotted to Indians was soon lost, including some of the best irrigated land. Around the turn of the century as much as 80 percent of the reservation was in non-Indian hands. Some Indians also established homesteads on original village sites off of the reservation. Despite government attempts to eradicate it, Indians retained their *Wáashat* (Longhouse) religion.

Dams (Bonneville, 1938; Grand Coulee, 1941; Dalles, 1956) destroyed the native fisheries. During the course of the twentieth century, the number of salmon and steelhead that returned to spawn in the Yakima River declined by about 99 percent. The issue of fishing rights remained an important and controversial one from the beginning of the reservation period through its resolution in the Boldt decision of 1974.

Well into the twentieth century, Yakimas contin-
ued much of their traditional subsistence and ceremonial activities. In the 1950s, their long-standing fishing place, Celilo Falls, was lost to a dam. A tribal renaissance began around that time, however. It included the development of several tribal industries such as a furniture factory, clothing manufactures, and a ceramic center as well as an all-Indian rodeo.

RELIGION   Yakima Indians believed in a creator as well as the existence of animal spirits. The latter could be helpful in life and were sought in remote places by adolescent boys. Shamans' powerful spirits allowed them to cure illness. Most important ceremonies had to do with first food (salmon, root, berry) feasts.

GOVERNMENT   Autonomous bands were led by leaders selected partly by merit and also by heredity. The bands came together under a head chief in times of celebration and danger.

CUSTOMS   Groups of families lived together in permanent winter villages, where they raced, gambled, and held festivals. During the rest of the year individual families dispersed to hunt, fish, and gather food. Corpses were buried in pits where they were sometimes cremated as well. Graves were marked by a ring of stones. More than one individual may have been buried and cremated at a time. Burials also occurred in rock slides, where they were marked with stakes.

DWELLINGS   The winter lodge consisted of a semisubterranean, rectangular, pole-frame structure covered with mats and earth. Skin-covered tipis were adopted during the eighteenth century.

DIET   Fish, especially salmon (five kinds), steelhead trout, eel, and sturgeon, was the staple. Fish was eaten fresh or dried, ground, and stored. People also ate game, roots, berries, and nuts.

KEY TECHNOLOGY   Men fished using platforms, weirs, dip nets, harpoons, and traps. They hunted using bow and arrow and deadfalls. Other technological items included skin bags, baskets (some watertight), and carved wooden utensils.

TRADE   Yakimas participated in aboriginal trade activities as well as the early-nineteenth-century fur trade. Prominent trade items included skins, shells, beads, feathers, baskets, and reed mats.

NOTABLE ARTS   Fine arts included tanned skins, decorated with shells, beads, and feathers, as well as baskets and reed mats.

TRANSPORTATION   People negotiated their territory using dugout canoes and snowshoes. Horses arrived in the early eighteenth century.

DRESS   Breechclouts, aprons, vests, and moccasins were made of skins. Fur robes were added in cold weather. Plains-style leggings and dresses became popular in the eighteenth century.

WAR AND WEAPONS   In the early nineteenth century the Yakima fought many wars with the Shoshone.

Contemporary Information

GOVERNMENT/RESERVATIONS   The Yakima Reservation and Trust Lands (1859) are located in Klikitat, Lewis, and Yakima Counties, Washington. They contain roughly 1.4 million acres. The 1990 Indian population was 6,296, of a total population of well over 27,000. The Yakima Nation is governed by a 14-member elected tribal council of both sexes.

Yakima Indians are also members of the Columbia River Indians, who live primarily in Priest Rapids, Cooks Landing, Billieville, and Georgeville, Washington; in Celilo, Oregon; and in non-Indian communities. The Council of Columbia River Chiefs meets in Celilo, Oregon. The community at Priest Rapids is directly descended from that of Smohalla, a founder of the Dreamer or Longhouse religion.

ECONOMY   Timber is the Yakima Nation's main income producer; its forest products industry includes a furniture manufacturing plant. The nation maintains extensive range and farmland. However, 80 percent of irrigated land remains leased by non-Indians. The Wapato Project provides the Indians with control over their own water. The tribe has spent over $50 million to purchase former lands.

The Yakima-Klickitat Fish Production Project, a cooperative effort between the Yakima Nation and Washington State, is a major fishery restoration/conservation venture. An industrial park contains Indian and non-Indian industries. The Yakima Land Enterprise operates fruit orchards and stands and a recreational vehicle park. Other employment is provided by the government and the nation as well as by small business enterprises. Still, unemployment fluctuates between about 30 and 60 percent, and up to 75 percent of the people live below the poverty level.

LEGAL STATUS   The Confederated Tribes and Bands of the Yakima Indian Nation is a federally recognized tribal entity. The Columbia River Indians are not federally recognized. Lawsuits over water use from the Yakima River system are pending.

DAILY LIFE   Many people follow the Longhouse (Seven Drums) religion as well as sweat house customs and first foods feasts. The four reservations longhouses serve as the locus of Indian identity and are used for ceremonial occasions. Longhouse families throughout the Plateau region are linked together, mostly through marriage. The Indian Shaker religion is also active on the reservation, as are several Christian churches.

Yakimas maintain many aspects of traditional culture, including family customs, service, and leadership. Although most live in nuclear families, elders remain of key importance to Yakima society. The language is alive and well, especially as part of religious ceremonies and among more traditional people. Adults and children may take classes to strengthen their native language skills. Yakima basketry is still an important art and craft.

The Yakima Reservation boasts a huge, full-service tribal cultural center, museum, and restaurant in addition to two community centers and an elders' retirement center. There is an emphasis on education, with the tribe providing incentives such as scholarships and summer programs. Children attend public school on the reservation. The reservation also sponsors a tribally run school; a private, accredited, four-year liberal arts college; tribal newspapers; and a radio station. It hosts an annual all-Indian rodeo, a powwow, a huckleberry festival, and several basketball tournaments. In 1972, the government restored about 22,000 acres of land to the Yakima Nation, including the sacred Pahto (Mt. Adams).

CHAPTER SIX

The Great Plains

Great Plains

Indians living on the Great Plains shared both a physical environment and, to a large degree, a lifestyle. Their natural resources changed relatively little from thousands of years ago until the late nineteenth century, when the great buffalo herds were destroyed. Wanton elimination of the roughly 30 million buffalo, in addition to millions more deer, antelope, and other game, brought an end to the Plains lifestyle as well, centered as it was, particularly after the various bands and tribes acquired horses, around the great, shaggy beasts.

The Great Plains is generally defined as a region of about 1.5 million square miles between the Mississippi River and the Rocky Mountains and from central Alberta and Saskatchewan to central Texas. The region's greatest river is the Missouri, which is fed by tributary rivers and streams originating in the Rocky Mountains. The lower area between the Mississippi and roughly 100 degrees longitude constitutes prairie rather than true high plains, which in the west may range up to a mile or more in altitude. For comparative cultural purposes, however, the prairie region is usually discussed as part of the Great Plains.

Climatologically, the high plains is a relatively dry region—the average 15 inches of annual rainfall did not permit native agriculture as did the better-watered and more humid prairie. The plains' generally flat terrain allows frigid polar air to enter the region in winter, whereas summers are often stiflingly hot. Dramatic weather events, from tornadoes and severe thunderstorms to blizzards, are regular occurrences. Grasses covered the region, shorter in the west and longer and more lush in the prairie.

In addition to grasses, cactus and sage grow in the western plains. Stands of trees, often willow, oak, box elder, and cottonwood, are found mostly in the river valleys. Scrub cedar and juniper dot prominent features like mesas and cliffs, whereas deciduous and coniferous trees grow in the lower Rockies. A number

of wild vegetable plants and fruits also grew in the region.

The horse, which came from the Spanish settlements in the south and west, represented a foreign influence on Indians of the Great Plains. Other influences, such as guns, soon followed, and non-native diseases, which rivaled and perhaps exceeded the horse in changing Indian circumstances, stalked the people from the sixteenth century on. Thus non-Indian influences were indispensable to the "classic" phase of Plains Indian culture, which lasted for about 100 to 250 years. Despite heroic resistance, however, by the late nineteenth century that culture—and more—was gone. Yet, like many other Indians, descendants of the prehistoric inhabitants of the Great Plains are determined to survive and prosper as Native Americans in twenty-first-century America.

The first bands of hunter-gatherers moved onto the Great Plains perhaps 40,000 years ago. About 10,000 years ago, as the last ice sheets melted and the Plains became drier, grass began to cover the region. Ancient species such as the horse, camel, mammoth, and bison disappeared and were gradually replaced by smaller bison from Mexico. Hunters found and killed these animals in accustomed watering places, but they were not yet able to pursue them freely across the vast expanse of the Plains.

Early prehistoric people stored wild fruits and vegetables in underground caches, and some people began to grow a few crops. Vast networks that focused on the exchange of goods and complex religious practices operated on the Plains during the first millennium, centered in the Ohio Valley Adena-Hopewell culture. But as the region became ever drier and less hospitable, the nomadic bands slowly followed the game and the water eastward until, by perhaps 1200, the Plains were virtually empty of human habitation.

Shortly after this period, however, a moderation in weather conditions combined with severe drought in the Southwest led to the gradual repopulation of the Plains. The people were drawn in part by the presence of buffalo and other game and, at least in the beginning, by the possibility of settlement without conquest. Caddoan tribes in east Texas, such as the Pawnee, may have been among the first to reenter the Plains. Shortly thereafter, Athapaskan bands from northern Canada began migrating southward along the eastern Rockies.

With the exception of the Kiowa and Comanche, the Shoshonean-speaking peoples remained on the western fringes of the Plains in the seventeenth century. Some of the agricultural Siouan peoples, motivated partly by aggressive Iroquois expansion and the dynamics of the French fur trade, migrated west from the Ohio Valley to the Mississippi and Missouri Valley regions, reaching the high plains in successive waves between the sixteenth and the nineteenth centuries. Late in the 1700s they composed about half of the total population of the Great Plains. Finally, Algonquian-speaking Indians such as the Cheyennes and Blackfeet arrived from the east between the sixteenth and eighteenth centuries.

Before the horse transformed life on the Plains, dogs pulled the travois. Buffalo were generally killed by driving them over cliffs or surrounding them on foot and shooting into the confused mass of animals. Even later, buffalo and other animals might be killed in this way or, especially in winter, by individual stalking.

With the arrival of the horse, generally in the late seventeenth to mid–eighteenth century, "classic" Plains Indian culture began to come into its own. Horses allowed the people to acquire more food by traveling farther and faster after buffalo. Horse-drawn travois also increased overall mobility and thus people's ability to follow the herds. Plains Indians soon became among the most skilled horsemen the world has ever seen. At their best, using only a modified halter, they could ride low enough over a horse's flanks both to shield themselves while shooting their own arrows under the horse's neck and to pick up fallen comrades on the fly. They also rode expertly in the midst of thundering buffalo herds.

At that time, there were three types of Indian groups on the Plains. Those like the Blackfeet had no agricultural traditions. Those like the Teton Dakota (Lakota) traded a farming life for that of the nomad, and those like the Mandan and the southern Siouans continued to grow crops while also hunting buffalo and other game.

The nomadic tribes generally lived in conical tipis that were relatively lightweight, easily manufactured from products of the hunt, and portable. Women sewed together between 6 and 18 buffalo skins and stretched them over a frame of poles. Tipis were about 14 feet high and about 14 feet in diameter on the ground and held on average between five and eight people. An adjustable smoke hole at the top kept the tipi free of smoke and well ventilated. The unfastened, east-facing seam at the front was the door. The bottom could be staked or weighted down or rolled up for increased air circulation.

Sacred places that mirrored the cosmos, tipis contained an interior stone altar for burning incense during prayers. In winter, they were insulated with pelts added to the walls. Since the wind most often blew from the west, tipis were also slanted slightly to the east to decrease overall wind pressure. Decorations might represent war exploits or visions.

People living in permanent or semipermanent villages also used tipis on the hunt but otherwise lived in square or rectangular (later circular) earth lodges holding up to 40 or more people. They depended to a greater or lesser degree on corn, beans, squash, and sunflowers, and some also grew tobacco. Among these people, scattered settlements gave way in time to more consolidated villages, located on high bluffs overlooking river valleys. These villages were often fortified by ditches and stockades. Both nomads and farmers ate large and small game such as buffalo, deer, elk, antelope, prairie chickens, and badgers, and most ate dogs, especially on special occasions. Some fished, and all gathered various wild nuts, fruits, and vegetables such as wild turnips and onions, gooseberries, and chokecherries.

Buffalo meat was eaten fresh or cut into strips, dried, and stored. Pemmican, consisting of cooked meat, fat, and berries, kept for months at least. Assuming that the buffalo herds were found during the autumn hunt, starvation was rarely a problem. Once the winter hit with its dangerous and unpredictable weather, the camp usually remained in a sheltered lowland location for up to five months. Horses could easily survive the winter on cottonwood bark.

Women made the clothing, generally from deer, mountain sheep, and/or buffalo skin. Tanning was an arduous process that consisted of stretching, scraping, treating (with a mixture of brains, fat, and other items), and soaking. Women wore a two-piece dress, with optional sleeves. For warmth, they also wore short leggings, moccasins, and buffalo robes. Men wore breechclouts and moccasins in warm weather, with a deerskin shirt, leggings, and a buffalo-hide robe in winter. Garments decorated with fringe and quillwork might reflect war honors. Plains Indians generally wore personal ornamentation such as necklaces and earrings made from bone, shell, hair, or feathers, as well as tattoos.

In addition to food, clothing, and shelter, the buffalo provided items such as bull-boats, parfleches, and other containers (hides and stomach); awls, hoes, and other tools (bones); rattles (hoof); bowstrings and thread (sinew); ropes and belts (hair); altars (skull); and spoons and cups (horn). The dried droppings even made excellent fuel. Other material items included saddles (although most people rode bareback) and riding gear, fish baskets and weirs, and elk antler or bone scrapers for tanning hides. Stone was also used as a raw material, particularly in earlier days. Plains Indians generally used two kinds of bow, a very fine one for buffalo hunting, and one for other purposes.

Plains Indians were noted for a wide-ranging artistic tradition. Ancient artifacts include birdstones and other items as early as 3000 B.C.E. and carved stone pipes as early as 700 C.E. More settled groups made pottery. Clothing and other items was decorated with porcupine-quill embroidery and, later, beadwork; both men and women painted leather goods such as tipis and parfleches.

For most Plains Indians, the circle was a sacred shape, the symbol of the interconnectedness of the universe. The sacred pipe, its bowl a circle, might be the property of one individual or the entire tribe. The use of a pipe in any kind of ceremony or agreement meant that an occasion was sacred and any associated vows or promises could not be broken. Sun and sky were foremost among a group of sacred natural beings and spirits known as *Wakan Tanka*, the Great Mystery.

Like many other Native Americans, Plains Indians also held vision quests, usually in a remote location and accompanied by personal deprivation. They took place only after purification in a sweat lodge and often at pivotal times, such as puberty or before war. Visions—also obtainable in dreams—were held to be direct communication with the world of sacred forces, which was considered ubiquitous. If successful, the vision quest resulted in the adoption of a guardian spirit.

Through their spirits, people received "medicine," or power, to be used in a variety of ways. Medicine often included certain behaviors, songs, and dances as well as the contents of a sacred bundle. Just as visions could benefit both individuals and the tribe as a whole, so also were medicine bundles the property of individuals or the entire tribe. Medicine bundles often conferred the power and the right to conduct a ceremony. They could be sold and the ceremonial rights transferred accordingly.

Although agricultural tribes conducted numerous ceremonies related to growing crops, the Sun Dance was the classic high plains Indian ceremony of the historic period. It originated during the early eighteenth century, although its antecedents predate that time. As the most important ceremony of the year, its purpose was to renew both nature and the well-being of the tribe. The dance was held in summer, when the various bands gathered for the communal buffalo hunt. During that period, the bands set up camp in a great circle, in which each band had a definite place and carefully proscribed behaviors. It was a time of socializing, courting, game playing, and generally reestablishing tribal unity.

Sponsored by a person seeking supernatural assistance, and led by a shaman, the Sun Dance itself lasted 12 days. Bands approached the Sun Dance circle over a four-day period. The four days following arrival of the bands was a time of ritual preparation. Marshals, children who would get their ears pierced, virginal female attendants, and people who obtained and prepared the Sacred Tree were all selected. This was a time of feasting and partying.

The ceremony itself took place over the following four days. It included mock battles with spirits, the "capture" and raising of the sacred tree and the mounting on it of a rawhide buffalo effigy, the erection of the sacred lodge, and sacred dancing and singing that included long periods of staring at the sun. As part of the ceremony, some tribes, such as the Teton Dakota, employed methods of self-torture, in which some participants implanted skewers in their chests or backs and danced until they ripped from the flesh. Other participants dragged buffalo skulls attached to skewers embedded in their chests around the field until the skewers ripped out. The purpose of the self-torture was to bring about visions for personal and tribal success.

Shamans, who were men and women possessing particularly powerful medicine, were intermediaries between the sacred and profane worlds. As such, they cured disease, helped people interpret their personal visions, and directed the hunt, since their powers were believed to influence both the herds and the hunters' safety. In addition, some enjoyed varying degrees of political power. Shamanic priests, who received special training, played a key role in ceremonies.

With the necessities of life freely available, trade was not as well developed on the Plains as it was in some regions. Still, the development of a universal sign language greatly facilitated the exchange of goods, ideas, and information. Articles of the hunt were often exchanged for agricultural goods. Parfleches were a common item of trade, and even items from as far away as the Pacific Ocean (dentalium shells), the Great Lakes (copper), and the Gulf Coast (shells) were exchanged on the Plains. Two early trade centers were located at the Mandan and Arikara villages. After the seventeenth century, most trade items originated with non-natives. Chief among these (in addition to horses) were metal goods, guns, cloth, and beads.

Among the nomadic tribes especially, daring and bravery, particularly during the hunt and in raiding and war, were among the most important virtues. Military leadership was provided by a young man seeking glory. Plains Indian fighting was no less deadly than war ever is, yet warriors generally considered that the highest form of bravery was not killing an enemy but touching him, stealing his horse in a particularly daring way, or some other difficult and brave accomplishment. This custom was called counting coup, or war honors. Among most Plains tribes scalping, a custom that may have originated with the Spanish, did not merit a high war honor. Its importance lay primarily in representing the spiritual death of the victim.

War honors, which had to be publicly announced and accepted, were reflected in various articles of dress, such as feathers and types of shirt fringe. Eagle feathers symbolized the highest war honors. Warbonnets were worn only in parade, as a dress costume, with other highly decorated items. Shields, sacred by virtue of their designs, were normally kept covered.

The fundamental unit of Plains Indian society was the extended family. Bands or villages of variable constituency, composed of up to several hundred people of related families, formed the tribe. Some mostly semisedentary tribes also recognized clans and/or dual divisions. Bands only came together as a tribe in summer, when they united under a much more centralized political leadership to hunt, socialize, trade, raid, make war, and perform religious ceremonies. During these times, the camp police, composed of elite warrior societies, kept order and punished offenders, especially during the hunt. Among the nomadic peoples, bands often separated back into constituent families in winter.

Band and kin group chiefs, generally older men, had to have led lives characterized by generosity, bravery, proven ability in the hunt and in war, spiritual accomplishment, and honorable actions in every sphere. The position was honorific rather than authoritative. That is, the chief's authority stemmed from his stature and lasted only as long as he could command respect. Each band often contained more than one chief. Among some semisedentary tribes the chieftainship had hereditary elements. Bands were also led by a council of older men.

Men's, women's, and children's cultural or military societies had their own particular ceremonies, songs, insignias, dances, and medicine bundles. Open societies, generally age graded, could be entered by anyone of the proper age who could purchase admission. Closed societies could only be entered by invitation. Societies were associated with different levels of status. Outside of the societies, status, which was generally fairly fluid on the Plains, might also be obtained by being a shaman or a berdache. In the case of semisedentary groups, status also had a hereditary component.

Entry into womanhood was marked by isolation for several days while performing typical female work. A girl might acquire a vision during this time. If her parents could afford it, a feast and the distribution of gifts followed her seclusion. There were generally no formal puberty ceremonies for boys. A series of events, such as a boy's first successful buffalo hunt, first war party, and certainly first vision quest, marked his passage to manhood. Marriages could be arranged as a union between families, but many were romantic, and many stories attest to sweet flute serenades and secret rendezvous.

Certain near relatives, such as other-sex siblings and in-laws, were generally avoided out of respect. In Plains Indian society there was always an obligation to provide for relatives; the extended family might number 30 people, each working to ensure the prosperity of the rest. Grandparents played a major role in culture transmittal and in day-to-day child rearing. Children were considered a blessing and were generally raised in what today might be considered a permissive manner. With the exception of the camp and hunt police, social order was generally maintained by peer pressure rather than any kind of systematic punishment. Early prehistoric traditions, particularly in the Ohio Valley, include mound burial. In later times, the dead were often buried in tree scaffolds or in the ground.

Even as the horse had transformed Plains Indian life, so disease epidemics—measles, influenza, and smallpox—decimated many Indian populations before the non-natives even arrived, thus setting up the "empty wilderness" that the latter came to covet. Beginning in the mid–nineteenth century, the presence of railroads and wagon trains disrupted the buffalo herds. Pioneers fought even friendly Indians. Their world under general attack, many of the warring tribes began to unite against the common enemy. Several major councils, particularly those at Fort Laramie in 1851 and 1868, produced treaties designed to strike a balance between Indian needs and non-native desires.

Later-nineteenth-century Plains Indian warfare retained its central role in ritual and status acquisition, but it also became a quest for survival and as such more brutal. Facing possible destruction and possessing superior horses and knowledge of the terrain, the Indians were successful at first. Ultimately, however, they were defeated by the sheer numbers of their opponents combined with their superior firepower.

The final "battle" took place on December 15, 1890, when U.S. soldiers wiped out up to 300 Indians, mostly women and children, at Wounded Knee, South Dakota. The massacre took place against the backdrop of the Ghost Dance, a new Indian religion that promised a return to a prewhite Indian paradise. The government had feared it could reignite widespread military resistance.

By 1900, non-Indians had deliberately and systematically destroyed the great buffalo herds. They had confined Plains Indians to reservations and taken most of their land. The 1877 Dawes Severalty Act was another major land-grab scheme as well as a frontal attack against the tribal way of life. The act allotted tribal land to individuals, the "surplus" (91 million acres total in the United States) to be opened to nonnative purchase. Later, thousands of Indians lost their allotments through tax default.

Through missionaries, the government began a full-scale assault on Indian culture. Their means of subsistence gone and their traditional leaders killed or undermined, Plains Indians went into a long period of extreme transition. Their situation became characterized by dependence and poverty. In Canada, Plains Indians were forced to take up farming but were denied decent land, land ownership, credit, and even, without the permission of the government bureaucracy, the right to sell their produce.

Plains Indians in the United States were under similar pressures and faced similar difficulties. Furthermore, at least among the former nomads, agriculture was for a long time considered socially unacceptable. Plains Indians were individualists, but their ethic of generosity frustrated the efforts of government officials determined to make them more selfish. Toward this end, the government began removing Indian children, often by force, from the family environment and shipping them to violent, culture-killing boarding schools. Early in the twentieth century, the Peyote religion (Native American Church), with its origins in Mexico, became popular among several Plains Indian groups.

In the 1930s, the Dawes Act was superseded by the Wheeler-Howard Act, also known as the Indian Reorganization Act (IRA). Among other provisions, the IRA allowed Indians to set up constitutional governments. Although allowing Indians to deal government-to-government with the United States, the act also further undermined the traditional political structure. In the 1950s, the federal "termination" policy was designed to abrogate all treaties unilaterally.

Also in the 1950s, the government again got into the business of forcibly relocating Indians, this time from reservations to urban centers. Ostensibly done in order to enhance economic opportunity, the result of this policy was the alienation of large numbers of Indians in urban ghettos and their permanent loss to the reservation community.

Policies of the "self-determination" era of the 1960s and 1970s, combined with Great Society antipoverty programs, helped Plains Indians begin to pull away from chronic poverty. This era also saw renewed Indian activism. The American Indian Movement (AIM) encouraged Indians to throw off internal corruption while holding the federal government to its trust obligations. Several tribal colleges were begun. However, renewed funding cutbacks in the 1980s and 1990s negated some of these gains. Despite the rise of casino gambling on several reservations, poverty continues to stalk many Plains Indian communities. Most Indian reservations suffer from a lack of capital, and, with few exceptions, economic development remains an elusive goal.

Although Plains Indians have assimilated in varying degrees to mainstream society, many continue to lead lives deeply rooted in their cultural and spiritual traditions. Reservation life, although economically difficult, provides a vital focus for these activities. Many native Plains languages are in regular use. The Sun Dance, once banned with other "heathen" ceremonies, has reemerged in a modified version. Giveaways, traditional healing and other ceremonies, and art, craft, and aesthetic traditions remain very much alive and vital. The refusal of some tribes to sell the Black Hills for any price (the current offer is over $200 million) symbolizes the unyielding regard for and the enduring place of their heritage in the lives of Plains Indians today.

Alabama-Coushatta
See Alabama (Chapter 7)

Apache, Plains
Plains Apache (U `pa ch ē) have also been known to non-natives as Kiowa Apaches, Prairie Apaches, Plains Lipans, and possibly Catakas, Palomas, Wetapahatos, and Paducas. Their self-designation is *Na-i-shan Dine,* "Our People." *See also* Kiowa.

LOCATION   In the late eighteenth century the Plains Apache were located along the upper Missouri River. Today, most live near the towns of Apache and Fort Cobb, Oklahoma.

POPULATION   The 1780 population was about 400. That number had declined to about 150 in 1900. By the early 1990s, there were about 1,400 people calling themselves Plains Apaches.

LANGUAGE   Plains Apaches spoke an Athapaskan language.

Historical Information

HISTORY   Tribal tradition notes a northern Plains origin. Ancestors of the historic Plains Apache may have lived in northeastern Wyoming and western South Dakota as early as the twelfth century. They may also have entered the Yellowstone Valley from Canada by 1600. The Kiowa, located just to their west, joined them in the early eighteenth century, having been displaced by the mounted Shoshone.

In the early eighteenth century, the Comanches on the west and the Pawnee on the east forced Apaches living on the central Plains south and southwest. Cut off from their fellow Apacheans around 1720, the people known as Plains Apaches may have joined the Kiowa for protection. Although they functioned effectively as a Kiowa band and were a Plains tribe in all senses, they maintained a separate language and never came under the jurisdiction of the Kiowa Tribal Council.

Kiowas and Kiowa Apaches, pressed by the Crow and the Wind River Shoshone, soon left Yellowstone Valley for the Black Hills, where they remained until about the end of the century. At the same time, some Kiowa moved south while others remained near the Black Hills with the Plains Apache. The northern group finally moved south, under pressure from the Teton Dakota, to join the larger group around 1805 in western Kansas.

Plains Apaches are probably the "Apaches del Norte" named in the historical record as that group of Apaches who arrived in New Mexico by the late eighteenth century. They moved back and forth between New Mexico and the upper Missouri area during the early nineteenth century, serving as trade intermediaries between New Mexico and upper Missouri tribes such as the Mandans and Arikaras.

With the Kiowa, Plains Apaches moved south to the Arkansas River area in the early nineteenth century. In the early 1850s, they were part of an unsuccessful effort of Arkansas River tribes to defeat a number of tribes encroaching from the east. By then they and the Kiowa were spending more time south rather than north of the Arkansas. They settled on the Kiowa-Comanche-Apache Reservation in 1868. In 1901, this reservation was allotted in 160-acre parcels to individual tribal members, with the "surplus" opened to non-native settlement.

RELIGION   With their associated ceremonies, sacred bundles were a focus of Kiowa religious practice. Plains Apaches adopted the Sun Dance in the eighteenth century, although they did not incorporate elements of self-mutilation into the ceremony.

Young men also fasted to produce guardian spirit visions.

GOVERNMENT   From the early eighteenth century on, the Plains Apaches functioned as a band of the Kiowa. As such they had their own peace and war chiefs. They joined the Kiowa as part of their summer camp.

CUSTOMS   From the nineteenth century on, there were four named categories of social rank. The highest was held by those who had attained war honors and were skilled horsemen, generous, and wealthy. Then came those men who met all the preceding criteria except war honors. The third group was people without property. At the bottom were men with neither property nor skills. War captives remained outside this ranking system. In general wealth remained in the family through inheritance.

Corpses were buried or left in a tipi on a hill. Former possessions were given away. Mourners cut their hair and mutilated themselves. A mourning family lived apart from the rest of the group.

DWELLINGS   Women built and owned skin tipis.

DIET   Before the people acquired horses, they hunted some nearby buffalo and ate local roots, berries, seeds, and bulbs. Buffalo became a staple after the mid–eighteenth century.

Men also hunted other large and small game. They did not eat bear or, usually, fish. Women gathered a variety of wild potatoes and other vegetables, fruits, nuts, and berries. Plains Apaches ate dried, pounded acorns and also made them into a drink. Cornmeal and dried fruit were acquired by trade.

KEY TECHNOLOGY   The buffalo and other animals provided the usual material items such as parfleches and other containers. Points for bird arrows came from prickly pear thorns. The cradle board was a bead-covered skin case attached to a V-shaped frame. Women made shallow coiled basketry gambling trays.

TRADE   During the eighteenth century, Plains Apaches traded extensively with the upper Missouri tribes (Mandans, Hidatsas, and Arikaras). There was also regular trade with New Mexico, where they exchanged meat, buffalo hides, and salt for cornmeal and dried fruit. During the nineteenth century they traded Comanche horses to the Osage and other tribes.

NOTABLE ARTS   Calendric skins and beadwork were two important artistic traditions.

TRANSPORTATION   The people acquired horses by the early eighteenth century.

DRESS   Women dressed buffalo, elk, and deer hides to make robes, moccasins, leggings, shirts, breechclouts, skirts, and blouses.

WAR AND WEAPONS   Plains Apaches took part in

the Plains war-and-raiding complex. There were numerous military societies. The tribe was allied with the Crow in the late seventeenth century and with the Comanche beginning around 1790. Enemies in the eighteenth and early nineteenth century included the Dakota, Cheyenne, and Osage.

Contemporary Information

GOVERNMENT/RESERVATIONS Because of their geographical location, contemporary Plains Apaches are sometimes referred to as the Cache Creek Apaches (located near Apache, Oklahoma) and the Washita Apaches (near Fort Cobb, Oklahoma). They organized a tribal government in the 1970s. The tribal administrative center is in Anadarko, Oklahoma.

ECONOMY Chronic high unemployment is a function of the lack of local economic opportunity.

LEGAL STATUS The Apache Tribe of Oklahoma is a federally recognized tribal entity.

DAILY LIFE Plains Apaches intermarry at a high rate with Indians of other tribes. Language classes and other educational and social programs are held in the administrative complex; ceremonials are held near Fort Cobb in June and August. The people are known for their extensive collection of traditional music, and their singers, drummers, and dancers are in demand at many tribal powwows. They have produced many excellent artists and craftspeople who work especially in beads, silver, wood, paints, and feathers.

ARAPAHO

Arapaho (U `ra pu h ō), probably from the Pawnee *tirapihu,* "trader," or the Kiowa and Spanish word for "tattered and dirty clothing." "Kanenavish" (various spellings), a term in use around 1800, was a corruption of the French *gens de vache* ("Buffalo People"). The Arapahos originally called themselves *Inuna-ina,* "Our People."

LOCATION The Arapahos probably migrated in the early eighteenth century from the Red River region of present-day Minnesota and North Dakota to the upper Missouri River region. Then, as Northern and Southern Arapaho, they moved in the nineteenth century to Wyoming (along the North Platte River) and eastern Colorado and western Kansas (along the Arkansas River).

POPULATION The total Arapaho population ranged between 3,000 and 5,000 people around 1800. There were about 6,500 Arapahos in 1993.

LANGUAGE Arapaho is an Algonquian language.

Historical Information

HISTORY At least 3,000 years ago the Arapaho, possibly united with the future Gros Ventres and other peoples, probably lived in the western Great Lakes region, where they grew corn and lived in permanent villages. They migrated by the eighteenth century to the upper Missouri River region, acquiring horses about that time.

In the nineteenth century, the groups separated and divided into Northern and Southern Arapaho. The northern branch settled around the North Platte River in Wyoming and the southern branch in the area of Bent's Fort on the Arkansas River in Colorado. The two groups remained in close contact. By this time, the Arapaho had adopted the classic Great Plains culture: They were master horsemen, buffalo hunters, and raiders.

Early Anglo traders found the Arapahos very friendly and disposed to trade. Although fur traders entered the area in the 1730s, they merely observed intertribal trade of items of European manufacture, especially knives and guns but also metal tools and other items. Furs were not an important trade commodity until around the turn of the century. Traders also brought alcohol and disease into the region, both to devastating effect. Still, powerful chiefs like Bear Tooth, favorably disposed to non-Indians, kept the peace in the early nineteenth century.

In 1837 a major war broke out, with the Southern Arapaho and Southern Cheyenne fighting against the Comanche. Peace was established in 1840, largely on Arapaho-Cheyenne terms. However, the opening of the Oregon Trail brought more non-Indians to the Plains and encouraged growing conflict, based on ignorance of Indian customs, land hunger, and race hatred.

Arapahos played a major role in the nineteenth-century wars for the Plains. The northern branch fought along with the Lakota and the southern branch with the Southern Cheyennes and occasionally with the Comanches and Kiowas. Although Arapahos signed the 1851 Fort Laramie Treaty, major gold finds in 1858–1859 caused further frictions between Indians and non-natives. In the 1859 Fort Wise Treaty, Arapahos and Cheyennes agreed to live peacefully in a delineated section of land while retaining subsistence rights throughout their territory.

Despite the existence of the treaty, in 1864 a group of Southern Arapaho and Cheyennes, mostly women and children, were attacked, massacred, and mutilated by U.S. Army troops at Sand Creek, Colorado, as part of a successful campaign to drive all Indians out of Colorado. Cut off from the rich Colorado buffalo herds and under further pressure from the United States, the Cheyennes and Arapahos in 1867 signed the Medicine Lodge Treaty, under which they formally ceded their lands north of the Arkansas River and were placed on a reservation in the Indian Territory (Oklahoma). Little Raven, a skilled orator and diplomat, represented his people in these negotiations.

By the terms of the Fort Laramie Treaty (1868), the Northern Arapaho were supposed to settle with the Lakota on the Pine Ridge Reservation in South Dakota. Holding out for their own reservation, the Northern Arapaho remained in Wyoming, refusing also to settle with the Southern Arapaho in the Indian Territory. They finally (1878) agreed to become part of the Eastern Shoshones' Wind River Reservation.

The Arapaho, especially those on the Wind River Reservation, adopted the Ghost Dance religion in the late 1880s. By this time the enormous buffalo herds had been virtually wiped out. In 1890, Arapahos and Southern Cheyennes agreed to exchange their 3.5-million-acre reservation for allotments of 160 acres each. The group formally organized in 1937 as the Cheyenne-Arapaho Tribe.

RELIGION Medicine bundles, containing various sacred objects, were said to have magical powers. An individual knew which objects to obtain for the bundle through knowledge gained in dreams or the (adult) vision quest. Medicine men (shamans or priests) used their bundles in ceremonies; other bundles belonged to secret societies or to the whole tribe.

A flat pipe some two feet long, wrapped in a bundle, was the most sacred object for the tribe. Tobacco was smoked in it only as part of the most sacred ceremonies and occasions. The lead rider carried it during a move.

In the eighteenth century, the annual Sun Dance became the most important single ceremony. Its purpose was the renewal of nature and tribal prosperity. Although it was in part a test of endurance, the Arapaho, unlike other tribes, did not include extreme acts of self-torture. Some Arapahos adopted the Peyote religion in the 1890s.

GOVERNMENT Each of four bands had a chief, but there was no principal chief.

CUSTOMS Bands wintered separately, along streams, and came together in summer to hunt buffalo and celebrate ceremonies. Although menstruating women were avoided, and the subject was taboo, there was no formal girls' puberty ceremony or menstrual seclusion. Men could marry more than one woman. Marriage was generally matrilocal. Children were generally nursed for four years. Blood relative and in-law taboos were strict. Extended family members, such as uncles and aunts, had specific responsibilities concerning their nieces and nephews.

Arapahos played the hoop-and-pole game and the cup-and-ball game and held athletic contests. Curing techniques included sweating in the sweat lodge and fumigation with roots, twigs, or herbs. There was one women's society in addition to the series of men's societies (see "War and Weapons"). The dead lay in state in fine clothing before being removed by horse and buried in a nearby hill. A favorite horse was killed. Mourners cut their hair, wore old clothes, and cut their arms and legs.

DWELLINGS At least since the nineteenth century, women made buffalo-skin tipis. Willow-framed beds covered with skins lined the interior walls. There were no permanent villages, as the tribe migrated with the herds.

DIET Buffalo had become a staple by the nineteenth century. Men also hunted elk, antelope, deer, and small animals. Meat was boiled in a hole in the ground filled with water and hot rocks. To preserve it for winter, women dried it and sometimes mixed it with fat and chokecherries to make pemmican. They also gathered wild mountain fruits, roots, berries, and tobacco.

KEY TECHNOLOGY Prehistoric Arapahos may have made ceramics. Most raw materials came from the buffalo or other animals. They carved items such as bowls from wood, some of which had artistic and/or religious significance. They smoked black stone pipes and made shallow basketry trays.

TRADE Mandan villages along the Knife River (North Dakota) were a primary regional trading center. By the early nineteenth century the Arapaho traded buffalo robes with Mexicans and Americans for items not provided by the buffalo. They also served as middlemen in trade between northern and southern Plains Indians.

NOTABLE ARTS Women decorated clothing, tipis, and other items with beautiful porcupine-quill embroidery and painting. Designs often included legends and spiritual beings. Designs, which often represented natural and celestial features, included diamonds with appendages such as forked trees (triangles atop a line).

TRANSPORTATION The Arapaho probably acquired horses in the early eighteenth century. Babies were carried on the back in a U-shaped, wood-framed buckskin cradle board. The people used oval snowshoes in winter.

DRESS Historic Arapaho dress was similar to that of other high plains tribes.

WAR AND WEAPONS Eight military societies were graded according to age. One, the Crazy Dog Society, was noted for its extreme bravery and valor. Traditional enemies included the Shoshones, Utes, Pawnees, Crows, Lakota, Comanche, and Kiowa. The latter three tribes had become allies, with the Southern Cheyenne, by the 1840s.

Counting coup, or touching the enemy with the hand or a stick, was highly prestigious, much more so than killing an enemy. Up to four people could count coup, in descending order of prestige, on the same enemy.

Contemporary Information

GOVERNMENT/RESERVATIONS The Wind River Reservation (1863; Shoshone and Arapaho tribes), Fremont and Hot Springs Counties, Wyoming, contains 2,268,008 acres. The 1990 Indian population was 5,674. Both tribes have business councils.

Roughly 3,000 (1993) Southern Arapahos live in western Oklahoma. They own no tribal land and live on the last of their allotments.

ECONOMY Major economic activities at Wind River are ranching and crafts. There are some jobs in the school district and within the tribal government. There are also a number of small businesses. Some people regularly hunt and fish, and there is income from mineral leases. Un- and underemployment is chronically high (up to 80 percent).

The unemployment rate for Southern Arapahos and Southern Cheyennes in Oklahoma hovers around 70 percent (1993). They operate a smoke shop and a casino.

LEGAL STATUS The Arapaho Tribe of the Wind River Reservation and the Cheyenne-Arapaho Tribe of Oklahoma are federally recognized tribal entities.

DAILY LIFE A Northern Arapaho family is keeper of the Scared Pipe, which remains the symbol of the tribe. Quasi-traditional religion remains important. The Sun Dance, held in July, has been explicitly Christianized and is now intertribal. Peyotism and sweat lodge ceremonies are popular. Giveaways, formerly related to public coup counting, are now associated with other occasions. Control of water rights has become an issue on the reservation.

High rates of substance abuse and suicide plague the reservation; related accidents have replaced disease as a primary killer. Outmigration remains a problem. Women have more freedom as well as political and social power, obtained in part through their participation in certain musical ceremonies. Wyoming Indian High School is Arapaho dominated; most Shoshone attend off-reservation public high schools. Traditional games such as the hand game, with its associated gambling, remain popular, especially at powwows.

Only a few people, mostly Southern Arapahos, still speak the language, despite the implementation of language programs at Wind River. There is still contact, particularly for ceremonies, between the northern and southern branches of the Arapaho tribe. Housing, most of which consists of modern "bungalows," is considered generally inadequate at Wind River. Canvas tipis are used for ceremonial purposes.

Arikara

Arikara (U `ri ku ru), "horn," referring to a traditional hairstyle. Their self-designation is *Tanish*, "Original People." In the historic period they were culturally similar to the Mandans.

LOCATION Arikaras migrated from the central Plains into central South Dakota in the seventeenth and eighteenth centuries. Today most live in western North Dakota.

POPULATION The late-eighteenth-century Arikara population was approximately 3,000–4,000. In the early 1990s, enrollment in the Three Affiliated Tribes was about 6,000 people.

LANGUAGE Arikara is a Caddoan language.

Historical Information

HISTORY Around the beginning of the seventeenth century, the Arikara separated from the Skidi Pawnee in Nebraska and moved north along the Missouri River, spreading knowledge of agriculture along the way. They arrived in the Dakotas in the late eighteenth century.

Contact with French traders was established in the 1730s. During the early to mid–eighteenth century they acquired horses and ranged even farther west, to eastern Montana, to hunt buffalo. In the 1780s the people suffered a smallpox epidemic but continued to live relatively well, despite harassment by Teton, Dakota, and other bands.

As a result of wars with the United States, the Arikara retreated south to join their Pawnee relatives on the Loup River in Nebraska from the early 1820s through about 1835. A devastating smallpox epidemic in 1837 brought them to the verge of extinction. About 1845, the weakened Arikara moved farther north and occupied land formerly under Mandan control (the latter having recently moved up the Missouri River with the Hidatsa).

In 1862, the Arikara also moved up the Missouri to the Mandan/Hidatsa village of Like-a-Fishhook and joined politically with those two tribes. Like-a-Fishhook Village was a center of trade and commerce at that time. The Fort Laramie Treaty of 1851 recognized tribal holdings of more than 12 million acres.

In 1870, the United States established the eight-million-acre Fort Berthold Reservation for the tribes. This land was reduced, mostly by allotment, to about one million acres during the 1880s. By this time, Like-a-Fishhook had been abandoned, the people scattering to form communities along the Missouri River. The Arikara lived in Nishu and Elbowwoods, on the east side of the river.

In the 1950s, against the tribes' vehement opposition, the United States built the Garrison Dam on the Missouri. The resulting Lake Sakakawea covered much of their land, farms, and homes. This event destroyed the tribes' economic base and permanently damaged their social structure.

RELIGION The Arikara believed in a supreme deity who shared power with four lesser gods. Most religious festivals were associated with corn, which they originally acquired from the south and southwest. Medicine men possessed particularly fine, generations-old ears of corn, within which resided the spirit of "mother corn."

Religious activity included fasting, acquiring visions, and the possession and use of personal sacred bundles. Certain religious positions, such as the priesthood and the keeper of the sacred tribal medicine bundles, were hereditary within families.

GOVERNMENT Political centralization was weak among the Arikara. Villages combined in a loose confederation of named bands. Village chiefs made up the band council, which assisted the head chief.

CUSTOMS The Arikara were excellent swimmers; hauling trees out of the Missouri River provided them with firewood in an area short of trees. The game of shinny was particularly popular, as were feats of dexterity, skill, and magic. The people enjoyed building toys and whistles for and otherwise entertaining their children.

Families owned farms and dogs as well as dwellings. There were a number of mens' societies, focused on the hunt and on keeping order, as well as women's societies. Men hunted and provided protection; women were in charge of vegetable foods (garden plots), preparing hides for clothing as well as baskets and pottery, and caring for the lodge. Descent was matrilineal and residence was matrilocal. Social rank was hereditary to a significant degree. The dead were buried sitting, wrapped in skins, their faces painted red. A year of mourning followed a death.

DWELLINGS Arikaras located their villages on bluffs over the Missouri River. Later villages were strongly reinforced by wooden stockades and ditches. Partially excavated earth lodges measured about 40 feet in diameter and held two or more extended families. A wooden framework supported woven willow branches and grass covered with earth. A lodge might last up to 20 years. A larger structure, around which residential lodges were grouped, served as the medicine or ceremonial lodge. Skin tipis served as temporary field dwellings.

DIET Women grew corn (small, highly nutritious ears), squash, beans, and sunflowers, fertilizing their crops and rotating their fields. They also cultivated tobacco. Men hunted buffalo and other large and small game. They also fished and gathered berries and other plants.

KEY TECHNOLOGY Material items included wil-
low weirs (fish traps); farm equipment, weapons, and utensils from buffalo parts; stone mortars; pottery cooking vessels; a variety of baskets; and leather pouches and other containers.

TRADE Women traded surplus crops to the Cheyenne, Kiowa, Lakota, and other groups for buffalo and other animal products. Later they traded with the French for European-made products. There was also some cultural and material exchange between the Arikara and the Mandan and the Hidatsa.

NOTABLE ARTS Pottery and basketry were traditional arts.

TRANSPORTATION People used boats constructed of buffalo hide stretched over a willow frame (bull-boats) to cross the Missouri. They also wore snowshoes and used dogs and later (mid–eighteenth century) horses to pull travois.

DRESS Women made blankets, robes, and moccasins of buffalo hide. They also made clothing of white weasel or ermine skin and made winter turbans of various animal skins.

WAR AND WEAPONS The Arikara were alternately friendly and at war with the Mandans and Hidatsas. After about the late eighteenth century, the Lakota fought the Arikaras, cutting off both trading parties and buffalo hunters. Weapons included various flint projectiles and buffalo-hide shields.

Contemporary Information

GOVERNMENT/RESERVATIONS The Three Affiliated Tribes (Arikara, Hidatsa, Mandan) live on the Fort Berthold Reservation (roughly 900,000 acres in Dunn, McKenzie, McLean, Mercer, Mountrail, and Ward Counties, North Dakota). The 1990 reservation Indian population was 2,999. More than half of the reservation is owned by non-Indians.

ECONOMY Tribal and federal governments are the largest employers. A few people have farms or ranches. The tribe opened a high-stakes casino in 1993. Unemployment remains very high.

LEGAL STATUS The Three Affiliated Tribes is a federally recognized tribal entity.

DAILY LIFE Most Arikaras live on the east side of Lake Sakakawea, near the towns of White Shield and Parshall. Their lifestyle is similar to that of their non-Indian neighbors.

Although politically united, the three tribes continue to maintain separate identities. The annual powwow held by each reservation community has become a focus for tribal activities. War Bonnet dances help maintain an Indian identity. Crafts include quilting and beadwork. Some Arikara practice sweat lodge ceremonies and are members of the Native American Church. Most consider themselves Christians.

Only elders speak the native language, despite attempts to institute regular language classes. The community operates several reservation schools, and it publishes the *Mandan, Hidatsa, and Arikara Times.* There is a museum at New Town.

Assiniboine

Assiniboine (U `sin u boin), "those who cook with stones" (Algonquian). Canadian Assiniboines are also known as Stoneys. Their traditional self-designation is unknown. *See also* Nakota.

LOCATION The Siouan people probably originated in the lower Mississippi Valley and moved north through Ohio and into the Lake Superior region (northern Minnesota/southwestern Ontario). In the seventeenth century, the Assiniboine lived near Lake Winnipeg. From the eighteenth century on they have lived in present-day Montana and Saskatchewan.

POPULATION The seventeenth-century population was roughly 10,000 people. In the 1990s about 8,000 Assiniboines, Gros Ventres, and Yanktonais lived on the two Montana reservations. There is also a Stoney population on Canadian reserves.

LANGUAGE Assiniboines/Yanktonais speak the Nakota dialect of Dakota, a Siouan language.

Historical Information

HISTORY Assiniboines separated from the northern Yanktonai by perhaps the late sixteenth century, moving north from the Ohio Valley through Wisconsin and Minnesota, along the edge of the Woodlands into southern and southwestern Ontario. They became involved in the French fur trade in the early seventeenth century.

By later in that century they had made peace with the Plains Cree, joining them near Lake Winnipeg, and were trading with Hudson's Bay Company posts there. Assiniboines ranged over an extremely wide territory during that period, from near the Arctic Circle to the upper Missouri River and from James Bay to the Rocky Mountains. When trade with the Hudson's Bay Company declined, in the later eighteenth century, the Assiniboine became fully nomadic, continuing the westward migration and hunting around the Saskatchewan and Assiniboine Rivers and across much of the northern Plains.

Major smallpox epidemics struck the people in 1780 and 1836, and alcohol and venereal disease also took a heavy toll. During that period, the Assiniboine divided into a lower and an upper division. Decimation of the buffalo herds as well as their own sharp population decline forced them to sign the 1851 Fort Laramie Treaty, limiting Assiniboine lands to parcels in western Montana.

Some Assiniboines worked as scouts for U.S. and Canadian armies in their Indian wars. In 1887, upper division Assiniboines (and the Gros Ventres) were confined to the new Fort Belknap Reservation; Fort Peck, which they shared with the Yanktonai, was created in 1873. Several hundred Assiniboine died of starvation at Fort Peck in 1883–1884.

Meanwhile, in Canada, unregulated whiskey sales were taking a great toll on Indian people. In 1877, as a result of national police intervention in the whiskey trade, the Stoneys and some other tribes signed Treaty Number 7, exchanging their traditional territory for reserves in Alberta and Saskatchewan, although some groups attempted to maintain their autonomy. Much of the reserve land was alienated in the early twentieth century owing to allotting and permitting of non-Indian homesteads.

RELIGION Male and female specialists provided religious leadership. Ceremonial implements and techniques included rattles, chants, charms, and songs. In the eighteenth century, the annual Sun Dance became the people's most important religious ceremony, although the custom of self-torture was not generally present.

Wakonda was worshiped as a primary deity, although the Assiniboine also recognized natural phenomena such as sun and thunder. Sweat lodge purification was an important religious practice. Spirit visions could be obtained through quests or in dreams. Some ceremonies featured masked clowns.

GOVERNMENT The Assiniboine were composed of up to 30 bands, each with its own chief. The chieftainship was based on leadership skills and personal contacts rather than heredity. Each band also had a council, whose decisions were enforced by the *akitcita*, or camp police.

CUSTOMS The people valued hospitality highly; they enjoyed visits with each other and with friendly tribes. There were a number of men's and women's dance societies with various social and ceremonial importance. There may have been clans.

The dead were placed on tree scaffolds with their feet to the west. When the scaffolds fell through age, the bones were buried and the skulls placed in a circle, facing inward. Cremation was also practiced. All burial areas were treated with great respect. Dead souls were said to inhabit a paradise to the south.

Dead warriors were dressed in their finest clothes. Their faces were painted red, their weapons placed beside them, and one of their horses was killed for use in the next life. Women's tools, such as those used for dressing skins, were placed beside them. Mourning practices included cutting hair, dressing in rags, and sometimes slashing limbs.

Pubescent girls were secluded for four days, during which time they observed dietary and behavioral restrictions. Brides were purchased. Marriage consisted of a simple gift-giving ceremony between parents. The people played lacrosse and games of skill and dexterity, such as shinny and the cup-and-ball game, and held athletic competitions. Most games were accompanied by gambling.

DWELLINGS A village might contain up to 200 skin lodges or tipis. The average, which held two to four families, had roughly a 30-foot circumference and was constructed of about 12 sewn buffalo hides. Assiniboine tipis had a three-pole foundation. A temporary brush field shelter was also used.

DIET Assiniboines on the high plains lived mainly on game such as buffalo, elk, and antelope. Women often accompanied hunters to butcher the animals and cut meat into strips to dry. Fresh meat was usually roasted on a spit, although it was sometimes boiled with hot rocks in a skin-lined hole. Other foods included wild berries, roots (turnip), fruits (grapes, plums), and nuts.

KEY TECHNOLOGY The buffalo was the basis of all technology. Most items, such as clothing, tools, and utensils, were made of buffalo and other animal products. The flageolet, or flute, was used in part to convey surreptitious messages between young lovers. Assiniboines also played the rasp and the drum.

TRADE The people were known as shrewd traders, especially in their role as middlemen with the Hudson's Bay Company. Before trade began with non-Indians, they generally traded pelts and meat with farming tribes for agricultural products.

NOTABLE ARTS Significant art included decorative beaded quillwork (nineteenth century) and designs on tree bark.

TRANSPORTATION Dogs (later horses) carried saddle bags and travois. The people acquired horses in about the 1730s. They also used snowshoes.

DRESS Dress on the high plains was similar to that of other tribes, particularly the Plains Cree. Men often wore their long hair coiled atop the head.

WAR AND WEAPONS The Plains Cree were traditional allies, with whom the Assiniboine regularly fought the Dakota, Crow, Gros Ventre, and Blackfeet. The Assiniboine were recognized as highly capable warriors. Counting coup was more important than killing an enemy; four people might count coup on the same enemy, in descending order of prestige. Weapons included war clubs (a stone in a leather pouch attached to a stick), bow and arrow, and buffalo-hide shields.

Contemporary Information

GOVERNMENT/RESERVATIONS Fort Belknap (Blaine and Philips Counties, Montana), established

in 1887, contains roughly 616,000 acres, about one-quarter of which are tribally owned. The 1990 Indian population was 2,332. The reservation is governed under an Indian Reorganization Act (IRA) constitution and by-laws.

Fort Peck (Daniels, Roosevelt, Sheridan, and Valley Counties, Montana), established in 1873, contains about 981,000 acres, about one-quarter of which are tribally owned. The 1990 Indian population was 5,782. Their 1927 constitution is not based on the IRA. The reservation adopted a representative government, the Tribal Executive Board, in 1960.

Canadian communities include Carry the Kettle, Pheasant Rump, and Ocean Man in Saskatchewan and Elexis, Paul, Wesley, Big Horn, and Eden Valley in Alberta.

ECONOMY Both reservations lease land to non-Indian farmers and ranchers. Fort Peck owns and operates a profitable oil well. It also contains other mineral resources and has encouraged industrial development.

LEGAL STATUS The Assiniboine and Sioux Tribes of the Fort Peck Reservation is a federally recognized tribal entity. The Fort Belknap Indian Community (Gros Ventre and Assiniboine-Sioux) is a federally recognized tribal entity.

DAILY LIFE Maintaining their cultural identity in a community shared with other tribes as well as non-Indians is a major challenge facing contemporary Assiniboines. The Bureau of Indian Affairs, which has long dominated the Fort Belknap Reservation, has traditionally viewed both Indian groups as one community, to the detriment of Indian cultural identity. Fort Peck has traditionally enjoyed stronger political leadership and consequently greater self-determination and economic opportunity.

Diabetes is an ongoing and serious health problem. Traditional religion is maintained in the form of the hand game and the Sun Dance. There are also a number of important ceremonies associated with funerals and sweat lodges. The sacred pipe remains central to Assiniboine religion. Some members of the tribe participate in the Native American Church as well as in Medicine Lodge (called Rain Dance in Canada) ceremonies. The Assiniboine language is spoken by young and old alike, although it is used primarily in ceremonies. Assiniboine women continue to make museum-quality star quilts for secular and religious purposes.

Atsina

See Gros Ventres

Blackfeet

The Blackfeet are a confederacy of three closely

related Plains tribes. These include the *Pikuni* (Pie-gan, known as Peigan in Canada), meaning "small robes" or "poorly dressed robes"; the *Kainah*, "Blood" or "many chiefs"; and the *Siksika*, the Blackfeet proper. *Siksika*, a Cree word meaning "Blackfoot People," may have referred to their moccasins, blackened by dye or by the ashes of prairie fires. All three tribes were called the *Sakoyitapix*, "Prairie People," or the *Nitsitapix*, "Real People." The Piegan were further divided into northern and southern branches. The Blackfeet Confederacy also included the Sarcees and, until 1861, the Gros Ventres.

LOCATION   Around 1800, the Blackfeet proper and the Bloods lived around the Saskatchewan, Battle, and Bow Rivers (Alberta), and the Piegan claimed the area south of the Marais River (Rocky Mountain foothills of north-central Montana). Today, Blackfeet live in northwestern Montana as well as in southern Alberta.

POPULATION   The Blackfeet Confederacy in 1780 numbered around 15,000 people. In 1993 the tribe had over 13,000 members.

LANGUAGE   The Blackfeet groups spoke Algonquian languages.

Historical Information

HISTORY   The Blackfeet people may have originated in the Great Lakes region but had migrated to between the Bow and North Saskatchewan Rivers well before the seventeenth century. During the eighteenth century they completed their move southward into Montana, displacing the Shoshones.

Like many peoples, the Blackfeet were transformed by the horse and the gun, both of which they acquired during the early to mid–eighteenth century. One result was that they had surplus buffalo products to offer for trade. Raiding, especially for horses, became an important activity. They joined in alliance with the Assiniboine, Arapaho, and Gros Ventre and were frequently at war during the historic period.

Blackfeet people first felt the influence of non-Indians in the seventeenth century. By the late eighteenth century they were engaged in the fur trade and were known as shrewd traders, playing American and British interests off against each other. The people experienced severe epidemics in 1781–1782, 1837, 1864, and 1869–1870. After one of their number was killed by a member of the Lewis and Clark expedition in 1804, the Blackfeet fought all Americans whenever possible until they began trading with them again in 1831.

The 1868 Fort Laramie Treaty gave the Blackfeet lands south of the Missouri River, although their traditional lands had all been north of the Missouri. Still, in various treaties between 1851 and 1878 they ceded land to the United States and Canada. Epidemics, the decline of the buffalo, and, later, whiskey hurt the Blackfeet more than anything, although in 1870 they were the victims of a U.S. Army massacre in which 173 peaceful Indians, mostly women and children, were killed.

The Blackfeet Reservation was established in 1855 in northern Montana. In exchange for the northern Montana plains, the Southern Piegan received fixed hunting grounds bordered by the Canadian, Missouri, and Musselshell Rivers and the Rocky Mountains; they also received promises of payments and annuities. Other Blackfeet groups considered themselves to be British and did not treat with the Americans.

From the 1870s into the 1890s, the United States took away much of the huge Blackfeet Reservation. In Treaty Number 7 (1877), the Blackfeet (and others) ceded much of southern Alberta for a number of small reserves. Roughly 600 Blackfeet, mostly Southern Piegan, died of starvation in 1883 after the last great buffalo herd was destroyed.

After a farming experiment failed, Piegans began a program of stock raising around 1890, on land individually assigned by the Bureau of Indian Affairs. A few Indians became prosperous, but the majority leased their land to non-Indians, who often did not pay. A combination of events in 1919 left the people in dire poverty and dependent on government rations. During this period, over 200,000 acres of Indian land were lost through nonpayment of taxes and allotments that were sold to fend off starvation. Blackfeet on both sides of the border were also subject to having their children kidnapped and sent to missionary boarding schools. Log houses replaced tipis during this time. Most Canadian Blackfeet lost large portions of their reserves from 1907 to 1921.

Stock raising returned during the 1920s, accompanied by grain farming and some subsistence gardening. U.S. Blackfeet adopted an Indian Reorganization Act constitution in 1930s. Income rose, as the government provided credit for ranching enterprises. After World War II, up to one-third of the population was living off-reservation. Conditions on the reservations began to improve at that time, a trend that accelerated during the 1960s. Among most people, English replaced Blackfeet as the daily language in the 1970s. At the same time, many traditions severely declined.

RELIGION   The Blackfeet envisioned a world inhabited by spirits, some good and some evil. Deities included sun and thunder as well as all animals. Religious feelings and practice were pervasive. Prayers were offered regularly throughout the day.

Some people had visions to benefit the tribe as a

whole. They became holy men, or medicine pipe men, because their medicine bundle was particularly sacred. Such bundles, including scared pipes, were owned by individuals, societies, and bands. They were thought to ensure a long, happy, successful life and thus could be quite valuable if sold.

Ceremonies included the Sun Dance, probably acquired from the Arapaho or the Gros Ventres around the mid–eighteenth century. Unlike most Plains tribes, women participated in the Blackfeet Sun Dance. Religious societies were responsible for healing and curing. Individual religious activity focused on the acquisition of guardian spirits through prayerful vision quests in remote places. Guardian spirits would bring various forms of luck and/or skills.

Sweating was considered a religious activity as well as a preparation for ceremonials. Women were generally not permitted access to the sweat lodge. Sacred bundles were also smudged or smoked in the sweat lodge.

GOVERNMENT The constituent tribes of the confederacy were completely autonomous, although all were closely related and occasionally acted in concert. The tribes were in turn organized into autonomous bands of between 20 and 30 families (200 people) before the early eighteenth century.

Each band had a civil headman, or chief, chosen on the basis of acts of bravery and generosity. The chief had the most influence regarding the band's movements and also acted as judge. Each band also had a war chief, who exerted power only during military situations. All headmen constituted a tribal council, which in turn selected a temporary tribal chief when the bands came together. All decisions were taken by consensus.

CUSTOMS The bands lived separately in winter but came together in summer to hunt buffalo and observe their ceremonies. They generally followed the buffalo in all seasons save winter. Originally egalitarian, levels of social prestige based on horse ownership emerged after the mid–eighteenth century.

Men were members of one of seven age-graded military societies. In addition, men and women could belong to numerous other religious, dance, and social societies, each with its own symbols and ceremonies. There was also a society exclusively for women. Membership in all societies was drawn from all bands and functioned mainly when the tribe came together in summer.

Virginity in women was held in high esteem. Depending on his wealth, a man might have more than one wife. Residence after marriage was generally patrilocal. Wedding formalities centered on gift giving. There was a mother-in-law taboo but none for a wife and her father-in-law. Divorce was possible on the grounds of laziness or infidelity (men) or cruelty or neglect (women).

Names were sometimes given by the mother but more often by a male family member based on his war experiences. Boys usually earned a new name around adolescence. Despite beliefs about the danger of contact with menstruating women, there was no particular ceremony when a girl reached puberty.

Public ridicule was generally an effective deterrent to socially unacceptable behavior. Winter nights might be filled with storytelling, gambling, or all-night smokes during which people sang their religious songs. Childrens' games included hide and seek, archery and other contests, throwing balls, playing with toys, or sledding.

The dead were placed on scaffolds in trees or in tipis if death took place there; horses were generally killed to help in the journey to the next world. Women mourners cut their hair, wailed ritualistically, and slashed their limbs. Men cut their hair and left the band for a while.

DWELLINGS Women constructed tipis from 12 to 14 buffalo skins over as many as 23 pine poles. There was a basic foundation of four poles upon which the others were laid. Tipis always faced east. Larger tipis, of up to 30 buffalo skins, were a sign of wealth. Tipis were smaller when dogs pulled the travois.

DIET Food was generally abundant, although droughts or blizzards could bring hunger or even starvation. Plains Blackfeet ate mostly buffalo but also other large as well as small game. Buffalo were driven over cliffs, surrounded on foot and shot, communally hunted with bow and arrow (most common after the Blackfeet acquired horses), and individually stalked. The Indians also ate waterfowl and their eggs. They did not eat fish or dog.

In addition to the usual wild fruits, nuts, and berries, Blackfeet women gathered camas roots, which they steamed in an underground oven. Some tobacco was grown for ceremonial purposes.

KEY TECHNOLOGY Early, pre-Plains Blackfeet may have made pottery. The buffalo provided more than 60 material items. Various skin containers were often decorated with painted designs. Musical instruments included a rattle of skin around wood as well as a flageolet (flute). The people also used stone pounding mauls and war clubs attached to wooden handles, chipped stone knives, and brushes of porcupine bristles or horsehair bound with rawhide. They also made backrests of willow sticks tied with sinew and supported by a tripod.

TRADE The Blackfeet traded as far south as Mexico in all seasons save winter.

NOTABLE ARTS Men painted tipis and other leather items with stars and designs such as battle events. Women made beaded quillwork, usually on clothing. In general, the people were known for the high quality of everyday items such as clothing, tools, tipis, and headdresses.

TRANSPORTATION Dogs pulled the travois until horses arrived in the early to mid–eighteenth century. Temporary hide rafts, towed by swimmers, were used to cross deep streams.

DRESS Women wore long, one-piece skin dresses, later fringed and beaded, and buffalo robes in winter. They wore their hair long and loose. Men dressed in skin shirts, leggings, and moccasins, as well as buffalo robes in winter. Men also wore their hair long down the back, with a lock of hair down their foreheads to their noses, and they plucked their faces. Young men might also paint their faces. Caps were made of bird or weasel skins.

WAR AND WEAPONS All men were members of age-graded military societies known as All Comrades. Although they were generally allied with the Gros Ventre and Sarcee, the Blackfeet fought most other Plains and Plateau tribes, including Salish/Flathead, Nez Percé, Kootenai, Assiniboine (after the nineteenth century), Shoshone, Crow, and Cree. Blackfeet Indians were considered among the best fighters, hunters, and raiders. Although the three divisions were politically autonomous, they acted in unison to fight their enemies.

Weapons included three-foot horn, sinew-backed bows, stone clubs, arrows (held in otter-skin quivers), and decorated buffalo-hide shields. Rather than counting coup with a stick, Blackfeet warriors gathered high war honors by wresting a gun or other weapon from an enemy. Taking a horse or a scalp merited honors but of relatively low caliber.

Contemporary Information

GOVERNMENT/RESERVATIONS The Blackfeet Reservation (Glacier and Pondera Counties, Montana), established in 1855, consists of roughly two million acres, of which the tribe owns about 70 percent individually or in common. The 1990 Indian population was 7,025. The reservation is governed by a tribal business council.

On all three Canadian reserves—Siksika, Blood, and Peigan—decisions of the tribal councils must be approved by the government, but this is considered a mere formality.

ECONOMY The Blackfeet Tribe owns Blackfeet National Bank and a pencil and pen company as well as grazing and mineral leases. The tribe received a settlement of $29 million in 1982 as compensation for unsound federal accounting practices over the years.

Their unemployment rate remains generally above 50 percent (nearer 80 percent in Canada). Most businesses and services are owned by non-Indians in the reservation town of Browning

In Canada, Indian-run businesses on the Siksika Reserve include a cafeteria, supermarket, video store, and furniture store. The Blood Reserve has a small mall and several service stations. There are several small stores and a crafts shop on the Peigan Reserve.

LEGAL STATUS The Blackfeet Tribe is a federally recognized tribal entity.

In Canada, the Blackfeet Tribe has changed its name to the Siksika Nation, and the Peigans are called both the Peigan Nation and the Pikuni Nation.

DAILY LIFE Many Blackfeet have intermarried with non-Blackfeet or non-Indians, and many have adopted Christian religions. Still, the Sun Dance is maintained, as are medicine bundle, sweat lodge, and guardian spirit traditions. Language classes are in place to keep the language alive. Blackfeet Indians are better educated and have more and better jobs than ever before. Nevertheless, the unemployment rate remains high, with attendant social problems. The Museum of the Plains Indian as well as Blackfeet Community College (established 1976) is located on the reservation. There is an annual Medicine Lodge ceremony and Sun Dance in July.

Canadian Bloods operate Red Crow College, and a local college offers courses on the Siksika Reserve. The University of Lethbridge has a Native Studies program based mostly on Blackfeet culture.

Blood

See Blackfeet

Cheyenne

Cheyenne (Sh ī `an), a word of Lakota origin meaning "red talkers" or "foreign talkers." Their self-designation is *Tse-tsehese-staestse*, "People."

LOCATION In the early nineteenth century, Cheyennes lived from the Yellowstone River to the upper Arkansas River. Today, most live in southeastern Montana and western Oklahoma as well as in cities throughout the West.

POPULATION The late-eighteenth-century population was about 3,500 people. In the 1990s there are about 11,000 Cheyennes.

LANGUAGE Cheyenne is an Algonquian language. There were at least two major dialects of Cheyenne in the early nineteenth century.

Historical Information

HISTORY The Algonquian people may have come north from the lower Mississippi Valley shortly after the last ice sheet receded. Late prehistoric (sixteenth and seventeenth century) Cheyennes lived in the upper Mississippi Valley (northern and western Minnesota) in permanent villages and grew corn, beans, and squash. They also fished and hunted game, including buffalo.

Some bands encountered René-Robert La Salle in 1680, on the Illinois River. The French fur trade in the Great Lakes region was responsible for arming local Indian groups such as the Ojibwa with guns; these groups began attacking Cheyenne villages, eventually forcing them to abandon the region and undertake a slow migration westward throughout the eighteenth century. They lived near the Shyenne River (North Dakota), where they built a fortified town and continued their agricultural patterns. They also hunted buffalo and other game on a growing herd of horses but had not yet abandoned the agricultural life.

By the end of the eighteenth century, however, well-armed Ojibwas (Anishinabe) had destroyed a main Cheyenne village. Surviving Cheyennes moved farther west, to the upper Missouri River, joining some of their number who had gone there several years earlier. During that period they associated with the Mandan, Arikara, and Hidatsa. They continued to plant some crops but relied increasingly on the buffalo.

By the early nineteenth century, raids from Siouan tribes forced the Cheyenne out onto the Plains, where they gave up farming entirely, becoming nomadic buffalo hunters as well as fierce fighters. Allied with the Arapaho, they settled primarily near the Black Hills and then in the upper Platte–Powder River area, where they eventually became allied with Lakota bands. It was also during that period that they absorbed another Algonquian group, the Sutaio tribe.

About 1832, some bands moved south, attracted by trade centered around Taos, New Mexico, as well as Bent's Fort on the Arkansas River in southern Colorado. The move precipitated a tribal split into Northern and Southern Cheyenne. In alliance with the Southern Arapaho, the Southern Cheyenne controlled most of the buffalo country between western Kansas and eastern Colorado and the Platte River.

In 1837 a major war broke out, with the Southern Arapaho and Southern Cheyenne fighting against the Comanche; peace was established in 1840, largely on Arapaho-Cheyenne terms. The Cheyenne signed the 1851 Fort Laramie Treaty, which reaffirmed their right to land between the North Platte and Arkansas Rivers. The treaty also formalized the separation of the Cheyenne groups. However, during the 1850s and 1860s they were regularly harassed by army troops and gold-seeking trespassers.

Meanwhile, non-Indian leaders of territorial Colorado had decided to force all Indians from that region. Pressure against the Southern Cheyenne was increased, especially after the Pike's Peak gold rush of 1859. Under Chief Black Kettle (Moketavato), the Southern Cheyenne repeatedly compromised in an effort to avoid war. However, the 1864 massacre and mutilation of several hundred of their people at Sand Creek, Colorado (where they had been told to camp under the protection of the U.S. Army and met the soldiers flying a white surrender and an American flag), forced the Southern Cheyenne to cede their lands in Colorado.

Black Kettle continued to seek peace but was shot down with his tribe, which offered no resistance, in the Washita Valley, Oklahoma, in 1868. At this point, the Cheyenne divided again. One group went north to the Powder River Country, and most of the rest settled on the Southern Cheyenne and Arapaho Reservation, established in 1869 in Indian Territory. This roughly four-million-acre reservation was eliminated through allotment and non-Indian settlement by 1902. Some Southern Cheyennes continued to fight with the Kiowa, Comanche, and Arapaho, until the few survivors were forced to surrender in 1875.

In the meantime, the Northern Cheyenne tried to resist the onslaught of the gold seekers and land grabbers who invaded their lands, ignoring the terms of the 1851 Fort Laramie Treaty. Formerly among the tribes who held out for peace, they turned to war following the Sand Creek massacre. Under chiefs like Roman Nose, some Northern Cheyennes fought with Red Cloud's Lakota in the successful effort to close the Bozeman Trail (1866–1868). The resulting Fort Laramie Treaty (1868) affirmed the exclusion of non-Indians from the Powder River region of Montana. In 1876, the Northern Cheyenne joined with other Plains Indians in defeating the United States in the Battle of the Little Bighorn.

Shortly thereafter, however, the U.S. Army caught and defeated the Northern Cheyennes, rounding up almost 1,000 and forcing them south to the Cheyenne-Arapaho Reservation in Indian Territory. Though exhausted after their forced march, sick and dying from malaria, and starving, roughly 300 desperate Northern Cheyennes under Dull Knife and Little Wolf escaped and headed toward home north of the North Platte River. Fighting valiantly for their freedom, they were pursued by soldiers and had to cross lands now inhabited by white farmers and ranchers. The people were recaptured with much loss of life and relocated to the Pine Ridge area of South Dakota in 1881. Three years later, the Tongue River Reservation in eastern Montana was established for this now-decimated people. Although this land was never opened to non-Indian purchase, allotments fragmented the reservation, causing long-term legal and cultural problems.

Christian missionaries, especially Mennonites, Catholics, and Southern Baptists, became active among the Cheyenne toward the end of the nineteenth century. Around the same time, the Peyote religion and the Ghost Dance became popular among the Northern Cheyennes. Following confinement to reservations, most Indians lived on government rations (often inadequate at best) and marginal gardening and wage labor. In 1911, the United States organized a 15-member Northern Cheyenne Business Council, largely under its control. The tribe adopted an Indian Reorganization Act (IRA) constitution in 1935. In 1918, Southern Cheyennes were among those who formally incorporated the Peyote religion into the Native American Church.

RELIGION The Cheyenne conceived of a universe divided into seven major levels, each with resident spiritual beings that were also associated with earthly plants and animals. They also believed in a creator of all life.

Through fasting and prayer, both men and women sought visions in remote places in order to acquire guardian spirit helpers. Spirit guides might appear during a vision quest or in a dream. They and their associated songs, prayers, and symbols would provide special skills or protection in times of crisis. Priests and doctors (shamans) used plants to cure disease.

Annual ceremonies included the Renewal of Sacred Arrows, the Sun Dance (New Life Lodge), and the annual, five-day Sacred Buffalo Hat ceremony. The first revolved around four scared arrows that were thought to have been given to the Cheyenne by their culture hero, Sweet Medicine, who had in turn received them from the Great Spirit. During the four-day ceremony, held at least every few years, the arrows were removed from the sacred bundle. They, and, by extension, the tribe, were restored to good condition and renewed.

GOVERNMENT On the Plains, traditional government consisted of the Council of Forty-Four: a group of 40 exceptionally wise, generous, brave, and able men, four from each of the 10 bands, plus four elders/religious authorities held over from the previous council. The latter four men, plus a tribal chief chosen by them, were known as the five sacred chiefs. Council terms were 10 years. Each band also had its own chief. Six military societies helped to carry out council directives and maintain strict internal discipline.

CUSTOMS Bands lived separately in winter so as to hunt more effectively in a wider space. In summer, the bands came together for the communal buffalo hunt and for sacred ceremonies. At these times, camp consisted of a large circle, within which each band had a designated position.

Murder was considered among the most reprehensible of crimes as well as a sin; murderers were ostracized for life or exiled. Bravery was highly valued, as was female chastity. Courtship was prolonged, with both families closely involved. Residence after marriage was generally matrilocal.

Games, generally accompanied by gambling, included lacrosse and the cup-and-ball game. In addition to the men's military societies, the highly prestigious buffalo society was open only to women who had embroidered at least 30 buffalo hides. Corpses were dressed in their best clothing, wrapped in robes, and placed on a scaffold, usually in a tree. Weapons and other items useful in the afterworld, including possibly a just-killed horse, were placed nearby.

DWELLINGS While still in the northern Mississippi Valley, Cheyennes lived in bark and, in North Dakota (Shyenne River area), earth lodges. By the late eighteenth century they had begun living in buffalo-hide tipis.

DIET Cheyennes grew corn, beans, and squash; gathered wild rice; fished; and hunted in the northern Mississippi and Shyenne valleys. From the late eighteenth century on, as the tribe became nomadic hunters, their diet depended largely on the buffalo. Women participated in all hunts, helping to drive the herds within range of the hunters. Women also cut the meat into strips to dry and dressed the skins. Cheyennes also ate other large game as well as dog. The Plains diet was supplemented by wild turnips, berries, and prickly pear cactus.

KEY TECHNOLOGY The Cheyenne made pottery prior to their move to the Plains. Once there, the buffalo provided most of their clothing, dwellings, tools, containers, and utensils. They also made small, shallow basketry trays, primarily used for gambling.

TRADE Cheyennes traded at both precontact trade centers of the northern Plains: Mandan villages on the Knife River and Arikara villages in present-day South Dakota. In the early nineteenth century, for instance, they were trading buffalo products for agricultural ones. They also traded for tobacco after they ceased growing it around 1800. Both divisions, especially the Southern Cheyenne, were highly skilled traders.

NOTABLE ARTS Traditional artists worked with leather, wood, quills, and feathers. They also carved pipes. Slender figures to divide space into five parts, especially on parfleches and other such items, was a regular artistic motif.

TRANSPORTATION Cheyennes acquired horses by the mid–eighteenth century.

DRESS Women dressed the skins for clothing. They made moccasins, leggings, breechclouts, shirts, and robes for men, and for themselves they made two-piece dresses and moccasins with leggings and robes in winter. Clothing was usually decorated with beaded quillwork.

WAR AND WEAPONS During the late eighteenth through the mid–nineteenth century, the Cheyennes were great warriors and raiders, plundering the Spanish and other Plains tribes as well. Six interband military societies, such as the prestigious Dog Soldiers, selected a war chief. Four members of each society also constituted a 24-member war council. Each society had its own rituals, objects, and symbols.

The Siouan tribes were enemies until they and the Northern Cheyennes joined forces in the mid–nineteenth century. The Southern Cheyennes fought many regional tribes, particularly the Kiowa and the Comanches, until they joined with these two tribes in about 1840 to fight the Crows, Pawnees, Shoshones, Utes, and Apaches. Cheyennes also fought alongside the Arapaho.

As Plains dwellers, counting coup in battle by touching an enemy counted for more prestige than killing him. Weapons included the horn bow, arrows, clubs, shields, and spears.

Contemporary Information

GOVERNMENT/RESERVATIONS The Northern Cheyenne Reservation (Big Horn and Rosebud Counties, Montana), established in 1884, consists of 436,948 acres. There are also Northern Cheyenne Trust Lands in Rosebud County, Montana, and Meade County, South Dakota. According to the 1935 IRA constitution, amended in 1960, the tribe is governed by a council in which the president is popularly elected. The 1990 Indian population was 3,542.

A 28-member elected business council governs the Cheyenne-Arapaho Tribe, formed in 1937. Most Southern Cheyennes live in cities and towns of western Oklahoma. Their estimated population in 1990 was about 5,000.

A modified Council of Forty-Four, composed of chiefs, religious leaders, and military society members, continues its authority over Northern and Southern Cheyennes. Their decisions do not always accord with those of the official tribal governments.

ECONOMY On the Northern Cheyenne Reservation, most jobs are provided by the tribal and federal governments, several power companies, a financial company, a construction company, and the Forest Service (seasonal fire fighting). Unemployment commonly ranges between about 50 and 90 percent. Additional tribal income comes from land use fees and leases.

Although the reservation contains a large coal reserve, many tribal members resist mining out of respect to traditional cultural values. Kerr-McGee strip mined coal, devastating vast stretches of the Northern Cheyenne Reservation, until the tribe canceled all leases in 1973.

Among the Southern Cheyenne, wheat, oil, ranching, and government-sponsored projects provide most individual income. The Southern Cheyenne also suffer from chronically high unemployment and very low average annual incomes.

LEGAL STATUS The Cheyenne-Arapaho Tribe of Oklahoma and the Northern Cheyenne Tribe of Montana are federally recognized tribal entities.

DAILY LIFE Both tribes are focused primarily on ensuring their cultural survival. In addition, they are working on providing economic opportunities and social services. Land reacquisition is another important goal. Most Northern Cheyennes live in almost 1,000 mobile homes or government housing, much of which is of substandard quality.

All reservation schools include Cheyenne language and culture courses. Southern Cheyenne children attend public schools. Northern Cheyenne youth, in particular, are plagued with social problems such as high drop-out rates, substance abuse, and violence. Dull Knife Memorial College was chartered in 1976 "to promote academic excellence and the Cheyenne way of life."

Many Cheyenne continue to employ traditional healing practices to restore spiritual as well as physical health. Many Cheyennes continue traditional religious beliefs and practices. The Sacred Buffalo Hat is kept among the Northern Cheyenne and the Sacred Arrow generally in Oklahoma. Many see ecological destruction, resulting from improper religious veneration, as heralding the end of the universe. Many Cheyennes are also Christians and members of the Native American Church. Cheyenne remains a living language, although few young people can speak it fluently.

A number of cooperative organizations, based on the old societies, include the military societies as well as women's groups such as Quillwork Society and War Mothers' Association. Cheyenne artists continue to work in traditional media, making items for ceremonial as well as tourist consumption. The Northern Cheyennes, with other signatories of the 1868 Fort Laramie Treaty, have refused any financial compensation for the Black Hills offered by the U.S. government. They insist on a return of the land. A congressional bill to this effect (financial compensation plus some land return) was filed in 1985. It was opposed by the South Dakota delegation and withdrawn in 1990.

Comanche

Comanche (Ku `man sh ē), a name derived from either the Ute *Komantcia,* "People Who Fight Us All the Time," or the Spanish *camino ancho,* "broad trail." Their self-designation was *Numinu,* "People." *See also* Shoshone, Eastern or Wind River (Chapter 4).

LOCATION The Comanche lived in the Rocky Mountain regions of Wyoming and northern Colorado until the mid– to late seventeenth century, when the people moved into the central and southern Great Plains. Today, most Comanches live in Oklahoma.

POPULATION In the late eighteenth century there were between 7,000 and 12,000 Comanches. Their population in the 1990s is about 8,500.

LANGUAGE Comanche is part of the Uto-Aztecan language. During the eighteenth and early nineteenth centuries, variations of Comanche were used as a common trade language throughout the southwestern Great Plains.

Historical Information

HISTORY The Comanche were originally part of the Eastern Shoshone, who had lived along Arizona's Gila River from about 3000 B.C.E. to about 500 B.C.E. At that time, a group of them began migrating north toward Utah, growing a high-altitude variety of corn that had been developed in Mexico. This group, who grew corn, beans, and squash and also hunted and gathered food, is known as the Sevier Complex.

In time, Sevier people moved north of the Great Salt Lake. When a drought struck the Great Basin in the thirteenth century, the Sevier people spread out north of the Great Salt Lake. Known then as Shoshones, they lived by hunting and gathering throughout much of the Great Basin.

By about the late seventeenth century, some Shoshone bands, from the mountainous regions of Wyoming and northern Colorado, later known as Comanche, had acquired horses. The bands began migrating into New Mexico and toward the Arkansas River on the central Plains. They adopted the cycle of buffalo hunting, raiding, and fighting characteristic of Plains life.

By about 1750 they had acquired vast horse herds and dominated the central high plains. Their population had increased considerably, in part owing to the capture and adoption of young women and the abundance of buffalo meat to feed the growing numbers of children. They were also trading directly with the French by this time, from whom they acquired a steady supply of guns.

In 1780–1781 the Comanche (as well as most other Plains tribes) lost a large number of their people, perhaps as many as half, to a smallpox epidemic.

In about 1790, several thousand northern Comanches and Kiowas joined together in a lasting alliance. There was a brief period of peace between the Spanish and the Comanche, roughly from 1787 to 1810, during which these two peoples were allied against the Apaches.

The Comanche continued southward throughout the eighteenth and into the early nineteenth century, pressured from the north by the Dakota/Lakota and other tribes and drawn by trade and raiding opportunities in the Southwest into New Spain/Mexico. During this period they continued to drive Apachean groups from the Plains. They also prevented the Spanish from colonizing Texas extensively, and they acted as a brake to French trade expansion into the Southwest.

By the mid–nineteenth century, Comanches were roughly separated into three divisions. The southern group lived between the Red and Colorado Rivers in Texas. The middle group wintered in Texas but followed the buffalo in summer north toward the Arkansas River. The northern group wintered on the Red River and wandered widely during the summer. In 1840, northern Comanches made peace with the Southern Cheyennes and Arapahos, after the latter had staged several successful raids against them. As part of this agreement, the Comanche gave up land in western Kansas north of the Arkansas River.

A cholera epidemic in 1849–1850 took a heavier toll on Comanche population than had all battles to date. During the 1840s and 1850s, the Comanche fought bitter wars with the Texans, the latter bent on exterminating all Indian groups. In 1853, the Comanche joined with some Apaches in a failed bid to destroy the Indians who had been settled since the 1830s on "their" lands in the Indian Territory.

The Comanche defeated Kit Carson in 1864, but they and the Kiowa signed a treaty in 1865 that reserved much of western Indian Territory (Oklahoma) for them and their allies. When the U.S. government failed to keep non-Indians out of these lands, the Indians rebelled. In the ensuing 1867 Medicine Lodge Treaty, some Comanche bands agreed to accept a reservation in southwestern Indian Territory with the Kiowa and Kiowa Apaches. Hostilities over non-Indian squatters and the difficulties of life in captivity continued for another eight years. However, by the late 1860s the Comanche were in serious trouble. The great buffalo herds had been hunted to near extinction and the U.S. Army was pursuing Indians relentlessly.

After the 1868 Battle of the Washita, in which the United States massacred a group of Cheyenne Indians, a few Comanche leaders surrendered their bands at Fort Cobb, Oklahoma; these roughly 2,500 people were later moved to Fort Sill, Oklahoma, and began farming corn. Several bands, however, remained on the Plains, holding on to the free life for several more years. The Comanche adopted a modified version of the Sun Dance in 1874. At about the same time, a short-lived religious movement led to an unsuccessful battle against the United States at Adobe Walls.

In 1874, War Chief Quanah Parker led the last free Comanche bands, along with some Kiowa and Cheyenne refugees from Fort Sill, into Palo Duro Canyon, Texas, site of the last great buffalo range. There they lived traditionally until the army found and destroyed their camp and horses. In 1875, Parker surrendered to mark the end of Comanche resistance.

Parker continued as an important leader on the reservation, overseeing favorable land leases and playing a major role in bringing the Peyote religion to the Comanche and many other Indian tribes after 1890. Reservation lands were allotted beginning in 1892. Nonallotted lands were sold to non-Indians, and nothing remained of the reservation by 1908.

RELIGION Comanche deities included numerous celestial objects such as the sun and moon. The Eagle Dance and Beaver ceremony were important, but they did not adopt the Sun Dance until 1874. Shamans interceded with the spirit world to cure the sick.

Young men undertook vision quests in remote places, hoping to attract a guardian spirit helper. When they returned, shamans helped them to interpret their visions, which included associated songs and taboos, and to prepare their personal medicine bundles.

GOVERNMENT Membership was fluid in each of the roughly 13 bands, including 4 major ones. Each band had a chief or headman, who was assisted by a council of the leading men of the band. Bands cooperated with each other, but there was no overall tribal organization or leadership, a fact that limited their nevertheless great effectiveness on the Plains.

CUSTOMS In contrast to most other Plains Indians, the fiercely independent Comanche maintained virtually no police to keep order in the camp. Leaders for buffalo hunts maintained authority for that hunt only. Men might have more than one wife. Corpses were dressed in their best clothing, face painted red and red clay on eyes, and buried in flexed position in a cave or shallow grave. Mourners cut their hair, arms, and legs; gave away their possessions; and burned the dead person's tipi, never mentioning his or her name again. After the move to the Plains, the custom of killing all of a man's horses when he died was replaced by that of killing only the best one, with the rest to be distributed among other people.

DWELLINGS Women made Plains-style buffalo-skin tipis.

DIET Buffalo was the main staple on the Plains. They were driven over cliffs, stalked individually, or, most popular after the people acquired horses, surrounded on horseback. Men also hunted other large and small game. Women gathered wild potatoes, fruit (plums, grapes, and currants), nuts, and berries.

KEY TECHNOLOGY Babies were cradled in beaded skin pockets attached to V-shaped frames. Comanches also made shallow basketry gambling trays.

TRADE Comanches frequented both northern Plains aboriginal trade centers. One was located in southern North Dakota, centered on the Knife River Mandan villages. The other was located north of the mouth of the Grand River, in present-day South Dakota, and centered on the Arikara villages there.

By the early eighteenth century, Comanches were also trading at Taos and Santa Fe, New Mexico, although they also raided these areas mercilessly. Other important eighteenth- and nineteenth-century trading partners included the Wichita and Osage, with whom the Comanche traded horses for guns, and Mexicans, from whom the Comanche obtained tobacco. Because of their wide range, the Comanche helped to spread the use of horses throughout the Plains.

NOTABLE ARTS Comanches were known for their silver and copper ornaments.

TRANSPORTATION Having acquired horses during the late sixteenth century, probably from the Utes, the Comanche became among the most highly skilled horsemen on the Plains. They were excellent breeders and trainers as well as raiders and maintained some of the largest horse herds on the Plains. Both boys and girls began riding around age five. During the eighteenth century they began using pack horses to pull travois.

DRESS Women made moccasins, leggings, breechclouts, shirts, and robes for men, and for themselves they made two-piece dresses and moccasins with leggings and robes in winter. Clothing was often decorated with beaded quillwork.

WAR AND WEAPONS Comanches used red paint for battle on their horses' heads and tails as well as themselves. Other battle gear included buffalo horn headdresses, high buffalo-hide boots, and horsehair extensions to their already long hair. Weapons included feathered lances, buffalo-hide shields, and bows, mainly of Osage orange wood. The people adopted military societies beginning in the eighteenth century as well as many other features of Plains warrior culture.

Traditional enemies of the Kiowa, the two groups made peace about 1790 and became raiding partners. Apaches became a favorite raiding target beginning in the late eighteenth century, as did groups such as the Ute (allies before about 1750), Navajo, Pawnee, Osage, and eastern Pueblos as well as non-Indians in the Southwest. Allies included Caddo-speaking tribes such as the Pawnee. About 1840 the Comanche joined in a loose confederacy with the Southern Cheyennes and Southern Arapahos.

Contemporary Information

GOVERNMENT/RESERVATIONS The Comanche Indian Tribe of Oklahoma is governed by a business committee under a 1967 constitution. The chair and other officials are popularly elected. They have no reservation or tribally owned land. Roughly 5,000 Comanches live near the tribal headquarters north of Lawton.

ECONOMY Craft sales and government programs represent the only alternative to the local economy.

LEGAL STATUS The Comanche Indian Tribe is a federally recognized tribal entity.

DAILY LIFE Many Comanches have intermarried with other Indian and non-Indian people. Perhaps 250 elderly Comanches spoke their language in 1993. Efforts, undertaken by tribal members as well as the University of Oklahoma, are under way to preserve the language from demise.

Since the Indian Self-Determination Act of 1975, Comanches have administered many of their own programs, such as education scholarships and assistance for the elderly. Continuing crafts include elaborate dance costumes characterized by fine feather and beadwork. The hand game, with its associated singing and gambling, is still widely played. Comanches participate in numerous local powwows, especially the Comanche Homecoming Powwow, held in July at Walters, Oklahoma. Most Comanches are Christians, although some are also members of the Native American Church.

Cree, Plains

Plains Cree (Kr ē), a division of the Cree Indians of central Canada. The name comes from the French *Kristenaux,* a corruption of a Cree self-designations. *See also* Cree (Chapter 9).

LOCATION Early in the seventeenth century, Crees inhabited the forests between Lake Superior and Hudson Bay. By the eighteenth and nineteenth centuries, groups of Crees had moved into western Saskatchewan and eastern Alberta and south to northern Montana. These were the northernmost of the Plains Indians.

POPULATION From an early-seventeenth-century total Cree population of about 15,000, there were roughly 4,000 Plains Cree in 1780. There are some 60,000 Cree today, mostly in Canada.

LANGUAGE All nine Cree dialects belong to the central division of the Algonquian language family.

Historical Information

HISTORY The earliest Algonquians may have come north from the lower Mississippi Valley shortly after the last ice sheet retreated from the Great Lakes and St. Lawrence River regions. Their population grew until a large number of them lived north and west of the Great Lakes. Crees probably originated in central and northern Manitoba around 1100. By 1500 they were located at the forest's edge along and south of the Saskatchewan River. Cree bands began acquiring guns and other goods from the French in the mid–seventeenth century, trading furs, especially beaver, for them. Hudson's Bay Company opened a post in Cree territory in 1667.

During the period of the French fur trade, many Cree and French intermarried. Many *voyageurs* and *coureurs de bois* were mixed French and Cree, as were the mixed-blood Métis. During the later seventeenth century, the quest for furs, as well as their own growing population, pushed the Cree on toward the west until they stretched from near Labrador in the east to the Great Slave Lake and south to Alberta, northern Montana, and North Dakota in the west. During these migrations they displaced their ancient enemies to the west, the Athapaskans, and pushed Dakota bands westward as well.

Crees formed a close alliance with the Assiniboine in the late seventeenth century. They experienced severe smallpox epidemics in 1737 and 1781, particularly in the Lake Winnipeg area. By the early eighteenth century, the Cree were roughly divided into Woodland (eastern and western) and Plains divisions, having reached Lake Winnipeg and beyond. During this period they still retained much of their old Woodland culture.

Plains Crees acquired horses in the mid– to late eighteenth century and adopted much of classic nomadic Plains Indian culture, including warring, raiding, and using the buffalo for food, clothing, shelter, tools, equipment, and fuel. Some also intermarried with Mohawk Indians who were serving as guides for non-Indian fur trading companies, which the Cree were provisioning with buffalo meat. By the early nineteenth century, Plains Crees controlled the area north of the Missouri River and were pressuring the Blackfeet to the west and south.

A sharp decline set in during the 1850s, however, owing primarily to smallpox epidemics and warfare with the Blackfeet. Canadian officials created Cree reserves in the 1870s, on which Crees were theoretically encouraged to turn to the agricultural life. In fact, the Indians themselves were aware that the buffalo life was soon to end and wanted help in making the change to agriculture. Though they might well have adapted to this change, most were denied access to key resources, such as implements and livestock (both promised in treaties). Such items, if they were issued at all, were generally inappropriate and/or of poor quality.

From the Indian point of view, they had given up their land for empty promises. Privation and even starvation stalked Indian communities. Government officials tended to blame Indian farming failures on their presumed idleness. Of course, non-Indians also had problems farming the Plains during these years, but they were free to move at will and were not subject to discrimination or undue restrictions in marketing their yield or obtaining loans, credit, and basic supplies.

Despite these obstacles, some bands did make a relative success of farming, to the extent that non-Indian farmers were complaining toward the end of the 1880s about unfair competition from Native Americans. In 1890, the Canadian government turned to a policy of peasant farming, in which the reserves were subdivided. Land was allotted in severalty, "surplus" land was sold to non-Indians, and mechanized farm equipment was taken away. With this policy, Canadian officials succeeded in dramatically reducing total land under Indian cultivation as well as the number of Indian farmers and in maintaining the reserves in poverty. Indian protests were routinely ignored or repressed.

In 1885, Poundmaker and Big Bear led the Cree in the Second Riel Rebellion (Louis Riel was a Métis nationalist leader). They and the Métis joined forces to try to stem the flow of non-Indian settlers to the vicinity of the Canadian Pacific Railway line in Saskatchewan and to create a native state. The Cree were not defeated but surrendered shortly after their Métis allies did. One group of Cree became associated at that time with Little Shell's band of Chippewas in Montana. Big Bear, a leader of the rebellion, escaped with 200 Cree to the United States, where they wandered for three decades in Montana until joining with a band of Chippewa under the leadership of Stone Child, or Rocky Boy. In 1916, the U.S. government created the Rocky Boy Reservation in the Bearpaw Mountains of Montana for these people. Little Shell's band eventually settled in nearby towns and reservations.

RELIGION   Adolescent boys undertook vision quests. Shamans used their spirit powers to cure illness. In midsummer, bands (either individually or collectively) celebrated the Sun Dance.

GOVERNMENT   There were from 8 to 12 bands of fluid composition among the Plains Cree, each with a headman and a loosely defined hunting territory. The leadership position required excellent hunting and speaking skills as well as the traits of bravery and generosity and could be hereditary. Each band also had a warrior society.

CUSTOMS   Newborn infants were dried with moss or soft wood and, after a few days, placed in a hide sack stuffed with moss. A baby later wore a small pouch containing the umbilical cord around the neck. Babies were named at a feast soon after birth by a same-sex relative. The child's name was associated with the name-givers' spirit vision. Most people also had nicknames. Names associated with supernatural power and with the dead were not commonly spoken.

Children were nursed for up to five years. Girls were secluded for four nights at the onset of puberty. During this time they performed various tasks, ate little, and scratched their heads with a stick. They also often acquired their spirit visions. A feast followed this initial period of seclusion. Married women also withdrew when menstruating. There were no male puberty ceremonies, except that boys were encouraged to fast and undertake a vision quest.

For marriage gifts, the bride's family gave the couple a fully equipped tipi. The groom received a horse from his father-in-law as well as moccasins from his new wife. Plains Crees observed the mother-in-law taboo.

Corpses were dressed in their best clothing, and their faces were painted. They were taken out the side of the tipi, not the door, and buried in the ground, in log chambers, or in tree scaffolds. Some eastern bands built gabled-roof grave houses. A filled pipe and a container of grease were buried with the body. Close relatives sliced their limbs and wore their hair loose until the mourning period ended. Bundles containing ancestral locks of hair were considered extremely important and were carried by the women when the camp moved. The possessions of the dead were given away.

The early Cree practiced tattooing with needles and leather threads. Shinny was widely played. Both men and women used tobacco, obtained from traders and mixed with dried bearberry leaves, for ceremonial purposes.

DWELLINGS   Plains Crees lived in buffalo-hide tipis with three-pole foundations.

DIET   Buffalo was the staple food. Men hunted in small groups during the winter and communally in summer. Buffalo were driven into brush impoundments or, in winter, into marshes or deep snow. Men also hunted other large game.

Women snared a variety of small game, fished, and caught birds (and gathered their eggs). They also gathered roots (such as prairie turnip), berries (such as Saskatoon berries), fruits, and tubers. Most of these were dried and stored for winter. At least as early as the early nineteenth century, some Plains Crees maintained gardens and even kept cattle to help ensure a constant food supply.

KEY TECHNOLOGY Plains Crees periodically burned the grasslands in autumn to encourage higher yield and earlier growth, thus helping to maintain the buffalo herd. They also used fire to drive a herd toward a particular area and to keep them away from key trade sites. In addition to the usual buffalo-based technology, Plains Crees fished using weirs, platforms, and spears.

TRADE Crees acted as intermediaries between non-Indian traders and Indian tribes such as the Blackfeet in the late seventeenth century.

NOTABLE ARTS Like many Plains Indians, the Cree made beaded quillwork and painted hides.

TRANSPORTATION Dogs carried extra goods with the help of a strap across the chest before the advent of the travois. Later, dog-drawn and, after about 1770, horse-drawn travois were used to transport goods. The Cree also used snowshoes and canoes, which they abandoned during the seventeenth and eighteenth centuries in favor of crude, temporary buffalo-hide rafts.

DRESS In general, the upper body remained bare except for a robe or ceremonial garments. The people also wore one-piece moccasins as well as rawhide visors against the sun.

WAR AND WEAPONS Each band had a warrior society. Early enemies included the Iroquois and Dakotas to the south as well as Athapaskan and Inuit tribes to the north. Later, they fought with the Blackfeet. Allies included the Ojibwa and the Assiniboine.

Unlike many Plains tribes, the Cree placed a high value on scalping. One customarily gave away much of the booty captured in a raid. Weapons included sinew-backed bows and war clubs consisting of a stone in a bag on the end of a stick.

Contemporary Information

GOVERNMENT/RESERVATIONS The Rocky Boy Chippewa-Cree Reservation (1,485 Indians in 1990) and Trust Lands (397 Indians in 1990) is located in Chouteau and Hill Counties, Montana. It was established in 1916 and contains 108,015 acres. The tribe is governed by the Chippewa-Cree Business Committee. Roughly half of the population lives off-reservation.

The Little Shell people, some of whom are of Cree descent, had a 1990 population of 3,300.

There are Cree reserves in Alberta, Saskatchewan, Manitoba, Ontario, and Quebec.

ECONOMY Activities in Montana include cattle grazing, wheat and barley farming, some logging and mining, and recreation and tourism. Unemployment regularly approaches 75 percent.

LEGAL STATUS The Chippewa-Cree Indians of the Rocky Boy Reservation, Montana, are a federally recognized tribal entity.

The Little Shell people have been seeking federal recognition since the 1920s. Other Montana Cree, such as the people of Hill 57, also remain landless and unrecognized.

DAILY LIFE The Chippewa-Crees opened Stone Child Community College in 1978. Crees along Lubicon Lake in Alberta, Canada, have had to contend with serious pollution caused by non-Indian oil drilling companies. Most children of landless Cree attend public schools. Many Chippewa-Crees are Christians. Many also participate in the Sun Dance, sweat lodge ceremonies, and the Native American Church. Cree is still spoken on the reservation and by some older people living off-reservation.

Crow

The Crow (Kr ō) self-designation was *Absaroke*, after a bird once native to the region. *See also* Hidatsa.

LOCATION The Crow traditional homeland was south of Lake Winnipeg. By the late eighteenth century they inhabited southwestern Montana and northern Wyoming. Today, most Crows live in Bighorn and Yellowstone Counties, Montana.

POPULATION There were about 4,000 Crows in the late eighteenth century. There were 8,491 enrolled members of the tribe in 1991.

LANGUAGE Crow/Hidatsa is a Siouan language.

Historical Information

HISTORY The Hidatsa-Crow lived originally in the Ohio country. From there, they moved to northern Illinois, through western Minnesota and into the Red River Valley, south of Lake Winnipeg. There they remained for at least several hundred years, beginning around the twelfth or thirteenth century, growing gardens and hunting buffalo.

Pressured by newly armed bands of Ojibwas and Crees, the group moved southwest to Devil's Lake in the mid–sixteenth century and then again toward the upper Missouri River, north of the Mandans, where they continued to hunt and grow corn. In the late seventeenth century, the Crow struck out on their own toward southwestern Montana and northern Wyoming and the vicinity of the Yellowstone, Powder, and Mussellshell Rivers. During this period, they separated into mountain (southern Montana and northern Wyoming) and river (lower Yellowstone region) divisions.

The Crow acquired horses, probably from the

Shoshone, and became full-fledged nomadic Plains Indians during the mid–eighteenth century. In addition to the Crows' warring and raiding activities, they also traded with the Shoshone and other Great Basin and Plateau groups for horses that they then exchanged with easterly tribes. Whenever possibly they avoided non-Indians. During that period they were considered a wealthy tribe with many horses. Their land between the Yellowstone River and Big Horn Mountains contained plenty of pasture as well as excellent natural defenses.

Major smallpox epidemics struck the people in 1781 and 1833. Crow boundaries under the 1851 Fort Laramie Treaty included about 38.5 million acres, mostly in the Yellowstone region. The Powder River country remained in dispute between them and the Lakota. However, their lands were drastically reduced in 1868 and again in subsequent years. During that period the Crows became seminomadic, building winter camps that included a few log cabins. In much of the 1860s and 1870s, Crows served the United States as scouts in the Indian wars, especially against the Lakota and the Nez Percé.

Despite their help to the United States, the U.S. government treated the Crow no differently than it did any other Indians. By the late 1880s the Crow had been forced to cede most of their remaining land. Catholic missionaries and boarding schools had made inroads into the reservation and into Crow culture. Many aspects of traditional Crow culture, such as giveaways and the Sun Dance, had been outlawed in 1884. It was also illegal to leave the reservation without permission and to sell a horse to another Indian. In the seven years from 1914 to 1921, Crow horse herds declined from roughly 35,000 to less than 1,000. Some leaders, like Chief Plenty Coups, urged accommodation, especially in the area of education.

Meanwhile, the Crow developed a tribal council that managed to keep the Bureau of Indian Affairs staff at arm's length and provide them with a semi-independent decision-making body. In the 1950s, the government coerced the Crow into selling their rights to the Bighorn Canyon, where it built the Yellowtail Dam, ironically named for one of its chief opponents. In 1981, legal ownership of the Bighorn River passed to the state of Montana.

RELIGION Like other Plains Indians, the Crow placed great importance in supernatural guardian helpers acquired in dreams or during vision quests. Their main ceremonies included the Sun Dance, the Medicine Lodge, and the triennial Tobacco Society ceremony, performed by both men and women in honor of the tribe's sacred plant.

The existence of the Tobacco Society conferred benefits on both planters and the tribe as a whole. Payment of a high fee entitled one to membership in the society and the right to learn and perform the associated songs and dances. The proper place for planting tobacco was determined by consultation over ranking members' dreams. Seed preparation and planting were highly ritualized, although the area was always burned over first.

Planting was followed by a dance and then a feast. In a subsequent ceremony, new members were adopted into the society; this ceremony was also highly ritualized and included fees paid for various honors, painting, dancing, singing, and sweating as well as the acquisition of medicine bundles. Members observed various behavior restrictions during the year. The harvest was also accompanied by ritual.

GOVERNMENT Each of about 13 matrilineal clans was led by a headman selected on the basis of his war record. A council of chiefs governed the tribe; one member of the council was head of the camp. Each spring, one of the men's military societies was appointed camp police force, which was charged with maintaining internal order, supervising the buffalo hunt, and regulating war parties.

CUSTOMS Generosity was highly valued among the Crow, as with most Plains tribes. For instance, the leader of a successful raid was entitled to all its plunder but was socially obligated to give it away.

Unlike most Plains nomads they were organized into matrilineal clans. Most girls married before puberty to men outside the clan, and most men purchased their wives. Pre- or extramarital sex was not punished, but female chastity was valued. Wives were also gained by inheritance and capture. Mother-in-law and father-in-law taboos were observed.

Parents spent a great deal of time nurturing, teaching, and encouraging their children to prepare for life as adults. There were no orphans, as orphans were immediately adopted by aunts or uncles. Children rarely, if ever, received corporal punishment. Instead, "joking relatives" used pointed humor to keep people in line.

Corpses were removed from the tipi through the side, dressed in their best clothes, painted, and placed on a scaffold. The bones were later buried among rocks or in a cave, except that tipis were erected over the scaffolds of great chiefs. Mourners cut their hair, gashed their limbs (or sometimes cut off their fingers), and gave away their property.

Games included the hand game, dice games, shinny, contests, and hoop and pole. Most games included gambling. Relatively high prices were commanded for various ceremonial privileges.

DWELLINGS When Crows lived near Lake Winnipeg and with the Hidatsa along the Missouri River, they built earth lodges. Later, women made four-pole,

25-foot-high (or higher) skin tipis of between 7 and 20 buffalo skins. The larger tipis could house as many as 40 people, but the average was about 12. The tipi owner or a special guest slept at the rear (opposite the door). A draft screen around the lower inside was painted with pictures of the owner's war feats.

DIET Pre-Plains Crows raised corn and other crops. Buffalo were hunted by driving them into impoundments or over cliffs or by means of the mounted surround. Men also hunted deer, antelope, and other large game, sometimes by wearing the skin of such an animal and stalking it. Meat was roasted over a fire, cooked in the ashes, or stone boiled in a skin-lined pit. It was also cut into strips, dried, and stored for the winter. Women dug roots and gathered berries, fruit, and other wild foods. The Crow grew their ceremonial tobacco but traded for the everyday variety.

KEY TECHNOLOGY Pottery predated the move to the Plains. Material goods included, in addition to the usual buffalo-based items, fire drills; bows from hickory, ash, or even elk antler; and stone scrapers and other tools. The cradle board, mostly a means of transportation, was U-shaped at the top and tapered at the bottom. Backrests for use within the tipi were made of willow sticks bound with sinew and hung from a tripod.

TRADE The Crow played the role of intermediary between the Mandans and Hidatsas to the east and Great Basin and Plateau tribes such as the Shoshone, Salish (Flathead), Nez Percé, and Ute. The Crow-Mandan trade continued until the early nineteenth century.

NOTABLE ARTS Weapons were extremely finely made, as were clothing, blankets, and leather items such as decorated parfleches. There were also various ceremonial carvings.

TRANSPORTATION Dogs carried movable goods and pulled travois. After the people acquired horses in the mid–eighteenth century, they became highly skilled horsemen and perhaps the best horse thieves on the Plains. They used skin rafts to cross rivers.

DRESS Typical Plains clothing included, for men, a shirt, hip-high leggings, moccasins, and a buffalo robe. Women wore a long dress, knee-high leggings, and moccasins. Both used rawhide visors against the sun. Before braiding became customary, the Crow parted their hair in the middle and wore it, sometimes with additions of horse hair, as low as ground level. In the later period, women's dresses were decorated with elks' teeth and fur trim.

WAR AND WEAPONS The various men's societies were voluntary and not age-graded, although some were more important than others. Most or all had military, hunt, or police-related functions. The Crazy Dogs were dedicated to unusual bravery in combat. Dog Soldiers were the camp police. Some societies occasionally engaged in annual wife capturing.

Traditional enemies included the Shoshone, Lakota (after circa 1800), and Blackfeet. Allies included the Mandan, Salish (Flathead), and Nez Percé. Crows preferred to count coup rather than to scalp. Four people could count coup against the same enemy, with diminishing honor. Four war activities worthy of formal honors were, in descending order: leading a successful party, touching an enemy, stealing a picketed horse, and taking a weapon in a hand-to-hand encounter. Weapons included wooden or horn bows and arrows, stone-headed war clubs, knives, and painted, feather-decorated shields.

Contemporary Information

GOVERNMENT/RESERVATIONS The Crow Reservation (Big Horn and Yellowstone Counties, Montana), established in 1868, is composed of over 1,500,000 acres, of which about 400,000 are tribally owned. The 1990 resident Indian population was 4,724. The constitution dates from 1948. All adults are members of the general council, which elects four tribal officers and various governing committees. The council governs the tribe, along with the tribal court. Almost half the land base is owned by non-Indians.

ECONOMY The reservation is rich in natural resources, such as coal, although the Crow for years had been unable to profit greatly from it. However, in 1993 the tribe concluded a settlement with the United States that called for the creation of a trust fund of up to $85 million in compensation for mismanaged mineral resource development. There are jobs with the tribal government, Little Bighorn College, and mining companies. Most agricultural land is leased to large corporations. There is also a visitor center and motel complex. Unemployment regularly tops 50 percent

LEGAL STATUS The Crow Tribe is a federally recognized tribal entity.

DAILY LIFE Most Crow people speak the native language. A matrilineal clan system and regular giveaways help maintain a semitraditional family structure. Other customs, such as traditional healing ceremonies, the giving of Indian names, and the use of medicine bundles in traditional prayers, are also maintained.

The annual fair in August, featuring feasting, rodeos, giveaways, and other traditional and semitraditional activities, is a time to renew social and family ties. Crows adorn their costumes and riding gear with expertly made beadwork, although they do not generally sell it to tourists.

Tribally controlled Little Bighorn College represents a continuing focus on educational achievement. Some Crows are Christians. Many also practice sweat lodge, Sun Dance, and Native American Church ceremonies. People still undertake vision quests, and the Tobacco Society remains active. The Crow continue to battle high unemployment and its associated social problems, such as substance abuse, as well as continuing racial discrimination.

Dakota

Dakota (Dä `k ō tä), a Siouan dialect spoken by the Eastern group of the tribe commonly referred to as Sioux. The divisions of the Eastern group include Sisseton ("swamp village," "lake village," or "fishscale village"), Wahpeton ("dwellers among the leaves"), Wahpekute ("shooters among the leaves"), and Mdewakanton ("People of the Mystic Lake"). The latter two divisions are also known as Santee (from *Isanati,* "knife.") and shared a closely related culture.

The Dakota refer to themselves as Dakota ("ally"), Dakotah Oyate ("Dakota People"), or *Ikce Wicasa* ("Natural" or "Free People"). The word "Sioux" is derived originally from an Ojibwa word, *Nadowe-is-iw,* meaning "lesser adder" ("enemy" is the implication), which was corrupted by French voyageurs to *Nadoussioux* and then shortened to *Sioux.* Today, many people use the term "Dakota" or, less commonly, "Lakota" to refer to all Sioux people.

All 13 subdivisions of Dakota-Lakota-Nakota speakers (Sioux) were known as *Oceti Sakowin,* or Seven Council Fires, a term referring to their seven political divisions: Teton (the Western group, speakers of Lakota); Sisseton, Wahpeton, Wahpekute, and Mdewakanton (the Eastern group, speakers of Dakota); and Yankton and Yanktonai (the Central, or Wiciyela, group, speakers of Dakota and Nakota). *See also* Lakota and Nakota.

LOCATION In the late seventeenth century, the Dakotas lived in Wisconsin and north-central Minnesota, around Mille Lacs. By the nineteenth century they had migrated to the prairies and eastern plains of Minnesota, Iowa, Nebraska, and eastern South Dakota. Today, most Dakotas live on reservations in the Dakotas, Nebraska, and Minnesota and in regional cities and towns.

POPULATION Dakota, Lakota, and Nakota speakers numbered about 25,000 in the late seventeenth century. At that time there were approximately 5,000 Dakota speakers. There were about 12,000–15,000 Dakota and Nakota speakers in the late eighteenth century. Today there are at least 6,000 Dakotas living in the United States and Canada.

LANGUAGE The Eastern group speaks the Dakota dialect of Dakota, a Siouan language.

Historical Information

HISTORY The Siouan linguistic family may have originated along the lower Mississippi River or in eastern Texas. Siouan speakers moved to, or may in fact have originated in, the Ohio Valley, where they lived in large agricultural settlements. They may have been related to the Mound Builder culture of the ninth through twelfth centuries. They may also have originated in the upper Mississippi Valley or even the Atlantic seaboard.

Siouan tribes still lived in the southeast, between Florida and Virginia, around the late sixteenth and early seventeenth century. All were destroyed either by attacks from Algonquian-speaking Indians or a combination of attacks from non-Indians and non-Indian diseases. Some fled and were absorbed by other tribes. Some were also sent as slaves to the West Indies.

Dakota-Lakota-Nakota speakers ranged throughout more than 100 million acres of the upper Mississippi region, including Minnesota and parts of Wisconsin, Iowa, and the Dakotas, from the sixteenth to the early seventeenth century. Some of these people encountered French explorers around Mille Lacs, Minnesota, in the late seventeenth century, and Santees were directly involved in the great British-French political and economic struggle. Around that time, conflict with the Cree and Anishinabe, who were well armed with French rifles, plus the lure of great buffalo herds to feed their expanding population, induced bands to begin moving west into the Plains. The people acquired horses around the mid–eighteenth century.

Dakotas were the last to leave, with most bands remaining in prairies of western Minnesota and eastern South Dakota. They also retained many eastern Woodland/western Great Lakes characteristics. Around 1800, the Wahpeton established villages above the mouth of the Minnesota River. Fifty years later they had moved farther upriver and broken into an upper and a lower division. The Mdewakanton and Wahpekute tribes (Santee) established villages around the Mississippi and lower Minnesota Rivers and began hunting buffalo communally, competing with the Sauk, Fox, and other tribes.

Dakotas ceded all land in Minnesota and Iowa in 1837 and 1851 (Mendota and Traverse des Sioux Treaties), except for a reservation along the Minnesota River. Santees were served by a lower agency, near Morton, and Sissetons and Wahpetons by an upper agency, near Granite Falls. At the mercy of dishonest agents and government officials, who cheated them out of food and money, and all but overrun by squatters, the Santees rebelled in 1862. Under the leadership of Ta-oya-te-duta (Little Crow), they killed hundreds of non-Indians.

Since many Wahpetons and Sissetons remained neutral (or, as in the case of Chief Wabasha, betrayed their people), and support for the rebellion was not deep, it shortly collapsed. In reprisal, the government hanged 38 Dakotas after President Lincoln pardoned over 250 others and confiscated all Dakota land and property in Minnesota. All previous treaties were unilaterally abrogated. Little Crow himself was killed by bounty hunters in 1863. His scalp and skull were placed on exhibition in St. Paul.

Many Santees fled to Canada and to the West, to join relatives at Fort Peck and elsewhere. Many more died of starvation and illness during this period. Mdewakanton and Wahpekute survivors were rounded up and finally settled at Crow Creek, South Dakota, a place of poor soil and little game, where hundreds of removed Dakotas died within one year. Thus ended the long Santee occupation of the eastern Woodlands/prairie region.

In 1866, Santees at Crow Creek were removed to the Santee Reservation, Nebraska, where living conditions were extremely poor. Most of the land was allotted in 1885. Missionaries, especially Congregationalists and Episcopalians, were influential well into the twentieth century. Most people lived by subsistence farming, hunting, fishing, and gathering.

Two reservations were established for Wahpetons and Sissetons around 1867: the Sisseton-Wahpeton Reservation, near Lake Traverse, South Dakota, and the Fort Totten Reservation, at Devil's Lake. By 1892, two-thirds of the Lake Traverse Reservation had been opened to non-Indians, with the remaining one-third, about 300,000 acres, allotted to individuals. In order not to starve, many sold their allotted land, so that more than half of the latter acreage was subsequently lost. For much of the early twentieth century, people eked out a living through subsistence farming combined with other subsistence activities as well as wages and trust-fund payments.

Several hundred Dakotas left the Santee Reservation in 1869 to settle on the Big Sioux River near Flandreau, South Dakota, renouncing tribal membership at that time. Some federal aid was arranged by a Presbyterian minister, but by and large these people lived without even the meager benefits provided to most Indians. Some Flandreau Indians eventually drifted back to form communities in Minnesota. The official status of these communities was uncertain well into the twentieth century.

RELIGION Male and female shamans provided religious leadership. Depending on the tribe, their duties might include leading hunting and war parties; curing the sick; foretelling the future, including the weather; and interpreting visions and dreams. Wahpeton shamans also divined the whereabouts of the enemy and lost objects. They performed feats of skill and magic in front of large audiences to impress the public with their powers.

Sissetons and Wahpetons believed in Wakan Tanka, the Great Spirit and creator of the universe, as well as other gods and spirits. The secret Wahpeton Medicine Lodge Society performed the Medicine Dance several times a year. Participants used drums, deer hoof rattles, whistles, and sacred pipes carved of pipestone. Other religious activities included vision quests and ritual purification in the sweat lodge. The Sisseton later adopted some Plains ceremonies, such as the Sun Dance.

GOVERNMENT All but the Wahpekute were divided into seven bands, each usually led by a chief. In more recent times that position was often hereditary. For the same three bands, the *akitcita* was an elite warrior group that maintained discipline at camp and on the hunt. This police society was distinctive of Siouans and may have originated with them. The Seven Council Fires met approximately annually to socialize and discuss matters of national importance.

CUSTOMS Mdewakantons wrapped their dead in skins or blankets and placed them on scaffolds. Remains were taken to a tribal burial grounds after a few months or years and buried in mounds with tools and weapons. Burial mounds were at least several feet high and up to 60 feet in diameter.

Sissetons treated their dead similarly but included tools, weapons, and utensils. Bodies with heads facing south were placed in scaffolds or trees. A horse might be killed for a dead warrior to use in the next life. Murder victims were placed face down in the ground. Mourners cut their hair and slashed their limbs.

Wahpetons buried their dead early on but changed to scaffolds, probably as a result of Sisseton influence. The Dakota bands may once have been clans. Favorite games, usually accompanied by gambling, included lacrosse and shinny. Descent was patrilineal.

DWELLINGS Dakotas built small, occasionally palisaded villages near lakes and rice swamps when they lived in the Wisconsin-Minnesota area. At that time they lived in large, heavily timbered bark houses with pitched roofs. In winter, some groups lived in small conical houses covered with skins. Both men and women helped build the houses. The Sisseton sometimes used tipis after their move to the prairies.

DIET Siouan people in the Ohio Valley farmed

corn, beans, and squash. While still in the Great Lakes region, women grew corn, beans, and squash. People ate turtles, fish, dogs, and large and small game and gathered wild rice. Buffalo, which roamed the area in small herds, was also an important food source. People burned grass around the range and forced the buffalo toward an ambush. The Sisseton, especially, turned more toward buffalo with their westward migration.

KEY TECHNOLOGY Bows and arrows were the main hunting weapons. The Sisseton carved pipestone (catlinite) ceremonial pipes and wove rushes into mats. The Wahpeton wove rushes into mats and also wove cedar and basswood fiber bags. All groups made pottery. Fish were either speared or shot with a bow and arrow. Iron-containing clays were pulverized in stone mortars and mixed with gluey material to make paint. Brushes were made of bone, horn, wood, or a tuft of antelope hair mounted on a stick. The flageolet was a common musical instrument.

TRADE Depending on time and location, Dakota tribes traded various woodland/prairie/plains goods. Items included wild rice, pottery, and skins and other animal products.

NOTABLE ARTS The Dakota made fine painted rawhide trunks. They incised and painted parfleches, pipe pouches, robes, and other items. Women tended to make geometric designs, whereas men made more realistic forms. Clothing was embroidered and, later, beaded.

TRANSPORTATION The Sisseton made dugout canoes, and the Wahpeton made birch-bark canoes. Most groups obtained horses beginning around 1760, but the eastern groups never had as many as did the western groups.

DRESS Most clothing was made from buckskin. In the Woodlands, the people wore breechclouts, dresses, leggings, and moccasins, with fur robes for extra warmth. On the Plains, they decorated their clothing with beads and quillwork in geometric and animal designs.

WAR AND WEAPONS The idea that the purpose of war was to bring glory to an individual rather than to acquire territory or destroy an enemy people was distinctive to the Siouan people and may have originated with them. Dakotas did not generally fight other Dakotas. The akitcita, known particularly among the Mdewakanton, was an elite warrior group that maintained discipline at camp and on the hunt. The Ojibwa were traditional enemies, at least around the seventeenth and eighteenth centuries.

Contemporary Information

GOVERNMENT/RESERVATIONS The Fort Peck Reservation, Roosevelt, Sheridan, and Valley Counties, Montana (Assiniboine-Sioux [Upper Yanktonai and Sisseton-Wahpeton]), established in 1873, consists of about one million acres, about one-quarter of which is tribally owned. Their 1927 constitution is not based on the Indian Reorganization Act (IRA). Their representative government, the Tribal Executive Board, dates from 1960. Enrollment in 1992 was 10,500, with 6,700 residents.

The Devil's Lake (formerly Fort Totten) Reservation, Benson, Eddy, Nelson and Ramsey Counties, North Dakota (Sisseton, Wahpeton, and Cuthead Yanktonai), established in 1867, consists of 53,239 acres, most of which have been allotted. There were 4,420 enrolled members in 1992, with about 2,900 in residence. The IRA constitution adopted in 1944 calls for elections to a tribal council.

The Lake Traverse Reservation, Richland and Sargent Counties, North Dakota, and Cadington, Day, Grant, Marshall, and Roberts Counties, South Dakota (Sisseton and Wahpeton), established in 1867, consists of about 105,000 acres. Under a 1934 constitution and by-laws, the people elect district representatives to a tribal council. Tribal enrollment was 10,073 in 1992, with a resident population of 5,306.

The Santee Sioux Reservation, Knox County, Nebraska (Santee), established in 1863, consists of about 3,600 acres. Enrollment in 1992 was about 2,000. In the same year there were 748 residents. A tribal council governs the reservation.

The Flandreau Santee Sioux Reservation, Moody County, South Dakota (Santee), established in 1935, consists of about 2,180 acres. The constitution and by-laws were approved in 1931 and then amended in 1936 to conform to the IRA. Enrolled membership in 1992 was 611 with about 230 residents. An executive committee governs the reservation.

The Lower Sioux Community, Redwood County, Minnesota (Santee), established in 1887, owns 1,742.93 acres. The 1992 enrollment was 750 with about 300 residents. The people elect a community council.

The Prairie Island Community, Goodhue County, Minnesota (Santee), established in 1887, consists of about 534 acres. Enrollment in 1992 was 440, with 56 residents in 1990. A community council is popularly elected.

The Upper Sioux Community, Yellow Medicine County, Minnesota (Sisseton, Wahpeton, Flandreau Santee, Santee, Yankton), established in 1938, consists of 743.57 acres. There were 43 residents in 1990. Political power is exercised by a board of trustees.

The Prior Lake (Shakopee) Community, Scott County, Minnesota (Santee), established in 1969, consists of about 293 acres. Enrollment in 1992 was 227, with 174 residents. A community council governs the community.

The Wabasha Community (Minnesota) consists of 110.24 acres. There are no residents. It was purchased in 1944 as part of the Upper Mississippi Fish and Wildlife Refuge.

Some Wahpetons and other Dakotas also live on Canadian reserves, such as Portage la Prairie, Sioux Valley, Pipestone, and Bird Tail in Manitoba and Fort Qu'appelle, Moose Wood, and Round Plain in Saskatchewan.

ECONOMY The Devil's Lake Sioux have a plant that makes nonviolent armaments such as camouflage nets. There are also a bingo hall and a casino. Lake Traverse has a bingo hall and casino as well as a plastic bag factory. With an inadequate land base and little industry, many residents of the Santee Sioux Reservation must seek employment in nearby cities and towns. A pharmaceutical company provides a small number of jobs.

The Flandreau Reservation opened the Royal River Casino in 1990. Fort Peck has a bingo hall, and land is leased to non-Indian farmers and ranchers. Fort Peck owns and operates a profitable oil well. They also have other mineral resources and have encouraged industrial development.

The Lower Sioux own a casino, as do Prairie Island (casino and bingo hall), Upper Sioux (casino), and Prior Lake (casino and bingo hall).

LEGAL STATUS The Assiniboine and Sioux Tribes of the Fort Peck Reservation, the Devils Lake Sioux Tribe, the Flandreau Santee Sioux Tribe, the Lower Sioux Indian Community of Minnesota Mdewakanton Sioux Indians, the Prairie Island Indian Community of Minnesota Mdewakanton Sioux Indians, the Santee Sioux Tribe, the Shakopee Mdewakanton Sioux Community (Prior Lake), the Sisseton-Wahpeton Sioux Tribe (Lake Traverse), and the Upper Sioux Indian Community are federally recognized tribal entities.

DAILY LIFE The Wahpeton and Sisseton people are closely related, in part through much intermarriage. At Lake Traverse, Sisseton-Wahpeton Community College opened in 1979, and Tiospa Zina High School emphasizes tribal values. Many people speak Dakota at Devil's Lake, which is a relatively traditional community. They sponsor a powwow in July. The Native American Church and Sacred Pipe ceremony, among other religious practices, remain active. People on the Santee Reservation resisted a casino in favor of cultural revival. Flandreau received new homes, irrigation, and health care facilities in the 1960s.

Gros Ventres

Gros Ventres (Gr ō vant) is French for "big belly," after a mistranslation of the sign language for their name. They were once known to non-Indians as Gros Ventres of the Prairie as opposed to the Gros Ventres of the Missouri (Hidatsa). The Blackfeet gave these people another of their common names, Atsina; their self-designation is *Haaninin*, "Lime People" or "White Clay People."

LOCATION In the late eighteenth century, Gros Ventres lived from north-central Montana to southern Saskatchewan. Today, most live in north-central Montana.

POPULATION The Gros Ventre population was about 3,000 in the late eighteenth century. It was approximately 2,900 in 1992.

LANGUAGE Gros Ventre is an Algonquian language.

Historical Information

HISTORY At least 3,000 years ago the Arapaho, possibly united with the future Gros Ventres and other peoples, probably lived in the western Great Lakes region to the Red River Valley, where they grew corn and lived in permanent villages. Under pressure from the Ojibwa (Anishinabe), they migrated to the upper Missouri River region in the early eighteenth century.

During the migration, perhaps around Devil's Lake, the Gros Ventre separated from the Arapaho. They acquired horses in the early to mid–eighteenth century. Shortly thereafter they became a Plains tribe and joined the Blackfeet Confederacy.

The people signed the 1851 Fort Laramie Treaty after spending a brief period of time with the Arapaho. Another treaty in 1855 led to further land cessions. In the early 1860s the Gros Ventres joined with their Crow enemies to fight their traditional friends, the Blackfeet, but were soundly defeated in 1867. Following a further decline caused mostly by disease, in 1888 survivors were placed on the Fort Belknap Reservation, which they shared with the Assiniboine, also former enemies.

The Gros Ventres filed a lawsuit in 1897 to gain compensation for lands seized under the 1855 treaty; during the twentieth century the tribe has received several land claims awards. Also around the turn of the century, members of the tribe sold under extreme duress a 28-square-mile strip of reservation land. Tuberculosis was a severe problem in the early twentieth century, affecting more than 90 percent of the tribal population.

RELIGION Two sacred pipes figured prominently in traditional Gros Ventre religion. Gros Ventres also observed other Plains religious customs such as vision quests, medicine bundles, and the Sun Dance.

GOVERNMENT There were 12 autonomous bands in historic times, each with its own chief.

CUSTOMS Bands camped separately in winter, coming together in summer for communal buffalo hunt and celebrations, including the Sun Dance. At this time they camped in a circle, with each band having a designated place.

Descent was patrilineal. People generally found marriage partners outside of the parents' band. Girls were often married by age 12, usually to men around 20. Polygamy and divorce were common. The mother-in-law taboo was in force.

Age-graded male societies had their own costumes, dances, and paraphernalia. Men moved through the various rankings with their peers, each group purchasing the regalia of the next-higher group, until the men at the top sold out and retired with a large amount of wealth. Healing, through medicines and ritual, was a job that one might attain by fasting and attaining special powers. Corpses were wrapped in robes and placed on a scaffold, in a cave, or on a high rock.

DWELLINGS On the Plains, groups of women made skin tipis with three-pole foundations.

DIET Buffalo were hunted by driving them into chutes; after about 1730, they were hunted on horseback. Women cut meat into strips and dried it or made pemmican. Fresh meat was roasted over the fire or boiled, using red-hot rocks in a water-filled hole. People also ate deer, elk, and puppies and gathered foods such as rhubarb, berries, and eggs. They did not eat fish.

KEY TECHNOLOGY Women dressed skins with brains and liver. Men made bows of ash or cherry wood and also of horn. Horn bows were covered with rattlesnake skin. Sewing equipment included buffalo sinew thread and bone awls.

TRADE Gros Ventres participated in the regional trade complex, trading horses and animal products for agricultural items and, later, non-Indian items.

NOTABLE ARTS Gros Ventres made fine painted leather items and tanned and embroidered clothing.

TRANSPORTATION Horses arrived around 1730. Both dogs and horses pulled the travois. People made makeshift rafts of tipi covers and poles.

DRESS Women made the clothing, usually of elk skin or deerskin. They wore dresses; men wore leggings, breechclouts, shirts, and moccasins. Both sexes wore buffalo-skin caps and mittens in winter.

WAR AND WEAPONS Weapons included buffalo-hide shields and bows and arrows. In the mid–nineteenth century, Gros Ventres fought Crows with the Blackfeet and then fought the Blackfeet in alliance with the Crow. Other enemies included the Shoshone, Salish (Flathead), and Assiniboine. Traditional allies included the Arapaho, Cheyenne, and Cree.

Contemporary Information

GOVERNMENT/RESERVATIONS The Fort Belknap Reservation (Blaine and Philips Counties, Montana),

established in 1887, contains roughly 616,000 acres, about one-quarter of which are tribally owned. The 1990 Indian population was 2,332. A constitution and by-laws based on the Indian Reorganization Act were approved in 1935. The community council has 12 elected members, 6 Gros Ventres and 6 Assiniboines, as well as 3 appointed officers.

ECONOMY Income is generated through land leases to non-Indian farmers and ranchers. There is also some reservation farming and ranching. The federal government is a major employer. Un- and underemployment is chronic.

Stores and a bingo hall provide more money, although some gambling money comes from tribal members who can least afford it. Interest from land claims payments is used for burial assistance as well as for annual direct family payments.

LEGAL STATUS The Fort Belknap Indian Community (Gros Ventre and Assiniboine-Sioux) is a federally recognized tribal entity.

DAILY LIFE The Bureau of Indian Affairs, which has long dominated the Fort Belknap Reservation, has traditionally viewed both native groups as one community, to the detriment of Indian self-determination and cultural identity. The strip of land sold in 1897 is now, still under protest, being mined for gold. The mines have severely contaminated the regional environment and are associated with health problems on the reservation.

As of 1993, the Gros Ventres were considering officially changing their name to Ah-ah-nee-nin, as well as instituting a confederation form of government, in the interests of preserving individual tribal identity. Most children attend reservation public schools. There is also a mission school, and some attend off-reservation boarding schools. Fort Belknap Community College, containing a library and tribal archives, opened in 1984. A museum is proposed.

Hardly anyone in the early 1990s spoke the language fluently, although it is taught at the elementary and community college levels, and language and cultural retention are a major priority. Traditional religion is still practiced. Many Gros Ventres are also Christians, especially Catholics. The reservation hosts annual powwows.

Hidatsa

Hidatsa (H ē `dät sä), possibly taken from the name of a former village. Called Gros Ventres of the Missouri by French traders, they have also been known as the *Minitaris* (Mandan for "they crossed the water").

LOCATION Most Hidatsas lived along the upper Missouri River in western North Dakota in the late eighteenth century. Today, most live in western North Dakota.

POPULATION The late-eighteenth-century Hidatsa population was about 2,500. In the early 1990s, there were about 6,000 enrolled members of the Three Affiliated Tribes.

LANGUAGE Hidatsa is a Siouan dialect.

Historical Information

HISTORY Siouan people may have lived originally along the lower Mississippi River, slowly migrating north through Tennessee and Kentucky and into Ohio. Some then went east across the Appalachian Mountains, but most continued northwest. Originally one people, the Hidatsa-Crow were perhaps the first Siouan group to leave the Ohio country. They moved to northern Illinois, through western Minnesota, and into the Red River Valley.

For at least 400 years, beginning around the twelfth or thirteenth century, they grew gardens and hunted buffalo south of Lake Winnipeg. Finally, pressured by newly armed bands of Ojibwas and Crees, the group moved southwest to Devil's Lake in the mid–sixteenth century. They then moved again toward the upper Missouri River, where they continued to hunt and grow corn, encouraged by receiving seeds and acquiring new techniques from the Mandans.

In the late seventeenth century, the Crow struck out on their own, leaving the Hidatsa behind. At this time, the latter associated with other agricultural tribes such as the Mandans and Arikaras. Non-Indians also traded regularly at Hidatsa villages, exchanging items of non-native manufacture for furs. Early non-Indian explorers, such as Meriwether Lewis and William Clark, also lived among the Hidatsa. The people lost significant population in the late eighteenth century through warfare, primarily with the Dakota, as well as smallpox epidemics. By about 1800 they had been reduced to a few villages along the Knife River.

The smallpox epidemic of 1837 devastated the tribe; surviving Hidatsas and Mandans regrouped by 1845 into a single village called Like-a-Fishhook, located near Fort Berthold, North Dakota. They were joined there by the Arikara in 1862. The Fort Berthold Reservation was created in 1871 for Hidatsas, Mandans, and Arikaras. Although the 1851 Fort Laramie Treaty recognized the tribes' claims to 12 million acres, the original reservation consisted of 8 million acres; by 1886 it had been reduced to about 1 million acres.

Like-a-Fishhook was an important regional commercial center until the 1880s, when most people left it to establish communities along the Missouri River. The Hidatsa lived on both sides of the river, in Lucky Mound, Shell Creek, and Independence. During the 1950s, against the tribes' vehement opposition, the United States built the Garrison Dam on the Missouri. The resulting Lake Sakakawea covered much of their land, farms, and homes. This event destroyed the tribes' economic base and severely damaged its social structure.

RELIGION The Corn Dance Feast of the Women was based on mythological concepts and offered as thanks for their crops. Elderly women hung dried meat on poles and then performed a dance. Younger women fed them meat and received grains of corn to eat in return. The dried meat would be left on the poles until harvest time. The Hidatsa also learned the Sun Dance.

There were a number of religious societies. The right to perform ceremonies was either inherited or purchased. The associated bundles were purchased, even from parents. Hidatsas undertook vision quests from an early age.

GOVERNMENT The tribe contained several bands, including the Hidatsa proper, the Awatixa, and the Awaxawi. Villages were ruled by a council, a chief, and a war chief. The chieftainship had a hereditary component.

CUSTOMS Descent was matrilineal, and the extended family was the primary economic unit. Land was held by groups of related families known as lineages, which were in turn organized into larger groups, with formal leadership usually provided by older men. Lineages remained within one village, but the larger groups crossed villages. Within villages, each larger group was divided into two divisions; this organization played a key role in village leadership as well as games and other competition. The Hidatsa also recognized about seven clans.

Women controlled the gardens and were in charge of harvest distribution to their families. The White Buffalo Society, which featured dancing to lure buffalo to the hunters, was open only to women. Age-graded men's societies had mainly military functions. Each group had its own dances, songs, and regalia, which were acquired by the youngest group and purchased en masse from the next-higher group, the buyers displacing the sellers as the latter also "moved up."

Social rank was hereditary to some degree. Most adults were excellent swimmers. "Joking relatives," whose fathers were in the same clan, teased or upbraided each other for deviating from normative conduct. This mechanism was very effective for maintaining social customs and proper behavior. Food, weapons, and personal items were placed on scaffolds along with corpses. Mourners cut their hair. When chiefs died, all lodge fires were extinguished.

DWELLINGS From around 1700 on, the people lived in permanent villages on bluffs overlooking the upper Missouri River. Groups of people erected circular, dome-shaped earth lodges about 40 feet in diameter. Each housed two to three families or up to about 40 people. A wooden framework supported interwoven willow branches and grass, covered with mud or clay. Posts, beams, and rafters were skillfully fitted together. Entrance was via a covered passageway. Floors may have been partially excavated. The lodges lasted from seven to ten years.

Cooking took place inside in winter and outside in summer. Cook kettles were suspended on poles over central fires. People slept on rawhide platform beds. Furniture also included willow back rests and buffalo-robe couches. Interior floors contained deep storage pits, with more storage behind beds and against walls. People also used smaller earth lodges in winter, when they took refuge in forests. Skin tipis were used while traveling or hunting.

DIET Women cooperated in growing corn, beans, squash, pumpkins, and sunflowers. Gardens were located in river bottoms below the villages. They stored corn in earth caches, lined with logs and grass and covered with grass. Corn was boiled and eaten fresh or shelled and dried for the winter, when it was pounded and eaten as meal with other vegetables and meat. Squash was cut into strips and sun dried. Crops were harvested in midsummer and especially in early fall.

Old men grew a small tobacco crop. Tobacco was sacred and some ritual surrounded its cultivation, harvesting, and use. Only elderly men generally smoked, in pipes and for ceremonial purposes.

Buffalo and other meat was acquired primarily through trade, although men did hunt buffalo and other animals. After the people acquired horses they tracked the buffalo farther onto the plains, into present-day South Dakota and Montana. Women also gathered berries, most of which were dried. Sugar came from box elder sap. Other foods included fish and dogs.

KEY TECHNOLOGY Many material items, such as agricultural implements (bone hoes and rakes) and horn utensils and tools were made of buffalo and elk parts. Mortars, pestles, and digging sticks were made of wood. Women made twilled plaited baskets and pottery. Especially before they acquired horses, people used tumplines and chest straps for carrying burdens on their backs.

People felled and burned trees in order to enrich the soil for growing. Garden plots were left fallow after about three years of cultivation. Cache pits (for crop storage) were about 8 feet deep, 2 or 3 feet wide at the top, and perhaps twice as wide at the bottom. Women placed ears of corn around the outside and shelled corn and squash in the center. They covered the pits with ashes, dirt, and grass. Entrance was via a ladder.

Painted rawhide trunks or boxes, more typical of Woodland tribes, were about 15 inches square and 10 inches high. The people also painted parfleches and built seven-hole flageolets from box elder wood with the pith removed. They also made music with rattles, rasps (notched wood), hand drums, or tambourines and by singing.

TRADE Village people traded agricultural products with nomads for meat and other animal products. Trade occupied an important position in Hidatsas' lives.

NOTABLE ARTS Artistic expression was particularly manifest in painted skins, baskets, and pottery.

TRANSPORTATION Serviceable boats were made of buffalo hides stretched over circular willow frames. Hidatsas tended to rely more on dogs than horses to pull their travois.

DRESS Women made clothing from skins and furs, particularly white weasel and ermine. Buffalo-hide blankets were the main cold-weather item. Tattoos were common.

WAR AND WEAPONS Traditional enemies included the Dakota and Shoshone, whereas the Hidatsa were often allied with the Mandan. The men's groups included Dog Soldiers, a military-police society.

Contemporary Information

GOVERNMENT/RESERVATIONS The Three Affiliated Tribes (Arikara, Hidatsa, Mandan) live on the Fort Berthold Reservation (roughly 900,000 acres in Dunn, McKenzie, McLean, Mercer, Mountrail, and Ward Counties, North Dakota). The 1990 reservation Indian population was 2,999. More than half of the reservation is owned by non-Indians. The governing structure was established during the 1930s.

ECONOMY The tribal and federal governments are the largest employers. A few people have farms or ranches. Although the tribe opened a high-stakes casino in 1993, unemployment remains very high. There is some tourism along Lake Sakakawea.

LEGAL STATUS The Three Affiliated Tribes is a federally recognized tribal entity.

DAILY LIFE Most Hidatsas live in the town of Mandaree. Their lifestyle is similar to that of their non-Indian neighbors. Only elders speak the native language, despite the attempt to institute regular language classes.

Some Indians practice sweat lodge ceremonies and are members of the Native American Church. Most consider themselves Christians.

Ceremonies called Warbonnet Dances also help maintain an Indian identity. Ongoing crafts include quilt making and beadwork. The annual powwow held by each reservation community has become a focus for tribal activities.

Although the three tribes continue to maintain separate identities, they operate several reservation schools and publish the *Mandan, Hidatsa, and Arikara Times*. There is a tribal museum at New Town.

Hunkpapa
See Lakota

Hunkpatina
See Nakota

Ioway
Ioway (ˈĪ ō ä), from *ayuhwa*, "sleepy ones." Their self-designation is *Pahoja*, "dusty noses." Along with tribes such as Otoes, Missourias, and Winnebagos, they had elements of both Plains and Woodland cultures.

LOCATION   In the seventeenth century, most Ioways lived in northern Iowa and southern Minnesota. Today, most live in extreme northeast Kansas and in central Oklahoma.

POPULATION   There were about 1,100 Ioways in 1760. In the early 1990s, tribal enrollment was roughly 2,000 in Kansas-Nebraska and about 350 in Oklahoma.

LANGUAGE   Iowa-Otoe-Missouria is a member of the Chiwere division of the Siouan language.

Historical Information
HISTORY   According to tradition, the Ioway, Winnebago, Missouria, and Otoe once lived together north of the Great Lakes. Migration toward their historic areas began in the sixteenth century. Moving south through Wisconsin, the Ioway crossed the Mississippi River in the late sixteenth and early seventeenth centuries and began building villages in northeastern Iowa, just south of Minnesota.

Shortly thereafter, they continued west to the Des Moines River area of northwestern Iowa and southwestern Minnesota. In the mid–seventeenth century, the Ioway, constantly on the move and under pressure from the Dakota, moved west again into northern Nebraska. By the late seventeenth century they had crossed the Missouri eastward back into Iowa.

After they acquired horses in the early to mid–eighteenth century, they began to range farther west and take on more characteristics of Plains Indians. They were heavily engaged in the fur trade in the eighteenth and early nineteenth centuries, when some bands were living as far west as the Platte River. Around 1800 they were engaged in territorial wars

with the Sauk, Fox, and Dakota tribes. They also suffered a major smallpox epidemic in 1803.

The tribe signed treaties with the United States in 1824, 1825, 1830, 1836, and 1837, eventually ceding all of their lands. In 1836, they were assigned a reservation along the Great Nemaha River (southeastern Nebraska and northeastern Kansas) that was subsequently reduced in size. In the 1870s, the tribe divided into two independent groups, the Southern Ioway, in Oklahoma, and the Northern Ioway, in Kansas and Nebraska. The former group preferred to live in the traditional way, on lands held in common, whereas the latter group accepted individual allotments of land. The Southern Ioways were assigned a reservation in the Indian Territory in 1883, but it was opened to non-Indian settlement several years later.

RELIGION   The Ioway practiced a ceremony similar to the Grand Medicine Dance of the Woodland tribes. A candidate for admission to the secret Ojibwa medicine society, for example, was "shot" with a shell and then "revived" by members. The Ioway offered the first puff of tobacco smoke to the sky spirit. In the late nineteenth century, the people adopted a semi-Christianized Peyote religion.

GOVERNMENT   Hereditary clan and war chiefs held positions of authority.

CUSTOMS   The people played lacrosse and the moccasin (guessing) game, games customarily played by Woodlands tribes. There was a dual tribal division. Patrilineal clans were divided into subclans.

DWELLINGS   Semipermanent villages contained earth lodges. When hunting and traveling, people used bark-covered pole-frame lodges as well as skin tipis.

DIET   The major crops were corn, beans, squash, melons, sunflowers, and pumpkins. Buffalo were taken, using the surround method, in two communal buffalo hunts a year. Men also hunted other animals such as deer, beaver, raccoon, otter, and bear. Women gathered plant foods such as nuts, berries, and roots. The Ioway also fished.

KEY TECHNOLOGY   Fishing equipment included spears and possibly weirs and basketry traps. Men made a combination quiver and bow case. After the eighteenth century, women dressed skins with elk-horn scrapers. They also wove reed floor mats over a bark-cord foundation. Like Woodland tribes, Iowas made soft-twilled buffalo-hair wallets and rawhide box containers or trunks.

TRADE   During the early eighteenth century, Ioways were selling Indian slaves, probably Pawnees, to French traders for resale to Gulf Coast plantation owners. They were actively involved in the fur trade at that time. They also traded pipes to other tribes.

NOTABLE ARTS Ioways were particularly adept at weaving and wood working.

TRANSPORTATION The Ioway acquired horses about 1730.

DRESS Women made clothing of tanned animal skins.

WAR AND WEAPONS After their adoption of many Plains traits in the eighteenth century, the people gave highest war honors to those who led several successful raids. In descending order, other honors included killing an enemy, touching an enemy, and scalping. They also created rival military clubs.

Contemporary Information

GOVERNMENT/RESERVATIONS The Iowa Reservation, Brown and Doniphan Counties, Kansas, and Richardson County, Missouri, established in 1836, contains about 1,500 acres of mixed Indian and non-Indian ownership. The 1990 Indian population was 83. Governing structures included a tribal council and an executive committee.

There are also about 1,300 acres of individually owned land in Oklahoma, mostly in Lincoln, Payne, and Logan Counties, plus about 200 acres held in trust. The Oklahoma tribe ratified an Indian Reorganization Act constitution and is administered by a business committee.

ECONOMY The Iowa Tribe of Kansas and Nebraska owns a dairy farm, gas station, bingo parlor, and grain processing operation. The Oklahoma tribe owns a bingo operation and leases most of its land to non-Indians for grazing or farming operations. Most wage work is in nearby towns. There is also some individual income from oil and gas leases. Both groups of Ioway received almost $8 million in land claims settlements in the 1970s.

LEGAL STATUS The Iowa Tribe of Kansas and Nebraska and the Iowa Tribe of Oklahoma are federally recognized tribal entities. The latter is a member of the United Indian Nations of Oklahoma.

DAILY LIFE Although both groups are largely assimilated, extended kinship groups still form a basis of community life, and a modified clan system persists in Oklahoma. Despite the existence of primers and a lexicon, few people speak the native language. Most Ioways consider themselves Christian, although some attend some traditional ceremonies such as sweats, funerals, and namings and are also members of the Native American Church. Some also participate in intertribal dances.

Among the northern group, reacquisition of the land base is a prime goal, as is economic self-reliance. The Oklahoma tribe contracts with the Potawatomis for food and health programs. They are fighting the development of a toxic waste dump, proposed by a subsidiary of Amoco, on the site of a burial ground. Each tribe sponsors an annual powwow, in part because factionalism prevents extensive contacts between the two groups. The Kansas Ioway also present a rodeo.

Itazipco (Sans Arcs)
See Lakota

Kansa
See Kaw

Kaw

Kaw (Kä), also known as the Kansa (or Konza) tribe. Their self-designation is *Hutanga,* "by the edge of the shore," referring to a mythical residence on the Atlantic Ocean.

LOCATION The Kaw migrated from the Ohio Valley in the fifteenth century to the Kaw Valley in the sixteenth century. Today, most Kaws live near Kaw City, Oklahoma.

POPULATION About 5,000 people in 1700, the 1993 enrollment was 1,678, including five fullbloods.

LANGUAGE With the Osage, Omaha, Ponca, and Quapaw, the Kaw spoke a dialect of the Dhegiha branch of the Siouan language family.

Historical Information

HISTORY Perhaps once one people with other southern Siouans such as the Quapaw, Omaha, Ponca, and Osage, the Kaw remained in the Wabash Valley until driven out, possibly by the Iroquois, with the others in the early sixteenth century. They traveled down the Ohio River to the Mississippi and then north to near present-day St. Louis.

Finding the lower Missouri Valley open, the Kaw moved north on that river to the Kaw Valley, where they stopped and built lodges. The Spanish explorer Juan de Oñate saw them there in 1601. They lived peacefully, at least for a while, with their Pawnee and Apache neighbors. The other tribes continued in various directions.

Direct trade with the French out of New Orleans began at least as early as 1719. During the eighteenth and nineteenth centuries, the Kaw were frequently at war with both Indians and non-Indians. In 1724, at the request of French officials but also out of their own self-interest, over 1,000 Kaw traveled to Apache villages on a successful peace mission. The Kaw acquired their first horses at that time, and a brief peace was also established between the Apache and the French, the latter hitherto actively engaged in the trade in Apache slaves.

Shortly after that summer, however, French

traders resumed their purchase of Apache slaves from, among others, the Kaw, the latter preferring good trade relations with the French to peace with the declining Apaches. A French trading post was built near their territory during the period, and the Kaw soon took over some land in western Kansas vacated by the departing Apaches. The Kaw acquired horses at that time and began to adopt the characteristics of Plains Indians.

By the late eighteenth century, the well-armed Kaw, along with other tribes such as the Osage, Pawnees, and Wichitas, represented the eastern boundary of the huge Comanche country. The Kaw ceded all of their Missouri land in 1825 in exchange for a two-million-acre reservation in Kansas. That land in turn was ceded in 1846, and they were removed to a 265,000-acre reservation farther west, at Council Grove, on the Neosho River. The United States took those lands in 1873, and the remaining Kaw were removed to the Indian Territory. Their remaining lands were allotted in 1902, and the tribe was legally dissolved. A significant number of the full-bloods, such as Chief Al-le-go-wa-ho, had opposed allotment, a situation that exacerbated factionalism and the legal struggles that followed tribal dissolution. An example of the "progressive" faction was congressman and later vice president Charles Curtis, who was largely responsible for the Kaw Allotment Act of 1902 that stripped the Kaw people of their tribal lands.

The tribe reconstituted itself in 1959 under the auspices of the Department of the Interior. Tribal holdings at that time included 260 acres near the mouth of Beaver Creek. In the mid-1960s, the U.S. Army built the Kaw Reservoir, flooding most of these lands. The cemetery and council house were moved, the latter to a 15-acre tract that was subsequently enlarged by Congress to 135.5 acres.

RELIGION Traditional religious belief held that spirits dwelt in aspects of nature, such as celestial objects. The sun was a deity to which prayers were offered and donations made, as were the wind and a sacred salt spring in northern Kansas. Pubescent boys were taken by their fathers to a remote spot for at least three days, where they sought visions via fasting and self-deprivation.

GOVERNMENT Each village was ruled by a council-elected chief; a head chief ruled over all the villages. War chiefs led military operations.

CUSTOMS Sixteen patrilineal clans, each including several families, combined into seven larger organizational units. There were also two tribal divisions, *Nata* and *Ictunga*.

Men were mostly concerned with war and hunting while women did most of the work around the village. Kaws placed an extremely high value on morality and also on the chastity of women. Dog Soldiers served as camp police and administered public punishments as needed. After being painted and covered with bark, corpses were buried in a sitting position facing west. Food and possessions were buried with them. The mourning lasted a year.

DWELLINGS Circular or oval lodges were framed in wood and covered with mats woven of reed, grass, or bark and then a layer of earth. They ranged up to 60 feet in diameter and housed five or six families. Smoke holes were placed in the center. Skin-covered wood platforms around sides served as beds. The people also used skin tipis on hunting trips.

DIET Buffalo, and other animals as well, were the most important food source. There were two large, communal buffalo hunts a year. Women grew corn, beans, squash, and sunflowers in valley bottomlands. There were generally two harvests, one in midsummer and another in early fall. Women also gathered prairie potatoes and other foods.

KEY TECHNOLOGY Farm implements included hoes, digging sticks, and rakes. Most items came from the buffalo, including utensils and the raw material for various woven items.

TRADE The Kaw traded in buffalo skins and products. They also supplied the French with slaves in exchange for guns and other items.

NOTABLE ARTS Weaving, skin tanning, and painting were the most important arts.

TRANSPORTATION Dogs carried burdens before horses, which were acquired from the Apache in 1724.

DRESS Kaws dressed in typical Plains skin clothing. The men plucked or shaved all of their hair except for a single lock at the back.

WAR AND WEAPONS Weapons included bows, arrows, and buffalo-hide shields. The people chose war chiefs as needed. Enemies, beginning in the eighteenth century, included the Sauk, Fox, Omaha, Osage, Ioway, Otoe, Pawnee, and Cheyenne.

Contemporary Information

GOVERNMENT/RESERVATIONS The Kaw Nation administers 135.5 acres as trust lands. Tribal headquarters is at Kaw City, Oklahoma. The present constitution was adopted in 1990. The tribe is governed by an elected seven-member executive committee.

ECONOMY The Kaw Nation owns and operates a bingo enterprise, a nursery, a truck stop, and discount tobacco shops. With the Pawnee, Tonkawa, Ponca, and Otoe-Missouria, the Kaw are members of the Chilocco Development Authority. The Kaw Enterprise Authority seeks to increase the Kaw land base in and develop the tribal economy on former tribal land in Kansas City, Kansas.

The Kaw Nation of Oklahoma is a federally recognized tribal entity.

DAILY LIFE Fewer than a dozen Kaws are fluent in their native language (1993); language preservation programs are under way. The tribe provides academic scholarships for tribal members as well as social service programs. Kaw Nation district and supreme courts were dedicated in 1992. There is a tribal powwow in August.

Kiowa

Kiowa (`K ī u wu), "Principal People," is a derivation of *Ka'i gwu*, their self-designation.

LOCATION The Kiowa migrated in the seventeenth century from the Gallatin-Madison Valleys in southwestern Montana to the Black Hills. By the early nineteenth century, their territory included southeast Colorado, extreme northeast New Mexico, southwest Kansas, northwest Oklahoma, and extreme north Texas.

POPULATION In the late eighteenth century there were around 2,000 Kiowas. Roughly 10,000 people were enrolled Kiowas in the early 1990s.

LANGUAGE Kiowa is considered a linguistic isolate that might be related to Tanoan, a Pueblo language, as well as Shoshonean.

Historical Information

HISTORY The Kiowa may have originated in Arizona or in the mountains of western Montana. They began drifting southeast from western Montana in the late seventeenth century, settling near the Crow. In the early eighteenth century, the Kiowa Apaches became cut off from their fellow Apacheans, at which time (if not a generation before) they joined the Kiowa for protection. Although they maintained a separate language and identity they functioned effectively as a Kiowa band.

Meanwhile, the Kiowa had acquired horses, probably through trade with upper Missouri tribes, and were living in the Black Hills as highly successful buffalo hunters, warriors, and horsemen. Individual Kiowas and Kiowa Apaches also lived in northern New Mexico, probably brought there originally by Comanches and others as prisoners or slaves. Later in the century, the Kiowa, still in the Black Hills, acted as trade intermediaries between Spanish (New Mexican) traders and the upper Missouri tribes.

The people suffered a smallpox epidemic in 1781, from which they gradually recovered. A large group of Kiowa and Kiowa Apache migrated south during that period, to be followed by the rest around the turn of the century. At that time, the Kiowa were pushed south to the Arkansas River area by Dakotas, Arapahos, and Cheyennes (southeastern Colorado), where they ran into the Comanche barrier. They were also drawn south by raiding opportunities provided by Spanish and Pueblo settlements in New Mexico and Mexico. In the early nineteenth century they ranged between New Mexico and the upper Missouri River area.

In 1814 they concluded a treaty with the Dakota defining the boundary between the two groups. Making peace also with the Comanche, these two groups raided for horses, guns, and food as far south as Durango, Mexico. They were known as fierce, effective, and wide-ranging raiders, fighting other Indian groups as well as Spanish, Mexicans, and Anglos. By the mid–nineteenth century, the Kiowa spent more time south of the Arkansas than north of it. In the 1830s they made peace with longtime Cheyenne, Osage, and Arapaho enemies.

In the early 1860s, the Kiowa strongly resisted non-native intruders, land thieves, and immigrants. In 1865 they agreed to a reservation south of the Arkansas River. In the 1867 Medicine Lodge Treaty, they ceded tribal lands and, in exchange for a shared reservation in the Indian Territory, agreed to hunt buffalo only south of the Arkansas and withdrew opposition to a railroad. After the U.S. massacre of Cheyennes called the Battle of the Washita (December 1868), Kiowas and others were ordered to Fort Cobb, Oklahoma. Kiowas, citing provisions in the Medicine Lodge Treaty that allowed then to continue to live and hunt south of the Arkansas, refused. During a peace meeting in 1869, the Kiowa negotiators, Satanta (White Bear) and Lone Wolf, were taken prisoner and placed under a death sentence unless the Kiowa surrendered, which they did.

Two thousand Kiowas and 2,500 Comanches were placed on a reservation at Fort Sill, Indian Territory (Oklahoma). The United States encouraged them to farm, but the Kiowa were not farmers. With starvation looming, the United States permitted them to hunt buffalo. In 1870 and 1871, the Kiowa went on a buffalo hunt and continued their old raiding practices to the south. Some argued for remaining free while others spoke for cooperating with the United States. In 1871, soldiers arrested Kiowa leaders Satanta, Satank, and Big Tree for murders committed during the raids. Satank was killed on the way to his trial in Texas. The other two were convicted and sentenced to life imprisonment. During a meeting in Washington the following year, Lone Wolf won their release as a condition for keeping the Kiowas peaceful.

In 1873, a party of Kiowas and Comanches raided in Mexico for horses. The following year, a group of Indians including Kiowas fought a losing battle against whites at Adobe Walls. By this time, most of the great buffalo herds, almost four million buffalo, had been killed by non-Indians. That summer, a large group of Kiowas and Comanches left Fort Sill for the last great buffalo range at Palo Duro Canyon, Texas, to live as traditional Indians once again. In the fall, U.S. soldiers hunted them down and killed 1,000 of their horses. Fleeing, scattered groups of Indians were hunted down in turn.

The last of these people surrendered in February 1875. They were kept in corrals. Satanta was returned to prison in Texas, and 26 others were exiled to Florida. Kicking Bird died mysteriously two days after the exiles he selected had departed, possibly poisoned by those who resented his friendship with the whites. Within a few years, the great leaders were all gone, and the power of the Kiowa was broken.

The late 1870s saw a major measles epidemic and the end of the Plains buffalo; more epidemics followed in 1895 and 1902. Many Kiowas took up the Ghost Dance in the late 1880s and early 1890s. In 1894, Kiowas offered to share their reservation with their old Apache enemies who were exiles in Florida; Geronimo and other Chiricahua Apaches lived out their lives there.

Almost 450,000 acres of the reservation were allotted to individuals in 1901, with the remaining more than two million acres then sold and opened for settlement to non-natives. Kiowas were among the group of Indians who organized the Native American Church in 1918, having adopted ritual peyote use around 1885. Thanks to the legacy of Kicking Bird and others, Kiowas in the twentieth century have concentrated on education, sending their children to boarding schools (including Riverside, still active in the 1990s) and several nearby mission schools.

RELIGION Kiowas gained religious status through shield society membership and/or guardianship of sacred tribal items, such as the Ten Grandmother Bundles. According to legend, the bundles originated with Sun Boy, the culture hero. With their associated ceremonies, they were a focus of Kiowa religious practice.

Kiowas adopted the Sun Dance in the eighteenth century, although they did not incorporate elements of self-mutilation into the ceremony. Young men also fasted to produce guardian spirit visions.

GOVERNMENT There were traditionally between 10 and 27 autonomous bands, including the Kiowa Apache, each with its own peace and war chiefs. Occasionally, especially later in their history, a tribal chief presided over all the bands.

CUSTOMS Beginning in the nineteenth century the Kiowa adopted a social system wherein rank was based especially on military exploits and also on wealth and religious power. There were four named categories of social rank. The highest was held by those who had attained war honors and were skilled horsemen, generous, and wealthy. Then came those men who met all the preceding criteria except war honors. The third group included people without property. At the bottom were men with neither property nor skills. War captives remained outside this ranking system.

Generosity was valued, and wealthy men regularly helped the less fortunate, but in general wealth remained in the family through inheritance. Sons from wealthy families could begin their military training earlier and thus, through military success, gain even more wealth. There were numerous specialized men's and women's societies.

Bands lived apart in winter but came together in summer to celebrate the Sun Dance. Corpses were buried or left in a tipi on a hill. Former possessions were given away. Mourners cut their hair and gashed themselves, even occasionally cutting off fingers. A mourning family lived apart during the appropriate period of time.

DWELLINGS Women built and owned skin tipis.

DIET Buffalo supplied most of the food, shelter, and clothing for Kiowas on the Plains. Buffalo hunts were highly organized and ritualized affairs. After the hunt, women cut the meat into strips to dry. Later, they mixed it with dried chokecherries and fat to make pemmican, which remained edible in skin bags for up to a year or more.

Men also hunted other large and small game. They did not eat bear or, usually, fish. Women gathered a variety of wild potatoes and other vegetables, fruits, nuts, and berries. Kiowas ate dried, pounded acorns and also made them into a drink. Cornmeal and dried fruit were acquired by trade.

KEY TECHNOLOGY Kiowas made pictographs on buffalo skins to record events of tribal history. They used the buffalo and other animals to provide the usual material items such as parfleches and other containers. Points for bird arrows came from prickly pear thorns. The cradle board was a bead-covered skin case attached to a V-shaped frame. Women made shallow coiled basketry gambling trays.

TRADE During the eighteenth century, Kiowas traded extensively with the upper Missouri tribes (Mandans, Hidatsas, and Arikaras). They exchanged meat, buffalo hides, and salt with Pueblo Indians for cornmeal and dried fruit. During the nineteenth century they traded Comanche horses to the Osage and other tribes.

NOTABLE ARTS Calendric skins and beadwork were two Kiowa artistic traditions.

TRANSPORTATION The people acquired horses by 1730.

DRESS Women dressed buffalo, elk, and deer hides to make robes, moccasins, leggings, shirts, breechclouts, skirts, and blouses.

WAR AND WEAPONS The highest status for men was achieved through warfare. Counting coup and leading a successful raid or fight were the most prestigious military activities. Raiding groups were usually drawn from kin groups, whereas revenge war parties were larger (up to 200 men) and formally organized following a Sun Dance. War honors were recounted following the fight and at any future event at which the recipients spoke formally.

The numerous military societies included the Principal Dogs (or Ten Bravest), a group of ten extremely brave and tested fighters. During battle, one of these warriors would drive a spear through his sash into the ground and fight from that spot, not moving until another Principal Dog removed the spear. Satank (Sitting Bear) was the leader of the Principal Dogs during the last phase of Kiowa resistance.

Kiowas beginning a raid sometimes appealed to a group of women for their prayers, feasting them upon their return. The tribe was allied with the Crow in the late seventeenth century, and the Comanche beginning around 1790. Enemies in the eighteenth and early nineteenth century included the Dakota, Cheyenne, and Osage.

Contemporary Information

GOVERNMENT/RESERVATIONS The Kiowa organized a tribal council in 1968. A 1970 constitution and by-laws divided power between the Kiowa Indian Council (all tribal members) and the eight-member elected Kiowa Business Committee. Tribal headquarters are located in Carnegie, Oklahoma.

The Kiowa land base is 208,396 acres in Caddo, Kiowa, Comanche, Tillman and Cotton Counties, Oklahoma. This land was first designated to them in 1867. Just over 7,000 acres are tribally owned.

ECONOMY Important sources of income include farming, raising livestock, and leasing oil rights.

LEGAL STATUS The Kiowa Tribe of Oklahoma is a federally recognized tribal entity.

DAILY LIFE Many prominent Kiowa artists have played an important part in the twentieth-century revival of Indian arts, beginning in 1927 with the introduction of the "Kiowa Five"—Spencer Asah, Jack Hokeah, Stephan Mopope, Monroe Tsatoke, and James Auchiah. In addition to painting, contemporary Kiowa artists are involved in media such as buckskin, beads, and silver. N. Scott Momaday, a distinguished novelist and professor, won the 1969 Pulitzer for his novel *House Made of Dawn*.

Most Kiowas are Christians, predominantly Baptists and Methodists. Many also belong to the Native American Church. As of the early 1990s, fewer than 400 spoke the native language, and almost all of these were over 50. Still, many elements of traditional culture have been preserved. Even the children's Rabbit Society, with its special songs and dances, endures. The tribe publishes the *Kiowa Indian News*.

Kiowa Apache

See Apache, Plains

Lakota

Lakota (Lä `k ō tä), a Siouan dialect spoken by the Western or Teton *(Titunwan,* "prairie dwellers") group of the tribe commonly referred to as Sioux. The subdivisions of the Western group include Oglala ("they scatter their own"), Sicangu ("burned thighs"; also known by the French name *Brulé*), Hunkpapa ("end village"), Minneconjou ("plant beside the stream"), Itazipco ("no bows"; also known by the French name *Sans Arcs*), Sihasapa ("black feet"), and O'ohenonpa ("two kettles").

The Lakota refer to themselves as Lakota ("ally"), as Lakotah Oyate ("Lakota People"), or as *Ikce Wicasa* ("Natural" or "Free People"). The word "Sioux" is derived originally from an Ojibwa word, *Nadowe-is-iw,* meaning "lesser adder" ("enemy" is the implication) that was corrupted by French voyageurs to *Nadousssioux* and then shortened to *Sioux*. Today, many people use the term "Dakota" or, less commonly, "Lakota" to refer to all Sioux people.

All 13 subdivisions of Dakota-Lakota-Nakota speakers ("Sioux") were known as *Oceti Sakowin*, or Seven Council Fires, a term referring to their seven political divisions: Teton (the Western group, speakers of Lakota); Sisseton, Wahpeton, Wahpukute, and Mdewakanton (the Eastern group, speakers of Dakota); and Yankton and Yanktonai (the Central, or Wiciyela, group, speakers of Dakota and Nakota). *See also* Dakota; Nakota.

LOCATION In the late seventeenth century, the Lakota lived in north-central Minnesota, around Mille Lacs, and parts of Wisconsin. By the mid–nineteenth century they had migrated to the western Dakotas, northwestern Nebraska, northeastern Wyoming, and southeastern Montana. Today, most Lakotas live on reservations in South Dakota as well in as regional and national cities. Many Lakotas leave the reservation to find work but return for summer visits and, often, to retire.

POPULATION Dakota, Lakota, and Nakota speakers numbered approximately 25,000 in the late eighteenth century; almost half of these were probably Lakotas. In the mid-1990s there were roughly 55,000 Lakotas living on U.S. reservations, mostly Oglalas at

Pine Ridge and Sicangus at Rosebud. There were 103,255 "Sioux" people in the United States, according to the 1990 census.

LANGUAGE The Western group speaks the Lakota dialect of Dakota, a Siouan language.

Historical Information

HISTORY The Siouan language family may have originated along the lower Mississippi River or in eastern Texas. They migrated to, or may have originated in, the Ohio Valley, where they lived in large agricultural settlements. They may have been related to the Mound Builder culture of the ninth through twelfth centuries. The Siouans may also have originated in the upper Mississippi Valley or even the Atlantic seaboard.

Siouan tribes still lived in the southeast, between Florida and Virginia, around the late sixteenth and early seventeenth century. All were destroyed either by attacks from Algonquian-speaking Indians and/or a combination of attacks from non-Indians and non-Indian diseases. Some fled and were absorbed by other tribes. Some were sent as slaves to the West Indies.

Dakota-Lakota-Nakota speakers inhabited over 100 million acres, mostly prairie, in the upper Mississippi region, including Minnesota and parts of Wisconsin, Iowa and the Dakotas, in the sixteenth to early seventeenth century. They largely kept clear of the British-French struggles. Conflict with the Cree and Anishinabe, who were well armed with French rifles, plus the lure of great buffalo herds to feed their expanding population, induced bands to begin moving west onto the Plains in the mid–seventeenth century. The Teton migration may have begun in the late seventeenth century, in the form of extended hunting parties into the James River basin.

Lakotas acquired horses around 1740; shortly after that time the first Teton bands crossed the Missouri River. They entered the Black Hills region around 1775, ultimately displacing the Cheyenne and Kiowa, and made it their spiritual center. As more and more Teton bands became Plains dwellers (almost all by 1830), they helped establish the classic Plains culture, which featured highly organized bands, almost complete dependence on the buffalo, and a central role for raiding and fighting. The Teton subdivided into their seven bands during that time.

In 1792 the Lakota defeated the Arikara Confederacy, allowing the Lakota to expand into the Missouri Valley and western South Dakota. In 1814 they concluded a treaty with the Kiowa marking boundaries between the two peoples, including recognition that the Lakota now controlled the Black Hills (known to

them as *Paha Sapa*). By that time, at the latest, the Lakota were well armed with rifles.

Around 1822, the Lakota joined with the Cheyenne to drive the Crow out of eastern Wyoming north of the Platte. During that period, Tetons were engaged in supplying furs for non-Indians, although contacts were usually limited to trading posts, particularly Fort Laramie after 1834 and the Oglala move to the Upper Platte region. In the 1840s, wagon trains passing through Teton territory began disrupting the buffalo herds, and the Indians began attacking the wagons. In the 1851 Fort Laramie Treaty, the Indians agreed to give the wagons free access in exchange for official recognition of Indian territory.

Conflict continued throughout the 1850s. In one series of incidents, in which a group of Sicangu ate and offered to pay for a stray Mormon cow, the U.S. Army attacked Sicangu villages and killed over 100 people. In the early to mid-1860s, the Oglala chief Red Cloud (Makhpiya-luta) led and ultimately won a brutal and protracted fight to force the United States to close the Bozeman Road through the Powder River country, the last great hunting ground of the Lakota. The road through it had been opened illegally as a route to newly discovered gold fields in Montana; it crossed Teton territory without their permission, in violation of the 1851 Fort Laramie Treaty. Fighting with the Tetons were Northern Cheyennes under their leader, Dull Knife, as well as Northern Arapahos.

The 1868 Fort Laramie Treaty was an admission by the United States of the Indian victory in the so-called Red Cloud's war. The government agreed to close the Bozeman Road and stay out of Teton territory. In exchange, the Indians agreed to stop their raids and remain on a "Great Sioux Reservation." Both Red Cloud and the Sicangu leader Spotted Tail remained committed to peace, although they often spoke against easy accommodation to U.S. terms.

In 1874, gold was discovered in the Black Hills during an illegal military expedition. This event brought swarms of miners and other non-Indians, in direct violation of the treaty. With Red Cloud and Spotted Tail settled on reservations, it fell to new leaders, young and free, such as the medicine man Sitting Bull (Tatanka Yotanka) and Crazy Horse (Tashunka Witco), to protect the sacred and legally recognized Teton lands against invasion. The United States rebuffed all Indian protests, and the Indians rejected U.S. efforts to purchase the Black Hills.

In 1876, army units ceased protecting the Black Hills against non-Indian interlopers and went after Teton bands who refused to settle (which they were under no obligation to do under the terms of the Fort Laramie Treaty). In March, Tetons under Crazy Horse repelled an attack led by Colonel Joseph Reynolds. At

Rosebud Creek the following June, Crazy Horse and his people routed a large force of soldiers as well as Crow and Shoshone scouts under the command of General George Crook. Later that month, Teton and Cheyenne Indians led by Oglalas under Crazy Horse and Hunkpapas under Sitting Bull and Gaul wiped out the U.S. Seventh Cavalry, under General George Custer, at the Little Bighorn River.

Here the Indian victories came to an end. The army defeated a large force of Cheyennes in July, and in September General Crook's soldiers captured a combined force of Oglalas and Minneconjous under American Horse. Two months later, Dull Knife and his Northern Cheyennes lost an important battle, and Crazy Horse himself was defeated in January 1877 by General Nelson Miles. Finally, Miles defeated Lame Deer's Minneconjou band in May 1877. Meanwhile, Sitting Bull, tired of the military harassment, had taken his people north to Canada. With his people tired and starving, Crazy Horse surrendered in April 1877. In August he was placed under arrest and was assassinated on September 5. He is still regarded as a symbol of the Lakotas' heroic resistance and as their greatest leader.

Defeated militarily and under threat of mass removal to the Indian Territory, Red Cloud, Spotted Tail, and the other Lakota and Santee chiefs signed the treaty ceding the Black Hills and the Powder River country. Shortly thereafter, the army confiscated all Lakota weapons and horses and then drove the people into exile to reservations along the Missouri River.

After unilateral "cessions" in 1877, the Great Sioux Reservation consisted of 35,000 square miles of land, but a coalition of non-Indians, including railroad promoters and land speculators, maneuvered to break up this parcel. Meanwhile, Canada proved completely inhospitable to the exiled Lakota, and gradually they began drifting back to the United States. Sitting Bull returned to formal surrender in 1881.

The giant land grab came in 1888, when the United States proposed to carve the great reservation up into six smaller ones, leaving about nine million acres open for non-Indian settlement. The government unsuccessfully offered the Lakota $.50 an acre for the land. They then offered $1.50 an acre and prepared to move unilaterally if this offer were to be rejected. The government needed three-quarters of the adult male votes for approval. Despite the opposition of Red Cloud, about half of the Oglalas signed the treaty. With Spotted Tail dead (he had been assassinated in 1881), most of the Sicangu signed. Sitting Bull was the loudest voice opposed, but he was physically restrained from attending a meeting presided over by accommodationist chiefs, and the signatures

were collected. The Great Sioux Reservation was no more.

Deprived of their livelihood, Lakotas quickly became dependent on inadequate and irregular U.S. rations. The United States also undermined traditional leadership and created their own subservient power structure. A crisis ensued in 1889 when the government cut off all rations. The general confusion provided fertile ground for the Ghost Dance.

In 1888, a Northern Paiute named Wovoka, building on previous traditions, popularized a new religion that came to be called the Ghost Dance (see Paiute, Northern [Chapter 4]). Wovoka foretold the return of an Indian paradise if people would pray, dance, and abandon the ways of non-Indians. The new religion gave hope to many Native Americans whose societies by this time had reached a crisis point, and it quickly spread over much of the West. Many Indians also thought special Ghost Shirts could stop bullets.

Fearing that the Ghost Dance would encourage a new Indian militancy and solidarity, white officials banned the practice. In defiance, Oglala leaders in 1890 planned a large gathering on the Pine Ridge Reservation. To keep Sitting Bull, the last strong Lakota leader, from attending, the Indian police arrested him in December. During the arrest he was shot and killed.

The Minneconjou leader Big Foot once supported the dance, and for this reason General Miles ordered his arrest. Big Foot led his band of about 350 people to Pine Ridge to join Red Cloud and others who advocated peace with the United States. The army intercepted him along the way and ordered him to stop at Wounded Knee Creek. The next morning (December 29) the soldiers moved in to disarm the Indians. When a rifle accidentally fired into the air, the soldiers opened fire with the four Hotchkiss cannon on the bluffs overlooking the camp, killing between 260 and 300 Indians, mostly women and children. The Wounded Knee massacre marked the symbolic end of large-scale Native American armed resistance in the United States.

From the 1880s into the 1950s, most Lakota children were forced to attend mission or Bureau of Indian Affairs (BIA) schools, There the children were taught menial skills, and their culture was violently repressed. During the twentieth century, tipis slowly gave way to government-issue tents and then log cabins. Many Lakotas became Catholics or Episcopalians, although traditional customs and religious practices also continued, including the officially banned Sun Dance.

Bands were broken up, in part by the allotment process. As the United States worked to replace traditional leadership, education, religion, and other cultural and political structures, Lakota society underwent a profound demoralization. Most Lakota were fed government-issue beef, which they had trouble eating after a steady diet of buffalo. In general, government rations were of low quality and quantity.

Lakotas were ordered to begin raising cattle. Despite some success in the early twentieth century, U.S. agents encouraged them in 1917 to sell their herds and lease their lands to non-Indians. When the lessees defaulted in 1921, the government urged Indians to sell their allotments for cash. By the 1930s, devoid of cattle and land, general destitution had set in.

Lakotas adopted the Indian Reorganization Act in 1934, after which reservations were governed by an elected tribal council, although the traditional system of chief-led *tiyospayes* (subbands) was still in place. A tribal court system handled minor problems; more serious offenses fell under the control of the U.S. court system.

Native Americans were part of the ethnic pride movement of the 1960s. The Red Power movement had its origins in the formation of the National Congress of American Indians (NCAI) in 1944. In 1972, many Lakotas participated in a march to Washington, D.C., called the Trail of Broken Treaties, during which they took over the BIA.

The following January, under the leadership of the American Indian Movement (AIM), several hundred Pine Ridge Lakotas attempted to end and reverse U.S.-sponsored corruption on Pine Ridge, particularly the strong-arm tactics of the tribal chair at that time. The context was decades of poverty and frustration on the reservation. The government responded with a massive show of force. During the 71-day siege, known as Wounded Knee II, two Indians were killed by federal agents. The event forged a new solidarity among Lakotas and other Indians but also left deep scars among the reservation population.

RELIGION According to legend, White Buffalo Calf Pipe Woman brought the people seven ceremonies: the Sweat Lodge *(Inipi),* Making of Relatives *(Hunka),* Vision Quest *(Hanbleceya),* Girls' Puberty Ritual *(Isnati alowanpi),* Throwing of the Ball *(Tapa wankayeyapi),* Keeping of the Soul ceremony *(Wakicagapi),* and the Sun Dance *(Wiwanyang wacipi).*

Given originally by a legendary personage, the Sacred Pipe is a symbol of the vitality of the nation and its relationship with the creative forces of the universe. It was removed from its pouch only on the most important occasions, such as famine or pledging peace. Pipes, carried by members of a special society, were used in peace ceremonies and to "sacredize"

decisions and agreements. Members of the society also had special responsibilities such as organizing camp moves, camping locations, and large hunts.

Shamans, or medicine people (men or women), were healers and curers as well as interpreters of visions. Curing ceremonies generally involved burning sage, sweet grass, and tobacco. Shamans danced and sang power songs. They could also cause illness. They also found lost objects, divined the future, and provided important leadership during war or hunts. They received their powers from especially powerful guardian spirits and had a particularly close relationship with all of the deities. They were especially familiar with all legends, symbols, rituals, ceremonies, and cosmology. Common ailments were generally cured with the use of herbs. Women generally had the greater knowledge of curing herbs.

A guardian spirit, usually in the guise of an animal, appeared to people on a vision quest, which was a period of self-deprivation in a remote place, or perhaps in a dream. Spirits were associated with particular songs, prayers, and symbols that, properly used, could bring the individual luck, skills, and/or protection from evil or danger. Women as well as men sought visions. Shamans assisted in preparing for and interpreting such visions. Not all visions were of equal potency, and not everyone received a vision, although people who did not generally kept trying. Women could receive visions but generally did not seek them. Personal medicine bundles were made up of objects dictated by the guardian spirit during the vision quest. They were kept on the person and provided special protection.

Shamans also led the Sun Dance, the most important of Plains ceremonies after about the mid–eighteenth century, when the horse transformed Plains dwellers into full-time nomadic buffalo hunters. Among the Lakota the Sun Dance brought together their most important beliefs about themselves and the universe. *Wakan Tanka,* or the Great Spirit, as the supreme creator of the universe, or the sacred hoop, was first among 16 gods representing forces of nature. The number four was particularly sacred to the Lakota, representing the four cardinal directions, the pantheon of gods (four groups of four), and the four stages of life. The highly symbolic, 12-day-long Sun Dance brought benefits both to the participants and the nation as a whole. Individually sponsored as the result of a vow taken the previous winter, the dance itself contained elements of dancing, feasting, praying, fasting, and self-torture.

GOVERNMENT Elected chiefs in the Woodlands gave way to leadership by warriors. The subdivisions became more autonomous, and themselves divided into bands and their basic units. These were known as *tiyospaye,* a group of fluid composition composed of relatives and led by a warrior-chief. Each had its own recognized hunting area.

Chiefs were older men who had distinguished themselves in hunting and battle and were noted for their wisdom, well-spokenness, and generosity. Each band also had a council of such men, who governed without any force to back them up except the respect engendered by their position and a consensus-style of decision making.

In the later historical period, the Oglala had a society composed of older men, which elected seven lifelong chiefs. In practice, authority was delegated to four highly respected "shirt-wearers," who also served for life. There were also four *wakikun,* or camp police, who were temporary officials assisted by the members of the *akitcita.*

The seven Teton divisions met regularly, ideally annually in summer, from at least the late eighteenth century to about 1850. At these times there was a Sun Dance, and people socialized and generally renewed acquaintances. A supreme council of four chiefs met to discuss national policies. Still, the nation was very decentralized, with no overall political or military coordination, and the supreme council's power was largely symbolic.

CUSTOMS On the Plains, patrilineal clans gave way to bilaterally descended extended families. The band, Oglala, for example, came together only for the summer activities. Otherwise it was divided into independent subbands, which themselves broke into even smaller groups during winter.

Generosity was highly valued, as were bravery, fortitude, wisdom, and fidelity. In the "giveaway" custom, people shared generously, especially with the less able or fortunate and during important times in their lives. Thus did people achieve prestige while actually reducing individual suffering and want.

In winter, people repaired their tools and weapons and made crafts and clothing. Social control was effected mostly by peer pressure and ridicule, although serious crimes were punished by revenge and/or adjudication by the council. Various voluntary societies included those for men (mostly war related); feast and dance societies, which included social groups of both sexes and groups for women only; dream cult societies (such as the Heyoka, or clown, society); and craft societies. Games included various guessing games, cup-and-ball, and competitions. Adult games were usually accompanied by gambling. Toys included conical tops and sleds. In general, storytelling was a favorite pastime.

Work was generally divided by gender but not by profession, except for medicine men and berdaches. Prestige was based less on wealth than on bravery,

generosity, oratorical ability, supernatural powers, and other factors. Wealth and kin connections did, however, play a part, and status ultimately rested on a combination of individual and family qualities.

Although premarital sex was frowned upon, the extent to which it occurred may be inferred by the fact that some Lakotas kept their young daughters in chastity belts at night. Polygamy was practiced, although it was expensive. Each wife might or might not have a separate tipi. Marriage was mainly a matter of parental agreement, often based on the couple's choice, and divorce was common and easy to obtain. Fidelity in marriage was an ideal, and disloyal women might have the end of their noses cut off.

Children, especially boys, were always welcomed. Infants spent their first few months swaddled in a cradleboard. They were allowed to nurse on demand. Children were treated with love and affection and were rarely struck. They were generally weaned after about four years, after which time their ears were pierced. Boys and girls (except for brothers and sisters) generally played together until puberty. Games revolved around future adult activities.

During menstruation, girls and women were secluded for a few days, as men considered them dangerous. Girls having their first period were seen only by women and instructed on proper womanly behavior. Several weeks later, fathers who were able gave a ceremony, presided over by a shaman, for their daughters. The relative lavishness of the ceremony reflected on the whole family. Girls who had reached puberty were considered marriageable.

Boys did not have a specific puberty ceremony. Their vision quests, first successful buffalo hunt, first war party, and so forth might be marked by feasts and gifts and were considered rites of passage. Men generally married slightly older than did women, having first to prove their manhood and perhaps acquire enough goods to distribute.

As a matter of respect there was no verbal communication between a man and his mother-in-law. Aged people were generally accorded a great deal of respect. When people reached what they considered to be the end of their functional lives, they might elect to remain behind the migrating band, although sometimes this action was taken involuntarily.

The dead were buried with their effects on high hills or in scaffolds in trees. In the prehistoric period remains were buried in an earth mound. In the late historical period a chief's favorite horse might be killed.

DWELLINGS Winter camps on the plains were places containing wood and water, such as valley cottonwood groves. People also needed forage for horses and some natural protection against weather and enemies. Winter camps were small, generally consisting of between 5 and 50 related families

In the Woodlands, Lakotas lived in pole-frame lodges covered with woven mats or bark. Once on the Plains, they shifted to conical buffalo-skin tipis in both summer and winter. The average tipi was made of about 12 buffalo skins, dressed and sewn together by women and placed over a pole framework. A tipi held one family. The interior fire was slightly off center. Two skin flaps at the top, attached to long poles, regulated the smoke hole. A small, elevated doorway was covered by a rawhide door.

Skin liners helped insulate against the cold and wind. Tanned buffalo robes served as beds and blankets and buffalo robes as carpeting. Women also erected and took down the tipis, which could be moved quickly and easily. Tipis were often painted with special symbols and war exploits and were also decorated with feathers, quills, or other items.

DIET Large and small game, wild rice, maple sugar, and fish constituted the bulk of the Woodland diet. On the Plains, people mostly ate buffalo. No part of the animal went to waste. The communal hunt, which was often but not always very successful, was accomplished by fire surrounds, shooting with bow and arrow, clubbing, or driving the animals off cliffs. Men also hunted individually or in family groups. Following the main hunt, which took place in summer, women butchered the meat and carried it back to camp. Meat was roasted on a spit, stone boiled in a buffalo stomach with dried berries and tubers, or cut into strips and dried. Pemmican (buffalo meat pounded with fat and dried chokecherries) was eaten on the hunt and in some ceremonies.

Lakotas also ate antelope, deer, and other large and small game as well as birds, eggs, turtles, tortoises, and fish. Young dog, considered a delicacy, was often eaten at feast times. Women gathered foods such as wild potatoes and turnips, berries, chokecherries, cactus, acorns, and wild onions. Some Teton women occasionally planted a little maize. There were also many medicinal herbs and plants.

KEY TECHNOLOGY On the Plains, most manufactured items came from the buffalo. Many tools were also made of stone, until iron became available from non-Indian traders. Bone fishhooks were fastened onto sinew lines attached to willow poles.

Women tanned the skins using elk antler scrapers with an attached stone (or iron) blade; the hair was either left on or soaked and scraped off. Rawhide was often used to attach items to each other, such as clubs and mauls. People made willow back rests for use in tipis.

TRADE Lakotas traded at Arikara villages, north of the mouth of the Grand River, in present-day South Dakota, until about 1800, when they completely subjugated the Arikara. They acted as intermediaries for the catlinite (red pipestone) trade between the Yankton and most northern Plains tribes. Part of an extensive trade complex stretching throughout the West, the Tetons traded buffalo products to the eastern Dakota for non-Indian goods the latter had obtained through the fur trade.

NOTABLE ARTS Art was integral to all Lakota materialism. Winter counts were pictographs on hides that recorded annual events. Clothing and bags were decorated with painting and porcupine quillwork, later beadwork. Bags, robes, and tipis were also painted.

Designs were either realistic (generally painting, often made by men) or geometrical (generally quillwork and beadwork, often made by women). Musical instruments included flageolets, rattles, rasps, and drums.

TRANSPORTATION Lakotas used birch-bark and dugout canoes and snowshoes in the Woodlands. On the Plains, dogs served as the first beast of burden; the original migrations of the seventeenth and early eighteenth centuries were accomplished with the aid of dogs pulling travois. They still played a role in transportation even after the Lakota acquired horses during the mid–eighteenth century, probably from the Arikaras. Tetons became extremely skilled riders. Horse travois carried tipis and other goods. Poles, carried along because wood was often hard to find on the plains, facilitated the travois structure.

DRESS Men wore deerskin or elk-skin breechclouts, leggings, and soft-sole moccasins. They braided their hair, and they often wore face and body paint. Some wore their hair in a roach. In winter, women wore long elk-skin dresses, knee-length leggings, and moccasins. They braided and parted their hair in the middle. They also wore face paint and earrings. Both sexes wore buffalo-hide robes. Some of the above clothing was discarded in summer.

Plains clothing often was fringed and decorated with colorful beadwork, especially in the later historical period and for ceremonial purposes. People made ornaments of bone, dentalium shell, elk and grizzly bear teeth, beads, copper and obsidian, and perhaps turquoise.

From about the mid–nineteenth century on, certain war leaders wore long eagle-feathered war bonnets for ceremonial purposes, although even before that period young men wore eagle feathers in their hair to signify achievements in battle. Chiefs and other people of authority also often wore special clothing and other paraphernalia at official occasions.

WAR AND WEAPONS Tetons were feared fighters

but did not fight each other. By 1800 they subjugated the Arikara, mostly by harassing the Kiowa and other important Arikara trade partners. They raided Mandans, Hidatsas, and most everyone else on the northern Plains, Indian or not.

The *akitcita* was an elite warrior society that kept order in camp and especially on the hunt. Severe penalties were meted out to those who disrupted the summer hunt.

Warfare and raiding were the primary means to gain prestige. Weapons included bows and arrows, buffalo-hide shields, war clubs, and lances. Military societies had their own songs, paraphernalia (such as feathered headgear), and ceremonies. War leaders, generally young men, had absolute authority but only over the war party while on a sortie. War and raiding parties were completely voluntary, motivated mainly by the desire to attain prestige. Men generally engaged in ritual purification in the sweat lodge before battle. Large battles involving hundreds of warriors occurred only in the late historical period.

As practiced in the early nineteenth century, counting coup meant achieving bravery in a hand-to-hand encounter with the enemy or some other feat of daring such as stealing a horse within a village. Killing and scalping generally merited less honor than did counting coup, although, in the nineteenth century, scalping was important to the Lakota for ritualistic purposes. There were several levels of coup, each with accompanying symbols, such as feathers, and corresponding levels of prestige. Lakotas were often allied with Cheyennes and Arapahos in the nineteenth century.

Contemporary Information

GOVERNMENT/RESERVATIONS Standing Rock Reservation, Sioux County, North Dakota, and Carson County, South Dakota (Hunkpapa, Sihasapa, Minneconjou, O'ohenonpa, and Yanktonai), established in 1868, contains 847,799 acres, almost 300,000 of which are tribally owned. In 1990 there were 4,866 Indian residents. Government is by tribal council.

Cheyenne River Reservation, Dewey and Ziebach Counties, South Dakota (Itazipco and Sihasapa), established in 1889, contains 1,419,499 acres, 911,000 of which are tribally owned. The 1990 Indian population was 5,100. Government is by tribal council.

Lower Brulé Reservation, Lyman and Stanley Counties, South Dakota (Sicangu and others), established in 1868, contains 114,219 acres, about 66,600 of which are tribally owned. The 1990 Indian population was 994. Government is by tribal council.

Crow Creek Reservation, Buffalo, Hughes, and Hyde Counties, South Dakota (Hunkpatina and oth-

ers), established in 1863, contains 125,483 acres. The 1990 Indian population was 1,531. Government is by tribal council.

Pine Ridge Reservation and Trust Lands, Jackson, Shannon, and Bennett Counties, South Dakota, and Sheridan County, Nebraska (Oglala), established in 1868, contains 2,778,000 acres, more than 372,000 of which are tribally owned. The 1990 Indian population was 11,180; 23,000 people (both Indians and non-Indians lived there in 1992. Government is by tribal council.

Rosebud Reservation and Trust Lands, Todd, Gregory, Lyman, Mellette, and Tripp Counties, South Dakota (Sicangu and O'ohenonpa), established in 1868, contains almost 1 million acres, about 409,000 of which are tribally owned. The 1990 Indian population was 1,160; 18,000 Indians and non-Indians lived there in 1992. Government is by tribal council.

Some Lakotas also live on the Standing Buffalo and the Wood Mountain Reserves in Saskatchewan, Canada.

ECONOMY Moccasins are manufactured at Pine Ridge. The Standing Rock Reservation leases land to Texas ranching firms. Pine Ridge has plans to open a casino.

Except for a few gas stations, convenience stores, and arts and crafts stores, most retail businesses on the reservations are owned by non-Indians. In general, land leasing is the most important economic activity. Unemployment on all Lakota reservations is commonly over 50 percent and has reached 80 percent. Federal commodities support continues.

LEGAL STATUS The Cheyenne River Sioux Tribe, the Crow Creek Sioux Tribe, the Lower Brulé Sioux Tribe, the Oglala Sioux Tribe, the Rosebud Sioux Tribe, and the Standing Rock Sioux Tribe are federally recognized tribal entities.

Lakotas continue to press for legal possession of the Black Hills. Modifications to the 1868 Fort Laramie Treaty required the signatures of a minimum of three-quarters of adult males. Although it did not have nearly enough signatures, the United States simply appropriated 7.7 million acres that included the Black Hills, the Lakota's holiest land. The Lakota began a series of legal actions to recover the land in 1920, as soon as it had legal standing to do so. After a number of complicated rulings from various courts, the U.S. Supreme Court ruled in 1980 that the Lakotas' treaty rights had been violated and that they were entitled to compensation of $17.5 million plus interest.

All eight tribes (the South Dakota Lakotas plus the Santees in Nebraska and the Fort Peck Sioux of Montana) have refused a cash award, holding out for congressional action that would return the land to them. A bill to that effect, opposed by the South Dakota delegation, died in the Senate in 1990. The Lakota succeeded in defeating a plan by the Honeywell Corporation to build a munitions testing facility in the Black Hills. In 1981, a group of Lakotas established Camp Yellow Thunder as an initial step toward reoccupying the Black Hills.

DAILY LIFE Such seminal mid- to late-nineteenth-century events as the Battle of the Greasy Grass (also known as Custer's Last Stand) and the Wounded Knee massacre remain very much in the hearts and minds of Lakotas, with many observing annual remembrance ceremonies and pilgrimages to sites.

There is ongoing tension between the tribal councils, dating from the 1930s, and traditional *tiyospaye* governing structure. According to Lakota custom, the latter voice is the stronger, but the U.S. government supports the former. Today, most *tiyospaye* are organized around Christian churches, which have also become associated with many traditional ceremonies.

Although many Lakotas consider themselves Christian, they continue to follow many traditional ceremonies and customs. Summer remains a time of traditional ceremonies and feasting, including the Sun Dance, which today lasts for four days, not including preparation time. Giveaways, which have their origin in the Keeping of the Soul ceremony, continue to act as expressions of traditional culture and family life. The original sacred pipe of the Lakota Nation is kept at the Cheyenne River Reservation.

In general, the Lakota reservations face problems associated with poverty, including relatively poor health related in part to substance abuse. Most reservations have hospitals and clinics. Schools feature classes in many aspects of Lakota culture and history. Lakota institutions of higher education include two-year colleges at Cheyenne River and Standing Rock in addition to the four-year Oglala Lakota College (Pine Ridge) and Sinte Gleska University (Rosebud). Lakotas rank among the best contemporary Native American artists.

In 1975, a Lakota and two Federal Bureau of Investigation (FBI) agents were killed during a confrontation near Wounded Knee, South Dakota. The incident stemmed from continuing unrest in the area following the battles between AIM and the corrupt Pine Ridge Tribal Council; these battles themselves grew out of the appalling level of violence directed against local Indians, in part by council-controlled thugs. In an extremely controversial trial, Leonard Peltier, an Anishinabe/Dakota Indian, was found guilty of killing the FBI agents and sentenced to two consecutive life sentences in federal prison. For many Lakotas and others, his case remains emblematic of the continuing mistreatment of Indians by the U.S. government.

Mandan

Mandan (`Man dan) is a Dakota word. Their self-designation was *Numakiki,* "People."

LOCATION For centuries before the coming of non-Indians, Mandans lived along the upper Missouri River and near the mouth of the Heart River, in central North Dakota. Today, most Mandans live in Dunn, McKenzie, McLean, Mercer, Mountrail, and Ward Counties, North Dakota.

POPULATION The early-eighteenth-century Mandan population was around 3,600. In the mid-1990s, enrollment in the Three Affiliated Tribes was about 6,000.

LANGUAGE Mandan, related to but unintelligible with Hidatsa, is a Siouan language.

Historical Information

HISTORY The Mandan arrived in the Missouri River region from the southeast (Ohio Valley) between about 1000 and the thirteenth century, perhaps as early as the seventh century. They gradually moved upriver and away from other Siouan-speaking people.

The first smallpox epidemics arrived in the early sixteenth century. The acquisition of horses in the early to mid–eighteenth century allowed the Mandan to expand their buffalo hunting, but they did not give up their sedentary lifestyle. During the mid–eighteenth century, the Mandan became intermediaries between French and Indian traders, dealing in furs, horses, guns, crops, and buffalo products.

The Mandan suffered a gradual decline beginning in the late eighteenth century, owing primarily to smallpox and warfare with the Dakota and other tribes. In the early nineteenth century, Mandans were friendly to non-Indians, even allowing visitors to study their religious ceremonies. In 1837, a major smallpox epidemic dropped the Mandan population by over 90 percent, to just about 125 people. In 1845, surviving Mandans joined the Hidatsa people to establish Like-a-Fishhook village on the Missouri. They were joined by the Arikara in 1862. Like-a-Fishhook was a significant commercial center at this time.

Although the 1851 Fort Laramie Treaty recognized native holdings of more than 12 million acres, the 1870 Fort Berthold Reservation, created for the Three Affiliated Tribes (Mandan, Hidatsa, and Arikara) consisted only of eight million acres, which was reduced, mostly by allotment, to about one million during the 1880s. By that time, the people had abandoned Like-a-Fishhook to form communities along the Missouri River.

In 1910, the United States unilaterally removed a large section of land from the reservation. During the 1950s, the United States built the Garrison Dam on the Missouri, against the tribes' vehement opposition. The resulting Lake Sakakawea covered much of their land, farms, and homes. This event destroyed the tribe's economic base and severely damaged its social structure as well as its infrastructure.

RELIGION Sacred or medicine bundles (called "Mother") symbolized fertility and crop productivity. They were owned by individual men who passed them down to their descendants or sold them. All bundles had a mythological component and were considered so sacred that the welfare of the entire village depended on their safety and proper care. They were associated with specific ceremonies, songs, and activities

The four-day Okipa ceremony, similar to and a likely precursor of the Sun Dance, was a ritual enactment of their worldview. Its dual purpose was tribal renewal and bringing the buffalo. Prompted by their vision, individuals pledged to offer the summer ceremony, which included periods of fasting and ritual self-torture. The preparation period lasted several months at least. The ceremony contained masked performers representing animals, and required a special lodge fronting the village plaza. Creation legends were told during this time but in an unintelligible language; the uninformed could pay for a translation. Participants hoped to receive a vision afterward.

People accepted as Okipa Makers (those entitled to sponsor the Okipa ceremony) were required to give feasts and to possess a certain quantity of material goods. In acquiring these goods they were assisted by members of their kin group, because individual honor reflected on the group.

Other agricultural and hunting festivals included the women's Corn Dance and the men's Buffalo Dance. Clan chiefs were in charge of ceremonial activities, aspects of which were overseen by dual (summer and winter) divisions. The Mandans also had secret religious societies.

GOVERNMENT There were nine villages in the early nineteenth century. Villages had two hereditary chiefs, one from each division, roughly the same as a war and a peace chief. The people were also governed by a council of older males who made decisions by consensus. In the eighteenth century there were about five bands, each speaking slightly different dialects. There was also a police group called the Black Mouth Society.

CUSTOMS Women grew the crops and processed animal skins into clothing. Descent was matrilineal, and residence was matrilocal. Households controlled the garden plots, but the land was actually held by lineages composed of several extended families. About 13 matrilineal clans, composed of extended family lineages, were loosely ranked by status, depending on

their ritual importance. The tribe was also divided into two groups, each producing a village leader, which competed against each other in games and contests.

Social class determined status to a far greater degree than did war deeds. High individual rank was affirmed through lavish giveaways and brave personal acts, but a high inherited status did not always need this sort of affirmation. Similarly, a commoner could not rise to be a chief despite the most extensive gift giving and remarkable personal exploits.

Age-graded societies and ranked social clubs united nonrelatives. Organized around hunting, dancing, or curing, membership was purchased from existing members, who then purchased their way up to the next level. Only a few reached the highest level, which in any case was open by invitation only.

Grandparents largely brought up the children. Marriage, which consisted of an exchange of gifts between the two families, took place outside of the division and clan. Corpses were buried in the earth, although the people adopted scaffold burial in later times. After a four-day mourning period, and when the bones had dried, people placed skulls in circles around the village.

DWELLINGS People lived where there was arable land and a supply of wood. Permanent villages, composed of between a dozen to as many as 150 earth lodges, were on high bluffs overlooking the river, often where tributary streams joining the Missouri were protected on two sides by the steep riverbanks. Heavily fortified with wooden stockades and barrier ditches, they were fairly impervious to attack. The central plaza was the focus of the village, the place where games were played and ceremonies took place. In the depth of winter, people sought shelter in more protected, wooded areas, where they built smaller, cruder earth lodges. They also used skin tipis for hunting and traveling.

The main lodges were semiexcavated. A heavy wooden frame was overlaid with willow branches and overlapping strips of sod and covered with an outer layer of earth. These lodges sheltered as many as 50 people but usually about 20–40 extended family members. The lodges were about 40 feet or more in diameter. A set of planks in front of the rawhide door further protected against cold winds. Animals occasionally stayed in the lodges as well.

Rawhide beds on raised platforms were placed next to the outer wall. The fire was in the center. Roofs were strong enough so that people regularly congregated on them and used them for storing and drying maize. Deep pits, wider at the base, were dug into the earth for crop storage. An altar and weapons storage area was located on the righthand side of the

lodge. Furniture included willow back rests and buffalo-robe couches.

DIET Men hunted elk, deer, and smaller mammals. Buffalo were hunted communally in summer as
well as individually. Before the people acquired
horses, they hunted buffalo by driving the herd into a
channel made of wood and stone that led to the edge
of a cliff or an enclosure.

Women grew maize, sunflowers, beans, squash,
and tobacco. Burned trees provided additional soil
fertilizer to the already rich bottomlands. Mandan
maize was a variety adapted by the people to their
short growing season. Women parched sunflower
seeds and then ground them into meal used for thick-
ening boiled dishes. Men also ate balls of this meal as
travel food.

Green corn was eaten freshly boiled and dried for
the winter. Squash was sliced and sun dried. The people also ate fish and gathered a variety of wild foods.
Dogs were eaten in times of want, although puppy
stew was considered a delicacy. Tobacco was considered sacred and grown only by the older men.

KEY TECHNOLOGY Material items included willow fish weirs, buffalo horn and bone utensils,
pointed digging sticks, antler or willow rakes, hoes
made from the shoulder blade of a buffalo or elk, and
clay and stone pipes. Women made baskets (twilled
plaited carrying and coiled gambling) and pottery.

TRADE Mandan villages on the Knife River were
a major center of aboriginal trade. They traded surplus agricultural products to the Assiniboine and
other nomadic tribes for hides and meat. As early as
1738, the Mandan had obtained guns from the Assiniboine as well as horses, which they used mostly for
trade. They traded with the Kiowa from the late eighteenth into the first years of the nineteenth century.

NOTABLE ARTS Mandans were famous for their
painted buffalo robes. They also made fine baskets.
Painted skins depicted battles and other significant
events.

TRANSPORTATION Horses began pulling sleds or
travois toboggans around 1745. Bull-boats were made
of hide stretched over a wooden framework. They
were paddled across rivers laden with a cargo of people, meat, and/or hides.

DRESS Women made the clothing, such as blankets, robes, and moccasins. In addition to buffalo,
deer, and elk, they also used white weasel or ermine
skin. The Mandan wore animal skin head wraps in
winter.

WAR AND WEAPONS Traditional allies were the
Hidatsa and the Crow. Enemies included Dakota
tribes from the eighteenth century on. Weapons
included bows and arrows, clubs, and buffalo-hide
shields.

Contemporary Information

GOVERNMENT/RESERVATIONS The Three Affili-
ated Tribes (Arikara, Hidatsa, Mandan) live on the
Fort Berthold Reservation (roughly 900,000 acres in
Dunn, McKenzie, McLean, Mercer, Mountrail, and
Ward Counties, North Dakota). The 1990 reservation
Indian population was 2,999. More than half of the
reservation is owned by non-Indians. The Indian
Reorganization Act constitution provides for govern-
ment by a business council.

ECONOMY Tribal government and the federal
government are the largest employers. A few people
own farms or ranches. The tribe opened a high-stakes
casino in 1993. Unemployment remains very high.

In 1992, the tribe received $143 million in addi-
tional compensation (on top of $12 million previ-
ously awarded) for damages caused by the Garrison
Dam.

LEGAL STATUS The Three Affiliated Tribes is a
federally recognized tribal entity.

DAILY LIFE Most Mandans live on the west side
of the reservoir, near the town of Twin Buttes. Their
lives are similar to those of their non-Indian neighbors.

The annual powwow held by each reservation
community has become a focus for tribal activities.
Ceremonies called Warbonnet Dances help maintain
an Indian identity. Some Indians practice sweat lodge
ceremonies and are members of the Native American
Church. Most consider themselves Christians.

Only elders speak the native language well, despite
the attempt to institute regular language classes. The
tribes operate several reservation schools and publish
the *Mandan, Hidatsa and Arikara Times*. Craft workers make quilts and beadwork. There is a museum at
New Town.

Mdewkanton
See Dakota

Métis
See Ojibwa, Plains

Minneconjou
See Lakota

Missouria

Missouria (Mi `zor ä) or Missouri, an Algonquian
term probably meaning "People with Dugout
Canoes." Their self-designation was *Niutachi*, or
"People of the River Mouth." They were closely
related to Poncas, Ioways, Otoes, and Winnebagos. All
Southern Siouans had elements of both Plains and
Woodland cultures.

LOCATION Located near the Missouri and Grand

Rivers in the late eighteenth century, today most Missourias live in the Red Rock region of Oklahoma and in regional cities and towns.

POPULATION There were about 1,000 Missourias in the late eighteenth century. Enrolled membership as of the mid-1990s was about 1,500.

LANGUAGE Iowa-Otoe-Missouria was a member of the Chiwere division of the Siouan language family.

Historical Information

HISTORY According to tradition, the Winnebago, Ioway, Missouria, and Otoe once lived together north of the Great Lakes. In the sixteenth century, the groups began migrating south toward their historic areas. The Otoe and Missouria continued past the Ioway and especially the Winnebago until they reached the junction of the Missouri and Grand Rivers around 1600. There the tribes had a falling out ascribed to a love affair between the two chiefs' children.

After the split, the Missouria were under constant attack from such tribes as the Sauk and Fox. They were also regularly struck by smallpox and other diseases. Jacques Marquette encountered the Missouria in 1673 by the Missouri and Grand Rivers. Trade with the French soon developed and continued for about a century.

In 1730, after the Sauk killed several hundred of their people, the Missouria moved across the Missouri River and settled near the Osage. After they acquired horses in the early to mid–eighteenth century, their lives became much more focused on hunting buffalo. The Missouria were nearly all killed in a 1798 Fox ambush on the Missouri River. Many rejoined the Otoe at that time. Some also went to live with the Osage and the Kaw. Several years later, the rest of the tribe, including the fewer than 100 survivors of the devastating 1829 smallpox epidemic, joined the Otoes.

Several difficult decades followed, during which the people continued to battle disease as well as Indians and non-Indians. By treaties in the 1830s and 1854, the Otoe-Missouria ceded all land and moved to a 162,000-acre reservation on the Kansas-Nebraska border, along the Big Blue River. Additional land cessions in occurred in 1876 and 1881.

Two factions developed in 1880 over the issue of acculturation. The Coyote, or traditional faction, moved to the Indian Territory (Oklahoma). The Quakers ceded their land for a 129,000-acre reservation near Red Rock in north-central Oklahoma. Most Coyotes joined them by 1890, having lived for a time in a separate village on the Iowa Reservation. The reservation was allotted by 1907.

The tribe established a court system for both civil and criminal cases by 1900. Many people lived by growing grains and potatoes. After oil was discovered on their land in 1912, the United States forced many Otoe-Missourias to give up their allotments. During the early to mid–twentieth century, intermarriage truly created one tribe. Many Indians left the region during the 1930s. The tribe received a $1.5 million land claim settlement in 1955 and another payment in 1964. Both were divided on a per capita basis.

RELIGION Wakonda was recognized as a universal spirit, to which the people could draw closer through fasting and vision seeking. There were secret curing and dance societies and a hereditary priesthood. As part of a Woodland ceremony related to the Ojibwa Midewiwin, members of a particular religious society "shot" a prospective member with a magic shell. The candidate was later restored by older shamans.

GOVERNMENT Political authority was vested in hereditary clan and war chiefs.

CUSTOMS Each of about ten patrilineal clans had specific social and religious responsibilities. The people played lacrosse, a Woodland game. Corpses were placed in a tree or buried in the ground. A four-day mourning period followed funerals, and a horse was sometimes killed so that the dead person's spirit might have transportation to the spirit world.

DWELLINGS Missourias lived in small farming villages of between 40 and 70 semiexcavated earth lodges. Each lodge measured about 40 feet in diameter and was constructed of interwoven brush and grass over a heavy wooden framework, with an outer earthen layer. From the eighteenth century on, the people used skin tipis on hunting trips.

DIET Women grew corn, beans, and squash in river bottomlands. Men assisted with the crops but mainly hunted buffalo (twice a year from the eighteenth century on), deer, and small game. Hunting, in fact, was a major occupation, and once on the Plains the Missouria gradually came to rely more on buffalo than on crops. The people also gathered plant foods such as nuts, berries, and roots, and they ate fish.

KEY TECHNOLOGY Crops were stored in underground bell-shaped caches. People speared fish or caught them in weirs and basketry traps. Women dressed skins with elk antler scrapers.

Material items included buffalo wool bags; reed floor mats woven over a bark-cord foundation; twined rectangular storage bags; rawhide trunks or containers, bent and sewn into place; and buffalo-hair wallets. The latter two items were more typical of Woodland tribes such as the Sauk and Fox.

TRADE During the late seventeenth and early eighteenth centuries, Missourias traded heavily with the French, supplying Indian slaves, among other items.

NOTABLE ARTS Woodworking was particularly well developed among the Missouria.

TRANSPORTATION The Missouria acquired horses during the early eighteenth century.

DRESS On the Plains, Missourias dressed similarly to other local Indians. Skins tanned by women formed the basis of most clothing. Men wore leggings and a breechclout; women wore a one-piece dress. Both wore moccasins. Cold-weather gear included shirts, robes, and fur caps.

WAR AND WEAPONS Missourias and Otoes were usually military allies. Traditional enemies included the Sauk, Fox, Pawnee, Omaha, and Dakota.

Contemporary Information

GOVERNMENT/RESERVATIONS About 800 Otoe-Missourias lived in Oklahoma's Red Rock region in the mid-1990s. The tribe is governed by a tribal council under a 1984 constitution.

ECONOMY Jobs are available in the local economy as well as through the various tribal enterprises, such as elderly and community health programs. There is also a tribal bingo parlor.

LEGAL STATUS The Otoe-Missouria tribe is a federally recognized tribal entity.

DAILY LIFE Traditional kinship and family ties remain alive and important. The tribe hosts a pow-wow in July. Other gatherings and ceremonies take place regularly, often in the cultural center. Children study the native language in school, assisted by a Chiwere grammar published in 1975.

The people began buying land and adding to their land base in the 1970s. At that time they received a series of federal grants to reconstruct tribal facilities and institute services. Religious affiliations include Protestant, Catholic, and the Native American Church.

Nakota

Nakota (Nä `k ō tä), a Siouan dialect spoken by the Central group—whose divisions include Yankton ("end village") and Yanktonai ("little end village")—of the tribe commonly referred to as Sioux. Yanktonai was divided into Upper Yanktonai and Lower Yanktonai (Hunkpatina), from which Assiniboine/Stoney was derived.

The Nakota refer to themselves as Nakota ("ally") or as *Ikce Wicasa* ("Natural" or "Free People"). The word "Sioux" is derived originally from an Ojibwa word, *Nadowe-is-iw*, meaning "lesser adder" ("enemy" is the implication) that was corrupted by French voyageurs to *Nadousssioux* and then short-ened to *Sioux*. Today, many people use the term

"Dakota" or, less commonly, "Lakota" to refer to all Sioux people.

All 13 subdivisions of Dakota-Lakota-Nakota speakers ("Sioux") were known as *Oceti Sakowin,* or Seven Council Fires, a term referring to their seven political divisions: Teton (the Western group, speakers of Lakota); Sisseton, Wahpeton, Wahpukute, and Mdewakanton (the Eastern group, speakers of Dakota); and Yankton and Yanktonai (the Central, or Wiciyela, group, speakers of Dakota and Nakota). *See also* Assiniboine; Dakota; Lakota.

LOCATION Nakota speakers migrated from north-central Minnesota, around Mille Lacs, in the early seventeenth century, to near the Missouri River in present-day eastern North and South Dakota, southwestern Minnesota, and southwestern Iowa in the nineteenth century. Today, Yanktons and Yank-tonais live on reservations in the Dakotas and Montana as well as in regional cities and towns.

POPULATION Dakota, Lakota, and Nakota speakers numbered approximately 25,000 in the late seventeenth century. At that time there were approximately 5,000 Nakota speakers. In the mid–nineteenth century there were about 3,000 Yanktons and 6,000 Yank-tonais. Today there are roughly 10,000 Yanktons and Yanktonais.

LANGUAGE Nakota is a dialect of Dakota, a Siouan language.

Historical Information

HISTORY The Siouan family may have originated along the lower Mississippi River or in eastern Texas. Siouan speakers moved to, or may have originated in, the Ohio Valley, where they lived in large agricultural settlements. They may have been related to the Mound Builder culture of the ninth through twelfth centuries. They may also have originated in the upper Mississippi Valley or even the Atlantic seaboard.

Siouan tribes still lived in the southeast, between Florida and Virginia, around the late sixteenth and early seventeenth century. All were destroyed either by attacks from Algonquian-speaking Indians or a combination of attacks from non-Indians and non-Indian diseases. Some fled and were absorbed by other tribes. Some were sent as slaves to the West Indies.

Dakota-Lakota-Nakota speakers ranged throughout more than 100 million acres in the upper Mississippi region, including Minnesota and parts of Wisconsin, Iowa, and the Dakotas, in the sixteenth to early seventeenth century. At this time the Yankton and Yanktonai were one tribe, the Assiniboine having separated from the Yankton/Yanktonai, probably by the mid–sixteenth century.

French explorers encountered Eastern group tribes around Mille Lacs, Minnesota, in the late seventeenth century. Shortly afterward, the latter probably became directly involved in the fur trade. But conflict with the Cree and Ojibwa, who were well armed with French rifles, plus the lure of great buffalo herds to feed their expanding population, induced bands to begin moving west onto the Plains.

The Yankton and Yanktonai separated near Leech Lake in the late seventeenth century. The Yankton had moved out of the northern Woodlands and onto the southern prairies (near the pipestone quarries of southwest Minnesota and then west of the Missouri in northwest Iowa) by the early eighteenth century. A hundred years later, Yanktons ranged north and northwest into Minnesota and South Dakota.

Meanwhile, the Yanktonai left their homes in Mille Lacs by the early eighteenth century to follow Teton tribes west, making winter villages on the James River (South Dakota) at least as early as 1725. They acquired horses in the mid– to late eighteenth century. By the early nineteenth century they were hunting buffalo between the Red and the Missouri Rivers and north to Devil's Lake.

A general Yankton decline set in during the 1830s. Its causes were smallpox, the growing scarcity of game, and war, particularly with the Pawnee, Otoe, and Omaha. Yanktons ceded their Iowa lands (2.2 million acres) to the United States in 1830 and 1837 treaties and ceded over 11 million acres in 1858. They did retain a 430,000-acre reservation near Fort Randall, South Dakota. They also claimed the 650-acre Pipestone Reservation in Minnesota.

By 1860, Yanktons had ceded all of their remaining lands. Most moved to the Yankton Reservation in South Dakota; others went to the Crow Creek and Lower Brulé Reservations in South Dakota and to the Fort Totten (now Devil's Lake) Reservation in North Dakota. The Yanktonai ceded their remaining lands in 1865. They were removed to a number of reservations, including Standing Rock (South Dakota), Devil's Lake (North Dakota), Crow Creek (South Dakota), and Fort Peck (Montana). In 1866 they replaced the Santee at Crow Creek when the latter were moved to Nebraska. Yanktons sold the Pipestone Reservation in 1929 for almost $330,000 plus guarantees of Indian access.

RELIGION Wakan Tanka was known as the great spirit and creator of the universe. There were other deities as well; Nakotas were a very prayerful people. Access to the supernatural world was provided in part by guardian spirits obtained through quests and in dreams. From the eighteenth century on, Nakotas performed the Sun Dance.

GOVERNMENT The Yankton were organized into eight bands. The upper division Yanktonai consisted of six bands, and the Hunkpatina had seven bands. The governing band council was composed of band chiefs and clan leaders. The Seven Council Fires met approximately annually to socialize and discuss matters of national importance.

CUSTOMS Nakota bands were composed of patrilineal clans. Around the mid–eighteenth century, Nakotas adopted many Plains customs. They wrapped their dead in skins and placed them on high scaffolds with their belongings. Belowground interment took place occasionally. Mourners cut their hair, wore white clay on their faces, and affected an unkempt appearance.

DWELLINGS Small villages were located near lakes and rice swamps when the people lived in the Wisconsin-Minnesota area. In summer they lived in large houses of timbered frames with pitched roofs and bark-covered sides, whereas in winter they lived in small mat-covered houses. From the mid– to late eighteenth century, the Yanktonai lived in earth lodges like the Arikara, as well as in tipis.

DIET While still in the Great Lakes region, women grew corn, beans, and squash. People also gathered wild rice and ate turtles, fish, and dogs. Large and small game, especially buffalo, which roamed the area in small herds, were also an important food source. Buffalo were hunted in part by burning grass around the range and forcing the animals toward an ambush. With the westward migration, buffalo became increasingly important, although men still hunted deer, elk, and antelope. Women also grew some corn, beans, and squash along river bottomlands and gathered fruits and berries.

KEY TECHNOLOGY In addition to the usual tools and other items made of animal parts, Nakotas caught fish with weirs and basket traps and wove mats and various containers. They also made pottery and pipes.

TRADE As the Missouri River trade developed, the Yankton controlled the catlinite, or red pipestone, quarry in southwest Minnesota, supplying its clay to most of the northern Plains groups. During the early nineteenth century, the Yanktonai traded along the Jones River, acting as intermediaries for British goods between the Sisseton and Wahpeton Dakota and the Tetons farther west.

NOTABLE ARTS Pottery, pipe carving, and skin tanning were well-developed arts.

TRANSPORTATION Nakotas plied the northern Woodlands in birch-bark and dugout canoes. On the Plains, horses replaced dogs as travois carriers around 1760. They also used round bull-boats when crossing water.

DRESS Most clothing was made from buckskin. In the Woodlands, the people wore breechclouts, dresses, leggings, and moccasins, with fur robes for extra warmth. On the Plains, they decorated their clothing with beads and quillwork in geometric and animal designs.

WAR AND WEAPONS The Plains warrior ideal—that the purpose of war was to bring glory to an individual rather than to acquire territory or destroy an enemy people—was distinctive to and may have originated with the Siouan people. Dakota people did not generally fight other Dakotas. The *akitcita* was an elite warrior group that maintained discipline at camp and on the communal hunt. Nakota enemies included the Ojibwa (seventeenth and eighteenth centuries).

Contemporary Information

GOVERNMENT/RESERVATIONS The Yankton Reservation, Charles Mix County, South Dakota (Yankton), established in 1853, contains roughly 36,000 acres. Enrollment in 1992 was about 6,000, with about 3,400 in residence. The original constitution was adopted in 1891; as of the late 1990s, the constitution does not conform to the Indian Reorganization Act (IRA). The reservation is governed by a business committee.

The Upper Sioux Community, Yellow Medicine County, Minnesota (Sisseton, Wahpeton, Flandreau Santee, Santee, Yankton), established in 1938, contains 743.57 acres. There were 43 residents in 1990. Political authority resides in a board of trustees.

The Fort Peck Reservation, Daniels, Roosevelt, Sheridan, and Valley Counties, Montana (Assiniboine-Sioux [Assiniboine, Upper Yanktonai, and Sisseton-Wahpeton]), established in 1873, contains about 1,000,000 acres, roughly one-quarter of which are tribally owned. Although their 1927 constitution is not based on the IRA, they adopted a representative government, the Tribal Executive Board, in 1960. Enrollment in 1992 was 10,500, with 6,700 residents.

The Devil's Lake Reservation (formerly Fort Totten), Benson, Eddy, Nelson, and Ramsey Counties, North Dakota (Sisseton, Wahpeton, and Cuthead Yanktonai), established in 1867, contains 53,239 acres, most of which are allotted. There were 4,420 people enrolled in 1992, with about 2,900 in residence. The IRA constitution adopted in 1944 calls for elections to a tribal council.

The Standing Rock Reservation, Sioux County, North Dakota, and Carson County, South Dakota (Hunkpapa, Blackfoot Lakota, Yanktonai), established in 1868, contains 847,799 acres, almost 300,000 of which are tribally owned. There were 4,866 Indian residents in 1990. Political authority is vested in a tribal council.

The Crow Creek Reservation, Buffalo, Hughes, and Hyde Counties, South Dakota (Hunkpatina), established in 1863, contains 125,483 acres. There were 3,521 enrolled members in 1992, with about 1,200 in residence. A 1923 constitution and by-laws, since revised, call for an elected tribal council.

ECONOMY The Devil's Lake people have a bingo hall and casino as well as a plant that makes nonviolent armaments such as camouflage nets. Income at Fort Peck is provided by a bingo hall and land leases to non-Indian farmers and ranchers. Fort Peck owns and operates a profitable oil well. The Indians also have other mineral resources and have encouraged industrial development.

At Crow Creek there is a tribal farm and the Lode Star Casino. Other sources of employment include a muffler plant, a boarding school, federal and tribal jobs, and off-reservation jobs. The people have received more than $5 million for land taken for dam projects. The Fort Randall Casino on the Yankton Reservation provides full employment for that community. Important economic activities at Standing Rock include cattle ranching and leasing land to Texas ranching firms.

LEGAL STATUS The Assiniboine and Sioux Tribes of the Fort Peck Reservation is a federally recognized tribal entity. The Devils Lake Sioux Tribe, the Standing Rock Sioux Tribe, the Crow Creek Sioux Tribe, the Yankton Sioux Tribe, and the Upper Sioux Indian Community are federally recognized tribal entities.

DAILY LIFE The Devil's Lake community remains relatively traditional. People perform sacred pipe ceremonies, and many speak Dakota. There is an active Native American Church. The powwow is held in July. At Crow Creek, religious observances include sacred pipe ceremonies as well as the Native American Church.

Standing Rock Community College was chartered in 1973. The reservation has a history of maintaining cultural integrity through relative isolation by resisting full federal funding as well as IRA compliance. Members of the Deloria family—including Philip J., Vine, Sr., Vine, Jr., and Ella Cara—of the Standing Rock community have achieved national and international prominence as writers, teachers, activists, and leaders.

There is also a community college at Fort Peck. That reservation has bucked the gambling tide, refusing to turn their bingo hall into a casino. They have enjoyed relatively effective political leadership. Many Yanktons and Yanktonais have achieved success as artists.

Oglala

See Lakota

Ojibwa, Plains

Plains Ojibwa (Ō `jib w ə), "puckered up," refers to a distinctive style of moccasin seam. They were also known as "Bungi." Their self-designation is *Anishinabe,* "First People." People of Ojibwa/ Cree/French ancestry are known as Métis, or Mitchif. The Plains Ojibwa are the westernmost branch of the large Ojibwa people, also known variously as Ojibwe, Ojibway, Chippewa, and Anishinabe. *See also* Anishinabe (Chapter 8).

LOCATION Located along the northern Lake Superior shore in the late seventeenth century, the proto–Plains Ojibwa migrated to the Red River Valley (Lake Winnipeg to the North Dakota–Minnesota border) in the eighteenth century. In the nineteenth century, the Plains Ojibwa were located in north-central Montana (vicinity of Milk and Judith Rivers). Today, most live on a reservation in Chouteau and Hill Counties, Montana; in nearby towns such as Havre, Great Falls, and Helena; and in eastern Montana and western North Dakota.

POPULATION There were roughly 35,000 Ojibwa in the mid–seventeenth century and about 3,000 Plains Ojibwa in the late eighteenth century. In the early 1990s there were roughly 3,100 enrolled members of the Rocky Boy Reservation, about 1,000 residents of the Montana Allotment Community, and about 25,000 enrolled members of the Turtle Mountain Reservation.

LANGUAGE Ojibwa is an Algonquian language.

Historical Information

HISTORY The Plains Ojibwa originated in the eastern Great Lakes region. The so-called Salteaux Anishinabe bands had their origin in the vicinity of Sault Sainte Marie. During the late sixteenth century, the people came into friendly, trade-based contact with Dakota bands west and south of Lake Superior. The first French traders and missionaries arrived in the early seventeenth century. Later in that century, the Anishinabe became heavily involved in the fur trade.

The Anishinabe also began to expand their territory during the seventeenth century, an event caused in part by pressure from the Iroquois as well as the overtrapping of food and pelts. One migration route was westward into northern Wisconsin and Minnesota (upper Mississippi basin)—displacing Dakotas, Sauks, Foxes, and Kickapoos along the way—where these people became influenced by the Cree. Wild rice became an important part of their diet during this time. This group emerged from the forest about 1690.

Anishinabe groups that continued into the Red River area (northwest Minnesota, northeast North Dakota, and Canada) during the eighteenth century, such as the Pembina band of Chippewa, were armed with French guns and thus able to displace Hidatsa, Arikara, and Cheyenne bands. From this base there were four separate migrations to Montana.

During the eighteenth century, Red River Valley Ojibwa, Cree, and Métis traveled west in response to the continued overtrapping of small game. They acquired horses in the late eighteenth century and became buffalo hunters, fully adapting to life on the Plains by the early nineteenth century. After a failed effort to establish a native state in Manitoba, Canada, in 1868, about 4,000 Chippewa-Cree from the Pembina Band moved into present-day Montana. During the 1880s, the United States forced many Cree out of the United States into Canada. Many Chippewa and Métis were also forced out; their homes were burned behind them.

In 1885, the Chippewa, Cree, and Métis, now back in Canada, again attempted to create a native state in Manitoba under the leadership of the Métis Louis Riel. When this effort failed, the Chippewa chief Stone Child, or Rocky Boy, led a group of people back into Montana. In the late 1870s another group of Chippewa-Cree followed the buffalo into Montana from the Turtle Mountain area in North Dakota. They generally moved between Montana and North Dakota Chippewa-Cree communities.

In 1882, the United States recognized the Turtle Mountain Band's claim to 20 townships in north-central North Dakota. Two years later, however, it decided that the reservation was too large. The Little Shell Band, away hunting buffalo in Montana, was excluded from a government census, as were all Métis, who were declared to be Canadian. Despite the existence of these roughly 5,000 people, the North Dakota Reservation was reduced by about 10 million acres, or about 90 percent.

Little Shell's people sought refuge and a reservation near their relatives at Fort Belknap, Montana. Some remained on that reservation, with others settling in towns such as Havre, Great Falls, and Helena. Little Shell himself worked from the 1880s to his death in 1900 to establish a reservation for his people in Montana. He also worked to restore the size of the Turtle Mountain Reservation and to reenroll the Métis.

In the early twentieth century, following the negotiations over the Turtle Mountain Reservation, many of those people were forced to accept allotments on the public domain in North and South Dakota and eastern Montana. In 1904 the United States paid the Turtle Mountain band $1 million for their land cession, or about 10 cents an acre, but they refused to reenroll the Métis. Cree Chief Little Bear's people joined the Indians already in the Rocky Boy community in 1910. The Rocky Boy Reservation was established in 1916.

By 1920, many of the exiled Turtle Mountain and Pembina Chippewas, having lost their allotments through tax foreclosure, returned to the North Dakota community. During the next several decades the situation became, if anything, worse, with the poverty-stricken people squeezed on an inadequate land base. Many left the reservation during those years in search of work, never to return. The Turtle Mountain people were saved from termination in the 1950s only by the deplorable example of the Menominee termination fiasco (*see* Menominee [Chapter 8]).

RELIGION Gitchi Manito, the Great Spirit, and other spirits pervaded all nature. Children were encouraged to attract guardian spirit helpers by fasting in remote places. The people adopted the Sun Dance in the nineteenth century.

The Midewiwin, or Medicine Lodge Society, included both men and women. Candidates, who usually had to have experienced dream spirit visions, were initiated in a dance ceremony lasting several days. The main event included being "shot" by a member with a white shell that, taken from the medicine bag, carried supernatural power into the initiate. Upon being "revived" by older members, the initiate would spit out the shell. Members "shot" at one another as well to demonstrate their magical power. The meeting events were recorded on birch-bark scrolls with bone awls dipped in red paint. Members wore special medicine bags, usually of otter skin.

GOVERNMENT While still living around Lake Superior, people lived in small hunting bands of about ten people, each with its own hunting area. On the Plains, government conformed largely to the Plains model, including the presence of soldier societies.

CUSTOMS On the Plains, patrilineal clans gave way to bilaterally descended extended families. Generosity was highly valued, as were bravery, fortitude, wisdom, and fidelity. People shared regularly, especially with the less able or fortunate. Thus did people achieve prestige while actually reducing individual suffering and want. Wealth and kin connections also played a part, however, and status ultimately rested on a combination of individual and family qualities.

Winter was generally a time for repairing tools and weapons and making crafts and clothing. Social control was effected mostly by peer pressure and ridicule, although serious crimes were punished by revenge and/or council action. Among the various

social and religious groups were men's dance societies. Games included various guessing games, cup-and-ball, and competitions. Adult games were usually accompanied by gambling. Toys included conical tops and sleds. In general, storytelling was a favorite pastime.

Polygamy was practiced, although it was expensive. Each wife might or might not have a separate tipi. Marriage was mainly a matter of parental agreement, often based on the couple's choice, and divorce was common and easy to obtain. Infants spent their first few months swaddled in a cradle board. Children were treated permissively. Boys and girls (except for brothers and sisters) generally played together until puberty. Games revolved around future adult activities.

During menstruation, girls and women were secluded for a few days, as men considered them dangerous. Several weeks later, fathers who were able gave a ceremony, presided over by a shaman, for their daughters. Girls who had reached puberty were considered marriageable. Boys did not have a specific puberty ceremony. Their vision quests, first successful buffalo hunt, first war party, and so forth might be marked by feasts and gifts and were considered rites of passage. Men generally married slightly older than did women, having first to prove their manhood and perhaps acquire enough goods to distribute.

As a matter of respect there was no verbal communication between a man and his mother-in-law. Aged people were generally accorded a great deal of respect. The dead were buried with their effects on high hills or in scaffolds in trees. In the prehistoric period remains were buried in an earth mound.

DWELLINGS Winter camps on the Plains were places containing wood and water, such as valley cottonwood groves. People also needed forage for horses and some natural protection against weather and enemies.

On the Plains, the people lived in conical buffalo-skin tipis in both summer and winter. The skins were dressed and sewn together by women and placed over a pole framework. A tipi held one family. Two skin flaps at the top, attached to long poles, regulated the smoke hole. A small, elevated doorway was covered by a rawhide door.

Skin liners helped insulate against the cold and wind. Tanned buffalo robes served as beds and blankets and buffalo robes as carpeting. Women erected and took down the tipis, which could be moved quickly and easily. Tipis were often painted with special symbols and war exploits and also decorated with feathers, quills, or other items.

DIET While in the vicinity of Lake Superior, rabbits and wild rice were staples. On the Plains, buffalo, hunted communally, became the main food. Men also hunted other large and small game. Women gathered local roots, berries, and nuts. Sugar syrup came from box elder or maple trees.

KEY TECHNOLOGY Bone fishhooks were fastened onto sinew lines attached to willow poles. Many tools were also made of stone, until iron became available from non-Indian traders. On the Plains, most manufactured items came from the buffalo.

Women tanned the skins using elk antler scrapers with an attached stone (or iron) blade; the hair was either left on or soaked and scraped off. Rawhide was often used to attach items to each other, such as two-piece clubs and mauls. People made willow back rests.

TRADE Plains Ojibwas exchanged sugar syrup with tribes that had no such traditions. Among the products they imported were pipes. Part of an extensive trade complex stretching throughout the West, Plains tribes traded buffalo products to eastern groups for non-Indian goods the latter had obtained through the fur trade.

NOTABLE ARTS Some people used a pointed tool (or, occasionally, pieces of wood) to cut into the inner layer of birch bark to produce line drawings; most such drawings related to the Midewiwin society. Such pictograms also combined to illustrate song texts. People occasionally used incised drawings to decorate prayer sticks and weapons. Some groups also used a different style of decoration, consisting of zigzags and bands of triangles combined with symbolic shapes. On the Plains, the people decorated clothing and hides with paint, beads, and quillwork. Nineteenth-century quillwork consisted mainly of floral designs. Carved pipes were also a notable Plains Ojibwa art form.

TRANSPORTATION Canoes were common in the Woodlands. The Plains Ojibwa acquired horses in the later eighteenth century.

DRESS On the Plains, women made tailored skin clothing and buffalo robes. They decorated the clothing with geometric designs and floral patterned beadwork. Both sexes wore hard-soled moccasins.

WAR AND WEAPONS The Ojibwa historically were fierce warriors. They adopted Plains-style soldier societies in the nineteenth century. Weapons included bows and arrows, clubs, and shields.

Contemporary Information

GOVERNMENT/RESERVATIONS Modern communities of Plains Ojibwa groups are as follows:

The Rocky Boy Chippewa-Cree Reservation (1,485 resident Indians in 1990) and Trust Lands (397 resident Indians in 1990), Chouteau and Hill Counties, Montana, established in 1916, contains 108,015 acres. The tribe is governed by a written constitution delegating authority to the Chippewa-Cree Business Committee. There is also a tribal court. Roughly half of the population lives off-reservation.

The Little Shell people, some of whom are of Cree descent, had a 1990 population of 3,300. They are governed by a tribal council under a constitution. Their main offices are in Havre and Helena, Montana.

There is also a community of Chippewa, established during the process of allotting the Turtle Mountain Reservation, living in eastern Montana. The seat of their government is in Trenton, North Dakota.

The Turtle Mountain Reservation and Trust Lands, Rolette, Burke, Cavalier, Divide, McLean, Mountrail, and Williams Counties, North Dakota, and Perkins County, South Dakota, established in 1882, contains over 45,000 acres, of which about 30 percent is controlled by non-Indians. The 1990 resident Indian population was 6,770. The reservation is governed by an elected nine-member Tribal Council under a 1959 constitution and by-laws.

ECONOMY The Rocky Boy Chippewa-Cree Development Company manages that tribe's economic resources. The tribe's beadwork is in high demand. The company organized a propane business and owns a casino as well as recreational facilities. The largest employers on the reservation are the tribal government, Stone Child Community College, and industry. Other activities include cattle grazing, wheat and barley farming, some logging and mining, and recreation/tourism. Unemployment regularly approaches 75 percent.

People in the Montana Allotment Community are integrated into the local economy. Turtle Mountain operates a casino.

LEGAL STATUS The Chippewa-Cree Indians of the Rocky Boy Reservation, Montana, are a federally recognized tribal entity.

The Turtle Mountain Band of Chippewa Indians is a federally recognized tribal entity.

The Saginaw Cippewa Tribe (Swan Creek and Black River Chippewa) is a federally recognized tribal entity.

The Little Shell Tribe of Chippewa Indians, as well as some of the "landless Chippewa," have been seeking federal recognition since the 1920s.

DAILY LIFE People from all four Montana Chippewa communities (Rocky Boy, Little Shell, Allotment Community, and "landless community") are generally related and often visit and move freely between locations. A renaissance of Montana Chippewa communities has taken place in the 1990s. The people look toward to a future well grounded in the past.

The Chippewa-Crees opened Stone Child Community College in 1978. Many Chippewa/Crees/Métis are Christians. Many also participate in the Sun Dance, sweat lodge ceremonies, and the Native American Church. Most Chippewa/Crees/Métis consider themselves one people and commonly intermarry. Indians living on the Rocky Boy Reservation speak English, Cree, and Métis.

Turtle Mountain Community College is located in Belcourt, North Dakota. At Turtle Mountain, the Chippewa and Métis languages are still spoken. Most people are Catholic. Some tribal members have received payments as part of a settlement regarding the unfairness of the original land claims payment. Turtle Mountain author Louise Erdrich has set many of her stories in the Turtle Mountain area. The Midewiwin Society remains active but has incorporated elements of Christianity.

Omaha

Omaha (`Ō m ə hä) comes from *Umon'hon,* "those going against the current," a reference to the people's migration down the Ohio River and then north on the Mississippi. They were closely related to the Ponca.

LOCATION The Omaha inhabited the Ohio and Wabash Valleys in the fifteenth century. In the late eighteenth century they had migrated to northeast Nebraska. Today, most Omahas live along the Iowa-Nebraska border.

POPULATION The late-eighteenth-century Omaha population was about 2,800 people. In the early 1990s, about 6,000 people were enrolled in the tribe.

LANGUAGE Omaha is a member of the Dhegiha division of the Siouan language family.

Historical Information

HISTORY The group of Siouan people known as Omaha left the Wabash and Ohio River regions in the early sixteenth century. Shortly thereafter, they reached the Mississippi River and split into five separate tribes. The initial exodus was prompted in part by pressure from the Iroquois. Those who continued north along the Mississippi became known as Osage, Kaw, Ponca, and Omaha; the people who headed south were known as Quapaw.

The Omaha and Ponca, accompanied by the Skidi Pawnee, followed the Des Moines River to its headwaters and then traveled overland toward the Minnesota catlinite (pipestone) quarries, where they lived until the early to mid–seventeenth century. Then, driven west by the Dakota, they moved to near Lake Andes, South Dakota, where the Omaha and Ponca briefly separated.

Reunited, the two tribes traveled south along the Missouri to Nebraska, where they separated once again, probably along the Niobrara River, in the late seventeenth century. The Omaha settled on Bow Creek, in northeast Nebraska. After acquiring horses about 1730, the people began to assume many characteristics of typical Plains Indians.

During the eighteenth century, the Omaha visited French posts as far north as Lake Winnipeg. Well supplied with horses (from the Pawnee) and guns (from French traders), the Omaha were able to resist Dakota attacks, even acting as trade intermediaries with their enemies. In 1791–1792, the two warring groups signed a peace treaty.

By the early nineteenth century, heavy involvement in the non-native trade had altered Omaha material culture. A severe smallpox epidemic in 1802 reduced the population to around 300. In 1854 they were forced to cede their land and, the following year, to take up residence on a reservation. In 1865 the government created the Winnebago Reservation from the northern Omaha Reservation. In 1882 the reservation was allotted.

By 1900 most Omahas knew English, and many spoke it well. All lived in houses, and nearly all wore nontraditional clothing. Most children attended school, and a significant number of adults were succeeding as farmers or in other occupations in the nontraditional economy. Still, throughout the twentieth century, the Omaha fought further encroachments on the reservation and tribal sovereignty. Well-known twentieth-century Omahas include Francis La Flesche, who coauthored the classic ethnographic study *The Omaha Tribe* (1911); Susan La Flesche Picotte, the first Native American woman to earn a medical degree; and Thomas L. Sloane, mayor of Pender, Nebraska, and president of the Society of American Indians in the 1920s.

RELIGION Wakonda was the supreme life force, through which all things were related. People sought connection to the supernatural world through visions, which were usually requisite for membership in a secret society.

Two pipes featuring mallard heads attached to the stems were the tribe's sacred objects. There were two religious organizations, the Shell and Pebble societies, which enacted a classic Woodlands ceremony of "shooting" a candidate with a shell and having him revived by the older members.

GOVERNMENT Each of the two tribal divisions, sky people and earth people, were represented by a head chief and a sacred pipe, symbolized by a sacred pole. A tribal council of seven chiefs acted as arbitrators of disputes, with the ability to pronounce sentences that included banishment and the death penalty, and as representatives to other tribes. They also chose the buffalo hunt leader and a group of camp and hunt police.

CUSTOMS The two divisions were each composed of five patrilineal clans. There were numerous social and secret societies. Marriage took place outside the division. A man might have as many as three wives. The dead were placed in trees or scaffolds or were buried in a sitting position facing east. In the latter case, mounds of earth covered the grave.

Homicide was considered a crime against the wronged family; murderers were generally banished but allowed to return when the aggrieved family relented. The people played shinny and other games, including guessing/gambling games. During the communal buffalo hunt, tipis were arranged by clan in a circle. People gained status both in war and through their generosity.

DWELLINGS In villages located along streams, men and women built earth lodges similar to those of (and probably adopted from) the Arikara. About 40 feet in diameter, they were built of willow branches tied together with cords around a heavy wooden frame. The whole was covered with grass and sod. Skin curtains covered either side of the 6-to-10-foot entranceway. The fireplace was located in the middle, with an opening at the top for smoke.

In the nineteenth century, the Omaha built embankments around four feet high around their villages when they learned of an impending attack. Women also built skin tipis, which were mostly used during hunting trips—including the tribal spring and late-summer buffalo hunt—or in sheltered winter camps.

DIET Women grew corn, beans, and squash. Dried produce was stored in underground caches. After planting their crops, people abandoned the villages to hunt buffalo. The spring and summer buffalo hunts provided meat as well as hides for robes and tipis and many other material items. Men also hunted deer and small game. The people ate fish.

KEY TECHNOLOGY Especially after the mid–eighteenth century, most material items were derived from buffalo parts. Hoes, for instance, came from buffalo shoulder blades. The Omaha made pottery until metal containers became available from non-Indian traders. They speared fish or shot them with tipless arrows. Nettle fibers were made into ropes. Bowls, mortars and pestles, and utensils were fashioned occasionally from horn but usually from wood. Hairbrushes were made of stiff grass.

TRADE In the eighteenth and nineteenth century, the Omaha traded regularly and often with French, British, and U.S. traders as well as local Indians.

NOTABLE ARTS Omaha artists made items using quills, paints, and beads. Black, red, and yellow were the traditional colors.

TRANSPORTATION Horses were acquired about 1730. The people used hide bull-boats to cross bodies of water.

DRESS Women dressed the skins for and made all clothing. They wore fringed tunics that left the arms free. Men wore leggings and breechclouts. Tattoos were used, especially ceremonially (such as a sun on the forehead and a star on the chest). Both sexes wore smoked skin moccasins as well as cold-weather gear such as robes, hats, and mittens.

WAR AND WEAPONS Men's warrior societies existed, although they were not as important as other religious and social organizations. Men fought with bow and arrow, clubs, spears, and hide shields. Enemies included the Dakota, at least from the eighteenth century on. The Skidi Pawnee were early (seventeenth-century) allies.

Contemporary Information

GOVERNMENT/RESERVATIONS The Omaha Reservation (Monona County, Iowa, and Burt, Cuming, and Thurston Counties, Nebraska), established in 1854, contains 26,792 acres, about 8,500 of which are tribally owned. There were 1,908 resident Indians in 1990. Authority is vested in an elected council of seven members plus a tribal chair.

ECONOMY The Omaha tribal farm raises livestock. There is also income from the Chief Big Elk Park recreation area.

LEGAL STATUS The Omaha Tribe is a federally recognized tribal entity. The tribe gained civil and criminal jurisdiction over the reservation from Nebraska in 1970.

DAILY LIFE Omaha children learn Omaha in schools, and roughly half of the people speak the language. Many former ceremonies have been lost. Some people are active in the Native American Church. Omahas also participate in traditional activities such as the hand game and the Gourd Dance. Traditional gift giving forms an important part of the annual tribal powwow. Omaha traditional music, especially warrior songs, has influenced the contemporary music of other Plains tribes.

In 1989, the tribe obtained the return of its sacred pole from Harvard's Peabody Museum. Two years later the people effected the return, from the Museum of the American Indian in New York, of their sacred White Buffalo Hide. Plans for an interpretive center to house these and other items and exhibits are under way. Omahas have also worked for the return from museums and schools of human remains.

O'ohenonpa (Two Kettles)

See Lakota

Osage

Osage (`Ō s ā j) is the French version of *Wazhazhe*, one of their three historical bands (Great Osage, Little Osage, and Arkansas Osage). Their self-designation was *Ni-U-Ko'n-Ska*, or "Children of the Middle Waters."

LOCATION   In the late seventeenth century, Osage Indians lived along the Osage River in western Missouri. Today, most live in Osage County, Oklahoma.

POPULATION   The early-eighteenth-century Osage population was about 1,000. The people had grown to over 6,000 within the century. In 1993, the Osage tribe had about 11,000 enrolled members.

LANGUAGE   Osage is a member of the Dhegiha division of the Siouan language family.

Historical Information

HISTORY   A group of Siouan people, known as Omaha, split into five separate tribes after they reached the Mississippi in the late sixteenth century from the Wabash and Ohio River regions. The initial exodus was prompted in part by pressure from the Iroquois. Those who continued north along the Mississippi and Missouri Rivers became known as Osage, Kaw, Ponca, and Omaha; the people who headed south were known as Quapaw.

The French explorers Jacques Marquette and Louis Joliet encountered the Osage in 1673, when the Indians were living in two villages along and nearby the south fork of the Osage River. Around 1700, the Osage acquired horses and began hunting buffalo. They organized a smaller hunt in June for about four weeks and a larger hunt in October and November. Nearly the whole tribe was involved in the fall hunt; only the very young and old stayed behind to guard the crops against birds and animals. Soon half of their food came from the buffalo, and they relied on that animal for material needs as well.

In the early eighteenth century, the Osage formed a strong alliance with the French, who gave them special trade treatment in exchange for pelts and slaves. The Osage captured the slaves from raids on Ponca and Pawnee villages. Osage warriors helped the French fight Fox Indians, the English, and various other enemies. During the mid–eighteenth century, the Osage were well armed and powerful, able both to defend their farming villages and to hunt buffalo on the western plains. The Spanish, a presence in the later eighteenth century, also tried to stay on good terms with the Osage, despite Osage raids on their outlying settlements.

In 1802, half of the Great Osage Band, under Chief Big Track, moved to the Arkansas River in Oklahoma to be near a trading post opened by the friendly Chouteau family. Thereafter they were known to non-Indians as the Arkansas Osages. In 1808, however, following the large-scale arrival of non-Indians in the region, the Osage ceded most of Missouri and northern Arkansas to the United States. The Little and Great Bands then moved to the Neosho River in Kansas.

By treaties in 1818 and 1825, the Osage ceded all of their lands except for a reservation in extreme southern Kansas, to which all bands had relocated by 1836. In the 1850s, in alliance with Plains tribes such as the Cheyenne, Kiowa, and Comanche, they fought and lost a battle to stem the tide of eastern bands, such as the Cherokee, Choctaw, and Chickasaw, who had been moved to their lands by the United States. The Osage fought for both the United States and the Confederacy during the Civil War. Following that war, Osage men scouted for the United States in its wars against the Cheyenne in 1868–1869.

By 1870, the Osage had sold their Kansas lands and bought roughly one million acres of land from the Cherokee in northeastern Indian Territory (Oklahoma). There, they settled in five villages and retained a structure of 24 clans and two divisions. Many Osage embraced the Native American Church in the 1890s.

Large oil deposits were discovered on the reservation in 1897, and the Osage became very wealthy during the 1920s. In 1906, influenced by the prospect of oil wealth, the Osage created and implemented a voluntary allotment plan, dividing the tribal land individually, with the tribe retaining mineral rights. By the 1960s, however, half of the allotted parcels were lost. Although the oil wealth conferred many benefits, it also brought a large measure of corruption, through which people were cheated out of land and money, as well as greatly increased substance abuse. There was a general decline in revenues during the Depression and a resurgence during the Arab oil embargo of the early 1970s.

RELIGION   Wakonda was the supreme life force, with which people might connect through the acquisition of supernatural visions. Shamans provided religious leadership. There was a secret religious society to which both men and women belonged. Ceremonies revolved around planting, peace, and war. The oral history of the tribe was recounted in the Rite of Chiefs.

GOVERNMENT   Each of two divisions (see "Customs") had a peace and a war chief. In certain cases, clan leadership was hereditary. There was also a council of older men to make laws and arbitrate disputes. From the nineteenth century on, the tribe was divided into three political divisions (bands): Great Osage, Little Osage, and Arkansas Osage. Discipline during the hunt was provided by the hunt/camp police, who could publicly whip offenders in order to maintain order.

CUSTOMS Two divisions, Sky/Peace *(Tzi-sho)* and Land/War *(Hunkah)* people, encompassed a total of 21 patrilineal clans, each of which held distinctive ceremonial and political functions. Marriage was exogamous. Men who married older sisters were entitled to marry the younger ones as well. At death, chiefs and other important people were placed in a sitting position, surrounded by rocks and logs, and covered with earth. Others were buried in the ground with food, water, and various possessions. From the eighteenth century on, mourning ceremonies required the promise of an enemy scalp.

DWELLINGS The Osage located their villages along wooded river valleys. They built oval or rectangular pole-frame houses, 36–100 feet long, 15–20 feet wide, and 10 feet high, covered with woven rush mats or bark. The arched poles were tied together on top and then interlaced with saplings. People lived in tipis while on buffalo hunts.

DIET Women grew corn, squash, pumpkins, and beans and gathered foods such as persimmons, wild fruits and berries, and acorns and other nuts. In addition to buffalo, men hunted deer, wild fowl, beaver, and wildcat. Before they acquired horses, men hunted buffalo by using fire and costumes to stampede them over cliffs.

KEY TECHNOLOGY Osage orange was considered the best wood for bows. The people also built carved wooden cradleboards, cattail and rush mats, and buffalo-hair bags.

TRADE By around 1700, the Osage were supplying the French with Indian (mainly Pawnee and then Apache) slaves in exchange for guns, among other items. In the later eighteenth and into the nineteenth century, Osages had a surplus of horses to trade, in part because they did not require as many as did the truly nomadic Plains buffalo hunters. Being short on winter pastureland, they generally traded most of their horses in the fall, restocking again in the spring. Osages acted as middlemen in the horse trade, moving Comanche horses to the Midwest markets. They also traded with Wichita and Comanche Indians, generally horses for guns.

NOTABLE ARTS Osages were particularly skilled at woodcarving and skin tanning.

TRANSPORTATION The people acquired horses around the late seventeenth century, probably from the Apache.

DRESS Most clothing was made of deerskin. Women wore a shirt and a cape; men wore leggings and a breechclout. They wore their hair in a roach. Men also wore body paint, jewelry, and scalp locks. Through acts of bravery, a warrior gained the privilege to tattoo himself and his wife and daughter(s).

WAR AND WEAPONS On the Plains, war was a way of life, and the Osage fought with most tribes on both sides of the Mississippi, especially nearby Plains and Caddoan-speaking peoples.

Contemporary Information

GOVERNMENT/RESERVATIONS Most Osage live in Osage County, Oklahoma. The administrative center is in Pawhuska. Only those people who have inherited land from the original (1906) allottees may vote in tribal elections.

ECONOMY Oil dollars have made the Osage tribe rich, although revenues have slipped in the 1990s, and the future of the oil fields is uncertain. Individual Osages work in the local economy. Some work in tribal administration or for the tribal bingo parlor; others farm or ranch.

LEGAL STATUS The Osage Tribe is a federally recognized tribal entity.

DAILY LIFE In the mid-1990s only about one-third of the parcels allotted in 1906 were still owned by Osage Indians. There are also three 160-acre community-held village sites (Pawhuska, Hominy, and Grayhorse) and a larger site for tribal administration and facilities. Any Osage can live free of charge in one of the villages.

By law, the oil wealth (and thus political power) must remain among inheritors of the original (1906) allottees. In the mid-1990s, the group of Osage Indians who did not meet these criteria constituted a majority of enrolled members. The effective disenfranchisement of these people is one reason that the concern over oil leases and payments still dominates the business of the tribal council.

Most Osages are Catholic, some are Protestant, and some are also members of the Native American Church. Fewer than 300 people spoke Osage fluently in 1993. Traditional dances are held in June, and Osage people attend many pan-Indian powwows across the country.

Otoe

Otoe (`Ō t ō), or Oto, from *Wahtohtata,* "lovers" or "lechers," referring to an alleged incident between the children of an Otoe and a Missouria chief. An earlier self-designation may have been *Che-wae-rae.* Otoes are closely related to Poncas, Ioways, Missourias, and Winnebagos. All Southern Siouans had elements of both Plains and Woodland cultures.

LOCATION Late-eighteenth-century Otoes lived along the Platte River in eastern Nebraska. In the 1990s, most lived in the Red Rock region of Oklahoma.

POPULATION Otoe population in 1780 was about 900. There were about 1,550 enrolled tribal members in the mid-1990s.

LANGUAGE Otoe-Iowa-Missouria is a member of the Chiwere division of the Siouan language family.

Historical Information

HISTORY According to tradition, the Winnebago, Ioway, Missouria, and Otoe once lived together north of the Great Lakes. In the sixteenth century, groups began migrating toward their historic areas. The Otoe and Missouria continued past the Ioway and especially the Winnebago until they reached the junction of the Missouri and Grand Rivers, in the late sixteenth to early seventeenth century.

There the two tribes had a falling out, traditionally ascribed to a love affair between the two chiefs' children. After the split, the Otoe moved west along the Missouri. Trade with the French began soon after Jacques Marquette and Louis Joliet encountered the Otoe in 1673 and continued for about a century. Between 1680 and 1717, the Otoe lived along the upper Iowa River and then the Blue Earth River. From 1717 to 1854 they lived along the Platte in various locations, including its mouth at the Missouri River. The people acquired horses early in that period and became much more involved in hunting buffalo.

The Otoe people absorbed the smallpox-decimated Missouria, with whom they had been fighting the Sauk and Foxes for years, in 1829. Several difficult decades followed, during which the people battled disease as well as Indians and non-Indians. By treaties in the 1830s and 1854, the Otoe-Missouria ceded all land and moved to a 162,000-acre reservation on the Kansas-Nebraska border, along the Big Blue River. Two more land cessions occurred in 1876 and 1881.

Two factions developed in 1880 over the issue of acculturation. The Coyote, or traditional faction, moved to the Indian Territory (Oklahoma). The Quakers ceded their land for a 129,000-acre reservation near Red Rock in north-central Oklahoma. Most Coyotes joined them by 1890, having lived for a time in a separate village on the Iowa Reservation. The reservation was allotted by 1907.

By 1900, the tribe had established a court system for both civil and criminal cases, Many individuals grew crops of grains and potatoes at that time. After oil was discovered on their land in 1912, the United States forced many Otoe-Missourias to give up their allotments. During the early to mid–twentieth cen-

tury, intermarriage truly created one tribe. Many Indians left the region during the 1930s. The tribe received a $1.5 million land claim settlement in 1955 and another payment in 1964. Both were divided on a per capita basis.

RELIGION Wakonda was the universal spirit, to which people could draw closer by fasting and acquiring visions. There were a number of secret curing and dance (religious) societies as well as a hereditary priesthood. In a ceremony related to the Ojibwa (Woodland) Midewiwin, members of a religious society "shot" an initiate with a magic shell. He was later "restored" by older shamans.

GOVERNMENT Political and military leadership was provided by hereditary clan and war chiefs.

Customs There were about ten patrilineal clans, each with particular responsibilities. The people played lacrosse, among other games. Corpses were placed in a tree or buried in ground. A four-day mourning period followed funerals, during which a horse was occasionally killed to provide transportation to the spirit world.

DWELLINGS Otoe villages were composed of from 40 to 70 semiexcavated earth lodges. Each lodge was about 40 feet in diameter. People caked clay or earth over a wooden framework interwoven with brush and grass. Skin tipis were used on hunting trips.

DIET Women grew corn, beans, and squash in river bottomlands. Men assisted in this work but mainly hunted buffalo (twice a year), deer, and small game. Hunting, in fact, was a major occupation, and once on the Plains the people gradually shifted to rely more on buffalo than on crops. Women gathered plant foods such as nuts, berries, and roots. The people also ate fish.

KEY TECHNOLOGY Crops were stored in underground, bell-shaped caches. Material items included buffalo wool bags; a combination quiver and bow case; twined rectangular storage bags; rawhide trunks or containers, bent and sewn into place; and soft-twilled buffalo-hair wallets. The latter two were items more typical of Woodland tribes such as the Sauk or Fox.

Fish were caught using spears and possibly weirs and basketry traps. Women used elkhorn scrapers (post–eighteenth century) in the tanning process. They also wove reed floor mats over a bark-cord foundation.

TRADE During the late seventeenth and early eighteenth centuries, Otoes traded heavily with the French, supplying Indian slaves, among other commodities.

NOTABLE ARTS Artistic endeavors including weaving and woodworking.

TRANSPORTATION Otoes acquired horses in the early eighteenth century.

DRESS On the Plains, Otoes dressed similarly to other local Indians. Skins tanned by women formed the basis of most clothing. Men wore leggings and breechclout, and women wore a one-piece dress. Both wore moccasins. Cold weather gear included shirts, robes, and fur caps.

WAR AND WEAPONS Traditional enemies included the Pawnee, Sauk, Fox, Omaha, and Dakota. Otoes often joined forced with the Missouria.

Contemporary Information

GOVERNMENT/RESERVATIONS About 800 Otoe-Missourias lived in Oklahoma's Red Rock region in the mid-1990s. The tribe is governed by a tribal council under a 1984 constitution.

ECONOMY Some jobs are provided by federal and tribal governmental projects. Most Otoes work within the local economy.

LEGAL STATUS The Otoe-Missouria tribe is a federally recognized tribal entity.

DAILY LIFE Children study the native language in school, assisted by a Chiwere grammar published in 1975. In the late 1970s, the people began buying land and adding to their land base. At that time they received a number of federal grants to reconstruct tribal facilities and institute certain services. Religious affiliations include Protestant, Catholic, and the Native American Church. Traditional kinship and family ties remain important. In addition to the annual powwow held in July, other ceremonies and gatherings take place regularly, often in the tribe's cultural center.

Pawnee

Pawnee (Pä`n ē) comes from the Caddoan *pariki,* or "horn," referring to the distinctive male hairstyle, or from *parisu,* "hunter." Their self-designation was *Chahiksichahiks,* "Men of Men." By about 1700, if not sooner, the Pawnee had divided into four independent subtribes: the Panimaha (Skidi), the Kitkehaki (Republican), the Chaui (Grand), and the Pitahauerat (Tappage). All but the Skidi spoke a similar dialect and were sometimes known as the Southern Pawnees. The Skidi were also known as Loups (French), Lobos (Spanish), and Wolves (English). The Pawnee were closely related to the Wichita and the Arikara and maintained attributes characteristic of southwestern and Mesoamerican cultures.

LOCATION In the sixteenth century, Pawnees were located along the Arkansas, Platte, and Loup Rivers and on the Republican Fork of the Kansas River (Skidi) in east-central Nebraska. Most Pawnees inhabited the Platte River Valley in the late eighteenth century. In the 1990s, Pawnees lived in Oklahoma and in other states.

POPULATION The late-eighteenth-century Pawnee population was about 10,000. The figure stood at about 2,500 in the early 1990s.

LANGUAGE Panian (Skidi Pawnee, Southern Pawnee, and Arikara) is a Caddoan language.

Historical Information

HISTORY Pawnee tradition has the people originating in the Southwest, but they may have their origin in the southeast, perhaps in the Gulf region of southern Texas, and may have been associated very early on with Iroquoian people. Caddoan people occupied the Plains, from Texas to the Arkansas River region of Oklahoma and Kansas, inconsistently for perhaps several thousand years. Caddoans had major ceremonial centers by 500, including large temple mounds.

Upon leaving east Texas (thirteenth century), the Skidi Pawnee separated from the other bands and traveled east across the Mississippi, following the trail of the Iroquois to the northeast and settling in the Ohio Valley. In the sixteenth century, pressured by the initial stages of Iroquois expansion, the Skidis headed down the Ohio. They were joined along the way by the Omaha. Together, the two people traveled to the Des Moines River, where the Skidi left the Omaha, continuing west to join their cousins and settling on the Loup fork of the Platte River.

Despite a separation of several hundred years, the Skidis reintegrated smoothly among the other Pawnee groups and soon became the largest and most powerful Pawnee tribe. They encountered the Spanish during the sixteenth century. Residents of western Pawnee villages were victims of Apache raiders from the mid–seventeenth century into the eighteenth century. The men were killed, and the women and children were sold as slaves. Thus occurred a gradual abandonment of Pawnee villages in western Nebraska and northeastern Colorado. The Illinois and other tribes also raided them for slaves in the eighteenth century.

Pawnees acquired a few horses around 1700, and within a generation they became great raiders and buffalo hunters, slowly relying less on crops and more on the buffalo for their food. Direct contact with French traders began in the early eighteenth century and expanded rapidly. By the 1750s, the French switched from buying Pawnees to buying Apaches, which the Pawnee, among other tribes, gladly provided. The guns they received in trade helped protect them against Apache attacks, which soon ended against them.

From about 1770 to 1800, the Skidi Pawnee,

reduced from eight villages to only one, lived with the Taovayas Band of Wichita Indians on the Red River in northeastern Texas. Pawnees first met Anglo-Americans, including Meriwether Lewis, William Clark, and Zebulon Pike, in the early nineteenth century. After the Louisiana Purchase, more and more Americans entered Pawnee land. Most generally received a friendly and peaceful welcome.

By the terms of the 1805 Treaty of Table Rock, all Pawnee were relocated to a reservation in Genoa, Nebraska. During the 1830s and 1840s, they often fought and raided in the vicinity of the Arkansas River in southeastern Colorado and southwestern Kansas. Many also served as scouts for the U.S. Army during that period and later. Presbyterian missionaries arrived in 1834. Three years later, the Pawnee suffered a major smallpox epidemic.

By 1850, cholera and warfare with the Dakota tribes had greatly reduced the Pawnee population. They held their last tribal hunt in 1873. Pressured in 1876 to cede their reservation, the tribe moved to a new one, of over 200,000 acres, in north-central Indian Territory (Oklahoma). Part of this reservation was allotted in 1892, with more than half then opened for non-Indian settlement. In 1906, the tribal population had declined 94 percent, to about 600 from about 10,000 just a century before. In 1966, the tribe won a land claims award of over $7 million, and in the 1970s they forced the return of tribal lands given by the United States to the city of Pawnee.

RELIGION *Tirawa,* the sun, was the great spirit or creator and ruler of lesser deities. Among the Skidi, the morning and evening stars represented the masculine and feminine elements respectively. The celestial bodies formed the basis of a complex mythology.

Much of the rich ceremonial life revolved around the heavenly bodies as well as planting, cultivating, and harvesting corn and hunting buffalo. In the Morning Star ceremony, a young girl, usually a captive, was ritually sacrificed (shot with arrows while tied to a wooden frame) to the morning star at the time of the summer solstice to ensure the success of their crops. Petalesharo (Man-Chief) was responsible in 1816 for forcing the priests to stop holding this ceremony.

Hereditary priests were a large and powerful class of people. They conducted the rituals, knew sacred songs and rituals, and were associated with the sacred bundles. Shamans obtained powers from supernatural beings. They performed a large ceremony in late summer or early fall at which they impressed people with feats such as handling live coals and plunging their hands in boiling water. Shamans were also priests insofar as they were trained to lead ceremonies.

Sacred bundles, connected with various rituals and associated with specific villages, dominated Pawnee life. Wrapped in buffalo skin, many bundles contained smoking materials, paints, feathers, and corn. Chiefs kept the bundles, but priests used them. There were also many secret societies, each with its own paraphernalia and rituals. Sacred animal lodges were associated with the Southern people.

GOVERNMENT The chieftaincy was inherited through the female line. Villages were political units, each of which had chiefs, priests, bundles, and a council. The four independent subtribes were united in a confederation.

Councils made all final civil and military decisions. They were established at the different levels of societal organization (village, tribe, confederacy). Each successive level of council was composed of members of the preceding level.

All but two of the Skidi villages were joined in a political and religious confederation before they were forced to consolidate into one village following the smallpox epidemic of 1780–1781. The Chaui had but one village.

CUSTOMS A dual division, winter and summer people, came into play during games and ceremonies. Descent was matrilineal. Most people married from within the village. Corpses were wrapped in matting and buried in a sitting position, usually on high ground away from the village. The grave was covered with mounds of dirt.

People owned the right to perform dances and ceremonies. A society of single and elderly women effected shabby dress and tortured prisoners of war. There were various men's societies as well, generally revolving around military and religious themes. Pawnees played various games, including contests, dice (women) and shinny, and hoop-and-pole (men). Only a few old female doctors were allowed to smoke.

DWELLINGS By 1500, some Pawnees were living in permanent villages of between 5 and 15 earth lodges. The lodges were round, semiexcavated, and about 40–60 feet in diameter. They featured a pole framework interwoven with brush and grass, covered with a thick layer of soil and clay. Some had separate sleeping areas partitioned by mats or wickerwork. Such lodges were designed to last eight to ten years. Religious ceremonies accompanied lodge construction.

By the early nineteenth century, most Pawnees used temporary semicircular summer tents that differed from standard tipis. After driving small, arched poles into the ground along the circumference, people placed four larger posts vertically across the front. They also used standard skin tipis on buffalo hunting trips.

DIET Unlike their neighbors who lived at similar longitudes, Pawnee women grew corn, beans, pumpkins, and sunflowers in small gardens. There were generally two harvests, one in midsummer, of green corn (boiled or roasted, shelled, dried, and stored in bags), and the main one in late summer to early fall.

The people also hunted buffalo in early summer and in winter. They preferred two or three small drives to one massive slaughter. Meat was quickly butchered and dried. Those less able stayed at the villages to protect the crops. Before they acquired horses, Pawnee men stampeded buffalo over cliffs or into swamps.

There was also at least one antelope drive each year, during which the animals were surrounded and clubbed or lanced. The people depended about equally on corn and buffalo, although more on buffalo in the nineteenth century. Men also hunted antelope, elk, deer, and small game, including fowl and birds. Women gathered roots, berries, plums, grapes, chokecherries, and nuts.

KEY TECHNOLOGY Women wove twilled, plaited baskets and shallow gambling trays as well as mats used for floor coverings and bedding. People used both pottery and buffalo-hide containers. Babies were wrapped in fur or fleece and tied with buckskin lacing onto decorated flat wooden cradle boards. Garden tools included hoes from buffalo or elk shoulders, digging sticks, and antler rakes.

TRADE Pre–seventeenth century Skidis traded with the Omaha and other related Siouan tribes. In the early to mid–eighteenth century, they exchanged Apache slaves, buffalo robes, and animal pelts with the New Orleans French for French guns, tools, and other items. By later in the century they were trading guns for Comanche horses, which they traded in turn to the Omaha, Ponca, and other tribes.

NOTABLE ARTS Pawnee art included basketry and incised pottery. They occasionally smoked their fine tanned hides. Tipis, robes, and shields were painted with heraldic designs.

TRANSPORTATION Dogs pulled the travois until they were slowly replaced by horses during the seventeenth century.

DRESS Women made most clothing of antelope or elk rather than buffalo hide. Men wore breechclouts and moccasins, plus leggings and a robe in the cold or on special occasions. They also tied a scarflike turban around their heads and plucked their facial hair. Women wore moccasins, a skirt and cape, and leggings and a robe in winter. Both sexes painted their faces. Warriors stiffened a lock of hair with paint and fat, making it curve like a horn (a style known as a roach).

WAR AND WEAPONS Enemies included the Apache (mid–seventeenth to eighteenth century), Dakota, Cheyenne, Arapaho, and Kiowa. The Pawnee raided a huge area, more or less the entire Plains. Allies included the Comanche and, later, the United States. On the Plains, the Pawnee adhered to the system of war honors known as counting coup. Weapons included the bow and arrow, club, and buffalo-hide shield.

Contemporary Information

GOVERNMENT/RESERVATIONS The Pawnee tribe still owns several hundred acres of land in Pawnee and Payne Counties, Oklahoma. The present tribal government was established in 1934. The tribe is governed by two eight-member bodies, the Nasharo (chiefs) Council, chosen by band, and an elected Business Council.

ECONOMY An annual annuity (from the 1857 treaty) and funds obtained from mineral (oil and gas) leases and agriculture are disbursed on a per capita basis. The tribe also sponsors bingo games. There is chronic high unemployment around Pawnee.

LEGAL STATUS The Pawnee Indian Tribe is a federally recognized tribal entity.

DAILY LIFE Administrative offices, ceremonial roundhouse, recreation room, community building, and campground are located on the tribal land. The tribe administers various social programs with the help of federal grants. Traditional activities surviving at least in modified form include various dances (war, ghost, round) and the hand game. However, the Pawnee language is approaching the point where complete decline may be irreversible. Most people are Christians; some are also members of the Native American Church. The many social clubs sponsor various activities. There is a four-day Pawnee homecoming in July.

Peigan
See Blackfeet

Piegan
See Blackfeet

Ponca
Ponca (`Pon ku) is a word possibly meaning "sacred head." The Ponca are linguistic and cultural relatives of the Omaha.

LOCATION Poncas inhabited present-day northeast Nebraska in the late seventeenth century. Today, Northern Poncas live mostly in Nebraska, South Dakota, and Iowa, and most Southern Poncas live in north-central Oklahoma.

POPULATION The late-seventeenth-century Ponca population was about 800. In 1993 there were about 2,360 Southern Poncas and perhaps 900 Northern Poncas.

LANGUAGE Ponca, with Kaw, Omaha, Osage, and Quapaw, is part of the Dhegiha division of the Siouan language family.

Historical Information

HISTORY Dhegiha speakers probably originated in the southeast and entered the Plains from the Ohio Valley. After arriving at the Mississippi in the mid–sixteenth century, the Ponca traveled upriver with the Kaw, Omaha, and Osage. Continuing north with the Omaha into Iowa and Minnesota, the groups settled on the Big Sioux River near the pipestone quarries.

Pressure from the Dakota forced them to the Lake Andres area of South Dakota, where they separated from the Omaha in the early to mid–seventeenth century. From there they traveled west to the Black Hills and then east again, rejoining the Omaha and moving south along the Missouri River to Nebraska. They settled on the mouth of the Niobrara River around 1763. The Omaha left them soon after to settle on Bow Creek.

Epidemics had reduced the Ponca population by over 90 percent by the time they encountered the Lewis and Clark expedition in 1804. Poncas were generally friendly with Americans and eager to trade. Treaties with the United States, beginning in 1817, cost them over two million acres of land. In 1858, the people accepted a reservation of about 100,000 acres and promises of protection against Lakota tribes. However, ten years later the Lakota successfully claimed most of this land in the 1868 Fort Laramie Treaty. Lakota attacks were worse then ever, since they now controlled the disputed land by treaty.

In contravention of the treaties and in the face of active resistance of the chiefs, the United States forced the Poncas to remove to the Indian Territory (Oklahoma). There the Indians received a reservation of just over 100,000 acres near the Arkansas and Salt Fork Rivers. Within a year, about a quarter of the tribe died in those new lands from hunger and disease.

In 1877, Chief Standing Bear and others led their people on a 500-mile walk back to the Niobrara River to bury their dead. They were arrested and detained, but a precedent-setting trial established their rights both to legal standing and to their Nebraska land, to which they soon returned. Fearing for the very survival of the reservation system, however, not to mention the corrupt system of supplying reservation Indians with substandard food and materials, the United States refused permission for the rest of the Poncas to return to Nebraska. From then on, Poncas

living in Nebraska were known as Northern Ponca, and the Southern Ponca remained in Oklahoma.

The Oklahoma land was allotted 1908. Most people later sold their allotments or leased them to non-Indians. Among the Southern Ponca, strong antiallotment sentiment led to factionalism within the tribe. Two Poncas were among those who established the Native American Church in the 1910s; the church's first president was a Ponca.

The Northern Ponca were formally "terminated" in the 1950s. By the mid-1960s, over 400 Poncas had lost all of their remaining 834 acres of land. The Ponca Clyde Warrior and a Paiute, Mel Thom, formed the National Indian Youth Council, a group dedicated to advancing Indian rights, in 1961.

RELIGION Wakanda was the Great Spirit or universal creator. All things had supernatural power, which could be accessed through guardian spirits obtained in vision quests. The original tribal Sacred Pipe was carved of catlinite when the Ponca lived in Minnesota. It was used in the Pipe Dance and on other occasions, as were its later replacements. Other important events included the Medicine Lodge ceremony, Sun Dance, and War Dance. The Ponca Sun Dance included self-torture. Shinny, a ball game, also had religious import.

GOVERNMENT Hereditary chiefs governed the clans. On the Plains, buffalo police kept order during the hunt.

CUSTOMS Two divisions, Chighu and Wazhazha, were each subdivided into four patrilineal clans. The people wrapped corpses in buffalo robes with food and other articles and buried them in graves. The people adopted scaffold burial with other aspects of Plains life. The mourning period lasted up to a year. The Ponca envisioned two afterworlds, a happy one for the worthy dead and an unhappy one for unworthy spirits.

DWELLINGS The Ponca built permanent villages on bluffs over rivers and fortified them with log and earth stockades. They lived in east-facing earth or hide-covered lodges. There was also a ceremonial earth lodge. Skin tipis were used on buffalo hunts.

DIET Women grew corn, beans, squash, pumpkins, and tobacco in gardens located on river bottomlands. There were two annual communal buffalo hunts. Before the people acquired horses, buffalo were often stampeded over cliffs. Men also hunted other large and small game. The people ate fish as well as a variety of wild foods.

KEY TECHNOLOGY Material goods included pottery, mats, baskets woven from willow and bullrush stems, and trunks and boxes of cut, folded, and sewn rawhide.

TRADE Poncas were involved in the early-eighteenth-century slave trade, selling mainly Pawnees to the French, from whom they received guns, among other items.

NOTABLE ARTS Notable art items included carved wooden goods, blue clay pottery, woven mats and baskets, and work in quills and beads in floral and geometric designs.

TRANSPORTATION Around 1730 the people acquired horses, which then began pulling the travois. They used rawhide bull-boats for crossing rivers.

DRESS Women tanned the skins and made the clothing. They wore a one-piece dress and moccasins. Men wore leggings and breechclout as well as moccasins. Cold weather gear included shirts, mittens, robes, and caps. On the Plains men wore their hair long, a custom they probably adopted from the Dakota.

WAR AND WEAPONS Weapons included the bow and arrow, buffalo-hide shield, and wooden war club. The Omaha were alternately allies and enemies. The Dakota were generally enemies. On the Plains, the Ponca acquired the institution of rival military clubs, probably from the Tetons.

Contemporary Information

GOVERNMENT/RESERVATIONS Since 1990, the Northern Ponca tribe has reacquired 413 acres of its former reservation and is continuing to add to its land base. The people are also involved in reestablishing a tribal government and constitution.

The Southern Ponca are located in north-central Oklahoma. They adopted a constitution and by-laws in 1950. The tribe is governed by a seven-member Tribal Business Committee.

ECONOMY High unemployment is endemic among the Northern Ponca. An economic development plan remained to be implemented in the late 1990s. The Southern Ponca run a bingo facility and a smoke shop.

LEGAL STATUS The Ponca Tribe of Nebraska (Northern Ponca) was federally rerecognized in 1990. The Ponca Tribe of Oklahoma (Southern Ponca) is a federally recognized tribal entity.

DAILY LIFE Termination cost the Northern Ponca a great deal in the way of cultural survival. Among these people, the War Dance Society survives. Annual powwows feature traditional singing and dancing. Members participate in Sun Dances held by other tribes. Few speak the native language, but it is closely related to Omaha, which is more widely spoken. The people, who suffer especially from diabetes and hypertension, are generally less healthy than are those of the nearby non-Indian community. The Northern Ponca would like formally to reestablish their reservation.

The Southern Ponca built many facilities in the 1970s, including a clinic, headquarters, cultural center, and gymnasium. The factionalism that beset these people in the 1970s and 1980s eased in the 1990s. The annual Southern Ponca powwow is intertribal in nature. The Ponca Indian War Dance Society, formed in the 1950s from old traditions, sponsors semiannual dances. The people also perform a scalp dance and various other dances. There are regular games of shinny, especially in the spring. A regional tribal center and museum are planned. Many Poncas are Christians and/or members of the Native American Church.

Quapaw

Quapaw (Kwu ˋpä) comes from *Ugakhpa,* "Downstream People," referring to their migration south along the Mississippi. The Quapaw were also known as Arkansas Indians.

LOCATION These people lived along the Ohio River, near the mouth of the Wabash, in the sixteenth century. By the late seventeenth century they had migrated to near the mouth of the Arkansas River. Today, most Quapaws live in northeast Oklahoma.

POPULATION The late-seventeenth-century population was about 15,000. In the mid-1980s, approximately 3,000 Indians called themselves Quapaws.

LANGUAGE Quapaw is a member of the Dhegiha division of the Siouan language family.

Historical Information

HISTORY Quapaw ancestors may have been the Indian Knoll people of Kentucky and vicinity, of about 500 C.E., who lived along rivers and ate mainly shellfish. In the sixteenth century, with the Omaha and other Siouan groups, the Quapaw migrated through the Ohio Valley to the Mississippi River. When the others continued north along the Mississippi, the Quapaw struck out toward the south.

Shortly after the people met Jacques Marquette and Louis Joliet in 1673, they were decimated by smallpox and ongoing warfare. They acquired horses in the early eighteenth century and adopted much of Plains buffalo culture. Although in general the Quapaw avoided taking sides in the regional European colonial struggles, they fought the Chickasaw in the eighteenth century as French allies as well as to avenge raids made against them.

In 1818 the Quapaw ceded their claims to southern Arkansas, southern Oklahoma, and northern Louisiana. They did reserve about one million acres of land in Arkansas but were forced to give that up by 1824. Landless now, they went to live with the Caddo south of the Red River, but following several crop failures as a result of floods they drifted back to Arkansas.

The Quapaw were forced to relocate to a reservation in the Indian Territory (Oklahoma and Kansas) in 1833. In 1867 they lost their Kansas lands when that territory became a state. The tribe voted in 1893 to liquidate the reservation by allotting 240 acres each to 230 tribal members. About this time, a variant of the Peyote religion was introduced to the people.

Rich mineral deposits (zinc and lead) were found on Quapaw land in 1905. For a few years non-Indians defrauded the Quapaw out of land and money. After the government finally stepped in and exercised its trust responsibility, considerable monetary benefits began to accrue, despite the fact that royalties were paid to the federal government and not to the tribe. Many individuals who managed to share in the wealth spent most or all of their money in the 1920s. The tribe received a land claims payment in the early 1960s of roughly $1 million.

RELIGION Wakonda was the great universal spirit who encompassed any number of other spirits or deities. Pipes featured prominently in their ceremonies, and the Green Corn Dance celebrated the beginning of the harvest. There were also numerous other agriculture-related ceremonies.

GOVERNMENT A hereditary chief and a council of elders governed each village. Beginning in the eighteenth century, the people created an overall tribal chief.

CUSTOMS Two divisions were subdivided into 22 patriarchal clans. People were buried with tools, weapons, and other items, both in and above the ground. If above, the graves were covered with rocks and dirt.

DWELLINGS Some villages were protected with palisades. Women built rectangular houses with domed roofs covered with cypress bark, grass, woven mats, and hides. Several families lived in each house.

DIET Women grew three crops of corn a year, plus beans, squash, and tobacco. They also gathered foods, including persimmons, walnuts, berries, and plums. Men hunted buffalo, fowl, and other large and small game. The people also ate fish.

KEY TECHNOLOGY Fish were captured in weirs. The people carved stone pipes, made pottery, wove mats, and stored corn in gourds or cane baskets.

TRADE Quapaws traded pottery and other items primarily to the Chickasaw, the Tunica, and, later, the French.

NOTABLE ARTS Painted and incised pottery was a Quapaw specialty.

TRANSPORTATION Before the onset of Plains culture, Quapaws made walnut and cypress dugout canoes. They acquired horses in the early eighteenth century.

DRESS Prior to the eighteenth century, men generally went naked, pierced their nose and ears, and wore their hair short. On the Plains, men and women adopted the typical dress, including breechclouts, leggings, shirts, dresses, and robes.

WAR AND WEAPONS Quapaws fought the Chickasaw in the eighteenth century. Their best bows were made of Osage orange wood.

Contemporary Information

GOVERNMENT/RESERVATIONS The new tribal headquarters is located near Quapaw, Oklahoma. The people elect a business committee. There were about 1,500 local Indian residents in the early 1990s.

ECONOMY Many Quapaws farm or work in local businesses. There are also a tribal bingo parlor and a gas station.

LEGAL STATUS The Quapaw Tribe is a federally recognized tribal entity.

DAILY LIFE Little traditional culture survives. A few people speak the native language. Most Quapaws are Christians. The Native American Church is a minor presence among the people. Their annual powwow, at which the people perform tribal dances, is nationally noted.

Santee
See Dakota

Saulteaux
See Ojibwa, Plains

Sicangu (Brulé)
See Lakota

Sihasapa (Blackfeet Teton)
See Lakota

Sioux
See Dakota; Lakota; Nakota

Sisseton
See Dakota

Stoney
See Assiniboine

Teton
See Lakota

Tonkawa
Tonkawa (`Ton k ǝ wä) is a Waco word possibly meaning "they all stay together." Their self-designa-

tion was *Titska Watitch,* possibly meaning "Most Human People."

LOCATION Tonkawas traditionally lived in east-central Texas. In the late twentieth century, most lived in and around Kay County, Oklahoma.

POPULATION From a fifteenth-century population of perhaps 5,000 people, their numbers declined to about 1,600 people in the late seventeenth century and 34 people in 1921. The 1993 Tonkawa population was 186 people.

LANGUAGE Tonkawan is considered a language isolate but may relate to the Hokan-Coahuiltecan group of languages.

Historical Information

HISTORY The Tonkawa may be descended from Indians who lived in southern Texas and northern Mexico. They had contact with the Spanish in the 1530s. Beginning in the late seventeenth century, the people were caught up in the colonial struggle between Spain and France for control of Texas. The Tonkawa lived around Mission San Gabriel in east Texas for a time before it was abandoned in 1758. They acquired horses in the late seventeenth or early eighteenth century.

El Mocho was a captured Apache who became a Tonkawa chief in the late eighteenth century. His dream was to unite the Apaches and the Tonkawas against the Spanish. At a council attended by over 4,000 Indians, the two peoples failed to resolve their differences. El Mocho was captured and killed by the Spanish.

After Mexican independence in 1821, the Tonkawa became allied with Anglo-Texans against the Comanche and Waco Indians. Along with other Texas tribes, the Tonkawa were assigned two small reservations on the Brazos River in 1855. Despite their past alliance with non-native Texans, in 1859 the Tonkawa were deported from Texas and relocated to Fort Cobb on the Washita River, Indian Territory (Oklahoma). From there some fought for the Confederacy during the Civil War, and in 1862 more than half of the tribe were killed in a raid by Unionist Caddo, Shawnee, and Delaware people.

Survivors returned to Texas, where they remained until 1884, when they were assigned to the former Nez Percé Reservation in the Indian Territory. This reservation was allotted in 1896. Some Tonkawas participated in the Pawnee Ghost Dance in the early twentieth century.

RELIGION The people recognized numerous deities. They may have engaged in cannibalism, possibly for religious reasons. Psychotropic plants also played a part in their religious practice.

GOVERNMENT There were at least 20 autonomous bands with loose, decentralized governing structures.

CUSTOMS The Tonkawa were excellent runners. For most of their existence they were nomadic hunters. Infants were tied in cradle boards, resulting in some possibly inadvertent head flattening.

DWELLINGS On the Plains, the people lived in skin tipis.

DIET Men hunted large and small game, especially buffalo and deer. Women gathered roots, seeds, nuts, prickly pear, and other wild foods. The people also ate fish, shellfish, and rattlesnake meat but neither wolf nor coyote.

KEY TECHNOLOGY Like all Plains tribes, most of their material goods came from the buffalo and other animals.

TRADE Tonkawas traded buffalo-derived materials for feathers and other items. They were also well-known horse traders. Pueblo groups were among their trade partners. They imported copper from the north.

NOTABLE ARTS Painting—of shields, tipis, and their own bodies—was a major part of Tonkawa art.

TRANSPORTATION The people acquired horses in the late seventeenth or early eighteenth century and soon became expert riders.

DRESS Women made all clothing from animal skins. They wore short wraparound skirts and either let their hair hang long or made one braid. Men wore long breechclouts and long, braided hair. Men also plucked their beards and eyebrows. Moccasins or fiber sandals were rarely worn. Both sexes wore buffalo robes, and both tattooed and painted their bodies and wore many personal ornaments.

WAR AND WEAPONS Tonkawa men had a reputation as fierce raiders, with many enemies, especially the Apache and Comanche. Their weapons included the bow and arrow, hide vests, feathered helmets, and hide shields. They were considered excellent shots. They painted for war in red, yellow, green, and black. Warriors may have cut their hair on the left side, leaving the long hair on the right to be tied with a thong.

Contemporary Information

GOVERNMENT/RESERVATIONS In the mid-1990s, the Tonkawa owned 398.74 acres, most of which were allotted, in Kay County, Oklahoma. They were governed by a 1938 constitution calling for elected officers. The tribal council meets monthly.

ECONOMY All jobs are provided by local small businesses.

LEGAL STATUS The Tonkawa Tribe, a federally recognized tribal entity, includes some members of a former Texas coast tribe known as Karankawas.

DAILY LIFE The native language is extinct, and

most traditional culture has been lost. Some people are members of the Native American Church. The people hold an annual powwow.

Wahpekute
See Dakota

Wahpeton
See Dakota

Wichita
Wichita (`Wi chi tä) is the name of one band of a loose confederacy of several tribes living in separate villages. The Spanish called them *Jumanos*. They have also been called Black Pawnee as well as by the names of related tribes such as Waco, Tawakoni, Tawehash, and Akwits. Their self-designation was *Kitikiti'sh*, meaning "Men."

LOCATION Wichitas lived in central and southeast Kansas, along the Great Bend of the Arkansas River, in the mid–sixteenth century. They migrated to the Kansas-Oklahoma border area in the early eighteenth century and to the Red River region of southeastern Oklahoma in the late eighteenth century. By the mid–nineteenth century they had moved to southwestern Oklahoma. Today, most live in Caddo County, Oklahoma.

POPULATION The Wichita population (including associated tribes) was at least 15,000 in the mid–sixteenth century. That number had dwindled to about 3,200 in the late eighteenth century. In the 1890s there were 153 Wichitas. There were 1,764 enrolled tribal members in 1993.

LANGUAGE Wichita is a Caddoan language.

Historical Information
HISTORY The people who were to become the historic Wichita split apart from the proto-Pawnee about 1,500 years ago. These people may have lived near the Washita River of western Oklahoma about 1,000 years ago. They probably moved north from eastern Texas in the fourteenth century to the Great Bend of the Arkansas River. There they were visited by Francisco Vasquez de Coronado in 1541, when he referred to their villages as Quivira. The people acquired horses by 1700.

During the eighteenth century, under pressure from the well-armed Osage, the Wichita began moving south toward Oklahoma and Texas. Trade with the French began after 1720; with the southern Pawnee, the Wichita dominated the gun trade out of New Orleans. However, in the mid– to late eighteenth century the French trade was suspended while the Wichita were engaged in periodic wars with the Spanish.

A severe smallpox epidemic crippled the people in 1801. Osage and non-Indian raids depleted their population even further in subsequent years. An 1835 treaty between the United States and the Wichita, Comanche, and several eastern tribes marked the first time that the Wichita were officially referred to by that name.

In 1854, several Wichita bands settled with the Shawnees and Delawares on a reservation on the Brazos River, although the non-native Texans soon forced them out. The United States established a Wichita reservation in Indian Territory (Oklahoma), south of the Canadian River, in 1859. Wichitas left the Indian Territory for Kansas (near present-day Wichita) during the Civil War but returned in 1867. They formally ceded all their nonreservation land in 1872 in exchange for a 743,000-acre reservation along the Washita River. However, the agreement was never ratified by Congress. Tribal lands were allotted in 1901. The government paid them $1.25 an acre for the "excess" and then opened that land to non-Indian settlement.

RELIGION Kinnikasus was the great creator. Other deities were recognized, too, particularly those related to the celestial bodies. The people held a deer dance three times a year. They also performed a calumet (pipe) ceremony. There were many secret societies, for both men and women, each with its own ceremonies and dances.

GOVERNMENT The Wichita were traditionally a loose confederation of several bands or tribes occupying independent villages. A chief and a subchief, chosen by a council of warriors, presided over each village.

CUSTOMS The smallest economic unit was the family. Descent was matriarchal. Corpses were buried in a nearby hill with various goods associated with their earthly activities. Mourners cut their hair and gave away some of their possessions.

DWELLINGS The various Wichita bands lived in separate villages near rivers. In the sixteenth century, settlements consisted of up to 1,000 round houses, each 15–30 feet in diameter and built of a pole framework tied with branches or reeds and thatched with grass. The houses had two doors, a smoke hole in the center, and sleeping platforms along the walls. The people also used ramadas in summer and for some occasions as well as skin tipis during the fall buffalo hunts.

DIET Women grew corn, beans, squash, and tobacco. Crops were stored in underground caches. Pumpkins were cut, dried, and woven into mats for storage. Women also gathered foods such as plums, grapes, and nuts. Men hunted buffalo, usually twice a year—in June and following the harvest—after they obtained horses. They also hunted deer, elk, rabbit, antelope, and bear.

KEY TECHNOLOGY Wichitas made items typical of agricultural societies, such as pottery, manos, and metates.

TRADE They traded agricultural goods to nomadic tribes in exchange for animal goods. Although the two societies did communicate, there was little trade with the New Mexico pueblos. After 1720, the Wichita acted as intermediaries between the French (tools, guns) and the western nomadic tribes (hides, furs). Following a 1746 friendship treaty, they traded guns to the Comanche for horses, which went eventually to the plantations on the lower Mississippi or southeastern states.

NOTABLE ARTS Native artists focused on making pottery and clothing as well as some items of personal ornamentation.

TRANSPORTATION The people acquired horses by 1700.

DRESS Women made all clothing of animal skins. Both sexes practiced extensive body and facial tattooing.

WAR AND WEAPONS War horses wore leather armor. Although the Wichita were generally a peaceful people, they did fight the Osage and the Apache. After 1746 they were allied with the Comanche.

Contemporary Information

GOVERNMENT/RESERVATIONS The Wichita tribe owns 10 acres of land and holds another 2,400 acres in joint trust with Caddos and Delawares in Caddo, Canadian, and Gray Counties, Oklahoma. They elect seven tribal officers. Tribal headquarters is located near Anadarko, Oklahoma.

ECONOMY The tribal government and the local clinic are major employers. The tribe also collects license and vendor fees.

LEGAL STATUS The Wichita Tribe is a federally recognized tribal entity.

DAILY LIFE The native language is almost extinct, although there are programs designed to save it. Most Wichitas are Baptists; some are members of the Native American Church. The Caddo-speaking tribes of Texas have a long history of ritual peyote use. There is an annual dance in August and an annual large-scale visit with the Pawnee, each tribe taking turns hosting the event.

Yankton

See Nakota

Yanktonai

See Nakota

CHAPTER SEVEN

The Southeast

Southeast

The Southeast cultural area may be thought of as comprising several distinct environmental zones. The Appalachian Mountains run northeast to southwest; their highest point is a 6,684-foot peak in North Carolina. Here such southern hardwoods as chestnut and hickory meet more northerly species, such as birch, sugar maple, and hemlock. The mountain region includes numerous well-watered plateaus and valleys, such as the Cumberland Plateau, the Appalachian Plateau, and, to the west, the Great Valley. Well west of the mountains is the great Mississippi River. Preeminent southeastern rivers include the Shenandoah, the James, the Savannah, the Roanoke, the Coosa, and the Tennessee.

East of the mountains, the Piedmont Plateau is located between the mountains and the coastal plain. Its heavy forests, mainly of oak, pine, sassafras, sycamore, and gum, contained a great quantity and diversity of animal life. Descending still lower, below the fall line, the mild, wet coastal plain itself extends inland for between 100 and 300 miles. Salt marsh, lagoons, and swamps characterize the coastal regions from the Atlantic to the Gulf of Mexico. Cypress, cane, and palmetto grow in the southern part of the plain, and cypress and red gum in the river valleys; conifers and scrub oak dominate the somewhat higher interior.

At least in the early historic period, the four major languages of southeastern Indians were Muskogean, spoken by, among others, Chickasaws, Choctaws, and Creeks; Algonquian, spoken mainly by coastal Indians of Virginia and North Carolina as well as the interior Shawnee; Iroquoian, spoken by the Cherokee and other tribes in the north and northeast of the region; and Siouan, spoken by people living in South Carolina and on the Louisiana and Mississippi coasts. There were several linguistic isolates as well.

At least 150,000 people, and perhaps ten times that number, probably lived in this region of over 400,000 square miles in the fifteenth century. In general, the area was hospitable to humans, providing a variety of large and small animals, fish, marine life, wild fruits, vegetables, and nuts. Most southeastern Indian tribes adopted large-scale agriculture after about 900, and some also developed large towns and highly centralized social and political structures.

Contact with non-natives began in the early sixteenth century. By the eighteenth century, extensive involvement with non-native traders, combined with population loss from disease and slave raiding, had fundamentally altered Native American societies. Radical dispossession occurred in the 1830s, after which most southeastern Indians rebuilt their lives in Indian Territory (Oklahoma). A relative few remained in the southeast, to continue living as Indians as best they could, but many of the old tribes simply disappeared.

The first people appeared in the southeast at least 11,000 years ago, perhaps from the north but more likely from the west. Early people hunted and then fished for and gathered their food. Initial game included species that have since become extinct. People constructed material items from stone, bone, and wood. Pottery appeared well into the onset of this period, around 2000 B.C.E.

The two definitive technological innovations of the period were the spear thrower, or atlatl, and the grinding stone. The former consisted of a wooden shaft used to provide extra force and range for a wooden spear tipped with a stone point. Armed with this implement, early hunters had little trouble bringing down white-tailed deer and other game. Grinding stones, made of stone or wood, along with stone pestles, were used to pulverize seeds and nuts prior to processing and cooking.

Depending on location and time of year, bands lived either in their constituent nuclear families or occasionally, after about 6000 B.C.E., together as a group. Tribal organization was unknown until the natural abundance of certain places was great enough to produce early civilizations such as Adena (circa 800 B.C.E. to 200 C.E.) and Hopewell (circa 300 B.C.E. to 700 C.E.). Both cultures peaked around the beginning of the present era. Although centered in the Ohio Valley (Adena) and Mississippi-Ohio Valleys (Hopewell), their influences were felt strongly in much of the southeast.

Adena and Hopewell people tended to live in permanent villages. Adena people built earthworks and burial mounds, some up to a quarter of a mile long and shaped like animals, over their dead, to whom much ritual attention was paid. These people enlisted the assistance of shamans to mediate between the human and nonhuman worlds. Copper ornaments and "stamped," or imprinted, pottery were produced. Society may have been hierarchically ordered. Hopewell was also characterized by mound building, advanced art, and, later, by extensive agriculture.

As early as 2500 B.C.E., but especially during the Adena and Hopewell periods, southeastern Indians participated in a number of interregional trade networks. Items such as Gulf Coast conch and other shells, mica and other stone, and clay items moved north into the Midwest, Northeast, and even the Far West. In exchange, obsidian, copper, iron, quartz crystals, and other goods moved back into the south. Most exchange took place between groups of related families rather than among professional, long-distance traders.

Corn was introduced into the southeast from the Midwest in the early part of the first millennium, although large-scale agriculture and its often-related societal centralization did not truly begin until about 900. The bow and arrow was also introduced into the region, probably from the eastern woodlands, around this time. By about 1200 many people were growing the famous triad of corn, beans, and squash.

Concurrent with the rise of large-scale agriculture, most southeast tribes had developed matrilineal clans, which were often grouped into two opposing divisions—red and white—to counter the tendency to overcentralize power. The tribes themselves, in fact, were loose aggregations of clans. Descent was reckoned through the mother's line, and her brothers were often more important to a child than was his or her biological father. Clan membership generally established one's role or position in rituals and in society in general.

Late in the first millennium, some tribes had built on technological advances such as the bow and arrow, flint hoes, and a hardier type of corn to construct highly centralized, hierarchically ranked societies (chiefdoms) led by powerful, even absolute, chiefs. Members of the elite classes received tribute in the form of goods and services from the common people. Palisaded urban centers of up to tens of thousands of people contained a ceremonial plaza with mounds on which the temple and chief's and priests' houses stood. The people built temples on mounds of up to 300 acres in size, grew fields of crops up to several square miles in area, and had a rich artistic and ceremonial life. These "Mississippian" cultures, which peaked between the eleventh and thirteenth centuries, were likely influenced by people from Mesoamerica.

Among the chiefdoms, religion was characterized by the existence of three cults, or modes of religious expression. One featured large, flat-topped temple mounds located in the ceremonial grounds. The Mound Builders expressed their core idea—the primacy of purity over pollution—by placing layers of white (purity) sand over red (disorder) clay. A second cult revolved around warfare and the glorification of the warrior; a third featured stone, wood, and clay figurines used to represent ancestral spirits.

By the dawn of the historical period, Mississippian culture was in general decline, although burial customs were still often elaborate. Most religious activity in the region was centered around the idea of the sun as life-giver and chief deity. A priesthood conducted rituals in which the sacred fire, as a representative of the sun, figured prominently, as did corn. Shamans, or conjurers, interceded with the spirit world to cure disease, divine the future, and control the weather. The ceremonial round began generally in the spring and culminated with the Green Corn Ceremony (described under the discussion of the nineteenth century), although various other dances might continue into the fall. Leaders conducted business and rituals in the ceremonial plaza, or Square Ground.

Most late prehistoric southeastern Indians lived in permanent villages, built in river valleys wherever possible. Towns, consisting of houses or groups of houses, with a social and ceremonial center, were often strung out for miles. The classic dwelling was made of pole frames covered with branches and vines and then a layer of mud or clay. Summer houses were generally rectangular, with gabled, thatched roofs. Circular winter "town" houses were plastered inside and out. Materials such as animal hides, grasses, bamboo, bark, woven mats, and palm leaves might also be used in their outer construction. Many people also built houselike storage structures in addition to the dwelling unit. Large towns contained huge town houses, with up to several hundred seats, for conducting business and rituals. Sweat houses were also common.

Most southeastern Indians were farmers of corn,

beans, squash, and sometimes sunflowers. Surplus grain was often stored in special granaries. Men hunted large (deer, bear, buffalo) and small (beaver, otter, squirrel) game. As in most native cultures, animal products such as sinew, oil, and horn were used extensively for various purposes in addition to food and clothing. Hunting took place between planting and harvest and especially in winter, when the people often left the villages in small hunting parties.

Important wild plant foods included hickory and other nuts, acorns, persimmons and other fruits, berries, wild rice, and mushrooms. Shellfish was an important staple in certain areas. Birds, especially the turkey, played an important role in diet as well as decoration. Depending on location, southeastern Indians used different techniques for capturing fish, including weirs, spears, and poison. Most cultures utilized tobacco.

Stone and bone remained important raw materials into the historical period; they were used to make mortars, clubs, scrapers, adzes, axes, and various other tools as well as arrowheads. People made wooden stools with legs. Cane was a widely employed raw material, used in making baskets and mats, houses, arrows and darts, containers, musical instruments, and many other items. Men and boys used blowguns and darts to bring down birds or small animals, and women manufactured pottery, twilled baskets, and wove mats. Cypress was the favored wood for canoe manufacture, although pine, poplar, and other woods were also suitable, and bark canoes were also used in the interior.

Although most clothing was made from skins, mainly deer, women also used the inner bark of the mulberry tree to make items such as hair nets and some textiles. Bear or buffalo robes were important winter garments. Some people also made ornate feather mantles or cloaks from turkeys and other birds. Men generally wore breechclouts and perhaps shirts, shawls, or cloaks. Leggings were more common around the Gulf region. Women generally wore a short skirt as well as a mantle or tunic, although there were considerable regional variations. Moccasins were used mainly for travel. Personal ornamentation, especially in the form of shell beads, pearls, and copper, was common. Body paint was generally reserved for special occasions, although elaborate tattooing was widespread.

Intercourse between the tribes included regular trade fairs. Items of the hunt—primarily hides, meat, and animal products—were exchanged for manufactured items such as pipes, bowls, dishes, and spoons. Also, coastal tribes offered shells, fish products, and "black drink" leaves to peoples of the interior, who provided red pigment, pottery, and feather cloaks.

Salt, copper, wood, and mica were other important items of exchange. Even catlinite pipes from Minnesota were seen at some trade fairs, which were also occasions to feast and visit. The Choctaws created a language that was used as a lingua franca in regional intertribal trade.

Clan vengeance was a primary motivation for war. Weapons included the bow and arrow and assorted clubs, spears, knives, and hatchets. Hide shields were also used. The practice of warfare varied from place to place, but there was often a great deal of ritual preparation, and warriors often left distinguishing signs to show who had committed the violent deeds. Some carried along a sacred war ark filled with various medicines. Prisoners, if there were any, were often taken home and tortured or sold into slavery. Scalping was common, at least in the early historic period; it constituted, along with other practices, war honors. War parties were often led by war chiefs.

A form of modern-day lacrosse was the most common game played by southeastern Indians. Indeed, more than a game, it had considerable significance in the realms of social custom and ceremony. Two sticks were generally used, as was a deer-hide ball. The sides consisted of different divisions or towns. Among some tribes, a great deal of ceremonial preparation took place for up to a week or more before a game, and medicine men played an important role before and during play. Gambling was extensive. Play was very rough, and severe injuries, sometimes leading to death, were not unusual. Most, although not all, such games were all male. There were separate games for women, and people of both sexes played many games besides stickball. In particular, chunkey, a variety of the hoop-and-pole game, was widely played.

By around 1600, the power of the chiefs, still mainly band leaders, ranged from advisory—with power, such as it was, being held mainly by a representative council—to absolute. Some tribes associated in confederacies, such as the Powhatan, Natchez, Calusa, Cofitachiqui, and Creek. Among the Creek, up to 50 or more towns spoke different Muskogean and even non-Muskogean languages. Professional interpreters were employed to maintain effective communication between the constituent elements. Towns assumed an identity characterized by war (red) or peace (white).

The arrival of Columbus in 1492 inaugurated the contact period in southeastern history. News of the effects of this event on the offshore native people—massive death, mistreatment, and enslavement—may have reached Florida well before the actual arrival of Europeans. By the time of the 1519 Juan Ponce de León expedition and other Spanish explorations well into the interior soon after, many Indians knew enough to fear the intruders. Despite efforts to protect themselves, many Indians suffered violence and death from non-native depredations and disease.

As contact between Indians and Europeans became more regular after the mid– to late sixteenth century, Indian culture itself began to change. Indian societies were drawn into increased trade with French and British adventurers, who arrived in the seventeenth century to join Spanish traders, missionaries, and colonists. At the same time, the Indians continued to die in large numbers from disease and were increasingly forced to deal with other problems, such as factionalism, fraud, land grabbing, and the introduction of alcohol. Several aspects of traditional culture, such as clan and political structure, began to break down, and overall conflict increased.

By the mid–eighteenth century there was a thriving regional trade in deerskin and other products. Hundreds of thousands of pounds of skins went to Europe every year. The effects of this trade completed an essential transformation in southeast native life. Native manufacture of certain items ceased, since they were more readily obtained through trade. As the deer disappeared, many Indians began to raise cattle for meat and skins. Also part of regional trade was the traffic in slaves, in which Indians participated as buyers and sellers as well as victims. Some southeastern tribes, but especially the Seminole, welcomed African Americans into the ranks of tribal membership. Populations moved or were moved to suit trade and political exigencies.

In some respects, however, native culture remained solidly rooted in its traditions. The classic Green Corn ceremony (or Busk), for example, which flourished in the nineteenth century, had its origins deep in Mound Builder culture. Held when the new late corn crop ripened, the four-day ceremony was a thanksgiving for the crop, a time for purifying or renewal, and a new year's festival. There were many variations on the ceremony, but, in general, the precise starting day was ascertained first of all. Housing was found or made for all visitors, followed by a great feast.

Men then repaired and cleaned the public places and women the homes. Men separated from women and children and began a fast while religious leaders prepared an emetic, high-caffeine black drink. All fires were extinguished. Then the priest and his assistants, dressed in special clothing, kindled a new sacred fire, from which all home fires were lit. The ceremony concluded with a sermon by the chief, the green corn dance itself, a ritual immersion in water, and a feast that included the new corn. Most past wrongs were forgiven, and most exiles could return.

Meanwhile, loss of native land accelerated, especially after the Indian defeat in the pivotal Battle of Horseshoe Creek in 1814. Despite the fact that at least the larger, so-called civilized tribes had adopted a lifestyle very similar to that of their non-native neighbors—including slave-based agriculture, literacy, Anglo-style government and laws, and, to some extent, Christianity—they were almost completely dispossessed in the 1830s. The Trail of Tears, a term originally depicting the removal of the Cherokee to Indian Territory (Oklahoma), is now applied to the removal of the Creek, Chickasaw, Choctaw, and Seminole as well (from their hideouts in Florida's Everglades, some Seminoles were able to resist removal). Tens of thousands of Indians were forcibly uprooted, and significant numbers of them died in transit or shortly after their arrival.

Indians rebuilt their lives out west, reestablishing their villages, towns, fields, and institutions. They fared poorly during and following the Civil War, in which many supported the Confederacy. Indian casualties were relatively high, and further dispossession and forcible removal followed the fighting. Missionaries redoubled their efforts. Toward the end of the century, the government decided to break up the reservations and terminate tribal governments. Oklahoma became a state in 1907. By the 1950s, much of the Indian-held land had been lost to non-natives, mostly through fraud and tax default. Oklahoma Indians became increasingly polarized. Wealthier people gravitated toward Anglo society, whereas poorer Indians continued to resist allotment and hold tenaciously to a more traditional Indian identity.

Today, most "southeast" Indians live in Oklahoma. Traditional culture is preserved in varying ways and to different degrees. Although most Indians are Christians, many tribes celebrate traditional rituals, such as the Green Corn ceremony, as well as pan-Indian ones. There are also tens of thousands of Indians in most southern states, notably Florida, North Carolina, and Mississippi. Even many contemporary southeastern tribes that are not federally recognized retain their Indian identities to varying degrees.

Alabama

Alabama (A li `ba mu) or Alibamu, "plant" or "medicine gatherers" or "thicket clearers." Alabamas were culturally related to the neighboring Creeks and Choctaws.

LOCATION Most fifteenth-century Alabamas lived along the upper Alabama River. By the seventeenth century they had moved to the lower course of that river. Today, most Alabamas live in Polk County, Texas; Allen Parish, Louisiana; and eastern Oklahoma.

POPULATION Alabamas numbered between 700 and 1,000 in the eighteenth century. In the 1990s there were about 400 living in Louisiana, about 800 enrolled in Texas, and 900 enrolled as part of the Creek Nation.

LANGUAGE Alabamas spoke a Muskogean language.

Historical Information

HISTORY Alabamas probably descended from Mound Builder cultures and may have originated north and west of the Mississippi. They encountered a hostile Spanish party under Hernando de Soto in 1540. By the early eighteenth century they had become allies of the French, who built Fort Toulouse in Alabama country in 1713.

Many Alabamas left their homeland following the French defeat in 1763. Some joined the Seminoles in Florida. Some resettled north of New Orleans, and later some of that group moved on to western Louisiana and Texas. Land given them in recognition of their contribution in the 1836 fight against Mexico was promptly stolen by non-natives. In 1842, the Alabamas and the Coushatta Indians were given a 1,280-acre reservation along the Trinity River. The United States added 3,081 acres to that reservation in 1928. In 1954 the tribe voluntarily terminated its relationship with the federal government, at which time the state took over control of the reservation. The tribe reverted to federal status in 1986.

Those who remained in Alabama fought unsuccessfully with the Creeks against non-natives in the 1813–1814 Creek war. Survivors of that conflict settled in the Alabama town of Tawasa. Most were resettled in Indian Territory (Oklahoma) with the Creeks in the 1830s. Part of the Creek Nation until 1938, the Alabama-Quassartes at that time received a federal charter, several hundred acres of land, and political, but not administrative, independence.

Louisiana Alabamas maintained a subsistence economy during the early twentieth century, gradually entering the labor market. Tourism and tourist-related sales of cane baskets and wood crafts began to grow in midcentury.

RELIGION The sun (fire) was worshiped, as were a host of lesser deities and beings. Alabamas celebrated the Green Corn ceremony as well as other ceremonies throughout the spring, summer, and fall. Dances might be social or ceremonial in nature. Most councils and ceremonies began with an emetic tea (black drink). Priests, doctors, and conjurers underwent a rigorous training period that included healing techniques, songs, and formulas.

GOVERNMENT Alabamas were part of the Creek Confederacy, although each village was politically sovereign. In most towns of the confederacy, a chief (miko), usually from a white clan, was chosen largely by merit. He was head of a democratic council that had ceremonial and diplomatic responsibilities. The nature of his power was to influence and to carry out certain duties, not to command. Decisions were taken by consensus. There were also a subchief and a war chief. A town crier announced the governmental decisions to the people.

CUSTOMS Chunkey was a popular game. One threw a pole after a rolling stone disc, scoring points by hitting the disc and coming closest to where it finally fell. There were also many other games, most of which involved gambling. The dead were buried with their heads to the east and sometimes a knife in the hand for fighting eagles on the way to the afterworld. Alabamas had over 50 clans in the eighteenth century, although probably fewer before contact. Infidelity in marriage was an offense punishable by public whipping and exile.

DWELLINGS Towns were laid out in a square and enclosed by walls up to several hundred feet long. By design, entrance and egress were difficult: On one side the gate was too low for a horse to enter, and another side might open onto a steep embankment. Many towns were surrounded by mud-covered wooden stockades. Their ceremonial centers included bark-covered, circular structures, a plaza, and a game field.

Dwellings were pole-frame structures with plastered walls and bark-covered or shingled, gabled roofs. The outer covering was of mud and grass or mats. Many families had a winter house and a summer house. They also had a two-story granary, one end of which was used for storing grain and roots (lower) and for meetings (upper). The other end, with open sides, was a general storage area (lower) and a reception area (upper). A fourth building, if one could afford it, was a storehouse for skins. The four buildings were placed to form a square, in the manner of the ceremonial Square Ground. Fires stood on the bare floor or on a stone hearth; there was usually a smoke hole in the roof.

DIET Alabamas ate fish, squirrels and other small game, deer and other large game, and their crops. The winter hunt, during which men traveled up to 250 miles or more, lasted from after the harvest until the spring planting. The less able remained behind in the villages.

KEY TECHNOLOGY Fish were taken with spears, bows and arrows, and poison. Women wove cane or palmetto baskets. Many points and knives were made of flint, although mortars and pestles were generally wooden. Bows were also made of wood (cedar was considered the best), with hide (perhaps bark in earlier times) strings. Men also hunted with blowguns and possibly spears. Other notable items included hide wrist guards, drums, and pottery.

TRADE Alabamas exported flint and animal products and imported pipes and shells. They participated in the general interior-coastal trade.

NOTABLE ARTS Women made pottery and wove geometric designs into their baskets. Artisans worked silver ornaments from the sixteenth century on.

TRANSPORTATION Most precontact transportation was via dugout pirogues.

DRESS Personal adornment included ornaments in pierced ears and noses, body paint, and various armbands, bracelets, and necklaces. In the late eighteenth century, women wore cloth skirts, as well as shawls, or capes, that covered one breast and were fastened over the left shoulder, made of the skin of buffalo calves. They parted their hair down the middle and tied each section off. Men generally had four braids, two behind and two in front. They wore breechclouts, cloaks or shirts, and bear or buffalo robes in winter.

WAR AND WEAPONS Alabamas often joined forces with the Coushatta people against the Tohome, among others. Men decorated their hair for war with buffalo horns. They fought with the war club and bow and arrow. The war chief carried along the sacred war ark or medicine bundle. Life (of one's own people) was considered precious, and warriors were extremely careful not to risk inopportune or imprudent fighting or capture.

Contemporary Information

GOVERNMENT/RESERVATIONS The Alabama-Coushatta Reservation, established in 1854, is located in Polk County, Texas. It consists of 4,400 acres and is governed by a tribal council. There were 477 Indian residents in 1990.

The 154-acre Coushatta Reservation is located in Allen Parish, Louisiana. About 400 people lived there in the early 1990s. Indian residents are often referred to as Koasati Indians. They are governed by a tribal council.

The Alabamas and Quassartes of Oklahoma live mostly near Weleetka, in Okfuskee County. Tribal headquarters is in Henryetta. They are still administered together with the Creek Nation.

ECONOMY Some Alabamas continue to make traditional arts and crafts. There is income from tourism, including camping and recreation, in Texas. The Coushatta in Louisiana own a Christmas tree farm and a bingo establishment.

LEGAL STATUS The Coushatta Tribe of Louisiana, the Alabama-Coushatta Tribe, and the Alabama-Quassarte Tribal Town of the Creek Nation are federally recognized tribal entities.

DAILY LIFE Most Alabamas are Protestants. The Alabama-Coushattas operate a tribal museum; they also host various dances as well as a June powwow. Both the Alabama and the Coushatta languages are still spoken in Texas. In Louisiana, federal money has helped the people improve sanitation and build schools, a health clinic, and a tribal center. Residents of Oklahoma often visit and intermarry with members of the other communities. A few older people in Oklahoma speak both languages.

Biloxi
See Tunica

Caddo

Caddo (`Ca d ō), "true chiefs," from Kadohadacho, a principal tribe. The Caddo Indians included people of the Natchitoches Confederacy (Louisiana), the Hasinai (Tejas or Texas) Confederacy (Texas), the Kadohadacho Confederacy (Texas and Arkansas), and the Adai and Eyish people. There were about 25 Caddo tribes in the eighteenth century.

LOCATION Traditionally, Caddos lived in a wide area from the Red River Valley (Louisiana and Arkansas) to the Brazos Valley in Texas. Today, the highest concentration of Caddo Indians is found in Caddo County, Oklahoma.

POPULATION Numbering around 8,000 people in the late seventeenth century, there were 3,371 enrolled Caddos in the early 1990s.

LANGUAGE Caddos spoke a Caddoan language.

Historical Information

HISTORY Caddoans are thought to have originated in the Southwest. They reached the Great Plains in the mid–twelfth century and the fringes of the Southeast cultural area shortly thereafter. They gave the Spanish under Hernando de Soto a mixed reception in 1541. Few of the Spanish missions in their country had any success.

Trade with the French began in the early seventeenth century. The Indians traded their crops for animal pelts, which they then traded to the French for guns and other items of non-native origin. During the eighteenth century, Caddo villages suffered from Spanish-French colonial battles. Many tribes were wiped out by disease during that period.

In 1835, the Caddos ceded their Louisiana land and moved to Texas. In the 1850s, however, nonnative Texans drove all Indians out of Texas, and the Caddos fled from their brutality to the Indian Territory (Oklahoma). In 1859, the United States confined them to a reservation along the Washita River, which the Wichitas and Delawares later joined.

Rather than support the Confederacy, most Caddos fled to Kansas during the Civil War, returning in 1868. Some scouted for the U.S. Army during the Plains wars, in part as a strategy of supporting farmers against nomads. The boundaries of their reservation were secured in 1872, but despite Caddo objections, most of the reservation was allotted around 1900. After extensive litigation and appeals, the tribe won over $1.5 million in land claim settlements in the 1980s.

RELIGION Their supreme deity was known as Ayanat Caddi. There were also other deities and spirits, including the sun. Most annual ceremonies revolved around the agricultural cycle.

GOVERNMENT Each Caddo tribe was headed by a powerful chief, who was assisted by other people of authority. Among the Hasinai (at least), a high priest had supreme authority.

CUSTOMS Clans were more hierarchical and social classes more pronounced among the western Caddo than in the east. Guests were greeted by ritual wailing and ceremonially washed. Shell beads were used as a medium of exchange. The people practiced frontal head deformation. Chiefs were carried on the shoulders of the people. Popular games included hoop and pole and also foot races. Men placed fowl down on their heads in preparation for feasts.

Premarital sexual liaisons were condoned. In some tribes, men were allowed to have more than one wife, although in others a woman might not allow it. Divorce was easily obtained and occurred regularly. The dead were buried with food and water as well as appropriate items (weapons for men, utensils for women). War dead were cremated. Six days after death, all spirits went southward to a pleasant house of the dead. Some tribes may have engaged in ritual murder.

DWELLINGS At least one seventeenth-century town had over 100 houses. Some villages may have been reinforced with towered stockades. Houses in the east were round, about 15 feet high and between 20 and 60 feet in diameter. They were constructed of a pole frame covered with grass thatch, through which smoke from the cooking fires exited; roofs came all the way to the ground. Western Caddos built earth lodges, with wooden frames and brush, grass, and mud walls reaching to the top. There were also outside arbors. Sacred fires always burned in circular temples.

Houses were generally grouped around an open plaza or game/ceremonial area. Cane beds, separated by mats, were raised about three feet off the ground. Doors usually faced east, although sometimes southeast or south. There were also indoor compartments near the entrance and outdoor areas to store dried corn and other items.

DIET Women grew two corn crops a year, as well as beans, pumpkins, sunflowers, and tobacco. They also gathered wild foods such as nuts, acorns, mulberries, strawberries, blackberries, plums, pomegranates, persimmons, and grapes. Agricultural products were most important in the diet, although buffalo grew in importance as the group moved westward. Men hunted deer, bear, raccoon, turkey, fowl, and snakes. They stalked deer using deer disguises. Dogs may have assisted them in the hunt. Fish were caught where possible.

KEY TECHNOLOGY Bows were made of Osage orange whenever possible. Most fish were taken in traps. Caddos made a variety of baskets and mats. Other important items included wood and horn dishes; wooden mortars, chests, and cradles; drums; rattles; and flutes (flageolets). Deer sinew was generally used as thread.

TRADE Caddos exported Osage orange wood and salt, which they obtained from local mines (licks) and boiled in earthen (later iron) kettles. They imported Quapaw wooden platters, among other items. The Texas Caddos traded with Chichimecs from Mexico.

NOTABLE ARTS Fine arts included basketry, pottery, and carved shells.

TRANSPORTATION Single-log dugout canoes and cane rafts were used to navigate bodies of water. The people acquired horses in the late seventeenth century.

DRESS Most clothing was made of deerskin. Men wore breechclouts, untailored shirts, and cloaks, Women wore skirts and a poncho-style upper garment and painted their bodies. They parted their hair in front and fastened it behind. Both wore blankets or buffalo robes and tattooed their faces and bodies, especially in floral and animal patterns. Girls wore grass or hay breechclouts from birth.

WAR AND WEAPONS Weapons included the bow and arrow and lances. Warriors underwent special ceremonies in a war house prior to battle; the house was burned down when the war party departed. Enemies included the Osage and Choctaw, whereas in the later period the people were often allied with the Delaware.

Contemporary Information

GOVERNMENT/RESERVATIONS Tribal facilities are located on 42.5 acres near Binger, Oklahoma. A constitution and by-laws were adopted in 1938 and revised in 1976. An elected eight-member tribal council with a chair governs the tribe. The people also claim almost 2,400 acres of land held in trust in Oklahoma with the Wichita and Delaware.

ECONOMY Unemployment often reaches 40 percent among Indians in Caddo County. Caddos participate in the local economy as professionals, ranchers, farmers, and workers of many kinds. The tribal economy relies heavily on oil, gas, and land leasing. With the other two tribes, the Caddo operate a smoke shop, a factory, and a bingo parlor.

LEGAL STATUS The Caddo Tribe of Oklahoma is a federally recognized tribal entity. The people are considering changing their name to the Caddo Nation in Oklahoma.

DAILY LIFE Tribal facilities include administrative offices, dance grounds, and several community centers. The tribe improved its housing in the 1990s and is seeking to build new program and activity buildings. The people have retained a significant amount of traditional culture, especially songs and dances, and there are many programs designed to revitalize Caddo traditions. There is an active Native American Church.

Catawba

The Catawba (C ə `täw bä) people were also known as Issa or Esaw, "People of the River."

LOCATION Catawbas traditionally lived along the North Carolina–South Carolina border, especially along the Catawba River. Today, most live near Rock Hill, South Carolina. Some live in Oklahoma, in Colorado, and in other states.

POPULATION The Catawba were the largest of the eastern Siouan tribes in the early seventeenth century, with a population of about 6,000. There were roughly 1,400 people enrolled in the tribe in the mid-1990s.

LANGUAGE Catawba is probably a Siouan language.

Historical Information

HISTORY Catawbas may have come to the Carolinas from the northwest. They first encountered non-natives—Spanish explorers—in the mid–sixteenth century. Extensive contact with British traders in the late seventeenth and early eighteenth centuries transformed their lives. A dependence on non-native goods caused them to hunt ever farther afield for pelts with which to purchase such goods. Encroachment on other peoples' hunting grounds combined with the heavy volume of goods carried along the trade routes encouraged increased attacks by enemy Indians. Catawbas also underwent severe depopulation from disease.

In order to maintain trade relations with the colonists, the Catawba took their side in a 1711–1713 war with the Tuscarora Indians. By 1715, however, some Catawbas had taken the Indian side in the Yamasee war, rebelling against unfair trade practices,

forced labor, and slave raids. The non-native victory in this conflict broke the power of the local Indians.

In the mid–eighteenth century smallpox epidemics almost wiped the tribe out: Their precontact population of about 6,000 had declined by over 90 percent to 500 or fewer. Alcohol sold and aggressively promoted by Anglo traders took many more lives. Catawbas tended to absorb local tribes who suffered the same fate, such as the Cheraw, Sugaree, Waxhaw, Congaree, Santee, Pedee, and Wateree.

In 1760–1761 the Catawbas were forced by their dependence on the state of South Carolina to fight against the powerful Cherokee in the French and Indian War. By 1763 they were confined within a 15-square-mile (144,000-acre) reservation, as non-natives continued to take their former lands. Part of the agreement creating the reservation stipulated that non-Indians would be evicted from it (which never happened) and that the Catawba continued to enjoy hunting rights outside the area. Their last great chief, Haigler, or Arataswa, died at that time.

The declining tribe took the patriot side in the American Revolution and began a long process of intermarriage with the Pamunkey of Virginia at that time. After the war, they granted many long-term renewable leases to non-natives. They also established two towns, Newtown and Turkeyhead, on both sides of the Catawba River.

Some of the few remaining, poverty-stricken Catawbas went to live with the Cherokee in western Carolina in the 1830s. In 1840 they signed a treaty with the state of South Carolina, agreeing to cede lands in that state and move to North Carolina. Unable to buy land there, however, most dispersed among the Cherokee and Pamunkey, although a very few remained in South Carolina.

In the 1850s, most Catawbas who had gone to live with the Cherokee returned to South Carolina. A few families moved to Arkansas, the Indian Territory, Colorado, Utah, or elsewhere. Those in South Carolina acquired a reservation of 630 (of the original 144,000) poor-quality acres. They also obtained the promise of annual payments from the state.

Many South Carolina Catawbas began sharecropping at that time but returned occasionally to live on the reservation. They also continued to speak their language and to make their traditional crafts. The Catawba Indian School opened in 1896 and ran until 1962. Mormons also played a large role in educating Catawba children beginning in the 1880s.

Many Catawbas worked in textile mills beginning after World War I. The Indians added to their reservation by purchasing land in the mid–twentieth century. By that time, however, traditional Catawba culture had all but expired. Although the federal trust relationship was formally begun only in 1943, as a result of Catawba legal pressure, in 1962 the tribe voluntarily ended its relationship with the federal government, at which time individuals took over possession of the recently purchased tribal lands.

RELIGION The people made use of wooden images in their ceremonies, which were relatively unconnected to the harvest. Enemies were killed to accompany the dead to an afterworld.

GOVERNMENT There were two bands in the early eighteenth century. Some of their chiefs—men and women—were quite powerful.

CUSTOMS Catawbas may have practiced frontal head deformation. The chunkey game was a variety of hoop and pole, played with a stone roller. They also played stickball, or lacrosse. At puberty, young women learned how properly to wear decorative feathers. Doctors and conjurers cured and detected thieves by consorting with spirits. Men alone were punished in cases of adultery. Divorce was easy to obtain, and widows could remarry at once. Corpses were buried under bark and earth; later, the bones of chiefs were dug up, cleaned, wrapped in deerskins, and redeposited in a crypt. Personal enemies may have been poisoned.

DWELLINGS Six early villages were located in river valleys. People lived in bark-covered pole-frame houses. The town houses were circular, as were the temples. Open arbors were used in summer.

DIET Women grew corn, beans, squash, and gourds. Men hunted widely for large and small game, including buffalo, deer, and bear. The people also ate fish, pigeons, acorns, and various other wild plant foods.

KEY TECHNOLOGY Blowguns with an average length of 5–6 feet and with an effective range of no more than 30 feet were used to bring down birds. Darts, about 8–10 inches long, were made of wood slivers. Scratchers, similar to combs, were made of a split reed with rattlesnake teeth. A number of clay items were made, including pipes.

TRADE The main regional aboriginal trade routes ran right through Catawba territory. The Catawba became heavily involved with British traders, especially in the mid–eighteenth century but beginning at least in 1673.

NOTABLE ARTS Pottery was an ancient and highly developed art. It was often stamped with a carved piece of wood before firing. Baskets were constructed of rushes, roots, or grasses.

TRANSPORTATION Rivers were navigated on dugout and possibly birch bark canoes.

DRESS Chiefs wore headdresses of wild turkey feathers. Women may have worn leggings as well as, when mourning, clothing made from tree moss.

WAR AND WEAPONS Traditional enemies included the Cherokee, Shawnee, and Iroquois, with whom they fought often. They also fought the Delaware in historic times. Catawba raiding parties traveled long distances, even to the Great Lakes.

Contemporary Information

GOVERNMENT/RESERVATIONS The Catawba State Reservation (650 acres) is located near Rock Hill (eastern York County), South Carolina. The tribe gained nonprofit corporate status in 1973 and elected an eight-member tribal council and executive committee at that time. The 1990 Indian population was 124.

ECONOMY The tribe is known for its pottery, which, unlike any other eastern tribe, they continue to make approximately in the ancient way. There is also individual and tribal income from the 1993 settlement (see "Legal Status"). The people are relatively well educated and enjoy a range of economic opportunities.

LEGAL STATUS The Catawba Indian Nation is a federally recognized tribal entity. The tribe claimed possession of its 144,000-acre colonial reservation, holding that the lands were never legally transferred. An agreement with the United States was effected in 1993, by the terms of which federal tribal status was reinstated and the tribe was paid $50 million.

DAILY LIFE Catawbas in Colorado and other western states, though not formally enrolled, communicate regularly with the Carolina people. Pottery making and training are still important activities. Other crafts include hide tanning, blowgun making, and beadwork. Most Catawbas are Mormons. The tribe sponsors an annual cultural festival and is involved with numerous local and regional museums. Efforts are under way to revive the native language. The old knowledge and ceremonies have long since disappeared.

Cherokee

Cherokee (`Cher ə k ə), probably from the Creek *tciloki*, "People Who Speak Differently." Their self-designation was *Ani-yun-wiya*, "Real People." With the Creek, Choctaw, Chickasaw, and Seminole, the Cherokee were one of the so-called Five Civilized Tribes; this non-native appellation arose because by the early nineteenth century these Indians dressed, farmed, and governed themselves so nearly like white Americans. At the time of contact the Cherokee were the largest tribe in the southeast. Cherokees were formerly known as Kituhwas.

LOCATION Between about 70 and 100 precontact villages were located in roughly 40,000 square miles of the southern Appalachian region, including parts of the present-day states of North Carolina, Kentucky, Tennessee, Virginia, South Carolina, Georgia, and Alabama. There were towns in the lower region (headwaters of the Savannah River), the middle region (headwaters of the Little Tennessee River), and the upper region (lower Little Tennessee River and the headwaters of the Hiwassee River). Today, most Cherokees live in northeastern Oklahoma. A sizable minority lives in western North Carolina.

POPULATION   There were roughly 29,000 Cherokees in the mid–sixteenth century and perhaps 22,000 in 1650. In 1990, 308,132 people identified themselves as Cherokees, although fewer than half belong to federally recognized groups.

LANGUAGE   Cherokee is an Iroquoian language. The lower towns spoke the Elati dialect; the middle towns spoke the Kituhwa dialect; the upper (overhill and valley) towns spoke the Atali dialect. The dialects were mutually intelligible with difficulty.

Historical Information

HISTORY   The Cherokee probably originated in the upper Ohio Valley, the Great Lakes region, or someplace else in the north. They may also have been related to the Mound Builders. The town of Echota, on the Little Tennessee River, may have been the ancient capital of the Cherokee Nation.

They encountered Hernando de Soto about 1540, probably not long after they arrived in their historic homeland. Spanish attacks against the Indians commenced shortly thereafter, although new diseases probably weakened the people even before Spanish soldiers began killing them. There were also contacts with the French and especially the British in the early seventeenth century. Traders brought guns around 1700, along with debilitating alcohol.

The Cherokee fought a series of wars with Tuscarora, Shawnee, Catawba, Creek, and Chickasaw Indians early in the eighteenth century. In 1760 the Cherokee, led by Chief Oconostota, fought the British as a protest against unfair trade practices and violence practiced against them as a group. Cherokees raided settlements and captured a British fort but were defeated after two years of fighting by the British scorched-earth policy. The peace treaty cost the Indians much of their eastern land, and, in fact, they never fully recovered their prominence after that time

Significant depopulation resulted from several mid–eighteenth century epidemics. Cherokee support for Britain during the American Revolution encouraged attacks by North Carolina militia. Finally, some Cherokees who lived near Chattanooga relocated in 1794 to Arkansas and Texas and in 1831 to Indian Territory (Oklahoma). These people eventually became known as the Western Cherokee.

After the American Revolution, Cherokees adopted British-style farming, cattle ranching, business, and government, becoming relatively cohesive and prosperous. They also owned slaves. They sided with the United States in the 1813 Creek war, during which a Cherokee saved Andrew Jackson's life. The tribe enjoyed a cultural renaissance between about 1800 and 1830, although they were under constant pressure for land cession and riven by internal political factionalism.

The Cherokee Nation was founded in 1827 with "western" democratic institutions and a written constitution (which specifically disenfranchised African Americans and women). By then, Cherokees were intermarrying regularly with non-natives and were receiving increased missionary activity, especially in education. Sequoyah (also known as George Gist) is credited with devising a Cherokee syllabary in 1821 and thus providing his people with a written language. During the late 1820s, the people began publishing a newspaper, the *Cherokee Phoenix.*

The discovery of gold in their territory led in part to the 1830 Indian Removal Act, requiring the Cherokee (among other tribes) to relocate west of the Mississippi River. Despite significant public pressure to let them remain, and despite a victory in the U.S. Supreme Court, President Andrew Jackson forced the Indians out. When a small minority of Cherokees signed the Treaty of New Echota, ceding the tribe's last remaining eastern lands, local non-natives immediately began appropriating the Indians' land and plundering their homes and possessions. Indians were forced into internment camps, where many died, although over 1,000 escaped to the mountains of North Carolina, where they became the progenitors of what came to be called the Eastern Band of Cherokees.

The removal, known as the Trail of Tears, began in 1838. The Indians were forced to walk 1,000 miles through severe weather without adequate food and clothing. About 4,000 Cherokees, almost a quarter of the total, died during the removal, and more died once the people reached the Indian Territory, where they joined—and largely absorbed—the group already there. Following their arrival in Indian Territory, the Cherokees quickly adopted another constitution and reestablished their institutions and facilities, including newspapers and schools. Under Chief John Ross, most Cherokees supported slavery and also supported the Confederate cause in the Civil War.

The huge "permanent" Indian territory was often reduced in size. When the northern region was removed to create the states of Kansas and Nebraska, Indians living there were again forcibly resettled. One result of the Dawes Act (late 1880s) was the "sale" (virtual appropriation) of roughly two million acres of Indian land in Oklahoma. Oklahoma became a territory in 1890 and a state in 1907. Although the Cherokees and other tribes resisted allotment, Congress forced them to acquiesce in 1898. Their land was individually allotted in 1902, at about the same time their native governments were officially "terminated."

Ten years after the Cherokee removal, the U.S. Congress ceased efforts to round up the Eastern Cherokee. The Indians received state (North Carolina) citizenship in 1866 and incorporated as the Eastern Band of Cherokee Indians in 1889. In the early twentieth century, many Eastern Cherokees were engaged in subsistence farming and in the local timber industry. Having resisted allotment, the tribe took steps to ensure that it would always own its land. Although the Cherokee suffered greatly during the Depression, the Great Smoky Mountain National Park (1930s) served as the center of a growing tourist industry.

In the 1930s, the United Keetoowah Band (UKB), a group of full-bloods opposed to assimilation, formally separated from the Oklahoma Cherokees. The group originated in the antiallotment battles at the end of the nineteenth century. In the early twentieth century the UKB reconstructed several traditional political structures, such as the seven clans and white towns, as well as some ancient cultural practices that did not survive the move west. The name Keetoowah derives from an ancient town in western North Carolina. They received federal recognition in 1946.

RELIGION The tribe's chief deity was the sun, which may have had a feminine identity. The people conceived of the cosmos as being divided into an upper world, this world, and a lower world. Each contained numerous spiritual beings that resided in specific places. The four cardinal directions were replete with social significance. Tribal mythology, symbols, and beliefs were complex, and there were also various associated taboos, customs, and social and personal rules.

Many ceremonies revolved around subsistence activities as well as healing. The primary one was the annual Green Corn ceremony (Busk), observed when the last corn crop ripened. Shamans were religious leaders and curers. The people thought of disease as being caused by dreams or animals, real or mythical. Cures consisted of herbal treatments, sweats, changes in diet, deep scratching, rubbing, and spiritual remedies.

Medicine people (men and women) were curers, conjurers, diviners, wizards, and witches. They could, by magical means, influence events and the lives and fortunes of people. Witches, when discovered, were summarily killed. Learning sorcery took a lifetime. Medicine powers could be used for good or evil, and the associated beads, crystals, and formulas were a regular part of many people's lives.

GOVERNMENT The various Cherokee villages formed a loose confederacy. There were two chiefs per village: a red, or war, chief and a white chief (Most Beloved Man or Woman), who was associated with civil, economic, religious, and juridical functions. The red chief was also in charge of lacrosse games. Chiefs could be male or female, and there was little or no hereditary component. There was also a village council, in which women sat, although usually only as observers. Its powers were fairly limited. The Cherokee were not a cohesive political entity until the late eighteenth century at the earliest.

CUSTOMS Men played intraclan lacrosse and chunkey. They also held athletic races and competitions. Lacrosse had serious ceremonial aspects and accompanying rituals, including dances and certain taboos. There were seven matrilineal clans in the early historic period. Cherokees regularly engaged in ceremonial purification, and they paid careful attention to their dreams.

Both men and women, married and single, enjoyed a high degree of sexual freedom. Divorce was possible; men who were thrown out returned to their mothers. Pregnant women were expected to pray and bathe every new moon for several months prior to delivery. Babies were bathed every morning, and young children bathed every morning for at least the first two years. Twins were accorded special treatment and were often raised to be wizards. Children were treated gently, and they behaved with decorum. In general, Cherokees, valuing harmony as well as generosity, tried to avoid conflict.

Intraclan, but not interclan, murder was a capital offense. Names were changed or added to frequently. As with chiefs, towns may also have been considered red and white. Women owned the houses and their contents; this custom, along with matrilineal descent and the clan system, weakened with increasing exposure to non-native society. Kinsmen avenged the death of their kinsmen, according to the law of retaliation.

People did not address each other directly. In place of public sanctions, Cherokees used ostracism and public scorn to enforce social norms. Burial with possessions took place in the earth or under piles of stone.

DWELLINGS Towns were located along rivers and streams. They contained a central ceremonial place and in the early historic period were often surrounded by palisades. People built rectangular summer houses of pole frames and wattle, walls of cane matting and clay plaster, and gabled bark or thatch roofs. The houses, about 60 or 70 feet by 15 feet, were often divided into three parts: a kitchen, a dining area, and bedrooms. Some were two stories high, with the upper walls open for ventilation. There was probably one door. Beds were made of rush mats over wood splints, and animal skins served as bedding.

Smaller, circular winter houses (which also served as sweat houses) were simply 20-foot-high pole-and-earth cones placed over pits. Cherokees also built domed town/council/ceremonial houses and seven-sided temples, the latter located on raised mounds in the village plaza, of earth over a post-and-beam frame. Some were large enough to hold 500 people. Tiered interior seats surrounded a center fire.

DIET   Cherokees were primarily farmers. Women grew corn (three kinds), beans, squash, sunflowers, and tobacco, the latter used ceremonially. Corn was roasted, boiled, and ground into flour and then baked into bread.

Wild foods included roots, crab apples, persimmons, plums, cherries, grapes, hickory nuts, walnuts, chestnuts, and berries. Men hunted various animals, including deer, bear, raccoon, rabbit, squirrel, turkey, and rattlesnake. They stalked deer using entire deerskins and deer calls. Hunting was preceded by the proper prayers and songs. Meat was broiled or boiled. They fished occasionally, and they collected maple syrup in earthen pots and boiled it into syrup.

KEY TECHNOLOGY   Fish were caught using spears, weirs, poison, and the hook-and-line. Hunting gear included the bow and arrow, stone hatchet, and flint knife. Smaller animals and birds were shot with darts blown out of hollow 9- to 10-foot-long cane stems; these blowguns were accurate up to 60 feet.

Other material items included cane and root baskets; stone pipes on wooden stems; pottery of various sizes and shapes, often "stamped" with carved wooden designs; wooden medicine boxes; reed arrows with bone or fish-scale points attached with deer sinew; and drums, flutes, and gourd rattles. Ovens were a hot, flat stone covered with an inverted dish.

TRADE   Cherokee pipes were widely admired and easily exported. The people also traded maple sugar and syrup. They imported shell wampum that was used as money.

NOTABLE ARTS   Plaited cane baskets, pottery, and masks carved of wood and gourds were especially fine. Pipes and moccasins may have been decorated with porcupine quills.

TRANSPORTATION   Men built 30- to 40-foot-long canoes of fire-hollowed pine or poplar logs. Each canoe could hold between 15 and 20 people. The people may also have used bark canoes.

DRESS   Women made most clothing of buckskin and other skins and furs as well as of mulberry bark fibers. Men wore breechclouts; women wore skirts. In winter, both wore bear or buffalo robes. Men also wore shirts and leggings, and women wore capes. Both sexes wore moccasins as well as nose ornaments, bracelets, and body paint. Men wore their hair in a roach; women wore it long. There were also ceremonial turkey and eagle feather headdresses and capes. Men slit their ears and stretched them with the use of copper wires.

WAR AND WEAPONS   Each village had a red (war) chief as well as a War Woman, who accompanied war parties. She fed the men, gave advice, and determined the fate of prisoners. Women also distinguished themselves in combat and often tortured prisoners of war. Cherokee enemies over time included the Catawba, Shawnee, Congaree, Tuscarora, Creek, and Iroquois. They were often allied with the Chickasaw. Weapons included the bow and arrow, knife, tomahawk, and darts, or short lances. The people often painted themselves, as well as their canoes and paddles, for war. The party carried an ark or medicine chest to war, and it left a war club engraved with its exploits in enemy territory.

Contemporary Information

GOVERNMENT/RESERVATIONS   Cherokee Tribal Headquarters is located in Tahlequah, Oklahoma. As of the early 1990s there were more than 122,000 enrolled members of the Cherokee Nation. The 61,000-plus acres of tribal land is not a reservation but an administrative entity. Governmental leaders have been popularly elected since the 1970s. The tribe adopted a new constitution in 1975 that mandates a tripartite form of government.

The Qualla Boundary Cherokee Reservation, established in 1874, is located in western North Carolina. The enrolled population in 1990 was almost 10,000, nearly two-thirds of whom lived on tribal lands. The group owns more than 56,000 acres of land in North Carolina, mostly in Jackson and Swain Counties, and more than 76 acres in eastern Tennessee. Individuals hold title to most of this land, but they may transfer it only to other tribal members. Tribal government is composed of executive (three offices, two of which are elected), legislative (popularly elected tribal council), and judicial branches. As part of its responsibilities as a trustee for tribal lands, the U.S. government manages schools, lands, and public health.

The United Keetoowah Band is located in northeastern Oklahoma. It is governed by a tribal council. There were 7,450 members in the early 1990s. As they are legally unable to obtain a land base within the Cherokee Nation, they are currently seeking one elsewhere.

ECONOMY Important economic activities include oil and gas sales and leases, arts and crafts, bingo, a utility company, and ranching, poultry, and woodcutting operations. In the early 1990s, the tribe was generating about half of its annual operating budget of over $65 million. It also anticipated payments from the settlement of disputed control of resources under the Arkansas riverbed, but this situation is still being argued, and no settlement has been achieved.

In North Carolina there are a craft factory, a lumber business, tourist enterprises, and numerous other businesses. People work seasonally in non-native tourist enterprises.

LEGAL STATUS The Eastern Band of Cherokee Indians, the Cherokee Nation of Oklahoma, and the United Keetoowah Band are federally recognized tribal entities. More than 50 other groups in 12 states also claim Cherokee identity.

DAILY LIFE Oklahoma and North Carolina Cherokees stage an annual presentation for tourists. Since the 1970s, two people, Ross Swimmer and Wilma Mankiller, have dominated Cherokee tribal politics. In Oklahoma, there is some division between rural "conservatives" and "progressives," who tend to be wealthier and more urban. Most people are Christians. Many live in fairly isolated hill communities. Of the three Cherokee dialects, the Atali (Overhill) is still spoken in Oklahoma by about 13,000 people and another (the Middle, or Kituhwa) in North Carolina by about 1,000 people, primarily in religious services. In the 1990s, the Cherokee Nation adopted its own tax code as well as various self-governance mechanisms. Its major celebrations are held over Labor Day weekend. The Keetoowah Society (or the Nighthawk Keetoowas) closely adheres to traditional religious practice.

Eastern Cherokees have created a vibrant, economically stable community secure in its Indian identity. Most of their high school students attend college. There are various celebrations in the fall that feature traditional games and dancing. Facilities include a reproduced ancient village and a museum. The people still speak the language and still practice traditional medicine. The Eastern Band and the Cherokee Nation meet in joint council every two years. The UKB continues to resist reintegration into the Cherokee Nation. They conduct their own cultural activities.

Chickasaw

Chickasaw (`Chi k ə sä), a Muskogean name referring to the act of sitting down. The Chickasaw were culturally similar to the Choctaw. Along with the Cherokee, Choctaw, Creek and Seminole, the Chickasaw were one of the so-called Five Civilized Tribes.

LOCATION Chickasaws traditionally lived in northeastern Mississippi as well as northern Alabama, eastern Arkansas, western Kentucky, western Tennessee, and throughout the Mississippi Valley. Many Chickasaws now live in southern Oklahoma.

POPULATION There were about 5,000 Chickasaws in 1600. In the mid-1990s, roughly 26,000 people identified themselves as Chickasaw.

LANGUAGE Chickasaw is a Muskogean language.

Historical Information

HISTORY The Chickasaw may once have been united with the Choctaw. The people encountered Hernando de Soto in 1541. At first welcoming, as their customs dictated, they ultimately attacked the Spanish when the latter tortured some of them and tried to enslave others.

In the late seventeenth and early eighteenth centuries, warfare increased with neighboring tribes as the Chickasaw expanded their already large hunting grounds to obtain more pelts and skins for the British trade. Increasingly dependent on this trade, they did not shrink from capturing other Indians, such as the Choctaws, and selling them to the British as slaves. In general, the Chickasaws' alliance with the British during the colonial period acted as a hindrance to French trade on the Mississippi.

Constant warfare with the French and their Choctaw allies during the eighteenth century sapped the people's vitality. In part to compensate, they began absorbing other peoples, such as several hundred Natchez as well as British traders. A pattern began to emerge in which descendants of British men and Chickasaw women (such as the Colbert family) became powerful tribal leaders. Missionaries began making significant numbers of converts during that time.

Tribal allegiance was divided during the American Revolution, with some members supporting one side, some the other, and some neither. The overall goal was to preserve traditional lands. The tribe did not rally behind Tecumseh in 1809 (*see* Shawnee entry in Chapter 8). With game growing scarce, many Chickasaws became exclusively farmers during the early to mid–nineteenth century. Some also began cotton plantations, and the tribe owned up to 1,000 African American slaves during that period. By 1830 they had a written code of laws (which banned whiskey) and a police force.

As non-native settlement of their lands increased during the 1820s, many Chickasaws migrated west, ceding land in several treaties (1805, 1816, 1818) during the period. Finally they ceded all lands east of the Mississippi in 1832. Roughly 3,000 Chickasaws were forcibly removed to Indian Territory (Oklahoma) after 1837, where many died of disease, hunger, and attacks by Plains Indians who resented the intrusion. The Chickasaw fared somewhat better than did the Cherokee, being able to purchase many supply items, including riverboat transportation, with tribal funds. Most settled in the western part of Choctaw lands.

Survivors of the ordeal resumed farming and soon, with the help of their slaves, grew a surplus of crops. However, as a tribe the people had lost most of their aboriginal culture. Their own reservation and government were formally established in 1855 and lasted until Oklahoma statehood in 1907. In the years before the Civil War, the people operated schools, mills, and blacksmith shops, and they had started a newspaper. Chickasaws fought for the Confederacy in the Civil War. Unlike some other Oklahoma tribes of southeast origin, the Chickasaw never adopted their freed slaves.

Their lands were allotted around 1900. All tribal governments in Oklahoma were dissolved by Congress in 1906. By 1920, of the roughly 4.7 million acres of preallotment Chickasaw land, only about 300 remained in tribal control, a situation that severely hampered tribal political and economic development well into the century. Many prominent twentieth-century Oklahoma politicians were mixed-blood Chickasaws. From the 1940s on, individuals received payments from the sale of land containing coal and asphalt deposits.

RELIGION The supreme deity was *Ababinili,* an aggregation of four celestial beings: Sun, Clouds, Clear Sky, and He That Lives in the Clear Sky. Fire, especially the sacred fire, was a manifestation of the supreme being. Rattlesnakes were also greatly revered, and the people recognized many other lesser gods as well as evil spirits.

Two head priests, or *hopaye,* presided over ceremonies and interpreted spiritual matters. They wore special clothing at such times. Healers *(aliktce),* who combated evil spirits by using various natural substances, and witches were two types of spiritual people. Men painted their faces for ceremonies. People used charms and observed various food taboos.

GOVERNMENT Political leadership was chosen in part according to hereditary claim but also according to merit. The head chief, chosen from the Minko clan, was known as the High Minko. Each clan also had a

chief. There was also a council of advisers, which included clan leaders and tribal elders. The fundamental units were local groups.

CUSTOMS Key Chickasaw values included hospitality and generosity, especially to those in need. Two divisions were in turn divided into many ranked matrilineal clans. The people played lacrosse, chunkey, and other games, most of which included gambling and had important ritual components. Tobacco was used ritually and medicinally. Murder was subject to retaliation. Chickasaws liked to dance, both on social and religious occasions.

Boys were toughened by winter plunges and special herbs. Women were secluded in special huts during their menstrual periods. There was some childhood betrothal. Marriage involved various gift exchanges, mainly food or clothing. A man might have more than one wife. Men avoided their mothers-in-law out of respect. In cases of adultery only the woman was punished, often by a beating or an ear or nose cropping. Chickasaws practiced frontal head deformation.

The dead were buried in graves under houses, along with their possessions, after an elaborate funeral rite. They were placed in a sitting position facing west, with their faces painted red. After death they were only vaguely alluded to and never directly by name. All social activities ceased for three days following a death in the village. Chickasaws maintained the concept of a heaven generally in the west, the direction of witchcraft and uneasy spirits.

DWELLINGS Chickasaws built their villages on high ground near stands of hardwood trees. They were often palisaded and more compact during periods of warfare.

Rectangular summer houses were of pole-frame construction, notched and lashed, and clapboard sides, with gabled roofs covered with cypress or pine-bark shingles. They were whitewashed in and out with powdered oyster shell or white clay. Outside materials included grass or cane thatch, bark, and hide. A small doorway, usually facing east, offered protection against insects. The people also built several outbuildings for fowl, corn, sweating, and other purposes.

Winter houses were semiexcavated and circular, about 25 feet in diameter, with a narrow, 4-foot-high door. They were plastered with at least 6 inches of clay and dried grass. Bark shingles or thatch covered conical roofs with no smoke holes. Furniture included couches and raised wood-frame beds, under which food was stored. Town houses or temples were of similar construction.

DIET Crops—corn, beans, squash, and sunflowers—were the staple foods. Corn was made into a variety of foods, including an unfermented drink. Men also hunted buffalo, deer, bear, and numerous kinds of small game, including rabbits but probably not beaver or opossum. Hunting techniques included shooting, trapping, and using animal calls and decoys. Birds and their eggs were included in the diet.

Women gathered nuts, acorns, honey, onions, persimmons, strawberries, grapes, and plums. Tea was made from sassafras root. Chickasaws ate a variety of fish, including the huge (up to 200 pounds) Mississippi catfish.

KEY TECHNOLOGY Earthen pots of various sizes and shapes served a number of purposes. Men stunned fish with buckeye or green walnut poison. Women wove mulberry bark in a frame and used the resulting textile in floor and table coverings. Other material items included stone axes, fire drills, wooden mortars, and various cane baskets, some of which could hold water. Musical instruments included drums (wet skins over clay pots), gourd rattles, and flutes.

TRADE Chickasaws traded as far away as Texas and perhaps even Mexico. Among other items, they traded deerskins for conch shell to use as wampum. Vermilion may have been counted as a basis of wealth.

NOTABLE ARTS Cloth items (from woven mulberry inner bark) were decorated with colorful animal and human figures and other designs. The people also made exceptional dyed and decorated cane baskets.

TRANSPORTATION Men hollowed dugout canoes out of hardwood trees. Caddo Indians brought horses in from the Red River region; some were also stolen from the early Spanish. Eventually, the Chickasaw developed a horse breed of their own. Some chiefs may have been carried in litters.

DRESS Most clothing was made of deerskin, although other hides, including beaver, were also used. Wild mulberry bark formed material for items of "cloth." Men wore breechclouts, with deerskin shirts and bearskin robes in cold weather. Most kept their hair in a roach soaked in bear grease. There were also high boots for hunting. Women wore long dresses and added buffalo robes or capes in winter. They tended to tie up their hair.

People generally went barefoot, although they did make moccasins of bear hide and occasionally elk skin. Women made turkey feather blankets. Some young men slit their ears and expanded them with the use of copper wire. Other personal ornamentation included nose rings, head bracelets, and body paint.

WAR AND WEAPONS Chickasaws were known as fierce, enthusiastic, and successful warriors. Their enemies included the Choctaw and the Caddo. In the early eighteenth century, the Chickasaws joined with the Cherokee to drive the Shawnees from the Cumberland Valley, but they often fought the Cherokee as well.

Raiding parties usually consisted of between 20 and 40 men, their faces painted for war. They engaged in ritual preparation before they departed as well as ritual celebration, which might include the bestowal of new war names, upon their return. Weapons included bows and (sometimes flaming) arrows, knives, clubs, spears, tomahawks, and shields. The party carried along a sacred war ark, or medicine bundle. Particularly respected warriors were tattooed, usually with the picture of an animal.

Contemporary Information

GOVERNMENT/RESERVATIONS Over 9,000 Chickasaws (mid-1990s) lived in a 13-county area in southern Oklahoma. Their headquarters is located in Ada, Oklahoma. Congress granted the right in 1970 to elect their own leadership. A 1983 constitution provides for a tripartite government, including a 13-member legislature. The Chickasaw Nation's land base, held in trust, is about 77,600 acres.

ECONOMY With a $15 million annual budget (1990), the Chickasaw Nation itself provides many employment opportunities. It owns recreational parks, tobacco shops, and bingo parlors. There is some industrial development. Payments are anticipated from the settlement of disputed control of resources under the Arkansas riverbed, but this situation is still being argued, and no settlement has been achieved. In the early 1990s, roughly 20 percent of Chickasaw families in Oklahoma were living below the poverty line.

LEGAL STATUS The Chickasaw Nation is a federally recognized tribal entity.

DAILY LIFE Most Chickasaws are Methodists or Baptists. About 500 mostly older people still speak the language, which is taught with the aid of a dictionary. Tribal celebrations, especially the annual festival in September/October, feature traditional foods such as cracked corn and pork, corn grits, and poke greens. There is a tribal museum and library, as well as a tribal newspaper, the *Chickasaw Times*. The Nation controls its own schools.

Chitimacha

Chitimacha (Chi ti `mä chä or Shi ti `mä shä) may have meant "those living on Grand River," "those who have pots," or "men altogether red." They may have comprised three or four separate tribes in the early sixteenth century.

LOCATION The Chitimacha traditionally lived along the lower Louisiana coast, especially around

Grand Lake, Grand River, and Bayou Teche. Today, most live in St. Mary Parish, Louisiana.

POPULATION   From about 3,000 people in 1700, the population dropped to 51 in the 1930 census. There were 720 enrolled members in the early 1990s.

LANGUAGE   Chitimacha may be an isolate, or it may be related to Tunican.

Historical Information

HISTORY   Resident in their historic area for at least 2,500 years, the Chitimacha may have migrated south from the region of Natchez at some early time and east from Texas still earlier. Their decline began with the French arrival in the late seventeenth century. French slaving among the Indians created a generally hostile climate between the two peoples, especially in the early eighteenth century. Peace was established in 1718, but by then the Chitimacha population had suffered great losses through warfare and disease. Survivors were forcibly relocated north or taken away as slaves.

The influx of French Acadians in the late eighteenth century led to intermarriage (with Acadians as well as with other surviving local Indian groups), further land thefts, and the increased influence of Catholicism. In 1917, the Indians' remaining land base was privately purchased and sold to the United States. Throughout the twentieth century, chiefs have continued to govern the people and struggle to retain tribal land and sovereignty.

RELIGION   Chitimachas recognized a sky god, possibly feminine in nature. Boys and girls sought and obtained guardian spirits through solitary quests. Priests oversaw religious life. A 12-foot-square temple on Grand Lake served as a center of religious activity, especially for the annual six-day midsummer festival. The main event here was the male adult initiation ceremony, during which the young men fasted and danced until exhausted.

GOVERNMENT   There was a chief in each town and a subchief in each village; leadership was largely hereditary. Head chiefs possessed a large measure of authority and power and were fed, at least in part, by others.

CUSTOMS   Among the different social classes, priests, headmen, and curers constituted a nobility. There may also have been clans. Women might obtain any religious or political position. The dead may have been laid on scaffolds, where special people (Buzzard Men) disposed of flesh and returned cleaned bones to families, where they were eventually buried under mounds of earth. The Buzzard Men may instead have burned the bones and buried the ashes in a basket under a mound. A special ceremony was conducted at the reburial of war chiefs' bones. The people played chunkey and other games. They practiced frontal head deformation. A man became known by his child's name as soon as the latter was born.

DWELLINGS   Village populations reached up to 500 in the early historic period. Pole-frame houses were covered with palmetto thatch. Smoke escaped through a hole in the roof. Walls were occasionally plastered with mud.

DIET   The people ate bear, alligators, turtles (and their eggs), and deer, among other animals. They were highly dependent on fish and shellfish. Women grew sweet potatoes as well as beans, squash, sunflowers, and possibly four varieties of corn. They also gathered water lily seeds, palmetto seeds, nuts, and various wild fruits and berries.

KEY TECHNOLOGY   Men used blowguns as well as bows and arrows for hunting. They caught fish with nets, basket traps, and hooks and lines. Cane baskets with fitted tops were used, among other things, for food storage. Women wove cane matting with various colors (red, yellow, and black) and designs, and they made pottery. The people also used the fire drill, dried alligator skin rasps, and gourd rattles.

TRADE   Exports included fish and salt; imports, mainly from inland tribes, included flint, stone beads, and arrow points. They traded often with the Atakapa and the Avoyel Indians.

NOTABLE ARTS   Patterned black-and-yellow cane baskets, made with a unique double weaving technique, were especially fine. Pottery was also of generally high quality.

TRANSPORTATION   Extensive canoe transportation was made easier by the natural harbor provided by Grand Lake.

DRESS   Nose ornaments, bracelets, and earrings were common personal adornments. Both sexes kept their fingernails long. Men wore their hair in roaches, or perhaps long, and decorated with feathers and lead weights.

WAR AND WEAPONS   The people may have poisoned their enemies. Warriors also used the bow and arrow. There were four or five war chiefs per village.

Contemporary Information

GOVERNMENT/RESERVATIONS   The Chitimacha Reservation (1830) consists of roughly 250 acres in St. Mary Parish, Louisiana. There were 212 resident Indians in 1990. The tribe operates its own housing program and is governed by a council.

ECONOMY   Tribal enterprises include a processing plant, a store, and a recreation/museum complex. They also lease land to oil companies. Most people work in the oil or fishing industries. Some people make cane baskets as well as traditional and generic "Indian" jewelry for the tourist trade.

LEGAL STATUS   The Chitimacha Tribe is a federally recognized tribal entity.

DAILY LIFE   The language no longer survives. There is a Bureau of Indian Affairs school in the reservation. Efforts continue to obtain compensation for land expropriations. The tribe supports ongoing training in traditional craft techniques. There is a tribal fair over the Fourth of July weekend.

Choctaw

Choctaw (`Chok tä or `Shok tä), originally Chahta. An early name for the tribe might have been *Pafallaya*, or "long hair." They were culturally related to the Chickasaws and Creeks. With the Cherokee, Chickasaw, Creek, and Seminole, they were regarded by whites as one of the Five Civilized Tribes.

LOCATION   In the sixteenth century, most Choctaws lived in southern and central Mississippi, as well as parts of Alabama, Georgia, and Louisiana. Today, most live in southeastern Oklahoma and east-central Mississippi.

POPULATION   There were probably between 15,000 and 20,000 Choctaws in the mid–sixteenth century. In 1984 almost 20,000 Choctaws lived in Oklahoma, and roughly 4,000 lived in Mississippi in 1990.

LANGUAGE   Choctaw is a Muskogean language.

Historical Information

HISTORY   Choctaws probably descended from Mississippian Temple Mound Builders. They may once have been united with the Chickasaw. Early encounters with the Spanish, starting with Hernando de Soto about 1540, were not peaceful, as de Soto generally burned Choctaw villages as he passed through the region.

The French established a presence in Choctaw territory in the late seventeenth century, and the two groups soon became important allies, although there was always a faction of Choctaws friendly to the British. Fighting along with the French and other Indian tribes, the Choctaws helped defeat the Natchez revolt of 1729. Bitter internal fighting around 1750 between French and British supporters was resolved generally in favor of the former.

Intertribal war continued with the Chickasaw and the Creek until in 1763 the French ceded all lands east of the Mississippi to Britain. Choctaws fought the Creeks even after that, until the United States took "possession" of greater "Louisiana" in the early nineteenth century. Small bands of Choctaws began settling in Louisiana in the late eighteenth century. At the same time, alcohol, supplied mainly by British traders, was taking a great toll on the people.

Largely under the influence of their leader, Push-mataha, the Choctaw refused to join the pan-Indian Tecumseh confederacy (*see* Shawnee [Chapter 8]). However, non-natives continued pushing into the Choctaws' territory. One strategy that non-natives used to gain Indian land was to encourage trade debt by offering unlimited credit. Under relentless pressure and threats, the Choctaw began ceding land in 1801. Although treaties usually called for an exchange of land, in practice the Indians seldom received the western land they were promised, in part because the United States traded land that was not the government's to give or that it had no intention of allowing the Indians to have.

By the 1820s, the Choctaw had adopted so many lifeways of the whites that the latter regarded them as a "civilized tribe." Nevertheless, and although the Choctaws had never fought the United States, President Andrew Jackson signed the Indian Removal Act of 1830, requiring the Choctaw and other southeast tribes to leave their homelands and relocate west of the Mississippi. A small minority of unrepresentative Choctaws signed the Treaty of Dancing Rabbit Creek, ceding all of their land in Mississippi, over 10 million acres. Articles in the treaty providing for Choctaws to remain in Mississippi were so full of loopholes that most of those who did so were ultimately dispossessed. At the same time, the state of Mississippi formally made the Indians subject to state laws, thus criminalizing tribal governments.

Removal of roughly 12,000 Choctaws took place between 1831 and 1834. Terrible conditions on this forced march of several hundred miles caused about a quarter of the Choctaws to die of fatigue, heartbreak, exposure, disease, and starvation. Many more died once they reached the Indian Territory (Oklahoma). Roughly 3,000–5,000 Choctaws escaped to the back country rather than join the removal. Many of these people were removed in the 1840s, but some remained. Although they continued living as squatters in a semitraditional manner, their condition declined. Officially illegal, they were plied with alcohol and relentlessly cheated, and they became disheartened.

The bulk of the people reestablished themselves out west and prospered in the years before the Civil War, with successful farms, missionary schools, and a constitutional government. Most Choctaws fought for the Confederacy; the war was a disaster for them and the other tribes. A relatively high percentage of Indians died in the war, and further relocations and dispossessions followed the fighting. After the war, the Choctaw paid for the removal of African Americans living on their territory, although most were eventually adopted into the tribe.

In the last two decades of the nineteenth century,

the General Allotment Act and the Curtis Act were passed over the opposition of the tribes. These laws deprived Oklahoma Indians, including the Choctaw, of most of their land. The "permanent" Indian Territory became the state of Oklahoma in 1907 (the name "Oklahoma," a Muskogean word for "Red People," was introduced by a Choctaw Indian), at which time the independent Choctaw Nation became subject to U.S. control. The tribe spent decades attempting to reassert control over its institutions.

After the Reconstruction period, the Mississippi and Louisiana Choctaws lived by sharecropping, subsistence hunting, some wage labor, and selling or bartering herbs and handicrafts. Their community and traditions were kept alive in part by the retention of their language and their rural isolation, both from Euro-Americans, who branded them nonwhite, and African Americans, with whom the Choctaw refused to identify.

The government finally recognized the Mississippi Choctaw in the early twentieth century, and the Bureau of Indian Affairs began providing services, such as schools and a hospital, during the 1920s and 1930s. It began purchasing land for them as well. Reservations were created in 1944, and the tribe adopted a constitution and by-laws in 1945. Educational and employment opportunities remained severely limited until the 1960s owing to the Mississippi's Jim Crow policies.

RELIGION Choctaws worshipped the sun and fire as well as a host of lesser deities and beings. They celebrated the Green Corn ceremony and other festivals, mainly in late summer and fall.

GOVERNMENT Three or four districts were each headed by a chief and a council. Also, each town had a lesser chief and a war chief. The power of these chiefs was relatively limited, and the Choctaw were among the most democratic of all southeastern Indians. Although there was no overall head chief, a national council did meet on occasion.

CUSTOMS The people placed a high priority on peace and harmony. Lacrosse, played with deerskin balls and raccoon-skin-thong stick nets, was a huge spectator sport as well as a means for settling disputes. Rituals and ceremonies began days before a game. There was always gambling; sometimes the stakes included a person's net worth. Players were assisted by shamans who tried to use spiritual power in the service of their team. Games could be quite dangerous, as they were played with few rules regarding physical contact. There were both male and female teams. The people also played chunkey and other games of chance.

Women adulterers were severely punished; some contributed to a class of prostitutes. Both men and women observed food taboos when a child was born. Infants' heads were generally shaped at birth. Maternal uncles taught and disciplined boys. At puberty, boys were tattooed, and some wore bear claws through their noses. Homosexuality was accepted.

Corpses were wrapped in skins and placed on a scaffold along with items the deceased might need, including food and drink, on the way to the land of the dead. Their skulls were painted red. A dog or, later, a pony might be killed to accompany the person in the afterlife. A ritual mourning or crying time took place at designated periods throughout the day. Paid mourners were also used. A person's house was burned and the possessions sold. After some one to six months, special bone pickers scraped the bones clean with long fingernails, disposed of any remaining flesh, and then placed the bones in a coffin that they returned to the family. Periodically, the people of each village buried their people's bones under mounds.

The tribe was organized into two divisions. Many people wrote music and poetry; new songs were often introduced at festivals. Names often referred to the weather. Healing techniques included bleeding and cupping. Both men and women used herbal and plant remedies to cure illness, many of which were quite effective. Doctors also chanted, danced, and used magical formulas.

DWELLINGS Perhaps 100 or more Choctaw villages (summer and winter) existed in the seventeenth century. Border towns, especially in the northeast, were generally fortified, whereas interior towns were more spread out. Towns, which were groups of villages and houses surrounded by farms, usually contained a public game/ceremonial area.

Men built pole-frame houses roofed with grass or cane-reed thatch and walled with a number of materials, including crushed shell, hide, bark (often pine or cypress), and matting. Doors may have faced south. Summer houses were oblong or oval with two smoke holes. The winter houses were circular and insulated with clay. Water poured over hot rocks provided steam for internal moisture.

DIET Choctaws farmed bottomland fields along the lower Mississippi. They often realized food surpluses. Women, with the assistance of men, grew corn, beans, squash, sunflowers, tobacco, and later potatoes and melon. Also, in the eighteenth century they grew leeks, garlic, cabbage, and other garden produce, the latter strictly for trade. Corn was also made into bread, as was sweet potato seed.

Large game, such as buffalo, deer, and bear (killed mainly for their fat), were particularly important when the harvest was poor. Men hunted deer with decoys and costumes. Small game included squirrel, turkey, beaver, otter, raccoon, opossum, and rabbit. Other foods included birds' eggs, fish, and wild fruits, nuts, seeds, and roots. Sassafras root was used for tea and as a thickener.

KEY TECHNOLOGY Fields were cleared using slash-and-burn technology. People fished using spears, nets, stunning poison, and buffalo-hide traps. They carved bows, mortars, and stools of wood; made skin-covered gourd and horn pouches; and wove bags from twisted tree bark. Women wove and dyed baskets. Spun buffalo wool was also used as a fabric. Cane, another important raw material, was used for such items as knives, blowguns, darts, and baskets. Musical instruments included drums of skins stretched over hollowed logs, rattles, and rasps.

TRADE Traders developed a regional trade language mixed with sign language for wide communication. They traded food, especially to the Chickasaw. In the eighteenth century this food included garden produce such as garlic, leeks, and cabbage; after the mid–eighteenth century it also included fowl and hogs. They imported soapstone pipes from the Minnesota quarries.

NOTABLE ARTS There were fine carvings on mortuary houses. Some of the dyed cane baskets were woven tight enough to hold water.

TRANSPORTATION The people used carved dugout canoes sparingly. Horses arrived as early as the sixteenth century. In time, the Choctaw and other tribes developed their own breeds.

DRESS Choctaws followed the general southeastern dress of deerskin breechclouts, skirts, and tunics and buffalo or bear robes and turkey-feather blankets for warmth. Some women made their skirts of spun buffalo wool plus a plant fiber. Both men and women wore long hair except, for men, in time of mourning. Both also tattooed their bodies.

WAR AND WEAPONS The Choctaw partook less of war than did many of their neighbors, although they did not shirk from defensive fighting. Above all, they did not value victory bought with many of their own dead. Weapons included bow and arrow, knives, clubs, hatchets, and shields. They fought the Chickasaw in the early historical period. Any captured property was divided completely among families who had lost warriors in that battle. Adult captives were regularly burned; others were enslaved. Men tattooed records of war feats on their bodies. Warriors celebrated pre- and postwar rituals.

Contemporary Information

GOVERNMENT/RESERVATIONS The Choctaw Nation is located in ten counties in Oklahoma. Their headquarters is in Durant, and their capital in Tuskahoma. The land base is roughly 145,000 acres.

The Mississippi Choctaw Reservation (17,819 acres, almost all tribally owned) was established in 1830. The Mississippi Band of Choctaw communities include Bogue Chitto, Bogue Homa, Conehatta, Pearl River, Redwater, Standing Pine, and Tucker, Mississippi. The reservation and trust lands are located in Attala, Jackson, Jones, Kemper, Leake, Neshoba, Newton, Scott, and Winston Counties. The band manages over 500 housing units. The 1990 Indian population was roughly 4,000 of an enrolled membership of roughly 8,000. The tribal government consists of an elected chief and council.

The Mowa Band of Choctaw Indians lives on roughly 300 acres in Mt. Vernon, Alabama. This community is governed by a tribal council.

ECONOMY Oklahoma Choctaws will share with the Cherokee a settlement regarding riverbed resources of the Arkansas River, but this situation is still being argued, and no settlement has been achieved. Other resources include bingo, a finishing company, a factory (Texas Instruments), a travel center, and a cattle ranch.

The Mississippi Band organized a private stock company in 1969 to oversee economic development. The main natural resource is timber. Its projects have included several construction projects and an industrial park. Profits are reinvested in new projects. Other businesses include wire harness, electronics, and several other companies as well as a resort and casino.

LEGAL STATUS The Choctaw Nation of Oklahoma, the Jena Band of Choctaw (Louisiana), and the Mississippi Band of Choctaws are federally recognized tribal entities.

The Choctaw-Apache Community of Ebard, Louisiana, has petitioned for federal recognition. It is governed by a tribal council and maintains an officially recognized Indian school. The Clifton Choctaw Indians in Louisiana and the Mowa Band of Choctaws in Alabama have also petitioned for federal recognition. The Washington City Band of Choctaw Indians of Southern Alabama was denied federal recognition in 1998.

DAILY LIFE In Oklahoma, most Choctaw children attend public school, although some attend Jones Academy, an Indian school. Most Oklahoma Choctaws are Baptists. The language survives, although mainly in hymns and dictionaries. The annual Labor Day festival features traditional foods, games, and dance. There is also a museum and a monthly newspaper, *Bishinik*.

The Mississippi Choctaws still play lacrosse. They also hold an annual fair. Many are Baptists. The language remains current, especially among older people. The tribe operates several schools, a small hospital, a radio station, and a monthly newspaper.

The Mowa Band of Choctaw Indians holds pow-wows and operates two schools.

Coushatta

See Alabama

Creek

Creek (Cr ē k), taken from Ochesee Creek, the British name for the Ocmulgee River. The so-called Creeks were actually composed of many tribes, each with a different name, the most powerful of which was called the Muskogee (or Mvskoke), itself a collection of tribes who probably migrated from the Northwest. With the Cherokee, Choctaw, Chickasaw, and Seminole, the Creeks became known by non-natives in the early nineteenth century as the Five Civilized Tribes.

The Creek Confederacy was a loose organization that united many Creek and non-Creek villages. Muskogee-speaking towns and tribes formed the core of the confederacy, although other groups joined as well. It was founded some time before 1540 but strengthened significantly in the seventeenth and eighteenth centuries. Tribes of the Creek Confederacy included the Alabama, Mikasuki, Yuchi, Shawnee, Natchez, Koasati, Tuskegee, Apalachicola, Okmulgee, Hitchiti, and Timucua, as well as many others. Through intermarriage or adoption, some of these people ultimately became part of Muskogee towns, whereas others, including escaped slaves and whites, lived among them as ethnic minorities.

LOCATION   Traditionally, Upper Creeks lived along the Coosa and Tallapoosa Rivers, in Alabama. Their two main towns were Tukabahchee and Abihkba. The Lower Creeks lived along the Flint and Chattahoochee Rivers in eastern Georgia and along the coast. Their main towns were Coweta and Kashita. Today, most Creeks live in east-central Oklahoma, with much smaller groups in Alabama and Florida.

POPULATION   There were perhaps 22,000 people in the Creek Confederacy in the mid–sixteenth century, of whom roughly 80 percent were Muskogeans. In 1990 there were about 30,000 enrolled Creeks, over half of whom lived in Oklahoma.

LANGUAGE   Creeks spoke two principal Muskogean languages.

Historical Information

HISTORY   Creek people probably descended from Mississippian Temple Mound Builders, entering their historic area from the west. Hernando de Soto passed through the region in 1540. In the colonial wars, Creeks were traditional allies of the British, although they were often successful in playing the European nations off against one another. Early on, the Creeks were grouped very informally into a "lower" section, located in eastern Georgia and more accommodating to Anglo society, and an "upper" section, more traditional and resistant to assimilation.

As British allies in the late seventeenth and early eighteenth centuries, the Creek fought the Spanish as well as other Indian tribes, such as the Apalachee, the Timucua, the Choctaw, and the Cherokee. They also absorbed some of the tribes they defeated in battle, such as part of the Apalachicola and the Apalachee about 1704. Creeks took part in the 1715 Yamasee war, as years of British abuse, including slaving, rape, and cheating, temporarily disrupted the Creek-British alliance. Following the Yamasee defeat, the bulk of the Creeks moved inland to the Chatta-hoochee River.

Creeks were more cautious about choosing sides in the French and Indian War and the American Revolution. Few favored the colonists, however, which was reason enough for the victors to demand land cessions after the fighting. In the late eighteenth century, the Creek leader Alexander McGillivray dominated the confederacy's diplomatic maneuvering and attempted to reorganize its political structure to his advantage. In 1790 he signed a treaty, later repudiated by the leaders of the confederacy, accepting U.S. protection and involvement in the people's internal affairs.

Many Creeks resisted joining Tecumseh's plan for a united Indian attack against the Americans, but in 1813 and 1814 they mounted their own military challenge. This was actually a civil war resulting from continuing diplomatic pressures and relentless encroachments from the Georgians as well as their own political and economic decline. The White Stick faction (mainly Lower Creeks) supported the United States and the Red Sticks the British. Despite early successes, the war was put down. As punishment, the Creeks, both Red and White, were made to sign the Treaty of Horseshoe Bend, ceding 23 million acres of land. Many Creeks migrated to Florida around that time to become part of the newly formed Seminole people.

In 1825, 13 chiefs ceded all remaining Creek lands to the state of Georgia. These chiefs were later condemned by their people for high treason, and two were shot. Although the treaty was illegal, the state of Georgia proceeded to act as if it owned the land, and the United States soon backed the state, calling for complete Indian removal. President Andrew Jackson signed the Indian Removal Act in 1830. Non-natives obtained the remaining Indian lands in the usual way: fraud, intimidation, and outright theft.

In 1832, Creeks signed the Treaty of Washington, ceding five million acres of land. Farcically, the treaty offered the Creeks a choice to remain or move and stated that white usurpers would be removed if the Indians chose to stay. In the mid-1830s, more Creeks joined the Seminoles in Florida while others made a last-ditch military stand. Forced relocation began in 1836. The Indians were taken to a place between the Canadian and the Arkansas Rivers. Of the roughly 14,000 who were relocated, almost 4,000 died of starvation, disease, exposure, and heartbreak during the march and shortly after their arrival in Indian Territory.

Once there, the people began to rebuild, accepting missionary schools and reestablishing towns, fields, and government. Christianization proceeded rapidly after removal. In 1856 the Creek lost over two million acres along the Canadian River to the Seminoles. Although the Creeks split in their allegiance during the Civil War, they suffered with the other Five Civilized Tribes, which had largely supported the South, and lost land, goods, crops, and political power.

The 1867 constitution of the Muskogee Nation reaffirmed the sovereignty of tribal towns and provided for a democratic governmental structure. Following the war, a full-blood, pronorthern, traditional faction that took a hard line on land cessions emerged, as did a moderate Muskogee Party and a number of other parties. Creeks also pressed for intertribal cooperation among Oklahoma tribes. Their land base was gradually whittled away until they lost all of it in 1907, as well as their political independence, when Oklahoma became a state.

From 1907 until 1970, the federal government recognized only the Creek Nation, an entity of the accommodationist Lower Creeks. Its principal chiefs were appointed by the U.S. government. Around 1900, an Upper Creek named Chitto Harjo (Crazy Snake) led a rebellion against allotment, the process that gave tribal holdings to individuals and made the "surplus" available for non-native purchase. In 1917, the Upper Creeks again took up arms as part of the Green Corn Rebellion, a movement of African Americans, Indians, and whites dedicated to obtaining federal help for the rural poor.

In the 1930s, three tribal towns, including the Alabama-Quassartes, opted out of the Creek Confederacy to accept charters under the Indian Reorganization Act. Many people left the Creek communities for cities during and after World War II. By 1970, 95 percent of preallotment tribal land was owned by non-natives, and non-natives held petroleum leases worth $50 billion. In 1970, a new law allowing for the democratic election of the principal chief gave rise to the Creek Nation of Oklahoma.

RELIGION The Green Corn ceremony, also called the Busk, marked the new year. It was both a thanksgiving ceremony and one of renewal. Some participants drank a black drink that was mainly caffeine and that induced vomiting when consumed in quantity; it was designed to purify the body. The ceremony also included dancing, fasting, feasting, games, and contests. It ended with a communal bath and an address from the head chief. Most crimes were forgiven at that time. Other ceremonies in spring and early summer included "stomp dances." Another group of feasts culminated in the late fall Dance of the Ancient People. Most dances were both social and ceremonial, and most councils and ceremonies began with the black drink (or "white drink," as they called it, reflecting its role in purification).

The supreme being, "master of breath," presided over the Land of the Blessed Dead. It received an offering of the first buck killed each season and also a morsel of flesh at each meal. Its representative on earth was the Busk fire. There were also many spiritual beings, particularly dwarfs, fairies, and giants. Priests and doctors underwent a rigorous training period that included healing techniques, songs, and formulas. Numerous diviners, weather control experts, and religious advisers claimed religious identity as well.

GOVERNMENT Tribal towns (talwas) were the main political unit. Each contained about 100 to over 1,000 people, and each was politically sovereign, the alliance among them determining the nature of the confederacy. Towns chiefs (mikos) were largely chosen by merit, although membership in a white clan was an advantage. The power of the chiefs was to influence (and to carry out certain duties), not to command. They were head of the democratic council, which had ceremonial and diplomatic responsibilities. Decisions were taken by consensus. There was also a subchief and a war chief. A town crier announced governmental decisions to the people.

The council met daily in the square ground or the town house. The people drank "black drink" and smoked tobacco before each important council meeting. Part of the council was a group of elders known as the Beloved Men. There were also Beloved Women, although women generally did not have formal power. Another council, composed of white clan members, oversaw internal public works affairs.

CUSTOMS A dual division within most tribes manifested itself in the existence of red towns and white towns. Red was associated with war, and white with peace. There were also about 40 matrilineal clans, unequal in prestige, with animal names. Clans were the fundamental social unit.

Lacrosse games were played between towns of different divisions, in part to relieve tensions. The many pregame ceremonies included preparations administered by medicine men. The goals were up to a quarter-mile apart; 60 or so people played on a side. Games were quite wide open and rough. They also had significant political and ritualistic significance. A great deal of personal wealth was often bet on games. In addition to games, people participated in archery and other contests.

Unmarried women had considerable sexual freedom. There was also a class of prostitutes. Men could marry more than one wife. Marriage was formalized by gift giving, repeatedly in the case of multiple wives. Divorce was unusual, especially if there were children. Both parties were killed or punished in cases of adultery, unless they could escape punishment until the next Busk. Rape, incest, and witchcraft were capital offenses, as was nonseclusion during a woman's periods. Infanticide was permitted within the first month of life. Widows or divorcées were obligated to remain single for four years, but a widower could remarry in four months. Men generally avoided their mothers-in-law out of deference.

People bathed before eating. Women made pottery, baskets, mats, and other such items; prepared food and skins; made clothing; helped with the communal fields; and grew all the garden crops. Men also helped with the communal fields, and they hunted, fished, fought, played ball games, led ceremonies, built houses and other structures, and made tools. Men also carried skin pouches containing medicines, tobacco, and knives that hung by their sides. The dead were buried with their possessions beneath houses, in a sitting position and with reddened hair. Only the worthy could made it to the land of the dead, located beyond the Milky Way. Strict mourning rites were observed.

DWELLINGS Fifty towns, each with between 30 and 100 houses and located on river or creek banks, formed the original core of the confederacy. Each town was organized around a central square or plaza, which contained several features: a circular town (or hot) house at least 200 feet around, with 12-foot walls, a 12-foot roof, no windows, a small smoke hole, and beds around the walls; a game field; and a summer ceremonial house, or square ground.

The square ground was actually four sheds around a square of one-half acre or so, in the center of which was the sacred fire. The single-story buildings were about 30 feet long and roughly 25 feet high; they had clay walls and a gabled bark roof. Walls came within about 2 feet of the roof, for circulation, and the front was left open. Some of the sheds were divided into compartments, and they also had tiered benches or beds. Supporting timbers were often painted or carved with human and animal designs.

In cold or bad weather, the council met in the hot house, around a spiral-shaped or circular fire, and ceremonies were also celebrated here. In summer the square ground served these purposes. Both the hot house and the square ground were built atop mounds prior to the eighteenth century.

Private homes were clustered in groups of up to four. They were pole framed with plastered walls and grass or mats on the outside. Gabled roofs were covered with bark or shingles. Each reasonably prosperous family had a winter house and a summer house, both generally rectangular. A third structure was a two-story granary, one end of which was used for storing grain and roots (lower) and for meetings (upper). The other end, with open sides, was a general storage area (lower) and a reception area (upper). A fourth building, if one could afford it, was a storehouse for skins. The four buildings were placed to form a square, after the ceremonial square ground design.

DIET Crops—corn, beans, and squash—were the staples. Corn was consumed in many, perhaps over 40, different ways. The people had both private gardens and communal fields. Women gathered persimmons, nuts, sweet potatoes, wild rice, acorns, and grapes, among other foods. Nut oil was used in food preparation. Hunting was important for meat and skins. Most men left the villages during winter to hunt. Women often accompanied the hunting parties, mostly to attend to the meat and skins along the way. The people also ate fish.

KEY TECHNOLOGY Hoes and digging sticks were the most important agricultural tools. Animals were shot, trapped, and snared. People fished with hook and lines, spears, bow and arrows, weirs, hand nets, baskets, and narcotic roots. Women made coiled pottery, wove mats, and spun material for clothing.

Other important technologies included the fire drill, steatite (soapstone) pipes and pots, flint points, and wooden and horn utensils. Bows were generally made of hickory, and arrows were pointed with fish bones and flint. Blowguns, 8–10 feet long, were used mostly for shooting small animals and birds. Musical instruments included drums, flutes, and tortoise-shell ankle rattles. Bead belts may have served as records of events. Baskets and other items were made of cane.

TRADE Creeks utilized the Choctaw trade language. Some groups exported flint and salt. Their pipes came from the Cherokee and Natchez, and/or they traded for catlinite pipes from the early eighteenth century on. In the early contact period, Creeks traded horses (obtained from Apalachee Indians) to British Carolinians for guns and other goods.

NOTABLE ARTS People in some towns carved figures of a nonreligious significance, perhaps to honor a dead warrior. A pictographic system represented historical events. Women made pottery, glazed with smoky pitch, and cane and hickory splint baskets.

TRANSPORTATION Men made large cypress dugout canoes. Some early chiefs may have been carried on litters. Creek horses came from Mexico and the Spanish southeast; Lower Creeks had no horses until the eighteenth century.

DRESS Creeks generally made a greater use of leggings than did many nearby peoples. Except on the Georgia coast, where they used tree moss, women made their clothes largely from skins and textiles. They also roached their hair. Only prostitutes painted their faces. Women sewed clothing with a bone awl and sinew thread. Skirts that reached below the knee were tied around the waist.

Men wore breechclouts and often leggings. Some young men wore nose ornaments and enlarged their ears with copper wire. Many men shaved their heads, except for two thin strips of hair running from temple to temple and straight down the top of the head. The hair at the ends was allowed to grow long. Some men wore moustaches. There were turkey feather cloaks for ceremonial purposes.

Both sexes wore buffalo- and deer-hide moccasins as well as extensive tattoos. Boys often went naked until puberty. Rank was reflected in clothing and adornment.

WAR AND WEAPONS There were three levels of warriors: war chiefs, big warriors, and little warriors, depending on their level of accomplishment. Most fighting took place in spring. The purpose was generally honor and revenge. Men painted their bodies black and red for war. In addition to their weapons, they brought blankets, cordage, leather for moccasin repair, corn, and the sacred ark with them. Weapons included bow and arrow, knife, tomahawk, war club, spear, and shield. There were a number of pre- and postwar rituals.

A successful war party left signs to indicate who had done the deeds. Parties that resulted in the loss of many men, no matter how successful otherwise (captured horses, war honors, and so on) were considered failures. Enemies were often scalped and dismembered; those remaining alive might be enslaved or whipped and otherwise tortured by the women, unless they could escape. Enemies in the historic period included the Apalachee, Cherokee, and Choctaw.

Contemporary Information

GOVERNMENT/RESERVATIONS Headquarters for the Creek Nation of Oklahoma is in Okmulgee, Oklahoma. The land base encompasses roughly 143,384 acres, all held in trust, in eight counties of northeast Oklahoma.

The Kialegee Creek Tribal Town is located in Wetumka, Oklahoma.

The Thlopthlocco Creek Tribal Town is located in Okemah, Oklahoma.

The Alabama-Quassarte Tribal Town is located in Henryetta, Oklahoma.

The Poarch Band Reservation is located near Atmore, in Elmore and Escambia Counties, Alabama. Established in 1984, it consists of 213 acres. Its total population was roughly 1,875 people in the early 1990s, although the 1990 Indian population was just 149.

ECONOMY Individuals may apply for funds for various emergencies and pressing needs. Most jobs are with the tribal government, farms, and bingo halls.

LEGAL STATUS The Creek Nation of Oklahoma, the Poarch Band, the Kialegee Tribal Town of the Creek Nation, the Thlopthlocco Tribal Town of the Creek Nation, and the Alabama-Quassarte Tribal Town (*see* Alabama) are federally recognized tribal entities.

Unrecognized Creek communities include the Principal Creek Indian Nation East of the Mississippi, in Florala, Alabama; the Lower Muskogee Creek Tribe East of the Mississippi, Inc., in Cairo, Georgia; the Creeks East of the Mississippi, in Molino, Florida; the MaChis Lower Alabama Creek Indian Tribe, in New Brockton, Alabama; the North Bay Clan of Lower Creek Muskogee Tribe, in Lynn Haven, Florida; the Star Clan of Muskogee Creek Tribe of Pike County, in Goshen, Alabama; and the Florida Tribe of East Creek Indians, in Bruce, Florida.

DAILY LIFE Several former tribal towns (*talwas*), now rural communities, retain some centuries-old traditions. The annual cycle of native activities revolves around a traditional stomp ground. Other activities include a rodeo and an annual festival. Facilities include an excellent health care complex, over a thousand new homes, a museum, and a library.

From his 1971 election as principal chief into the 1990s, Claude Cox, a Methodist church leader, created a political party with a base of Lower Creeks that has dominated the Creek Nation and led it into a quasi-alliance with the Republican Party. The mainly Upper Creek opposition held that the Creek Nation was illegal under the 1867 constitution, but the dominant faction simply rewrote the constitution; the new document was adopted in 1979. Members of both groups sit in the National Council.

There is little trace of aboriginal culture among the Poarch Band. They receive federal grants for education, health care, and economic development. Their

Thanksgiving powwow is based mainly on Plains Indian traditions.

Houma

Houma (`Ū mä), or Ouma. The word means "red" in Choctaw and Chickasaw, but it may have been a shortened form of Chakchiuma, a tribe from whom they probably descended. It may also be an abbreviation of their tribal symbol, *sakti homma,* or "red crawfish." Many Houma prefer simply the word "Indian" as a self-designation.

LOCATION In the late seventeenth century, Houmas lived on the east side of the Mississippi River, opposite the mouth of the Red River. Today, most live in the southeastern Louisiana marshes.

POPULATION There were perhaps 1,000 Houmas in 1650 and between 600 and 700 around 1700. There were about 11,000 enrolled members in the early 1990s.

LANGUAGE Houma is a Muskogean language.

Historical Information

HISTORY Shortly after they made their initial alliance with the French, in 1686, more than half the tribe was killed by disease. Catholic missionaries began operating among the Indians after 1700. The Tunica Indians, to whom the Houma had given permission to settle in the area in 1706, soon killed more than half of their hosts. The survivors moved south after the massacre.

In 1718, shortly after the conclusion of the Chitimacha war, the Houma joined some Chitimachas and members of other tribes and migrated south again, to the vicinity of New Orleans, and then north again to present-day Ascension parish. After the Natchez defeat at the hands of the French, Houmas, who aided the Indian refugees, were in their turn attacked by French forces; hundreds were captured and sold as slaves in New Orleans.

By the early eighteenth century the Houma had begun a process of absorbing some smaller, neighboring tribes, such as the Acolapissa, Bayogoula, Biloxi, and Chitimacha. Beginning some time in the early nineteenth century, the people still in Ascension parish moved south and settled on the Gulf Coast (present-day Lafourche and Terrebonne parishes). Other portions of the tribe intermarried with the Atakapa and moved to their territory or migrated to Oklahoma or to the north, toward their original homeland, and became lost to history.

The Houma remained generally isolated well into the twentieth century. In the 1930s, oil speculators began taking advantage of the Indians' illiteracy and lack of understanding in order to obtain their land. In response, local Indian leaders pushed their people to learn English. Still, most Houmas did not attend school until after World War II. Schools in the area were desegregated in the 1960s. Centuries of intermarriage thoroughly integrated Catholicism and the French language into Houma identity.

RELIGION Temples were fronted with carved wooden figures. There may also have been earthen images of deities inside. The people probably worshiped a number of gods, in particular the sun, thunder, and fire. Young people may have sought guardian spirits through quests.

GOVERNMENT Houma head chiefs, if they existed at all, were less powerful than the Natchez Suns. Women were known to have served as war chiefs.

CUSTOMS Corpses were placed on scaffolds. After a certain period of time, special workers cleaned the bones and placed them in a chest, in which they were subsequently buried. The people played chunkey and other games. They practiced head flattening, which they probably learned from the Natchez when the Houma migrated south.

DWELLINGS Each town may have had over 100 cabins, possibly arrayed in a circle. Houses were square, pole-frame structures, from 15 to more than 30 feet on a side, and with walls of adobe and Spanish moss. They were covered with cane matting inside and out and then by grass thatch without. Doors were less than 4 feet high. There were no smoke holes.

DIET Traditionally horticulturists, the Houma grew corn and other crops. They also collected shrimp and other marine food as well as a variety of wild plant food, and they ate muskrat and other small game.

KEY TECHNOLOGY Palmetto was used in the manufacture of baskets, mats, and other items. Hunters used a two-piece blowgun. Musical instruments included clay-pot drums with skins stretched over the top.

TRADE The Caddo were significant trade partners. Marine food was an important export. The people probably imported flint and bow wood. They may also have traded in salt and bird feathers.

NOTABLE ARTS Houmas carved wooden satyrs and animals, some in relief, and painted in black, white, red, and yellow on their temple vestibules.

TRANSPORTATION The primary method of transportation was by pirogue, or hollowed-out canoe.

DRESS Men wore deerskin cloaks or went naked. Some men and women wore turkey-feather or woven muskrat-skin mantles. They may also have worn skin leggings and moccasins and possibly bearskin blankets in winter. Girls, from about eight to ten years of age until marriage or the loss of their virginity, may have worn a waist-to-ankle–length mulberry thread netting garment, fringed and ornamented. Their clothing may have been colored red and/or yellow and/or white. Most men wore their hair long.

WAR AND WEAPONS Allies included the Okelousa, and enemies included the Bayogoula, at least in the late seventeenth century. The Houma fought with bows and arrows, knives, and clubs.

Contemporary Information

GOVERNMENT/RESERVATIONS Most Houmas live in Terrebonne and Lafourche parishes, Louisiana, and particularly in the Dulac–Grand Caillou and Golden Meadow communities. They are governed through an elected tribal council. There is no tribal land base.

ECONOMY Fishing, trapping, and hunting are still important. People also work in nearby oil fields. The people have been unable legally to substantiate their claims to oil-rich land.

LEGAL STATUS The United Houma Nation, Inc. (1979), was denied federal recognition in 1998.

DAILY LIFE Few Houma Indians interacted with their non-native neighbors until after the 1960s. Around that time, traditional shrimping and muskrat trapping were being undermined, by technologically advanced competition in the former case and by competition and ecological problems in the latter. Despite intermarriage with both whites and African Americans, and although the three races live and work in close proximity, there remains some racially based tension among them and within the Indian community.

Ongoing traditional palmetto crafts include baskets, mats, dolls, and fans. Kinship patterns also remain as do healing and other cultural traditions. Healers often use native methods combined with Christian prayers. French is the first language, with English second. Only a few words still exist of Houma, which was probably in sharp decline in the middle of the last century. The lack of a land base, among other things, has worked against community cohesion.

Lumbee

Lumbee (`Lum b ē), a historical Indian tribe whose ancestors were Indians of indeterminate tribal affiliations, Anglos, and African Americans. The name is taken from the Lumber (formerly Lumbee) River.

LOCATION From colonial times to the present, Lumbee Indians have lived in and near Robeson County, in southeastern North Carolina, and also in several counties in northeastern South Carolina. This region was formerly characterized by extensive marshland. There are also Lumbee communities in Baltimore, Philadelphia, and Detroit.

POPULATION In the mid-1990s there were about 48,000 members of the Lumbee Indian tribe.

LANGUAGE The Lumbee have always spoken English.

Historical Information

HISTORY Lumbee Indians have lived in North Carolina since at least the mid–eighteenth century. Their origins are obscure. They are probably descended from Cheraw Indians and other local Siouan speakers. Their ancestors may also include British settlers from the "lost" colony of Roanoke, Virginia (1587), who may have joined Hatteras Indians living on Croatoan Sound. There are at least 20 surnames of Roanoke colonists among contemporary Lumbees. Their ancestors may also include Cherokee, Tuscarora, and Croatoan Indians.

The marshy character of the Lumber and Pee Dee River area made it a likely haven for refugees of all sorts. Lumbee Indians, free frontier farmers, were first encountered by British and Scots settlers in the early eighteenth century. At that time they had no Indian traditions or customs, although their skin color was suggestive of an Indian origin. They maintained little contact with Anglo settlers, most of whom were more interested in the better and more accessible land farther west.

In the 1760s, the Lumbee experienced increasing competition with Highland Scots settlers. Land incursions were resisted where possible, but Lumbees soon lost much land to the Scots and to the tidewater planters, often by fraudulent means. The state of North Carolina formally disenfranchised them, along with other "persons of color," in 1835.

During the Civil War, Lumbees were conscripted into service as forced labor; when they resisted they were attacked by soldiers. Lumbee resistance to this oppression was led by Henry Berry Lowry (or Lowerie), who led raids on plantations to feed the poor of all races. Lowry kept up his campaign for justice even after the war, taking on as well the Republican (Reconstruction) Party, which sided with the Democrats and branded Lowry's organization as bandits. He eluded capture at least until his disappearance in 1872.

The Lumbees pressed their claim for state and federal recognition after war's end, but with the defeat of the multicultural Lowry movement, their identity turned more inward. They accepted a status as a third racial caste, with more rights than African Americans but not as many as whites. In 1885 the North Carolina General Assembly recognized them as "Croatoan Indians" and allowed them to operate their own schools, segregated from whites but apart from African Americans. A normal (teacher training) school was also opened, which later became a college and, around 1970, Pembroke State University. In 1911 the North Carolina legislature dubbed them "Robeson County Indians." This was changed to "Cherokee Indians of Robeson County" until protests by the Cherokees forced a withdrawal of that name. The people filed an unsuccessful request for federal recognition as the Siouan Tribes of the Lumber River.

Most Lumbees continued farming until after World War II. They were recognized by the state of North Carolina as Lumbee Indians in 1953. Partial federal recognition came in 1956, although the tribe was prohibited from receiving federal benefits. In 1958, thousands of Lumbees stood up to the Ku Klux Klan and drove them from Robeson County. They lost control of their school system in the 1960s. The tribe formed the Lumbee River Regional Development Association, a nonprofit corporation, in 1968.

Contemporary Information

GOVERNMENT/RESERVATIONS The Lumbee River Regional Development Association is located in Robeson County, North Carolina. Fourteen elected directors represent nine county districts. The directors elect their officers.

ECONOMY Lumbees are integrated into the local economy at all levels.

LEGAL STATUS Lumbees have been federally acknowledged since 1956, but they are not fully recognized by the Bureau of Indian Affairs (BIA) and do not receive most federal services. The Lumbee Regional Development Association, Inc., has been determined to be ineligible to petition for official BIA recognition. The Lumbee Indians have been recognized by the state of North Carolina since 1953.

DAILY LIFE Lumbees have held important political offices, including that of mayor, in Pembroke. Kinship networks help the people maintain a Native American identity. Most Robeson County Lumbees belong to all-Indian Protestant churches. The annual homecoming and parade in July bring thousands of people together from all over the country. Local schools (students and teachers) are mostly Lumbee. There is a community newspaper. As members of the Eastern Seaboard Coalition of Native Americans, the Lumbees (and other un- or incompletely recognized tribes) attempt to obtain some BIA benefits.

Miccosukee
See Seminole

Muskogee
See Creek

Natchez

Natchez (`Nat ches), an extinct tribe that had a marked similarity to Mississippian Mound Builder culture in the early historic period. They were the largest, most powerful tribe on the Mississippi in the mid–sixteenth century.

LOCATION The early historic location of the Natchez was along St. Catherine's Creek, near present-day Natchez, Mississippi. Their lands were fertile but protected against chronic flooding.

POPULATION The Natchez population was about 4,000 to 4,500 in 1650 and 300 in 1731.

LANGUAGE Natchezean languages may have been related to the Muskogean language family, with possible Tunican influences.

Historical Information

HISTORY With other Muskogean people, the Natchez may have come to their historical territory from the northwest. The Natchez had clear cultural ties to the Mississippian Mound Builder civilization, which may in turn have been influenced by Mesoamerican Indian cultures.

Contact with the Hernando de Soto party in 1542 was likely casual and not particularly friendly. French explorers entered the region in the later seventeenth century, and Catholic missionaries soon followed. The little nation soon divided its loyalties between France and Britain. By 1715 it was raiding nearby Indians such as the Chawasha in the service of British slave traders.

The Natchez population was greatly reduced by wars with the French beginning in 1716. The final conflict began when a governor of Louisiana moved to take over the site of the Natchez Great Village. In late 1729, partly at British instigation, Natchez warriors sacked Fort Rosalie and other French settlements, killing and capturing hundreds of people. The Yazoo Indians soon joined in, but the Choctaw sided with the French. In 1731 the French achieved a decisive victory. They killed many people and sold even more (including the last Great Sun) into slavery. Some people managed to escape to local tribes, especially to the Chickasaw and also to the Creek and Cherokee.

Three to five Natchez towns continued among the Creek into the nineteenth century. After removal to Oklahoma, Natchez descendants formed communities in the eastern part of the reservation. By about 1900, intermarriage had ended a distinct Natchez identity. The Natchez held their last formal ceremony in 1976; the last native speaker died in 1965. Some traces of Natchez ceremony and culture remain among various groups, such as the Muskogee Creeks of the Arbeka Stomp

Grounds and the Cherokee Red Bird Smith Ceremonial Ground.

RELIGION The sun was the supreme deity. Its son was said to be responsible for Natchez culture, and its authority was continued in the sun caste. The people also recognized many minor servant spirits. Natchez society was a theocracy. An absolute monarch called the Great Sun wore a crown of red-tasseled swan feathers. Sitting on a throne of goose feathers and furs high on a mound, he directed some ceremonies and guided the sun every morning.

A ceremonial center in the main village included a partitioned, rectangular sun temple and the house of the Great Sun, each built on mounds of adobe and covered with woven mats. A fire, tended by a select group of eight people, always burned within the temple, and the roof was decorated with three carved and painted birds. The door faced east. Other villages had smaller ceremonial centers as well.

The Natchez also offered human sacrifices, especially upon the death of a chief. They observed the Great Corn ceremony, which corresponded to the Creek Busk, in mid to late summer. Most ceremonies were led by the Great Sun and/or other suns. There was also a priesthood, whose members shaved their heads. Doctors acquired supernatural powers by fasting for nine days in a cabin while shaking a gourd rattle. Failure to cure or to correctly foretell the weather might be met with death. Curing consisted of sweating, bleeding, dancing, singing, and evoking spirits of plants or animals. There were also many plant medicines. Curers were usually old men, but women might be herbalists.

GOVERNMENT The Great Sun was a hereditary monarch. Although his power was absolute, it was tempered in part by his personal abilities as well as by his respect for the opinions of the council.

CUSTOMS The Natchez recognized two social classes, nobles and commoners. The former included the king, or Great Sun; the king's brothers and uncles (little suns), from whom were chosen the war chief and head priest; hereditary nobles; and honored men and women, a status obtainable by merit. Commoners (or Stinkards) farmed, built the mounds, and did most of the manual labor. They gave food and other presents to the suns, and the Great Sun redistributed some of it.

There were elaborate deferential codes of behavior and speech between the classes. Members of the higher classes, even the Great Sun, were required to marry commoners. The offspring of a male of high rank and a commoner were a step below the man's rank, but the offspring of a highly ranked woman and a male commoner kept the mother's rank.

When a person of high rank died, his or her com-moner spouse, if there was one, and several servants were killed for companions in the afterlife. Much ritual attended the deaths of nobility. Dead suns were placed in the temple, their bones preserved and later buried nearby. Dead nobles were dried on platforms; commoners were buried in the earth or placed on a scaffold and enclosed in a plaster vault, to which food and water were periodically brought. Houses of the dead were burned. The afterlife destination was based on earthly conduct: There was a paradise of equality and freedom from want and a hell full of mosquitoes.

Women enjoyed a high degree of sexual license before marriage, although fidelity after marriage was the norm, and divorce was rare. Men occasionally lent their wives to other men. Women generally married around age 25. The Natchez practiced infant head flattening. Babies nursed until they stopped voluntarily or the mother became pregnant. Children's bodies were rubbed with bear oil, in part to keep off flies. Older male relatives were responsible for boys' discipline and education. People older than three bathed at least daily.

Men engaged in generally cooperative work, such as hunting, fishing, cultivating the sacred fields, fighting, playing games, dressing skins, building houses, and making canoes and weapons. They were fed before women and generally enjoyed a higher status. Women prepared food; kept the fires going; made pottery, baskets, mats, clothing, and beadwork; and tended crops. Much of their work was performed alone. Berdaches assumed women's economic as well as sexual roles.

As part of the Great Corn ceremony, men played a hand ball game with as many as 1,000 or more players, the object of which was to keep the ball from touching the ground. They also played chunkey and staged an occasional deer surround for sporting or diversionary purposes. Women played dice or split cane games. There were also contests and many games of chance.

DWELLINGS Nine villages were scattered among woods and fields. Low, windowless square adobe houses with domed, thatched roofs over cane matting were built in rows around a central plaza. Platform beds stood along the walls. There were no smoke holes.

DIET Diet was agriculture based. Men and women grew corn as well as pumpkins and beans and also melons and peaches in the historic period. They made corn into at least 42 different dishes, including gruel (hominy) and bread. Sowing and harvesting were highly ritualistic activities. The people also grew a particular grain-bearing grass as well as tobacco.

Women gathered wild rice, nuts, berries, grapes, mushrooms, and persimmons; the latter were made into bread. Men hunted deer, turkey, and buffalo as well as a host of other game. They stalked deer with deer head disguises and went on communal buffalo hunts in the fall. Hibernating bears were routed with fire shot into their hollows. Bear fat oil was an important seasoning. The people also ate duck, other fowl, fish, and shellfish. Fish and meat were preserved by smoking and cooking. The people may have eaten dog on ceremonial occasions.

KEY TECHNOLOGY Wooden items, carved and/or hollowed by fire, included mortars, stools, and bowls. Bows were fashioned of black locust wood, their strings of sinew and tree bark. Arrow tips were fire hardened or made of bone. Men used cane spears, perhaps with flint tips, for hunting large game. Many other items were made of cane as well. Fish were netted or harpooned. Women made pottery, mats, and baskets. Curved hickory sticks as well as buffalo shoulder blades became hoes. Bead belts recorded certain significant information, such as the line of Great Suns. Food was stored in pottery or gourd containers.

TRADE Natchez Indians participated in local trading. Among other items, they obtained salt from Caddo tribes to the northwest.

NOTABLE ARTS Women made incised pottery, dyed cane baskets and mats, and white fabric from the inner bark of mulberry trees. They also wove baskets and nets. Men carved and painted religious figures, such as birds and rattlesnakes. They also made pipes from a black stone, especially in the later eighteenth century.

TRANSPORTATION Men burned logs to fashion dugout canoes, some up to 40 feet long. Travelers used cane rafts to cross bodies of water. Women transported goods using bearskin shoulder straps or tumplines. Chiefs and high nobles were carried on litters.

DRESS Clothing and personal adornment indicated differences in rank. Most clothing was made of mulberry tree inner bark fabric and/or deerskin. Women wore a knee-length skirt. Men wore a deerskin breechclout. Both wore high, laced moccasins, a long deerskin shirt, and leggings in colder weather. Other winter wear included buffalo robes and feather mantles. Girls remained naked until about age 10, when they wore a two-piece tasseled mulberry net apron. When they were no longer virgins, the garment was replaced with the standard skirt. Boys remained naked until puberty, when they donned the buckskin breechclout.

Both sexes painted and tattooed faces and bodies. Women also blackened their teeth with tobacco and ash and wore spike-shaped earrings. Warriors were tattooed from head to foot; they slit the lower part of their ears and decorated them with wire. Some men roached their hair and some wore it long, at least on one side. Women wore their hair long, tied in a queue with mulberry netting and tassels. Belts and garters were made of spun and woven buffalo and opossum hair. The Great Sun wore a crown of feathers in a beaded cap. Children, depending on their social rank, wore shell and pearl ornaments.

WAR AND WEAPONS The Natchez recognized three classes of warriors, and war was seen a means of social advancement. Most war parties were led by the head war chief. Warriors wore breechclouts, belts, and ear pendants and carried rattles. Weapons included war clubs, bows and arrows with garfish points, axes, and sometimes shields. There were various prewar rituals, including drinking an emetic, feasting on dog meat, dancing and relating war stories, and planting the war post. Warriors carried fetishes of war spirits with them. Male captives were generally scalped and burned alive, whereas women were kept as slaves.

Pamunkey

See Powhatan

Powhatan

Powhatan (`Pow u `tan or Pow `ha t ə n), "falls in a current of water," part of a group of Algonquian speakers from North Carolina to New Jersey known as Renápe ("human beings") or Lenápe in the L dialect. The Powhatan tribes (Renápe of Virginia) were culturally intermediate between the southeast and northeast regions.

Powhatan was also the main tribe and village of the roughly 30-tribe Powhatan Confederacy. Other prominent tribes included the Pamunkey, Chickahominy, and Mattaponi.

LOCATION Powhatans traditionally lived in the Chesapeake Bay region of present-day Virginia. Today, most live in the Delaware Valley of Pennsylvania and New Jersey as well as in Oklahoma and Canada.

POPULATION The confederacy numbered between 9,000 and 14,000 people in the early seventeenth century. That number had declined to about 500 in 1705. Today, about 600 people claim membership in the Powhatan-Renápe Nation. There were roughly 450 Pamunkeys in the early 1990s.

LANGUAGE Powhatan Indians spoke an Algonquian language.

Historical Information

HISTORY Aside from a short-lived Spanish mission in 1570, the British were the first European power in the region. By 1607, Chief Wahunsonacock (known to early British colonists as Powhatan) had expanded the confederacy by conquest from 6 or 8 tribes to more than 30. Shortly after the establishment of the Jamestown colony in 1607, the settlers began wide-scale cultivation of tobacco to sell in Europe. Because tobacco rapidly depletes the soil, the British constantly needed more land and did not shrink from obtaining it by fraud and trickery from the Indians.

According to legend, Pocahontas, daughter of Chief Wahunsonacock, intervened with her father to save the life of the leader of the Jamestown colonists, Captain John Smith. Smith was among a group captured in part because of Wahunsonacock's anger at the colonists' land grabbing and released after Wahunsonacock was crowned king in a British-style ceremony. Meanwhile, the colonists had captured Pocahontas and held her as surety against the other prisoners' release. During her captivity she converted to Christianity and married a settler, inaugurating a period of peace between the two groups. Pocahontas traveled to Britain and died there in 1617, and Wahunsonacock died shortly thereafter.

In 1622, the Powhatans determined to break the cycle of land thefts. Now led by Opechancanough, Wahunsonacock's brother, they organized a revolt that killed almost 350 colonists and destroyed all settlements except Jamestown. In response, the colonial militia began a push to sweep the Indians farther inland. At one point, the British attacked a group of Indians who had come to attend a peace council. After years of bitter fighting, during which the Powhatans lost many people, peace was restored in 1636, but Opechancanough organized another revolt in 1644, at which time he may have been over 100 years old. Over 500 colonists died during this campaign. After Opechancanough was captured and shot in 1644, his people were forced out of Virginia or placed on reservations, and the confederacy came to an end.

Powhatan people were attacked by whites in 1675 after being falsely accused of depredations; the following year the whites massacred a large number of Powhatan men, women, and children living at a fort near Richmond. By this time, most Powhatan people and towns had disappeared. The people lost several of their reservations in the early eighteenth century. In 1722, Iroquois Indians agreed to stop attacking the Powhatans. Beginning in the 1770s, surviving Powhatans began migrating north to New Jersey, a movement that accelerated during and after the Civil War.

Pamunkey and Mattaponi reservations of about 800 and 1,000 acres, respectively, remained in 1800. The reservations existed as a result of treaties signed with colonial governments. In 1831, most surviving Powhatans, many of whom had intermarried with African Americans, were chased away by whites in the aftermath of the Nat Turner slave rebellion. Few Powhatan Indians fought in the Civil War; those that did mainly did so on the Union side.

Following the Civil War, Virginia's Indians fought successfully for a social—and legal—status higher than that of African Americans; the result was a three-way segregation system. This negotiation affected their legal identity as Indians. For instance, during World War I, Pamunkey and Mattaponi Indians protested the fact that they were drafted, since they were not citizens. The courts ruled in their favor. Having made their legal point, many proceeded to enlist.

Prior to World War II, many Pamunkeys continued to live by fishing, hunting, and trapping. Also during that time, attention paid to Virginia Indians by anthropologists stimulated a renewal of their ethnic identity and political organization, although this soon provoked a fierce white backlash. Powhatans began a community in the Philadelphia-Camden area, maintaining their native identity in part through a close network of families. They frequently intermarried with Nanticokes of Delaware and members of other tribes. Formal organization began in the 1930s, culminating in the emergence of the Powhatan Indians of the Delaware Valley in the 1960s and the Powhatan-Renápe Nation in the 1970s.

RELIGION The chief deity was known as Okee. There were carved images of various kings and deities in the temples, as well as carved idols, dressed in various clothing and ornaments. There were at least one priest and temple in every village. Priests as well as conjurers were considered holy men. Chiefs had their own, private temples. Constructed like the houses, and partitioned with mats, these were used for worship as well as for burials of kings and for storehouses.

Priests made sacrifices of meat and tobacco at outdoor stone altars. Two or three children may have been sacrificed annually to propitiate the gods. There were regular communal ceremonies, including singing and dance, especially in times of triumph or crisis and at the harvest. Common people were thought to have no afterlife, but chiefs and priests were said to inhabit a western paradise until they were born again.

GOVERNMENT Each town, or kingdom, was led by a chief, or king. Sometimes, when kings controlled more than one town, a regent did the king's bidding in his absence and paid him tribute. Chiefly descent was mainly matrilineal. Chiefs regularly poisoned their rivals.

The Powhatan Confederacy was an alliance of

about 30 tribes (200 villages) at its peak in the early seventeenth century. Wahunsonacock, at least, was an absolute authority and inflicted torture or death at will. He also took a high tribute or tax from the people and was well guarded around the clock.

CUSTOMS Children were bathed daily in cold water for strengthening. Also for this purpose, various concoctions were rubbed into their skin. Furthermore, male children may have been beaten as part of a general toughening ceremony. Some of these young men may have been killed, perhaps as a sacrifice to the gods, while others were cast out into the wilderness for nine months, afterward to become priests or conjurers.

Men provided animal food, conducted ceremonies, fought, and probably made tools and weapons as well as houses and canoes. Women (except upper-class women) prepared food; grew and harvested crops; dressed skins; made mats, baskets, pots, and (perhaps) mortars; and carried burdens. As a rule, men and women did not eat together. Murder, certain thefts, and adultery were capital crimes. Goods and food were stored in holes in the ground. Doctors could cure certain wounds quite well. Sweating cured some sicknesses.

Corpses of commoners were wrapped in mats and buried in the ground, following which women wailed for a full day. Dead chiefs were ornamented with necklaces of beads and pearls. Baskets containing their valuables were placed at their feet. They were then wrapped in mats and placed on a scaffold. There was a period of public mourning, followed by a feast. Later, their bones were collected, hung from their houses, and buried with the remains of the houses when the latter fell apart or were destroyed.

Men had many wives; Wahunsonacock is said to have had over 100. Men announced their intentions by bringing the women a quantity of fresh food. After her family received presents and promises of more to come, the women was brought to the man for a small wedding ceremony, followed by a feast. Once she had a baby, the king's wife was given a quantity of goods and dismissed, after which she was free to marry someone else; the child was taken from her and raised in the king's household.

DWELLINGS Villages, often palisaded in the early seventeenth century, were usually located along a river. There were between 2 and about 100 houses and between 50 and 500 families per village/kingdom. Houses were constructed by bending and tying off saplings and then covering them with bark or woven mats. Roofs were rounded, with a smoke hole over the central fire. There were generally two mat doors that may have faced east. Beds, with skin covers, were placed along the walls.

Houses were generally built under trees. They may have had windows. Some elongated houses may have reached more than 100 feet in length, but most were much smaller. Several families lived in each house. There may also have been a combination raised storage/drying area under which men congregated.

DIET Fish and shellfish constituted a major part of the diet. Agriculture was somewhat less intensive than in other parts of the southeast. Women grew corn (three varieties), beans, and squash in fields of up to 200 acres. Corn was roasted or boiled and eaten fresh or pounded into cornmeal cakes. The people also gathered acorns and other nuts, fruits, and berries. Some nuts and fruits were dried and stored for winter. A milky drink was made from walnuts. Men hunted deer, beaver, opossums, otters, squirrels, and turkeys, among other animals. Meat was broiled on a spit or boiled. The people also ate birds' eggs.

KEY TECHNOLOGY Men hunted using bows and arrows, spears, clubs, snares, and rings of fire. They speared and netted fish from their canoes; nets came from tree bark or grass woven with sinew. Digging sticks and hoes were the main farming tools. Women pounded grain in wooden mortars. Pottery, baskets, and mats were used for many purposes. Reeds and shells were fashioned into razors. Men carved pots and platters from wood. Musical instruments included rattles, drums, and reed flutes. Pipes were of both clay and stone. The people also built wooden bridges over creeks.

TRADE Powhatans traded dried oysters for various furs and skins, deer fat cakes, vegetables, and possibly buffalo-horn spoons.

NOTABLE ARTS The main arts were basketry, beadwork, and pottery as well as ceremonial clothing woven from turkey feathers. Men carved religious images from wood.

TRANSPORTATION Dugout canoes were up to 50 feet long.

DRESS Women made the clothing, mostly from skins. Married women wore hairstyles that were different—longer in front—than those of unmarried women. They may have worn flowers and feathers in their hair. Men wore their hair long on the left side. They also wore earrings of bone and pearl as well as animal parts. Both sexes painted their bodies, particularly black, yellow, and red. The chief priests wore turkey feather cloaks and snake and weasel skin headdresses. Priests, but not common men, may have worn beards.

WAR AND WEAPONS Weapons included tomahawks, bows and arrows, clubs, and shields. Priests had the final say about making war. The war chief and soldiers were generally appointed. The purpose of warfare was generally for revenge and to capture women and children; men were killed, often after torture. Women prepared the warriors' hair with bear grease and special ornamentation, and they painted their faces. War parties left signs marking their presence and deeds.

Contemporary Information

GOVERNMENT/RESERVATIONS The Pamunkey State Reservation, located in King William County, Virginia, was established in 1658. It consists of about 1,200 acres and was home to about 30 families in the mid-1990s. The 1990 Indian population was 35. Other Pamunkeys live in nearby cities and towns and in New York, New Jersey, and Pennsylvania. Government consists of an all-male seven-member tribal council, six non-Indian appointed trustees, and several committees. There is also a Pamunkey Indian Baptist Church governing board.

The Mattaponi State Reservation, King William County, Virginia, was established in 1658 and consists of 150 acres. There were 65 Indian residents in 1990.

A group of Chickahominy Indians lives along the Chickahominy River in New Kent and Charles Counties, Virginia.

The Powhatan-Renápe Nation is a group of about 600 Chickahominys, Eastern Chickahominys, Mattaponis, Pamunkeys, Nansemonds, Nanticokes, Upper Mattaponis, and Rappahannocks living in the Delaware Valley of New Jersey and Pennsylvania. The Nation acquired a 350-acre reservation (the Rankokus Reservation) in 1981 from the state of New Jersey.

ECONOMY Pamunkeys and Powhatan-Renápes are fully integrated into the regional economy.

LEGAL STATUS The Powhatan-Renápe Nation is a state-recognized, nonprofit tribal entity. The Pamunkey Nation is recognized by the state of Virginia. The Eastern Chickahominy Indian Tribe, the Chickahominy Indian Tribe, and the Nansemond Indian Tribal Association are state-recognized tribal entities. The Upper Mattaponi Indian Tribe is recognized by the state of Virginia and has petitioned for federal recognition. The United Rappahannock Tribe and the Nanticoke Lenni-Lenápe Indians of New Jersey are state recognized and have petitioned for federal recognition.

DAILY LIFE Facilities on the Powhatan-Renápe Nation Reservation include an education center, conference center, art gallery, nature center, museum, and reconstructed traditional village. The people hold various crafts, language, and traditional culture classes. There is also an annual arts festival.

As mandated in the 1677 treaty on which their reservation is based, the Pamunkey continue every fall to deliver a quantity of fresh game to the Virginia legislature. This tribe won a land claim settlement in 1979; other cases are pending. The Pamunkey Indian museum, completed in 1979, forms the core of the people's efforts to preserve their traditions. The Pamunkey Pottery Guild has helped revitalize pottery traditions and market the product.

Although many or most Powhatans resemble their non-native neighbors in looks and lifestyle, there is still an awareness of the key role of their Indian identity. The nature of this identity remains for many a matter of very personal negotiation. The Chickahominy hold a fall festival in September.

Renápe
See Powhatan

Seminole

Seminole (`Se mi n ō l) means "pioneer," or "runaway," possibly from the Spanish *cimarrón,* "wild." The Seminoles, known as such by 1775, formed in the eighteenth century from members of other Indian peoples, mainly Creeks, but also Oconee, Yamasee, and others. Their traditional culture was similar to that of the Creeks. The Creek, Choctaw, Chickasaw, and Cherokee, and Seminole were known by non-natives in the nineteenth century as the Five Civilized Tribes.

Until 1962, the Miccosukee Indians were part of the Seminoles. According to their traditions, they were descended from Chiaha Indians. The name Miccosukee means "Red Person."

LOCATION Located in north Florida in the early eighteenth century, the Seminole and Miccosukee were forced southward into the swamps, and west to Oklahoma, from the mid–nineteenth century on.

POPULATION From a population of perhaps 1,500 in 1800, the tribe grew to about 5,000 in 1821. Roughly 400 Miccosukees and 2,000 Florida Seminoles were enrolled in the early 1990s. There were also roughly 10,500 Oklahoma Seminoles in 1991.

LANGUAGE Seminoles spoke two mutually unintelligible Muskogean languages: Hitchiti, spoken by Oconee Indians and today mostly by Miccosukees, and Muskogee.

Historical Information

HISTORY Apalachee and Timucua Indians were the original inhabitants of north Florida. By about 1700, most had been killed by disease and raids by more northerly tribes. Non-Muskogee Oconee Indians from south Georgia, who moved south during the early eighteenth century, formed the kernel of the Seminole people. They were joined by Yamasee refugees from the Carolina Yamasee war, 1715–1716, as well as by some Apalachicola, Calusa, Hitchiti, and

Chiaha Indians, and escaped slaves. The Chiaha were known by the late eighteenth century as Miccosukee. Several small Muskogean groups joined the nascent Seminoles in the late eighteenth century.

Seminoles considered themselves Creek; they supported Creeks in war and often attended their councils. They experienced considerable population growth after the 1814 Creek war, mainly from Muskogeans from Upper Creek towns. From this time on the dominant language among the Seminoles was Muskogee, or Creek. However, Seminole settlements, mainly between the Apalachicola and the Suwannee Rivers, were too scattered to permit the reestablishment of Creek towns and clan structures.

Prior to the Civil War some Seminoles owned slaves, but the slaves' obligations were minimal, and Seminoles welcomed escaped slaves into their communities. Until 1821, U.S. slaves might flee across an international boundary to Florida. Even after that year, the region remained a haven for escaped slaves because of the presence of free African American and mixed African American and Seminole communities.

Seminoles first organized to fight the United States in 1817–1818. The conflict was begun by state militias chasing runaway slaves and resulted in the Spanish cession of Florida. Southern whites feared the possibility of an African American–Indian military alliance, and they were aware of the numbers of escaped slaves living in the area. Despite the best U.S. efforts, which included burning villages and other such tactics, the Seminole did not fall.

In the Treaty of Moultrie Creek (1823), the Seminole traded their north Florida land for a reservation in central Florida. The 1832 Treaty of Payne's Landing, which was signed by unrepresentative chiefs and was not supported by most Seminoles, called for the tribe to relocate west to Indian Territory. By 1838, up to 1,500 Seminoles had been rounded up and penned in concentration camps. These people were forcibly marched west, during which time as many as 1,000 died from disease, starvation, fatigue, heartbreak, and attacks from whites. Although under pressure to do so, the Seminole consistently refused to give up the considerable number of African Americans among them. In 1856, the western Seminole were given a strip of land of about two million acres west of the Creeks.

Resistance to relocation and to white slave-capturing raids led to the second Seminole war of 1835–1842. Under Osceola, Jumper, and other leaders, the Seminole waged a guerrilla war against the United States, retreating deep into the southern swamps. Although Osceola was captured (at a peace conference) and soon died in captivity, and although at war's end most Seminoles, about 4,500 people,

were forced into Indian Territory, the Seminole were not militarily defeated. The war ended because the United States decided not to spend more than the $30 million it had already spent or to lose more than the 1,500 soldiers that had already been killed.

Most of the several hundred remaining Seminoles were either Cow Creek Indians (Muskogees) or Big Cypress Indians (Miccosukees).

A third Seminole war took place from 1855 to 1858. From their redoubt in the Everglades, the Indians attacked non-native surveyors and settlers. The army, through its own attacks and by bringing in some Oklahoma Seminoles, succeeded in persuading another 100 or so Seminoles to relocate, but about 300 remained, undefeated, in Florida. There was never a formal peace treaty.

In the 1870s, as the first non-natives began moving south of Lake Okeechobee, there was another call for Seminole removal, but the government decided against an attempt. In the late nineteenth century, a great demand for Seminole trade items led to close relationships being formed between Florida Indians and non-native traders.

Western Seminoles settled in present-day Seminole County, Oklahoma, in 1866. By the 1890s the people had formed 14 bands, including two composed of freedmen, or Black Seminoles. Each band was self-governing and had representation on the tribal council. Most of the western Seminole reservation, almost 350,000 acres, was allotted in the early twentieth century. Through fraud and other questionable and illegal means, non-natives by 1920 had acquired about 80 percent of the land originally deeded to Indians. Tribal governments were unilaterally dissolved when Oklahoma became a state in 1907. An oil field opened on Seminole land in 1923, but few Indians benefited. Many Oklahoma Seminoles moved away from the community during and after World War II in search of jobs.

Indian Baptists from Oklahoma achieved the first large-scale successes in Christianizing Florida Seminoles in the early twentieth century. Most Florida Seminoles lived by subsistence hunting, trapping, and fishing, as well as by trading, until non-natives overhunted and out-trapped the region. Around the time of World War I, the subsistence economy disintegrated even further as Florida began to drain the swamps and promote agriculture. By the 1920s, the new land boom, in conjunction with the drainage projects, led to significant Indian impoverishment and displacement.

Most Seminoles relocated to reservations during the 1930s and 1940s. There they quickly acculturated, adopting cattle herding, wage labor, schools, and Christianity. With the help of Florida's congressional delegation, the tribe avoided termination in the 1950s. At that time they adopted an Indian Reorganization Act–style corporate charter. Formal federal recognition came in 1957. By the 1950s, a group of more traditional Mikasuki-speaking Indians, mostly living deep in the Everglades, moved to separate themselves from the Seminole, whom they regarded as having largely renounced their Indian traditions. After a great deal of struggle, the Miccosukees were given official permission by the federal government to form their own government, the Miccosukee Tribe, which they did in 1962.

RELIGION The Seminoles considered themselves children of the sun. They observed the Green Corn ceremony as early as May or June. This ritual helped to unify the tribe after the wars. It began with the presentation of buckskin-wrapped medicine bundles, which contained items such as crystals, ginseng, horn, and white deer hair, all individually wrapped in buckskin. Medicine bundles were considered central to the identity of the people.

Seminoles believed that a person's soul exited the body when he or she slept. Illness occurred when the soul failed to return, in which case a priest was called to coax the soul back.

GOVERNMENT Before the wars, Seminole towns had chiefs and councils of elders. Afterward, there were three bands, based on language (two Miccosukee and one Creek). Each had its own chief and council of elders.

CUSTOMS Matrilineal clans helped provide cultural continuity among widely scattered bands after the wars. There was also a dual division among the people. Particularly after 1817, the Seminole lived in small extended families. Oklahoma Seminoles retained more of traditional Creek social and religious structures, such as the *talwas,* or band/towns, than did the Florida people. Lacrosse and other Creek games played a similar social and ceremonial role. Snakes were not killed out of fear of their spirits. Bloodletting through scratching was thought to alleviate illness or troublesome behavior.

DWELLINGS Owing to a fairly mobile and decentralized existence, early towns were much less organized than were those of the Creeks. For example, there were no chunkey yards and only a vague public square. People living in these towns generally owned a longhouse, divided by mats into a kitchen, dining area, and sleeping area, and another, smaller house of two stories, similar to the Creek granary.

People in south Florida built their villages on hammocks and near rivers. Houses, or chickees, had pole foundations of palmetto trunks and palmetto-thatched roofs, platforms raised about three feet off the ground, and open walls. The thatch was water-tight and could resist very strong winds. A small attic provided storage space. Cotton cloths were occasionally suspended around sleeping areas for privacy and insect protection. Utensils hung from the poles or from stakes driven in the ground. One cook hut sufficed for the village; fires burned in it continuously, and women cooked for everyone.

DIET Women grew corn, beans, squash, and also tobacco. They made hominy and flour from corn and "coontie" from certain roots. They also grew such non-native crops as sweet potatoes, bananas, peanuts, lemons, melons, and oranges. The fields often were on different hammocks, up to a day's journey distant from their homes. They also gathered wild rice; cabbage palmetto; various roots and wild foods, such as persimmon, plum, honey, and sugarcane; and nuts, such as hickory and acorns.

Men hunted alligator, bear, opossum, rabbit, squirrel, wild fowl, manatee, and turkeys (using calls for the turkeys). The people ate fish, turtles, and shellfish. Turtles were often roasted alive over a fire. Favorite dishes included *sofkee* (corn soup) and boiled hominy with wood ash (for flavor). From the beginning they traded with non-natives for coffee and other items.

KEY TECHNOLOGY Spears were used to kill fish and alligators. Baskets, such as winnowing baskets, were fashioned of palmetto and cane. Many items were made from the palmetto tree, such as house frames and platforms from the trunk and roof thatch and beds from the leaves. Arrows of cane and wood were tipped with iron, 4- to 6-foot bows were made from mulberry or other woods, and deer rawhide was used for bowstrings. Before matches, fire was kindled with flint and steel on a bit of gunpowder and tinder. The people also had drums, flutes, and rattles.

TRADE Traditional trade items included alligator hides, otter pelts, bird plumes, and foods. Bird plumes and alligator hides in particular were very much in demand in the late nineteenth century. The people imported firearms, canned foods, clothing, cloth, and hand-operated sewing machines.

NOTABLE ARTS Seminoles were known for their patchwork clothing and baskets. Their geometric designs were often in the pattern of a snake. Ribbon appliqué, previously consisting mainly of bands of triangles along borders, became much more elaborate during the later nineteenth century.

TRANSPORTATION Men built fire-hollowed cypress dugout canoes, often poled from a stern platform. Canoes were relatively flat to accommodate the shallow, still water of the swamps. Some had sails, for journeys on Lake Okeechobee and even to the Bahamas. Their horses may have been of Mexican origin. The Seminoles eventually developed their own breed.

DRESS Women made patchwork clothing beginning around 1900. It consisted of colorful pieces of material sewed into strips that were in turn sewn into garments. Some clothing was made of tanned deerskin as well. Women wore short shirts and long skirts, both generally of cloth. In cool weather they added a cotton shawl. They also wore as many as 200 bead necklaces around the neck.

Men, especially among the Miccosukee, wore turbans made of wrapped shawls. Some had silver bands with bird feathers in them. Other clothing included shirts, neckerchiefs, breechclouts, and, occasionally, buckskin moccasins. Belts held up pockets containing hunting items and supported a long knife. Young children generally went naked, with older children wearing shirts (boys) and skirts (girls). Both sexes wore ornaments of silver and other metals and painted their faces and upper bodies.

WAR AND WEAPONS There was no intertribal warfare: Seminoles fought only with the U.S. Army and local non-native settlers. Quartz crystals were thought to ward off bullets and to bring success in warfare, hunting, and other pursuits.

Contemporary Information

GOVERNMENT/RESERVATIONS The Seminole Tribe of Florida elects a tribal council with representation from all reservations. It also elects a board of directors to supervise business affairs.

Big Cypress Reservation (Seminole) is located in Broward and Hendry Counties, Florida. It consists of 42,700 acres. The 1990 Indian population was 447.

Brighton Reservation (Seminole) is located in Glades County, Florida. It consists of 35,805 acres. The 1990 Indian population was 402.

Hollywood (formerly Dania) Reservation (Seminole) is located in Broward County, Florida. It consists of 480 acres. The 1990 Indian population was 481.

Miccosukee Reservation (Miccosukee) is located in Broward and Dade Counties, Florida. It consists of 333 acres. The 1990 Indian population was 94. Leadership is elected but is traditionally dominated by certain families and clans.

The Florida State Reservation (Miccosukee and Seminole) is located in Broward County, Florida. It consists of 104,000 acres; there are no residents.

There is also a Seminole community in Tampa, Florida.

Most Oklahoma Seminoles live in Seminole County, Oklahoma. Tribal headquarters is located near Wewoka. Other tribal buildings are south of Seminole, Oklahoma. Roughly 35,000 acres remain in Seminole hands. A new 1970 constitution calls for an elected chief, an assistant chief, and a tribal council that represents all 14 bands.

ECONOMY The large Florida reservations, Big Cypress and Brighton, are home to large cattle and farming (citrus) enterprises. Other important economic activities include tourism (sales of patchwork clothing, baskets, and other crafts), small business, and forestry. The Florida Seminole also have hunting and fishing rights on the Florida State Reservation.

The Seminole Tribe of Florida, Inc., oversees tribal business activity, such as tax-free cigarette sales and high-stakes bingo. These two activities provide the bulk of tribal income and fund various services as well as a per capita dividend. Miccosukee enterprises include a restaurant/service station, cultural center, and bingo hall and casino.

In Oklahoma, unemployment is chronically high. There are some jobs in the oil industry, retail, small business, and agriculture.

LEGAL STATUS The Seminole Tribe of Florida, including each of the four constituent reservations, and the Seminole Nation of Oklahoma are federally recognized tribal entities. The Oklewaha Band of Seminole Indians (Florida) has petitioned for federal recognition.

DAILY LIFE Most Florida Seminoles continue to speak Mikasuki and Muskogee, or Creek, whereas most Miccosukees speak Mikasuki. The Miccosukees live in modern housing about 40 miles west of Miami or in suburban Miami. They offer classes, provide health and recreation services, and have their own police and court system. The tribe controls about 200,000 acres of wetlands. It also holds an annual arts festival. The people were relatively traditional as late as the 1950s, but today's Miccosukees wonder if the allure of Miami and modern society will destroy the old ways forever. The severe pollution and reduction in area of the Everglades has significantly impacted the Miccosukees' and Seminoles' traditional life.

Seminole reservations feature recreation facilities and community centers. Almost all Seminoles live in modern housing. The Hollywood Reservation contains a re-created traditional village, and ceremonials are held there in mid-July. Most children attend public school; there is also a tribal elementary school at Big Cypress. Clan and kinship structures remain in place, although traditional knowledge is in danger of being lost.

After years of internal disputes regarding the allocation of a $16 million land claims victory in 1976, the Oklahoma Seminole decided on a compromise in 1990. Hitchiti is no longer spoken in Oklahoma, but many Oklahoma Seminoles speak Muskogee. Although most Oklahoma Seminoles are Christians, most also retain many traditional cultural and religious practices and, except for jobs and schools, remain apart from non-native life. There are three stomp grounds; these, plus several located among the Creek, serve as the focus of traditional religious activities, especially the Green Corn Dance. The clan structure has been severely weakened, although band descent remains matrilineal.

Tunica

Tunica (`T ū ni kä), "Those Who Are the People." They were culturally similar to the Yazoo.

LOCATION The people lived anciently in northwestern Mississippi and Arkansas as far as the Washita River. By the later seventeenth century they had migrated to the Lower Yazoo River in present-day Mississippi. Today, most live in Avoyelles Parish, Louisiana.

POPULATION From about 2,000 in the late seventeenth century, their population declined to no more than 30 in 1800. There were 430 members of the Tunica-Biloxi tribe in the early 1990s.

LANGUAGE Tunica was one of several Tunican languages.

Historical Information

HISTORY Tunicas had ancient links to southern Hopewell culture. Hernando de Soto came through their territory in 1541. Around 1700, the French claimed the lower Mississippi area, at which time Jesuit missionaries established a presence. The Tunica became loyal French allies, in part to counter pro-British Chickasaw slave traders.

Out of fear of the Chickasaw and other tribes, the Tunica moved south to a Houma town, opposite the mouth of the Red River, around 1705. Despite being given a friendly reception, after several years they killed most of their hosts and forced the others to move away. The Tunica were important French allies in the 1729 Natchez war and fought the Yazoo and several other tribes in 1731.

The Tunica fought the British as part of the Pontiac uprising when the French lost political control of the region in 1763. For years after that event, the Tunicas attempted to maintain a delicate diplomatic balance between the European powers. They sided with Spain and the colonies in the American Revolution. Their existence and their rights ignored, at best, by the U.S. government, the Tunicas dispersed in the later eighteenth century, moving up the Red River to the Avoyelles prairie. Others joined the Atakapa, and still others joined the Choctaws in Indian Territory.

The tribe hired a lawyer to protect its interests in the early nineteenth century. Still, ignoring federal law, the United States denied the Tunicas long-established title to their land. The Indians lived in relative harmony with their neighbors, however, until their chief was murdered in 1841 for resisting the theft of tribal land. In a state trial, centering on the land dispute, the Indians were formally awarded some of their own land, which became the basis of their reservation.

The Tunica continued to hunt, farm, fish, and practice traditional healing and religion into the twentieth century. They merged with the Biloxi, a small Siouan tribe, in the 1920s. Participation in several court cases in the early twentieth century underscored the need for literacy and formal recognition. Faced with a severely diminished population, one chief proposed in the 1940s to sell all tribal lands and move the people to Texas, for which he was removed from office. The last chief died in 1976.

RELIGION Tunicas worshiped the sun, among other deities. They celebrated the Green Corn feast. Clay figures stood inside thatched temples built atop mounds. They may have engaged in sacrificial killing.

GOVERNMENT Chiefs were relatively authoritarian, although not at the level of the Natchez.

CUSTOMS Men planted, harvested, and dressed skins. Women made pottery, clothing, and mulberry tree–bark fabric. The people buried their dead in the ground with their heads facing east. A four-day fasting and mourning period followed the funeral, after which participants bathed in the river. Cemeteries were located on hills and were guarded. The custom of infant head deformation was probably acquired in the late prehistoric period. If personally witnessed, adultery was severely punished. The Tunica played stickball and enjoyed various dances.

DWELLINGS Villages were located on the Mississippi floodplain in the mid–sixteenth century but on the bluffs overlooking the floodplain in the late seventeenth century. At least in the early eighteenth century, towns were laid out in a circle. Thatched houses were partly square and partly round and contained no smoke holes. Granaries, possibly square, were built on posts. A square chief's cabin was decorated with carved wooden images.

DIET The Tunica economy was based on agriculture. Men and women grew corn as well as pumpkins and beans. They integrated crops such as melons and peaches after contact with non-natives. Corn was made into at least 42 different dishes, including gruel (hominy) and bread. The people also grew a particular grain-bearing grass.

Women gathered wild rice, berries, fruits, grapes, mushrooms, and nuts. In season, persimmon bread was a staple food item for at least a month. Deer, turkey, and buffalo were the most important animal foods. Men stalked deer with deer head disguises and went on communal buffalo hunts in fall. They used fire to rout hibernating bears out of their hollows. Bear fat oil was an important seasoning. Other foods included ducks and other fowl, fish, and possibly dogs.

KEY TECHNOLOGY Cloth fabric woven from mulberry bark was used in a number of items. Women also made pottery and pine straw baskets. Men hollowed logs for mortars and cut saplings for pestles.

TRADE Tunicas mined and boiled down salt from licks to trade with other tribes, particularly the Quapaw and Taensa.

NOTABLE ARTS The people made very fine pottery as well as well-dressed skins.

TRANSPORTATION Carved dugout canoes enabled the people to move around the many rivers and lakes.

DRESS Most clothing was made from deerskins. Men wore breechclouts, and women wore a wrapped waist-to-knee skirt made from deerskin or mulberry cloth. Mantles or cloaks were made from turkey feathers or muskrat skins. Girls wore a two-piece tasseled mulberry-net apron, like those of the Natchez. Most men wore their hair long. Women blackened their teeth. Both sexes tattooed their bodies.

WAR AND WEAPONS Traditional enemies included the Chickasaw, Alabama, and Houma. War parties visited the temple before they departed and after they returned. Weapons included the bow and arrow, club, and knife.

Contemporary Information

GOVERNMENT/RESERVATIONS The Tunica-Biloxi Reservation is located in Avoyelles Parish, near Marksville, Louisiana. It consists of 130 acres and had 16 resident Indians in 1990. There is an elected tribal council.

ECONOMY The tribe operates a housing authority and owns a cattle herd and a pecan-processing plant. It is developing a program to facilitate crafts training and marketing.

LEGAL STATUS Since the 1980s, the Tunica-Biloxi tribe has been a federally recognized tribal entity.

DAILY LIFE The Tunica language is no longer spoken. The people continue to celebrate the New Corn ceremony. They also hold a parallel, secular festival around the same time, which features craft sales, dancing, and ball play. Tribal leaders are active in local and national Indian affairs. There is a tribal museum.

Tuscarora

Tuscarora (Tu sku ˋr ō r ə), from *Skaroo'ren,* "hemp gatherers," their self-designation and possibly the name of one of the constituent tribes or villages. *See also* Oneida (Chapter 8).

LOCATION In the sixteenth century, the Tus-carora were living near Cape Hattaras on the Roanoake, Neuse, Tar, and Pamlico Rivers, in North Carolina. The people migrated to New York in the early eighteenth century.

POPULATION There were about 5,000 Tuscaroras in 1500. In the early 1990s there were roughly 1,400 enrolled members living in New York, of a total of around 3,000 in the United States, as well as an additional 1,200 living in Canada.

LANGUAGE Tuscaroras spoke an Iroquoian language that changed markedly following the northward migration.

Historical Information

HISTORY The Tuscarora people came originally from the north, perhaps around the St. Lawrence Valley–Great Lakes region. They may have moved southward as late as around 1400. In the sixteenth century, and for some time thereafter, they were the dominant tribe in eastern North Carolina, despite losing upward of 80 percent of their population to European diseases during the seventeenth and early eighteenth centuries. Their somewhat inland location kept them from extensive contact with non-native settlers until the mid–seventeenth century.

Tuscaroras were traditionally friendly to the British settlers, even to the point of helping them fight other Indians. Active involvement in the deerskin, rum, and slave trade led to a growing factionalism within the tribe, which was most intense in villages closest to trade centers. Involvement with rum also contributed significantly to a general decline of the people. Throughout the seventeenth and into the eighteenth century, non-natives regularly took advantage of Indian generosity, taking their best lands, cheating them in trade, and stealing their children for slaves.

War between the two groups broke out in 1711. It was largely a reaction to years of British abuse and to continuing population loss due to disease. Led by Chief Hancock, the Indians raided settlements and killed perhaps 200 British, who took their revenge as they could. Some Tuscarora villages remained neutral because of especially pro-British contact and sympathies; the "neutral" and "hostile" camps each had their Indian allies from other tribes. Freed African Americans played a significant role in construction of European-style forts among the Indians.

The conflict soon became a general war, with some tribes, such as the Coree and Pamlico, fighting with the Tuscaroras and others, mainly Algonquians, fighting with the Carolina militias. In 1713, as a result of a betrayal by Tuscarora leader Tom Blount, Carolina soldiers killed or captured almost 1,000 Tuscaroras. Many of the captives were sold into slavery.

Most survivors migrated to New York to live among their Iroquoian-speaking relatives. Those who did not join the initial exodus lived for some additional years on the Susquehannah and Juniata Rivers, and some neutrals continued to live for a time in North Carolina. Virtually all Tuscaroras had left by 1802.

In 1722 or 1723, under the sponsorship of the Oneida, the Tuscarora were formally admitted into the Iroquois League, although their chiefs were not made official sachem chiefs. The former southerners soon adopted much of northern Iroquois culture. With the Oneidas, most Tuscaroras remained neutral or sided with the colonists in the American Revolution, although the rest of the league supported the British. The Seneca and a non-native land company donated land to the Tuscarora consisting of three square miles near Niagara Falls. The tribe purchased over 4,000 acres in 1804. It also received over $3,000 from the North Carolina legislature from the sale of Tuscarora land in that state.

Most Tuscaroras had become farmers and Christians by the end of the nineteenth century. Meanwhile, those loyal to Britain in the war settled in Oshweken, Ontario, on the Six Nations Reserve. The Tuscarora rejected the Indian Reorganization Act in the 1930s. In the 1950s, the government proposed that a massive reservoir be built on their land. The Indians' refusal to sell led to many protests and a court battle. Although they ultimately lost, and the reservoir was constructed, the process contributed significantly to their own, as well as other tribes', sense of empowerment and national identity.

RELIGION Tuscaroras believed that after death the immortal soul traveled to a western paradise. They buried their dead on scaffolds; bones were later placed in a village repository. Eventually the people adopted the practice of ground burial in bark, cane, or woven rush coffins. There were a number of planting and harvest festivals. Priests addressed every large gathering of any purpose.

GOVERNMENT The "tribe" was a collection of autonomous villages, each with its own chief, or headman, and council. The office of chief may or may not have been hereditary. Women served in some political capacity. Ultimate political authority was vested in the people and the council. The Tuscaroras were at first represented by the Oneida in the Iroquois League's annual council.

CUSTOMS Clan descent was matrilineal. There were eight clans in New York. Women nominated the clan chiefs. For five or six weeks, once in their lives, older children were secluded in a cabin and tortured with hunger and emetic plants. Some died from this treatment, which was ostensibly done to toughen them. The people may have played a mathematical

reed game, in which high-stakes gambling figured prominently. At least in the historical period, villagers moved to hunting locations in late fall; such quarters were often within a day's walk of their permanent villages.

A great deal of ceremony was associated with the burial of men, the degree of ritual and expense being related to a person's social standing. The corpse lay in state for a day or so, in a cane hut, in which relatives cried, mourned, and painted their faces black. Then the bodies were wrapped in blankets, covered with mats, and placed within a woven reed or cane shroud. One or more shamans conducted the funeral, at which they delivered lengthy eulogies. A small house was raised over the grave, which was then covered with earth. Chiefs were later disinterred. Their bones were cleaned and reassembled, and, dressed in white deerskins, they were buried in a crypt or house with other past chiefs.

Curing methods included shaking gourd rattles, sucking blood and fluids, and using snakes. Curers also used many herbal and plant medicines. The cures were often quite effective, and early non-native observers noted that these Indians were generally much healthier than were the colonists and other Europeans.

DWELLINGS Some villages were palisaded, at least in the early historical period. A village might have hundreds of houses; the average early-eighteenth-century village population was around 400. A village consisted of several "hamlets," or cabins near an open ceremonial area surrounded by fields. People who lived in "the country" had more distant neighbors.

Houses were ridged-roof pole lodges covered with cypress, cedar, or pine bark. There was a center fire and no smoke hole. Mats or deerskins served as bedding. In the north, multifamily longhouses were divided into compartments, each with its own fire, beds, and storage.

DIET Corn was the staple food, north and south. People also grew beans and squash. Women gathered wild fruits, nuts, berries, and roots. Men hunted game, including deer, bear, beaver, otter, rabbit, cougar, opossum, raccoon, partridge, pheasant, geese, and ducks. Seafood also played an important dietary role.

KEY TECHNOLOGY Bows were carved from black locust wood whenever possible. Animal bones were used as hoes. Men made bowls, dishes, spoons, and utensils from tulip, gum, and other wood. Women made pottery and wove baskets of bark and hemp as well as mats of rush and cane. In the north, the people acquired many of their material goods by trade.

TRADE Tuscaroras were very active traders, at

least in the early to mid–seventeenth century. Inter-tribal trade included wooden bowls and utensils, and possibly white clay tobacco pipes, for raw skins. They also imported copper from the west.

NOTABLE ARTS Tuscarora arts included carved wooden items, woven mats and baskets, and pottery.

TRANSPORTATION The people navigated rivers and marshes in cypress log canoes. They acquired horses in the mid– to late seventeenth century.

DRESS Men wore hand-tanned breechclouts; women wore a wraparound skirt and a tunic. Both were made from Spanish moss or softened tree bark. Outerwear consisted of turkey feather, fur, or deer-skin mantles. Men, especially among the wealthy, wore copper bracelets and other ornaments. Both men and women painted their bodies extensively.

WAR AND WEAPONS The people celebrated both war and peace. Traditional enemies included the Catawba, Creek, and Cherokee (the latter may also have been allies). Allies included the Coree, Pamlico, and Machapunga. During the Tuscarora war, the people built and lived in forts about a mile apart.

Contemporary Information

GOVERNMENT/RESERVATIONS The Tuscarora Reservation is located in Niagara County, New York. Established in 1784, it contains roughly 5,700 acres and had a 1990 resident population of 310 Indians (of an enrolled population of about 1,200). Each clan is represented on the council of chiefs. Titles are conferred by Iroquois Confederacy sachems.

Tuscaroras (about 200 in the mid-1990s) also live on the Six Nations Reserve, Ontario, Canada.

ECONOMY There is little or no employment specific to Indians. Most jobs are located in the Buffalo and Niagara Falls areas, especially in construction and heavy industry but also in business and the professions.

LEGAL STATUS The Tuscarora Nation is a federally recognized tribal entity.

DAILY LIFE Most Tuscaroras are Christian, and most of these are Protestant. The Longhouse religion is also active. Local issues include the status of non-natives living on the reservation as well as individual efforts to sell tax-free cigarettes and gasoline and to open gambling establishments. Language classes are held at the Tuscarora Indian School. The people join in pan-Iroquois festivals. A field day in July and a community fair in October are both open to non-natives.

Yuchi

Yuchi (`Y ū ch ē), possibly "from far away" or possibly Hitchiti for "People of Another Language." The tribe consisted of several distinct, named bands,

one of which may have been called Chisca. They were culturally similar to the Catawba Indians. *See also* Creek.

LOCATION Yuchis lived in the eastern Tennessee hills in the mid–sixteenth century. In the seventeenth century they built towns on the Ohio River and in Illinois. By later in that century they had expanded into the Savannah River region and into parts of Tennessee, North and South Carolina, Georgia, and Florida. Today, most Yuchis live in Oklahoma.

POPULATION There were at least 2,500 Yuchis in the mid–seventeenth century and around 1,500 in the early 1990s.

LANGUAGE Yuchean was an linguistic isolate, possibly related to the Siouan language family.

Historical Information

HISTORY Yuchis may have descended from Siouan peoples. They may have encountered Hernando de Soto around 1540 but were certainly attacked by the Spanish in 1566. In the 1630s, Yuchi bands began a process of leaving the Appalachian highlands to raid Spanish settlements in Florida. Some of these bands remained in the south, settling in west Florida among the Upper Creeks. The people encountered British settlers in Tennessee and North Carolina in the 1670s.

In the mid– to late seventeenth century, under pressure by the Shawnee, many Yuchi bands left the high country and followed the Savannah River toward coastal Georgia. They joined Yuchis who had migrated there earlier. With the Creek, both groups became British allies, conducting slave raids for them on Spanish settlements and among other tribes, such as the Apalachee, Timucua, Calusa, Guale, and Cusabo. This wave was soon driven away from the Savannah, however, and moved west toward the Chattahoochee River in central Alabama. A final wave of Yuchis migrated south in the early eighteenth century. By the late 1700s, most Yuchis were living near the Coosa and Tallapoosa Rivers, although some remained in southeast Georgia.

By the nineteenth century, the Yuchi no longer existed as a tribe, having combined with other peoples. Yuchis in Tennessee and North Carolina merged with the Cherokee. Georgia Yuchis joined the Creeks, and Florida Yuchis joined the Seminoles. As many as 900 Yuchis were removed with the Creeks to Indian Territory in 1836. They formed 11 communities in present-day Creek County, Oklahoma.

In the early twentieth century, the Yuchis remained legally united with the Creeks but maintained their own stomp grounds and churches. They refused their own charter in 1938, fearing the motives of the federal government. They maintained their own language and customs, as well as ties to religious sites in Georgia, through the 1950s.

RELIGION The sun was recognized as the chief deity and power. The three-day corn harvest festival included dancing, a new fire ceremony, and male deep scarring. The Green Corn festival included a stickball game as well as the formal initiation of boys into manhood. Disease was said to be caused by offended animal spirits; shamans cured with herbs, chants, and dancing. One of the four souls possessed by each person could pass to another life.

GOVERNMENT Each band had its own chief and leadership structure.

CUSTOMS Yuchis belonged to one of two societies, chief and warrior. Membership was determined by patrilineal descent. Babies were named on the fourth day of life. Matrilineal clans may or may not antedate their associations with the Creeks.

DWELLINGS Yuchis built their villages—stockaded in the mid–seventeenth century—near streams. They grouped their houses around a central square used for ceremonial and social purposes. Houses were wood-frame structures covered with clay or woven mats and roofed with cypress bark or shingles.

DIET Corn, beans, and squash were planted in river valleys. Corn was the staple food. It was served in many ways and often mixed with other foods, including powdered hickory nuts and meat. Wood ash was added for flavor. Men hunted buffalo, bear, elk, deer, turkey, and birds. They used calls to attract deer and turkey and possibly fire to drive deer. Game might be roasted on a cottonwood stick over an open fire. Women gathered a number of wild foods, including fruits, nuts, and berries. Hickory nut oil was preserved and used in cooking or as a beverage.

KEY TECHNOLOGY Men hunted using bows and arrows and blowguns (for birds and small game). Bows were made of Osage orange, sassafras, hickory, or other woods, with squirrel skin, deer sinew, or rawhide strings. Arrows were wooden or cane, pointed with stone and feathered with hawk and turkey tail feathers. Dogs assisted on the hunt. Fish were taken with willow and hickory traps, cane harpoons, various hook devices, wooden spears, and poisons.

Most men owned two large leather pouches decorated with beads and slung over the shoulder on straps. Turkey-feather fans were used mostly by men to keep insects away and as a sign of leadership. Log mortars and wooden pestles may also have had religious significance. Sewing awls were made of deer antler with bone points. The people also made pottery, baskets, and assorted wooden utensils and tools.

TRADE The Yuchi may have been a link in moving copper south from the Great Lakes. Some groups, using the Choctaw trade language, traded in flint or salt. Their pipes came from the Cherokee and Natchez, and they also traded for catlinite pipes from the early eighteenth century on. In the early contact period they also traded horses for other non-native goods.

NOTABLE ARTS Especially fine pottery included pipes and decorated bowls. Women also made fine cane and split hickory baskets. Turtles and snakes were a common design. Other design motifs included geometric diamonds made of Vs and Ws.

TRANSPORTATION Canoes were hollowed out of logs and may also have been made of bark.

DRESS Men wore deerskin leggings, sashes, and moccasins, although they frequently went barefoot. In the later eighteenth century they wore bright-colored cloth shirts and jackets, modified breech-clouts, leggings tied to a belt, cloth turbans, and various ornaments. Women wore cloth dresses, short leggings, belts, moccasins, and personal ornaments.

Men wore their hair in a roach with a fringe of hair along the forehead. Only unmarried women painted their faces, although the practice later became widespread. A male's face paint pattern was related to his particular society. It was worn on ceremonial occasions, including ball games, and at death.

WAR AND WEAPONS Little is known about aboriginal Yuchi war practices. Weapons probably included the bow and arrow as well as knives, clubs, hatchets, and possibly shields. They attacked and raided many neighboring tribes as British allies in the seventeenth century.

Contemporary Information

GOVERNMENT/RESERVATIONS Yuchis maintain three traditional ceremonial grounds in Oklahoma: Polecat, Sand Creek, and Duck Creek. The headquarters of the Yuchi Tribal Organization is in Sapulpa, Oklahoma.

ECONOMY Yuchis are fully integrated into the local mixed-farming economy.

LEGAL STATUS The Yuchi Tribal Organization is presently unrecognized. The Yuchi Nation was provisionally denied federal recognition in 1998.

DAILY LIFE Many Christian Yuchis belong to the Pickett Prairie Methodist Church. There is also a Yuchi chapter of the Native American Church. Yuchi is still spoken.

CHAPTER EIGHT

The Northeast Woodlands

Northeast Woodlands

The area known as the Northeast Woodlands encompasses close to one million square miles. Bordered by the Atlantic Ocean on the east, its northern frontier is the start of the boreal forest. To the west, the trees themselves separate the woodlands from prairie and plains, although fringe tribes hunted buffalo and shared other characteristics of Plains Indians. The region shades almost imperceptibly into the Southeast cultural area, which tends to be characterized by increased social stratification, denser populations, and a greater reliance on agriculture.

Aboriginal populations are difficult to establish, since disease epidemics began so long ago, but probably some two million Indians lived in the Northeast Woodlands in the sixteenth century. Southern New England and the mid-Atlantic region had the highest population densities. Thick forest covers the hilly Northeast Woodlands except in the far western regions, where relatively flat forest and prairie predominate. The highest mountain is Mount Washington (6,288 feet). The Appalachian Mountain chain and the Great Lakes dominate the region geologically. The entire area is well watered by an abundance of rivers and lakes. Major rivers include the Hudson, Ohio, Susquehannah, and St. Lawrence.

The region's temperate climate is moderated along the coast by Gulf Stream influences. Winters in the northern parts are particularly severe; summers, although pleasantly warm, are also relatively short. Conifers mix with deciduous trees, replacing them in the more northern locations and the higher elevations.

All northeastern Indians but the Siouan Winnebagos spoke either Algonquian or Iroquoian languages. (Besides being a major northeastern language group, Algonquian was also spoken by former Woodlands and well-known Plains tribes such as the Arapaho, Blackfeet, and Cheyenne. Even the Californian Yuroks spoke an Algonquian language.) Most northeastern Indians cultivated corn and other aboriginal crops using slash-and-burn agriculture. They also hunted, fished, and gathered wild plant foods to varying degrees.

Non-natives arrived in this region before they came to any other place in the New World. Norse explorers from Scandinavia visited coastal areas from about Newfoundland to Cape Cod. However, the Norse apparently left little of permanent influence. It was the trade in beaver furs as well as disease epidemics, beginning around 1600, that transformed life in the northeast. By the mid–nineteenth century, many Indian groups had simply disappeared, and most of those who remained had been militarily defeated and largely resettled on reservations, some of which were located far from home. On the other hand, there are more Indians in the northeast today than many people realize. Although the Indians are largely acculturated, many proudly maintain an Indian identity. On both sides of the international border, Native Americans continue to struggle for recognition, land, economic development, and sovereignty.

People have lived in the Northeast Woodlands for at least 12,000 years. The first residents may have come from the Southwest and moved north and east as the glaciers receded. During the Paleo-Indian stage, small bands pursued ancient species of large game. Although the Archaic period begins with the disappearance of the last of the Canadian ice (as well as the ancient large game) about 6000 B.C.E., the environment was still changing dramatically during those years, and people did not become fully established in the northeast until around 3,000 years later. Hunter-fisher-gatherer subsistence patterns and material culture from that period lasted into the seventeenth century among some interior Algonquian people. The first Mesoamerican influences entered the region about 2000 B.C.E. in the form of pottery and polished stone items.

The great eastern prehistoric civilizations influenced northeastern people during the Woodland period (circa 1000 B.C.E.–1500 C.E.). The Adena culture flourished around Kentucky and Ohio between about 800 B.C.E. and 200 C.E. These people cultivated crops, produced pottery, and cremated their dead or buried them in a flexed position under mounds. They also used copper tools and evolved considerable artistic traditions. The use of red ocher in burial customs was also associated with Adena culture. It is important to note that all Woodland cultural influences manifested themselves in ways that were highly specific yet variable in terms of time and place.

Hopewell cultures (circa 300 B.C.E.–700 C.E.) extended from the Great Lakes to the Gulf Coast and west of the Appalachians to the Great Plains. They also focused on complex death rituals, including mounds, and are known for their stamped pottery and other types of fine art. Hopewell was marked by larger population centers and the establishment of vast trade networks that extended throughout most of the present-day United States east of the Rocky Mountains. These people were excellent metal workers as well as weavers and craftspeople.

Most influential in western parts of the region, Mississippian Culture (circa 700–1500) was characterized by intensive agriculture, fine pottery, distinctive art themes, stockaded villages, and flat-topped pyramid mounds. There was an important Mississippian center at Cahokia, near present-day St. Louis, whose influence extended north into Wisconsin. Other late prehistoric cultural complexes include Fort Ancient and Monongahela Woodland, both located in the Ohio Valley.

Aboriginal trade generally took place between local groups. Trade patterns favored the exchange of Iroquoian agricultural products and Algonquian animal products, especially in the north. Birch items also went to those groups south of the primary birch area. Other trade items included pottery, shell objects, and copper as well as foods. There was some limited specialization, such as Iroquois pipes and Nanticoke beads.

Algonquians tended to use swift and light birch-bark canoes, in contrast to slower Iroquoian elm-bark models. The Iroquois proper did much of their traveling over land. Men made small canoes for use on rivers and large ones (holding up to ten people or more) for lakes. Styles were based on expected wind and water conditions. Canoes were often framed with cedar and trimmed with maple. Bark was sewn onto the frame with spruce roots and caulked with pine pitch or spruce resin. Some groups, particularly those who needed seaworthy crafts, hollowed out tree trunks for dugout canoes as well.

Other material items included grass, root, and bark baskets; cords and rope hand-spun and braided from plant fibers; woven hempen and basswood bags; and soapstone and carved wood bowls and utensils. Women made ceramic vessels for cooking, serving, and storage. Some Great Lakes groups made (and traded) tools of native copper. In addition to food and raw materials, wild plants provided hundreds of medicines. Wampum—strung shell beads—of native manufacture was originally used for tribal records and ceremonial purposes; its use was broadened into money and treaty confirmation in the historical period.

Artistic expression in the northeast ranged from baskets decorated with dyed fibers and woven in geometric patterns to painted and incised pottery to finely carved wooden bowls, spoons, and cups. The Iroquois carved wooden masks for use in certain curing ceremonials. Some women were expert at decorating clothing using softened porcupine quills.

Political organization varied across the region. Among most groups, chiefs (sachems, sagamores) led bands or groups of bands. Some chiefs were stronger than others; however, village councils acting in unanimity often decided important matters. Although among most groups political leadership had a hereditary component, social stratification in general was strongest in southern New England.

In the west, central Algonquians created parallel civil and military political organizations. Many of these tribes were divided into two distinct groupings that played important roles in games and celebrations. Most western tribes also had warrior organizations to perform policing activities. Women held formal political power in some western groups, such as the Miami, Shawnee, and Potawatomi.

In general, religious activities reinforced core values of generosity, bravery, and loyalty to the community. Iroquoian religion was based on the belief in a creator or creative life force balanced by the forces of evil and destruction. Algonquians, too, took notice of a host of evil spirits that might be used or abused by sorcerers. For these people, spirits were ubiquitous. They had human attributes and in fact could assume human form. The spirits included cannibal giants as well as the great creative spirit, Manitou, which was occasionally identified with the sky or the sun.

Among many groups, puberty was the time to undertake a vision quest, which included fasting and isolation, in order to attract the lifelong assistance of a spirit power. Dreaming was important for many Woodland Indians, because in dreams the human soul was thought to be able to leave the body and assume different shapes. Indians believed in life after death or the perpetual existence of the soul. Most cultures also recognized mythic culture heroes/transformers, such as Gluskap among the Micmac.

In addition to conducting ceremonies, religious specialists or shamans often had subspecialties, such as curing and divining. They performed their various feats with the help of their spirit powers. Shamans cured by sucking or blowing illness out of the body.

Important ceremonies among different groups included the Midewiwin, the feast of the dead, medicine dances, and the Green Corn festival. The Midewiwin may be aboriginal but most likely evolved in response to the unprecedented degree of disease and death endured by Indians beginning in about the sixteenth century.

Practitioners among the Ojibwa kept written records of proceedings on birch-bark scrolls. Some western groups had sacred bundles, whose medicines were associated with special powers. Especially among Great Lakes peoples, the pipe, or calumet—usually made of pipestone (catlinite)—was an especially sacred object and was associated with utmost solemnity and honesty. Religious significance also accrued to various games, such as lacrosse, especially among the Iroquois.

Algonquians typically lived in dome- or cone-shaped wigwams. These tended to be made of bark strips or woven mats or reeds attached to a frame of bent saplings tied together with spruce roots. Woven mats also covered interior walls and floors. Sleeping platforms were located around the perimeter; skins and furs were placed over the platforms as bedding. Smoke holes could be closed with a flap. There were usually two doors.

Summer and winter wigwams were of similar construction, but the latter tended to be smaller. Some Algonquian groups also used rectangular, multifamily houses with peaked roofs. Other buildings included menstrual huts, sweat houses, and temporary brush shelters at special hunting and fishing areas. Some Great Lakes groups built large wooden council houses in the center of their villages.

By the twelfth century, Iroquoians had developed longhouses. In the early historical period they were about 25 feet wide and up to 200 feet long, although most averaged less than 100 feet. Constructed of pieces of bark over a curved sapling frame, the longhouses were divided into six to eight two-room sections, each sharing a fire and housing one family. Storage bins divided the sections. Residents were generally members of the same maternal lineage. Inside the apartments were low platforms covered with skins or mats. Eastern longhouses tended to be covered with elm bark and western with cedar bark. Both had vaulted roofs.

The forests provided a home for a great variety of large and small creatures. Deer was generally the most important food animal, but people also hunted moose, caribou, bear, elk, beaver, muskrat, otter, wolf, fox, and rabbit. Fowl, especially turkey, were common in many areas.

Among some groups, saltwater and freshwater fish, turtles, shellfish, and marine mammals played an important dietary role. Fish was often smoked to preserve it for the winter. Depending on location, different groups used a variety of other food sources, such as maple sap (a sweetener), fresh greens, nuts, berries, honey, and roots.

After around 1000, or even as late as 1400 around parts of the Great Lakes, corn, followed by beans and squash, became an important food. In parts of the Great Lakes region, wild rice—really a grain—took the place of corn as a staple food source. Some groups also grew sunflowers, and most grew tobacco, although, unlike the other crops, doing so was considered the province of men. In general, people wintered in small groups, generally in hunting grounds, and summered in large ones, near their fields.

Women made most clothing from the hides of white-tailed deer. In general, clothing consisted of breechclouts, skirts, leggings, and moccasins. Additional clothing, such as fur robes, was worn in winter. Women decorated the clothing with softened and dyed porcupine quills and/or paint. Some groups also wore fringed garments. Shell and stone jewelry, tattoos, and body paint were common among most groups.

Warfare was endemic among most prehistoric Woodland Indians. The Iroquois revered war, although from about 1500 on, give or take 50 years or so, it was reserved for non-natives and tribes outside of the Iroquois League. The ritual torture of captives was common. Some groups also engaged in cannibalism. Both of these activities were associated with sun sacrifice and may show Mesoamerican influences. Among many groups, captives were frequently adopted to make up for population losses.

Coastal groups and the Iroquois developed gradually into the historic period. Cultural developments generally occurred in situ. Technological changes, such as ceramics, agriculture, and the use of shellfish, slowly advanced to their natural limits. The situation differed in the upper Great Lakes and in Illinois and the Ohio Valley, however, where ethnic continuity between prehistoric and historic peoples is speculative. Little-known residents of the Ohio Valley were gone by the mid–seventeenth century as a result of warfare and fast-moving epidemics. The region was later repopulated by historic tribes from other locations.

Half a millennium passed between the Norse visits

and the arrival of other Europeans. Indians of coastal Maine were using items of non-native manufacture by 1602, and many Europeans arriving even in the early contact days met Indians already familiar with their goods and knowledgeable in sophisticated trade practices.

Profound changes in Indian life followed the arrival of non-natives. The rate of change was uneven, but the most rapid and common impact was the decimation of Indian populations owing to epidemics of smallpox, typhus, and other diseases. Some tribes experienced as much as 95 percent population loss in the initial rounds (early seventeenth century in the east) alone. Furthermore, with the growing European demand for furs from the mid–sixteenth century on, the New World became a new center of competitiveness between France and Britain, and Native Americans soon became a part of both the trade and the rivalry.

The intrusion and eventual domination of fur trapping led to a dependence on alternate sources of food and technology. It even led to famine in some cases, as groups dependent on marine foods were cut off from the coast and spent more time trapping inland. Many groups eventually relocated to be near trade centers, even if the new locations were detrimental to their traditional subsistence activities. Time formerly spent making items was spent in trade-related activities, resulting in the decline of native arts and material culture. Early trade items of non-native manufacture included cloth, iron nails, knives, glass beads, and brass kettles, not to mention firearms.

Political and social structures were also affected. For their own convenience, non-natives promoted more centralized political authority among Indian groups. Some "trade chiefs" divided group land into distinct territories. This practice had several results, including an increase in individual ownership of subsistence areas, a breakdown in reciprocal arrangements and sharing, and increased social stratification. Indians also suffered further population decline, as well as a serious deterioration of traditional mores, from the introduction of alcohol and the accompanying sharp increase of venereal disease. They were as unprepared for liquor as they were for smallpox, and unscrupulous traders took full advantage of the fact.

Along the coast, once Indians taught non-natives how to survive in the New World, the latter quickly moved from friendliness to slave raiding, robbery, extortion, and demands for land and religious conversion. The Pequot war and King Philip's war stemmed at least in part from colonial opposition to acts of Indian self-determination, such as selling land and making independent alliances. Both involved the slaughter of hundreds of Indian women and children and the ensuing cession/capture of much Indian land.

Numerous other conflicts stemmed from non-native lust for land, outright brutality practiced against Indians (often justified with recourse to Christian values), trade-related issues, and simple fear and misunderstanding. All took place within the context of the wider international struggle between France and Great Britain. Warfare, both interracial and among Indians themselves, occasionally escalated into attempted genocide: More than once smallpox-infected blankets were intentionally traded to "troublesome" Indians, and some Indian groups, notably the Iroquois, succeeded in virtually annihilating other tribes. In short, ritual warfare was transformed slowly into economic and political warfare as a result of the fur trade and competition over land.

One important aspect of non-native influence was a steady pressure, almost from the beginning, to accept Christianity. Although relatively few Indians truly accepted Christian doctrine before the nineteenth century, a significant number did convert, mainly to Catholicism. Reasons for taking this action included not only genuine personal conviction but also the hope for trade and/or political advantage. Indians were well aware, for instance, that the French would trade firearms only to Christians.

Many Indians attempted to hold on to traditional beliefs and religious practice despite the breakdown of religious structures. Those in this camp often came to accept neotraditional beliefs such as the Handsome Lake (Longhouse) religion and, later, the Native American Church. With these new religions, Indians found a way to blend the old with the new without feeling that they had abandoned their heritage.

In general, Algonquians tended to favor the French whereas Iroquoians were pro-British. After the French defeat in 1763, many Algonquian tribes, recognizing the threat to their lands, fought with the British against the colonists. Most upper Great Lakes Indians supported the British in the American Revolution. Indians also acted on their own or in multitribal coalitions (Pontiac, 1763; Little Turtle, circa 1790; Tecumseh, 1810; and Black Hawk, 1832), in vain efforts to stem the tide of westward emigration.

The first half of the nineteenth century saw the cession of practically all remaining Indian land east of the Mississippi and the consolidation of tribes on reservations. After relocating several times, most western tribes ended up in Indian Territory, although some groups refused to leave their homes and were able to remain in scattered pockets. Some also accepted reserves in Canada (the word "Canada" is derived from an Iroquoian word meaning "settlement" or "village"). Many of these Indians carried on in a semitraditional way until the fur trade finally drew to an end around 1900.

Into the twentieth century, Indian life, especially in the west but even in the east, was characterized by an inadequacy of food, shelter, and employment and by continuing assaults on the people's land, culture, and self-determination. Indians resisted as best they could. Their fortunes tended to rise and fall along with the general state of the U.S. economy as well as the prevailing Indian policy. In the east, job opportunities off of the reservation or community tended to encourage cultural assimilation. Cultural preservation was generally less difficult in Canada than in the United States.

As is the case with most North American Indians, the goal of self-determination remains paramount. On Cape Cod, Wampanoag Indians battle non-native vacationers and developers for the right to control their land. Recognition is also an issue for these people, as it is for the Houlton Band of Maliseet, the Pokanoket, and other Northeast Indians. Many are still trying to settle land claims and obtain reservation status for communities both recognized and unrecognized.

Indians in the northeast as well as Woodland descendants in Oklahoma seek economic development as well as housing and adequate medical care. Craft traditions remain strong but are not generally sufficient to provide a decent standard of living. Many communities remain riven by factionalism: The Mohawk, for example, are deeply divided over the issues of gaming and the nature of their political leadership—"traditional" or "progressive." Many groups have initiated various programs and gatherings in order to focus or refocus on their traditions. Among those groups whose native traditions have long since been lost, pan-Indianism has become important.

In Canada, at least six different governmental agencies have controlled Indian affairs since 1867, with the result that a consistent and effective policy has yet to be developed. Canadian Indians, especially the thousands of Métis (or mixed Indian and Anglo-French descendants) in Canada's southeast, face continuing problems of recognition. In both countries, despite almost 500 years of contact with non-natives and extremely strong pressures during those centuries to abandon their traditions and culture, many descendants of the forest dwellers remain Indians. Far removed from the life of their ancestors, they insist upon their identity as they continue to adapt their deeply rooted traditions.

Abenaki

Abenaki (`Ä bə `nä kē), more properly Wabenaki, "Dawn Land People" or "easterners," were a group of Algonquian tribes. They are sometimes discussed as Eastern Abenaki (including Kennebec, Penobscot, Arosagunticook, and Pigwacket) and Western Abenaki (including Penacook, Winnipesaukee, and Sokoki). There was also a seventeenth- and eighteenth-century Abenaki Confederacy consisting of these and other tribes, such as the Maliseet, Micmac, and Passamaquoddy. *See also* Maliseet; Micmac; Passamaquoddy; Penobscot.

LOCATION Abenakis lived near major rivers of northern New England and southern Quebec in the early seventeenth century. Today, there are Micmac, Penobscot, and Passamaquoddy Reservations in northern and eastern Maine. Maliseets live in northern Maine and southeastern Quebec, and Abenakis live in northern Vermont and southern Quebec.

POPULATION There were perhaps 10,000 Eastern and 5,000 Western Abenakis in the early seventeenth century. In 1990, around 1,700 Western Abenakis lived in northern Vermont, about 800 lived in New Hampshire, and roughly 1,800 lived in Quebec, Canada. There were about 2,000 Penobscots in the early 1990s.

LANGUAGE Abenakis spoke dialects of Eastern Algonquian languages.

Historical Information

HISTORY Abenakis originally came from the Southwest, according to their legends. They may have met early explorers such as Giovanni da Verrazano in the sixteenth century. They were definitely visited by Samuel de Champlain and others, including missionaries, early in the seventeenth century, shortly after which time the Abenakis became heavily involved in the fur trade. Western groups traded with the Dutch and entered the fur trade later than the eastern groups.

Almost immediately, many eastern villages disappeared as a result of war (mostly Micmac attacks) and disease. Among the survivors, material culture and subsistence economy changed rapidly with the availability of non-native items. Indians and French regularly intermarried. Western groups came in conflict with the Iroquois from the mid– to late seventeenth century. Abenakis first arrived in Quebec from Maine in the late seventeenth century. They lived on the banks of the Chaudière River before moving to their present territory in the early eighteenth century.

Abenakis were staunch allies of the French in the colonial wars, although eastern groups needed to cover their bases with the British in the interest of preserving trade. Fierce Abenaki fighters sacked many British settlements throughout New England in the late seventeenth century and early eighteenth century. The Western Abenakis, in particular, played a significant role in much of the history of New France, including fur trading, exploring, and fighting the Seneca and Mohawk.

The Indians steadily lost land during the late seventeenth and eighteenth centuries. The Penobscot slowly emerged as the strongest eastern tribe. When the town of Norridgewalk fell to the British in 1724, many Eastern Abenakis withdrew to Quebec. Although Penobscots urged Abenaki neutrality in the French and Indian War, other Eastern Abenakis, now living in Quebec, fought with the French. The Penobscots were eventually drawn in: The treaty of 1763 marked the British victory as well as the Penobscot defeat. Meanwhile, after the fighting ended in 1763, Western Abenakis returned to their territory to find British squatters. They abandoned most of these lands after 1783, settling near a reserve on the Ste. Francois River in Quebec.

In the nineteenth and early twentieth centuries, most Western Abenakis sought to avoid anti-Indian sentiment by speaking French, selling ash-splint baskets to tourists, and keeping to themselves. Some hunted in a large territory north of the St. Lawrence River, and some returned to northern New England for seasonal cash work and subsistence activities. Many Western Abenakis attended Dartmouth College in the nineteenth century.

In 1941, the establishment of a wildlife refuge by the state of Vermont ended the people's ancient hunting and fishing rights. A postwar resurgence of the western group was based on controversies over fishing and hunting rights and a lack of official recognition. These groups held fish-ins to dramatize their situation. State recognition in 1976 was withdrawn the following year.

RELIGION Western groups tended to believe in a supreme creator, and both Eastern and Western Abenakis enjoyed a rich mythology. Many ceremonies were based on crops or the hunt as well as on greeting visitors, weddings, and funerals. At least among the western group, boys might seek the help of supernatural beings by obtaining a guardian spirit through a vision quest around the time of puberty. Dances were often associated with the spirit power. Shamans, often employing drums, foretold the future, located game, and cured illness.

GOVERNMENT Authority was gained as a result of leadership qualities, although there was also an element of patrilineal descent. Eastern chiefs of extended families were also sometimes shamans and after the seventeenth century were known as sagamores. Western groups recognized lifelong civil and war chiefs as well as a council of elders. The chiefs' powers were relatively limited.

CUSTOMS Several related nuclear families living together made up a household, which was the basic social and economic unit. Descent was patrilineal.

Social status was somewhat hierarchical, especially in the east, where chiefs might have more than one wife. Shamans or special healers were brought in when herbal or plant-based cures and sweats failed.

In general, men provided animal foods, fought, and made tools and houses; women grew crops, gathered foods, prepared and cooked food, made clothing, and took care of children. Men engaged in frequent races and archery contests. They also played ball games, including lacrosse. People kept dogs as pets and used them to track game.

The use of stories and gentle group pressure was sufficient to discipline children. Boys gave away their first big game animal kills (all men gave away their first kill of the season). Marriage, considered official after gifts were given to the bride's family, was celebrated by feasting and dancing (as were many occasions). The dead were buried as soon as possible with weapons and/or tools for use in the afterlife. The western group put bodies in bark coffins and placed east-facing triangular structures over the graves.

DWELLINGS Villages were located along streams and, among the western group, near meadows. Easterners lived in dome-shaped and square houses with pyramid roofs shingled with bark. There were smoke holes at the top, and deerskins covered two doors. At least in the early historical period villages were palisaded. Westerners tended to live in birch-bark longhouses with arched roofs. Several families lived in each house. They also built dome-shaped sweat lodges.

DIET A shorter growing season and poorer soil meant that Abenakis depended less on crops than did southern Algonquians. In small family groups they hunted caribou, deer, and bear and trapped beaver and other small game as well as birds. Western groups called and ran down moose.

Women gathered berries, nuts, potatoes, and wild cherries and other fruits. They also boiled maple and birch sap for syrup and sugar. In spring, the eastern group fished along the coast for salmon, shad, eel, sturgeon, smelt, and other fish. They also gathered shellfish and other marine foods and hunted sea mammals. Fish were also important to the western group, who grew more corn, beans, squash, and tobacco.

KEY TECHNOLOGY Men fished using hooks, nets, spears, and weirs and hunted using the bow and arrow, lance, and knife. Hunting bags, some made of woodchuck skin, included fire-making tools and pipe (clay and stone) and tobacco. Important tools included knives, awls, gouges, adzes, wooden and stone scrapers, and pounders. Some groups made carved wooden dishes and utensils as well as pottery.

Containers were made of folded bark, rushes, or grasses. Some were decorated with porcupine quills.

From the early seventeenth century on, wampum beads were used to record treaties and major council decisions.

Trade Abenakis generally traded with neighboring groups until the beginning of the fur trade period, when they traded furs for corn from southern New England. At that time, wampum became a medium of exchange and political status.

NOTABLE ARTS Many items, including pottery, were carefully decorated. Bark containers, for example, were often decorated with incised, curved designs. Ash-splint baskets became popular after contact with non-natives, although the people may have woven some baskets aboriginally.

TRANSPORTATION Men made birch-bark and dugout canoes, snowshoes, and toboggans.

DRESS Women tanned skins to make most clothing. Men wore beaver-pelt breechclouts and belts. Western women wore skirts and blouses in addition to cold-weather gear. Both wore moccasins, leggings, moose hide coats, and fur robes and caps. Tunics were also common. Both sexes painted their faces and bodies and wore their hair long.

WAR AND WEAPONS Before they joined the confederacy. Micmacs often fought eastern Abenakis. The western group often clashed with the Iroquois but were generally friendly with Algonquians. Weapons included the bow and arrow, knife, spear, and club. Among the western group, the question of war was discussed at a general council that all people attended and in which all could participate. If war was agreed upon, the war chief called for volunteers. Warriors painted their faces and bodies.

Contemporary Information

GOVERNMENT/RESERVATIONS There are Western Abenaki communities in Odanak (St. Francis; 607.02 hectares) and Wôlinak (Bécancour; 79 hectares), Quebec, Canada. The Odanak reserve had a 1994 population of 1,458, of whom 267 lived within the territory. The Wôlinak reserve had a 1994 population of 311, of whom 114 lived within the territory. There are communities in northern Vermont near Highgate and St. Albans (Traditional Abenaki of Mazipskwik). The community at St. Albans, also known as the St. Francis–Sokoki Band, is governed by a tribal council. The Quebec communities are governed by band councils and represented by the Grand Council of the Waban-Aki Nation. The Abenaki Indian Village is located in Lake George, New York.

ECONOMY Most Abenakis work mainly in the local non-native economy. Canadian Abenakis have begun setting up an outfitting business by filing a claim for exclusive local hunting and fishing rights. Basketry also generates income for the two communities.

LEGAL STATUS The St. Francis–Sokoki Band of the Abenaki Nation of Vermont has petitioned for federal recognition. The Penobscot Nation and the Passamaquoddy tribe are federally recognized tribal entities. The Odanak and Wôlinak reserves are federally and provincially recognized.

DAILY LIFE The Abenaki Self-Help Association attempts to meet people's health and housing needs. Many Western Abenakis maintain their family-based culture. Ongoing cultural events include a harvest dinner in October and traditional dances and ceremonies at late spring/early summer powwows. A few people still speak the native language in Quebec. Abenakis are working to have the language taught in local public schools. Two Canadian institutions, the Société Historique (Odanak Historical Society) and the Musée des Abénaquis (Abenaki Museum) represent the culture of the people to the world. Penobscots, Maliseets, and Passamaquoddys have intermarried considerably. Penobscot children attend their own elementary school.

Algonquin

Algonquin (Al `gon kin or Al `gon kwin) or Algonkin, probably from a Micmac word meaning "at the place of spearing fish and eels from the bow of a canoe," is the name of a northeastern group of bands that also gave its name to an important language family. The original self-designation was *Anishinabeg*, or "true men." Principal Algonquin bands included the Weskarini (Algonquin proper), Abitibi, and Temiskaming. *See also* Anishinabe; Ottawa; Wyandotte.

LOCATION In the early seventeenth century, Algonquins lived in the Ottawa Valley of Quebec and Ontario, particularly along the northern tributary rivers. Today they live on reserves in Ontario and Quebec and in regional cities and towns.

POPULATION There were roughly 6,000 Algonquins in the early seventeenth century and about 8,000 in the mid-1990s. Of the roughly 7,300 Quebec Algonquins, about 4,300 live among nine communities.

LANGUAGE Algonquins spoke an Algonquian language.

Historical Information

HISTORY Algonquins lived on the north shore of the St. Lawrence River from about 1550 to 1650. They began trading with the French in the early sixteenth century and later became important French allies. Trade frictions soon provoked a war with the Mohawk. The Algonquin won that skirmish with assistance provided by the French in order to maintain an important trade partner.

However, the French had made a powerful enemy in the Mohawk, and within a few decades the local military situation had been reversed, with the Iroquois now firmly in control. Meanwhile, the Huron had replaced the Algonquin as the key French trade partner. The Mohawk, needing to expand their trapping area, soon attacked again. The Algonquin were forced to abandon the upper St. Lawrence and, after about 1650, the Ottawa Valley. They returned in the 1660s when peace was reestablished. An epidemic in the 1670s left them further weakened.

During the late seventeenth century, some Algonquin bands merged with the Ottawa Indians. French trading posts were established, and missionaries became a permanent presence in their territory by the early eighteenth century. Some Algonquins traveled to the far west to trap for Canadian companies. After the final French defeat in 1763, the Algonquin became staunch British allies. Reserves for the group were created in the nineteenth century, when their lands were overrun by British settlers. The decline of the fur trade and of their hunting grounds (mainly owing to local logging operations) as well as a growing dependence on non-natives led many Algonquins to adopt a sedentary lifestyle.

RELIGION The people believed in a great creator spirit and a host of lesser spirits, both good and evil. Both shamans and hunters sought guardian spirits to help them with their work, which included interpreting dreams and healing the sick. After death, the spirits of hunters were thought to pursue the spirits of animals.

GOVERNMENT Small bands were composed of one or more clans with local chiefs. People smoked tobacco silently before council meetings.

CUSTOMS Algonquins entertained visitors with the annual Feast of the Dead, a dance with a war theme. When entertaining guests, the host did not eat. Clan descent as well as the inheritance of hunting territories may have been patrilineal. Bands tended to come together in summer and disperse in winter. People placed wooden rooflike structures with painted self-images at one end over the graves of high-status people. People were reluctant to mention their real names for fear of misuse by witches.

DWELLINGS People lived in cone-shaped, tipilike dwellings. They also built rectangular birch-bark hunting shelters.

DIET Men fished in both summer and winter (through holes cut in the ice). They hunted game such as moose, deer, caribou, and beaver. Agricultural crops played a small role in their diet. Some bands made maple sugar. Dog was eaten on occasion.

KEY TECHNOLOGY Important material items included birch-bark containers sewn with spruce roots, basswood bags and mats, wooden cradleboards, bows and arrows, and double-headed drums.

TRADE Algonquins imported fish nets and cornmeal from Hurons and also traded extensively with Iroquoian tribes. They traded animal pelts and porcupine quills to nearby groups in exchange for corn, tobacco, fishing gear, and wampum.

NOTABLE ARTS The people decorated many birch-bark items with the use of templates. Decorative styles included zigzag bands and floral motifs. Most designs were symmetrical. Southern bands decorated items with porcupine quillwork.

TRANSPORTATION Men made birch-bark canoes, snowshoes, and toboggans.

DRESS Dress varied according to location. Most clothing was made of buckskin or moose skin. Clothing included breechclouts, skirts, ponchos, leggings, robes, and moccasins; moccasins were often dyed black. Fur garments were added in cold weather. Both men and women tended to wear their hair long and braided.

WAR AND WEAPONS Algonquins fought with bows and arrows, spears, and knives; they were early allies with the Huron. They dominated the Iroquois before the latter banded together in their great confederacy.

Contemporary Information

GOVERNMENT/RESERVATIONS The two Algonquin communities in Ontario are Golden Lake and Wahgoshig. Quebec communities include Abitibiwinni (90.5 hectares; 674 people in 1994, of whom 388 lived within the territory), Barrière Lake (28 hectares; 520 people in 1994, of whom 409 lived within the territory), Eagle Village–Kipewa (21.49 hectares; 494 people in 1994, of whom 170 lived within the territory), Kitcisakik (12.14 hectares; 302 people in 1994, of whom 272 lived within the territory), Kitigan Zibi Anishinabeg (11,165.14 hectares; 2,094 people in 1994, of whom 1,313 lived within the territory), Lac Simon (275.01 hectares; 1,104 people in 1994, of whom 874 lived within the territory), Long Point (37.84 hectares; 558 people in 1994, of whom 273 lived within the territory), Témiscamigue (2,428.08 hectares; 1,241 people in 1994, of whom 473 lived within the territory), and Wolf Lake (Hunter's Point; 4 hectares; 185 people in 1994, of whom 7 lived within the territory). Canadian communities are governed by band councils. Algonquin communities are also represented by the Anishinabe Algonquin Nation Council and the Algonquin Nation Programs and Services Secretariat.

Algonquins also live on Gibson Reserve, Ontario, primarily a home to Iroquois people.

ECONOMY Some people raise gardens, and some

serve as guides to visiting sportsmen. Some maintain a traditional hunting and trapping life. Important local industries include construction, forestry, and transportation. The Algonquin Development Association provides support for the initiation of economic projects.

LEGAL STATUS The Canadian communities listed under "Government/Reservations" are legally recognized tribal entities. Long Point and Kitcisakik do not have the status of a reserve. In 1994, a framework for negotiations was reached between the people of Golden Lake and provincial officials concerning a land claim for 3,400 square kilometers of land in Ontario.

DAILY LIFE Many Algonquins have intermarried with non-natives and merged with non-native society. Still, at least 60 percent of Quebec Algonquins probably speak their ancestral language. The community of Kitigan Zibi Anishinabeg has a primary and secondary school, a women's shelter, a youth center, and other resources. The Matciteeia Society is an Algonquin cultural organization.

Anishinabe

Anishinabe (Ä nish i n`ä b ā), "People," are also variously known by the band names Ojibwe/ Ojibwa/Ojibway/Chippewa, Mississauga, and Salteaux. The name Ojibwa means "puckered up," probably a reference to a style of sewn moccasin. With the Potawatomi and Ottawa, with whom they may once have been united, some groups were part of the Council of Three Fires in the nineteenth century. Northern groups had a Subarctic as well as a Woodlands cultural orientation (see Chapter 9, especially Cree). See also Ojibwa, Plains (Chapter 6); Ottawa.

LOCATION Anishinabe groups lived north of Lake Huron and northeast of Lake Superior (present-day Ontario, Canada) in the early seventeenth century. In the eighteenth century, northern Ojibwas lived between the Great Lakes and Hudson Bay, and the Lake Winnipeg Salteaux lived just east and south of that body of water.

Today, there are Anishinabe communities and reservations in central and northern Michigan, including the Upper Peninsula; northern Wisconsin; northern and central Minnesota; northern North Dakota; northern Montana; and southern Ontario. Anishinabe also live in regional cities and towns.

POPULATION The people numbered at least 35,000, but perhaps more than double that figure, in the early seventeenth century. There were roughly 125,000 enrolled Anishinabe in the United States in the mid-1990s, including about 48,000 in Minnesota, at least 30,000 in Michigan, 25,000 members of the Turtle Mountain Band in North Dakota, 16,500 in

Wisconsin, and 3,100 at Rocky Boy Reservation in Montana, plus other communities in Montana and elsewhere in the United States. There were about 60,000 Anishinabe in Canada in the mid-1990s, excluding Métis.

LANGUAGE The various Anishinabe groups spoke dialects of Algonquian languages.

Historical Information

HISTORY The Anishinabe probably came to their historical location from the northeast and had arrived by about 1200. They encountered Frenchmen in the early seventeenth century and soon became reliable French allies. From the later seventeenth century on, the people experienced great changes in their material and economic culture as they became dependent on guns, beads, cloth, metal items, and alcohol.

Pressures related to the fur trade, including Iroquois attacks, drove the Anishinabe to expand their territory by the late seventeenth century. With French firearms, they pressured the Dakota to move west toward the Great Plains. They also drove tribes such as the Sauk, Fox, and Kickapoo from Michigan and replaced the Huron in lower Michigan and extreme southeast Ontario. With the westward march of British and especially French trading posts, Ojibwa bands also moved into Minnesota and north-central Canada (Lake of the Woods and the Red River area), displacing Siouan and other Algonquian groups (such as the Cheyenne).

As early as the late seventeenth century, Anishinabe bands had moved west into the Lake Winnipeg/North Dakota region. Many people intermarried with Cree Indians and French trappers and became known as Métis, or Mitchif. By the eighteenth century, Anishinabe bands stretched from Lake Huron to the Missouri River.

The people were most deeply involved in the fur (especially beaver) trade during the eighteenth century. They fought the British in the French and Indian War and in Pontiac's rebellion. In 1769, in alliance with neighboring tribes, they utterly defeated the Illinois Indians. They fought with the British in the Revolutionary War. Following this loss, they kept up anti-American military pressure, engaging the non-natives in Little Turtle's war, Tecumseh's rebellion, and the War of 1812.

By the early nineteenth century, scattered, small hunter-fisher-gatherer bands of northern Ojibwa and Salteaux were located north and west of the Great Lakes. These people experienced significant changes from the early nineteenth century, such as a greater reliance on fish and hare products and on non-native material goods.

The Plains Ojibwe (Bungi) had moved west as far as southern Saskatchewan and Manitoba and North Dakota and Montana. They adopted much of Great Plains culture. The southeastern Ojibwe (Mississauga), living in northern and southern Michigan and nearby Ontario, were hunters, fishers, gatherers, and gardeners. They also made maple sugar and, on occasion, used wild rice. Their summer villages were relatively large. Finally, the southwestern Ojibwe had moved into northern Wisconsin and Minnesota following the departing Dakotas. They depended on wild rice as well as hunting, fishing, gathering, gardening. and maple sugaring.

Anishinabe living in the United States ceded much of their eastern land to that government in 1815 upon the final British defeat. Land cessions and the establishment of reservations in Wisconsin and Minnesota followed during the early to mid–nineteenth century. Two small bands went to Kansas in 1839. In the 1860s, some groups settled with the Ottawa, Munsee, and Potawatomi in the Indian Territory.

Michigan and Minnesota Anishinabe groups (with the exception of the Red Lake people) lost most of their land (90 percent or more in many cases) to allotment, fraud, and other irregularities in the mid–to late nineteenth century. They also suffered significant culture loss as a result of government policies encouraging forced assimilation. In the late nineteenth century, many southwestern Ojibwe worked as lumberjacks. Many in the southeast concentrated more on farming, although they continued other traditional subsistence activities when possible. Transition to non-native styles of housing, clothing, and political organization was confirmed during this period.

Plains Ojibwa took part in the Métis rebellion of Louis Riel in 1869–1870. These groups were finally settled on the Turtle Mountain Reservation in the late nineteenth century and on the Rocky Boy Reservation in the early twentieth century. Around the turn of the century, the Turtle Mountain Chippewa, led by Chief Little Shell, worked to regain land lost in 1884 and to reenroll thousands of Métis whom the United States had unilaterally excluded from the tribal rolls. In 1904, the tribe received $1 million for a 10-million-acre land claim, a settlement of 10 cents an acre. Soon thereafter, most of the Turtle Mountain land was allotted. One result of that action was that many people, denied adequate land, were forced to scatter across the Dakotas and Montana. Most of the allotments were later lost to tax foreclosure, after which the tribal members, now landless, drifted back to Turtle Mountain.

The growing poverty of Michigan bands was partially reversed after most accepted the Indian Reorganization Act (IRA) in the 1930s and the United States reassumed its trust relationship with them. Many of these people moved to the industrial cities of the Midwest, especially in Michigan and Wisconsin, after World War II, although most retained close ties with the reservation communities.

Among the northern Ojibwa, bands had made treaties with the Canadian government since the mid–nineteenth century. The Canadian Pacific Railway was completed in the 1880s and the Canadian National Railway around 1920. Supply operations changed again during the 1930s, when "bush planes" began flying. Many people began growing small gardens at that time as well.

RELIGION Some groups may have believed in the existence of an overarching supreme creative power. All animate and inanimate objects had spirits that could be good or evil (the latter, like the cannibalistic Windigo, were greatly feared). People attempted to keep the spirits happy through prayer and by the ritual use of tobacco and the intervention of shamans. Tobacco played a significant role in many rituals.

By fasting and dreaming in a remote place, young men sought a guardian spirit that would assist them throughout their lives. In general, dreams were considered of extreme importance. There was probably little religious ceremonialism before people began dying in unprecedented numbers as a result of hitherto unknown diseases of Old World origin. The Midewiwin or Medicine Dance was a graded curing society that probably arose, except among the northern Ojibwa, in response to this development.

Membership in the Midewiwin was gained by experiencing particular visions or dreams. Candidates received a period of instruction and paid certain fees. Once a year, a secret meeting lasting several days was held in a special long lodge to initiate new members, who could be men or women. Initiates were shot with a sacred white shell, through which supernatural power entered the body, and were then restored by a priest. One member recorded the proceedings by carving and painting bark scrolls. Members wore special medicine bags around their necks. Initiates did not become shamans, but many were cured through entering the society; members also achieved greater supernatural power as well as prestige.

Bears were revered and were the focus of a special ceremony. Shamans, usually older men, cured the sick with recourse to spiritual power, and herbalists offered effective cures using hundreds of local plants. Several degrees of shaman were recognized. Among the Lake Winnipeg Salteaux, shamans cured disease by using sucking tubes, sometimes after communicating with their spirit helpers in a special shaking tent. These shamans engaged in contests for authority by showing off their evil powers. People also observed special first-fruits ceremonies over wild rice and bear.

GOVERNMENT Men led autonomous bands of perhaps 300–400 people on the basis of both family and ability. Bands were related by marriage but never politically united. Band headman were often war captains but had little direct authority before the fur trade period; for their own advantage, traders worked to increase the power of the headman. These efforts ultimately led to the creation of a patrilineal line of chiefs.

CUSTOMS About 15–23 patrilineal clans were linked into the larger divisions. Bands came together in villages during summer and dispersed for the winter hunting season. Within the context of a social organization that was relatively egalitarian, there were people with higher status than others, such as chiefs, accomplished warriors, and shamans.

Infants spent most of their first year on a cradle board with a moss "mattress." Names were ultimately spirit derived. A close relationship existed between the namer and the named. Children were raised with little harsh discipline.

Although a special feast was held to celebrate a boy's first kill, the major male puberty rite was the vision quest, which entailed a four-day fast deep in the forest to await a propitious dream. At that time he received a guardian spirit power that could be used for good or evil; with the spirit came various names and songs. Contact with the spirit was maintained throughout the man's life by means of food offerings and tobacco. Girls might also have visions, but they were not generally required to undergo a quest.

Girls were chaperoned at all times. A man might play a flute to court a prospective wife, who was likely chosen by his parents. A man brought food to the future wife's family to formalize the engagement. Eventually they moved into their own lodge. Important men might have more than one wife. Divorce was easy to obtain on grounds as basic as incompatibility.

Corpses were washed and well presented. Wrapped in birch bark, they were removed from the wigwam, after a period of lying in state, through an opening in the west side. A priest gave a funeral ceremony, after which the body was buried with tools and equipment. The soul was said to travel for four days to a happy location in the west. The mourning period lasted one year.

The Anishinabe enjoyed regular visiting as well as social dancing (although on such occasions men often danced apart from women). They also enjoyed various sports, such as lacrosse and a game in which they threw a pole along frozen snow, and contests;

gambling invariably played a part in these activities. Lacrosse was rough and carried religious overtones.

DWELLINGS The traditional Anishinabe dwelling was a domed wigwam of cattail mats or birch bark over a pole frame. There was a smoke hole in the center over the fire. The doorway was covered with bark, hide, or a blanket. Mats and furs were placed around the sides for sleeping and storage. Floors were covered with cedar inner bark, bullrush mats, or, in the north, boughs.

There were also larger, elliptical wigwams that housed several families. These had a fireplace at either end. Hunters also used temporary bark-covered A-frame lodges, and people built smaller sweat lodges, used for purification or curing, as well as menstrual huts and Midewiwin lodges.

DIET Women grew small gardens of corn, beans, and squash in the south. Men hunted and trapped a variety of large and small game, mostly in winter, as well as birds and fowl. Meat was roasted, stone boiled, or dried and stored. Some was dried and mixed with fat and chokecherries to make pemmican, an extremely nourishing, long-lasting food. Men fished year round, especially for sturgeon, sometimes at night by the light of flaming birch-bark torches. People also ate shellfish where available. Dog was often served at feasts.

In the fall, women in canoes gathered wild rice, which became a staple in the Anishinabe southwest and important as well around Lake Winnipeg. Wild rice was actually a grass with an edible seed that could be knocked into the canoe with sticks. It was stored and eaten after being dried, parched, and winnowed. They also gathered a variety of berries, fruits, and nuts, and some groups collected maple sap for sugar, which they used as a seasoning and in water. Northern Ojibwas had access neither to wild rice nor to maple sap.

KEY TECHNOLOGY Most items were made of wood and birch bark, but people also used stone, bone, and possibly some pottery. Important material items included birch-bark containers and dishes; water drums, flutes, tambourines, and rattles; cattail, cedar, and bulrush mats; and basswood twine and bags. Fishing equipment included nets, spears, and wood or bone lures and hooks. Lake Winnipeg people made distinctive black steatite pipes as well as sturgeon-skin containers.

TRADE Trade items included elm-bark bags and assorted birch-bark goods, carved wooden bowls, food, and maple sugar. As they expanded west, the people began to trade Woodland items for buffalo-derived products.

NOTABLE ARTS Clothing and medicine bags were decorated with quillwork. Men carved wooden utilitarian as well as religious items (figurines). Pattern designs were bitten into thin birch-bark sheets. The Anishinabe were also known for their soft elm-bark bags. Lake Winnipeg women made fine moose-hide mittens, richly decorated in beads. As with many native peoples, storytelling evolved to a fine art.

TRANSPORTATION Men made birch-bark canoes and snowshoes. Horses were acquired in the late eighteenth century. Northern Ojibwas used toboggans and canoe-sleds, sometimes hauled by large dogs, from the nineteenth century on.

DRESS Dress varied according to location. Most clothing was made of buckskin. Ojibways tended to color their clothing with red, yellow, blue, and green dyes. In the southwestern areas, women wore woven fiber shirts under a sleeveless dress. Other clothing included breechclouts, leggings, robes, and moccasins, the last often dyed and featuring a distinctive puckered seam. Fur garments were added in cold weather. Both men and women tended to wear their hair long and braided.

WAR AND WEAPONS The Anishinabe were generally effective but unenthusiastic fighters. They were traditional allies of the Ottawa and Potawatomi; their enemies included the Iroquois and Dakota. Battles were fought on land as well as occasionally from canoes. Weapons included the knobbed wooden war club, bow and arrow, knife, and moose-hide shield. Enemies were generally killed in battle. Some were ritually eaten. Warriors sometimes exchanged their long hair for a scalp lock.

Contemporary Information

GOVERNMENT/RESERVATIONS The following are Anishinabe reservations in Michigan:

L'Anse Reservation (Keweenaw Bay, L'Anse, and Otonagan Bands), Baraga County, established in 1854, consists of about 13,000 acres of land, almost two-thirds of which is allotted. There were about 3,100 enrolled members in the early 1990s. The 1990 Indian population was 724.

The Lac Vieux Desert Reservation, Gogebic County, consists of 104 acres of land. The 1990 Indian population was 119. This band had an enrollment of about 240 in the early 1990s. The reservation remains officially unrecognized.

The Bay Mills Indian Reservation (Bay Mills and Sault Ste. Marie Bands), Chippewa County, established in 1850, consists of 2,209 acres of land. The 1990 Indian population was 403. Enrolled membership was about 950 in the early 1990s.

The Sault Ste. Marie Reservation (Sault Ste. Marie Band), Alger, Chippewa, Mackinac, and Schoolcraft Counties, owns 293 acres of land. The 1990 Indian population was 554. There were about 20,630 enrolled band members in the early 1990s. The reservation remains officially unrecognized.

Isabella Reservation and Trust Lands, Isabella and Aranac Counties (Saginaw Chippewa Tribe), established in 1864, contains 1,184 acres, about half of which is tribally owned. A ten-member tribal council is elected at large. The 1990 Indian population was 790. This band had almost 2,200 enrolled members in the early 1990s.

The Grand Traverse Reservation (Ottawa and Chippewa), Leelanau County, consists of about 600 acres of land. The 1990 Indian population was 208. The tribe had about 2,300 members in the early 1990s. The reservation remains officially unrecognized.

The Burt Lake (State) Reservation (Ottawa and Chippewa), Brutus County, consists of about 20 acres. There were over 500 enrolled Chippewas and Ottawas in the early 1990s.

The Anishinabe communities in Minnesota, which are member reservations of the Minnesota Chippewa Tribe, are self-governed by an elected tribal council or business committee, in cooperation with local councils. Each community is also represented in an overall tribal executive committee, headquartered at Cass Lake community, Leech Lake. Red Lake Reservation is self-governing. The communities are as follows:

Nett Lake (Bois Forte) Reservation (Deer Creek Band), Koochiching and St. Louis Counties, established in 1854, consists of almost 42,000 acres. The 1990 Indian population was 345.

Fond du Lac Reservation, Carlton and St. Louis Counties, established in 1854, consists of almost 22,000 acres. The 1990 Indian population was 1,102.

Grand Portage Reservation, Cook County, established in 1854, consists of almost 45,000 acres. The 1990 Indian population was 206.

Leech Lake Reservation (Mississippi and Pilanger Bands), Beltrami, Cass, Hubbard, and Itasca Counties, established in 1855, consists of roughly 27,500 acres. The 1990 Indian population was 3,390.

Mille Lacs Reservation, Aitkin, Crow Wing, Kanabec, Mille Lacs, and Pine Counties, established in 1855, consists of almost 4,000 acres. The 1990 Indian population was 428.

White Earth Reservation, Blecker, Clearwater, and Mahnomen Counties, established in 1867, consists of roughly 56,000 acres. The 1990 Indian population was 2,759.

Red Lake Reservation, Beltrami, Clearwater, Koochiching, Lake of the Woods, Marshall, Pennington, Polk, Red Lake, and Roseau Counties, established in 1863, consists of roughly 564,000 acres of land. There were almost 8,000 enrolled members of this band in the early 1990s. The 1990 Indian population was 3,601.

The following are reservations of the Lake Superior Tribe (Wisconsin) of Chippewa Indians. Each is governed and administered by an IRA-style tribal council of from 5 to 12 members, headed by an executive officer. Tribal courts are also in the process of expanding their authority to cover welfare and environmental issues. The communities are also members of regional organizations such as the Great Lakes Inter-Tribal Council.

Bad River Reservation, Ashland and Iron Counties, established in 1854, consists of about 56,000 acres, less than half of which is tribally owned. The 1990 Indian population was 868. Tribal membership in the early 1990s was about 4,500 people.

Lac Courte Oreilles Reservation and Trust Lands, Sawyer, Burnett, and Washburn Counties, established in 1854, consists of about 48,000 acres, less than half of which is tribally owned. The 1990 Indian population was 1,769. Tribal membership in the early 1990s was about 4,000 people.

Lac du Flambeau Reservation, Iron, Oneida, and Vilas Counties, established in 1854, consists of almost 45,000 acres, about two-thirds of which is tribally owned. The 1990 Indian population was 1,431. Tribal membership in the early 1990s was about 2,700 people.

Red Cliff Reservation and Trust Lands, Bayfield County, established in 1854, consists of almost 75,000 acres, about three-quarters of which is tribally owned. The 1990 Indian population was 727. Tribal membership in the early 1990s was about 2,800 people.

The St. Croix Reservation and the Sokaogon Community and Trust Lands are also located in Wisconsin. St. Croix Reservation, Barron, Burnett, and Polk Counties, established in 1938, consists of about 2,200 acres, all of which is tribally owned. The 1990 Indian population was 459. Tribal membership in the early 1990s was about 750 people. The community is governed by a tribal council with officers.

Sokaogon Community and Trust Lands (Mole Lake Band), Forest County, established in 1938, consists of about 1,900 acres, all of which is tribally owned. The 1990 Indian population was 311. Tribal membership in the early 1990s was about 1,400 people. The community is governed by a tribal council with officers.

Other communities are in Montana and the Dakotas. The Rocky Boy Chippewa-Cree Reservation (1,485 resident Indians in 1990) and Trust Lands (397 resident Indians in 1990), located in Chouteau and Hill Counties, Montana, established in 1916, contains 108,015 acres. The tribe is governed by a written constitution delegating authority to the Chippewa-Cree Business Committee. There is also a tribal court. Roughly half of the population lives off of the reservation.

The Little Shell people, some of whom are of Cree descent, had a 1990 population of 3,300. They are governed by a tribal council under a constitution. Their main offices are in Havre and Helena, Montana. They are related to scattered groups of landless Chippewas living in and near Lewistown, Montana.

There is also a community of Chippewa, established during the process of allotting the Turtle Mountain Reservation, living in eastern Montana. The seat of their government is in Trenton, North Dakota.

The Turtle Mountain Reservation and Trust Lands, Rolette, Burke, Cavalier, Divide, McLean, Mountrail, and Williams Counties, North Dakota, and Perkins County, South Dakota, established in 1882, contains over 45,000 acres, of which about 30 percent is controlled by non-Indians. The 1990 resident Indian population was 6,770. The reservation is governed by an elected nine-member tribal council under a 1959 constitution and by-laws. Headquarters are located in Belcourt, North Dakota.

Canada recognizes over 130 Indian communities that are wholly or in part Anishinabe. They are located in Alberta, Manitoba, Ontario, and Saskatchewan and include Walpole Island (Ontario), where Anishinabe Indians live with some Potawatomis and Ottawas.

ECONOMY All of the acknowledged Michigan tribes operate successful casinos. Minnesota reservations operate at least one casino each. There is a women's cooperative that produces and sells wild rice and crafts at White Earth, Minnesota, and there is a fisheries cooperative at Red Lake, Minnesota. All Wisconsin reservations operate casinos. Forestry is an important industry. Many people are also part of local off-reservation economies. Unemployment is often around 50 percent.

The Rocky Boy Chippewa-Cree Development Company manages that tribe's economic resources. The tribe's beadwork is in high demand. The company organized a propane company and owns a casino as well as recreational facilities. The largest employers on the reservation are the tribal government, Stone Child Community College, and industry. Other activities include cattle grazing, wheat and barley farming, some logging and mining, and recreation/tourism. Unemployment regularly approaches 75 percent.

People in the Montana Allotment Community are integrated into the local economy. Turtle Mountain operates a casino, a manufacturing company, and a shopping center.

Many northern Ojibwas work at seasonal or part-time employment in industries such as construction, logging, and tourism. Fire fighting and tree planting offer some employment possibilities. There has also been an increase in government assistance.

LEGAL STATUS The following are federally recognized tribal entities in Michigan: the Bay Mills Indian Community of the Sault Ste. Marie Band of Chippewa Indians, Grand Traverse Band of Ottawa and Chippewa, Keweenaw Bay Indian Community of L'Anse of Chippewa Indians, Keweenaw Bay Indian Community of Lac Vieux Desert of Chippewa Indians, Keweenaw Bay Indian Community of Ontonagon Bands of Chippewa, Sault Ste. Marie Band of Chippewa Indians, and Saginaw Chippewa Indian Tribe.

In Minnesota, the federally recognized tribal entities are the Minnesota Chippewa Tribe (Bois Forte [Nett Lake] Band, Fond du Lac Band, Grand Portage Band, Leech Lake Band, Mille Lacs Band, and White Earth Band) and the Red Lake Band of Chippewa.

The Chippewa-Cree Indians of Rocky Boy Reservation is a federally recognized tribal entity in Montana.

The Turtle Mountain Band of Chippewa Indians is a federally recognized tribal entity in North Dakota.

The following are federally recognized tribal entities in Wisconsin: the Lake Superior Tribe of Chippewa (Bad River Band, Lac Courte Oreilles Band, Lac du Flambeau Band, and Red Cliff Band), the St. Croix Chippewa Indians, and the Sokaogon Band of Chippewa Community of the Mole Lake Band of Chippewa Indians.

The Burt Lake Band of Ottawa and Chippewa Indians is recognized by the state of Michigan and is pursuing federal acknowledgment. The Lake Superior Chippewa of Marquette Tribal Council (Michigan) has petitioned for federal recognition. The Consolidated Bahwetig Ojibwas and Mackinac Tribe (Michigan) has petitioned for federal recognition. The Kah-Bay Kah-Nong (Warroad) Chippewa (Minnesota) have petitioned for federal recognition.

The Little Shell Tribe of Chippewa Indians (North Dakota and Montana), as well as some of the "landless Chippewa" in Montana, have been seeking federal recognition since the 1920s. The Christian Pembina Chippewa Indians have also petitioned for federal recognition. Other officially unrecognized communities include the NI-MI-WIN Ojibweys (Minnesota), the Sandy Lake Band of Ojibwe (Minnesota), and the Swan Creek and Black River Chippewa (Montana).

The following are officially recognized northern Ojibwa bands in Ontario: Angling Lake, Bearskin Lake, Big Trout Lake, Caribou Lake, Cat Lake, Deer Lake, Fort Hope, Kasabonika lake, Kingfisher, Martin Falls, Muskrat Dam Lake, Osnaburgh, Sachigo Lake, and Wunnumin. Manitoba bands included Garden Hill, Red Sucker Lake, St. Theresa Point, and Wasagamack. Total population in 1980 was around 10,000.

Lake Winnipeg Salteaux bands in Ontario include Pikangikum, Islington, Grassy Narrows, Shoal Lake No. 39, Shoal Lake No. 40, Northwest Angle No. 33, Northwest Angle No. 37, Dalles, Rat Portage, Whitefish Bay, Eagle Lake, Wabigoon, Wabauskang, Lac Seul, Big Island, Big Grassy, and Sabaskong. Manitoba bands include Little Black River, Bloodvein, Hole River, Brokenhead, Roseau River, Berens River, Fort Alexander, Peguis, Little Grand Rapids, Jackhead, Fairford, Lake St. Martin, and Poplar River. Total population in 1980 was around 19,000.

DAILY LIFE The Michigan Anishinabe retain hunting and gathering rights on some ceded land. The Midewiwin society remains active in most communities, and most tribes maintain an active schedule of traditional or semitraditional events such as powwows, sweat lodges, and conferences. The Bay Mills Community operates its own community college. The Sault Ste. Marie tribe hosts two powwows and publishes a newspaper.

In Minnesota, most people retain their Indian identity in a number of important ways. A community college at Fond du Lac emphasizes tribal culture. People are pursuing several land reacquisition projects and subsistence rights cases. There are a number of powwows and other traditional and semitraditional activities throughout the state. The Ojibwa language, which roughly 30,000 people speak, is taught in schools and colleges. Authors continue a tradition of writing about their culture. Artists and craftspeople continue to produce moccasins, clothing, baskets, and other items. Leech Lake hosts five annual powwows, operates a school and a tribal college, and publishes a newsletter.

Although about half of Wisconsin Anishinabes live in mostly non-native cities and towns, most retain close ties to their home communities. The people maintain their Indian identity through events such as powwows, athletic contests, and traditional subsistence activities. Since a landmark court case in 1983 reaffirmed their subsistence rights on ceded land, the people have redoubled their efforts to defend those rights against a non-native backlash. Toward this end, they have established a number of environmental organizations, such as the Great Lakes Indian Fish and Wildlife Commission, to manage their natural resources and provide other related enforcement and public relations services.

Lac Courte Oreilles Community College provides crucial educational services to Wisconsin's Indians, including a radio station and courses on native language and cultures. Ongoing cultural traditions include Midewiwin lodges, the Drum Society (a late-nineteenth-century phenomenon), and subsistence activities. Although most are less than fluent, many people continue to speak the language.

Turtle Mountain Community College, which administers many tribal and federal social, health, and educational programs, is an important part of the Turtle Mountain, North Dakota, community. Ojibwe and Métis are still spoken. Most of these people are Catholic. Economic self-sufficiency remains a high priority.

In 1968, three Anishinabe founded the American Indian Movement (AIM), a self-help organization that proceeded to fight both quietly and openly for Indian rights. Important AIM actions have included the 1969 takeover of Alcatraz Island, the 1972 occupation of the Bureau of Indian Affairs in Washington, and the 1973 defense of Wounded Knee, South Dakota.

Northern Ojibwas in Canada have enjoyed decent health care facilities and educational opportunities since the 1950s. Trapping remains important but considerably less so than in the past. Many people live near their relatives. Many people are Christians.

Many Lake Winnipeg Salteaux people in Canada have intermarried with Cree Indians. The native religion has practically disappeared. Christianity, including some fundamentalist sects, has largely taken over, with one result being a high degree of factionalism. Roads have connected the people to the outside world only since the 1950s.

Brothertown

See Pequot

Cayuga

The Cayuga (K ī ` ū gä), from their word for "People of Oiogouen," were one of the five original tribes of the Iroquois League. The name Iroquois ("real adders") comes from the French adaptation of the Algonquian name for these people. Their self-designation was *Kanonsionni*, "League of the United (Extended) Households." Iroquois today refer to themselves as *Haudenosaunee*, "People of the Longhouse." *See also* Seneca.

LOCATION In the early historical period, the Cayuga lived in upstate New York, especially between Cayuga and Owasco Lakes, land between that of the Onondaga and the Seneca. At the height of their power, the Iroquois controlled land from the Hudson to the Illinois Rivers and the Ottawa to the Tennessee Rivers. Today, Cayugas live in Canada, western New York, Wisconsin, and Oklahoma.

POPULATION There were about 1,500 Cayuga in 1660 and possibly as many as several thousand or more a century earlier, of perhaps 20,000 members of the Iroquois League. In the 1990s fewer than 500 Cayugas lived in New York, about 3,000 lived in Canada, and about 2,500 Seneca-Cayugas lived in Oklahoma. There were roughly 70,000 Iroquois Indians living in the United States and Canada in the mid-1990s.

LANGUAGE Cayugas spoke a Northern Iroquois dialect.

Historical Information

HISTORY The Iroquois began cultivating crops shortly after the first phase of their culture in New York was established around 800. Deganawida, a Huron prophet, and Hiawatha, a Mohawk shaman living among the Onondaga, founded the Iroquois League or Confederacy some time between 1450 and 1600. It originally consisted of five tribes: Cayuga, Mohawk, Oneida, Onondaga, and Seneca; the Tuscarora joined in the early eighteenth century. The league's purpose was to end centuries of debilitating intertribal war and work for the common good. Both Deganawida and Hiawatha may have been actual or mythological people.

Iroquois first met non-natives in the sixteenth century. There were sporadic Jesuit missions in Cayuga country throughout the mid–seventeenth century. During those years, the Cayuga were more friendly toward the French than were some other Iroquois tribes. The people became heavily involved in the fur trade during the seventeenth and eighteenth centuries. Trading, fighting, and political intrigue characterized those years. Although they were good at playing the European powers off against each other, the Iroquois increasingly became British allies in trade and in the colonial wars and were instrumental in the ultimate British victory over the French.

Diplomatic success allowed the Iroquois to concentrate on expanding their trapping territory and increasing their trade advantages, mainly by fighting many tribes to their west and south. The Cayuga warpath led as far south as Virginia. Iroquois power blocked European westward expansion. Two Siouan tribes, the Tutelo and the Saponi, joined the Cayuga in 1753.

The British victory in 1763 meant that the Iroquois no longer controlled the regional balance of power. Despite their long-standing allegiance, some Indians joined anti-British rebellions in an effort to protect their land. One such rebellion took place in 1774 and was led by Logan, a Cayuga chief of the Iroquoian Mingos of Pennsylvania.

The confederacy split its allegiance in the Revolutionary War, with most Cayugas siding with the British. This split resulted in the council fire's being extinguished for the first time in some 200 years. The Iroquois suffered a major defeat in 1779. After the final U.S. victory, many Cayugas migrated to Ontario, Canada, where they established two villages on the Six Nations Reserve. Others settled with the Seneca in western New York. Still others remained for several more years in their homelands. However, by 1807 the Cayuga had sold all their land to the United States. After the Buffalo Creek and Tonawanda Reservations were sold in 1842, Indians who had been living there, including many Cayugas, relocated to the Cattaraugus and Allegany Reservations. Most Cayugas went to Cattaraugus.

The Iroquois Council officially split into two parts during that time. One branch was located at the Six Nations Reserve and the other at Buffalo Creek. Gradually, internal reservation affairs as well as relations with the United States and Canada assumed more significance than intraconfederacy matters. In the 1840s, when the Buffalo Creek Reservation was sold, the fire there was rekindled at Onondaga.

In Canada, the Cayugas, known with the Onondagas and Senecas as the "lower tribes," tended to retain more of their traditional beliefs than did the "upper" Iroquois tribes. Many subsequently adopted the Handsome Lake religion. Traditional structures were further weakened by the allotment of reservation lands in the 1840s; the requirement under Canadian law, from 1869 on, of patrilineal descent; and the transition of league councils and other political structures to a municipal government. In 1924, the Canadian government terminated confederacy rule entirely, mandating an (all male) elected system of government on the reserve.

The native economy gradually shifted from primarily hunting to farming, dependence on annuities received for the sale of land, and some wage labor. The people faced increasing pressure from non-natives to adopt Christianity and sell more land. The old religion declined during that time, although on some reservations the Handsome Lake religion grew in importance.

In 1817, some of the New York Cayuga, along with other Iroquois and Delaware Indians, moved west to near the Sandusky River in Ohio. They were removed to Indian Territory (Oklahoma) in 1831. Some other Cayugas moved to Wisconsin in 1832 with a group of Oneidas. The Cayuga maintained a separate tribal government in Oklahoma until 1937. Mainly because of fraud and outright theft, their 65,000-acre reservation had been reduced to 140 acres of tribal land by 1936. In 1937, the Seneca-Cayuga incorporated under Oklahoma law, adopting a constitution and by-laws

and electing a business committee. Although their land base quickly grew, almost 300 acres were later taken away as a result of reservoir construction. The tribe successfully resisted termination in the 1950s. With other members of the confederacy, the Cayuga resisted the 1924 citizenship act, selective service, and all federal and state intrusions on their sovereignty.

RELIGION The Cayuga recognized *Orenda*, a supreme creator. Other animate and inanimate objects and natural forces were also considered of a spiritual nature. They held important festivals to celebrate maple sap and strawberries as well as corn planting, ripening (Green Corn ceremony), and harvest. These festivals often included singing, male dancing, game playing, gambling, feasting, and food distribution.

The eight-day new year's festival may have been most important of all. Held in midwinter, it was a time to give thanks, to forget past wrongs, and to kindle new fires, with much attention paid to new and old dreams. A condolence ceremony had quasi-religious components. Curing societies also conducted ceremonies, since illness was thought to be of supernatural origin.

In the early nineteenth century, many Iroquois embraced the teachings of Handsome Lake. This religion was born during the general religious ferment known as the Second Great Awakening and came directly out of the radical breakdown of Iroquois life. Beginning in 1799, the Seneca Handsome Lake spoke of Jesus and called upon Iroquois to give up alcohol and a host of negative behaviors, such as witchcraft and sexual promiscuity. He also exhorted them to maintain their traditional religious celebrations. A blend of traditional and Christian teachings, the Handsome Lake religion had the effect of facilitating the cultural transition occurring at the time.

GOVERNMENT The Iroquois League comprised 50 hereditary chiefs, or sachems, from the constituent tribes. Each position was named for the original holder and had specific responsibilities. Sachems were men, except where a woman acted as regent, but they were appointed by women. The Cayuga sent ten sachems to meetings of the Iroquois Great Council, which met in the fall and for emergencies. Their symbol at this gathering was the Great Pipe.

Tribes were divided into two divisions within the league, the Cayuga belonging to the "younger brothers." Debates within the great council were a matter of strict clan, division, and tribal protocols, in a complex system of checks and balances. Politically, individual league members often pursued their own best interests while maintaining an essential solidarity with the other members. The creators of the U.S. government used the Iroquois League as a model of democracy.

Locally, the village structure was governed by a headman and a council of elders (clan chiefs, elders, wise men). Matters before the local councils were handled according to a definite protocol based on the clan and division memberships of the chiefs. Village chiefs were chosen from groups as small as a single household. Women nominated and recalled clan chiefs. Tribal chiefs represented the village and the nation at the general council of the league. The entire system was hierarchical and intertwined, from the family up to the great council. Decisions at all levels were reached by consensus.

There were also a number of nonhereditary chiefs ("pine tree" or "merit" chiefs), some of whom had no voting power. This may have been a postcontact phenomenon.

CUSTOMS The Cayuga recognized a dual division, each composed of two more matrilineal, animal-named clans. The clans in turn were composed of matrilineal lineages. The Cayuga probably had nine clans. Each owned a set number of personal names, some of which were linked with particular activities and responsibilities.

Women enjoyed a high degree of prestige, being largely equated with the "three sisters" (corn, beans, and squash), and they were in charge of most village activities, including marriage. Great intravillage lacrosse games included heavy gambling. Other games included snowsnake, or sliding a spear along a trench in the snow for distance. Food was shared so that everyone had roughly the same to eat.

Personal health and luck were maintained by performing various individual rituals, including singing and dancing, learned in dreams. Members of the False Face medicine society wore wooden masks carved from trees and used rattles and tobacco. Shamans also used up to 200 or more plant medicines to cure illness. People committed suicide on occasion for specific reasons (men who lost prestige; women who were abandoned; children who were treated harshly). Murder could be revenged or paid for with sufficient gifts.

The dead were buried in a sitting position, with food and tools for use on the way to the land of the dead. A ceremony was held after ten days. The condolence ceremony mourned dead league chiefs and installed successors. A modified version also applied to common people.

DWELLINGS In the early eighteenth century, Cayugas lived in at least three villages of 30 or more longhouses, each village with 500 or more people. The people built their villages near water and often on a hill after about 1300. Some villages were palisaded. Other Iroquois villages had up to 150 longhouses and 1,000 or more people. Villages were moved about twice in a generation, when firewood and soil were exhausted.

Iroquois Indians built elm-bark longhouses, 50–100 feet long, depending on how many people lived there, from about the twelfth century on. The longhouses held 2 or 3 or as many as 20 families, related maternally (lineage segments), as well as their dogs. There were smoke holes over each two-family fire. Beds were raised platforms; people slept on mats, their feet to the fire, covered by pelts. Upper platforms were used for food and gear storage. Roofs were shingled with elm bark. The people also built some single-family houses.

DIET Women grew corn, beans, squash, and gourds. Corn was the staple and was used in soups, stews, breads, and puddings. It was stored in bark-lined cellars. Women also gathered a variety of greens, nuts, seeds, roots, berries, fruits, and mushrooms. Tobacco was grown for ceremonial and social smoking.

After the harvest, men and some women took to the woods for several months to hunt and dry meat. Men hunted large game and trapped smaller game, mostly for the fur. Hunting was a source of potential prestige. They also caught waterfowl and other birds, and they fished. The people grew peaches, pears, and apples in orchards from the eighteenth century on.

KEY TECHNOLOGY Iroquois used porcupine quills and wampum belts as a record of events. Wampum was also used as a gift connoting sincerity and, later, as trade money. These shell disks, strung or woven into belts, were probably a postcontact technological innovation.

Hunting equipment included snares, bow and arrow, stone knife, and bentwood pack frame. Fish were caught using traps, nets, bone hooks, and spears. Farming tools were made of stone, bone, wood (spades), and antler. Women wove tobacco trays, mats, and baskets.

Other important material items included elm-bark containers, cordage from inner tree bark and fibers, and levers to move timbers. Men steamed wood or bent green wood to make many items, including lacrosse sticks.

TRADE Cayugas obtained birch-bark products from the Huron. They imported copper and shells. They were extensively involved in the trade in beaver furs from the seventeenth century on.

NOTABLE ARTS Men carved wooden masks worn by the Society of Faces in their curing ceremonies. Women decorated clothing with dyed porcupine quills.

TRANSPORTATION Unstable elm-bark canoes were roughly 25 feet long. The people were also great runners and preferred to travel on land. They used snowshoes in winter.

DRESS Women made most clothing from deerskins. Men wore breechclouts and shirts; women wore skirts. Both wore leggings, moccasins, and cornhusk slippers in summer. Clothing was decorated with feathers and porcupine quills. Both men and women tattooed their bodies extensively.

WAR AND WEAPONS Boys began developing war skills at a young age. Prestige and leadership were often gained through war, which was in many ways the most important activity. The title of Pine Tree Chief was a historical invention to honor especially brave warriors.

All aspects of warfare, from the initiation to the conclusion, were highly ritualized. War could be decided as a matter of policy or undertaken as a vendetta. Women had a large, sometimes decisive, say in the question of whether or not to fight. During war season, generally the fall, Iroquois war parties ranged over hundreds of miles. Their weapons included the bow and arrow, ball-headed club, shield, rod armor, and guns after 1640.

Male prisoners were often forced to run the gauntlet: Those who made it through were adopted, but those who did not might be tortured by widows. Women and children prisoners were regularly adopted. Some captives were eaten.

Contemporary Information

GOVERNMENT/RESERVATIONS The Cayuga have no reservation. Most live on the three Seneca reservations—Allegany, Oil Spring, and especially Cattaraugus—and on the Onondaga Reservation. The tribe is governed by a council of hereditary chiefs. Their headquarters is located in Versailles, New York.

Cayugas also live on the Six Nations/Grand River Reserve, Ontario, Canada. Established in 1784, it is governed by both an elected and a hereditary council, although only the first is federally recognized.

The Seneca-Cayuga Tribe is located in Ottawa County, Oklahoma. The tribe owned roughly 4,000 acres of trust and allotted land in 1993.

ECONOMY There is generally high unemployment in New York and Canada. Many Cayugas are integrated into local economies, especially in construction, the trades, and the service industries. Oklahoma Cayugas work in ranching and in nearby cities.

LEGAL STATUS The Cayuga Nation of New York and the Seneca-Cayuga Tribe of Oklahoma are federally recognized tribal entities. There are ongoing negotiations with the federal government over land claims; in one such case, a federal court ruled against the state of New York in 1991.

DAILY LIFE Traditional political and social (clan) structures remain intact, as does the language. One major exception is caused by Canada's requirement that band membership be reckoned patrilineally. The tribe generally meets annually in Versailles and in the Buffalo area. Cayugas and Senecas have yet to resolve issues of Cayuga land ownership on the Cattaraugus reservation. Cayugas may avail themselves of health, education, and other programs of the Seneca Nation.

Cayugas gather with other Iroquois Indians for various festivals, such as the Six Nations festival held on Labor Day weekend. They make some traditional foods, such as hulled corn soup, especially for special occasions. The political structure of the Iroquois League continues to be a source of controversy for many Iroquois (Haudensaunee). Some recognize two seats—at Onondaga and Six Nations—whereas others consider the government at Six Nations a reflection of or a corollary to the traditional seat at Onondaga. Important issues concerning the confederacy in the later twentieth century include Indian burial sites, sovereignty, gambling casinos, and land claims.

The Six Nations Reserve is still marked by the existence of "progressive" and "traditional" factions, with the former generally supporting the elected band council and following the Christian faith and the latter supporting the confederacy and the Longhouse religion. Traditional Iroquois Indians, many of whom are Cayugas, celebrate at least ten traditional or quasi-traditional ceremonies, including the Midwinter, Green Corn, and Strawberry. Oklahoma Cayugas maintain ties with their northeastern relatives. They celebrate the Green Corn and other ceremonies and maintain a longhouse.

Chippewa
See Anishinabe

Delaware
See Lenápe

Fox

Fox (Fäks), possibly from one of the tribe's clans. Their self-designation was *Mesquaki,* "Red Earth People." The Fox were culturally related to the Kickapoo. *See also* Sauk.

LOCATION In the seventeenth century, the Fox were located in a wide area on the border between the Woodlands and the prairie, centered in eastern Wisconsin near Lake Winnebago. By the eighteenth century the Anishinabe had forced them into extreme southwest Wisconsin, extreme northwest Illinois, and northern Iowa. Today, most Fox Indians live in central Iowa. Headquarters for the Sac and Fox Nation is in Lincoln County, Oklahoma.

POPULATION   There were about 2,500 Fox in the mid–seventeenth century. The tribe had approximately 1,000 enrolled members in the early 1990s.

LANGUAGE   The Fox people speak an Algonquian language.

Historical Information

HISTORY   The Fox may once have lived just west and/or south of Lake Erie and, before that, along the southern shore of Lake Superior. They were driven by Iroquois raids into the upper Fox River–Chicago River area, perhaps in the early seventeenth century.

After non-natives first appeared among them in the mid–seventeenth century, the Fox quickly joined the fur trade. Unlike most Algonquians, however, they refused to settle near trading posts or missions. They also made enemies by requiring a toll from French traders plying the Fox River and were even able to block French access to the Mississippi if and when they chose.

The Fox fought the French and their Indian allies in the early to mid–eighteenth century, armed primarily with British weapons. They were almost destroyed during that period by warfare and disease, which was in fact the goal of French forces. Survivors took refuge with the Sauk in 1733, beginning an alliance that lasted until the 1850s. Refusing to give up their Fox friends, in 1735 the Sauk held off French attackers, and both tribes escaped to Iowa. The French pardoned both tribes in 1737, and shortly thereafter they returned to Wisconsin.

In 1769, the Sauk, Fox, and other tribes dealt a permanent defeat to the Illinois tribes and moved south and west into some of their former territory and ultimately back into Iowa. By that time they had become highly capable buffalo hunters. Hunting parties traveled far west of the Mississippi in search of the herds, and they adopted many aspects of typical Great Plains buffalo-hunting culture.

The Fox took an active part in Little Turtle's war (1790–1794) and in Tecumseh's rebellion (1809–1811), two defensive actions in which the tribes of the old west made a last-ditch effort to hold onto their lands. Lead mines near Dubuque, Iowa, at which the Fox had been mining up to two tons of lead a year, were illegally seized by non-native interests in the early nineteenth century. In 1842, the Sauk and Fox ceded their remaining lands and were relocated to a reservation in Kansas.

Some Fox remained with the Sauk in Kansas and went with them in 1869 to the Indian Territory (Oklahoma). However, after a series of disputes with the Sauk, most Fox returned to Iowa in the late 1850s, settling near Tama and acquiring land there. Ownership of their own land prevented future allotment

and enabled the people to maintain their physical boundaries and thus much of their traditional culture. The people generally refused to enroll their children when the Bureau of Indian Affairs opened a boarding school in the late nineteenth century, but they did accept a day school after 1912. They adopted an Indian Reorganization Act–based government in 1937.

RELIGION   The Fox recognized an upper and a lower region. The former was ruled by the great or gentle manitou. There were also any number of other nature-related spirits, or manitous, the most important of which were connected with the four directions. People might gain the attention and assistance of the manitous by offering tobacco, blackening the face with charcoal, fasting, and wailing.

The vision quest, undertaken at puberty, was another way to attract spiritual power. Those who were especially successful assembled a medicine pack or bundle; certain packs represented power that affected and were the property of entire lineages. Two annual ceremonies were related to the medicine packs.

The Midewiwin was a key ceremony. Others included the Green Corn and Adoption ceremonies. As part of the latter, a person was formally adopted to take the place of someone who had died or been killed. The calumet, or sacred pipe, played a vital role in all sacred activities, including peace negotiations. A head shaman instructed others in curing, hunting, agricultural, and other ceremonies.

GOVERNMENT   Fox society was divided into bands or villages, of fluid composition, that formed in summer but broke up in winter. There were dual political divisions of peace and war. Officers were the main chief, subchiefs, and criers.

A hereditary peace chief held authority over gatherings, treaties, peace councils, intertribal negotiations, and rituals. In return for access to his property, the people regularly gave him gifts. War chiefs were chosen by other warriors on the basis of merit, although there may have been a hereditary component. These people commanded the camp police and presided over councils during war when a stricter, more disciplined organization was needed.

CUSTOMS   The Fox recognized about 14 patrilineal clans. Membership in one of the two tribal divisions was determined by birth order. Each summer house was an economic unit as well as a social one. The families of murder victims usually accepted compensation, but they were at liberty to require blood vengeance. Lacrosse was a popular game.

Birth took place in special lodges in the company of only women; the mother remained subject to special postpartum restrictions for up to a year or more.

The baby was named by an elderly relative, who could choose from among the stock of clan names. As adults, people might acquire additional, nonclan names as a result of dreams or warfare. Parents rarely inflicted corporal punishment upon their children.

At the onset of puberty, girls were secluded for ten days and were subject to various restrictions. Both sexes marked puberty by undertaking a vision quest. Vermilion face paint indicated an adult status. Marriages were generally arranged by the couple in question and were formalized when the families exchanged gifts. The couple lived with the wife's family for a year before establishing their own household. Some men had more than one wife. Adultery was generally cause for divorce.

Burial took place after various rituals had been performed. Warriors might be buried in a sitting position. All people were buried in their finest clothing, wrapped in bark or mats with their feet toward the west. Sacred tobacco was placed on the graves. A dog might be killed as a companion on the way to the land of the dead. The mourning period lasted for at least six months, during which time mourners were subject to a variety of behavioral restrictions.

DWELLINGS Summer villages were located near crop fields in river bottoms. Extended families of some ten people lived in houses about 50 feet long by 20 feet wide and covered with elm bark. These houses were oriented in an east-west direction and were built in parallel rows, with an open game and ceremonial area in between. People moved the villages when firewood became scarce or when attacks forced them to move. When in their winter camps, people lived in small, dome-shaped wigwams covered with reed mats and located in sheltered river valleys. The camps ranged in size from just one or two families to an entire band.

DIET Fox women grew corn, beans, squash, and tobacco. They also gathered a number of wild plant foods, including nuts, honey, berries, fruits, and tubers. Men hunted a variety of large and small game, especially deer, as well as buffalo from at least the eighteenth century until about 1820.

KEY TECHNOLOGY Pipes were made of carved pipestone (catlinite) and wooden or reed stems. Most tools and utensils were made of wood, grasses, stone, or bone. The people also made bark containers.

TRADE The Fox exported deerskins and tallow as well as lead.

NOTABLE ARTS The people made silk appliqué from the mid–eighteenth century on.

TRANSPORTATION Men made bark and dugout canoes.

DRESS Clothing was generally light and consisted mainly of buckskin breechclouts, dresses or aprons, leggings, and moccasins. Hide or fur robes were added for extra warmth. The people also tattooed and painted their bodies.

WAR AND WEAPONS Reasons for war included conflict over territory, retaliation, and the achievement of status. War parties had to be authorized by the war council. Leaders of war parties began by fasting to obtain a vision and undertook several more ritualistic activities before the party departed. The leader carried his sacred ark, which was said to provide the party with spiritual power. Warriors were subject to a number of rituals on their return as well.

Prisoners were often adopted. War calumets were decorated with red feathers and peace calumets with white feathers. Traditional enemies included the Anishinabe and occasionally the Dakota; allies were the Sauk from the early eighteenth century on and the Kickapoo.

Contemporary Information

GOVERNMENT/RESERVATIONS The Mesquaki Nation lives on or near their own settlement established in 1856 and located near Tama, Tama County, Iowa. The nation holds roughly 5,000 acres of land, none of which has been allotted. The 1990 Indian population was 563. Government is by a seven-member tribal council with officers, all of whom must be enrolled in the tribe and living in the community. Some members still recognize the authority of the hereditary chief.

ECONOMY There is some corn and soybean farming, some farmwork or wage work in neighboring towns, and some income from land leased to nonnatives. There is also bingo, and a casino and other tourist-related enterprises are planned.

LEGAL STATUS The Sac and Fox Tribe of the Mississippi in Iowa (Mesquaki Nation) is a federally recognized tribal entity.

DAILY LIFE "Traditional" and "progressive" factions have struggled for control of the tribe for much of the twentieth century. Traditional kinship ties remain important, and the language remains vital. The Sac and Fox Settlement School, bilingual and bicultural, enrolls children from kindergarten through the eighth grade. Christian sects, the Native American Church, and the Drum religion are all active, as are elements of traditional Fox religion. The annual powwow is held in August.

Huron

See Wyandotte

Illinois

Illinois (I li `noy) were a group of bands, probably all Algonquians, that included but were not limited to the Cahokia, Kaskaskia, Michigamea, Moingwena, Peoria, and Tamaroa. The word "Illinois" is a French adaptation of their self-designation, *Inoca*. The Illinois were a borderline Eastern Woodlands group, with much of their territory consisting of prairie. They were culturally similar to the Miami.

LOCATION The Illinois lived south of Lake Michigan in the early seventeenth century. Later in that century they were located in present-day Illinois, western Missouri, northern Arkansas, and eastern Iowa, especially along the Illinois River. Today, most surviving Peorias live in northeastern Oklahoma.

POPULATION There were about 10,000 Illinois in 1650 and approximately 2,000 Peorias in the mid-1990s.

LANGUAGE Illinois was an Algonquian language.

Historical Information

HISTORY The Illinois may have come to their historic territory from the northeast. They may have mixed with the Cahokian (Mississippian) people when they moved into Illinois in the mid–seventeenth century. The people fought two major wars with the Winnebago from about 1630 to 1645: They lost the first and won the second. In the mid–seventeenth century, the Illinois also attacked the Miamis and pushed them northward out of northern Illinois.

Iroquois attacks drove the people west of the Mississippi in about 1660. They did not return until pushed east by the Dakota after 1870. After this time they began slaving raids on Siouan and Pawnee tribes west of the Mississippi. The Illinois tribes first met French explorers in the 1670s and became French allies shortly thereafter. The Iroquois, aided by the Miami, kept up their attacks against the Illinois until at least the late seventeenth century.

Abandonment of the Illinois River region and a southward movement began around 1700, marking a general defeat at the hands of tribes such as the Kickapoo, Fox, and Sauk, who also sought French favor. With the exception of the Peoria, who held out in the north until the later eighteenth century, most Illinois tribes became associated with specific French agricultural settlements. By 1800, the Michigamea, Cahokia, and Tamaroa merged with the Kaskaskia and Peoria.

The Wisconsin tribes maintained more or less continuous pressure on the Illinois tribes during the eighteenth century. The final battle may have come after an Illinois Indian, said to be in the pay of Britain, killed Chief Pontiac in 1769. In any case, those Illinois still free of French protection were all but wiped out, suffering upward of 90 percent casualties. Meanwhile, the southern Illinois, through their contact with the French, had become missionized, poor, and alcoholic.

Survivors of the wars with the Great Lakes Algonquians, mainly members of the Kaskaskia and Peoria Bands, signed treaties in the early nineteenth century ceding their lands to the United States. Their culture practically gone, these people moved to eastern Kansas in 1833, where they lived with the Wea and Piankashaw (Miami) Bands until 1867, when they all bought land in northeastern Oklahoma. In 1873 they took the name United Peoria and Miami. Their lands were allotted in 1893, and any remaining tribal land was lost when Oklahoma became a state in 1907. The group reincorporated as the Peoria Tribe of Oklahoma in 1940. They were terminated in 1950 but restored in 1978.

RELIGION Manitou, a supreme being or creator, dwelled to the east and may have been identified with the sun. Men probably undertook a vision quest at adolescence, during which they hoped to attract a personal guardian spirit. At the onset of puberty, girls fasted in a special lodge until they received a personal guardian spirit. Shamans, or medicine people (they could be men or women and were usually older), conducted religious ceremonies. They acquired their powers from powerful animal spirits. Most ceremonies included dancing and smoking tobacco from a sacred pipe, or calumet. There were regular summer ceremonies involving the ritual death and revival of a patient.

GOVERNMENT Each tribe was an independent entity and lived either in a separate village or in a separate section of a multitribe village. There may have been peace and war chiefs as well as criers to make announcements. Camp police during the summer buffalo hunt enforced strict discipline.

CUSTOMS Illinois tribes recognized patrilineal clans. Hospitality was a primary value. A ritual feast followed a boy's first game kill. Boys who showed such an inclination might become berdaches, or men who dressed like women and assumed all of their roles. Berdaches were regarded as having a particularly sacred element: They attended all ceremonies, and their advice was sought at council meetings. Murderers were either killed or were allowed to pay retribution. Lacrosse was a popular game.

Men usually refrained from marriage until they had proven themselves as warriors and hunters. Marriage negotiations were held in clearly defined ways between the two families and revolved around gift exchange. Men often had more than one wife. Women could destroy the property of men who attempted to marry without the proper lineage controls. Female adultery was punished by death, mutilation, or mass rape. A man who killed his wife's lover was subject to blood retribution.

Each sex was responsible for burying its own dead. After their face and hair were painted, corpses were dressed in fine clothing, wrapped in skins, and buried in the ground or on scaffolds. Tools, pipes, and other goods were set by the grave, which was marked by two forked sticks with a cross-stick or, in the case of a chief, by a painted log. Various ceremonies were then performed that honored the dead by reenacting a favorite activity. Souls or spirits were said to travel to an afterlife. Property exchange also accompanied death. The official mourning period lasted about a year.

DWELLINGS The Illinois built semipermanent summer villages strung out for miles along river banks. The villages consisted of up to 300 or more lodges, each with one to four fireplaces and housing up to 12 families. There were also small menstrual/birth huts and possibly an additional structure used for political or ceremonial purposes.

Large, rectangular summer houses were built of woven mats over a pole frame. Mats were also placed on the ground as floors. The people also built temporary summer and winter hunting camps. Summer huts were bark-covered buildings, whereas winter lodges were covered with rush mats.

DIET Meat formed the most important part of the Illinois diet. Men hunted elk, bear, deer, mountain lion, turkey, beaver, and other animals. They also hunted buffalo on the nearby prairies. Communal hunts took place in summer. Before they acquired horses, Illinois men generally surrounded buffalo with a ring of fire and then shot them with a bow and arrow. Women and children went along on the hunt to dry the meat and pack it home. Women grew corn, beans, and squash. They also gathered a variety of wild fruits, nuts, berries, and roots.

KEY TECHNOLOGY Wood was the basic material, but tools and other items were also made from bone, stone, and shell. Women made a variety of mats and bags with yarn spun of buffalo and bear hair.

TRADE The people exported animal and wood products, crops, and some woven items.

NOTABLE ARTS Illinois found artistic expression in painting buffalo robes, weaving, woodcarving, and doing quillwork.

TRANSPORTATION Men fashioned dugout canoes of up to 50 feet in length from butternut trees.

DRESS Men wore breechclouts; women wore long dresses. Both sexes wore buffalo robes and blankets. They also tattooed and painted their bodies and wore various personal adornments of animal teeth, colored stones, feathers, and other items.

WAR AND WEAPONS The Illinois were considered relatively poor fighters and were mainly unenthusiastic about war. Raiding parties were generally small, although there were large ones accompanied by women. Birds were the supernatural spirit related to war, and each warrior kept bird skins in a special reed mat. Raids were led by a person who sponsored a dog feast; the group then engaged in an all-night ceremony designed to propitiate the bird spirits. Personal bird cries accompanied the actual attack. Success was defined by the relative loss of warriors, and leaders had to compensate relatives for lost men.

Illinois enemies included the Iroquois, Dakota, Quapaw, Pawnee, and Osage in the seventeenth century and the Great Lakes Algonquians and the Chickasaw in the eighteenth century. Otoes were occasional allies. Weapons included bows and flint-tipped arrows, spears, clubs, flint knives, and long buffalo-hide shields. Berdaches fought with clubs rather than bows.

Capturing prisoners rated higher war honors than killing them. Male prisoners were usually burned and eaten, whereas women and children were distributed among the population. Some were ultimately adopted, but some maintained a slavelike identity.

Contemporary Information

GOVERNMENT/RESERVATIONS Peoria tribal headquarters is located in Miami (Ottawa County), Oklahoma. A 1981 constitution provides for an elected business council plus officers. The tribe includes descendants of the Miami bands as well as bands of the Illinois Confederacy. It owns almost 40 acres of land.

ECONOMY Tribal members own local businesses. Some people work in Tulsa. The unemployment rate among tribal members regularly approaches 90 percent.

LEGAL STATUS The Peoria Tribe of Oklahoma is a federally recognized tribal entity.

DAILY LIFE Peorias work with neighboring tribes (Seneca, Miami, Quapaw, and Ottawa) in areas of common interest. Most are assimilated into mainstream life. Tribal members participate in local and regional Indian celebrations, such as Indian Heritage Days, held in June. Although most traditional culture has disappeared, including the language, some members know some old songs and dances, and there is an effort to revive the Calumet Dance as well as traditional arts and crafts.

Iroquois

See Cayuga; Mohawk; Oneida; Onondaga; Seneca. *See also* Tuscarora (Chapter 7).

Kickapoo

Kickapoo (`Kik ə p ū), possibly from *kiwegapaw*, "he moves about, standing now here, now there." The

Kickapoo were culturally similar to the Sauk and Fox and may once have been united with the Shawnee.

LOCATION   The Kickapoo lived around the Fox and Wisconsin Rivers (present-day southern Wisconsin) in the mid–seventeenth century, although they inhabited present-day Michigan and Ohio earlier and Illinois and Kansas somewhat later. Today, Kickapoos live in northeast Kansas, central Oklahoma, and northern Mexico.

POPULATION   There were between 2,000 and 3,000 Kickapoos in the mid–seventeenth century and approximately 3,000 in the 1990s.

LANGUAGE   Kickapoos spoke an Algonquian language similar to Sauk and Fox.

Historical Information

HISTORY   The Kickapoo may have originated in southeast Michigan. In the seventeenth century, pressure from the Iroquois drove them west to southern Wisconsin, where they encountered French missionaries. They may have shared villages with the Miami at that time.

Kickapoos entered the fur trade, but throughout the later seventeenth century and early eighteenth century resisted pressure to assimilate and cede their lands. They were often at war with the French during that period, although the two groups established an alliance in 1729. They also fought various Indian tribes.

In the early eighteenth century, the Kickapoo joined tribes such as the Ojibwa, Ottawa, Sauk, and Fox to defeat the Illinois Confederacy and occupy their territory. The Kickapoo moved south to the Illinois River, where the tribe soon divided. One group headed farther south to the Sangamon River. Known as the Prairie Band, they increased their buffalo hunting. The other group moved east toward the Vermillion Branch of the Wabash River. This band retained their forest hunting practices. The band also absorbed the Mascouten, or Prairie Potawatomi, tribe of Indians.

Part of the Prairie Band moved into southwest Missouri in the mid-1760s. Following the French defeat in 1763, the Kickapoo transferred their allegiance to the Spanish. They participated in Pontiac's rebellion and later accepted British aid against the United States, with whom they never had good relations.

The early nineteenth century saw greatly increased non-native settlement in the region. Most Kickapoos participated in Little Turtle's war. The Vermillion Band also supported Tecumseh's rebellion, which the Prairie Band opposed. Both groups, however, were drawn into the War of 1812. Some chiefs of each band ceded the people's Illinois land in 1819, a move that forced most Kickapoos to join the group already living in Missouri.

Some Kickapoos, however, under Chief Mecina and the prophet Kenakuk, continued to resist relocation by passive means as well as guerrilla tactics. They were finally forced to move to Kansas in the early 1830s following their defeat in Black Hawk's war (see Sauk). Most Missouri Kickapoos had accepted a reservation in Kansas in 1832. Some later fought with the United States against the Seminole in 1837.

From their base in Kansas, the tribe broke into several smaller groups, some remaining in Kansas and some migrating to Oklahoma; Texas, where they settled on the Sabine River with a group of Indians from several tribes; and Mexico. Horse-stealing raids, particularly in Texas, were an important activity throughout much of the nineteenth century. In 1862, some Kickapoo land was allotted and some was sold to a railroad company.

In the early to mid-1860s, fighting erupted between Mexican Kickapoos and Texas Rangers attempting to prevent some Kansas Kickapoos from crossing Texas to join their relatives. In the 1870s, the U.S. Army illegally crossed the Mexican border and destroyed the main Kickapoo village in Mexico. They also brought a group of women and children back to the Indian Territory as hostages; many men then agreed to leave Mexico and join them there.

In 1883, these people were granted a 100,000-acre reservation in Oklahoma. However, when that reservation was allotted ten years later, and pressure to assimilate increased, many people returned to Mexico, first to Nacimiento and then to northern Sonora. In 1908, the Kansas reservation was allotted to individuals. In 1937, the Kansas Kickapoos reorganized under the Indian Reorganization Act. They successfully resisted termination in the 1950s.

RELIGION   All things, animate and inanimate, contained spirits, or manitou. Kicitiata, the supreme manitou, or creator, dwelled in the sky. Tobacco facilitated communication with the manitous. Young people may have undertaken vision quests. Dreams, which may have been encouraged by fasts, also had spiritual significance.

The main ceremony was a weeklong renewal and thanksgiving in early spring, at which time sacred bundles were opened and repaired. The people also celebrated the Green Corn and Buffalo Dances. Priests were in charge of religious observances. There may have been a ritual office, held by a woman, that gave approval to hold certain ceremonies. In the 1830s, the prophet Kenakuk preached a Christian-influenced religion that emphasized acculturation and prohibited alcohol, polygyny, and warfare. His message attracted some Kickapoos and Potawatomis.

GOVERNMENT The Kickapoo were divided into constituent bands, which were probably led by chiefs. A council of clan heads took decisions by consensus.

CUSTOMS Kickapoo society was organized in patrilineal clans. Furthermore, a dual division formed the basis for various cultural features such as joking (informal enforcement of social norms), games, races, and ritual seating. People played dice and ball games (such as lacrosse), held archery contests, and danced socially. They may have eaten human flesh.

Personal names were tied to dreams or visions. Menstrual seclusion was particularly long and rigorous the first time, at which time the woman was advised by older women on how to behave as an adult. After killing their first game, boys were given a feast, which included songs and prayers.

Courting may have involved the use of a flute. Marriage was finalized by gift giving between the families. Funeral or death ceremonies included feasting, song, and prayer as well as quiet moments. The dead were dressed in travel clothing and buried with tobacco, wooden spoons, food, and water in stone slabs or log vaults. Their feet faced west, the direction of the land of the dead. Graveyards were in or near villages. People left the village for four days following a death, after which time ceremonial adoptions were often performed.

DWELLINGS Rectangular summer and round or oval winter houses were framed with green saplings. Summer houses were covered with elm bark and were often attached to an arbor. Sleeping platforms lay along the sides. Doors faced east, and there was a smoke hole in the roof. Temporary winter houses were covered with woven cattail or tule mats. The people also built separate cook and menstrual/birth huts.

DIET Kickapoos were heavily dependent on crops. Women grew corn, beans, and squash, and they gathered various wild foods. Men hunted deer, bear, and other game, including some buffalo, and they fished.

KEY TECHNOLOGY Carved wooden prayer sticks recorded prayers and myths as well as events. Pottery containers could hold water. There were many wooden items, such as utensils, bowls, and cradle boards. Spoons held particular significance.

TRADE Kickapoos served as intermediaries in the mid–nineteenth century Comanche horse trade.

NOTABLE ARTS Important art objects included pottery and carved and decorated (with porcupine quills) wooden items. Silk appliqué was popular from the mid–eighteenth century on as clothing decoration.

TRANSPORTATION The people acquired the horse earlier than most Indians of the northeast, probably in the early eighteenth century.

DRESS Kickapoo dress depended largely on their location. Basic items were breechclout, dress or apron, leggings, and moccasins, although they tended to borrow local customs, especially with regard to personal ornamentation.

WAR AND WEAPONS Kickapoo warriors were known as extremely fierce, able, and enthusiastic fighters. Among their seventeenth- and early-eighteenth-century enemies were the Chickasaw, Osage, Dakota, Iroquois, Fox, and Illinois. They were periodically allied with the Sauk, Fox, and other tribes as well as with the French after 1730. Their warfare and raiding took them from New York and Pennsylvania into Georgia and Alabama, throughout the entire Great Lakes and prairie regions, and into Texas and Mexico.

Contemporary Information

GOVERNMENT/RESERVATIONS The Kickapoo Reservation in Brown County, Kansas, contains 19,200 acres of land, slightly more than a third of which are owned by Indians. Of this land, about half is held by individuals. The 1990 reservation Indian population was 368, although almost 200 Kickapoos lived nearby.

Oklahoma Kickapoos live in Lincoln, Potawatomi, and Oklahoma Counties. Tribal offices are located near the town of McCloud. The people are governed by a five-member business committee. Of the 22,000 acres originally allotted, individuals now own roughly 6,000 acres of land. There were about 1,900 tribal members in the early 1990s.

The Texas (Mexican) Kickapoos live in El Nacimiento Rancheria, Coahuilla, Mexico, on roughly 17,000 acres of land. Their village is located under the international bridge over the Rio Grande. A small group also lives in the state of Sonora. In 1984, the Kickapoo Trust Land Acquisition Committee purchased 125 acres of land along the Rio Grande in Texas, about eight miles south of Eagle Pass, but so far the people have preferred to remain in their old village. Band population in the mid-1980s was roughly 650.

ECONOMY In Kansas, much of the allotted land is leased to non-natives. There is also a tribal farm and ranch, as well as a buffalo herd, on lands purchased with land claims settlement money. Some people work for the tribe or the Bureau of Indian Affairs. Unemployment remains around 40 percent, and more than a third of the people lived below the federal poverty level in the early 1990s. The tribe is attempting to build a gambling casino.

In Oklahoma, most land is leased to non-natives. Kickapoos in Mexico lived a traditional subsistence lifestyle until after World War II; now many work in the United States as migrant laborers. Unemployment is extremely high in Oklahoma, Texas, and Mexico.

LEGAL STATUS   The Kickapoo Tribe in Kansas, the Kickapoo Tribe of Oklahoma, and the Texas Band of Kickapoo (Kickapoo Traditional Tribe in Texas) are federally recognized tribal entities. In 1983, the United States recognized the Texas Band as a self-governing entity within the Oklahoma tribe and extended to them federal benefits that included the right to move freely across the international border. About one-quarter of this group are U.S. citizens.

DAILY LIFE   The Kansas Kickapoo own a gymnasium, day care center, and housing and other facilities for seniors. There is also a Kickapoo Nation school serving grades K–12. Few people have college degrees. The language is no longer spoken. Many Kansas Kickapoos have married neighboring Prairie Band Potawatomis. Ongoing traditions include the Kenakuk religion, the Drum religion (Dream Dance), and the Native American Church.

The Oklahoma and Texas Kickapoo regard themselves as one people. Kickapoos in Mexico migrate to the United States to work as farm laborers from spring through fall and then return to their villages for the winter ceremonial season. In Mexico, they live in cardboard and cane houses. The native religion remains intact in Mexico, as does much else of traditional culture. It centers on a seasonal round of ceremonies that are attended by many Kickapoos from Oklahoma. Many Oklahoma Kickapoos speak only Kickapoo; only a small number of them, mostly young people, are fluent in English.

Lenápe

Lenápe (Le `nä p ā), or Leni Lenápe, "Human Beings" or "Real People" in the Unami dialect, were part of a group of Algonquian speakers from North Carolina to New York. The Lenápe tribes who lived around the Delaware River are more commonly known as Delaware Indians (from Baron De La Warre, governor of Virginia). This central group of northeastern Algonquian Indians was referred to as "grandfather" by other Algonquian tribes, in recognition of its position as the group from which many local Algonquian tribes diverged.

LOCATION   In the sixteenth century, the Lenápe were located in the Delaware River area, both along the coast and inland. The Unami lived in southeastern Pennsylvania and northern Delaware; the Munsee lived in northern New Jersey, extreme southern New York, and southeastern Connecticut. A quasi-division known as Unalachtigo lived mainly in New Jersey. Late-twentieth-century Lenápe communities were located in New Jersey, Pennsylvania, Wisconsin, Oklahoma, Kansas, and Ontario, Canada.

POPULATION   There were roughly 10,000 Lenápe in 1600. The present-day Lenápe population is hard to determine, but it is probably around 16,000 people.

LANGUAGE   Munsee and Unami are Algonquian languages.

Historical Information

HISTORY   According to the Walum Olum (see "Key Technology"), the Lenápe may have originated to the northeast, possibly in Labrador, where they were united with the Shawnee and the Nanticoke. They may have passed through the eastern Great Lakes region and the Ohio Valley, where they met and possibly defeated Hopewell Mound Builder people. They likely encountered non-natives in the early to mid–sixteenth century.

Contact with Henry Hudson in 1609 was followed by the people's rapid involvement in the fur trade. In short order, their dependence on items of non-native manufacture, such as metal items, guns, and cloth, fundamentally altered their economy as well as their relations with neighboring peoples. Other changes in material culture included the introduction of new foods such as pigs, chickens, and melons. In 1626, the Manhattan Band of Lenápe traded the use of Manhattan Island to a Dutchman for about $24 worth of goods. This arrangement was quickly interpreted as a sale by the Dutch, who, unlike the Lenápe, valued property ownership.

Growing numbers of non-natives, Indian land cessions and pressure for more, and intertribal rivalries brought on by competition over furs led to conflict with the Dutch from the 1640s until the British took possession of the colony in 1663. In 1683, the Lenápe people, represented by Chief Tamanend (from whose name the designation of Tammany Hall was taken), signed a treaty of friendship with the Quaker William Penn (who gave his name to the state of Pennsylvania).

By the late seventeenth century, the Lenápe population had been decimated by disease and warfare. In the early eighteenth century, the Iroquois Confederacy dominated the Lenápe people, even going so far as to sell some of their land to the British. By the middle of that century, more and more Lenápes had moved into western Pennsylvania and the Ohio River Valley. A group of Lenápe established farms in eastern Ohio, but hostilities with non-natives increased as the frontier moved west. About 100 Lenápes were slaughtered by Kentucky frontiersmen at a Moravian mission in 1782.

Unami speakers living in the lower Allegheny and

upper Ohio Valleys in the mid–eighteenth century formed the nucleus of the emerging Lenápe or Delaware tribe. These people were organized into three groups, or clans—Turkey, Turtle, and Wolf—each with a chief living in a main village. One of the chiefs acted as tribal spokesman. The Lenápe fought the British in the French and Indian War and were generally divided in the Revolutionary War. In 1762, a Lenápe medicine man called Delaware Prophet helped to unite the local Indians to fight in Pontiac's rebellion. Some Lenápe also participated in Little Turtle's war (1790–1794) and in Tecumseh's rebellion (1809–1811).

As the non-natives kept coming, groups of Lenápe continued west into Missouri and even Texas, where they remained until forced into western Oklahoma in 1859. These "absentee Delaware" began hunting buffalo and assumed some aspects of Plains life.

After the Lenápe remaining in Ohio were defeated, with their Indian allies, in the 1794 Battle of Fallen Timbers, they moved to Indiana, Missouri, and Kansas. From their base in Kansas they fought with the Pawnee, who claimed their land, as well as with other Plains tribes. Many also served as scouts in the U.S. Army. After living in Kansas for a couple of generations as farmers, trappers, and guides, they were forced to relocate to Oklahoma in the 1860s. Following a court battle, these Lenápe became citizens of the Cherokee Nation.

Meanwhile, groups of Munsee speakers had joined the Stockbridge Indians in Massachusetts and New York and moved with them to a reservation in Wisconsin. Others joined the Cayuga in New York and migrated with them to the Six Nations Reserve in Ontario in the late eighteenth century. Still others moved to Canada as well, one group founding a Moravian village in 1792 along the Thames River and another group living at Munceytown. Yet another group joined the Swan Lake and Black River Chippewa near Ottawa, Kansas.

RELIGION Like many Algonquins, the Lenápe believed in a great spirit (manitou) as well as the presence of other spirits in all living things. Personal guardian spirits were acquired in adolescence and were said to be connected with future success.

The fortnight-long bear sacrifice, held in midwinter, was the most important of at least five annual religious festivals. Others revolved around foods, such as maple sugar (early spring), corn (late spring and late summer), and strawberries (early summer), as well as curing. Many festivals were held in a long wooden structure that had 12 ceremonial masks carved on its posts. The festivals included singing and dancing as well as drumming on deerskin drums and shaking turtleshell rattles.

After death, spirits were said to travel to an afterlife. Names were given with the benefit of a personal vision by the name giver, which enhanced his or her status. Chiefs often served as religious as well as political leaders of the village. Shamans of both sexes were responsible for holding the curing ceremonies.

GOVERNMENT Each of the three autonomous divisions maintained its own territory; there was never any political unity. Each village group of several hundred people had its own hereditary chief (sachem or sagamore). The chief had no coercive powers, instead acting as mediator, adviser, and hunt leader. With the chief, other lineage leaders and elders formed a council.

Village groups were autonomous, but they often acted in concert for purposes of hunting drives and defense. There were also specific rules governing shared resource use areas and social contacts.

CUSTOMS There were traditionally three matrilineal clans. Women grew and prepared foods, took care of children, gathered firewood, and prepared skins. Men hunted, fished, traded, fought, cured, made houses and most tools, and served as chiefs. People from the coast tended to visit the interior in the spring, when they moved to fishing and hunting camps, whereas people from the interior visited the coast in summer. Murder was generally expiated by a payment.

Infants were kept on a cradle board, which mothers wore on their backs supported with tumplines, for most of the first year. Girls were secluded and observed strict behavioral taboos during their periods. Premarital sexual relations were condoned, but adultery was not, except where consent was given, such as in wife lending on the part of a polygynous chief. There was a yearlong betrothal period. Intermarriage was frequent between the village groups. Divorce was easily and frequently obtained. Corpses were buried in a sitting position with some possessions. Mourners blackened their faces and visited the grave annually. Widowers could marry again after making a payment to the former wife's family.

DWELLINGS Each of 30–40 villages, located on river and tributary meadows, was surrounded by fields and hunting grounds. Houses were circular, domed wigwams or 30- to 60-foot (but up to 100 foot) multifamily, grass or bark-covered, single doorway longhouses with both pitched and arched roofs. Both dwellings contained smoke holes. Interior longhouses may have been palisaded in times of war. Bark partitions did not meet the opposite wall, leaving room for a structure-long corridor. Multilevel wall platforms served as seats, beds, and storage areas. Woven reed mats were placed on floors and hung on walls for added insulation. Crops were strung on the ceiling to dry. Most interior people left the villages in winter, when they retired to the woods to live generally in small dwellings.

DIET From at least circa 1300, inland groups depended mostly on corn; beans and squash were also important. Corn was prepared to make soup, bread, dumplings, and many other dishes. Game hunted in seasonal trips included deer, elk, bear, raccoons, rabbit, wolves, squirrel, and fowl. Fire surrounds were used as part of a general practice of burning the undergrowth of certain lands. Men also trapped various small mammals, turkeys, and other birds. Fresh meat and fish were boiled or fire roasted. Coastal people depended mainly on fish and shellfish (generally dried and preserved), seaweed, birds, berries, and meat and oil from stranded whales. Women gathered various roots, greens, wild fruits, and nuts as well as maple sap. Tobacco was also grown.

KEY TECHNOLOGY The Walum Olum ("red score") was a pictographic history, painted or engraved on wood or bark, of the people's legends and early migrations. A later manuscript, the only one that survives in any form, interpreted the pictographs in the Lenápe language.

Fishing equipment included various types of nets as well as spears, traps, bow and arrow, and weirs. Women made rush (coast) and corn-husk (interior) baskets. Along the coast, people used fish bones as needles and sharp mollusk shell edges as blades; sharp rocks served as blades in the interior. Old people generally made pottery, fishnets, and other items. Men hunted using bows and arrows, traps, fire surrounds, and drives.

People carved dishes and bowls from wood or simply used gourds. Hollowed stumps served as mortars, with wood or stone pestles. Plant fibers or the inner bark from particular trees supplied cordage material. Corn was stored in mat-lined pits. Most cutting tools were made of stone. Men affixed stone, bone, horn, or tooth arrowheads with fish glue or resin.

TRADE The Lenápe traded in, among other items, rounded-bottom pots; grass mats, bags, and baskets; wampum (polished shell); and bark and skin containers. Summer was the main trade season.

NOTABLE ARTS Woven items, such as baskets, were decorated with painted spruce roots or porcupine quills.

TRANSPORTATION Men made dugout and bark canoes.

DRESS Women made clothing of deerskins and furs. People generally wore few clothes, such as breechclouts for men and skin kilts for women, in warm weather. Both added leggings, deerskin moccasins, and robes of bear or other skins in winter (women sometimes wore feather robes). Other items of clothing included turkey feather cloaks, leather belts, and temporary cornhusk footwear. Men also wore snakeskin or feather headbands.

Some clothing was painted or tasseled and fringed. People dressed their hair and bodies with bear or raccoon grease mixed with onion, in part as a protection against the sun and insects. Women tended to wear braids, whereas men roached their hair. Various personal adornments included earrings and necklaces, tattoos, and body paint.

WAR AND WEAPONS There was some fighting between Lenápe villages. Most Lenápe warfare was limited in nature. Warriors painted their faces, wore special attire, and used a special jargon. Weapons included the bow and arrow, wooden helmet, wooden war club, and large wooden or moose-hide shield. Captives were generally adopted or tortured and killed. Special war dances were associated with wars and raids. Intertribal confederacies were occasionally formed in times of major wars.

Contemporary Information

GOVERNMENT/RESERVATIONS The Delaware Tribe of Indians, Washington, Nowata, Craig, and Delaware Counties, Oklahoma, is governed by the Delaware Tribal Business Committee. Tribal population was about 10,000 in the early 1990s.

The Delaware Tribe of Western Oklahoma, established in 1866, is located near Anadarko, Oklahoma. Their land area is roughly 63,600 acres, held with the Wichita and Caddo tribes. Fewer than 3,000 acres are tribally owned. Tribal enrollment was around 1,000 in 1990.

A small number of Citizen Delaware (Munsee and Ojibwa) live near Ottawa, Kansas.

The Stockbridge-Munsee Reservation, Shawano County, Wisconsin (established in 1856), consists of approximately 46,000 acres of land, roughly one-third of which is held in trust by the federal government. The 1990 Indian population was 447, with about an additional 1,000 people also enrolled. The tribe is governed by a seven-member elected tribal council.

Other U.S. communities include the Ramapough Mountain Indians in New Jersey (about 2,500 people), the Powhatan-Renápe Nation at Rancocas, New Jersey (about 600 people), the Brotherton Indians (Wisconsin), and the Eastern Lenápe Nation (Pennsylvania).

The Six Nations Reserve, Ontario, was home to roughly 350 mixed Lenápe in the early 1990s. Delaware Indians also live on the following three Ontario reserves: Delaware of Grand River, Moravians of the Thames, and Muncey of the Thames.

The Moravians of the Thames Reserve, Kent County, Ontario, consists of roughly 1,200 hectares and is home to roughly 500 mixed Lenápe.

Roughly 200 Muncee Indians live on the Muncey of the Thames Reserve near London, Ontario, on about 2,700 acres.

ECONOMY In Oklahoma, most Lenápe are integrated with the non-native population. Tribal enterprises include bingo and tobacco sales. The Oklahoma Delawares received a land claims settlement of about $15 million in the late 1970s.

LEGAL STATUS The Delaware Tribe of Indians, the Delaware Tribe of Western Oklahoma (Absentee), and the Stockbridge-Munsee Band of Mohican Indians of Wisconsin are federally recognized tribal entities.

Other tribal organizations include the Native Delaware Indians (New Jersey), the Nanticoke Lenni-Lenápe Indians (New Jersey), the Delaware-Munsee (Kansas), the Powhatan-Renápe Nation (New Jersey), the Munsee Thames River Delaware Tribal Council (Colorado), the Eastern Lenápe Nation (Pennsylvania), and the Nanticoke Indian Association (Delaware). The Ramapough Mountain Indians (New Jersey) have been denied federal recognition (1997).

DAILY LIFE Most Lenápe are Christians, and some belong to the Native American Church, especially in Oklahoma. Each Oklahoma community hosts a powwow in summer. Some communities still hold "secular" naming ceremonies. The native language remains alive but not in common use, and there are programs in Oklahoma devoted to maintaining and building an awareness of some traditional culture. The Delaware Nation Grand Council of North America, incorporated in 1992, coordinates ongoing relations between the scattered groups of Lenápe.

Mahican

Mahican (Mu `h ē k ə n), from *Muh-he-con-ne-ok*, "People of the Waters That Are Never Still." This tribe is often confused with the Mohegans, a Connecticut tribe, in part because of the J. F. Cooper book *Last of the Mohicans*, a fictional story about a fictional tribe of Indians. There were originally several members of the Mahican confederacy, including, in the late seventeenth century, the Housatonic, Wyachtonoc, and Wappinger.

LOCATION The Mahican proper lived on both sides of the northern Hudson (Mahicanituck) River, in present-day eastern New York and western Vermont. The confederacy was centered around Schodac, near present-day Albany, and included tribes living along the lower Hudson River as well as in western Massachusetts and Connecticut. Today, Mahican descendants live in north-central Wisconsin and Oklahoma.

POPULATION There were between 4,000 and 5,000 Mahicans in 1600 and around 500 in 1700. There were approximately 1,500 Stockbridge-Munsees in the early 1990s.

LANGUAGE Mahican was an Algonquian language.

Historical Information

HISTORY The Mahicans were drawn into the fur trade shortly after they encountered Henry Hudson in 1609. They soon began collecting tribute from the Mohawk for access to a Dutch trade post established in Mahican country in 1614. Shell beads, or wampum, came into use at that time as currency. For a time the Mahicans, trading with Algonquians to the north, monopolized the regional fur trade.

As nearby fur areas became trapped out, the European powers had some success encouraging their Indian partners to expand through intertribal conflict. With the help of French firearms, for instance, Mohawks drove the Mahicans east of the Hudson River Valley in 1628. The latter reestablished their council fire to the north, around Schaghticoke. Some defeated New England tribes joined this group in the 1670s.

Throughout the late seventeenth century, the Mahican fought the Munsee, Iroquois, and others in the Piedmont and the Ohio Valley in their quest for pelts. They even ranged as far west as Miami territory, where some of them remained. By 1700 or so, Mahican culture was in retreat, and the people began to sell or otherwise abandon traditional lands to non-natives. Traditional social and political structures, such as localized clan and lineage patterns (see "Government"), began to break down owing to the demands of the fur trade, as did traditional manufacture and economies. The people also underwent a general moral breakdown, due in part to the influence of alcohol and the general cultural disruption.

In the 1670s, some groups withdrew to live among the Housatonic Band of Mahicans, in Westenhunk, although Mahicans also remained in the Hudson River Valley. Some Mahicans also merged with the Saint Francis Abenaki in the Saint Lawrence Valley and joined other Indian communities as well. In the mid-1730s, a group migrated to Wyoming, Pennsylvania, and some resettled in the mission town of Stockbridge, Massachusetts. The so-called Stockbridge Indians fought with the British in the French and Indian War and with the patriots in the American Revolution. In the mid-1740s, Moravian missionaries persuaded local Indians to remove to the area of

Bethlehem, Pennsylvania. This group ultimately settled in Ottawa, Canada.

By the mid– to late eighteenth century, the Indians had completely lost their subsistence economy. Most survived by selling splint baskets, other crafts, and their labor. Despite assisting the colonies in their various wars of this period, the Stockbridge Mahicans were soon dispossessed, and many joined their relatives in the Susquehanna River area in Pennsylvania, there to merge with other tribes, especially the Algonquian Delaware.

By the end of the American Revolution, most of the dispirited remnant of the Mahican Nation had left Stockbridge and nearby areas and settled near the Oneida Indians in New York, where they established a thriving non-native–style farm and craft community. Between 1818 and 1829, these Indians left the Oneida country and migrated west to Wisconsin, where missionaries had purchased land for them. They moved again several years later, after the Wisconsin Indians repudiated their land sales.

Some of this group dispersed to Kansas or died along the way after an abortive move to the Missouri River in 1839. In 1856, they were granted a reservation in Wisconsin, with the Munsee Band of Delaware Indians and, later, a group of Brothertown Indians (*see* Pequot). The community was marked by factionalism and various removals for years.

The tribe lost a significant amount of land in the post-1887 allotment process. It was officially terminated in 1910. In the 1930s, the Stockbridge-Munsee, landless and destitute, reorganized under the Indian Reorganization Act and acquired 2,250 acres of land.

RELIGION Manitou—the Great Spirit—was present in all things. Some families owned sacred dolls, which were feasted so that their spirit would protect the owners. The Mahican celebrated the Green Corn Dance at the beginning of harvest season as well as various first fruits and first game rituals. They believed that the soul did not die with the body.

GOVERNMENT Each autonomous village had its own chief and councilors. The positions of lineage leaders and clan chiefs (who may also have been village chiefs) were inherited matrilineally. The head chief, or sachem, kept the tribal bag of peace, which contained wampum, at least in the historical period. As Mahican local and regional power grew, the sachem acquired three assistants: owl, or orator and town crier; runner, or messenger; and hero, or war chief.

CUSTOMS The three matrilineal clans may have inhabited separate villages. Men helped women with the harvest after celebrating the Green Corn festival. Families scattered into the woods in late fall and remained through midwinter, when they returned to the villages. Old people remained in the villages all winter long, generally doing craft work. There may have been a recognized system of social status. People were buried in a sitting position and then covered with wood and stones. Graves were stocked with provisions such as food, dishes, and weapons for use in the afterlife.

DWELLINGS Villages were often located on a hill near a river. At least from the seventeenth century on they were often palisaded. Roughly 200 people lived in a village. Each village contained from 3 to 16 long, rectangular bark lodges, as well as domed wigwams, framed with hickory saplings and covered with birch, elm, or basswood bark pressed flat. Longhouses averaged three fireplaces and as many nuclear families. Animal skins were hung on interior walls for insulation. Villages were moved every ten years or so owing to exhaustion of land and firewood.

DIET The Mahican practiced slash-and-burn field clearing and regular rotation of fields. They used fish and ash as fertilizer. Women grew beans, squash, probably sunflowers, and several varieties of corn. Corn was used in bread, soup, and other dishes. Cornmeal mixed with maple sap and water made a trail food for hunters and warriors. Crops were the most important food. Women also gathered waterlily roots, greens, mushrooms, nuts, and berries and made sassafras and wintergreen tea. Maple sap may have been boiled into sugar.

Men hunted game such as bear, deer, moose, beaver, rabbit, otter, squirrel, raccoon, turkey, passenger pigeons, and many other birds. Deer were hunted in fall, moose in spring. In summer, men gathered mussels and caught herring, shad, and other fish. Fish as well as meat was eaten fresh or dried and smoked.

KEY TECHNOLOGY Corn was stored in bark containers or bark-lined pits. Men caught fish with bone hooks, weirs, and nets. They hunted with spears and traps in addition to the bow and arrow. Their bows were made of hickory or red cedar, and they used flint arrowheads. Most Mahican technology was wood based: Wooden or bark items included bowls, utensils, and containers. Mortars were fire-hollowed stumps. Women made pottery and wove baskets, bags, and mats.

TRADE Mahicans acted as intermediaries in the shell bead trade from the coast to the Saint Lawrence Valley. Major trade partners included Algonquins to the east and south.

NOTABLE ARTS Containers and clothing were decorated with porcupine quills and paints.

TRANSPORTATION Men made dugout and birchbark canoes as well as snowshoes.

DRESS Women made most clothing of finely tanned skins. Men wore breechclouts, and women wore skirts. Both wore shirts, blankets, high leggings, and moccasins. Both also wore long braids dressed with bear grease and tattooed their faces.

WAR AND WEAPONS War season began after the harvest was in. Warriors sometimes burned or plucked out their hair except for a strip down the middle. Mahican enemies included Iroquois tribes, especially the Mohawk, although this relationship sometimes became an alliance in the mid–seventeenth century.

Contemporary Information

GOVERNMENT/RESERVATIONS The Stockbridge-Munsee Reservation, Shawano County, Wisconsin (established in 1856), consists of approximately 46,000 acres of land, roughly one-third of which is held in trust by the federal government. The 1990 Indian population was 447. The community is governed by a seven-member elected tribal council.

ECONOMY The casino is a major employer on the Stockbridge-Munsee Reservation. Other tribal members have jobs associated with tribal facilities and programs as well as small tribal businesses. Some people work in the local non-native economy.

LEGAL STATUS The Stockbridge-Munsee Band of Mohican Indians is a federally recognized tribal entity.

DAILY LIFE Longtime president of the tribe Arvid Miller helped establish the Great Lakes Intertribal Council in the 1960s. The tribe, along with Menominee Indians and neighboring non-natives, has been fighting a huge low-level radiation dump since the late 1970s. Tribal facilities include offices, a health center, residential and recreational facilities for the elderly, a library and museum, a campground, and a casino.

The people observe a traditional 12-day new year celebration. Most Stockbridge-Munsees are Christians, although some participate in sweat lodge ceremonies. Some people study the Munsee-Mahican language and would like to teach it. Most traditional culture has been lost. The tribe hosts a large powwow in early August.

Maliseet

Maliseet (`Mal ə s ē t), or Malicite, probably a Micmac word for "lazy speakers" or "broken talkers." The tribe may have derived from people of Passamaquoddy (maritime) and Natick (inland) extraction. Together with the Passamaquoddy they have also been known as the Etchemin tribe. *See also* Abenaki; Micmac; Passamaquoddy.

LOCATION The Maliseet traditionally lived along the Saint John River drainage in present-day New Brunswick, Canada, as well as in northeastern Maine.

Today, Maliseets live on and near reserves in extreme southeast Canada, including the Gaspé, as well as in nearby and regional cities and towns.

POPULATION With the Passamaquoddy, the Maliseet numbered about 1,000 in the early seventeenth century. In the early 1990s, the Malecites of Viger (Malecite First Nation) (Quebec) had a population of 425 out of a total Maliseet population of around 3,000.

LANGUAGE Maliseets and Passamaquoddys spoke dialects of the same Algonquian language.

Historical Information

HISTORY The Maliseet people may have come to their historical territory from the southwest, where they probably had contact with the Ohio Mound Builders in ancient times. They may also have been united with the Passamaquoddy in the distant past. Their first contact with non-natives probably occurred in the early seventeenth century when they met Samuel de Champlain, although they may have encountered fishermen from northern and western Europe as much as a century earlier.

A growing involvement in the French fur trade led to a parallel dependence on items of non-native manufacture. The people also accepted Catholic missionaries in the seventeenth century. Throughout the eighteenth century, the Maliseet population declined sharply as a result of disease, abuse of alcohol, and loss of land. They joined the pro-French Abenaki Confederacy in the mid–eighteenth century. They also sided with the French in the colonial wars and intermarried with them.

By the late eighteenth century, British settlers had pushed the Maliseet out of many of their best subsistence areas, and the traditional annual round of subsistence activities had been seriously disrupted. Reserves were established from 1876 on, although the Maliseet resisted a sedentary lifestyle for a long time. In the mid– to late nineteenth century, many Maliseets worked as loggers, stevedores, craftspeople, guides, and farm laborers. Logging and potato farming transformed the region in the 1870s. Local Maliseets, such as the several families who roamed around Houlton, Maine, also worked as house cleaners and in the mills, made baskets, and hunted, fished, and gathered foods where possible.

In the twentieth century, some old communities were abandoned, as many people congregated in a few reservations or moved off the reservations altogether. Along with other landless Indians, Maliseets formed the Association of Aroostook Indians in 1970.

RELIGION Guardian spirits gave people the ability to protect subsistence areas from trespass. They also gave shamans the power to cure, which they did by chanting, blowing, and possibly sucking. Sweat lodges and dances were associated with spiritual power.

GOVERNMENT Skilled hunters generally provided local leadership. In the seventeenth century there was a supreme hereditary chief who lived at the main village. In general, leadership was more formalized under the confederacy, with graduated civil offices and a war chief. The Maliseets were part of the Abenaki Confederacy from the mid–eighteenth century to the mid– to late nineteenth century, when the confederacy ceased to exist.

CUSTOMS The people came together in large villages in summer and dispersed into small hunting camps in winter. They preferred football, a kicking game, to lacrosse. They also played any number of dice gambling games. Herb doctors could be men or women.

Men served their prospective in-laws for at least a year before marriage. During this period, the woman made the man's clothing and footgear. Weddings were marked by feasting, oratory, and the formal recognition of the groom's ancestry. At least in the historical period, sexual mores were strict, and divorce was rare. Children were generally treated gently and with a high degree of freedom, at least when compared with the early French in the area. Boys could sit in council with the older men after killing their first moose. When death was expected, it was sometimes hastened by pouring cold water on the victim, who may also have been buried alive.

DWELLINGS Some summer villages were palisaded. They included multi- and single-family dwellings. The former were conical, pole-frame wigwams covered with birch bark; the latter, as well as council houses, were rectangular log-frame structures with birch-bark roofs. Council houses could hold up to 100 people.

DIET Farming, especially corn, was the key economic activity. Harvested corn was either stored or taken on the winter hunts. Men hunted inland animals such as moose, bear, otter, and muskrat. They also fished for salmon, bass, and sturgeon. This, with wild grapes and roots gathered by the women, made up most of the summer diet. Women also gathered fiddlehead ferns in early spring.

KEY TECHNOLOGY Corn was stored in bark-lined pits. Various birch-bark items included canoes, containers, baskets, dishes, and boxes, some of which were decorated with porcupine quills. Cordage came from spruce roots or cedar bark. The crooked knife was an important woodworking tool. Men summoned moose with a birch-bark calling instrument. Musical instruments included boards (for beating time), drums, rattles, flageolets, and flutes.

TRADE Although part of a wide-ranging network, Maliseets traded mainly among local groups. They exported corn and birch-bark products, mainly to people living to the south.

NOTABLE ARTS Many items were decorated with porcupine-quill embroidery. Maliseets made excellent ash-splint baskets and beadwork in the historical era.

TRANSPORTATION Men made lightweight canoes of birch bark, moose hide, or spruce bark. They also made snowshoes.

DRESS The basic dress was breechclouts for men, dresses for women, and moccasins. Furs and heavy skins were used in cold weather. Beaverskin caps protected people's heads from the cold. There were also temporary raincoats made of birch bark.

WAR AND WEAPONS War chiefs may have predated the historical era. This position was never inherited or elected. The war chief had responsibility for attracting followers for a raid. Weapons included the bow and arrow and the spear.

Contemporary Information

GOVERNMENT/RESERVATIONS The Houlton Band of Maliseet Indians, Houlton, Maine, had a population of around 550 in the early 1990s. At the same time, its land base was around 800 acres. It is governed by an elected tribal council.

Canadian Maliseets had a population in the early 1990s of about 2,500. New Brunswick communities include Oromocto, Devon (St. Mary's), Kingsclear (Pilick), Woodstock, Tobique, and St. Basile (Madawaska First Nation). Nobody lives on the Quebec reserves of Whitworth (173 hectares) and Cacouna (.17 hectares), but Quebec Maliseets are members of the Malecite First Nation (Viger). Canadian Maliseets are organized into a number of nonprofit corporations.

ECONOMY Unemployment seldom dipped below 50 percent in the early to mid-1990s. The band provides some jobs, primarily in administration, economic development, and housing projects. There is seasonal work with potatoes and blueberries.

LEGAL STATUS The Houlton Band of Maliseet Indians is a federally recognized tribal entity. The Canadian bands listed under "Government/Reservations" are federally and provincially recognized.

DAILY LIFE State of Maine services date from 1973. Although the Houlton Band receives numerous benefits as a party to the 1980 Maine Indian Land Claims Settlement Act, such as cash, land, and access to federal services, many unaffiliated Maliseet families remain without services or recognition. Facilities in Houlton include a new tribal center. Maliseets and Passamaquoddys have long enjoyed close relations and continue to intermarry. Canadian Maliseets have largely assimilated into French society. Few people outside of New Brunswick speak the native language fluently. The Tobique Reservation operates its own school as well as shops selling locally made arts and crafts. The Wabanaki Aboriginal Music Festival is held there over Labor Day weekend. Saint-Anne Day is celebrated in July.

Menominee

Menominee (Me `no m ə n ē), from *Manomini*, Anishinabe for "Wild Rice People." The Menominee were culturally related to the Winnebago and Anishinabe.

LOCATION The Menominee controlled nearly 10 million acres along the northwestern shore of Lake Michigan and west into central Wisconsin. Today, most live on a reservation on the Wolf River in northern Wisconsin.

POPULATION From a population of perhaps 3,000 in the early seventeenth century, the Menominee have grown to around 7,000 people in the early 1990s.

LANGUAGE Menominees speak an Algonquian language.

Historical Information

HISTORY Shortly after the first non-natives made contact with the Menominee people in the mid–seventeenth century, Iroquois warriors drove the Menominees into the Green Bay area, possibly from Michilimackinac. Jesuit missionaries arrived among them in 1671. The people maintained generally friendly relations with non-natives, especially the French, with whom they occasionally intermarried.

Participation in the fur trade from the late seventeenth century through the early nineteenth century broke the tribe into small, mobile bands of hunters-trappers. They avoided many of the colonial and other wars of the eighteenth and nineteenth centuries, although some sided with the British in the American Revolution and the War of 1812. With the fur-bearing animals depleted, and under pressure from non-natives, the Menominee in 1854 ceded all of their remaining lands except for a reservation on the Wolf River in north-central Wisconsin.

On the reservation, a split soon developed between pagans and Christians, traditionalists and progressives. Some people tried farming in the later nineteenth century, but as this was generally unsuccessful, many soon turned to lumbering. In the early twentieth century, with the help of the U.S. Forest Service, the Menominee began harvesting their prime timber resources for sustained yield. Their sawmill became the center of economic activity and the tribe's most important employer.

Despite the government's mismanagement of the tribe's timber resources (for which the tribe won a legal judgment and collected an award of over $7.5 million in 1951), the Menominee were among the country's most economically stable and prosperous tribes by the early 1950s. Suddenly, they learned that they were to experience the effects of a new government policy. The tribe was officially terminated, or removed from its special relationship with the federal government, in 1961. The reservation became a county and the tribe a corporation.

The Menominee are perhaps the classic termination disaster. Termination-related expenses soon depleted their cash reserves. When the hospital was forced to close, the people experienced a sharp rise in tuberculosis and other health problems. The low tax base could not finance needed government services, and the tribe, once self-sufficient, sank into poverty. Faced with total financial collapse, it was forced in the late 1960s to sell off prime waterfront real estate to non-natives. Many people began to judge the intent of termination by its effects: the destruction of a relatively prosperous Indian group and the further transfer of its prime land to non-natives.

In reaction to these developments and to the related possibility that non-natives would make up a majority of the county's voters, a new organization, the Determination of Rights and Unity for Menominee Shareholders (DRUMS), called for a new federal trust relationship for the tribe as well as tribal self-determination. Although termination was reversed in 1973, and most of the former reservation was restored, the tribe has yet to recover from the devastating effects of the termination.

RELIGION Mecawetok, who may have been identified with the sun, was the Great Spirit and supreme creative force. There were many levels of deities and spirits, some friendly and some evil; the latter were assumed to reside below the earth. Most people sought to obtain spiritual power with the help of a guardian spirit, which one acquired in a vision through fasting and dreaming. Dreams were in some ways the entire basis of living: They determined an individual's sacred songs, dances, and ceremonies. One's power was said to increase with age.

Medicine bundles contained various personal sacred charms. There may have been several old religious cults made up of medicine men or people with outstanding power. People with particularly strong powers included witches and "jugglers." The latter were curers and diviners.

The Midewiwin (medicine lodge) Society was a secret society of shamans. Membership was by invitation or inheritance; initiation was highly ritualized. Each member possessed a medicine bag as well as strong and benevolent medicines.

The Dream Dance or Drum Dance contained some precontact elements. Membership was relatively unrestricted. Members petitioned the sacred spirits with drums and related rituals to obtain supernatural power. The ceremonies were highly ritualized, and codes of behavior were associated with what essentially was a religion.

GOVERNMENT Clan chiefs were probably hereditary. Chiefs of the Bear Clan served as tribal chiefs, and the various lineage chiefs made up the village council. Nonhereditary chiefs achieved status through their dreams or war exploits. These people might be war leaders, lead public celebrations, or enjoy other duties and responsibilities.

A band system replaced clans and villages during the late seventeenth century and early eighteenth century. Bands tended to follow clan lines but were mostly based on friendships. The hereditary system of leadership became less important, replaced by skills such as excellence in trapping and an ability to negotiate with non-natives. There was also a tribal council from this time on.

CUSTOMS The Menominee were divided into two divisions, Bear and Thunderbird. Each was in turn divided into patrilineal clans. Smoking tobacco accompanied nearly every important activity. Certain relatives were allowed or encouraged to joke with each other as a means of maintaining social mores and order.

The male sphere included ceremonies, tool and weapon manufacture, and war. Women saw to the home and children; grew, collected, and prepared all food; were responsible for firewood, water, and carrying goods; and made clothing and items associated with food and the home. Women could also participate in many male activities, such as fishing, hunting, dancing, and some power ceremonies.

Boys and girls undertook ten-day dream fasts at puberty; these were the culmination of short childhood fasts. There was also a feast following a boy's first game kill. Children were toughened by icy plunges and other such means. Women were isolated during their menstrual periods and after childbirth because they were thought to threaten the balance of spiritual power.

Marriages were generally arranged by elders, who took their lead from a couple to a greater or lesser degree. They were probably formalized by an exchange of gifts. Men might have more than one wife. Corpses were placed on scaffolds, but in the later historical period they were painted red and placed in birch-bark coffins, along with personal items. Mourners blackened their faces with charcoal,

but funerals were accompanied by feasting and sport.

DWELLINGS Winter houses were domed wigwams, with cattail and reed mats placed over bent saplings. These structures were especially used after contact with non-natives in winter hunting camps. Rectangular summer houses were made of bark over a pole framework. Other hut-type buildings were used for sweat lodges, for women's seclusion, and for ceremonial purposes. Permanent villages usually contained a lacrosse field.

DIET Wild rice—which is not rice but a grass seed—gave this tribe its name and was a staple, along with fish. It was collected in summer by people, usually women, in canoes. The method entailed bending the plants over and knocking them with paddles; the seeds fell into the bottom of the canoes. They were then dried, pounded, and winnowed, with the grain boiled and served in a stew or with maple syrup.

Men hunted large game, such as deer and buffalo. They also hunted small game from canoes. They relied more on hunting once they became involved in the fur trade. Bundles or charms helped ensure cooperation from spirits. Men also fished for sturgeon and other fish in Green Bay and in nearby streams. They fished through the ice in winter. Women grew small gardens of corn, beans, squash, and tobacco. They also gathered berries and maple sap.

KEY TECHNOLOGY Fish were caught using traps, hooks, spears, and woven bark-fiber gill nets. Women wove pouches of plant fibers and buffalo hair. These items served many purposes, such as food storage and protection of ceremonial items. They also wove and dyed cattail, rush, or cedar-bark mats and winnowing trays, and they made pottery. Hunting equipment and weapons of war included the bow and arrow, clubs, and knives made of a variety of materials such as bone, stone, and copper. The people also used stone axes.

TRADE Wild rice was a major export, as were items made of stone and wood. The people imported buffalo hides and other prairie items, catlinite (pipestone), and copper.

NOTABLE ARTS Menominee women made especially fine pottery, pouches, and clothing decorated with porcupine quills and animal hair. Motifs included geometric figures and sacred beings.

TRANSPORTATION Men made bark and dugout canoes as well as snowshoes.

Dress Men wore deerskin breechclouts, shirts, leggings, and moccasins. Women wore woven nettle shirts as well as deerskin robes, leggings, and moccasins. Both decorated their clothing with paint and porcupine quills. Both also wore copper jewelry and rubbed oil and grease on their hair and bodies.

WAR AND WEAPONS The Menominee were not

known for their aggressiveness. Nevertheless, they were often at war. They were generally friendly with the Winnebago and occasionally enemies with the Sauk and Fox. Weapons were similar to hunting tools.

Contemporary Information

GOVERNMENT/RESERVATIONS The Menominee Reservation, Menominee and Shawano Counties, Wisconsin (established in 1848) consists of roughly 230,000 acres of land. The 1990 Indian population was nearly 3,200. A 1977 constitution and by-laws call for an elected nine-member legislature as well as a tribal chair, a judiciary, and a general council.

ECONOMY Gaming operations are central to the new tribal economy; profits underwrite a host of social and health services.

LEGAL STATUS The Menominee Indian Tribe of Wisconsin is a federally recognized tribal entity.

DAILY LIFE Most tribal members are Christians, although the Big Drum religion is also popular, as are the Ojibwa-based Warrior's Dance, the Native American Church, and Medicine Lodge ceremonies. A renewed clan structure exists among the people. The language is in use and taught in school. The College of the Menominee Nation is located in Keshena. The people host an annual powwow. Substance abuse remains a daunting challenge. The tribe is committed to maintaining its sovereignty and its Indian identity.

Miami

Miami (Mī `a mē), possibly from the Ojibwa word Omaumeg, "People of the Peninsula," or from their own word for pigeon. Their original name may have been Twaatwaa, in imitation of a crane. The traditional bands were Atchatchakangouen, Kilatika, Mengakonkia, Pepicokia, Wea, and Piankashaw. Miamis were culturally and linguistically related to the Illinois.

LOCATION From a position possibly south of Lake Michigan, the Miami moved into northern Illinois and southern Wisconsin in the mid–seventeenth century. Within a few generations, they moved south of Lake Michigan, roughly between the Wabash and the Ohio Rivers, and especially along the St. Joseph River. Today Miamis live in Ottawa County, Oklahoma, and in Allen, Huntington, and Miami Counties, Indiana.

POPULATION There were approximately 4,500 Miamis in the mid–seventeenth century. In the early 1990s, about 6,000 lived in Indiana. In the mid-1990s about 4,500 lived in Oklahoma.

LANGUAGE Miami is an Algonquian language.

Historical Information

HISTORY Miami culture evolved at least in part from the prehistoric Ohio Mound Builders. In the mid–seventeenth century, the people effected a temporary retreat west of the Mississippi in the face of Iroquois war parties; Dakota pressure, including a huge military defeat, sent them back east (with French assistance). Peace was established between the Miami and the Iroquois in 1701.

Miamis traded with the French from the mid–seventeenth century on but tended to side with the British in the colonial wars. Some Miamis guided Jacques Marquette and Louis Joliet down the Mississippi in the 1670s. The tribe experienced early factionalism over the issue of Christianity. The Miami participated in Pontiac's rebellion (1763), after which they ceded most of their Ohio lands and concentrated in Indiana. They fought with the British against the Americans in the Revolutionary War.

The Miami war, also known as Little Turtle's war, was led by the great strategist Michikinikwa, or Little Turtle. The Indian coalition included Objibwas, Ottawas, Lenápes, Shawnees, Potawatomis, and Illinois as well as Miamis. The war was a defensive one, fought to contain non-native settlement of the Ohio Valley. The coalition enjoyed significant victories in the early years, thanks mainly to Michikinikwa's strategy of guerrilla warfare. In the end, however, sheer numbers of non-native soldiers wore the Indians down. Although Michikinikwa foresaw the inevitable defeat and advised a cessation of hostilities, the coalition replaced him with another leader and was decisively defeated at the Battle of Fallen Timbers in 1794. The ensuing Treaty of Greenville forced local Indians to cede all of Ohio and most of Indiana to the United States.

The Miami underwent a dramatic population decline beginning in the late eighteenth century. Groups of Wea and Piankashaw began moving to Missouri as early as 1814. The United States forcibly removed a group of about 600 Miami to Kansas in 1846. In 1854, these groups came together to join the remnants of the Illinois tribe, forming the Confederated Peoria Tribe. They were later relocated to Oklahoma. There, in 1873, the Miami joined that confederacy, which changed its name to the United Peoria and Miami. The group that remained in Indiana consisted of about 1,500 people whose chiefs had been granted private land.

By the early twentieth century, Miami land in both Oklahoma and Indiana had largely been lost through allotment and tax foreclosure. Through the process of losing their lands, both communities, but especially that in Indiana, suffered significant population loss, as people moved away to try to survive. Forty years after the Indiana Miami lost federal recognition in 1897, they organized a nonprofit corporation in an effort to maintain their identity.

RELIGION The sun was the supreme deity, possibly the revered master of life central to Miami religion. There were also lesser manitou, or spirits, which were involved in a vision quest complex. Both sexes undertook a vision quest at puberty, for which they began training by fasting at a young age. Some men were directed by their guardian spirit to act and dress like women; this role was generally accepted, although if they engaged in warfare they did so as men.

Priests who cured with magic powers made up the Midewiwin or Grand Medicine Society. There were also shamans who cured with herbs and plant medicines. The most important ceremonies focused on the harvest and the return from the winter hunt. In both cases, celebrations included feasting, dancing, games, and music.

GOVERNMENT The six traditional bands had consolidated by the eighteenth century into four: the Miami proper, the Pepicokia, the Wea, and the Piankashaw. Of these, the second soon merged into the last two, which by the nineteenth century acted as separate tribes. Even in the nineteenth century, each of the three Miami tribes was divided into bands.

Each village had a council made up of clan chiefs; the council in turn confirmed a village chief, generally a patrilineally inherited position, who was responsible for civil functions and was in turn supported by the people. There was also a war chief who oversaw war rituals. This person generally inherited his position but might obtain it by merit (as was the case with Little Turtle). There were also parallel female peace and war chiefs: The former supervised feasts, and the latter provisioned war parties and could demand an end to various types of hostilities.

The village council also sent delegates to the band council, which in turn sent delegates to the tribal council. All leaders enjoyed respect and a great deal of authority. In fact, early tribal chiefs may have had a semidivine status, reflecting the influence of Mound Builder culture.

CUSTOMS The Miami recognized roughly five patrilineal clans and possibly a dual division. Elderly women may have named children based on dreams. Names were clan specific, although adults might change names to alter their luck or to avert bad luck. Children were rarely punished; parental instruction and discipline consisted mostly of lectures and behavior modeling. Adult status was indicated by face painting. Adults enjoyed athletic competitions, especially footraces.

Marriages were either arranged or initiated by couples. The formalities included a gift exchange. Newly married couples generally lived with the father's family. Killing an adulterous wife (or clipping off the end of her nose) or an abusive husband was condoned; however, other murders were either avenged by blood or by money or property.

Burial, either extended or seated, took place on scaffolds, in hollowed-out logs, and in small, sealed huts. Only food and water and perhaps some personal adornments went with the corpse. Postfuneral activities included a performance of the dead's favorite dance or activity and, if a parent, a ceremonial adoption of a new parent a year later.

DWELLINGS The people built small summer villages along river valleys. Private houses were made of an oval pole framework covered with woven cattail or rush mats. There were also village council houses. Structures in winter hunting camps tended to be covered with elm bark or hides.

DIET Miamis developed and grew a particularly fine variety of corn, in addition to beans, squash, and, later, melons. Men hunted buffalo on the open prairies, using fire surrounds and bow and arrow before they acquired horses. The whole village, except the old and infirm, would accompany the hunters, with the women and children helping to prepare and pack the meat for the trip home. Women also gathered wild roots and other plant food.

KEY TECHNOLOGY Men made pipes of Minnesota pipestone (catlinite). Musical instruments included drums, rattles, flutes, and whistles. Women made bags from spun buffalo hair.

TRADE Miamis exported agricultural products, pipes, and buffalo products. They imported shell beads, among other items.

NOTABLE ARTS Some items of clothing were decorated by quillwork with bands in a twining or geometric pattern. Buffalo robes were also painted with representational and geometric designs. The people made silk appliqué from the mid–eighteenth century on. Red was a favorite color for decoration.

TRANSPORTATION Dugout canoes were often made of butternut trees, although the people traveled mainly on land.

DRESS Except for soft-soled moccasins, men often went naked in summer; women wore a wraparound skirt, leggings, and a poncho. In winter, men wore deerskin shirts and breechclouts. Both occasionally wore painted animal robes, especially during ceremonies. Knife sheaths were attached to leather or woven belts. Men wore their hair in a roach and were extensively painted and tattooed.

WAR AND WEAPONS With the help of the council, war chiefs decided the issue of whether or not to wage war. Traditional allies included the Kickapoo, whereas enemies included the Dakota (until the eighteenth century) as well as the Chickasaw and other southeastern tribes. The people held a ceremony to ensure the safe return of the war party. War rituals, such as the all-night war dance and the homecoming of a successful war party, were clan based, and leaders of war parties were not considered responsible for deaths or members of their own clan. Warriors carried large buffalo-hide shields.

Contemporary Information

GOVERNMENT/RESERVATIONS Headquarters for the Miami Tribe of Oklahoma is located in Miami, Oklahoma. The people own 38 acres of land. Their constitution provides for a principal chief, other officers, and a council. There is an annual meeting of all tribal members.

The Miami Nation of Indiana is located near Peru. A powerful principal chief and elders council are chosen by clans and serve for life. There is also a vice chief, a principal chiefress (female chief), and a spiritual leader. About 2,500 tribal members lived in Indiana in the early 1990s.

ECONOMY In Indiana, bingo provides most tribal funds. Tribal resources in Oklahoma include a trucking company, gasoline reserves, a motel and supper club, bingo, and tourism.

LEGAL STATUS The Miami Tribe of Oklahoma is a federally recognized tribal entity. The Miami Nation of Indiana asked for summary action to overturn their 1897 termination and reinstate tribal recognition. Their recognition petition was rejected in 1992.

DAILY LIFE The Indiana Miami meet twice annually and hold an annual picnic in August. Their agenda for years has focused on reinstating federal recognition, reacquiring land, and economic development. Facilities include three buildings, which house the tribal headquarters, a museum, a day care center, various social programs, and a gymnasium.

Facilities in Oklahoma include the tribal headquarters, a common room, a library, and a community kitchen and dining area for elders. There is also a brick longhouse, at which tribal meetings are held. Both Miami tribes helped found the Minnetrista Council for Great Lakes Native American Studies, in Muncie, Indiana, an organization dedicated to preserving and promoting Woodlands culture.

Micmac

Micmac (`Mik mak), or Mi'kmaq, "allies." The Micmac called their land Megumaage and may have called themselves *Souriquois*. They were members of the Abenaki Confederacy in the eighteenth and nineteenth centuries. Culturally similar to the Maliseet, Penobscot, and Passamaquoddy, they were known to the seventeenth-century British as Tarantines, possibly meaning "traders."

LOCATION The people were traditionally located in southeast Quebec, the Maritime Provinces, and the Gaspé Peninsula of eastern Canada, a region of forests, lakes, rivers, and a rugged coast. They lived there and in northern Maine in the late twentieth century.

POPULATION The Micmac population was between 3,000 and 5,000 in the sixteenth century. There were approximately 20,000 registered Canadian Micmacs in 1993, including about 15,000 in the Maritimes and 4,000 in Quebec, and several thousand more in the United States.

LANGUAGE Micmac was an Algonquian language.

Historical Information

HISTORY The Micmac were originally from the Great Lakes area, where they probably had contact with the Ohio Mound Builders and were exposed to agriculture. They may have encountered Vikings around 1000. The Cabots, early explorers, captured three Micmacs at their first encounter. Friendly meetings with Jacques Cartier (1523) and Samuel de Champlain (1603) led to a long-term French alliance.

The Micmac were involved with the fur trade by the seventeenth century, becoming intermediaries between the French and Indian tribes to the south. A growing reliance on non-native manufactured metal goods and foods changed their cultural and economic patterns, and war, alcohol, and disease vastly diminished their population. In 1610, the grand chief Membertou converted to Catholicism after being cured by priests.

In the eighteenth century, the French armed Micmacs with flintlocks and encouraged them, with scalp bounties, to kill people from the neighboring Beothuk tribe. This they did to great effect, nearly annihilating those Indians, after which they occupied their former territory in Newfoundland. British attempts at genocide against the Indians included feeding them poisoned food, trading them disease-contaminated cloth, and indiscriminate individual and mass murder.

By the mid–eighteenth century, most Micmacs had become Catholics. They continued fighting the British until 1763. Much of this fighting took place at sea, where the people showed their excellent nautical skills. Following the American Revolution and the end of the fur trade, Micmacs remained in their much-diminished traditional area, which was increasingly invaded by non-natives.

In the nineteenth century, Micmacs were forced to accept non-Indian approval of their leadership as well as a general trimming of lands guaranteed by treaty. The people continued some traditional subsistence activities during the nineteenth century but also moved toward working in the lumber, construction, and shipping industries and as migrant farm labor. They were generally excluded from skilled or permanent (higher-paying) jobs. Starvation and disease also stalked the people during those years.

Micmacs had lost most of their Canadian reserves by the early 1900s. Schools were located on many of those that remained. Hockey and baseball became very popular before the Depression. Significant economic activities in the early to mid–twentieth century included logging, selling splint baskets, and local seasonal labor, such as blueberry raking and potato picking. An administrative centralization of reserves in the 1950s led to increased factionalism and population flight.

In the 1960s, many Micmac men began working in high-steel construction, on projects mainly in Boston. Women used vocational training to find work as nurses, teachers, and social workers. They also became increasingly active in band politics. Canadian Micmacs formed the Union of New Brunswick Indians and the Union of Nova Scotia Indians in 1969 to coordinate service programs and document land claims. They and other landless tribes formed the Association of Aroostook Indians in 1970 to try to raise their standard of living and fight discrimination. The tribe formed the Aroostook Micmac Council in 1982.

RELIGION Manitou, the ubiquitous creative spirit, was identified with the sun. Other deities in human form could be prevailed upon to assist mortals. All animals, but especially bears, were treated with respect, in part because it was believed that they could transform themselves into other species. The Micmacs' rich mythology included Gluscap, the culture hero, as well as several types and levels of magical beings, including cannibalistic giants. Shamans were generally men and could be quite powerful. They cured, predicted the future, and advised hunters.

GOVERNMENT Small winter hunting groups, composed of households, came together in summer as bands, within seven defined districts. They also joined forces for war. Bands were identified in part through the use of distinctive symbols. There were three levels of chiefs, all with relatively little authority. Local hunting groups of at least 30 to 40 people were led by a hereditary headman (sagamore), usually an eldest son of an important family. These groups were loosely defined and of flexible membership. Chiefs of local groups provided dogs for the hunt, canoes, and food reserves. Sagamores also kept all game killed by unmarried men, and some of the game killed by married men.

There were also chiefs of the traditional seven districts. These leaders called district council meetings, entertained visiting chiefs, and participated in the grand council. At the top of the pyramid, at least from the nineteenth century on, there was also a grand chief or sagamore. In summer, this leader conferred grand councils to consider treaties as well as issues of war and peace.

CUSTOMS The general Micmac worldview valued moderation, equality, generosity, bravery, and respect for all living things. When the people gathered together from spring through fall, each group camped at a traditional place along the coast. There was a recognized social ranking in which commoners came below three levels of chiefs but above slaves, who were taken in war.

Children were welcomed and treated indulgently. A newborn's first meal was bear or seal grease. Women resumed normal activities immediately after giving birth. They generally avoided new pregnancies for several years, until the child had been weaned. Children as well as the elderly were treated with respect and affection, although little or no effort was made to help ill or old people remain alive.

There were many occasions for feasting and dancing, especially as part of life-cycle events. The Micmac probably observed a woman's puberty ceremony; boys were considered men when they had killed their first large game. There were elaborate menstrual taboos, including seclusion. Women's tasks included gathering firewood, making clothing and bark containers, bringing game into camp, and setting up the wigwam. Older brothers and sisters generally avoided each other. Men used the sweat lodge for purification.

Marriages were generally arranged. A prospective husband, usually at least age 20, spent at least two years working for his future father-in-law as a hunter and general provider. After the probationary period, he provided game for a big wedding feast, including dancing (first marriages only). The birth of children formalized a marriage. Adultery was rare, although polygyny was practiced.

Longevity (life spans over 100 years) was not unusual before contact with Europeans. People gave their own funeral orations shortly before they died, if possible. Burial and a feast followed a three-day general mourning period. In some locations, corpses were wrapped in bark and buried with personal effects on an uninhabited island. There was also scaffold burial. Close relatives cut their hair and observed a yearlong mourning period.

DWELLINGS Micmacs built their inland winter camps near streams. Single extended families lived in conical wigwams of birch bark, skins or woven mats. Each had a central indoor fireplace. The inside was divided into several compartments for cooking, eating, sleeping, and other activities. Floors were covered with boughs, and fur-covered boughs served as beds.

The people may have had rectangular, open, multi-family summer houses.

DIET In winter, small bands hunted game such as moose, bear, caribou, and porcupine. They also trapped smaller game such as beaver, otter, and rabbit and ate land and water birds (and their eggs). Moose were stalked with disguises and attracted with callers. Dogs helped in the hunt. Meat and fish were eaten fresh, roasted, broiled, boiled, or smoked. Pounded moose bones yielded a nutritious "butter."

People fished in spring and summer for eel, salmon, cod, herring, sturgeon, and smelt. They also collected shellfish and hunted seals and other marine animals. Salmon and fowl were sometimes speared at night with the light of birch-bark torches. The sea provided most of the summer diet.

They also gathered a number of wild berries, roots, and nuts. They occasionally ate dog, especially at funeral feasts, but they generally avoided snakes, amphibians, and skunks.

KEY TECHNOLOGY Men made birch-bark moose calls and boxes. They also made double-edged moose-bone-blade spears and bows and stone-point arrows for hunting as well as snares and deadfalls for trapping. They fished with nets, bone hooks, weirs, and bone-tipped harpoons.

Meat was boiled with hot stones in hollowed wooden troughs. Women made reed and coiled spruce-root baskets, woven mats, and possibly pottery.

TRADE Micmacs generally served as intermediaries between northern hunters and southern farmers.

NOTABLE ARTS Women decorated clothing and containers with dyed porcupine quillwork. Wigwams were sometimes carefully painted, especially with symbols distinctive to each band.

TRANSPORTATION Men built 8- to 10-foot-long, seaworthy birch-bark and caribou-skin canoes. They made two types of square-toed snowshoes, one for powder and one for frozen surfaces. Women carried burdens using backpacks and tumplines.

DRESS People dressed in skin robes fastened with one (men) or two (women) belts, moose-skin or deerskin leggings, and moccasins. Men also wore loincloths. Both sexes wore their hair long. People tattooed band symbols on their bodies.

WAR AND WEAPONS Small population groups came together as bands for war. The people were allied with southern Algonquians as members of the Abenaki Confederacy. Their traditional enemies included the Beothuk, Labrador Eskimo, Maliseet (occasionally), Iroquois (especially Mohawk) around the St. Lawrence River, and New England Algonquians.

The Micmac adopted some Iroquois war customs, such as the torture of prisoners by women. Their weapons included bows, poisoned arrows, spears with moose-bone blades, and possibly stone tomahawks. There was some interband fighting (intraband disputes were generally resolved by individual fighting or wrestling). Captives were taken as slaves, tortured and killed, or, especially in the case of young women, adopted.

Contemporary Information

GOVERNMENT/RESERVATIONS The Aroostook Band of Micmacs is governed by an elected board of directors. Headquarters for the tribal council is in Presque Isle, Maine. Band membership was slightly less than 500 in 1991.

The approximately 28 Canadian reserves include Pictou Landing, Eskasoni, and Shubenacadie in Nova Scotia and Burnt Church, Eel River Bar, Pabineau, Red Bank, Eel Ground, Indian Island, Bouctouche, Fort Folly, and Big Cove in New Brunswick. The three Micmac communities in Quebec are Listuguj (3,663.22 hectares; 2,621 people in 1994, of whom 1,641 live within the territory), Gesgapegiag (182.26 hectares; 936 people in 1994, of whom 432 live within the territory), and Gaspé (no area; 435 people in 1994).

Each is governed by a band council. Some are represented by captains of the Grand Council. The Grand Council, traditional government of the Micmac Nation, unites the six districts of Micmac territory (Quebec's Gaspé Peninsula, northern and eastern New Brunswick, Nova Scotia, Newfoundland, and Prince Edward Island).

ECONOMY Fishing, especially for salmon, remains important. Maine Micmacs operate a mail-order crafts cooperative. There have been some land claims victories in Canada, particularly a $35 million settlement to the Micmac of the Pictou Landing reserve.

LEGAL STATUS The Aroostook Band of Micmacs is a federally recognized tribal entity. Excluded from the giant 1980 Maine Indian land claim settlement, the tribe persuaded the federal government in 1991 to pass the Aroostook Band of Micmacs Settlement Act, which provided it with land and a tax fund as well as federal benefits. Newfoundland Indians organized in 1973 and were recognized under the Indian Act in 1984.

DAILY LIFE Many Micmacs still speak the native language. Most are Catholics. Micmacs tend to be active in various pan-Indian organizations. There have been some gains in Canadian Micmacs' quest to regain their hunting and fishing rights. Canadian Micmacs still face severe problems such as substance abuse, discrimination, and a high suicide rate. Roughly 40 percent of Canadian Micmacs speak their ancestral language.

Mohawk

Mohawk (`M ō häk), Algonquian for "eaters of men," one of the five original tribes of the Iroquois League. The Mohawk self-designation was *Kaniengehawa*, "People of the Place of Flint." They were the Keepers of the Eastern Door of the Iroquois League. The name Iroquois ("real adders") comes from the French adaptation of the Algonquian name for these people. Their self-designation was *Kanonsionni*, "League of the United (Extended) Households." Iroquois today refer to themselves as *Haudenosaunee*, "People of the Longhouse."

LOCATION The Mohawk were located mainly along the middle Mohawk River Valley but also north into the Adirondack Mountains and south nearly to Oneonta. At the height of their power, the Iroquois controlled land from the Hudson to the Illinois Rivers and the Ottawa to the Tennessee Rivers. Today, Mohawks live in southern Quebec and Ontario, Canada, and extreme northern New York.

POPULATION There were perhaps 15,000–20,000 members of the Iroquois League around 1500 and roughly 4,000 Mohawks in the mid–seventeenth century. About 70,000 Iroquois Indians were living in the United States and Canada in the mid-1990s. Of these, about 28,000 were Mohawks: about 13,000 in Canada and 15,000 in the United States.

LANGUAGE Mohawks spoke a Northern Iroquois dialect.

Historical Information

HISTORY The Iroquois began cultivating crops shortly after the first phase of their culture in New York was established around 800. Deganawida, a Huron prophet, and Hiawatha, a Mohawk shaman living among the Onondaga, founded the Iroquois League or Confederacy some time between 1450 and 1600. It originally consisted of five tribes: Cayuga, Mohawk, Oneida, Onondaga, and Seneca; the Tuscarora joined in the early eighteenth century. The league's purpose was to end centuries of debilitating intertribal war and work for the common good. Both Deganawida and Hiawatha may have been actual or mythological people.

Iroquois first met non-natives in the sixteenth century. There were sporadic Jesuit missions in Mohawk country throughout the mid–seventeenth century. During these and subsequent years, the people became heavily involved in the fur trade. Trading, fighting, and political intrigue characterized that period. Although they were good at playing the European powers off against each other, the Iroquois increasingly became British allies in trade and in the colonial wars and were instrumental in the ultimate British victory over the French.

Shortly after 1667, a year in which peace was concluded with the French, a group of Mohawk and Oneida Indians migrated north to La Prairie, a Jesuit mission on the south side of the St. Lawrence River. This group eventually settled south of Montreal at Sault Saint Louis, or Kahnnawake (Caughnawaga). Although they were heavily influenced by the French, most even adopting Catholicism, and tended to split their military allegiance between France and Britain, they remained part of the Iroquois League. Some of this group and other Iroquois eventually moved to Ohio, where they became known as the Seneca of Sandusky. They ultimately settled in Indian Territory (Oklahoma).

At about the same time, a group of Iroquois settled on the island of Montreal and became known as Iroquois of the Mountain. Like the people at Caughnawaga, they drew increasingly close to the French. The community moved in 1721 to the Lake of Two Mountains and was joined by other Indians at that time. This community later became the Oka reserve. Other Mohawks traveled to the far west as trappers and guides and merged with Indian tribes there.

Early in the eighteenth century, the first big push of non-native settlers drove into Mohawk country. Mohawks at that time had two principal settlements and were relatively prosperous from their fur trade activities. The establishment of St. Regis in the mid–eighteenth century by some Iroquois from Caughnawaga all but completed the migration to the St. Lawrence area. Most of these people joined the French in the French and Indian War, and their allegiance was split during the American Revolution.

The British victory in 1763 meant that the Iroquois no longer controlled the balance of power in the region. Despite the long-standing British alliance, some Indians joined anti-British rebellions as a defensive gesture. The confederacy split its allegiance in the Revolutionary War, with most Mohawks, at the urging of Theyendanegea, or Joseph Brant, siding with the British. This split resulted in the council fire's being extinguished for the first time in roughly 200 years.

The British-educated Mohawk Joseph Brant proved an able military leader in the American Revolutionary War. Despite his leadership and that of others, however, the Mohawks suffered depredations throughout the war, and by war's end their villages had been permanently destroyed. When the 1783 Treaty of Paris divided Indian land between Britain and the United States, British Canadian officials established the Six Nations Reserve for their loyal allies, to which most Mohawks repaired. Others went to a reserve at the Bay of Quinté, which later became Tyendinaga (Deseronto) Reserve.

The Iroquois council officially split into two parts during that time. One branch was located at the Six Nations Reserve and the other at Buffalo Creek. Gradually, the reservations as well as relations with the United States and Canada assumed more significance than intraconfederacy matters. In the 1840s, when the Buffalo Creek Reservation was sold, the fire there was rekindled at Onondaga.

In Canada, traditional structures were further weakened by the allotment of reservation lands in the 1840s; the requirement under Canadian law, from 1869 on, of patrilineal descent; and the transition of league councils and other political structures to a municipal government. In 1924, the Canadian government terminated confederacy rule entirely, mandating an (all male) elected system of government on the reserve.

The native economy gradually shifted from primarily hunting to farming, dependence on annuities received for the sale of land, and some wage labor. The people faced increasing pressure from non-natives to adopt Christianity and sell more land. The old religion declined during that time, although on some reservations the Handsome Lake religion grew in importance. During the nineteenth century, Mohawks worked as oarsmen with shipping companies, at one point leading an expedition up the Nile in Egypt. They also began working in construction during that period, particularly on high scaffolding.

At Akwesasne (see "Government/Reservations"), most people farmed, fished, and trapped during the nineteenth century. Almost all resident Indians were Catholic. Government was provided by three U.S.-appointed trustees and, in Canada, by a mandated elected council. With other members of the confederacy, Mohawks resisted the 1924 citizenship act, selective service, and all federal and state intrusions on their sovereignty.

RELIGION The Mohawk recognized Orenda as the supreme creator. Other animate and inanimate objects and natural forces were also considered to be of a spiritual nature. The Mohawk held important festivals to celebrate maple sap and strawberries as well as corn planting, ripening (Green Corn ceremony), and harvest. These festivals often included singing, male dancing, game playing, gambling, feasting, and food distribution.

The eight-day new year's festival may have been most important of all. Held in midwinter, it was a time to give thanks, to forget past wrongs, and to kindle new fires, with much attention paid to new and old dreams. A condolence ceremony had quasi-religious components. Medicine groups such as the False Face Society, whose members wore carved wooden masks, and the Medicine, Dark Dance, and Death Feast Societies (the last two controlled by women) also conducted ceremonies, since most illness was thought to be of supernatural origin.

In the early nineteenth century, many Iroquois embraced the teachings of Handsome Lake. This religion was born during the general religious ferment known as the Second Great Awakening and came directly out of the radical breakdown of Iroquois life. Beginning in 1799, the Seneca Handsome Lake spoke of Jesus and called upon Iroquois to give up alcohol and a host of negative behaviors, such as witchcraft and sexual promiscuity. He also exhorted them to maintain their traditional religious celebrations. A blend of traditional and Christian teachings, the Handsome Lake religion had the effect of facilitating the cultural transition occurring at the time.

GOVERNMENT The Iroquois League comprised 50 hereditary chiefs, or sachems, from the constituent tribes. Each position was named for the original holder and had specific responsibilities. Sachems were men, except where a woman acted as regent, but they were appointed by women. The Mohawk sent nine sachems (three from each clan) to meetings of the Iroquois Great Council, which met in the fall and for emergencies. Their symbol at this gathering was the shield.

Debates within the great council were a matter of strict clan, division, and tribal protocols, in a complex system of checks and balances. Politically, individual league members often pursued their own best interests while maintaining an essential solidarity with the other members. The creators of the U.S. government used the Iroquois League as a model of democracy.

Locally, the village structure was governed by a headman and a council of elders (clan chiefs, elders, wise men). Matters before the local councils were handled according to a definite protocol based on the clan and division memberships of the chiefs. Village chiefs were chosen from groups as small as a single household. Women nominated and recalled clan chiefs. Tribal chiefs represented the village and the nation at the general council of the league. The entire system was hierarchical and intertwined, from the family up to the great council. Decisions at all levels were reached by consensus.

There were also a number of nonhereditary chiefs ("pine tree" or "merit" chiefs), some of whom had no voting power. This may have been a postcontact phenomenon.

CUSTOMS The Mohawk recognized a dual division, each composed of three matrilineal, animal-named clans (Wolf, Bear, and Turtle). The clans in turn were composed of matrilineal lineages. Each owned a set number of personal names, some of which were linked with particular activities and responsibilities.

Women enjoyed a high degree of prestige, being largely equated with the "three sisters" (corn, beans, and squash), and they were in charge of most village activities, including marriage. Great intravillage lacrosse games included heavy gambling. Other games included snowsnake, or sliding a spear along a trench in the snow for distance. Food was shared so that everyone had roughly the same to eat.

Personal health and luck were maintained by performing various individual rituals, including singing and dancing, learned in dreams. Members of the False Face medicine society wore wooden masks carved from trees and used rattles and tobacco. Shamans also used up to 200 or more plant medicines to cure illness. People committed suicide on occasion for specific reasons (men who lost prestige; women who were abandoned; children who were treated harshly). Murder could be revenged or paid for with sufficient gifts.

Young men's mothers arranged marriages with a prospective bride's mother. Divorce was possible but not readily obtained because it was considered a discredit. The dead were buried in sitting position, with food and tools for use on the way to the land of the dead. A ceremony was held after ten days. The condolence ceremony mourned dead league chiefs and installed successors. A modified version also applied to common people.

DWELLINGS In the seventeenth century, Mohawks lived in three villages (Caughnawaga, Kanagaro, and Tionnontoguen) of 30 or more longhouses, each village with 500 or more people, as well as roughly five to eight smaller villages. The people built their villages near water and often on a hill after circa 1300. Some villages were palisaded. Other Iroquois villages had up to 150 longhouses and 1,000 or more people. Villages were moved about twice in a generation, when firewood and soil were exhausted.

Iroquois Indians built elm-bark longhouses, 50–100 feet long, depending on how many people lived there, from about the twelfth century on. They held around 2 or 3 but as many as 20 families, related maternally (lineage segments), as well as their dogs. There were smoke holes over each two-family fire. Beds were raised platforms; people slept on mats, their feet to the fire, covered by pelts. Upper platforms were used for food and gear storage. Roofs were shingled with elm bark. The people also built some single-family houses.

DIET Women grew corn, beans, squash, and gourds. Corn was the staple and was used in soups, stews, breads, and puddings. It was stored in bark-lined cellars. Women also gathered a variety of greens, nuts, seeds, roots, berries, fruits, and mushrooms. Tobacco was grown for ceremonial and social smoking.

After the harvest, men and some women took to the woods for several months to hunt and dry meat. Men hunted large game and trapped smaller game, mostly for the fur. Hunting was a source of potential prestige. They also caught waterfowl and other birds, and they fished. The people grew peaches, pears, and apples in orchards from the eighteenth century on.

KEY TECHNOLOGY Iroquois used porcupine quills and wampum belts as a record of events. Wampum was also used as a gift connoting sincerity and, later, as trade money. These shell disks, strung or woven into belts, were probably a postcontact technological innovation.

Hunting equipment included snares, bow and arrow, stone knife, and bentwood pack frame. Fish were caught using traps, nets, bone hooks, and spears. Farming tools were made of stone, bone, wood (spades), and antler. Women wove corn-husk dolls, tobacco trays, mats, and baskets.

Other important material items included elm-bark containers, cordage from inner tree bark and fibers, and levers to move timbers. Men steamed wood or bent green wood to make many items, including lacrosse sticks.

TRADE Mohawks obtained birch-bark products from the Huron. They imported copper and shells and exported carved wooden and stone pipes. They were extensively involved in the trade in beaver furs from the seventeenth century on.

NOTABLE ARTS Men carved wooden masks worn by the Society of Faces in their curing ceremonies. Women decorated clothing with dyed porcupine quills or moose-hair embroidery.

TRANSPORTATION Unstable elm bark canoes were roughly 25 feet long. The people were also great runners and preferred to travel on land. Women used woven and decorated tumplines to support their burdens. They used snowshoes in winter.

DRESS Women made most clothing from deerskins. Men wore shirts and short breechclouts and a tunic in cooler weather; women wore skirts. Both wore leggings, moccasins, and corn-husk slippers in summer. Robes were made of lighter or heavier skins or pelts, depending on the season. These were often painted. Clothing was decorated with feathers and porcupine quills. Both men and women tattooed their bodies extensively. Men often wore their hair in a roach, whereas women wore theirs in a single braid doubled up and fastened with a thong. Some men wore feather caps or, in winter, fur hoods.

WAR AND WEAPONS Boys began developing war skills at a young age. Prestige and leadership were often gained through war, which was in many ways the most important activity. The title of Pine Tree Chief was a historical invention to honor especially brave warriors. Mohawks were known as particularly fierce fighters. Their enemies included Algonquins, Montagnais, Ojibwas, Crees, and tribes of the Abenaki Confederacy. In traditional warfare, at least among the Mohawk, large groups met face to face and fired a few arrows after a period of jeering, then engaged in another period of hand-to-hand combat using clubs and spears.

Weapons included the bow and arrow, ball-headed club, shield, rod armor, and guns after 1640. All aspects of warfare, from the initiation to the conclusion, were highly ritualized. War could be decided as a matter of policy or undertaken as a vendetta. Women had a large, sometimes decisive, say in the question of whether or not to fight. During war season, generally the fall, Iroquois war parties ranged up to 1,000 miles or more. Male prisoners were often forced to run the gauntlet: Those who made it through were adopted, but those who did not might be tortured by widows. Women and children prisoners were regularly adopted. Some captives were eaten.

Contemporary Information

GOVERNMENT/RESERVATIONS Kahnawake/Caughnawaga (5,0599.17 hectares) and Doncaster (7,896.2 hectares) Reserves, Quebec, Canada, were established in 1667 as a Jesuit mission for mostly Oneida and Mohawk Indians. The mid-1990s population was about 6,500, of a total population of almost 8,000. The reserves are administered by a band council.

Oka/Kanesatake/Lake of Two Mountains, Quebec, Canada, established in 1676 by residents of Kahnawake, is populated mainly by Algonquians and several Iroquois tribes. It is roughly 10 square kilometers in size and is governed by a band council. The mid-1990s Mohawk population was about 1,800.

Gibson Reserve (Watha Mohawk Nation), Ontario, Canada, was established in 1881 at Georgian Bay by people from Oka/Kanesatake who resented resistance offered by the Sulpician Catholics to their cutting timber from the home reserve. The mid-1990s population was about 800.

St. Regis Reservation/Akwesasne Reserve, Franklin County, New York, and Quebec and Ontario, Canada, was formerly a mission established on the St. Lawrence River in the mid–eighteenth century for Mohawks and other groups. The resident Indian population in 1990 was 1,923, but the enrolled population approached 13,000. A tribal council provides local self-government. The 14,600 acres of this community straddle the international border.

Six Nations/Grand River, Ontario, Canada, was established in 1784. It is governed by both an elected and a hereditary council, although only the first is officially recognized by Canada.

Tyendinega Reserve (Deseronto), Hastings County, Ontario, Canada, is mainly a Mohawk reserve. The mid-1990s population was around 3,000.

Ganienkeh Reservation, Altoona, New York, had a mid-1990s population of about 300.

There is a small population of Mohawk high-steel workers in Brooklyn, New York.

In 1993, a small group from Akwesasne reestablished a Mohawk presence in New York's Mohawk Valley, for the first time in 200 years. Known as Kanatsioharehe, the Mohawk population in the mid-1990s was about 50.

The Mohawk (Kahniakehaka) Nation does not recognize the U.S.-Canadian border, nor do they consider themselves U.S. or Canadian citizens. Their communities are governed under authority of the Grand Council of the Haudenosaunee Confederacy.

ECONOMY At Kahnawake/Caughnawaga, most people engage in small-scale farming, high-steel work, factory work, and reservation government. There are also four schools on the reserve as well as a radio station, a newspaper, a hospital, and a credit union. At St. Regis/Akwesasne there is mainly high-steel work; small businesses, including bingo halls; and tribal government.

LEGAL STATUS The St. Regis Band of Mohawk Indians is a federally recognized tribal entity. The Canadian reserves listed under "Government/ Reservations" are provincially and federally recognized.

DAILY LIFE Mohawks, particularly those from Kahnawake, have earned a first-rate reputation as high-steel workers throughout the United States since the late nineteenth century. People from Kahnawake have pursued self-determination particularly strongly. In 1990 there was a major incident, sparked by the expansion of a golf course, that resulted in an armed standoff involving local non-natives and the communities of Oka, Kahnawake, and Kanesatake. Akwesasne Mohawks have continued to battle the U.S. and Canadian governments over a number of issues. In 1968, by blocking the Cornwall International Bridge, they won concessions making it easier for them to cross the international border. The same year, a Mohawk school boycott brought attention to the failure of Indian education. In 1974, they and others established a territory called Ganienkeh on a parcel of disputed land. In 1977, New York established the Ganienkeh Reservation in Altoona.

The Akwesasne community has also been beset by fighting from within. In 1980, after the New York State Police averted a bloody showdown between traditionalists and "progressives," that body replaced the tribal police. In the late 1980s, violence was rampant over the issue of gambling. This situation had quieted but had not been resolved by the mid-1990s. Community leaders have had difficulty uniting around these and other divisive issues such as state sales and cigarette taxes, pollution, sovereignty, and land claims.

As a result of generations that have worked in high steel, Mohawk communities exist in some northeastern cities. Most of these people remain spiritually tied to their traditions, however, and frequently return to the reserves to participate in ceremonies, including Longhouse ceremonies, which have been active at least since the 1930s.

Akwesasne Mohawks publish an important journal, *Akwesasne Notes.* There is a museum and library at St. Regis. Many Mohawks still speak the native language, which remains the people's official language. Akwesasne Mohawks face a barrage of administrative barriers, owing to their location in two U.S. counties and two Canadian provinces. Since the 1968 boycott, dropout rates have plunged from about 80 percent to about 10 percent. Major educational reforms have included the establishment of the Akwesasne Freedom School, the North American Indian Traveling College, language and culture courses, and an Indian library.

In general, traditional political and social (clan) structures remain intact. One major exception is caused by Canada's requirement that band membership be reckoned patrilineally. The political structure of the Iroquois League continues to be a source of controversy for many Iroquois (Haudenosaunee). Some recognize two seats—at Onondaga and Six Nations—whereas others consider the government at Six Nations a reflection of or a corollary to the traditional seat at Onondaga. Important issues concerning the confederacy in the later twentieth century include Indian burial sites, sovereignty, gambling casinos, and land claims.

The Six Nations Reserve is still marked by the existence of "progressive" and "traditional" factions, with the former generally supporting the elected band council and following the Christian faith and the latter supporting the confederacy and the Longhouse religion. Traditional Iroquois Indians celebrate at least ten traditional or quasi-traditional events, including the midwinter, green corn, and strawberry ceremonies. Iroquois still observe condolence cere-

monies as one way to hold the league together after roughly 500 years of existence. The code of Handsome Lake, as well as the Longhouse religion, based on traditional thanksgiving ceremonies, is alive on the Six Nations Reserve and other Iroquois communities. Roughly 15 percent of Canadian Mohawks speak their native language.

Mohegan
See Mahican; Pequot

Nanticoke
Nanticoke (`Nan t ə c ō k), from *Nentego,* "Tidewater People," one of a group of similar Algonquian Indian tribes that also included the Choptank, Assateague, Pocomoke, Patuxent, Conoy, and Piscataway. *See also* Lenápe.

LOCATION In the seventeenth century, Nanticokes lived on the peninsula between Delaware and Chesapeake Bays. Today, most live in Canada, Oklahoma, and Delaware.

POPULATION The Nanticoke and neighboring tribes numbered around 12,000 people in 1600, although the Nanticoke proper made up only slightly more than 10 percent of this number. In the 1990s there were about 1,000 Nanticokes in Delaware.

LANGUAGE Nanticokes and their neighbors spoke Algonquian languages.

Historical Information
HISTORY The Nanticoke may have originated to the northeast, possibly in Labrador, with the Shawnee and the Lenápe. They may also have passed through the eastern Great Lakes region and the Ohio Valley, where they met and possibly defeated Hopewell Mound Builder people.

Contact in 1608 with British Captain John Smith probably came a generation or two later than their neighbors' encounters with earlier British and Spanish explorers. In any case, the people soon became involved in the local beaver trade. Some groups allied themselves with the British as protection against Iroquois raids. In eastern Maryland, some groups, including the Nanticoke, continued to have problems with the British, based on the presence of alcohol and disease, throughout most of seventeenth century.

British settlers granted the Nanticokes a reservation in 1684 between Chicacoan Creek and the Nanticoke River. The British also reserved the right to confirm Nanticoke leaders and to collect a formal tribute. Other groups signed similar treaties during the later seventeenth century. Nanticokes and other neighboring tribes also became subordinate to the Iroquois Confederacy during that time.

After non-natives usurped their original reservation, in 1707 the people obtained a 3,000-acre tract on Delaware's Broad Creek, which was sold in 1768. In 1742, they were forced to eliminate the position of grand chief. In 1744, with Iroquois permission, they settled near Wyoming, Pennsylvania, and along the Juniata River, although ten years later they were living farther up the Susquehanna in a former Onondaga town. At about that time they merged with the Piscataway and became administratively linked with the Iroquois Confederacy.

Nanticokes (and many Conoys who had joined them in the 1740s) remained neutral in the French and Indian War, but they did side with the British during the American Revolution. In 1778, about 200 Nanticokes moved to Fort Niagara and subsequently to the Six Nations Reserve in Canada. Some Nanticokes also remained at Buffalo Creek, New York, while another group of Nanticokes and Conoys went west with the Lenápe, ending up in Kansas and, after 1867, Oklahoma.

Throughout the later nineteenth century and into the twentieth century, the Nanticoke remaining in Delaware gradually lost their official tribal status and were in danger of losing their Indian identity completely. In 1922, Delaware Nanticokes incorporated the Nanticoke Indian Association. They elected a chief and assistant chief and began to recapture interest in some of their former traditions. The annual powwow dates from that time.

RELIGION The people recognized good and evil deities. There may have been a formal priesthood. First fruits ceremonies were directed at a benevolent deity.

GOVERNMENT A great chief or sachem was the overall leader. Each village may also have been ruled by a lesser chief, who might be a woman. The office of chief was probably inherited. The people also recognized war captains.

CUSTOMS Descent was matrilineal. There may have been a social hierarchy, with the chiefs and their councilors having more material worth and respect and better clothing. The people poisoned their enemies and even other tribal members; poisoners were often considered witches. Shell bead money could be used to compensate for crimes and to purchase trade goods. The people may have observed a male puberty ceremony as well as polygyny.

Corpses were buried or placed on scaffolds. In the historical period, their bones were stored temporarily in log houses, whose shelves also held pipes and other personal belongings. Bones of up to several hundred people were later buried to the accompaniment of a spirit dance, which was meant to send them off to the afterlife. Chiefs' bones were preserved in temples.

DWELLINGS There were at least five Nanticoke towns in the early seventeenth century. These were built along stream banks, and some were palisaded, especially those closest to the Iroquois. Houses may have been at least 20-foot rectangles with barrel roofs, covered with bark or mats. There was a smoke hole over the central fire and mat-covered shelves along the sides for beds.

DIET Women planted corn, beans, and pumpkins. They pounded corn in mortars to make meat, fish, or vegetable hominy. They also gathered nuts and other wild foods. Fishing and shellfishing took place in summer. The whole village removed to the woods for the fall hunt, which included deer, bear, turkey, squirrel, and other small game and fowl. Meat was roasted on a spit or stewed.

KEY TECHNOLOGY Men glued bone, antler, or stone arrowheads to wooden shafts. They built springpole snares and set traps on trees felled across a river. Women used a hollowed log mortar and a wooden pestle. They made yucca and rush baskets as well as pottery. Bowls were made of wood.

TRADE The Nanticoke were notable traders. Shell bead money could be used to purchase trade goods

NOTABLE ARTS Nanticoke art included pottery, woven baskets, and carved wood bowls. Baskets were decorated with spruce or porcupine quills. The people also made shell necklaces and similar items.

TRANSPORTATION The people used mainly dugout canoes, although bark canoes were used for trips beyond the fall line.

DRESS Skin clothing consisted of breechclouts and knee-length aprons fastened with a belt. Children generally remained naked. People wore fur cloaks in winter and cloaks without fur in summer. They painted their faces and bodies and covered themselves with bear grease. Various personal ornaments included bird claws, animal teeth, and shells.

WAR AND WEAPONS Weapons included bow and arrow, wooden war clubs, and poisoned arrows.

Contemporary Information

GOVERNMENT/RESERVATIONS The Nanticoke in Delaware (Nanticoke Indian Association) live in a community near Millsboro. There may also be other small communities of Nanticoke descendants scattered around the region.

ECONOMY Nanticokes participate fully in the non-native economy.

LEGAL STATUS The Nanticoke Tribe has requested federal recognition. Other organizations include the Nanticoke Lenni-Lenápe Indians (recognized by the state of New Jersey) and the Eastern Lenápe Nation.

DAILY LIFE The Nanticoke Indian Heritage Project, dating from 1977, established a tribal museum and encourages continued exploration of Indian traditions. The Nanticoke Lenni-Lenápe Indians maintain a museum and library, and they host an annual powwow.

Narragansett

Narragansett (Na r ə `gan sit), "People of the Small Point," was the name both of a specific tribe and a group of tribes—such as Shawomet, Pawtuxet, Coweset (Nipmuc), and eastern Niantic—dominated by Narragansett sachems. *See also* Pequot.

LOCATION In the sixteenth century, the Narragansett proper were located in south-central Rhode Island, although the greater Narragansett territory extended throughout all but northwest and extreme southwest Rhode Island. Today, most Narragansetts live in southern Rhode Island.

POPULATION There may have been about 3,000 Narragansetts in 1600. There were at least 2,400 in the mid-1990s.

LANGUAGE Narragansetts spoke an Eastern Algonquian language.

Historical Information

HISTORY This group may have originated well to the southwest of their historical territory. They were the most powerful New England tribe until 1675, dominating neighbors such as the Niantic and Nipmuc. They may have encountered non-natives in 1524, although there was no significant contact for another century or so afterward.

Trade with the British and Dutch was under way by 1623. Although the Narragansetts largely avoided the epidemics of 1617–1619, smallpox and other diseases dramatically weakened the people in 1633 and thereafter. As British allies, some Narragansetts fought against the Indians in the Pequot war of 1636–1637. In 1636, the grand sachem Canonicus sold land to Roger Williams, on which he established the future state of Rhode Island.

In an effort to protect themselves from non-native depredations, the tribe voluntarily submitted to Britain in 1644. Despite Williams's entreaties to treat the Indians fairly, many British remained extremely hostile. Eventually, they forced the Narragansett people to join the Nipmucs and Wampanoags in King Philip's war (1675–1676). A huge defeat in December 1675, in which more than 600 Narragansetts were killed and hundreds more captured and sold into slavery, signaled the beginning of the end of the war as well as the virtual destruction of the tribe itself.

After the war, survivors dispersed among the Mahican, Abenaki, and Niantic, the last group thenceforth assuming the name Narragansett. Some

of the Mahicans joined the Brotherton Indians in 1788 (*see* Pequot) and later moved with them to Wisconsin. Those who remained in Rhode Island (probably fewer than 100) worked as servants or slaves of the non-native settlers, who moved quickly to occupy the vacated Narragansett lands.

The people underwent a general conversion to Christianity in the mid–eighteenth century, at which time a Christian reservation community was established in Charlestown. After the last hereditary sachem died during that period, government changed to an elected president and council. The last native speaker died in the early nineteenth century. A constitution was adopted in 1849. All of the Narragansett Reservation, except for two acres, was sold in 1880, and the tribe was terminated by the state at that time. The Rhode Island Narragansett incorporated in 1934 under the terms of the Indian Reorganization Act.

RELIGION Cautantowwit, the supreme deity, lived to the southwest. There were also numerous other spirits or deities, who could and did communicate with people through dreams and visions. Priests or medicine men (powwows) were in charge of religious matters. They were usually men who realized their profession in a dream or a vision experience. Their main responsibilities included curing, bringing rain, and ensuring success in war. A harvest ritual was held in a longhouse near the sachem's house. At one important ceremony, possibly held in winter, participants burned their material possessions.

GOVERNMENT Narragansetts recognized a dual (junior and senior) chief or sagamore. Power was shared with a council of elders, sachems, powwows, and other leaders. Sachems were responsible for seeing to the public welfare and defense and for administering punishment. The office of sagamore may have been inheritable and was occasionally held by a woman. Within the larger administrative body there were smaller groups presided over by lesser sachems.

CUSTOMS People changed their names at various life-cycle ceremonies. They were generally monogamous. The dead were wrapped in skins or woven mats and then buried with tools and weapons to accompany them to an afterworld located to the southwest. Only good souls joined the creator there; bad souls wandered aimlessly forever.

Women mostly assumed agricultural duties, set up the houses, made carrying and cooking items, and gathered wild foods and shellfish. Men made house poles and canoes and also hunted, fished, and fought. Some men also made tools and wampum, and old men made turkey-feather mantles.

DWELLINGS Narragansetts lived in dome-shaped, circular wigwams about 10–20 feet in diameter, covered with birch and chestnut bark in summer and mats in winter. Smoke passed through an opening at the top. Winter hunting lodges were small and built of bark and rushes. People erected temporary field houses where they stayed when guarding the crops. Villages were often stockaded.

DIET Women grew corn, beans, squash, and sunflowers; men grew tobacco. The men also hunted moose, bear, deer, wolves, and other game and trapped beaver, squirrels, and other small animals and fowl. Deer were stalked and may have been hunted communally. People fished in freshwater and salt water. They gathered much marine life, including the occasional stranded whale, as well as strawberries and a number of other wild foods.

KEY TECHNOLOGY Crops were dried and stored in underground pits. Fish weirs were often made of stone. Needles were made from bone; necklaces and wampum from shell. Women made twined baskets, pottery, and mats.

TRADE The Narragansett were notable traders. They dealt in wampum, skins, clay pots, carved bowls, and chestnuts. They imported carved stone and wooden pipes from the Mohawk.

NOTABLE ARTS Clothing was decorated with quillwork and wampum beads.

TRANSPORTATION Canoes were mainly of the dugout variety.

DRESS People generally wore deerskin breechclouts, skirts, and leggings. They might also wear turkey-feather mantles and moccasins. In winter they donned bear- and rabbit-skin robes, caps, and mittens.

WAR AND WEAPONS Enemies at times included the Pokanoket (Wampanoag) and Pequot, and allies included the Niantic. Surprise attacks were favored, as were small attacks, although large-scale fights did occur. The people built forts within their territory; as a last resort they withdrew into swamps. Weapons were generally identical with hunting tools.

Contemporary Information

GOVERNMENT/RESERVATIONS In Charleston, Rhode Island, the Narragansett have 1,800 acres held in federal trust. They also own several hundred acres, acquired in 1991 from a private donation, in Westerly. Under its by-laws, the tribe recognizes an elected tribal council, a chief sachem, a medicine man, and a Christian leader (or prophet). A number of committees deal with various matters. Major decisions require the approval of the entire community.

ECONOMY A fishery and high-stakes gambling were under consideration in the late 1990s, the latter being especially controversial.

LEGAL STATUS The Narragansett Tribe is a federally recognized tribal entity.

DAILY LIFE In 1985, the state of Rhode Island returned two pieces of land of about 900 acres each. The August annual meeting and powwow have been held for the last 250 or more years on the old meeting ground in Charlestown. Other ceremonies are both religious (such as the Fall Harvest Festival held in the longhouse) and secular (such as the commemoration of the 1675 battle) in nature. There are tribal programs for the elderly and for children. Tribal representatives are involved in local non-native cultural and educational programs.

Ojibwe

See Anishinabe

Oneida

Oneida (Ō `n ī dä), "People of the Standing Stone," one of the five original tribes of the Iroquois League. Their name refers to a large boulder near their main village. The name Iroquois ("real adders") comes from the French adaptation of the Algonquian name for these people. Their self-designation was *Kanonsionni*, "League of the United (Extended) Households." Iroquois today refer to themselves as *Haudenosaunee*, "People of the Longhouse."

LOCATION The Oneida were located between the Mohawk and the Onondaga, between Lake Ontario and the upper Susquehanna River, and especially around Oneida Creek. At the height of their power, the Iroquois controlled land from the Hudson to the Illinois Rivers and the Ottawa to the Tennessee Rivers. Today most Oneidas live around Green Bay, Wisconsin; in Ontario, Canada; and around Oneida and the Onondaga Reservation in New York.

POPULATION There were perhaps 15,000–20,000 members of the Iroquois League around 1500, and roughly 1,000 Oneidas in the mid–seventeenth century. In the early 1990s, there were 11,000 members of the Wisconsin Oneida tribe, 4,600 Oneidas in Ontario, and about 700 in New York. The total number of Iroquois Indians approached 70,000.

LANGUAGE The Oneida spoke a Northern Iroquois dialect.

Historical Information

HISTORY The Iroquois began cultivating crops shortly after the first phase of their culture in New York was established around 800. Deganawida, a Huron prophet, and Hiawatha, a Mohawk shaman living among the Onondaga, founded the Iroquois League or Confederacy some time between 1450 and 1600. It originally consisted of five tribes: Cayuga, Mohawk, Oneida, Onondaga, and Seneca; the Tuscarora joined in the early eighteenth century. The league's purpose was to end centuries of debilitating intertribal war and work for the common good. Both Deganawida and Hiawatha may have been actual or mythological people.

Iroquois first met non-natives in the sixteenth century. During these and subsequent years, the people became heavily involved in the fur trade. Trading, fighting, and political intrigue characterized the period. Although they were good at playing the European powers off against each other, the Iroquois increasingly became British allies in trade and in the colonial wars and were instrumental in the ultimate British victory over the French.

In the late seventeenth century, battles with the French and allied Indian tribes as well as disease epidemics severely reduced the Oneidas' already small population. As much as two-thirds of the tribe in those years was made up of enemies such as Hurons and Algonquins. Following the Tuscarora wars in 1711–1713, people of that tribe began resettling on Oneida land. The Oneida sponsored the Tuscarora tribe as the sixth member of the Iroquois Confederacy in the early 1720s. Some Oneidas began to drift into the Ohio Valley as early as the mid–eighteenth century. By that time, longhouse living had seriously declined, with houses of nuclear families taking their places.

The British victory in 1763 meant that the Iroquois no longer controlled the balance of power in the region. Despite the long-standing British alliance, some Indians joined anti-British rebellions as a defensive gesture. From 1767 on, evangelical missionaries provided a theoretical/religious basis for the new Pine Tree Chiefs/warriors, such as the Susquehannock Shenendoah, to oppose the traditional chiefs. The missionaries attacked traditional religion and politics, and in this were aided by the warriors, who saw a way to topple control by the clan mothers and traditional chiefs. The 1760s were also a time of famine, increased pressure from non-natives for land, and growing alcohol abuse, all of which provided fertile ground for the missionaries and their new converts.

The confederacy split its allegiance in the Revolutionary War, with most Oneidas (and Tuscaroras), after a period of neutrality, siding with the patriots at the warriors' urging. This split resulted in the council fire's being extinguished for the first time in roughly 200 years. Oneidas participated in American attacks on Onondaga, Cayuga, and Seneca villages. The Iroquois suffered a defeat in 1779 that broke the power of the confederacy. The Oneida ended the war a scattered people, alienated from their fellow Iroquois, with little food and their traditional social, political, and economic systems in ruins.

The Oneidas welcomed two more groups of Indi-ans in the late eighteenth century. Stockbridge Indians arrived to build the community of New Stockbridge, New York, in 1785. Three years later, a group of Mohegans, Mahicans, Narragansetts, Pequots, Montauks, and other Algonquian Indians, as well as some Oneidas, formed the Brothertown Community near New Stockbridge.

Following the Revolutionary War, New York state and the new U.S. government guaranteed the territorial integrity of nearly six million acres of Oneida land. However, the Oneida bowed to pressure and sold most of their lands in New York, gradually relocating westward. Under the influence of an Episcopal missionary and despite the objections of most Oneidas, about half of the tribe settled around Green Bay, Wisconsin, in the 1820s and 1830s, on land they purchased from the Menominee tribe. Following the Treaty of Buffalo Creek (1838), which called for the removal of all Iroquois from New York to Kansas, other Oneidas moved to the Six Nations Reserve in Ontario, Canada; the Thames River near London, Ontario; the Onondaga Reservation near Syracuse; and their original territory near Utica.

The Iroquois council officially split into two parts during that time. One branch was located at the new Six Nations Reserve and the other at Buffalo Creek. Gradually, the reservations as well as relations with the United States and Canada assumed more significance than intraconfederacy matters. In the 1840s, when the Buffalo Creek Reservation was sold, the fire there was rekindled at Onondaga.

In Wisconsin, most people practiced Christianity, with few elements of their traditional religion. Political leadership was based mainly on personal qualities and affiliations, although a hereditary council maintained considerable power. Most land had been allotted by 1908; as usual, the allotments were lost through tax default and foreclosure. At the same time, municipal governments began to replace the tribal structures. Although many people left the community permanently or seasonally to find work, Indian life remained centered on family, medicine societies, church, and several associations.

The Oneida community in Ontario reestablished the traditional tribal council shortly after they arrived in 1839 (although most power was exercised by a general assembly). Clan leaders also represented the tribe at the Council held at the Six Nations Reserve. Kinship ties and traditional medicine societies remained strong. Most people farmed throughout the nineteenth century, with perhaps seasonal lumbering in winter. In the twentieth century, the economic focus shifted to wage labor in white communities. This development led to increased factionalism and the eventual creation of a parallel tribal council supported by adherents of the Longhouse religion. After a third faction arose in the 1930s, the Canadian government unilaterally mandated an elective system. With other members of the confederacy, the Oneida have tried to resist governmental intrusions on their sovereignty.

RELIGION The Oneida recognized Orenda as the supreme creator. Other animate and inanimate objects and natural forces were also considered of a spiritual nature. They held important festivals to celebrate maple sap and strawberries as well as corn planting, ripening (Green Corn ceremony), and harvest. These festivals often included singing, male dancing, game playing, gambling, feasting, and food distribution.

The eight-day new year's festival may have been most important of all. Held in midwinter, it was a time to give thanks, to forget past wrongs, and to kindle new fires, with much attention paid to new and old dreams. A condolence ceremony had quasi-religious components. Medicine groups such as the False Face Society, which wore carved wooden masks, and the Medicine, Dark Dance, and Death Feast Societies (the last two controlled by women) also conducted ceremonies, since most illness was thought to be of supernatural origin.

In the early nineteenth century, many Iroquois embraced the teachings of Handsome Lake. This religion was born during the general religious ferment known as the Second Great Awakening and came directly out of the radical breakdown of Iroquois life. Beginning in 1799, the Seneca Handsome Lake spoke of Jesus and called upon Iroquois to give up alcohol and a host of negative behaviors, such as witchcraft and sexual promiscuity. He also exhorted them to maintain their traditional religious celebrations. A blend of traditional and Christian teachings, the Handsome Lake religion had the effect of facilitating the cultural transition occurring at the time. Among the Oneida, however, this movement lost out to a revitalization of traditional religious beliefs in the early nineteenth century.

GOVERNMENT The Iroquois League comprised 50 hereditary chiefs, or sachems, from the constituent tribes. Each position was named for the original holder and had specific responsibilities. Sachems were men, except where a woman acted as regent, but they were appointed by women. The Oneida sent nine sachems to meetings of the Iroquois Great Council, which met in the fall and for emergencies. Their symbol at this gathering was the great tree.

Debates within the great council were a matter of strict clan, division, and tribal protocols, in a complex system of checks and balances. Politically, individual league members often pursued their own best inter-

ests while maintaining an essential solidarity with the other members. The creators of the U.S. government used the Iroquois League as a model of democracy.

Locally, the village structure was governed by a headman and a council of elders (clan chiefs, elders, wise men). Matters before the local councils were handled according to a definite protocol based on the clan and division memberships of the chiefs. Village chiefs were chosen from groups as small as a single household. Women nominated and recalled clan chiefs. Tribal chiefs represented the village and the nation at the general council of the league. The entire system was hierarchical and intertwined, from the family up to the great council. Decisions at all levels were reached by consensus.

There were also a number of nonhereditary chiefs ("pine tree" or "merit" chiefs), some of whom had no voting power. This may have been a postcontact phenomenon.

CUSTOMS The Oneida recognized a dual division, each composed of probably three matrilineal, animal-named clans. The clans in turn were composed of matrilineal lineages. Each owned a set number of personal names, some of which were linked with particular activities and responsibilities.

Women enjoyed a high degree of prestige, being largely equated with the "three sisters" (corn, beans, and squash), and they were in charge of most village activities, including marriage. Great intravillage lacrosse games included heavy gambling. Other games included snowsnake, or sliding a spear along a trench in the snow for distance. Food was shared so that everyone had roughly the same to eat.

Personal health and luck were maintained by performing various individual rituals, including singing and dancing, learned in dreams. Members of the False Face medicine society wore wooden masks carved from trees and used rattles and tobacco. Shamans also used up to 200 or more plant medicines to cure illness. People committed suicide on occasion for specific reasons (men who lost prestige; women who were abandoned; children who were treated harshly). Murder could be revenged or paid for with sufficient gifts.

Young men's mothers arranged marriages with a prospective bride's mother. Divorce was possible but not readily obtained because it was considered a discredit. The dead were buried in a sitting position, with food and tools for use on the way to the land of the dead. A ceremony was held after ten days. The condolence ceremony mourned dead league chiefs and installed successors. A modified version also applied to common people.

DWELLINGS The main aboriginal village, Oneniote, had over 60 longhouses and was palisaded. The people built their villages near water and often on a hill after circa 1300. Some Iroquois villages had up to 150 longhouses and 1,000 or more people. Villages were moved about twice in a generation, when firewood and soil were exhausted.

Iroquois Indians built elm-bark longhouses, 50–100 feet long, depending on how many people lived there, from about the twelfth century on. They held around 2 or 3 but as many as 20 families, related maternally (lineage segments), as well as their dogs. There were smoke holes over each two-family fire. Beds were raised platforms; people slept on mats, their feet to the fire, covered by pelts. Upper platforms were used for food and gear storage. Roofs were shingled with elm bark. Painted animal figures marked the clan of the inhabitants. The people also built some single-family houses.

DIET Women grew corn, beans, squash, and gourds. Corn was the staple and was used in soups, stews, breads, and puddings. It was stored in bark-lined cellars. Women also gathered a variety of greens, nuts, seeds, roots, berries, fruits, and mushrooms. Tobacco was grown for ceremonial and social smoking.

After the harvest, men and some women took to the woods for several months to hunt and dry meat. Men hunted large game and trapped smaller game, mostly for the fur. Hunting was a source of potential prestige. They also caught waterfowl and other birds, and they fished. The people grew peaches, pears, and apples in orchards from the eighteenth century on.

KEY TECHNOLOGY Iroquois used porcupine quills and wampum belts as a record of events. Wampum was also used as a gift connoting sincerity and, later, as trade money. These shell disks, strung or woven into belts, were probably a postcontact technological innovation.

Hunting equipment included snares, bow and arrow, stone knife, and bentwood pack frame. Fish were caught using traps, nets, bone hooks, and spears. Farming tools were made of stone, bone, wood (spades), and antler. Women wove corn-husk dolls, tobacco trays, mats, and baskets.

Other important material items included elm-bark containers, cordage from inner tree bark and fibers, and levers to move timbers. Men steamed wood or bent green wood to make many items, including lacrosse sticks.

TRADE Oneidas obtained birch-bark products from the Huron. They imported copper and shells and exported carved wooden and stone pipes as well as dried salmon. They also raised and traded ginseng with other tribes. They were extensively involved in the trade in beaver furs from the seventeenth century on.

NOTABLE ARTS Men carved wooden masks worn by the Society of Faces in their curing ceremonies. Women decorated clothing with dyed porcupine quills or moose-hair embroidery.

TRANSPORTATION Unstable elm bark canoes were roughly 25 feet long. The people were also great runners and preferred to travel on land. They used snowshoes in winter.

DRESS Women made most clothing from deerskins. Men wore shirts and short breechclouts and a tunic in cooler weather; women wore skirts. Both wore leggings, moccasins, and corn-husk slippers in summer. Robes were made of lighter or heavier skins or pelts, depending on the season. These were often painted. Clothing was decorated with feathers and porcupine quills. Both men and women tattooed their bodies extensively. Men often wore their hair in a roach; women wore theirs in a single braid doubled up and fastened with a thong. Some men wore feather caps or, in winter, fur hoods.

WAR AND WEAPONS Boys began developing war skills at a young age. Prestige and leadership were often gained through war, which was in many ways the most important activity. The title of Pine Tree Chief was a historical invention to honor especially brave warriors. Oneidas were known as particularly fierce fighters. In traditional warfare, large groups met face to face and fired a few arrows after a period of jeering, then engaged in another period of hand-to-hand combat using clubs and spears. Population losses were partially offset by the adoption of captives. Former enemies became Oneidas because they were brought in to fill specific roles in specific lineages; the clan mothers could order the death of anyone who did not do what was expected of him.

Weapons included the bow and arrow, ball-headed club, shield, rod armor, and guns after 1640. All aspects of warfare, from the initiation to the conclusion, were highly ritualized. War could be decided as a matter of policy or undertaken as a vendetta. Women had a large, sometimes decisive, say in the question of whether or not to fight. During war season, generally the fall, Iroquois war parties ranged up to 1,000 miles or more. Male prisoners were often forced to run the gauntlet: Those who made it through were adopted, but those who did not might be tortured by widows. Some captives were eaten.

Contemporary Information

GOVERNMENT/RESERVATIONS The checkerboard Oneida Reservation (established in 1838) is located in Brown and Outagamie Counties, Wisconsin. In the mid-1990s it contained roughly 2,500 acres, most of which had been repurchased since the 1930s by the federal government. The 1990 Indian population was

2,447. The community is governed under an Indian Reorganization Act constitution by an elected business committee, which itself is subject to the general assembly.

The New York Oneida community owns 32 acres of land in Madison County, near Oneida. The land, acquired in 1794, is not recognized as a reservation by either the state or federal governments. The 1990 Indian population was 37, but about 700 live in the community at large. Some Oneidas also live on the Onondaga Reservation, New York.

Ontario Oneidas live on the Six Nations/Grand River Reserve (1,800 Indian residents in the mid-1990s) and Oneida of the Thames, near London (2,800 Indian residents in the mid-1990s). The Six Nations/Grand River Reserve was established in 1784. It is governed by both an elected and a hereditary council, although only the first is federally recognized. In 1934, Canada mandated a political system consisting of elected councilors and an elected chief, although adherents of the Longhouse religion maintain their own hereditary council.

ECONOMY   The two U.S. communities have gaming establishments. The proceeds go in part to reacquiring land, building new facilities, and sponsoring activities. The Wisconsin tribe employs 2,000 tribal members in its various enterprises, including a hotel. The Canadian Oneidas are largely dependent on government funding.

LEGAL STATUS   The Oneida Nation of New York and the Oneida Tribe of Wisconsin are federally recognized tribal entities. The Oneida people in all three communities are involved in an extended lawsuit over land against two New York counties.

DAILY LIFE   Descent is bilateral in Wisconsin, where most Oneidas are either Episcopalians or Methodists. Some follow the Longhouse religion. Few people speak Oneida, although the tribal school teaches classes in the native language. Important crafts include beadwork, wood carving, and silver work. There is an annual powwow.

Although most people are Christian, there are also many adherents of the Handsome Lake religion among the Ontario Oneida community. Descent is patrilineal by Canadian law, and clan identification has lost much of its significance.

In New York, leadership has been in dispute since at least the 1950s, when a newly organized elective system was more or less successfully challenged by traditionalists. Sachems and clan mothers now hold the leadership positions. Most members are Christians, although many are also members of the Longhouse religion. The nation operates a health center, youth and elderly programs, and a housing development. Facilities include a pool and recreation center

and a museum/cultural center. The community also publishes a newsletter. Some New York Oneidas still speak the language.

The political structure of the Iroquois League continues to be a source of controversy for many Iroquois (Haudenosaunee). Some recognize two seats—at Onondaga and Six Nations—whereas others consider the government at Six Nations a reflection of or a corollary to the traditional seat at Onondaga. Important issues concerning the confederacy in the later twentieth century include Indian burial sites, sovereignty, gambling casinos, and land claims. The Six Nations Reserve is still marked by the existence of "progressive" and "traditional" factions, with the former generally supporting the elected band council and following the Christian faith and the latter supporting the confederacy and the Longhouse religion.

Traditional Iroquois Indians also celebrate at least ten traditional or quasi-traditional ceremonies, including the midwinter, green corn, and strawberry. Iroquois still observe condolence ceremonies as one way to hold the league together after roughly 500 years of existence. Many Iroquois continue to see their relationship with the Canadian and U.S. governments as one between independent nations and allies, as opposed to one marked by paternalism and dependence.

Onondaga

Onondaga (`O n ə n `dä gä), "People of the Hill," were one of the five original tribes of the Iroquois League. As Keepers of the Council Fire, they hosted the annual great council. The name Iroquois ("real adders") comes from the French adaptation of the Algonquian name for these people. Their self-designation was *Kanonsionni*, "League of the United (Extended) Households." Iroquois today refer to themselves as *Haudenosaunee*, "People of the Longhouse."

LOCATION   The Onondaga were the geographically central tribe of the Iroquois confederacy, located near Onondaga Lake and the Oswego River, near present-day Syracuse. At the height of their power, the Iroquois controlled land from the Hudson to the Illinois Rivers and the Ottawa to the Tennessee Rivers. Most Onondagas today live on the Six Nations Reserve in Ontario, Canada, and in Onondaga County, New York.

POPULATION   There were perhaps 15,000–20,000 members of the Iroquois League around 1500, and approximately 1,000 Onondaga in the mid–seventeenth century. Of perhaps 70,000 Iroquois living in the United States and Canada in the mid-1990s, roughly 1,600 Onondagas lived in the United States and another 3,000 lived in Canada.

LANGUAGE   Onondagas spoke a Northern Iroquois dialect.

Historical Information

HISTORY   There were Indians in upper New York at least 10,000 years ago. The Iroquois began cultivating crops shortly after the first phase of their culture in New York was established around 800. Deganawida, a Huron prophet, and Hiawatha, a Mohawk shaman living among the Onondaga, founded the Iroquois League or Confederacy some time between 1450 and 1600. It originally consisted of five tribes: Cayuga, Mohawk, Oneida, Onondaga, and Seneca; the Tuscarora joined in the early eighteenth century. The league's purpose was to end centuries of debilitating intertribal war and work for the common good. Both Deganawida and Hiawatha may have been actual or mythological people.

Iroquois first met non-natives in the sixteenth century. During those and subsequent years, the people became heavily involved in the fur trade. Trading, fighting, and political intrigue characterized the period. Although they were good at playing the European powers off against each other, the Iroquois increasingly became British allies in trade and in the colonial wars and were instrumental in the ultimate British victory over the French.

Still, as a result of trade-motivated efforts to make peace with the French, a pro-French faction existed at Onondaga from the mid–seventeenth century on. The French also established a Catholic mission in their territory about that time. By the mid–seventeenth century, war with the Susquehannock was taking a heavy toll on the Onondaga and other Iroquois tribes. In fact, captive foreigners outnumbered Onondagas in the tribe by the time the war ended in 1675.

Fighting with the French at the end of the seventeenth century led to the torching and temporary abandonment of the main Onondaga village. In the mid–eighteenth century, a number of Onondagas and other Iroquois went to live at Oswegatchie, a mission on the upper Saint Lawrence River. These people became French allies in the French and Indian War, although they sided with the British in the American Revolutionary War.

The British victory in 1763 meant that the Iroquois no longer controlled the balance of power in the region. Despite the long-standing British alliance, some Indians joined anti-British rebellions as a defensive gesture. The Onondaga and the confederacy as a whole split their allegiance in the Revolutionary War. This split resulted in the council fire's being extinguished for the first time in roughly 200 years.

The Iroquois suffered a defeat in 1779 that broke the power of the confederacy. By war's end most of their villages had been destroyed. When the 1783 Treaty of Paris divided Indian land between Britain and the United States, British Canadian officials established the Six Nations Reserve for their loyal allies, to which over 200 Onondagas repaired. Several hundred others moved to Buffalo Creek, New York, where groups of Senecas and Cayugas were living. A 100-square-mile Onondaga Reservation was established in 1788, although most of it had been lost by the early nineteenth century. In 1806, the Oswegatchies were removed. They scattered to St. Regis, Onondaga, and elsewhere in New York.

The Iroquois council officially split into two parts during that time. One branch was located at the Six Nations Reserve and the other at Buffalo Creek. Gradually, the reservations as well as relations with the United States and Canada assumed more significance than intraconfederacy matters. In the 1840s, when the Buffalo Creek Reservation was sold, the fire there was rekindled at Onondaga.

In Canada, the Onondagas, referred to along with the Cayugas and Senecas as the "lower tribes," tended to retain more of their traditional beliefs than did the "upper" Iroquois tribes. Many subsequently adopted the Handsome Lake religion. Slowly, the general influence of non-natives increased, as tribal councils, consensus decision making, and other aspects of traditional culture fell by the wayside. Traditional structures were further weakened by the allotment of reservation lands in the 1840s. The council eventually came to resemble a municipal government. In 1924, the Canadian government terminated confederacy rule entirely, mandating an (all male) elected system of government on the reserve.

In the mid–nineteenth century there were significant Onondaga communities at Onondaga (Onondaga Reservation), on the Six Nations Reserve, and on Seneca and Tuscarora land, especially the Allegany Reservation. The native economy gradually shifted from primarily hunting to farming, dependence on annuities received for the sale of land, and some wage labor. There was also increasing pressure for Indians to sell more land and adopt Christianity, although the Onondaga remained fairly resistant to both. The old religion declined in importance during that time, although among some Iroquois, including many Onondaga, the Handsome Lake religion grew in importance.

In 1898, the wampum belts remaining among the Onondaga were placed in the keeping of the New York State Museum. With other members of the confederacy, the Onondaga resisted the 1924 citizenship act, selective service, the Indian Reorganization Act, and all federal and state intrusions on their sovereignty.

RELIGION The Onondaga recognized Ha-wah-ne-u as the supreme creator. Other animate and inanimate objects and natural forces were also considered of a spiritual nature. They held important festivals to celebrate maple sap and strawberries as well as corn planting, ripening (Green Corn ceremony), and harvest. These festivals often included singing, male dancing, game playing, gambling, feasting, and food distribution.

The eight-day new year's festival may have been most important of all. Held in midwinter, it was a time to give thanks, to forget past wrongs, and to kindle new fires, with much attention paid to new and old dreams. A condolence ceremony had quasi-religious components. Medicine groups such as the False Face Society, which wore carved wooden masks, and the Medicine, Dark Dance and Death Feast Societies (the last two controlled by women) also conducted ceremonies, since most illness was thought to be of supernatural origin.

In the early nineteenth century, many Iroquois embraced the teachings of Handsome Lake. This religion was born during the general religious ferment known as the Second Great Awakening and came directly out of the radical breakdown of Iroquois life. Beginning in 1799, the Seneca Handsome Lake spoke of Jesus and called upon Iroquois to give up alcohol and a host of negative behaviors, such as witchcraft and sexual promiscuity. He also exhorted them to maintain their traditional religious celebrations. A blend of traditional (especially thanksgiving ceremonies) and Christian teachings, the Handsome Lake religion had the effect of facilitating the cultural transition occurring at the time.

GOVERNMENT The Iroquois League comprised 50 hereditary chiefs, or sachems, from the constituent tribes. Each position was named for the original holder and had specific responsibilities. Sachems were men, except where a woman acted as regent, but they were appointed by women. The head of the council was always an Onondaga. This person was assisted by a council of two other Onondagas, and a third Onondaga kept the council wampum. The Onondaga sent 14 sachems to meetings of the Iroquois Great Council, which met in the fall and for emergencies.

Debates within the great council were a matter of strict clan, division, and tribal protocols, in a complex system of checks and balances. Politically, individual league members often pursued their own best interests while maintaining an essential solidarity with the other members. The creators of the U.S. government used the Iroquois League as a model of democracy.

Locally, the village structure was governed by a headman and a council of elders (clan chiefs, elders, wise men). Matters before the local councils were handled according to a definite protocol based on the clan and division memberships of the chiefs. Village chiefs were chosen from groups as small as a single household. Women nominated and recalled clan chiefs. Tribal chiefs represented the village and the nation at the general council of the league. The entire system was hierarchical and intertwined, from the family up to the great council. Decisions at all levels were reached by consensus.

There were also a number of nonhereditary chiefs ("pine tree" or "merit" chiefs), some of whom had no voting power. This may have been a postcontact phenomenon.

CUSTOMS The Onondaga probably recognized a dual division, each composed of eight matrilineal, animal-named clans. The clans in turn were composed of matrilineal lineages. Each owned a set number of personal names, some of which were linked with particular activities and responsibilities.

Women enjoyed a high degree of prestige, being largely equated with the "three sisters" (corn, beans, and squash), and they were in charge of most village activities, including marriage. Great intravillage lacrosse games included heavy gambling. Other games included snowsnake, or sliding a spear along a trench in the snow for distance. Food was shared so that everyone had roughly the same to eat.

Personal health and luck were maintained by performing various individual rituals, including singing and dancing, learned in dreams. Members of the False Face medicine society wore wooden masks carved from trees and used rattles and tobacco. Shamans also used up to 200 or more plant medicines to cure illness. People committed suicide on occasion for specific reasons (men who lost prestige; women who were abandoned; children who were treated harshly). Murder could be revenged or paid for with sufficient gifts.

Dancing was popular; the Onondaga had up to 30 or more different types of dances. Young men's mothers arranged marriages with a prospective bride's mother. Divorce was possible but not readily obtained because it was considered a discredit. The dead were buried in a sitting position, with food and tools for use on the way to the land of the dead. A ceremony was held after ten days. The condolence ceremony mourned dead league chiefs and installed successors. A modified version also applied to common people.

DWELLINGS In the seventeenth century, Onondagas probably lived in two villages, a large one (roughly 140 longhouses) and a small one (roughly 24 longhouses). The people built their villages near water and often on a hill after circa 1300. Some villages were palisaded. Other Iroquois villages had up to 150 longhouses and 1,000 or more people. Villages were moved about twice in a generation, when firewood and soil were exhausted.

Iroquois Indians built elm-bark longhouses, 50–100 feet long, depending on how many people lived there, from about the twelfth century on. They held around 2 or 3 but as many as 20 families, related maternally (lineage segments), as well as their dogs. There were smoke holes over each two-family fire. Beds were raised platforms; people slept on mats, their feet to the fire, covered by pelts. Upper platforms were used for food and gear storage. Roofs were shingled with elm bark. The people also built some single-family houses.

DIET Women grew corn, beans, squash, and gourds. Corn was the staple and was used in soups, stews, breads, and puddings. It was stored in bark-lined cellars. Women also gathered a variety of greens, nuts, seeds, roots, berries, fruits, and mushrooms. Tobacco was grown for ceremonial and social smoking.

After the harvest, men and some women took to the woods for several months to hunt and dry meat. Men hunted large game and trapped smaller game, mostly for the fur. Hunting was a source of potential prestige. They also caught waterfowl and other birds, and they fished. The people grew peaches, pears, and apples in orchards from the eighteenth century on.

KEY TECHNOLOGY Iroquois used porcupine quills and wampum belts as a record of events. Wampum was also used as a gift connoting sincerity and, later, as trade money. These shell disks, strung or woven into belts, were probably a postcontact technological innovation.

Hunting equipment included snares, bow and arrow, stone knife, and bentwood pack frame. Fish were caught using traps, nets, bone hooks, and spears. Farming tools were made of stone, bone, wood (spades), and antler. Women wove corn-husk dolls, tobacco trays, mats, and baskets.

Other important material items included elm-bark containers, cordage from inner tree bark and fibers, and levers to move timbers. Men steamed wood or bent green wood to make many items, including lacrosse sticks.

TRADE Onondagas obtained birch-bark products from the Huron. They imported copper and shells and exported carved wooden and stone pipes. They were extensively involved in the trade in beaver furs from the seventeenth century on.

NOTABLE ARTS Men carved wooden masks worn by the Society of Faces in their curing ceremonies. Women decorated clothing with dyed porcupine quills and moose-hair embroidery.

TRANSPORTATION Unstable elm-bark canoes were roughly 25 feet long. The people were also great runners and preferred to travel on land. They used snowshoes in winter.

DRESS Women made most clothing from deerskins. Men wore shirts and short breechclouts and a tunic in cooler weather; women wore skirts. Both wore leggings, moccasins, and corn-husk slippers in summer. Robes were made of lighter or heavier skins or pelts, depending on the season. These were often painted. Clothing was decorated with feathers and porcupine quills. Both men and women tattooed their bodies extensively. Men often wore their hair in a roach; women wore theirs in a single braid doubled up and fastened with a thong. Some men wore feather caps or, in winter, fur hoods.

WAR AND WEAPONS Boys began developing war skills at a young age. Prestige and leadership were often gained through war, which was in many ways the most important activity. The title of Pine Tree Chief was a historical invention to honor especially brave warriors. Enemies included Algonquins, Montagnais, Ojibwas, Crees, and tribes of the Abenaki Confederacy. In traditional warfare, large groups met face to face and fired a few arrows after a period of jeering, then engaged in another period of hand-to-hand combat using clubs and spears.

Weapons included the bow and arrow, ball-headed club, shield, rod armor, and guns after 1640. All aspects of warfare, from the initiation to the conclusion, were highly ritualized. War could be decided as a matter of policy or undertaken as a vendetta. Women had a large, sometimes decisive, say in the question of whether or not to fight. During war season, generally the fall, Iroquois war parties ranged up to 1,000 miles or more. Male prisoners were often forced to run the gauntlet: Those who made it through were adopted, but those who did not might be tortured by widows. Women and children prisoners were regularly adopted. Some captives were eaten.

Contemporary Information

GOVERNMENT/RESERVATIONS The Onondaga Reservation, Onondaga County, New York, contains 7,300 acres, all of which is tribally owned. The Indian population was about 1,600 in the mid-1990s. Government is by a council of hereditary chiefs, selected by the clan mothers.

The Six Nations/Grand River Reserve, Ontario, Canada, was established in 1784. It is governed by both an elected and a hereditary council, although only the first is federally recognized.

ECONOMY Like most Indians, the Onondaga face high unemployment. Many people work in Syracuse, especially in the construction (high-steel especially) and service industries.

LEGAL STATUS The Onondaga Nation of New York is a federally recognized tribal entity. The Six Nations/Grand River Reserve is provincially and federally recognized.

DAILY LIFE Onondagas are considered to be the most conservative of the Six Nations. The Onondaga Reservation is again the capital of the Iroquois Confederacy. The leader of the Iroquois League, who alone can summon meetings of the Great Council, is always an Onondaga. Recent political activism has resulted in the return of wampum belts, education reforms, and the prevention of acquisition of reservation land for road widening by New York State. In 1994 the tribe ceased seeking or accepting federal grants.

There is a K–8 school on the reservation. Although most Onondagas are Christian, all chiefs must adhere to the Longhouse religion. This requirement ties them to other Iroquois Longhouse communities throughout the United States and Canada. A hereditary council heads both political and religious life. Many people speak Onondaga, although English is the official tribal language. The community is known for its artists and athletes, especially its lacrosse players. Mutual aid remains strong.

In general, traditional political and social (clan) structures remain intact. One major exception is caused by Canada's requirement that band membership be reckoned patrilineally. The political structure of the Iroquois League continues to be a source of contrversy for many Iroquois (Haudenosaunee). Some recognize two seats—at Onondaga and Six Nations—whereas others consider the government at Six Nations a reflection of or a corollary to the traditional seat at Onondaga. Important issues concerning the confederacy in the later twentieth century include Indian burial sites, sovereignty, gambling casinos, and land claims.

The Six Nations Reserve is still marked by the existence of "progressive" and "traditional" factions, with the former generally supporting the elected band council and following the Christian faith and the latter supporting the confederacy and the Longhouse religion. Traditional Iroquois Indians celebrate at least ten traditional or quasi-traditional events, including the midwinter, green corn, and strawberry ceremonies. Iroquois still observe condolence ceremonies as one way to hold the league together after roughly 500 years of existence.

Many Iroquois continue to see their relationship with the Canadian and U.S. governments as one between independent nations and allies, as opposed to one marked by paternalism and dependence.

Occasionally, the frustrations inherent in this type of situation boil over into serious confrontation.

Ottawa

Ottawa (`Ä tu wu) or Odawa, from *adawe,* "to trade." Before about 1600, the name was loosely applied to several groups of upper Algonquians. Their self-designation was Anishinabe ("People"). *See also* Anishinabe.

LOCATION Ottawas lived in the northern Lake Huron region, specifically Manitoulin Island, Georgian Bay, and the Bruce Peninsula, in the early seventeenth century. By the end of the century most were living in Michigan's lower peninsula. Today, most live in northern lower Michigan and southern Ontario. There are also scattered populations in Oklahoma and Wisconsin.

POPULATION There were approximately 8,000 Ottawas in about 1600 and about 10,000 in the mid-1990s, of whom about 4,000 lived in Canada and perhaps 6,000 in Michigan.

LANGUAGE Ottawas spoke a dialect of Anishinabe, an Algonquian language.

Historical Information

HISTORY According to legend, the Ottawa migrated from the Northwest as one people with the Anishinabe and the Potawatomi. They probably arrived on the east side of Lake Huron in about 1400. They first encountered non-natives in 1615, in the person of Samuel de Champlain. The people traded furs to Huron intermediaries, in exchange for European goods, until the 1649 Iroquois defeat of the Huron. At that point, the Ottawa took over direct trade with the French, taking their canoes up the St. Lawrence river to Montreal.

In 1660, the Ottawa suffered their own military defeat at the hands of the Dutch-armed Iroquois, at which time they moved west to the Green Bay area. Some groups continued even farther west, to around Lake Superior and the Mississippi River (these were soon driven back by Dakota warriors). With a guarantee of French protection, many returned to their old homes in 1670. By 1680, most had joined the Huron at Mackinaw. There were many Ottawa settlements around Lakes Michigan and Huron in the eighteenth century.

Like most Algonquins, the Ottawa took the French side in the colonial wars. The Ottawa chief Pontiac led a coalition of regional Indians in an anti-British rebellion in 1763, after the latter's decisive victory over French forces. Pontiac and Delaware Prophet convinced many Indians of the need for unity. The coalition at first enjoyed much success, forcing the British to abandon many of their posts and killing thousands of non-natives. However, it failed to take the two most important British forts, Pitt and Detroit, in part because the defenders of Fort Pitt spread smallpox among the Indians by using infected blankets. Other reasons for the ultimate Indian defeat were the lack of French support, factionalism, and the need of the warriors to provide for their families for the coming winter. Pontiac surrendered and obtained a British pardon in 1766, only to be killed three years later by an Illinois Indian, probably under British orders.

The people tried to remain neutral during the American Revolution, although some actively sided with the Americans; they were similarly divided in the War of 1812. Most Ottawas had converted to Catholicism by the early nineteenth century. By the terms of an 1833 treaty, Ottawas south and west of Lake Michigan, about 500 people, were relocated to Iowa and Kansas with some Chippewas and Potawatomis, with whom they had united in an alliance called the Three Fires.

Other groups, forced to move by the scarcity of game and pressure from non-natives, relocated to the Lake Huron islands or to Michigan reservations or allotments. In 1867, most Kansas Ottawa bought land on the Quapaw Reservation in Indian Territory (Oklahoma). This land was allotted in severalty in the 1890s. The tribe was officially terminated in 1956 but was reinstated in 1978. In 1965, the people received just over $400,000 in land claims settlements pertaining to their time in Kansas.

During the mid– and later nineteenth century, when many Ottawa groups merged or otherwise became associated with Ojibwa and Potawatomi Indians, the United States created an ersatz tribal entity called the Ottawa and Chippewa Bands. This bogus "tribe" was the basis on which the Michigan Ottawa were wrongly but effectively assumed to have been officially terminated. These people have been seeking redress for losses of various benefits and payments for over 100 years. The government has consistently refused to recognize them, even under the Indian Reorganization Act.

Northern Ottawas farmed or worked in lumbering throughout most of the twentieth century. After World War II, however, many moved from local communities to regional cities in search of employment. In 1948 the people created the Northern Michigan Ottawa Association (NMOA) to represent them in all litigation.

RELIGION The Ottawa recognized Manitou, the great spirit, along with many lesser spirits, both good and evil. Around puberty, boys and girls sought visions through dreams or in isolated areas. There were three religious cults, as well as the Midewiwin

medicine society; the latter, open to both men and women initiates, was designed to channel spiritual power toward the well-being of members. Shamans cured through intercession with the spirits.

GOVERNMENT At least four, or possibly up to seven bands, had their own relatively weak chief or chiefs. These bands were composed of local villages, each with their own leadership.

CUSTOMS Small hunting groups left the villages during winter, returning to plant crops in spring. Men might have more than one wife. The dead were cremated, buried, or placed on scaffolds. A feast honoring the dead was held every year or so. Mourners blackened and scratched their faces.

DWELLINGS Permanent villages were sometimes palisaded. The Ottawa built longhouses of fir or cedar bark on pole frames with barrel roofs. They also used temporary mat-covered conical lodges while on trips.

DIET Men hunted and trapped large and small game and birds. Game was often taken in fire drives. Meat and fish were smoked, fried, roasted, and boiled. Fishing was of key importance, especially around the lake shores. Women gathered various berries and other plant food. They also grew corn, beans, and squash and collected maple sap. They baked cornmeal bread in ashes and hot sand.

KEY TECHNOLOGY The people fished with nets and used wooden digging sticks in their fields. Women ground grain using log mortars and wooden pestles. They also wove and decorated rush mats. Other material items included birch-bark and hide containers and pouches.

TRADE The Ottawa were heavily engaged in trade from precontact days on, mainly between the Huron and tribes hundreds of miles to the west. Among other items, they traded rush mats for shells, paints, and pottery. They also dealt in furs, cornmeal, herbs, copper, tobacco, and sunflower oil.

NOTABLE ARTS Men carved various wooden objects. The Ottawa were also known for their woven mats. The people decorated many birch-bark items with the use of templates. Decorative styles included zigzag bands and floral motifs. Most designs were symmetrical. Southern bands decorated items with porcupine quillwork. Robes were often painted.

TRANSPORTATION People navigated lakes and rivers in birch-bark canoes. They wore two kinds of snowshoes—round for women and children and tailed for men—when traveling in snow.

DRESS In summer, men went naked or wore a light robe; they added fitted, decorated breechclouts for special occasions. They added leggings and heavier robes made of skin or pelts in winter. They wore their hair short and brushed up in front. Women wore wraparound skirts, with added ponchos and robes in winter. They generally wore their hair in one braid wrapped with fur or snakeskin. Moccasins were of deer or moose skin, with attached retractable cuffs. Both sexes tattooed their bodies and faces and wore ornaments of copper, stone, and shell in pierced noses and ears.

WAR AND WEAPONS Ottawa warriors fought with bows and arrows, war clubs, and large hide shields. Allies included the neighboring Algonquian tribes as well as the Wyandotte. Despite a close trade relationship, relations with the Huron were often strained. Other enemies included the Iroquois and the Dakota.

Contemporary Information

GOVERNMENT/RESERVATIONS The following bands live in Michigan: Burt Lake (Charlevoix, Cheboygan, and Emmet Counties), Grand River (Kent, Ottawa, and Muskegon Counties), Grand Traverse (Benzie, Grand Traverse, Kalkaska, Leelanau, and Manistee Counties), Little River (Manistee and Mason Counties), and Little Traverse Bay (Charlevoix, Delta, Emmet, Mackinac, and Schoolcraft Counties).

The Grand Traverse Band of Ottawa and Chippewa Indians owns 12.5 acres of land in Peshawbestown, Michigan; reservation status was achieved in 1982.

Most Canadian Ottawas (about 4,000 in the mid-1990s) live with the Ontario First Nations on Cockburn, Manitoulin, and Walpole Islands.

Most of the roughly 400 Oklahoma Ottawas live near Miami, Oklahoma. Their constitution provides for a chief and a tribal council.

ECONOMY Many people are engaged making crafts for the tourist trade. In general, the people work in sawmills and as farmers and fishing guides. Poor economic opportunities and low wages characterize life in Michigan. Most Oklahoma Ottawa are engaged in business and agriculture.

LEGAL STATUS The Grand Traverse Band of Ottawa and Chippewa Indians has been a federally recognized tribal entity since 1980. The Ottawa Tribe of Oklahoma, the Little River Band of Ottawa Indians, and the Little Traverse Bay Band of Odawa Indians are federally recognized tribal entities.

The Burt Lake Band of Ottawa and Chippewa Indians is recognized by the state of Michigan and has petitioned for federal recognition. Other unrecognized Ottawa groups in the United States (there are over 20 in total) include the Grand River Band of the Ottawa National Council and the 9,000-member Northern Michigan Ottawa Association.

DAILY LIFE Michigan Ottawas have regularly suffered arrest and other actions for asserting their treaty rights to hunt and fish. The language survives in Michigan mainly among elders, although the people have instituted various language and cultural preservation programs (many Ontario Ottawas speak their native Algonquian language). Most Michigan Ottawas are Christian, although some celebrate quasi-traditional feasts, naming ceremonies, and other festivals. Michigan Ottawas are active in producing quasi-traditional and contemporary crafts such as birch-bark containers, sweetgrass baskets, buckskin clothing, and maple sugar candy. Contemporary issues focus on the continuing fight for federal recognition and economic development.

The Oklahoma Ottawa are highly acculturated. Few people speak the native language. The annual powwow is held over Labor Day weekend.

Passamaquoddy

Passamaquoddy (Pa su mu `kwä d ē), "those who pursue the pollack" or "pollack-spearing place." Together with the Maliseet, they have also been known as the Etchemin tribe. *See also* Abenaki; Maliseet; Penobscot.

LOCATION The traditional location of the Passamaquoddy is in the vicinity of Passamaquoddy Bay and the St. Croix River. Many contemporary Passamaquoddys also live on the Penobscot Reservation at Old Town, Maine, as well as in industrial centers of New England.

POPULATION With the Maliseet, their population reached about 1,000 in the early seventeenth century. There were approximately 2,500 tribal members in the early 1990s.

LANGUAGE Maliseets and Passamaquoddys spoke dialects of the same Algonquian language.

Historical Information

HISTORY The Passamaquoddy may once have been united with the Maliseet. First contact with nonnatives probably occurred with Samuel de Champlain in the early seventeenth century, although the people may have met fishermen from northern and western Europe as much as a century earlier.

With their growing involvement in the French fur trade, the people soon became dependent on items of non-native manufacture. They also accepted Catholic missionaries. Their population declined severely throughout the eighteenth century, owing to disease, abuse of alcohol, and loss of land.

They joined the pro-French Abenaki Confederacy in the mid–eighteenth century. Many Passamaquoddys married French men and women. By the late eighteenth century, British settlers had pushed them out of many of their best subsistence areas, and the traditional annual round of subsistence activites had been seriously disrupted. The state of Massachusetts set aside 23,000 acres of land for them in 1794 as part of a treaty never ratified by the federal government. The two reservations were founded around 1850 by competing political factions, the "progressive" one based at Sipayik and the conservatives at Motahkok-mikuk.

In the mid– to late nineteenth century, many Passamaquoddys worked in sea-related industries and as farmers, loggers, and guides. They also worked as migrant laborers (potatoes, blueberries) and made baskets, paddles, moccasins, and other items for sale to the tourist trade. Both reservations became enclaves of poverty in a poor region, and by the 1960s many Indians had left to pursue economic opportunities elsewhere. During World War II, the government used part of Indian Township as a German prisoner of war camp; this land was later sold to non-natives. This and other such actions ignited the native rights struggle in Maine and led ultimately to the Maine Indian Claims Settlement Act.

RELIGION Guardian spirits, acquired through vision quests, gave shamans the power to cure and regular people the ability to protect subsistence areas from trespass. Shamans cured by chanting, blowing, and possibly sucking. Sweat lodges were also associated with spiritual power. Any number of supernatural beings included Kuloscap, the culture hero. Dances were mainly associated with spiritual power.

GOVERNMENT Skilled hunters provided local leadership. The people recognized a supreme hereditary chief in the seventeenth century who lived at the main village. The last such chief died in the 1870s. Leadership became more formalized under the confederacy, with graduated civil offices and a war chief. The people remained part of the Abenaki Confederacy from the mid–eighteenth century to the mid– to late nineteenth century, when the confederacy ceased to exist.

CUSTOMS The people came together in large villages in summer and dispersed into small hunting camps in winter. They preferred football, a kicking game, to lacrosse. They also enjoyed any number of dice gambling games.

Men served their prospective in-laws for at least a year before marriage. During that period, the woman made the man's clothing and footgear. Weddings were marked by feasting and oratory recognizing the groom's ancestry. At least after contact, sexual mores were strict, and divorce was rare. Children were generally treated gently and with a high degree of freedom, at least when compared with the region's early French. Boys could sit in council with the older men after killing their first moose. When death was expected, it was sometimes hastened by pouring cold

water on the victim, who may also have been buried alive. Herb doctors could be men or women.

DWELLINGS Summer villages were sometimes palisaded. They included multi- and single-family dwellings. The former were conical pole-frame wigwams covered with birch bark; the latter as well as council houses were rectangular log-frame structures with birch-bark roofs. Council houses could hold up to 100 people.

DIET Farming, especially of corn, was the key economic activity. Harvested corn was stored and taken on the winter hunts. There was some hunting of inland animals such as moose, bear, otter, and muskrat. More important was the capture of marine animals such as seal and porpoise. The people also ate stranded whales as well as other marine foods, including lobster, shellfish, and sea birds and their eggs. Marine mammals were hunted in canoe teams. They also fished for salmon, bass, and sturgeon and gathered wild grapes, roots, and fiddlehead ferns. Maple sugaring may have predated contact with non-natives.

KEY TECHNOLOGY Fish were generally speared. Corn was stored in bark-lined pits. Various birch-bark items included canoes, containers, baskets, dishes, and boxes. Some were decorated with porcupine quills. Cordage came from spruce roots or cedar bark. The crooked knife was an important woodworking tool. The people also made a birch-bark moose call.

TRADE Locally traded goods included birch-bark items, corn, and shells. They also exported porpoise and seal oil and skins.

NOTABLE ARTS Clothing and other items were decorated with porcupine quill embroidery. The people made excellent ash-splint baskets and beadwork from the eighteenth century on.

TRANSPORTATION Lightweight canoes were made of birch bark, moose hide, or spruce bark. Snowshoes were worn in winter.

DRESS Clothing was made from skins. Beaver-skin caps shielded people's heads from the cold. They also wore temporary birch-bark raincoats.

WAR AND WEAPONS War chiefs existed at least from the eighteenth century on. This position was never inherited or elected. The war chief could attract followers for raids.

Contemporary Information

GOVERNMENT/RESERVATIONS The Pleasant Point State Reservation is home to Sipayik, the main Passamaquoddy village since 1770. Population in the early 1990s was about 560 people. The reservation consists of about 225 acres in Washington County, Maine.

Indian Township State Reservation is the site of the town of Motahkokmikuk, population about 550 in the early 1990s. The town has two distinct neighborhoods: Peter Dana Point and the Strip. The reservation contains about 23,000 acres on the Schoodic Lakes in Maine.

The tribe also owns over 130,000 acres of trust land in Maine. Each reservation elects a government that includes a six-member council. A joint tribal council is led by the governors of both reservations. In addition, each reservation alternately selects a representative to the state legislature.

ECONOMY   The tribe sold a cement plant for a $60 million profit in 1988. It has also invested in a blueberry farm and owns a high-stakes bingo establishment, media outlets, several small businesses, and a patent for a coal-emissions scrubber. The tribe itself is the largest employer of Passamaquoddy Indians. Tribal members receive quarterly per capita payments.

LEGAL STATUS   The Passamaquoddys are a federally recognized tribal entity. In 1981, they and the Penobscots (and the Houlton Band of Maliseet Indians) settled a landmark federal and state land claims case against the state of Maine. The Indians won millions of dollars with which they purchased 150,000 acres as trust land. They also gained a unique status as both a federally recognized tribe and a municipality.

DAILY LIFE   Tribal facilities include many new buildings, such as offices, schools, homes, and a museum. The people enjoy free health care. The native language is falling into disuse, with most speakers among the older population. It is taught in school, as are traditional crafts and tribal history. Alcoholism, high unemployment, and anti-Indian prejudice are obstacles that remain to be fully conquered. Most Passamaquoddys are Catholic. The tribe holds an annual festival.

Penobscot

Penobscot (P ə `nob scot), "where the rocks widen," refers to falls on the Penobscot River. The Penobscot were members of the Abenaki Confederacy and are sometimes referred to as being among the Eastern Abenaki people (others include the Kennebec, Arosagunticook, and Pigwacket). They are culturally similar to the Micmac and Passamaquoddy. *See also* Abenaki.

LOCATION   Penobscots traditionally lived along the Penobscot River, from the headwaters to the mouth, including tributaries. Today, most Penobscots live in east-central Maine, although many live in various cities and towns throughout New England and elsewhere.

POPULATION   There were perhaps 10,000 Eastern Abenakis around 1600 and about 1,000 Penobscots in the early eighteenth century. The 1992 Penobscot population was approximately 2,000.

LANGUAGE   Penobscots spoke an Eastern Algonquian language.

Historical Information

HISTORY   Tribal tradition has these people originating in the Southwest. Shortly after their first encounter with non-natives, in the sixteenth century, a story began to circulate in parts of Europe about Norumbega, a fantastic (and mythical) Penobscot town. This tale greatly encouraged British interest in the region.

Because early British visitors mistreated the Indians, the Penobscots showed a preference for contacts with French traders. Intertribal war with the Micmac ended in 1615, about the same time that devastating epidemics drastically reduced the local Indian population. Involvement in the fur trade from the seventeenth century on signaled the virtual end of many aspects of traditional material culture, as the Indians became dependent on cloth, glass beads, corn, metal items, guns, and items of non-native manufacture. Wampum became a currency as well as an important status symbol.

Winter dispersal into the forests and summer trips to the shore became less necessary, as village Indians could eat corn and other foods obtained in trade for furs. Some groups started growing their own corn at that time. Penobscots were often at war with the British, some of whom were pushing into Penobscot territory, during the later seventeenth and the eighteenth centuries. However, since they needed the British as trade partners, they refrained from establishing a full-blown alliance with the French until the mid–eighteenth century, when they joined the Abenaki Confederacy. By that time, many Penobscots had exchanged their traditional dwellings for log cabins. Much of western Maine was in British hands, and other Eastern Abenakis had left the area for residence in Quebec.

Although the Penobscots tried to remain neutral in the French and Indian War, British bounties on their scalps pushed them into the French camp. The British victory ended their access to the ocean, among other calamities. Around that time, the Penobscots joined a confederacy of former French allies whose center was at Caughnawaga, Quebec. They remained members until 1862, when regional intertribal affairs could no longer hold their interest sufficiently.

Although Penobscots fought with the patriots in the American Revolution, Massachusetts took possession of most of their land in the late eighteenth century in exchange for in-kind payments (food, blankets, ammunition, and so on). An Indian agent appointed by the state of Maine was responsible for conducting the tribe's business after 1820.

In 1833, the tribe sold all but about 5,000 acres to Maine. Their traditional economy in ruins, Penobscots became farmers, seasonal wage laborers (loggers, hunting guides), artisans (snowshoes, canoes, moccasins), and basket makers for the tourist trade. Traditional government was superseded by state-mandated elections in 1866, and the last sagamore (chief) died in 1870.

In the 1920s, the tribe actively sought to bring tourists to the reservation by means of pamphlets and pageants. They also benefited from increasing work in local industries (canoes, shoes, textiles). With other Maine Indians, the Penobscot in the 1960s pushed for and won improved services through a new state Indian Affairs department.

RELIGION Summer was the time for religious ceremonies. Shamans were religious leaders. They led ceremonies and cured illness of spiritual origin by blowing and dancing. Common ailments (those without a spiritual component) were cured with herbs and plant medicines.

GOVERNMENT Tribal organization traditionally consisted of a loose grouping of villages, each with its own sagamore. These leaders, who might or might not be shamans, consolidated their power through multiple marriage and by supporting and making alliances with nonrelatives. Leaders were chosen by merit, although there was a weak hereditary component. Sagamores had various social obligations that included feasting the band.

The Eastern Abenaki were politically united, prior to and through the time of the first European contact, under one chief sagamore named Bashabes. Penobscots had a chief sagamore, sometimes in name only, from at least the early seventeenth century to 1870.

CUSTOMS Penobscots were divided into patrilineal lineages, each with its own winter hunting territory that became more strictly defined in the fur trade era. They may have recognized a dual division. The tribe broke into small hunting groups in winter but came together in summer villages along rivers.

Most socializing, such as playing the hoop and pole game, took place in summer gatherings. Women were secluded during their menstrual periods. The first kill of the season was given away, as was the first kill of any boy. Gifts to the bride's family formalized a marriage; the quantity and quality of the gifts reflected the desirability of the bride and the status of her family. Leading men might have more than one wife.

Common illness was treated by means of sweating, herbs, and plant medicines. An anticipated death might be hastened by starvation. Those material goods not given away before death were buried with the body.

DWELLINGS There were no permanent villages until at least the eighteenth century. Some villages were palisaded, at least in the historical period. People lived in both square houses with pyramid roofs and cone-shaped wigwams. Both were covered with birch-bark sheets and were about 12 feet in diameter. They featured two deerskin-covered doors and a top smoke hole.

DIET Men hunted and trapped deer, moose, bears, beaver, otter, and other animals, especially in winter. Hunters wore deerskin disguises. Most meat and fish were dried and stored for winter. Eaten fresh, they were either roasted or boiled.

The people boiled maple sap for syrup. They gathered wild tubers, fruits, and berries, and they fished. On spring and summer trips to the ocean, they gathered shellfish and hunted porpoise, seals, and fowl. There may have been a small amount of corn cultivation.

KEY TECHNOLOGY Hunting equipment included bows and arrows, knives, deadfalls, clubs, snares, and spears. Fishermen used harpoons, nets, weirs, and basketry traps. Birch bark was a key material; in addition to houses and canoes, the people made it into folded containers, baskets, and other important items. They also made smaller containers of bark, sweetgrass, and hide.

Pipes might be made of clay or stone, but most vessels were of clay. Utensils were carved of wood. The fire kit consisted of iron pyrite and pieces of chert (silica). Items were sewn with basswood inner bark, split spruce, or cedar roots. Lashings were generally of rawhide.

TRADE Penobscots were part of a trade network that reached past the Mississippi to the west, almost to the Gulf Coast to the south, and north into Labrador. Still, most trade was local and included items such as canoes, pipes, pottery, and birch-bark goods.

NOTABLE ARTS Clothing was decorated in curvilinear designs with dyed quills and braided moose hair.

TRANSPORTATION Men built canoes of birch bark (and occasionally moose hide) "skin" over cedar ribs and keel. The sheets were sewn together with basswood inner bark; pitch caulking made the seams watertight. They also made ash and moose-hide snowshoes and toboggans.

DRESS Most clothing, such as tunics, breechclouts, long skirts, and moccasins, came from tanned skins. In winter people wore removable sleeves and leggings and moose-hide coats. Beaver pelts were sometimes used for breechclouts and robes. Sagamores might wear special headgear. Men and women also engaged in extensive face and body painting.

WAR AND WEAPONS Penobscot enemies included the Mohawk and Micmac. From the eighteenth century on, the Penobscot were part of the Abenaki Confederacy, which also included the Abenaki, Maliseet, Passamaquoddy, and Micmac.

Contemporary Information

GOVERNMENT/RESERVATIONS The Penobscot Reservation, Penobscot County, Maine, established in 1820, consists of about 4,400 acres of land on about 200 islands in the Penobscot River. The only regularly inhabited one, Indian Island, is home to the main village of Old Town. The people elect tribal officers, a 12-member tribal council, and a nonvoting delegate to the Maine legislature. The 1990 Indian population was 417. The tribe also owns about 55,000 acres of trust land in Penobscot County and in western Maine as well as roughly 69,000 acres of other land.

ECONOMY Tribal members receive per capita payments from their share (over $40 million) of a 1980 land claims settlement. The money was also used to reacquire land (the trust land described under "Government/Reservations"), to provide for the tribe's elderly, and to finance development projects. Other income comes from land leased to logging companies and an audiocassette manufacturing plant. Although unemployment is relatively low (for an Indian reservation), poverty is still a problem.

LEGAL STATUS The Penobscot Tribe is a federally recognized tribal entity.

DAILY LIFE There is a tribal police force and court as well as a primary school. Recognition in 1980 brought a host of new projects and improvements in infrastructure and standards of living. Substance abuse remains a significant problem. There is some interest in traditional crafts and religious ideas, although most traditional culture was lost over 100 years ago. Although only a few elders still know the native language, the people are attempting to preserve that language. Most Penobscots are Catholic. The people regularly intermarry with Maliseets and Passamaquoddys as well as with people from other tribes and non-natives.

Peoria

See Illinois

Pequot

Pequot (`P ē kwot), "destroyers." The tribe known as Mohegan ("wolf") sprang from a Pequot faction in the early seventeenth century. *See also* Narragansett.

LOCATION Pequots lived in eastern Connecticut and extreme northeastern Rhode Island in the early seventeenth century. Their main villages were situated on the Thames and Mystic Rivers. Today, most Pequots live in southern Connecticut. Brotherton Indians, who include Pequot descendants, live in Milwaukee, Racine, and Green Bay, Wisconsin. There are other descendants among the Schaghticoke tribe in northwestern Connecticut.

POPULATION There were approximately 4,000 Pequots in 1600 and about 25 Mashantucket Pequots in 1907. In the mid-1990s there were a handful of families on the Schaghticoke Reservation; 1,650 Brotherton Indians; about 600 Paucatuck Pequots; about 300 Mashantucket Pequots; and about 1,000 Mohegans.

LANGUAGE Pequots spoke an Eastern Algonquian language.

Historical Information

HISTORY The Pequot may have arrived in their historical territory from the Hudson River Valley–Lake Champlain area, wresting land from the Narragansett and the Niantic in the late sixteenth century. In the early seventeenth century, the grand sachem Sassacus dominated 26 subordinate sagamores. However, the people were driven out of Rhode Island by the Narragansett in 1635. About that time Uncas, son-in-law of Sassacus, led a group of Pequot to establish another village on the Thames River; that group became known as Mohegans.

Soon after the Dutch arrived in the region, they began trade with the Pequots, who sold them land at the future site of Hartford. However, control of that land had been disputed, and the British favored more local Indians. As tensions worsened, the Mohegan saw a chance to end their subordinate status. In 1637, they and the Narragansett aided British forces in attacking a Pequot village, killing between 300 and 600 people. The rest of the tribe fled to the southwest. Many were captured, however, and sold into slavery or given to allied tribes as slaves. Some did escape to Long Island and Massachusetts, where they settled with other Algonquins.

Surviving Pequots were forced to pay tribute to the Massachusetts Bay Colony and were prohibited from using the name Pequot. Sassacus and a large group of followers were killed by Mohawks while trying to escape. Uncas then became chief of the Pequots and Mohegans, now all known as Mohegans. He remained firm in his friendship with the colonists, fighting the Narragansett in 1657 and Britain's enemies in King Philip's war.

Although the Pequot/Mohegan survived that conflict, they and other local Indians were severely diminished, and they ceased to have a significant independent role other than as servants or indigents. Some joined other Indian tribes, such as those who passed through Schaghticoke in upstate New York to join the western Abenaki. In 1655, freed Pequot slaves in New England resettled on the Mystic River. The people suffered a continuing decline until well into the twentieth century.

The tribe divided in the later seventeenth century, into an eastern group (Paucatucks) and a western group (Mashantuckets). The former received a reservation in 1683, and the latter were granted land in 1666. Most of their land was later leased to non-natives and lost to Indian control.

In the 1770s, some Mohegans joined a group of Narragansetts, Mahicans, Wappingers, and Montauks in creating the Brotherton (or Brothertown) tribe in Oneida territory (New York). The community was led by Samson Occom, an Indian minister. In the early nineteenth century, this community, joined by groups of Oneidas and Stockbridge (Mahican) Indians, was forced to migrate to Wisconsin, where they received a reservation on Lake Winnebago that they shared with the Munsee band of Delaware Indians. The reservation was later divided and sold.

By the early twentieth century, most Brotherton Indians had been dispossessed, but the community remained intact, mainly because members kept in close contact and returned regularly for gatherings and reunions. Mohegan Indians began a political revival in the early twentieth century, forming the Mohegan Indian Council and becoming involved with the Algonquin Indian Council of New England.

RELIGION The people recognized a supreme deity as well as lesser deities. Medicine men called powwows used herbs, sweats, plants, and songs to cure illness and banish evil spirits. The people also celebrated a variety of the Green Corn festival.

GOVERNMENT Village bands were led by sagamores, or chiefs, who maintained their influence through generosity and good judgment. A council of important men together took all major decisions. There may have been a hereditary component to the position of village sagamore. There may or may not have been a grand sachem who led the bands in pre-contact times. Certainly, that was the case in the early seventeenth century, when Sassacus dominated the Pequot as well as some Long Island bands.

CUSTOMS Unlike many northeastern tribes, the Pequot dispersed in summer to designated resource sites such as fishing weirs, shellfish gathering places, gardens, and marshlands and came together in winter villages. They also dispersed in early winter to hunting camps. Leading men might have more than one wife, in part so that they could entertain more fre-

quently and more lavishly and in part to built alliances with other families. Corpses were wrapped in skins and woven mats and buried in the ground with weapons, tools, and food. The ultimate destination was the land of the dead. Houses were abandoned after a death.

DWELLINGS Villages were usually located on a hill and were often palisaded. Consisting of at least several houses, they were moved when the supply of firewood was exhausted. People lived in bark or woven mat houses, framed with saplings or poles bent and lashed together. Smaller houses (roughly 15 feet in diameter) held two families. Square openings in the roof provided barely adequate ventilation. Doorways were low and mat covered. Larger bark-covered longhouses (up to 100 feet long and 30 feet wide) with multiple fires held up to 50 people.

Bedding consisted of skins and mats laid directly on the floor or on platforms raised 12–18 inches off the ground. Cooking pots were placed on poles suspended on forked sticks driven into the ground. There was a central village plaza for games and meetings. Temporary villages were located along the coast in summer and in the woods in winter.

DIET Women grew corn, beans, and squash; men grew tobacco. Corn was used in stew; cornmeal was also made into cakes and baked in hot ashes. The people gathered shellfish along the coast in summer. They also ate an occasional beached whale. Although deer was the animal staple, men hunted an enormous variety of large and small game as well as fowl, the latter including turkey, quail, pigeon, and geese. Deer were stalked and may have been hunted in communal drives. Fish and wild vegetables, nuts, and berries complemented the diet.

KEY TECHNOLOGY The Pequots used hickory or witch hazel bows and arrows tipped with flint, bone, shell, or eagle claws. Fish were caught with nets, spears, and bone hooks. Other key items included rush baskets, carved wood bowls and utensils, Indian hemp cordage and twined baskets, wooden mortars, pottery jars, and stone woodworking tools.

TRADE The Pequot were part of long-standing ancient trade networks. They engaged in little long-distance trade. Trade items included clay pots, carved wood bowls, chestnuts, and wampum (whelk and quahog shells that were ground into beads using stone drills). Wampum had ceremonial and mnemonic uses before it became a symbol of status and a medium of exchange in the postcontact period.

NOTABLE ARTS Porcupine quills were soaked, softened, and dyed and then used to decorate clothing. Jewelry was made from shell, bone, and other material. Pottery was generally basic although often decorated by incision.

TRANSPORTATION Canoes were of the birch bark and especially the dugout variety.

DRESS Deer, especially the white-tailed deer, furnished most of the people's clothing. Men generally wore breechclouts, leggings (in winter), and moccasins; women wore skirts or dresses and moccasins. Both donned fur robes in cold weather. Clothing was often decorated with quillwork as well as feathers, paints, and shells.

WAR AND WEAPONS The bow and arrow were the basic weapon, along with spears and clubs. Enemies included the Long Island Montauk, the Narragansett, and the Niantic. The people had few known allies.

Contemporary Information

GOVERNMENT/RESERVATIONS The Mashantucket (western) Pequots own about 1,800 acres of land in New London County (Ledyard), Connecticut, which they acquired in 1667. Their 1974 constitution calls for an elected tribal council with a chair. The 1990 Indian population was 55.

The Paucatuck (eastern) Pequots occupy the approximately 226-acre Lantern Hill State Reservation in New London County (North Stonington), Connecticut (established in 1623). The 1990 Indian population was 15.

The Golden Hill Reservation (Paugussett Tribe [Pequot and Mohegan]), New London and Fairfield Counties, Connecticut, was established in 1886. The people are governed by an elected tribal council and officers. The community has purchased roughly 700 acres on the Thames River and hopes to acquire Fort Shantok State Park. The 1990 resident Indian population was two.

Schaghticoke State Reservation, Litchfield County, Connecticut, was established in 1792. It consists of about 400 acres and is governed by a tribal council. About five families lived on the reservation in the mid-1990s.

The Brotherton Tribe maintains a headquarters in Fond du Lac, Wisconsin, and is governed by an elected, nine-member tribal council.

ECONOMY The Mashantucket economy is dominated by an enormously successful bingo operation and casino. The Mohegans operate a casino as well.

LEGAL STATUS The Mashantucket Pequot Tribal Nation and the Mohegan Indian Tribe are federally recognized tribal entities. The Paucatuck Pequots are recognized by the state of Connecticut and have applied for federal recognition. The Schaghticoke Tribal Nation is recognized as a self-governing entity and has applied for full federal recognition. The Brotherton Indians of Wisconsin have petitioned for federal recognition. The Golden Hill Paugussett Tribe has been denied federal recognition.

DAILY LIFE Paucatuck Pequots continue to fight for full federal recognition as well as full recognition by the state of Connecticut of their rights and land claims. They are also attempting to ease the factionalism that has troubled them for some time. The Mashantucket Pequots were recognized and their land claims settled by Congress in 1983. A museum and cultural center are planned. They publish the *Pequot Times.*

Elements of the Pequot language exist on paper and are known by some people, especially tribal elders. Various gatherings and family reunions continue among the Brotherton people of Wisconsin. The spiritual center of the tribe is in Gresham, Wisconsin. Traditional culture has disappeared, but these people remain proud of their heritage.

The Mohegan have a land claim pending against the state of Connecticut for roughly 600 acres of land alienated in the seventeenth century. The Tantaquidgeon museum is a central point of reference for the tribe, as is the Mohegan church (1831) and the Fort Shantok burial ground. The people celebrate the wigwam festival or powwow, which has its origins in the Green Corn festival of ancient times.

Pokanoket
See Wampanoag

Potawatomi

Potawatomi (Po tǝ ˋwä tǝ mē), a word of uncertain meaning. The commonly ascribed translation, "People of the Place of Fire" or "Keeper of the Fire" is probably apocryphal and refers to their traditional obligation to maintain a council fire uniting them with the Ottawa and Anishinabe. Their own self-designation was *Weshnabek,* "the People." *See also* Anishinabe; Ottawa.

LOCATION In the early seventeenth century, the Potawatomi lived in southwest Michigan. The people were located west of Lake Michigan, near Green Bay, in the later seventeenth century. By 1800, they lived all around the lower part of Lake Michigan; from Green Bay south and west to the Mississippi River; east into northern Illinois, Indiana, and extreme northwestern Ohio; and north to the Grand River and Detroit. Today, most Potawatomis live in Kansas and Oklahoma, with other communities in Indiana, Michigan, Wisconsin, and Ontario, Canada.

POPULATION There were about 8,000 Potawatomis in the early seventeenth century and at least 10,000 in the early nineteenth century. In the mid-1990s there were some 22,000 Potawatomis in the United States and Canada. This number included almost 1,100 on the Kansas reservation; 836 members of the Hannaville Community; almost 18,000 members of the Citizen Band; roughly 750 members of the Wisconsin Band; and several hundred living in southern Michigan.

LANGUAGE Potawatomi is an Algonquian language.

Historical Information

HISTORY Tradition has the people, once united with the Anishinabe and the Ottawa, coming to their historical territory from the northeast. Driven from southwest Michigan around 1640 by the Iroquois, Huron, and others, the Potawatomi took refuge in upper Michigan and then the Green Bay area, where they met other refugee groups and built advantageous alliances and partnerships, notably with the French but also with other tribes. At this time they occupied a single village and became known to history as a single tribe with their present name.

By the late seventeenth century, however, having consolidated their position as French trade and political allies, the single village had collapsed, mainly under trade pressures. Forced by Dakota raiding parties, Potawatomi groups began moving southward to occupy former lands of the Illinois Confederacy and the Miami. By the early eighteenth century there were multiclan Potawatomi villages in northern Illinois and southern Michigan. By the mid–eighteenth century, southern groups had acquired enough horses to make buffalo hunting a significant activity.

The French alliance remained in effect until 1763. The Potawatomi fought the British in Pontiac's rebellion. They also joined the coalition of tribes to administer the final defeat to the Illinois about that time, evicting them from northern Illinois and moving into the region themselves. The Potawatomi fought on the side of the British, however, in the Revolutionary War and continued to fight the American invasion of their territory in a series of wars in the late eighteenth and early nineteenth centuries that included Little Turtle's war (1790–1794); Tecumseh's rebellion (1809–1811), and the Black Hawk war of 1832. By that time, many southern Potawatomis had intermarried with non-natives.

After all these Indian losses, the victorious non-natives demanded and won significant land cessions (the people ultimately signed at least 53 treaties with the United States). The Potawatomis were forced to remove west of the Mississippi. Bands from the Illinois-Wisconsin area went to southwest Iowa while Michigan and Indiana Potawatomis went to eastern Kansas. In 1846 both groups were placed on a reservation near Topeka, Kansas. Some remained in Michigan and Wisconsin, however, and some managed to return there from the west. Others joined the Kickapoo in Mexico, and still other went to Canada.

Some Potawatomi in Kansas became relatively successful merchants and farmers. In 1861, a group of these people formed the Citizen Band as a separate entity from the Prairie Band. They were moved to Indian Territory in the 1870s, and their land there was allotted by 1890. Since much of the land was of marginal quality, however, people tended to leave the community in the early to mid–twentieth century. Many Citizen Band Potawatomis were educated in Catholic boarding schools in the early twentieth century.

The Prairie Potawatomi remained in Kansas. Despite their strong resistance, lands along the Kaw River in Kansas were allotted by 1895. The tribal council disbanded by 1900, and all government annuities ended in 1909. By 1962, less than one-quarter of their former lands remained in their possession, and much of this was leased to non-natives. The tribe rejected the 1934 Indian Reorganization Act (IRA) and was able to avoid termination in the 1950s.

Among those who refused to leave their homelands, a large group of Potawatomi refugees was still in Wisconsin in the mid–nineteenth century. These people had been joined by several Ottawa and Anishinabe families. With the help of an Anishinabe man, they obtained land and money to build a community, called Hannaville, in the 1880s. The U.S. Congress purchased additional land for them in 1913. The community adopted an IRA constitution and by-laws in 1936. Most people were farmers, and many also worked seasonally in the lumber industry. By the early twentieth century, the land was exhausted, the lumber industry had declined, and the state refused them all services, contributing to the onset of widespread poverty and exacerbating anti-Indian prejudice.

In 1839, Huron Potawatomis who had escaped removal purchased land for a community. The state of Michigan added another 40 acres in 1848. The Methodist Episcopal church served as the focus of community life. Near Waterviliet, Michigan, members of the future Pokagon Band bought land near Catholic churches. They continued a subsistence economy based on small-game hunting; gathering berries, maple sap, and other resources; and small-scale farming. They also worked on nearby farms when necessary. They created a formal government as early as 1866, which later pursued land claims against the United States. They and the Huron Potawatomis were denied federal recognition in the 1940s based on an arbitrary administrative ruling.

RELIGION The people may have recognized a chief deity that corresponded with the sun. Religion was based mainly on obtaining guardian spirits through fasting. Sacred bundles were probably part of religious practice from prehistoric times on; at some point they became associated with the supernatural power of clans. There were three types of shamans: doctors, diviners, and adviser-magicians. The people observed the calumet (peace pipe) ceremony. Other festivals included the Midewiwin Dance, the War Dance, and the Sacred Bundle ceremony.

GOVERNMENT There were clan chiefs, but the decision makers were generally the clan's warriors, elders, and shamans. Chiefs of semiautonomous villages, who were chosen from among several candidates of the appropriate clans, lacked authority, since the democratic impulse was strong among the Potawatomi. There was no overall tribal chief, although a village chief, through his personal prestige, might lead a large number of villages. The chief was aided by a council of men. Women occasionally served as village chiefs. There was also an intratribal warrior society that exercised police functions in the villages.

CUSTOMS At least 30 patrilineal clans owned certain supernatural powers, names, and ritual items. Over time, clans died out, and new ones were created. They were a source of a child's name as well as part of his or her personal spirit power. They also had important ceremonial functions. A dual division by birth order had significance in games and some rituals. Lacrosse was a popular game, as were the woman's double ball game and dice games.

After the harvest, people generally broke into small hunting camps for the winter. Polygyny was common. Marriages were formalized by gift exchange between clans and by the approval of senior clan members. After the wedding, a man lived with his wife's family for a year, after which time the couple established their own household.

Women gave birth assisted by other women in special huts. They remained secluded with the infant for a month. Babies were named after a year and weaned after several years. Both sexes were recognized as adults at puberty. Both were isolated around that time, women during their periods and men to fast and seek a vision. Young women might also have visions at this time.

Corpses were dressed in their best clothes and buried in an east-west alignment (one clan practiced cremation) with considerable grave goods that included food, tools, and weapons. Graves were marked with painted or incised posts. Souls were said to travel to an afterworld located to the west.

DWELLINGS Summer villages, numbering up to 1,500 people of several clans, were built along lakes and rivers and often contained members of Anishinabe and Ottawa groups. Small winter camps lay in sheltered valleys. Some villages may have been palisaded.

Summer houses were bark-covered rectangular structures with peaked roofs. The people built smaller, dome-shaped wigwams with mats covering a pole framework for their winter dwellings. They also built ramadas with roofs of bark or limbs for use as cooking shelters. Rush-mat menstrual huts were built away from the main part of the village. There was also a nearby playing field.

DIET Women grew corn, beans, squash, and tobacco. Squash and meat were smoked or sun dried. Women also gathered wild rice, maple sap for sugar, beechnuts (which were pounded into flour), berries, roots, and other wild plant foods. Cranberries were smoked, as were fowl, after first being pickled. Men fished and hunted buffalo (especially from the eighteenth century on), deer, bear, elk, beaver, and many other animals, including fowl. Dogs were eaten mainly at rituals.

KEY TECHNOLOGY Men hunted mainly with bows and arrows. Fishing equipment included nets, weirs and traps, hooks, and harpoons. People also made bark food storage containers, pottery, and stone or fired-clay pipes with wooden or reed stems. Pictographs on birch-bark scrolls served as mnemonic devices.

TRADE Potawatomis imported copper and Atlantic coast shells. Intervillage trade helped to keep the people's identity intact.

NOTABLE ARTS Clothing was decorated with quillwork and paint. Silk appliqué was an important art from the mid–eighteenth century on.

TRANSPORTATION Potawatomis used both dugout and bark-frame canoes. The latter were up to 25 feet long; construction and ownership of these vessels were limited. Horses were acquired well before 1800. A litter slung between two horses could carry materials or ill people; woven rush-mat saddlebags also held goods.

DRESS Clothing was made of skins and furs. Men were tattooed. Both sexes painted their bodies. They wore personal adornments made of native copper and shell.

WAR AND WEAPONS Potawatomi warriors fought with bows and arrows, war clubs, and hide shields. Allies included the Ottawa and other neighboring Algonquian tribes. Enemies included the Iroquois and the Dakota.

Contemporary Information

GOVERNMENT/RESERVATIONS The Potawatomi Reservation (Prairie Band), located in Jackson County, Kansas, consists of 121 square miles of land. The 1976 constitution calls for a tribal council. The 1990 Indian population was 503 (less than half of the total enrolled population).

The Citizen Band of Potawatomis owns land south of Shawnee, Oklahoma. Tribal lands consist of roughly 300 acres held in trust. They are governed by a five-person tribal council and an elected business committee.

The Pine Creek Reservation, Huron (Nottawaseppi-huron) Band, Barry and Allegan Counties, Michigan (established in 1845), consists of 120 acres of land. The 1990 Indian population was 20. The community is governed by an elected band council.

The Pokagon (Potawatomi Indian Nation) Potawatomi live in Berrien, Cass, and Van Buren Counties, Michigan, and St. Joseph County, Indiana. They are governed by a band council.

Hannaville community and trust lands, Delta and Menominee Counties, Michigan (established in 1913), contain roughly 3,200 acres of trust land. The 1990 Indian population was 173. They are governed by an elected tribal council.

The Forest County Potawatomi, Wisconsin, have almost 12,000 acres of land, most of which is tribally owned. About 460 Indians live in the three towns of Stone Lake, Blackwell, and Wabeno/Carter (mid-1990s). The general council elects an executive council annually.

There are numerous Potawatomi communities in Ontario, including Walpole Island, Sarnia, Saugeen, Kettle Point, Manitoulin Island, and Cape Croker. There are also other groups of Potawatomi living in the region.

ECONOMY The Kansas Potawatomi own a bingo establishment and are seeking to build a casino. Unemployment is chronically high. Hannaville has important farm, wildlife, and forest resources. A casino provides regular employment. The Citizen Band owns several businesses, including a bank, a museum and gift shop, a restaurant, and a golf course. It also owns a bingo establishment and is building a casino. The Wisconsin Potawatomi own two casinos and several small businesses. Tourism and lumbering are also important economic activities.

LEGAL STATUS The Prairie Band of Potawatomi, the Citizen Band Potawatomi, the Hannaville Indian Community, the Nottawaseppi-Huron Potawatomi Band, the Potawatomi Indian Nation (Pokagon Band), and the Forest County Potawatomi Community are federally recognized tribal entities. The Mash-she-pe-nash-she-wish Indian Tribe (Michigan) has been granted provisional federal recognition (1998).

DAILY LIFE Income and educational levels among the Prairie Band remain low. The band is considered culturally conservative: Many people still speak the native language, and most belong either to the Drum religion, the Dream Dance, or the Native American Church.

The Hannaville Community maintains various social service programs. Grounded in traditional precepts and culture, they are expanding the number of native language speakers beyond a core of elders. People practice traditional or quasi-traditional religions as well as Christianity. They host the Great Lakes powwow.

The Methodist Episcopal Church still serves as a focus of the Huron Potawatomi. The band also hosts an annual powwow. Among the Pokagon band, the Catholic church has served as a similar focus. The band has worked hard for over 100 years to reestablish a government-to-government relationship with the United States. In addition to political considerations, both band councils emphasize economic development and social programs for their members.

In Oklahoma, the Citizen Band is noted for its entrepreneurial ethos. In addition to its many businesses, the tribe administers a variety of social and health services, including a summer program for young people. Most of the people are Christian and relatively assimilated. There are a tribal museum, a tribal newsletter, and an annual powwow held in June.

The Forest County Potawatomi retain a significant measure of their traditional culture. Many people speak the native language, and many traditional and semitraditional religions and ceremonies, such as the Medicine Drum Society, Native American Church, Dream Dance, War Dance, and naming feasts, remain vibrant.

Sauk

Sauk (Sok), or Sac, from *Osakiwugi*, "People of the Outlet," or "Yellow Earth People." The Sauk were culturally related to the Kickapoo and Potawatomi. *See also* Fox.

LOCATION For much of their history, the Sauk straddled the area between the Northeast Woodlands and the Prairie. In the sixteenth century they lived around Saginaw Bay in eastern Michigan. In the mid–seventeenth century they lived in the vicinity of Green Bay, Wisconsin. Today they live in Lincoln County, Oklahoma, and on the Missouri-Nebraska line.

POPULATION There were approximately 3,500 Sauk in the mid–seventeenth century and about 2,200 enrolled members of the Sac and Fox Tribe of Oklahoma in the early 1990s.

LANGUAGE Sauk is an Algonquian language.

Historical Information

HISTORY The Sauk may once have been united

with the Fox and the Kickapoo. The Anishinabe and/or the Iroquois pushed the Sauk out of eastern Michigan and toward the lower Fox River sometime in the late sixteenth or early seventeenth century. French explorers arrived around 1667.

The Sauk got along well with the British. The people also maintained good relations with the French until they began sheltering the Fox and other French enemies. Fox Indians fleeing the French took refuge with the Sauk in 1733, beginning an alliance that lasted until the 1850s. At that time, the Sauk and Fox moved away from the Green Bay area into eastern Iowa. They moved back to northern Illinois and southern Michigan after peace with the French was established in 1737.

In 1769 the Sauk, Fox, and other tribes, under pressure from the French as well as the Menominee and Anishinabe, dealt a permanent defeat to the Illinois tribes. At that point the Sauk and Fox moved south and west into some of the Illinois tribes' former territory. Later they headed back into Iowa, where they adapted rapidly to a prairie/plains existence, becoming highly capable buffalo hunters. Their parties traveled far to the west of the Mississippi in search of the herds. They also continued to grow corn.

In 1804, one Sauk band (the Missouri Band) ceded all tribal lands, although they claimed they were only ceding a small parcel of land. The action was not binding, however, because the tribal council, in whom authority for land cessions was vested, refused to ratify the treaty. Anger at this treaty on the part of the rest of the Sauk people forced the Missouri Band to remain separate from the main group, ultimately settling on the eastern border of Kansas and Nebraska.

The Sauk took an active part in Little Turtle's war (1790–1794), but most remained neutral in Tecumseh's rebellion (1809–1811). They sided with the British in the War of 1812. After the war, the Sauk divided into two factions. Black Hawk headed the anti-U.S. band, which refused to accept the treaty of 1804, and Keokuk headed the accommodationist party. In the 1820s, the United States exercised an increasingly important role in Sauk internal politics, ultimately vesting Keokuk as tribal chief, a man with no hereditary claim to the position.

Black Hawk's war (1832) resulted directly from the controversy over the 1804 treaty. Black Hawk (Makataimeshekiakiak), a Saukenuk (Rock Island) Sauk leader, attempted to form a pan-Indian alliance to defend his homeland against illegal non-native usurpation. Despite the fact that Keokuk had agreed to relocate west of the Mississippi, Black Hawk and his people were determined to occupy their own lands. Some fighting ensued, after which the Sauk decided to retreat beyond the Mississippi. However, a U.S. steamer caught up with and shelled the Indians, many of whom were women and children, as they attempted to cross the river in rafts, slaughtering hundreds. Black Hawk himself surrendered several months later. Following his release from prison in 1833, he toured several cities and dictated his autobiography.

The Sauk and Fox soon defeated Dakota warriors in Iowa (who had themselves killed many of the survivors of the Mississippi shelling) and occupied their land. Over the next few years, the factions hardened, and relations became strained with the Fox, who resented the U.S.-backed Keokuk's control over the tribe. In 1842, the people were forced to cede their lands in Iowa and were relocated to a reservation in Kansas. They were joined by some members of the Missouri Band at that time. Most Fox returned to Iowa in the late 1850s. In 1867, the Sauk were forced into Indian Territory (Oklahoma). In 1890, most of the reservation was allotted in severalty, with the rest, almost 400,000 acres, opened to non-native settlement.

RELIGION The Sauk recognized any number of nature-related spirits, or manitous, the most important of which were Wisaka, founder of the Medicine Dance, and those connected with the four directions. People might gain the attention and assistance of the manitous by offering tobacco, blackening the face with charcoal, fasting, and wailing.

A vision quest at puberty was meant to attract manitous. Those who obtained especially powerful spirits assembled a medicine pack or bundle; certain packs represented spiritual power that affected and were the property of entire lineages. Two annual ceremonies were related to the vision packs.

The Midewiwin was a key ceremony. Others included green corn, naming, and adoption. In the last, there was a formal adoption to replace a family member who had died. The calumet, or sacred pipe, played a key role in all solemn activities, including peace negotiations. A head shaman instructed others in curing, hunting, and agricultural and other ceremonies.

GOVERNMENT The Sauk were divided into bands or villages, of fluid composition, that came together as one unit in summer. The chief of any one band was considered the tribal chief. Other officers were subchiefs and criers. A religious leader was in charge of ceremonies.

There was also a dual "peace and war" political division. A hereditary, clan-based village peace chief held authority over gatherings, treaties, peace councils, intertribal negotiations, and rituals. In return for access to his property, the people regularly gave him gifts. Two war chiefs were chosen by other warriors on the basis of merit, although there may have been a hereditary component. The war chief commanded the camp police and presided over war councils. He also assumed greater overall authority during war when a stricter, more disciplined organization was needed.

CUSTOMS Sauks recognized about 12 patrilineal clans. Membership in the dual division—peace/white and war/black—was determined by birth order. The families of murder victims usually accepted compensation, but they were at liberty to require blood vengeance. Lacrosse was a popular game.

Birth took place in special lodges in the company of only women; the mother remained subject to special postpartum restrictions for up to a year or more. An elderly relative named a baby from the stock of clan names. As adults, people might acquire additional, nonclan names as a result of dreams or warfare.

Parents rarely engaged in corporal punishment of their children. At the onset of puberty, girls were secluded for ten days and were subject to various other restrictions. Boys marked puberty by undertaking a vision quest. Girls also sought visions, although not in seclusion. Vermilion face paint indicated adult status.

Marriages were generally arranged by the couple and were formalized when the families exchanged gifts. The couple lived with the wife's family for a year before establishing their own household. Some men had more than one wife. Adultery usually led only to divorce.

Burial took place after various rituals had been performed. Warriors might be buried in a sitting position. All people were buried in their finest clothing and wrapped in bark or mats with their feet toward the west. Sacred tobacco was placed on the graves. A dog might be killed as a companion on the way to the land of the dead. The mourning period lasted for at least six months, during which time mourners were subject to a variety of behavioral restrictions.

DWELLINGS Summer villages were located near fields in river bottoms. At least in the early nineteenth century, almost the entire tribe assembled at the summer villages. Each summer house was an economic unit as well. Extended families of some ten people lived in houses about 50 feet long and 20 feet wide and covered with elm bark. Houses were oriented in an east-west direction and were built in parallel rows, with an open game and ceremonial area in between. Villages were moved when firewood became scarce or when attacks forced the people to move.

In their winter camps, people lived in small, dome-shaped wigwams covered with reed mats and skins and located in sheltered river valleys. The camps ranged in size from one or two families to an entire band.

DIET Women grew corn, beans, squash, and tobacco. They also gathered a number of wild plant foods, including nuts, honey, berries, fruits, and tubers. Men hunted a variety of large and small game, especially deer, as well as buffalo until about 1820. There were fall, spring, and summer hunts.

KEY TECHNOLOGY Men hunted mainly with bows and arrows and spears. They made carved pipes of pipestone (catlinite) attached to wooden or reed stems. Bark containers and bone needles were heavily used items.

TRADE The Sauk mined and traded lead. They also exported corn. They imported deer tallow, feathers, and beeswax.

NOTABLE ARTS The people decorated their clothing with quillwork and paint. Art objects also included pottery and carved and quilled wooden items. Silk appliqué was an important art from the mid–eighteenth century on.

TRANSPORTATION Water transportation was by bark and dugout canoe.

DRESS Clothing was made of skin and furs and consisted mainly of breechcouts, dresses, leggings, and moccasins. Body tattooing and painting were common.

WAR AND WEAPONS Reasons for war included conflict over territory, retaliation, and the achievement of status. Military adventures had to be authorized by the war council. Leaders of war parties began by fasting to obtain a vision and undertook several more ritualistic activities before they and their men departed. The leader carried his sacred ark, which was said to provide the party with spiritual power. Warriors were subject to a number of rituals on their return as well.

Weapons included the bow and arrow, spear, and war club. Most prisoners were adopted into the tribe. War calumets were decorated with red feathers, whereas peace calumets featured white feathers. Traditional enemies included the Anishinabe, Iroquois, Illinois, and later the Osage and Dakota. Allies included the Fox from the early eighteenth century on as well as the Kickapoo.

Contemporary Information

GOVERNMENT/RESERVATIONS The Sac and Fox Tribe of Oklahoma (Sac and Fox Nation) is located on over 16,000 acres of land in Lincoln County, Oklahoma, almost 1,000 of which is tribally owned. About 1,500 of the roughly 2,200 tribal members lived in the community in 1992. Under the 1987 constitution (successor to the original Indian Reorganization Act constitution of 1934), the tribe is governed by a governing council (every adult), which elects a five-member business committee and other committees. There are two main communities, one near Shawnee and a smaller one near Cushing.

The Sac and Fox Reservation (Sac and Fox of Missouri), Brown County, Kansas, and Richardson County, Nebraska, was established in 1842 and contains 354 acres. The 1990 Indian population was 48.

ECONOMY Tribal members are generally assimilated into the regional economy. The oil industry has provided fluctuating benefits and advantages. There are also a bingo facility and tobacco shops in Oklahoma.

LEGAL STATUS The Sac and Fox Nation (so called since 1988) and the Sac and Fox Nation of Missouri in Kansas and Nebraska are federally recognized tribal entities.

DAILY LIFE Eleven clans remain in existence. Classes will increase the number of people who speak the native language, now estimated at about 200. Many traditions continue, including seasonal ceremonies, adoptions, and naming. Crafts include appliqué, beadwork, basketry, and featherwork. Most people are Christians, but many adhere to the Native American Church.

Tribal facilities in Oklahoma include offices, a health center, a library and archives, and a community building. The tribe maintains its own police and court system. It publishes the *Sac and Fox News*. Local groundwater has been contaminated by oil. There is an annual all-Indian stampede and rodeo.

Most of the Kansas Sauks are acculturated and assimilated into the local economy.

Schaghticoke

See Pequot

Seneca

Seneca (`Se n ə ku) were the largest, most powerful, and westernmost of the five original tribes of the Iroquois League. Their self-designation was *Onotowaka*, "Great Hill People." The name Iroquois ("real adders") comes from the French adaptation of the Algonquian name for these people. Their self-designation was *Kanonsionni*, "League of the United (Extended) Households." Iroquois today refer to themselves as *Haudenosaunee*, "People of the Longhouse." *See also* Cayuga.

LOCATION The Seneca homeland stretched north to south from Lake Ontario to the upper Allegheny and Susquehanna Rivers and west to east from Lake Erie to Seneca Lake, but especially from Lake Canandaigua to the Genesee River. At the height of their power, the Iroquois controlled land from the Hudson to the Illinois Rivers and the Ottawa to the Tennessee Rivers. In the 1990s, most Senecas continue to live in upstate New York near their traditional land. Some live in Ontario, Canada, and northeastern Oklahoma.

POPULATION There were perhaps 15,000–20,000 members of the Iroquois League around 1500 and about 5,000 Senecas in the mid–seventeenth century. In the mid-1990s, there were approximately 8,000 members of the Seneca Nation of Indians in the United States, including members of the Tonawanda Band; 2,500 Seneca-Cayugas; and some 1,000 Seneca in Canada. There were about 70,000 Iroquois Indians living in the United States and Canada in the mid-1990s.

LANGUAGE The Seneca spoke a Northern Iroquois dialect.

Historical Information

HISTORY The Iroquois began cultivating crops shortly after the first phase of their culture in New York was established around 800. Deganawida, a Huron prophet, and Hiawatha, a Mohawk shaman living among the Onondaga, founded the Iroquois League or Confederacy some time between 1450 and 1600. It originally consisted of five tribes: Cayuga, Mohawk, Oneida, Onondaga, and Seneca; the Tuscarora joined in the early eighteenth century. The league's purpose was to end centuries of debilitating intertribal war and work for the common good. Both Deganawida and Hiawatha may have been actual or mythological people.

There were two Seneca groups in the sixteenth century and perhaps as early as the founding of the league, each of which had its own large village. The people first encountered Jesuit missionaries shortly before the latter established a mission in Seneca country in 1668. During the seventeenth and eighteenth centuries, the people became heavily involved in the fur trade. Trading, fighting, and political intrigue characterized this period.

In the course of their expansion to get more furs, especially beaver, the Iroquois, often led by the Seneca, wiped out tribes such as the Huron and Erie and fought many generally pro-French Algonquian tribes, such as the Algonquin, Ottawa, Miami, and Potawatomi. The Iroquois also fought and defeated the Iroquoian Susquehanna (or Conestoga) Indians during the early to mid–seventeenth century. Their power effectively blocked European westward expansion.

Although they were good at playing the European powers off against each other, the Iroquois increasingly became British allies in trade and in the colonial wars and were instrumental in the ultimate British victory over the French. The western Seneca (Chenussios) remained pro-French, however, even in the French and Indian War and Pontiac's uprising of 1763.

The British victory in 1763 meant that the Iroquois no longer controlled the balance of power in the region. Despite the long-standing British alliance, some Indians joined anti-British rebellions as a defensive gesture. The confederacy split its allegiance in the Revolutionary War, with most Seneca siding with the British. This split resulted in the council fire's being extinguished for the first time in roughly 200 years.

Despite the leadership of Cornplanter and others, however, the Seneca suffered depredations throughout the war, and by war's end their villages had been permanently destroyed. When the 1783 Treaty of Paris divided Indian land between Britain and the United States, British Canadian officials established the Six Nations Reserve for their loyal allies, to which many Seneca repaired.

Seneca lands were formally defined in the 1794 Canandaigua or Pickering Treaty. Most Seneca lands (except for 310 square miles) were sold in 1797. This action was the genesis of the Buffalo Creek, Tonawanda, Allegheny, Cattaraugus, and several other small reservations, most of which were soon sold. Chief Cornplanter also received a land grant from the Commonwealth of Pennsylvania around that time, in consideration of services rendered during the war. After the war, both Cornplanter and the Pine Tree Chief Red Jacket recognized the sovereignty of the United States. Cornplanter favored alliance with the new government, whereas Red Jacket urged his people to continue to live as traditionally as possible.

The Iroquois council officially split into two parts during that time. One branch was located at the Six Nations Reserve and the other at Buffalo Creek. Gradually, the reservations as well as relations with the United States and Canada assumed more significance than intraconfederacy matters. In the 1840s, when the Buffalo Creek Reservation was sold, the fire there was rekindled at Onondaga. Some Seneca who had settled with the Cayuga at Buffalo Creek traveled to Ohio and were removed from there to the Indian Territory (Oklahoma) in the early 1830s.

The Seneca Handsome Lake (half-brother of Cornplanter) founded the Longhouse religion in 1799 (see "Religion"). In 1838, the U.S. Seneca lost of their remaining land in a fraudulent procedure. Four years later, a new treaty replaced the fraudulent one. However, it still included the sale of the Buffalo Creek and Tonawanda Reservations.

In 1848, an internal dispute over the payment of annuities led to the formal creation of the Seneca Nation of Indians (Allegany and Cattaraugus) and the adoption of a U.S.-style constitution and government. With this action the people effectively withdrew from the Iroquois Confederacy and separated from the Tonawanda Reservation as well. In 1857, the Tonawanda Seneca won a long-standing fight to retain their reservation; part of it was bought back with the money that was originally intended to be used for their removal to Kansas. In the mid–nineteenth century, illegal land leases led to the formation of several non-native towns on the Allegany reservation, the largest being Salamanca.

In Canada, the Seneca, referred to along with the Onondaga and Cayuga as the "lower tribes," tended to retain more of their traditional beliefs than did the "upper" Iroquois tribes. Many subsequently adopted the Handsome Lake religion. Slowly, the general influence of non-natives increased, as tribal councils, consensus decision making, and other aspects of traditional culture fell by the wayside. Traditional structures were further weakened by the allotment of reservation lands in the 1840s; the requirement under Canadian law, from 1869 on, of patrilineal descent; and the transition of league councils and other political structures to a municipal government. In 1924, the Canadian government terminated confederacy rule entirely, mandating an (all male) elected system of government on the reserve.

In 1869, the Seneca Donehogawa (Ely Parker), a general in the U.S. Army, became the first Native American Commissioner of Indian Affairs. He stood for peace with the western tribes and fairness in general, shaking up the corrupt "Indian Ring." However, trumped-up charges, of which he was fully exonerated, led to a congressional investigation and ultimately to his resignation in 1871.

The native economy gradually shifted from primarily hunting to farming, dependence on annuities received for the sale of land, and some wage labor. By 1900 there were a number of missionary and state-supported schools on the reservations. Although there were also several churches, relatively few Seneca attended services. Instead, longhouses served as the place where the old ceremonies were maintained and continue to fill that role today. Most Seneca spoke English by that time. With other members of the confederacy, the Seneca resisted the 1924 citizenship act, selective service, and all federal and state intrusions on their sovereignty.

The Seneca in Oklahoma elected a tribal council from the 1870s to 1937. By that time their land base had shrunk, mostly through allotment and outright theft, from about 65,000 acres to 140 acres. At that time they incorporated under state law as the Seneca-Cayuga tribe, adopted a constitution and by-laws, and elected a business committee. The tribe resisted termination in the 1950s.

In the 1960s, despite massive protests, the army flooded over 9,000 acres of the Cornplanter tract and the Allegany Reservation to build the Kinzua Dam. Many important cultural and religious sites were lost. The tribe eventually received over $15 million in damages.

RELIGION The Seneca recognized an "earth holder" as well as other animate and inanimate objects and natural forces of a spiritual nature. They held important festivals to celebrate maple sap and strawberries as well as corn planting, ripening (Green Corn ceremony), and harvest. These festivals often included singing, male dancing, game playing, gambling, feasting, and food distribution.

The eight-day new year's festival may have been most important of all. Held in midwinter, it was a time to give thanks, to forget past wrongs, and to kindle new fires, with much attention paid to new and old dreams. A condolence ceremony had quasi-religious components. Medicine groups such as the False Face Society, which wore carved wooden masks, and the Medicine, Dark Dance and Death Feast Societies (the last two controlled by women) also conducted ceremonies, since most illness was thought to be of supernatural origin.

In the early nineteenth century, many Iroquois embraced the teachings of Handsome Lake. This religion was born during the general religious ferment known as the Second Great Awakening and came directly out of the radical breakdown of Iroquois life. Beginning in 1799, the Seneca Handsome Lake spoke of Jesus and called upon Iroquois to give up alcohol and a host of negative behaviors, such as witchcraft and sexual promiscuity. He also exhorted them to maintain their traditional religious celebrations. A blend of traditional and Christian teachings, the Handsome Lake religion had the effect of facilitating the cultural transition occurring at the time.

GOVERNMENT The Iroquois League comprised 50 hereditary chiefs, or sachems, from the constituent tribes. Each position was named for the original holder and had specific responsibilities. Sachems were men, except where a woman acted as regent, but they were appointed by women. The Seneca sent eight sachems to meetings of the Iroquois Great Council, which met in the fall and for emergencies.

Debates within the great council were a matter of strict clan, division, and tribal protocols, in a complex system of checks and balances. Politically, individual league members often pursued their own best interests while maintaining an essential solidarity with the other members. The creators of the U.S. government used the Iroquois League as a model of democracy.

Locally, the village structure was governed by a headman and a council of elders (clan chiefs, elders, wise men). Matters before the local councils were handled according to a definite protocol based on the clan and division memberships of the chiefs. Village chiefs were chosen from groups as small as a single household. Women nominated and recalled clan chiefs. Tribal chiefs represented the village and the nation at the general council of the league. The entire system was hierarchical and intertwined, from the family up to the great council. Decisions at all levels were reached by consensus.

There were also a number of nonhereditary chiefs ("pine tree" or "merit" chiefs), some of whom had no voting power. This may have been a postcontact phenomenon.

CUSTOMS The Seneca recognized a dual division, each composed of eight matrilineal, animal-named clans. The clans in turn were composed of matrilineal lineages. Each owned a set number of personal names, some of which were linked with particular activities and responsibilities.

Women enjoyed a high degree of prestige, being largely equated with the "three sisters" (corn, beans, and squash), and they were in charge of most village activities, including marriage. Great intravillage lacrosse games included heavy gambling. Other games included snowsnake, or sliding a spear along a trench in the snow for distance. Food was shared so that everyone had roughly the same to eat.

Personal health and luck were maintained by performing various individual rituals, including singing and dancing, learned in dreams. Members of the False Face medicine society wore wooden masks carved from trees and used rattles and tobacco. Shamans also used up to 200 or more plant medicines to cure illness. People committed suicide on occasion for specific reasons (men who lost prestige; women who were abandoned; children who were treated harshly). Murder could be revenged or paid for with sufficient gifts.

Young men's mothers arranged marriages with a prospective bride's mother. Divorce was possible but not readily obtained because it was considered a discredit. The dead were buried in a sitting position, with food and tools for use on the way to the land of the dead. A ceremony was held after ten days. The condolence ceremony mourned dead league chiefs and installed successors. A modified version also applied to common people.

DWELLINGS From the early sixteenth century on, scattered Seneca villages were consolidated into two large (100 or more houses) villages (one eastern and one western) and one or two smaller (about 25 houses) ones. Gandagaro, the large eastern village, was also the main tribal village. The people built their villages near water and often on a hill after circa 1300. Some villages were palisaded. Other Iroquois villages had up to 150 longhouses and 1,000 or more people. Villages were moved about twice in a generation, when firewood and soil were exhausted.

Iroquois Indians built elm-bark longhouses, 50–100 feet long, depending on how many people lived there, from about the twelfth century on. They held around 2 or 3 but as many as 20 families, related maternally (lineage segments), as well as their dogs. There were smoke holes over each two-family fire. Beds were raised platforms; people slept on mats, their feet to the fire, covered by pelts. Upper platforms were used for food and gear storage. Roofs were shingled with elm bark. The people also built some single-family houses.

DIET Women grew corn, beans, squash, and gourds. Corn was the staple and was used in soups, stews, breads, and puddings. It was stored in bark-lined cellars. Women also gathered a variety of greens, nuts, seeds, roots, berries, fruits, and mushrooms. Tobacco was grown for ceremonial and social smoking.

After the harvest, men and some women took to the woods for several months to hunt and dry meat. Men hunted large game and trapped smaller game, mostly for the fur. Hunting was a source of potential prestige. They also caught waterfowl and other birds, and they fished. The people grew peaches, pears, and apples in orchards from the eighteenth century on.

KEY TECHNOLOGY Iroquois used porcupine quills and wampum belts as a record of events. Wampum was also used as a gift connoting sincerity and, later, as trade money. These shell disks, strung or woven into belts, were probably a postcontact technological innovation.

Hunting equipment included snares, bow and arrow, stone knife, and bentwood pack frame. Fish were caught using traps, nets, bone hooks, and spears. Farming tools were made of stone, bone, wood (spades), and antler. Women wove corn-husk dolls, tobacco trays, mats, and baskets.

Other important material items included elm-bark containers, cordage from inner tree bark and fibers, and levers to move timbers. Men steamed wood or bent green wood to make many items, including lacrosse sticks.

TRADE Summer was the main trading season. The people obtained birch-bark products from the Huron. They imported copper and shells and exported carved wooden and stone pipes. They were extensively involved in the trade in beaver furs from the seventeenth century on.

NOTABLE ARTS Men carved wooden masks worn by the Society of Faces in their curing ceremonies. Women decorated clothing with dyed porcupine quills or moose-hair embroidery. The Seneca also made artistic baskets.

TRANSPORTATION Unstable elm-bark canoes were roughly 25 feet long. The people were also great runners and preferred to travel on land. They used snowshoes in winter and wooden frame backpacks to carry heavy loads such as fresh meat.

DRESS Women made most clothing from deerskins. Men wore shirts and short breechclouts and a tunic in cooler weather; women wore skirts. Both wore leggings, moccasins, and corn-husk slippers in summer. Robes were made of lighter or heavier skins or pelts, depending on the season. These were often painted. Clothing was decorated with feathers and porcupine quills. Both men and women tattooed their bodies extensively. Men often wore their hair in a roach; women wore theirs in a single braid doubled up and fastened with a thong. Some men wore feather caps or, in winter, fur hoods.

WAR AND WEAPONS Boys began developing war skills at a young age. Prestige and leadership were often gained through war, which was in many ways the most important activity. The title of Pine Tree Chief was a historical invention to honor especially brave warriors. Weapons included the bow and arrow, ball-headed club, shield, rod armor, and guns after 1640. All aspects of warfare, from the initiation to the conclusion, were highly ritualized. War could be decided as a matter of policy or undertaken as a vendetta. Women had a large, sometimes decisive, say in the question of whether or not to fight. During war season, generally the fall, Iroquois war parties ranged up to 1,000 miles or more. Male prisoners were often forced to run the gauntlet: Those who made it through were adopted, but those who did not might be tortured by widows. Women and children prisoners were regularly adopted. Some captives were eaten.

Contemporary Information

GOVERNMENT/RESERVATIONS Allegany Reservation, Cattaraugus County, New York (Seneca Nation of Indians), established in 1794, consists of about 20,000 acres (excluding the area of the Kinzua Dam). The 1990 Indian population was 1,059.

Cattaraugus Reservation, Cattaraugus, Chatauqua, and Erie Counties, New York (Seneca Nation of Indians with Cayuga and Munsee), established in 1794, consists of about 21,600 acres. The 1990 Indian population was 2,051. The Seneca Nation of Indians (Allegany and Cattaraugus) is governed by a constitution with elected officials.

Oil Springs Reservation, Allegany and Cattaraugus Counties, New York (Seneca Nation of Indians), established in 1877, consists of 640 acres (a square mile). There were no residents in 1990.

Tonawanda Reservation, Erie, Genesee, and Niagara Counties, New York (Tonawanda Band), established in 1863, consists of 7,550 acres. The 1990 Indian population was 453. The community is governed by a tribal council of eight chiefs.

Six Nations/Grand River, Ontario, Canada, was established in 1784. It is governed by both an elected and a hereditary council, although only the first is federally recognized.

The Seneca-Cayuga Tribe is located in Ottawa County, Oklahoma. The reservation consists of about 4,000 acres, about one-quarter of which is tribally owned. Roughly 800 tribal members lived in northeastern Oklahoma in the mid-1990s.

There is also a small (roughly 100 of the original 9,000 acre) parcel of land located in Pennsylvania, near the Allegany Reservation, that belongs to the descendants of Cornplanter.

ECONOMY The tribe received a federal settlement of $35 million in 1990 and a state settlement of $25 million in 1992. Many people work in Rochester and Buffalo. Tribal businesses include minimarts as well as bingo on the Allegany and Cattaraugus Reservations. Its natural resources include timber, sand and gravel, and natural gas. The tribe itself also provides a number of jobs. Many Seneca-Cayugas work in Tulsa and Oklahoma City. Some also work in the ranching industry.

LEGAL STATUS The Seneca Nation of Indians, the Tonawanda Band of Seneca, and the Seneca-Cayuga Tribe of Oklahoma are federally recognized tribal entities.

DAILY LIFE The Seneca have recently renegotiated thousands of leases in and around the town of Salamanca, New York, which is located on the Allegany Reservation. The possibility of casino gambling remains controversial. The Seneca Nation Health Department provides quality health care services. The Seneca Nation Education Department provides a number of quality educational programs. Children attend public schools, and the tribe offers scholarships to students interested in higher education.

Traditional political and social (clan) structures remain intact, as does the language, with the exception of Canada's requirement that band membership be reckoned patrilineally. The people participate in Longhouse and many other celebrations, such as the midwinter, maple, green corn, and harvest ceremonies. Not all are observed at all reservations, and of those that are, there are some local differences. A number of medicine ceremonies also continue to be performed.

There are a museum and library on the Allegany Reservation. The Cattaraugus Reservation features a museum, a library, and a sports arena. The community hosts a fall festival, an Indian fair, and two bazaars. Cayugas and Senecas have yet to resolve issues of Cayuga land ownership on the Cattaraugus Reservation. Few people there speak the native language, but the community does retain various traditional ceremonies.

The political structure of the Iroquois League continues to be a source of controversy for many Iroquois (Haudenosaunee). Some recognize two seats—at Onondaga and Six Nations—whereas others consider the government at Six Nations a reflection of or a corollary to the traditional seat at Onondaga. Important issues concerning the confederacy in the later twentieth century include Indian burial sites, sovereignty, gambling casinos, and land claims. The Six Nations Reserve is still marked by the existence of "progressive" and "traditional" factions, with the former generally supporting the elected band council and following the Christian faith and the latter supporting the confederacy and the Longhouse religion.

Many Iroquois continue to see their relationship with the Canadian and U.S. governments as one between independent nations and allies, as opposed to one marked by paternalism and dependence. Occasionally, the frustrations inherent in this type of situation boil over into serious confrontation.

Shawnee

Shawnee (Shä `n ē), from *Shawanwa*, "southerner," their self-designation. These people acted in many ways as agents of cultural change and adaptation between the northeast Woodlands and the southeastern and prairie tribes. They were variously known to non-natives as Ouchaouanag, Chaouanons, Satanas, and Shawano. They were culturally related to the Sauk, Fox, and Kickapoo.

LOCATION The Shawnee migrated often, but their territory in the late seventeenth century may have ranged from the Illinois River east to the Delaware, Susquehannah, and Savannah Rivers. Some scholars place them on the Cumberland River at or before that time. Shawnee villages have been located within an enormous area, ranging from the present states of New York and Illinois south to South Carolina, Georgia, and Alabama. Their aboriginal home may have been around the south shore of Lake Erie, and they lived in southern Ohio during the second half of the eighteenth century. Today, most Shawnees live in Oklahoma. There is also a significant community in and around Ohio.

POPULATION There may have been as many as 50,000 or more Shawnee in the sixteenth century.

Their population dropped to about 3,000 in 1650. In the mid-1990s, there were about 600 in Ohio and almost 12,000 in Oklahoma.

LANGUAGE Shawnees spoke an Algonquian language.

Historical Information

HISTORY According to tradition, the Shawnee people were once united with the Lenápe and the Nanticoke, perhaps in Labrador. They may have originated north of or in the Ohio Valley. They were probably associated with the Fort Ancient cultural complex (1000–1700), which was characterized by a mixed subsistence economy, including agriculture, with fortified villages having central courtyards. Many tools were made of bone, and the people also made pottery. Town populations may have ranged up to 1,000 people.

The Iroquois may have begun pushing scattered Shawnee bands south into Ohio as early as the sixteenth century. Iroquois attacks on Shawnees in Ohio lasted until the mid– to late eighteenth century, when the Iroquois forced the last Shawnees out of that area. Shawnees pushed into Pennsylvania in the late seventeenth century, and a population center was established on the Savannah River by that time as well. In the early eighteenth century, bands began a general westward movement again, settling on the north bank of the Ohio River. By about 1750 most Shawnee had come to that location, with Iroquois permission. Some groups also joined the Creek Nation in Alabama about that time.

Heavy involvement in the fur trade from the early eighteenth century on soon left many Shawnee in the clutches of alcohol and debt. Most Shawnee bands were pro-French in the colonial wars, but some were steadfast British trade partners and military allies, especially those bands that came under the control of the Iroquois. Most Shawnees participated in Pontiac's rebellion of 1763–1764. Under Chief Cornstalk, they also fought the British later in 1764 over the issue of land. Pressured by the colonies to cede land, the Shawnee joined the British cause in the American Revolution, hoping that the country that promulgated the Proclamation Line of 1763 would defend their interests against the rapacious colonials. The loss in that war and in Little Turtle's war (1794) led to further land cessions in Ohio and Indiana. In the 1790s, a group of Shawnee and Lenápe moved to Missouri to occupy a Spanish land grant.

In the early nineteenth century, two Shawnees— twins by birth—achieved renown as among the last great military defenders of Indian land in the entire region. The shaman Tenskwatawa, or Shawnee Prophet, encouraged his people to return to their tra-

ditions and eschew all non-native elements, particularly Christianity and alcohol. He also claimed to have special medicine that would help repulse the whites. His brother was Tecumseh, a brilliant orator and military strategist. Envisioning an Indian country from Canada to the Gulf of Mexico, he encouraged pan-Indian solidarity and resistance to the domination of the United States. In particular, he believed that no single Native American had the moral right to sell or cede any Indian land.

Unlike many Indian military leaders, Tecumseh did not hate non-natives. He studied their history and admired aspects of their cultures. Furthermore, he insisted on fair treatment of prisoners of war. He traveled constantly throughout the Midwest and southeast in order to build his multitribal alliance. Slowly he began to win the support of even those groups whose strong feelings of tribal identity worked against pan-Indianism. Paradoxically, however, many Shawnee refused to join the coalition.

In 1812, Tenskwatawa foolishly moved against a non-native military expedition before the alliance was complete. The Indian forces were defeated, and Tenskwatawa's power proved to be ineffective. This action fatally disrupted the alliance before it had a chance to coalesce. Tecumseh quickly joined the British cause in the War of 1812, hoping that what remained of his alliance, in conjunction with British forces, could defeat the Americans. Although as a general in the British Army he led many successful campaigns, many Indians refused to join the war. Tecumseh was fatally shot in October 1833.

Their power broken, many Ohio tribes, including the Shawnee, became refugees, drifting in scattered bands throughout Kansas, Missouri, Arkansas, Oklahoma, and Texas. Meanwhile, the Missouri Shawnee living on Spanish land were slowly joined by other Shawnee groups. Resulting tensions forced the groups apart once again. About 1845, groups of Shawnees gathered near Oklahoma's Canadian River and later became known as the Absentee Shawnee (this tribe was composed mostly of the former divisions of Hathawekela, Kispokotha, and Piqua). Most members accepted allotments soon after the reservation was officially established in 1872, and by 1900 most had assimilated into the dominant society. Factionalism between "progressives" and "traditionals" kept the two sides apart throughout the early twentieth century.

In 1825 the United States established a reservation in Kansas for those Indians still living on the Spanish land grant. Shawnees still in Ohio moved there in the early to mid–1830s, although they were forced into Oklahoma, where the groups split up. One part joined the Cherokee (known thereafter as the Cherokee [or Loyal, from their Unionist stance during the Civil War] Shawnee), and the other joined the Absentee Shawnee.

In 1831, a group of Shawnees and Senecas who had been living in Ohio settled in Ottawa County, Oklahoma. When the groups separated in 1867, the Shawnee became known as the Eastern Shawnee. They organized formally as the Eastern Shawnee Tribe of Oklahoma in 1937, when they officially broke apart from the Seneca. Despite their loyalty to the Union in the Civil War, most Shawnee were forced out of Kansas and into Oklahoma, where they merged with the Cherokee in 1869. During the nineteenth and twentieth centuries, scattered Shawnee communities in Ohio and Indiana retained their Indian identity and some of their traditions. These communities came together politically in 1971 as the United Remnant Band.

RELIGION A supreme deity, possibly female identified, controlled a large number of other deities, which in turn all had their places in Shawnee mythology. The people recognized 12 fundamental laws with religious/mythological origins. The Piqua division of the tribe was in charge of religious ceremonies. Each division was conceived of as ritually discrete, and each held a sacred pack.

Important communal ceremonies included the Bread Dance, held at planting and harvest times and organized by women. The ceremony featured dancing and a feast of meat hunted by 12 men and cooked by 12 women. The people also celebrated the Green Corn Dance (a harvest/thanksgiving/renewal ceremony) and various other sacred ceremonies.

Prayer accompanied many life-cycle and cyclical events. Women might conduct ceremonies and often cured disease through their knowledge of medicinal plants. Young (less than age ten) boys and girls fasted to obtain spirit visions. Opposition in ceremonial activities, such as ball games, was based on gender.

GOVERNMENT The five Shawnee divisions were Chillikothe, Kispokotha, Piqua, Hathawekela, and Spitotha. They were linked through specific responsibilities, such as politics, ceremonialism, and war, and were associated both with specific territories and towns. Division membership was inherited patrilineally. This arrangement broke down with time.

Political functions fell under either the peace or war organization. Tribal, clan, and division chiefs were hereditary (clan chiefs may have been associated more with ritual than politics) prior to the nineteenth century, although the office of war chief also had a merit component. There was also a tribal council made up of the chiefs as well as elderly men. Town councils probably existed as well.

Women related to male leaders could be chiefs on the town level. Women were also associated with peace and war organizations. Among their prerogatives were the right to ask for the cancellation of a war party, the right to spare prisoners, and direction over feasts and planting crops.

Another type of tribal division was geographical in nature. These groups were fluid in number, size, and composition as the tribe shifted its territory. This system was eventually responsible for the three formal Shawnee divisions of the late nineteenth century.

CUSTOMS Up to 12 patrilineal clans controlled names; certain qualities associated with certain names also belonged to particular clans. Ritual and political appointments might follow from these qualities and were thus associated with clans. Women were in charge of the crops, of the game after it was killed, and of gathering wood and cooking. Murder could be redeemed by blood or by payment, with a women commanding more than twice the price of a man. The people enjoyed a number of social dances.

Birth occurred in a special, secluded hut, where mother and child remained for ten days, after which a naming ceremony was held. Marriage was probably arranged, at least in part, and was associated with gift giving. In a departure from tradition, divorce had become easy to obtain by the nineteenth century.

Only men buried Shawnee men, but both men and women buried women. The dead's possessions were divided among relatives, except for some that went to reward friends who played a prominent role in the funeral. Corpses were buried in their best clothing and usually prone, with the head facing west. Tobacco was sprinkled over the body. The mourning period of 12 days was bracketed with two feasts (spouses mourned for up to a year). Diverse death customs might include a condolence ceremony and, if a husband died, a replacement ceremony, when the widow chose a new husband about a year after the death.

DWELLINGS The Shawnee created various house styles, depending on period and location. Typical summer dwellings were bark-covered extended lodges. Town organization by division included ceremonial aspects as well, on the southeast "town" model. Each Shawnee town had a large, wooden council house used for a number of purposes, including sacred and secular group functions and ritual seclusion for warriors after fighting. In the eighteenth century such houses occasionally served as forts. Towns varied in size according to time and location, but the largest consisted of hundreds of houses and over 1,000 people.

DIET Women grew several varieties of corn. Household fields were grouped together. They also gathered a number of foods, including berries, cherries, and persimmon, and they tapped maple trees for their sap. Men hunted deer, bear, buffalo, and turkey. They also trapped a number of smaller mammals. The people left their summer towns in fall to establish winter camps. From there, able-bodied men and women left on months-long hunting trips. There was also a summer deer hunt. The Shawnee diet also included fish.

KEY TECHNOLOGY Musical instruments included drums and deer-hoof rattles. Pottery vessels held water and served other functions.

TRADE Shawnees had many trade partners throughout their various locations. They exported items such as pottery, corn, and other foods and manufactured goods from plants and animals; they imported feathers and minerals. In the historical period they also traded in horses.

NOTABLE ARTS The wandering Shawnee did not develop much of an artistic tradition, with the exception of some pottery, carved wood containers, and quill-decorated clothing.

TRANSPORTATION Although Shawnees did most of their traveling overland, they built dugout canoes to navigate local waterways.

DRESS The people generally adopted the clothing of their neighbors, incorporating some styles of their former environs as well. In general, they wore little clothing. Items included buckskin breechclouts, aprons, and moccasins. Body painting and tattooing were extensively practiced. Personal ornamentation varied according to location.

WAR AND WEAPONS Tribal and divisional war chiefs were selected by merit within certain clans and divisions. War chiefs announced the decision of the tribal council for war, subject to the possible review by a female chief. Female chiefs also had the power to spare prisoners.

War parties usually included a shaman/curer. The group held a dance before departing. There were also a feast and a dance upon arrival home, after which the warriors remained secluded for four days. Prisoners were either killed or distributed as slaves or for adoption. Generally, Shawnee enemies included the Chickasaw, Cherokee, Catawba, and Iroquois. Allies included the Lenápe from the late seventeenth century on and the Cherokee from the nineteenth century on. There was also an ancient association with the Creek.

Contemporary Information

GOVERNMENT/RESERVATIONS The Absentee Shawnee are located near Shawnee, Oklahoma. They are governed under a constitution that calls for an executive committee headed by a governor. Tribal

membership was about 2,000 in the mid-1990s. The land base is roughly 13,500 acres.

The Eastern Shawnee live in West Seneca, Ottawa County, Oklahoma. The people adopted a constitution and by-laws in 1937. They are governed by a business committee. There were about 1,500 members in the mid-1990s. The tribe owns almost 100 acres of land on their reservation of almost 800 acres.

The Cherokee (or Loyal) Shawnee are located mainly in Whiteoak, Oklahoma, although members live throughout the United States. They are enrolled Cherokee citizens, although they maintain distinct rolls for their tribal membership of about 8,000. The tribe maintains a business committee consisting of officers and members. There is also a general council that passes judgment on membership eligibility.

The Shawnee Nation United Remnant Band (URB) live in and around Ohio. In the early 1990s, the tribe owned 117 acres of land at Shawandasse and another 63 acres at Chillicothe. The tribe recognizes a chief.

ECONOMY The Absentee Shawnee gain income through farming, ranching, taxes on oil and gas contracts, small businesses, bingo, and tax-free sales. Among the Eastern Shawnee, some jobs are available with the tribe, in the bingo facility, and among the general population.

LEGAL STATUS The Absentee Shawnee and the Eastern Shawnee Tribe are federally recognized tribal entities. The Shawnee Nation United Remnant Band is recognized by the state of Ohio and has petitioned for federal recognition. The Piqua Sect of Ohio Shawnee Indians has petitioned for federal recognition. The Loyal Shawnee have received state recognition.

DAILY LIFE The URB continues to purchase more land. Their main holdings now serve not as a residence but as a ceremonial and cultural center, where the tribe conducts powwows, youth programs, and ceremonies. Most are well integrated into the surrounding non-native population. The Absentee Shawnee maintain a police force, a tribal court system, and a clinic. Most of the people are Christians, especially Baptists and Quakers. The native language is still spoken. The more traditional Big Jim Band holds quasi-traditional dances every year.

Facilities of the Eastern Shawnee include a tribal headquarters, a recreational park, and an eye clinic. The tribe also runs a nutrition clinic for the elderly, provides most of its own health care, and publishes a newsletter. Few speak their native language. The Loyal Shawnee maintain a cultural center and several traditions, such as the bread, green corn, and buffalo dances. The native language among these people is practically defunct.

Stockbridge-Munsee
See Mahican

Tuscarora
See Chapter 7.

Wampanoag
Wampanoag (Wäm pu `n ō ag), "Eastern People." They were formerly known as Pokanoket, which originally was the name of Massasoit's village but came to be the designation of all territory and people under that great sachem. The Wampanoag or Pokanoket also included the Nauset of Cape Cod, the Sakonnet of Rhode Island, and various tribes of the offshore islands. *See also* Narragansett.

LOCATION Traditionally, Wampanoags lived in southern New England from just north of Cape Cod, but including Nantucket and Martha's Vineyard, to Narragansett Bay. Today, there are Wampanoag communities in southeastern Massachusetts and around Bristol, Rhode Island.

POPULATION There were approximately 6,500 Wampanoags in 1600, including tributary island tribes. The contemporary (mid-1990s) population is about 2,700.

LANGUAGE Wampanoags spoke the Massachusett dialect of an Algonquian language.

Historical Information
HISTORY Wampanoag/Pokanoket culture developed steadily in their approximate historical location for about 8,000 years. The people have lived in their historic territory at least since the fifteenth century. They had already been weakened from disease and war with the Penobscot when they encountered nonnatives in the early seventeenth century. They had also been forced by the Narragansett to accept tributary status.

The people greeted the Pilgrims in 1620, although there had been contact with the British some years earlier. The Grand Sachem Massasoit made a treaty of friendship with the British. His people helped the Europeans survive by showing them how to grow crops and otherwise survive in a land alien to them. Men named Squanto and Samoset are especially known in this regard. Largely as a result of Massasoit's influence, the Wampanoags remained neutral in the Pequot war of 1636. Many Indian residents of Cape Cod and the islands of Nantucket and Martha's Vineyard were Christianized during the mid-seventeenth century.

Massasoit died in 1662. At that time his second son, Metacomet, also known as Philip, renewed the peace. However, relations were strained by British abuses such as the illegal occupation of land; trickery, often involving the use of alcohol; and the destruction of resources, including forests and game. Diseases also continued to take a toll on the population.

Finally, local tribes reached the breaking point. The Pokanoket, now mainly relocated to the Bristol, Rhode Island, area and led by Metacomet, took the lead in uniting Indians from southern and central New England in King Philip's war (1675–1676). This was an attempt by the Wampanoag, Narragansett, and other tribes to drive the British out of their territory. However, the fighting began before all the preparations had been completed. In the end, hundreds of non-native settlers died, but the two main Indian tribes were nearly exterminated. The tribal name of Pokanoket was also officially banned.

Most Wampanoags were either enslaved or killed. Survivors fled into the interior or onto the Cape and the islands, whose tribes had not participated in the war. Some also fled to the Great Lakes region and Canada. For centuries following this event, local Indians were cheated, discriminated against, used as servants, or, at best, ignored.

The Indian population on Nantucket Island declined from possibly 1,500 in 1600 to 358 in 1763 to 20 in 1792, mainly owing to disease. The last of the indigenous population died in 1855. Indians at Mashpee, on Cape Cod, were assigned 50 square miles of land in 1660. Self-government continued until 1788, when the state of Massachusetts placed the Indians under its control. Most of their lands were allotted in 1842. Trespass by non-natives was a large problem during the entire period. Near Mashpee, the 2,500-acre Herring Pond Reservation was allotted in 1850.

Indian land in Fall River was divided into lots in 1707, and a 160-acre reservation was created in 1709. The people's right of self-government was abrogated in the early nineteenth century. The reservation was eliminated entirely in 1907. Of the three reservations on Martha's Vineyard in the nineteenth century—Chappaquiddick, Christiantown, and Gay Head—only the latter remained by 1900. This group was never governed by non-native overseers, and its isolation allowed the people to retain their identity and cohesion to a far greater extent than other Wampanoag communities.

Other groups of Wampanoag descendants maintained a separate existence until the nineteenth century, when most became fully assimilated. The Wampanoag Nation was founded in 1928 in response to the pan-Indian movement of the times.

RELIGION The people recognized a supreme deity and many lesser deities. Priests, or medicine men (powwows), provided religious leadership. Their duties included mediating with the spirit world in order to cure, forecast the weather, and conduct ceremonies.

GOVERNMENT A hereditary chief sachem led the tribe. In theory his power was absolute, but in practice he was advised by a council of village and clan chiefs (sagamores). The village was the main political unit. Villages were led by chiefs with limited power; important decisions were made in consultation with influential men of the village. There was a hereditary element to village leadership. This factor may be responsible for the existence of women chiefs. Villages may have made their own temporary alliances. Overall political structure consolidated and became more hierarchical after the epidemics of 1616–1619.

CUSTOMS Wampanoags were organized into a number of clans. Their annual round of activities took them from winter villages to gathering sites at summer fields. Women had clearly defined and significant political rights. Social stratification was reflected in leadership and marriage arrangements. Leading men might have more than one wife. The dead were wrapped in mats and buried with various possessions. Mourners blackened their faces. The souls of the dead were said to travel west.

DWELLINGS There were at least 30 villages in the early seventeenth century, most of which were located by water. People lived in wigwams, both circular and rectangular. The largest measured up to 100 feet long; smaller ones were about 15 feet in diameter. The houses consisted of pole frames covered with birch bark, hickory bark, or woven mats. There were smoke holes in the roofs. The wigwams were often semiexcavated and lined with cattails, pine needles, or other such material.

Wigwams tended to have central fires, but longhouses featured rows of several fires. Some houses may have been palisaded. Their larger structures were probably built in winter villages. Mat beds stood on platforms against the walls or directly on the ground. Skins served as bedding. All towns featured a central open space used for ceremonies and meetings. The people also built sweat houses.

DIET Men hunted fowl and small and large game, with the white-tailed deer being the most important. They stalked, trapped, and snared deer and may have hunted them in communal drives. They also grew tobacco. The people ate seals and beached whales, and they gathered shellfish, often steaming them over hot rocks. They fished for freshwater and saltwater species in winter (through the ice) and summer. Women gathered roots, wild fruits, berries, and nuts as well as maple sap for sugar. Women began growing corn, beans, and squash in the late prehistoric period. Fish may have been used as fertilizer. Dried corn was stored in underground caches.

KEY TECHNOLOGY Hunting equipment included traps, snares, nets, witch hazel bows, and arrows. People caught fish with nets, bone hooks, and weirs. Cordage was made mainly of Indian hemp. Hoes were made of hardwood and clamshell. Women wove mats and baskets of rushes and grasses, including Indian hemp. Other material items included stone, bone, and shell tools; wooden bowls; and dishes and other items of stone and clay. Shell wampum was used for adornment and later for trade.

TRADE Wampanoags were part of regional trade networks. There were few professional or long-distance traders; most trade was very local. Items traded included wampum, agricultural products, chestnuts, skins, pottery, and wooden bowls.

NOTABLE ARTS Carved wooden items, such as bowls, were especially fine.

TRANSPORTATION Dugout canoes could hold up to 40 men, with the average being 10–15. There may have been some number of birch-bark canoes. Women carried burdens on their backs.

DRESS Women wore skirts and poncho-style blouses as well as soft-soled moccasins. They donned rabbit and beaver robes in cold weather. Men wore skin leggings and breechclouts and soft-soled moccasins. They also wore turkey-feather cloaks and bone and shell necklaces. They tended to pull out all their hair except for a scalp lock.

WAR AND WEAPONS Allies included the Massachusett; enemies included the Penobscot and Narragansett. The main weapons consisted of witch hazel bows; wooden arrows with stone, bone, eagle claw, and crab tail tips; and ball-headed war clubs. Men painted their faces for war.

Contemporary Information

GOVERNMENT/RESERVATIONS The Wampanoag Nation is divided into five groups: Gay Head, Mashpee, Assonet, Herring Pond, and Nemasket, each with a written constitution, a chief, and an elected tribal council. There is also a council of chiefs, and the mainland groups recognize a supreme medicine man.

The Wampanoag Reservation (Gay Head Wampanoags), also known as Aquinnah, is located at Gay Head on Martha's Vineyard, Massachusetts. Fewer than half of the roughly 600 members live on the island. The tribe owns several parcels of land— about 150 acres—in trust.

More than half of the approximately 1,000 Mashpee Wampanoag live in the town of Mashpee, Massachusetts. The Pokanoket Tribe of Wampanoag Nation is located in Bristol, Rhode Island.

ECONOMY Most Wampanoags are integrated into local economies. At Gay Head, tourism and small Indian-owned businesses are important.

LEGAL STATUS The Gay Head Wampanoags are a federally recognized tribal entity. The Mashpee Wampanoags have petitioned for federal recognition. The Pokanoket Tribe of Wampanoag Nation plans to petition for federal recognition.

DAILY LIFE Contemporary Wampanoag events, many of which have both sacred and secular/public components, include a powwow on the Fourth of July (Mashpee), Indian Day and Cranberry Day (Gay Head), and new year's ceremony and the Strawberry Festival (Assonet). Many Gay Head people have left the island, but many also plan to return. Recent construction on the island includes housing and a multi-purpose building. The people hope to make remaining on the island a viable option.

In 1978, the Mashpee people lost a court case in which they sought the return to tribal ownership of the entire town of Mashpee. They continue to seek a land base and hope that federal recognition will advance their prospects. The community is in the process of working out a fair relationship with the increasingly non-native population of the town.

The Pokanoket tribe, led by descendants of Massasoit, seek federal recognition and as well as stewardship of 267 acres of land in Bristol, Rhode Island.

Winnebago

Winnebago (Wi n ə ˋb ā g ō) is Algonquin for "People of the Filthy Water," referring to the lower Fox River and Lake Winnebago, which became clogged with dead fish every summer. This name was translated by the French into *Puants* and back into English as "Stinkards." The people's self-designation was *Hochungra*, "People of the Big (Real, or Parent) Speech (Voices)" or "Great Fish (Trout) Nation." Today they are known as the Ho-Chunk Nation.

The Winnebago shared cultural characteristics with Plains Siouans such as the Otoe, Ioway, and Missouria as well as with Woodland/prairie Algonquians such as the Sauk, Fox, and Menominee. Little is known of Winnebago culture prior to their brush with annihilation in the early seventeenth century.

LOCATION In the early seventeenth century the people were located in Wisconsin on the Door Peninsula, Green Bay, just south of the Menominee. The Winnebago may also once have lived in west-central Wisconsin. By the early nineteenth century they lived in southwestern Wisconsin and northwestern Illinois. Today, there are communities in northeast Nebraska and central Wisconsin and in regional cities and towns.

POPULATION From about 3,800 in the mid–seventeenth century or earlier, the Winnebago have grown to approximately 7,000 in 1990.

LANGUAGE Winnebago belongs or is related to the Chiwere division of the Siouan language family.

Historical Information

HISTORY According to tradition, the Winnebago were united with the Chiwere Siouans in the distant past, perhaps in Kentucky. Their ancestors were in Wisconsin as early as around 700. As the groups moved north and west, and then south and west, the Winnebago may have remained in the forest while the other Chiwere speakers moved onto the prairie and plains in the early to mid–seventeenth century. They probably participated in the fifteenth-century Mound Builder culture. They were also probably allied with—and borrowed some cultural elements (perhaps including cannibalism) of—sixteenth-century Temple Mound people based at Cahokia, near present-day St. Louis. A colony of these people apparently lived near the Winnebago, at a settlement called Aztalan.

The Winnebago may have defeated the Illinois in the early seventeenth century. Shortly after the French arrival, around 1634, Michigan-area Algonquians fleeing from Iroquois attacks swarmed into Winnebago territory. Winnebago warfare against these people led to the defeat of most of these refugee groups. Despite their strength and military capability, by the mid–seventeenth century the Winnebago had been reduced to near extinction by disease and war with the Illinois, Ottawa, and other Algonquian tribes. At that point, the Winnebago were forced to sue for peace with their enemies, adopting and marrying many of them to make up for their losses and in the process incorporating many aspects of Algonquian culture.

They became involved in the fur trade from the mid– to late seventeenth century. That development tended to disperse the tribe west and south of Lake Winnebago. Material changes and technological dependence soon followed. They were French allies during the colonial wars, but pro-British in the American Revolution. They participated in Tecumseh's rebellion (1809–1811) and tentatively in Black Hawk's war (1832).

Unstable relations between the European and Euro-American powers had aided the Indian cause. The end of fighting between the United States and Britain in 1815 ushered in the era of land cessions and removals for the Winnebago. They were powerless to prevent the United States from pressuring the Menominee to cede land traditionally belonging to the Winnebago so that Indians from New York might have a home in the west.

Crowding by non-natives and pressure from the U.S. government led the Winnebago to cede their Wisconsin lands between 1825 and 1837 (at least the final treaty was blatantly fraudulent). By then two factions had developed within the tribe: those agreeing to removal and those determined not to leave. The former group, determined to acculturate, soon moved onto several successive reservations in Iowa, Minnesota, South Dakota, and finally Nebraska. Up to one-third of the people died during the removals, particularly on the move to South Dakota. There was an especially severe smallpox epidemic in 1836.

In Nebraska, people continued to grow gardens and hunt. Most of the land was allotted by 1900. Allotments were generally leased to non-natives, who profited by the towns that grew up in the area, most notably the town of Winnebago. In the early twentieth century, most Winnebago land was sold to non-natives. At the same time, forced attendance at boarding schools had a particularly destructive effect on the Winnebago. Demoralization set in, and factionalism, based on religious differences (such as Christian sects and the Native American Church), rent the tribe. As was the case so often, educational and employment opportunities were closed to Indians.

The tribe reorganized in 1936 under the Indian Reorganization Act but was unable to stem the tide of despair, poverty, and growing social problems. Many aspects of traditional culture had vanished by that time. The government soon began a program of purchasing homes in scattered counties for tribal members. In the 1960s, the tribe benefited from both federal antipoverty programs and its own community development work.

Meanwhile, by the 1870s over half of the tribe had returned to Wisconsin, which some members had never left. In the 1880s, many members received scattered 40-acre parcels of land under the Homestead Act, most of which were later sold. The people lived in a semitraditional manner until well into the twentieth century, despite the growing presence of missionaries and missionary schools. In 1906, the people lost much of their land to tax foreclosure.

In 1908, many Wisconsin Winnebagos became involved with the Native American Church. As in Nebraska, the tribe soon developed bitter factions based at least in part on religious differences. The people continued to gather berries and harvest fruit and vegetables from non-native farms. Tourism—mainly craft sales (especially ash-splint baskets)—became increasingly important after World War I.

RELIGION The primary deity was the sun or earth maker. The people also recognized other deities, some sex identified, and many lesser spirits. Winnebago cosmology was intricate and complex, and although most people were unfamiliar with the details, most also observed the various rituals associated with aspects of traditional religious belief having to do with personal visions, clan membership, and life-cycle events.

Young people undertook vision quests in order to acquire guardian spirits. These were said to provide luck and success in hunting, war, or curing. The Midewiwin ceremony differed from the Algonquian version in that it dealt mainly with life and death as well as life after death. Clan feasts focused on making offerings to the clan animal. There was also a winter feast.

War bundle ceremonies, held under clan auspices, resulted from particular visions. They included ritual offerings and were meant to enhance the spiritual power of the military enterprise. There were several kinds of shamans: Those associated with war and curing were considered good, but those associated with hunting might be good or bad (witches). Certain older people used both medicinal plants and spiritual power to cure disease.

GOVERNMENT There was a hereditary head chief in former times. As the population dispersed during the eighteenth century, population centers became more autonomous. Dual chieftainships (peace and war chiefs) existed in villages and among head chiefs. The peace chief was always inclined toward peace and reconciliation. He was generous, strove for consensus in decision making, and tried to discourage most war parties. Civil chiefs came from a clan of the air division. War chiefs came from a clan of the earth division. They were concerned with rule breaking and punishment. Both civil and war chiefs were selected from hereditary candidates according to merit. One clan—the Bear—served as a tribal police force.

CUSTOMS Generosity may have been the people's highest value. The tribe was organized into two divisions, earth and air. There were also 12 patrilineal clans, 4 among the air division and 8 among the earth division. Clans were related to animals and were represented by mounds in the shape of animals. They governed marriage, leadership, and games such as lacrosse. Each clan also owned certain names, ceremonies, responsibilities, and restrictions. Descent may have been matrilineal in the distant past.

There may have been a social ranking, although the basis is unclear. Berdaches (transvestites), thought to be divinely inspired, were accorded respect. The mother's brother(s) played an important role in raising a boy. Although menstruating women were isolated, some degree of courtship may have taken place at those times. Marriages were often arranged by close male relatives of a woman. In-laws were generally avoided out of respect.

People enjoyed various sports, such as lacrosse, as well as gambling games such as the moccasin game. The Winnebago were cannibals. At four-night wakes held for the dead, people told stories and gambled for the souls of enemies, which would later assist the dead on their way to the afterlife. Corpses were buried on scaffolds.

DWELLINGS The few large late-seventeenth-century villages became 40 or so scattered settlements by the early nineteenth century. People lived in rectangular bark- or mat-covered lodges. There was also a rectangular council house for meetings and ceremonies and similarly built sweat houses. From the eighteenth century on, as populations became less concentrated, people began to build domed wigwams.

DIET Women grew gardens of corn, beans, and squash as well as tobacco. Corn was steamed in a pit layered with husks. It was also stored in pits or fiber bags. Men hunted buffalo communally on the nearby prairie and trapped small game. Other large game included deer and bear. Hunting parties probably included women. Runners traveled between winter hunting parties and the villages, exchanging fresh meat for dried vegetables. Fish was often taken at night by the light of pine-pitch torches. Women gathered fruit, berries, and tubers as well as wild rice from canoes.

KEY TECHNOLOGY Fishing gear included spears, bow and arrow, and weirs. Carved hickory calendar sticks marked celestial occurrences. People also carved wooden bowls. Women made pottery jars and wove baskets and bags.

TRADE Among other transactions, the Winnebago traded buffalo robes with the Menominee for wild rice. They also exported corn and pottery items.

NOTABLE ARTS Leather goods were decorated with dyed porcupine quills and feathers. Other arts included beadwork, woven baskets, and carved wooden bowls.

TRANSPORTATION People traveled over water in birch-bark and dugout canoes. They used snowshoes in winter.

DRESS Most clothing was made from tanned buckskin. Men wore deer-hair headdresses dyed red. They also wore breechclouts, leggings, and soft-soled moccasins, possibly fringed and/or decorated with quillwork. Women wore sleeveless dresses (consisting of two skins sewed together at the shoulder and belted) over a nettle-fiber undershirt, leggings, and moccasins with a distinctive flap over the toe. Both wore buckskin robes in cold weather.

WAR AND WEAPONS Winnebagos were known as enthusiastic fighters. Captured enemies were regularly eaten. Allies included the Menominee, Sauk, Fox, and Kickapoo; enemies included the Anishinabe, Dakota, and sometimes the Fox. Clans owned sacred war bundles, which contained items dictated in a vision by a particular war-related spirit. One clan—the Hawk—had the power of life and death over prisoners of war. War honors included counting coup. The people engaged in a celebratory dance when a war party returned.

Contemporary Information

GOVERNMENT/RESERVATIONS The Winnebago Reservation, Dixon and Thurston Counties, Nebraska, established in 1865, consists of over 27,000 acres. The 1990 Indian population was 1,151 of a total enrollment of roughly 4,000. Government consisted of a tribal council with officers.

The Winnebago Nation in Wisconsin includes the communities of Black River Falls, Wisconsin Dells, Tomah–La Crosse, Wittenberg, and Wisconsin Rapids. The community recognizes two types of government, a "progressive" business committee and a traditional chief-clan structure.

The Ho Chunk (Winnebago) Reservation, Dane, Jackson, Juneau, Monroe, Sauk, Shawana, and Wood Counties, Wisconsin, was established in 1875 on lands repurchased from aboriginal territory. The reservation consists of approximately 4,200 acres. The 1990 Indian population was 465, with an additional 101 Indians located on the trust lands (Adams, Clark, Crawford, Jackson, Juneau, La Crosse, Marathon, Monroe, Shawana, and Wood Counties). Total enrollment at that time was about 5,000.

ECONOMY In Nebraska, a $4.6 million land claim settlement in 1975 was divided 65/35 between the tribe as a whole and per capita payments. Important programs that were developed with these funds include credit facilitation, land acquisition, and funerary programs. Other important economic activities include a casino and several small businesses. The tribe is seeking economic self-sufficiency. The Wisconsin Winnebago operate bingo establishments and casinos. The people also work in the general economy.

LEGAL STATUS The Winnebago Tribe of Nebraska and the Wisconsin Winnebago Indian Tribe are federally recognized tribal entities.

DAILY LIFE The Nebraska Winnebago have a tribal court system. Community facilities include a hospital, tribal offices, and public schools. There is also a local campus of Nebraska Community College. The native language is spoken by relatively few people. Most Winnebagos are Christian. Diabetes is a serious health problem. The tribe hosts an annual powwow in July.

The Wisconsin Winnebago have retained their

clan structure within the context of the two divisions, earth and air (or sky). Many people still observe traditional religious ceremonies such as the vision quest and various festivals. They celebrate a powwow around Labor Day. Gaming remains controversial, but even traditionalists defend it on grounds of sovereignty. Wisconsin Winnebagos are known in part for their dedicated service in the U.S. armed forces. The Native American Church remains popular in both locations.

Wyandotte

Wyandotte or Wyandot (`W ī un dot), from *Wendat*, "islanders," or "People of the Peninsula," the self-designation of the Huron people. The Wyandottes are a successor tribe to the Huron Confederacy, which was destroyed in 1650 and which consisted of four or five tribes: Attignaouantan (People of the Bear), Attigneenongnahac (Barking Dogs or People of the Cord), Arendahronon (People of the Rock), Tohontaenrat (People of the Deer), and possibly Ataronchronon (People of the Marshes). The name Huron is taken from a French word meaning "boar-like" or "boorish" and refers to the roached hair style. Contemporary Canadian Hurons are known as Hurons-Wendat.

LOCATION   In the sixteenth century, Hurons lived in the St. Lawrence River Valley. By 1600 at the latest, they inhabited an area known as Huronia, which included land between Georgian Bay (Lake Huron) and Lake Ontario. Today, most Wyandottes live in Wyandotte County, Kansas; Ottawa County, Oklahoma; and near Quebec City, Canada.

POPULATION   From between 16,000 and 30,000 people in the early seventeenth century, the Huron population dropped to about 10,000 in the mid–seventeenth century and to fewer than 200 in Canada in the early nineteenth century. There were around 500 Wyandottes in the Great Lakes region in the mid– to late seventeenth century. In the mid-1990s, about 2,000 tribal members lived in Oklahoma and Kansas. About 2,700 live in Quebec, Canada.

LANGUAGE   Huron/Wyandottes spoke mutually intelligible dialects of a Northern Iroquoian language.

Historical Information

HISTORY   The Huron probably originated with other Iroquoians in the Mississippi Valley. They encountered Jacques Cartier in 1534 and Samuel de Champlain in 1609. The Iroquois wars probably began sometime in the sixteenth century, if not earlier, when those people drove the Huron tribes out of the St. Lawrence Valley, lands that they may originally have taken by warfare from the Iroquois. Thereafter the Huron sided with the Algonquians against the Iroquois.

The people entered the fur trade in the early seventeenth century, mainly as intermediaries between the French and other tribes. Catholic missionaries soon followed the traders, as did venereal disease and alcohol. Until the late 1640s, the Huron dominated the French beaver pelt trade. The French, however, were reluctant to sell arms to unconverted Hurons, a policy that was to have disastrous consequences. Severe epidemics in the late 1630s were followed by more Christian conversions and increased factionalism.

The Iroquois, armed with Dutch firearms, launched their final invasion in 1648. These tribes were allied with the British and sought to expand their trapping area and their control over neighboring tribes. Within two years they had destroyed the Huron. Some Hurons escaped to Lorette, near Quebec City, where they were granted land. They continued to grow crops, hunt, and trap until the end of the nineteenth century, when craft sales and factory work became the most important economic activities. They also intermarried regularly with the French.

Other Hurons settled among tribes such as the Erie, who were themselves later destroyed by the Iroquois. Many were adopted by the victorious Iroquois nations. Some Hurons escaped to the west, where they joined with the Tionotati (Petun, or Tobacco Nation), a related tribe. Under continuing pressure from the Iroquois, they began wandering around the Michilimackinac–Green Bay region, where they hunted and remained active in the fur trade. Although never a large tribe, membership in various alliances allowed them to play an important role in regional affairs.

Jesuits continued to minister to these people, who migrated to Detroit around 1700. They split into pro-British (at Sandusky) and pro-French groups in the mid–eighteenth century. The latter group became known as the Wyandotte and claimed territory north of the Ohio River, where they allowed Shawnee and Lenápe bands to settle. Wyandottes fought the British in Pontiac's rebellion (1763).

Land cessions to non-natives began in 1745 and continued into the nineteenth century. Wyandottes sold their lands on the Canadian side of the Detroit River in 1790 in exchange for reserves, most of which were ceded in the early nineteenth century; the rest were allotted in severalty later in the century. These people sided with the British in the Revolutionary War and split their allegiance in the War of 1812.

Their land in Ohio and Michigan was recognized by the United States after the War of 1812, but the tribe ceded most of it by 1819. With the decline of the fur trade, many Wyandottes began farming and acculturating to non-native society. More land was ceded in 1832, and in 1842 the people had ceded all Ohio and Michigan lands and moved to the Indian Territory (Kansas), on land purchased from the Lenápe and on individual sections. During this period, the question of slavery increased factionalism among tribal members; some were slaveholders, whereas others were adamant abolitionists.

An 1855 treaty provided for land allotment (most allotments were soon alienated) and divided the tribe into citizens and noncitizens. Three years later, roughly 200 Wyandottes settled on the Seneca Reservation. The more traditional group (noncitizen) relocated to the new Indian Territory (Oklahoma) in 1867, after the Seneca-Cayuga agreed to donate part of their reservation there. This reservation was allotted in 1893. The Wyandotte Tribe of Oklahoma was created in 1937. It was terminated in the 1950s but was rerecognized in 1978. The "citizen" group remained in Kansas, incorporating as the Wyandot Nation of Kansas in 1959.

RELIGION The Huron recognized an almost unlimited number of spirits and deities, the most powerful of which were the sun and sky. Dreams were considered important as foreshadowing good or evil. There were four types of annual religious feasts: prewar singing, the departure of a dying man, thanksgiving, and healing. Of these, the last were related to medicine societies. Women participated in several formal dances.

Disease was caused by wounds and other obvious causes as well as by witches and soul loss (psychological disturbance). Dreams were important in curing problems of the latter type; otherwise, curers used magic, dancing, and other spiritual methods. Every winter, a three-day ceremony in which people feigned madness was held. There were also three types of shamans: conjurers, who were associated with the weather; diviners, who foretold the future and found lost objects; and healers.

The Dance of the Fire, which involved physical contact with boiling water and hot stones or coals, was meant to attract the assistance of a curing spirit. The most important celebration was the Feast of the Dead, held every ten years or so. Relatives cleaned, rewrapped, and buried bones in a common tribal grave. Then they feasted and honored their ancestors' lives in story. This ceremony was accompanied by games, contests, and gift giving.

GOVERNMENT The tribes of the Huron Confederacy were led by a council of chiefs from each tribe. This council had no jurisdiction in purely local matters. The position of chief was inherited matrilineally,

but within that context it was subject to merit criteria and a confirmation process.

Large villages were governed by clan civil and war chiefs. The chiefs' male relatives acted as their councilors. Decisions were taken by consensus and were not, strictly speaking, binding on individuals or, if a tribal-level decision, on villages.

CUSTOMS Generosity was highly valued: Stinginess could leave one open to charges of witchcraft, a capital offense. Constituent clan families were led by the senior mother. These women also selected the chiefs from within the appropriate families. Certain lineages within clans were more important than others; holding feasts was a means to achieve status.

Crimes against the body politic, such as witchcraft or treason, were punishable by death, but serious crimes like murder were subject to settlement, including compensation. Popular diversions included lacrosse and gambling games.

Premarital sexual relations, beginning shortly after puberty, were common and accepted, within certain clan restrictions. A couple need not marry in the eyes of society, but if they chose to, marriages were apparently monogamous. Both the couple and their parents had to approve a marriage. Divorce was unusual after children had been born. In such cases, the children probably remained with the mother.

Corpses, wrapped in furs, lay in state for several days, during which time people gave speeches and feasted. The body was then laid on a scaffold and a small hut built over it. Gifts (food and tools) were placed near the body to help the spirit in the afterworld, which was regarded as similar to the world of the living. A mourning period lasted a year, during which time a surviving spouse could not remarry. Every ten years or so the tribe held a feast of the dead (see "Religion").

DWELLINGS There were at least 18 villages in the early seventeenth century. Villages were located on high ground near waterways and woods. The larger ones were often palisaded with up to five rows of sharpened stakes. Public spaces were located between the longhouses. Larger villages had up to 100 longhouses and 2,000 people or more; the average size was perhaps 800 people. Villages were moved every 10 to 20 years, after the soil and/or firewood was exhausted.

The people built pole-frame, bark (elm, cedar, or ash) houses, 25–30 feet wide and high and about 100–150 (even up to 240) feet long. Roofs were vaulted with closable smoke holes. A center passageway divided the house. Sleeping platforms ran along the sides, but people slept on the floor near the fire in winter. Rush mats served as doors and floors. There were both large central hearths and smaller cooking fires.

Each longhouse was home to 8–24 families, with an average of about six people per family. The longhouses tended to be smoky, and fleas and mice were particular pests. The larger house of chiefs also served as council/ceremonial houses. Villages were economically self-sufficient.

DIET Women grew corn, beans, squash, and sunflowers. Men may have grown some tobacco. Corn, the staple food, was eaten mainly as soup with some added foods. Women also gathered blueberries, nuts, and fruits as well as acorns in times of famine.

Men hunted deer, bear, numerous other large and small game, and fowl. Deer were hunted in part by driving them into rivers or enclosures where they were shot with the bow and arrow. Bear were occasionally trapped and then fattened for a year or two before being eaten for special feasts. Dog was also eaten. The people fished throughout the year for whitefish, catfish, pike, and other species. Other aquatic foods included clams, crabs, and turtles.

KEY TECHNOLOGY The digging stick and an antler or bone hoe were the primary agricultural tools. Men hunted with bows and arrows, snares, and spears. Fishing equipment included bone hooks and harpoons as well as large (up to 1,200 feet long) nets woven from nettles. Women wove mats, baskets, and nets of Indian hemp, reeds, bark, and corn husks. They also made leather bags; these and the baskets were painted or decorated with porcupine quills. Men made wooden items such as utensils, bowls, and shields as well as stone or clay pipes and heavy stone tools such as axes. Pottery and wooden mortars were related to food preparation.

TRADE Most people traded to acquire goods to give away and thus acquire status. The Huron were important traders even before the French arrived. They had a monopoly on corn and tobacco. They also dealt in furs and chert, wampum beads, dried berries, mats, fish, and hemp. Important trading partners included the Petun (tobacco) and northern Algonquian people. The Nipissing were also important trade partners; they traded fish and furs for Huron corn. Extensive trade routes took the Huron all over much of the eastern Great Lakes and the St. Lawrence River region and kept their society rich and stable.

Trade routes were owned or controlled by the people who had made them as well as by other members of their lineage. Intratribal use of the trails entailed payment of a fee. Intertribal use was prohibited. June through September was the main trading season, during which time most men were away from the villages. The people also imported gourds.

NOTABLE ARTS Pottery and twined bags were two important arts. The people also wove belts and other items from native fibers. Designs were mostly geometric. Moccasins and other items were embroidered or appliquéd with moose hair.

TRANSPORTATION Rivers were navigated via birch-bark canoe. Most intervillage communication was overland.

DRESS Women made clothing from buckskin. It consisted generally of shirts, breechclouts, leggings, skirts, and moccasins. Fur capes were added in winter. Clothing was decorated with fringe and brightly painted designs. Face painting and tattooing were popular, especially among men.

WAR AND WEAPONS Hurons never achieved the kind of unity of purpose and command essential for defeating or even realistically engaging an enemy as powerful as the Iroquois. People fought mainly for blood revenge as well as to gain personal status. War chiefs usually organized and led raiding parties, which might include up to 600 men.

Most fighting was practiced by surprise attacks on small groups. The main Huron enemies were the Iroquois, especially the Seneca. Hurons were allied with local Algonquian groups, especially the Ottawa, as well as the Susquehannock. Weapons included the bow and arrow, war clubs, wooden shield, and rod armor. Captives were often ritually tortured and sometimes eaten. Some, especially women and children, might be adopted.

Contemporary Information

GOVERNMENT/RESERVATIONS The Wyandotte Tribe, Ottawa County, Oklahoma, is governed under a constitution that calls for a chief, elected officers, and a tribal council. The land base consists of 192 acres of land in addition to individual allotments.

The Wyandot Nation of Kansas (1959), formerly the "citizen" or "absentee" Wyandottes, is located near Kansas City.

Huron Village (Wendake), Quebec, Canada, consists of 67 hectares. There were about 1,000 residents in the mid-1990s, of a total population of about 2,600. The community is governed by a band council.

ECONOMY A casino is planned in Kansas. Many people are integrated into the local economy.

In Canada, many people still make and sell crafts such as snowshoes, moccasins, and canoes. One Huron group operates a bed-and-breakfast. A museum draws tourists in summer. The local economy is extensive and provides jobs for hundreds of non-natives.

LEGAL STATUS The Wyandotte Tribe of Oklahoma is a federally recognized tribal entity. The Wyandot Nation of Kansas is state recognized and has petitioned for federal recognition. Quebec Hurons-Wendats are provincially and federally recognized.

DAILY LIFE The tribe in Oklahoma provides several important services, including student scholarships and meals for the elderly. Facilities include housing, a tribal center, and a preschool. A museum and cultural center are planned. The people are working on identifying and preserving aspects of their cultural traditions.

Hurons of Lorette (Quebec) are all Catholic and part French. The Canadian National Railway bisects the reserve. Most Indians own property. Children attend school on the reserve through grade four. The reserve is similar to neighboring towns in Quebec. There is some effort to revive the native language. The artistic custom of moose-hair appliqué persisted here longer than in the south.

CHAPTER NINE

The Subarctic

Subarctic

The vast Subarctic region stretches from the Atlantic Ocean in the east to the Rocky Mountains and the Alaska coast in the west and from the northern Great Lakes region and Great Plains to the tundra. Over two million square miles in area, the Subarctic is commonly divided into different geological zones, such as Canadian Shield (Hudson Bay and Mackenzie River lowlands), Cordillera (northern Rocky Mountain region), Alaska Plateau (central interior Alaska, including major river drainages), and Alaska Coast (primarily Cook Inlet and Copper River).

The boreal forest is the region's chief distinguishing physiographic feature. With the exceptions of birch and aspen, most trees, such as spruce, pine, fir, and tamarack, are conifers. There are thousands of streams and freshwater lakes, including Lake Winnipeg, Great Bear Lake, and Great Slave Lake, as well as Hudson Bay and coasts on two oceans. Low hills and rock outcroppings characterize much of the east. High mountains with glaciers, as well as plains, mark the far west. Major rivers include the Mackenzie, Peace, Churchill, Yukon, and Athabaska.

Despite its size and the variety of physical features, much of the region can be forbidding. Its continental climate is characterized by short, mild-to-hot summers (up to 38° Celsius/100° Fahrenheit) and long, bitterly cold winters (down to at least −38° Celsius/−100° Fahrenheit). Precipitation is generally low, except along the Alaska coast and in some mountain regions, and it falls mainly as snow. The short spring is marked by ice breakup and snow melt out as well as plagues of mosquitoes, black flies, and other insects. Travel is limited in spring and also during fall freeze up. Food, mainly in the form of game and fish, could be plentiful, but starvation was also a regular feature of life in the Subarctic.

The sheer difficulty of living in the Subarctic accounts for its low aboriginal population. Probably no more than 100,000 people ever lived in the region at any one time. These hunter-gatherers spoke Athapaskan (mostly in the west) and Algonquian languages. Some southern groups blend almost imperceptibly into other cultural regions. For instance, the Anishinabe (Northern Ojibwa and Salteaux) are often discussed (as in this encyclopedia) with Northeast Indians, whereas Carrier and Chilcotin are sometimes grouped in the Plateau region. Alternatively, people such as the Shuswap, discussed in this book as Plateau Indians, are occasionally placed in the Subarctic region.

The arrival of non-natives—around 1500 in the extreme southeast and not until the nineteenth century in some western interior regions—affected Indian groups in different ways. Like Native Americans everywhere, however, all suffered sharp population losses. Most Subarctic Indians today mix Christianity, to different degrees, with significant elements of traditional belief and spirituality. Acculturation levels vary widely. Many people continue to hunt, fish, and trap, although giant hydroelectric and mining projects both claim and pollute the land. Contemporary Subarctic Indians still fight to regain their sovereignty. As people for whom traditions remain vital, they struggle to redefine their identities in the face of a global economy and culture that are increasingly part of their lives.

The first people entered the Subarctic region about the time that the frozen Bering Straits provided a land corridor between Asia and North America. This migration occurred at least 12,000 years ago but possibly as long as 25,000 or more years ago. Shallow lakes covered much of today's lowlands, and glacial ice persisted in some areas up to 7,000 years ago. On the other hand, southern grasslands and the boreal forest extended farther north than they do today, as did animal species like bison and caribou. Some of the earliest northwestern people used tools like stone microblades, which were straight-sided and flat. They probably had spears, snares, snowshoes, and canoes but not the bow and arrow.

Athapaskan speakers descend from a Northern Archaic culture that existed at least 6,000 years ago. About the same time, and over the next several thousand years, the Shield culture diverged in the east, as far as Labrador, from more ancient ones. Local technology changed only slowly until the first non-native influences arrived. People acquired the bow and arrow around 1,000 or perhaps 2,000 years ago. The Taltheilei tradition began about 2,600 years ago from Great Bear Lake to Lake Athabaska and the Churchill River.

The Laurel Culture of Manitoba and northern Ontario, characterized in part by a ceramic tradition acquired from the south, lasted from about 1000 B.C.E. to about 800 C.E. Laurel pots were coiled, impressed, incised, and then fired. Some were later painted red. Some people living in the extreme south built mounds over their dead. Later prehistoric cultures included the Selkirk and Blackduck Cree, who also made pottery, beginning about 1,500 years ago. Selkirk ceramics are fabric impressed.

Names of contemporary Indian tribes bear little relationship to aboriginal nomenclature or political organization. In general, the basic unit was the local group, which generally consisted of from 10 to 20 related people but could be up to 75 or so. Membership was fluid and nonbinding, in deference both to values of autonomy and the need for flexibility in a difficult environment. Leadership was extremely informal and nonauthoritarian, with the exception of those groups most influenced by Northwest Coast cultures. When conditions permitted, probably not quite every summer, local groups might come together as loosely constructed regional bands of several hundred people to socialize and renew family ties.

In parts of the Cordillera, the memorial potlatch was a major ceremonial event. Consisting of public celebration as well as ritual display of crests and distribution of wealth, it was used to enhance rank when the fur trade generated greater wealth. Even so, chiefs were recognized only among their own clan or lineage. Despite official opposition by non-natives in the nineteenth century, potlatches actually grew in importance.

Warfare was generally a local matter. Although some groups sought women, most people fought over revenge for trespass or a prior blood transgression. Warfare was better developed in the far west than in other regions. Weapons there included antler clubs soaked in grease, armor, and spears as well as the bow and arrow. Nowhere did large, regional groups conduct full-scale wars.

Trade, which occurred at least as early as 10,000 years ago, provided a peaceful reason for travel and human interaction. Both goods and services, such as curing, were exchanged. Most material trade was in animal products. Northwest Coast peoples and Cordillerans exchanged animal products for marine products, including dentalium, salmon, and eulachon oil. Other trade goods included raw materials, such as birch bark, obsidian, copper, fused tuff, and manufactured goods, such as birch-bark containers, snowshoes, baskets, and clothing. Ancient trade also existed between Alaska and Asia. Except for the western Cordillera and Alaska Plateau, the existence of large, multitribal trade fairs remains a matter of speculation.

Religious conceptions and ceremonial innovation varied considerably throughout the Subarctic. Nearly everyone believed in the existence of various natural powers. In order to tap into those powers, they fasted, dreamed, and/or held vigils to attract guardian spirits, mainly animal related, that might provide individual assistance. Respect for all nature, especially animals and particularly food animals, was a key part of Subarctic religion and ceremonialism, as was a belief in reincarnation. Most groups had also formulated rich mythologies as well as conceptions of malevolent supernatural beings that were greatly to be feared.

Illness was generally associated with soul loss. Cures might be effected by shamans, men and/or women with particularly strong spirit powers. Shamans were also said to be able to find lost things, including game, and to foretell the future. Their methods included scapulimancy, or looking at burn marks on an animal's shoulder blade, and communing with spirits in a shaking tent. Most people believed that shamans could also use their powers for ill.

Since the entire Subarctic is north of the limits of native agriculture, people fed themselves by hunting, fishing, and, to a variable extent, gathering berries and other plant foods. Unfortunately, many groups depended on a single species, such as moose or caribou, for the bulk of their diet. When game was plentiful this practice was not a problem, but since the population of key resources was subject to natural fluctuation, groups regularly suffered hunger and even starvation.

Caribou were often captured by means of large surrounds or corrals or were driven through fence systems into lakes, where they were shot. They were also stalked and snared, as were moose. In the extreme north, people brought firewood, tent stakes, and canoes out onto the Barren Grounds for the summer caribou hunt, thanks mainly to the strength and endurance of women. Fowl and smaller animals, such as hare, marmot, beaver, and muskrat, were also snared and shot. People caught fish with a variety of devices, depending on location, such as nets, traps, gaffs, hooks, and weirs. Coastal people relied also on sea mammals and shellfish. In the west, some groups, such as the Beaver, even hunted buffalo.

Subarctic natives generally used animal parts as well as wood, bark, roots, and stone (including, in some areas, native copper) as their raw materials. With a limited local tool kit, many groups borrowed liberally from neighbors, such as Northwest Coast Indians or Inuit. One key item, especially in the west, was babiche, or semisoftened rawhide. This material was used for everything from snares to netting to bowstrings. Although overland travel was preferred, the people did build bark canoes and, in some cases, moose-hide boats. They used bark, skin, or woven roots to make containers, including those that held water. In a successful effort to encourage certain microhabitats and environments, many Subarctic Indians also practiced controlled burning.

Shelter was remarkably homogeneous across the region. The most common type was the domed or conical lodge, consisting of poles covered with skins, boughs, or birch bark. Groups nearest Northwest Coast people built plank houses. Some northwestern groups built frame houses partially below the earth, using earth and moss as insulating materials, as well as bark-covered rectangular houses at fishing camps. Some groups used shelters with a double A-ridgepole framework and containing multiple fires. Drying racks, sweat houses, caches, menstrual huts, and other structures were also commonly built.

Women generally made the clothing, which came from moose, caribou, hare, or other skins, with trim of beaver or other fur. Winter items, such as parkas, hats, and mittens, were also made of fur. Hides were tanned, generally with brains or grease, and often dehaired. Many people wore leggings with attached moccasins. Clothing was variously decorated with fringe, paint, quills, claws, or down.

The general status of women varied according to local custom. Female infanticide was not unknown throughout much of the region. Women were generally subject to menstrual taboos, some quite rigorous. Some served essentially as pack animals while getting little to eat. On the other hand, benefiting from a general tradition of autonomy, some also attained both authority and power.

In this harsh climate, generosity and good humor were two key virtues. In most societies, newly married men were required to live with and serve their in-laws for a period of at least a year before establishing their own households. Descent was generally matrilineal,

although this custom was neither important nor rigorously followed. Corpses were often cremated.

Indians living in the extreme east and southeast of the region may have encountered Vikings a thousand years ago. They certainly met Basques, Bretons, and other Europeans fishing in the Gulf of St. Lawrence around 1500. Indians of the interior Cordillera, however, did not actually encounter non-natives until the early to mid–nineteenth century, although items of non-native manufacture had reached them much earlier through aboriginal trade networks. The fur trade became the basis of interracial relations. The Hudson's Bay Company was chartered in 1670 and the Northwest Company in 1787. The two merged in 1821. Russian trade forts were founded in Alaska as early as the 1780s.

Throughout the region, the non-native presence profoundly affected Indians in several ways. Hitherto unknown diseases, such as smallpox, measles, scarlet fever, influenza, and syphilis, not to mention alcoholism and alcohol-related deaths, reduced populations by up to 90 percent or even 100 percent in some locations. Local economies slowly changed from subsistence to trade based, resulting in a decline in native manufacture and an accompanying loss of knowledge. A few more isolated groups rejected the attraction of trade, preferring to maintain their traditional patterns.

Another result of the non-native presence was increased hunger and poor nutrition, as big game dwindled in numbers and items such as white flour and refined sugar increasingly replaced healthy traditional foods. Social and political structures began to change as well in response to the demands of fur traders and, later, non-native governments. Especially in the nineteenth century, missionaries worked to eliminate native customs and beliefs and ultimately Christianized most Subarctic Indians, although, among many groups, traditional beliefs coexist with Christianity to varying degrees. Generosity, reciprocity, and autonomy were increasingly threatened by individualism and dependence.

Among the first actions of the Dominion of Canada (1867) was instituting federal control over First Nations (as Indian bands are called in Canada). Under the various Indian Acts, the Canadian government required the election of band leaders; controlled Indian finances; undermined Indian religion and spirituality; and regulated Indians' movement, mobility, organizing abilities, and their very identity (for instance, Indian women who married non-natives officially lost their Indian "status"). The Indian departments were highly corrupt. Indian land was often alienated by methods that were quasi-legal at best.

The Canadian government signed 11 "numbered" treaties with Indian groups (with the general exception of those living in British Columbia and Yukon Territory) from 1871 to 1921. A common feature was the exchange of land rights for payments and other benefits. Informal groups of Indians accustomed to living near trading posts were officially recorded as fixed, legal bands with chiefs legitimized by the Canadian and U.S. governments. The treaties generally ignored the rights of Métis, or descendants of Indian–non-native unions. The federal and certain provincial governments fought over jurisdictional issues until 1927. Since the United States stopped treating with Indian groups after 1871, the question of land ownership in Alaska remained even nominally unresolved until well after the end of World War II.

By 1900, the numbers of missionaries, construction crews, miners, and other adventurers continued to grow. Railroads and steamboats reached isolated areas. Even groups that retained a nomadic lifestyle tended to congregate around the trading posts for Christian holidays. Indian groups began to use dog teams for winter transport. That development made trapping more efficient, but it also contributed to the sedentary lifestyle by increasing the need for fish (used as dog food). Although still few in number, there were growing job opportunities in industries such as transportation, mining, and forestry.

The 1940s were a watershed in Subarctic native history. The Alaska Highway was completed in 1943. It changed life dramatically for many natives, not least by ushering in a period of severe epidemics. Air service—for example, for medical treatment—to towns and even large cities became widely available. Educational opportunities as well as wide-ranging health and social services increased markedly. About the same time, fur prices collapsed. Seasonal trading post communities turned into permanent villages and towns. Native populations, after generally reaching their nadir in the 1920s, began to grow.

The post–World War II era has also been characterized by the creation of giant mining and hydroelectric projects. Inevitably, the interests of corporations and people have clashed, and the results have been ambiguous at best. For instance, the James Bay and Northern Quebec Agreement of the mid-1970s allowed the massive flooding of Cree lands. Although the people gained unprecedented (for the modern era) control over their internal affairs, they have had to cope with an equally unprecedented loss of territory, widespread pollution, and promises that remain unfulfilled.

Farther west, a proposed pipeline through Indian land spurred heightened consciousness and political unity. The Dene Nation successfully resisted that project and continues to fight for political sovereignty. In Alaska, the Alaska Federation of Natives was founded in 1966. That group was instrumental in passing the 1971 Alaska Native Claims Settlement Act, in which natives traded aboriginal rights for land and money. The people also agreed to subsume their political identities into local and regional corporations, the latter of which have tended to become enmired in legal entanglements. Some villages have Indian Reorganization Act–style governments, whereas others are incorporated or have reservation status. The eleven contemporary Alaskan Athapaskan groups are Ahtena, Han, Holikachuk, Ingalik (Deg Hit'an), Koyukon, Kutchin (Gwich'in), Tanacross, Tanaina (Dena'ina), Tanana, Upper Kuskokwim, and Upper Tanana.

The debates over Quebec independence and related constitutional issues have provided First Nations with an opportunity to press even more strongly for self-government. In fact, this goal has been achieved to a significant extent. Since the 1970s, for instance, schools, including curricula, have come increasingly under the control of local Indian organizations. In the 1980s, sections of the Indian Act dealing with federal control of band membership were repealed. At least in theory, native self-governance is now also the goal of the Canadian government. However, most federal policies are still taken without significant Indian input.

Today, some Subarctic Indians continue to trap, hunt, gather, and fish, although few remain long in the bush. Those who do often depend on snowmobiles and boats with outboard motors to get them where they need to go. Most live in towns and work for wages and/or receive government payments. Job opportunities remain limited. Many native languages survive, but despite efforts to slow or reverse the process, they are increasingly threatened. Electronic communication increasingly removes the younger generations from the world of their grandparents.

The statistical profile of Subarctic Indians shows high mortality rates, inadequate housing, health problems, and other ills. However, in many ways optimism and renewal are taking over. Native-owned businesses are on the rise. Substance-abuse programs are proliferating and are increasingly linked with successful and local social programs. Educational levels are rising sharply. On the crucial issue of sovereignty the people still have an uphill battle, but they are perhaps better prepared—and more willing—to wage that battle than they ever have been before.

Beaver

Beaver, from *Tsattine*, "dwellers among the beaver." Today the people refer to themselves as

Deneza or *Dunne-za,* "Real People." They were culturally similar to the Chipewyan and Sekani.

LOCATION Traditional Beaver territory (in the mid–eighteenth century) is the prairies south of the Peace River and east of the Rocky Mountains and on the upper Peace River (present-day Alberta and British Columbia). They may once also have lived in the Lake Claire area and the upper parts of the Athapaska River.

POPULATION The Beaver population may have been between 1,000 and 1,500 in the seventeenth century. In 1990 there were approximately 800 officially recognized Beaver Indians.

LANGUAGE The Beaver people speak a Northern Athapaskan language.

Historical Information

HISTORY Ancestors of the Beaver were in their historical territory 10,000 years ago. The Beaver and Sekani people may once have been united. By the mid–eighteenth century, Cree Indians, armed with guns, had confined the Beaver to the Peace River basin. At that time, eastern Beaver groups joined the Cree, adopting many of their customs and habits, while western groups moved farther up the Peace River, toward the eastern slopes of the Rocky Mountains. The Sarcee probably branched off from the Beaver about that time as well.

In 1799, the leader Makenunatane (Swan Chief) sought to attract both missionaries and a trading post. The people became more and more involved in the fur trade during the nineteenth century. Catholic missionaries arrived around 1845; most people had accepted Catholicism by about 1900, although many retained a core of their former religious ideas.

Although they had been obtaining arms and other items of non-native manufacture for years, direct contact between the people and non-native traders occurred only in 1876. New foods were introduced, and for the first time the subsistence activities of the people were fundamentally altered. Since some of the Peace River area was arable, non-native farmers began displacing the people as early as the 1890s. The Beaver signed Treaty 8 with Canada in 1899, under which the Indians accepted reserves but retained extensive subsistence rights. Canadian officials began appointing nominal chiefs after that.

In the early twentieth century, some Beaver were raising horses and trapping for a living. By 1930, non-native farmers had settled much of their territory. Construction of the Alaska Highway in the early 1940s disrupted the nomadic life of the last traditional Beaver bands. Oil and gas became major regional industries in the 1950s and 1960s.

RELIGION A well-defined cosmology and mythology were intimately connected with vision quests. Young people fasted to acquire guardian spirits, mainly in dreams. Various food and behavioral taboos, as well as songs and medicine bundles, were associated with a particular animal spirit. The people recognized a spiritual connection between people and animals, with the latter entitled to respect on an equal level with people.

The most important festival took place twice a year and involved the fire sacrifice of food to ensure continued bounty. Dreamers, or prophets—people in touch through dreams with the past and future—had special powers. Shamans were those who had acquired especially powerful guardian spirits. They cured by singing, blowing, and sucking illness-linked objects from the body.

GOVERNMENT Three or four independent bands had their own hunting areas and leaders. Leadership was based on skill and knowledge, which was in turn gained partly through experience and partly through dreaming. Bands were composed of hunting groups of roughly 30 people; the size and composition of the bands were variable. Groups grew in size during summer and broke into constituent parts in winter and early spring.

CUSTOMS Bands occasionally came together in summer to socialize. Festivities consisted in part of group singing and dancing around a fire, during which seating was ritually regulated. The people established a well-defined and close kinship system within which everyone was related on some level. Hunters fed the entire camp based on need. People slept facing east.

Men might have more than one wife. Newlyweds lived with the woman's family and served her parents for a period of time, but descent was patriarchal. Corpses were placed on birch-bark strips and buried in tree scaffolds or on platforms. Mourners gave away their possessions and grieved loudly and publicly. Men often cut their bodies and went to war; women cut their hair as well as part of a finger.

DWELLINGS The typical dwelling was a three-pole conical moose- or caribou-skin tipi. There were also winter lodges of logs covered with moss and earth. In summer, people mainly lived in conical brush shelters or simple lean-tos.

DIET The Beaver were basically nomadic hunters of moose, caribou, beaver, and other animals. Men drove buffalo into enclosures as late as the early nineteenth century. Fish were not an important part of the diet except in emergencies. People also snared smaller animals, such as rabbits, and women gathered berries and other plant food.

KEY TECHNOLOGY Food was often hot-rock boiled in containers of spruce or birch bark or woven spruce roots. Bags were generally made of moose and caribou skins. Bark containers were important as well. Arrowheads were mostly flint, as were knife blades, although people also used moose horn or beaver teeth for this purpose. Fish were caught with rawhide (babiche) line and bone hook, nets, and stone weirs. Hunters used cone-shaped calls to summon moose. Food was served on birch-bark dishes. In order to encourage certain plants and animals, people regularly burned parts of the prairie.

TRADE   Favorite trade locations included Vermilion and the mouth of the Smoky River. Trade partners included the Chipewyan, Slavey, Sekani, and Cree. Buffalo products were a main trade item. In general, the Beaver did not particularly focus on acquiring material goods.

NOTABLE ARTS   The relation of oral tradition was taken very seriously and considered a fine art. Clothing was decorated with porcupine-quill embroidery. The people also made fine bark containers.

TRANSPORTATION   Women drew toboggans before the advent of dog power in the twentieth century. People traveled in spruce-bark and birch-bark canoes as well as on snowshoes.

DRESS   Women made most clothing from moose skin. Clothing consisted of shirts, leggings, fur-lined moccasins, and a knee-length coat. Men added breechclouts after being influenced by the Cree. Women sometimes wore a short apron.

Items of personal adornment included horn and bone bracelets. Hunters wore grizzly bear claws around their necks. Both sexes painted their bodies and wore marmot or hare robes, caps, and mittens in winter.

WAR AND WEAPONS   Weapons were spears and the bow and arrow. The Sekani were occasional enemies, as were the Cree.

Contemporary Information

GOVERNMENT/RESERVATIONS   The Blueberry River (formerly Fort St. John) Band owns two reserves with a total land area of 1,148 hectares. There were 263 members in the mid-1990s, of whom 151 lived on the reserves. The band is affiliated with the Treaty Eight Tribal Council. A chief and councilors are elected according to provisions of the Indian Act.

The Doig River (formerly Fort St. John) Band owns two reserves with a total land area of 1,348 hectares. There were 195 members in the mid-1990s, of whom 94 lived on the reserves. The band is affiliated with the Treaty Eight Tribal Council. A chief and councilors are elected according to provisions of the Indian Act.

The Halfway River Band owns one reserve with a total land area of 3,989 hectares. Band membership in

the mid-1990s was 184, of whom 145 lived on the reserves. A chief and councilors are elected according to provisions of the Indian Act. The band is affiliated with the Treaty Eight Tribal Council.

The West Moberly First Nations (formerly part of Hudson Hope Band) own one reserve with a total land area of 2,034 hectares. Band membership in the mid-1990s was 116, of whom 69 lived on the reserves. A chief and councilors are elected according to custom. The band is affiliated with the Treaty Eight Tribal Council.

The Saulteau First Nation (Beaver and Cree) owns one reserve with a total land area of 3,026 hectares. Band membership in the mid-1990s was 628, of whom 325 lived on the reserve. A chief and councilors are elected according to custom. The band is affiliated with the Treaty Eight Tribal Council.

Other reserve communities include Clear Hills, Horse Lakes, Child Lake, and Boyer, all in Alberta. The local town is Fort St. John, British Columbia.

ECONOMY   There is minimal hunting and trapping, but some people work as guides and maintaining roads. At Doig River there is farming and cattle raising, fire fighting, trapping, and road maintenance. At Halfway River there is seasonal work, farming, trapping, guiding, forestry, and fire fighting. West Moberly offers logging, trapping, and a backhoe business, and at Saulteau there is a cattle ranch and farm, forestry, and a gravel operation.

LEGAL STATUS   The bands listed under "Government/Reservations" are provincially and federally recognized. Legal action continues on Canada's attempt to remove a key parcel of land from Beaver control.

DAILY LIFE   The ancient prophet tradition has waned in recent years, although dreamers' songs remain the basis for much ceremonialism as well as an important part of the summer gatherings known as Treaty 8 Days. The Alaska and Mackenzie Highway has separated the Beavers of Alberta and British Columbia from one another. Most younger people are literate in English, although Beaver remains the first language for most.

Effective rule by Indian agents came to an end in the 1980s, when the people began to administer their own affairs through such organizations as the Treaty Eight Tribal Association. Children attend band and/or provincial and/or private schools. Most people have high school educations. In general, housing and social services are considered adequate.

Blueberry River Band facilities include a cultural center, a drop-in center, offices, and a school. Doig River facilities include offices, a community hall, a store, a kindergarten, and a garage. Halfway River facilities include offices, a community hall, a school, and a store. West Moberly facilities include offices and a community center. Saulteau's facilities include offices, a community hall, and a healing center.

Carrier

Carrier, from the French *Porteur,* originally from a Sekani word referring to the custom among certain bands for widows to carry their dead husbands' bones on their backs in a birch-bark container. They called themselves *Takulli* ("People Who Go upon the Water") in the nineteenth century, apparently a word given to them from without. The people usually refer to themselves by the subtribe or band name.

The Carrier were strongly influenced by Northwest Coast tribes and were culturally similar to the Sekani and the Chilcotin. They are sometimes located by anthropologists in the Plateau culture area (see Chapter 5).

LOCATION Carrier territory is the region of Eutsuk, Francis, Babine, and Stuart Lakes and the upper Skeena and Fraser Rivers in north-central British Columbia.

POPULATION From perhaps 8,500 in the late eighteenth century, the Carrier population in the mid-1990s stood at about 9,800.

LANGUAGE Carriers spoke dialects (lower, central, and upper) of a northern Athapaskan language.

Historical Information

HISTORY The Carrier may have originated east of the Rocky Mountains and were probably in their historic location for at least several centuries before contact with non-natives. Major epidemics began in the late eighteenth century, about the time they met the Scotch trader and explorer Alexander Mackenzie (1793).

Beginning in the late eighteenth century, the Carrier began to acquire iron and other items of non-native manufacture, first through coastal intermediaries such as the Gitksan (north) and Bella Coola (south) and then directly. With the growing value of interior animal (beaver, marten, and lynx) pelts, Carrier wealth increased with their ability to export these products. Carrier control of some local trade networks in the early nineteenth century allowed some chiefs to amass wealth and power. Some high-ranking people began to intermarry with Bella Coola and Gitksan families around this time, as Northwest Coast cultural influences became much more pronounced.

The first local trade fort (James) was built in 1806 at Stuart Lake. A quasi-Christian prophet movement arose among the Carrier beginning in the 1830s. An entire band was exterminated by smallpox in 1837. Catholic missionaries arrived in the 1840s. Penetra-

tion by miners, farmers, and ranchers from the mid–nineteenth century on led to increased disease and general problems for the Indians.

Another ramification of increased contact was the decline of the potlatching complex. Retention of material goods became more important than status gained by giving them away. Also, there was a growing need to accumulate items of non-native manufacture just to survive, so giving them away became difficult. The Catholic church also worked to eliminate potlatching

Wage work, such as ranch, guide, cannery, sawmill, and construction work, began to take the place of traditional subsistence activities. The Carrier were prevented by law from preempting land after 1866. The Canadian Pacific Railway, completed in 1885, bisects Carrier territory. Most reserves were created in the later nineteenth century, although additional ones were established in the early twentieth century. Subsistence activities were increasingly government regulated by then.

Another railway line, completed in 1914, led to an influx of settlers and speculators. Commercial mining and lumbering began in the early twentieth century. Lumbering, including clear-cutting, expanded sharply after World War II. In the 1970s, the Carrier began organizing politically over the chronically unresolved issues of native land title and rights.

RELIGION Traditional religious belief may have included recognition of a supreme deity in the sky. Most important were a host of supernatural beings, mostly animal based, with whom the people tried to communicate through fasting and dreams. Through their rituals, the people sought to gain the favor and power of these spiritual beings. The people also believed in life after death, perhaps in a land to the west. Some especially Tsimshian-influenced groups adopted a secret cannibal society.

Young men fasted and dreamed in remote places in an effort to attract a guardian spirit protector (optional in southern regions). Those with special power became shamans. These people could cure illness, although they themselves might be killed if a patient died. Shamans could also retrieve lost souls and forecast the future. Their gear included carved wooden masks, wood rattles, grizzly bear claw and beaver tooth necklaces, and cloaks.

GOVERNMENT Each of roughly 15 independent subtribes/regional bands was composed of one or more villages/local bands. The subtribes were associated with specific subsistence areas. In the south, leaders were heads of extended families who acted as spokesmen and subsistence coordinators. Shamans were also politically important in the south.

Roughly 20 hereditary matrilineal clans were the

most important political unit in central and northern areas. They were divided into houses, which had hereditary chiefs who supervised subsistence areas, provided for the poor, and represented clan interests in councils.

Hereditary chiefs of up to five larger divisions came from constituent clans. These people controlled the various subsistence areas within the division and settled disputes. Hereditary village chiefs were leaders of the most important divisions. They consulted other leaders, such as the clan leaders within their division and the other divisional chiefs, before making important decisions.

CUSTOMS Society was divided into ranked, hereditary social classes of nobles, commoners, and a few slaves. Depending on specific location, descent could be through the mother's or father's line. Except on the Tsimshian border, commoners had the possibility of obtaining sufficient goods to give potlatches and attain the noble rank. The nobility had crests and defined privileges, such as specific seating at dances or the right to recount certain stories. Crests were displayed on totem poles, houses, and regalia. Crests, titles, and honors were considered clan property and could usually be bought and sold. These customs varied according to geographical location and the customs of neighboring tribes.

Trespass was considered a serious offense, but chiefs could often work out an arrangement or decide on appropriate compensation. The extended family was the main social and economic unit. Several related families made up a band, which might have one or more villages.

Potlatching occurred in the north. Feasts were given and presents distributed at important life-cycle events. The installation of a new chief was considered the most important occasion of all, requiring numerous potlatches. The entire potlatch complex became especially important from the late eighteenth century through the late nineteenth century.

Women were responsible for most domestic tasks, such as carrying water and firewood, cooking, tanning skins, and sewing clothing. Men made houses, tools, and weapons; fought; and acquired animal foods. Women gave birth in a specially constructed hut assisted by their husbands and/or other women. Names were taken from a hereditary stock, if available, or from dreams if not.

At adolescence, boys were encouraged to increase their level of physical activity, whereas girls were secluded and their activity restricted for up to two years. They were subject to numerous food and behavioral taboos and were considered marriageable after the end of their seclusion. Young women selected a mate with their parents' assistance. The

couple was engaged after the man gave valuable items to his prospective mother-in-law and married after the couple spent the night together at a later date. They lived with the woman's parents for up to a year while the new husband helped provide for his new in-laws.

Corpses were cremated. Widows were expected to hold their husband's burning body for as long as they could. In the east, women carried the charred bones of their husbands on their backs for several years.

DWELLINGS Semipermanent villages served as bases for hunting and fishing expeditions. Rectangular winter houses were built of pole frames covered with spruce bark. Gabled roofs extended to the ground. These houses held several families. Some southern groups built underground winter lodges similar to those of the Chilcotin and Shuswap.

Summer houses had low, plank walls and plank or bark gabled roofs. Some high-status men carved their crests into house pillars. Chiefs and their extended families lived in particularly large, semicommunal houses. There were also specialty menstrual, fishing, sweat, and smoking structures.

DIET Fish, especially salmon, was perhaps the most important item in the diet, although this was less true in the south. People fished through the ice for carp and other species. Fish was smoke dried and cached. Before the snow fell, men hunted caribou, mountain goats, and bear as well as smaller game such as beaver, marmot, and hare. Women gathered a number of roots, bulbs, greens, and berries.

KEY TECHNOLOGY Cooking vessels were made of birch bark. To capture animals, men used bows with sinew strings; babiche nets; several types of snares, some strong enough to capture big game; and deadfalls. Caribou were also driven along fences into corrals. People fished using weirs, traps, wooden rakes, willow and alder bark and nettle-fiber nets, hooks, and harpoons. Wood was an important raw material, as were bone and hide. Pestles and axes were among the few stone tools. Fire was made with the fire drill.

TRADE Important trade partners included the Gitksan and Bella Coola. The Carrier imported woven baskets from the Bella Coola, Chilcotin, and Shuswap; Chilkat blankets, cedar boxes, and stone labrets from the Tsimshian; and wooden cooking boxes, eulachon oil, shell ornaments, and copper bracelets from other coast tribes. There was also some intratribal trade. The people mainly exported prepared hides and furs.

NOTABLE ARTS Crests were carved, painted, and tattooed on house posts, graves, clothing, and bodies. Some groups erected totem poles.

TRANSPORTATION Men made spruce- and birch-bark canoes as well as cottonwood dugouts. Goods were carried overland with the help of tumpline and backpacks. Snowshoes and toboggans arrived with the non-natives.

DRESS   Skin clothing consisted of robes, leggings, and moccasins, with fur caps and mittens added in colder weather. In warm weather, men sometimes went naked; women wore a knee-length apron. High-status men wore Chilkat blankets for special occasions, and similarly ranked northern women wore wooden labrets in their mouths. Other ornaments were made of dentalium, bone, and haliotis shell.

WAR AND WEAPONS   Weapons included the bow and arrow, spear, club, and knife. Some groups had "armor" made of wooden slats or moose hide covered with small pebbles; others used oval shields and a bow "bayonet."

Contemporary Information

GOVERNMENT/RESERVATIONS   The Broman Lake Band owns 11 reserves with a total land area of 620 hectares. There were 144 members in the mid-1990s, of whom 69 lived on the reserves. A chief and councilors are elected according to custom. The band is affiliated with the Carrier-Sekani Tribal Council.

The Burns Lake Band owns four reserves with a total land area of about 170 hectares. Band population was 72 in the mid-1990s, of whom 25 lived on the reserves. A chief and councilors are elected according to provisions of the Indian Act. The band is affiliated with the Carrier-Sekani Tribal Council.

The Cheslatta Carrier Nation owns eight reserves with a total land area of 1,403 hectares. Population was 218 in the mid-1990s, 89 of whom lived on the reserves. A chief and councilors are elected according to custom. The nation is affiliated with the Carrier-Sekani Tribal Council.

The Hagwilget Band owns two reserves with a total land area of 168.8 hectares. Population was 575 in the mid-1990s, of whom 207 lived on the reserves. A chief and councilors are elected according to provisions of the Indian Act. The band is affiliated with the Gitksan Wet'suwet'en Local Services Society.

The Kluskus Band owns 17 reserves with a total land area of 1,653 hectares. Population was 150 in the mid-1990s, of whom 68 lived on the reserves. A chief and councilors are elected according to custom. The band is affiliated with the Carrier-Chilcotin Tribal Council.

The Moricetown Band population was 1,437 in the mid-1990s, of whom 674 lived on the reserves. A chief and councilors are elected according to provisions of the Indian Act. The band is affiliated with the Gitksan Wet'suwet'en Local Services Society.

The Nadleh Whuten (formerly Fraser Lake) Band owns seven reserves with a total land area of 966 hectares. Population was 338 in the mid-1990s, of whom 197 lived on the reserves. A chief and councilors are elected according to provisions of the Indian Act. The band is affiliated with the Carrier-Sekani Tribal Council.

The Nak'azdli (formerly Necoslie) Band owns 16 reserves with a total land area of 1,460 hectares. Population was 1,333 in the mid-1990s, of whom 545 lived on the reserves. A chief and councilors are elected according to custom. The band is affiliated with the Carrier-Sekani Tribal Council.

The Nazko Band owns 18 reserves with a total land area of 1,844 hectares. Population was 261 in the mid-1990s, of whom 232 lived on the reserves. A chief and councilors are elected according to provisions of the Indian Act. The band is affiliated with the Carrier-Chilcotin Tribal Council.

The Nee-tahi-buhn (Moricetown) Band owns seven reserves with a total land area of 1,421 hectares. Population was 192 in the mid-1990s, of whom 66 lived on the reserves. A chief and councilors are elected according to custom. The band is affiliated with the Gitksan Wet'suwet'en Local Services Society.

The Red Bluff (formerly Quesnel) Band owns four reserves with a total land area of 683 hectares. Population was 109 in the mid-1990s, of whom 58 lived on the reserves. A chief and councilors are elected according to provisions of the Indian Act. The band is affiliated with the Carrier-Chilcotin Tribal Council.

The Stellat'en First Nation owns two reserves with a total land area of 834 hectares. Population was 297 in the mid-1990s, of whom 196 lived on the reserves. A chief and councilors are elected according to custom. The band is affiliated with the Carrier-Sekani Tribal Council.

The Stony Creek Band owns ten reserves with a total land area of 3,236 hectares. Population was 706 in the mid-1990s, of whom 433 lived on the reserves. A chief and councilors are elected according to provisions of the Indian Act. The band is affiliated with the Carrier-Sekani Tribal Council.

The Takla Lake Band owns 17 reserves with a total land area of 807 hectares. Population was 496 in the mid-1990s, of whom 254 lived on the reserves. A chief and councilors are elected according to custom.

The Tl'azt'en Nations owns 19 reserves with a total land area of 2,277 hectares. Population was 1,343 in the mid-1990s, of whom 922 lived on the reserves. A chief and councilors are elected according to custom. The band is affiliated with the Carrier-Sekani Tribal Council.

The Ulkatcho Band owns 20 reserves with a total land area of 3,213 hectares. Population was 683 in the mid-1990s, of whom 513 lived on the reserves. A chief and councilors are elected according to custom. The band is affiliated with the Carrier-Chilcotin Tribal Council.

ECONOMY Although fish and game have become much scarcer in recent years, there is still some trapping, fishing, and hunting and also some small farming. Pollution has spawned some opposition to the lumbering industry in spite of employment possibilities. There is also some railroad work and spot and seasonal work in local industries such as ranching, fisheries, and tourism. There are some small businesses. People also avail themselves of government assistance.

LEGAL STATUS The bands listed under "Government/Reservations" are federally recognized tribal entities.

DAILY LIFE Most Carriers today live in individual houses. Many still speak Carrier. Clans exist today, especially among northern and central groups, although they are vastly less important than they used to be. Potlatch privileges and responsibilities are rarely observed except among those groups nearest the Tsimshian people. Most people are Christian, at least nominally, although ancient beliefs linger as well, including the power of dreams and the efficacy of shamans. Children attend band and/or provincial and/or private schools.

Local anti-Indian sentiment remains deeply entrenched. Carrier bands along the Nechako River have strongly opposed the completion of a hydroelectric project, the initial stages of which created forced relocations and other hardships for the people beginning in the 1950s. Struggles also continue over issues such as land title and rights. One example is the development of the so-called Mackenzie Grease Trail, which continues against Indian wishes and portrays them (when they are not ignored entirely) as little more than tourist attractions. Members of the Cheslatta Nation are negotiating with Alcan Aluminum for unflooded portions of their former reserves.

Band facilities include offices and a community center (Broman Lake); offices (Burns Lake); offices, workshops, and a recreation hall (Cheslatta); offices, a community hall, a clinic, a nursery school, and a fire station (Hagwilget); a school (Kluskus); offices, a maintenance yard, a community hall, a fire station, a recreation center, a clinic, a school, and a store (Moricetown); offices, a school, a store, and a community hall (Nadleh Whuten); offices, a gymnasium, a school, a garage, and a crafts store (Nak'azdli); offices, a community hall, a workshop, a warehouse, and a nursery school (Nazko); offices, a community hall, a wood shop, and a fishery research station (Neetahi-buhn); offices, a barn, and a store (Red Bluff); offices and a community hall (Stallat'en); a store, a cultural center, a school, offices, a community hall,

and elders' and adult centers (Stony Creek); offices, a community hall, a clinic, and an elders' center (Takla Lake); schools, clinics, offices, and a community hall (Tl'azt'en Nations); and offices, a store, a dormitory, and a school (Ulkatcho).

Chilcotin

Chilcotin (`Tsil k ō t ə n), "inhabitants of Young Man's River." The Chilcotin were culturally related to the Carrier, the interior Salish tribes, the Bella Coola, and the Kwakiutl. They are occasionally classified among Plateau groups.

LOCATION The territory of the Chilcotin is along the headwaters of the Chilcotin River and the Anahim Lake district and from the Coast Range to near the Fraser River, British Columbia.

POPULATION The Chilcotin population stood at approximately 1,500 in the seventeenth century. It increased to possibly 3,500 in the late eighteenth century. There were about 500 Chilcotins in the mid-1990s.

LANGUAGE Chilcotin is an Northern Athapaskan language.

Historical Information

HISTORY Chilcotins first encountered nonnatives in either 1793 or 1815. Fort Alexandria, a trading post, was established in 1821. A gold strike around the Fraser River around 1860 led to the largescale invasion of Indian lands and widespread destruction of resources, with no compensation. Indian villages and even graves were looted by the newcomers.

There was a serious smallpox epidemic in about 1862. Chilcotins sent out war parties to attack road builders. Several warriors, including Chiefs Tellot, Elexis, and Klatsassin, were captured and hanged. After the epidemics and the fighting, many survivors worked on non-native–owned ranches, since Indians were explicitly excluded from preempting land, and much of their land was confiscated.

Missionaries helped established villages that became reserves. They also significantly influenced the selection of chiefs, or headmen. Some groups merged with the Shuswap and Carrier on the Fraser River at that time. Most were located on three reserves by 1900 and were largely acculturated. "Stonies," or Stone Chilcotin bands, remained semi-traditional in the western mountains. In the early twentieth century, most people hayed and/or sold a few head of cattle or some furs for a living. There was little contact with the outside world until the 1960s.

RELIGION Boys, and girls to some extent, went into seclusion at adolescence to acquire a guardian spirit. Spirits could be any natural phenomenon and gave the person songs and dances as well as protective power. A person who acquired many spirits might become a shaman and engage in curing and seeing what most people could not.

Shamans could use their power for evil as well as good, although evil against an individual was generally considered to be practiced only for the general good. Illnesses that were not soul related were treated by medical specialists. Souls were said to be capable of leaving the body.

GOVERNMENT Three or four autonomous bands were each composed of camp groups. Bands were defined as people sharing a wintering territory. There was no overall leadership, and the people never came or acted together.

CUSTOMS Bands were divided into social classes of nobles, commoners, and slaves. Nobles and commoners were arranged into clans, the most powerful of which was Raven. Descent was bilateral.

Although sharing was highly valued, some people accumulated more material goods than did others. In those cases, the surplus was generally given away—effectively exchanged for prestige—in feasts. High rank was obtained by giving potlatches. When a member of the nobility died, clans gave large potlatches, at which they gave away most of his possessions.

Early adolescence was a time for adult training. Boys focused on endurance and survival skills. Girls were isolated during their first menstrual period, at which time they observed several behavioral restrictions and performed domestic tasks. Marriage occurred shortly after this adult training. Most marriages were arranged by parents with input from the children.

Women generally did all the camp work; men were responsible for getting animal foods, fighting, and making tools. The dead were buried in the ground, cremated, or simply left under a pile of rocks or branches. People amused themselves by playing bone and dice games, snowsnake (sliding a spear along a trench in the snow for distance), ring and arrow, and athletic contests. Social control was largely internalized. Extreme violators were ostracized or, rarely, killed.

DWELLINGS People generally lived in rectangular, pole-framed, earth-covered lodges with bark or brush walls and gable roofs. An open space at the top served as a smoke hole. There were also small, subterranean winter houses and dome-shaped sweat houses.

DIET Men hunted a variety of animals including caribou, elk, mountain goat, sheep, and sometimes bear. Smaller animals like marmots, beaver, and rabbits were trapped, as were fowl. Men and women caught fish such as trout, whitefish, and salmon.

Women gathered camas and other roots as well a variety of berries.

KEY TECHNOLOGY Baskets and water containers were made primarily of birch bark. Women wove rush mats and learned from the Shuswap to make coiled baskets. Fish were taken using a variety of nets and spears. Hunting equipment included the bow and arrow and stone-tipped spear. A digging stick helped women to gather camas and other roots. Food-related equipment included horn spoons, bone knives, and wooden pestles. Other tools, such as scrapers, adzes, and awls, were made mainly of bone and stone. The people also had the fire drill and made drums and flutes.

TRADE Chilcotins acquired salmon from the Shuswap and Bella Coola. They also imported shell ornaments, cedar-bark headbands, wooden containers, and stone pestles from the Bella Coola. They sent dried berries, paints, and furs to the Bella Coola and furs, dentalium shells, and goat-hair blankets woven by the Bella Coola to other tribes. Snowshoes were exported in the later historical period.

NOTABLE ARTS The people made fine coiled basketry with designs of humans and animals as well as geometric shapes.

TRANSPORTATION Although most travel was overland, men carved spruce-bark and dugout canoes, some with pointed prows like those of the interior Salish. Snowshoes were used for winter travel. Goods were carried in skin sacks with tumplines.

DRESS Dress generally consisted of moccasins, buckskin aprons, belts, and leggings. Cold-weather gear included caps; robes of marmot, hare, or beaver; and woven wool and fur blankets. Men's hair was generally no longer than shoulder length, although women grew their hair long and often wore it in two braids. The people used a number of personal ornaments of bone, shell, teeth, and claws. Both men and women painted or tattooed their faces and greased their bodies, face, and hair in cold, windy weather.

WAR AND WEAPONS Weapons included clubs with stone heads, the bow and arrow, spears, and daggers. There was some use of hide or slat armor. Chilcotin enemies included the Carrier and Shuswap, although there was much friendly intercourse as well with these groups. Trespass was a reason to fight, as were murder and feuding. Fighters wore red and black face paint. Ritual purification, including vomiting, took place after a raid. Those who had killed lived apart from others for a time.

Contemporary Information

GOVERNMENT/RESERVATIONS The Alexandria Band owns 13 reserves with a total of 1,142 hectares of land. Band population in the mid-1990s was 135, with 59 living on reserves. The band is affiliated with the Ts'ilhqot'in Tribal Council. A chief and councilors are elected according to provisions of the Indian Act.

The Alexis Creek Tribal Government owns 37 reserves on almost 4,000 hectares of land. Band population in the mid-1990s was 496, with 345 living on reserves. A chief and councilors are elected according to provisions of the Indian Act.

The Stone Band owns five reserves on 2,146 hectares of land. Band population in the mid-1990s was 304, with 189 living on reserves. A chief and councilors are elected according to provisions of the Indian Act. The band is affiliated with the Ts'ilhqot'in National Government.

The Tl'etinqox-t'in Government (formerly the Anaham Band) owns 19 reserves on 5,656 hectares of land. Band population in the mid-1990s was 1,111, with 599 living on reserves. A chief and councilors are elected according to provisions of the Indian Act. The band is affiliated with the Ts'ilhqot'in National Government.

The Toosey Band owns four reserves on 2,582 hectares of land. Band population in the mid-1990s was 201, with 95 living on reserves. A chief and councilors are elected according to provisions of the Indian Act. The band is affiliated with the Carrier-Chilcotin Tribal Council.

The Xeni Gwet'in First Nations Government (formerly the Neneiah Valley Band) owns eight reserves on 1,383 hectares of land. Band population in the mid-1990s was 350, with 259 living on reserves. A chief and councilors are elected according to custom. The band is affiliated with the Ts'ilhqot'in National Government.

ECONOMY The following are important economic activities for the band members: Alexandria Band—farming and forestry; Alexis Creek and Stone Bands—farming, cattle, ranching, and forestry; Tl'etinqox-t'in Government and Xeni Gwet'in First Nations Government—farming, cattle ranching, and trapping; Toosey Band—individual farming and cattle ranching, a heavy equipment company, and trapping.

LEGAL STATUS The bands listed under "Government/Reservations" are recognized by Canada.

DAILY LIFE The westernmost people still cross the mountains to visit the Bella Coola. Public lands containing natural resources from which Chilcotins traditionally derived subsistence have steadily decreased since the 1960s. Children attend various band and/or provincial and/or private schools. Band facilities include an office (Alexandria Band); offices, a community hall, warehouses, and schools (Alexis Creek Band); a community center, schools, offices, and a fire station (Stone Band); offices, a community hall, schools, a carpentry building, and the Native

Law Center (Tl'etinqox-t'in Government); offices, a community hall, a fire station, and a machine shed (Toosey Band); and offices, a community hall, and a rodeo field (Xeni Gwet'in).

Chipewyan

Chipewyan (Chi pu `w ī an), "pointed skins," from the Cree word *chipwayanewok*, referring to a style of drying beaver skins that left shirts pointed at the bottom. Their self-designation was *Dene*, "the People." Geographical divisions included the Athabaska (Chipewyan proper), Desnedekenade, Ethaneldi (Caribou Eaters), and Thilanottine. The Yellowknife (Tatsanottine) are sometimes considered to be a Chipewyan division. The people were known to the French as Montagnais, not to be confused with the people of eastern Canada.

LOCATION In the early eighteenth century, Chipewyans occupied a huge expanse north of the Churchill River between the Great Slave Lake and Hudson Bay, in present-day Northwest Territories and northern Manitoba, Alberta, and Saskatchewan. In the later eighteenth century they filtered south and west to the Churchill River area and Lake Athabaska. Chipewyan land straddled the northernmost taiga and the southern tundra.

POPULATION There were probably between 4,000–5,000 Chipewyans in the seventeenth century. The 1990 population was approximately 1,000.

LANGUAGE The people spoke an Athapaskan language. The word "Athapascan" is taken from one of their divisions.

Historical Information

HISTORY The Chipewyan may have originated in the Rocky Mountains. The Hudson's Bay Company forced an uneasy truce between Chipewyans and Crees to their south in 1715, although fighting remained intermittent for another 45 years. In 1717, the Hudson's Bay Company established a post at Churchill in Chipewyan territory.

The Chipewyan soon acquired firearms, after which time they expanded north at the expense of the coast Inuit. They also harassed the Dogrib and the Yellowknife by excluding them from the fort, cheating them of goods, and kidnapping women. Chipewyans generally served as intermediaries in the fur trade between the British and the Yellowknife and Dogrib until their monopoly was ended in the late eighteenth century. Chipewyans such as the guides Thanadelther and Matonabbee helped non-natives explore the northland.

The people suffered a mortality rate of up to 90 percent in a 1781 smallpox epidemic. Survivors continued to trade at Fort Chipewyan, a closer North West Company fort, after 1788. Some groups moved into the boreal forest, where there were more fur-bearing animals, but in so doing they gave up their traditional dependence on the caribou.

Their subsequent lives were characterized by dependence on non-native goods and poor health caused by malnutrition and disease. Missionaries worked among them from the mid–nineteenth century. They accepted reserves and five-dollar per capita annuities in treaties signed from 1876 through 1906. Log cabin settlements were established in the 1920s. The post–World War II era saw increased school attendance, better health care, and the spread of social services among the people. In the 1960s, forcible relocation brought severe disruption to the most traditional group, the Caribou Eaters.

RELIGION Communication with the spirit world through dreams and visions provided success in hunting and other activities. Owing to the harsh environment there were no herbal curers: All illness was considered a function of witchcraft, and shamans, by virtue of their spirit powers, acted as curers. After death, only good souls were said to inhabit an island full of game.

GOVERNMENT There were many autonomous bands of various sizes within each division. Regional bands (at least 200–400 people) came together during caribou migration periods and broke into smaller local bands (perhaps 50 or so people) at other times. Bands were associated with particular subsistence areas. Leaders had little or no authority beyond an immediate activity such as hunting or war.

CUSTOMS When families met after the winter, they generally sat apart and listened to the old people tell about the recent deaths and problems. After the women wailed in mourning, the groups exchanged greetings. Men were named after seasons, animals, or places, but women's names always included the word for "marten."

In general, weaker men were at the mercy of the stronger, and women fared worst of all. They were separated from boys around late childhood, did most of the hardest work, and were the first to go without food in lean times. Women were segregated during their first menstrual periods and on subsequent occasions were subjected to behavioral taboos. Women were married at the onset of adolescence, often to considerably older men.

Good hunters had more than one wife. Old and/or sick people were often abandoned to starve to death. The dead were generally left on the ground. When someone died, their property was destroyed. Widows cut off their hair and observed a yearlong mourning period. Games of chance, such as ring and pin and the hand game, were popular.

DWELLINGS People lived in temporary encampments in open country in summer and in the woods in winter. Dwellings were conical caribou-skin tents with a smoke hole at the top. Spruce boughs and caribou skins served as floors. The tipis were semi-insulated with snow around the base in winter.

DIET The annual round of subsistence activities revolved around following the caribou, which was the main food for all Chipewyan groups. Caribou were driven into pounds, snared with ropes, and shot from canoes or by men on foot. Men also hunted buffalo, deer, bear, musk oxen, and moose. Some groups mixed dried meat with fat to make pemmican, which they stored in caribou intestines. Otherwise, meat was eaten boiled, roasted, smoked, and raw (the latter possibly learned from the Inuit).

The people also snared and trapped small game and fowl. They fished for trout, whitefish, and pike. Most fish were smoked or sun dried. There were also some plant foods, such as moss and lichen (the latter generally eaten fermented in an animal's stomach).

KEY TECHNOLOGY Men hunted with spears and birch bows with arrows and babiche strings. Caribou were often hunted by means of a chute and pound up to a mile or more in circumference, within which snares were set. Fishing equipment included babiche nets, wooden and stone weirs, spears, clubs, and bone hooks.

Most tools were of stone and bone. The use of copper for tools such as hatchets, awls, knives, and arrow and spearheads probably came from the Yellowknife people. Water could be stone boiled in birch-bark and caribou-skin pots. The Chipewyan language contains counting systems. Moss was used for baby diapers. The people also made drums.

TRADE Birch-bark items were acquired from the Cree. The people also imported shell, including dentalium, mainly for decorative purposes. There was some trade in copper in the late prehistoric period. Trade chiefs ("captains") emerged in the mid–eighteenth century.

NOTABLE ARTS The people made relatively crude wood paintings. They also used porcupine quills and moose hair to decorate clothing and bags, often with complex designs.

TRANSPORTATION Birch-bark and spruce-bark canoes served as river transport. Snowshoes made from summer tent poles featured right and left sides. Women dragged heavy toboggans in winter and served as pack animals in summer, carrying goods, food, and skins on their backs. Dogs were not widely used as pack animals until the twentieth century.

DRESS Well-tanned caribou-skin clothing consisted of shirts, leggings (sometimes joined to moccasins), breechclouts (men), dresses (women), caps, and mittens. Caribou robes were hooded and trimmed with fur. The hair on the hides was shaved off in summer but left on and worn on the inside in winter. Children wore body suits of rabbit skin. People tattooed their faces with parallel lines on the cheek. Women wore their hair very long. Some men wore beards.

WAR AND WEAPONS Enemies were often massacred, although afterward the murderers underwent numerous purification rites. Enemies included the Cree and Inuit. Weapons included shields painted with fighters' spirit symbols.

Contemporary Information

GOVERNMENT/RESERVATIONS There are currently five reserves in Alberta, six in Saskatchewan, two in Manitoba, and two in the Northwest Territories. The total reserve land base is about 337,000 acres. Bands include Barren Lands, Churchill, Cold Lake, English River, Fond du Lac, (Fort) Chipewyan, Fort McKay, Fort McMurray, Janvier, Lac le Hache, Peter Pond Lake, Portage, LaRoche, Resolution, Snowdrift, Stony Rapids, and Yellowknife.

ECONOMY There is some commercial fishing and sporadic wage labor. Hunting and trapping are still important. Many people depend on government annuities and payments.

LEGAL STATUS The bands listed under "Government/Reservations" are federally and/or provincially recognized tribal entities.

DAILY LIFE Hunting, fishing, and trapping remain important activities, although the bands live in permanent village of log or frame houses. Most people are at least nominal Christians. Most people still speak Chipewyan as their first language. Some groups have moved from the more settled communities they were forced to inhabit back to more traditional areas, mainly to be closer to caribou.

Cree

Cree (Kr ē), from *Kristeneaux,* a French word for the name (possibly Kenistenoag) of a small Cree band. The self-designation is *Ininiw,* "person," or, among the Woodland Cree, *Nehiyawak,* "those who speak the same language"; *Atheneuwuck,* "People"; or *Sackaweé-thinyoowuk,* "Bush People." Crees are commonly divided into Woodland (or Western Woods) Cree (west) and Muskegon (from *Omaskekow*), Swampy, or West Main Cree (east). Another division, the Plains Cree, is described in Chapter 6. (*See* Naskapi/Montagnais; *see also* Anishinabe [Chapter 8]). The East Cree, who live just east of James Bay, are generally regarded as being a division of the Naskapi/Montagnais (Innu). Cree speakers whose territory included land northwest of Quebec and Trois Rivières are known as Tête-de-Boule, or

Attikamek. It should be noted, however, that all such labels are spurious and that originally such groups consisted of autonomous groups or "nations."

Three divisions make up the Woodland Cree: Rocky Cree, Western Swampy Cree, and Strongwoods Cree. Information about the traditional lives of these people should be considered sketchy and incomplete. There may also have been a fourth group, the Athabaska-Cree. Traditional Swampy Cree bands include Abitibi, Albany, Attawapiskat, Monsoni, Moose River (Mousousipiou), Nipigon, Piscotagami, Severn, Winisk, and Winnipeg.

LOCATION Around 1700, the Cree lived from south of James Bay westward into eastern Alberta, north to around Fort Churchill and Lake Athabaska, and south to a line running roughly from just north of Lake of the Woods to the Lesser Slave Lake. Swampy Cree land was roughly the easternmost 330 kilometers of this territory, including a considerable portion of coastline along James and Hudson Bays.

By about 1800, the people lived from Labrador in the east to Lubicon Lake in the west (includes the East Cree; *see* Naskapi/Montagnais), north almost to the Great Slave Lake, and south into North Dakota and Montana (includes Plains Cree; *see* Chapter 6).

Today, there are Cree reserves in practically all of this area. There are also Cree or Iroquois/Cree communities near Edmonton, Alberta, and in the Rocky Mountain foothills. These groups are descended from people who acted as guides for the fur companies.

POPULATION There were at least 20,000 Crees in the sixteenth century and at least 120,000 in the mid-1990s. Most Crees live in Ontario and Quebec.

LANGUAGE Crees spoke dialects of a Central Algonquian language.

Historical Information

HISTORY The Cree and Anishinabe probably share a common origin. Crees have been in their known aboriginal territory for at least 4,000 years. They first encountered non-natives when the Henry Hudson exploration arrived in 1610.

The first trade forts were founded among the Swampy Cree beginning around 1670 and in the west from the mid–eighteenth century on. Crees serving as guides and trappers increased their importance to local fur trade companies. French and Scottish trappers and traders regularly intermarried with Cree Indians. The mixed-race offspring, known as Métis, eventually developed their own culture. Some fought two wars with Canada in the mid– to late nineteenth century over the issues of land rights and sovereignty (*see* Cree, Plains entry in Chapter 6).

In the early trade days (seventeenth century in the east and mid–eighteenth to early nineteenth century in the west), the Indians prospered in part by playing the French and British off against each other. Their acquisition of firearms from the Hudson's Bay Company, as well as the completion of an alliance with the Assiniboine, precipitated a tremendous expansion almost to the Arctic Sea, the Rocky Mountains, and the Red River region. Groups of Crees arriving on the Great Plains, near the end of the seventeenth century, adopted many elements of classic Plains culture, especially including dependence on the buffalo.

Jesuit missionaries began working among the Swampy Cree for a short time in the late seventeenth century. The region was devoid of missionaries, however, from then until 1823, when the Church of England established a presence. By 1717, the Swampy Cree had become dependent on non-native traders for necessities such as cloth, blankets, and even food, in addition to trade goods. New foods included sugar and flour; alcohol and tobacco were also valued. Many traditional customs changed or disappeared during the trade period.

The people were devastated by smallpox in the early 1780s. Survivors succumbed to alcohol and were often attacked by enemies, including the Blackfeet Confederacy. Furthermore, the Cree's strong trade position led to overtrapping as well as depletion of the moose and caribou herds by the early nineteenth century. Although the effects were partially offset by the Indians' growing dependence on items of non-native manufacture, these trends combined to shrink the Indians' land base. Also about that time, western Crees, now using an iron chisel and moving on dogsleds, began taking more of an interest in fishing.

When the Hudson's Bay Company and the North West Company merged in 1821, many Cree began to abandon their traditional nomadic lives in favor of settlement at or near trade posts. Eventually, all-Indian communities arose in these areas. There was a second devastating smallpox epidemic in 1838. The people never fully recovered from this event. Severe tuberculosis and influenza epidemics struck in the early twentieth century as well.

Heavy missionary activity began in the mid–nineteenth century. Most Indians were at least nominally Christian by the mid–twentieth century, although many western groups retained a core of traditional beliefs and practices. In the mid–nineteenth century, northern and eastern groups adopted a missionary-devised syllabary that soon gained wide acceptance. Parallel to this development was the elimination of practically all traditional religion in favor of the Churches of Rome and England.

The treaty and reserve period began in the 1870s. People began slowly to settle into all-native log cabin communities, and the election of chiefs was made mandatory in the 1920s. Although their land and resources were being gradually but steadily whittled away, Crees were able to use their land in at least a semitraditional way well into the twentieth century.

After World War II, however, many Swampy Crees, their land essentially trapped out, began working in local cities and towns such as Moosonee and Churchill. Many Woodland Crees altered their lives fundamentally for the first time, attending school, using non-native medicine, accepting government financial assistance, and becoming connected to the outside world via road and air links. The advent of relatively extensive roads and rail lines in the 1950s and 1960s, as well as the expansion of the forestry industry, greatly increased pollution. At the same time there was a dramatic reduction in game animals. In 1975, the eastern Cree and Inuit ceded over 640,000 square kilometers of land to the James Bay Hydroelectric Project, in exchange for promises of hundreds of millions of dollars and various other provisions.

RELIGION Woodland Crees believed in the ubiquitous presence of Manitou, the great spirit power. Some coastal people also believed in a number of powerful creatures such as dwarfs and cannibalistic giants (Windigo). Some groups may have had the Midewiwin, which they probably borrowed from the Anishinabe.

Adolescents fasted and secluded themselves to obtain dream visions; the guardian spirits that they obtained in these visions were said to provide luck. Secret religious societies were dedicated to propitiating animal spirits. Special ceremonies followed the killing of a bear. Shamans, or conjurers, wielded much authority, in part because of the general fear that they would use their powers for evil purposes (sorcery). Several degrees of shaman were recognized. Their legitimate functions were to divine the future and cure illness. The latter activity was often associated with a "shaking tent" ritual. Both men and women could become shamans. (Herbalists also cured illness.)

GOVERNMENT Small local bands, consisting of several extended families, were the basic political units. Bands remained separated during all but the summer season, at which time they united on lake shores for ceremonies and councils. Band membership was fluid, and the bands probably had no clearly defined hunting territories. All groups were politically autonomous.

During the summer gatherings, temporary regional bands were led by chiefs. Band leaders had no explicit power; their authority was based on merit as well as the possession of spiritual power. In the contact period, specialty chiefs, who might have been band leaders, took charge of trade among their people.

CUSTOMS   In the west, local band chiefs might have as many as seven wives. Parents had a great deal of influence regarding their childrens' mates. Girls were often married before they reached puberty. Newly married men worked for their wives' parents for a period of time. Among the eastern people, divorce was easily obtained. Men might temporarily exchange their wives with others and/or "lend" them to strangers as an act of hospitality, although adultery by the wife was severely punished.

Babies kept on cradle boards used diapers of dried moss. Both twins were not permitted to live: If twins were of both sexes, the girl was killed (infant girls may have been killed under other circumstances as well). Children were generally raised with great affection and without physical punishment. Girls were subjected to isolation and a number of behavioral restrictions during and immediately following their first menstrual periods; a feast was held when a young man killed his first big game.

Widows and orphans were protected by the group. Death was not generally feared, and the very old or sick were often abandoned or killed. Corpses were wrapped in bark and buried in the ground or on a scaffold. Some weapons and tools were placed on the grave. The people held an annual feast of the dead.

Murder was avenged by relatives. Crees were forced into cannibalism during periods of starvation. They learned tobacco smoking from people of the St. Lawrence valley, and this custom became important among some groups. Eastern games included cup-and-pin, football, lacrosse, and string figures. All groups also held numerous athletic contests and games of skill. Singing and dancing occurred both socially and for luck (as in hunting).

DWELLINGS   Toward the south, the people lived in conical or dome-shaped birch-bark wigwams with a three-pole foundation. Farther north and west, the lodges were covered with pine bark or caribou, elk, or moose skin. They sheltered extended families of ten or more people.

Floors were sometimes partially excavated. Doors faced south. Some groups also built rectangular bark- or skin-covered lodges with two fires inside. There were also sweat lodges, used in curing and for cleanliness, and menstrual lodges as well as various caches and ceremonial pavilions.

DIET   Cree men were considered superb hunters. They targeted caribou, elk, moose, and beaver. They killed bear when they could get them, and hare when they could not. Some southern groups also hunted buffalo. There were many behavioral taboos and customs designed to mollify spirits related to the hunt.

Every hunter carried his personal medicine pouch, and hides were often painted with red stripes and dots.

Meat was generally stone boiled. It was also dried and mixed with fat and berries to make pemmican. Fowl were plentiful, especially in certain areas. Woodland people fished only out of necessity, but Swampy Cree relied on fish such as lake trout, pike, whitefish, and pickerel. People on the coast occasionally ate seals and beluga whales, spearing them with harpoons. Seal fat was often added to meat and fish in the east.

KEY TECHNOLOGY   The primary hunting equipment included bows (strung with bark or babiche) and arrows and spears (fitted with stone, bone, or antler points). Animals were also trapped, snared (willow-bark hare snares were popular,) or caught in deadfalls. Fishing gear (in the east) included bone and spruce hooks, nets, and weirs. Other tools included bone awls and fleshers, stone axes, and beaver tooth chisels.

The people made birch-bark cooking vessels, except in the east, where woven spruce-root or soapstone (around James Bay) pots were used. Some vessels were also made of clay. Other food-related items included carved wood spoons, bowls, and trays.

Some groups used an Inuit-style curved knife for scraping hides, although farther west the women used a Plains-style tool shaped more like a chisel. A balancing stick was used while walking on snowshoes or pulling toboggans. People carved soapstone pipes and made birch-bark moose calls. Cordage came from spruce roots, hide, willow bark, and sinew. Fire was generally kept alive as coals in a birch-bark container.

TRADE   Most trade was local, with groups such as the Chipewyan. The Cree traded in elm-bark bags and assorted birch-bark goods, carved wooden bowls, and food items. As they expanded west, the people began to trade Woodland items for buffalo-derived products. They played an important role in the fur trade, and their acquisition through trade of firearms allowed them to expand their territory greatly.

NOTABLE ARTS   Artistic expression took the forms of fine moose-hair and bird- and porcupine-quill embroidery, carved wood items, and face and body tattooing and painting. Clothing generally contained painted geometric patterns and, later, beaded floral designs. There was some rock painting of both realistic and stylized animals, people, and mythological personages.

TRANSPORTATION   People made birch-bark canoes, toboggans (of juniper in the west), and elongated birch-frame snowshoes. Many groups had horses by the mid–eighteenth century. The people adopted dogsleds beginning in the twentieth century.

DRESS Moose-, caribou-, or elk-skin clothing was often fringed. Clothing generally consisted of breechclouts (belted in the east), shirts, dresses, belts, moccasins (extended in winter), and long leggings. Winter gear included beaver and caribou robes, socks, mittens, and hats as well as woven hare-skin coats and blankets and caribou coats. Women generally tattooed the corners of their mouths and men their entire bodies. Eastern men and women plucked facial hair. Hair was often braided. Cree men, especially, paid close attention to their various hairstyles. Ornaments were worn in pierced ears.

WAR AND WEAPONS Allies included the Assiniboine (Stoney), the Blackfeet Confederacy before about 1800, and the Ojibwa. Enemies included the Blackfeet Confederacy after about 1800, the Gros Ventres, Iroquois, Dakota, and Inuit as well as western Athapaskan tribes.

Contemporary Information

GOVERNMENT/RESERVATIONS Contemporary Swampy Cree bands include Albany, Attawapiskat, Churchill, Fort Severn, Fox Lake, Moose Factory, New Post, Shamattawa, Weenusk, and York Factory.

There were more than 60 official Western Woods Cree bands in 1980 with a total population of over 35,000. However, this information excludes Métis, and there are many "unofficial" bands or groups as well.

There are Cree reserves in Quebec, Ontario, Manitoba, Alberta, and Saskatchewan, Canada. Plains Crees live on the Rocky Boy Chippewa-Cree Reservation, Chouteau and Hill Counties, Montana.

The following are Attikamek reserves in Quebec: Manawan (771.36 hectares; 1,600 people in 1994, of whom 1,378 lived within the territory), Obedjiwan (926.76 hectares; 1,719 people in 1994, of whom 1,536 lived within the territory), and Weymontachie/Coucoucache (2,982.8 hectares; 1,056 people in 1994, of whom 866 lived within the territory). These communities are governed by band councils.

The following Cree communities fall under the aegis of the Grand Council of the Crees (established in 1974), the political voice of the James Bay Crees: Mistissini (1,380.43 square kilometers; 2,445 people in 1994, of whom 2,295 lived within the territory), Waswanipi (598.5 square kilometers; 1,249 people in 1994, of whom 864 lived within the territory), Eastmain (489.53 square kilometers; 483 people in 1994, of whom 432 lived within the territory), Wemindji (512.82 square kilometers; 1,048 people in 1994, of whom 925 lived within the territory), Waskaganish (784.76 square kilometers; 1,832 people in 1994, of whom 1,364 lived within the territory), Chisasibi (1,309.56 square kilometers; 2,715 people in 1994, of whom 2,634 lived within the territory), Nemaska (152.8 square kilometers; 306 people in 1994, of whom 292 lived within the territory), Whapmagootsui (316.2 square kilometers; 581 people in 1994, of whom 563 lived within the territory), and Oujé-Bougoumou (area still to be determined; 559 people in 1994, of whom 390 lived within the territory).

ECONOMY Hunting and fishing are still important. A few people raise horses. Important industries include mining, transportation, logging, and commercial fishing. There is some employment with the James Bay Project. Craftwork, particularly bark baskets made by women, provides some income. People also work in administrative services and programs and receive government subsidies. Unemployment and underemployment are quite high throughout the region.

LEGAL STATUS Federally recognized Cree bands are listed in Appendix 1. The 1984 Cree-Naskapi Act provides for local self-government.

DAILY LIFE In recent years, Crees have attained greater control over local services and resources and the ability to maintain legal pressure on non-native governments. The Cree school system in Quebec is under native control. Perhaps half of all Crees speak their native language. Yet the people face several crises, including the destruction of natural resources, the need for appropriate economic development, and the need to forge a viable relationship with provincial and national governments. Crees still face severe morale problems stemming from over a century of chronic disease, ill treatment at the hands of nonnatives, and a diminished capability to pursue their traditional way of life. Clear- and overcutting of forests have also negatively affected Cree hunting and trapping lands.

The Lubicon Band of Treaty Eight area never received the reserve promised them in 1939. The region around Lubicon Lake, in northern Alberta, is rich in oil. In the 1970s, the band unsuccessfully fought to prevent road construction into the drilling site. By the early 1980s there were hundreds of oil wells in and near the community, creating dangerous levels of pollution.

The band is pressing for compensation for "irreparable damage to their way of life." Once a self-sustaining hunting community, its people now depend on welfare in order to survive. However, two subgroups have settled with the government. The newly created Woodland Cree Band (unrecognized by treaty chiefs) received a reserve of 142 square kilometers and a financial settlement of almost $50 million. The Loon Lake people are negotiating for a $30 million settlement.

The James Bay hydroelectric project was allowed

to proceed in 1972 over the objections of the Grand Council of the Crees. A 1975 agreement called for an Indian cession of over 640,000 square kilometers of land. In exchange, the people were promised a cash settlement of over $230 million and special concessions, including land ownership of over 3,300 square kilometers, subsistence rights on over 20,000 square miles more, and a veto over mineral exploitation.

However, not all of the money was allocated, an epidemic of childhood diarrhea was caused by the pollution of vital water supplies, and Indians are often excluded from many of the better jobs. The final project—the completion of which the Cree still oppose—is expected to affect a land area of over 360,000 square kilometers.

Dogrib

Dogrib, from their self-designation, *Thlingchadinne,* "Dog Flank People," signifying their legendary descent from a dog. The people also call themselves *Done,* "men" or "People." They are culturally related to the Slavey.

LOCATION In the nineteenth and twentieth centuries, Dogribs lived between Great Slave and Great Bear Lakes, Northwest Territories, an area that included both forest and tundra.

POPULATION There were perhaps 1,250 Dogribs in the late seventeenth century. The mid-1990s population was about 3,000.

LANGUAGE Dogrib is a Northeastern Athapaskan language.

Historical Information

HISTORY The people may have come to their historic location from the south and east. They first encountered non-natives in either 1744 or 1771. The first trade posts were built in the 1790s.

The fur trade and provisioning were the dominant economic activities throughout the nineteenth century, during which time the people gradually began settling around trade posts. Fort Rae (1852) marked the first permanent local post and the beginning of extensive contact for most Dogribs with non-natives. Fur trading became much more important at that time, especially after 1900 and the end of the Hudson's Bay Company monopoly. In addition to the usual fur-bearing animals, musk-ox robes were also in demand.

The people suffered severe epidemics from 1859 onward. Most Dogribs had been baptized Catholic by 1870. The first treaty with Canada was signed in 1900. In 1920, the Dogrib stopped accepting government payments as a protest against hunting and fishing restrictions. This issue was resolved when they accepted a special designation, but the signed agreement was later lost.

As part of a 1921 treaty, the leader Monphwi became a "government chief," and band leaders formed an official council. There was a brief local gold rush, at Great Bear Lake, in 1930. The people were largely monolingual and semitraditional through the 1940s.

RELIGION People acquired guardian spirits in dreams. They also made offerings to spirits that inhabited bodies of water. Shamans caused and cured disease and foretold the future.

GOVERNMENT There were traditionally four autonomous bands, or divisions (Lintchanre, Takfwelottine, Tsantieottine, and Tseottine). Band leadership was informal; a chief hunter had helpful spiritual power but little authority. Bands were composed of local hunting groups. Membership in all groups was fluid.

CUSTOMS When a young man killed his first game, his peers would strip him and wish him continued good luck. Only indirect address was considered polite. The people enjoyed games and dancing; the latter was often accompanied by group male singing.

People's names often changed at the birth of their children. Brothers and sisters remained reserved with each other, as did a man with his brother-in-law and father-in-law. Men might have more than one wife, but they were required to serve their new in-laws for a period of time after the marriage. There may have been a practice of wrestling for wives as well as some female infanticide.

The elderly or ill were often abandoned. Streamers attached to burial scaffolds were meant to placate spirits of the dead. Mourners destroyed most of their property, and the women slashed their bodies. A memorial feast was held a year following the death.

DWELLINGS Dogribs lived in conical tipis covered with as many as 40 caribou skins sewn together with sinew or babiche. The sides were covered with snow in winter. There were also some rectangular pole-and-brush winter huts. In the coldest weather, people often slept outside in skin bags to avoid the interior drafts.

DIET Men hunted mainly caribou, which they snared in pounds and speared in lakes, in the forests, and on short trips onto the tundra. They also hunted musk ox, moose, hare and other small game, fowl, and birds. There was some fishing; later, with decreasing game in the nineteenth century, fish gradually assumed a greater importance in the diet. Fish and meat were roasted, stone boiled (in caribou stomach–lined holes), smoked, dried in strips, or mixed with marrow and perhaps berries and made into pemmican.

Women gathered some berries and other plant

foods as well as poplar sap. Food taboos included the weasel, wolf, skunk, and dog.

KEY TECHNOLOGY   Fish were taken with the use of dams, weirs, and willow-bark fishnets. Men hunted with bows and arrows and snares. Food was wrapped in hide and cached on poles or platforms. The main raw materials were caribou parts and wood.

TRADE   The people exported native copper to the Slavey and Yellowknife, among other groups. They also traded in caribou skins, flint, chert, and pyrites as well as Inuit bone and ivory knives. They exported moose and fish products.

NOTABLE ARTS   Women decorated a number of items, such as moccasins, shirts, and bags, with woven quillwork or moose hair. Musical instruments included drums and caribou-hoof rattles.

TRANSPORTATION   Most transportation was overland using sleds and snowshoes. Burdens were carried with a tumpline and chest strap. Birch-bark canoes were caulked with spruce gum.

DRESS   Typical clothing included a tailored skin shirt, breechclout, leggings, and moccasins. The latter two were separate. Winter items included moose-hide blankets, fur robes, hats, and mittens.

WAR AND WEAPONS   Enemies included the Yellowknife, Chipewyan, and Cree. A decisive military victory in 1823 destroyed the threat from the first group. War leaders were chosen on an ad-hoc basis. All enemies, except young women, were killed whenever possible.

Contemporary Information

GOVERNMENT/RESERVATIONS   Contemporary bands include Follow the Shore People, Filth Lake People, Edge of the Woods People, People Next to Another People, Bear Lake Dogrib, and Connie River People. Roughly 70 percent of the population lives at Rae. Other population centers include Yellowknife, Fort Franklin, and Edzo, Northwest Territories. A strong chief and council have been elected since the 1970s.

ECONOMY   Hunting, fishing, and trapping remain important. There is some wage labor as fishing guides and construction laborers. Women work at producing crafts.

LEGAL STATUS   The bands listed under "Government/Reservations" are federally recognized. The Treaty 11 Dogrib, formerly part of the larger Dene/Métis claim (*see* Kutchin), filed their own land claim in 1992. According to two interim agreements in 1994, the people will win the withdrawal of about 13,000 square kilometers of land from around four Dogrib communities as well as participation in the decision-making process concerning the North Slave region.

DAILY LIFE   Band membership is still recognized

and considered important. Although the language is still in use, there is a high degree of acculturation among the people. Modern housing, non-native education, welfare eligibility, and medical services date from the 1960s. Most Dogribs are Catholic. Their lands are being rapidly developed, mainly by mineral extraction industries, without Dogrib input. This had led to a decision to negotiate a land claim settlement with the Canadian government in an effort to gain some control over development.

Han

See Ingalik; Kutchin

Hare

The name Hare comes from the people's reliance on the Arctic or snowshoe hare. Their self-designation was *Kawchottine*, "People of the Great Hares," or *Kasogotine*, "Big Willow People." They were culturally similar to the Kutchin and Dogrib. This description of "aboriginal" culture includes some postcontact influences as well.

LOCATION   Hare Indians lived and continue to live west (to just past the Mackenzie River) and northwest of Great Bear Lake, present-day Northwest Territories. They ranged in parts of Alberta, Yukon, and Alaska. This territory includes tundra, taiga, mountains, and intermediary areas.

POPULATION   There were probably no more than 800 Hares in the early eighteenth century, and there are about the same number (or somewhat fewer) today.

LANGUAGE   Hare is a Northern Athapaskan language.

Historical Information

HISTORY   Shortly after the people encountered Alexander Mackenzie in 1789, the North West Company built Fort Good Hope (1806) in the area. Rapid involvement in the fur trade brought dependence on items of non-native manufacture. Non-native traders created trade chiefs among the people, so that their political organization eventually became more hierarchical.

The people were decimated by epidemics throughout the nineteenth century. A local Catholic church was built around 1866. Gradually, nomadic band life was mitigated in favor of growing concentration around the trade posts. As the government created "bands" for administrative purposes and assigned subsistence areas for such groups, ethnic and group identity became stronger The people were largely acculturated, as Hare Indians, by 1900.

Treaties signed with the Canadian government in the early twentieth century provided for payments and services in exchange for land title, although the

Indians retained the right to use land for subsistence activities. Children began attending Catholic boarding school in 1926. Tuberculosis was rampant between the 1930s and the 1960s, and the people suffered periodic outbreaks of other diseases as well.

During the 1920s, many people built log homes and left native manufacture further and further behind. The fur trade continued to flourish until World War II. People increasingly worked at seasonal wage labor after the war, mainly in the oil and construction industries. The more traditional Colville Lake community dates from around 1960.

RELIGION Guardian spirits formed the basis of Hare religious belief. Spirit helpers were not formally sought out but appeared in dreams. Shamans were able to attract particularly powerful guardians through dreams and visions. They were said to be able to summon game, defeat enemies, and cure illness. Cures were effected by using medicinal plants, singing, and sucking. Shamans sometimes hung by ropes from trees or tent poles when communicating with the spirits. Religious feasts included a memorial to the dead a year after death and on the occasion of a new moon. Singing and dancing formed a part of these ceremonies.

GOVERNMENT There were perhaps five to seven small, autonomous, nomadic bands of fluid size and composition. The bands had defined hunting territories but informal leaders with little authority other than respect for their hunting and/or curing abilities.

CUSTOMS Sharing and generosity were highly valued. The bands gathered together several times a year for ceremonies, socializing, and hunting and fishing during migration and spawning seasons. Girls entering puberty were isolated in special huts and required to observe food and behavior taboos. Certain of these taboos, such as those regarding fish and animals, were continued during every monthly period. A feast would be held for young men who killed their first big game.

Intermarriage was common with several peoples, such as Bearlake Mountain (Kaska and other tribes) and Kutchin Indians. Marriage occurred in the early teens and was generally arranged, although divorce was readily available. There was some period of bride service after marriage.

The elderly as well as some female babies were killed or left to die. Corpses were wrapped in blankets or moose skin and placed in above-ground enclosures. Relatives cut their hair and disposed of their property. Ghosts were feared and provided with offerings to keep them at bay. Souls were said to be reborn at a later date.

DWELLINGS People lived in rectangular or A-frame winter pole-frame houses with gabled roofs, covered with spruce boughs, brush, and snow. Caribou-hide tipis date from the nineteenth century. Summer lean-tos were common as well.

DIET Caribou and musk ox were staples, although small animals (especially hare) and fish (such as trout and whitefish) contributed the bulk of the diet. Meat was generally roasted or stone boiled. Meat and fish were also pounded and mixed with grease and berries to make pemmican. Surpluses might be frozen or smoke dried. There was a severe lack of food every seven years or so when hares became scarce.

Women gathered a few plant foods, such as berries and material predigested by caribou and other animals. Mosses and lichens were used as beverages and medicines. Wolves and dogs were not eaten.

KEY TECHNOLOGY Stone tools included adzes and knives, the latter having a beaver-tooth blade. The main hunting and fishing equipment included bows and arrows as well as babiche snares, willow-bark nets, hooks, weirs, and spears. People made caribou ice chisels and wood or bark dishes. Willow and spruce-root baskets served as cooking vessels.

TRADE Trade partners probably included fellow Athapaskans such as Yellowknife, Dogrib, Beaver, and Slavey Indians. Items exchanged included animal skins, copper, and various minerals. There may have been some trade in Inuit knives.

NOTABLE ARTS Women decorated a number of items, such as moccasins, shirts, belts, and bags, with fringe and woven quillwork or moose hair. Musical instruments included drums and caribou-hoof rattles. Beads, dentalium shell, and then silk floral patterns and ribbon appliqué replaced more traditional decorative styles by the nineteenth century.

TRANSPORTATION Most travel was overland. Snowshoes were used in winter. Women pulled wooden toboggans before dogs took over in the twentieth century. Men also made spruce, birch-bark, and occasionally moose-hide canoes.

DRESS Most clothing came from hare pelts, supplemented by caribou and moose hides. The standard summer wardrobe was shirt, leggings, moccasins, and possibly a breechclout. In winter, the people wore robes, mittens, and hats and added hoods to their shirts. Clothing was often decorated with porcupine-quill embroidery. They wore caribou or hare hairbands. There was very little personal ornamentation except for facial tattooing and painting.

WAR AND WEAPONS Hares fought the Inuit and Yellowknife, although the people generally took pains not to fight at all. They were allied with the Dogrib and Kutchin. Prisoners were staked to the ground and their hearts cut out for the women to eat.

Contemporary Information

GOVERNMENT/RESERVATIONS Contemporary

bands are located at Fort Franklin, Colville Lake, and Fort Good Hope. Some local bands are ethnically mixed and consist of Slavey and Bearlake as well as Hare Indians.

ECONOMY   The Colville Lake people rely mainly on traditional subsistence activities. People at Good Hope live mostly on part-time, seasonal, and some full-time wage labor as well as government payments.

LEGAL STATUS   The Colville Lake and Good Hope communities are federally recognized entities.

DAILY LIFE   Full access to western culture has led to increased levels of acculturation and a comparable decline of traditional knowledge and practice. The Colville Lake and Good Hope communities remain in close touch.

Ingalik

Ingalik (`Ēn gä l ē k), from the Russian via an Inuit word for "Indian." The name has been loosely used to include such culturally related—but separate—tribes as Koyukon, Tanana, and Han. Their self-designation is *Deg Hit'an,* "People from Here." They were heavily influenced by their Yup'ik neighbors.

LOCATION   The Ingalik shared eastern parts of their traditional territory—the banks of the Anvik, Innoko, Kuskokwim, Holitna, and lower Yukon Rivers—with the Kuskowagamiut Inuit. The land consists of river valleys as well as forest and tundra. The Holikachuk, a related though distinct people, lived to their north.

POPULATION   There were between 1,000 and 1,500 Ingalik in the nineteenth century. Population in the early 1990s was roughly 650.

LANGUAGE   Ingaliks speak a northern Athapaskan language. However, by the later twentieth century most Kuskokwim Ingalik spoke the language of their Kuskowagamiut Inuit relatives.

Historical Information

HISTORY   The people probably originated in Canada. They were driven west by the Cree to settle in present-day Alaska around 1200. They encountered Russian explorers in 1833. A trade post was constructed either around then or in 1867. There were Russian Orthodox missionaries in the region during that period. The major epidemics began in 1838–1839.

Steamboats began operating on the Yukon, expanding the fur trade, beginning in about 1867, the year the United States took possession of Alaska. Catholic and Anglican missionaries arrived in the 1880s and soon opened boarding schools. The caribou disappeared in the 1870s, leading to even more fishing and closer ties with the Kuskowagamiut Inuit. Non-natives flooded into the region during the Yukon gold rush of the late 1890s. Most Ingaliks had accepted Christianity by the mid–twentieth century.

RELIGION   Everything, animate or inanimate, was thought to have had spirits. The Ingalik universe consisted of four levels, one higher and two lower than earth. Spirits of the dead might travel to any of the levels, depending on the method of death. A creator, spirits associated with nature, and various spiritual and superhuman beings, as well as people, inhabited the four worlds.

Most ceremonies were designed to maintain equilibrium with the spirit world. They included the two- to three-week Animals ceremony, the Bladder ceremony, the Doll ceremony, and four potlatch-type events with other villages. The single-village Bladder and Doll ceremonies involved paying respects to animal spirits and learning the future. Of the potlatch ceremonies, the Midwinter Death potlatch was the most solemn. The purpose was to honor a dead relative, usually a father, to gain status, and to maintain reciprocal giving arrangements with other families. Accompanying this ceremony was the so-called Hot Dance, a night of revelry.

The feast of the animals, involving songs, dances, costumes, and masks, was most important. Major roles were inherited. It involved a ritual enactment of hunting and fishing, with a clown providing comic relief. Other, more minor, ceremonies involved sharing food and occurred at life-cycle events and on occasions such as eclipses.

Songs, or spells, helped keep the human, animal, and spiritual worlds in harmony. They could be purchased from older people. Songs were also associated with amulets, which could be bought, inherited, or made. Male and female shamans were said to have more powerful souls than other people. They acquired their powers through animal dream visions. Shamans' powerful songs, or spells, could be used for good or evil.

GOVERNMENT   Each of four geographical groups contained at least one village that included a defined territory and a chief.

CUSTOMS   Society was divided into ranked status groups or social classes known as wealthy, common people, and idlers. People in the first group were expected to be generous with their surpluses and did hold potlatches as a redistributive method. Members could lead ceremonies. The idlers were considered virtually unmarriageable; however, the classes tended to be fluid and were noninherited. Wealth consisted mostly of fish but also of items such as furs, meat, and any particularly well-wrought item, such as a carved bowl, a canoe, or a drum.

Ingaliks often intermarried with, and borrowed culturally from, the nearby Inuit. Marriage depended in part on the ability of the man to perform bride service. With a first wife's permission, a wealthy man might have two wives. Both parents observed food and behavioral restrictions for at least three weeks following a birth. Young women endured segregation for a year at the onset of adolescence, during which time they mastered all the traditionally female tasks.

Punishments for inappropriate social behavior, such as theft, included banishment or death. This was a group decision, on the part of the men and older women, whereas murder required individual blood revenge. Corpses were placed in wooden coffins and buried in the ground or in vaults. Cremation was practiced on rare occasions. Personal property was disposed of. Following funerals, the people observed a 20-day mourning period and often held memorial potlatches.

DWELLINGS Ingaliks maintained summer and winter villages as well as canoe or spring camps. The winter dwelling was dome shaped and covered with earth and grass. Partially underground, it housed from one to three nuclear families. Ten to 12 such houses made up a winter village. Men used a larger, rectangular, semisubterranean communal house for sleeping, eating, working, sweating, and conducting ceremonies. This "kashim" was adapted from their Yup'ik neighbors. Canoe and sled racks were placed in front of houses.

Canoe camps, containing cone-shaped spruce-pole and bough shelters, were built while people went in search of fresh fish. Summer houses were built of spruce plank, spruce bark, or cottonwood logs. There were also gabled-roof smoke houses and fish-drying racks. Temporary brush houses were located away from the village.

DIET Among most groups, fish were the most important part of the diet. Species included lamprey eels, caught under ice, as well as salmon, trout, whitefish, pike, and blackfish. The people also ate a variety of large and small animals. Caribou, hunted by communal surround, were the most important. Others included moose, bear, sheep, and numerous fur-bearing animals, especially hare.

Ingaliks also ate birds, mainly waterfowl, and their eggs, as well as berries and other plant foods. "Ice cream," a mixture of cottonwood pods, oil, snow, and berries, was eaten ceremonially and with some restrictions on who could receive it from whom. Food was generally cached in logs on posts.

KEY TECHNOLOGY Hunting equipment included bows and arrows, spears, deadfalls, and snares. Fish were taken using a variety of nets, spears, traps, and hook (bone) and line (sinew). Stone tools included axes and wedges. The Ingalik made stone, horn, and wood knives, wooden bowls, and pottery as well as sewn birch-bark and twined grass and willow-bark baskets.

TRADE The Ingalik did not trade extensively because they possessed rich natural resources. When they did exchange goods, it was mostly with Inuit groups, exporting wooden bowls, wolverine skins, and furs for seal products and caribou hides. They might also trade furs, wolverine skins, spruce gum, and birch-bark canoes for fish products and dentalia.

NOTABLE ARTS Hide and birch baskets were probably this group's most important material artistic achievement.

TRANSPORTATION Ingaliks moved around in birch-bark canoes and on sleds and snowshoes.

DRESS Most clothing was made from squirrel and other skins. Shirts and pants were common. as were parkas. Women's moccasins were attached to their pants; the men's were separate. Personal adornment included dentalium earrings and nose and neck decorations.

WAR AND WEAPONS The Ingalik were a relatively peaceful people. When they did fight, their enemies included most neighboring tribes, especially the Koyukon and other Athapaskan tribes.

Contemporary Information

GOVERNMENT/RESERVATIONS Contemporary villages include Anvik, Holy Cross, and Shageluk.

ECONOMY Most people still engage in traditional subsistence activities, supplemented with some wage work as fishing and hunting guides. There is also some government, seasonal, and utility work.

LEGAL STATUS Doyon, Inc., is the legal entity representing Ingalik villages in the ANCSA.

DAILY LIFE For most people, life still revolves around the seasons. Frame or log houses have replaced traditional structures. Although many people struggle with a number of social problems related to high unemployment and cultural upheaval, and the people retain little aboriginal culture, traditional values remain palpable among the Ingalik.

Innu

See Naskapi/Montagnais

Kaska

Kaska (`Kas k ə) is taken from the local name for McDame Creek. The Kaska were culturally related to the Sekani. They are also known, or included, with the Tahltan and others, among the people called Nahani (Nahane) or Mackenzie Mountain People.

LOCATION Kaskas lived and continue to live in northern British Columbia and southern Yukon Territory, in a rough triangle from the Pelly River south to Dease Lake and east to the Fort Nelson River.

POPULATION The Kaska probably numbered around 500 before contact with non-natives. Their official 1991 population was 705.

LANGUAGE Kaska, along with Tahltan and Tagish, is a Northern Athapaskan language.

Historical Information

HISTORY The people traded with non-natives through Tlingit intermediaries until Fort Simpson, on the Laird and Mackenzie Rivers, was established in the early nineteenth century as the local trade center. Forts Laird and Nelson opened soon afterward. Fort Halkett, the first trade fort located directly in Kaska territory, was established soon after 1821. The people gradually came to rely on metal pots, nails, wire, and tools as well as items such as flour, soap, candles, guns and ammunition, and kerosene.

Kaska territory was invaded by gold seekers in the 1870s and again during the Klondike gold rush of 1897, seriously disrupting their traditional way of life. A Catholic mission was established in 1926. In the early 1940s the Alaskan Highway was built through their territory. Trapping remained important well into the contemporary period.

RELIGION Young men and women fasted in order to acquire animal guardian spirits in dreams and visions. Illness was said to be caused by breaking taboos. Shamans cured and foretold the future with recourse to their powerful spirit guides. Curing methods included blowing water onto the body or transferring the illness to another object.

GOVERNMENT There were at least four divisions. Each was composed of independent regional bands that had no fixed membership but generally consisted of local bands of extended families. Local band leadership was provided by the best hunters. Women occasionally served in important leadership positions.

CUSTOMS Two matrilineal clans, Wolf and Raven, were borrowed from coastal tribes, as was the institution of the memorial potlatch. Also from coastal cultures, women acquired the custom of attacking symbolic enemies while their husbands were away at war.

Birth took place apart from the community out of fear of spiritual contamination. From late childhood on, boys began training for the vision quest, as well building strength, with icy plunges and other physically demanding activities. Women were secluded and observed various taboos during their menstrual periods. Girls married in their mid-teens, boys slightly later or as soon as they could provide for a family. Men served their prospective in-laws for a year before the wedding; thereafter, they avoided speaking to one another. Though frowned upon, divorce was common. The dead were wrapped in skins and left under a pile of brush; later the tribe adopted cremation and underground burial.

The people enjoyed many games and contests. Most life-cycle events were marked by feasts. Names were inherited, as were some material items. Peer pressure usually sufficed as a means of social control; more serious offenses might be dealt with by exile, payments, or revenge.

DWELLINGS Two or more families lived in conical or A-frame lodges covered with sod, brush, or skin. Most people used simple brush lean-tos in summer.

DIET Men hunted mainly caribou, but also buffalo, mountain goat, bighorn sheep, and numerous smaller game. They drove large game into pounds, snared them, or caught them in deadfalls or pitfalls. Beaver were clubbed to death. Meat was generally boiled, often in a dried moose stomach, but could be sun dried and stored. It was rarely eaten raw. Salmon and other fish were caught in summer. Women gathered berries and a few other wild plant foods such as mushrooms, onions, lily bulbs, and rhubarb.

KEY TECHNOLOGY From coastal groups, Kaskas learned to weave blankets and ropes of sheep wool and goat hair. Babies were carried in skin bags padded with moss and rabbit fur. Men hunted with the bow and arrow as well as with spears, clubs, and especially babiche snares. Some groups may have used the atlatl.

Other important items included fishing nets, weirs, and clubs; woven spruce baskets for cooking; horn or wood spoons; wood or birch-bark dishes; cordage of sinew, spruce root, and willow bark; and tools, such as axes, knives, and scrapers, made of stone, bone, antler, and horn. Skins were prepared and tanned in various ways.

TRADE Kaskas traded with the Tahltan, Tlingit, and other groups along or near the coast.

NOTABLE ARTS Clothing was decorated with porcupine-quill and moose-hair embroidery. Some groups developed the custom of carving wooden animal masks for potlatches.

TRANSPORTATION Men built dugouts and spruce-bark canoes; sewn caribou-skin toboggans; two different types of snowshoes, depending on the quality of the snow; and moose-skin boats. Gas-powered boats and dogsleds have been in wide use since the 1940s.

DRESS Most clothing was made of sewn caribou skins. Both sexes wore belted breechclouts, skin shirt (hooded in winter), and leggings, belted and fastened to moccasins in winter. Other winter gear included mittens and hide robes. Clothing was often decorated with porcupine-quill embroidery, sewn fringe, and hard material obtained from moose stomach. People tattooed their bodies and wore ear and nose rings for personal ornamentation.

WAR AND WEAPONS Wars were fought either to

steal women or to avenge violent acts performed by strangers. War party leadership was selected on an ad hoc basis. Younger men carried the supplies while seasoned warriors did the fighting. There was some limited ceremonial cannibalism.

Contemporary Information

GOVERNMENT/RESERVATIONS Kaska bands include Laird River, Dease River, Lower Post, and Ross River. The Ross River Dena Council and the Laird First Nation are part of the Kaska Tribal Council.

ECONOMY Important economic activities include fishing, trapping, and professional guiding and other wage labor.

LEGAL STATUS The bands listed under "Government/Reservations" are federally recognized.

DAILY LIFE Kaskas have spoken English for several generations. Most are Catholic.

Koyukon

See Ingalik

Kutchin

Kutchin (`Ku chin) or Gwich'in, "People." The Kutchin were a group of tribes or bands who called themselves by various names, each having the suffix "-kutchin." The name of one band—Tukkuth, or "People of the Slanting Eyes"—was translated by the French to *Loucheux,* a name now commonly used to designate the Kutchin people. Their self-designation is *Dindjie,* "person." They were culturally related to the Han, Tutchone, and Tanana and were culturally influenced by the Inuit as well as the Tlingit.

LOCATION Kutchin territory is the Peel River Basin to its junction with the Mackenzie River as well as the Yukon River drainage (Alaska and Yukon).

POPULATION The Kutchin population, between 3,000 and 5,000 in the eighteenth century, declined to around 1,300 in the mid–nineteenth century and around 700 in the mid-1970s. In the mid-1990s there were around 2,000 Gwich'in people in Canada and an additional 600 in Alaska.

LANGUAGE Kutchin people spoke dialects of Kutchin, a Northern Athapaskan language.

Historical Information

HISTORY Kutchin people encountered the Mackenzie expedition in 1789. The North West Company founded Fort Good Hope in 1806; other trading posts followed in 1839 (Fort MacPherson) and 1847 (Fort Yukon). Fur trapping gained in importance among the people during the nineteenth century. Catholic and Protestant (Church of England) missions worked in Kutchin territory from the mid–nineteenth century on. Missionaries introduced a system of reading and writing (called Tukudh) in the 1870s.

Major epidemics stalked the people during the 1860s and 1870s, and again in 1897 and into the twentieth century. Many Kutchins left their immediate region to take advantage of the local whaling boom at the end of the nineteenth century. The Klondike gold rush (1896) brought an influx of non-natives into the region, many of whom abused the Indians and stole their land. Religious residential schools existed from 1905.

RELIGION Shamans acquired spiritual power through fasting and dreaming. They could foretell the future, cure illness, and control the weather. They were quite powerful in the west but less so in the east. In general, most people seldom came in "official" contact with the shamans.

Spirits inhabiting nature were mollified with offerings of beads. Hunters prayed to moon-related deities, offering pieces of caribou fat thrown into the fire. Ceremonial feasts, including singing and dancing, were held on various occasion. The main ceremonies revolved around life-cycle events, lunar eclipses, and memorial potlatches. There was a general fear of giants and other monsters. Bear and caribou were considered to be especially deserving of respect, in part owing to a supposed physical connection (shared hearts) between people and caribou.

GOVERNMENT Kutchin bands included the Kutcha (Yukon Flats), Nakotcho (Mackenzie Flats or Arctic Red River), Natsit (Chandalor River), Tatlit (Peel River), Tennuth (Birch Creek), Tukkuth (Upper Porcupine River), Tranjik (Black River), Vunta (Crow Flats), and Dihai (Downriver People).

Tribal chiefs were chosen for their leadership qualities or wealth. In some cases the positions were hereditary, but leaders had no real power. Local groups (two or so extended families) lived in a defined area and used its resources.

CUSTOMS Animal-associated matrilineal clans declined in importance from west to east. The clans had marriage and ceremonial functions, playing significant roles in feasts and games. There were three social classes that may have been ranked: the "dark people" (Crow), "fair people" (Wolf), and "halfway people" (no crest). There were also some slaves, although they probably were not purchased. Among the distinct socioeconomic levels, the wealthy were considered better in every way.

Women carried babies in their coats or in birch-bark containers. They also performed most hard work (except for cooking, which men did) and ate only after the men had finished. Women generally selected husbands for their daughters. Female infants, as well as the elderly, were sometimes killed. From shortly before puberty until marriage, young men moved away from their parents to live in a lodge with other such young men. This was a period of self-denial and skill sharpening. Men without family might attach themselves to other families as servants.

Young women were segregated during their menstrual periods. At that time they observed many taboos, such as not looking at others, designed to prevent others being "contaminated" by their "condition." The dead were cremated. Their ashes were hung in bags from poles or, if the person were particularly influential, placed in coffins in trees until decayed and then burned. Relatives destroyed their property and cut their bodies.

Hospitality was a key value. The nuclear family was the basic unit, but grandparents might sleep in a lodge near the family and spend a lot of time with them. Items of value included dentalium shell beads, wolverine skins, and caribou products. Rich men of certain tribes gave potlatches but usually only at funerals. Everyone enjoyed singing, dancing, games, and contests. Games included stick and hand games, ball games, and athletic contests. Witches were greatly feared.

DWELLINGS Dome-shaped, caribou-skin tents were stretched over curved spruce poles painted red. These portable lodges were about 12 to 14 feet long and 6 to 8 feet high. There was a smoke hole at the top, fir boughs for flooring, and bough and snow insulation. Some groups covered the lodges with birch bark rather than caribou skin. Some groups built semisubterranean dwellings of moss blocks covering a wood frame, with gabled roofs. When traveling, men sometimes built dugout snow houses glazed with fire.

DIET Fishing took place mainly in summer. Pike and whitefish were important fish species. There were salmon along the Yukon River and moose along its banks. Men hunted mainly caribou but also moose, hare, beaver, muskrat, and other game. Dogs often assisted in the hunt. People also ate waterfowl and plant foods, such as berries, rhubarb, and roots.

KEY TECHNOLOGY Many items were derived from the caribou. Bows, generally of birch, were made in several sections and bound with sinew or willow shoots. Men hunted with bows and arrows, deadfalls, and babiche snares. They also used caribou pounds or corrals. Fishing equipment included hooks, lures, spears, dip nets, and willow baskets.

Other important items included wooden and birch-bark trays, woven spruce and tamarack-root baskets and cooking vessels, and other containers made of bent wood and birch bark. There were any number of tools with which to work hides, bone, and wood. Blades were mostly of stone and bone. Musical instruments included wooden gongs, drums, and willow whistles.

TRADE Trade partners included the Tanana, the Koyukon, the Inuvialuit, and the Inupiat as well as the Tlingit. Imported dentalium shell was used as a currency. The people also imported some copper blades. As intermediaries, they relayed Arctic coast oil, bon, and tusks to inland groups. They exported furs even before contact with non-natives.

NOTABLE ARTS Containers and clothing were decorated with porcupine quills. Skins were finely tanned.

TRANSPORTATION Sleds were made with high-framed runners, which might be covered with bone or frozen sod coated with water or blood. Inuit-style birch-bark canoes had flat bottoms and nearly straight sides. The people also used moose-skin canoes, toboggans, and particularly well-made long, narrow snowshoes with babiche netting.

DRESS Most clothing came from white caribou skin as well as furs. Shirts were pointed both front and rear. Wide (Inuit-style) leggings attached to moccasins were beaded or embroidered with porcupine-quill designs along the sides. Winter gear included long mittens, headbands, fur hats, and winter hoods. Most clothing was fringed and/or decorated with seeds or dentalium shell beads and/or painted and embroidered with porcupine quills.

Both sexes, but especially men, wore quill and dentalium shell personal ornamentation. Men also skewered their noses; women simply wore nose decorations. People took particular care with their hair. Men applied a large amount of grease and wore it in a ball at the neck, covered with bird down and feathers. They also painted their faces red and black. Women tattooed lines on their chins.

WAR AND WEAPONS The Kutchin were a relatively aggressive people. Kutchin enemies included the Inuvialuit and Inupiat and sometimes the Tanana and the Koyukon Indians. Enemies, with the occasional exception of young women, were generally killed. There was some ritual cannibalism.

Contemporary Information

GOVERNMENT/RESERVATIONS Alaska Kutchins live in villages such as Arctic Village, Chalkyitsik, Circle, and Venetie. Some of these villages are shared with Inuits. Fort Yukon, Alaska, ranks as a town, the only Gwich'in population center to boast of the presence of roads. Villages corporations with elected boards of directors administer Alaska Native Claims Settlement Act (ANCSA) assets.

ECONOMY Most people still rely on traditional subsistence activities as well as fur trapping and barter.

LEGAL STATUS   According to the terms of the Dene/Métis Western Arctic Land Claim Agreement (1992), the Dene surrendered aboriginal and treaty rights in return for surface rights on about 24,000 square kilometers of land, some subsurface rights, and about $75 million in cash as well as hunting and fishing rights. The groups also participate in decision making about renewable resources, land use planning, and other environmental and development issues. In the early 1990s, the Mackenzie Delta Gwich'in broke away from the Dene Nation and Métis Association over this issue. They concluded a separate agreement with the Canadian government in 1991 for land and cash. Most Kutchin became members of the Doyon Corporation under the ANCSA.

The Vuntut Gwitch'in First Nation is included in an umbrella land claims settlement (1993) with the Council of Yukon First Nations. Its terms are similar to those of other Canadian/First Nation land claims settlements: land, a mixture of surface and subsurface rights, cash, and participation in the overall decision-making process concerning development, land use, and other environmental issues.

DAILY LIFE   Some groups live in small wood-frame houses. Although some have access to modern inventions such as snowmobiles, televisions, and satellite dishes, more than most other Indians the Kutchin have been able to retain a semiaboriginal lifestyle and culture, including religious beliefs, to a considerable degree (although less so in Fort Yukon). Most are fluent in English, although there are efforts to retain the native language. The people are fighting to maintain the health and existence of the Porcupine caribou herd, which is threatened by development-related resource destruction.

Loucheux
See Kutchin

Mackenzie Mountain People
See Kaska

Nahani
See Kaska; Tahltan

Naskapi/Montagnais
Naskapi/Montagnais (`Nas ku p ē /`Mon tun y ā). Naskapi is a Montagnais word that may mean "rude or uncivilized people." Montagnais is French for "mountaineers." Their self-designation was *Nenenot,* "the People." Contemporary Naskapi and Montagnais refer to themselves as *Innu. See also* Cree (especially discussion of East Cree).

LOCATION   The territory of these groups, including the East Cree, ran from the Gulf of St. Lawrence to James Bay, along the northeastern coast of Hudson Bay to Ungava Bay, and east to the Labrador Sea. The division was more or less that the East Cree occupied the west of this region, the Naskapi the north, and the Montagnais the south and east. Much of this territory is extremely rugged and remote. Moose lived in the wooded Montagnais country, whereas Naskapi country, more open and grassy, was favored by caribou.

POPULATION   There were perhaps 4,000 Montagnais and 1,500 Naskapis in the fifteenth century. A centuries-long population decline began to reverse itself only after World War II. In the mid-1990s the Innu population stood at approximately 16,000, including a small percentage who had moved away from eastern Quebec and Labrador (known also as Nitassinan).

LANGUAGE   Montagnais and Naskapi are dialects of Cree, an Algonquian language.

Historical Information
HISTORY   Humans—likely direct ancestors of the Naskapi/Montagnais—have lived on the Labrador Peninsula for at least 5,000 years. Indians may have lived peacefully alongside the Inuit in ancient times. These people were among the first North American groups to come in contact with non-natives, probably Basque and other European fishermen, in the early sixteenth century.

The Montagnais welcomed Champlain in 1603; his French muskets proved to be of some help against crippling Iroquois war parties. The people soon became heavily involved in the fur trade. They found it very competitive and profitable and soon began acquiring a large number of non-native goods. Europeans created Indian trade chiefs, or "captains." Missionaries arrived among the Montagnais in 1615. Tadoussac remained a key trade town from the mid–sixteenth century until Quebec was founded in 1608.

However, both moose and caribou were soon overhunted. As food supplies became less certain, some starvation ensued. Problems with alcohol abuse exacerbated the situation. The people were able to trade furs for supplies until non-natives took over the best trapping grounds. Devastating disease epidemics reduced and weakened the Indian population. Further mass deaths resulted from relocating to the coast at the urging of missionaries.

The fur trade remained important during the eighteenth and early nineteenth centuries. The Naskapi became involved in the fur trade during that period. As they quickly increased their dependence on the trading posts and forsook the caribou hunt, they began to lose important elements of their traditional lives. By the mid–nineteenth century, traditional small local bands had generally become associated with a particular Hudson's Bay Company trading post. As forestry operations began replacing the fur trade, and non-natives continued to move into the St. Lawrence Valley, the people's hunting grounds became severely diminished. At that time the government created the first official Indian villages.

By the mid–twentieth century, the trading post communities were being replaced by larger, permanent settlements. Also, well-defined trapping areas of at least several hundred square miles had evolved. People generally remained around a settlement in summer, retiring to their territory in small groups (10–20 people) to hunt and trap during the other seasons.

Since 1940, Canada has built over 20 hydroelectric dams and plants in Labrador. The government created several new reserves in the 1950s. In 1975, the Eastern Cree and Inuit ceded over 640,000 square kilometers of land to the James Bay Hydroelectric Project, in exchange for promises of hundreds of millions of dollars and various other provisions.

RELIGION People may have believed in a great sky spirit to whom pipe smoke was occasionally offered. The people certainly believed in any number of spirits or supernatural beings. The key to Naskapi/Montagnais religion was to maintain a healthy and respectful relationship with the spirit world. This could be done both by observing the various taboos and by acquiring certain techniques.

They especially attempted not to offend the spirits or souls of the animals upon which they depended for food, mainly by being as respectful as possible toward them. Other primary concerns were good health and successful births. Ceremonies included the Mokosjan, in which people ate caribou bone marrow. Feasting was also considered a religious practice, as was drumming.

Prayer was always offered before beginning any important activity. Boys fasted to obtain spirit helpers. Male and female shamans cured and kept away evil spirits. Shamans sometimes demonstrated their magic powers. In the shaking tent rite, shamans communicated with their spirits in specially built lodges to learn of good hunting areas. People feared cannibalistic monsters called Windigo (Montagnais) or Atsan (Naskapi).

GOVERNMENT Society consisted of perhaps 25–30 small, independent hunting (winter) bands related by marriage. There were several lodge groups (families of 15–20 people) to a band. A named band, or division, probably consisted of two or three of these winter bands (up to 300 people or so) who shared a general area. Several named bands came together in summer on lake shores or river mouths

for fishing, group hunting, and socializing. These gatherings might consist of between 1,000 and 2,000 people. In all cases, band affiliation was fluid. Traditional chiefs or headmen had little or no formal authority, and all decisions were taken by consensus.

CUSTOMS Within the context of group cooperation for survival, individuals answered to no one about their personal behavior. Most people were generous, patient, and good natured. Joking, or kidding, was effective in maintaining social mores, because real criticism was taken very seriously and avoided if possible. Montagnais had defined and patrilineally inherited family hunting grounds. Although groups were associated with specific subsistence areas, in lean times they readily gave permission to share.

Within the lodge groups there was no real dependence of one individual on another, since sexual relations were not limited to marriage, divorce was easy to obtain, and children were in many ways considered a group responsibility. These structures and relations encouraged a general egalitarianism.

Although gender roles were not especially rigid, men generally worked with wood and stone and women with leather. Men hunted big game while women set snares and gathered berries. Women were secluded during their menstrual periods. Parents generally arranged marriages. Men tended to marry in their early twenties, and women in their late teens. Some men had two wives, but a few had more. Men were obligated to perform bride service for a year or so. Joking, or familiar, relationships with cousins sometimes led to marriages.

Children were raised with tolerance and gentleness by both men and women, regardless of whether or not they were "legitimate." The old and sick were sometimes killed out of a sense of compassion. Dead Montagnais were wrapped in birch bark and buried in the ground. A memorial feast followed the funeral. Naskapis placed their dead on platforms or in trees.

DWELLINGS Conical dwellings were covered mainly in birch bark (Montagnais) and caribou skin (Naskapi). They held between 15–20 people and featured central fires with top smoke holes. The ground was covered with branches and then mats or skins. The people also used temporary lean-tos, some made of snow.

The Naskapi also built large A-frame or rectangular lodges to house several families and for winter dancing. This structure was covered with caribou skins and floored with boughs. There were several fires in these structures. Caribou-skin coverings of more traditional lodges were not sewn but rather overlapped.

DIET Men hunted primarily moose (Montagnais), caribou (Naskapi), and fowl as well as bear and other animals. The people used canoes to pursue big game after driving the animals into water and also wore snowshoes to run the game down. Meat was generally stone boiled or roasted. Small game, snared by women and sometimes men, included hares, porcupines, and beaver. The people also fished for salmon, eels, and trout. The Montagnais and Naskapi of Labrador also harpooned seals (among other things, seal oil repelled mosquitoes) and fished through the ice, both activities probably borrowed from the Inuit.

Some Montagnais had gardens and may have made maple syrup. Wild foods, such as berries, grapes, apples, and bulbs, played a small role in people's diet. Food was unsparingly shared when necessary. Meals were generally eaten silently. Before they were pushed north by non-natives, the Montagnais of the Saint Lawrence region had a greater variety of food resources than their more northerly kin.

KEY TECHNOLOGY Babies were carried in moss-bag carriers and used moss diapers. Men hunted using the bow and arrow, deadfalls, nets, snares, and spears. Some groups attracted moose with a birchbark call. The crooked knife was a basic tool from at least the early nineteenth century on. Most aboriginal tools were made from bone, antler, bark, wood, and stone. People fashioned birch bark or animal skins into storage containers and bone and sinew into needles and thread.

TRADE The Montagnais traded meat and skins at Tadoussac and other places with Great Lakes people for tobacco, corn, and even some wild rice. This location became key during the fur trade period. Northern bands acquired cedar to use for canoe ribbing. Some groups also traded for birch bark.

NOTABLE ARTS Red ochre and greasepaint were applied to clothing in geometrical patterns with bone or antler pens or stamps. Skin objects, including clothing and bags, were painted with groups of parallel lines, triangles, and leaf shapes.

TRANSPORTATION The people made several varieties of snowshoes and birch-bark canoes as well as some log rafts. They used a canoe-sled with runners in spring. Toboggans were dragged with a cord across the chest. Dogsleds were used after around 1900.

DRESS The Naskapi wore clothing of caribou skin that had been dressed, smoked, and sewn. Some southern groups wore breechclouts; leggings (sometimes attached with a belt); bear, moose, or beaver robes; and moccasins as well as attachable sleeves for winter wear. Clothing also included fur pants, sewn hare blankets, fur or hide headbands, and hide caps.

In the north, hooded winter coats had fur inside. Moccasins in the north were sometimes made of seal-skin. Unlike many neighboring groups, who ran a charcoal-coated thread through the skin, the Naskapi tattooed themselves by simply rubbing charcoal or soot into a cut on the skin.

WAR AND WEAPONS Warrior councils made military decisions. Weapons included bows and arrows, spears, and knives. The Montagnais also used clubs and shields, the latter custom probably borrowed from the Iroquois. They also adopted Iroquois methods of torture and cruelty.

Montagnais enemies included Micmac and Iroquois. They were allied with the Algonquin and the Maliseet. The Naskapi fought only with the Inuit to their east. They took few prisoners except that they might marry the women.

Contemporary Information

GOVERNMENT/RESERVATIONS Contemporary Innu communities in Quebec include Betsiamites (25,536.57 hectares; 2,752 people in 1994, of whom 2,352 lived within the territory), Kawawachikamach [Naskapi] (326.34 square kilometers; 526 people in 1994, of whom 456 lived within the territory), La Romaine (40.47 hectares; 832 people in 1994, of whom 812 lived within the territory), Essipit (formerly Les Escoumins; 38.5 hectares; 366 people in 1994, of whom 184 lived within the territory), Mashteuiatsh (3,150.99 hectares; 4,016 people in 1994, of whom 1,708 lived within the territory), Schefferville (Matimekosh [15.91 hectares] and Lac-John [23.5 hectares]; 660 people in 1994, of whom 608 lived within the territory), Mingan (3,887.82 hectares; 416 people in 1994, of whom 398 lived within the territory), Natashquan (20.63 hectares; 690 people in 1994, of whom 616 lived within the territory), Pakuashipi (Settlement of St. Augustin; 4.47 hectares; 217 people in 1994, of whom 216 lived within the territory), and Uashat (108.31 hectares) and Maliotenam (499.28 hectares) (total of 2,758 people in 1994, of whom 2,221 lived within the territory). Communities in Labrador include Sheshatshiu and Utshimassit (Davis Inlet; about 300 square miles; roughly 500 people in 1994). Government is generally by elected chief and councilors as well as an appointed band manager.

The Mushuau Innu (Davis Inlet), a community of around 535 people, are governed by a chief and the Mushuau Innu Band Council.

Sheshatshiu and Utshimassit (Davis Inlet) are represented politically by the Innu Nation. Other regional representational groups include Mamuitun, on the Quebec North Shore (Betsiamites, Essipit, Mashteuiatsh, Uashat-Maliotenam), and Mammit Innuat (La Romaine, Mingan, Natashquan, and Pakuashipi (St. Augustin).

ECONOMY   Among the East Cree, there are some jobs with the Hudson's Bay Company and oil and other companies. There is also some community-based service employment as well as some mainly short-term jobs in construction. Many people still hunt, fish, and trap. Some also work as guides, outfitters, and woodcutters. The salmon industry is important among some communities. The Naskapi Adventure Club is a northern travel agency. Government support is important.

LEGAL STATUS   The communities listed under "Government/Reservations" are federally recognized, although Pakuashipi (St. Augustine) does not have reserve status. The Northeastern Quebec Agreement between the Innu of Schefferville, Hydro-Quebec, and provincial and federal governments (1978) pertained to the great regional dam projects. In exchange for payments of $9 million, confirmed land ownership, and land use rights, the people will see over 10,000 square kilometers of land flooded and tens of thousands more acres altered. A framework for negotiation was reached in 1995 between the Innu Nation and provincial officials concerning the former's claim of large portions of Labrador. Other land claims are under negotiation.

DAILY LIFE   Among the East Cree, many people retain elements of traditional religious belief either along with or instead of Christianity. Parts of these people's territory, such as north-central Labrador, has only recently been explored by non-natives. Most Innu, however, are Christian. In a marked departure from the precontact period, they have discarded former ideas about personal independence and duty to the group in favor of duty to individuals (women must obey men, children their parents, people their leaders). Few people remain self-sufficient.

Southeastern bands live in permanent framehouse villages. Hunting and trapping trips into the interior are far less important than they used to be, yet the cooperative ethic remains strong. Most people wear non-native dress, and most children go to non-native schools and are largely acculturated.

The Cree-Naskapi Act of Quebec (1984) replaced the Indian Act and provides for local self-government. The Labrador Innu (North West River) won an injunction in 1989, later overturned, preventing the military from continuing low-flying exercises of their region. The Naskapi-Montagnais Innu Association work for, among other issues, the sovereignty of the Davis Inlet Innu and the Sheshatshiu Montagnais. The Conseil Attikamek/Montagnais (12 bands in Quebec) is also negotiating for specific rights with the Canadian government.

In 1974, the people formed the Grand Council of the Crees (of Quebec) to deal with the ramifications of the James Bay hydroelectric project, which had been allowed to proceed over Indian opposition. The James Bay and Northern Quebec Agreement, ratified in 1975 but controversial ever since, called for cession of over 640,000 square kilometers of Indian land. In return, the people were promised a cash settlement of over $230 million and special concessions, including land ownership of over 3,300 square kilometers, subsistence rights on over 32,000 square kilometers more, and a veto over mineral exploitation.

However, not all of the money was allocated. An epidemic of childhood diarrhea was caused by the pollution of vital water supplies, and Indians are often excluded from many of the better jobs. The Cree still oppose the final stages of the project.

The people of Davis Inlet, led by the Mushuau Innu Band Council and the Mushuau Innu Renewal Committee (1993), have worked to address serious health and safety issues. They have constructed and renovated houses, instituted job training, and increased social services. Furthermore, in 1995 a multilateral agreement was signed calling for the return of the provincial court to Davis Inlet. This is part of the community's plan to assume greater responsibility in policing its own affairs.

Ojibwa, Northern
See Anishinabe (Chapter 8)

Salteaux
See Anishinabe (Chapter 8)

Sekani
Sekani (Se `kä n ē), "People of the Rocks" (Rocky Mountains), from their own self-designation. They were culturally related to the Beaver and the Kaska.

LOCATION   Traditional Sekani territory is the Parsnip and Finlay River Basins, British Columbia. An eighteenth-century expansion to the south was largely checked by the Shuswap. In the nineteenth century, some groups had moved west into areas draining into the Pacific Ocean (Bear Lake and northern Takla Lake) to gain access to salmon. The people also gave up large parts of their eastern territory.

POPULATION   There were probably around 3,000 Sekani in the eighteenth century and around 200 in the early nineteenth century, not counting 300 or so people in groups living west of the Arctic-Pacific divide. The 1991 Sekani population was 630, exclusive of Indians officially considered "non-status."

LANGUAGE   Sekanis spoke an Athapaskan language.

Historical Information
HISTORY   The Sekani may have originated east of the mountains and been driven west by the Cree.

They may once have been united with the Beaver. They probably first encountered non-natives in 1793. Around the same time, Shuswaps stopped the southward expansion of the people.

The North West Company established two posts in 1805, including Trout Lake (Fort McLeod). Trade forts continued to be established for the next several decades. The people began a decline shortly after the trade posts opened that was mainly linked with alcohol abuse and disease.

The Omineca gold rush occurred in 1861. By 1870, over 1,000 non-native trappers and miners had occupied the territory of the Senaki. Environmental degradation and the decline of natural resources, including game animals, were the result. In consequence of these trends, mal- and undernourishment were added to the people's woes, and their population declined even more sharply. Still armed mainly with traditional weapons, the people at that time were forced to give up their winter grounds east of the Rocky Mountains to the Beaver and Cree, who had access to firearms. Catholic missionaries were active in the area from about 1870 on.

Two new bands or groups created around the turn of the century were the T'lotona (Sasuchans intermarried with Gitksans) and Davie's Band (Otzane), people organized around the son of a French Canadian man and a Sasuchan woman. A large dam created in the 1960s displaced many bands and separated several traditionally linked Sekani groups.

RELIGION Young men fasted and dreamed alone in the wilderness to acquire supernatural guides, which were associated with animals or birds. These guides were only of help in emergencies. However, men might obtain other guides later in life, associated with either animals or natural forces, that might provide more regular assistance. These men became shamans, who were able to cause and cure disease, the latter for pay.

Women could not become curers but they could, through dreaming, acquire the power to foretell the future. Disease was considered to be caused by soul loss, taboo breaking, or malice. Some people were influenced by a quasi-Christian cult in the 1830s.

GOVERNMENT Several autonomous bands were led by a headman of little real authority. Sekani was the name of one such band. Regional bands in the nineteenth century were, from north to south, Tseloni, Sasuchan, Yutuwichan, and Tsekani. Other groups may have been Meadow Indians and Baucanne (Says-Thau-Dennehs). Bands owned hunting territories.

CUSTOMS Names were derived ultimately from guardian spirits. Most children were nursed for about three years. At puberty, girls were secluded and forced to observe special food and behavioral taboos, all designed to keep them apart from men and animals. Boys fasted and dreamed for spirit guides.

Men might have more than one wife, especially if the wives were sisters. Newly married men served their in-laws for a year or so but lived apart from them during that time. The dead may anciently have been buried in the ground or covered in brush huts; they were later cremated. Chiefs or other people of authority were placed in hollow-log coffins deposited in trees or on platforms. Daily mourning (wailing) could last for years after a death. The Sekani adopted matrilineal divisions and even quasi-potlatches for a short time in the nineteenth century, in imitation of the Carrier and Gitksan.

DWELLINGS Temporary conical lodges were covered with spruce bark or, later, moose hide. The people also built lean-tos covered with brush, bark, or skins as well as brush menstrual huts.

DIET Large game, such as moose, caribou, mountain sheep, and bear, constituted the bulk of the Sekani diet. Many other animals were also hunted, including porcupine, beaver, and marmot. There was some buffalo hunting, at least around 1800, in the eastern foothills and prairies. Some groups hunted in both summer and winter. Meat was boiled, roasted, or smoke dried.

Trout and whitefish were the most important fish species. Fish were occasionally taken at night, from canoes, in the light of pine torches. Other foods included fowl and berries. Surplus food was cached in trees.

KEY TECHNOLOGY Hunting tools and war weapons included the bow and arrow, club (fashioned from a moose jawbone), and spear. The people also used deadfalls and babiche snares to take both large and small game. They caught fish with willow bark or nettle-fiber nets, bone hooks, spears, and some weirs. Most tools were made of bone, wood, and antler, with some stone for points and blades. They made spruce-bark or woven spruce-root containers and hide or netting bags. Babies were carried in bags lined with groundhog or rabbit fur.

TRADE The Sekani traded with Carrier groups. They exported mainly products of the hunt.

NOTABLE ARTS Sekanis decorated their clothing with porcupine-quill and moose-hair embroidery.

TRANSPORTATION Most people traveled overland, carrying their possessions on their backs. They used snowshoes in winter and, occasionally, some spruce-bark canoes.

DRESS Men wore a sleeveless skin shirt, which they sometimes laced together between their legs, high skin leggings, and moccasins lined with fur. They added a breechclout after sustained contact with the Cree. Women wore similar clothing, although their leggings were shorter and their shirts were longer. Sometimes they wore a short apron as well.

Items of personal adornment included horn and bone bracelets. Hunters wore grizzly bear claws around their necks. Both sexes painted their bodies and wore marmot or hare robes, caps, and mittens in winter.

WAR AND WEAPONS Enemies included the Cree, Beaver, and Shuswap. The Carrier were mostly friends, with notable exceptions. There was also some interband fighting. Bows were tipped with stone point "bayonets" for stabbing at close range.

Contemporary Information

GOVERNMENT/RESERVATIONS The Fort Ware Band owns three reserves with a total land area of 391 hectares. There were 328 band members in the mid-1990s, of whom 277 lived on the reserves. A chief and councilors are elected by custom. The band is affiliated with the Kaska Dene Tribal Council.

The Tsay Keh Dine Band (formerly known as Ingenika, a part [with Fort Ware] of the Finlay River Band [Tseloni and Sasuchan Bands]) owns five reserves with a total land area of 201 hectares. There were 282 band members in the mid-1990s, of whom 2 lived on the reserves (much of their land was flooded by BC Hydro) and a number on Crown lands. A chief and councilors are elected by custom. The band is affiliated with the Carrier Sekani Tribal Council.

The McLeod Lake Band is located in British Columbia.

ECONOMY Important economic activities include freighting, trapping, guiding, logging, and construction.

LEGAL STATUS The above bands listed under "Government/Reservations" are federally recognized.

DAILY LIFE Children attend federal and/or band and/or provincial schools. Fort Ware Band facilities include offices, a school, a community hall, a store, a clinic, and a motel. Tsay Keh Dine facilities include an airstrip, a school, offices, a fire station, and a community center.

Slavey

Slavey (`Sl ā v ē), or Slave, is a translation of a name *(Awakanak)* given by the Cree enemies of these people. Their self-designation was *Dine'é,* "People." They were also known as *Etchareottine,* "People Dwelling in the Shelter." They are culturally related to the Dogrib and, like them, were not considered a "tribe" until relatively recently.

LOCATION In the early eighteenth century, Slaveys lived between Lake Athabaska and Great Slave Lake. Their mid-nineteenth-century territory included the Mackenzie and Laird River Basins, from western Great Slave Lake south to around Hay Lake and north to Fort Norman, boreal forestland in present-day northeast British Columbia, northwest Alberta, and southwest Northwest Territories. The people live on reserves in this area today.

POPULATION The Slavey population was possibly 1,250 in the late seventeenth century and was officially 5,120 in 1991.

LANGUAGE Slaveys spoke dialects of a northeastern Athapaskan language.

Historical Information

HISTORY The Cree, carrying firearms, drove the people north from the Lake Athabaska area in the late eighteenth century. They encountered Alexander Mackenzie in 1789. The first trade post in the area was built in 1796, with additional posts following in the next 15 years. Anglican and Catholic missionaries arrived in 1858; Christianization was virtually complete by 1902.

Treaties signed with Canada in 1900, 1911, 1921, and 1922 generally called for land cessions in return for payments, services, and reserves. The high cost of trade items, as well as the relatively limited nonnative presence in the area, kept the people from dramatically changing many aspects of their culture until well into the twentieth century. Slaveys adopted nonnative material goods (such as metal items, firearms, flour, and tobacco) on a large scale after World War I, when many began trapping for income for the first time. At about the same time, groups began gathering for the summer at trade posts rather than at traditional lakeshore places, and gatherings were added for Christmas and Easter.

Permanent, significant governmental intrusion began only after World War II for some more remote groups, when the fur market collapsed. Oil and gas exploitation replaced furs as the region's most important commercial resource at about the same time. By the 1960s, most people had moved from the bush into towns and had enrolled their children in schools.

RELIGION People sought to acquire a guardian animal spirit in a dream, which would provide them with luck and assistance. Special songs usually accompanied powers provided by the guardian spirits. There were also malevolent spirits or supernatural beings, such as giants, who abducted young children. Quasi-medicine bundles, or collections of items inspired by the dream vision, were kept in a pouch or a box. With few herbal remedies, medicine men were primary curers through removing physical manifestations of illness from a patient. Souls were said to live again after death.

GOVERNMENT People with little real authority led several autonomous bands, each with perhaps 200 people, that came together only in summer, and even then only when conditions permitted. The bands were composed of local hunting groups of 10–15 people, within which food and other items were shared. Membership in all groups was fluid. An informal council of hunters settled disputes.

CUSTOMS Within the local group, all people fared roughly equally well or poorly in terms of subsistence. Most personal disputes were settled by compensation or, in extreme cases, banishment. Local groups often resolved differences by playing a game, such as the hand game, or through ritual competition by medicine men. The meeting of two local groups might be an occasion to feast and dance.

Individuals chose their own marriage partners, although parents also played a key role. A yearlong bride service for men followed a wedding. Men sometimes engaged in the custom of wrestling each other for their wives. Divorce was rare.

Women generally gave birth in a kneeling position attended only by women. There was some female infanticide. At her first menstrual period, a young woman left the camp and lived in a separate shelter for about ten days; she returned to the shelter every month. During this time she was subject to several food and behavioral taboos, such as avoiding eye contact with others and not traveling on an existing trail. Boys marked the passage into adulthood by making their first big game kill.

Unlike many groups, men did much of the hard work, such as obtaining firewood and preparing the lodge, in addition to hunting and fighting. Grandparents were important in the lives of children, often "joking" with them to teach proper behavior. The elderly and ill were rarely abandoned. Many people confessed wrongs on their deathbeds. The entire camp remained awake to witness a person's death. Death was greatly feared and was considered, with illness, to be the result of sorcery. Corpses were placed on scaffolds or covered with leaves and snow and placed with their property under a hut.

DWELLINGS The winter dwelling was a low pole-frame structure covered with moss, with a pitched spruce-bough roof and two doorways. There was an open smoke hole at the top. These structures might be 20 feet long and 10 feet wide and were inhabited by extended families. In summer, people built conical spruce, moose-hide, bark, or brush lodges.

DIET Men hunted mainly moose, but they also hunted woodland caribou, running them down and shooting them with bow and arrow in spring and snaring them with the help of dogs in summer and winter. Beaver were caught in wooden traps in fall and speared or clubbed in winter. Men also hunted numerous small animals as well as birds. Fish were also very important.

Meat and fish were either roasted, boiled, smoked, dried, or made into pemmican. Women gathered berries, roots, and some other plant foods. Food to be stored was cached in the ground (winter) or hung in a bag from a pole.

KEY TECHNOLOGY Most animals were caught with babiche or sinew snares. Other hunting gear consisted of the bow and arrow, clubs, and spears. People fished with twisted willow bark or babiche nets and weirs as well as with hook and line. Other important items included stone adzes, beaver-tooth knives, bone or antler projectile points, woven spruce-root or -bark cooking vessels, and moose-hide, calf-skin, or hare-pelt diapers. Babies were carried in moose-hide bags lined with moss.

TRADE Slaveys imported some native copper from the Yellowknife and Dogrib people. They also imported some caribou skins, flint, chert, and pyrites as well as Inuit bone and ivory knives. They exported moose and fish products.

NOTABLE ARTS There was some geometric-style painting and dyed porcupine-quill embroidery. The people made music from drums and caribou-hoof rattles.

TRANSPORTATION The people used two types of snowshoes, beaver-hide or birch toboggans, birch or spruce-bark canoes, and some moose-hide rafts. Much travel took place overland, with goods carried on a person's back by means of a tumpline around the forehead.

DRESS Clothing was mainly of moose skins and consisted of pointed shirts and coats, leggings joined to moccasins, tassels (men), dresses (women), robes, caps, and mittens. In some areas, women's clothing was made mostly of woven hare skins. Clothing was heavily fringed, with moose-hair and porcupine-quill decoration. People also wore moose-hide and rabbit-skin blankets.

Faces were tattooed with parallel lines on the cheek. Women wore woven spruce-root caps. Men plucked their facial hair and skewered their noses with wood or goose quills. Both sexes wore embroidered leather waist, wrist, and arm ornaments.

WAR AND WEAPONS Despite their peaceful reputation, the Slavey were known to massacre Kaskas and other mountain Indian enemies. Neighboring tribes were reluctant to attack them for fear of witchcraft reprisals. The people also fought the Cree. War garments included bear-claw headdresses or feather caps. Weapons included willow-twig shields. War leaders were chosen on an ad hoc basis.

Contemporary Information

GOVERNMENT/RESERVATIONS Slavey communities include Hay River, Fort Laird, Fort Norman, Fort

Providence, Fort Simpson, and Fort Wrigley in the Northwest Territories; Fort Nelson in British Columbia; and Hay Lakes Region in Alberta. The people own roughly 40,500 reserve hectares.

Fort Nelson (formerly the Slave Indian) Band owns four reserves with a total land area of 9,558 hectares. Total population was 575 in the mid-1990s, of whom 284 lived on the reserves. Local government is provided by an elected chief and councilors. The band is affiliated with the Treaty Eight Tribal Council.

Prophet River (formerly part of the Fort Nelson) Band owns one reserve with a total land area of 374 hectares. Total population was 151 in the mid-1990s, of whom 84 lived on the reserve. Local government is provided by a chief and councilors elected according to custom. The band is affiliated with the Treaty Eight Tribal Council.

ECONOMY Government payments have largely taken the place of traditional strategies that provided long-term economic independence. There are seasonal jobs in oil and gas. At Fort Nelson, people engage in trapping, oil work, forestry, construction, guiding, road building, and freighting, and they collect gas royalties. Trapping, guiding, and work at a fur depot are the main activities at Prophet River.

LEGAL STATUS The Slavey are a federally recognized tribe.

DAILY LIFE Traditional nomadic patterns have been replaced by a sedentary existence, especially since the 1960s. Since about the same time, the Slavey have become politically active to maintain control of their own affairs. The nature of local development, such as the proposed controversial oil and gas pipeline, may be the biggest issue of all.

Contemporary life is marked in part by a number of problems, including substance abuse and general ill health, substandard housing, limited educational and economic opportunities, crime, and racism. Most of these problems can be attributed to the tension between the loss of traditional culture and replacement by spiritually and materially inadequate non-native institutions, programs, and attitudes.

Facilities at Fort Nelson include offices, a community hall, a clinic, a school, and a garage. Facilities at Prophet River include offices and a store.

Tahltan

Tahltan (`Täl tan), from the Tlingit for "basin-shaped hollow," referring to a place at the mouth of the Tahltan River. There are also other possible origins and meanings of the name. Their self-designation was *Titcakhanotene*, "People of Titcakhan." They are sometimes classified, with the Kaska, as Nahani Indians and were culturally related to the Carrier.

LOCATION The Tahltan lived, and continue to live, in northwest British Columbia, specifically the upper Stikine River drainage. They also shared the Stikine River Valley below Telegraph Creek with the Tlingit. The Tahltan hunted in the region in winter, whereas the Tlingit fished and gathered there in summer.

POPULATION There were perhaps 2,000 Tahltans in the late eighteenth century and officially 1,330 in 1991.

LANGUAGE Tahltan is a dialect of Tahltan-Kaska, an Athapaskan language.

Historical Information

HISTORY Tahltan history is in part a process of continuous adaptation of their native Athapaskan traditions to those of Pacific Coast cultures. Tahltans probably moved into their known territory in the seventeenth century. The rich natural resources of the region encouraged population growth, larger and more permanent habitations, acquisition of more material goods, increased social stratification, and a more complex culture in general.

Tlingit-Tahltan contact intensified after non-natives established a presence along the coast in the early nineteenth century. At that time, trade and the production of furs became increasingly important. As wealth grew, stratification became more pronounced. At the same time, with so many people dying, opportunities were rife for social mobility.

Major epidemics began in the early nineteenth century when coastal people brought germs into the interior. Up to 75 percent or more of Tahltans died from epidemics during the nineteenth century. Sustained contact with non-natives came when gold was discovered below Glenora in 1861 and especially after the 1874 gold strike at Cassiar. At that point, the Tahltan no longer controlled the Stikine River territory. In the late nineteenth century, survivors of various bands coalesced into one unit, or tribe, with a head chief. They built Tahltan village, a log house community.

The trend toward loss of land and control over their own destinies became even stronger following the Klondike gold rush of 1898, as thousands of non-native prospectors, missionaries, tourists, and entrepreneurs rushed into the region. Although many people were drawn into the wage economy as guides, wranglers, and government employees, most Indians remained engaged in traditional subsistence activities through the mid–twentieth century. Major employment opportunities during and after World War II included highway construction and asbestos mining.

RELIGION The people recognized a sky god and a sun god. Adolescent boys fasted in wilderness vision quests to obtain guardian animal or bird spirits and songs. Shamans dreamed powerful guardian animal spirits.

GOVERNMENT Six autonomous bands were each associated with a particular hunting territory. Leadership was relatively weak, and band membership was fluid. Eventually, under Tlingit influence, the bands became clans, which were led by a chief who inherited his office through his mother's line. (In the mid–eighteenth century a seventh clan was created, but it remained more of a Tlingit than a Tahltan entity.) Family and possibly clan leaders might be women. Clan leaders constituted an informal council. In about 1875, a single "tribal" leader emerged.

CUSTOMS Two matrilineal divisions, Raven and Wolf, each contained three of the clans. Eventually, the three clans in each division came to share hunting territories. People were socially ranked as either nobles, commoners, or slaves. The latter category was permanent, and the children of slaves were born slaves.

Commoners, however, could enter the nobility by accumulating wealth and giving potlatches and/or through marriage. Titles, which confirmed social status, could be inherited but also had to be earned, mainly by potlatching. Three kinds of potlatches existed among the Tahltans: those given by parents to acknowledge their childrens' rank, those given by rivals to increase their status, and memorial potlatches.

Men toughened themselves with icy plunges and by self-flagellation with willow switches. Girls reaching adolescence remained secluded for up to two years, receiving intensive training in the female tasks during that time and enduring a number of food and behavior taboos, such as keeping their faces covered. Young men served a prospective wife's family for a period of time before the wedding.

Widowers often married a sister of their late wife. Women were supported by—and often married—their nephews when their husbands died. The dead were cremated, after which the bones were placed on a post or within a small box raised off the ground. Death chants were sung for the dying and the dead. When a prominent person died, one of his slaves might be killed or, alternatively, freed.

DWELLINGS Tahltans lived in pole-frame leantos with bark roofs and earth-and-bough packing. Those who could covered the poles with moose hide. At semipermanent fishing villages, the people built bark-roofed huts with straight sapling walls and gabled roofs. In the main village, clans built structures up to 100 or more feet long that housed the clan's main families and served as a ceremonial hall. There were also special living and club houses for young, unmarried men.

DIET Tahltans ate mainly game, including caribou, moose, bear, buffalo, and a range of smaller animals, such as marmot and beaver. Dogs assisted in hunting. Fish, especially salmon, were an important part of the diet. Women gathered roots, berries, and other plant foods.

KEY TECHNOLOGY Men hunted using bows and arrows, snares, deadfalls, spears, and traps. Caribou were caught in surrounds. People fished using weirs and a variety of nets. Women made various sized babiche net bags as well as bark cooking vessels. Babies were carried in leather bags.

TRADE Tahltans had long-standing trade and other personal contacts with Tlingit, Kaska, and Sekani groups. They imported eulachon and salmon oil, dentalium and abalone shells and ornaments, stone axes, woven blankets, and slaves (who originated among the Haida). Exports included moose and caribou products (such as cured hides and babiche) and furs.

NOTABLE ARTS Tahltans ornamented everyday objects, often with geometric designs.

TRANSPORTATION The people made a few relatively poor quality spruce-bark canoes and temporary rafts. When people traveled overland, which they preferred to water travel, they might use snowshoes and carry baskets with tumplines. Women pulled a rough toboggan.

DRESS Tanned skin and fur clothing included shirts and leggings, often with attached moccasins, for men and dresses (long shirts), leggings, and moccasins for women. Both sexes wore goat-skin and woven rabbit-fur robes as well as various personal adornments. Clothing was often decorated with quillwork.

WAR AND WEAPONS Tahltans periodically fought the Inland Tlingit, Taku River Tlingit, and the Tsimshian (Ness River branch), mostly over trade and the use of subsistence areas. Weapons included bows and arrows, spears, and knives as well as antler bayonets. Warriors also used goat-skin helmets and armor. They took scalps and held women prisoners for ransom. There was also some ceremonial cannibalism. Allies included other Tlingit groups, the Dease River Kaska, and the Bear Lake Sekani.

Contemporary Information

GOVERNMENT/RESERVATIONS The Tahltan Band, located at Telegraph Creek, owns 11 reserves with a total land area of 3,230 hectares. Band population in the mid-1990s was 1,309, of whom 238 lived on the reserves. A chief and councilors are elected according to provisions of the Indian Act. The band is unaffiliated.

The Iskut Band is of Sekani origin.

ECONOMY Hunting, fishing, and trapping are still important. There is also some work as sport guides and miscellaneous seasonal and government wage work.

LEGAL STATUS The bands listed under "Government/Reservations" are federally recognized.

DAILY LIFE Children attend band and provincial schools. Tahltan band facilities include a community hall, an arts and crafts center, and stores.

Tanaina

Tanaina (Tu `n ī nu), or Dena'ina, "the People." They were also known as *Knaiakhotana*. Designation as a tribe is a non-native convention, the people having consisted traditionally of various related tribes, or divisions, such as Kachemak, Kenai-tyonek, Upper Inlet, and Iliamna-susitna. They were culturally related to local Northwest Coast tribes such as the Tlingit.

LOCATION Before contact with non-natives, Tanainas lived around the drainage of Cook Inlet, Alaska. Today, most Tanainas still live in cities, towns, and villages in the area as well as in other U.S. cities, particularly in the Northwest.

POPULATION From perhaps 4,500 in the mid–eighteenth century, the Tanaina population dropped to around 3,000 in 1800. There were 400 Tanaina Indians in the United States in 1990.

LANGUAGE Tanaina includes two major divisions—Upper Inlet and Lower Inlet—as well as many subdialects. It is an Athapaskan language.

Historical Information

HISTORY Captain James Cook entered the area in 1778, followed by more British traders. Local Indian groups already possessed iron and other items of non-native manufacture when Cook arrived. Although Indians welcomed the Europeans as traders, they strongly and, for some time, successfully opposed non-native settlement.

Russians built the first trading posts in the later eighteenth century. Relations between the Russians and Native Americans were difficult, even though the two groups regularly intermarried. Russians often attacked the native people and took them as hostages, ultimately turning many Indian and Inuit groups into forced labor. Russian control was generally brutal. As the violence subsided and more posts were built in the early to mid–nineteenth century, many native people became active in the fur trade.

A severe smallpox epidemic in 1838 took thousands of Indian lives. Other non-native diseases such as syphilis and tuberculosis also killed many Indians. The people had guns by the 1840s. Russian Orthodox missionaries arrived in force about 1845; the people were nominally converted within two generations, especially along the coast.

Although population decline and game shortages caused interior groups to consolidate their villages, the late nineteenth century was generally a time of increasing prosperity, owing mainly to the extension of credit and growing involvement in the fur trade. The peak years were between 1867 (when the United States purchased Alaska) and the fur market crash of 1897. As a consequence, traditional "rich men," or Indian trade leaders, became even wealthier and more powerful. One consequence of the U.S. purchase of Alaska was that the Tanaina lost legal rights as Russian citizens. U.S. citizenship was not granted until 1924.

The discovery of gold in the area around 1900 brought a flood of miners and other non-natives. Other factors, such as the growth of commercial fishing and canning industries (with their attendant pollution and resource monopolization), improved transportation, and continuing population declines and game shortages, weakened social distinctions and contributed to the people's general decline.

These developments also hastened the transition from a subsistence to a wage economy. Canneries and commercial salmon fishing boomed by the mid–twentieth century. Schools, at least through the eighth grade, have been available to most Tanainas since the 1960s.

RELIGION Everything in nature was said to have a spirit. The people recognized three groups of beings in particular: mythological beings; supernatural beings, such as giants and tree people; and beings that interacted closely with people, such as loon, bear, and wolf spirits. There was also a fourth group of creatures known as Hairy Man and Big Fish. Ceremonies included memorial potlatches and first salmon rites.

Male and female shamans mediated between the human and spiritual worlds, using spirit powers acquired in dreams to cure illness and divine the future. To cure illness, shamans wore carved wooden masks and used dolls to locate and exorcise evil spirits. Shamanic power could be used for good or for evil. In addition to their spiritual power, many shamans enjoyed a great deal of political power, occasionally serving as the village leader ("rich man").

GOVERNMENT Tanainas traditionally organized into three distinct societies: Kenai, Susitna, and Interior. The three developed separately because of the difficulty of communicating across the hazardous Cook Inlet. The village was the main political unit. It was headed by one or more leaders ("rich men"), usually the wealthiest members of their clan lineage groups. Leadership functioned mainly as a redistributive mechanism, wherein goods flowed to the "rich man" and were redistributed by him according to need. The leader was also responsible for the moral upkeep of his people.

The power of these leaders was noncoercive, and their "followers" were bound to them only out of respect. Leadership qualities, in addition to wealth, included generosity, bravery, and hunting ability. A man who aspired to this position needed help and material support from his relatives.

Russians began appointing chiefs in the nineteenth century. These people were invested by the non-natives with the power to speak formally for their people. They acted as intermediaries between the non-natives and their people, especially in trade matters.

CUSTOMS Relatively stable winter villages gave rise to social hierarchy and other complex organizations. A dual societal division was further broken into matrilineal clans, approximately five in one division and ten in the other. Clans owned most property and controlled marriage as well as most hunting and fishing areas. Social control was maintained primarily by peer pressure, although revenge, physical retribution, and payments played a role also.

"Rich men" gave potlatches as an important means of economic redistribution and to increase or maintain their prestige. They were provided crucial support by their relatives. Potlatch occasions included life-cycle events as well as other opportunities to express generosity. Dentalium shells, certain furs, and, later, glass beads were the primary symbols of prestige. "Rich men" had several wives as well as slaves. The latter were generally well treated and not kept for more then several years. In general, women had a relatively high degree of prestige and honor and could become wealthy in their own right.

Men served their future in-laws for at least a year. Children were born in a separate house. Adoption was common. Puberty recognition was accorded to both sexes. Boys fasted, either in a room (Interior) or in the woods (Susitna), and ran in the morning. Girls were confined for the better part of a year, during which time they learned appropriate skills and proper behavior. They also endured various behavioral taboos during this time, including the prohibition against looking directly at anyone else.

People made loud noises around the sick and dying to keep malevolent spirits at bay. Corpses were cremated. Their ashes were placed either in boxes on posts or buried, and their possessions were destroyed or given away. Members of another clan were responsible for making all funeral arrangements. A mourning period of several weeks followed funerals. Memorial potlatches were held about a year after death.

DWELLINGS Winter villages consisted of from one to ten or more partially excavated houses with a tunnel entry. Winter village population averaged between 50 and 200 people. These rectangular houses had log walls covered with grass and dirt. Spruce-bark or planked gabled roofs were also covered with dirt. There was a large main room with several side sleeping chambers. The total length ranged from 10 to 100 feet.

The houses featured rooms for several families, including a main room with a fire and sleeping platforms for adolescent boys. Compartments for married couples and their young children as well as adolescent girls were located underneath the platforms. Other chambers were for sweating, menstrual isolation, and sleeping for the elderly. Villages were often concealed or camouflaged against enemy attack.

Summer houses were similarly designed, but lighter. The people also built temporary houses, such as birch-bark or skin tents or log and sod structures, at fish and hunting camps. These houses held only nuclear or small extended families. House styles began to change in the nineteenth century with Russian influence.

DIET There was a wide dietary divergence between groups. Some, such as those in the extreme south, depended mainly on marine life, whereas the northern interior people were mainly hunters and fishers. Most groups depended on fish, especially all five kinds of salmon. Other important species included eulachon, halibut, and catfish.

Important sea animals included seals, otter, and beluga whale. Land animals included caribou, bear, moose, beaver, and rabbit. Caribou herds were driven into lakes and speared or shot, or they were channeled with fences into snares and surrounds. The people also ate birds and fowl as well as various roots and berries. Coastal people gathered shellfish.

KEY TECHNOLOGY Fish were taken with nets, weirs, basket traps, and antler spears. Hunting equipment included spruce bows, deadfalls, traps, knives, clubs, and spears. Women wove spruce-root baskets. Babies rested in birch-bark cradles with moss diapers inside. There was some pottery.

TRADE The Tanaina acquired kayaks and umiaks from the Alutiiq, serving also as intermediaries between those people and interior groups. The Tanaina participated in regional trade networks stretching across Alaska. Informally and at trade fairs, they traded with other Tanaina groups as well as with groups farther away. Wealthy men with established trade partners were especially successful. Traditional exports included wolverine skins, porcupine quills, and moose products. Imports included copper, dentalium shell, and cedar arrow shafts.

NOTABLE ARTS Men carved and decorated wooden bowls. Clothing was decorated with quills, shells, and ermine tails.

TRANSPORTATION Water transportation included birch-bark canoes and moose-skin boats as well as Inuit-style sealskin kayaks and umiaks. People traveled overland in winter on foot (snowshoe); dogsleds dated from the mid–nineteenth century.

DRESS Tailored clothing was made of tanned caribou or sheepskins. Both sexes wore a knee-length undergarment, a shirt, and boots. Fur coats and shirts were added in winter. Rain gear included a whale-membrane parka and waterproof salmon-skin boots. In winter, the long undergarment had knee-high bear or beluga whale–soled boots attached. Blankets were made of sewn rabbit skins. Skin shirts were worn in summer.

Clothing was often dyed brown or red, embroidered with porcupine quills, and decorated with fur trim and shells. Decoration often reflected social rank. Tattooing and face painting were common, especially among the wealthy. Women wore bone labrets in their lower lips. Both sexes pierced their ears and septa for shell decorations.

WAR AND WEAPONS Enemies included the Alutiiq and occasionally the Ingalik. Villages were generally camouflaged to discourage attack. Captives on both sides were taken and sold as slaves.

Contemporary Information

GOVERNMENT/RESERVATIONS Tanaina population centers include Nondalton (roughly 160 native residents in 1990), which is governed by the seven-member elected Nondalton Tribal Council and a seven-member elected city council); Pedro Bay (roughly 40 native residents in 1990), which is governed by the seven-member elected Pedro Bay Village Council); Anchorage; and Tyonek. The first two fall under the purview of the Bristol Bay Native Corporation and are members of the Lake and Peninsula Borough. Nondalton is located between Lake Clark and Lake Iliamna, and Pedro Bay is located on Lake Iliamna.

Moquawkie Reserve consists of 26,918 acres. Government is by village council, with elected officials such as mayor or president. The institution of "rich man" began to decline after about 1900. There have been no "rich men" in the traditional sense since the 1960s. Village corporations with elected boards of directors administer Alaska Native Claims Settlement Act (ANCSA) assets.

ECONOMY Important economic activities include commercial fishing, including canning; construction; trapping; air transportation; and the oil industry. Tanainas also work as fishing and hunting guides. Tyonek village collects investments from oil revenues. Subsistence hunting and fishing also remain important.

LEGAL STATUS The Tanaina are represented by the Cook Inlet Region Corporation and the Bristol Bay Regional Corporation for the purposes of the ANCSA.

DAILY LIFE Tanainas are generally acculturated, although many retain a strong pride in their heritage and traditions. The three traditional societies are no longer distinct. The clan system is still important in most areas. Most people are Russian Orthodox Christians, although some elements of traditional religion survive. Tyonek used revenue from oil leases in part to modernize village facilities. Local concerns include bridge construction and road improvement. A Tanaina Athapaskan Indian cultural facility has been proposed, perhaps to be built in Iliamna.

Tanana
See Ingalik

Tlingit, Inland
See Tlingit (Chapter 3)

Tutchone
See Kutchin

Yellowknife
See Chipewyan

CHAPTER TEN

The Arctic

Arctic

For people who have never lived there (and for some who have), the word "Arctic" conjures up a landscape almost incredibly forbidding. The Inuit, however, over the course of thousands of years, learned to live successfully in that cold, rugged country. Inuit (plural of Inuk) means "People" in the native language. In recent years, and especially in Canada and Greenland, it has replaced Eskimo, an Algonquian word meaning "eaters of raw meat" and one that many Inuit find offensive. The Unangan, or Aleut, are also generally considered to be Arctic, rather than Subarctic, residents.

The Arctic is a remarkable region in several ways. It stretches 5,000 miles from Asia (Siberia) to Greenland and 1,800 miles from southeast Labrador to the Queen Elizabeth Islands. It encompasses well over 2,000 miles of the Alaska coast and is generally considered to include the 1,000-mile-long Aleutian Island chain. Another way to think of the vastness of the Arctic region is that it is roughly 12,000 miles (20,000 kilometers) from the eastern Aleutian Islands and along the coast of northern Alaska and Canada to Greenland. The total aboriginal population—including perhaps 15,000 Unangans, 31,000 Yup'iks, and 35,000 Inuits—was probably in the vicinity of 80,000 people. Four modern nations claim Arctic lands: Canada, Denmark, Russia, and the United States.

Arctic winters are long, dark, and extremely cold, except less cold right along the Pacific Ocean and adjacent waters. Although the interior may be colder in winter, fierce winds blow relentlessly along the coast. The flat tundra is covered with ice and snow in winter, but owing to poor drainage and the presence of permafrost it becomes boggy in summer, a perfect environment for mosquitoes, black flies, and other such insects. Although there are few or no trees in most of the Arctic, there are, during the brief summer, dwarf flowers, mosses, and lichens. As little as four inches of precipitation may fall in a year, except

for Labrador and especially southwest Alaska. It is fortunate that ocean ice tends to lose its salinity after a year or so; otherwise finding fresh water would have been a serious problem for many Arctic residents.

All native Arctic people speak languages belonging to the same family, known as Eskimo-Aleut, or Eskaleut. Aleut is considered a separate language with two main dialects. The Eskimo language is made up of Inuit-Inupiaq (Eastern Eskimo), or Inuktitut, and Yup'ik. Yup'ik is divided into five branch languages and several dialects, whereas Inuktitut is broken merely into mutually intelligible dialects. The Inuit also maintained a nonverbal language based on body expression and other cues.

Some Arctic peoples were forced to deal with nonnatives in the 1780s, whereas others did not experience direct contact until almost the twentieth century. The initial results of contact were mixed: They included disease epidemics, the breakdown of traditional structures and morality, and growing economic dependence as well as a new and acceptable religion and helpful trade goods. In many cases, native people continued to live in at least a semitraditional way until after World War II. Since then they have experienced many changes but not, as in the south, genocidal wars and the wholesale confiscation of their land.

Anthropologists remain uncertain whether the various native Arctic people came directly from Siberia or adapted to their environment from the Subarctic. Many believe that ancestors of the Inuit arrived in North America far later than did ancestral American Indians—perhaps only about 4,000 years ago—and in fact were preceded by at least 10,000 years by paleo-Indians. Along the Alaskan Peninsula and parts of the Aleutians, two cultures—Kodiak (circa 2500 B.C.E.) and Aleutian (circa 2000 B.C.E.)—continued approximately unchanged until the Russians arrived in the eighteenth century. Both were characterized by the use of poisoned lances for whaling, detachable barbed-head harpoons, an emphasis on clothing and personal decoration, and the development of woodworking, painting, and weaving.

Meanwhile, a hunting tradition known as Arctic Small Tool (Denbigh) arose around the Bering Sea from the Paleo-Arctic peoples of the rest of Alaska and northern Canada around 5,000 years ago. After about 1,000 years it had diffused throughout much of Alaska and Canada. These people made small flint blades, skin-covered boats, bows and arrows, needles, semiexcavated houses, and stone lamps. In the east, this complex was further refined into the somewhat more sea-oriented Dorset Tradition by about 1000 B.C.E. Dorset people also adapted well to snow and ice, possibly originating the snow house.

Again beginning in the Bering Sea area, the Norton culture materialized about 2,000 years ago. It in turn gave way to the Thule culture, which gradually overtook all other cultural traditions save the Aleutian by about the twelfth century. Thule people had dogs and sleds, umiaks and kayaks, the bow and arrow, and the harpoon thrower (atlatl), and they hunted whales. Through increased specialization and adaptation to local environments, this culture led directly to those found by non-natives.

With the possible exception of Native Alaskans, Arctic peoples were not organized into tribes. Instead, they saw themselves as members of groups that were tied to the land but whose definition nevertheless depended on perspective. These groups carried the suffix -miut, "people of." The smallest and most basic unit was the nuclear family. The extended family generally formed a household. Camps, or settlements, were seasonal constructions comprising one or more households. The larger of these groups might be considered bands.

Leadership was generally undeveloped in the Arctic. In certain temporary situations, such as whaling expeditions, strong leaders emerged, but there was little formal structure. Leaders were usually older, experienced men who might be heads of leading households and excellent hunters and who, in whaling cultures, probably owned an umiak. Authority was more formalized in southwest Alaska, owing partly to the influence of Northwest Coast cultures.

Hunting sea mammals—ringed and bearded seals, walrus, narwhal, and whales—was the main occupation of most Inuit men. Hunting walrus was considered inordinately dangerous, owing to the animals' size and aggressive nature. (Polar bears presented the same problem and were taken, if at all, mainly for their hides.) Most men hunted seals from ice floes in winter. This was an extremely demanding task. Seals must come up for air, so men waited with their dogs and various equipment (see discussion of key technologies that applied to hunting) at breathing holes. In order to catch one seal, a man might have to guard a hole for hours, motionless in the dark and bitter cold. Breathing-hole sealing was done communally, so that a number of holes could be covered at once.

Whaling was a special occupation practiced mainly in northwest Alaska. The whaling umiaks were led by a captain and chief harpooner. Once the great animal was fatigued by the initial thrust and from the drags, it would slow down enough for other men to spear it to death. The whale was then either towed to shore or left to drift back. In the case of seals and whales, the kill was divided according to very precise and respected formulas.

In other seasons, a number of subsistence activities took place. Men stalked seals on the ice or harpooned them on open water from kayaks. Birds such as ptarmigan, ducks, and geese were taken, as were their eggs. In some areas, people gathered berries. Fishing was a three-season or in some areas a four-season activity.

Among the land animals, caribou were by far the most important source of food. Most groups took advantage of the great seasonal migrations, particularly those in late summer and fall. Men working together generally shot or speared the beasts from land or from kayaks as they crossed bodies of water or forced them, with corrals and/or stone cairns, into narrow places and shot them there. Other land animals used for meat and/or fur included musk ox, wolf, fox, wolverine, and squirrel.

In addition to food, caribou also provided the single most important source of raw material. From the caribou, and other animals as well, came clothing, shelter, bedding, boats, thread, and lines (sinew). The people made a variety of tools and weapons, such as harpoons, bow and arrow, needles, thimbles, knives, axes, adzes, drills, scrapers, and shovels, primarily from bone and antler. The defining women's tools, reflecting their main activities, were the ivory or bone needle, the semilunar, sinew-backed knife, and the stone skin scraper.

People used a number of chipped stone (flint, slate, or quartz) items, such as points, blades, pots, and scrapers. Some copper was also used around Coronation Gulf. Many people depended on soapstone (pottery in southwest Alaska) oil- or blubber-burning lamps with moss wicks for heat and cooking. Wood, mainly driftwood, might provide boat and house frames, boxes, tool and weapon handles, and dishes. Depending on location, baleen could also be worked into boxes or other items. Other key technologies included movement indicators (for breathing-hole sealing), various types of harpoons (especially with detachable heads), throwers (atlatls), seal nets, bird bolas, three-pronged spears, fishhooks, stone fish weirs, and small animal traps and snares. Most people started a fire either by striking two pieces of pyrite or by friction generated with a thong drill.

Chipped stone work was well developed among the Native Arctic people, but they were particularly adept at carving figurines, amulets, toys, and other items out of bone, antler, and ivory. Tailored clothing was decorated with finely sewn furs. Some groups, mainly in Alaska, carved and painted wooden ceremonial and dance masks. Baskets were particularly fine among the Unangan, but people in southwest Alaska and in Labrador made them as well. In some areas, music and storytelling were considered high arts.

Although kayaks varied somewhat from place to place, they were basically one-man, closed-deck hunting canoes. They were made of a wooden frame lashed with sinew and covered with sewn seal or caribou skin. Men propelled them with double-bladed paddles and used them mainly for hunting. Skin-covered umiaks were larger, open boats, used either for whale hunting or simply for transportation, depending on the region. In the latter case they were rowed or paddled by women. Sleds, pulled by dogs and/or people, were used for winter travel. These were built of a wood frame lashed together with rawhide. The wood, hide, or bone runners were often covered with moss and then ice to ensure a smooth ride.

Inuit built two basic types of winter houses, depending on location. Primarily in the central region, snow houses were the rule. Two men could build one in a hour or so. Snow blocks were cut, placed on a circle about 10 to 15 feet in diameter, stacked in an inward-moving spiral, and knocked into place. Small porches were generally used for storage. Women chinked the gaps with snow. People entered through a passageway built underground to trap the cold air and keep it out. A sheet of clear ice or gut served as a window. Benches and tables were made of snow. Snow platforms, covered with willow twigs or baleen and then thick, warm skins and furs, served as beds. Women tended the lamp, over which was placed a cooking pot or drying rack. Snow houses often were attached to one another in the interests of sociability and added warmth. They were also used temporarily by travelers and hunters in other parts of the Arctic.

The other major winter house type was the semi-excavated nonsnow dwelling. This square or oblong house was constructed of a wood or whale bone frame covered by sod and snow. As with the snow house, entrance was generally gained through an underground or tunnel-like passageway. In some areas people entered these houses through the roof. Other structures included the *kashim*, or men's large ceremonial house, and summer tents of seal or caribou skin over bone or wood frames.

Dress, as might be imagined, was well constructed for warmth. Most clothing was made of tailored caribou skin, although polar bear, wolverine, squirrel, or even bird or fish skins were occasionally used by some groups. In general, people wore both inner and outer garments in winter, with the inner garment fur side in and the outer garment fur side out, although in summer only the inner garment was worn, fur side out. Outer shirts (parkas) were cut away at the sides and featured a long tail at the rear and a hood, which women wore extra large to shelter babies. Both sexes wore pants, stockings, insulated mittens, and sealskin boots or low shoes, depending on the season. Raincoats were carefully sewn of waterproof gut. Clothing was often decorated with colored furs or fringe. Items of personal adornment included labrets (lip plugs), ear pendants, nose rings, and tattoos.

Although regional variations must be acknowledged, some common threads concerning religious belief among native Arctic people may be discerned. Most people believed that all things, animate and inanimate, had souls, or spirits. These beings varied in appearance. In order to maintain a positive and respectful relationship with them, particularly with the spirits of game animals, people observed any number of taboos or behavioral proscriptions and rules. Observing the taboos was considered an essential aspect of health maintenance. In order to enlist the aid of helpful spirits or to ward off bad spirits, people also used magic or wore amulets (identified with specific spirits and functions). The loss of an individual's soul not only gave offense to other souls or spirits but might also cause illness or death.

Female and especially male shamans were in touch with and could control various beings of the spirit world. A long period of training was required before one could be considered a shaman. Shamans cured individual disease, and they saw to the overall health of the community, in part by ascertaining who broke which taboo when disaster befell the community. Performance was central to their method. They also exercised a degree of leadership in the community group. Their authority, however, was inspired more by fear than respect, as they were thought to be able to harm people through the agency of their supernatural powers.

In a more general sense, most native Arctic people recognized a dichotomy between the worlds of the land and the sea. There were various rules against using the same weapons to hunt land and sea animals, for example, and other taboos designed to maintain separation between the two realms. (This is one reason why the polar bear, which inhabited both land and sea, was considered so awesome.) There was also a general recognition (except in western Alaska and northwestern Hudson Bay) of an undersea female deity. Some western Alaska communities observed the Bladder and the Memorial Feasts. The Midwinter Feast was central to the ceremonial season in the central Arctic.

In terms of family and social customs, descent was generally bilateral. Kinship was of primary importance to these people, so much so that "strangers"— those who could not immediately document kin affiliations—were perceived as potentially hostile and might be summarily killed. Other groups of people subject to willful death were infants, especially females, and old people. Suicide was not uncommon, nor was cannibalism, but only in the most extreme cases of need. Prospective husbands often served a future bride's parents for a period of time (bride service). Wife stealing, committed in the overall competition for supremacy, might end in death, as might other conflicts, although murders were subject to revenge. Corpses were generally wrapped in skins and left on the ground. In southwest Alaska and the Aleutians, mummification was also practiced. Pastimes included kickball, acrobatics, string games, and storytelling.

Formal nonkin partnerships were a distinctive feature of most native societies in the Arctic. This custom stemmed from the need for nonkin members to work cooperatively. Partners might cooperate in a number of areas, including hunting, trade, and even death vengeance. Within certain male partnerships, wives might be exchanged for a more or less temporary period of time. Any children who resulted from such an arrangement were considered fully legitimate. Other types of formal nonkin relationships were formed between "joking partners" and people who shared the same name (though they might or might not be the same gender).

The direct encounter with non-natives began at widely divergent times in the Arctic; perhaps 500 years ago on Baffin Island and the Labrador coast to as little as 75 or so years ago east and north of the Mackenzie Delta. (Norse people may have met some northeastern Inuit as early as circa 1000.) Europeans came looking for the mythical northwest passage, a water route through the continent to Asia. Non-natives also came to exploit marine and land resources such as sea otter, whale, and walrus. In most cases, the initial period of contact was marked by some two-way trade, in which the natives received mainly metal products (and, later, rifles and ammunition), and the initiation of severe disease epidemics.

Occasionally, natives served as guides and played other important roles in the exploration of the far north.

Traditional life began to change for most Arctic natives only with the introduction of fox fur trapping in the late nineteenth and early twentieth centuries. Trading posts sprang up in many native communities. Credit for food and other items extended in the fall was repaid with fox pelts in the spring. With more and more effort and resources going into trapping, and as opportunities for wage labor slowly increased, people began to drift away from their traditional lives. Residential areas around the posts grew in size, although most remained small until after World War II. Most included missionaries and, in Canada, a detachment of the Royal Canadian Mounted Police (RCMP). The former opened schools and clinics, and both worked to reduce violence among the Inuit.

Meanwhile, Russians had colonized southwestern Alaska and parts of the Aleutian Islands from the mid–eighteenth century on. The natives put up a fierce resistance to the Russians' general brutality. After becoming wealthy from sea otters and seals, and defeating the people into the bargain, the Russians "sold" Alaska to the United States in 1867. By then, Yankee whalers were plying the north Alaska coast, bringing alcohol, disease, and trade items as well as some jobs and a measure of cosmopolitanism to the natives.

The near extinction of the whale population by the early twentieth century coincided with the beginning of fox trapping, commercial fishing and canning, and various gold rushes. These activities all brought severe disruption to Native Alaskans, along with some employment. At about the same time, the U.S. government required all native children to be removed from their families and educated at remote boarding schools. It also attempted to force the people to "settle down" by pressuring them to maintain domestic reindeer herds—not to farm, as was the case with Native Americans to the south.

The market proved to be at least as mysterious and intractable a force as were the elements. When fox fur prices dropped sharply in the 1930s, many Arctic natives were devastated. Soon, however, military activity in response to World War II and the Cold War formed the basis for a recovery. Natives in both Canada and Alaska found jobs in construction and with government projects, although, at least in Alaska, many natives migrated to urban centers such as Anchorage and Fairbanks. In 1959, Alaska became the forty-ninth state of the United States.

At about the same time, the Canadian government, under the auspices of the Department of Northern Affairs and Natural Resources (DNANR;

1954), assumed responsibility for comprehensive public assistance as well as compulsory education and health care. As part of these programs, it encouraged natives to settle down in permanent communities. In theory, settlements were self-governing, but decisions were subject to review by Canadian officials. School curricula were culturally and practically inappropriate. Local jobs, where they existed, were generally unskilled and poorly paid. Progress with diseases such as tuberculosis was gradually offset by the rise of substance abuse and other health problems caused by a less healthy diet as well as a general moral breakdown.

Since the 1960s, native people of the Arctic have become increasing active politically. In Canada, organizations like the Committee for Original People's Entitlement (COPE, 1970) and the Inuit Tapirisat of Canada (ITC, 1971) have taken the lead in advocating for land claims, appropriate resource management, language and educational rights, and other similar issues. In 1993, the Tungavik Federation of Nunavut (an outgrowth of the ITC) convinced the Canadian government to divide the Northwest Territories at the tree line and to establish in 1999 a new, mainly Inuit territory of roughly 350,000 square kilometers—roughly one-fifth of the land mass of Canada—to be known as Nunavut ("our land"). The settlement also includes over $1 billion in compensation as well as a strong Inuit role in decision making regarding land use and resource royalties. Other groups have claims pending as well.

Huge oil deposits were located on Alaska's North Slope in the 1960s, and plans for an 800-mile pipeline were begun. People began to organize around this and other issues, such as their exclusion from discussions about Alaska's native land claims as well as the low levels of opportunity for and the degree of poverty experienced by both rural and urban natives. In 1966, eight regional native organizations joined together to form the Alaska Federation of Natives (AFN) and proceeded to push a claim for almost 400 million acres of land.

In 1971, all sides resolved their interests with the signing of the landmark Alaska Native Claims Settlement Act (ANCSA). In brief, roughly 41,000 natives agreed to cede their aboriginal (including subsistence) rights in exchange for corporate ownership of 44 million acres and almost $1 billion in compensation for lands lost. Of the cash settlement, 10 percent went toward per capita payments and the rest toward the establishment of various capitalist ventures under the administration of 12 (later 13) regional and more than 200 village corporations. Corporate interests including mining, real estate, seafood processing, construction, and numerous other fields. There are

also 12 nonprofit corporations, through which human service funding is channeled. The act has been amended several times, most notably in 1987.

The practical results of ANCSA have been mixed for the native population. Interpretation has given rise to seemingly endless legal and administrative entanglements. Stock ownership is subject to sale, a provision that recalls the 1887 Dawes Severalty Act. The issue of subsistence rights, in particular, has been very problematic, as have the issues of sovereignty and self-determination. Furthermore, not all corporations have been profitable. Native groups continue to act independently to advance what they perceive as their legitimate interests ignored by ANCSA.

Despite the growth of local cities and towns, most of the roughly 70,000 (1990) native Arctic people living on the Aleutian Islands and in Alaska (45,000) and Canada (25,000) still live in small communities in or near their traditional lands. Communities generally feature frame houses with all modern amenities. For reasons of survival as well as identity, many people still engage in subsistence activities, although guns, power boats, and snowmobiles have radically changed the hunting dynamic. Important economic activities in the far north also include commercial fishing, guiding, tourism, oil-related work, mining, construction, and government work and assistance. Various cooperative and traditionally organized businesses increase access to markets as well as goods and services. Arts and crafts, including sculpture, carvings, prints, and woven items, are a key part of the native economy.

In Canada, Inuktitut is spoken in all Inuit communities. Education is locally controlled, as it is in Alaska. Health problems, including substance abuse, death by accident and violence, malnutrition, and infectious disease, persist among Canadian Inuit. In general, Native Alaskans have access to good stores, transportation, and infrastructure. They face many of the same problems as do Canadian Inuit, however.

Building on a tradition of Inuit cooperation, and as part of a general pan-Inuit movement, the Inuit Circumpolar Conference (ICC) held its first assembly in Barrow, Alaska, in June 1977. The ICC holds NGO (nongovernmental organization) status within the United Nations. It represents the interests of native Arctic people of Greenland (Denmark), Scandinavia, Canada, Alaska, and Russia. Major issues facing Arctic natives include land claims, sustainable economic development, environmental pollution, climate change, and sovereignty. Pollution—mainly from oil spillage, industrial chemicals such as PCBs, nuclear waste, and other sources—remains a big threat and a major issue in the Arctic. Despite the vast size of the Arctic, regional cooperation may offer the best hope for these people to make significant gains in the twin goals of political sovereignty and economic self-sufficiency.

Aleut

See Alutiiq; Unangan

Alutiiq

The word Alutiiq (A `lu t ē k) means "a Pacific Eskimo person"; the plural form is Alutiit. The Alutiiq were a maritime people. The people are also known as Pacific Eskimos, Pacific Yup'ik, South Alaska Inuit, Yuit (with the Yup'ik), or Aleut; however, Aleut is easily confused with the culturally and linguistically separate native people of the Aleutian Islands. The word "Aleut" is of Russian origin.

The self-designation of the Alutiiq people is *Sugpiaq* ("real person"). The three traditional subgroups are Chugachmiut (Prince William Sound), Unegkurmiut (lower Kenai Peninsula), and Qikertarmiut, or Koniagmiut (Kodiak Island). There are many similarities to Unangan culture.

LOCATION   Alutiit lived and continue to live along coastal southern Alaska, between Prince William Sound and Bristol Bay. Kodiak Island was one of the most densely populated places north of Mexico.

POPULATION   The aboriginal (mid– to late eighteenth century) population was between 10,000 and 20,000 people. There were about 2,000 Alutiit in 1850 and roughly 5,000 in the 1990s.

LANGUAGE   Alutiit spoke the Sugcestun, or Suk, dialect of the Pacific Gulf Yup'ik branch of Eskimo, an Eskaleut language.

Historical Information

HISTORY   The Alutiiq people had been living in their historic territory for at least 2,000 and perhaps as many as 7,000 years when the Dane Vitus Bering, working for Russia, arrived in 1741. Although he may not have actually encountered any people, contact became regular in the 1760s and 1770s. It was generally resisted by the Alutiiq. The first permanent Russian settlement was established in 1784, on Kodiak Island. By that time British and Spanish seamen had also visited the area.

In part by keeping their children as hostages, Russians soon forced the natives to hunt sea otter pelts and do other work for them. Disease and general oppression soon cut the Alutiiq population dramatically. Many people were acculturated to the Russian religion and customs when the United States gained political control of Alaska in 1867.

At that time there began a renewed push for acculturation in another direction. Children were soon sent to mission and Bureau of Indian Affairs boarding schools, where they were forced on pain of punishment to accommodate to the U.S. model. Economically, canneries and commercial fishing dominated the region from the late nineteenth century on.

Several Alutiiq villages suffered a devastating earthquake and tsunami in 1964. The Alaska Native Claims Settlement Act (ANCSA, 1971) had a profound influence on the people. The act established 12 formal culture areas, of which 3 fell in Alutiiq territory. In 1989 the *Exxon Valdez* ran aground and spilled nearly 11 million gallons of crude oil in Alutiiq territory, resulting in a tremendous loss of sea life, among other things.

RELIGION   The people recognized one or several chief deities as well as numerous supernatural beings. Success in hunting required a positive relationship with the spirits of game animals. Human spirits were reincarnated through birth and naming. Trances, as well as certain masks and dolls, allowed contact with the supernatural.

A large variety of dances, ceremonies, and rituals, including masked performances, songs, and feasts, began in early winter. Specific ceremonies included a memorial feast, a ritual to increase the animal population, the Messenger's Feast (a potlatchlike affair that took place between two closely related villages), life-cycle events, the selection of chiefs, and preparation for the whale hunt. Wise men (Kodiak Island) were in charge of most religious ceremonies, although a dance leader might direct ceremonies and instruct children in dances.

Male and female shamans forecast weather and other events, and they cured disease. Berdaches were often shamans as well. Women also acted as healers through bloodletting and herbal cures.

GOVERNMENT   Despite the existence of 50 or more villages or local groups, there was no strong central government. Most important decisions were taken by consensus agreement of a council. Village leaders were chosen on the basis of merit, although there was a hereditary component. They were expected to earn respect and retained their offices by giving gifts and advice. Some controlled more than one village. Their primary responsibilities were to lead in war and guide subsistence activities. From the nineteenth century on, chiefs *(toyuq)* and secondary chiefs *(sukashiq)* were appointed by a consensus of elders.

CUSTOMS   Descent was weakly matrilineal. Women generally had relatively high status, although they did not participate in formal governing structures such as councils. Society was divided into ranked classes: noble, commoner, and slave. Slaves might be acquired through trade or war, especially among the Chugach and the Koniag. High-stakes gambling was a favorite pastime.

Women were secluded in special huts during their menstrual periods and at the birth or death of a child. Seclusion during the initial menstrual period could extend for several months or more. Women's chins were tattooed when they reached puberty. Male transvestites were esteemed and performed the woman's role for life. Some girls were also raised as boys and performed male roles.

Marriage was formalized when gifts were accepted and the man went to live, temporarily, with his wife's family. A woman might have two husbands, although the second would have very low status. Men might also have multiple wives. Divorce and remarriage were possible. Babies' heads were flattened in the cradle, perhaps intentionally for aesthetic purposes. Children were generally raised gently, with no corporal punishment, but toughened with icy plunges.

Corpses were wrapped in seal or sea lion skin and kept in a special death house. High-status people were mummified. Slaves were sometimes killed and buried with a person of high rank. Mourners blackened their faces, cut their hair, and removed themselves from society. Graveside ceremonies went on for a month or more. Pieces of the corpse of a great whale hunter were sometimes cut up and rubbed on arrow points or used as talismans on hunting boats.

DWELLINGS Houses were semisubterranean, with planked walls and sod and straw-covered roofs. A common main room also served as kitchen and workshop. Side sleeping rooms, heated with hot rocks, were also used by both sexes for ritual and recreational sweats. Up to 20 people (several families) lived in each house. Winter villages were composed of up to ten or so houses. Some villages had large ceremonial halls *(kashims)*. In fishing and other temporary camps, people lived in bark shelters or even under skin boats.

DIET Salmon was a staple, although other fish, such as herring, halibut, cod, and eulachon, were also important. Sea mammals, such as whales, porpoises, sea lions, sea otters, and seals, were also key. Seals were hunted in part by the use of decoys and calls. Dead whales were not pulled ashore but were allowed to drift in the hope that they would come back to camp. Whale darts may have been poisoned.

The people also ate sea birds. There was some gathering of shellfish and seaweed as well as greens, roots, and berries. Land mammals, such as caribou, moose, squirrel, mountain goat, and hare, also played a part in the diet.

KEY TECHNOLOGY A foot-long slate dart on a five-foot-long shaft, possibly poisoned, was used for killing whales. A bow and arrow as well as several kinds of darts, spears, clubs, and harpoons sufficed to kill other marine and land mammals. Some land mammals were also snared or trapped. Seals and sea birds were also netted.

Fishing gear included hooks, weirs, harpoons, and rakes. Lines were made of certain algae and/or of sinew. Women wove spruce-root baskets and hats and sewed bags and clothing. Other tools were made of stone and wood. Some iron, probably acquired from shipwrecks, was also used. Lamps burned whale oil and grass. Bladders stretched over hoops served as drums.

TRADE The Alutiiq acquired dentalia and slaves from the Northwest Coast. They exported caribou, mountain goats, and marmot parts. Messenger Feasts/potlatches also involved trade.

NOTABLE ARTS Woven spruce-root baskets were decorated with grass and fern embroidery. Men carved and painted wooden dance masks.

TRANSPORTATION Two-hatch skin kayaks were the main vehicle for transportation, whaling, and sealing. They were made of sealskin stretched over branches. The people also used some dugout canoes, umiaks, and plank toboggans pulled by dogs.

DRESS Alutiiq people wore long parkas of fur (squirrel or sea lion) and bird skin, sewn eagle-skin or -intestine rain parkas, and sea lion–, salmon-, or bear-skin boots in cold weather. Men's conical bentwood or woven spruce-root hats, worn at sea, may reflect a Tlingit influence. Men also wore Unangan-style wooden visors.

Women wore labrets and nose pins. Men also wore ornaments, such as sea lion whiskers, in their ears and noses. Other types of ornaments included coral, shell, and bone. Men braided their long hair, whereas women wore it tied up on their heads.

WAR AND WEAPONS There was some fighting among Alutiiq groups and between Alutiit and nearby Indian tribes, particularly the Tlingit and Tanaina. Slave raiding was part of that activity. Men were generally killed or tortured, whereas women and children might be taken prisoner as slaves. Surprise attack was the preferred method of fighting. Weapons included slat armor, bow and arrow, and quivers.

Contemporary Information

GOVERNMENT/RESERVATIONS Five villages, all located on the south shore of the Alaskan Peninsula, fall under the purview of the Bristol Bay Native Corporation. Chignik Bay, 103 native residents, is governed by seven elected representatives to the Chignik Bay Village Council as well as seven elected members of the city council. Chignik Lagoon, 46 native residents, is governed by eight elected representative to the Chignik Lagoon Village Council. Chignik Lake, 122 native residents, is governed by seven elected representatives to the Chignik Lake Village Council. Ivanof Bay, 33 native residents, is governed by five elected representatives to the Ivanof Bay Village Council. Perryville, 114 native residents, is governed by five representatives to the native village of Perryville Village Tribal Council (Indian Reorganization Act [IRA]). The first four villages are also members of the Lake and Peninsula Borough. Some of these villages also have Unangan residents. Population figures are as of the early 1990s.

Other villages include Afognak, Akhiok, Kaguyak, Karluk, Larsen Bay, Old Harbor, Ouzinkie, and Port Lions (Kodiak Island) and English Bay, Port Graham, and Tatitlek (Kenai Peninsula). Villages are governed by elected tribal councils, some IRA-derived and some structured according to tradition. Towns, or communities within urban centers, are located in Anchorage, Cordova, Kodiak, Seward, and Valdez.

ECONOMY The most important sources of income are commercial and subsistence salmon fishing and payments from the Alaska Native Land Fund.

LEGAL STATUS Under ANCSA, the Alutiiq people are represented by the Chugach Alaska Corporation, Koniag, Inc., and the Bristol Bay Native Corporation. The many village governments have government-to-government relationships with the United States. Tribal consortia representing village governments contract with the United States for health, education, and social services. These include the Bristol Bay Native Association, Chugachmiut (formerly North Pacific Rim), and the Kodiak Area Native Association.

DAILY LIFE Many villages are only accessibly by air or water. Most people are Russian Orthodox, many older people speak Russian (along with English and Alutiiq), and there are considerable other Russian influences. Most village social activities are church related.

Some Alutiit are more identified with the ANCSA corporate entities than as Alutiit. Village concerns include protecting the local fisheries, road construction, and the construction of a boat harbor. Efforts to preserve the native culture include the formation of the Kodiak Alutiiq Dancers, language classes, oral histories, and craft (woodworking and kayak making) projects.

Eskimo, Bering Strait
See Inupiat

Eskimo, Kotzebue Sound
See Inupiat

Eskimo, Nunivak
See Yup'ik

Eskimo, Pacific
See Alutiiq

Eskimo, South Alaska
See Yup'ik

Eskimo, Southwest Alaska
See Yup'ik

Eskimo, St. Lawrence Island
See Yup'ik

Eskimo, West Alaska
See Yup'ik

Iglulik

Iglulik (I `gl ū lik), a name derived (with their main settlement, Igloolik) from the custom of living in snow houses, or igloos. *See also* Inuit, Baffinland.

LOCATION Traditional Iglulik territory is north of Hudson Bay, including northern Baffin Island, the Melville Peninsula, Southhampton Island, and part of Roes Welcome Sound. It lies within the central Arctic, or Kitikmeot.

POPULATION Estimated at 500 in the early nineteenth century, the 1990 Iglulik population was about 2,400.

LANGUAGE Igluliks speak a dialect of Inuit-Inupiaq (Inuktitut), a member of the Eskaleut language family.

Historical Information

HISTORY The people encountered Scottish whalers early in the nineteenth century. Eventually, Scottish celebrations came to supplant traditional ones in part. By the time American whalers arrived in the 1860s, the Iglulik had acquired whaleboats, guns, iron items, tea, and tobacco. Later in the century, the people became involved with fox trapping and musk ox hunting. They also intermarried with non-natives and acquired high rates of alcoholism and venereal disease.

Regular contact with other Inuit, such as the Netsilik, was established at local trading posts and missions. These arrived in the early twentieth century, as did a permanent presence of the Royal Canadian Mounted Police (RCMP). Improved medical care followed these inroads of non-native influence.

The far north took on strategic importance during the Cold War, about the same time that vast mineral reserves became known and technologically possible to exploit. These developments encouraged population movements. Also, as non-natives increased their influence, such aspects of traditional culture as shamanism, wife exchange, and murders began to disappear. In 1954 the federal Department of Northern Affairs and Natural Resources officially encouraged Inuit to abandon nomadic life. It built housing developments, schools, and clinics. Local political decisions were made by a community council subject to non-native approval and review.

The snowmobile, introduced in early 1960s, increased the potential trapping and hunting area and diminished the need for meat (fewer dogs to feed). Such employment as Inuit could obtain was generally unskilled and menial. With radical diet changes (including flour and sugar), the adoption of a sedentary life, and the appearance of drugs and alcohol, the people's health declined markedly.

RELIGION Religious belief and practice were based on the need to appease spirit entities found in nature. Hunting, and specifically the land-sea dichotomy, was the focus of most rituals and taboos, such as that prohibiting sewing caribou skin clothing in certain seasons. The people also recognized generative spirits, conceived of as female and identified with natural forces and cycles. A rich body of legends was related during the long, dark nights.

Male and female shamans *(angakok)* provided religious leadership by virtue of their connection with guardian spirits. They could also control the weather, improve conditions for hunting, cure disease, and divine the future. Illness was due to soul loss and/or violation of taboos and/or the anger of the dead. Curing methods included interrogation about taboo adherence, trancelike communication with spirit helpers, and performance.

GOVERNMENT There was no real political organization; nuclear families came together in the fall to form local groups, or settlements, that in turn were grouped into three divisions—Iglulingmiut, Aivilingmiut, and Tununermiut—associated with geographical areas *(-miuts)*. Local group leaders were usually older men, with little formal authority and no power. Leaders generally embodied Inuit values, such as generosity, and were also good hunters.

CUSTOMS Sharing was paramount in Inuit society. Descent was bilateral. People came together in larger group gatherings in late autumn; that was a time to sew and mend clothing and renew kinship ties. Spring was also a time for visiting and travel.

People married simply by announcing their intentions, although infants were regularly betrothed. Prospective husbands often served their future inlaws for a period of time. Men might have more than

one wife, but most had only one. Divorce was easy to obtain. The people also recognized many other types of formal and informal partnerships and relationships. Some of these included wife exchanges.

A woman gave birth in a special shelter and lived in another special shelter, in which she observed various taboos, for some time after the birth. Because infant mortality was high, infanticide was rare, and usually practiced against females. Babies were generally named after a deceased relative. Children were highly valued and loved, especially males. They were generally given a high degree of freedom. After puberty, siblings of the opposite sex acted with reserve toward each other. This reached an extreme in the case of brothers- and sisters-in-law.

The sick or aged were sometimes abandoned, especially in times of scarcity, or the aged might commit suicide. Corpses lay in state for three days, after which they were wrapped in skins, taken out through the rear of the house, and buried in the snow. The tools of the deceased were left with him or her. No activities, including hunting, were permitted for six days following a death.

Feuds, with blood vendettas, were a regular feature of traditional life. Tensions were relieved through games; duels of drums and songs, in which the competing people tried to outdo each other in parody and song; some joking relationships; and athletic contests. Outdoor games included ball, hide-and-seek, and contests. There were many indoor games as well. These activities also took place on regular social occasions, such as visits. Ostracism and even death were reserved for the most serious cases of socially inappropriate behavior.

DWELLINGS The people lived in domed snow houses for part of the winter. They entered through an above-ground tunnel that trapped the warm air inside. Snow houses featured porches for storage and sometimes had more than one room. Ice or gut skin served as windows. Some groups lined the snow house with sealskins. Snow houses were often joined together at porches to form multifamily dwellings. People slept on raised packed snow platforms on caribou hide bedding. Some larger snow houses were built for social and ceremonial purposes. People generally lived in sealskin tents in summer. In spring and fall some groups used stone houses reinforced with whalebone and sod and roofed with skins.

DIET The Iglulik were nomadic hunters. The most important game animals were seals, whales, walrus, and narwhal. Men hunted seals at their breathing holes in winter and from boats in summer, as they did whales and walrus. In summer, the people traveled inland to hunt caribou, musk ox, and birds and to fish, especially for salmon and trout. Other foods included some berries and birds and their eggs. Meat, which might not be very fresh, was cooked in soapstone pots over soapstone blubber lamps or eaten raw or frozen. In summer, people burned oil-soaked bones for cooking fuel.

KEY TECHNOLOGY Men used bone knives to cut blocks for snow houses. Other tools and equipment included harpoons, spears, snares, lances, bow and arrow, and bolas. They caught fox and wolf in stone or ice traps. Bows were made of spruce with sealskin and sinew backing. Some were also made of musk ox horn or antler. Many tools were made from caribou antlers as well as stone, bone, and driftwood. Blades were made of bone or copper. Fires were started with flint and pyrite or a wooden drill.

Fishing equipment included hooks, wooden or stone weirs and traps, and a variety of spears and harpoons. The people carved soapstone cooking pots and seal-oil lamps as well as wooden utensils, trays, dishes, spoons, and other objects. Women sewed with bone needles and sinew thread and used curved knives and scrapers to prepare skins.

TRADE Material goods were exchanged with nearby neighbors, both Iglulik and non-Iglulik, mostly in summer.

NOTABLE ARTS The people carved wooden and ivory objects and made finely tanned skin clothing decorated with bands of color.

TRANSPORTATION Men hunted in one- or two-person sealskin kayaks. Occasionally, several might be lashed together to form a raft. Umiaks were larger, skin-covered open boats. Dogs pulled wooden sleds, the whalebone or wood runners of which were covered with ice. Dogs also carried small packs during seasonal travel.

DRESS Women sewed most clothing from caribou skins, although sealskins were commonly used on boots. Apparel included men's long, gut sealing coats and light swallowtail ceremonial coats. The people wore a double skin suit in winter and only the inner layer in summer. Most men's parkas had a long flap in the back; the woman's had two long, narrow flaps. Women's clothing featured large shoulders and hoods as well as one-piece, attached leggings and boots. They wore high caribou skin and sealskin boots containing square pouches. Men wore small loon-beak dancing caps with weasel-skin tassels. They sometimes shaved their foreheads. Both sexes wore tattoos and ivory or bone snow goggles.

WAR AND WEAPONS There was some intragroup fighting and some fighting as well with the Netsilik. Hunting equipment generally doubled as weapons of war.

Contemporary Information

GOVERNMENT/RESERVATIONS Contemporary communities include: Ausuittuq (Grise Ford), Iglulik (Igloolik), Ikpiarjuk/Tununirusiq (Arctic Bay), Iqaluit, Mittimatalik/Tununiq (Pond Inlet), Qausuittuq (Resolute Bay), and Sanirajuk (Hall Beach). Government is by locally elected community council.

ECONOMY There is some employment in oil fields and mines. Government assistance is an important source of income for many Iglulik. The Iglulik economy today is mainly money based. Unemployment was officially pegged at 30 percent in 1994.

Native-owned and -operated cooperatives have been an important part of the Inuit economy for some time. Activities range from arts and crafts to retail to commercial fishing to construction. Woodcarving is particularly important among the Iglulik.

LEGAL STATUS Inuit are considered "nonstatus" native people. Most Inuit communities are incorporated as hamlets and are officially recognized. Baffin Island is slated to become a part of the new territory of Nunavut.

DAILY LIFE The Baffin Regional Association was formed to press for political rights. In 1993, the Tungavik Federation of Nunavut (TFN), an outgrowth of the Inuit Tapirisat of Canada (ITC), signed an agreement with Canada providing for the establishment in 1999 of a new, mostly Inuit, territory on roughly 36,000 square kilometers of land, including Baffin Island.

The people never abandoned their land, which is still central to their identity. Traditional and modern coexist, sometimes uneasily, for many Inuit. Although people use television (there is even radio and television programming in Inuktitut), snowmobiles, and manufactured items, women also carry babies in the traditional hooded parkas, chew caribou skin to make it soft, and use the semilunar knives to cut seal meat. Full-time doctors are rare in the communities. Housing is often of poor quality. Most people are Christians. Culturally, although many stabilizing patterns of traditional culture have been destroyed, many remain. Many people live as part of extended families. Adoption is widely practiced. Decisions are often taken by consensus. However, with access to the world at large, social problems, including substance abuse and suicide among the young, have increased. Fewer than half of the people finish high school.

Politically, community councils have gained considerably more autonomy over the past decade or two. There is also a significant Inuit presence in the Northwest Territories Legislative Assembly and some presence at the federal level as well. The disastrous effects of government-run schools have been mitigated to some degree by local control of education, including more culturally relevant curricula in schools. Many people still speak Inuktitut, which is also taught in most schools, especially in the earlier grades. Children attend school in their community through grade nine; the high school is in Frobisher Bay. Adult education is also available.

Inuit, Baffinland

Baffinland Inuit (`I ny ū it), "People." The people call themselves *Nunatsiaqmiut,* "People of the Beautiful Land." The Baffin region today, including Baffin Island, and the eastern High Arctic Islands, is known as Qikiqtaaluk.

LOCATION The Baffinland Inuit live on mainly coastal parts of southern and central Baffin Island, eastern Northwest Territories. The land is rugged and includes mountains, plains, rolling hills, fjords, lakes, and rivers. The weather is also rugged and extreme, and the tides, especially in the east, are very high.

POPULATION There were approximately 2,700 Baffinland Inuit in the mid–eighteenth century, most of whom lived on Cumberland Sound. The mid-1990s Qikiqtaaluk Inuit population was about 11,300.

LANGUAGE The native language is Inuit-Inupiaq (Inuktitut), a member of the Eskaleut language family.

Historical Information

HISTORY Parts of Baffin Island were settled over 4,000 years ago. The Thule, or pre-Inuit culture, entered the region circa 1200. Norsemen may have visited Baffin Island around the year 1000, but definite contact with non-natives was not established until the people met early explorers in the late sixteenth century.

Non-native whaling began in the east (Davis Strait) in the eighteenth century. The Inuit people shortly began to experience high rates of tuberculosis and other diseases, such as measles. Whaling centers established in the nineteenth century employed Inuit and slowly changed their economy, marking the shift to dependency.

Anglican missionaries arrived in the early twentieth century and conducted the first baptisms. A missionary-derived syllabary was created and persisted well into the twentieth century. The Hudson's Bay Company built trading posts from 1911 on, signaling the end of whaling and the beginning of fur trapping as the most important economic activity. This period also saw the beginning of outside control of the people's lives by traders, missionaries, and police.

The far north took on strategic importance dur-ing the Cold War, about the same time that vast mineral reserves became known and technologically possible to exploit. The federal Department of Northern Affairs and Natural Resources (1954) encouraged the Inuit to abandon their nomadic life. It saw to the construction of housing developments, schools, and a general infrastructure. Local political decisions were made by a community council subject to non-native approval and review. Inuit found generally menial and poorly paying employment. With radical diet changes, the adoption of a sedentary life, and the appearance of drugs and alcohol, health declined markedly.

RELIGION Religious belief and practice were based on spirit entities found in nature and needing to be treated with respect. Rituals showing respect to an animal just killed focused on these beliefs, which were also the basis of most taboos and the use of amulets. People could acquire the spirits of objects as protectors. There were also more overarching, generative spirits identified with natural forces and cycles. These were largely female identified. Souls were said to be reincarnated.

Male and female shamans *(angakok)* provided religious leadership by virtue of their direct connection with guardian spirits. They led group religious activities. They could also cure disease and see into the future. Illness was perceived as having to do with soul loss and/or violation of taboos. Curing methods included interrogation about taboo adherence, trancelike communication with spirit helpers, and performance.

GOVERNMENT There was no formal political organization; instead, nuclear families combined to form villages in distinct geographical areas *(-miuts).* Villages occasionally came together as small, fluid, kinship-related bands. The bands were also geographically identified—their names carried the *-miut* suffix—although other groups were not specifically excluded. Larger but ill-defined population regions included Sikosuilarmiut, Akuliarmiut, Qaumauangmiut, Nugumiut, Oqomiut, Padlimiut, and Akudnirmiut.

Band leaders *(isumataq)* were usually older men with little formal authority and no power. Leaders embodied Inuit values, such as generosity, and were also good hunters.

CUSTOMS Sharing was paramount in Inuit society. All aspects of a person's life were controlled by kinship relationships. People married by announcing their intentions, although infants were regularly betrothed. Some men might have more than one wife. Divorce was easy to obtain. Wife exchange was practiced as part of formal male partnerships. Infanticide was rare and usually practiced against females. Names were taken from deceased people and given by elders. A person might have several names, each denoting a kinship relationship and particular behaviors. Names were not sex specific. Children were generally raised gently. Men hunted, made and repaired weapons and tools, and build kayaks, sleds, and shelter. Women prepared skins and made clothing, sewed hides for coverings, caught and prepared fish, raised children, and gathered moss, berries, and other items.

The sick or aged were sometimes abandoned, especially in times of scarcity. Corpses were wrapped in skins and covered with rocks. People brought weapons and food to the grave after four days. No work, including hunting, was performed during the days of mourning. Tensions were relieved through games, such as feats of strength, and duels of drums and songs, in which one person tried to outdo another in parody and song. Joking relationships also helped keep people's emotions in check. Games included ring-and-pin and cat's cradle. Children liked to play games, including tag and hide-and-seek. Ostracism and even death were reserved for the most serious cases of socially inappropriate behavior.

DWELLINGS Domed snow houses were used in winter, although people might also build stone houses covered with skin and plant material. Entrance through a tunnel kept the warm air inside. These houses sometimes had more than one room and had storage porches as well. Beds were raised snow platforms covered with branches and skins. The people also built some larger snow or sod and bone houses for ceremonial purposes. Skin tents were generally used in summer.

DIET Baffinland Inuit were nomadic hunters. The most important marine animals were seals and beluga whales, but they also hunted walrus, narwhal, and polar bear. Seals were hunted at their breathing holes and also on floe ice. In summer, the people traveled inland to hunt caribou and birds (and eggs) as well as some small game. They fished year-round and gathered some berries, roots, and shellfish.

KEY TECHNOLOGY Men used bone knives to cut snow blocks for houses. Hunting equipment included harpoons, lances, spears, and the bow (driftwood or antler) and arrow. Wood and leather floats and drags were also used in whale hunting. Birds (their bones made excellent needles) were caught with wood and leather nets as well as whalebone snares; fish were caught with hooks and stone weirs. Most tools were made of caribou antlers as well as stone, bone, and driftwood. Sinew served nicely as thread. Other important items included carved soapstone cooking pots and lamps that burned seal oil/blubber and carved wooden trays, dishes, spoons, and other objects.

TRADE Baffinland Inuit engaged in some trade and other intercourse with nearby neighbors; for instance, the people of Cumberland Sound were in contact with the Iglulik Inuit and those of southern Baffin Island with Inuit of Labrador (Ungava), where they obtained wood for their kayaks and umiaks. Other trade items included copper and ivory.

NOTABLE ARTS Some groups carved wooden and ivory figurines. Storytelling was also considered a high art. Drum dancing, a performance art, combined music, story, dance, and song. Some Inuit women also practiced a form of singing known as throat singing.

TRANSPORTATION Men hunted using one- or two-person kayaks of driftwood frames and sealskin. Umiaks were larger, skin-covered open boats. Wooden sleds carried people and belongings to and from the interior. Dog traction dates generally from the early twentieth century to the 1960s.

DRESS Most clothing consisted of caribou-skin and sealskin clothing and boots. Women's sealskin parkas had a larger hood for accommodating an infant. Some people were able to acquire polar bear–skin pants. Waterproof seal-intestine suits, partially lined with dog fur, were used for whale hunting. Women coiled or braided their hair.

WAR AND WEAPONS Conflicts were local in nature. They generally took the form of raids. Hunting equipment such as spears and bows and arrows doubled as weapons of war.

Contemporary Information

GOVERNMENT/RESERVATIONS Population centers include Kangiqtugaapik (Clyde River), Broughton Island, Panniqtuuq (Pangnirtung), Frobisher Bay, Kimmirik (Lake Harbour), and Kinngait (Cape Dorset). There are also five small (fewer than 30 people) hunting villages. Government is by locally elected community councils.

ECONOMY Subsistence hunting, trapping, and fishing are still important, as are various kinds of wage work and government assistance. Possible future developments include oil and gas exploration as well as tanker traffic. Cape Dorset artists are well known and relatively successful.

Native-owned and -operated cooperatives have been an important part of the Inuit economy for some time. Activities range from arts and crafts to retail to commercial fishing to construction.

LEGAL STATUS Inuit are considered "nonstatus" native people. Most Inuit communities are incorporated as hamlets and are officially recognized. Baffin Island is slated to become a part of the new territory of Nunavut.

DAILY LIFE The Baffin Regional Association was

formed to press for political rights. In 1993, the Tungavik Federation of Nunavut (TFN), an outgrowth of the Inuit Tapirisat of Canada (ITC), signed an agreement with Canada providing for the establishment in 1999 of a new, mostly Inuit, territory on roughly 36,000 square kilometers of land, including Baffin Island.

The people never abandoned their land, which is still central to their identity. Traditional and modern coexist, sometimes uneasily, for many Inuit. Although people use television (there is even radio and television programming in Inuktitut), snowmobiles, and manufactured items, women also carry babies in the traditional hooded parkas, chew caribou skin to make it soft, and use the semilunar knives to cut seal meat. Full-time doctors are rare in the communities. Housing is often of poor quality. Most people are Christians. Culturally, although many stabilizing patterns of traditional culture have been destroyed, many remain. Many people live as part of extended families. Adoption is widely practiced. Decisions are often taken by consensus.

Politically, community councils have gained considerably more autonomy over the past decade or two. There is also a significant Inuit presence in the Northwest Territories Legislative Assembly and some presence at the federal level as well. The disastrous effects of government-run schools have been mitigated to some degree by local control of education, including more culturally relevant curricula in schools. Many people still speak Inuktitut, which is also taught in most schools, especially in the earlier grades. Children attend school in their community through grade nine; the high school is in Frobisher Bay. Adult education is also available.

Inuit, Caribou

Caribou Inuit (`I ny ū it) is a non-native term reflecting the people's reliance on caribou. The Inuit self-designation was *Nunamiut,* "inlanders."

LOCATION   The Caribou Inuit homeland is located on the southern Barren Grounds west of Hudson Bay (Keewatin District, Northwest Territories). The early population centered along the coast, near Whale Cove. As population grew during the nineteenth century, the trend was to expand to the north, south, and west (interior), especially as the Chipewyan Indians abandoned the latter region. This windy land consists mainly of gently rolling plains. It is very well watered, although little plant life exists there.

POPULATION   There were between 300 and 500 Caribou Inuit in the late eighteenth century. The population had grown to around 1,500 in 1915. In the mid-1990s there were approximately 6,900 Inuit in the Keewatin District (Kivalliq).

LANGUAGE   The Caribou Inuit speak a dialect of Inuit-Inupiaq (Inuktitut), part of the Eskaleut language family.

Historical Information

HISTORY   The historic Caribou Inuit descended directly from ancient Thule people, in local residence since about the twelfth century. The first non-native explorers arrived in the early seventeenth century, although there may not have been direct contact between the two peoples.

Regular trade with non-natives began shortly after the people were first visited by Hudson's Bay Company representatives in 1717. Ships brought foreign goods from Churchill, and the Inuit traded for items such as metal knives and axes, beads, tobacco, and, later, guns and powder. At that time they often acted as intermediaries between non-natives and the Iglulik, Netsilik, and Copper Inuit. Regular trade began at Churchill in 1790.

By the early nineteenth century, Caribou Inuit society had begun to reorient itself, with southerners focusing on the Churchill area and the non-native trade, and northerners making stronger ties with the Aivilik Iglulik Inuit. The two groups divided in about 1810. Shortly thereafter, the two societies became five.

The Hudson's Bay Company conducted commercial whaling from about 1860 to 1915. The Inuit people killed seals and whales each summer, trading most oil and other products, while shifting to almost total dependence on caribou as well as musk ox and fish to a lesser extent.

Canada established a formal presence in 1903. Trading posts and Catholic missionaries arrived in 1912, followed by various non-native settlements in the region. A severe famine from 1915 to around 1924 killed perhaps two-thirds of the people. After that event, the people turned to trapping (mainly fox fur) and the wage/trade economy as a means of survival. This marked the end of their essential independence.

Gradually, continuing hunger and epidemics began to fragment the societies, as the population continued to decline. The situation attracted governmental intervention in the 1950s. Administrative centers were established. Most people relocated by choice to one of five settlements, most of which contained a minority of Caribou Inuit (although a majority of Inuit).

The shift to towns was completed in the 1960s. The people lived in prefabricated housing, generally wore nontraditional clothing, and ate nontraditional foods. With the breakdown of the traditional economy, and nothing to take its place, many experienced for the first time problems of substance abuse. Children began learning English in school but little about their traditional culture. Acculturation quickly became established among the young. The arrival of television in the 1970s and then other electronic media accelerated these trends.

RELIGION The Caribou Inuit recognized a supreme creative force that took an interest in the affairs of people. This deity may have been associated with the female caribou. The souls of people who had lived well (observed all the taboos, of which there were many) were thought to rejoin this force when they died, thence to be reincarnated on earth. The souls of those who had not lived well were said to be eternally damned.

Religion was essentially hunting based. Respect was owed to all things in nature but especially game animals. People left offerings for the spirits of slain animals. A number of ceremonial danced reinforced these ideas. Shamans specialized in spiritual matters, acting as intermediary between the two worlds. They could find out, by communicating with the spirits, who had broken which taboo and how a problem situation could be rectified (curing).

GOVERNMENT Political leadership, such as it was, took place within the context of the family. The leader was generally an older man who sat atop the family kinship network. He was also likely to be strong, wise, highly skilled in hunting, and familiar with the spirit world. Other than this, informal, ad hoc leaders advised small groups on hunting matters and when to move camp.

There were five bands or societies in the mid–nineteenth century: Paatlirmiut, Qairnitmuit, Ahiarmiut, Hauniqturmiut, and Harvaqturmiut. The societies were separate although related by marriage and descent.

CUSTOMS Betrothal took place as early as infancy. Cross cousins (children of a mother's brothers or a father's sisters) were regarded as highly desirable marriage partners. There was some regular intermarriage with other Inuit groups such as the Netsilik and Iglulik. There was little or no marriage ceremony. Newly married couples might live with either set of parents. Men might have more than one wife; widows, especially, tended to marry their brothers-in-law.

Occasional temporary partner swapping—considered a type of marriage—established further obligations and social ties. Other alternative relationships were known as dancing partners. This arrangement consisted of partners beating each other until one surrendered, after which time presents were bestowed. Later, they danced together to the sound of beating drums. These people generally lived apart but visited regularly.

Although children were highly valued and gener-

ally treated very well, and although childless couples often adopted children, there was some female infanticide. Corpses were wrapped in skins and placed within a circle of stones, along with various possessions. The mourning period was highly ritualized.

The extended family was the basic unit. The people displayed a distinct fondness for singing, feasting, and social drum dancing, sometimes in a large snow house or tent. They played several games, many of which included gambling, and took part in athletic contests. The art of making string figures was well developed.

DWELLINGS For most of their prehistory, coastal people used stone winter houses, chinked with moss and dirt and covered with snow. Around 1880 they learned, from the Iglulik, to build domed snow houses. These houses generally held ten people at most. A clear ice window was placed over the door. Storage was available on the sides of a long entryway, which itself was placed below ground level to keep the cold drafts out. Furniture consisted of snow platforms covered with skins and willow mats. Some people built a small connected kitchen with a smoke hole, although many cooked, when they cooked at all, outside on fires of moss and willow. There was generally no heat. Houses of family members might be linked by tunnels.

The people used conical skin (hair side out for waterproofing) tents as well as temporary brush windbreaks in other seasons. Most settlements were occupied by only one extended family, although groups might grow in size in spring and summer.

DIET Men engaged in extensive summer seal, walrus, and whale hunting before the early to mid–nineteenth century. A few coastal people continued these activities even after that time. Meat was sun dried and stored in sealskin bags and retained for winter use.

Especially from the mid–nineteenth century on, the people depended almost totally on migrating herds of caribou, which reached their peak numbers in autumn. People intercepted the animals at water crossings, drove them into lakes, and directed them down courseways where hunters waited. The men continued to hunt while women processed the meat and skins. Excess meat was covered with skins and hidden under rocks. Men also hunted musk ox when necessary, especially when the caribou meat began to run out. These were hunted to extinction by about 1900.

Most winter food was eaten frozen and raw. Fishing took place mostly in winter and spring. Other foods included birds and their eggs, some summer berries, and the plant foods inside of caribou stomachs. Winter food stores often ran quite low toward the end of the season. Sharing of food was well developed, to the point where hunters were not considered to own their own kills.

KEY TECHNOLOGY   Most material items, such as tools, scrapers, needles, hooks, and arrowheads, were derived from the caribou. Men used bone or antler snow knives to cut blocks of snow for winter houses. They hunted with bow and arrow, snares, pitfalls, lances, and harpoons. Stone weirs and hook and line were the most common fishing equipment. Other raw materials included wood and soapstone. Small, weak lamps burned caribou fat or fish oil. Cooking fires burned dwarf shrubbery. Musical instruments included drums, tambourine, and voice.

TRADE   All trade took place in summer. The people traded caribou skins and soapstone with the Chipewyan and Cree for snowshoes, moccasins, and pyrite. They also traded with the Aivilik Iglulik Inuit from about 1800 on. Exports included driftwood and seal dog traces and boot soles, among other items.

NOTABLE ARTS   Caribou Inuit may have learned quill embroidery from the Chipewyan and/or Cree Indians.

TRANSPORTATION   Long, narrow, skin-covered kayaks were sometimes tied together to form rafts for crossing larger bodies of water. After around 1800, the people used dogsleds whose runners were coated with ice-covered peat. Most transportation was overland with the help of tumplines, the Caribou Inuit being particularly strong walkers.

DRESS   Six to eight caribou skins provided an adult suit of well-tailored clothing, including pants, boots, mittens, and outer and inner parkas. Furs and fur trim came from polar bears, wolves, wolverines, and foxes. Women wore bone or copper headbands. Women's parka hoods were extra large to accommodate babies carried high on the back. Wet clothing was dried only with great difficulty in winter.

WAR AND WEAPONS   Enemies of the Caribou Inuit included the Chipewyan (at least to the mid–eighteenth century) and Dogrib Athapaskans. Hunting implements doubled as weapons.

Contemporary Information

GOVERNMENT/RESERVATIONS   Contemporary population centers include Arviat (Eskimo Point), Igluliagaarjuq (Chesterfield Inlet), Kangiqliniq (Rankin Inlet), Naujaat/Aivilik (Repulse Bay), Qamanittuaq (Baker Lake), Salliq (Coral Harbour), and Tikirarjuaq (Whale Cove). Government is based on elected councils.

The Caribou Inuit have pushed hard and successfully for the creation of an all-Inuit territory, Nunavut, which will include their territory. They are also active in the Inummarilirijikkut, or Inuit Central Institute.

ECONOMY   Hunting and fishing remain important subsistence activities. Wage labor includes trapping; some crafts, especially woodcarving; mining; working as support personnel; and government assistance.

Native-owned and -operated cooperatives have been an important part of the Inuit economy for some time. Activities range from arts and crafts to retail to commercial fishing to construction.

LEGAL STATUS   Inuit are considered "nonstatus" native people. Most Inuit communities are incorporated as hamlets and are officially recognized. Baffin Island is slated to become a part of the new territory of Nunavut.

DAILY LIFE   The people never abandoned their land, which is still central to their identity. Traditional and modern coexist, sometimes uneasily, for many Inuit. Although people use television (there is even radio and television programming in Inuktitut), snowmobiles, and manufactured items, women also carry babies in the traditional hooded parkas, chew caribou skin to make it soft, and use the semilunar knives to cut seal meat. Full-time doctors are rare in the communities. Housing is often of poor quality. Most people are Christians. Culturally, although many stabilizing patterns of traditional culture have been destroyed, many remain. Many people live as part of extended families. Adoption is widely practiced. Decisions are often taken by consensus. Intermarriage between Inuit groups in the five population centers has blurred ethnic identity; people now tend to identify with their settlement.

Politically, community councils have gained considerably more autonomy over the past decade or two. There is also a significant Inuit presence in the Northwest Territories Legislative Assembly and some presence at the federal level as well. The disastrous effects of government-run schools have been mitigated to some degree by local control of education, including more culturally relevant curricula in schools. Many people still speak Inuktitut, which is also taught in most schools, especially in the earlier grades. Children attend school in their community through grade nine; the high school is in Frobisher Bay. Adult education is also available. Caribou overhunting has prompted increased government regulations, which are resisted by the Caribou Inuit, who still identify to a significant extent with the caribou.

Inuit, Copper

Copper Inuit (ʻI ny ū it), "People." The people received this name from non-native explorers who found them using native copper in tools and weapons. See also Netsilik.

LOCATION   In the eighteenth century the Copper

Inuit were living between Cape Parry and Queen Maude Gulf, especially on southern Victoria Island and along Coronation Gulf. The region is almost entirely tundra, except for some forest to the south and along the Coppermine River. Many Copper Inuit still live in this area of the central Arctic, known as Kitikmeot.

POPULATION The native population was probably between 800 and 1,300 in the late eighteenth century. In 1990 there were around 2,000 Inuit in the local communities, most of whom were Copper Inuit. The mid-1990s population of the Kitikmeot Region (Copper and Netsilik Inuit) was roughly 4,000.

LANGUAGE Copper Inuits speak a dialect of Inuit-Inupiaq (Inuktitut), a member of the Eskaleut language family.

Historical Information

HISTORY Historical Copper Inuit people are descended from ancient pre-Dorset, Dorset, and Thule cultures. They first encountered non-natives in the late eighteenth and early nineteenth centuries. Although they obtained some non-native trade goods, such as iron, and caught new diseases, traditional life remained relatively unchanged for some time thereafter.

Local trading posts were established in the 1920s, bringing items such as rifles, fish nets, and steel traps as well as cloth, tea and flour. These material changes had the result of extending the caribou season and generally reorienting the people away from the sea. This development, plus the regular presence of trade ships, began to undermine traditional self-sufficiency and social structures. The region's first missionaries arrived at about the same time, as did a permanent presence of the Royal Canadian Mounted Police (RCMP).

It was not until the 1950s, however, that the root aspects of traditional culture began to disappear. Some mixing with western Inuit newcomers occurred during that time. The far north took on strategic importance during the Cold War, about the same time that vast mineral reserves became known and technologically possible to exploit. These two industries offered some wage labor and contributed to the decline of nomadic life. Other factors contributed as well, such as the decline of the caribou herds.

The federal Department of Northern Affairs and Natural Resources (1954) began constructing wood-frame housing developments, clinics, and schools and encouraged resettlement in these permanent communities. Local political decisions were made by a community council subject to non-native approval and review. Population centralization was largely completed by the 1970s. Most job opportunities for Inuit were unskilled and menial, although hunting and trapping remained important. With radical diet changes, the adoption of a sedentary life, and the appearance of drugs and alcohol, health declined markedly.

RELIGION Religious belief and practice were based on the need to appease spirit entities found in nature. Hunting, and specifically the land-sea dichotomy, was the focus of most rituals and taboos, such as that prohibiting sewing caribou-skin clothing in certain seasons. The people also recognized generative spirits, conceived of as female and identified with natural forces and cycles.

Male and female shamans (angakok) provided religious leadership by virtue of their connection with guardian spirits. They could also control the weather, improve conditions for hunting, cure disease, and divine the future. Illness was due to soul loss and/or violation of taboos and/or the anger of the dead. Curing methods included interrogation about taboo adherence, trancelike communication with spirit helpers, and performance.

GOVERNMENT Nuclear families were the basic economic and political unit. Families were led by the oldest man. They were loosely organized into small local groups associated with geographical areas (-miuts). Local groups occasionally came together as perhaps six or seven small, fluid bands. The bands were also geographically identified, their names carrying the -miut suffix as well.

CUSTOMS Sharing was paramount in Inuit society. All aspects of a person's life were controlled by kinship relationships. The people recognized many types of formal and informal partnerships and relationships. Some of these included wife exchanges. People came together in larger group gatherings in late autumn; this was a time to sew and mend clothing and renew kinship ties. Men hunted, made and repaired weapons and tools, and build kayaks, sleds, and shelter. Women prepared skins and made clothing, sewed hides for coverings, caught and prepared fish, raised children, and gathered moss, berries, and other items.

Descent was bilateral. People married simply by announcing their intentions, although infants were regularly betrothed. Prospective husbands often served their future in-laws for a period of time. Men might have more than one wife, but most had only one. Divorce was easy to obtain. Names were taken from deceased people and given by elders. A person might have several names, each denoting a kinship relationship and particular behaviors. Names were not sex specific.

People often adopted orphans. Children were highly valued and loved, especially males. When a boy

Nunavut.

DAILY LIFE The people never abandoned their land, which is still central to their identity. Traditional and modern coexist, sometimes uneasily, for many Inuit. Although people use television (there is even radio and television programming in Inuktitut), snowmobiles, and manufactured items, women also carry babies in the traditional hooded parkas, chew caribou skin to make it soft, and use the semilunar knives to cut seal meat. Full-time doctors are rare in the communities. Housing is often of poor quality. Most people are Christians. Culturally, although many stabilizing patterns of traditional culture have been destroyed, many remain. Many people live as part of extended families. Adoption is widely practiced. Decisions are often taken by consensus.

Politically, community councils have gained considerably more autonomy over the past decade or two. There is also a significant Inuit presence in the Northwest Territories Legislative Assembly and some presence at the federal level as well. In 1993, the Tungavik Federation of Nunavut (TFN), an outgrowth of the Inuit Tapirisat of Canada (ITC), signed an agreement with Canada providing for the establishment, in 1999, of a new, mostly Inuit, territory on roughly 36,000 square kilometers of land, including Kitikmeot.

The disastrous effects of government-run schools have been mitigated to some degree by local control of education, including more culturally relevant curricula in schools. Many people still speak Inuktitut, which is also taught in most schools, especially in the earlier grades. Children attend school in their community through grade nine; there is a high school in Frobisher Bay. Adult education is also available.

Inuit, Labrador or Ungava

Labrador or Ungava Inuit (`I ny ū it), actually two groups of northeastern Inuit once differentiated by dialect and custom. Reflecting recent political developments, many people of the latter group now refer to themselves as *Inuit Kapaimiut*, "People of Quebec."

LOCATION From the late sixteenth century on, these people have lived on the northern half of the Labrador peninsula, especially along the coasts and the offshore islands. There is some controversy as to whether or not Inuit groups ever occupied land bordering the Gulf of St. Lawrence. Contemporary communities are either located in Labrador or Nunavik (Quebec north of the 55th parallel).

POPULATION The Labrador Inuit population in the mid–eighteenth century was between 3,000 and 4,200, about two-thirds of whom lived in the south. The mid-1990s Inuit population of Labrador and Nunavik was approximately 12,000 people.

LANGUAGE The people speak dialects of Inuit-Inupiaq (Inuktitut), a member of the Eskaleut language family.

Historical Information

HISTORY This region has been occupied since about 2500 B.C.E., probably at first by people emigrating in waves from the Northwest. Norse explorers arrived circa 1000 C.E. The ancient Dorset culture lasted until around the fourteenth century, when it was displaced by Thule immigrants from Baffin Island. Around 1500, some Thule groups began a slow migration to the southern Labrador coast.

The people encountered Basque and other European whalers in the late fifteenth century. Inuit whaling technology was more advanced at that time. Contacts with non-native explorers, particularly those looking for the fabled northwest passage to Asia, continued throughout the sixteenth century. Early contacts between the Inuit and non-natives were generally hostile.

Whale and caribou overhunting, combined with the introduction of non-native diseases, led to population declines in the north by the late seventeenth century. The first trade centers were established in the north during the eighteenth century, although trade did not become regular there until close to the mid–nineteenth century.

In the eighteenth century, especially after the 1740s, sporadic trade began with the French fishery in the south. Moravian missions, schools, and trading posts, especially to the south, gradually became Inuit population centers after the mid– to late eighteenth century. Missionization began in Arctic Quebec in the 1860s. A mixed British-Inuit population (known as "settlers") also became established in the south from the mid–eighteenth century on. This influential group slowly grew in size and spread northward as well. Increased trade activity in the south in the mid–nineteenth century led to Inuit population declines as a result of alcohol use and disease epidemics. Fox trapping for the fur trade began in the early nineteenth century.

In the north, by later in the century, some families intermarried with non-native traders and otherwise established close relations with them. Fur trade posts became widespread in the north in the early twentieth century. Native technology began to change fundamentally and permanently during that period. Shamanism, too had all but disappeared, as most people had by then accepted Christianity, although not without much social convulsion.

In the south, the Moravians turned the Inuit trade over to the Hudson's Bay Company in 1926. There was an increasing government presence in the 1930s and 1940s. Few or no inland groups remained in Arctic Quebec after 1930, the people having moved to the coast. About the same time, the bottom dropped out of the fox fur market. Trade posts disappeared, and many people went back to a semitraditional mode of subsistence and technology.

The far north took on strategic importance during the Cold War, about the same time that vast mineral reserves became known and technologically possible to exploit. The federal Department of Northern Affairs and Natural Resources (1954) encouraged the Inuit to abandon their nomadic life. Extensive Canadian government services and payments date from that time. Local Moravian missions ceded authority to the government when Labrador and Newfoundland entered the Canadian confederation in 1949.

Some of Labrador's native communities were officially closed in the 1950s and their residents relocated. Most wage employment was of the unskilled and menial variety. By the 1960s, most people had abandoned the old ways. With radical diet changes, the adoption of a sedentary life, and the appearance of drugs and alcohol, their health declined markedly.

The entire region has experienced growing ethnopolitical awareness and activism since the 1970s. During that period, the Labrador Inuit Association (LIA) reached an accommodation with local biracial residents ("settlers") regarding representation and rights. The LIA is associated with the Inuit Tapirisat of Canada (ITC). This advocacy group works to settle land claims and to facilitate interracial cooperation. It also supports and funds local programs and services, including those relating to Inuit culture.

RELIGION Religious belief and practice were based on the need to appease spirit entities found in nature. Hunting, and specifically the land-sea dichotomy, was the focus of most rituals and taboos, such as that prohibiting sewing caribou-kin clothing in certain seasons. The people also recognized generative spirits, conceived of as female and identified with natural forces and cycles. Their rich cosmogony and mythology was filled with spirits and beings of various sizes, some superhuman and some subhuman.

Male and female shamans (*angakok*) provided religious leadership by virtue of their connection with guardian spirits. They could also control the weather, improve conditions for hunting, cure disease, and divine the future. Illness was perceived as stemming from soul loss and/or the violation of taboos and/or the anger of the dead. Curing methods included interrogation about taboo adherence, trancelike communication with spirit helpers, and performance.

GOVERNMENT Nuclear families were loosely organized into local groups of 20 to 30 people associated with geographical areas (*-miuts*). These groups occasionally came together as roughly 25 (perhaps 10 among the Ungava) small, fluid bands that were also geographically identified. The Ungava Inuit also recognized three regional bands (Siqinirmiut, Tarramiut, Itivimiut) that were identified by intermarriage and linguistic and cultural similarities.

The harpooner or boat owner provided leadership for whaling expeditions. The best hunters were often the de facto group leaders. Abuse of their authority was likely to get them killed. Still, competition for leadership positions was active, with people dueling through song and woman exchange. Women also competed with each other through singing. Local (settlement) councils helped resolve conflicts that arose in situations without a strong leader, especially in the south.

CUSTOMS Women were in charge of child rearing as well as skin and food preparation. They made the clothes, fished, hunted small animals, gathered plant material, and tended the oil lamps. Men hunted and had overall responsibility for all forms of transportation. They made and repaired utensils, weapons, and tools. They also built the houses.

Children were named for dead relatives regardless of sex; they were generally expected to take on the sex roles of their namesake, as opposed to those of their own sex. Children were occasionally brought up in the roles of the opposite gender for economic reasons. Adults occasionally married transvestites.

People married simply by announcing their intentions, although infants were regularly betrothed. Good hunters might have more than one wife (especially in the south), but most had only one. Divorce was easy to effect. Some wife exchanges were permitted within defined family partnerships; these relationships were considered as a kind of marriage.

Infanticide was rare and usually practiced against females; cannibalism, too, occasionally occurred during periods of starvation. Children were highly valued and loved, especially males. Adoption was common. The sick or aged were sometimes abandoned, especially in times of scarcity. Corpses were buried in stone graves covered by broken personal items.

Tensions were relieved through games; duels of drums and songs, in which the competing people tried to outdo each other in parody; and some "joking" relationships. Ostracism and even death were reserved for the most serious cases of socially inappropriate behavior. Murders led to ongoing blood feuds.

DWELLINGS The typical winter house was semi-excavated and made of stone, whalebone, and wood frames filled with sod and stone with a skin roof. Floors were also stone; windows were made of gut. Each house held up to 20 people; spaces were separated by skin partitions. The people also built mainly temporary domed snow houses. Conical and/or domed sealskin or caribou-skin tents served as summer housing. There were also large ceremonial and social structures (*kashim*) as well.

DIET Labrador Inuit were nomadic hunters, taking game both individually and collectively. Depending on location, they engaged in a number of subsistence activities, such as late summer and fall caribou hunting, whaling, and breathing-hole sealing in winter. They hunted seals from kayaks in spring and summer. Men and women fished year-round. People also ate birds and their eggs as well as walrus and bear (polar and black). Women gathered numerous berries and some roots as well as some shellfish and sea vegetables. Coastal hunters traveled into the interior in spring to hunt caribou, reemerging on the coast in the fall.

The results of a hunt were divided roughly equally, with those who played more important roles getting somewhat better (but not generally larger) shares. Food was eaten any number of ways, including frozen, raw, decayed, partially or fully boiled, and dried. Drinks included blood and water. There was some ritual division of "first fruits," particularly those obtained by adolescent boys or girls.

KEY TECHNOLOGY Special harpoons, floats, and drags were used in whaling. Caribou were generally shot with bow and arrow or speared from kayaks. Birds were shot, snared, or brought down with bolas. Fish were caught with hooks, weirs, and spears.

Most tools were fashioned from caribou antlers as well as stone, bone, and driftwood. Specific tools included bone or ivory needles; thread of sinew, gut, or tendon; sealskin containers; whalebone and wooden utensils; wooden goggles with narrow eye slits; the bow drill; and soapstone (steatite) pots.

Soapstone lamps burned beluga oil (north) or caribou fat (south and interior). The latter provided light but not much heat. In the interior and more southern areas, people also molded caribou tallow candles in goose-leg skins. They started fires with pyrite, flint, and moss. Coiled baskets and woven willow mats were made around Hudson Bay.

TRADE Southeastern groups imported wood for bows and arrows from the Beothuk Indians of Newfoundland. Inlanders and coastal residents exchanged dogs, ivory, caribou, and sealskins. The Inuit of present-day Quebec and those of modern Labrador engaged in regular trade. There was limited trade and contact between southern groups and the nearby Naskapi/Montagnais (Innu).

NOTABLE ARTS Art objects included woven grass baskets and carved ivory figures. There were also some petroglyphs in steatite quarries.

TRANSPORTATION Travel was fairly well developed, allowing people to move with relative ease to exploit the various regions of their territory. Several types of kayaks were used generally for hunting sea mammals, birds, and caribou. Umiaks (larger, skin-covered open boats that might hold up to 30 people) were generally rowed by women on visits to offshore islands or during seasonal migrations. They were also used in the south for autumn whale hunting. Wooden sleds were pulled by dogs, who also carried some gear. Temporary boats might be made of caribou skin stuffed with branches. Long-distance walking, on snowshoes in winter, was common (snowshoes may not be native).

DRESS Dress throughout Labrador was originally similar to that of the Baffinland Inuit. It consisted mainly of caribou-skin and sealskin clothing and boots. Skins of other animals were used as needed. Some island people made clothing of bird skins, especially those of ducks.

Coats probably had long flaps at the rear. Waterproof outerwear was made from gut. Other gear included sealskin boots (women of some groups wore theirs hip high) and mittens. In some areas, boots had corrugated soles made of looped leather strips.

Better hunters had newer and better clothing. Decoration was also age- and sex-appropriate. Ivory, wood, and other materials were used in clothing decoration. Some items were used as amulets or charms, whereas others were basically decorative. Women generally tattooed their faces, arms, and breasts after reaching puberty. Men occasionally tattooed noses or shoulders when they had killed a whale. Both men and women wore hair long, but women braided, rolled, and knotted theirs.

WAR AND WEAPONS Inuit and Indians generally avoided each other out of mutual fear. The East Cree killed Inuit whenever possible. Intergroup and intragroup conflict regularly led to bloodshed. Hunting equipment doubled as weapons.

Contemporary Information

GOVERNMENT/RESERVATIONS Major Inuit communities in Labrador include Aqvituq (Hopedale), Nunainguk (Nain), Marruvik (Makkovik), Kikiak (Rigolet), Northwest River, Qipuqqaq (Postville), and Happy Valley/Goose Bay. Government is by locally elected community council, some dominated by "settlers."

Nunavik communities include Aupaluk, Chisasibi (also Cree), Ivujivik, Kangirsujuaq, Kangirsuk, Kangiqsualujjuaq, Kuujjuarapik, Kuujjuaq, Puvirni-

killed his first seal, the seal's body was ritually dragged over his. The sick or aged were sometimes abandoned, especially in times of scarcity. Corpses were wrapped in skins and buried in stone or snow vaults or, later, left outside within a ring of stones. The tools of the deceased were left with him or her. People brought weapons and food to the grave after four days. No work, including hunting, was performed during the days of mourning.

Tensions were relieved through games, such as feats of strength, and duels of drums and songs, in which one person tried to outdo another in parody and song. Joking relationships also helped keep people's emotions in check. Games included ring-and-pin and cat's cradle. Children liked to play games, including tag and hide-and-seek. Ostracism and even death were reserved for the most serious cases of socially inappropriate behavior.

DWELLINGS   Men built domed snow houses in winter. Entrance through a straight-sided, flat-topped tunnel kept the warm air inside. Some houses had more than one room. Snow platforms covered with caribou, musk ox, or bearskins served as beds. The people used larger snow or sod and bone houses for ceremonial purposes. They also used caribou-skin and sealskin tents built over raised sod rings in summer and over pits in autumn.

DIET   Copper Inuits were nomadic hunters. The most important game animals were seals and whales. Dogs helped roughly eight large bands of 50 to 200 people hunt seals at their breathing holes in winter. Some polar bears were caught in winter as well.

The people also hunted caribou, musk ox, small game, and fowl, mainly in small groups in summer and autumn. Women and children chased caribou through stone runways to where the men were waiting with bows and lances. Caribou were also hunted from kayaks. The meat was sun dried or frozen and cached for the winter. Fishing was a year-round activity. Some berries were available in summer.

KEY TECHNOLOGY   Men used bone knives to cut blocks for snow houses. Other tools and equipment included harpoons, spears, snares, lances, bow and arrow, and bolas. Bows were made of spruce with sealskin and sinew backing. Some were also made of musk-ox horn or antler. Many tools were made from caribou antlers as well as stone, bone, and driftwood. Blades were made of bone or copper.

Fishing equipment included hooks, wooden or stone weirs and traps, and a variety of spears and harpoons. The people carved soapstone cooking pots and seal-oil lamps as well as wooden utensils, trays, dishes, spoons, and other objects. Women sewed with bone needles and sinew thread.

TRADE   Summer was trade season. The people exchanged goods, particularly copper and driftwood, with the Inuvialuit, the Caribou Inuit, and the Netsilik. There were occasional contacts with Athapaskan Indians to their south.

NOTABLE ARTS   The most important artistic traditions were carved wooden and ivory figurines. Clothing decoration consisted mainly of bands of white fur or skin. There was some skin fringing.

TRANSPORTATION   One- or two-person kayaks, propelled with a double-bladed paddle, were generally used for hunting. Several men could hunt whales in umiaks, which were larger, skin-covered open boats. Dogs carried burdens in summer and pulled wooden sleds in winter. The sleds had wooden runners covered with whalebone, mud, or peat and then ice. Toboggans were occasionally made of skin.

DRESS   Women sewed most clothing from caribou skins, although sealskins were commonly used on boots. Apparel included men's long, gut sealing coats and light swallowtail ceremonial coats. The people wore a double skin suit in winter and only the inner layer in summer. Women's clothing featured large shoulders and hoods as well as one-piece, attached leggings and boots. Their coattails were long and narrow. Men wore small loon-beak dancing caps with weasel-skin tassels. They sometimes shaved their foreheads. Both sexes wore tattoos and ivory or bone snow goggles.

WAR AND WEAPONS   Spears and arrowheads were copper tipped. Most fighting was local and small-scale in nature.

Contemporary Information

GOVERNMENT/RESERVATIONS   Contemporary Copper Inuit communities include Iqaluktuuttiaq (Cambridge Bay), Qingauq (Bathurst Inlet), Qurluqtuuq (Coppermine), Umingmaktuuq, and Taloyoak. Government is by locally elected council.

ECONOMY   Subsistence hunting, trapping, and fishing are still important, as are various types of wage work and government assistance. Possible future developments include oil and gas exploration as well as tanker traffic. Cape Dorset artists are well known and relatively successful.

Native-owned and -operated cooperatives have been an important part of the Inuit economy for some time. Activities range from arts and crafts to retail to commercial fishing to construction.

LEGAL STATUS   Inuit are considered "nonstatus" native people. Most Inuit communities are incorporated as hamlets and are officially recognized. Kitikmeot is slated to become a part of the new territory of

tuq, Salluit, Tasiujaq, and Umiujaq. The Kativiq Regional Government is responsible for municipal services and various policies. There is also a local school board.

ECONOMY Art, craft, food, and many other cooperatives date from the late 1950s. The Torngat Fish Producers Cooperative Society runs local fisheries operations. The Makivik Corporation, set up under the James Bay and Northern Quebec Agreement (JBNQA) (see "Daily Life"), manages tens of millions of dollars in development funds and represents the Inuit of northern Quebec on environmental, resource, and constitutional issues. Other JBNQA corporations manage interests in air transport, construction, communications, and cultural activities. Many people depend on government employment and assistance. Subsistence, especially fishing, is most important in northern Labrador. Associated cultural behaviors and traditions, such as sharing, remain correspondingly relatively strong.

LEGAL STATUS Inuit are considered "nonstatus" native people. Most Inuit communities are incorporated as hamlets and are officially recognized. The communities listed under "Government/Reservations" are provincially and federally recognized.

DAILY LIFE The Northern Quebec Inuit Association (1971) approved the JBNQA in 1975. It provided for local and regional administrative power as well as some special rights in the areas of land use, education, and justice. There was also monetary compensation. This controversial agreement divided the Inuit on the issue of aboriginal land rights. The opposition, centered in the locally based cooperative movement, formed the Inuit Tungavingat Nunami (ITN). This group rejects the JBNQA, including the financial compensations, carrying on its opposition activities through local levies on carvings.

A cultural revival beginning in the 1980s led to the creation of museums, cultural centers, and various studies and programs. Newspapers, air communication, television, and telephone reach even remote villages. Education is locally controlled from grades 1–12, although the curriculum differs little from those in non-native communities. Issues there include mineral and other development versus protecting renewable resources. Many local committees and associations, such as the Labrador Women's Group (1978), provide needed social, recreational, and other services. Many Labrador Inuit still experience some ongoing racial conflict.

Traditional and modern coexist, sometimes uneasily, for many Inuit. Full-time doctors are rare in the communities. Housing is often of poor quality. Most people are Christians. Culturally, although many stabilizing patterns of traditional culture have been destroyed, many remain. Many people live as part of extended families. Adoption is widely practiced. Decisions are often taken by consensus.

Inuit, Mackenzie Delta
See Inuvialuit

Inuit, North Alaska
See Inupiat

Inupiat

Inupiat (In `ū p ē ut) "the People," an Inuit name covering the Eskimo or Inuit groups formerly known to anthropologists as Bering Strait, Kotzebue Sound, sometimes West Alaska, and North Alaska Eskimos. The last group has also been divided into two groups: coastal people, or Tareumiut, and the land-oriented Nuunamiut.

LOCATION The Inupiat lived in northwest and northern Alaska, from about Norton Sound and the Seward Peninsula (with offshore islands) north and east to about the Canadian border, including the North Slope–Barrow region. This is considered to have been one of the world's most productive sea mammal regions. Many Inupiat still live in this area.

POPULATION There were perhaps 9,500 Inupiat in the mid–nineteenth century. The population in the early 1990s was approximately 12,000.

LANGUAGE Inupiat people spoke dialects of Inupiaq (Inuktitut), an Eskaleut language. Some Bering Strait Inuit spoke Yup'ik dialects.

Historical Information

HISTORY The historic Nuunamiut (interior North Alaska people) moved into their region from the south and west from circa 1400 through about 1800. Russian explorers and traders arrived in the early to mid–eighteenth century and remained for the next 100 years or so. Whalers and traders from other countries plied the local waters from about the 1840s on (1880s in the far north). Among other things, they introduced alcohol, tobacco, and non-native diseases. Traditional patterns began to break down as well after that time.

The Nuunamiut began a sharp decline from the mid–nineteenth century on, largely owing to disease and starvation (smaller caribou herds). Most families had left the interior by 1820, drawn to the coast, although a few families began moving back around 1840. There were severe epidemics throughout the region in the 1870s and 1880s. A severe famine struck the Kotzebue Sound region in 1880–1881.

Mining began in the Bering Strait area in the

1880s. Meanwhile, imported reindeer herding, fur trapping, missionaries, and schools began to attract people to local settlements from the mid– to late nineteenth century on. Reindeer herding proved ultimately to be unsuccessful in the area. The Nome gold rush of 1898 saw the migration of many Inuit to the Nome area to sell crafts and, eventually, to work and to attend school. Anti-Inuit sentiment remained strong in Nome for some time thereafter.

Fur traders arrived around 1900, about the time of a severe measles epidemic and the near-depletion of the caribou herds. Another severe influenza epidemic struck in 1918. In the early twentieth century, the federal government assumed responsibility for Inuit education. To a greater extent even than the churches, the government increased the pressure to acculturate. For instance, government schools punished people severely for speaking their native language. The only high schools were located away from Inupiat-speaking centers.

The people experienced a general population growth after World War II, attributable to the return of the caribou, the introduction of moose into the region, and government efforts against disease. The far north took on strategic importance during the Cold War, about the same time that vast mineral reserves became known and technologically possible to exploit. Oil was discovered on the North Slope in 1968. Most jobs that Inuit were able to obtain were unskilled menial. Furthermore, with radical diet changes, the adoption of a sedentary life, and the appearance of drugs and alcohol, their health declined markedly.

In the late 1950s, Inupiat people began organizing politically over the U.S. government's threat to use nuclear weapons to build a deep-water port as well as over bird hunting restrictions. The Seward Peninsula Native Association, Alaska Federation of Natives, Inupiat Paitot, Northwest Alaska Native Association, and North Slope Native Association formed as a result of this activism. Land issues also gave rise to the Alaska Native Claims Settlement Act (ANCSA) in 1971. The settlement gave the people legal rights to millions of acres of land and shares in corporations worth millions of dollars in exchange for their cession of aboriginal title. Major land conservation laws were enacted in 1980.

RELIGION Religious belief was based on the existence of spirit entities found in nature. In particular, the spirits of game animals allowed themselves to be caught only if they were treated properly. Respect was expressed in behaviors such as maintaining a separation between land and sea hunting, opening the head of an animal just killed in order to allow its spirit to escape, speaking well of game animals, offering sea mammals a drink of cold water and land animals knives or needles, and many other taboos, rituals, and ceremonies as well as certain songs and charms.

Among whale hunters, personal spirit songs that were purchased or inherited were used to make the hunt more successful. Whale and caribou hunters and their wives were required to observe many rituals and taboos. Whaling ceremonies along the north coast and caribou ceremonies inland were the most important rituals, representing a sort of world renewal.

Male and older female shamans (*angakok*) provided religious leadership by virtue of their connection with the spirit world. They also participated in regular economic activities. They could cure disease and see into the future. Illness was seen as owing to soul loss and/or violation of taboos. Curing methods included interrogation about taboo adherence, trancelike communication with spirit helpers, and performance, including singing and sucking. (Nonspiritual ailments included infected eyes and respiratory problems, stomach diseases, boils, and lice.) Shamans might also be accused of and killed for causing a death.

GOVERNMENT Nuclear or small extended families were loosely organized into fluid local groups (*-miuts*) associated with geographical areas. These local groups occasionally came together as small, fluid, autonomous bands (family groups; tribes) of between 20 and 200 bilaterally related people. The bands were also geographically identified but were not political entities; their names carried the *-miut* suffix. People within them depended on each other for subsistence support and spoke the same subdialect. Several distinct societies of bands had formed in the interior north by the mid–nineteenth century.

Family heads (*umialik,* literally umiak captain, or whaling leader) were usually older men, with little formal authority and no power. Leaders generally embodied Inuit values, such as generosity, and were also good hunters. Within the context of a basically egalitarian society, they were relatively wealthier (owing to their following) and had more status than other men. Their main responsibilities included directing hunt, trade, and diplomatic activities. The *umialik* and his wife were also responsible for food redistribution.

Among the northern Inupiat, leaders might also impose their will on women as well. Potential leaders often competed with each other to hold their crews or hunters by such means as wife exchange and gift giving. Additional wives generally meant additional followers, wealth, and power. Leaders there might oversee not only the hunt but also religious ceremonies, festivals, and trade.

The northern Inupiat came together briefly for

larger hunting (sea and land) forays, but mainly they remained in family groups. The Bering Strait and Kotzebue Sound tribes had principal winter villages. Each had one or more chiefs for each local group residing in the village. The chief(s) and a council oversaw local and intertribal affairs.

CUSTOMS Kinship networks were the most important social structure as well as the key to survival in terms of mutual aid and cooperative activity. This arrangement also led to ongoing blood feuds: An injury to one was perceived as an injury to the whole kin group and called for revenge.

Nonkin men teamed up for hunting or trade purposes. Such defined partnerships might include temporary wife exchanges, which were considered as a kind of marriage (interestingly, at least among the Bering Strait people, relations considered adulterous were harshly dealt with). Joking relationships between unrelated men also furthered mutual aid and support and served to reduce tension and conflict. Nonkin relationships also included adopted people and people who had the same name.

In some Bering Strait Inuit villages, family groups lived on patrilineally inherited plots of land. In larger groups, food was generally turned over to the *umialik* and his wife, who redistributed it according to various priorities. Generosity was highly valued. When hunters brought in a whale or caribou, no one went hungry. Hard work and individual freedom were other key values, the latter within the context of kinship associations.

Southerners especially celebrated fall and winter Messenger Feasts, in which a neighboring group was invited to feast and dance. Social status was related to largesse on these occasions, which were similar to potlatches. They brought some north Alaska Inuit together with some Athapaskan Indians.

People married simply by announcing their intentions, although infants were regularly betrothed. Marriage was considered to be mainly a kinship-building exercise. Successful hunters might have more than one wife, but most had only one. Divorce, or the end of cohabitation, was easy to obtain, especially before many children had been born. It was also the case that men might try to dominate women, including raping them, in their or another's household. In this endeavor the "bully" was usually backed by members of his kinship group (as, in fact, older women might occasionally, by virtue of their supposed magical powers, capture a young man for a husband).

Infanticide was rare and usually practiced against females. Children were highly valued and loved, especially males. They were raised by the women with a great deal of liberty. Names, usually of dead relatives,

were associated with specific food taboos. The sick or aged were sometimes abandoned, especially in times of scarcity. Death was attended by a minimum of ritual. Corpses were removed through skylights and left on the tundra. A mourning period of four or five days ensued, during which all activity ceased, and a feast was often held a year after a relative's death.

Tensions were relieved by playing games, joking, and competitive song duels, in which men took turns insulting each other in witty songs. Ostracism and even death were reserved for the most serious cases of socially inappropriate behavior, although punishment by death often led to blood feuds. Amusements included competitive gambling games, song contests, dancing, wrestling, and storytelling, especially in midwinter in the men's houses called *kashims.*

DWELLINGS The regular winter dwelling was a semiexcavated, domed, driftwood and sod house, roughly 12–15 feet long. Moss was placed between the interior walls and the sod for insulation. There was a separate kitchen with a smoke hole and storage niches off the entrance tunnel, which descended into a meat cellar and ended at a well that led up to the main room. The houses held from 8 to 12 people (two families). Inside were raised sleeping platforms and suspended drying racks. Stretched gut or ice served as windows.

Some groups also used a dome-shaped wooden structure covered with skins or bark and also temporary snow or ice houses. Interior groups also used willow-frame dome tents covered with caribou skin, bark, or grass. Some Bering Strait people built wood frame summer houses.

Larger men's houses *(kashim)* were present in communities with more than a few families. Reserved for men and boys by day, they became a family social center at night. They were also used for ceremonies and other activities and, along the coast, were associated with whaling crews.

DIET The Tareumiut and some Bering Strait and Kotzebue Sound people depended mainly on marine life such as seals, bowhead and beluga whales, and walrus, whereas the Nuunamiut hunted mainly caribou. Whale meat was stored in the permafrost and generally provided a reliable food source from season to season. Northern groups hunted whales from umiaks in spring and seal and walrus through the ice in winter.

The Kotzebue Sound and some Bering Strait people had a mixed land and marine hunting economy. Game animals included fowl, mountain sheep, bear, wolves, wolverines, hares, squirrels, and foxes. Men and women fished year-round.

Game was generally divided among the hunting party according to a precise set of rules. Food was often boiled, often with fat or blubber, although fish was also eaten frozen. Dogs were often fed walrus or human feces mixed with oil. The Bering Strait and Kotzebue Sound people also gathered a variety of greens, berries, and roots in summer.

KEY TECHNOLOGY   Stone-tipped, toggle-headed harpoons were attached to wooden floats and inflated sealskins to create drag on a submerging whale. Floats were also used to keep a slain whale from sinking before it could be towed to shore.

Hunting equipment included spears, bow and arrow, bolas (strings attached to stone balls to bring down birds), deadfalls, traps, and snares. The atlatl was used to throw sealing darts or harpoons. Fishing equipment included hooks, weirs, nets, traps, and spears. People used a variety of mainly stone and ivory butchering tools; some were fashioned of antler and driftwood as well. The key women's tool was a crescent-shaped knife. The Bering Strait people made some grass baskets and mats.

Boiling pots might be made of driftwood or pottery. Other important items included baleen seal nets; bone needles and sinew thread; carved wooden trays, dishes, spoons, and other objects; a bow drill to start fires and drill holes; sun goggles; and carved soapstone (north) or pottery (Bering Strait and Kotzebue Sound) cooking pots and lamps (the latter burned seal oil using moss wicks). Local stone around Kotzebue Sound included chert, slate, and jade. There was also some birch bark around Kotzebue Sound that the people made into containers.

TRADE   The two groups of northern Inupiat were mutually dependent, trading whale products, such as skin, oil, and blubber, for caribou skins on a regular basis. Other trade items included fish, driftwood, other skins, and ivory labrets.

Summer trade fairs were widely attended. The one at Sheshalik, on Kotzebue Sound, may have attracted 2,000 or more people. The other large northern Alaska trade fair was held in Nigalik (Colville River Delta) and was attended by Yup'ik people as well as Athapaskan Indians. In addition to trade, fairs included private contact between various partners, dancing, feasts, and competitions.

Kotzebue trade fairs were also attended by Siberians, who exchanged jade, pottery, reindeer skins, and beads for local products. Native Siberians (Chukchi) also provided Russian goods from the late seventeenth century on.

NOTABLE ARTS   Most art objects were ceremonial in nature. They included carved wooden and ivory objects, such as labrets, masks, and marionettes.

TRANSPORTATION   The basic hunting vehicle was the one- or two-person closed skin kayak. Several men could hunt whales in umiaks (skin-covered open boats with a driftwood frame between 15 and 50 feet long). Umiaks might also hold 2,000 pounds of cargo. The people also used wooden sleds with iced runners. Dogs pulled (or helped pull) the sleds after about 1500. Some interior people used snowshoes.

DRESS   Women tanned skins and made sealskin and caribou-skin clothing, some with fur trim. In winter, people wore two suits of parkas and pants: The inner suit was worn with the fur turned in, whereas the outer had the fur turned out. Other winter clothing included mittens and hoods (women's were extra large for carrying babies). Clothing in the Kotzebue Sound area was sewn from untanned skins.

Other items of clothing included skin socks, boots of caribou skin and chewed seal-hide soles, and waterproof outer jackets of sewn sea mammal intestine. Men wore labrets, the lip being pierced around puberty. Many women had three lined tattoos down the chin. Babies wore moss and ptarmigan feather diapers. In general, clothing in this area exhibited considerable regional diversity.

WAR AND WEAPONS   Fighting was generally a matter of kin group involvement and remained limited in scope if not in time. Strangers outside of the kinship or alliance system were considered potential enemies and could be killed on sight, their goods and women taken. Blood feuds were the result of the lack of overall conflict-resolution structures. Fighting also took place among rival trade groups. Also, territory was defended against neighboring groups. The enemies of the Bering Strait people included Siberian Inuit and also nearby Athapaskan Indians. Some interior north Alaska groups were friendly with Athapaskan Koyukon and unfriendly with Athapaskan Kutchin. Hunting equipment generally doubled as weapons, except that some groups also wore armor.

Contemporary Information

GOVERNMENT/RESERVATIONS   Regional political structures include the North Slope Borough (1972) and the Northwest Arctic Borough (1986). There are 11 permanent villages of the Kotzebue region, all of which have electricity and telephone service. Government is by elected mayors and city councils. There is also a northern interior village of Anaktuvuk Pass, which has been settled mainly since the early 1950s. Barrow and Kotzebue are far-northern cities.

ECONOMY   Important sources of income among Northwest Arctic Borough people include the Red Dog Mine, the school system, and the government. Among people in the North Slope Borough, sources of income are mainly local government and the oil industry. Employment opportunities also exist in the cities of Kotzebue and Barrow. Many people also count on government assistance. Chukchi Sea Trading Company is a cooperative of Inuit women from Point Hope who sell arts and crafts on the World Wide Web. In general, because most subsistence activities take place in winter, and most wage work is available in summer, the Inupiat have made a relatively successful adaptation to new economic opportunities while maintaining traditional subsistence activities.

LEGAL STATUS   The regional corporations under ANCSA are Arctic Slope, Bering Straits, and Nana. Other ANCSA entities include the Maniilaq and Inupiat Community Nonprofit Corporations of the Arctic Slope Regional Corporation.

DAILY LIFE   In response to severe problems with substance abuse, several communities have restricted or eliminated the sale of alcohol. Other efforts to remedy the problems are ongoing. Severe radioactive pollution exists around the Cape Thompson area. This is caused by the use by the Atomic Energy Commission (predecessor to the Nuclear Regulatory Commission) of the area as a nuclear dump and its conduct of nuclear experiments using local plant and animal life as well as by Soviet nuclear waste dumping. Negotiations over cleanup are ongoing.

Curricula and, in fact, control of education, shifted to local authorities beginning in the 1970s. Preservation and instruction of native culture are part of this effort. The native trade fair in Kotzebue follows the Fourth of July celebration, and the Messenger Feast is held in Barrow in January.

Most Inupiat people have access to all modern air and electronic transportation and communication. Most speak English as a first language, although most adults are bilingual. With the construction of roads from Anaktuvuk Pass to the North Slope oil fields, many people think that that town will some day be abandoned.

Inuvialuit

Inuvialuit (I `n ū v ē a `l ū it) is the Inuit name for the people formerly known as Mackenzie Delta Eskimo or western (Canadian) Arctic Eskimo.

LOCATION   The homeland of this group is the Mackenzie Delta region, specifically from Herschel Island to the Baillie Islands, northwest Northwest Territories.

POPULATION   From between 2,000 and 2,500 people in the mid–eighteenth century, the Inuvialuit population was reduced to about 150 in 1910 and perhaps 10 in 1930. The mid-1990s Inuit population was about 5,000.

LANGUAGE   Inuvialuits speak a dialect of Inuit-Inupiaq (Inuktitut), a member of the Eskaleut language family.

Historical Information

HISTORY   The people offered a generally friendly reception when they first met non-native traders in the late eighteenth and early nineteenth century. However, relations soon soured. Missionaries were active in the region by mid–nineteenth century, although few Inuvialuit accepted Christianity before 1900.

The heyday of the whaling period began in 1888, when some 1,000 non-native whalers wintered near the Mackenzie River; the region soon became a trade center as well as a haven for "frontier living" that included alcohol abuse, sexual promiscuity, and death from firearms. Traditional life declined sharply, as did the population, which was further beset by a host of hitherto unknown diseases such as scarlet fever, syphilis, smallpox, and influenza. By 1920 the Inuvialuit had all but disappeared from the Yukon. Most modern Inuvialuit are descended from Inupiat groups who moved east from Alaska about that time. Indians and non-natives moved in as well.

The far north took on strategic importance during the Cold War. In 1954, the federal Department of Northern Affairs and Natural Resources encouraged the Inuit to abandon their nomadic life. The department oversaw the construction of housing developments, schools, and clinics. Local political decisions were made by a community council subject to non-native approval and review. In 1959, the "government" town of Inuvik was founded as an administrative center.

Inuits generally found only unskilled and menial work. They also survived through dependence on government payments. With radical diet changes, the adoption of a sedentary life, and the appearance of drugs and alcohol, health declined markedly. The Committee for Original People's Entitlement (COPE), founded in 1969, soon became the political voice of the Inuvialuit. Oil and gas deposits were found in the Beaufort Sea in the 1970s.

RELIGION   Religious belief and practice were based on the need to appease spirit entities found in nature. Hunting, and specifically the land-sea dichotomy, was the focus of most rituals and taboos, such as that prohibiting sewing caribou skin clothing in certain seasons. The people also recognized generative spirits, conceived of as female and identified with natural forces and cycles.

Male and female shamans (angakok) provided religious leadership by virtue of their connection with guardian spirits. They could also control the weather, improve conditions for hunting, cure disease, and divine the future. Illness was perceived as stemming from soul loss and/or the violation of taboos and/or the anger of the dead. Curing methods included interrogation about taboo adherence, trancelike communication with spirit helpers, and performance.

GOVERNMENT Nuclear families were loosely organized into local groups associated with geographical areas (-miuts). These groups occasionally came together as perhaps five small, fluid bands or subgroups: Kittegaryumiut, Kupugmiut, Kigirktarugmiut, Nuvouigmiut, and Avvagmiut. The bands were also geographically identified. Informal or ad hoc village leaders (isumataq) were usually older men, with little formal authority and no power. They embodied Inuit values, such as generosity, and were also good hunters, perhaps especially good whalers.

Contact with neighboring Inuit groups may have influenced the development of a somewhat stronger village leadership structure, including inheritance in the male line, around the time of contact. The Inuvialuit population was generally less dispersed than that of other Inuit groups. Their largest summer village, for instance, contained up to 1,000 people.

CUSTOMS Descent was bilateral. Intermarriage was common between members of the five bands. People married simply by announcing their intentions, although infants were regularly betrothed. Men might have more than one wife, but most had only one. Divorce was easy to obtain. Some wife exchanges took place within defined partnerships between men; the relationship between a man and his partner's wife was considered as a kind of marriage.

Infanticide was rare and, when practiced, was usually directed against females. Children were highly valued and loved, especially males. Their names generally came from deceased relatives and were bestowed by shamans. Male adolescents had some teeth filed down and their cheeks and earlobes pierced. The sick or aged were sometimes abandoned, especially in times of scarcity. Corpses were not removed from houses through the door but rather through a specially made hole in the wall. They were then placed on the ground and covered with driftwood. Personal items were placed on top of the grave.

Tensions were relieved through games; duels of drums and songs, in which the competing people tried to outdo each other in parody; and some "joking" relationships. Ostracism and even death were reserved for the most serious cases of socially inappropriate behavior, such as murder, wife stealing, and theft. Relations between the Inuvialuit and their Indian neighbors were both cordial, including intermarriage, and hostile. Regular social gatherings might feature drum dances and bouncing on stretched walrus skins.

DWELLINGS The typical winter dwelling was a semiexcavated, rectangular, turf-covered, log frame-work house. Each one held about three families. Sleeping chambers were appended, giving the whole a cross shape. Each family had a separate cooking area as well. Entrance was via an underground tunnel. Houses were named. Windows or skylights were made of gut. Storage was located along the tunnel or in niches within.

The people occasionally used temporary domed snow houses in winter, mainly when traveling. Entrance was gained through a door. There were some larger open-roofed sod and wood houses as well for ceremonial purposes, although these may reflect a later Inupiat influence. Conical caribou-skin tents used in summer were strengthened by a hoop lashed to the frame about 6 feet from the ground. Also, each village had a men's house (kashim) up to 60 feet long.

DIET The Inuvialuit were nomadic hunters. The most important game animals were seals and baleen whales, especially beluga. Whales were hunted communally by driving up to 200 of them into shallow water with kayaks. Seals were netted on the edges of ice floes and hunted at their breathing holes in winter.

The people also hunted caribou (fall drives), moose, mountain sheep, hares, bears, musk ox, muskrat, beaver, and birds. Fishing took place especially in spring and summer, mainly for whitefish and herring. Most fish and meat were dried, frozen, or preserved in oil and stored for winter. Other than fish, which was often eaten raw, food was boiled or roasted and eaten with various oils and fats. Other foods included berries and some roots. People generally drank water or stock.

KEY TECHNOLOGY Hunting equipment included several kinds of whale harpoons, lances, and spears as well as bow and arrow, knives, and bird bolas. Seals were also netted under the ice. Fishing equipment included hooks and weirs. Most tools were made from caribou antler tools as well as wood (including driftwood), ivory, and bone. There were some stone items as well, especially steatite (soapstone) ornaments and pots.

The people used some carved steatite lamps (that burned seal oil), although most cooking was done over an outdoor wood fire. They also carved wooden trays, dishes, spoons, and other objects. Bow drills were used to make fire. Wolves and foxes were killed when they ate sharpened baleen spring traps placed in fat.

TRADE Goods were exchanged with the Kutchin and Hare Indians as well as with the Inupiat to the west. Individual formal trade partnerships were a part of this process. The people exported wood, which they procured in the southern part of their territory.

NOTABLE ARTS Sewn clothing and carved wooden and ivory figurines were developed to artistic levels.

TRANSPORTATION One- or two-person kayaks were used mostly for sea mammal hunting. Several men hunted whales in umiaks, or larger open boats covered with beluga skin. Overland travel was facilitated by the use of wooden dogsleds with iced-over runners of bone or antler.

DRESS Clothing consisted mainly of sewn caribou skins. Men and women wore two layers, the under layer with the hair turned in and the outer layer with the hair turned out. Coats and pants were trimmed with fur, as were parka hoods. Men's hoods were made from caribou or wolf-head skin, the latter with the ears left on. Women's parkas were knee length and double flapped, as opposed to mens', which ended at the hip. Women's parka hoods were also made bigger to cover their double bun–shaped hairstyles. Other clothing included caribou-leg boots with beluga-skin soles and caribou mittens.

In summer, most people wore old inner garments with the hair turned out. Men who had killed a bear wore pieces of stone or ivory through their cheeks. Most men also wore polished stone or ivory labrets in their lips. Both sexes wore ornaments in pierced ears and nasal septa. Both men and women applied small tattoos on their faces and bodies. Children who had reached puberty had their teeth filed down; boys' cheeks and ears were pierced as well.

WAR AND WEAPONS The Inuvialuit fought mainly with nearby Athapaskan Indians. Hunting equipment generally doubled as war weapons.

Contemporary Information

GOVERNMENT/RESERVATIONS Contemporary communities include Aklaavik, Ikaahuk (Sachs Harbour), Paulatuuq, Uluksartuuq (Homlan), and Tuktuujaqtuuq (Tuktoyaktuk). Government is provided by locally elected councils. These communities control the Inuvialuit Regional Corporation (IRC), formed in 1985 to administer the Inuvialuit Final Agreement (IFA) (see "Legal Status").

ECONOMY The Inuvialuit Development Corporation (IDC) owns a multimillion-dollar transportation concern as well as air, energy, manufacturing, and real estate businesses. It also works to provide markets for musk ox meat and wool. The IDC also pays individuals annuities from corporate profits.

Subsistence hunting, trapping, and fishing are still important, as are various types of wage work and government assistance. Native-owned and -operated cooperatives have been an important part of the Inuit economy for some time. Activities range from arts and crafts to retail to commercial fishing to construction.

LEGAL STATUS The Western Arctic Claim Agreement (or IFA), signed in 1984, was the first comprehensive land claims settlement worked out by natives living in the Northwest Territories. It provides for the extinguishing of aboriginal title to the western Canadian Arctic in exchange for native ownership of approximately 91,000 square kilometers of land and payments of $45 million in benefits and $10 million for economic development, the latter to be administered by the IDC. However, federal and territorial laws apply in the region; the people have yet to work out a framework for self-government.

DAILY LIFE The people never abandoned their land, which is still central to their identity. Traditional and modern coexist, sometimes uneasily, for many Inuit. Although people use television (there is even radio and television programming in Inuktitut), snowmobiles, and manufactured items, women also carry babies in the traditional hooded parkas, chew caribou skin to make it soft, and use the semilunar knives to cut seal meat. Full-time doctors are rare in the communities. Housing is often of poor quality. Most people are Christians. Culturally, although many stabilizing patterns of traditional culture have been destroyed, many remain. Many people live as part of extended families. Adoption is widely practiced. Decisions are often taken by consensus.

Politically, community councils have gained considerably more autonomy over the past decade or two. There is also a significant Inuit presence in the Northwest Territories Legislative Assembly and some presence at the federal level as well. The disastrous effects of government-run schools have been mitigated to some degree by local control of education, including more culturally relevant curricula in schools. Many people still speak Inuktitut, which is also taught in most schools, especially in the earlier grades. Children attend school in their community through grade nine; the high school is in Frobisher Bay. Adult education is also available.

Netsilik

Netsilik (`Net sil ik), "People of the Seal" or "there are seals." See also Inuit, Copper.

LOCATION Netsilik territory is north of Hudson Bay, especially from Committee Bay in the east to Victoria Strait in the west, north to Bellot Strait, and south to Garry Lake. It is entirely within the Arctic Circle. The sea begins to freeze as early as September, and the thaw is generally not completed until the end of July. The summer tundra remains wet, since permafrost not far below the surface prevents drainage. Many Netsilik Inuit still live in this area of the central Arctic, known as Kitikmeot.

POPULATION From about 500 in the late nineteenth century, the Netsilik population grew to around 1,300 in 1980, although this number included some non-Netsilik Inuit. The mid-1990s population of the Kitikmeot Region (Netsilik and Copper Inuit) was approximately 4,000.

LANGUAGE   The native language is a dialect of Inuit-Inupiaq (Inuktitut), a member of the Eskaleut language family.

Historical Information

HISTORY   Netsiliks are descended from the ancient Thule culture. In about 1830 they encountered non-natives looking for the northwest passage. Still, contact with non-natives remained only sporadic until the early twentieth century. About that time, the people obtained firearms from the neighboring Iglulik. More productive hunting enabled them to keep more dogs, changing their migration and subsistence patterns.

The establishment of trading posts in their territory around 1920 heralded the economic switch to white fox fur trapping and trade for additional items of non-native manufacture, such as woolen clothing, tobacco, steel traps, fishing nets, canoes (which replaced kayaks), tea, and canvas tents. Game killed with rifles came to belong to the hunter, a practice that eroded and ultimately destroyed traditional exchange.

Missions established in the 1930s soon became permanent settlements. The Netsilik quickly accepted Christianity (Anglicanism and Catholicism), ending the taboo system and shamanic practices, not to mention infanticide and other social practices. The authority of traders, missionaries, and eventually the Royal Canadian Mounted Police (RCMP) undermined traditional leadership, such as it was.

The far north took on strategic importance during the Cold War, about the same time that vast mineral reserves became known and technologically possible to exploit. In 1954, the federal Department of Northern Affairs and Natural Resources began a program of population consolidation and acculturation. Coastal settlements were abandoned, and all people moved to one of three towns. The department oversaw the construction of housing developments, schools, and a general infrastructure. Local political decisions were made by a community council subject to non-native approval and review. The natives were offered generally unskilled employment. With radical diet changes, the adoption of a sedentary life, and the appearance of drugs and alcohol, their health declined markedly.

RELIGION   Overarching, generative, female-identified deities or spirits were associated with natural forces and cycles. Another level of spirit entities were human and animal souls or spirits. Most religious activities were designed to propitiate the spirits of game animals specifically and potentially dangerous supernatural forces in general. Hunting and life-cycle events, particularly childbirth and death, were the basis of most taboos.

Magic spells, generally applicable to a single subject, were personal and secret and could be purchased or transmitted between generations. Souls were considered to be immortal. Those of people who died violently, including by their own hand, as well as those of good hunters and beautifully tattooed women were able to inhabit a paradise. The souls of lazy hunters and women without tattoos went to a sad and hungry place. Yet another type of supernatural being was numerous monsters and ghosts.

Male and female shamans (angakok) provided religious leadership by virtue of their connection with personal guardian spirits. They led group religious activities. They could also cure disease, see into the future (including such things as the location of game), and harm people. Training took place under the tutelage of an older shaman. Illness was said to be owing to soul loss and/or violation of taboos. Curing methods included interrogation about taboo adherence, trancelike communication with spirit helpers, and performance.

GOVERNMENT   Nuclear families loosely combined into extended families or local groups associated with geographical areas (-miuts). Local group leaders (isumataq) were usually older men with little formal authority and no power. Leaders embodied Inuit values, such as generosity, and were also good hunters. Older women played a leadership role in food distribution.

Local groups occasionally traveled together as fluid hunting regional bands. The bands were also geographically identified and included Arvertormiut, Arviligjuarmiut, Ilivilermiut, Kitdlinermiut; Kungmiut, Netsilingmiut, and Qegertarmiut.

CUSTOMS   Although the nuclear family was the basic social unit, survival required the regular association of extended families and, in fact, the existence of numerous complex relationships. For instance, although the people were generally monogamous, wives were exchanged within various defined male partnerships, such as song partnerships; these relationships were considered as a kind of marriage. The precise workings of wife (and husband) exchange were varied and ranged from short to long (or even permanent) and from willing to acrimonious.

Young women married around age 14 or 15, boys around age 20. People married simply by announcing their intentions, although infants and even fetuses were regularly betrothed. Women usually moved in with the husband's household. Men might have more than one wife, but most had only one. Divorce was easy to obtain. In general, the Netsilik enjoyed a high degree of sexual freedom. There was some in-law avoidance.

Infanticide was usually practiced against females, but the high rate of adult male mortality somewhat evened the gender balance. Children were highly valued and loved, especially males. Adoption was common. The sick or aged were sometimes abandoned, especially in times of scarcity. Suicide for those and other reasons, such as a general sense of insecurity or perceived weakness, was a regular occurrence as well. Corpses were abandoned, as the camp generally moved after a death. No work, including hunting, could be done within several days following a death.

Food was generally shared within the extended family or local group. In cases of collaborative hunting, such as winter sealing, food was shared according to precise rules. Tensions were relieved through games, duels of drums and songs (not the same as song partnerships, but contests of insulting songs sung by the wives), and some "joking" relationships. Tension was also occasionally resolved through physical separation, fights, and murder, although the latter inevitably brought on revenge. Ostracism and even execution were reserved for the most serious offenders of social norms. Strangers or people without direct relatives were feared and might be summarily killed.

DWELLINGS Villages of domed snow houses contained around 50 people but could hold up to 100. Entrance to the houses was gained through a tunnel that kept the warm air inside. Windows were made of freshwater ice. Two related nuclear families generally occupied a snow house, which had more than one room, and even a porch. The average house size was between 9 and 15 feet in diameter, although sizes varied widely. People slept on raised packed snow platforms covered with skins and furs.

Other structures included large ceremonial or dance snow houses, a platform for storing dog feed, and a toilet room or outhouse. Some groups built ice houses in the fall. People used a combination snow house and skin tent in spring; these were snow houses with a skin roof. Summer dwellings were conical sealskin tents held down by stones.

DIET The Netsilik were nomadic hunters. The most important game animals were seals, which were hunted communally at their breathing holes in winter and stalked in spring. A hunter might have to stand motionless next to a breathing hole for hours in the dark and bitter cold. The people also hunted caribou, polar bear, and musk ox (in the east). The caribou were speared from kayaks as they crossed bodies of water during fall migrations or stalked and shot on land. Smaller animals included fox and squirrel. Meat was eaten raw, frozen, or, preferably, cooked. Large animals' stomach contents were eaten as well.

Fishing, particularly for salmon trout (Arctic char) and lake trout, occurred mainly in summer and autumn, individually or communally at inland weirs. Fish was mainly eaten raw, although it might be boiled or dried and cached for winter. Other food resources included fowl, gulls, and some berries. In winter, people drank melted old sea ice, which loses its salinity after a year or so. Blood was another common drink.

KEY TECHNOLOGY Womens' semilunar knives were used mainly for skin preparation and fish cleaning. Men used antler knives to cut snow blocks for houses and to butcher caribou. Hunting equipment included various harpoons, spears, the bow and arrow, breathing-hole finders and protectors, down or horn seal motion indicators (also used for breathing-hole sealing), and other hunting equipment. Fish were caught with hooks, spears, prongs, weirs, and traps.

Most tools were made from caribou antlers as well as stone (including flint and soapstone) and bone. Wood was very scarce but when available was used for kayak frames, trays, handles, and other items. Other key tools included bone-tipped ice chisels, snow shovels made of sealskin lashed to antler, bone needles and caribou-sinew thread, the bow drill for tool manufacture and fire starting, and containers made of fowl skin, sealskin, and salmon skin. Sealskin thongs also provided cordage.

Men carved soapstone cooking pots and lamps (the latter burned seal oil or blubber and moss). Drying racks were placed above the lamps. Summer fires burned heather or mosses

TRADE Netsiliks engaged in some trade with Iglulik bands. Western groups traded with their neighbors for items such as pots and lamps. Some groups imported copper and driftwood from the Copper Inuit and wood from the Caribou Inuit.

NOTABLE ARTS Some people carved fine wooden and ivory figurines. In the early postcontact period, women decorated clothing with beaded fringe and pieces of metal.

TRANSPORTATION Men hunted seals and caribou from long, slender, one-person kayaks covered with sealskin. Umiaks were larger, skin-covered open boats. There were some wooden dogsleds, with runners covered with ice-coated peat or made of fish wrapped in sealskin. Polar bear skins were also used for sleds, especially in the east and in spring when the snow deteriorated. Winter travel was extremely difficult.

DRESS Men skinned the caribou, and women did most of the hide preparation and sewed the clothing. They also prepared sealskins for summer clothing as well as boots and mittens. About 20 caribou skins were needed to outfit a family of four.

Mens' coats had short, fringed flaps, and womens' coats had long wide flaps. All were two-layered and had pointed hoods. The hair of the inner layer was turned in, and that of the outer layer was turned out. The outer coat had a sewn-in hood, although for women both layers had extra-large shoulders and sewn-in hoods to fit over babies, which were carried in a pouch at the back of a coat.

Four layers of caribou fur—socks, stockings, boots, and shoes—protected people's feet in winter. Men wore knee-length, two-layered pants; women made do with one layer. All outer coats (parkas) and womens' pants might be decorated with white fur. Women often braided their hair around two sticks. They also tattooed their faces and limbs. Childrens' clothing was often a one-piece suit.

WAR AND WEAPONS Neighbors tended to avoid the Netsilik in part because of their reputation for strength and magic.

Contemporary Information

GOVERNMENT/RESERVATIONS Netsilik communities include Arvilikjuak (Pelly Bay) and Uqsuqtuuq (Gjoa Haven). Government is provided by locally elected community councils.

ECONOMY People still engage in some sealing and caribou hunting, although the caribou stock has been seriously overhunted. There is also government assistance and some wage work. Native-owned and -operated cooperatives have been an important part of the Inuit economy for some time. Activities range from arts and crafts to retail to commercial fishing to construction.

LEGAL STATUS Inuit are considered "nonstatus" native people. Most Inuit communities are incorporated as hamlets and are officially recognized. Baffin Island is slated to become a part of the new territory of Nunavut.

DAILY LIFE In 1993, the Tungavik Federation of Nunavut (TFN), an outgrowth of the Inuit Tapirisat of Canada (ITC), signed an agreement with Canada providing for the establishment in 1999 of a new, mostly Inuit, territory on roughly 36,000 square kilometers of land, including Kitikmeot.

The people never abandoned their land, which is still central to their identity. Traditional and modern coexist, sometimes uneasily, for many Inuit. Although people use television (there is even radio and television programming in Inuktitut), snowmobiles, and manufactured items, women also carry babies in the traditional hooded parkas, chew caribou skin to make it soft, and use the semilunar knives to cut seal meat. Full-time doctors are rare in the communities. Housing is often of poor quality. Most people are Christians. Culturally, although many stabilizing patterns of traditional culture have been destroyed, many remain. Many people live as part of extended families. Adoption is widely practiced. Decisions are often taken by consensus.

Politically, community councils have gained considerably more autonomy over the past decade or two. There is also a significant Inuit presence in the Northwest Territories Legislative Assembly and some presence at the federal level as well. The disastrous effects of government-run schools have been mitigated to some degree by local control of education, including more culturally relevant curricula in schools. Many people still speak Inuktitut, which is also taught in most schools, especially in the earlier grades. Children attend school in their community through grade nine; the high school is in Frobisher Bay. Adult education is also available.

Unangan

Unangan (Ū `nän g ə n), "People." The Unangan were formerly and are occasionally known as Aleut, possibly meaning "island" in a Siberian language. The Unangan consisted of perhaps nine named subdivisions, each of which spoke an eastern, a central, or a western dialect.

LOCATION Unangan territory included the Pribilof, Shumagin, and Aleutian (west to the International Date Line) Islands and the extreme west of the Alaska Peninsula. Fog and wind, perhaps more than anything else, characterized the climate. In contrast to most of the Arctic region, the ocean remains ice free year-round.

POPULATION The Unangan population was between 16,000 and 20,000 people, although there may have been fewer, in the early eighteenth century. There were about 4,000 Unangan in the early 1990s, of whom perhaps half lived away from their traditional lands. The Unangan people are known to have enjoyed relatively great longevity.

LANGUAGE Unangans spoke three dialects of Aleut, a member of the Eskaleut language family.

Historical Information

HISTORY Ancestors of the Unangan probably moved east and then south across the Bering land bridge and then west from western Alaska to arrive in their historical location, where people have lived for at least 7,000 years. Direct cultural relationships have been established to people living in the region as long ago as 4,000 years.

The Russians, arriving in the 1740s, quickly recognized the value of sea otter and other animal pelts. For a period of about a generation, they tried to compel the Unangan to hunt for them, mainly by taking hostages and threatening death. The natives resisted, and there was much bloodshed during that time. However, after losing between a third and half of their total population they gave up the struggle and were made to do the Russians' bidding. Unangan men were forced to hunt sea mammals from Alaska to southern California for the Russian-American company. Large-scale population movements date from that period and lasted well into the twentieth century.

The strong influence of Russian culture dates from that period and includes conversion to the Russian Orthodox church by the early nineteenth century, when the worst of the Russian excesses ended. Other significant Russian influences include metal tools, steam baths, and larger kayaks, with sails. An Unangan orthography was created about that time, allowing the people to read and write in their own language.

Unangan hunters had come into increasing conflict with their Inuit and Indian neighbors as they were forced to go farther and farther afield for pelts. By the early nineteenth century, disease as well as warfare had diminished their population by about 80 percent. Survivors were consolidated onto 16 islands in 1831, but, by that time, Unangan culture had suffered a near-fatal blow.

The Russians left and the Americans took over around 1867, increasing fur hunting and driving the sea otter practically to extinction. The town of Unalaska had become an important commercial center by 1890. Fox trapping and canneries had become important to the local economy by the early twentieth century. Much of the Aleutian chain was designated as a national park in 1913. Some religious and government schools were opened in the early to mid–twentieth century. Still, the people endured high tuberculosis rates in the 1920s through the 1940s, and there were few, if any, village doctors.

The Japanese attacked the Aleutian Islands during World War II, capturing residents of Attu. The United States removed almost all Unangans west of Unimak Island, interning them in camps in southeast Alaska. Many people, especially elders who normally transmitted cultural beliefs and practices to the young, died during that period owing to the poor conditions in the camps. When the people returned home after the war, they found that many of their homes and possessions had been destroyed. As a result, many villages were abandoned.

The commercial fishing and cash economy grew sharply after the war. Most Unangan worked at the lowest levels of the economy. By then, Unangan children were attending high school in Sitka (Bureau of Indian Affairs) and Anchorage. Alaska received statehood in 1958. Nine years later, the native people founded the Alaska Federation of Natives (AFN) and the Aleut League. Unangan were included in the 1971 Alaska Native Claims Settlement Act (ANCSA), after initial rejection because of their high percentage of Russian blood.

RELIGION The people may have recognized a generative deity associated with the sun that had overall responsibility for souls as well as hunting success. They also recognized good and evil spirits, including animal spirits. These were the supernatural beings that influenced people's lives on a day-to-day basis. Adult men made offerings to the spirits at special sacred places and used a number of various charms, talismans, and amulets for protection. They also undertook spirit dances, although mainly to intimidate women and children into proper behavior

Souls were said to migrate between three worlds: earth, an upper sphere, and a lower sphere. Shamans mediated between the material and spiritual worlds. Their vocations were considered to be predetermined; that is, they did not seek a shamanic career. They had the usual responsibilities concerning hunting, weather, and curing.

Various winter masked dances and ceremonies were designed to propitiate the spirits. Perhaps the major ceremony was a memorial feast held 40 days following a death. Death was an important rite of passage. Some groups mummified dead bodies in order to preserve that person's spiritual power. A whaler might even remove a piece of the mummy for assistance, but this custom was also considered potentially dangerous.

GOVERNMENT The eldest man usually led independent house groups, although all household leaders functioned as a council. One house group in a village was generally considered first among equals, the head of that group functioning as village chief if he merited the position. These leaders had little or no coercive power but mainly coordinated decision making over issues of war and peace and camp moves. They might become wealthy in part from receiving a share of subordinates' catch (wealth consisted not only of furs and skins but also of dentalium shells, amber, and slaves). This position could be inherited in the male line. In addition, there were also special leaders known as strong men. These people received special training but tended to die early.

CUSTOMS Among the Unangan, descent was probably matrilineal. Their class structure was probably derived from Northwest Coast cultures. The three hereditary classes were wealthy people (chiefs and nobles), commoners, and a small number of slaves, mainly women. The first two groups were usually related. Harmony, patience, and hard work were key values. Speech was judicious in nature, and silence was generally respected.

Villages claimed certain subsistence areas and evicted or attacked trespassers. Numerous formal partnerships between both men and women served to bind the community together. Berdaches were men who lived and worked as women. Women sewed and processed and prepared food. Truly incorrigible people might be put to death upon agreement by the village elders.

Boys moved from their mother's to their maternal uncle's home in mid-childhood. The uncle took over primary responsibility for raising the boy, with the father playing more of a supporting role. Boys were strengthened, toughened, and rigorously trained from a very early age for the life of a kayak hunter. When a girl began menstruating, she was confined for 40 days, during which time her joints were bound, in theory so they would not ache in her old age. She was also subject to a number of food and behavioral restrictions and admonishments and was allowed to cure minor illness, the people believing that she possessed special curative powers during these times.

Girls could marry even before they reached puberty, but boys were expected to wait until they were at least 18; that is, when they were capable providers. Most marriages were monogamous, except that particularly wealthy men might have more than one wife. Men performed a one- or two-year bride service. Cross cousins (children of a mother's brothers or a father's sisters) were considered potential, even preferred, spouses. Divorce was rare.

Winter was the time for ceremonies as well as social visits between communities. Village chiefs invited another community and extended great hospitality toward their guests. These visits featured wrestling, storytelling, and dance contests. Some dancers wore wooden masks to invoke spirits.

Some men paddled out to sea at the end of their lives, never to return. In fact, suicide tended to be seen in a positive light for a number of reasons. The insides of most corpses were removed and replaced with grass. Following this procedure, bodies would remain in the house, either in a corner or in a cradle over the bed, for up to several months. They were eventually buried in a flexed position in the house, either under the floor or within the walls. Central and eastern people also mummified some corpses, caching the mummies in warm, dry, volcanic caves. Widows and widowers were subject to a period of special behavioral restrictions, including some joint binding.

DWELLINGS Typical villages contained roughly 200 people, although up to 2,000 people may have populated some eastern communities. Rectangular, semiexcavated houses (*barabara*) were made of a driftwood and whalebone frame covered with matting and turf. Sizes varied widely. The average may have been about 35 to 60 feet long by about 15 to 30 feet wide. These houses held perhaps 40 people or several nuclear families related through the male line. The largest houses may have been up to 240 feet long by 40 feet wide, holding up to 150 people.

Sleeping compartments separated by grass mats ringed a large central room. Mats also served as flooring. Entrance was gained via a ladder placed through an opening in the roof. Cooking was generally outside the house. Large houses also served as dance halls.

DIET Depending on location, the people ate mainly sea lions, but also seals, sea otter, octopus, and some walrus. Most sea mammals were hunted by men in kayaks. Sea otters were hunted communally, in a surround, or clubbed on shore. Men who hunted sea otter avoided women for a month prior to the hunt.

There was also some whaling, especially in the west. Whaling was highly ritualized. For instance, men who had harpooned a whale retired to a special hut to feign illness, so that the whale would fall ill. Whaling privileges and powers could be inherited through the male line.

Other types of food included large and small game on the eastern islands and mainland. Important fish species included cod, flounder, halibut, herring, trout, and salmon. People ate birds, fowl, and their eggs, the latter gained mainly by climbing up or down steep cliffs. They also gathered seaweed, shellfish, roots, and berries, depending on location. Unangans tended to eat much of their food raw, although there was some pit cooking.

KEY TECHNOLOGY Sea mammals were harpooned or clubbed. Atlatls helped give velocity to a harpoon throw. Eastern people hunted large game with the bow and arrow. Whale lances may have had poison tips. Fishing equipment included spears, nets, and wooden and tooth hooks. Birds were taken with bolas and darts, although puffins were snared and netted. Women used chipped stone semilunar knives for hide preparation and fish cleaning.

Most tools were made from stone and bone. Other important material items included sewn skin bags and pouches, some wooden buckets and bowls, sea lion stomach containers, tambourine drums, and spruce-root and grass baskets. Stone lamps burned sea lion blubber for light and heat. Cordage came from braided kelp or sea lion sinew. The people started fires with a wooden drill and flint sparks on sulphur and bird down. A highly developed counting system allowed them to reckon in five figures.

TRADE Unagnan people traded both goods and ideas with Northwest Coast groups such as the Tlingit and Haida as well as with Yup'ik and Alutiiq peoples. Exports included baskets, sea products, and walrus ivory. The people imported items such as shells, slaves, blankets, and hides.

NOTABLE ARTS Art objects included carved wooden dancing masks and decorative bags. Women wove fine spruce-root and grass baskets and decorated mats with geometric designs. Ivory carvings of the great creative spirit were hung from ceiling beams in houses, and other objects were decorated with ivory carvings as well. The Unangan were also known for their painted wooden hats. Storytelling was highly developed. Clothing decoration included feathers, whiskers, and fringe. Some items were painted, mainly with geometric patterns.

TRANSPORTATION Men hunted in one- or possibly two-person kayaks. Larger skin-covered open boats were used for travel and trade but not for whaling.

DRESS Women and men wore long parkas of sea otter or bird skin (men wore only the latter material). The women's version had no hood, only a collar. Men also wore waterproof slickers made of sewn sea lion gut, esophagus, or other such material. Particularly in the east, sealskin boots had soles of sea lion flipper. Boots were less common in the west. The people used grass for socks.

Men also wore wooden visors, painted and decorated with sea lion whiskers. They wore painted conical wooden hats on ceremonial occasions. Other ceremonial clothing was made of colorful puffin skins. Both sexes wore labrets of various materials. They tattooed their faces and hands and wore bone or ivory nose pins. Women wore sea otter capes.

WAR AND WEAPONS The Unangan fought their Inuit neighbors, especially the Alutiiq, as well as themselves (especially those who spoke different dialects). Small parties often launched raids for women and children slaves or to avenge past wrongs. The people used stone and bone weapons, such as the bow and arrow, lances, wooden shields, and slat armor. Slain enemies were often dismembered, in the belief that an intact body, though dead, could still be dangerous. Prisoners might be tortured. On the other hand, high-status captives might be held for ransom or used as slaves.

Contemporary Information

GOVERNMENT/RESERVATIONS Unangan live on the Alaska coast, Aleutian Islands, Pribilof Islands, and Commander Islands. Communities include Atka, Akutan, Belkofski, Cold Bay, False Pass, Ivanof Bay

(*see* Alutiiq), King Cove, Nelson Lagoon, Nikolski, Paulof Harbor, St. George Island, St. Paul Island, Sand Point, Squaw Harbor, and Unalaska. There are various forms of government, including traditional structures and those modeled on the Indian Reorganization Act. Elected village governments own no land.

ECONOMY Economic development is recognized as key to survival. Many villages are in economic partnerships with seafood companies. Most jobs may be found with the fishing and military industries as well as other governmental bodies at lower levels.

LEGAL STATUS ANCSA granted some traditional lands to the Aleut Corporation and to village corporations but not to the tribes. The Aleut Corporation represents Unangans under ANCSA.

DAILY LIFE Most Unangan are of the Russian Orthodox faith. Most also live in wood frame houses. There is a considerable degree of intermarriage with non-Unangans. The position of the corporations vis-à-vis the tribes has made for some bitter interfamily and intervillage divisions. Political sovereignty remains a major goal for most people. Some public schools feature courses in the Unangan language. A cultural facility on Bristol Bay is planned.

Yup'ik

Yup'ik (`Y ū p ik), "Real People." The Yup'ik people were formerly known as Nunivak Inuit (or Eskimo), St. Lawrence Island Eskimo, West Alaska Eskimo, South Alaska Eskimo, and Southwest Alaska Eskimo. They are also known as Bering Sea Yuit and, with the Alutiiq (Pacific Eskimo), simply as Yuit. The St. Lawrence Islanders were culturally similar to Siberian Eskimos. *See also* Alutiiq.

LOCATION Yup'ik territory was located in southwestern Alaska, between Bristol Bay and Norton Sound, including Nunivak and St. Lawrence Islands.

POPULATION The early-nineteenth-century Yup'ik population was between about 15,000 and 18,000. It was approximately 18,000 in the early 1990s.

LANGUAGE The people spoke the Yuk or Central Alaskan Yup'ik (including St. Lawrence Island or Central Siberian Yup'ik) branch of Yup'ik. With Inuit-Inupiaq (Inuktitut), Yup'ik, or Western Eskimo, constitutes the Eskimo division of the Eskaleut language family.

Historical Information

HISTORY People have lived on Nunivak Island since at least 150 B.C.E. They made pottery and used mainly stone tools. The mainland has been inhabited for at least 4,000 years, with cultural continuity since circa 300 B.C.E.

Most groups avoided direct contact with non-natives until Russian traders established trading posts in Yup'ik territory, generally in the early nineteenth century. The Russians exchanged clothing, metal tools, and beads for beaver pelts. The Inuit began spending more time trapping beaver and less time on subsistence activities, eventually becoming dependent on the posts even for food. In general, Russian Orthodox missionaries followed the early traders. Most Inuit had accepted Christianity by the 1860s.

This process was uneven throughout the region. St. Lawrence Island people first met non-natives in the 1850s, whereas people on the Yukon Delta did not do so until the late nineteenth century. About 1,000 people (roughly two-thirds of the total population) of St. Lawrence Island died in 1878 from a combination of natural causes combined with a high incidence of alcohol abuse. Nunivak Island was similarly insulated (contact occurred in 1821 but perhaps not again until 1874), in part owing to the shallowness of the surrounding sea. The first trading post, which included a reindeer herd, was established there in 1920; missionaries and schools dated from about the 1930s. The people experienced various epidemics throughout the early to mid–twentieth century.

Little changed with the sale of Alaska to the United States until the advent of commercial fishing in Bristol Bay in the 1880s. Moravian missionaries appeared on the Kuskokwim River in 1885; those of other sects soon followed. Like most missionary schools, theirs forbade children to speak their native language. In an effort to undermine the traditional lifestyle, the U.S. government introduced reindeer to the region around 1900.

In addition to commercial fishing, fox hunting for the fur trade plus the manufacture of baleen and carved ivory objects formed the basis of a local cash economy from the late nineteenth century through the early twentieth century. Nunivak Islanders experienced the full cash economy only after World War II. By then the people had incorporated under the Indian Reorganization Act (IRA). The Bureau of Indian Affairs managed their reindeer herd.

The far north took on strategic importance during the Cold War, about the same time that mineral reserves became known and technologically possible to exploit. St. Lawrence Island became exposed to mainland life and tied to Alaska only after military installations were built there in the 1950s. Inuits generally found only unskilled menial labor. With radical diet changes, the adoption of a sedentary life, and the appearance of drugs and alcohol, health declined markedly. The Alaska Native Claims Settlement Act (ANCSA) was passed in 1971.

RELIGION Religious belief and practice were based on the conception of spirit entities found in nature and needing to be treated with respect. Most rituals focused on this belief, such as those that showed respect to an animal just killed. It was also the basis of most taboos as well as related objects and songs.

Souls were said to be reincarnated through naming. Spirits not yet reincarnated also needed to be treated with respect lest they cause harm. In some areas, secret, spirit-based knowledge, objects, and songs, all thought to bring success in hunting, were passed on from father to son. The people also believed in various nonhuman, nonanimal supernatural beings.

Male and female shamans (angakok) provided religious leadership by virtue of their connection with guardian spirits. They led group religious activities. They could also cure disease and see into the future. Illness was thought to be due to soul loss and/or the violation of taboos. Professional curing methods included interrogation about taboo adherence, trancelike communication with spirit helpers, extraction (such as sucking), and performance, including masked dances. Shamans were relatively powerful people, in part owing to their ability to use their spirit power to harm people.

The Messenger Feast, a major ceremony, included dancing and gift exchange between two villages. St. Lawrence Islanders held a spring whaling ceremony. When the successful crew returned, the umiak owner's wife offered the whale a drink of water as a token of respect. Then followed another feast and a thanksgiving ceremony. Some groups held memorial feasts about a year following a death.

In general, Yup'iks living along the Bering Sea had their main ceremonial season in the winter and early spring. The festivities featured spirit masks and dances. The Bladder Feast was another important ceremony dedicated to respect for animals, in this case, seals. This festival also underscored the ritual sexual division in society.

GOVERNMENT Nuclear families were loosely organized into extended families or local groups associated with geographical areas (-miuts). Local groups on the mainland occasionally came together as perhaps seven small, fluid subgroups or bands. From north to south, they were Kuigpagmiut, Maarmiut, Kayaligmiut, Kukquqvagmiut, Kiatagmiut, Tuyuryarmiut, and Aglurmiut. Older men, with little formal authority and no power, led kashims (men's houses) and kin groups (generally the same as villages on St. Lawrence Island). These leaders generally embodied Inuit values, such as generosity, and were also good hunters.

CUSTOMS The family was the most important

economic and political unit. Descent was bilateral, except patrilineal on St. Lawrence Island. There, secret songs, ceremonies, house ownership, and hunting group membership were passed through patrilineal clans and lineages. Status was formally ranked within the *kashim* and depended on hunting and leadership skills.

People married simply by announcing their intentions, although infants were regularly betrothed. Men might have more than one wife, but most had only one. Divorce was easy to obtain. Both men and women remained respectful and distant toward their in-laws. Wife exchange was a part of certain defined male partnerships, such as mutual aid, "joking," and trade. Some of these relationships were inheritable. The alliance between the wife and the exchanged husband was considered as a kind of marriage. Formal female partnerships existed as well.

Infanticide was rare and usually practiced against females. Children were highly valued and loved, especially males. Adoption was common. Life-cycle events, such as berry picking and grass gathering by girls and seal killing by boys, were recognized by the community. Childbirth, girls' puberty, and death were the occasions for special taboos.

The sick or aged were sometimes abandoned, especially in times of scarcity. Corpses were generally removed through an alternate exit (not the door) and left on the ground with certain grave goods. Along the Bering Sea, some groups placed their dead in painted wooden coffins and erected carved wooden memorial poles to keep their spirits at bay. The mourning period generally lasted four or five days, during which time activities, including hunting, were severely restricted.

Work was fairly gender specific. Women made food and clothing and cared for children; men provided fish and land animals. Use of the real name was generally avoided, perhaps for religious reasons. Tensions were relieved through games; duels of drums and songs, in which the competing people tried to outdo each other in parody; and some "joking" relationships. Ostracism and even death were reserved for the most serious cases of socially inappropriate behavior.

DWELLINGS The people created larger settlements in winter to take advantage of group subsistence activities. Villages ranged in size from just two to more than a dozen houses, plus one or more *kashims* and storehouses.

There were several kinds of dwellings throughout the area, depending on location. Houses were generally of the semiexcavated variety, roughly 12 to 15 feet by 15 feet and made of sod, grass, and/or bark over wooden posts and beams. They were mainly inhab-

ited by related women and children. Some might have plank walls with benches placed along them. Entrance was via an anteroom connected to the main room by an underground tunnel. A hearth and cooking area stood at one end of the open main room and raised sleeping platforms were at the other end. Windows were often made of sewn fish skins.

Except on St. Lawrence Island, men worked, bathed, slept, and ate in larger houses, or *kashims*. Women delivered the food. *Kashims* were also used as ceremonial houses. Political decisions were made there as well. Most villages contained at least one. Some groups built cut-sod spring camp houses, about 100 square feet in size. Skin tents were generally the norm in summer. Other structures included drying racks and food caches.

DIET Yup'ik people were nomadic hunters with either a land or a sea orientation, although most people also exploited the region opposite their own. The most important game animals were seals, walrus (especially St. Lawrence and Nunivak Island), and whales. Men hunted seals at their breathing holes in winter. On Nunivak, men hunted them from kayaks in spring and with nets under shore ice in fall. Some groups also hunted caribou (especially away from the coast and major rivers and on Nunivak Island until about 1900) and moose, especially in fall.

Fish, especially salmon, trout, smelt, and whitefish, were the most important dietary item in many locations and were generally taken in all seasons but winter. Fish were especially important inland, with marine mammals more important on the coasts and islands. Shellfish was gathered where possible. Birds and fowl, such as ptarmigan, were speared or netted and their eggs gathered. Some groups were able to obtain berries, roots, and greens.

KEY TECHNOLOGY Hunting equipment consisted of various harpoons, spears, bows and arrows, and bone arrowheads. Caribou were snared or shot with the bow and arrow. Birds were netted, snared, speared, or captured with bolas. Fish were caught with hooks, spears, stone weirs, and caribou-skin or willow-bark nets.

Most tools were fashioned from caribou antlers as well as stone, bone, and driftwood (on St. Lawrence and Nunivak Islands, many items were made from walrus parts). Men and women had their own specialty stone knives. People cooked in pottery pots and burned seal or walrus oil in saucer-shaped pottery lamps. They carved wooden trays, boxes, dishes, spoons, and other objects.

Various kinds of containers were made out of gut, wood, and clay. St. Lawrence Islanders often used baleen as a raw material. Some groups made twined and coiled baskets of grasses and birch bark. In fact, grass was used extensively for items such as mats, baskets, socks, and rope, although some cordage also came from beluga sinew. The ceremonial tambourine drum was made of seal gut stretched over a wooden frame.

TRADE   The Yup'ik engaged in a general coastal-interior interregional trade, including trade with Unangan and Northwest Coast peoples. St. Lawrence Island people traditionally traded and otherwise interacted with those from Siberia.

NOTABLE ARTS   The people made finely carved wooden and ivory figurines. Men painted designs, especially of animals, on wooden objects. Women decorated clothing borders, baskets, and pottery items.

TRANSPORTATION   Men hunted from one- or two-person sealskin-covered kayaks. Umiaks were larger, skin-covered open boats; several men could hunt whales or walrus in these. They were also used for trade voyages. Wooden sleds were used for overland winter travel. Some interior groups also used canoes.

DRESS   Women made most clothing of caribou and sealskin. Yup'ik clothing tended to fit relatively loosely. Some groups used skins of other animals, such as marmot and muskrat, as well as bird and even fish skins. Most people wore long hooded parkas and inner shirts and pants. Women's parkas were often shorter and featured front and rear flaps. Other items included sealskin (some groups used salmon skin) boots and mittens, skin or grass socks, fish-skin parkas and pants in summer, waterproof gut raincoats, and wooden snow goggles.

Men on St. Lawrence Island wore distinctive hairdos in which they shaved the tops of their heads but retained a circle of hair around the forehead. Women generally tattooed three lines on their chins. Personal ornaments included labrets and other items of walrus and bird parts.

WAR AND WEAPONS   The people regularly engaged in interregional raids. Victims were generally killed. Hunting equipment doubled as weapons of war.

Contemporary Information

GOVERNMENT/RESERVATIONS   Villages represented by the Bristol Bay Native Corporation (BBNC) include Egegik (86 native residents; governed by the Egegik Village Council and a seven-member city council), Pilot Point (91 native residents; governed by the Pilot Point Village Council and a seven-member elected city council), Port Heiden (86 native residents; governed by the Port Heiden Village Council and a seven-member elected city council), and Ugashik (six native residents; governed by the Ugashik Traditional Village Council and a five-mem-

ber elected city council). These villages are all members of the Lake and Peninsula Borough and are located on the east side of Bristol Bay on the Alaska Peninsula (Chignik area).

BBNC villages located in the western portion of Bristol Bay (Togiak area) include Manokotak (368 native residents; governed by the seven-member Manokotak Traditional Council and an eight-member city council), Togiak (535 native residents; governed by the seven-member Togiak Traditional Council as well as six city councilors and a mayor), and Twin Hills (61 native residents; governed by the five-member Twin Hills Village Council as well as a traditional elders' council).

BBNC villages located in the Iliamna area include Igiugig (26 native residents; governed by the five-member elected Igiugig Tribal Council), Iliamna (62 native residents; governed by the five-member elected Iliamna Village Council), Kokhanok (137 native residents; governed by the five-member elected Kokhanok Village Council), Levelock (87 native residents; governed by the five-member elected Levelock Village Council), and Newhalen (151 native residents; governed by the seven-member elected Newhalen Tribal Council as well as a seven-member elected city council). All of these villages are also members of the Lake and Peninsula Borough. In addition, the villages of Nondalton and Pedro Bay are described in the Tanaina entry in Chapter 9.

BBNC villages in the Kvichak Bay area include King Salmon (108 native members; governed by the five-member elected King Salmon Village Council), Naknek (236 native residents; governed by the five-member Naknek Village Council), and South Naknek (108 native residents; governed by the five-member South Naknek Traditional Council). All of these villages are also members of the Bristol Bay Borough.

BBNC villages in the Nushagak Bay area include Aleknagik (154 native residents; governed by the seven-member Aleknagik Traditional Council and a seven-member city council), Clark's Point (53 native residents; governed by the five-member Clark's Point Traditional Council and a seven-member city council), Dillingham (1,125 native residents; governed by the five-member Dillingham Native Village Council and by an elected mayor and six city councilors), Ekuk (two native residents; governed by the three-member Ekuk Village Council), Ekwok (67 native residents; governed by the seven-member Ekwok Tribal Council and a seven-member city council), Koliganek (174 native residents; governed by the seven-member Koliganek Traditional Council), New Stuyahok (375 native residents; governed by the seven-member New Stuyahok Traditional Council and a seven-member city council), and Portage Creek (three native residents; governed by the three-member Portage Creek Village Council).

All BBNC village population figures are as of the early 1990s. Some villages have significant numbers of Alutiiq residents.

Regional population centers include Bethel, Dillingham, and St. Michael. The Association of Village Council Presidents (AVCP) is a regional non-profit corporation representing 56 villages. Through it, some people hope to establish a regional tribal government.

On St. Lawrence Island there are three levels of local government: an IRA council, a state-mandated city council, and ANCSA village corporations.

ECONOMY Commercial fishing is probably the most important single industry. Except in the Bristol Bay region, traditional subsistence activities remain very important. The people also do some muskrat and mink trapping in the Kuskokwim Delta region. Lake Iliamna has one of only two populations of freshwater seals in the world (the other is in Lake Baikal, Russia). Traditional crafts are an important industry on Nunivak Island. Many people depend on government payments. There is also some tourism, especially in the Nuchagak Bay area.

LEGAL STATUS Three ANCSA regional corporations serve Yup'ik territory: Bering Straits Corporation, Calista Corporation, and Bristol Bay Native Corporation. Nunivak Island is a national wildlife refuge in which local residents may carry out subsistence activities. Under ANCSA, St. Lawrence Island is owned by the native residents but managed by corporations.

DAILY LIFE Bilingual education has been in force since the 1970s; most Yup'ik people still speak the native language. The Yukon Kuskokwim Health Corporation serves the people's health needs with culturally appropriate programs and care.

Some communities have been more severely disrupted and are consequently less cohesive than others. Most St. Lawrence Islanders had been converted to Christianity by the mid–twentieth century, although many of the old ideas still resonate for the people.

The issue of subsistence hunting rights remains very important to the Yup'ik. Chignik area villages share certain concerns, such as the decline of the local caribou herd, possibly owing to excess sport hunting, and the threat to subsistence activities of industrial development. Togiak area villages are pressing for permission from the state of Alaska to conduct a permanent annual walrus hunt on Round Island and for funds to maintain their reindeer herd. They are also trying to prevent desecration of ancient burial sites.

Local concerns in the Iliamna area include road improvement, bridge construction, and air links. Concerns in the Kvichak Bay area include the maintenance of subsistence fishing rights, the use and contamination cleanup of the former air force base site, the construction and management of a visitor center at Katmai National Park, and the decline of the local caribou herd. Issues in the Nushagak Bay area include the possible formation of a Nuchagak and Togiak area borough, land allotments within Wood-Tikchik State Park, and proper management of the local caribou herd.

Note: FR = French; SP = Spanish.

Ak chin farming: Farming based on an irrigation method consisting of the collection and channeling of floodwaters from arroyo mouths.

Allotment: A term denoting the government action of carving up communally held tribal land and granting sections of it to individual Indians. This activity characterized the General Allotment Act of 1887 (the Dawes Act).

Annual round: The annual cycle of activities engaged in by traditional societies.

Arroyo (U `rō yō, SP): A dry, sandy wash, prone to flash flooding during storms.

Atlatl (Ăt `lät l): A tool used to increase the leverage of the human arm in order for hunters to throw spears with greater velocity and accuracy.

Babiche (Bä `bēsh, FR): Semisoftened rawhide, used mainly in the far north for a number of purposes such as snares, nets, bowstrings, and line.

Baleen: A growth in the upper jaw of certain whales. Baleen is light, strong, and flexible. It serves the whales as a strainer and has been used by people to make tools and ceremonial objects.

Bent-corner boxes: An art form in which men steamed, bent, and then carved and/or painted pieces of red cedar. Bent-corner boxes were characteristic of Northwest Coast people.

Berdache (B ə r `d ə sh, FR): Literally "male prostitute," the term refers to any person participating in the cross-cultural practice of gender crossing. In general, females acting the male role were always considered women, whereas men were generally "reclassified."

Bola: A hunting weapon consisting of stone weights attached to thongs. When thrown, the bola entangles the feet of small animals and the wings of birds.

Breechclout: A piece of material, usually deerskin, used to cover the loins. It is also called a breechcloth or loincloth.

Bride service: The act of serving a new bride's parents, as a condition of marriage, for a period of time. Such service mainly consisted of obtaining food and other necessities.

Bureau of Indian Affairs (BIA): Founded in 1824 and referred to until the mid–twentieth century as the Office of Indian Affairs or the Indian Service, the BIA is the main bureaucratic arm of the U.S. government devoted to Indian affairs. In 1849 its jurisdiction was transferred from the War Department to the Interior Department. The Commissioner of Indian Affairs reports directly to the Secretary of the Interior.

Catlinite: *See* pipestone.

Clan: A group of families that traces descent through a common ancestor.

Coppers: Decorated, named plates of European copper that were important in later Northwest potlatching. A copper was worth the value of goods distributed at a potlatch and could only be bought at double that price. Coppers also played a role in rival potlatches: When one chief destroyed a copper, his rival was obliged to do the same or admit his social inferiority.

Coup (Kū, FR): Literally "blow," the term refers to a type of war honors common among early historical Plains cultures in which credit was earned (coup was counted) for acts of bravery and daring such as touching an enemy with a stick or knocking him off his horse.

Coureurs de bois (Cū `rūr de `bwä, FR): Independent, unlicensed fur traders and trappers who played an important role in early trade and exploration of later-seventeenth-century New France.

Datura: Also known as Jimsonweed, this tall, poisonous plant is sometimes used for ceremonial or medicinal purposes by certain Indians of California and the Southwest.

Deadfall: A type of trap in which a heavy object is rigged to fall upon prey.

Dentalium: A type of shell common to parts of the Pacific Northwest. With a natural hole that made threading easy, it was widely traded and highly valued for jewelry and exchange.

Enrollment: A category of tribal membership generally constituting formal acceptance by the U.S. or Canadian governments. Because of various laws and policies excluding certain groups of people, a given tribe might recognize as members far more people than a government recognizes as enrolled.

Exogamy: The custom of marrying outside a particular group (such as a clan).

Fiesta (Fē `es ta, SP): A celebration, usually religious in nature, featuring processions and dances.

Fire drill: A device for making fire in which a stick is twirled rapidly on another piece of wood. The resulting friction is sufficient to ignite bark or grass tinder.

First Nation: A term often used to refer to Canadian Indian bands.

Fiscales (Fēs `kä läs, SP): One of several officials of Spanish-mandated Pueblo governments, the *fiscales* were church assistants. Most Pueblo groups adopted these offices after 1620, when the Spanish began requiring them, but retained their own traditional and vastly more meaningful political and religious structures as well.

Games: An important part of most traditional Native American cultures, often having spiritual, ceremonial, and/or social implications. Games were often taken very seriously and were marked by intensive preparation, rigid codes of conduct, and wagering. Some of the most common and popular games were chunkey, the grass game, shinny, lacrosse (a running ball game played with web-pocketed sticks), and the hand game (a guessing game).

General Allotment Act of 1887 (Dawes Act): An act calling for the allotment of tribal land in severalty (a certain amount going to individual family heads), with the surplus to be opened for non-native settlement.

Grid plan of settlement: Houses laid out more or less evenly along ordered streets.

Hacienda (Hä cē `en dä, SP): A tract of land held by individual title; a plantation. Under the hacienda system, the dominant political, economic, and social system in nineteenth-century Mexico, the landowner maintained complete control over the land and the people on it. The system fostered peonage and the eradication of cultural differences.

Indian Act: The name applied to the body of Canadian federal laws pertaining to Indian affairs. The first Indian Act was passed in 1876. The act is regularly revised and updated.

Indian Reorganization Act (IRA): Legislation in 1934 that prohibited further allotment, which had been disastrous for most Indian groups, in favor of Indian self-government. Its provisions included the volun-

tary adoption of tribal councils within representative, constitutional governments.

Jerk (as meat): Jerking is the process of sun drying and/or smoking strips of meat.

Katsina (Kat `sē nä): Also known as kachinas, these are supernatural beings that figure prominently in the religion of Pueblo Indians. Katsina dolls and masks are used ceremonially to bestow blessings and teach proper behavior.

Kiva: An underground ceremonial chamber characteristic of Pueblo cultures.

L dialect: A dialect spoken by some bands/tribes in which the letter L was substituted for one letter of a word, commonly R or D. Thus Renápe becomes Lenápe and Dakota becomes Lakota in the L dialect (Dakota becomes Nakota in the Siouan N dialect).

Labret: A decorative plug worn in the lip.

Mano (`Mä nō, SP): The handheld upper millstone for grinding corn and other grains.

Matrilineal: Relating to descent through the maternal line.

Matrilocal: Relating to the residence of a wife's kin group.

Mesoamerica: Literally "middle America," the region between the continents of North and South America.

Mestiso/a: A man or woman of mixed European and American Indian ancestry.

Metate (M ə tä tä): A stone with a concave surface. Together with a mano, it is used for grinding corn and other grains.

Métis (Mä tē, FR): A people of mixed Cree-French or Cree-Scotch descent. By the nineteenth century, the Métis had developed a lifestyle with elements, including language and religion, drawn from both Indian and non-native traditions. The Métis were concentrated along the Red River of the North (Lake Winnipeg to the Minnesota River). Led by Louis Riel, they fought a series of unsuccessful wars in the mid–nineteenth century to defend their land rights.

Mother-in-law taboo: The custom in which a man avoided contact with his mother-in-law out of respect to her.

Olla (`Ō yä, SP): A container, usually a pot or a basket, for carrying or holding water.

Palisade: A high fence of pointed sticks enclosing an area for defensive purposes.

Parfleche (Pär `flesh, FR): Common mainly among Plains Indians, these were rawhide storage bags generally used to hold food.

Patrilineal: Relating to descent through the paternal line.

Patrilocal: Relating to the residence of a husband's kin group.

Pipestone: A type of clay, mainly found in Minnesota, widely used for making pipes. It is also referred to as catlinite after the painter George Catlin.

Polygamy: Having more than one wife or husband at a time.

Polygyny: Having more than one wife at a single time.

Powwow: Commonly used to describe a gathering at which native people dance, sing, tell stories, and exchange goods, the term also refers (in a mainly Algonquian context) to a healer or a healing ceremony.

Pueblo: Spanish for "village," the word refers to a style of architecture common among some southwestern Indian groups and characterized by multistory adobe or stone apartmentlike dwellings connected with ladders. The word also refers to the people and culture associated with that style of architecture.

Quillwork: Decoration, often on clothing, bags, and other items, made from dyed porcupine quills.

Ramada (R ə `mä da, SP): A covered yard or plaza.

Rancheria (Ranch ə `rē ä, SP): A settlement composed of spatially separated dwellings of nuclear or extended family units. In the California context, a rancheria is a parcel of Indian land and may be as large as a settlement or as small as a small cemetery.

Rasp: An instrument resembling a notched stick, used as a musical instrument among certain Indian groups, especially in the upper Great Plains.

Sachem: The chief of an (Algonquin) tribe or confederacy.

Sagamore: An (Algonquin) chief or leader with somewhat lesser status than a sachem.

Sandpainting: An art form associated mainly with the Navajo and some other southwestern Indian groups, sandpainting, or dry painting—the creation of designs from sand, cornmeal, and pollen—carries with it rich and complex religious and spiritual implications. Sandpaintings were destroyed immediately after their ceremonial use.

Shaman (`Shä m ə n): A traditional healer or holy man or woman.

Status Indians: Status is the term conferred by the Canadian government to those people who meet the official definition of Indian.

Taiga: The subarctic evergreen forest.

Termination: Federal Indian policy of the mid- to late 1950s that sought to end the relationship guaranteed by treaty between the government and Indian tribes.

Tipi (`Tē pē): A conical hide (usually buffalo) dwelling characteristic of Plains Indians. The tipi design had important cosmological implications.

Toloache: Any of several plants of the genus *Datura*, especially a narcotic annual herb used ceremonially by some California Indians.

Totem: A natural object or being serving as the emblem of a family or clan by virtue of a presumed shared ancestry with that object or being.

Travois (Trav `wä, FR): A transportation device common to Plains nomads. It consisted of two long poles (often lodgepole pines) connected by planks or hide webbing that supported goods and sometimes people. Dogs and, later, horses pulled the travois as the people migrated from place to place.

Tribe: A term, often misused, referring to the organization of a group of Indians. Tribes are generally composed of a number of constituent parts, such as bands or villages, and may share history, culture, and territory.

Tribelet: A single Indian group with a small territory, comprising a main settlement and one or more satellite villages. The tribelet's name was usually that of the principal town. The entire group often recognized a chief. Tribelets were autonomous but often acted as a unit in matters of land ownership, major ceremonies, and reaction to trespass and war. This form of political organization was most common in aboriginal California.

Tule (Tū lē): A type of reed used as a raw material by some southwestern and Californian Indians.

Tumpline: A strap across the forehead or chest that also supports a burden carried on the back.

Tundra: A treeless, Arctic region in which the ground is continually frozen no less than a few inches from the surface (permafrost). Various mosses and lichens will grow on tundra.

Voyageurs (Vō yä `jūr, FR): A group or class of Frenchmen who handled canoes and performed other trade-related tasks for the big fur companies in North America, primarily in the eighteenth and nineteenth centuries.

Wampum: An Algonquian word, wampum originally referred to strings or belts of shell (especially Quahog). They were used to record significant events as well as to communicate messages of peace or war between Indian groups. Shortly after non-natives arrived, wampum, now made increasingly of glass beads, was used as a medium of exchange and eventually as a form of money.

Wickiup (`Wi kē up): Dome-shaped, pole-framed dwellings covered with brush, grass, or reeds. Wickiups were often used by Apacheans.

Wigwam: A dwelling similar to a wickiup, although covered with products more reflective of their use among Algonquian people, such as skins, bark, or woven mats.

The following books are recommended for further study about native North Americans. I have omitted books on specific tribes or groups as well as the many helpful locations on the Internet. A growing number of tribes are also posting home pages on the World Wide Web.

General

Boxberger, Daniel. *Native North Americans: An Ethnohistorical Approach.* Dubuque, IA: Kendall/Hunt Publishing, 1990.

Champagne, Duane, ed. *The Native North American Almanac.* Detroit: Gale Research, 1994.

———. *Native America: Portrait of the Peoples.* Detroit: Visible Ink Press, 1994.

Confederated American Indians. *Indian Reservations.* Jefferson, NC: McFarland, 1986.

Davis, Mary. *Native America in the Twentieth Century.* New York: Garland Publishing, 1994.

Debo, Angie. *A History of Indians of the United States.* Norman: University of Oklahoma Press, 1970.

Dickason, Olive. *Canada's First Nations.* Norman: University of Oklahoma Press, 1992.

Dictionary of Indian Tribes of the Americas. Newport Beach, CA: American Indian Publishers, 1980.

Feest, Christian. *Native Arts of North America.* London: Thames and Hudson, 1992.

Frideres, James. *Native People in Canada.* Scarborough, Ontario: Prentice Hall Canada, 1983.

Gill, Sam, and Irene Sullivan. *Dictionary of Native American Mythology.* New York: Oxford University Press, 1992.

Hirschfelder, Arlene. *Native American Almanac.* New York: Prentice Hall, 1993.

Hoxie, Frederick, ed. *Encyclopedia of North American Indians.* Boston: Houghton Mifflin, 1996.

Jaimes, M. Annette. *The State of Native America.* Boston: South End Press, 1992.

Jenness, Diamond. *Indians of Canada.* 7th ed. Toronto: University of Toronto Press, 1977.

Johnson, Michael. *The Native Tribes of North America.* New York: Macmillan, 1995.

Jorgenson, Joseph J., ed. *Native America and Energy Development II.* Boston: Anthropological Research Center and Seventh Generation Fund, 1984.

Kehoe, Alice. *North American Indians.* Englewood Cliffs, NJ: Prentice Hall, 1981.

Klein, Barry. *Reference Encyclopedia of the American Indian.* 7th ed. West Nyack, NY: Todd Publications, 1995.

LePoer, Barbara Leitch. *Concise Dictionary of Indian Tribes of North America.* Algonac, MI: Reference Publications, 1979.

Markowitz, Harvey, ed. *American Indians.* Pasadena, CA: Salem Press, 1995.

Martin, Paul. *Indians before Columbus.* Chicago: University of Chicago Press, 1947.

Morrison, R. Bruce, and C. Roderick Wilson. *Native Peoples: The Canadian Experience.* 2d ed. Toronto: McClelland and Stewart, 1995.

O'Brien, Sharon. *American Indian Tribal Governments.* Norman: University of Oklahoma Press, 1989.

Paterek, Josephine. *Encyclopedia of American Indian Costume.* Santa Barbara, CA: ABC-CLIO, 1994.

Reddy, Marlita, ed. *Statistical Record of Native North Americans.* Detroit: Gale Research, 1993.

Spencer, Robert. *The Native Americans.* 2d ed. New York: Harper and Row, 1977.

Spicer, Eric. *A Short History of the Indians of the United States.* Malabar, FL: Robert E. Krieger Publishing, 1983.

Stewart, David E. *Glimpses of the Ancient Southwest.* Santa Fe, NM: Ancient City Press, 1985.

Sturtevant, William, ed. *Handbook of North American Indians.* Washington, DC: Smithsonian Institution, 1978.

Terrell, John W. *American Indian Almanac.* New York: World Publishing, 1971.

Thompson, William. *Native American Issues.*

Santa Barbara, CA: ABC-CLIO, 1996.

Waldman, Carl. *Encyclopedia of Native American Tribes.* New York: Facts on File, 1988.

———. *Atlas of the North American Indian.* New York: Facts on File, 1985.

Wells, Robert, Jr. *Native American Resurgence and Renewal.* Metuchen, NJ: Scarecrow Press, 1994.

Wright, J. V. *A History of the Native People of Canada.* Hull, Quebec: Canadian Museum of Civilization, 1995.

Chapter 1: The Southwest

Beck, Peggy, and A. Walters. *The Sacred.* Tsaile, AZ: Navajo Community College Press, 1977.

Dutton, Bertha. *American Indians of the Southwest.* Albuquerque: University of New Mexico Press, 1983.

Ford, Richard I. *The Ethnographic American Southwest.* New York: Garland Publishing, 1985.

Gumerman, George, ed. *Themes in Southwest Prehistory.* Santa Fe, NM: School of American Research Press, 1994.

Minnis, Paul, and Charles Redman. *Perspectives on Southwestern Prehistory.* Boulder, CO: Westview Press, 1990.

Ortiz, Alfonso. *The Tewa World.* Chicago: University of Chicago Press, 1969.

Reid, J. Jefferson, and David Doyel. *Emil W. Haury's Prehistory of the American Southwest.* Tucson: University of Arizona Press, 1986.

Trimble, Stephen. *The People.* Santa Fe, NM: School of American Research Press, 1993.

Waters, Frank. *Book of the Hopi.* New York: Ballantine Books, 1963.

Chapter 2: California

Bean, Lowell, and Thomas Blakburn. *Native Californians.* Socorro, NM: Ballena Press, 1976.

Heizer, R., and M. Whipple. *California Indians.* Berkeley: University of California Press, 1951.

Kroeber, A. L. *Handbook of the Indians of California.* Washington, DC: Government Printing Office, 1925.

Thomas, David H. *Spanish Borderlands Sourcebooks.* New York: Garland Publishing, 1991.

Chapter 3: The Northwest Coast

Brown, Vincent. *Native Americans of the Pacific Coast.* Happy Camp, CA: Naturegraph, 1985.

Brugmann, M. *Indians of the Northwest Coast.* New York: Facts on File, 1989.

Drucker, Philip. *Cultures of the North Pacific Coast.* San Francisco: Chandler Publishing, 1965.

———. *Indians of the Northwest Coast.* New York: McGraw-Hill, 1955.

Gunther, Erna. *Indian Life of the Northwest Coast of North America.* Chicago: University of Chicago Press, 1972.

Lyman, R. Lee. *Prehistory of the Oregon Coast.* San Diego: Academic Press, 1991.

Ruby, Robert H., and John A. Brown. *A Guide to the Indian Tribes of the Pacific Northwest.* Rev. ed. Norman: University of Oklahoma Press, 1992.

Chapter 4: The Great Basin

Bennyhoff, James A. *Shell Beads and Ornament Exchange Networks between California and the Western Great Basin.* New York: American Museum of Natural History, 1987.

Hughes, J. Donald. *American Indians in Colorado.* Boulder, CO: Pruett Publishing, 1977.

Jennings, Jesse. *Prehistory of Utah and the Eastern Great Basin.* Salt Lake City: University of Utah Press, 1978.

Strong, Emory. *Stone Age in the Great Basin.* Portland, OR: Bimfords and Mort, 1969.

Sutton, Mark. *Insects as Food.* Menlo Park, CA: Ballena Press, 1988.

Thomas, David H. *A Great Basin Shoshonean Sourcebook.* New York: Garland Publishers, 1986.

Vander, Judith. *Shoshone Ghost Dance Religion: Poetry, Songs and Great Basin Context.* Urbana: University of Illinois Press, 1997.

Chapter 5: The Plateau

Ackerman, Lillian. *A Song to the Creator: Traditional Arts of Native American Women of the Plateau.* Norman: University of Oklahoma Press, 1996.

Schwartz, E. A. *The Rogue River War and Its Aftermath.* Norman: University of Oklahoma Press, 1997 [also applies to California and Northwest Coast].

Stern, Theodore. *Chiefs and Change in the Oregon Country.* Corvallis: Oregon State University Press, 1996.

———. *Chiefs and Chief Traders.* Corvallis: Oregon State University Press, 1993.

Tennant, Paul. *Aboriginal Peoples and Politics.* Vancouver: University of British Columbia Press, 1990.

Walker, Deward E. *Indians of Idaho.* Moscow: University of Idaho Press, 1978.

Chapter 6: The Great Plains

Bancroft-Hunt, Norman. *The Indians of the Great Plains.* Norman: University of Oklahoma Press, 1981.

Brown, Dee. *Bury My Heart at Wounded Knee.* New York: Holt, Rinehart & Winston, 1971.

Driben, Paul. *We Are Metis.* New York: AMS Press, 1985.

Dugan, Kathleen M. *The Vision Quest of the Plains Indians.* Lewiston, NY: The Edwin Mellen Press, 1985.

Ewers, John C. *Plains Indian History and Culture.* Norman: University of Oklahoma Press, 1997.

Haines, F. *The Plains Indians.* New York: Crowell, 1976.

Hassrick, Royal B. *The Sioux.* Norman: University of Oklahoma Press, 1964.

Iverson, Peter, ed. *The Plains Indians of the Twentieth Century.* Norman: University of Oklahoma Press, 1985.

Lowie, R. *Indians of the Plains.* New York: McGraw-Hill, 1954.

Matthiessen, Peter. *In the Spirit of Crazy Horse.* New York: Viking Press, 1980.

Schlesier, Karl. *Plains Indians.* Norman: University of Oklahoma Press, 1994.

Chapter 7: The Southeast

Binford, Lewis. *Cultural Diversity among Aboriginal Cultures of Coastal Virginia and North Carolina.* New York: Garland Publishing Company, 1991.

Burt, J., and R. Ferguson. *Indians of the Southeast.* Nashville: Abingdon Press, 1962.

Cotterrill, Robert Spencer. *The Southern Indians.* Norman: University of Oklahoma Press, 1954.

Debo, Angie. *And Still the Waters Run.* New York: Gordion Press, 1966.

Hudson, Charles. *The Southeastern Indians.* Knoxville: University of Tennessee Press, 1976.

———. *Four Centuries of Southern Indians.* Athens: University of Georgia Press, 1975.

Paredes, J. Anthony, ed. *Indians of the Southeastern United States in the Late Twentieth Century.* Tuscaloosa: University of Alabama Press, 1992.

Swanton, John. *The Indians of the Southeastern United States.* Washington, DC: U.S. Government Printing Office, 1946.

Williams, Walt. *Southeastern Indians since the Removal Era.* Athens: University of Georgia Press, 1979.

Chapter 8: The Northeast Woodlands

Bragdon, Kathleen. *Native People of Southern New England 1500–1650.* Norman: University of Oklahoma Press, 1996.

Custer, Jay. *Late Woodland Cultures of the Middle Atlantic Region.* Newark: University of Delaware Press, 1986.

Danziger, Edmund. *The Chippewas of Lake Superior.* Norman: University of Oklahoma Press, 1979.

Hyde, George. *Indians of the Woodlands.* Norman: University of Oklahoma Press, 1962.

Simmons, William. *Spirit of the New England Tribes.* Hanover, NH: University Press of New England, 1986.

Webb, William, and Charles Snow. *The Adena People.* Knoxville: University of Tennessee Press, 1974.

Chapters 9 and 10: The Subarctic and the Arctic

Balikci, Asen. *The Netsilik Eskimo.* Garden City, NY: Natural History Press, 1970.

Birket-Smith, Kaj. *Eskimos.* New York: Crown, 1971.

Clark, Donald. *Western Subarctic Prehistory.* Hull, Quebec: Canadian Museum of Civilization, 1991.

Crowe, Keith. *A History of the Original Peoples of Northern Canada.* Montreal: McGill-Queen's University Press for the Arctic Institute of North America, 1974.

Dumond, Donald. *The Eskimos and Aleuts.* London: Thames and Hudson, 1987.

Elias, Peter D. *Northern Aborginal Communities.* North York, Ontario: Captus Press, 1995.

Holmberg, H. *Holmberg's Ethnographic Sketches.* Translated by Fritz Jaensch. Fairbanks: University of Alaska Press, 1985.

Langdon, Steve. *The Native People of Alaska.* 3d ed., rev. Anchorage: Greenland Graphics, 1993.

Laughlin, William. *Aleuts, Survivors of the Bering Land Bridge.* New York: Holt, Rinehart & Winston, 1980.

Mitchell, Donald C. *Sold American: The Story of Alaska Natives and Their Land, 1867–1959.* Hanover, NH: University Press of New England, 1997.

Tuck, James. *Newfoundland and Labrador Prehistory.* Toronto: Van Nostrand Reinhold, 1976.

Vaudrin, Bill. *Tanaina Tales from Alaska.* Norman: University of Oklahoma Press, 1969.

Yerbury, J. C. *The Subarctic Indians and the Fur Trade.* Vancouver: University of British Columbia Press, 1986.

Alaska Native Villages, by Language

VILLAGE	REGIONAL CORPORATION	NATIVE POPULATION	TRIBAL STATUS	VILLAGE	REGIONAL CORPORATION	NATIVE POPULATION	TRIBAL STATUS
Inupiaq				Chefornak	Calista	312	Traditional
Atqusuk	Arctic Slope	201	Traditional	Chevak	Calista	556	Traditional
Barrow	Arctic Slope	2,217	Traditional	Crooked Creek	Calista	96	Traditional
Kaktovik	Arctic Slope	189	Traditional	Eek	Calista	243	Traditional
Nuiqsut	Arctic Slope	328	Traditional	Emmonak	Calista	591	Traditional
Point Hope	Arctic Slope	587	IRA[1]	Georgetown	Calista	2	Traditional
Point Lay	Arctic Slope	113	IRA	Goodnews Bay	Calista	231	Traditional
Wainright	Arctic Slope	464	Traditional	Hamilton	Calista	N/A	Traditional
Ambler	Nana	279	Traditional	Hooper Bay	Calista	811	Traditional
Buckland	Nana	302	IRA	Kalskag	Calista	146	Traditional
Deering	Nana	148	IRA	Kasigluk	Calista	405	Traditional
Kiana	Nana	360	Traditional	Kipnuk	Calista	458	Traditional
Kivalina	Nana	309	IRA	Kongiganak	Calista	286	Traditional
Kobuk	Nana	62	Traditional	Kotlik	Calista	447	Traditional
Kotzebue	Nana	2,067	IRA	Kwethluk	Calista	586	IRA
Noatak	Nana	322	IRA	Kwigillingok	Calista	264	IRA
Noorvik	Nana	498	IRA	Lime Village	Calista	40	Traditional
Selawik	Nana	569	IRA	Lower Kalskag	Calista	286	Traditional
Shungnak	Nana	211	IRA	Marshall	Calista	253	Traditional
Elim	Bering Straits	242	IRA	Mekoryuk	Calista	176	IRA
Brevig Mission	Bering Straits	183	Traditional	Mountain Village/			
Golovin (Chinik)	Bering Straits	118	Traditional	Asa'carsarmiut	Calista	611	Traditional
Inalik	Bering Straits	136	N/A[2]	Napaimute	Calista	4	Traditional
Koyuk	Bering Straits	219	IRA	Napakiak	Calista	300	IRA
Shaktoolik[3]	Bering Straits	168	IRA	Napaskiak	Calista	211	Traditional
Shishmaref	Bering Straits	431	IRA	Newtok	Calista	193	Traditional
Solomon	Bering Straits	4	Traditional	Nightmute	Calista	146	Traditional
Teller	Bering Straits	131	Traditional	Nunapitchuk	Calista	367	IRA
Wales	Bering Straits	143	IRA	Ohogamiut	Calista	N/A	Traditional
White Mountain	Bering Straits	158	IRA	Oscarville	Calista	52	Traditional
				Paimiut	Calista	1	Traditional
Yup'ik				Pilot Station	Calista	440	Traditional
St. Michael	Bering Straits	269	IRA	Pitka's Point	Calista	129	Traditional
Stebbins	Bering Straits	379	IRA	Platinum	Calista	59	Traditional
Unalakleet	Bering Straits	534	IRA	Quinhagak	Calista	401	IRA
Akiachak	Calista	457	IRA	Red Devil	Calista	27	Traditional
Akiak	Calista	277	IRA	Russian			
Alakanuk	Calista	521	Traditional	Mission KU	Calista	233	Traditional
Andreafsky	Calista	93	Traditional	Russian			
Aniak	Calista	382	Traditional	Mission YU	Calista	159	Traditional
Atmautluak	Calista	250	Traditional	St.Mary's/			
Bethel/Orutsararmiut	Calista	2,986		Algaaciq	Calista	366	Traditional
Traditional				Scammon Bay	Calista	331	Traditional
Bill Moore's Slough	Calista	N/A		Sheldon's Point	Calista	101	Traditional
Traditional				Sleetmute	Calista	92	Traditional

VILLAGE	REGIONAL CORPORATION	NATIVE POPULATION	TRIBAL STATUS	VILLAGE	REGIONAL CORPORATION	NATIVE POPULATION	TRIBAL STATUS
Stony River	Calista	45	Traditional	Traditional			
Toksook Bay	Calista	401	Traditional	Nelson Lagoon	Aleut	167	Traditional
Tuluksak	Calista	342	IRA	Nikolski	Aleut	29	IRA
Tuntutuliak	Calista	290	Traditional	Pauloff Harbor	Aleut	N/A	Traditional
Tununak	Calista	304	IRA	St. George	Aleut	131	IRA
Aleknagik	Bristol Bay	154	Traditional	St. Paul	Aleut	504	IRA
Clark's Point	Bristol Bay	53	Traditional	Sand Point/Qagan			
Dillingham	Bristol Bay	1,125	Traditional	Tayagungin	Aleut	433	Traditional
Egegik[3]	Bristol Bay	86	Traditional	Unalaska/			
Ekuk	Bristol Bay	6	Traditional	Qawalangin	Aleut	259	Traditional
Ekwok	Bristol Bay	67	Traditional	Unga	Aleut	N/A	Traditional
Igiugig	Bristol Bay	26	Traditional				
Iliamna	Bristol Bay	62	Traditional	**Tlingit**			
Ivanof Bay	Bristol Bay	33	Traditional	Angoon	Sealaska	525	IRA
Kokhanok	Bristol Bay	137	Traditional	Chilkat	Sealaska	113	IRA
Koliganek	Bristol Bay	174	Traditional	Hoonah	Sealaska	534	IRA
Levelock	Bristol Bay	87	Traditional	Kake	Sealaska	514	IRA
Manokotak	Bristol Bay	368	Traditional	Yakutat	Sealaska	294	Traditional
Naknek	Bristol Bay	236	Traditional				
Newhalen	Bristol Bay	151	Traditional	**Haida**			
New Stuyahok	Bristol Bay	375	Traditional	Craig	Sealaska	288	IRA
Nondalton	Bristol Bay	159	Traditional	Hydaburg	Sealaska	342	IRA
Pedro Bay	Bristol Bay	38	Traditional	Kasaan	Sealaska	29	IRA
Pilot Point[3]	Bristol Bay	45	Traditional	Klawock	Sealaska	392	IRA
Portage Creek	Bristol Bay	44	Traditional				
South Naknek	Bristol Bay	108	Traditional	**Tsimshian**			
Togiak	Bristol Bay	535	Traditional	Saxman	Sealaska	284	IRA
Twin Hills	Bristol Bay	61	Traditional				
Ugashik[3]	Bristol Bay	11	Traditional	**Ahtna**			
				Chistochina	Ahtna	37	Traditional
Alutiiq				Chitina	Ahtna	23	Traditional
Chignik	Bristol Bay	85	Traditional	Copper Ctr/Kluti-kaah	Ahtna	155	
Chignik Lagoon	Bristol Bay	30	Traditional	Traditional			
Chignik Lake	Bristol Bay	122	Traditional	Gakona	Ahtna	0	Traditional
Perryville	Bristol Bay	102	IRA	Gulkana	Ahtna	61	Traditional
Port Heiden/				Mentasta Lake	Ahtna	70	Traditional
Meshick	Bristol Bay	86	Traditional	Slana	Ahtna	4	N/A
Afognak	Koniag	3	Traditional	Tazlina	Ahtna	4	Traditional
Akhiok	Koniag	72	Traditional				
Kaguyak	Koniag	N/A	Traditional	**Tanaina**			
Karluk	Koniag	65	IRA	Alexander	Cook Inlet	2	
Larsen Bay	Koniag	124	Traditional	Eklutna	Cook Inlet	42	Traditional
Old Harbor	Koniag	252	Traditional	Knik	Cook Inlet	31	Traditional
Ouzinkie	Koniag	178	Traditional	Ninilchik	Cook Inlet	58	Traditional
Port Lions	Koniag	150	Traditional	Salamatof	Cook Inlet	104	Traditional
Uyak	Koniag	N/A	N/A	Seldovia	Cook Inlet	48	IRA
Woody Island/Lesnoi	Koniag	3		Tyonek	Cook Inlet	142	IRA
Traditional							
English Bay/Nanwalek	Chugach	144		**Tanana**			
Traditional				Cantwell[3]	Ahtna	33	Traditional
Port Graham	Chugash	150	Traditional	Dot Lake	Doyon	38	Traditional
Tatitlek	Chugash	103	IRA	Healy Lake	Doyon	40	Traditional
				Manley Hot Springs	Doyon	14	
Unangan/Aleut (excluding western islands)				Traditional			
Akutan	Aleut	80	Traditional	Minto	Doyon	212	IRA
Atka	Aleut	67	IRA	Nenana	Doyon	188	Traditional
Belkofski	Aleut	10	Traditional	Northway	Doyon	79	Traditional
False Pass	Aleut	52	Traditional	Rampart	Doyon	64	Traditional
King Cove/Agdaagux	Aleut	177		Tanacross	Doyon	100	IRA

VILLAGE	REGIONAL CORPORATION	NATIVE POPULATION	TRIBAL STATUS
Tanana	Doyon	270	IRA
Tetlin	Doyon	83	IRA
Han			
Circle	Doyon	63	IRA
Eagle	Doyon	5	IRA
Kutchin (Gwich'in)			
Anaktuvuk Pass	Arctic Slope	220	Traditional
Arctic Village	Doyon	90	Traditional
Beaver	Doyon	98	Traditional
Birch Creek	Doyon	38	Traditional
Chalkyitsik	Doyon	83	Traditional
Evansville	Doyon	19	Traditional
Fort Yukon	Doyon	493	IRA
Stevens Village	Doyon	93	IRA
Venetie	Doyon	171	Traditional
Koyukon			
Alatna[3]	Doyon	29	Traditional
Allakaket[3]	Doyon	160	Traditional
Galena/Louden	Doyon	377	Traditional

VILLAGE	REGIONAL CORPORATION	NATIVE POPULATION	TRIBAL STATUS
Hughes	Doyon	50	Traditional
Huslia	Doyon	188	Traditional
Kaltag	Doyon	222	Traditional
Koyukuk	Doyon	123	Traditional
Nulato	Doyon	348	Traditional
Ruby	Doyon	126	Traditional
Holikachuk			
Grayling/Holikachuk IRA	Doyon	194	
Takotna[3]	Doyon	17	Traditional
Kolchan (Upper Kuskokwim)			
Nikolai[3]	Doyon	97	Traditional
Telida[3]	Doyon	32	Traditional
Ingalik			
Anvik	Doyon	75	Traditional
Holy Cross	Doyon	259	Traditional
McGrath[3]	Doyon	248	Traditional
Shageluk	Doyon	132	IRA

1. Indian Reorganization Act
2. Unavailable or not relevant
3. Status uncertain

Anca Village Corporations

(data are as of 1980)

Ahtna Region
Atna, Incorporated
Chitina Native Corporation
Aleut Region
Akutan Corporation
Atxam Corporation
Belkofski Corporation
Cahluka Corporation
Isanotski Corporation
King Cove Corporation
Nelson Lagoon Corporation
Ounalashka Corporation
Sanak Corporation
Shumagin Corporation
St. George Tanaq Corporation
Tanadgusix Corporation
Unga Corporation
Arctic Slope Region
Atqusuk Corporation
Cully Corporation
Kaktovik Inpiat Corporation
Kuukpik Corporation
Nunamiut Corporation
Olgoonik Corporation
Tigara Corporation
Ukpeagvik Inupiat Corporation
Bering Straits Region
Brevig Mission Native Corporation
Council Native Corporation
Elim Native Corporation
Golovin Native Corporation
King Island Native Corporation
Koyuk Native Corporation
Mary's Igloo Native Corporation
Savoonga Native Corporation
Shaktoolik Native Corporation
Shishmaref Native Corporation
Sitnasuak Native Corporation
Sivuqaq Incorporated
Solomon Native Corporation
Stebbins Native Corporation
St. Michael Native Corporation
Teller Native Corporation
Unalakleet Native Corporation
Wales Native Corporation

White Mountain Native Corporation
Bristol Bay Region
Alaska Peninsula Corporation
Aleknagik Natives, Ltd.
Bay View Incorporated
Becharof Corporation
Chignik Lagoon Corporation
Chignik River, Ltd.
Choggiung, Ltd.
Ekwok Natives, Ltd.
Far West Incorporated
Igiugig Native Corporation
Iliamna Natives Limited
Kijik Corporation
Koliganek Natives, Ltd.
Levelock Natives, Ltd.
Manokotak Natives, Ltd.
Oceanside Corporation
Olsonville, Incorporated
Paug-vik Incorporated, Ltd.
Pedro Bay Native Corporation
Pilot Point Native Corporation
Saguyak Incorporated
Stuyahok, Ltd.
Tanalian, Inc.
Togiak Natives, Ltd.
Twin Hills Native Corporation
Calista Region
Akiachak, Limited
Alakanuk Native Corporation
Arviq Incorporated
Askinuk Corporation
Atmautluak, Limited
Azachorok, Incorporated
Bethel Native Corporation
Chefarnmute, Incorporated
Chevak Company Corporation
Chinuruk, Incorporated
Chuloonawick Corporation
Emmonak Corporation
Iqfijouaq Company
Kasigluk, Incorporated
Kokarmuit Corporation
Kongniglnilkomuit Yuita Corporation
Kotlik Yupik Corporation

Kugkaktlik, Incorporated
Kuitsarak, Incorporated
Kuskokwim Corporation
Kwethluk Incorporated
Kwik, Incorporated
Lime Village Company
Maserculiq, Incorporated
Napakiak Corporation
Napaskiak Corporation
Nerkilikmute Native Corporation
Newtok Corporation
Nima Corporation
Nunakauiak Yupik Corporation
Nunapiglluraq Corporation
Nunapitchuk, Limited
Oscarville Native Corporation
Paimuit Corporation
Pilot Station, Incorporated
Pitka's Point Native Corporation
Qanirtuuq, Incorporated
Qemirtalek Coast Corporation
Russian Mission Native Corporation
Sea Lion Corporation
St. Mary's Native Corporation
Swan Lake Corporation
Tulkisarmute, Incorporated
Tuntunrmiut Rinit Corporation
Tuntutuliak Land, Limited
Chugach Region
Chenega Corporation
English Bay Corporation
Eyak Corporation
Port Graham Corporation
Tatitlek Corporation
Grouse Creek Corporation (regional group)
Mt. Marathon Native Association (regional group)
Valdez Native Association (regional group)
Cook Inlet Region
Chickalook-Moose Creek Native Association, Inc.
Eklutna, Incorporated
Knikatnu, Incorporated

Ninilchik Native Association, Inc.
Salamatof Native Association, Inc.
Seldovia Native Association, Inc.
Tyonek Native Corporation
Alexander Creek, Incorporated (regional group)
Caswell Native Association (regional group)
Gold Creek-Susitna (regional group)
Montana Creek Native Association (regional group)
Point Possession, Inc. (regional group)
Kenai Native Association (historic village)

Doyon Region
Baan-O-Yeel Kon Corporation
Bean Ridge Corporation
Beaver Kwit'chin Corporation
Chalkyitsik Native Corporation
Danzhit Hanlaii Corporation
Deloycheet, Inc.
Dineega Corporation
Dinyea Corporation
Dot Lake Native Corporation
Evansville, Inc.
Gana-a 'Yoo, Ltd.
Gungwitchin Corporation
Gwitchyaa Zhee Corporation
Hee-Yea Lindge Corporation
Ingalik, Inc.
K'oyitl'ots'ina, Ltd.
Mendas Chaag Native Corporation
MTNT, Ltd.
Northway Natives, Inc.
Seth-de-ya-ah Corporation

Tanacross, Inc.
Tihteet'aii, Inc.
Toghotthele Corporation
Tozitna, Ltd.
Zho-Tse, Inc.

Koniag Region
Afognak Native Corporation
Akhiok-Kaguyak, Inc.
Anton Larsen, Inc.
Ayakulik, Inc.
Bells Flats Natives, Inc.
Leisnoi, Inc.
Litnik, Inc.
Natives of Kiodiak, Inc.
Old Harbor Native Corporation
Ouzinkie Native Corporation
Shuyak, Inc.
Uganik Natives, Inc.
Uyak, Inc.

Nana Region
Kikiktagruk Inupiat Corporation
Nana Corporation

Sealaska Region
Cape Fox Corporation
Goldbelt, Incorporated
Haida Corporation
Huna Totem Corporation
Kake Tribal Corporation
Kavilco, Incorporated
Klawock Heenya Corporation
Klukwan, Incorporated
Kootznoowoo, Incorporated
Shaan Seet, Incorporated
Shee Atika, Incorporated
Yak-tat-kwaan, Incorporated